# Pragmatism and Classical American Philosophy

## ESSENTIAL READINGS AND INTERPRETIVE ESSAYS

Second Edition

*Edited by*

John J. Stuhr

New York • Oxford
OXFORD UNIVERSITY PRESS
2000

**Oxford University Press**

Oxford   New York
Athens   Auckland   Bangkok   Bogotá   Buenos Aires   Calcutta
Cape Town   Chennai   Dar es Salaam   Delhi   Florence   Hong Kong
Istanbul   Karachi   Kuala Lumpur   Madrid   Melbourne   Mexico City   Mumbai
Nairobi   Paris   São Paulo   Singapore   Taipei   Tokyo   Toronto   Warsaw

*and associated companies in*
Berlin   Ibadan

Copyright © 2000 by Oxford University Press, Inc.

Published by Oxford University Press, Inc.,
198 Madison Avenue, New York, New York, 10016
http://www.oup-usa.org
1-800-334-4249

**Library of Congress Cataloging-in-Publication Data**

Pragmatism and classical American philosophy : essential readings and
   interpretive essays / edited by John J. Stuhr. — 2nd ed.
      p.   cm.
   Includes bibliographical references and index.
   ISBN-13 978-0-19-511829-2 (cloth); ISBN-13 978-0-19-511830-8(pbk.)
   ISBN 0-19-511829-4 (cloth); ISBN 0-19-511830-8(pbk.)
   (pbk. : alk. paper)
      1. Pragmatism.   2. Philosophy, American.   I. Stuhr. John J.
   B944.P72P72   1999
144'.3'0973—dc21                                    98-41475
                                                    CIP

9 8 7 6 5

Printed in the United States of America
on acid-free paper

*For my parents*

# CONTENTS

## III. Contexts

# PREFACE

This book seeks to: (1) present the essential writings of Charles Sanders Peirce, William James, Josiah Royce, George Santayana, John Dewey, and George Herbert Mead, the major figures of classical American philosophy; (2) include introductions to these writing that are illuminating for both beginning and advanced readers; (3) provide the beginnings of a larger philosophical and historical context, as well as a variety of critical perspectives, on classical American philosophy through the philosophical writings of other major, often equally important, American writers from the same time but different, though related, philosophical traditions and cultural positions; and (4) offer suggestions for further reading and study. Ultimately, this book aims to contribute to our understanding of the classical American philosophical tradition and spirit, to increase our ability to appropriate the insights and dominant commitments of this philosophy in dealing with contemporary issues and problems, and to prepare us to reconstruct critically those insights and commitments as the press of these new issues and problems requires.

In pursuit of these goals, I have included significant portions of the work of all the central classical American philosophers. Essential readings are present, and present almost always in their entirety and across the full scope of each of these writer's complete works. I have utilized selections drawn from the very best editorial work to date: The Peirce Edition's *Writings of Charles. S. Peirce: Chronological Edition,* now being published by Indiana University Press; *The Works of William James,* published by Harvard University Press; the Santayana Edition volumes now being published by MIT Press; Southern Illinois University's *John Dewey: Early, Middle, and Later Works;* and, the University of Chicago editions of George Herbert Mead's work. I have also included introductory interpretive and critical essays by leading scholars. These original essays provide biographical and cultural context, philosophical overview, and critical reflection about the vision, strengths, difficulties, and contemporary vitality of the writings that follow. Further, classical American philosophy is a philosophy of context, and so it is important to understand this philosophy in the context of its philosophical predecessors—such as Emerson—and in the contexts of some of its most important contemporaries—American idealists and personalists, American naturalists and realists, early feminists and women writers in America, and African-American thinkers. (By including this philosophical context, I realize, of course, that I provide an opening for two sorts of critics. Some, perhaps yearning for absolute and neat identity, may claim that these writers and other traditions have nothing much to do with classical American philosophy. However, this simply is not the case: The concerns of idealists, personalists, naturalists, realists, feminists, women writers, African-American philosophers are taken up explicitly time after time by classical American philosophers themselves, and these concerns, both when explicit and when implicit, overlap, underlie, criss-cross, and identify classical American philosophy at every turn. Others, perhaps seeking absolute difference [and thus rejecting any account of "classical," "American," or even "philosophical" work], may claim that to present these traditions and writers as context for classical American philosophy is to marginalize or discredit them. However, this too simply is not the case: Classical American philosophy is a philosophically coherent and historically cohering intellectual tradition, but, as it frequently and loudly remarks, it is not the only, and never can be the final, philosophy. There are many philosophies, neither wholly identical to nor wholly different from classical American philosophy. To each of them, classical American philosophers respond pragmatically and pluralistically: Help us reconstruct.

In undertaking this second, revised edition of this book, I have been assisted by many people. This book clearly would not have been possible without the deep insights and collegial efforts of its contributors: John J. McDermott, John Lachs, Jacquelyn Ann K. Kegley, Vincent Colapietro, James Campbell, Charlene Haddock Seigfried, John Ryder, Leonard Harris, and Thomas O. Buford. Robert Miller at Oxford University Press has provided constant support and wise assistance. I have benefited immensely from the enthusiasm, understanding, and good ideas that my students have brought to American philosophy courses at Penn State, the University of Oregon, and Whitman College. I thank my wife, Eloise, and my children, Jennifer and Robert, for their good spirits, patience, and late night chocolate-chip cookies. Once again, I dedicate this book to my parents—to my mother, Ruth Stuhr, and now to the memory of my father, Robert Stuhr—for creating and nurturing my interest in classical American philosophy and for ceaseless support of every sort. This rededication makes clear one of the principal messages of classical American philosophy: Life is precarious. There is never enough time to convey thanks enough times.

*Port Matilda, Pennsylvania*
*11 April 1998*

# ACKNOWLEDGMENTS

Selections from the manuscripts of Charles Sanders Peirce are reprinted by permission of Indiana University Press.

Selections from *The Works of William James* are reprinted by permission of Harvard University Press.

Selections from *The Problem of Christianity* and from *The Philosophy of Loyalty* are reprinted by permission of Mr. Josiah Royce III.

Selections from *Obiter Scripta*, from *Realms of Being*, from *Scepticism and Animal Faith*, and from *Winds of Doctrine* are reprinted by permission of the MIT Press.

The selection from *Physical Order and Moral Liberty* is reprinted by permission of Vanderbilt University Press.

Selections from *John Dewey: The Early Works, 1882–1898*, from *John Dewey: The Middle Works, 1899–1924*, and from *John Dewey: The Later Works, 1925–1953* are reprinted by permission of Southern Illinois University Press.

Selections from *Mind, Self, and Society: From the Standpoint of a Social Behaviorist, from Movements of Thought in the Nineteenth Century*, from *The Philosophy of the Act*, from *The Philosophy of the Present*, and from *Selected Writings: George Herbert Mead* are reprinted by permission of the University of Chicago Press.

The selection from *Nature and Historical Experience* is reprinted by permission of Columbia University Press.

# CONTRIBUTORS

**Thomas O. Buford,** Professor of Philosophy at Furman University, wrote the introduction to American Idealism and Personalism. The founding editor of *The Personalist Forum,* he has written extensively on philosophical, social, and educational issues in American life. His books include: *In Search of a Calling: The College's Role in Shaping Identity; Toward a Philosophy of Education; Philosophy for Adults;* and, *Essays on Other Minds.*

**James Campbell,** who wrote the introduction to George Herbert Mead, received his Ph.D. in philosophy from the State University of New York at Stony Brook and is Professor of Philosophy at the University of Toledo. In addition to many articles and essays on Mead, John Dewey, and social philosophy, he is the author of *The Community Reconstructs: The Meaning of Pragmatic Social Thought, Understanding John Dewey,* and *Recovering Benjamin Franklin,* and editor of *Selected Writings of James Hayden Tufts.*

**Vincent M. Colapietro,** author of the introduction to Charles S. Peirce, earned his Ph.D. in philosophy at Marquette University and is Professor of Philosophy at the Pennsylvania State University. A co-editor of *The Journal of Speculative Philosophy,* he has published many articles and essays in American philosophy. In addition, he is the author of *Peirce's Approach to the Self* and *A Glossary of Semiotics,* and co-editor of *Peirce's Doctrine of Signs, Peirce's Philosophical Perspectives,* and *Reason, Experience, and God.*

**Jacquelyn Ann K. Kegley,** a Professor in the Department of Philosophy and Religious Studies and the Kegley Institute of Ethics at California State University, Bakersfield, wrote the introduction to Josiah Royce. She received her Ph.D. in philosophy from Columbia University, and has co-authored a logic text and edited several volumes dealing with contemporary social, educational, and family problems. Her extensive writings on American philosophy and Royce include *Genuine Individuals and Genuine Communities: A Roycean Public Philosophy* and *Genetic Knowledge, Human Value and Responsibility.*

**Leonard Harris,** who wrote the introduction to African-American philosophy, is a Professor of Philosophy and former Director of the African American Studies and Research Center at Purdue University. He has written extensively on contemporary social and political issues and on African-American philosophy, and has edited *Philosophy Born of Struggle: Anthology of Afro-American Philosophy from 1917, Philosophy of Alain Locke: Harlem Renaissance and Beyond,* and, forthcoming, *Alain Locke and Value.*

**John Lachs,** author of the introduction to George Santayana, is Centennial Professor of Philosophy at Vanderbilt University. He earned his Ph.D. at Yale University, and is a founder and past President of the Society for the Advancement of American Philosophy. The author of scores of articles and essays on American philosophy, Marxism, philosophy of mind, and moral and issues, his books include: *Intermediate Man; George Santayana; Mind and Philosophers; The Relevance of Philosophy to Life;* and, *In Love with Life.*

**John J. McDermott** wrote the introduction to William James. He is Distinguished Professor of Philosophy at Texas A & M University, a founder and past President of the Society for the Advancement of American Philosophy, and co-founder and advisory editor of the Harvard University critical edition of *The Works of William James.* An editor of the writings of James, Royce, and Dewey, he has written extensively on American philosophy and culture, including: *The Culture of Experience: Essays in the American Grain;* and *Streams of Experience: Reflections on the History and Philosophy of American Culture.*

**John Ryder,** Dean of Arts and Sciences at the State University of New York College at Cortland, wrote the introduction to American naturalism. He received his Ph.D. in philosophy at the State University of New York at Stony Brook, and has published on topics that range from pragmatism to Marxism, American philosophy to Russian philosophy, naturalism to postmodernism, and metaphysics to politics. He is the editor of *American Philosophic Naturalism in the Twentieth Century* and author of *Interpreting America.*

**Charlene Haddock Seigfried,** author of the introduction to feminism and the writings of American women, is Professor of Philosophy and a member of the American Studies and Women's Studies Committees at Purdue University. She received her Ph.D. from Loyola University, Chicago, and has written many articles, essays, and chapters on American philosophy, feminist theory, aesthetics, and philosophical psychology. She is the author of *Pragmatism and Feminism: Reweaving the Social Fabric,* and two books on James—*Chaos and Context* and *William James's Radical Reconstruction of Philosophy.*

**John J. Stuhr,** editor of the volume and author of the introductions to classical American philosophy and to John Dewey, is Professor and Head of the Department of Philosophy at the Pennsylvania State University. He received his Ph.D. from Vanderbilt University, and was the founding Director of the University of Oregon Humanities Center. He has published extensively on American and European philosophy, politics, education, and ethics, and has edited three books on ethical issues in the professions. Co-editor of *The Journal of Speculative Philosophy* and *Studies in American and European Philosophy,* he is the editor of *Philosophy and the Reconstruction of Culture* and author of *Genealogical Pragmatism, John Dewey,* as well as the forthcoming *Experience and Criticism.*

# CLASSICAL AMERICAN PHILOSOPHY

## Introduction by John J. Stuhr

Taken individually, Charles Sanders Peirce, William James, Josiah Royce, George Santayana, John Dewey, and George Herbert Mead are original, insightful, important thinkers. Taken collectively, they constitute the core of the period, perspective, and philosophical tradition that is classical American philosophy.[1] This tradition has a living, as well as historical, importance: Today it speaks directly, imaginatively, critically, and wisely to our contemporary global society, its massive and pressing problems, and its distant possibilities for real improvement.

These problems are clear enough in general outline. Our world is a world of possible nuclear self-destruction, a world in which this unthinkable prospect must not fail to be thought as long as it remains possible. Against this background, wars, invasions, occupations, suppressions, "covert operations," and self-righteous, absolutist, international terrorism are the norm. We live in—or, at least, if we are fortunate, near—hunger, malnutrition, disease, deformity, and pain. Our environment, increasingly polluted and plundered, now faces the demands of a rapidly expanding population. Social life is marked by inequity, crime, physical and psychological violence in both individual and institutional forms, and the absence of personal growth, enriching relationships, and genuine community. We see poverty and unfulfillment in the lives of many, and the poverty of fulfillment in the lives of a few others. None of this, of course, is shocking; these facts, at least in the abstract, are commonplace, and they are so horrible, terrifying, and depressing that we have had to become insensitive, in some measure, to them.

Still, the prospective reader is entitled to a suspicious grin or weary laugh—for this is another book, another book of philosophy, another book of the writings of several dead thinkers. What does it have to offer us as we confront these problems? This is an important question: though it is seldom posed and less frequently addressed, it is *the* pragmatic question *for* (if not *in*) philosophy. It is this question which makes clear the triviality of much contemporary thought—a triviality rooted not in subject matter but in a poverty of approach, form, self-understanding, and, above all, results.[2] The resulting suspicion, scepticism, and smile, however, are well known to the classical American philosophers. Thus, for example, George Santayana begins his *Scepticism and Animal Faith:*

> Here is one more system of philosophy. If the reader is tempted to smile, I can assure him that I smile with him, and that my system . . . differs widely in spirit and pretensions from what usually goes by that name. . . . I am merely attempting to express for the reader the principles to which he appeals when he smiles.[3]

So, too, Dewey confronts our suspicions and sceptical smiles:

> The chief intellectual characteristic of the present age is its despair of any constructive philosophy—not just in its technical meaning, but in the sense of any integrated outlook and attitude. The developments of the last century have gone so far that we are now aware of the shock and overturn

in older beliefs. But the formation of a new, coherent view of nature and man based upon facts consonant with science and actual social conditions is still to be had.[4]

He continues:

It is in such a context that a thoroughgoing philosophy of experience, framed in light of science and technique, has its significance. For it, the breakdown of traditional ideas is an opportunity. The possibility of producing the kind of experience in which science and the arts are brought unitedly to bear upon industry, politics, religion, domestic life, and human relations in general, is itself something novel. We are not accustomed to it even as an idea. But faith in it is neither a dream nor a demonstrated failure. It is a faith. Realization of the faith so that we may work in larger measure by sight of things achieved, is in the future. . . . A philosophic faith, being a tendency to action, can be tried and tested only in action. I know of no viable alternative in the present day to such a philosophy [of experience] as has been indicated.[5]

The writings that follow are presented in this spirit: they constitute an opportunity, a call to action, and a smile at self-contained intellectual systems, self-certain doctrines, and self-proclaimed absolute truths. Be forewarned, then: classical American philosophy offers no formula for salvation independent of human endeavor in time and nature; no method for infallibility, exactitude, or finality; no claim to truth or account of reality void of intrinsic historical and cultural connection; and no imperative to overcome the finite, unfinished, local, transient, pluralistic character of experience.

The introductory essays below provide the necessary personal, intellectual, and cultural contexts for the writings that follow, and the classical American philosophers (and all the writers included in this volume) speak clearly and effectively for themselves. Accordingly, there is no need for, or value in, an introductory "summary" of this material. On the other hand, a general characterization of its dominant features may be needed as a preliminary to assessing its contemporary value and viability.

Historically, we may identify classical American philosophy with a particular period in America, with particular individuals who influenced and in turn were influenced by each other's thought, and with the particular relation of this philosophy to both earlier and later thought in America. Understood in this manner, classical American philosophy is philosophy in America from approximately 1870 to roughly 1945, from the initial setting forth of pragmatism at the early meetings of the Cambridge "Metaphysical Club" (founded by Peirce, James, and others) to the final work of Dewey after World War II and the deaths of Dewey and Santayana in the early 1950s. In this historical sense, it is a philosophy forged in and through the personal and professional relationships of Peirce, James, Royce, Santayana, Dewey, and Mead, as well as others:[6] their lives overlapped (at, for example, Johns Hopkins, Harvard, Michigan, and Chicago, and at many other places on numerous, briefer occassions); their work and thoughts overlapped even more frequently and importantly, as evidenced by conversations, correspondence, written references, reviews (both positive and negative), and testimonies to the personal importance of the work of one or more of the others. Finally, understood in this historical fashion, classical American philosophy is classically American: it is the critical articulation (in a more complete, consistent, and self-aware manner) of attitudes, outlooks, and forms of life embedded in the culture from and in which it arose.[7] It marks a fruition and unified development of earlier thought, and stands as a point of departure and reference for later philosophical work.

Classical American philosophy may also be characterized in a more thematic or philosophical manner. In this sense, it may be defined by its exponents' common attitudes, purposes, philosophical problems, procedures, terminology, and beliefs. It is in virtue of such a shared complex of features that we identify, understand, and differentiate philosophical developments, movements, and "schools of thought." Such a unity of character, we must recognize, is not a single and simple essence, some necessary and sufficient feature of classical American philosophy, some property present always and only in classical American philosophy. Instead, it is an identifiable configuration, a characteristic shape, a resemblance, an overlapping and interweaving of features (present to differing degrees in the writings of the individual philosophers) that, as a relational whole, pervades and constitutes this philosophy and these philosophers.

What are these defining characteristics and commitments that, as such, must be the basis of claims for the contemporary cultural significance of classical American philosophy? The following themes, briefly listed here but articulated and developed in detail in the writings contained in this volume, appear both central to the classical American philosophical vision, and important for us today:

1. *The rejection of modern philosophy.* Classical American philosophy confronted and largely dismissed the categories, language, and notions central to earlier thought. This thought was fundamentally dualistic: problems arose and positions were articulated and defended in terms of dichotomies such as percept/concept, reason/will, thought/purpose, intellect/emotion, immediate knowledge/inferential knowledge, mind/matter, appearance/reality, experience/nature, belief/action, theory/practice, facts/values, means/ends, divine/human, self/others, individual/community, and so on. Classical American philosophers did not refuse to use these terms; instead, their point was that these notions refer to distinctions made in thought rather than to different kinds of being or levels of existence. That is, these terms have a functional rather than an ontological status: they stand for useful distinctions made within reflection, and not for different kinds of being, discrete and separate prior to reflection. This is crucial because it is bound up with the wholesale rejection of the central problems of modern philosophy, problems which presuppose the above dualistic categories. Classical American philosophers, that is, did not attempt to provide better answers to traditional problems (the "enduring problems" of so many introductory philosophy texts) as much as they sought to dissolve, dismiss, and undercut these problems altogether by denying the metaphysical assumptions which gave rise to them. In doing this, they rejected as well the image of philosophy itself embedded in modern philosophy. Philosophy no longer was to be understood as a purely theoretical quest for eternal truths or knowledge of an ultimate and unchanging reality. Its job no longer was to analyze experience into the real and unreal, the substantial and the insubstantial. Instead, it must be practical, critical, and reconstructive; it must aim at the successful transformation or amelioration of the experienced problems which call it forth and intrinsically situate it, and its success must be measured in terms of this goal. Thus, for the classical American philosophers, philosophy is primarily an instrument for the ongoing critical reconstruction of daily practice. In a world where daily life is frequently distant from intelligent self-examination and its fruits, a philosophy which removes itself (in subject matter or application) from the genuine problems of life is an unaffordable luxury. Classical American philosophy pursues a different course.

2. *Fallibilism.* For the classical American philosophers, fallibility is an irreducible dimension of the human condition: empirical belief can never be certain, exact, absolute, final. The abandoned "quest for certainty" is replaced by piecemeal, multi-directional efforts to verify and warrant beliefs. The possibility of belief revision is never erased. Fallibilism, however, does not signify a failing or shortcoming. It marks not the absence of omniscience, but the vulnerability of all dogma, the significance of inquiry and experiment, and the future-directed, eventual character of life. It is, for example, in this spirit that Santayana attacks the view of knowledge as certainty, a view central to both traditional metaphysics and scepticism. It is in this spirit that he asks instead for an *honest* philosophy. Similarly, Peirce identifies fallibilism as the spirit of science, and commands us not to block the way of inquiry. In a world saddled with policies and actions rooted in absolutist commitments and ideologies quarantined from examination, fallibilism seems ever more attractive.

3. *Pluralism.* Classical American philosophy is committed to pluralism in its view of reality and human values. Ontologically, experiences occur pluralistically: our transactions with the natural environment are individual and qualitatively unique, though all are equally real. These experiences are irreducibly personal, individual, "owned." We find not experience (in the abstract) but experiences (in the concrete). Morally, values and meanings are genuinely plural: experienced values, no matter how varied and messy, are real insofar as they are experienced. Concern for intellectual neatness aside, experience provides no transcendent position or principle of order for overcoming the varieties of experiences or the experiences of varied values. It is in this spirit that James, perhaps *the* philosopher of pluralism, writes:

> . . . whereas absolutism thinks that . . . substance becomes fully divine only in the form of totality, and is not its real self in any form but the *all*-form, the pluralistic view which I prefer to adopt is willing to believe that there may ultimately never be an all-form at all, that the substance of reality may never get totally collected, that some of it may remain outside of the largest combination of it ever made, and that a distributive form of reality, the *each*-form, is logically as acceptable and empirically as probable as the all-form commonly acquiesced in as so obviously the self-evident thing. . . .
>
> For pluralism, all that we are required to admit as the constitution of reality is what we ourselves find empirically realized in every minimum of finite life.[8]

What we find, for James, are differing experiences, values, and temperaments; accordingly, differing philosophies appear rational—call forth the "sentiment of rationality"—in differing individuals. The search for total, final, literal philosophic agreement, James concludes, *must* fail; a philosophy may not be ultimate and "strait-laced," for "individuality outruns all classification."[9] It is in this same light that Santayana contrasts the philosopher's supposed desire for truth with his or her defense of some "vested illusion." In "The Genteel Tradition in American Philosophy," he writes:

> No system would have ever been framed if people had been simply interested in knowing what is true, whatever it may be. What produces systems is the interest in maintaining against all comers that some favourite or inherited idea of ours is sufficient or right. A system may contain an account of many things which, in detail, are true enough; but as a system, covering infinite possibilities that neither our experience nor our logic can prejudge, it must be a work of imagination and a piece of human soliloquy. It may be expressive of human experience, it may be poetical; but how should any one who really coveted truth suppose that it was true?[10]

Local, regional, national, and global differences and conflicts abound. We need a philosophy that centrally recognizes those differences and seeks a harmonious pluralism; intellectual attempts to deny, impose on, or transcend this plurality are no longer innocuous, if they ever were.

4. *Radical empiricism.* A fundamental aspect of classical American philosophy is its radical view of experience, and its development of the implications of this view. The classical American philosophers reject traditional empiricism because it is not sufficiently empirical, not radically empirical. These concerns are developed most fully by James in *Essays in Radical Empiricism*[11] and by Dewey in "The Need for a Recovery of Philosophy"[12] and *Experience and Nature;*[13] they insist that experience is an active, ongoing affair in which experienc*ing* subject and experienc*ed* object constitute a primal, integral, relational unity. Experience is not an interaction of separate subject and object, a point of connection between a subjective realm of the experiencer and the objective order of nature. Instead, experience is existentially inclusive, continuous, unified: it is that interaction of subject and object which *constitutes* subject and object—as partial features of this active, yet unanalyzed, totality. Experience, then, is not an

"interaction" but a "transaction" in which the whole constitutes its interrelated aspects. Experience is primal or pure, and contains no "inner duplicity." Thus, the separation of it into knowing consciousness and known content can be explained, writes James, "as a particular sort of relation towards one another into which portions of pure experience may enter. The relation itself is a part of pure experience; one of its 'terms' becomes the subject or bearer of the knowledge, the knower, the other becomes the object known."[14] The implications of this view are many and profound. Negatively, radical empiricism is the basis for the rejection of modern philosophy described above: it demonstrates the artificiality of philosophical problems of somehow uniting man and world, experience and nature, self and not-self, mental and physical, and so on. Positively, it points to a new direction for philosophy: philosophy must examine the conditions under which the preceding distinctions are made and applied, and it must critically examine the values served by these distinctions. It is this aim that motivates Dewey, for example, in his writings on ethics, education, politics, and aesthetic and religious experience: today we are in desperate need of a philosophy that separates not experience from reality, but rather "blind, slavish, meaningless action" from "action that is free, significant, directed, and responsible."[15]

5. *The continuity of science and philosophy.* The classical American philosophers, especially Peirce, Dewey, and Mead, were greatly influenced by science, and in many ways sought to link philosophy to science. First, classical American philosophers rejected the view of philosophy as "queen of the sciences," as a discipline, in opposition to the sciences, concerned with transcendent reality, ultimate causes, absolute origins, and final, infallible truths. Second, as such, philosophy itself was understood as experimental: pragmatism and instrumentalism are, at base, efforts to connect meaning, truth, and epistemological justification of ideas, beliefs, and theories with the results of experience, experiment, and practice. For example, in "The Experimental Theory of Knowledge," Dewey writes:

> That truth denotes *truths,* that is, specific verifications, combinations of meanings and outcomes reflectively viewed, is, one may say, the central point of the experimental theory. Truth, in general or in the abstract, is a just name for an experienced relation among the things of experience: that sort of relation in which intents are retrospectively viewed from the standpoint of the fulfillment which they secure through their own natural operation or incitement. Thus the experimental theory explains directly and simply the absolutistic tendency to translate concrete true things into the general relationship, Truth, and then to hypostatize this abstraction into identity with real being, Truth *per se* and *in se,* of which all transitory things and events—that is, all experienced realities—are only shadowy futile approximations.[16]

In classical American philosophy, as in the sciences, the results of experimental inquiry are the measure of theory. Here science is understood in terms of a method of inquiry (rather than, for example, a particular subject matter), and, since proper results depend upon proper methods of inquiry, an understanding and critical examination of the nature of inquiry is fundamental. Accordingly, these philosophers were concerned with developing accounts of the nature of scientific method and logical reasoning. The writings below by Peirce, for example, on the nature of science and the theory of science[17] demonstrate the philosophical importance of these issues, as well as his own "saturation" by the spirit of the sciences; and, the influence of this work on the writings of the others demonstrates the centrality of these issues to classical American philosophy as a whole. Third, though scientific in the above senses, classical American philosophy is not reductionistic: the "world" of science is not "more real" than our commonsense, everyday life world; indeed, there is no ontological conflict at all between the objects of scientific activities and the objects of other endeavors. Insisting on radical empiricism, and viewing science as an inquiring (rather than spectating or copying or "mirroring") activity, classical American philosophers reject the premises of efforts to identify the mental with the physical, reduce the experiential to the material, and assimilate the human to the nonhuman. Inquiry into the conditions upon which the occurrence of immediate, qualitative experience depends presupposes, and so cannot call into question, the reality of that experience itself; the object of original experience has been transformed in being made the object of a later knowledge experience (which ignores qualitative features of the object while focusing on its causal relationships), but it has not been replaced or made "less real." Mead makes this clear in "The Nature of Scientific Knowledge,"[18] concluding that "the experimental scientist, apart from some philosophical bias, is not a positivist." In *The Philosophy of The Act,* Mead goes on to demolish popular, naive distinctions (rooted in modern philosophy) between the objective and the subjective, and primary and secondary qualities of existence. The ontological assumptions of science, as evident especially in contemporary physics and chemistry, converge on radical empiricism; Mead writes: "so-called objects which lie beyond the range of possible experience are in reality complex procedures in the control of actual experience."[19] In this age of science and increasing control of nature and society, we do not need a philosophy that seeks to deny or usurp the functions and results of science. Classical American philosophy, by contrast, offers us an understanding of scientific method and insight into the difference between science and pseudoscience, ideology, and dogma. It turns our attention, moreover, to the critical task of evaluating particular uses, users, and results of science.

6. *Pragmatism and meliorism.* Classical American philosophy is often pragmatic: its emphasis is on practical results of human activity, and the evaluation of theory by its instrumental function in resolving the problem situation at hand. As such, it is committed not to optimism or pessimism, but to meliorism—the view that human action can improve the human condition. James states this most directly and explicitly, contrasting meliorism with "intellectualism":

> 'Intellectualism' is the belief that our mind comes upon a world complete in itself, and has the duty of ascertaining its contents; but has no power of re-determining its character, for that is already given. . . . It implies the will to insist on a universe of intellectualist constitution, and the willingness to stand in the way of a pluralistic universe's success, such success requiring the good will and active faith, theoretical as well as practical, of all concerned to make it 'come true.' . . .[20]

The reality of this pluralistic or melioristic universe would require human action. James continues:

> The melioristic universe is conceived after a *social* analogy, as a pluralism of independent powers. It will succeed just in proportion as more of these work for its success. If none work, it will fail. If each does his best, it will not fail. Its destiny thus hangs on an *if,* or on a lot of *ifs*—which amounts to saying . . . that, the world being as yet unfinished, its total character can be expressed only by *hypothetical* and not by *categorical* propositions.[21]

This meliorism is clearly evident in Dewey's writings: he is concerned ultimately and in detail with liberating and extending the religious and aesthetic dimensions of experience, with securing effective individuality and community in social life, and with restructuring human relations and institutions so as to foster lifelong growth and education. This melioristic spirit pervades Royce's later writings, which focus on the nature and need for loyalty and community: the moral life require an ideal to which one is devoted and, above all, the expression of this devotion "in some *sustained and practical way,* by acting steadily."[22] This is an important, politically far-reaching message for individuals accustomed and resigned to the difficulties and institutional roadblocks that face such efforts, for such resignation rapidly turns problematic situations into metaphysically necessary conditions of "fate." Classical American philosophy offers no promise of success, but it directs us to make the effort. Reality, James tells us, is congenial to human powers.[23]

7. *The centrality of community and the social.* It is obvious that we live with others, that our actions are connected to and must take account of others, that we inhabit and form habits in a social environment. For the classical American philosophers, existence is social in a deeper, ontologically more important sense as well: the individual is intrinsically *constituted* by and in his or her social relations; the self is fundamentally a social self. Even James and Santayana, who champion the individual, recognize that cultural conditions enter into the very being of that individual. Mead develops this most fully: the self is "essentially a social structure, and it arises in social experience"; it is thus impossible to conceive to a self arising outside of a social context.[24] Mead continues:

> The unity and structure of the complete self reflects the unity and structure of the social process as a whole; . . . The organization and unification of a social group is identical with the organization and unification of any one of the selves arising within the social process in which that group is engaged, or which it is carrying on.[25]

Mead details how such a self arises in his account (included in the selections below) of language and communication, play, and the generalized other. Practically, two crucial points emerge from this discussion: first, the emergence of the self requires a social process of development—individuality is a social creation, not something innate, fixed, and sure; second, the individual and the social community implicate one another in experience—contrary both to metaphysical schemes which oppose self and society, and to abstract political philosophies, which assume a necessary opposition of private and public interest. These points are central to Dewey's efforts to establish both a new individualism and a genuine public or integrated community of association. And, they emerge powerfully in Royce's accounts of individual and social experience, and the development of local (or "provincial"), national, and international (or "great") communities. We are "saved through the community," through union,[26] Royce writes; individual fulfillment requires not detachment but devotion to communal cause. It is in this context that Royce, during World War I, sought to apply principles drawn from the business of insurance to the actions and associations of nations:

> Were any group of nations to begin in a businesslike and practicable way to do what the individual fellow members of a social order have now the means of doing, namely, to insure against risks of some insurable sort, we should have a good reason to expect that analogous and beneficent indirect workings would ere long follow from even a modest beginning in the art of international insurance.[27]

Despite our own best efforts to "get ahead," our lives often contain little personal fulfillment. Classical American philosophy links the attainment of this individuality with the creation of community and instructs us that the actualization of community requires difficult, imaginative action. Let Santayana have the last word:

> All traditions have been founded on practice: in practice the most ideal of them regain their authority, when practice really deals with reality, and faces the world squarely, in the interests of the whole soul. To bring the whole soul to expression is what all civilization is after. We must be patient, for the task is long; but the fields are always white for the harvest, and the yield cannot be insignificant when labourers go forth into the harvest with the high and diligent spirit which we divine in you.[28]

# Notes

1. For the history of American philosophy see: Elizabeth Flower and Murray Murphey, *A History of Philosophy in America,* 2 vols. (New York: Putnam, 1977); Bruce Kuklick, *The Rise of American Philosophy: Cam-*

*bridge, Massachusetts, 1860–1930* (New Haven, Conn.: Yale University Press, 1977) and *Churchmen and Philosophers: From Jonathan Edwards to John Dewey* (New Haven, Conn.: Yale University Press, 1985). Amelie Rorty, ed., *Pragmatic Philosophy* (Garden City, N.Y.: Anchor/Doubleday, 1966) is a collection of some key writings by pragmatists and their critics. H. S. Thayer, *Meaning and Action: A Critical History of Pragmatism* (Indianapolis, Ind.: Hackett, 1981) provides a sympathetic overview of the development of pragmatism, while John Patrick Diggins, *The Promise of Pragmatism: Modernism and the Crisis of Knowledge and Authority* (Chicago: University of Chicago Press, 1994) is a more critical survey. There are several strong collections of essays on classical American philosophy: Marcus Singer, ed., *American Philosophy* (New York: Cambridge University Press, 1985); Douglas Anderson, Carl Hausman, and Sandra Rosenthal, eds., *Classical American Pragmatism* (Urbana, Ill.: University of Illinois Press, 1999); and, Robert W. Burch and Herman J. Saatkamp, Jr., eds., *Frontiers in American Philosophy,* 2 vols. (College Station, Tex.: Texas A & M University Press, 1992). Finally, for books that extend classical American philosophy in new directions, see, for example: Cornel West, *The American Evasion of Philosophy: A Genealogy of Pragmatism* (Madison, Wis.: University of Wisconsin Press, 1989); Richard Shusterman, *Practicing Philosophy: Pragmatism and the Philosophical Life* (New York: Routledge, 1997); and, John J. Stuhr, *Genealogical Pragmatism: Philosophy, Experience, and Community* (Albany: State University of New York Press, 1997).

2. See my "Do American Philosophers Exist?: Visions of American Philosophy and Culture," *Genealogical Pragmatism: Philosophy, Experience* and Community (Albany: State University of New York Press, 1997), pp. 21–44.

3. George Santayana, *Scepticism and Animal Faith* (New York: Dover, 1955), p. v.

4. John Dewey, "What I Believe" in *John Dewey: The Later Works, 1925–1953,* Vol. 5, Jo Ann Boydston, ed. (Carbondale and Edwardsville, Ill.: Southern Illinois University Press, 1984), pp. 276–277.

5. Ibid., p. 278.

6. Autobiographical writings by all these authors make clear these personal influences. For a brief overview, see Max H. Fisch, "The Classic Period in American Philosophy," in his *Classic American Philosophers* (Englewood Cliffs, N.J.: Prentice-Hall, 1951), pp. 1–8.

7. This point has been made by a number of authors. In addition to the essays by Stuhr and Fisch cited above, see the following: John J. McDermott, *The Culture of Experience: Philosophical Essays in the American Grain* (New York: New York University Press, 1976), pp. 1–20; H. S. Thayer, *Meaning and Action: A Critical History of Pragmatism* (Indianapolis: Hackett, 1981), pp. 432–448; John E. Smith, *The Spirit of American Philosophy* (Albany: State University Press of New York, 1983), pp. 187–206. In addition to these and essays by other authors, many of Santayana's writings on America speak to these issues.

8. William James, *A Pluralistic Universe. The Works of William James,* Frederick Burkhardt, ed. (Cambridge, Mass.: Harvard University Press, 1977), pp. 20, 145.

9. Ibid., p. 7. See also William James, "The Sentiment of Rationality," in *The Will To Believe and Other Essays in Popular Philosophy. The Works of William James,* Frederick Burkhardt, ed., (Cambridge, Mass.: Harvard University Press, 1979), p. 89.

10. George Santayana, "The Genteel Tradition in American Philosophy," in *Winds of Doctrine* (New York: Charles Scribner's Sons, 1913), pp. 198–199.

11. See "A World of Pure Experience," p. 181, below.

12. See "The Need for a Recovery of Philosophy," p. 445, below.

13. See "Experience and Philosophic Method," "Existence as Precarious and Stable," and "Nature, Communication and Meaning," pp. 460, 471, and 476, below.

14. William James, "Does 'Consciousness' Exist?," in *Essays in Radical Empiricism. The Works of William James,* Frederick Burkhardt, ed. (Cambridge, Mass.: Harvard University Press, 1976), pp. 4–5.

15. John Dewey, *Experience and Nature in John Dewey: The Later Works, 1925–1953,* Vol. 1, Jo Ann Boydston, ed. (Carbondale and Edwardsville, Ill.: Southern Illinois University, 1981), p. 324. See also John Dewey and Arthur F. Bentley, *Knowing and the Known* in John Dewey, The Later Works, 1925–1953, vol. 16.

16. John Dewey, "The Experimental Theory of Knowledge," in *John Dewey: The Middle Works, 1899–1924,* Jo Ann Boydston, ed., (Carbondale and Edwardsville, Ill.: Southern Illinois University Press, 1977), pp. 108–109.

17. See pp. 54, 67, 77, and 88 below.

18. George Herbert Mead, "The Nature of Scientific Knowledge," in *The Philosophy of the Act,* Charles W. Morris, ed. (in collaboration with John M. Brewster, Albert M. Dunham, and David L. Miller) (Chicago: The University of Chicago Press, 1938), pp. 45–62.

19. Ibid., pp. 291–292.

20. William James, "Faith and the Right to Believe," in *The Writings of William James,* John J. McDermott, ed. (Chicago: The University of Chicago Press, 1977), pp. 735, 737. See also the concluding pages of *A Pluralistic Universe.*

21. James, "Faith and the Right to Believe," op. cit., p. 739.
22. Josiah Royce, *The Philosophy of Loyalty* (New York: Macmillan, 1908), p. 14.
23. William James, "The Sentiment of Rationality," op. cit., p. 73.
24. George Herbert Mead, *Mind, Self, and Society: From the Standpoint of a Social Behaviorist,* Charles W. Morris, ed. (Chicago: The University of Chicago Press, 1934), p. 140.
25. Ibid., p. 144.
26. Josiah Royce, *The Hope of the Great Community* (New York: Macmillan, 1916), p. 131.
27. Ibid., p. 75.
28. George Santayana, "Tradition and Practice," reprinted in *Santayana on America,* Richard Colton Lyon, ed. (New York: Harcourt, Brace & World, Inc., 1968), p. 35.

# PART I
## PROLOGUE

# RALPH WALDO EMERSON

## Introduction: "Emerson," a memorial address by William James

The pathos of death is this, that when the days of one's life are ended, those days that were so crowded with business and felt so heavy in their passing, what remains of one in memory should usually be so slight a thing. The phantom of an attitude, the echo of a certain mode of thought, a few pages of print, some invention, or some victory we gained in a brief critical hour, are all that can survive the best of us. It is as if the whole of a man's significance had now shrunk into a mere musical note or phrase, suggestive of his singularity—happy are those whose singularity gives a note so clear as to be victorious over the inevitable pity of such a diminution and abridgment.

An ideal wraith like this, of Emerson's singularity, hovers over all Concord today, taking in the minds of those of you who were his neighbors and intimates a somewhat fuller shape, remaining more abstract in the younger generation, but bringing home to all of us the notion of a spirit indescribably precious. The form that so lately moved upon these streets and country roads, or awaited in these fields and woods the beloved Muse's visits, is now dust; but the soul's note, the spiritual voice, rises strong and clear above the uproar of the times, and seems securely destined to exert an ennobling influence over future generations.

What gave a flavor so matchless to Emerson's individuality was, even more than his rich mental gifts, their combination. Rarely has a man so known the limits of his genius or so unfailingly kept within them. "Stand by your order," he used to say to youthful students; and perhaps the paramount impression one gets of his life is of his loyalty to his own type and mission. The type was that of what he liked to call the scholar, the perceiver of pure truth, and the mission was that of the reporter in worthy form of each perception. The day is good, he said, in which we have the most perceptions. There are times when the cawing of a crow, a weed, a snow-flake, or a farmer planting in his field, become symbols to the intellect of truths equal to those which the most majestic phenomena can open. Let me mind my own charge, then, walk alone, consult the sky, the field and forest, sedulously waiting every morning for the news concerning the structure of the universe which the good Spirit will give me.

This was the first half of Emerson, but only half; for his genius was insatiate for expression, and his truth had to be clad in the right verbal garment. The form of the garment was so vital with Emerson that it is impossible to separate it from the matter. They form a chemical combination,—thoughts which would be trivial expressed otherwise are important through the nouns and verbs to which he married them. The style is the man, it has been said; the man Emerson's mission culminated in his style, and if we must define him in one word, we have to call him Artist. He was an artist whose medium was verbal and who wrought in spiritual material.

This duty of spiritual seeing and reporting determined the whole tenor of his life. It was to shield it from invasion and distraction that he dwelt in the country, and that he consistently

From *The Works of William James—Essays in Religion and Morality,* ed. Frederick Burkhardt (Cambridge, Mass.: Harvard University Press, 1982 [1903]) pp. 109–115.

declined to entangle himself with associations or to encumber himself with functions which, however he might believe in them, he felt were duties for other men and not for him. Even the care of his garden, "with its stoopings and fingerings in a few yards of space," he found "narrowing and poisoning," and took to long free walks and saunterings instead, without apology. "Causes" innumerable sought to enlist him as their "worker"—all got his smile and word of sympathy, but none entrapped him into service. The struggle against slavery itself, deeply as it appealed to him, found him firm: "God must govern his own world, and knows his way out of this pit without my desertion of my post, which has none to guard it but me. I have quite other slaves to free than those negroes, to wit, imprisoned thoughts far back in the brain of man, and which have no watchman or lover or defender but me." This in reply to the possible questions of his conscience. To hot-blooded moralists with more objective ideas of duty, such a fidelity to the limits of his genius must often have made him seem provokingly remote and unavailable; but we who can see things in more liberal perspective must unqualifiedly approve the results. The faultless tact with which he kept his safe limits while he so dauntlessly asserted himself within them is an example fitted to give heart to other theorists and artists the world over.

The insight and creed from which Emerson's life followed can be best summed up in his own verse:

> *"So nigh is grandeur to our dust,*
> *So near is God to man!"*

Through the individual fact there ever shone for him the effulgence of the Universal Reason. The great Cosmic Intellect terminates and houses itself in mortal men and passing hours. Each of us is an angle of its eternal vision, and the only way to be true to our Maker is to be loyal to ourselves. "O rich and various Man!" he cries, "thou palace of sight and sound, carrying in thy senses the morning and the night and the unfathomable galaxy; in thy brain, the geometry of the City of God; in thy heart, the bower of love and the realms of right and wrong."

If the individual open thus directly into the Absolute, it follows that there is something in each and all of us, even the lowliest, that ought not to consent to borrowing traditions and living at second hand. "If John was perfect, why are you and I alive?" writes Emerson. "As long as any man exists, there is some need of him; let him fight for his own." This faith that in a life at first hand there is something sacred is perhaps the most characteristic note in Emerson's writings. The hottest side of him is this non-conformist persuasion, and if his temper could ever verge on common irascibility, it would be by reason of the passionate character of his feelings on this point. The world is still new and untried. In seeing freshly, and not in hearing of what others saw, shall a man find what truth is. "Each one of us can bask in the great morning which rises out of the eastern sea, and be himself one of the children of the light." "Trust thyself: every heart vibrates to that iron string. . . . There is a time in every man's education when he arrives at the conviction that . . . imitation is suicide; that he must take himself for better or worse as his portion; and know that though the wide universe is full of good, no kernel of nourishing corn can come to him but through his toil bestowed on that plot of ground which is given to him to till."

The matchless eloquence with which Emerson proclaimed the sovereignty of the living individual electrified and emancipated his generation, and this bugle-blast will doubtless be regarded by future critics as the soul of his message. The present man is the aboriginal reality, the Institution is derivative, and the past man is irrelevant and obliterate for present issues. If anyone would lay an axe to your tree with a text from 1 John, v. 7, or a sentence from Saint Paul, say to him, Emerson wrote, " 'My tree is Ygdrasil—the tree of life.' . . . Let him know by your security that your conviction is clear and sufficient, and if he were Paul himself, that you also are here, and with your Creator." "Cleave ever to God," he insisted, "against the name of God";—and so, in spite of the intensely religious character of his total thought, when he began his career it seemed to many of his brethren in the clerical profession that he was little more than an iconoclast and desecrator.

Emerson's belief that the individual must in reason be adequate to the vocation for which the Spirit of the world has called him into being is the source of those sublime pages, hearteners and sustainers of our youth, in which he urges his hearers to be incorruptibly true to their own private conscience. Nothing can harm the man who rests in his appointed place and character. Such a man is invulnerable; he balances the universe, balances it as much by keeping small when he is small as by being great and spreading when he is great. "I love and honor Epaminondas," said Emerson, "but I do not wish to be Epaminondas. I hold it more just to love the world of this hour, than the world of his hour. Nor can you, if I am true, excite me to the least uneasiness by saying, 'He acted, and thou sittest still.' I see action to be good, when the need is, and sitting still to be also good. Epaminondas, if he was the man I take him for, would have sat still with joy and peace, if his lot had been mine. Heaven is large, and affords space for all modes of love and fortitude." "The fact that I am here certainly shows me that the soul had need of an organ here. Shall I not assume the post?"

The vanity of all super-serviceableness and pretense was never more happily set forth than by Emerson in the many passages in which he develops this aspect of his philosophy. Character infallibly proclaims itself. "Hide your thoughts! Hide the sun and moon. They publish themselves to the universe. They will speak through you though you were dumb. They will flow out of your actions, your manners, and your face. . . . Don't *say* things. What you *are* stands over you the while, and thunders so that I cannot hear what you say to the contrary. . . . What a man *is* engraves itself upon him in letters of light. Concealment avails him nothing; boasting nothing. There is confession in the glances of our eyes; in our smiles; in salutations; and the grasp of hands. His sin bedaubs him, mars all his good impression. Men know not why they do not trust him; but they do not trust him. His vice glasses his eye, cuts lines of mean expression in his cheek, pinches the nose, sets the mark of the beast on the back of the head, and writes O fool! fool! on the forehead of a king. If you would not be known to do any thing, never do it. A man may play the fool in the drifts of a desert, but every grain of sand shall seem to see. . . . How can a man be concealed! How can a man be concealed!"

On the other hand, never was a sincere word or a sincere thought utterly lost. "Never a magnanimity fell to the ground, but there is some heart to greet and accept it unexpectedly. . . . The hero fears not, that, if he withhold the avowal of a just and brave act, it will go unwitnessed and unloved. One knows it,—himself,—and is pledged by it to sweetness of peace, and to nobleness of aim, which will prove in the end a better proclamation than the relating of the incident."

The same indefeasible right to be exactly what one is, provided one only be authentic, spreads itself, in Emerson's way of thinking, from persons to things and to times and places. No date, no position is insignificant, if the life that fills it out be only genuine:—

"In solitude, in a remote village, the ardent youth loiters and mourns. With inflamed eye, in this sleeping wilderness, he has read the story of the Emperor Charles the Fifth, until his fancy has brought home to the surrounding woods, the faint roar of cannonades in the Milanese, and marches in Germany. He is curious concerning that man's day. What filled it? The crowded orders, the stern decisions, the foreign despatches, the Castilian etiquette? The soul answers— Behold his day here! In the sighing of these woods, in the quiet of these gray fields, in the cool breeze that sings out of these northern mountains; in the workmen, the boys, the maidens you meet,—in the hopes of the morning, the ennui of noon, and sauntering of the afternoon; in the disquieting comparisons; in the regrets at want of vigor; in the great idea, and the puny execution;—behold Charles the Fifth's day; another, yet the same; behold Chatham's, Hampden's,

Bayard's, Alfred's, Scipio's, Pericles's day,—day of all that are born of women. The difference of circumstance is merely costume. I am tasting the self-same life,—its sweetness, its greatness, its pain, which I so admire in other men. Do not foolishly ask of the inscrutable, obliterated past, what it cannot tell,—the details of that nature, of that day, called Byron, or Burke;—but ask it of the enveloping Now. . . . Be lord of a day, and you can put up your history books."

Thus does "the deep today which all men scorn" receive from Emerson superb revindication. "Other world! there is no other world." All God's life opens into the individual particular, and here and now, or nowhere, is reality. The present hour is the decisive hour, and every day is doomsday.

Such a conviction that Divinity is everywhere may easily make of one an optimist of the sentimental type that refuses to speak ill of anything. Emerson's drastic perception of differences kept him at the opposite pole from this weakness. After you have seen men a few times, he could say, you find most of them as alike as their barns and pantries, and soon as musty and as dreary. Never was such a fastidious lover of significance and distinction, and never an eye so keen for their discovery. His optimism had nothing in common with that indiscriminate hurrahing for the Universe with which Walt Whitman has made us familiar. For Emerson, the individual fact and moment were indeed suffused with absolute radiance, but it was upon a condition that saved the situation—they must be worthy specimens,—sincere, authentic, archetypal; they must have made connection with what he calls the Moral Sentiment, they must in some way act as symbolic mouthpieces of the Universe's meaning. To know just which thing does act in this way, and which thing fails to make the true connection, is the secret (somewhat incommunicable, it must be confessed) of seership, and doubtless we must not expect of the seer too rigorous a consistency. Emerson himself was a real seer. He could perceive the full squalor of the individual fact, but he could also see the transfiguration. He might easily have found himself saying of some present-day agitator against our Philippine conquest what he said of this or that reformer of his own time. He might have called him, as a private person, a tedious bore and canter. But he would infallibly have added what he then added: "It is strange and horrible to say this, . . . for I feel that under him and his partiality and exclusiveness is the earth and the sea and all that in them is, and the axis around which the universe revolves passes through his body where he stands."

Be it how it may, then, this is Emerson's revelation:—The point of any pen can be an epitome of reality; the commonest person's act, if genuinely actuated, can lay hold on eternity. This vision is the head-spring of all his outpourings; and it is for this truth, given to no previous literary artist to express in such penetratingly persuasive tones, that posterity will reckon him a prophet, and, perhaps neglecting other pages, piously turn to those that convey this message. His life was one long conversation with the invisible divine, expressing itself through individuals and particulars:—"So nigh is grandeur to our dust, so near is God to man!"

I spoke of how shrunken the wraith, how thin the echo, of men is after they are departed. Emerson's wraith comes to me now as if it were but the very voice of this victorious argument. His words to this effect are certain to be quoted and extracted more and more as time goes on, and to take their place among the Scriptures of humanity. "'Gainst death and all oblivious enmity shall you pace forth," beloved Master. As long as our English language lasts, men's hearts will be cheered and their souls strengthened and liberated by the noble and musical pages with which you have enriched it.

# The American Scholar

MR. PRESIDENT AND GENTLEMEN:

I greet you on the recommencement of our literary year. Our anniversary is one of hope, and, perhaps, not enough of labor. We do not meet for games of strength or skill, for the recitation of histories, tragedies, and odes, like the ancient Greeks; for parliaments of love and poesy, like the Troubadours; nor for the advancement of science, like our contemporaries in the British and European capitals. Thus far, our holiday has been simply a friendly sign of the survival of the love of letters amongst a people too busy to give to letters any more. As such it is precious as the sign of an indestructible instinct. Perhaps the time is already come when it ought to be, and will be, something else; when the sluggard intellect of this continent will look from under its iron lids and fill the postponed expectation of the world with something better than the exertions of mechanical skill. Our day of dependence, our long apprenticeship to the learning of other lands, draws to a close. The millions that around us are rushing into life, cannot always be fed on the sere remains of foreign harvests. Events, actions arise, that must be sung, that will sing themselves. Who can doubt that poetry will revive and lead in a new age, as the star in the constellation Harp, which now flames in our zenith, astronomers announce, shall one day be the pole-star for a thousand years?

In this hope I accept the topic which not only usage but the nature of our association seem to prescribe to this day—the AMERICAN SCHOLAR. Year by year we come up hither to read one more chapter of his biography. Let us inquire what light new days and events have thrown on his character and his hopes.

It is one of those fables which out of an unknown antiquity convey an unlooked-for wisdom, that the gods, in the beginning, divided Man into men, that he might be more helpful to himself; just as the hand was divided into fingers, the better to answer its end.

The old fable covers a doctrine ever new and sublime; that there is One Man—present to all particular men only partially, or through one faculty; and that you must take the whole society to find the whole man. Man is not a farmer, or a professor, or an engineer, but he is all. Man is priest, and scholar, and statesman, and producer, and soldier. In the *divided* or social state these functions are parceled out to individuals, each of whom aims to do his stint of the joint work, whilest each other performs his. The fable implies that the individual, to possess himself, must sometimes return from his own labor to embrace all the other laborers. But, unfortunately, this original unit, this fountain of power, has been so distributed to multitudes, has been so minutely subdivided and peddled out, that it is spilled into drops, and cannot be gathered. The state of society is one in which the members have suffered amputation from the trunk, and strut about so many walking monsters—a good finger, a neck, a stomach, an elbow, but never a man.

Man is thus metamorphosed into a thing, into many things. The planter, who is Man sent out into the field to gather food, is seldom cheered by any idea of the true dignity of his ministry. He sees his bushel and his cart, and nothing beyond, and sinks into the farmer, instead of Man on the farm. The tradesman scarcely ever gives an ideal worth to his work, but is ridden by the routine of his craft, and the soul is subject to dollars. The priest becomes a form; the attorney a statute-book; the mechanic a machine; the sailor a rope of the ship.

In this distribution of functions the scholar is the delegated intellect. In the right state he is *Man Thinking*. In the degenerate state, when the victim of society, he tends to become a mere thinker, or still worse, the parrot of other men's thinking.

From *Nature, Addresses, and Lectures,* Vol I, Centenary Edition (Boston: Houghton, Mifflin, and Company, (1904 [1837]), pp. 41–63.

In this view of him, as Man Thinking, the theory of his office is contained. Him Nature solicits with all her placid, all her monitory pictures; him the past instructs; him the future invites. Is not indeed every man a student, and do not all things exist for the student's behoof? And, finally, is not the true scholar the only true master? But the old oracle said, "All things have two handles; beware of the wrong one." In life, too often, the scholar errs with mankind and forfeits his privilege. Let us see him in his school, and consider him in reference to the main influences he receives.

I. The first in time and the first in importance of the influences upon the mind is that of nature. Every day, the sun; and, after sunset, Night and her stars. Ever the winds blow; ever the grass grows. Every day, men and women, conversing—beholding and beholden. The scholar is he of all men whom this spectacle most engages. He must settle its value in his mind. What is nature to him? There is never a beginning, there is never an end, to the inexplicable continuity of this web of God, but always circular power returning into itself. Therein it resembles his own spirit, whose beginning, whose ending, he never can find— so entire, so boundless. Far too as her splendors shine, system on system shooting like rays, upward, downward, without center, without circumference—in the mass and in the particle, Nature hastens to render account of herself to the mind. Classification begins. To the young mind every thing is individual, stands by itself. By and by, it finds how to join two things and see in them one nature; then three, then three thousand; and so, tyrannized over by its own unifying instinct, it goes on tying things together, diminishing anomalies, discovering roots running under ground whereby contrary and remote things cohere and flower out from one stem. It presently learns that since the dawn of history there has been a constant accumulation and classifying of facts. But what is classification but the perceiving that these objects are not chaotic, and are not foreign, but have a law which is also a law of the human mind? The astronomer discovers that geometry, a pure abstraction of the human mind, is the measure of planetary motion. The chemist finds proportions and intelligible method throughout matter; and science is nothing but the finding of analogy, identity, in the most remote parts. The ambitious soul sits down before each refractory fact; one after another reduces all strange constitutions, all new powers, to their class and their law, and goes on forever to animate the last fiber of organization, the outskirts of nature, by insight.

Thus to him, to this schoolboy under the bending dome of day, is suggested that he and it proceed from one root; one is leaf and one is flower; relation, sympathy, stirring in every vein. And what is that root? Is not that the soul of his soul? A thought too bold; a dream too wild. Yet when this spiritual light shall have revealed the law of more earthly natures— when he has learned to worship the soul, and to see that the natural philosophy that now is, is only the first gropings of its gigantic hand, he shall look forward to an ever expanding knowledge as to a becoming creator. He shall see that nature is the opposite of the soul, answering to it part for part. One is seal and one is print. Its beauty is the beauty of his own mind. Its laws are the laws of his own mind. Nature then becomes to him the measure of his attainments. So much of nature as he is ignorant of, so much of his own mind does he not yet possess. And, in fine, the ancient precept, "Know thyself," and the modern precept, "Study nature," become at last one maxim.

II. The next great influence into the spirit of the scholar is the mind of the Past—in whatever form, whether of literature, of art, of institutions, that mind is inscribed. Books are the best type of the influence of the past, and perhaps we shall get at the truth—learn the amount of this influence more conveniently— by considering their value alone.

The theory of books is noble. The scholar of the first age received into him the world around; brooded thereon; gave it the new arrangement of his own mind, and uttered it again. It came into him life; it went out from him truth. It came to him short-lived actions; it went out from him immortal thoughts. It came to him business; it went from him poetry. It was dead fact; now, it is quick thought. It can stand, and it can go. It now endures, it now flies, it now inspires. Precisely in proportion to the depth of mind from which it issued, so high does it soar, so long does it sing.

Or, I might say, it depends on how far the process had gone, of transmuting life into truth. In proportion to the completeness of the distillation, so will the purity and imperishableness of the product be. But none is quite perfect. As no air-pump can by any means make a perfect vacuum, so neither can any artist entirely exclude the conventional, the local, the perishable from his book, or write a book of pure thought, that shall be as efficient, in all respects, to a remote posterity, as to contemporaries, or rather to the second age. Each age, it is found, must write its own books; or rather, each generation for the next succeeding. The books of an older period will not fit this.

Yet hence arises a grave mischief. The sacredness which attaches to the act of creation, the act of thought, is transferred to the record. The poet chanting was felt to be a divine man henceforth the chant is divine also. The writer was a just and wise spirit: henceforward it is settled the book is perfect; as love of the hero corrupts into worship of his statue. Instantly the book becomes noxious: the guide is a tyrant. The sluggish and perverted mind of the multitude, slow to open to the incursions of Reason, having once so opened, having once received this book, stands upon it, and makes an outcry if it is disparaged. Colleges are built on it. Books are written on it by thinkers, not by Man Thinking; by men of talent, that is, who start wrong, who set out from accepted dogmas, not from their own sight of principles. Meek young men grow up in libraries, believing it their duty to accept the views which Cicero, which Locke, which Bacon, have given; forgetful that Cicero, Locke, and Bacon were only young men in libraries when they wrote these books.

Hence, instead of Man Thinking, we have the bookworm. Hence the book-learned class, who value books, as such; not as related to

nature and the human constitution, but as making a sort of Third Estate with the world and the soul. Hence the restorers of readings, the emendators, the bibliomaniacs of all degrees.

Books are the best of things, well used; abused, among the worst. What is the right use? What is the one end which all means go to effect? They are for nothing but to inspire. I had better never see a book than to be warped by its attraction clean out of my own orbit, and made a satellite instead of a system. The one thing in the world, of value, is the active soul. This every man is entitled to; this every man contains within him, although in almost all men obstructed and as yet unborn. The soul active sees absolute truth and utters truth, or creates. In this action it is genius; not the privilege of here and there a favorite, but the sound estate of every man. In its essence it is progressive. The book, the college, the school of art, the institution of any kind, stop with some past utterance of genius. This is good, say they—let us hold by this. They pin me down. They look backward and not forward. But genius looks forward: the eyes of man are set in his forehead, not in his hindhead: man hopes: genius creates. Whatever talents may be, if the man create not, the pure efflux of the Deity is not his;—cinders and smoke there may be, but not yet flame. There are creative manners, there are creative actions, and creative words; manners, actions, words, that is, indicative of no custom or authority, but springing spontaneous from the mind's own sense of good and fair.

On the other part, instead of being its own seer, let it receive from another mind its truth, though it were in torrents of light, without periods of solitude, inquest, and self-recovery, and a fatal disservice is done. Genius is always sufficiently the enemy of genius by over-influence. The literature of every nation bears me witness. The English dramatic poets have Shakspearized now for two hundred years.

Undoubtedly there is a right way of reading, so it be sternly subordinated. Man Thinking must not be subdued by his instruments. Books are for the scholar's idle times. When he can read God directly, the hour is too precious to be wasted in other men's transcripts of their readings. But when the intervals of darkness come, as come they must—when the sun is hid and the stars withdraw their shining—we repair to the lamps which were kindled by their way, to guide our steps to the East again, where the dawn is. We hear, that we may speak. The Arabian proverb says, "A fig tree, looking on a fig tree, becometh fruitful."

It is remarkable, the character of the pleasure we derive from the best books. They impress us with the conviction that one nature wrote and the same reads. We read the verses of one of the great English poets, of Chaucer, of Marvell, of Dryden, with the most modern joy—with a pleasure, I mean, which is in great part caused by the abstraction of all *time* from their verses. There is some awe mixed with the joy of our surprise, when this poet, who lived in some past world, two or three hundred years ago, says that which lies close to my own soul, that which I also had well-nigh thought and said. But for the evidence thence afforded to the philosophical doctrine of the identity of all minds, we should suppose some pre-established harmony, some foresight of souls that were to be, and some preparation of stores for their future wants, like the fact observed in insects, who lay up food before death for the young grub they shall never see.

I would not be hurried by any love of system, by any exaggeration of instincts, to underrate the Book. We all know, that as the human body can be nourished on any food, though it were boiled grass and the broth of shoes, so the human mind can be fed by any knowledge. And great and heroic men have existed who had almost no other information than by the printed page. I only would say that it needs a strong head to bear that diet. One must be an inventor to read well. As the proverb says, "He that would bring home the wealth of the Indies, must carry out the wealth of the Indies." There is then creative reading as well as creative writing. When the mind is braced by labor and invention, the page of whatever book we read becomes luminous with manifold allusion. Every sentence is dou-

bly significant, and the sense of our author is as broad as the world. We then see, what is always true, that as the seer's hour of vision is short and rare among heavy days and months, so is its record, perchance, the least part of his volume. The discerning will read, in his Plato or Shakspeare, only that least part— only the authentic utterances of the oracle;— all the rest he rejects, were it never so many times Plato's and Shakspeare's.

Of course there is a portion of reading quite indispensable to a wise man. History and exact science he must learn by laborious reading. Colleges, in like manner, have their indispensable office—to teach elements. But they can only highly serve us when they aim not to drill, but to create; when they gather from far every ray of various genius to their hospitable halls, and by the concentrated fires, set the hearts of their youth on flame. Thought and knowledge are natures in which apparatus and pretension avail nothing. Gowns and pecuniary foundations, though of towns of gold, can never countervail the least sentence or syllable of wit. Forget this, and our American colleges will recede in their public importance, whilst they grow richer every year.

III. There goes in the world a notion that the scholar should be a recluse, a valetudinarian—as unfit for any handiwork or public labor as a penknife for an axe. The so-called "practical men" sneer at speculative men, as if, because they speculate or *see,* they could do nothing. I have heard it said that the clergy— who are always, more universally than any other class, the scholars of their day—are addressed as women; that the rough, spontaneous conversation of men they do not hear, but only a mincing and diluted speech. They are often virtually disfranchised; and indeed there are advocates for their celibacy. As far as this is true of the studious classes, it is not just and wise. Action is with the scholar subordinate, but it is essential. Without it he is not yet man. Without it thought can never ripen into truth. Whilst the world hangs before the eye as a cloud of beauty, we cannot even see its beauty. Inaction is cowardice, but there can be no scholar without the heroic mind. The preamble of thought, the transition through which it passes from the unconscious to the conscious, is action. Only so much do I know, as I have lived. Instantly we know whose words are loaded with life, and whose not.

The world—this shadow of the soul, or *other me*—lies wide around. Its attractions are the keys which unlock my thoughts and make me acquainted with myself. I run eagerly into this resounding tumult. I grasp the hands of those next me, and take my place in the ring to suffer and to work, taught by an instinct that so shall the dumb abyss be vocal with speech. I pierce its order; I dissipate its fear; I dispose of it within the circuit of my expanding life. So much only of life as I know by experience, so much of the wilderness have I vanquished and planted, or so far have I extended my being, my dominion. I do not see how any man can afford, for the sake of his nerves and his nap, to spare any action in which he can partake. It is pearls and rubies to his discourse. Drudgery, calamity, exasperation, want, are instructors in eloquence and wisdom. The true scholar grudges every opportunity of action past by, as a loss of power. It is the raw material out of which the intellect molds her splendid products. A strange process too, this by which experience is converted into thought, as a mulberry leaf is converted into satin. The manufacture goes forward at all hours.

The actions and events of our childhood and youth are now matters of calmest observation. They lie like fair pictures in the air. Not so with our recent actions—with the business which we now have in hand. On this we are quite unable to speculate. Our affections as yet circulate through it. We no more feel or know it than we feel the feet, or the hand, or the brain of our body. The new deed is yet a part of life—remains for a time immersed in our unconscious life. In some contemplative hour it detaches itself from the life like a ripe fruit, to become a thought of the mind. Instantly it is raised, transfigured; the corruptible has put on incorruption. Henceforth it is an object of beauty, however base its origin and neighborhood. Observe too the impossibility of antedating this act. In its grub state, it cannot fly, it

cannot shine, it is a dull grub. But suddenly, without observation, the selfsame thing unfurls beautiful wings, and is an angel of wisdom. So is there no fact, no event, in our private history, which shall not, sooner or later, lose its adhesive, inert form, and astonish us by soaring from our body into the empyrean. Cradle and infancy, school and playground, the fear of boys, and dogs, and ferules, the love of little maids and berries, and many another fact that once filled the whole sky, are gone already; friend and relative, profession and party, town and country, nation and world, must also soar and sing.

Of course, he who has put forth his total strength in fit actions has the richest return of wisdom. I will not shut myself out of this globe of action, and transplant an oak into a flowerpot, there to hunger and pine; nor trust the revenue of some single faculty, and exhaust one vein of thought, much like those Savoyards, who, getting their livelihood by carving shepherds, shepherdesses, and smoking Dutchmen, for all Europe, went out one day to the mountain to find stock, and discovered that they had whittled up the last of their pine trees. Authors we have, in numbers, who have written out their vein, and who, moved by a commendable prudence, sail for Greece or Palestine, follow the trapper into the prairie, or ramble round Algiers, to replenish their merchantable stock.

If it were only for a vocabulary, the scholar would be covetous of action. Life is our dictionary. Years are well spent in country labors; in town; in the insight into trades and manufactures; in frank intercourse with many men and women; in science; in art; to the one end of mastering in all their facts a language by which to illustrate and embody our perceptions. I learn immediately from any speaker how much he has already lived, through the poverty or the splendor of his speech. Life lies behind us as the quarry from whence we get tiles and copestones for the masonry of to-day. This is the way to learn grammar. Colleges and books only copy the language which the field and the work-yard made.

But the final value of action, like that of books, and better than books, is that it is a resource. That great principle of Undulation in nature, that shows itself in the inspiring and expiring of the breath; in desire and satiety; in the ebb and flow of the sea; in day and night; in heat and cold; and, as yet more deeply ingrained in every atom and every fluid, is known to us under the name of Polarity—these "fits of easy transmission and reflection," as Newton called them, are the law of nature because they are the law of spirit.

The mind now thinks, now acts, and each fit reproduces the other. When the artist has exhausted his materials, when the fancy no longer paints, when thoughts are no longer apprehended and books are a weariness—he has always the resource *to live*. Character is higher than intellect. Thinking is the function. Living is the functionary. The stream retreats to its source. A great soul will be strong to live, as well as strong to think. Does he lack organ or medium to impart his truths? He can still fall back on this elemental force of living them. This is a total act. Thinking is a partial act. Let the grandeur of justice shine in his affairs. Let the beauty of affection cheer his lowly roof. Those "far from fame," who dwell and act with him, will feel the force of his constitution in the doings and passages of the day better than it can be measured by any public and designed display. Time shall teach him that the scholar loses no hour which the man lives. Herein he unfolds the sacred germ of his instinct, screened from influence. What is lost in seemliness is gained in strength. Not out of those on whom systems of education have exhausted their culture, comes the helpful giant to destroy the old or to build the new, but out of unhandselled savage nature; out of terrible Druids and Berserkers come at last Alfred and Shakspeare.

I hear therefore with joy whatever is beginning to be said of the dignity and necessity of labor to every citizen. There is virtue yet in the hoe and the spade, for learned as well as for unlearned hands. And labor is everywhere welcome; always we are invited to work; only be this limitation observed, that a man shall not for the sake of wider activity sacrifice any opinion to the popular judgments and modes of action.

I have now spoken of the education of the scholar by nature, by books, and by action. It remains to say somewhat of his duties.

They are such as become Man Thinking. They may all be comprised in self-trust. The office of the scholar is to cheer, to raise, and to guide men by showing them facts amidst appearances. He plies the slow, unhonored, and unpaid task of observation. Flamsteed and Herschel, in their glazed observatories, may catalogue the stars with the praise of all men, and the results being splendid and useful, honor is sure. But he, in his private observatory, cataloguing obscure and nebulous stars of the human mind, which as yet no man has thought of as such—watching days and months sometimes for a few facts; correcting still his old records;—must relinquish display and immediate fame. In the long period of his preparation he must betray often an ignorance and shiftlessness in popular arts, incurring the disdain of the able who shoulder him aside. Long he must stammer in his speech; often forego the living for the dead. Worse yet, he must accept—how often!—poverty and solitude. For the ease and pleasure of treading the old road, accepting the fashions, the education, the religion of society, he takes the cross of making his own, and, of course, the self-accusation, the faint heart, the frequent uncertainty and loss of time, which are the nettles and tangling vines in the way of the self-relying and self-directed; and the state of virtual hostility in which he seems to stand to society, and especially to educated society. For all this loss and scorn, what offset? He is to find consolation in exercising the highest functions of human nature. He is one who raises himself from private considerations and breathes and lives on public and illustrious thoughts. He is the world's eye. He is the world's heart. He is to resist the vulgar prosperity that retrogrades ever to barbarism, by preserving and communicating heroic sentiments, noble biographies, melodious verse, and the conclusions of history. Whatsoever oracles the human heart, in all emergencies, in all solemn hours, has uttered as its commentary on the world of actions—these he shall receive and impart. And whatsoever new verdict Reason from her inviolable seat pronounces on the passing men and events of today—this he shall hear and promulgate.

These being his functions, it becomes him to feel all confidence in himself, and to defer never to the popular cry. He and he only knows the world. The world of any moment is the merest appearance. Some great decorum, some fetish of a government, some ephemeral trade, or war, or man, is cried up by half mankind and cried down by the other half, as if all depended on this particular up or down. The odds are that the whole question is not worth the poorest thought which the scholar has lost in listening to the controversy. Let him not quit his belief that a popgun is a popgun, though the ancient and honorable of the earth affirm it to be the crack of doom. In silence, in steadiness, in severe abstraction, let him hold by himself; add observation to observation, patient of neglect, patient of reproach, and bide his own time—happy enough if he can satisfy himself alone that this day he has seen something truly. Success treads on every right step. For the instinct is sure, that prompts him to tell his brother what he thinks. He then learns that in going down into the secrets of his own mind he has descended into the secrets of all minds. He learns that he who has mastered any law in his private thoughts, is master to that extent of all men whose language he speaks, and of all into whose language his own can be translated. The poet, in utter solitude remembering his spontaneous thoughts and recording them, is found to have recorded that which men in crowded cities find true for them also. The orator distrusts at first the fitness of his frank confessions, his want of knowledge of the persons he addresses, until he finds that he is the complement of his hearers;—that they drink his words because he fulfills for them their own nature; the deeper he dives into his privatest, secretest presentiment, to his wonder he finds this is the most acceptable, most public, and

universally true. The people delight in it; the better part of every man feels, This is my music; this is myself.

In self-trust all the virtues are comprehended. Free should the scholar be—free and brave. Free even to the definition of freedom, "without any hindrance that does not arise out of his own constitution." Brave; for fear is a thing which a scholar by his very function puts behind him. Fear always springs from ignorance. It is a shame to him if his tranquillity, amid dangerous times, arise from the presumption that like children and women his is a protected class; or if he seek a temporary peace by the diversion of his thoughts from politics or vexed questions, hiding his head like an ostrich in the flowering bushes, peeping into microscopes, and turning rhymes, as a boy whistles to keep his courage up. So is the danger a danger still; so is the fear worse. Manlike let him turn and face it. Let him look into its eye and search its nature, inspect its origin—see the whelping of this lion—which lies no great way back; he will then find in himself a perfect comprehension of its nature and extent; he will have made his hands meet on the other side, and can henceforth defy it and pass on superior. The world is his who can see through its pretension. What deafness, what stoneblind custom, what overgrown error you behold is there only by sufferance—by your sufferance. See it to be a lie, and you have already dealt it its mortal blow.

Yes, we are the cowed—we the trustless. It is a mischievous notion that we are come late into nature; that the world was finished a long time ago. As the world was plastic and fluid in the hands of God, so it is ever to so much of his attributes as we bring to it. To ignorance and sin, it is flint. They adapt themselves to it as they may; but in proportion as a man has anything in him divine, the firmament flows before him and takes his signet and form. Not he is great who can alter matter, but he who can alter my state of mind. They are the kings of the world who give the color of their present thought to all nature and all art, and persuade men by the cheerful serenity of their carrying the matter, that this thing which they do is the apple which the ages have desired to pluck, now at last ripe, and inviting nations to the harvest. The great man makes the great thing. Wherever Macdonald sits, there is the head of the table. Linnaeus makes botany the most alluring of studies, and wins it from the farmer and the herb-woman; Davy, chemistry; and Cuvier, fossils. The day is always his who works in it with serenity and great aims. The unstable estimates of men crowd to him whose mind is filled with a truth, as the heaped waves of the Atlantic follow the moon.

For this self-trust, the reason is deeper than can be fathomed—darker than can be enlightened. I might not carry with me the feeling of my audience in stating my own belief. But I have already shown the ground of my hope, in adverting to the doctrine that man is one. I believe man has been wronged; he has wronged himself. He has almost lost the light that can lead him back to his prerogatives. Men are become of no account. Men in history, men in the world of to-day, are bugs, are spawn, and are called "the mass" and "the herd." In a century, in a millennium, one or two men; that is to say, one or two approximations to the right state of every man. All the rest behold in the hero or the poet their own green and crude being—ripened; yes, and are content to be less, so *that* may attain to its full stature. What a testimony, full of grandeur, full of pity, is borne to the demands of his own nature, by the poor clansman, the poor partisan, who rejoices in the glory of his chief. The poor and the low find some amends to their immense moral capacity, for their acquiescence in a political and social inferiority. They are content to be brushed like flies from the path of a great person, so that justice shall be done by him to that common nature which it is the dearest desire of all to see enlarged and glorified. They sun themselves in the great man's light, and feel it to be their own element. They cast the dignity of man from their down-trod selves upon the shoulders of a hero, and will perish to add one drop of blood to make that great heart beat, those giant sinews combat and conquer. He lives for us, and we live in him.

Men, such as they are, very naturally seek money or power; and power because it is as good as money—the "spoils," so called, "of office." And why not? for they aspire to the highest, and this in their sleep-walking they dream is highest. Wake them and they shall quit the false good and leap to the true, and leave governments to clerks and desks. This revolution is to be wrought by the gradual domestication of the idea of Culture. The main enterprise of the world for splendor, for extent, is the upbuilding of a man. Here are the materials strewn along the ground. The private life of one man shall be a more illustrious monarchy, more formidable to its enemy, more sweet and serene in its influence to its friend, than any kingdom in history. For a man, rightly viewed, comprehendeth the particular natures of all men. Each philosopher, each bard, each actor has only one for me, as by a delegate, what one day I can do for myself. The books which once we valued more than the apple of the eye, we have quite exhausted. What is that but saying that we have come up with the point of view which the universal mind took through the eyes of one scribe; we have been that man, and have passed on. First, one, then another, we drain all cisterns, and waxing greater by all these supplies, we crave a better and more abundant food. The man has ever lived that can feed us ever. The human mind cannot be enshrined in a person who shall set a barrier on any one side to this unbounded, unboundable empire. It is one central fire, which, flaming now out of the lips of Etna, lightens the capes of Sicily, and now out of the throat of Vesuvius, illuminates the towers and vineyards of Naples. It one light which beams out of a thousand stars. It is one soul which animates all men.

But I have dwelt perhaps tediously upon this abstraction of the Scholar. I ought not delay longer to add what I have to say of nearer reference to the time and to this country.

Historically, there is thought to be a difference in the ideas which predominate over successive epochs, and there are data for marking the genius of the Classic, of the Romantic, and now of the Reflective or Philosophical age. With the views I have intimated of the oneness or the identity of the mind through all individuals, I do not much dwell on these differences. In fact, I believe each individual passes through all three. The boy is a Greek; the youth, romantic; the adult, reflective. I deny not, however, that a revolution in the leading idea may be distinctly enough traced.

Our age is bewailed as the age of Introversion. Must that needs be evil? We, it seems, are critical; we are embarrassed with second thoughts; we cannot enjoy anything for hankering to know whereof the pleasure consists; we are lined with eyes; we see with our feet; the time is infected with Hamlet's unhappiness—

> "Sicklied o'er with the pale cast of thought."

It is so bad then? Sight is the last thing to be pitied. Would we be blind? Do we fear lest we should outsee nature and God, and drink truth dry? I look upon the discontent of the literary class as a mere announcement of the fact that they find themselves not in the state of mind of their fathers, and regret the coming state as untried; as a boy dreads the water before he has learned that he can swim. If there is any period one would desire to be born in, is it not the age of Revolution; when the old and the new stand side by side and admit of being compared; when the energies of all men are searched by fear and by hope; when the historic glories of the old can be compensated by the rich possibilities of the new era? This time, like all times, is a very good one, if we but know what to do with it.

I read with some joy of the auspicious signs of the coming days, as they glimmer already through poetry and art, through philosophy and science, through church and state.

One of these signs is the fact that the same movement which effected the elevation of what was called the lowest class in the state, assumed in literature a very marked and as benign an aspect. Instead of the sublime and beautiful, the near, the low, the common, was explored and poetized. That which had been negligently trodden under foot by those who were harnessing and provisioning themselves for long journeys into far countries, is suddenly found to be richer than all foreign parts. The literature of the poor, the feelings of the child, the philosophy of the street, the meaning of household life, are the topics of the time. It is a great stride. It is a sign—is it not?—of new vigor when the extremities are made active, when currents of warm life run into the hands and the feet. I ask not for the great, the remote, the romantic; what is doing in Italy or Arabia; what is Greek art, or Provençal minstrelsy; I embrace the common, I explore and sit at the feet of the familiar, the low. Give me insight into to-day, and you may have the antique and future worlds. What would we really know the meaning of? The meal in the firkin; the milk in the pan; the ballad in the street; the news of the boat; the glance of the eye; the form and the gait of the body;—show me the ultimate reason of these matters; show me the sublime presence of the highest spiritual cause lurking, as always it does lurk, in these suburbs and extremities of nature; let me see every trifle bristling with the polarity that ranges it instantly on an eternal law; and the shop, the plough, and the ledger referred to the like cause by which light undulates and poets sing;—and the world lies no longer a dull miscellany and lumber-room, but has form and order; there is no trifle, there is no puzzle, but one design unites and animates the farthest pinnacle and the lowest trench.

This idea has inspired the genius of Goldsmith, Burns, Cowper, and, in a newer time, of Goethe, Wordsworth, and Carlyle. This idea they have differently followed and with various success. In contrast with their writing, the style of Pope, of Johnson, of Gibbon, looks cold and pedantic. This writing is blood-warm. Man is surprised to find that things near are not less beautiful and wondrous than things remote. The near explains the far. The drop is a small ocean. A man is related to all nature. This perception of the worth of the vulgar is fruitful in discoveries. Goethe, in this very thing the most modern of the moderns, has shown us, as none ever did, the genius of the ancients.

There is one man of genius who has done much for this philosophy of life, whose literary value has never yet been rightly estimated;—I mean Emanuel Swedenborg. The most imaginative of men, yet writing with the precision of a mathematician, he endeavored to engraft a purely philosophical Ethics on the popular Christianity of his time. Such an attempt of course must have difficulty which no genius could surmount. But he saw and showed the connection between nature and the affections of the soul. He pierced the emblematic or spiritual character of the visible, audible, tangible world. Especially did his shade-loving muse hover over and interpret the lower parts of nature; he showed the mysterious bond that allies moral evil to the foul material forms, and has given in epical parables a theory of insanity, of beasts, of unclean and fearful things.

Another sign of our times, also marked by an analogous political movement, is the new importance given to the single person. Everything that tends to insulate the individual—to surround him with barriers of natural respect, so that each man shall feel the world is his, and man shall treat with man as a sovereign state with a sovereign state—tends to true union as well as greatness. "I learned," said the melancholy Pestalozzi, "that no man in God's wide earth is either willing or able to help any other man." Help must come from the bosom alone. The scholar is that man who must take up into himself all the ability of the time, all the contributions of the past, all the hopes of the future. He must be an university of knowledges. If there be one lesson more than another which should pierce his ear, it is, The world is nothing, the man is all; in yourself is the law of all nature, and you know not yet how a globule of sap ascends; in yourself slumbers the whole of Reason; it is for you to know all; it is for you to dare all. Mr. President and Gentlemen, this confidence in the unsearched might of man belongs, by all motives, by all prophecy, by all

preparation, to the American Scholar. We have listened too long to the courtly muses of Europe. The spirit of the American freeman is already suspected to be timid, imitative, tame. Public and private avarice make the air we breathe thick and fat. The scholar is decent, indolent, complaisant. See already the tragic consequence. The mind of this country, taught to aim at low objects, eats upon itself. There is no work for any but the decorous and the complaisant. Young men of the fairest promise, who begin life upon our shores, inflated by the mountain winds, shined upon by all the stars of God, find the earth below not in unison with these, but are hindered from action by the disgust which the principles on which business is managed inspire, and turn drudges, or die of disgust, some of them suicides. What is the remedy? They did not yet see, and thousands of young men as hopeful now crowding to the barriers for the career do not yet see, that if the single man plant himself indomitably on his instincts, and there abide, the huge world will come round to him. Patience—patience; with the shades of all the good and great for company; and for solace the perspective of your own infinite life; and for work the study and the communication of principles, the making those instincts prevalent, the conversion of the world. Is it not the chief disgrace in the world, not to be an unit;—not to be reckoned one character;—not to yield that peculiar fruit which each man was created to bear, but to be reckoned in the gross, in the hundred, or the thousand, of the party, the section, to which we belong; and our opinion predicted geographically, as the north, or the south? Not so, brothers and friends—please God, ours shall not be so. We will walk on our own feet; we will work with our own hands; we will speak our own minds. The study of letters shall be no longer a name for pity, for doubt, and for sensual indulgence. The dread of man and the love of man shall be a wall of defense and a wreath of joy around all. A nation of men will for the first time exist, because each believes himself inspired by the Divine Soul which also inspires all men.

# Self-Reliance

"Ne te quæsiveris extra." [Lest you have to search outside]

"Man is his own star; and the soul that can
Render an honest and a perfect man,
Commands all light, all influence, all fate;
   Nothing to him falls early or too late.
Our acts our angels are, or good or ill,
Our fatal shadows that walk by us still."
*       Epilogue to Beaumont and Fletcher's
       Honest Man's Fortune.*

Cast the bantling on the rocks,
Suckle him with the she-wolf's teat;
Wintered with the hawk and fox,
Power and speed be hands and feet.

I read the other day some verses written by an eminent painter which were original and not conventional. The soul always hears an admonition in such lines, let the subject be what it may. The sentiment they instil is of more value than any thought they may contain. To believe your own thought, to believe that what is true for you in your private heart is true for all men,—that is genius. Speak your latent conviction, and it shall be the universal sense; for the inmost in due time becomes the outmost,—and our first thought is rendered back to us by the trumpets of the Last Judgment. Familiar as the voice of the mind is to each, the highest merit we ascribe to Moses, Plato, and Milton is, that they set at naught books and traditions, and spoke not what men but what they thought. A man should learn to detect and watch that gleam of light which flashes across his mind from within, more than the lustre of the firmament of bards and sages. Yet he dismisses without notice his thought, because it is his. In every work of genius we recognize our own rejected thoughts: they come back to us with a certain alienated majesty. Great works of art have no more affecting lesson for us than this. They teach us to abide by our spontaneous impression with good-humored inflexibility then most when the whole cry of voices is on the other side. Else, tomorrow a stranger will say with masterly good sense precisely what we have thought and felt all the time, and we shall be forced to take with shame our own opinion from another.

There is a time in every man's education when he arrives at the conviction that envy is ignorance; that imitation is suicide; that he must take himself for better, for worse, as his portion; that though the wide universe is full of good, no kernel of nourishing corn can come to him but through his toil bestowed on that plot of ground which is given to him to till. The power which resides in him is new in nature, and none but he knows what that is which he can do nor does he know until he has tried. Not for nothing one face, one character, one fact, makes much impression on him, and another none. This sculpture in the memory is not without pre-established harmony. The eye was placed where one ray should fall, that it might testify of that particular ray. We but half express ourselves, and are ashamed of that divine idea which each of us represents. It may be safely trusted as proportionate and of good issues, so it be faithfully imparted, but God will not have his work made manifest by cowards. A man is relieved and gay when he has put his heart into his work and done his best; but what he has said or done otherwise, shall give him no peace. It is a deliverance which does not deliver. In the attempt his genius deserts him; no muse befriends; no invention, no hope.

Trust thyself: every heart vibrates to that iron string. Accept the place the divine providence has found for you, the society of your contemporaries, the connection of events.

From *Essays* (London: J. Fraser, 1841), pp. 82–111.

Great men have always done so, and confided themselves childlike to the genius of their age, betraying their perception that the absolutely trustworthy was seated at their heart, working through their hands, predominating in all their being. And we are now men, and must accept in the highest mind the same transcendent destiny; and not minors and invalids in a protected corner, not cowards fleeing before a revolution, but guides, redeemers, and benefactors, obeying the Almighty effort, and advancing on Chaos and the Dark.

What pretty oracles nature yields us on this text, in the face and behavior of children, babes, and even brutes! That divided and rebel mind, that distrust of a sentiment because our arithmetic has computed the strength and means opposed to our purpose, these have not. Their mind being whole, their eye is as yet unconquered, and when we look in their faces we are disconcerted. Infancy conforms to nobody: all conform to it, so that one babe commonly makes four or five out of the adults who prattle and play to it. So God has armed youth and puberty and manhood no less with its own piquancy and charm, and made it enviable and gracious and its claims not to be put by, if it will stand by itself. Do not think the youth has no force, because he cannot speak to you and me. Hark! in the next room his voice is sufficiently clear and emphatic. It seems he knows how to speak to his contemporaries. Bashful or bold, then, he will know how to make us seniors very unnecessary.

The nonchalance of boys who are sure of a dinner, and would disdain as much as a lord to do or say aught to conciliate one, is the healthy attitude of human nature. A boy is in the parlor what the pit is in the playhouse; independent, irresponsible, looking out from his corner on such people and facts as pass by, he tries and sentences them on their merits, in the swift, summary way of boys, as good, bad, interesting, silly, eloquent, troublesome. He cumbers himself never about consequences, about interests: he gives an independent, genuine verdict. You must court him: he does not court you. But the man is, as it were, clapped

into jail by his consciousness. As soon as he has once acted or spoken with eclat, he is a committed person, watched by the sympathy or the hatred of hundreds, whose affections must now enter into his account. There is no Lethe for this. Ah, that he could pass again into his neutrality! Who can thus avoid all pledges, and having observed, observe again from the same unaffected, unbiassed, unbribable, unaffrighted innocence, must always be formidable. He would utter opinions on all passing affairs, which being seen to be not private, but necessary, would sink like darts into the ear of men, and put them in fear.

These are the voices which we hear in solitude, but they grow faint and inaudible as we enter into the world. Society everywhere is in conspiracy against the manhood of every one of its members. Society is a joint-stock company, in which the members agree, for the better securing of his bread to each shareholder, to surrender the liberty and culture of the eater. The virtue in most request is conformity. Self-reliance is its aversion. It loves not realities and creators, but names and customs.

Whoso would be a man must be a nonconformist. He who would gather immortal palms must not be hindered by the name of goodness, but must explore if it be goodness. Nothing is at last sacred but the integrity of your own mind. Absolve you to yourself, and you shall have the suffrage of the world. I remember an answer which when quite young I was prompted to make a valued adviser, who was wont to importune me with the dear old doctrines of the church. On my saying, What have I to do with the sacredness of traditions, if I live wholly from within? my friend suggested: "But these impulses may be from below, not from above." I replied: "They do not seem to me to be such; but if I am the Devil's child, I will live then from the Devil." No law can be sacred to me but that of my nature. Good and bad are but names very readily transferable to that or this; the only right is what is after my constitution, the only wrong what is against it. A man is to carry himself in the presence of all opposition, as if everything were titular and ephemeral but he. I am ashamed to think how easily we capitulate to badges and names, to large societies and dead institutions. Every decent and well-spoken individual affects and sways me more than is right. I ought to go upright and vital, and speak the rude truth in all ways. If malice and vanity wear the coat of philanthropy, shall that pass? If an angry bigot assumes this bountiful cause of Abolition, and comes to me with his last news from Barbadoes, why should I not say to him: 'Go love thy infant; love thy wood-chopper: be good-natured and modest: have that grace; and never varnish your hard, uncharitable ambition with this incredible tenderness for black folk a thousand miles off. Thy love afar is spite at home.' Rough and graceless would be such greeting, but truth is handsomer than the affectation of love. Your goodness must have some edge to it,—else it is none. The doctrine of hatred must be preached as the counteraction of the doctrine of love when that pules and whines. I shun father and mother and wife and brother, when my genius calls me. I would write on the lintels of the door-post, *Whim*. I hope it is somewhat better than whim at last, but we cannot spend the day in explanation. Expect me not to show cause why I seek or why I exclude company. Then, again, do not tell me, as a good man did to-day, of my obligation to put all poor men in good situations. Are they *my* poor? I tell thee, thou foolish philanthropist, that I grudge the dollar, the dime, the cent, I give to such men as do not belong to me and to whom I do not belong. There is a class of persons to whom by all spiritual affinity I am bought and sold; for them I will go to prison, if need be; but your miscellaneous popular charities; the education at college of fools; the building of meeting-houses to the vain end to which many now stand; alms to sots; and the thousand-fold Relief Societies;—though I confess with shame I sometimes succumb and give the dollar, it is a wicked dollar which by and by I shall have the manhood to withhold.

Virtues are, in the popular estimate, rather the exception than the rule. There is the man *and* his virtues. Men do what is called a good action, as some piece of courage or charity, much as they would pay a fine in expiation of daily non-appearance on parade. Their works are done as an apology or extenuation of their living in the world,—as invalids and the insane pay a high board. Their virtues are penances. I do not wish to expiate, but to live. My life is for itself and not for a spectacle. I much prefer that it should be of a lower strain, so it be genuine and equal, than that it should be glittering and unsteady. I wish it to be sound and sweet, and not to need diet and bleeding. I ask primary evidence that you are a man, and refuse this appeal from the man to his actions. I know that for myself it makes no difference whether I do or forbear those actions which are reckoned excellent. I cannot consent to pay for a privilege where I have intrinsic right. Few and mean as my gifts may be, I actually am, and do not need for my own assurance or the assurance of my fellows any secondary testimony.

What I must do is all that concerns me, not what the people think. This rule, equally arduous in actual and in intellectual life, may serve for the whole distinction between greatness and meanness. It is the harder, because you will always find those who think they know what is your duty better than you know it. It is easy in the world to live after the world's opinion; it is easy in solitude to live after our own; but the great man is he who in the midst of the crowd keeps with perfect sweetness the independence of solitude.

The objection to conforming to usages that have become dead to you is, that it scatters your force. It loses your time and blurs the impression of your character. If you maintain a dead church, contribute to a dead Bible society, vote with a great party either for the government or against it, spread your table like base housekeepers,—under all these screens I have difficulty to detect the precise man you are. And, of course, so much force is withdrawn from your proper life. But do your work, and I shall know you. Do your work, and you shall reinforce yourself. A man must consider what a blind-man's-buff is this game of conformity. If I know your sect, I anticipate your argument. I hear a preacher announce for his text and topic the expediency of one of the institutions of his church. Do I not know before-hand that not possibly can he say a new and spontaneous word? Do I not know that, with all this ostentation of examining the grounds of the institution, he will do no such thing? Do I not know that he is pledged to himself not to look but at one side,—the permitted side, not as a man, but as a parish minister? He is a retained attorney, and these airs of the bench are the emptiest affectation. Well, most men have bound their eyes with one or another handkerchief, and attached themselves to some one of these communities of opinion. This conformity makes them not false in a few particulars, authors of a few lies, but false in all particulars. Their every truth is not quite true. Their two is not the real two, their four not the real four; so that every word they say chagrins us, and we know not where to begin to set them right. Meantime nature is not slow to equip us in the prison-uniform of the party to which we adhere. We come to wear one cut of face and figure, and acquire by degrees the gentlest asinine expression. There is a mortifying experience in particular, which does not fail to wreak itself also in the general history; I mean "the foolish face of praise," the forced smile which we put on in company where we do not feel at ease in answer to conversation which does not interest us. The muscles, not spontaneously moved, but moved by a low usurping wilfulness, grow tight about the outline of the face with the most disagreeable sensation.

For non-conformity the world whips you with its displeasure. And therefore a man must know how to estimate a sour face. The bystanders look askance on him in the public street or in the friend's parlor. If this aversation had its origin in contempt and resistance like his own, he might well go home with a sad countenance; but the sour faces of the multitude, like their sweet faces, have no deep cause, but are put on and off as the wind blows and a newspaper directs. Yet is the discontent of the multitude more formidable than that of the senate and the college. It is easy enough for a firm man who knows the world to brook the rage of the cultivated classes. Their rage is decorous and prudent, for they are timid as being very vulnerable themselves. But when to their feminine rage the indignation of the people is added, when the ignorant and the poor are aroused, when the unintelligent brute force that lies at the bottom of society is made to growl and mow, it needs the habit of magnanimity and religion to treat it godlike as a trifle of no concernment.

The other terror that scares us from self-trust is our consistency; a reverence for our past act or word, because the eyes of others have no other data for computing our orbit than our past acts, and we are loath to disappoint them.

But why should you keep your head over your shoulder? Why drag about this corpse of your memory, lest you contradict somewhat you have stated in this or that public place? Suppose you should contradict yourself; what then? It seems to be a rule of wisdom never to rely on your memory alone, scarcely even in acts of pure memory, but to bring the past for judgment into the thousand-eyed present, and live ever in a new day. In your metaphysics you have denied personality to the Deity: yet when the devout motions of the soul come, yield to them heart and life, though they should clothe God with shape and color. Leave your theory, as Joseph his coat in the hand of the harlot, and flee.

A foolish consistency is the hobgoblin of little minds, adored by little statesmen and philosophers and divines. With consistency a great soul has simply nothing to do. He may as well concern himself with his shadow on the wall. Speak what you think now in hard words and to-morrow speak what to-morrow thinks in hard words again, though it contradict everything you said to-day.—'Ah, so you shall be sure to be misunderstood?'—Is it so bad, then, to be misunderstood? Pythagoras was misunderstood, and Socrates, and Jesus, and Luther, and Copernicus, and Galileo, and Newton, and every pure and wise spirit that ever took flesh. To be great is to be misunderstood.

I suppose no man can violate his nature. All the sallies of his will are rounded in by the law of his being, as the inequalities of Andes and Himmaleh are insignificant in the curve of the sphere. Nor does it matter how you gauge and try him. A character is like an acrostic or Alexandrian stanza;—read it forward, backward, or across, it still spells the same thing. In this pleasing, contrite wood-life which God allows me, let me record day by day my honest thought without prospect or retrospect, and, I cannot doubt, it will be found symmetrical, though I mean it not and see it not. My book should smell of pines and resound with the hum of insects. The swallow over my window should interweave that thread or straw he carries in his bill into my web also. We pass for what we are. Character teaches above our wills. Men imagine that they communicate their virtue or vice only by overt actions, and do not see that virtue or vice emit a breath every moment.

There will be an agreement in whatever variety of actions, so they be each honest and natural in their hour. For of one will, the actions will be harmonious, however unlike they seem. These varieties are lost sight of at a little distance, at a little height of thought. One tendency unites them all. The voyage of the best ship is a zigzag line of a hundred tacks. See the line from a sufficient distance, and it straightens itself to the average tendency. Your genuine action will explain itself, and will explain your other genuine actions. Your conformity explains nothing. Act singly, and what you have already done singly will justify you now. Greatness appeals to the future. If I can be firm enough to-day to do right, and scorn eyes, I must have done so much right before as to defend me now. Be it how it will, do right now. Always scorn appearances, and you always may. The force of character is cumulative. All the foregone days of virtue work their health into this. What makes the majesty of the heroes of the senate and the field, which so fills the imagination? The consciousness of a train of great days and victories behind. They shed an united light on the advancing actor. He is attended as by a visible escort of angels. That is it which throws thunder into Chatham's voice, and dignity into Washington's port, and America into Adams's eye. Honor is venerable to us because it is no ephemeris. It is always ancient virtue. We worship it to-day because it is not of to-day. We love it and pay it homage, because it is not a trap for our love and homage, but is self-dependent, self-derived, and therefore of an old immaculate pedigree, even if shown in a young person.

I hope in these days we have heard the last of conformity and consistency. Let the words be gazetted and ridiculous henceforward. Instead of the gong for dinner, let us hear a whistle from the Spartan fife. Let us never bow and apologize more. A great man is coming to eat at my house. I do not wish to please him; I wish that he should wish to please me. I will stand here for humanity, and though I would make it kind, I would make it true. Let us affront and reprimand the smooth mediocrity and squalid contentment of the times, and hurl in the face of custom, and trade, and office, the fact which is the upshot of all history, that there is a great responsible Thinker and Actor working wherever a man works; that a true man belongs to no other time or place, but is the centre of things. Where he is, there is nature. He measures you, and all men, and all events. Ordinarily, everybody in society reminds us of somewhat else, or of some other person. Character, reality, reminds you of nothing else; it takes place of the whole creation. The man must be so much, that he must make all circumstances indifferent. Every true man is a cause, a country, and an age; requires infinite spaces and numbers and time fully to accomplish his design;—and posterity seems to follow his steps as a train of clients. A man Cæsar is born, and for ages after we have a Roman Empire. Christ is born, and millions of minds so grow and cleave to his genius, that he is confounded with virtue and the possible of man. An institution is the lengthened shadow of one man; as Monachism, of the Hermit Antony; the Reformation, of Luther; Quakerism, of Fox; Methodism, of Wesley; Abolition, of Clarkson. Scipio, Milton called "the height of Rome"; and all history resolves itself very easily into the biography of a few stout and earnest persons.

Let a man then know his worth, and keep things under his feet. Let him not peep or steal, or skulk up and down with the air of a charity-boy, a bastard, or an interloper, in the world which exists for him. But the man in the street, finding no worth in himself which corresponds to the force which built a tower or sculptured a marble god, feels poor when he looks on these. To him a palace, a statue, or a costly book have an alien and forbidding air, much like a gay equipage, and seems to say like that, 'Who are you, sir?' Yet they all are his suitors for his notice, petitioners to his faculties that they will come out and take possession. The picture waits for my verdict: it is not to command me, but I am to settle its claims to praise. That popular fable of the sot who was picked up dead drunk in the street, carried to the duke's house, washed and dressed and laid in the duke's bed, and, on his waking, treated with all obsequious ceremony like the duke, and assured that he had been insane, owes its popularity to the fact, that it symbolizes so well the state of man, who is in the world a sort of sot, but now and then wakes up, exercises his reason and finds himself a true prince.

Our reading is mendicant and sycophantic. In history, our imagination plays us false. Kingdom and lordship, power and estate, are a gaudier vocabulary than private John and Edward in a small house and common day's work; but the things of life are the same to both; the sum total of both are the same. Why all this deference to Alfred, and Scanderbeg, and Gustavus? Suppose they were virtuous; did they wear out virtue? As great a stake depends on your private act to-day, as followed their public and renowned steps. When private men shall act with original views, the lustre will be transferred from the actions of kings to those of gentlemen.

The world has been instructed by its kings, who have so magnetized the eyes of nations. It has been taught by this colossal symbol the mutual reverence that is due from man to man. The joyful loyalty with which men have everywhere suffered the king, the noble, or the great proprietor to walk among them by a law of his own, make his own scale of men and things and reverse theirs, pay for benefits not with money but with honor, and represent the law in his person, was the hieroglyphic by which they obscurely signified their consciousness of their own right and comeliness, the right of every man.

The magnetism which all original action exerts is explained when we inquire the reason of self-trust. Who is the Trustee? What is the aboriginal Self, on which a universal reliance may be grounded? What is the nature and power of that science-baffling star, without parallax, without calculable elements, which shoots a ray of beauty even into trivial and impure actions, if the least mark of independence appear? The inquiry leads us to that source, at once the essence of genius, of virtue, and of life; which we call Spontaneity or Instinct. We denote this primary wisdom as Intuition, whilst all later teachings are tuitions. In that deep force, the last fact behind which analysis cannot go, all things find their common origin. For, the sense of being which in calm hours rises, we know not how, in the soul, is not diverse from things, from space, from light, from time, from man, but one with them, and proceeds obviously from the same source whence their life and being also proceed. We first share the life by which things exist, and afterwards see them as appearances in nature, and forget that we have shared their cause. Here is the fountain of action and of thought. Here are the lungs of that inspiration which giveth man wisdom, and which cannot be denied without impiety and atheism. We lie in the lap of immense intelligence, which makes us receivers of its truth and organs of its activity. When we discern justice, when we discern truth, we do nothing of ourselves, but allow a passage to its beams. If we ask whence this comes, if we seek to pry into the soul that causes, all philosophy is at fault. Its presence or its absence is all we can affirm. Every man discriminates between the voluntary acts of his mind, and his involuntary perceptions, and knows that to his involuntary perceptions a perfect faith is due. He may err in the expression of them, but he knows that these things are so, like day and night, not to be disputed. My wilful actions and acquisitions are but roving;—the idlest revery, the faintest native emotion, command my curiosity and respect. Thoughtless people contradict as readily the statement of perceptions as of opinions, or rather much more readily; for, they do not distinguish between perception and notion. They fancy that I choose to see this or that thing. But perception is not whimsical, but fatal. If I see a trait, my children will see it after me, and in course of time, all mankind,—although it may chance that no one has seen it before me. For my perception of it is as much a fact as the sun.

The relations of the soul to the divine spirit are so pure, that it is profane to seek to interpose helps. It must be that when God speaketh he should communicate, not one thing, but all things; should fill the world with his voice; should scatter forth light, nature, time, souls, from the centre of the present thought; and new date and new create the whole. Whenever a mind is simple, and receives a divine wisdom, old things pass away,—means, teachers, texts, temples fall; it lives now, and absorbs past and future into the present hour. All things are made sacred by relation to it,—one as much as another. All things are dissolved to their centre by their cause, and, in the universal miracle, petty and particular miracles disappear. If, therefore, a man claims to know and speak of God, and carries you backward to the phraseology of some old mouldered nation in another country, in another world, believe him not. Is the acorn better than the oak which is its fulness and completion? Is the parent better than the child into whom he has cast his ripened being? Whence, then, this worship of the past? The centuries are conspirators against the sanity and authority of the soul. Time and space are but physiological colors which the eye makes, but the soul is light; where it is, is day; where it was, is night; and history is an impertinence and an injury, if it be anything more than a cheerful apologue or parable of my being and becoming.

Man is timid and apologetic; he is no longer upright; he dares not say 'I think,' 'I am,' but quotes some saint or sage. He is ashamed before the blade of grass or the blowing rose. These roses under my window make no reference to former roses or to better ones; they are for what they are; they exist with God to-day. There is no time to them. There is simply the rose; it is perfect in every moment of its existence. Before a leaf-bud has burst, its whole life acts; in the full-blown flower there is no more; in the leafless root there is no less. Its nature is satisfied, and it satisfies nature, in all moments alike. But man postpones or remembers; he does not live in the present, but with reverted eye laments the past, or, heedless of the riches that surround him, stands on tiptoe to foresee the future. He cannot be happy and strong until he too lives with nature in the present, above time.

This should be plain enough. Yet see what strong intellects dare not yet hear God himself, unless he speak the phraseology of I know not what David, or Jeremiah, or Paul. We shall not always set so great a price on a few texts, on a few lives. We are like children who repeat by rote the sentences of grandames and tutors, and, as they grow older, of the men of talents and character they chance to see,— painfully recollecting the exact words they spoke; afterwards, when they come into the point of view which those had who uttered these sayings, they understand them, and are willing to let the words go; for, at any time, they can use words as good when occasion comes. If we live truly, we shall see truly. It is as easy for the strong man to be strong, as it is for the weak to be weak. When we have new perception, we shall gladly disburden the memory of its hoarded treasures as old rubbish. When a man lives with God, his voice shall be as sweet as the murmur of the brook and the rustle of the corn.

And now at last the highest truth on this subject remains unsaid; probably cannot be said; for all that we say is the far-off remembering of the intuition. That thought, by what I can now nearest approach to say it, is this. When good is near you, when you have life in yourself, it is not by any known or accustomed way; you shall not discern the footprints of any other; you shall not see the face of man; you shall not hear any name; the way, the thought, the good, shall be wholly strange and new. It shall exclude example and experience. You take the way from man, not to man. All persons that ever existed are its forgotten ministers. Fear and hope are alike beneath it. There is somewhat low even in hope. In the hour of vision, there is nothing that can be called gratitude, nor properly joy. The soul raised over passion beholds identity and eternal causation, perceives the self-existence of Truth and Right, and calms itself with knowing that all things go well. Vast spaces of nature, the Atlantic Ocean, the South Sea,— long intervals of time, years, centuries,—are of no account. This which I think and feel underlay every former state of life and circumstances, as it does underlie my present, and what is called life, and what is called death.

Life only avails, not the having lived. Power ceases in the instant of repose; it resides in the moment of transition from a past to a new state, in the shooting of the gulf, in the darting to an aim. This one fact the world hates, that the soul *becomes;* for that forever degrades the past, turns all riches to poverty, all reputation to a shame, confounds the saint with the rogue, shoves Jesus and Judas equally aside. Why, then, do we prate of self-reliance? Inasmuch as the soul is present, there will be power not confident but agent. To talk of reliance is a poor external way of speaking. Speak rather of that which relies, because it works and is. Who has more obedience than I masters me, though he should not raise his finger. Round him I must revolve by the gravitation of spirits. We fancy it rhetoric, when we speak of eminent virtue. We do not yet see that virtue is Height, and that a man or a company of men, plastic and permeable to principles, by the law of nature must overpower and ride all cities, nations, kings, rich men, poets, who are not.

This is the ultimate fact which we so quickly reach on this, as on every topic, the resolution of all into the ever-blessed ONE. Self-existence is the attribute of the Supreme Cause, and it constitutes the measure of good by the degree in which it enters into all lower forms. All things real are so by so much virtue as they contain. Commerce, husbandry, hunting, whaling, war, eloquence, personal weight, are somewhat, and engage my respect as examples of its presence and impure action. I see the same law working in nature for conservation and growth. Power is in nature the essential measure of right. Nature suffers nothing to remain in her kingdoms which cannot help itself. The genesis and maturation of a planet, its poise and orbit, the bended tree recovering itself from the strong wind, the vital resources of every animal and vegetable, are demonstrations of the self-sufficing, and therefore self-relying soul.

Thus all concentrates: let us not rove; let us sit at home with the cause. Let us stun and astonish the intruding rabble of men and books and institutions, by a simple declaration of the divine fact. Bid the invaders take the shoes from off their feet, for God is here within. Let our simplicity judge them, and our docility to our own law demonstrate the poverty of nature and fortune beside our native riches.

But now we are a mob. Man does not stand in awe of man, nor is his genius admonished to stay at home, to put itself in communication with the internal ocean, but it goes abroad to beg a cup of water of the urns of other men. We must go alone. I like the silent church before the service begins, better than any preaching. How far off, how cool, how chaste the persons look, begirt each one with a precinct or sanctuary! So let us always sit. Why should we assume the faults of our friend, or wife, or father, or child, because they sit around our hearth, or are said to have the same blood? All men have my blood, and I have all men's. Not for that will I adopt their petulance or folly, even to the extent of being ashamed of it. But your isolation must not be mechanical, but spiritual, that is, must be elevation. At times the whole world seems to be in conspiracy to importune you with emphatic trifles. Friend, client, child, sickness, fear, want, charity, all knock at once at thy closet door, and say,

'Come out unto us.' But keep thy state; come not into their confusion. The power men possess to annoy me, I give them by a weak curiosity. No man can come near me but through my act. "What we love that we have, but by desire we bereave ourselves of the love."

If we cannot at once rise to the sanctities of obedience and faith, let us at least resist our temptations; let us enter into the state of war, and wake Thor and Woden, courage and constancy in our Saxon breasts. This is to be done in our smooth times by speaking the truth. Check this lying hospitality and lying affection. Live no longer to the expectation of these deceived and deceiving people with whom we converse. Say to them, 'O father, O mother, O wife, O brother, O friend, I have lived with you after appearances hitherto. Henceforward I am the truth's. Be it known unto you that henceforward I obey no law less than the eternal law. I will have no convenants but proximities. I shall endeavor to nourish my parents, to support my family, to be the chaste husband of one wife,—but these relations I must fill after a new and unprecedented way. I appeal from your customs. I must be myself. I cannot break myself any longer for you, or you. If you can love me for what I am, we shall be the happier. If you cannot, I will still seek to deserve that you should. I will not hide my tastes or aversions. I will so trust that what is deep is holy, that I will do strongly before the sun and moon whatever inly rejoices me, and the heart appoints. If you are noble, I will love you; if you are not, I will not hurt you and myself by hypocritical attentions. If you are true, but not in the same truth with me, cleave to your companions; I will seek my own. I do this not selfishly, but humbly and truly. It is alike your interest, and mine, and all men's, however long we have dwelt in lies, to live in truth. Does this sound harsh to-day? You will soon love what is dictated by your nature as well as mine, and, if we follow the truth, it will bring us out safe at last.' But so you may give these friends pain. Yes, but I cannot sell my liberty and my power, to save their sensibility. Besides, all persons have their moments of reason, when they look out into the region of absolute truth; then will they justify me, and do the same thing.

The populace think that your rejection of popular standards is a rejection of all standard, and mere antinomianism; and the bold sensualist will use the name of philosophy to gild his crimes. But the law of consciousness abides. There are two confessionals, in one or the other of which we must be shriven. You may fulfil your round of duties by clearing yourself in the *direct,* or in the *reflex* way. Consider whether you have satisfied your relations to father, mother, cousin, neighbor, town, cat, and dog; whether any of these can upbraid you. But I may also neglect this reflex standard, and absolve me to myself. I have my own stern claims and perfect circle. It denies the name of duty to many offices that are called duties. But if I can discharge its debts, it enables me to dispense with the popular code. If any one imagines that this law is lax, let him keep its commandment one day.

And truly it demands something godlike in him who has cast off the common motives of humanity, and has ventured to trust himself for a taskmaster. High be his heart, faithful his will, clear his sight, that he may in good earnest be doctrine, society, law, to himself, that a simple purpose may be to him as strong as iron necessity is to others!

If any man consider the present aspects of what is called by distinction *society,* he will see the need of these ethics. The sinew and heart of man seem to be drawn out, and we are become timorous, desponding whimperers. We are afraid of truth, afraid of fortune, afraid of death, and afraid of each other. Our age yields no great and perfect persons. We want men and women who shall renovate life and our social state, but we see that most natures are insolvent, cannot satisfy their own wants, have an ambition out of all proportion to their practical force, and do lean and beg day and night continually. Our housekeeping is mendicant, our arts, our occupations, our marriages, our religions, we have not chosen, but society has chosen for us. We are parlor soldiers. We shun the rugged battle of fate, where strength is born.

If our young men miscarry in their first enterprises, they lose all heart. If the young merchant fails, men say he is *ruined*. If the finest genius studies at one of our colleges, and is not installed in an office within one year afterwards in the cities or suburbs of Boston or New York, it seems to his friends and to himself that he is right in being disheartened, and in complaining the rest of his life. A sturdy lad from New Hampshire or Vermont, who in turn tries all the professions, who *teams it, farms it, peddles,* keeps a school, preaches, edits a newspaper, goes to Congress, buys a township, and so forth, in successive years, and always, like a cat, falls on his feet, is worth a hundred of these city dolls. He walks abreast with his days, and feels no shame in not 'studying a profession,' for he does not postpone his life, but lives already. He has not one chance, but a hundred chances. Let a Stoic open the resources of man, and tell men they are not leaning willows, but can and must detach themselves; that with the exercise of self-trust, new powers shall appear; that a man is the word made flesh, born to shed healing to the nations, that he should be ashamed of our compassion, and that the moment he acts from himself, tossing the laws, the books, idolatries, and customs out of the window, we pity him no more, but thank and revere him,—and that teacher shall restore the life of man to splendor, and make his name dear to all history.

It is easy to see that a greater self-reliance must work a revolution in all the offices and relations of men; in their religion; in their education; in their pursuits; their modes of living; their association; in their property; in their speculative views.

1. In what prayers do men allow themselves! That which they call a holy office is not so much as brave and manly. Prayer looks abroad and asks for some foreign addition to come through some foreign virtue, and loses itself in endless mazes of natural and supernatural, and mediatorial and miraculous. Prayer that craves a particular commodity,—anything less than all good,—is vicious. Prayer is the contemplation of the facts of life from the highest point of view. It is the soliloquy of a beholding and jubilant soul. It is the spirit of God pronouncing his works good. But prayer as a means to effect a private end is meanness and theft. It supposes dualism and not unity in nature and consciousness. As soon as the man is at one with God, he will not beg. He will then see prayer in all action. The prayer of the farmer kneeling in his field to weed it, the prayer of the rower kneeling with the stroke of his oar, are true prayers heard throughout nature though for cheap ends. Caratach, in Fletcher's Bonduca, when admonished to inquire the mind of the god Audate, replies,—

*"His hidden meaning lies in our endeavors;*
*Our valors are our best gods."*

Another sort of false prayers are our regrets. Discontent is the want of self-reliance: it is infirmity of will. Regret calamities, if you can thereby help the sufferer; if not, attend your own work, and already the evil begins to be repaired. Our sympathy is just as base. We come to them who weep foolishly, and sit down and cry for company, instead of imparting to them truth and health in rough electric shocks, putting them once more in communication with their own reason. The secret of fortune is joy in our hands. Welcome evermore to gods and men is the self-helping man. For him all doors are flung wide: him all tongues greet, all honors crown, all eyes follow with desire. Our love goes out to him and embraces him, because he did not need it. We solicitously and apologetically caress and celebrate him, because he held on his way and scorned our disapprobation. The gods love him because men hated him. "To the persevering mortal," said Zoroaster, "the blessed Immortals are swift."

As men's prayers are a disease of the will, so are their creeds a disease of the intellect. They say with those foolish Israelites, 'Let not God speak to us, lest we die. Speak thou, speak any man with us, and we will obey.' Everywhere I am hindered of meeting God in my brother, because he has shut his own temple doors, and recites fables merely of his brother's, or his brother's brother's God. Every new mind is a new classification. If it prove a mind of uncommon activity and power, a Locke, a Lavoisier, a Hutton, a Bentham, a Fourier, it imposes its classification on other men, and lo! a new system. In proportion to the depth of the thought, and so to the number of the objects it touches and brings within reach of the pupil, is his complacency. But chiefly is this apparent in creeds and churches, which are also classifications of some powerful mind acting on the elemental thought of duty, and man's relation to the Highest. Such is Calvinism, Quakerism, Swedenborgism. The pupil takes the same delight in subordinating everything to the new terminology, as a girl who has just learned botany in seeing a new earth and new seasons thereby. It will happen for a time, that the pupil will find his intellectual power has grown by the study of his master's mind. But in all unbalanced minds, the classification is idolized, passes for the end, and not for a speedily exhaustible means, so that the walls of the system blend to their eye in the remote horizon with the walls of the universe; the luminaries of heaven seem to them hung on the arch their master built. They cannot imagine how you aliens have any right to see,—how you can see; 'It must be somehow that you stole the light from us.' They do not yet perceive, that light, unsystematic, indomitable, will break into any cabin, even into theirs. Let them chirp awhile and call it their own. If they are honest and do well, presently their neat new pinfold will be too strait and low, will crack, will lean, will rot and vanish, and the immortal light, all young and joyful, million-orbed, million-colored, will beam over the universe as on the first morning.

2. It is for want of self-culture that the superstition of Travelling, whose idols are Italy, England, Egypt, retains its fascination for all educated Americans. They who made England, Italy, or Greece venerable in the imagination did so by sticking fast where they were, like an axis of the earth. In manly hours, we feel that duty is our place. The soul is no traveller; the wise man stays at home, and

when his necessities, his duties, on any occasion call him from his house, or into foreign lands, he is at home still, and shall make men sensible by the expression of his countenance, that he goes the missionary of wisdom and virtue, and visits cities and men like a sovereign, and not like an interloper or a valet.

I have no churlish objection to the circumnavigation of the globe, for the purposes of art, of study, and benevolence, so that the man is first domesticated, or does not go abroad with the hope of finding somewhat greater than he knows. He who travels to be amused, or to get somewhat which he does not carry, travels away from himself, and grows old even in youth among old things. In Thebes, in Palmyra, his will and mind have become old and dilapidated as they. He carries ruins to ruins.

Travelling is a fool's paradise. Our first journeys discover to us the indifference of places. At home I dream that at Naples, at Rome, I can be intoxicated with beauty, and lose my sadness. I pack my trunk, embrace my friends, embark on the sea, and at last wake up in Naples, and there beside me is the stern fact, the sad self, unrelenting, identical, that I fled from. I seek the Vatican, and the palaces. I affect to be intoxicated with sights and suggestions, but I am not intoxicated. My giant goes with me wherever I go.

3. But the rage of travelling is a symptom of a deeper unsoundness affecting the whole intellectual action. The intellect is vagabond, and our system of education fosters restlessness. Our minds travel when our bodies are forced to stay at home. We imitate; and what is imitation but the travelling of the mind? Our houses are built with foreign taste; our shelves are garnished with foreign ornaments; our opinions, our tastes, our faculties, lean, and follow the Past and the Distant. The soul created the arts wherever they have flourished. It was in his own mind that the artist sought his model. It was an application of his own thought to the thing to be done and the conditions to be observed. And why need we copy the Doric or the Gothic model? Beauty, convenience, grandeur of thought, and quaint

expression are as near to us as to any, and if the American artist will study with hope and love the precise thing to be done by him, considering the climate, the soil, the length of the day, the wants of the people, the habit and form of the government, he will create a house in which all these will find themselves fitted, and taste and sentiment will be satisfied also.

Insist on yourself; never imitate. Your own gift you can present every moment with the cumulative force of a whole life's cultivation; but of the adopted talent of another, you have only an extemporaneous, half possession. That which each can do best, none but his Maker can teach him. No man yet knows what it is, nor can, till that person has exhibited it. Where is the master who could have taught Shakespeare? Where is the master who could have instructed Franklin, or Washington, or Bacon, or Newton? Every great man is a unique. The Scipionism of Scipio is precisely that part he could not borrow. Shakespeare will never be made by the study of Shakespeare. Do that which is assigned you, and you cannot hope too much or dare too much. There is at this moment for you an utterance brave and grand as that of the colossal chisel of Phidias, or trowel of the Egyptians, or the pen of Moses, or Dante, but different from all these. Not possibly will the soul all rich, all eloquent, with thousand-cloven tongue, design to repeat itself; but if you can hear what these patriarchs say, surely you can reply to them in the same pitch of voice; for the ear and the tongue are two organs of one nature. Abide in the simple and noble regions of thy life, obey thy heart, and thou shalt reproduce the Foreworld again.

4. As our Religion, our Education, our Art look abroad, so does our spirit of society. All men plume themselves on the improvement of society, and no man improves.

Society never advances. It recedes as fast on one side as it gains on the other. It undergoes continual changes; it is barbarous, it is civilized, it is Christianized, it is rich, it is scientific; but this change is not amelioration. For everything that is given, something is taken. Society acquires new arts, and loses old instincts. What a contrast between the well-clad, reading, writing, thinking American, with a watch, a pencil, and a bill of exchange in his pocket, and the naked New Zealander, whose property is a club, a spear, a mat, and an undivided twentieth of a shed to sleep under! But compare the health of the two men, and you shall see that the white man has lost his aboriginal strength. If the traveller tell us truly, strike the savage with a broad axe, and in a day or two the flesh shall unite and heal as if you struck the blow into soft pitch, and the same blow shall send the white man to his grave.

The civilized man has built a coach, but has lost the use of his feet. He is supported on crutches, but lacks so much support of muscle. He has a fine Geneva watch, but he fails of the skill to tell the hour by the sun. A Greenwich nautical almanac he has, and so being sure of the information when he wants it, the man in the street does not know a star in the sky. The solstice he does not observe; the equinox he knows as little; and the whole bright calendar of the year is without a dial in his mind. His note-books impair his memory; his libraries overload his wit; the insurance office increases the number of accidents; and it may be a question whether machinery does not encumber; whether we have not lost by refinement some energy, by a Christianity intrenched in establishments and forms, some vigor of wild virtue. For every Stoic was a Stoic; but in Christendom where is the Christian?

There is no more deviation in the moral standard than in the standard of height or bulk. No greater men are now than ever were. A singular equality may be observed between the great men of the first and of the last ages; nor can all the science, art, religion, and philosophy of the nineteenth century avail to educate greater men than Plutarch's heroes, three or four and twenty centuries ago. Not in time is the race progressive. Phocion, Socrates, Anaxagoras, Diogenes, are great men, but they leave no class. He who is really of their class will not be called by their name, but will be his own man, and, in his turn, the founder of a sect. The arts and inventions of each period are only its costume, and do not invigorate men. The harm of the improved machinery may compensate its good. Hudson and Behring accomplished so much in their fishing-boats, as to astonish Parry and Franklin, whose equipment exhausted the resources of science and art. Galileo, with an opera-glass, discovered a more splendid series of celestial phenomena than any one since. Columbus found the New World in an undecked boat. It is curious to see the periodical disuse and perishing of means and machinery, which were introduced with loud laudation a few years or centuries before. The great genius returns to essential man. We reckoned the improvements of the art of war among the triumphs of science, and yet Napoleon conquered Europe by the bivouac, which consisted of falling back on naked valor, and disencumbering it of all aids. The Emperor held it impossible to make a perfect army, says Las Casas, "without abolishing our arms, magazines, commissaries, and carriages, until, in imitation of the Roman custom, the soldier should receive his supply of corn, grind it in his hand-mill, and bake his bread himself."

Society is a wave. The wave moves onward, but the water of which it is composed does not. The same particle does not rise from the valley to the ridge. Its unity is only phenomenal. The persons who make up a nation to-day, next year die, and their experience with them.

And so the reliance on Property, including the reliance on governments which protect it, is the want of self-reliance. Men have looked away from themselves and at things so long, that they have come to esteem the religious, learned, and civil institutions as guards of property, and they deprecate assaults on these, because they feel them to be assaults on property. They measure their esteem of each other by what each has, and not by what each is. But a cultivated man becomes ashamed of his property, out of new respect for his nature. Especially he hates what he has, if he see that it is accidental,—came to him by inheritance, or gift, or crime; then he feels that it is not having; it does not belong to him, has no root in him, and merely lies there, because no revolution or no robber takes it away. But that which a man is does always by necessity acquire, and what the man acquires is living property,

which does not wait the beck of rulers, or mobs, or revolutions, or fire, or storm, or bankruptcies, but perpetually renews itself wherever the man breathes. "Thy lot or portion of life," said the Caliph Ali, "is seeking after thee; therefore be at rest from seeking after it." Our dependence on these foreign goods leads us to our slavish respect for numbers. The political parties meet in numerous conventions; the greater the concourse, and with each new uproar of announcement, The delegation from Essex! The Democrats from New Hampshire! The Whigs of Maine! the young patriot feels himself stronger than before by a new thousand of eyes and arms. In like manner the reformers summon conventions, and vote and resolve in multitude. Not so, O friends, will the God deign to enter and inhabit you, but by a method precisely the reverse. It is only as a man puts off all foreign support, and stands alone, that I see him to be strong and to prevail. He is weaker by every recruit to his banner. Is not a man better than a town? Ask nothing of men, and in the endless mutation, thou only firm column must presently appear the upholder of all that surrounds thee. He who knows that power is inborn, that he is weak because he has looked for good out of him and elsewhere, and so perceiving, throws himself unhesitatingly on his thought, instantly rights himself, stands in the erect position, commands his limbs, works miracles; just as a man who stands on his feet is stronger than a man who stands on his head.

So use all that is called Fortune. Most men gamble with her, and gain all, and lose all, as her wheel rolls. But do thou leave as unlawful these winnings, and deal with Cause and Effect, the chancellors of God. In the Will work and acquire, and thou hast chained the wheel of Chance, and shalt sit hereafter out of fear from her rotations. A political victory, a rise of rents, the recovery of your sick, or the return of your absent friend, or some other favorable event, raises your spirits, and you think good days are preparing for you. Do not believe it. Nothing can bring you peace but yourself. Nothing can bring you peace but the triumph of principles.

## *Suggestions for Further Reading*

### Works by Emerson

*Collected Poems and Translations* (New York: Penguin Books, 1994).

*The Collected Works of Ralph Waldo Emerson* (Cambridge, Mass.: Belknap Press, Harvard University Press, 1971).

*The Complete Sermons of Ralph Waldo Emerson* (Columbia, Mo.: University of Missouri Press, 1989–92).

*The Complete Works,* Centenary Edition (Boston: Houghton, Mifflin and Company, 1903–4).

*The Letters of Ralph Waldo Emerson* (New York: Columbia University Press, 1959).

### Anthologies

*Emerson: A Modern Anthology,* eds. A. Kazin and D. Aaron (Boston: Houghton, Mifflin and Company, 1959).

*The Portable Emerson,* ed. C. Bode and M. Cowley (New York: Viking Press, 1981).

*Selected Writings of Emerson,* ed. D. McQuade (New York: Random House, 1981).

### Essential Works on Emerson

Evelyn Barish, *Emerson: The Roots of Prophecy* (Princeton, N.J.: Princeton University Press, 1989).

Mark Bauerlein, *The Pragmatic Mind: Explorations in the Psychology of Belief* (Durham, N.C.: Duke University Press, 1997).

Van Wyck Brooks, *The Life of Emerson* (New York: Dutton, 1932).

Russell Goodman, *American Philosophy and the Romantic Tradition* (New York: Cambridge University Press, 1990).

Milton R. Konitz and Stephen E. Whichler, eds., *Emerson: A Collection of Critical Essays* (Englewood Cliffs, N.J.: Prentice Hall, 1962).

F. O. Mathiessen, *American Renaissance: Art and Expression in the Age of Emerson and Whitman* (New York: Oxford University Press, 1968).

Perry Miller, *The Transcendentalists* (Cambridge, Mass.: Harvard University Press, 1950).

Richard Poirier, *Poetry and Pragmatism* (Cambridge, Mass.: Harvard University Press, 1992).

George Santayana, *Interpretations of Poetry and Religion* (New York: Charles Scribner's Sons, 1990).

Cornel West, *The American Evasion of Philosophy* (Madison, Wisc.: University of Wisconsin Press, 1989).

# PART II
# CLASSICAL AMERICAN PHILOSOPHY

# CHARLES SANDERS PEIRCE

## Introduction by Vincent Colapietro

### Peirce's Life: Cultural Context and Philosophical Background

Charles Sanders Peirce was born on September 13, 1839, the second child of Benjamin Peirce and Sarah Hunt Mills Peirce. Benjamin, a major influence on his son's intellectual development, taught mathematics and physics at Harvard. Charles graduated from Harvard College in 1859, the year in which the cultural shock waves of Charles Darwin's *Origin of Species* were first felt (and the year in which John Dewey, Henri Bergson, and Edmund Husserl were born). Shortly after graduation, Peirce went to "the wilds of Louisiana," where he was engaged in biological research as part of a team organized by Louis Agassiz. Upon his return, he again studied at Harvard, receiving an M.A. in 1862 and, a year later, a B.S. *summa cum laude* from the newly founded Lawrence Scientific School at Harvard. Often listing his occupation as chemist, he was always proud to identify himself as a scientist, and indeed worked as a scientist, both at the Harvard Observatory and the U.S. Coast and Geodetic Survey. In 1862, even before finishing his scientific training, he married Harriet Melusina (Zina) Fay. They were officially divorced twenty years later, but lived apart for most of their "marriage." Almost immediately upon his divorce from Zina, Peirce married Juliette Pourtalai, a French woman about whom not much is known even now. From 1879 until his abrupt dismissal in 1884, he lectured at Johns Hopkins University, where he attracted a small group of very able students. Earlier (1865–66 and 1869–70) he had secured temporary lectureships at Harvard in logic.

In 1887, upon the death of his mother (his father had died in 1882), he received his family inheritance and, shortly afterwards, another small bequest came from one of his aunts. He invested this money in a home in Milford, PA, which he called Arisbe after the region to which ancient cosmological speculation of an embryonically scientific character can be traced. He also speculated in other pieces of real estate, but in 1893 was devastated financially—and emotionally—by the most severe economic depression in the history of the United States. Because he was forced in 1891 to resign from the U.S. Coast and Geodetic Survey, his only source of a steady income, this imposed an especially great hardship. In his last years, while suffering severely from cancer, he was forced to rely on the charity of friends (including the largesse of William James) to purchase the bare necessities. For the last twenty years of his life, from the crash in 1893 until his death on April 19, 1914, he lived a progressively secluded and impoverished life in a home which had fallen into disrepair and was never completed in its original design (a symbol of so many of Peirce's intellectual projects).

Even so, his death did receive public notice. To the editor of *The Nation,* a publication to which Peirce had contributed numerous pieces, Joseph Jastrow expressed his "desire to record a word of tribute to one of the master minds of America."[1] He went on to note that: "The recent death of Charles S. Peirce removes a heroic figure from the field of American learning. Living for the most part in retirement, he was known to a relatively small circle. Yet where known, his name was spoken with exalted respect . . ." He concluded by suggesting that Peirce's "memory invites not only the personal tribute, but is a reminder of our neglect of the true worth of genius" (CN: III, 306). But one of Peirce's own nephews wrote on an obituary clipped from a Boston newspaper that his uncle "loved & hated and quarreled with almost everyone he came in contact with, wives, relatives, & associates."[2] This side of Peirce's character was something to which even one of the public notices of his death alluded: "A man at once of extraordinary acumen and originality, and of a phenomenal range of intellectual interests, there was in Charles Peirce a vein of the erratic, perhaps one may say the unstable, which seems to account for his achievements having fallen far short of what might have been expected of his unquestionably splendid powers" (CN III, 304).

Outwardly, then, Peirce's life stands in marked contrast to the lives of William James and John Dewey. The two later pragmatists attained in their own lifetime international fame, whereas Peirce has for the most part achieved such fame only posthumously. James at Harvard and Dewey at Chicago and Columbia secured for themselves an institutional home, whereas Peirce was dismissed in his fifth year from his lectureship at the newly founded Johns Hopkins University. Both James and Dewey published books in which the outlines of their positions were broadly sketched and the details finely elaborated, while Peirce, despite numerous articles, published only one book, *Photometric Researches* (1878), or two if one counts *Studies in Logic* (1883), the volume of mostly students papers which he edited while at Johns Hopkins. Obviously, neither the scope nor depth of Peirce's thought are conveyed by these books. In its published form, his thought was most fully articulated in several series of articles, chronologically separated. James pitted himself against Hegel and never tired of attacking the Absolute; and while Dewey developed an empirical naturalism far removed from Hegelian idealism, Peirce in the end confessed his own affinity to the Hegelianism he had for years so strenuously denounced. "My own philosophy," he wrote, "resuscitates Hegel, though in a strange costume" (1.42).[3] Though he, like James, suffered from a severe emotional crisis in early adulthood, Peirce's preoccupations, unlike James, were not principally existential. Though he, like Dewey, was finely attuned to the radical social and economic transformations being wrought by late modernity, Peirce had, unlike Dewey, only a secondary interest in political and economic institutions.

Peirce was concerned, first and foremost, with advancing the cause of inquiry. His interest in the logic and history of science needs to be seen as an expression of this concern, and his understanding of science itself needs to be understood in an inclusive and vital sense (a sense inclusive of philosophy). His work *as a philosopher* was one with his interest in the history and logic of science, for he was concerned to show how philosophical reflection might make a significant contribution to the ongoing work of scientific inquiry. He certainly was aware that science is not the whole of life, and that much outside of science is precious, even more precious than much of what is embodied in, or revealed by, the practice of science itself. But he believed that a strict division of intellectual labor, by which the boundaries of those practices aiming at the disclosure of truth could be demarcated from those practices animated by other concerns, was desirable. As a laboratory-trained investigator, he was especially concerned with rescuing philosophical reflection from seminary-trained thinkers—and also wresting it from literary clutches! In this he proved himself to be a typically *modern* philosopher, though one in other respects deeply at odds with philosophical modernity.

## Peirce's Critique of Cartesianism

René Descartes is acknowledged by virtually everyone to be the father of modern European philosophy. Richard J. Bernstein has wittily remarked that if Descartes is to be taken as the father of modern European philosophy, "this title can best be understood in a Freudian sense." Within modern philosophy, especially during its later phases (including the classical period of American philosophy), the offspring of Descartes "have sought to overthrow and dethrone the father."[4] This is manifestly true of Peirce.

Indeed, Peirce's critique of Cartesianism is of great importance for understanding not only his philosophical development but also his final outlook. But we miss the importance of this critique if we conceive its target too narrowly. Many of the claims regarding the nature of consciousness and foundations of knowledge that Peirce attacked were claims found in classical British empiricism as well as modern European rationalism. So, Peirce did not think that he was contesting only a single tradition within modern philosophy. He thought he was offering a radical critique of philosophical modernity *in its entirety*.

Thus, like Descartes himself, Peirce *revolted* against an inherited outlook. Yet even the youthful Peirce was reluctant to pride himself on being a rebel. Indeed, he took the modern tendency of self-celebrating rebelliousness as part of what needed to be overcome. The spirit of rebellion and opposition undeniably has an indispensable role within any vital community of honest inquirers, but it must operate *within* such a community and not underwrite the pretensions of individuals who, narrowly shut up within themselves, presume to be the ultimate arbiters of intellectual disputes. Moreover, the boundaries of such communities must not be narrowly drawn; they must be conceived as including our intellectual ancestors as well as successors. Originality is not to be valued for its own sake, at least in the context of inquiry. The value of doubt, of calling into question what has not been questioned thus far, is itself beyond doubt; but it is a double illusion to suppose that (1) we can simultaneously call everything into question and (2) having done so, can establish some truth once and for all. As doubters, we can profitably go into the retail business, but are destined to bankrupt ourselves by trying to erect a wholesale outlet. As knowers, the quest for apodictic certainty can pave the way only to an enervating scepticism. Originality, opposition, doubt, certainty, clarity—as important as each one of these is— must be historically contextualized, seen as integral parts of an ongoing tradition of shared human inquiry. When individuals presume to possess, *within themselves* and *apart from others,* the cognitive ability to make absolute pronouncements, then originality, opposition, doubt, and certainty take on an extreme, unwarranted form. It does not matter whether such pronouncements take the form of absolute denial (e.g., that there is *no* possibility of human beings ever knowing anything at all) or absolute assertion ("I think, and in the act of thinking am absolutely assured of my own existence"); what matters rather is that the isolated knower mistakenly presumes to be in possession of such absolute power.

As one who had not yet himself grown old, Peirce noted that: "Descartes marks the period when Philosophy put off childish things and began to be a conceited young man. By the time the young man has grown to be an old man, he will have learned that traditions are precious treasures, while iconoclastic inventions are always cheap and often nasty" (CP 4.71). The all too powerful, because all too unrecognized, tradition of anti-traditionalism needed to be exposed for what it was: a self-concealed tradition and mixed blessing (mixed because while it encourages individuality in theory, it undermines in practice its possibilities).

In connection with Peirce's desired reformation of philosophy, two somewhat technical points need to be treated. The first concerns the critique of what has come to be called *foundationalism;* the second concerns what Peirce himself called *semeiotic* (his name for the general theory of signs).[5]

*Foundationalism.* In his effort to vanquish scepticism once and for all, Descartes sought to secure unshakable *foundations* upon which an elaborate edifice of human knowledge could be constructed. He believed that he had secured such foundations, first, with the absolute certainty of his own existence and, then, with the equally certain demonstrations of God's existence (an all-perfect being who would not be a deceiver nor even allow for human beings to be deceived, provided that they were sufficiently circumspect in their judgments—i.e., provided that they used Descartes' own method!). Most readers of Descartes, however, find his proofs for God's existence less than compelling (though he intended them as demonstrative, or knock-down, arguments). More importantly, the principal weapon by which Descartes believed himself to have defeated scepticism—*Cogito, ergo sum*—was purchased at an extremely high price: the cost of the Cartesian thinker's own embodied existence. For the being who triumphs over scepticism in the *Meditations* is one without hands or feet, head or genitalia, arms or legs. Descartes is quite explicit on this point: When he asserts that he knows with absolute certainty *that* he exists, he also acknowledges that he does not yet know *what* he is. In the course of doubting everything, he has lost his world and his body along with it, but not his mind, at least not as something self-enclosed and self-possessed and able to take possession of its own contents and control of its own judgments. Is it possible to lose one's world and even one's own body without losing one's mind? Here is a difference that divides Cartesians and pragmatists, for the pragmatist says "No" while the Cartesian answers "Yes." Descartes explicitly rules out, at the early stage of his efforts to recoup his world, that he knows with sufficient certainty that there is any intimate connection between his triumphant consciousness and the animal body with which, prior to the process of doubt, he identified himself. The "I" standing with its foot upon the throat of the sceptic, alas, turns out to be a being without feet: *It* (since Descartes' self at this point in his *Meditations* also lacks genitalia and any stable habits encoding the cultural responses called forth by genitalia and other biological markers of human sexuality, *it* seems more appropriate than *he*) is assured of its existence only as an unsituated, disembodied consciousness (allegedly) capable of entertaining radical doubts and, even in the midst of such doubts, making at least one absolute assertion (I exist).

The Peircean critique of this Cartesian foundationalism operates on two levels. *On the first level,* Peirce denies that individual consciousness could ever provide unshakable foundations for human knowledge. Peirce seems to offer his critique as much on moral as on theoretical grounds, for he stresses that "to make single individuals absolute judges of truth is most *pernicious*" (CP 5.265; emphasis added). In addition, it is possible to observe, throughout human history, efforts to establish an infallible authority. The authority of sacred scripture and, derived from this, the authority of those entrusted with interpreting the true meaning of these writings are two examples of such purported authority. Part of Peirce's critique of modernity is, however, that the shift from scholastic to Cartesian philosophy is too small: The traditional notion of infallible authority has not been jettisoned, simply internalized. Hence, Peirce asks: "Now, what if our internal authority should meet the same fate, in the history of opinions, as that external authority has met?" (CP 5.215). In fact, he supposed that he and his contemporaries were witnessing just this fate.

We do not need to choose between apodictic certainty and wholesale scepticism. Grant that our knowledge of anything whatsoever, including our own feelings, is exceedingly fallible. Nonetheless, "there is a world of difference between fallible knowledge and no knowledge at all" (CP 1.37). In fact, scepticism is simply the shadow cast by the fantastic requirement that absolute certitude is a defining feature of human knowledge. The sceptic is, in other words, the inconsolably disappointed infallibilist. Human knowers are obviously fallible beings; nonetheless, such beings are capable of constructing more or less accurate and, thus, reliable maps of their world. For the fulfillment of our purposes, then, not all opinions are equal. Though human knowers are never anything more than fallible cartographers, some of their maps are remarkably intricate and reliable. To deny the possibility of knowing anything at all, *because* there is not anything which can be known with complete certainty, seems an excessive reaction to what is after all an infantile demand. We actually do know countless things about ourselves and our world, and any philosophy which would convict us of ignorance, simply by exposing the uncertainty inherent in our most securely established hypotheses, discredits not us but itself. "A person may, it is true, in the course of his studies, find reason to doubt what he began by believing; but in that case he doubts because he has a positive reason for it, and not on account of the Cartesian maxim. Let us not pretend to doubt in philosophy what we do not doubt in our hearts" (CP 5.265). From these considerations, it should be clear why Peirce came to call his position regarding knowledge by the name of "fallibilism" and identified himself as a "critical commonsensist."

At one level, then, the Peircean critique of Cartesian foundationalism focuses on the insufficiency of consciousness to provide a foundation of knowledge. *At a second and deeper level,* it calls into question the aptness of the metaphor controlling the Cartesian understanding of knowledge.[6] The construction of a map suggests trips to be taken (perhaps to parts which have not yet been mapped, to places beginning where our maps leave off), whereas the drawing of a blueprint or floorplan suggests an edifice to be built. Houses and other buildings clearly require foundations. Is it equally clear that human knowledge is sufficiently like an architectural structure that it too needs to rest upon something?

If the metaphor of foundations is rejected or seen to be quite limited, then the emphasis shifts. It shifts *from* securing indubitable starting points for our cognitive quests *to* devising, *in medias res,* the means by which we might in the course of our own exertions detect and correct errors of various sorts. That is, the emphasis shifts *from* identifying self-certifying intuitions *to* crafting self-corrective methods. It does not matter whether these intuitions take the form of the intellectual principles championed by the rationalists or forwarded by the so-called empiricists; what matters is simply the claim that there must be self-warranting intuitions, of whatever form. Peirce shrewdly begins his critique of Cartesianism by asking, how these intuitions are themselves known, intuitively or only by reliance on mediating factors or signs? He concludes that, even if there are intuitions, they can never be intuitively known as such. This is the wedge to open a crack in Cartesianism.

Corrigibility comes to be seen as a condition of knowledge; and *actual* mistakes can be seen as being of the utmost value in inquiry earnestly undertaken, rather than abstractly discussed. What is crucial is not where we commence; nor in a sense even where we conclude. What is crucial is rather *how* we proceed, how we comport ourselves as inquirers. Here we see in Peirce what will become two hallmarks of pragmatism in general: first, the shift of attention away from origins and toward outcomes; and, second, the emphasis on method. Hence, if our knowledge required foundations, consciousness could not provide them. But, more fundamentally, knowledge is more like a journey in which the unreliability of our maps is revealed in the course of the journey itself than like the construction of either a physical building or a Euclidean proof. To suppose then that knowledge does require foundations is to persist in relying upon one of the most unreliable maps we have inherited from our philosophical ancestors. In trying *to make our way* around the terrain of knowledge, the use of this map cannot help but lead us astray.

Peirce's anti-foundationalism and anti-intuitionism are tightly intertwined. For to deny intuitions is tantamount to denying the foundations of knowledge. But Peirce was concerned (1) to examine, in its own right, the case for intuitive knowledge, (2) to resist drawing any sceptical conclusion from the denial of there being any such knowledge, and (3) to show in general that all human knowledge is mediated and in detail just how different kinds of signs (e.g., icons, indices, and symbols) mediate between human agents and their environing world. Intuition, one of the faculties traditionally claimed for humans, is denied by Peirce. This means that even our most immediate forms of awareness are complexly mediated by bodily organs, implicit expectations, and social systems of communication. But this does *not* mean that the mediating factors fall between our consciousness and the world as a screen behind which we cannot peek.

*Semeiotic.* In denying any foundational role to intuitive (or immediate) knowledge, Peirce was in effect granting a ubiquitous role to signs. Later, he went so far as to suggest that the universe itself is, if not entirely composed of signs, at least accurately describable as a perfusion of signs. Though it might seem that here Peirce's semeiotic has become a wild cosmological speculation, his purpose was ordinarily far more modest: to detail the specific ways in which human cognition is mediated by perceptual and other signs, some of which we can control, others of which we cannot.

At all levels, human consciousness is, accordingly, always semiotic consciousness. It relies upon signs to such a degree that it cannot be pried apart from these signs and still be recognizable as human consciousness. It is a mode of awareness always mediated by something "immediate" functioning as a sign of something else. Peirce put this point quite sharply by simply insisting that we cannot think without signs. Our disposition to recognize a sequence of sounds, or a configuration of shapes, as a sign (e.g., "dog" in its role as a common noun designating countless varieties of canines) indicates that our immersion in a world of signs can have relatively lasting effects. (What is the world of any identifiably human culture but a world of incessant semiotic exchange?) Signs are ordinarily not marks written in water, effacing themselves in the instant of their inscription; rather they often leave their mark, primarily in the relatively stable form of memories and habits. Peirce used the term "interpretant" to designate the outcome of a sign-process, and used the term "semiosis" to designate such a process. The linguistic habits formed as the cumulative result of countless linguistic exchanges would be examples of interpretants (though not the only examples), for these habits are the results of the impact of signs. Any lasting memory of a conversation would also be an illustration of an interpretant.

The notion of habit occupies a central place in Peirce's pragmatic philosophy, as it does also in Dewey's. So what might easily look like an ethereal, disembodied process of one sign leading to another, *ad infinitum,* turns out to be an utterly concrete, incarnate process of signs both expressing the tendencies of things and also shaping those tendencies, especially in the case of such highly modifiable organisms as human beings. We might attend ever more carefully to how things are disposed to act and, in turn, how we ourselves are disposed to react to their characteristic tendencies. We might even take the *general* modes of observable behavior to be an indispensable key to understanding anything whatsoever, so that we only feel confident that we know what we mean when we can translate our descriptions of things into descriptions of their general modes of acting.

## The Pragmatic Maxim: Thematizing the Implicit Norms of Objective Inquiry

Though we cannot think without signs, we do not characteristically think *about* them, at least in any explicit and formal way. What ordinarily operates at a level below awareness can be made into the object of attention. That is, signs may be *thematized* (i.e., made into the objects of focal and explicit awareness). So too can the grammatical rules we, in ordinary circumstances, unconsciously follow. The operation of these rules suggests that we are in some respects quite efficient not only at interpreting isolated signs (the gnawing feeling, growing in intensity, is a hunger pang, a sign that my body requires nutrition) but also at stringing signs together in ever more complex and comprehensive arrangements (the grammatically formed utterance becomes part of a conversation and, in turn, the conversation comes to be seen as an important episode in a still unfolding drama and also as a sign of friendship or estrangement or some other overarching, hence inclusive, theme). There are norms—grammatical, logical, and rhetorical—*inherent in* the ways we actually speak. The locus of these norms is the set of practices in which they operate. For example, grammatical norms are located nowhere other than in actual languages— the linguistic habits and formal codifications of these habits in "Grammars" and other textual artifacts. Their *immanence in* practice does not preclude *control over* the practices in which they inhere. Immanent norms do not cease to be norms by virtue of their immanence; indeed, only as inherent features of a distinctive form of human conduct (e.g., speaking, inquiring, judging, etc.) could they have the capacity to function as norms. Like the other pragmatists, Peirce strove to show how the norms immanent in a practice (for him, the practices of communication, interpretation, and investigation were of greatest significance) not only govern that practice but also provide the resources for effective critical evaluation and reconstruction of that practice.

Peirce's views of these and other matters were significantly developed in reference to Charles Darwin and Immanuel Kant. He was self-consciously both a post-Darwinian and post-Kantian philosopher. As a post-Darwinian, Peirce realized that, whatever else human inquirers are, they are human organisms whose bodily structures and capacities are, in effect, living testimonies to complex series of cosmic accidents and biological adaptations. From this same perspective, he also realized that the disembodied *cogito* could never suffice to carry on the actual work of human inquiry; only an embodied agent ("flesh-and-blood experimenters") would suffice for this. As a post-Kantian, Peirce knew that the only possible meaning which could be given to "objectivity" is one spelled out in terms of the possibilities of *our* experience (his anti-Cartesianism can be see in his stress on *our,* rather than *my,* experience; on the communal, rather than private). That is, whatever else "objectivity" might mean, it can only mean what *we,* equipped with certain organic capacities and trained within certain intellectual disciplines, *can* experience. Like the other pragmatists, he supposed that human experience has only barely suggested the scope of possibilities inherent in it.

Human inquirers have proven to be a contentious lot, so much so that the denial of the possibility of knowing anything at all, or the denial of the possibility of inquiry ever truly making progress, or that inquirers can ever arrive at a rational consensus, is a respectable position. Nonetheless, Peirce thought that what the actual history of our experimental inquiries shows is that such progress is discernible and such consensus attainable. We can, after all, construct reliable maps; we can identify the causes of some diseases, the laws governing some phenomena, the mechanisms responsible for some reactions, etc. Let us not deny in our philosophy what we accomplish in our garages and laboratories—our ability to know, in an utterly piecemeal and fallible way, some features of our world. The reliability of our maps is a function to be measured solely in reference to purely human purpose and experience. It bespeaks not the way the world is, *apart from us,* but rather the way the world is *for us.* Yet Peirce was unwilling to concede that this qualification required us to jettison the notion of objectivity. In a self-dramatizing rhetoric, we might proclaim (as Nietzsche did) that there are no facts, only interpretations. In a more modest, workaday tone, however, we might acknowledge that the only facts we are ever entitled to recognize as such are ones secured through inquiry (the very word *fact,* derived from *factum,* suggests that in a sense we make facts up), but that the pinging sound made by the engine of one's car is a real sign of real trouble. In some respects, philosophers know far less than their mechanics; but they do both themselves and their mechanics a grave disservice by offering no way of accounting for the widely accredited competency of *experienced* mechanics. Peirce's pragmatism was designed to avoid slighting the actual achievements and accredited competencies of those who have mastered a still evolving practice, be it the repair of mechanical devices or the discovery of natural laws.

By making explicit the implicit norms inherent in those human practices aiming at the objective disclosure of some feature of reality, Peirce hoped to assist the work of objective inquiry. How are we as inquirers to conduct the business of inquiry? It would be difficult to exaggerate the heuristic preoccupation of Peirce's intellectual life; at virtually very turn, he was concerned to guide and goad inquiry in new directions, along new paths. The first rule of reason is that, in order to learn, you must desire to learn; from this rule follows the corollary which should be "inscribed upon every wall in the city of philosophy: Do not block the road of inquiry" (CP 1.135).

In 1898, William James traveled to the University of California at Berkeley, where he launched American pragmatism as a truly public movement. The ideas he put forth in "Philosophical Conceptions and Practical Results" were ones hammered out, first, in the informal meetings of a small coterie of largely Boston intellectuals and, later, in several of Peirce's earliest but also best known publications (such as "The Fixation of Belief" and "How to Make Our Ideas Clear"). James was explicit in acknowledging and generous in praising Peirce's contribution. But it was James' address in 1898, not Peirce's essays of 1877–78, that publicly launched the pragmatic movement. James and others, most notably Schiller in England and Dewey at Chicago, took pragmatism in directions with which its originator became increasingly uncomfortable. After 1898, Peirce came to reformulate his views regarding pragmatism; his principal target was as much his own youthful self as the other pragmatists. The numerous late manuscripts, most of them still unpublished, in which Peirce undertook this reformulation are unsurpassed by any of his other writings. In "What Pragmatism Is," Peirce rechristened his doctrine. He noted "the merciless way that words have to expect [to be treated] when they fall into literary clutches" (CP 5.414). Finding his word "pragmatism" used to designate what it was designed to exclude (above all, a facile relativism and self-insulating subjectivism that could not but make itself invulnerable to criticism), he came to feel it was time to kiss his child good-by and let the spirit of the times blow it where it will; however, for "the precise purpose of expressing the original definition," he announced "the birth of the word 'pragmaticism,' which is ugly enough to be safe from kidnappers" (CP 5.414).

Even in its most mature formulations (in fact, *especially* there), Peirce's pragmatism is the *explication* of the norms implicit in any possible form of objective inquiry, a process of making explicit the norms and procedures actually used in such inquiry. In his own case, this explication was undertaken *by* an already committed inquirer *for the sake* of ongoing investigation. As a participant in the practice of investigation, he hoped to contribute to the methodological self-understanding of anyone committed to objective inquiry. But pragmatism was only one of several positions that Peirce defended. Whereas pragmatism was part of Peirce's methodology, his normative account of the method to be recommended to those willing to commit themselves to the rigorous demands of objective inquiry, scholastic realism was part of his metaphysics, his account of the cosmos insofar as it was known via such inquiry.

## Peirce's Guess at the Riddle of the Universe

Peirce's interests were by no means exclusively logical and methodological. They were also scientific and cosmological. The defense of substantive positions as well as methodological principles is part of Peirce's guess at the riddle of the universe. By presenting scholastic realism, and other doctrines Peirce defended, we can get a sense of just how he actually articulated this vision.

*Scholastic Realism.* In opposition to nominalism (the view that individuals alone exist and that universals or—as Peirce preferred to say—generals of any sort are merely mental constructions, having no basis in reality), Peirce advocated a version of scholastic realism, realism of the *general* ways in which things act and react and are, in some cases, not explicable without attributing generality to reality itself. In short, the general is real, though its mode of being (for which Peirce tended to reserve the word "reality") is quite different from the mode of being exhibited by mere possibilities and especially by actualities in their dynamic, energetic opposition to one another and all other forms of being. While strictly speaking only individuals do *exist,* existents (i.e., individuals) are only one of three possible types of being. In order to account for what is encountered in experience and discovered through investigation, the *possible* and the *general* need to be accorded an ontological status along with the *actual* or *existent.* While the nominalist refuses to recognize any mode of being other than that of the individual existent, supposing that all other modes are reducible to this one, the scholastic realist insists, at least on Peirce's interpretation, upon recognizing three irreducible modes of being: possibility, actuality, and generality or reality.

*Tychism.* In opposition to determinism or what in the nineteenth century was often called necessitarianism (the position that every natural event is one absolutely determined by its antecedent conditions and the laws, such as the law of universal gravitation, governing such occurrences), Peirce championed indeterminism or what he called *tychism* (from the Greek word τυχη meaning chance). Whereas the necessitarian believes that every event is *in principle* predictable (if we only knew with sufficient thoroughness the conditions antecedent to an event and the laws governing it, we could predict everything about it), the *tychist,* or indeterminist, supposes that some occurrences are really random and, thus, nature is not wholly predicable, even in principle. Chance is not simply a function of our ignorance, such that in knowing every-thing about nature we would never be surprised by anything; it is rather an objective feature of the natural world.

*Synechism.* In opposition to metaphysical atomism (the view that the really real is to be iden-tified as absolutely discrete units—or atoms, points not themselves composite—having an integrity and character of their own, apart from their relationships and connections to other things), Peirce espoused *synechism* (the view that continuity or connectedness is not a deriva-tive but rather a primordial and thus irreducible feature of anything that deserves to be called real). We do not start with particulars each in itself separable from all others; rather we start with continua or fields (such as space or time) in which whatever can be individuated from its sur-roundings and from other individuated things is, nonetheless, seen to be essentially connected to these other things. Whereas the atomist would start with the point and contends that the unbroken, seamless continuity of the line results from compacting together what are in them-selves unconnected units, the synechist would begin with the line as the more basic unit out of which points are constructed. Thus, the atomist contends that continuity is derivative: it derives from the connections forged among originally separate units. In contrast, the synechist argues that continuity is primordial or basic: individuality is a function of individuation and, in turn, individuation only ever occurs as a differentiation within a field of connectedness (in a word, a continuum). The whole is, according to synechism, more than the sum of its parts.

*Evolutionism and Agapism.* Peirce went so far as to claim that within the continua or fields most accessible to us—the natural world, human history in its most immediately personal form (one's own autobiographical sense of one's own life) and in its more encompassing forms (the history of a relationship, family, nation, etc.)—one cannot help but observe inherent, dynamic tendencies toward integration and even intimacy. The connections already in place make possi-ble more complex, intricate but also precarious connections. Of course such tendencies operate alongside other ones, such as those of dissipation, disintegration, dissolution, etc. But nature is a scene in which things not only wind down into undifferentiated, quiescent states of spent energy, but also evolve toward ever greater complexity. Evolution and growth are no less real than entropy and dissolution. In this ongoing process of cosmic evolution, chance plays a cru-cial role, as does of course continuity. But Peirce's evolutionism also includes the principle of *agapé* which brings order out of chaos, harmony out of conflict, deeper intimacy out of the rent-ing alienations likely to befall any dynamic union. Peirce viewed *agapé,* like chance, as such a force. So, his evolutionism took the form and name of agapism, a view he developed in an essay entitled "Evolutionary Love."

The world of mechanistic determinism, the scientific orthodoxy of the nineteenth century, which Peirce no less than James set out to undermine, is a world which precludes not only free-dom but also evolution and life and (as sentimental as it sounds) love. On its own terms, the story of the cosmos is the story of a machine wearing itself out so thoroughly that even the materials out of which it is made will eventually be worn to nothing. But how did the machine construct itself? Granting (if only for the sake of argument) its self-devolving character, is it not necessary to suppose that behind its present form is a self-evolving process? What we see today is the result of a process at the earlier stages of which not merely life forms on earth but the "size" and shape of the cosmos itself were different. Is it possible to account for the evolution of the cosmos on strictly deterministic grounds? Is not the introduction of chance needed here? In addition to chance, do not complexity and inherent, dynamic forces driving toward wider and deeper connections also have to be acknowledged? What is it but the tyrannical authority of our unexamined metaphysical prejudices which undercuts the responsibility to take seriously the facts of growing complexity and even intimacy?[7]

*Critical Commonsensism.* Some of this must seem like wild speculation rather than the responsibly framed hypotheses of a consistently self-critical inquirer. But this appearance might be deceiving. Moreover, for anyone who knows anything about the history of science, it is manifest that Peirce is right when he claims that science utterly depends upon imagination. But Peirce did not think that deliberately flying in the face of common sense makes good scientific sense, just as refusing to part with common sense spells scientific suicide. "Any view that wholly abandons common sense is," as Paul Weiss notes, "at best a fiction or a fantasy. Any view that refuses to examine it is at best uncritical and dogmatic. Reflection and reason require one to stand somewhere between these two extremes."[8] This is where Peirce the critical commonsensist also takes his stand. The massive stock of our commonsensical beliefs makes critical inquiry possible; it itself is in one or another of its particulars susceptible, on countless occasions, of criticism and correction; but it alone provides the unexamined background out of which the examined life and, more restrictedly, critical intelligence can emerge. This is not a scaffold that can be dismantled once the edifice of our knowledge attains a level of structural soundness. As we have seen, knowledge is only misleadingly conceived in architectural terms; thus, common sense is no removable scaffold, but a positively guiding force, even when it needs to be radically amended.

*Theism.* While philosophers tend to think that the vague cannot but be vacuous or empty of meaning, Peirce, in conjunction with his defense of commonsensism, also championed vagueness. In addition he thought that, given his longstanding and deep-rooted character, the belief in God could not lightly be dismissed. The character of the cosmos suggests that it has its origin and destiny in a beginning "vaguely like a man." Many today would suppose that such a claim is vague to the point of being completely vacuous; Peirce would concede only that it is *almost* as vacuous as that, but not completely so. The self-evolving cosmos is interlaced, in Peirce's mind, with an infinite God who nonetheless grows in concert with the cosmos itself. Like James, Peirce wanted to use his own intellectual authority to defend ordinary persons from being browbeaten out of their traditional religious beliefs by militant agnostics and positivists insisting that the success of science spelled the death of religion. Also like James, he was convinced that questions concerning the reality of God are to be decided only in terms of our experience; to defend religion by forsaking experience would be, for these two pragmatists, religious as well as intellectual suicide.

## Conclusion: The Phenomenological Recovery of Everyday Experience

Peirce believed that philosophers cannot know anything at all about reality except by making guesses about it and then trying to find how their guesses stand up to the disclosures of experience. He described his own *philosophy* as "the attempt of a physicist to make such conjecture as to the constitution of the universe as the methods of science may permit, with the aid of all that has been done by previous philosophers" (CP 1.7). In brief, his philosophy in its entirety had in his own eyes only the status of a hypothesis. He took the demonstrations put forth throughout the history of philosophy and in his own day to be "moonshine." Demonstrations (knock-down arguments which establish, once and for all, the truth of some claim) are counter-feit coins; philosophers should not be trading in them, and thus not be duped into accepting them. The painstaking, ongoing work of formulating, testing, revising, and rejecting hypothe-ses is the only form of responsible inquiry. The course of such inquiry often cuts the most cir-cuitous paths, ones doubling back upon themselves; it makes necessary considering afresh posi-tions thought to have been completely discredited. Moreover, it depends as much upon imagination as upon anything else (see, e.g., CP 1.46–47).

In Peirce's judgment, however, philosophical inquiry differed from the special sciences such as physics chemistry, and biology (i.e., from disciplines he subsumed under the name, follow-ing Jeremy Bentham, of idioscopy) in that it limited itself almost exclusively to what is observ-able in everyday human experience, whereas these sciences characteristically require instru-ments, travel, or some other means of attaining experiences that are quite rare. The phenomena to which philosophers properly attend "are as hard or harder to see [than the relatively rare phe-nomena with which the special sciences are concerned], simply because they surround us on every hand; we are immersed in them and have no background against which to view them" (CP 6.562). Peirce believed that in despising or even just failing to value highly "everyday experi-ence," we exhibit "an oversecure, not to say ridiculous, contempt" for what is truly precious (CP 6.563). And he believed that this was especially the case with Americans: "Young America will call familiar phenomena [so many] squeezed lemons, whatever they had to teach already learned, things to be left behind in pressing on to things new; and it will recall dazzling inven-tions sprung from recondite experiences, gunpowder, mariner's compass, steam engine, electric telegraph, India rubber, anaesthtics, sewing machine, telephone, electric light" (CP 6.564). The far more remarkable innovations of our own day have only reinforced the tendency Peirce observed over a century ago. Along with the other pragmatists, however, Peirce further believed that a phenomenologically attentive return to everyday experience reveals the phenomena encountered there to be not so many squeezed lemons but inexhaustible resources for philo-sophical reflection. Just as the special scientists cannot learn anything at all by "gazing on nature with a vacant eye, that is, in passive perception unassisted by thought" (CP 1.34), so philo-sophical inquirers cannot learn anything from blankly staring at the ubiquitous phenomena of everyday life. But, as a result of ongoing self-interrogation and critical dialogue with other inquirers (philosophical and otherwise), philosophers can craft the means to attend ever more carefully to the disclosures of their own lived experience. This experience is, above all else, the course of life itself and the cumulative result of that ongoing career.

The means enabling us to discern what has taken shape and is even now taking form before our very minds (for Peirce, the phaneron or phenomenon is what stands *before* the mind, not what appears *in* consciousness) are concepts. Among our conceptual resources are concepts deliberately designed to grasp phenomena so delicately as not to destroy what is grasped. These are what traditionally have been called categories; they are the concepts of widest applicability (CP 5.43). What is crucial to appreciate here is that one of Peirce's most technical doctrines, his doctrine of the categories of firstness, secondness, and thirdness, was explicitly designed to guide and goad inquiry in all fields, but most especially in the field of philosophy, in which phe-nomena prove so hard to see. All his categories "pretend to do" is to suggest ways of thinking, including ways of approaching the familiar from unfamiliar angles (CP 1.351). They are of a piece with his attempt to recover phenomenologically the inherent significance as well as minute details of our ordinary experience.

In this attempt, (despite differences which he may even have exaggerated) Peirce shows him-self to be in league with James and Dewey. The story of American pragmatism (which, important as it is, ought not to be equated with the story of American philosophy) is among other things the story of the phenomenological recovery of human experience. Each of the pragmatists made a unique contribution to this recovery. The texts in this section have been selected to show some of the most important ways in which Peirce's contribution here, and in other contexts, is allied with, and differs from, other philosophers—especially his fellow pragmatists. But their ultimate value resides in their heuristic power and fecundity, their capacity to focus attention on what is all too easily overlooked, and their power to generate fruitful questions, observations, and reflections in the mind of anyone truly committed to the practice of inquiry.

## Notes

1. *Charles Sanders Peirce: Contributions to the Nation,* Part II: 1901–1908, edited by Kenneth Laine Ketner and James Edward Cook (Lubbock, TX: Texas tech Press, 1979), p. 305. Hereafter all citations in text as CN: III, [page number].
2. Quoted in Joseph Brent, *Charles Sanders Peirce: A Life* (Bloomington, IN: Indiana University Press 1993), p. 319.
3. All references to *Collected Papers of Charles Sanders Peirce* will be in accord with established procedure, e.g., 1.42 refers to volume 1, paragraph 42 of the CP.
4. Richard J. Bernstein, *Praxis and Action* (Philadelphia: University of Pennsylvania Press, 1971), p. 5.
5. Whereas linguistics is the study of language, i.e., complex systems of *linguistic* signs, and whereas symptomatology is that branch of medicine concerned with bodily signs as symptoms or illness, etc., semeiotic is the attempt to frame a general and comprehensive theory of signs.
6. Specifically in reference to the topics we have been considering, H. S. Thayer suggests in *Meaning and Action: A Study of American Pragmatism* (Indianapolis, IN: Bobbs-Merrill Co., 1973) that: "Here, as so often in the study of philosophic argument, it is illuminating to watch the use of metaphors and similes" (p. 44).
7. "Find a scientific man who proposes to get along without any metaphysics—not by any means every man who holds the ordinary reasonings of metaphysicians in scorn—and you have found one whose doctrines are thoroughly vitiated by the crude and uncriticized metaphysics with which they are packed" (CP 1.129).
8. Paul Weiss, "Common Sense and Beyond" in *Determinism and Freedom,* edited by Sidney Hook (NY: Collier Books, 1958), p. 232.

# Some Consequences of Four Incapacities

Descartes is the father of modern philosophy, and the spirit of Cartesianism—that which principally distinguishes it from the scholasticism which it displaced—may be compendiously stated as follows:

1. It teaches that philosophy must begin with universal doubt; whereas scholasticism had never questioned fundamentals.

2. It teaches that the ultimate test of certainty is to be found in the individual consciousness; whereas scholasticism had rested on the testimony of sages and of the Catholic Church.

3. The multiform argumentation of the middle ages is replaced by a single thread of inference depending often upon inconspicuous premises.

From *The Journal of Speculative Philosophy,* vol. 2 1868, pp. 140–157.

4. Scholasticism had its mysteries of faith, but undertook to explain all created things. But there are many facts which Cartesianism not only does not explain, but renders absolutely inexplicable, unless to say that "God makes them so" is to be regarded as an explanation.

In some, or all of these respects, most modern philosophers have been, in effect, Cartesians. Now without wishing to return to scholasticism, it seems to me that modern science and modern logic require us to stand upon a very different platform from this.

1. We cannot begin with complete doubt. We must begin with all the prejudices which we actually have when we enter upon the study of philosophy. These prejudices are not to be dispelled by a maxim, for they are things which it does not occur to us *can* be questioned. Hence this initial scepticism will be a mere self-deception, and not real doubt; and no one who follows the Cartesian method will ever be satisfied until he has formally recovered all those beliefs which in form he has given up. It is, therefore, as useless a preliminary as going to the North Pole would be in order to get to Constantinople by coming down regularly upon a meridian. A person may, it is true, in the course of his studies, find reason to doubt what he began by believing; but in that case he doubts because he has a positive reason for it, and not on account of the Cartesian maxim. Let us not pretend to doubt in philosophy what we do not doubt in our hearts.

2. The same formalism appears in the Cartesian criterion, which amounts to this: "Whatever I am clearly convinced of, is true." If I were really convinced, I should have done with reasoning, and should require no test of certainty. But thus to make single individuals absolute judges of truth is most pernicious. The result is that metaphysicians will all agree that metaphysics has reached a pitch of certainty far beyond that of the physical sciences;—only they can agree upon nothing else. In sciences in which men come to agreement, when a theory has been broached, it is considered to be on probation until this agreement is reached. After it is reached, the question of certainty becomes an idle one, because there is no one left who doubts it. We individually cannot reasonably hope to attain the ultimate philosophy which we pursue; we can only seek it, therefore, for the *community* of philosophers. Hence, if disciplined and candid minds carefully examine a theory and refuse to accept it, this ought to create doubts in the mind of the author of the theory himself.

3. Philosophy ought to imitate the successful sciences in its methods, so far as to proceed only from tangible premises which can be subjected to careful scrutiny, and to trust rather to the multitude and variety of its arguments than to the conclusiveness of any one. Its reasoning should not form a chain which is no stronger than its weakest link, but a cable whose fibres may be ever so slender, provided they are sufficiently numerous and intimately connected.

4. Every unidealistic philosophy supposes some absolutely inexplicable, unanalyzable ultimate; in short, something, resulting from mediation itself not susceptible of mediation. Now that anything *is* thus inexplicable can only be known by reasoning from signs. But the only justification of an inference from signs is that the conclusion explains the fact. To suppose the fact absolutely inexplicable, is not to explain it, and hence this supposition is never allowable.

In the last number of this journal will be found a piece entitled "Questions concerning certain Faculties claimed for Man," which has been written in this spirit of opposition to Cartesianism. That criticism of certain faculties resulted in four denials, which for convenience may here be repeated:

1. We have no power of Introspection, but all knowledge of the internal world is derived by hypothetical reasoning from our knowledge of external facts.
2. We have no power of Intuition, but every cognition is determined logically by previous cognitions.

3. We have no power of thinking without signs.
4. We have no conception of the absolutely incognizable.

These propositions cannot be regarded as certain; and, in order to bring them to a further test, it is now proposed to trace them out to their consequences. We may first consider the first alone; then trace the consequences of the first and second; then see what else will result from assuming the third also; and, finally, add the fourth to our hypothetical premises.

In accepting the first proposition, we must put aside all prejudices derived from a philosophy which bases our knowledge of the external world on our self-consciousness. We can admit no statement concerning what passes within us except as a hypothesis necessary to explain what takes place in what we commonly call the external world. Moreover when we have upon such grounds assumed one faculty or mode of action of the mind, we cannot, of course, adopt any other hypothesis for the purpose of explaining any fact which can be explained by our first supposition, but must carry the latter as far as it will go. In other words, we must, as far as we can do so without additional hypotheses, reduce all kinds of mental action to one general type.

The class of modifications of consciousness with which we must commence our inquiry must be one whose existence is indubitable, and whose laws are best known, and, therefore (since this knowledge comes from the outside), which most closely follows external facts; that is, it must be some kind of cognition. Here we may hypothetically admit the second proposition of the former paper, according to which there is no absolutely first cognition of any object, but cognition arises by a continuous process. We must begin, then, with a *process* of cognition, and with that process whose laws are best understood and most closely follow external facts. This is no other than the process of valid inference, which proceeds from its premiss, A, to its conclusion, B, only if, as a matter of fact, such a proposition as B is always or usually true

when such a proposition as A is true. It is a consequence, then, of the first two principles whose results we are to trace out, that we must, as far as we can, without any other supposition than that the mind reasons, reduce all mental action to the formula of valid reasoning.

But does the mind in fact go through the syllogistic process? It is certainly very doubtful whether a conclusion—as something existing in the mind independently, like an image—suddenly displaces two premises existing in the mind in a similar way. But it is a matter of constant experience, that if a man is made to believe in the premises, in the sense that he will act from them and will say that they are true, under favourable conditions he will also be ready to act from the conclusion and to say that that is true. Something, therefore, takes place within the organism which is equivalent to the syllogistic process . . .

The third principle whose consequences we have to deduce is, that, whenever we think, we have present to the consciousness some feeling, image, conception, or other representation, which serves as a sign. But it follows from our own existence (which is proved by the occurrence of ignorance and error) that everything which is present to us is a phenomenal manifestation of ourselves. This does not prevent its being a phenomenon of something without us, just as a rainbow is at once a manifestation both of the sun and of the rain. When we think, then, we ourselves, as we are at that moment, appear as a sign. Now a sign has, as such, three references: 1st, it is a sign *to* some thought which interprets it; 2d, it is a sign *for* some object to which in that thought it is equivalent; 3d, it is a sign, *in* some respect or quality, which brings it into connection with its object. Let us ask what the three correlates are to which a thought-sign refers.

1. When we think, to what thought does that thought-sign which is ourself address itself? It may, through the medium of outward expression, which it reaches perhaps only after considerable internal development, come to address itself to thought of another person. But whether this happens or not, it is always

interpreted by a subsequent thought of our own. If, after any thought, the current of ideas flows on freely, it follows the law of mental association. In that case, each former thought suggests something to the thought which follows it i.e., is the sign of something to this latter. Our train of thought may, it is true, be interrupted. But we must remember that, in addition to the principal element of thought at any moment, there are a hundred things in our mind to which but a small fraction of attention or consciousness is conceded. It does not, therefore, follow, because a new constituent of thought gets the uppermost, that the train of thought which it displaces is broken off altogether. On the contrary, from our second principle, that there is no intuition or cognition not determined by previous cognitions, it follows that the striking in of a new experience is never an instantaneous affair, but is an *event* occupying time, and coming to pass by a continuous process. Its prominence in consciousness, therefore, must probably be the consummation of a growing process; and if so, there is no sufficient cause for the thought which had been the leading one just before, to cease abruptly and instantaneously. But if a train of thought ceases by gradually dying out, it freely follows its own law of association as long as it lasts, and there is no moment at which there is a thought belonging to this series, subsequently to which there is not a thought which interprets or repeats it. There is no exception, therefore, to the law that every thought-sign is translated or interpreted in a subsequent one, unless it be that all thought comes to an abrupt and final end in death.

2. The next question is: For what does the thought-sign stand—what does it name— what is its *suppositum?* The outward thing, undoubtedly, when a real outward thing is thought of. But still, as the thought is determined by a previous thought of the same object, it only refers to the thing through denoting this previous thought. Let us suppose, for example, that Toussaint is thought of, and first thought of as a *negro,* but not distinctly as a man. If this distinctness is afterwards added, it is through the thought that a *negro* is a *man;* that is to say, the subsequent thought, *man,* refers to the outward thing by being predicated of that previous thought, *negro,* which has been had of that thing. If we afterwards think of Toussaint as a general, then we think that this negro, this man, was a general. And so in every case the subsequent thought denotes what was thought in the previous thought.

3. The thought-sign stands for its object in the respect which is thought; that is to say, this respect is the immediate object of consciousness in the thought, or, in other words, it is the thought itself, or at least what the thought is thought to be in the subsequent thought to which it is a sign.

We must now consider two other properties of signs which are of great importance in the theory of cognition. Since a sign is not identical with the thing signified, but differs from the latter in some respects, it must plainly have some characters which belong to it in itself, and have nothing to do with its representative function. These I call the *material* qualities of the sign. As examples of such qualities, take in the word "man" its consisting of three letters—in a picture, its being flat and without relief. In the second place, a sign must be capable of being connected (not in the reason but really) with another sign of the same object, or with the object itself. Thus, words would be of no value at all unless they could be connected into sentences by means of a real copula which joins signs of the same thing. The usefulness of some signs—as a weathercock, a tally, etc.—consists wholly in their being really connected with the very things they signify. In the case of a picture such a connection is not evident, but it exists in the power of association which connects the picture with the brain-sign which labels it. This real, physical connection of a sign with its object, either immediately or by its connection with another sign, I call the *pure demonstrative application* of the sign. Now the representative function of a sign lies neither in its material quality nor in its pure demonstrative application; because it is something which the sign is, not in itself or in a real relation to its object, but which it is *to a thought,* while both of the characters just defined belong to the sign independently of its addressing any thought. And yet if I take all the things which have certain qualities and physically connect them with another series of things, each to each, they become fit to be signs. If they are not regarded as such they are not actually signs, but they are so in the same sense, for example, in which an unseen flower can be said to be *red,* this being also a term relative to a mental affection.

Consider a state of mind which is a conception. It is a conception by virtue of having a *meaning,* a logical comprehension; and if it is applicable to any object, it is because that object has the characters contained in the comprehension of this conception. Now the logical comprehension of a thought is usually said to consist of the thoughts contained in it; but thoughts are events, acts of the mind. Two thoughts are two events separated in time, and one cannot literally be contained in the other. It may be said that all thoughts exactly similar are regarded as one; and that to say that one thought contains another, means that it contains one exactly similar to that other. But how can two thoughts be similar? Two objects can only be *regarded* as similar if they are compared and brought together in the mind. Thoughts have no existence except in the mind; only as they are regarded do they exist. Hence, two thoughts cannot *be* similar unless they are brought together in the mind. But, as to their existence, two thoughts are separated by an interval of time. We are too apt to imagine that we can frame a thought similar to a past thought, by matching it with the latter, as though this past thought were still present to us. But it is plain that the knowledge that one thought is similar to or in any way truly representative of another, cannot be derived from immediate perception, but must be an hypothesis (unquestionably fully justifiable by facts), and that therefore the formation of such a representing thought must be dependent upon a real effective force behind consciousness, and not merely upon a mental comparison. What we must mean, therefore, by saying that one

concept is contained in another, is that we normally represent one to be in the other; that is, that we form a particular kind of judgment, of which the subject signifies one concept and the predicate the other.

No thought in itself, then, no feeling in itself, contains any others, but is absolutely simple and unanalyzable; and to say that it is composed of other thoughts and feelings, is like saying that a movement upon a straight line is composed of the two movements of which it is the resultant; that is to say, it is a metaphor, or fiction, parallel to the truth. Every thought, however artificial and complex, is, so far as it is immediately present, a mere sensation without parts, and therefore, in itself, without similarity to any other, but incomparable with any other and absolutely *sui generis.* Whatever is wholly incomparable with anything else is wholly inexplicable, because explanation consists in bringing things under general laws or under natural classes. Hence every thought, in so far as it is a feeling of a peculiar sort, is simply an ultimate, inexplicable fact. Yet this does not conflict with my postulate that that fact should be allowed to stand as inexplicable; for, on the one hand, we never can think, "This is present to me," since, before we have time to make the reflection, the sensation is past, and, on the other hand, when once past, we can never bring back the quality of the feeling as it was *in and for itself,* or know what it was like *in itself,* or even discover the existence of this quality except by a corollary from our general theory of ourselves, and then not in its idiosyncrasy, but only as something present. But, as something present, feelings are all alike and require no explanation, since they contain only what is universal. So that nothing which we can truly predicate of feelings is left inexplicable, but only something which we cannot reflectively know. So that we do not fall into the contradiction of making the Mediate immediate. Finally, no present actual thought (which is a mere feeling) has any meaning, any intellectual value; for this lies not in what is actually thought, but in what this thought may be connected with in representation by subsequent thoughts; so that the meaning of a thought is altogether something virtual. It may be objected, that if no thought has any meaning, all thought is without meaning. But this is a fallacy similar to saying, that, if in no one of the successive spaces which a body fills there is room for motion, there is no room for motion throughout the whole. At no one instant in my state of mind is there cognition or representation, but in the relation of my states of mind at different instants there is.[1] In short, the Immediate (and therefore in itself unsusceptible of mediation—the Unanalyzable, the Inexplicable, the Unintellectual) runs in a continuous stream through our lives; it is the sum total of consciousness, whose mediation, which is the continuity of it, is brought about by a real effective force behind consciousness.   ✳ ✳ ✳

Thus, we have in thought three elements: 1st, the representative function which makes it a _representation;_ 2d, the pure denotative application, or real connection, which brings one thought into _relation_ with another; and 3d, the material quality, or how it feels, which gives thought its _quality_.

That a sensation is not necessarily an intuition, or first impression of sense, is very evident in the case of the sense of beauty. . . . When the sensation beautiful is determined by previous cognitions, it always arises as a predicate; that is, we think that something is beautiful. Whenever a sensation thus arises in consequence of others, induction shows that those others are more or less complicated. Thus, the sensation of a particular kind of sound arises in consequence of impressions upon the various nerves of the ear being combined in a particular way, and following one another with a certain rapidity. A sensation of colour depends upon impressions upon the eye following one another in a regular manner, and with a certain rapidity. The sensation of beauty arises upon a manifold of other impressions. And this will be found to hold good in all cases. Secondly, all these sensations are in themselves simple, or more so than the sensations which give rise to them. Accordingly, a sensation is a simple predicate taken in place

of a complex predicate; in other words, it fulfills the function of an hypothesis. But the general principle that every thing to which such and such a sensation belongs, has such and such a complicated series of predicates, is not one determined by reason (as we have seen), but is of an arbitrary nature. Hence, the class of hypothetic inferences which the arising of a sensation resembles, is that of reasoning from definition to definitum, in which the major premiss is of an arbitrary nature. Only in this mode of reasoning, this premiss is determined by the conventions of language, and expresses the occasion upon which a word is to be used; and in the formation of a sensation, it is determined by the constitution of our nature, and expresses the occasions upon which sensation, or a natural mental sign, arises. Thus, the sensation, so far as it represents something, is determined, according to a logical law, by previous cognitions; that is to say, these cognitions determine that there shall be a sensation. But so far as the sensation is a mere feeling of a particular sort, it is determined only by an inexplicable, occult power; and so far, it is not a representation, but only the material quality of a representation. For just as in reasoning from definition to definitum, it is indifferent to the logician how the defined word shall sound, or how many letters it shall contain, so in the case of this constitutional word, it is not determined by an inward law how it shall feel in itself. A feeling, therefore, as a feeling, is merely the _material quality_ of a mental sign.

But there is no feeling which is not also a representation, a predicate of something determined logically by the feelings which precede it. For if there are any such feelings not predicates, they are the emotions. Now every emotion has a subject. If a man is angry, he is saying to himself that this or that is vile and outrageous. If he is in joy, he is saying "this is delicious." If he is wondering, he is saying "this is strange." In short, whenever a man feels, he is thinking of _something_. Even those passions which have no definite object—as melancholy—only come to consciousness through tinging the _objects of thought_. That which makes us look upon the emotions more as affections of self than other cognitions, is that we have found them more dependent upon our accidental situation at the moment than other cognitions; but that is only to say that they are cognitions too narrow to be useful. The emotions, as a little observation will show, arise when our attention is strongly drawn to complex and inconceivable circumstances. Fear arises when we cannot predict our fate; joy, in the case of certain indescribable and peculiarly complex sensations. If there are some indications that something greatly for my interest, and which I have anticipated would happen, may not happen; and if, after weighing probabilities, and inventing safeguards, and straining for further information, I find myself unable to come to any fixed conclusion in reference to the future, in the place of that intellectual hypothetic inference which I seek, the feeling of *anxiety* arises. When something happens for which I cannot account, I *wonder.* When I endeavour to realize to myself what I never can do, a pleasure in the future, I *hope.* "I do not understand you," is the phrase of an angry man. The indescribable, the ineffable, the incomprehensible, commonly excite emotion; but nothing is so chilling as a scientific explanation. Thus an emotion is always a simple predicate substituted by an operation of the mind for a highly complicated predicate. Now if we consider that a very complex predicate demands explanation by means of an hypothesis, that that hypothesis must be a simpler predicate substituted for that complex one; and that when we have an emotion, an hypothesis, strictly speaking, is hardly possible—the analogy of the parts played by emotion and hypothesis is very striking. There is, it is true, this difference between an emotion and an intellectual hypothesis, that we have reason to say in the case of the latter, that to whatever the simple hypothetic predicate can be applied, of that the complex predicate is true; whereas, in the case of an emotion this is a proposition for which no reason can be given, but which is determined merely by our emotional constitution. But this corresponds precisely to the differ-

ence between hypothesis and reasoning from definition to definitum, and thus it would appear that emotion is nothing but sensation. There appears to be a difference, however, between emotion and sensation, and I would state it as follows:

There is some reason to think that, corresponding to every feeling within us, some motion takes place in our bodies. This property of the thought-sign, since it has no rational dependence upon the meaning of the sign, may be compared with what I have called the material quality of the sign; but it differs from the latter inasmuch as it is not essentially necessary that it should be felt in order that there should be any thought-sign. In the case of a sensation, the manifold of impressions which precede and determine it are not of a kind, the bodily motion corresponding to which comes from any large ganglion or from the brain, and probably for this reason the sensation produces no great commotion in the bodily organism; and the sensation itself is not a thought which has a very strong influence upon the current of thought except by virtue of the information it may serve to afford. An emotion, on the other hand, comes much later in the development of thought—I mean, further from the first beginning of the cognition of its object—and the thoughts which determine it already have motions corresponding to them in the brain, or the chief ganglion; consequently, it produces large movements in the body, and, independently of its representative value, strongly affects the current of thought. The animal motions to which I allude, are, in the first place and obviously, blushing, blenching, staring, smiling, scowling, pouting, laughing, weeping, sobbing, wriggling, flinching, trembling, being petrified, sighing, sniffing, shrugging, groaning, heartsinking, trepidation, swelling of the heart, etc. etc. To these may, perhaps, be added, in the second place, other more complicated actions, which nevertheless spring from a direct impulse and not from deliberation.

That which distinguishes both sensations proper and emotions from the feeling of a thought, is that in the case of the two former the material quality is made prominent, because the thought has no relation of reason to the thoughts which determine it, which exists in the last case and detracts from the attention given to the mere feeling. By there being no relation of reason to the determining thoughts, I mean that there is nothing in the content of the thought which explains why it should arise only on occasion of these determining thoughts. If there is such a relation of reason, if the thought is essentially limited in its application to these objects, then the thought comprehends a thought other than itself; in other words, it is then a complex thought. An incomplex thought can, therefore, be nothing but a sensation or emotion, having no rational character. This is very different from the ordinary doctrine, according to which the very highest and most metaphysical conceptions are absolutely simple. I shall be asked how such a conception of a *being* is to be analyzed, or whether I can ever define *one, two,* and *three,* without a diallelon. Now I shall admit at once that neither of these conceptions can be separated into two others higher than itself; and in that sense, therefore, I fully admit that certain very metaphysical and eminently intellectual notions are absolutely simple. But though these concepts cannot be defined by genus and difference, there is another way in which they can be defined. All determination is by negation; we can first recognize any character only by putting an object which possesses it into comparison with an object which possesses it not. A conception, therefore, which was quite universal in every respect would be unrecognizable and impossible. We do not obtain the conception of Being, in the sense implied in the copula, by observing that all the things which we can think of have something in common, for there is no such thing to be observed. We get it by reflecting upon signs—words or thoughts;—we observe that different predicates may be attached to the same subject, and that each makes some conception applicable to the subject; then we imagine that a subject has something true of it merely because a predicate (no matter what) is attached to it,—and that we call Being. The conception of being is, therefore, a conception about a sign—a thought, or word;—and since it is not applicable to every sign, it is not primarily universal, although it is so in its mediate application to things. Being, therefore, may be defined; it may be defined, for example, as that which is common to the objects included in any class, and to the objects not included in the same class. But it is nothing new to say that metaphysical conceptions are primarily and at bottom thoughts about words, or thoughts about thoughts; it is the doctrine both of Aristotle (whose categories are parts of speech) and of Kant (whose categories are the characters of different kinds of propositions).

Sensation and the power of abstraction or attention may be regarded as, in one sense, the sole constituents of all thought. Having considered the former, let us now attempt some analysis of the latter. By the force of attention, an emphasis is put upon one of the objective elements of consciousness. This emphasis is, therefore, not itself an object of immediate consciousness; and in this respect it differs entirely from a feeling. Therefore, since the emphasis, nevertheless, consists in some effect upon consciousness, and so can exist only so far as it affects our knowledge; and since an act cannot be supposed to determine that which precedes it in time, this act can consist only in the capacity which the cognition emphasized has for producing an effect upon memory, or otherwise influencing subsequent thought. This is confirmed by the fact that attention is a matter of continuous quantity; for continuous quantity, so far as we know it, reduces itself in the last analysis to time. Accordingly, we find that attention does, in fact, produce a very great effect upon subsequent thought. In the first place, it strongly affects memory, a thought being remembered for a longer time the greater the attention originally paid to it. In the second place, the greater the attention, the closer the connection and the more accurate the logical sequence of thought. In the third place, by attention a thought may be recovered which has been forgotten. From these facts, we gather that attention is the power by which thought at one time is connected with and made to relate to thought at another time; or, to apply the conception of thought as a sign, that it is the *pure demonstrative application* of a thought-sign.

Attention is roused when the same phenomenon presents itself repeatedly on different occasions, or the same predicate in different subjects. We see that *A* has a certain character, that *B* has the same, *C* has the same; and this excites our attention, so that we say, "*These* have this character." Thus attention is an act of induction; but it is an induction which does not increase our knowledge, because our "these" covers nothing but the instances experienced. It is, in short, an argument from enumeration.

Attention produces effects upon the nervous system. These effects are habits, or nervous associations. A habit arises, when, having had the sensation of performing a certain act, *m*, on several occasions *a*, *b*, *c*, we come to do it upon every occurrence of the general event, *l*, of which *a*, *b* and *c* are special cases. That is to say, by the cognition that

Every case of *a*, *b*, or *c*, is a case of *m*,

is determined the cognition that

Every case of *l* is a case of *m*.

Thus the formation of a habit is an induction, and is therefore necessarily connected with attention or abstraction. Voluntary actions result from the sensations produced by habits, as instinctive actions result from our original nature.

We have thus seen that every sort of modification of consciousness—Attention, Sensation, and Understanding—is an inference. But the objection may be made that inference deals only with general terms, and that an image, or absolutely singular representation, cannot therefore be inferred.

"Singular" and "individual" are equivocal terms. A singular may mean that which can be but in one place at one time. In this sense it is not opposed to general. *The sun* is a singular in this sense, but, as is explained in every good treatise on logic, it is a general term. I may have a very general conception of Hermolaus Barbarus, but still I conceive him only as able

to be in one place at one time. When an image is said to be singular, it is meant that it is absolutely determinate in all respects. Every possible character, or the negative thereof, must be true of such an image. In the words of the most eminent expounder of the doctrine, the image of a man "must be either of a white, or a black, or a tawny; a straight, or a crooked; a tall, or a low, or a middle-sized man." It must be of a man with his mouth open or his mouth shut, whose hair is precisely of such and such a shade, and whose figure has precisely such and such proportions. No statement of Locke has been so scouted by all friends of images as his denial that the "idea" of a triangle must be either of an obtuse-angled, right-angled, or acute-angled triangle. In fact, the image of a triangle must be of one, each of whose angles is of a certain number of degrees, minutes, and seconds.

This being so, it is apparent that no man has a *true* image of the road to his office, or of any other real thing. Indeed he has no image of it at all unless he can not only recognize it, but imagines it (truly or falsely) in all its infinite details. This being the case, it becomes very doubtful whether we ever have any such thing as an image in our imagination. Please, reader, to look at a bright red book, or other brightly coloured object, and then to shut your eyes and say whether you *see* that colour, whether brightly or faintly—whether, indeed, there is anything like sight there. Hume and the other followers of Berkeley maintain that there is no difference between the sight and the memory of the red book except in "their different degrees of force and vivacity." "The colours which the memory employs," says Hume, "are faint and dull compared with those in which our original perceptions are clothed." If this were a correct statement of the difference, we should remember the book as being less red than it is; whereas, in fact, we remember the colour with very great precision for a few moments (please to test this point, reader), although we do not see any thing like it. We carry away absolutely nothing of the colour except the *consciousness that we could recognize it*. As a further proof of this, I will request the reader to try a little experiment. Let him call up, if he can, the image of a horse—not of one which he has ever seen, but of an imaginary one—and before reading further let him by contemplation fix the image in his memory . . . [sic]. Has the reader done as requested? for I protest that it is not fair play to read further without doing so.—Now, the reader can say in general of what colour that horse was, whether grey, bay, or black. But he probably cannot say *precisely* of what shade it was. He cannot state this as exactly as he could just after having *seen* such a horse. But why, if he had an image in his mind which no more had the general colour than it had the particular shade, has the latter vanished so instantaneously from his memory while the former still remains? It may be replied, that we always forget the details before we do the more general characters; but that this answer is insufficient is, I think, shown by the extreme disproportion between the length of time that the exact shade of something looked at is remembered as compared with that instantaneous oblivion to the exact shade of the thing imagined, and the but slightly superior vividness of the memory of the thing seen as compared with the memory of the thing imagined.

The nominalists, I suspect, confound together thinking a triangle without thinking that it is either equilateral, isosceles, or scalene, and thinking a triangle without thinking whether it is equilateral, isosceles, or scalene.

It is important to remember that we have no intuitive power of distinguishing between one subjective mode of cognition and another; and hence often think that something is presented to us as a picture, while it is really constructed from slight data by the understanding. This is the case with dreams, as is shown by the frequent impossibility of giving an intelligible account of one without adding something which we feel was not in the dream itself. Many dreams, of which the waking memory makes elaborate and consistent stories, must probably have been in fact mere jumbles of these feelings of the ability to recognize this and that which I have just alluded to.

I will now go so far as to say that we have no images even in actual perception. It will be suf-

ficient to prove this in the case of vision; for if no picture is seen when we look at an object, it will not be claimed that hearing, touch, and the other senses, are superior to sight in this respect. That the picture is not painted on the nerves of the retina is absolutely certain, if, as physiologists inform us, these nerves are needle-points pointing to the light and at distances considerably greater than the *minimum visibile.* The same thing is shown by our not being able to perceive that there is a large blind spot near the middle of the retina. If, then, we have a picture before us when we see, it is one constructed by the mind at the suggestion of previous sensations. Supposing these sensations to be signs, the understanding by reasoning from them could attain all the knowledge of outward things which we derive from sight, while the sensations are quite inadequate to forming an image or representation absolutely determinate. If we have such an image or picture, we must have in our minds a representation of a surface which is only a part of every surface we see, and we must see that each part, however small, has such and such a colour. If we look from some distance at a speckled surface, it seems as if we did not see whether it were speckled or not; but if we have an image before us, it must appear to us either as speckled, or as not speckled. Again, the eye by education comes to distinguish minute differences of colour; but if we see only absolutely determinate images, we must, no less before our eyes are trained than afterwards, see each colour as particularly such and such a shade. Thus to suppose that we have an image before us when we see, is not only a hypothesis which explains nothing whatever, but is one which actually creates difficulties which require new hypotheses in order to explain them away.

One of these difficulties arises from the fact that the details are less easily distinguished than, and forgotten before, the general circumstances. Upon this theory, the general features exist in the details: the details are, in fact, the whole picture. It seems, then, very strange that that which exists only secondarily in the picture should make more impression than the picture itself. It is true that in an old painting the details are not easily made out; but this is because we know that the blackness is the result of time, and is no part of the picture itself. There is no difficulty in making out the details of the picture as it looks at present; the only difficulty is in guessing what it used to be. But if we have a picture on the retina, the minutest details are there as much as, nay, more than, the general outline and significancy of it. Yet that which must actually be seen, it is extremely difficult to recognize; while that which is only abstracted from what is seen is very obvious.

But the conclusive argument against our having any images, or absolutely determinate representations in perception, is that in that case we have the materials in each such representation for an infinite amount of conscious cognition, which we yet never become aware of. Now there is no meaning in saying that we have something in our minds which never has the least effect on what we are conscious of knowing. The most that can be said is, that when we see we are put in a condition in which we are able to get a very large and perhaps indefinitely great amount of knowledge of the visible qualities of objects.

Moreover, that perceptions are not absolutely determinate and singular is obvious from the fact that each sense is an abstracting mechanism. Sight by itself informs us only of colours and forms. No one can pretend that the images of sight are determinate in reference to taste. They are, therefore, so far general that they are neither sweet nor non-sweet, bitter nor non-bitter, having savour nor insipid.

The next question is whether we have any general conceptions except in judgments. In perception, where we know a thing as existing, it is plain that there is a judgment that the thing exists, since a mere general concept of a thing is in no case a cognition of it as existing. It has usually been said, however, that we can call up any concept without making any judgment; but it seems that in this case we only arbitrarily suppose ourselves to have an experience. In order to conceive the number 7, I suppose, that is, I arbitrarily make the hypothesis or judgment, that there are certain points

before my eyes, and I judge that these are seven. This seems to be the most simple and rational view of the matter, and I may add that it is the one which has been adopted by the best logicians. If this be the case, what goes by the name of the association of images is in reality an association of judgments. The association of ideas is said to proceed according to three principles—those of resemblance, of contiguity, and of causality. But it would be equally true to say that signs denote what they do on the three principles of resemblance, contiguity, and causality. There can be no question that anything *is* a sign of whatever is associated with it by resemblance, by contiguity, or by causality: nor can there be any doubt that any sign recalls the thing signified. So, then, the association of ideas consists in this, that a judgment occasions another judgment, of which it is the sign. Now this is nothing less nor more than inference.

Everything in which we take the least interest creates in us its own particular emotion, however slight this may be. This emotion is a sign and a predicate of the thing. Now, when a thing resembling this thing is presented to us, a similar emotion arises; hence, we immediately infer that the latter is like the former. A formal logician of the old school may say, that in logic no term can enter into the conclusion which had not been contained in the premisses, and that therefore the suggestion of something new must be essentially different from inference. But I reply that that rule of logic applies only to those arguments which are technically called completed. We can and do reason—

> Elias was a man;
> ∴ He was mortal.

And this argument is just as valid as the full syllogism, although it is so only because the major premiss of the latter happens to be true. If to pass from the judgment "Elias was a man" to the judgment "Elias was mortal," without actually saying to one's self that "All men are mortal," is not inference, then the term "inference" is used in so restricted a sense that inferences hardly occur outside of a logic-book.

What is here said of association by resemblance is true of all association. All association is by signs. Everything has its subjective or emotional qualities, which are attributed either absolutely or relatively, or by conventional imputation to anything which is a sign of it. And so we reason,

The sign is such and such;
∴. The sign is that thing.

This conclusion receiving, however, a modification, owing to other considerations, so as to become—

The sign is almost (is representative of )
that thing.

We come now to the consideration of the last of the four principles whose consequences we were to trace; namely, that the absolutely incognizable is absolutely inconceivable. That upon Cartesian principles the very realities of things can never be known in the least, most competent persons must long ago have been convinced. Hence the breaking forth of idealism, which is essentially anti-Cartesian, in every direction, whether among empiricists (Berkeley, Hume), or among noölogists (Hegel, Fichte). The principle now brought under discussion is directly idealistic; for, since the meaning of a word is the conception it conveys, the absolutely incognizable has no meaning because no conception attaches to it. It is, therefore, a meaningless word; and, consequently, whatever is meant by any term as "the real" is cognizable in some degree, and so is of the nature of a cognition, in the objective sense of that term.

At any moment we are in possession of certain information, that is, of cognitions which have been logically derived by induction and hypothesis from previous cognitions which are less general, less distinct, and of which we have a less lively consciousness. These in their turn have been derived from others still less general, less distinct, and less vivid; and so on back to the ideal first, which is quite singular, and quite out of consciousness. This ideal first is the particular thing-in-itself. It does not exist *as such*. That is, there is no thing which

is in-itself in the sense of not being relative to the mind, though things which are relative to the mind doubtless are, apart from that relation. The cognitions which thus reach us by this infinite series of inductions and hypotheses (which though infinite *a parte ante logice* [from the standpoint of logic], is yet as one continuous process not without a beginning *in time*) are of two kinds, the true and the untrue, or cognitions whose objects are *real* and those whose objects are *unreal*. And what do we mean by the real? It is a conception which we must first have had when we discovered that there was an unreal, an illusion; that is, when we first corrected ourselves. Now the distinction for which alone this fact logically called, was between an *ens* relative to private inward determinations, to the negations belonging to idiosyncrasy, and an *ens* such as would stand in the long run. The real, then, is that which, sooner or later, information and reasoning would finally result in, and which is therefore independent of the vagaries of me and you. Thus, the very origin of the conception of reality shows that this conception essentially involves the notion of a COMMUNITY without definite limits, and capable of a definite increase of knowledge. And so those two series of cognitions—the real and the unreal—consist of those which, at a time sufficiently future, the community will always continue to re-affirm; and of those which, under the same conditions, will ever after be denied. Now, a proposition whose falsity can never be discovered, and the error of which therefore is absolutely incognizable, contains, upon our principle, absolutely no error. Consequently, that which is thought in these cognitions is the real, as it really is. There is nothing, then, to prevent our knowing outward things as they really are, and it is most likely that we do thus know them in numberless cases, although we can never be absolutely certain of doing so in any special case.

But it follows that since no cognition of ours is absolutely determinate, generals must have a real existence. Now this scholastic realism is usually set down as a belief in metaphysical fictions. But, in fact, a realist is simply one who knows no more recondite reality than that which is represented in a true representation. Since, therefore, the word "man" is true of something, that which "man" means is real. The nominalist must admit that man is truly applicable to something; but he believes that there is beneath this a thing in itself, an incognizable reality. His is the metaphysical figment. Modern nominalists are mostly superficial men, who do not know, as the more thorough Roscellinus and Ockham did, that a reality which has no representation is one which has no relation and no quality. The great argument for nominalism is that there is no man unless there is some particular man. That, however, does not affect the realism of Scotus; for although there is no man of whom all further determination can be denied, yet there is a man, abstraction being made of all further determination. There is a real difference between man irrespective of what the other determinations may be, and man with this or that particular series of determinations, although undoubtedly this difference is only relative to the mind and not *in re.* Such is the position of Scotus. Ockham's great objection is, there can be no real distinction which is not *in re,* in the thing-in-itself; but this begs the question, for it is itself based only on the notion that reality is something independent of representative relation.

Such being the nature of reality in general, in what does the reality of the mind consist? We have seen that the content of consciousness, the entire phenomenal manifestation of mind, is a sign resulting from inference. Upon our principle, therefore, that the absolutely incognizable does not exist, so that the phenomenal manifestation of a substance is the substance, we must conclude that the mind is a sign developing according to the laws of inference. What distinguishes a man from a word? There is a distinction doubtless. The material qualities, the forces which constitute the pure denotative application, and the meaning of the human sign, are all exceedingly complicated in comparison with those of the word. But these differences are only relative. What other is there? It may be said that man is

conscious, while a word is not. But consciousness is a very vague term. It may mean that emotion which accompanies the reflection that we have animal life. This is a consciousness which is dimmed when animal life is at its ebb in old age, or sleep, but which is not dimmed when the spiritual life is at its ebb; which is the more lively the better *animal* a man is, but which is not so, the better *man* he is. We do not attribute this sensation to words, because we have reason to believe that it is dependent upon the possession of an animal body. But this consciousness, being a mere sensation, is only a part of the *material quality* of the man-sign. Again, consciousness is sometimes used to signify the *I think,* or unity in thought; but the unity is nothing but consistency, or the recognition of it. Consistency belongs to every sign, so far as it is a sign; and therefore every sign, since it signifies primarily that it is a sign, signifies its own consistency. The man-sign acquires information, and comes to mean more than he did before. But so do words. Does not electricity mean more now than it did in the days of Franklin? Man makes the word, and the word means nothing which the man has not made it mean, and that only to some man. But since man can think only by means of words or other external symbols, these might turn round and say: "You mean nothing which we have not taught you, and then only so far as you address some word as the interpretant of your thought." In fact, therefore, men and words reciprocally educate each other; each increase of a man's information involves and is involved by, a corresponding increase of a word's information.

Without fatiguing the reader by stretching this parallelism too far, it is sufficient to say that there is no element whatever of man's consciousness which has not something corresponding to it in the word; and the reason is obvious. It is that the word or sign which man uses *is* the man himself. For, as the fact that every thought is a sign, taken in conjunction with the fact that life is a train of thought, proves that man is a sign; so, that every thought is an *external* sign, proves that man is an external sign. That is to say, the man and the external sign are identical, in the same sense in which the words *homo* and *man* are identical. Thus my language is the sum total of myself; for the man is the thought.

It is hard for man to understand this, because he persists in identifying himself with his will, his power over the animal organism, with brute force. Now the organism is only an instrument of thought. But the identity of a man consists in the *consistency* of what he does and thinks, and consistency is the intellectual character of a thing; that is, is its expressing something.

Finally, as what anything really is, is what it may finally come to be known to be in the ideal state of complete information, so that reality depends on the ultimate decision of the community; so thought is what it is, only by virtue of its addressing a future thought which is in its value as thought identical with it, though more developed. In this way, the exis-

tence of thought now, depends on what is to be hereafter; so that it has only a potential existence, dependent on the future thought of the community.

The individual man, since his separate existence is manifested only by ignorance and error, so far as he is anything apart from his fellows, and from what he and they are to be, is only a negation. This is man,

> . . . *proud man,*
> *Most ignorant of what he's most assured,*
> *His glassy essence.*

### Note

1. Accordingly, just as we say that a body is in motion, and not that motion is in a body we ought to say that we are in thought, and not that thoughts are in us.

# The Fixation of Belief

## I

Few persons care to study logic, because everybody conceives himself to be proficient enough in the art of reasoning already. But I observe that this satisfaction is limited to one's own ratiocination, and does not extend to that of other men.

We come to the full possession of our power of drawing inferences the last of all our faculties, for it is not so much a natural gift as a long and difficult art. The history of its practice would make a grand subject for a book. The mediæval schoolman, following the Romans, made logic the earliest of a boy's studies after grammar, as being very easy. So it was as they understood it. Its fundamental principle, according to them, was that all

knowledge rests on either authority or reason; but that whatever is deduced by reason depends ultimately on a premise derived from authority. Accordingly, as soon as a boy was perfect in the syllogistic procedure, his intellectual kit of tools was held to be complete.

To Roger Bacon, that remarkable mind who in the middle of the thirteenth century was almost a scientific man, the schoolmen's conception of reasoning appeared only an obstacle to truth. He saw that experience alone teaches anything—a proposition which to us seems easy to understand, because a distinct conception of experience has been handed down to us from former generations; which to him also seemed perfectly clear, because its difficulties had not yet unfolded themselves. Of all kinds of experience, the best, he

From *Popular Science Monthly,* vol. 12, 1877, pp. 1–15.

thought, was interior illumination, which teaches many things about nature which the external senses could never discover, such as the transubstantiation of bread.

Four centuries later, the more celebrated Bacon, in the first book of his *Novum Organum,* gave his clear account of experience as something which must be opened to verification and re-examination. But, superior as Lord Bacon's conception is to earlier notions, a modern reader who is not in awe of his grandiloquence is chiefly struck by the inadequacy of his view of scientific procedure. That we have only to make some crude experiments, to draw up briefs of the results in certain blank forms, to go through these by rule, checking off everything disproved and setting down the alternatives, and that thus in a few years physical science would be finished up— what an idea! "He wrote on science like a Lord Chancellor,"[1] indeed, as Harvey, a genuine man of science, said.

The early scientists, Copernicus, Tycho Brahe, Kepler, Galileo, Harvey, and Gilbert, had methods more like those of their modern brethren. Kepler[2] undertook to draw a curve through the places of Mars; and his greatest service to science was in impressing on men's minds that this was the thing to be done if they wished to improve astronomy; that they were not to content themselves with inquiring whether one system of epicycles was better than another but that they were to sit down by the figures and find out what the curve, in truth, was. He accomplished this by his incomparable energy and courage, blundering along in the most inconceivable way (to us), from one irrational hypothesis to another, until, after trying twenty-two of these, he fell, by the mere exhaustion of his invention, upon the orbit which a mind well furnished with the weapons of modern logic would have tried almost at the outset.

In the same way, every work of science great enough to be remembered for a few generations affords some exemplification of the defective state of the art of reasoning of the time when it was written; and each chief step in science has been a lesson in logic. It was so when Lavoisier and his contemporaries took up the study of Chemistry. The old chemist's maxim had been *Lege, lege, lege, labora, ora, et relege.* Lavoisier's method was not to read and pray, not to dream that some long and complicated chemical process would have a certain effect, to put it into practice with dull patience, after its inevitable failure to dream that with some modification it would have another result, and to end by publishing the last dream as a fact: his way was to carry his mind into his laboratory, and to make of his alembics and cucurbits instruments of thought, giving a new conception of reasoning as something which was to be done with one's eyes open, by manipulating real things instead of words and fancies.

The Darwinian controversy is, in large part, a question of logic. Mr. Darwin proposed to apply the statistical method to biology. The same thing has been done in a widely different branch of science, the theory of gases. Though unable to say what the movement of any particular molecule of gas would be on a certain hypothesis regarding the constitution of this class of bodies, Clausius and Maxwell were yet able, by the application of the doctrine of probabilities, to predict that in the long run such and such a proportion of the molecules would, under given circumstances, acquire such and such velocities; that there would take place, every second, such and such a number of collisions, etc.; and from these propositions they were able to deduce certain properties of gases, especially in regard to their heat-relations. In like manner, Darwin, while unable to say what the operation of variation and natural selection in every individual case will be, demonstrates that in the long run they will adapt animals to their circumstances. Whether or not existing animal forms are due to such action, or what position the theory ought to take, forms the subject of a discussion in which questions of fact and questions of logic are curiously interlaced.

## II

The object of reasoning is to find out, from the consideration of what we already know, something else which we do not know. Consequently, reasoning is good if it be such as to give a true conclusion from true premises, and not otherwise. Thus, the question of validity is purely one of fact and not of thinking. A being the premises and B being the conclusion, the question is, whether these facts are really so related that if A is B is. If so, the inference is valid; if not, not. It is not in the least the question whether, when the premises are accepted by the mind, we feel an impulse to accept the conclusion also. It is true that we do generally reason correctly by nature. But that is an accident; the true conclusion would remain true if we had no impulse to accept it; and the false one would remain false, though we could not resist the tendency to believe in it.

We are, doubtless, in the main logical animals, but we are not perfectly so. Most of us, for example, are naturally more sanguine and hopeful than logic would justify. We seem to be so constituted that in the absence of any facts to go upon we are happy and self-satisfied; so that the effect of experience is continually to counteract our hopes and aspirations. Yet a lifetime of the application of this corrective does not usually eradicate our sanguine disposition. Where hope is unchecked by any experience, it is likely that our optimism is extravagant. Logicality in regard to practical matters is the most useful quality an animal can possess, and might, therefore, result from the action of natural selection; but outside of these it is probably of more advantage to the animal to have his mind filled with pleasing and encouraging visions, independently of their truth; and thus, upon unpractical subjects, natural selection might occasion a fallacious tendency of thought.

That which determines us, from given premises, to draw one inference rather than another is some habit of mind, whether it be constitutional or acquired. The habit is good or otherwise, according as it produces true conclusions from true premises or not; and an inference is regarded as valid or not, without reference to the truth or falsity of its conclusion specially, but according as the habit which determines it is such as to produce true conclusions in general or not. The particular habit of mind which governs this or that inference may be formulated in a proposition whose truth depends on the validity of the inferences which the habit determines; and such a formula is called a *guiding principle* of inference. Suppose, for example, that we observe that a rotating disk of copper quickly comes to rest when placed between the poles of a magnet, and we infer that this will happen with every disk of copper. The guiding principle is that what is true of one piece of copper is true of another. Such a guiding principle with regard to copper would be much safer than with regard to many other substances—brass, for example.

A book might be written to signalize all the most important of these guiding principles of reasoning. It would probably be, we must confess, of no service to a person whose thought is directed wholly to practical subjects, and whose activity moves along thoroughly beaten paths. The problems which present themselves to such a mind are matters of routine which he has learned once for all to handle in learning his business. But let a man venture into an unfamiliar field, or where his results are not continually checked by experience, and all history shows that the most masculine intellect will ofttimes lose his orientation and waste his efforts in directions which bring him no nearer to his goal, or even carry him entirely astray. He is like a ship on the open sea, with no one on board who understands the rules of navigation. And in such a case some general study of the guiding principles of reasoning would be sure to be found useful.

The subject could hardly be treated, however, without being first limited; since almost any fact may serve as a guiding principle. But it so happens that there exists a division among facts, such that in one class are all those which are absolutely essential as guiding principles, while in the other are all those which have any other interest as objects of research. This division is between those which are necessarily taken for granted in asking whether a certain conclusion follows from certain premises, and those which are not implied in that question. A moment's thought will show that a variety of facts are already assumed when the logical question is first asked. It is implied, for instance, that there are such states of mind as doubt and belief—that a passage from one to the other is possible, the object of thought remaining the same, and that this transition is subject to some rules which all minds are alike bound by. As these are facts which we must already know before we can have any clear conception of reasoning at all, it cannot be supposed to be any longer of much interest to inquire into their truth or falsity. On the other hand, it is easy to believe that those rules of reasoning which are deduced from the very idea of the process are the ones which are the most essential; and, indeed, that so long as it conforms to these it will, at least, not lead to false conclusions from true premises. In point of fact, the importance of what may be deduced from the assumptions involved in the logical question turns out to be greater than might be supposed, and this for reasons which it is difficult to exhibit at the outset. The only one which I shall here mention is that conceptions which are really products of logical reflections, without being readily seen to be so, mingle with our ordinary thoughts, and are frequently the causes of great confusion. This is the case, for example, with the conception of quality. A quality as such is never an object of observation. We can see that a thing is blue or green, but the quality of being blue and the quality of being green are not things which we see; they are products of logical reflections. The truth is that common sense, or thought as it first emerges above the level of the narrowly practical, is deeply inbued with that bad logical quality to which the epithet *metaphysical* is commonly applied; and nothing can clear it up but a severe course of logic.

### III

We generally know when we wish to ask a question and when we wish to pronounce a judgment, for there is a dissimilarity between the sensation of doubting and that of believing.

But this is not all which distinguishes doubt from belief. There is a practical difference.

Our beliefs guide our desires and shape our actions. The Assassins, or followers of the Old Man of the Mountain, used to rush into death at his least command, because they believed that obedience to him would insure everlasting felicity. Had they doubted this, they would not have acted as they did. So it is with every belief, according to its degree. The feeling of believing is a more or less sure indication of there being established in our nature some habit which will determine our actions. Doubt never has such an effect.

Nor must we overlook a third point of difference. Doubt is an uneasy and dissatisfied state from which we struggle to free ourselves and pass into the state of belief; while the latter is a calm and satisfactory state which we do not wish to avoid, or to change to a belief in anything else.[3] On the contrary, we cling tenaciously, not merely to believing, but to believing just what we do believe.

Thus, both doubt and belief have positive effects upon us, though very different ones. Belief does not make us act at once, but puts us into such a condition that we shall behave in a certain way, when the occasion arises. Doubt has not the least effect of this sort, but stimulates us to action until it is destroyed. This reminds us of the irritation of a nerve and the reflex action produced thereby; while for the analogue of belief, in the nervous system, we must look to what are called nervous associations—for example, to that habit of the nerves in consequence of which the smell of a peach will make the mouth water.

### IV

The irritation of doubt causes a struggle to attain a state of belief. I shall term this struggle *inquiry,* though it must be admitted that this is sometimes not a very apt designation.

The irritation of doubt is the only immediate motive for the struggle to attain belief. It is certainly best for us that our beliefs should be such as may truly guide our actions so as to satisfy our desires; and this reflection will make us reject any belief which does not seem to have been so formed as to insure this result.

But it will only do so by creating a doubt in the place of that belief. With the doubt, therefore, the struggle begins, and with the cessation of doubt it ends. Hence, the sole object of inquiry is the settlement of opinion. We may fancy that this is not enough for us, and that we seek not merely an opinion, but a true opinion. But put this fancy to the test, and it proves groundless; for as soon as a firm belief is reached we are entirely satisfied, whether the belief be false or true. And it is clear that nothing out of the sphere of our knowledge can be our object, for nothing which does not affect the mind can be a motive for a mental effort. The most that can be maintained is that we seek for a belief that we shall *think* to be true. But we think each one of our beliefs to be true, and, indeed, it is mere tautology to say so.

That the settlement of opinion is the sole end of inquiry is a very important proposition. It sweeps away, at once, various vague and erroneous conceptions of proof. A few of these may be noticed here.

1. Some philosophers have imagined that to start an inquiry it was only necessary to utter or question or set it down on paper, and have even recommended us to begin our studies with questioning everything! But the mere putting of a proposition into the interrogative form does not stimulate the mind to any struggle after belief. There must be a real and living doubt, and without all this, discussion is idle.

2. It is a very common idea that a demonstration must rest on some ultimate and absolutely indubitable propositions. These, according to one school, are first principles of a general nature; according to another, are first sensations. But, in point of fact, an inquiry, to have that completely satisfactory result called demonstration, has only to start with propositions perfectly free from all actual doubt. If the premises are not in fact doubted at all, they cannot be more satisfactory than they are.

3. Some people seem to love to argue a point after all the world is fully convinced of it. But no further advance can be made. When doubt ceases, mental action on the subject comes to an end; and, if it did go on, it would be without a purpose, except that of self-criticism.

## V

If the settlement of opinion is the sole object of inquiry, and if belief is of the nature of a habit, why should we not attain the desired end, by taking any answer to a question, which we may fancy, and constantly reiterating it to ourselves, dwelling on all which may conduce to that belief, and learning to turn with contempt and hatred from anything which might disturb it? This simple and direct method is really pursued by many men. I remember once being entreated not to read a certain newspaper lest it might change my opinion upon free-trade. "Lest I might be entrapped by its fallacies and misstatements" was the form of expression. "You are not," my friend said, "a special student of political economy. You might, therefore, easily be deceived by fallacious arguments upon the subject. You might, then, if you read this paper, be led to believe in protection. But you admit that free-trade is the true doctrine; and you do not wish to believe what is not true." I have often known this system to be deliberately adopted. Still oftener, the instinctive dislike of an undecided state of mind, exaggerated into a vague dread of doubt, makes men cling spasmodically to the views they already take. The man feels that if he only holds to his belief without wavering, it will be entirely satisfactory. Nor can it be denied that a steady and immovable faith yields great peace of mind. It may, indeed, give rise to inconveniences, as if a man should resolutely continue to believe that fire would not burn him, or that he would be eternally damned if he received his *ingesta* otherwise than through a stomach-pump. But then the man who adopts this method will not allow that its inconveniences are greater than its advantages. He will say, "I hold steadfastly to the truth and the truth is always wholesome." And in many cases it may very well be that the pleasure he derives from his calm faith overbalances any inconveniences resulting from its deceptive character. Thus, if it be true that death is annihilation, then the man who believes that he will certainly go straight to heaven when he dies, provided he have fulfilled certain simple observances in this life, has a cheap pleasure which will not be followed by the least disappointment. A similar consideration seems to have weight with many persons in religious topics, for we frequently hear it said, "Oh, I could not believe so-and-so, because I should be wretched if I did." When an ostrich buries its head in the sand as danger approaches, it very likely takes the happiest course. It hides the danger, and then calmly says there is no danger; and, if it feels perfectly sure there is none, why should it raise its head to see? A man may go through life, systematically keeping out of view all that might cause a change in his opinions, and if he only succeeds—basing his method, as he does, on two fundamental psychological laws—I do not see what can be said against his doing so. It would be an egotistical impertinence to object that this his procedure is irrational, for that only amounts to saying that his method of settling belief is not ours. He does not propose to himself to be rational, and indeed, will often talk with scorn of man's weak and illusive reason. So let him think as he pleases.

But this method of fixing belief, which may be called the method of tenacity, will be unable to hold its ground in practice. The social impulse is against it. The man who adopts it will find that other men think differently from him, and it will be apt to occur to him in some saner moment that their opinions are quite as good as his own, and this will shake his confidence in his belief. This conception, that another man's thought or sentiment may be equivalent to one's own, is a distinctly new step, and a highly important one. It arises from an impulse too strong in man to be suppressed, without danger of destroying the human species. Unless we make ourselves hermits, we shall necessarily influence each other's opinions; so that the problem becomes how to fix belief, not in the individual merely, but in the community.

Let the will of the state act, then, instead of that of the individual. Let an institution be created which shall have for its object to keep correct doctrines before the attention of the people, to reiterate them perpetually, and to teach them to the young; having at the same time power to prevent contrary doctrines from being taught, advocated, or expressed. Let all possible causes of a change of mind be removed from men's apprehensions. Let them be kept ignorant, lest they should learn of some reason to think otherwise than they do. Let their passions be enlisted, so that they may regard private and unusual opinions with hatred and horror. Then, let all men who reject the established belief be terrified into silence. Let the people turn out and tar-and-feather such men, or let inquisitions be made into the manner of thinking of suspected persons, and, when they are found guilty of forbidden beliefs, let them be subjected to some signal punishment. When complete agreement could not otherwise be reached, a general massacre of all who have not thought in a certain way has proved a very effective means of settling opinion in a country. If the power to do this be wanting, let a list of opinions be drawn up, to which no man of the least independence of thought can assent, and let the faithful be required to accept all these propositions, in order to segregate them as radically as possible from the influence of the rest of the world.

This method has, from the earliest times, been one of the chief means of upholding correct theological and political doctrines, and of preserving their universal or catholic character. In Rome, especially, it has been practiced from the days of Numa Pompilius to those of Pius Nonus. This is the most perfect example in history; but wherever there is a priesthood—and no religion has been without one—this method has been more or less made use of. Wherever there is aristocracy, or a guild, or any association of a class of men whose interests depend or are supposed to depend on certain propositions, there will be inevitably found some traces of this natural product of social feeling. Cruelties always accompany this system; and when it is consistently carried out, they become atrocities of the most horrible kind in the eyes of any rational man. Nor should this occasion surprise, for the officer of a society does not feel justified in surrendering the interests of that society for the sake of mercy, as he might his own private interests. It is natural, therefore, that sympathy and fellowship should thus produce a most ruthless power.

In judging this method of fixing belief, which may be called the method of authority, we must, in the first place, allow its immeasurable mental and moral superiority to the method of tenacity. Its success is proportionally greater; and in fact it has over and over again worked the most majestic results. The mere structures of stone which it has caused to be put together—in Siam, for example, in Egypt, and in Europe—have many of them a sublimity hardly more than rivaled by the greatest works of nature. And, except the geological epochs, there are no periods of time so vast as those which are measured by some of these organized faiths. If we scrutinize the matter closely, we shall find that there has not been one of their creeds which has remained always the same; yet the change is so slow as to be imperceptible during one person's life, so that individual belief remains sensibly fixed. For the mass of mankind, then, there is perhaps no better method than this. If it is their highest impulse to be intellectual slaves, then slaves they ought to remain.

But no institution can undertake to regulate opinions upon every subject. Only the most important ones can be attended to, and on the rest men's minds must be left to the action of natural causes. This imperfection will be no source of weakness so long as men are in such a state of culture that one opinion does not influence another—that is, so long as they cannot put two and two together. But in the most priest-ridden states some individuals will be found who are raised above that condition. These men possess a wider sort of social feeling; they see that men in other countries and in other ages have held to very different doctrines from those which they themselves have been brought up to believe; and they cannot help seeing that it is the mere accident of their having been taught as they have, and of their having been surrounded with the manners and associations they have, that has caused them to believe as they do and not far differently. And their candor cannot resist the reflection that there is no reason to rate their own views at a higher value than those of other nations and other centuries; and this gives rise to doubts in their minds.

They will further perceive that such doubts as these must exist in their minds with reference to every belief which seems to be determined by the caprice either of themselves or of those who originated the popular opinions. The willful adherence to a belief, and the arbitrary forcing of it upon others, must, therefore, both be given up and a new method of settling opinions must be adopted, which shall not only produce an impulse to believe, but shall also decide what proposition it is which is to be believed. Let the action of natural preferences be unimpeded, then, and under their influence let men conversing together and regarding matters in different lights, gradually develop beliefs in harmony with natural causes. This method resembles that by which conceptions of art have been brought to maturity. The most perfect example of it is to be found in the history of metaphysical philosophy. Systems of this sort have not usually rested upon observed facts, at least not in any great degree. They have been chiefly adopted because their fundamental propositions seemed "agreeable to reason." This is an apt expression; it does not mean that which agrees with experience, but that which we find ourselves inclined to believe. Plato, for example, finds it agreeable to reason that the distances of the celestial spheres from one another should be proportional to the different lengths of strings which produce harmonious chords. Many philosophers have been led to their main conclusions by considerations like this; but this is the lowest and least developed form which the method takes, for it is clear that another man might find Kepler's [earlier] theory, that the celestial spheres are proportional to the inscribed and circumscribed spheres of the different regular solids, more agreeable to *his* reason. But the shock of opinions will soon lead men to rest on preferences of a far more universal nature. Take, for example, the doctrine that man only acts selfishly—that is, from the consideration that acting in one way will afford him more pleasure than acting in another. This rests on no fact in the world, but it has had a wide acceptance as being the only reasonable theory.

This method is far more intellectual and respectable from the point of view of reason than either of the others which we have noticed. But its failure has been the most manifest. It makes of inquiry something similar to the development of taste; but taste, unfortunately, is always more or less a matter of fashion, and accordingly, metaphysicians have never come to any fixed agreement, but the pendulum has swung backward and forward between a more material and a more spiritual philosophy, from the earliest times to the latest. And so from this, which has been called the *a priori* method, we are driven, in Lord Bacon's phrase, to a true induction. We have examined into this *a priori* method as something which promised to deliver our opinions from their accidental and capricious element. But development, while it is a process which eliminates the effect of some casual circumstances, only magnifies that of others. This method, therefore, does not differ in a very essential way from that of authority. The government may not have lifted its finger to influence my convictions; I may have been left outwardly quite free to choose, we will say, between monogamy and polygamy, and appealing to my conscience only, I may have concluded that the latter practice is in itself licentious. But when I come to see that the chief obstacle to the spread of Christianity among a people of as high culture as the Hindoos has been a conviction of the immorality of our way of treating women, I cannot help seeing that, though governments do not interfere, sentiments in their development will be very greatly determined by accidental causes. Now, there are some people, among whom I must suppose that my reader is to be found, who, when they see that any belief of theirs is determined by any circumstance extraneous to the facts, will from that moment not merely admit in words that that belief is doubtful, but will experience a real doubt of it, so that it ceases in some degree at least to be a belief.

To satisfy our doubts, therefore, it is necessary that a method should be found by which our beliefs may be caused by nothing human, but by some external permanency—by something upon which our thinking has no effect. Some mystics imagine that they have such a method in a private inspiration from on high. But that is only a form of the method of tenacity, in which the conception of truth as something public is not yet developed. Our external permanency would not be external, in our sense, if it was restricted in its influence to one individual. It must be something which affects, or might affect, every man. And, though these affections are necessarily as various as are individual conditions, yet the method must be such that the ultimate conclusion of every man shall be the same, or would be the same if inquiry were sufficiently persisted in. Such is the method of science. Its fundamental hypothesis, restated in more familiar language, is this: There are real things, whose characters are entirely independent of our opinions about them; those realities affect our senses according to regular laws, and, though our sensations are as different as our relations to the objects, yet, by taking advantage of the laws of perception, we can ascertain by reasoning how things really are, and any man, if he have sufficient experience and reason enough about it, will be led to the one true conclusion. The new conception here involved is that of reality. It may be asked how I know that there are any realities. If this hypothesis is the sole support of my method of inquiry, my method of inquiry must not be used to support my hypothesis. The reply is this: (1) If investigation cannot be regarded as proving that there are real things, it at least does not lead to a contrary conclusion; but the method and the conception on which it is based remain ever in harmony. No doubts of the method, therefore, necessarily arise from its practice, as is the case with all the others. (2) The feeling which gives rise to any method of fixing belief is a dissatisfaction at two repugnant propositions. But here already is a vague concession that there is some *one* thing to which a proposition should conform. Nobody, therefore, can really doubt that there are realities, or, if he did, doubt would not be a source of dissatisfaction. The hypothesis, therefore, is one which every mind admits. So that the social impulse does not cause men to doubt it. (3) Everybody uses the scientific method about a great many things, and only ceases to use it when he does not know how to apply it. (4) Experience of the method has not led us to doubt it, but, on the contrary, scientific investigation has had the most wonderful triumphs in the way of settling opinion. These afford the explanation of my not doubting the method or the hypothesis which it supposes; and not having any doubt, nor believing that anybody else whom I could influence has, it would be the merest babble for me to say more about it. If there be anybody with a living doubt upon the subject, let him consider it.

To describe the method of scientific investigation is the object of this series of papers. At present I have only room to notice some points of contrast between it and other methods of fixing belief.

This is the only one of the four methods which presents any distinction of a right and a wrong way. If I adopt the method of tenacity and shut myself out from all influences, whatever I think necessary to doing this is necessary according to that method. So with the method of authority: the state may try to put down heresy by means which, from a scientific point of view, seems very ill-calculated to accomplish its purposes; but the only test *on that method* is what the state thinks, so that it cannot pursue the method wrongly. So with the a priori method. The very essence of it is to think as one is inclined to think. All metaphysicians will be sure to do that, however they may be inclined to judge each other to be perversely wrong. The Hegelian system recognizes every natural tendency of thought as logical, although it is certain to be abolished by counter-tendencies. Hegel thinks there is a regular system in the succession of these tendencies, in consequence of which, after drifting one way and the other for a long time, opinion will at last go right. And it is true that metaphysicians get the right ideas at last; Hegel's system of Nature represents tolerably the science of his day; and one may be sure that whatever scientific investigation has put out of

doubt will presently receive a priori demonstration on the part of the metaphysicians. But with the scientific method the case is different. I may start with known and observed facts to proceed to the unknown; and yet the rules which I follow in doing so may not be such as investigation would approve. The test of whether I am truly following the method is not an immediate appeal to my feelings and purposes, but, on the contrary, itself involves the application of the method. Hence it is that bad reasoning as well as good reasoning is possible; and this fact is the foundation of the practical side of logic.

It is not to be supposed that the first three methods of settling opinion present no advantage whatever over the scientific method. On the contrary, each has some peculiar convenience of its own. The a priori method is distinguished for its comfortable conclusions. It is the nature of the process to adopt whatever belief we are inclined to, and there are certain flatteries to one's vanities which we all believe by nature, until we are awakened from our pleasing dream by rough facts. The method of authority will always govern the mass of mankind; and those who wield the various forms of organized force in the state will never be convinced that dangerous reasoning ought not to be suppressed in some way. If liberty of speech is to be untrammeled from the grosser forms of constraint, then uniformity of opinion will be secured by a moral terrorism to which the respectability of society will give its thorough approval. Following the method of authority is the path of peace. Certain nonconformities are permitted; certain others (considered unsafe) are forbidden. These are different in different countries and in different ages; but, wherever you are let it be known that you seriously hold a tabooed belief, and you may be perfectly sure of being treated with a cruelty no less brutal but more refined than hunting you like a wolf. Thus, the greatest intellectual benefactors of mankind have never dared, and dare not now, to utter the whole of their thought; and thus a shade of *prima facie* doubt is cast upon every proposition which is considered essential to the security of society. Singularly enough, the persecution does not all come from without; but a man torments himself and is oftentimes most distressed at finding himself believing propositions which he has been brought up to regard with aversion. The peaceful and sympathetic man will, therefore, find it hard to resist the temptation to submit his opinions to authority. But most of all I admire the method of tenacity for its strength, simplicity, and directness. Men who pursue it are distinguished for their decision of character, which becomes very easy with such a mental rule. They do not waste time in trying to make up their minds to what they want, but, fastening like lightning upon whatever alternative comes first, they hold to it to the end, whatever happens, without an instant's irresolution. This is one of the splendid qualities which generally accompany brilliant, unlasting success. It is impossible not to envy the man who can dismiss reason, although we know how it must turn out at last.

Such are the advantages which the other methods of settling opinions have over scientific investigation. A man should consider well of them; and then he should consider that, after all, he wishes his opinions to coincide with the fact, and that there is no reason why the results of those first three methods should do so. To bring about this effect is the prerogative of the method of science. Upon such considerations he has to make his choice—a choice which is far more than the adoption of any intellectual opinion, which is one of the ruling decisions of his life, to which when once made he is bound to adhere. The force of habit will sometimes cause a man to hold on to old beliefs after he is in a condition to see that they have no sound basis. But reflection upon the state of the case will overcome these habits, and he ought to allow reflection full weight. People sometimes shrink from doing this, having an idea that beliefs are wholesome which they cannot help feeling rest on nothing. But let such persons suppose an analogous though different case from their own. Let them ask themselves what they would say to a reformed Mussulman who should hesitate to

give up his old notions in regard to the relations of the sexes; or to a reformed Catholic who should still shrink from the Bible. Would they not say that these persons ought to consider the matter fully, and clearly understand the new doctrine, and then ought to embrace it in its entirety? But, above all, let it be considered that what is more wholesome than any particular belief is integrity of belief; and that to avoid looking into the support of any belief from a fear that it may turn out rotten is quite as immoral as it is disadvantageous. The person who confesses that there is such a thing as truth, which is distinguished from falsehood simply by this, that if acted on it should, on full consideration, carry us to the point we aim at and not astray, and then, though convinced of this, dares not know the truth and seeks to avoid it, is in a sorry state of mind, indeed.

Yes, the other methods do have their merits: a clear logical conscience does cost something—just as any virtue, just as all that we cherish, costs us dear. But, we should not desire it to be otherwise. The genius of a man's logical method should be loved and reverenced as his bride, whom he has chosen from all the world. He need not condemn the others; on the contrary, he may honor them deeply, and in doing so he only honors her the more. But she is the one that he has chosen, and he knows that he was right in making that choice. And having made it, he will work and fight for her, and will not complain that there are blows to take, hoping that there may be as many and as hard to give, and will strive to be the worthy knight and champion of her from the blaze of whose splendors he draws his inspiration and his courage.

## Notes

1. Cf. J. Aubrey's *Brief Lives* (Oxford, ed. 1898), I, 299.
2. Not quite so, but as nearly as can be told in a few words.
3. I am not speaking of secondary effects occasionally produced by the interference of other impulses.

# How to Make Our Ideas Clear

## I

Whoever has looked into a modern treatise on logic of the common sort, will doubtless remember the two distinctions between *clear* and *obscure* conceptions, and between *distinct* and *confused* conceptions. They have lain in the books now for nigh two centuries, unimproved and unmodified, and are generally reckoned by logicians as among the gems of their doctrine.

A clear idea is defined as one which is so apprehended that it will be recognized wherever it is met with, and so that no other will be mistaken for it. If it fails of this clearness, it is said to be obscure.

This is rather a neat bit of philosophical terminology; yet, since it is clearness that they were defining, I wish the logicians had made their definition a little more plain. Never to fail to recognize an idea, and under no circumstances to mistake another for it, let it come in how recondite a form it may, would indeed imply such prodigious force and clearness of intellect as is seldom met with in this world. On the other hand, merely to have such an acquaintance with the idea as to have become familiar with it, and to have lost all hesitancy in recognizing it in ordinary cases, hardly seems to deserve the name of clearness of apprehension, since after all it only amounts to a subjective feeling of mastery which may be entirely mistaken. I take it, however, that when the logicians speak of "clearness," they mean nothing more than such a familiarity with an idea, since they regard the quality as but a small merit, which needs to be supplemented by another, which they call *distinctness.*

A distinct idea is defined as one which contains nothing which is not clear. This is technical language; by the *contents* of an idea logicians understand whatever is contained in its definition. So that an idea is *distinctly* apprehended, according to them, when we can give a precise definition of it, in abstract terms. Here the professional logicians leave the subject; and I would not have troubled the reader with what they have to say if it were not such a striking example of how they have been slumbering through ages of intellectual activity, listlessly disregarding the enginery of modern thought, and never dreaming of applying its lessons to the improvement of logic. It is easy to show that the doctrine that familiar use and abstract distinctness make the perfection of apprehension, has its only true place in philosophies which have long been extinct; and it is now time to formulate the method of attaining to a more perfect clearness of thought, such as we see and admire in the thinkers of our own time.

When Descartes set about the reconstruction of philosophy, his first step was to (theoretically) permit skepticism and to discard the practice of the schoolmen of looking to authority as the ultimate source of truth. That done, he sought a more natural fountain of true principles, and professed to find it in the human mind; thus passing, in the directest way, from the method of authority to that of apriority, as described in my first paper. Self-consciousness was to furnish us with our fundamental truths, and to decide what was agreeable to reason. But since, evidently, not all ideas are true, he was led to note, as the first condition of infallibility, that they must be clear. The distinction between an idea *seeming* clear and really being so, never occurred to him. Trusting to introspection, as he did, even for a knowledge of external things, why should he question its testimony in respect to the contents of our own minds? But then, I suppose, seeing men, who seemed to be quite clear and positive, holding opposite opinions upon fundamental principles, he was further

From *Popular Science Monthly* vol. 12, 1878, pp. 286–302.

led to say that clearness of ideas is not sufficient, but that they need also to be distinct, i.e., to have nothing unclear about them. What he probably meant by this (for he did not explain himself with precision) was that they must sustain the test of dialectical examination; that they must not only seem clear at the outset, but that discussion must never be able to bring to light points of obscurity connected with them.

Such was the distinction of Descartes, and one sees that it was precisely on the level of his philosophy. It was somewhat developed by Leibniz. This great and singular genius was as remarkable for what he failed to see as for what he saw. That a piece of mechanism could not do work perpetually without being fed with power in some form, was a thing perfectly apparent to him; yet he did not understand that the machinery of the mind can only transform knowledge, but never originate it, unless it be fed with facts of observation. He thus missed the most essential point of the Cartesian philosophy, which is, that to accept propositions which seem perfectly evident to us is a thing which, whether it be logical or illogical, we cannot help doing. Instead of regarding the matter in this way, he sought to reduce the first principles of science to formulas which cannot be denied without self-contradiction, and was apparently unaware of the great difference between his position and that of Descartes. So he reverted to the old formalities of logic, and, above all, abstract definitions played a great part in his philosophy. It was quite natural, therefore, that on observing that the method of Descartes labored under the difficulty that we may seem to ourselves to have clear apprehensions of ideas which in truth are very hazy, no better remedy occurred to him than to require an abstract definition of every important term. Accordingly, in adopting the distinction of *clear* and *distinct* notions, he described the latter quality as the clear apprehension of everything contained in the definition; and the books have ever since copied his words. There is no danger that his chimerical scheme will ever again be overvalued. Nothing new can ever be learned by analyzing definitions. Nevertheless, our existing beliefs can be set in order by this

process, and order is an essential element of intellectual economy, as of every other. It may be acknowledged, therefore, that the books are right in making familiarity with a notion the first step toward clearness of apprehension, and the defining of it the second. But in omitting all mention of any higher perspicuity of thought, they simply mirror a philosophy which was exploded a hundred years ago. That much-admired "ornament of logic"—the doctrine of clearness and distinctness—may be pretty enough, but it is high time to relegate to our cabinet of curiosities the antique *bijou,* and to wear about us something better adapted to modern uses.

The very first lesson that we have a right to demand that logic shall teach us is how to make our ideas clear; and a most important one it is, depreciated only by minds who stand in need of it. To know what we think, to be masters of our own meaning, will make a solid foundation for great and weighty thought. It is most easily learned by those whose ideas are meagre and restricted; and far happier they than such as wallow helplessly in a rich mud of conceptions. A nation, it is true, may, in the course of generations, overcome the disadvantage of an excessive wealth of language and its natural concomitant, a vast, unfathomable deep of ideas. We may see it in history, slowly perfecting its literary forms, sloughing at length its metaphysics, and, by virtue of the untirable patience which is often a compensation, attaining great excellence in every branch of mental acquirement. The page of history is not yet unrolled which is to tell us whether such a people will or will not in the long run prevail over one whose ideas (like the words of their language) are few, but which possesses a wonderful mastery over those which it has. For an individual, however, there can be no question that a few clear ideas are worth more than many confused ones. A young man would hardly be persuaded to sacrifice the greater part of his thoughts to save the rest; and the muddled head is the least apt to see the necessity of such a sacrifice. Him we can usually only commiserate, as a person with a congenital defect. Time will help him, but intellectual maturity with regard to clearness comes rather late, an unfortunate arrangement of nature, inasmuch as clearness is of less use to a man settled in life, whose errors have in great measure had their effect, than it would be to one whose path lies before him. It is terrible to see how a single unclear idea, a single formula without meaning, lurking in a young man's head, will sometimes act like an obstruction of inert matter in an artery, hindering the nutrition of the brain, and condemning its victim to pine away in the fullness of his intellectual vigor and in the midst of intellectual plenty. Many a man has cherished for years as his hobby some vague shadow of an idea, too meaningless to be positively false; he has, nevertheless, passionately loved it, has made it his companion by day and by night, and has given to it his strength and his life, leaving all other occupations for its sake, and in short has lived with it and for it, until it has become, as it were, flesh of his flesh and bone of his bone; and then he has waked up some bright morning to find it gone, clean vanished away like the beautiful Melusina of the fable, and the essence of his life gone with it. I have myself known such a man; and who can tell how many histories of circle-squarers, metaphysicians, astrologers, and what not, may not be told in the old German story?

## II

The principles set forth in the first of these papers lead, at once, to a method of reaching a clearness of thought of a far higher grade than the "distinctness" of the logicians. We have there found that the action of thought is excited by the irritation of doubt, and ceases when belief is attained; so that the production of belief is the sole function of thought. All these words, however, are too strong for my purpose. It is as if I had described the phenomena as they appear under a mental microscope. Doubt and Belief, as the words are commonly employed, relate to religious or other grave discussions. But here I use them to designate the starting of any question, no matter how small or how great, and the resolution of it. If, for instance, in a horse-car, I pull out my purse and find a five-cent nickel and five coppers, I decide, while my hand is going to the purse, in which way I will pay my fare. To call such a question Doubt, and my decision Belief, is certainly to use words very disproportionate to the occasion. To speak of such a doubt as causing an irritation which needs to be appeased, suggests a temper which is uncomfortable to the verge of insanity. Yet, looking at the matter minutely, it must be admitted that, if there is the least hesitation as to whether I shall pay the five coppers or the nickel (as there will be sure to be, unless I act from some previously contracted habit in the matter), though irritation is too strong a word, yet I am excited to such small mental activity as may be necessary to deciding how I shall act. Most frequently doubts arise from some indecision, however momentary, in our action. Sometimes it is not so. I have, for example, to wait in a railway-station, and to pass the time I read the advertisements on the walls, I compare the advantages of different trains and different routes which I never expect to take, merely fancying myself to be in a state of hesitancy, because I am bored with having nothing to trouble me. Feigned hesitancy, whether feigned for mere amusement or with a lofty purpose, plays a great part in the production of scientific inquiry. However the doubt may originate, it stimulates the mind to an activity which may be slight or energetic, calm or turbulent. Images pass rapidly through consciousness, one incessantly melting into another, until at last, when all is over—it may be in a fraction of a second, in an hour, or after long years—we find ourselves decided as to how we should act under such circumstances as those which occasioned our hesitation. In other words, we have attained belief.

In this process we observe two sorts of elements of consciousness, the distinction between which may best be made clear by means of an illustration. In a piece of music there are the separate notes, and there is the air. A single tone may be prolonged for an hour or a day, and it exists as perfectly in each second of that time as in the whole taken together; so that, as long as it is sounding, it might be present to a sense from which everything in the past was as completely absent as the future itself. But it is different with the air, the performance of which occupies a certain time, during the portions of which only portions of it are played. It consists in an orderliness in the succession of sounds which strike the ear at different times; and to perceive it there must be some continuity of consciousness which makes the events of a lapse of time present to us. We certainly only perceive the air by hearing the separate notes; yet we cannot be said to directly hear it, for we hear only what is present at the instant, and an orderliness of succession cannot exist in an instant. These two sorts of objects, what we are *immediately* conscious of and what we are *mediately* conscious of, are found in all consciousness. Some elements (the sensations) are completely present at every instant so long as they last, while others (like thought) are actions having beginning, middle, and end, and consist in a congruence in the succession of sensations which flow through the mind. They cannot be immediately present to us, but must cover some portion of the past or future. Thought is a thread of melody running through the succession of our sensations.

We may add that just as a piece of music may be written in parts, each part having its own air, so various systems of relationship of succession subsist together between the same sensations. These different systems are distinguished by having different motives, ideas, or functions. Thought is only one such system; for its sole motive, idea, and function is to produce belief, and whatever does not concern that purpose belongs to some other system of relations. The action of thinking may incidentally have other results. It may serve to amuse us, for example, and among *dilettanti* it is not rare to find those who have so perverted thought to the purposes of pleasure that it seems to vex them to think that the questions upon which they delight to exercise it may ever get finally settled; and a positive discovery which takes a favorite subject out of the arena of literary debate is met with ill-concealed dislike. This disposition is the very debauchery of thought. But the soul and meaning of thought, abstracted from the other elements which accompany it, though it may be voluntarily thwarted, can never be made to direct itself toward anything but the production of belief. Thought in action has for its only possible motive the attainment of thought at rest; and whatever does not refer to belief is no part of the thought itself.

And what, then, is belief? It is the demi-cadence which closes a musical phrase in the symphony of our intellectual life. We have seen that it has just three properties: first, it is something that we are aware of; second, it appeases the irritation of doubt; and, third, it involves the establishment in our nature of a rule of action, or, say for short, a *habit*. As it appeases the irritation of doubt, which is the motive for thinking, thought relaxes, and comes to rest for a moment when belief is reached. But, since belief is a rule for action, the application of which involves further doubt and further thought, at the same time that it is a stopping-place, it is also a new starting-place for thought. That is why I have permitted myself to call it thought at rest, although thought is essentially an action. The *final* upshot of thinking is the exercise of volition, and of this thought no longer forms a part; but belief is only a stadium of mental action, an effect upon our nature due to thought, which will influence future thinking.

The essence of belief is the establishment of a habit, and different beliefs are distinguished by the different modes of action to which they give rise. If beliefs do not differ in this respect, if they appease the same doubt by producing the same rule of action, then no mere differences in the manner of consciousness of them can make them different beliefs, any more than playing a tune in different keys is playing different tunes. Imaginary distinctions are often drawn between beliefs which differ only in their mode of expression—the wrangling which ensues is real enough, however. To believe that any objects are arranged among themselves as in Fig. 1, and to believe

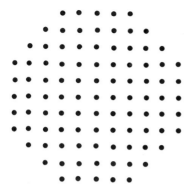

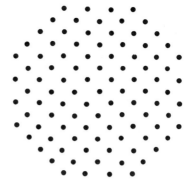

Fig. 1.                                           Fig. 2.

that they are arranged as in Fig. 2, are one and the same belief; yet it is conceivable that a man should assert one proposition and deny the other. Such false distinctions do as much harm as the confusion of beliefs really different, and are among the pitfalls of which we ought constantly to beware, especially when we are upon metaphysical ground. One singular deception of this sort, which often occurs, is to mistake the sensation produced by our own unclearness of thought for a character of the object we are thinking. Instead of perceiving that the obscurity is purely subjective, we fancy that we contemplate a quality of the object which is essentially mysterious; and if our conception be afterward presented to us in a clear from we do not recognize it as the same, owing to the absence of the feeling of unintelligibility. So long as this deception lasts, it obviously puts an impassable barrier in the way of perspicuous thinking; so that it equally interests the opponents of rational thought to perpetuate it, and its adherents to guard against it.

Another such deception is to mistake a mere difference in the grammatical construction of two words for a distinction between the ideas they express. In this pedantic age, when the general mob of writers attend so much more to words than to things, this error is common enough. When I just said that thought is an *action,* and that it consists in a *relation,* although a person performs an action but not a relation, which can only be the result of an

action, yet there was no inconsistency in what I said, but only a grammatical vagueness.

From all these sophisms we shall be perfectly safe so long as we reflect that the whole function of thought is to produce habits of action; and that whatever there is connected with a thought, but irrelevant to its purpose, is an accretion to it, but no part of it. If there be a unity among our sensations which has no reference to how we shall act on a given occasion, as when we listen to a piece of music, why, we do not call that thinking. To develop its meaning, we have, therefore, simply to determine what habits it produces, for what a thing means is simply what habits it involves. Now, the identity of a habit depends on how it might lead us to act, not merely under such circumstances as are likely to arise, but under such as might possibly occur, no matter how improbable they may be. What the habit is depends on *when* and *how* it causes us to act. As for the *when,* every stimulus to action is derived from perception; as for the *how,* every purpose of action is to produce some sensible result. Thus, we come down to what is tangible and practical as the root of every real distinction of thought, no matter how subtle it may be; and there is no distinction of meaning so fine as to consist in anything but a possible difference of practice.

To see what this principle leads to, consider in the light of it such a doctrine as that of transubstantiation. The Protestant churches generally hold that the elements of the sacrament are flesh and blood only in a tropical sense; they nourish our souls as meat and the juice of it would our bodies. But the Catholics maintain that they are literally just that, meat and blood; although they possess all the sensible qualities of wafer-cakes and diluted wine. But we can have no conception of wine except what may enter into a belief, either—

1. That this, that, or the other, is wine; or,
2. That wine possesses certain properties.

Such beliefs are nothing but self-notifications that we should, upon occasion, act in regard to such things as we believe to be wine according to the qualities which we believe wine to possess. The occasion of such action would be some sensible perception, the motive of it to produce some sensible result. Thus our action has exclusive reference to what affects the senses, our habit has the same bearing as our action, our belief the same as our habit, our conception the same as our belief; and we can consequently mean nothing by wine but what has certain effects, direct or indirect, upon our senses; and to talk of something as having all the sensible characters of wine, yet being in reality blood, is senseless jargon. Now, it is not my object to pursue the theological question; and having used it as a logical example I drop it, without caring to anticipate the theologian's reply. I only desire to point out how impossible it is that we should have an idea in our minds which relates to anything but conceived sensible effects of things. Our idea of anything *is* our idea of its sensible effects; and if we fancy that we have any other we deceive ourselves, and mistake a mere sensation accompanying the thought for a part of the thought itself. It is absurd to say that thought has any meaning unrelated to its only function. It is foolish for Catholics and Protestants to fancy themselves in disagreement about the elements of the sacrament, if they agree in regard to all their sensible effects, here or hereafter.

It appears, then, that the rule for attaining the third grade of clearness of apprehension is as follows: consider what effects, which might conceivably have practical bearings, we conceive the object of our conception to have. Then, our conception of these effects is the whole of our conception of the object.

# III

Let us illustrate this rule by some examples; and, to begin with the simplest one possible, let us ask what we mean by calling a thing *hard*. Evidently that it will not be scratched by many other substances. The whole conception of this quality, as of every other, lies in its conceived effects. There is absolutely no difference between a hard thing and a soft thing so long as they are not brought to the test. Suppose, then, that a diamond could be crystallized in the midst of a cushion of soft cotton, and should remain there until it was finally burned up. Would it be false to say that that diamond was soft? This seems a foolish question, and would be so, in fact, except in the realm of logic. There such questions are often of the greatest utility as serving to bring logical principles into sharper relief than real discussions ever could. In studying logic we must not put them aside with hasty answers, but must consider them with attentive care, in order to make out the principles involved. We may, in the present case, modify our question, and ask what prevents us from saying that all hard bodies remain perfectly soft until they are touched, when their hardness increases with the pressure until they are scratched. Reflection will show that the reply is this: there would be no *falsity* in such modes of speech. They would involve a modification of our present usage of speech with regard to the words "hard" and "soft," but not of their meanings. For they represent no fact to be different from what it is; only they involve arrangements of facts which would be exceedingly maladroit. This leads us to remark that the question of what would occur under circumstances which do not actually arise is not a question of fact, but only of the most perspicuous arrangement of them. For example, the question of free-will and fate in its simplest form, stripped of verbiage, is something like this: I have done something of which I am ashamed; could I, by an effort of the will, have resisted the temptation, and done otherwise? The philosophical reply is that this is not a question of fact, but only of the [possible] arrangement of facts. Arranging them so as to exhibit what is particularly pertinent to my question—namely, that I ought to blame myself for having done wrong—it is perfectly true to say that, if I had willed to do otherwise than I did, I should have done otherwise. On the other hand, arranging the facts so as to exhibit another important consideration, it is equally true that when a temptation has once been allowed to work, it will, if it has a certain force, produce its effect, let me struggle how I may. There is no objection to a contradiction in what would result from a false supposition. The *reductio ad absurdum* consists in showing that contradictory results would follow from a hypothesis which is consequently judged to be false. Many questions are involved in the free-will discussion, and I am far from desiring to say that both sides are equally right. On the contrary, I am of opinion that one side [determinism] denies important facts, and that the other does not. But what I do say is that the above single question was the origin of the whole doubt; that, had it not been for this question, the controversy would never have arisen; and that this question is perfectly solved in the manner which I have indicated.

Let us next seek a clear idea of Weight. This is another very easy case. To say that a body is heavy means simply that, in the absence of opposing force, it will fall. This (neglecting certain specifications of how it will fall, etc., which exist in the mind of the physicist who uses the word) is evidently the whole conception of weight. It is a fair question whether some particular facts may not *account* for gravity; but what we mean by the force itself is completely involved in its effects.

This leads us to undertake an account of the idea of Force in general. This is the great conception which, developed in the early part of the seventeenth century from the rude idea of a cause, and, constantly improved upon since,

has shown us how to explain all the changes of motion which bodies experience, and how to think about all physical phenomena; which has given birth to modern science, and changed the face of the globe; and which, aside from its more special uses, has played a principal part in directing the course of modern thought, and in furthering modern social development. It is, therefore, worth some pains to comprehend it. According to our rule, we must begin by asking what is the immediate use of thinking about force; and the answer is that we thus account for changes of motion. If bodies were left to themselves, without the intervention of forces, every motion would continue unchanged both in velocity and in direction. Furthermore, change of motion never takes place abruptly; if its direction is changed, it is always through a curve without angles; if its velocity alters, it is by degrees. The gradual changes which are constantly taking place are conceived by geometers to be compounded together according to the rules of the parallelogram of forces. If the reader does not already know what this is, he will find it, I hope, to his advantage to endeavor to follow the following explanation; but if mathematics are insupportable to him, pray let him skip three paragraphs rather than that we should part company here.

A *path* is a line whose beginning and end are distinguished. Two paths are considered to be equivalent, which, beginning at the same point, lead to the same point. Thus the two paths, *A B C D E* and *A F G H E* (Fig. 3), are equivalent. Paths which do *not* begin at the same point are considered to be equivalent, provided that, on moving either of them without turning it, but keeping it always parallel to its original position, [so that] when its beginning coincides with that of the other path, the ends also coincide. Paths are considered as geometrically added together, when one begins where the other ends; thus the path *A E* is conceived to be a sum of *A B, B C, C D*, and *D E*. In the parallelogram of Fig. 4 the diagonal *A C* is the sum of *A B* and *B C*; or, since *A D* is geometrically equivalent to *B C, A C* is the geometrical sum of *A B* and *A D*.

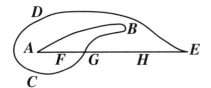

Fig. 3.

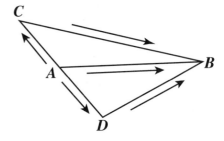

Fig. 5.

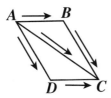

Fig. 4.

All this is purely conventional. It simply amounts to this: that we choose to call paths having the relations I have described equal or added. But, though it is a convention, it is a convention with a good reason. The rule for geometrical addition may be applied not only to paths, but to any other things which can be represented by paths. Now, as a path is determined by the varying direction and distance of the point which moves over it from the starting-point, it follows that anything which from its beginning to its end is determined by a varying direction and a varying magnitude is capable of being represented by a line. Accordingly, *velocities* may be represented by lines, for they have only directions and rates. The same thing is true of *accelerations,* or changes of velocities. This is evident enough in the case of velocities; and it becomes evident for accelerations if we consider that precisely what velocities are to positions—namely, states of change of them—that accelerations are to velocities.

The so-called "parallelogram of forces" is simply a rule for compounding accelerations. The rule is, to represent the accelerations by paths, and then to geometrically add the paths. The geometers, however, not only use the "parallelogram of forces" to compound different accelerations, but also to resolve one

acceleration into a sum of several. Let *A B* (Fig. 5) be the path which represents a certain acceleration—say, such a change in the motion of a body that at the end of one second the body will, under the influence of that change, be in a position different from what it would have had if its motion had continued unchanged, such that a path equivalent to *A B* would lead from the latter position to the former. This acceleration may be considered as the sum of the accelerations represented by *A C* and *C B*. It may also be considered as the sum of the very different accelerations represented by *A D* and *D B*, where *A D* is almost the opposite of *A C*. And it is clear that there is an immense variety of ways in which *A B* might be resolved into the sum of two accelerations.

After this tedious explanation, which I hope, in view of the extraordinary interest of the conception of force, may not have exhausted the reader's patience, we are prepared at last to state the grand fact which this conception embodies. This fact is that if the actual changes of motion which the different particles of bodies experience are each resolved in its appropriate way, each component acceleration is precisely such as is prescribed by a certain law of Nature, according to which bodies in the relative positions which the bodies in question actually have at the moment,[1] always receive certain accelerations, which, being compounded by geometrical addition, give the acceleration which the body actually experiences.

This is the only fact which the idea of force represents, and whoever will take the trouble clearly to apprehend what this fact is perfectly comprehends what force is. Whether we ought to say that a force *is* an acceleration, or that it *causes* an acceleration, is a mere question of propriety of language, which has no more to do with our real meaning than the difference between the French idiom "*Il fait froid*" and its English equivalent "*It is cold.*" Yet it is surprising to see how this simple affair has muddled men's minds. In how many profound treatises is not force spoken of as a "mysterious entity," which seems to be only a way of confessing that the author despairs of ever getting a clear notion of what the word means! In a recent, admired work on *Analytic Mechanics* [by Kirchhoff] it is stated that we understand precisely the effect of force, but what force itself is we do not understand! This is simply a self-contradiction. The idea which the word "force" excites in our minds has no other function than to affect our actions, and these actions can have no reference to force otherwise than through its effects. Consequently, if we know what the effects of force are, we are acquainted with every fact which is implied in saying that a force exists, and there is nothing more to know. The truth is, there is some vague notion afloat that a question may mean something which the mind cannot conceive; and when some hair-splitting philosophers have been confronted with the absurdity of such a view, they have invented an empty distinction between positive and negative conceptions, in the attempt to give their non-idea a form not obviously nonsensical. The nullity of it is sufficiently plain from the considerations given a few pages back; and, apart from those considerations, the quibbling character of the distinction must have struck every mind accustomed to real thinking.

## IV

Let us now approach the subject of logic, and consider a conception which particularly concerns it, that of *reality*. Taking clearness in the sense of familiarity, no idea could be clearer than this. Every child uses it with perfect confidence, never dreaming that he does not understand it. As for clearness in its second grade, however, it would probably puzzle most men, even among those of a reflective turn of mind, to give an abstract definition of the real. Yet such a definition may perhaps be reached by considering the points of difference between reality and its opposite, fiction. A figment is a product of somebody's imagination; it has such characters as his thought impresses upon it. That those characters are independent of how you or I think is an external reality. There are, however, phenomena within our own minds, dependent upon our thought, which are at the same time real in the sense that we really think them. But though their characters depend on how we think, they do not depend on what we think those characters to be. Thus, a dream has a real existence as a mental phenomenon, if somebody has really dreamt it; that he dreamt so and so, does not depend on what anybody thinks was dreamt, but is completely independent of all opinion on the subject. On the other hand, considering, not the fact of dreaming, but the thing dreamt, it retains its peculiarities by virtue of no other fact than that it was dreamt to possess them. Thus we may define the real as that whose characters are independent of what anybody may think them to be.

But, however satisfactory such a definition may be found, it would be a great mistake to suppose that it makes the idea of reality perfectly clear. Here, then, let us apply our rules. According to them, reality, like every other quality, consists in the peculiar, sensible effects which things partaking of it produce. The only effect which real things have is to cause belief, for all the sensations which they excite emerge into consciousness in the form of beliefs. The question, therefore, is, how is true belief (or belief in the real) distinguished from false belief (or belief in fiction). Now, as we have seen in the former paper, the ideas of truth and falsehood, in their full development, appertain exclusively to the scientific method of settling opinion. A person who arbitrarily chooses the propositions which he will adopt can use the word truth only to emphasize the expression of his determination to hold on to his choice. Of course, the method of tenacity never prevailed exclusively; reason is too natural to men for that. But in the literature of the Dark Ages we find some fine examples of it. When Scotus Erigena is commenting upon a poetical passage in which hellebore is spoken of as having caused the death of Socrates, he does not hesitate to inform the inquiring reader that Helleborus and Socrates were two eminent Greek philosophers, and that the latter having been overcome in argument by the former took the matter to heart and died of it! What sort of an idea of truth could a man have who could adopt and teach, without the qualification of a "perhaps," an opinion taken so entirely at random? The real spirit of Socrates, who I hope would have been delighted to have been "overcome in argument," because he would have learned something by it, is in curious contrast with the naïve idea of the glossist, for whom (as for the "born missionary" of today) discussion would seem to have been simply a struggle. When philosophy began to awake from its long slumber, and before theology completely dominated it, the practice seems to have been for each professor to seize upon any philosophical position he found unoccupied and which seemed a strong one, to intrench himself in it, and to sally forth from time to time to give battle to the others. Thus, even the scanty records we possess of those disputes enable us to make out a dozen or more opinions held by different teachers at one time concerning the question of nominalism and realism. Read the opening part of the *Historia Calamitatum* of Abélard, who was certainly as philosophical as any of his contemporaries, and see the spirit of combat which it breathes. For him, the truth is simply his particular stronghold. When the method of authority prevailed, the truth meant little more than the Catholic faith. All the efforts of the scholastic doctors are directed toward harmonizing their faith in Aristotle and their faith in the Church, and one may search their ponderous folios through without finding an argument which

goes any further. It is noticeable that where different faiths flourish side by side, renegades are looked upon with contempt even by the party whose belief they adopt; so completely has the idea of loyalty replaced that of truth-seeking. Since the time of Descartes, the defect in the conception of truth has been less apparent. Still, it will sometimes strike a scientific man that the philosophers have been less intent on finding out what the facts are than on inquiring what belief is most in harmony with their system. It is hard to convince a follower of the *a priori* method by adducing facts; but show him that an opinion he is defending is inconsistent with what he has laid down elsewhere, and he will be very apt to retract it. These minds do not seem to believe that disputation is ever to cease; they seem to think that the opinion which is natural for one man is not so for another, and that belief will, consequently, never be settled. In contenting themselves with fixing their own opinions by a method which would lead another man to a different result, they betray their feeble hold of the conception of what truth is.

On the other hand, all the followers of science are fully persuaded that the processes of investigation, if only pushed far enough, will give one certain solution to each question to which they can be applied. One man may investigate the velocity of light by studying the transits of Venus and the aberration of the stars; another by the oppositions of Mars and the eclipses of Jupiter's satellites; a third by the method of Fizeau; a fourth by that of Foucault; a fifth by the motions of the curves of Lissajous; a sixth, a seventh, an eighth, and a ninth, may follow the different methods of comparing the measures of statical and dynamical electricity. They may at first obtain different results, but, as each perfects his method and his processes, the results will move steadily together toward a destined center. So with all scientific research. Different minds may set out with the most antagonistic views, but the progress of investigation carries them by a force outside of themselves to one and the same conclusion. This activity of thought by which we are carried, not where we wish, but to a foreordained goal, is like the operation of destiny. No modification of the point of view taken, no selection of other facts for study, no natural bent of mind even, can enable a man to escape the predestinate opinion. This great law is embodied in the conception of truth and reality. The opinion which is fated[2] to be ultimately agreed to by all who investigate is what we mean by the truth, and the object represented in this opinion is the real. That is the way I would explain reality.

But it may be said that this view is directly opposed to the abstract definition which we have given of reality, inasmuch as it makes the characters of the real depend on what is ultimately thought about them. But the answer to this is that, on the one hand, reality is independent, not necessarily of thought in general, but only of what you or I or any finite number of men may think about it; and that, on the other hand, though the object of the final opinion depends on what that opinion is, yet what that opinion is does not depend on what you or I or any man thinks. Our perversity and that of others may indefinitely postpone the settlement of opinion; it might even conceivably cause an arbitrary proposition to be universally accepted as long as the human race should last. Yet even that would not change the nature of the belief, which alone could be the result of investigation carried sufficiently far; and if, after the extinction of our race, another should arise with faculties and disposition for investigation, that true opinion must be the one which they would ultimately come to. "Truth crushed to earth shall rise again," and the opinion which would finally result from investigation does not depend on how anybody may actually think. But the reality of that which is real does depend on the real fact that investigation is destined to lead, at last, if continued long enough, to a belief in it.

But I may be asked what I have to say to all the minute facts of history, forgotten never to be recovered, to the lost books of the ancients, to the buried secrets.

*"Full many a gem of purest ray serene*
*The dark, unfathomed caves of ocean bear;*

*Full many a flower is born to blush unseen,*
*And waste its sweetness on the desert air."*

Do these things not really exist because they are hopelessly beyond the reach of our knowledge? And then, after the universe is dead (according to the prediction of some scientists), and all life has ceased forever, will not the shock of atoms continue though there will be no mind to know it? To this I reply that, though in no possible state of knowledge can any number be great enough to express the relation between the amount of what rests unknown to the amount of the known, yet it is unphilosophical to suppose that, with regard to any given question (which has any clear meaning), investigation would not bring forth a solution of it, if it were carried far enough. Who would have said, a few years ago, that we could ever know of what substances stars are made whose light may have been longer in reaching us than the human race has existed? Who can be sure of what we shall not know in a few hundred years? Who can guess what would be the result of continuing the pursuit of science for ten thousand years, with the activity of the last hundred? And if it were to go on for a million, or a billion, or any number of years you please, how is it possible to say that there is any question which might not ultimately be solved?

But it may be objected, "Why make so much of these remote considerations, especially when it is your principle that only practical distinctions have a meaning?" Well, I must confess that it makes very little difference whether we say that a stone on the bottom of the ocean, in complete darkness, is brilliant or not—that is to say, that it *probably* makes no difference, remembering always that that stone *may* be fished up tomorrow. But that there are gems at the bottom of the sea, flowers in the untraveled desert, etc., are propositions which, like that about a diamond being hard when it is not pressed, concern much more the arrangement of our language than they do the meaning of our ideas.

It seems to me, however, that we have, by the application of our rule, reached so clear an apprehension of what we mean by reality, and of the fact which the idea rests on, that we should not, perhaps, be making a pretension so presumptuous as it would be singular, if we were to offer a metaphysical theory of existence for universal acceptance among those who employ the scientific method of fixing belief. However, as metaphysics is a subject much more curious than useful, the knowledge of which, like that of a sunken reef, serves chiefly to enable us to keep clear of it, I will not trouble the reader with any more Ontology at this moment. I have already been led much further into that path than I should have desired; and I have given the reader such a dose of mathematics, psychology, and all that is most abstruse, that I fear he may already have left me, and that what I am now writing is for the compositor and proofreader exclusively. I trusted to the importance of the subject. There is no royal road to logic, and really valuable ideas can only be had at the price of close attention. But I know that in the matter of ideas the public prefer the cheap and nasty; and in my next paper I am going to return to the easily intelligible, and not wander from it again. The reader who has been at the pains of wading through this paper shall be rewarded in the next one by seeing how beautifully what has been developed in this tedious way can be applied to the ascertainment of the rules of scientific reasoning.

We have, hitherto, not crossed the threshold of scientific logic. It is certainly important to know how to make our ideas clear, but they may be ever so clear without being true. How to make them so, we have next to study. How to give birth to those vital and procreative ideas which multiply into a thousand forms and diffuse themselves everywhere, advancing civilization and making the dignity of man, is an art not yet reduced to rules, but of the secret of which the history of science affords some hints.

### Notes

1. Possibly the velocities also have to be taken into account.
2. Fate means merely that which is sure to come true, and can nohow be avoided. It is a superstition to suppose that a certain sort of events are ever fated, and it is another to suppose that the word "fate" can never be freed from its superstitious taint. We are all fated to die.

# The Doctrine of Necessity Examined

I propose here to examine the common belief that every single fact in the universe is precisely determined by law. It must not be supposed that this is a doctrine accepted everywhere and at all times by all rational men. Its first advocate appears to have been Democritus, the atomist, who was led to it, as we are informed, by reflecting upon the "impenetrability, translation, and impact of matter (ἀντιτυπία καί φορά καί πληγή τῆς ὕλης)." That is to say, having restricted his attention to a field where no influence other than mechanical constraint could possibly come before his notice, he straightway jumped to the conclusion that throughout the universe that was the sole principle of action—a style of reasoning so usual in our day with men not unreflecting as to be more than excusable in the infancy of thought. But Epicurus, in revising the atomic doctrine and repairing its defences, found himself obliged to suppose that atoms swerve from their courses by spontaneous chance;

From *The Monist,* vol. 12, 1892, pp. 321–337.

and thereby he conferred upon the theory life and entelechy. For we now see clearly that the peculiar function of the molecular hypothesis in physics is to open an entry for the calculus of probabilities. Already, the prince of philosophers had repeatedly and emphatically condemned the dictum of Democritus (especially in the *Physics,* Book II, chapters 4, 5, 6), holding that events come to pass in three ways, namely, (1) by external compulsion, or the action of efficient causes, (2) by virtue of an inward nature, or the influence of final causes, and (3) irregularly without definite cause, but just by absolute chance; and this doctrine is of the inmost essence of Aristotelianism. It affords, at any rate, a valuable enumeration of the possible ways in which anything can be supposed to have come about. The freedom of the will, too, was admitted both by Aristotle and by Epicurus. But the Stoa, which in every department seized upon the most tangible, hard, and lifeless element, and blindly denied the existence of every other, which, for example, impugned the validity of the inductive method and wished to fill its place with the *reductio ad absurdum,* very naturally became the one school of ancient philosophy to stand by a strict necessitarianism, thus returning to a single principle of Democritus that Epicurus had been unable to swallow. Necessitarianism and materialism with the Stoics went hand in hand, as by affinity they should. At the revival of learning, Stoicism met with considerable favour, partly because it departed just enough from Aristotle to give it the spice of novelty, and partly because its superficialities well adapted it for acceptance by students of literature and art who wanted their philosophy drawn mild. Afterwards, the great discoveries in mechanics inspired the hope that mechanical principles might suffice to explain the universe; and, though without logical justification, this hope has since been continually stimulated by subsequent advances in physics. Nevertheless, the doctrine was in too evident conflict with the freedom of the will and with miracles to be generally acceptable, at first. But meantime there arose that most widely spread of philo-

sophical blunders, the notion that associationalism belongs intrinsically to the materialistic family of doctrines; and thus was evolved the theory of motives; and libertarianism became weakened. At present, historical criticism has almost exploded, the miracles, great and small; so that the doctrine of necessity has never been in so great vogue as now.

The proposition in question is that the state of things existing . . . at any time, together with certain immutable laws, completely determine the state of things at every other time (for a limitation to *future* time is indefensible). Thus, given the state of the universe in the original nebula, and given the laws of mechanics, a sufficiently powerful mind could deduce from these data the precise form of every curlicue of every letter I am now writing.

Whoever holds that every act of the will as well as every idea of the mind is under the rigid governance of a necessity co-ordinated with that of the physical world, will logically be carried to the proposition that minds are part of the physical world in such a sense that the laws of mechanics determine everything that happens according to immutable attractions and repulsions. In that case, that instantaneous state of things from which every other state of things is calculable consists in the positions and velocities of all the particles at any instant. This, the usual and most logical form of necessitarianism, is called the mechanical philosophy.

When I have asked thinking men what reason they had to believe that every fact in the universe is precisely determined by law, the first answer has usually been that the proposition is a "presupposition" or postulate of scientific reasoning. Well, if that is the best that can be said for it, the belief is doomed. Suppose it be "postulated": that does not make it true, nor so much as afford the slightest rational motive for yielding it any credence. It is as if a man should come to borrow money, and when asked for his security, should reply he "postulated" the loan. To "postulate" a proposition is no more than to hope it is true. There are, indeed, practical emergencies in which we act upon assumptions of certain propositions as true, because if they are not so, it can make no difference how we act. But all such propositions I take to be hypotheses of individual facts. For it is manifest that no universal principle can in its universality be comprised in a special case or can be requisite for the validity of any ordinary inference. To say, for instance, that the demonstration by Archimedes of the property of the lever would fall to the ground if men were endowed with freewill, is extravagant; yet this is implied by those who make a proposition incompatible with the freedom of the will the postulate of all inference. Considering, too, that the conclusions of science make no pretense to being more than probable, and considering that a probable inference can at most only suppose something to be most frequently, or otherwise approximately, true, but never that anything is precisely true without exception throughout the universe, we see how far this proposition in truth is from being so postulated.

But the whole notion of a postulate being involved in reasoning appertains to a by-gone and false conception of logic. Non-deductive, or ampliative inference, is of three kinds: induction, hypothesis, and analogy. If there be any other modes, they must be extremely unusual and highly complicated, and may be assumed with little doubt to be of the same nature as those enumerated. For induction, hypothesis, and analogy, as far as their ampliative character goes, that is, so far as they conclude something not implied in the premises, depend upon one principle and involve the same procedure. All are essentially inferences from sampling. Suppose a ship arrives at Liverpool laden with wheat in bulk. Suppose that by some machinery the whole cargo be stirred up with great thoroughness. Suppose that twenty-seven thimblefuls be taken equally from the forward, midships, and aft parts, from the starboard, center, and larboard parts, and from the top, half depth, and lower parts of her hold, and that these being mixed and the grains counted, four-fifths of the latter are found to be of quality *A*. Then we infer, experientially and provisionally, that approxi-

mately four-fifths of all the grain in the cargo is of the same quality. I say we infer this *experientially* and *provisionally*. By saying that we infer it *experientially,* I mean that our conclusion makes no pretension to knowledge of wheat-in-itself, our *alétheia* [truth], as the derivation of that word implies, has nothing to do with *latent* wheat. We are dealing only with the matter of possible experience—experience in the full acceptation of the term as something not merely affecting the senses but also as the subject of thought. If there be any wheat hidden on the ship, so that it can neither turn up in the sample nor be heard of subsequently from purchasers—or if it be half-hidden, so that it may, indeed, turn up, but is less likely to do so than the rest—or if it can affect our senses and our pockets, but from some strange cause or causelessness cannot be reasoned about—all such wheat is to be excluded (or have only its proportional weight) in calculating that true proportion of quality *A*, to which our inference seeks to approximate. By saying that we draw the inference *provisionally,* I mean that we do not hold that we have reached any assigned degree of approximation as yet, but only hold that if our experience be indefinitely extended, and if every fact of whatever nature, as fast as it presents itself, be duly applied, according to the inductive method, in correcting the inferred ratio, then our approximation will become indefinitely close in the long run; that is to say, close to the experience *to come* (not merely close by the exhaustion of a finite collection) so that if experience in general is to fluctuate irregularly to and fro, in a manner to deprive the ratio sought of all definite value, we shall be able to find out approximately within what limits it fluctuates, and if, after having one definite value, it changes and assumes another, we shall be able to find that out, and in short, whatever may be the variations of this ratio in experience, experience indefinitely extended will enable us to detect them, so as to predict rightly, at last, what its ultimate value may be, if it have any ultimate value, or what the ultimate law of succession of values may be, if there be any such ultimate law, or that it ultimately fluctuates irregularly within certain limits, if it do so ultimately fluctuate. Now our inference, claiming to be no more than thus experiential and provisional, manifestly involves no postulate whatever.

For what is a postulate? It is the formulation of a material fact which we are not entitled to assume as a premise, but the truth of which is requisite to the validity of an inference. Any fact, then, which might be supposed postulated, must either be such that it would ultimately present itself in experience, or not. If it will present itself, we need not postulate it now in our provisional inference, since we shall ultimately be entitled to use it as a premise. But if it never would present itself in experience, our conclusion is valid but for the possibility of this fact being otherwise than assumed, that is, it is valid as far as possible experience goes, and that is all that we claim. Thus, every postulate is cut off, either by the provisionality or by the experientiality of our inference. For instance, it has been said that induction postulates that if an indefinite succession of samples be drawn, examined, and thrown back each before the next is drawn, then in the long run every grain will be drawn as often as any other, that is to say, postulates that the ratio of the numbers of times in which any two are drawn will indefinitely approximate to unity. But no such postulate is made; for if, on the one hand, we are to have no other experience of the wheat than from such drawings, it is the ratio that presents itself in those drawings and not the ratio which belongs to the wheat in its latent existence that we are endeavoring to determine; while if, on the other hand, there is some other mode by which the wheat is to come under our knowledge, equivalent to another kind of sampling, so that after all our care in stirring up the wheat, some experiential grains will present themselves in the first sampling operation more often than others in the long run, this very singular fact will be sure to get discovered by the inductive method, which must avail itself of every sort of experience; and our inference, which was only provisional, corrects itself at last. Again, it has been said, that induction postulates that

under like circumstances like events will happen, and that this postulate is at bottom the same as the principle of universal causation. But this is a blunder, or *bévue,* due to thinking exclusively of inductions where the concluded ratio is either 1 or 0. If any such proposition were postulated, it would be that under like circumstances (the circumstances of drawing the different samples) different events occur in the same proportions in all the different sets— a proposition which is false and even absurd. But in truth no such thing is postulated, the experiential character of the inference reducing the condition of validity to this, that if a certain result does not occur, the opposite result will be manifested, a condition assured by the provisionality of the inference. But it may be asked whether it is not conceivable that every instance of a certain class destined to be ever employed as a datum of induction should have one character, while every instance destined not to be so employed should have the opposite character. The answer is that in that case, the instances excluded from being subjects of reasoning would not be experienced in the full sense of the word, but would be among these *latent* individuals of which our conclusion does not pretend to speak.

To this account of the rationale of induction I know of but one objection worth mention: it is that I thus fail to deduce the full degree of force which this mode of inference in fact possesses; that according to my view, no matter how thorough and elaborate the stirring and mixing process had been, the examination of a single handful of grain would not give me any assurance, sufficient to risk money upon, that the next handful would not greatly modify the concluded value of the ratio under inquiry, while, in fact, the assurance would be very high that this ratio was not greatly in error. If the true ratio of grains of quality $A$ were 0.80 and the handful contained a thousand grains, nine such handfuls out of every ten would contain from 780 to 820 grains of quality $A$. The answer to this is that the calculation given is correct when we know that the units of this handful and the quality inquired into have the normal independence of one another, if for instance the stirring has been complete and the character sampled for has been settled upon in advance of the examination of the sample. But in so far as these conditions are not known to be complied with, the above figures cease to be applicable. Random sampling and predesignation of the character sampled for should always be striven after in inductive reasoning, but when they cannot be attained, so long as it is conducted honestly, the inference retains some value. When we cannot ascertain how the sampling has been done or the sample-character selected, induction still has the essential validity which my present account of it shows it to have.

I do not think a man who combines a willingness to be convinced with a power of appreciating an argument upon a difficult subject can resist the reasons which have been given to show that the principle of universal necessity cannot be defended as being a postulate of reasoning. But then the question immediately arises whether it is not proved to be true, or at least rendered highly probable, by observation of nature.

Still, this question ought not long to arrest a person accustomed to reflect upon the force of scientific reasoning. For the essence of the necessitarian position is that certain continuous quantities have certain exact values. Now, how can observation determine the value of such a quantity with a probable error absolutely *nil?* To one who is behind the scenes, and knows that the most refined comparisons of masses, lengths, and angles, far surpassing in precision all other measurements, yet fall behind the accuracy of bank accounts, and that the ordinary determinations of physical constants, such as appear from month to month in the journals, are about on a par with an upholsterer's measurements of carpets and curtains, the idea of mathematical exactitude being demonstrated in the laboratory will appear simply ridiculous. There is a recognized method of estimating the probable magnitudes of errors in physics—the method of least squares. It is universally admitted that this method makes the errors smaller than they

really are; yet even according to that theory an error indefinitely small is indefinitely improbable; so that any statement to the effect that a certain continuous quantity has a certain exact value, if well-founded at all, must be founded on something other than observation.

Still, I am obliged to admit that this rule is subject to a certain qualification. Namely, it only applies to continuous[1] quantity. Now, certain kinds of continuous quantity are discontinuous at one or at two limits, and for such limits the rule must be modified. Thus, the length of a line cannot be less than zero. Suppose, then, the question arises how long a line a certain person had drawn from a marked point on a piece of paper. If no line at all can be seen, the observed length is zero; and the only conclusion this observation warrants is that the length of the line is less than the smallest length visible with the optical power employed. But indirect observations—for example, that the person supposed to have drawn the line was never within fifty feet of the paper—may make it probable that no line at all was made, so that the concluded length will be strictly zero. In like manner, experience no doubt would warrant the conclusion that there is absolutely *no* indigo in a given ear of wheat, and absolutely *no* attar in a given lichen. But such inferences can only be rendered valid by positive experiential evidence, direct or remote, and cannot rest upon a mere inability to detect the quantity in question. We have reason to think there is no indigo in the wheat, because we have remarked that wherever indigo is produced it is produced in considerable quantities, to mention only one argument. We have reason to think there is no attar in the lichen, because essential oils seem to be in general peculiar to single species. If the question had been whether there was iron in the wheat or the lichen, though chemical analysis should fail to detect its presence, we should think some of it probably was there, since iron is almost everywhere. Without any such information, one way or the other, we could only abstain from any opinion as to the presence of the substance in question. It cannot, I conceive, be maintained that we are in any *better* position than this in regard to the presence of the element of chance or spontaneous departures from law in nature.

Those observations which are generally adduced in favor of mechanical causation simply prove that there is an element of regularity in nature, and have no bearing whatever upon the question of whether such regularity is exact and universal, or not. Nay, in regard to this *exactitude,* all observation is directly *opposed* to it; and the most that can be said is that a good deal of this observation can be explained away. Try to verify any law of nature, and you will find that the more precise your observations, the more certain they will be to show irregular departures from the law. We are accustomed to ascribe these, and I do not say wrongly, to errors of observation; yet we cannot usually account for such errors in any antecedently probable way. Trace their causes back far enough, and you will be forced to admit they are always due to arbitrary determination, or chance.

But it may be asked whether if there were an element of real chance in the universe it must not occasionally be productive of signal effects such as could not pass unobserved. In answer to this question, without stopping to point out that there is an abundance of great events which one might be tempted to suppose were of that nature, it will be simplest to remark that physicists hold that the particles of gases are moving about irregularly, substantially as if by real chance, and that by the principles of probabilities there must occasionally happen to be concentrations of heat in the gases contrary to the second law of thermodynamics, and these concentrations, occurring in explosive mixtures, must sometimes have tremendous effects. Here, then, is in substance the very situation supposed; yet no phenomena ever have resulted which we are forced to attribute to such chance concentration of heat, or which anybody, wise or foolish, has ever dreamed of accounting for in that manner.

In view of all these considerations, I do not believe that anybody, not in a state of case-hardened ignorance respecting the logic of science, can maintain that the precise and universal conformity of facts to law is clearly proved, or even rendered particularly probable, by any observations hitherto made. In this way, the determined advocate of exact regularity will soon find himself driven to *a priori* reasons to support his thesis. These received such a socdolager from Stuart Mill in his Examination of Hamilton, that holding to them now seems to me to denote a high degree of imperviousness to reason; so that I shall pass them by with little notice.

To say that we cannot help believing a given proposition is no argument, but it is a conclusive fact if it be true; and with the substitution of "I" for "we," it is true in the mouths of several classes of minds, the blindly passionate, the unreflecting and ignorant, and the person who has overwhelming evidence before his eyes. But that which has been inconceivable today has often turned out indisputable on the morrow. Inability to conceive is only a stage through which every man must pass in regard to a number of beliefs—unless endowed with extraordinary obstinacy and obtuseness. His understanding is enslaved to some blind compulsion which a vigorous mind is pretty sure soon to cast off.

Some seek to back up the *a priori* position with empirical arguments. They say that the exact regularity of the world is a natural belief, and that natural beliefs have generally been confirmed by experience. There is some reason in this. Natural beliefs, however, if they generally have a foundation of truth, also require correction and purification from natural illusions. The principles of mechanics are undoubtedly natural beliefs; but, for all that, the early formulations of them were exceedingly erroneous. The general approximation to truth in natural beliefs is, in fact, a case of the general adaptation of genetic products to recognizable utilities or ends. Now, the adaptations of nature, beautiful and often marvelous as they verily are, are never found to be quite perfect; so that the argument is quite *against* the absolute exactitude of any natural belief, including that of the principle of causation.

Another argument, or convenient commonplace, is that absolute chance is *inconceivable.*

(This word has eight current significations. The *Century Dictionary* enumerates six.) Those who talk like this will hardly be persuaded to say in what sense they mean that chance is inconceivable. Should they do so, it would easily be shown either that they have no sufficient reason for the statement or that the inconceivability is of a kind which does not prove that chance is non-existent.

Another *a priori* argument is that chance is unintelligible; that is to say, while it may perhaps be conceivable, it does not disclose to the eye of reason the how or why of things; and since a hypothesis can only be justified so far as it renders some phenomenon intelligible, we never can have any right to suppose absolute chance to enter into the production of anything in nature. This argument may be considered in connection with two others. Namely, instead of going so far as to say that the supposition of chance can *never* properly be used to explain any observed fact, it may be alleged merely that no facts are known which such a supposition could in any way help in explaining. Or again, the allegation being still further weakened, it may be said that since departures from law are not unmistakably observed, chance is not a *vera causa,* and ought not unnecessarily to be introduced into a hypothesis.

These are no mean arguments, and require us to examine the matter a little more closely. Come, my superior opponent, let me learn from your wisdom. It seems to me that every throw of sixes with a pair of dice is a manifest instance of chance.

"While you would hold a throw of deuce-ace to be brought about by necessity?" (The opponent's supposed remarks are placed in quotation marks.)

Clearly one throw is as much chance as another.

"Do you think throws of dice are of a different nature from other events?"

I see that I must say that *all* the diversity and specificalness of events is attributable to chance.

"Would you, then, deny that there is any regularity in the world?"

That is clearly undeniable. I must acknowledge there is an approximate regularity, and that every event is influenced by it. But the diversification, specificalness, and irregularity of things I suppose is chance. A throw of sixes appears to me a case in which this element is particularly obtrusive.

"If you reflect more deeply, you will come to see that *chance* is only a name for a cause that is unknown to us."

Do you mean that we have no idea whatever what kind of causes could bring about a throw of sixes?

"On the contrary, each die moves under the influence of precise mechanical laws."

But it appears to me that it is not these *laws* which made the die turn up sixes; for these laws act just the same when other throws come up. The chance lies in the diversity of throws; and this diversity cannot be due to laws which are immutable.

"The diversity is due to the diverse circumstances under which the laws act. The dice lie differently in the box, and the motion given to the box is different. These are the unknown causes which produce the throws, and to which we give the name of chance; not the mechanical law which regulates the operation of these causes. You see you are already beginning to think more clearly about this subject."

Does the operation of mechanical law not increase the diversity?

"Properly not. You must know that the instantaneous state of a system of particles is defined by six times as many numbers as there are particles, three for the co-ordinates of each particle's position, and three more for the components of its velocity. This number of numbers, which expresses the amount of diversity in the system, remains the same at all times. There may be, to be sure, some kind of relation between the co-ordinates and component velocities of the different particles, by means of which the state of the system might be expressed by a smaller number of numbers. But, if this is the case, a precisely corresponding relationship must exist between the co-ordinates and component velocities at any other time, though it may doubtless be a relation less obvious to us. Thus, the intrinsic complexity of the system is the same at all times."

Very well, my obliging opponent, we have now reached an issue. You think all the arbitrary specifications of the universe were introduced in one dose, in the beginning, if there was a beginning, and that the variety and complication of nature has always been just as much as it is now. But I, for my part, think that the diversification, the specification, has been continually taking place. Should you condescend to ask me why I so think, I should give my reasons as follows:

(1) Question any science which deals with the course of time. Consider the life of an individual animal or plant, or of a mind. Glance at the history of states, of institutions, of language, of ideas. Examine the successions of forms shown by paleontology, the history of the globe as set forth in geology, of what the astronomer is able to make out concerning the changes of stellar systems. Everywhere the main fact is growth and increasing complexity. Death and corruption are mere accidents or secondary phenomena. Among some of the lower organisms, it is a moot point with biologists whether there be anything which ought to be called death. Races, at any rate, do not die out except under unfavorable circumstances. From these broad and ubiquitous facts we may fairly infer, by the most unexceptionable logic, that there is probably in nature some agency by which the complexity and diversity of things can be increased; and that consequently the rule of mechanical necessity meets in some way with interference.

(2) By thus admitting pure spontaneity or life as a character of the universe, acting always and everywhere though restrained within narrow bounds by law, producing infinitesimal departures from law continually, and great ones with infinite infrequency, I account for all the variety and diversity of the universe, in the only sense in which the really *sui generis* and new can be said to be accounted for. The ordinary view has to admit the inexhaustible multitudinous variety of the world,

has to admit that its mechanical law cannot account for this in the least, that variety can spring only from spontaneity, and yet denies without any evidence or reason the existence of this spontaneity, or else shoves it back to the beginning of time and supposes it dead ever since. The superior logic of my view appears to me not easily controverted.

(3) When I ask the necessitarian how he would explain the diversity and irregularity of the universe, he replies to me out of the treasury of his wisdom that irregularity is something which from the nature of things we must not seek to explain. Abashed at this, I seek to cover my confusion by asking how he would explain the uniformity and regularity of the universe, whereupon he tells me that the laws of nature are immutable and ultimate facts, and no account is to be given of them. But my hypothesis of spontaneity does explain irregularity, in a certain sense; that is, it explains the general fact of irregularity, though not, of course, what each lawless event is to be. At the same time, by thus loosening the bond of necessity, it gives room for the influence of another kind of causation, such as seems to be operative in the mind in the formation of associations, and enables us to understand how the uniformity of nature could have been brought about. That single events should be hard and unintelligible, logic will permit without difficulty: we do not expect to make the shock of a personally experienced earthquake appear natural and reasonable by any amount of cogitation. But logic does expect things *general* to be understandable. To say that there is a universal law, and that it is a hard, ultimate, unintelligible fact, the why and wherefore of which can never be inquired into, at this a sound logic will revolt; and will pass over at once to a method of philosophizing which does not thus barricade the road of discovery.

(4) Necessitarianism cannot logically stop short of making the whole action of the mind a part of the physical universe. Our notion that we decide what we are going to do, if as the necessitarian says, it has been calculable since the earliest times, is reduced to illusion.

Indeed, consciousness in general thus becomes a mere illusory aspect of a material system. What we call red, green, and violet are in reality only different rates of vibration. The sole reality is the distribution of qualities of matter in space and time. Brain-matter is protoplasm in a certain degree and kind of complication—a certain arrangement of mechanical particles. Its feeling is but an inward aspect, a phantom. For, from the positions and velocities of the particles at any one instant, and the knowledge of the immutable forces, the positions at all other times are calculable; so that the universe of space, time, and matter is a rounded system uninterfered with from elsewhere. But from the state of feeling at any instant, there is no reason to suppose the states of feeling at all other instants are thus exactly calculable; so that feeling is, as I said, a mere fragmentary and illusive aspect of the universe. This is the way, then, that necessitarianism has to make up its accounts. It enters consciousness under the head of sundries, as a forgotten trifle; its scheme of the universe would be more satisfactory if this little fact could be dropped out of sight. On the other hand, by supposing the rigid exactitude of causation to yield, I care not how little—be it but by a strictly infinitesimal amount—we gain room to insert mind into our scheme, and to put it into the place where it is needed, into the position which, as the sole self-intelligible thing, it is entitled to occupy, that of the fountain of existence; and in so doing we resolve the problem of the connection of soul and body.

(5) But I must leave undeveloped the chief of my reasons, and can only adumbrate it. The hypothesis of chance-spontaneity is one whose inevitable consequences are capable of being traced out with mathematical precision into considerable detail. Much of this I have done and find the consequences to agree with observed facts to an extent which seems to me remarkable. But the matter and methods of reasoning are novel, and I have no right to promise that other mathematicians shall find my deductions as satisfactory as I myself do, so that the strongest reason for my belief must for the present remain a private reason of my own, and cannot influence others. I mention it to explain my own position; and partly to indicate to future mathematical speculators a veritable gold mine, should time and circumstances and the abridger of all joys prevent my opening it to the world.

If now I, in my turn, inquire of the necessitarian why he prefers to suppose that all specification goes back to the beginning of things, he will answer me with one of those last three arguments which I left unanswered.

First, he may say that chance is a thing absolutely unintelligible, and, therefore, that we never can be entitled to make such a supposition. But does not this objection smack of naïve impudence? It is not mine, it is his own conception of the universe which leads abruptly up to hard, ultimate, inexplicable, immutable law, on the one hand, and to inexplicable specification and diversification of circumstances on the other. My view, on the contrary, hypothetizes nothing at all, unless it be hypothesis to say that all specification came about in some sense, and is not to be accepted as unaccountable. To undertake to account for anything by saying boldly that it is due to chance would, indeed, be futile. But this I do not do. I make use of chance chiefly to make room for a principle of generalization, or tendency to form habits, which I hold has produced all regularities. The mechanical philosopher leaves the whole specification of the world utterly unaccounted for, which is pretty nearly as bad as to boldly attribute it to chance. I attribute it altogether to chance, it is true, but to chance in the form of a spontaneity which is to some degree regular. It seems to me clear at any rate that one of these two positions must be taken, or else specification must be supposed due to a spontaneity which develops itself in a certain and not in a chance way, by an objective logic like that of Hegel. This last way I leave as an open possibility, for the present; for it is as much opposed to the necessitarian scheme of existence as my own theory is.

Secondly, the necessitarian may say there are, at any rate, no observed phenomena which the hypothesis of chance could aid in explaining. In reply, I point first to the phenomenon of growth and developing complexity, which appears to be universal, and which though it may possibly be an affair of mechanism perhaps, certainly presents all the appearance of increasing diversification. Then, there is variety itself, beyond comparison the most obtrusive character of the universe: no mechanism can account for this. Then, there is the very fact the necessitarian most insists upon, the regularity of the universe which for him serves only to block the road of inquiry. Then, there are the regular relationships between the laws of nature—similarities and comparative characters, which appeal to our intelligence as its cousins, and call upon us for a reason. Finally, there is consciousness, feeling, a patent fact enough, but a very inconvenient one to the mechanical philosopher.

Thirdly, the necessitarian may say that chance is not a *vera causa,* that we cannot know positively there is any such element in the universe. But the doctrine of the *vera causa* has nothing to do with elementary conceptions. Pushed to that extreme, it at once cuts off belief in the existence of a material universe; and without that necessitarianism could hardly maintain its ground. Besides, variety is a fact

which must be admitted; and the theory of chance merely consists in supposing this diversification does not antedate all time. Moreover, the avoidance of hypotheses involving causes nowhere positively known to act—is only a recommendation of logic, not a positive command. It cannot be formulated in any precise terms without at once betraying its untenable character—I mean as rigid rule, for as a recommendation it is wholesome enough.

I believe I have thus subjected to fair examination all the important reasons for adhering to the theory of universal necessity, and have shown their nullity. I earnestly beg that whoever may detect any flaw in my reasoning will point it out to me, either privately or publicly; for if I am wrong, it much concerns me to be set right speedily. If my argument remains unrefuted, it will be time, I think, to doubt the absolute truth of the principle of universal law; and when once such a doubt has obtained a living root in any man's mind, my cause with him, I am persuaded, is gained.

## Notes

1. *Continuous* is not exactly the right word, but I let it go to avoid a long and irrelevant discussion.

# The Categories and the Study of Signs

. . . I will today explain the outlines of my Classification of signs. . . . I was long ago (1867) led, after only three or four years' study, to throw all ideas into the three classes of Firstness, of Secondness, and of Thirdness. This sort of notion is as distasteful to me as to anybody; and for years, I endeavored to pooh-pooh and refute it; but it long ago conquered me completely. Disagreeable as it is to attribute such meaning to numbers, & to a triad above all, it is as true as it is disagreeable. The ideas of Firstness, Secondness, and Thirdness

Letters to Lady Welby, 1904, 1906 and 1908. From *Charles S. Peirce: Selected Writings,* ed. Philip Wiener (New York: Dover, 1958), pp. 382–393, and *The Essential Peirce,* vol. 2, ed. Nathan Houser and Christian Kloesel (Bloomington: Indiana University Press, 1998).

are simple enough. Giving to being the broadest possible sense, to include ideas as well as things, and ideas that we fancy we have just as much as ideas we do have, I should define Firstness, Secondness, and Thirdness thus:

Firstness is the mode of being of that which is such as it is, positively and without reference to anything else.

Secondness is the mode of being of that which is such as it is, with respect to a second but regardless of any third.

Thirdness is the mode of being of that which is such as it is, in bringing a second and third into relation to each other.

I call these three ideas the cenopythagorean categories.

The typical ideas of Firstness are qualities of feeling, or mere appearances. The scarlet of your royal liveries, the quality itself, independently of its being perceived or remembered, is an example, by which I do not mean that you are to imagine that you *do not* perceive or remember it, but that you are to drop out of account that which may be attached to it in perceiving or in remembering, but which does not belong to the quality. For example, when you remember it, your idea is said to be *dim* and when it is before your eyes, it is *vivid.* But dimness or vividness do not belong to your idea of the quality. They *might* no doubt, if considered simply as a feeling; but when you think of vividness you do not consider it from that point of view. You think of it as a degree of disturbance of your consciousness. The quality of red is not thought of as belonging to you, or as attached to liveries. It is simply a peculiar positive possibility regardless of anything else. If you ask a mineralogist what hardness is, he will say that it is what one predicates of a body that one cannot scratch with a knife. But a simple person will think of hardness as a simple positive possibility the *realization* of which causes a body to be like a flint. That idea of hardness is an idea of Firstness. The unanalyzed total impression made by any manifold not thought of as actual fact, but simply as a quality as simple positive possibility of appearance is an idea of Firstness. Notice the *naïveté* of Firstness. The cenopy-

thagorean categories are doubtless another attempt to characterize what Hegel sought to characterize as his three stages of thought. They also correspond to the three categories of each of the four triads of Kant's table. But the fact that these different attempts were independent of one another (the resemblance of these Categories to Hegel's stages was not remarked for many years after the list had been under study, owing to my antipathy to Hegel) only goes to show that there really are three such elements. The idea of the present instant, which, whether it exists or not, is naturally thought as a point of time in which no thought can take place or any detail be separated, is an idea of Firstness.

The type of an idea of Secondness is the experience of effort, prescinded from the idea of a purpose. It may be said that there is no such experience, that a purpose is always in view as long as the effort is cognized. This may be open to doubt; for in sustained effort we soon let the purpose drop out of view. However, I abstain from psychology which has nothing to do with ideoscopy. The existence of the word *effort* is sufficient proof that people think they have such an idea; and that is enough. The experience of effort cannot exist without the experience of resistance. Effort only is effort by virtue of its being opposed; and no third element enters. Note that I speak of the *experience,* not of the *feeling,* of effort. Imagine yourself to be seated alone at night in the basket of a balloon, far above earth, calmly enjoying the absolute calm and stillness. Suddenly the piercing shriek of a steam-whistle breaks upon you, and continues for a good while. The impression of stillness was an idea of Firstness, a quality of feeling. The piercing whistle does not allow you to think or do anything but suffer. So that too is absolutely simple. Another Firstness. But the breaking of the silence by the noise was an experience. The person in his inertness identifies himself with the precedent state of feeling, and the new feeling which comes in spite of him is the non-ego. He has a two-sided consciousness of an ego and a non-ego. That consciousness of the action of a new feeling in destroying the old feeling is what I call an *experience*. Experience generally is what the course of life has *compelled* me to think. Secondness is either genuine or degenerate. There are many degrees of genuineness. Generally speaking genuine secondness consists in one thing acting upon another, brute action. I say brute, because so far as the idea of any *law* or *reason* comes in, Thirdness comes in. When a stone falls to the ground, the law of gravitation does not act to make it fall. The law of gravitation is the judge upon the bench who may pronounce the law till doomsday, but unless the strong arm of the law, the brutal sheriff, gives effect to the law, it amounts to nothing. True, the judge can create a sheriff if need be; but he must have one. The stone's actually falling is purely the affair of the stone and the earth at the time. This is a case of *reaction*. So is *existence* which is the mode of being of that which reacts with other things. But there is also action without reaction. *Such is the action of the previous upon the subsequent*. It is a difficult question whether the idea of this one-sided determination is a pure idea of secondness or whether it involves thirdness. At present, the former view seems to me correct. I suppose that when Kant made Time a form of the internal sense alone, he was influenced by some such considerations as the following. The relation between the previous and the subsequent consists in the previous being determinate and fixed for the subsequent, and the subsequent being indeterminate for the previous. But indeterminacy belongs only to ideas; the existent is determinate in every respect; and this is just what the law of causation consists in. Accordingly, the relation of time concerns only ideas. It may also be argued that, according to the law of the conservation of energy, there is nothing in the physical universe corresponding to our idea that the previous determines the subsequent in any way in which the subsequent does not determine the previous. For, according to that law, all that happens in the physical universe consists in the exchange of just so much *vis viva* $1/2m (ds/dt)^2$ for so much displacement. Now the square of a negative quantity being

positive, it follows that if all the velocities were reversed at any instant, everything would go on just the same, only time going backward as it were. Everything that had happened would happen again in reverse order. These seem to me to be strong arguments to prove that temporal causation (a very different thing from physical dynamic action) is an action upon ideas and not upon existents. But since our idea of the past is precisely the idea of that which is absolutely determinate, fixed, *fait accompli,* and dead, as against the future which is living, plastic, and determinable, it appears to me that the idea of one-sided action, in so far as it concerns the being of the determinate, is a pure idea of Secondness; and I think that great errors of metaphysics are due to looking at the future as something that will have been past. I cannot admit that the idea of the future can be so translated into the Secundal ideas of the past. To say that a given Kind of event never will happen is to deny that there is any date at which its happening will be past; but it is not equivalent to any affirmation about a past relative to any assignable date. When we pass from the idea of an event to saying that it never will happen, or will happen in endless repetition, or introduce in any way the idea of endless repetition, I will say the idea is *mellonized* (*méllon,* about to be, do, or suffer). When I conceive a fact as acting but not capable of being acted upon, I will say that it is *parelélythose* (past) and the mode of being which consists in such action I will call *parelelythosine* (-ine = einai, being). I regard the former as an idea of Thirdness, the latter as an idea of Secondness. I consider the idea of any dyadic relation not involving any third as an idea of Secondness; and I should not call any completely degenerate except the relation of identity. But similarity which is the only possible identity of Firsts is very near to that. Dyadic relations have been classified by me in a great variety of ways; but the most important are first with regard to the nature of the Second in itself and second with regard to the nature of its first. The Second, or *Relate* is, in itself, either a *Referate,* if it is intrinsically a possibility, such as a Quality or it is a *Revelate* if it is of its own nature an Existent. In respect to its first, the Second is divisible either in regard to the dynamic first or to the immediate first. In regard to its dynamic first, a Second is determined either by virtue of its own intrinsic nature, or by virtue of a real relation to that second (an action). Its immediate second is either a Quality or an Existent.

I now come to Thirdness. To me, who have for forty years considered the matter from every point of view that I could discover, the inadequacy of Secondness to cover all that is in our minds is so evident that I scarce know how to begin to persuade any person of it who is not already convinced of it. . . . Even in the most degenerate form of Thirdness, and Thirdness has two grades of degeneracy, something may be detected which is not mere secondness. If you take any ordinary triadic relation, you will always find a *mental* element in it. Brute action is secondness, any mentality involves thirdness. Analyze for instance the relation involved in "A gives B to C." Now what is giving? It does not consist A's putting B away from him and C's subsequently taking B up. It is not necessary that any material transfer should take place. It consists in A's making C the possessor according to *Law.* There must be some kind of law before there can be any kind of giving—be it but the law of the strongest. But now suppose that giving *did* consist merely in A's laying down the B which C subsequently picks up. That would be a degenerate form of Thirdness in which the thirdness is externally appended. In A's putting away B, there is no thirdness. In C's taking B, there is no thirdness. But if you say that these two acts constitute a single operation by virtue of the identity of the B, you transcend the mere brute fact, you introduce a mental element. . . . For every combination of relatives to make a new relative is a triadic relation irreducible to dyadic relations. Its *inadequacy* is shown in other ways, but in this way it is in a conflict with itself *if it be regarded,* as I never did regard it, *as sufficient for the expression of all relations.* . . . I have not sufficiently applied myself to the study of the degenerate forms of Thirdness, though I

think I see that it has two distinct grades of degeneracy. In its genuine form, Thirdness is the triadic relation existing between a sign, its object, and the interpreting thought, itself a sign, considered as constituting the mode of being of a sign. A sign mediates between the *interpretant* sign and its object. Taking sign in its broadest sense, its interpretant is not necessarily a sign. Any concept is a sign, of course. Ockham, Hobbes, and Leibniz have sufficiently said that. But we may take a sign in so broad a sense that the interpretant of it is not a thought, but an action or experience, or we may even so enlarge the meaning of sign that its interpretant is a mere quality of feeling. A *Third* is something which brings a First into relation to a Second. A sign is a sort of Third. How shall we characterize it? Shall we say that a Sign brings a Second, its Object, into *cognitive* relation to a Third? That a Sign brings a Second into the same relation to a first in which it stands itself to that First? If we insist on *consciousness,* we must say what we mean by consciousness of an object. Shall we say we mean Feeling? Shall we say we mean association, or Habit? These are, on the face of them, psychological distinctions, which I am particular to avoid. What is the essential difference between a sign that is communicated to a mind, and one that is not so communicated? If the question were simply what we *do* mean by a sign, it might soon be resolved. But that is not the point. We are in the situation of a zoologist who wants to know what ought to be the meaning of "fish" in order to make fishes one of the great classes of vertebrates. It appears to me that the essential function of a sign is to render inefficient relations efficient—not to set them into action, but to establish a habit or general rule whereby they will act on occasion. According to the physical doctrine, nothing ever happens but the continued rectilinear velocities with the accelerations that accompany different relative positions of the particles. All other relations, of which we know so many, are inefficient. Knowledge in some way renders them efficient; and a sign is something by knowing which we know something more. With the exception of knowledge, in the present instant, of the contents of consciousness in that instant (the existence of which knowledge is open to doubt) all our thought & knowledge is by signs. A sign therefore is an object which is in relation to its object on the one hand and to an interpretant on the other in such a way as to bring the interpretant into a relation to the object, corresponding to its own relation to the object. I might say "similar to its own," for a correspondence consists in a similarity; but perhaps correspondence is narrower.

I am now prepared to give my division of signs, as soon as I have pointed out that a sign has two objects, its object as it is represented and its object in itself. It has also three interpretants, its interpretant as represented or meant to be understood, its interpretant as it is produced, and its interpretant in itself. Now signs may be divided as to their own material nature, as to their relations to their objects, and as to their relations to their interpretants.

As it is in itself, a sign is either of the nature of an appearance, when I call it a *qualisign*; or secondly, it is an individual object or event, when I call it a *sinsign* (the syllable *sin* being the first syllable of *sem*el, *sim*ul, *sin*gular, etc.); or thirdly, it is of the nature of a general type, when I call it a *legisign*. As we use the term "word" in most cases, saying that "the" is one "word" and "an" is a second "word," a "word" is a legisign. But when we say of a page in a book, that it has 250 "words" upon it, of which twenty are "the's," the "word" is a sinsign. A sinsign so embodying a legisign, I term a "replica" [token] of the legisign. The difference between a legisign and a qualisign, neither of which is an individual thing, is that a legisign has a definite identity, though usually admitting a great variety of appearances. Thus, &, *and,* and the sound are all one word. The qualisign, on the other hand, has no identity. It is the mere quality of an appearance & is not exactly the same throughout a second. Instead of identity, it has *great similarity,* & cannot differ much without being called quite another qualisign.

In respect to their relations to their dynamic objects, I divide signs into Icons, Indices, and Symbols (a division I gave in 1867). I define an Icon as a sign which is determined by its dynamic object by virtue of its own internal nature. Such is any qualisign, like a vision— or the sentiment excited by a piece of music considered as representing what the composer intended. Such may be a sinsign, like an individual diagram; say, a curve of the distribution of errors. I define an Index as a sign determined by its Dynamic object by virtue of being in a real relation to it. Such is a Proper Name (a legisign); such is the occurrence of a symptom of a disease (the Symptom itself is a legisign, a general type of a definite character. The occurrence in a particular case is a sinsign). I define a Symbol as a sign which is determined by its dynamic object only in the sense that it will be so interpreted. It thus depends either upon a convention, a habit, or a natural disposition of its interpretant, or of the field of its interpretant (that of which the interpretant is a determination). Every symbol is necessarily a legisign, for it is inaccurate to call a replica of a legisign a symbol.

In respect to its immediate object a sign may either be a sign of a quality, of an existent, or of a law.

In regard to its relation to its signified interpretant, a sign is either a Rheme, a Dicent, or an Argument. This corresponds to the old triune Term, Proposition, & Argument, modified so as to be applicable to signs generally. A *Term* is simply a class-name or proper-name. I do not regard the common noun as an essentially necessary part of speech. Indeed, it is only fully developed as a separate part of speech in the Aryan languages & the Basque—possibly in some other out-of-the-way tongues. In the Shemitic languages it is generally in form a verbal affair, & usually is so in substance too. As well as I can make out, such it is in most languages. In my universal algebra of logic there is no common noun. A rheme is any sign that is not true nor false, like almost any single word except "yes" and "no," which are almost peculiar to modern languages. A *proposition* as I use that term, is a dicent symbol. A dicent is not an assertion, but is a sign *capable* of being asserted. But an assertion is a dicent. According to my present view (I may see more light in future) the act of assertion is not a pure act of signification. It is an exhibition of the fact that one subjects one-self to the penalties visited on a liar if the proposition asserted is not true. An act of judgment is the self-recognition of a belief; and a belief consists in the acceptance of a proposition as a basis of conduct deliberately. But I think this position is open to doubt. It is simply a question of which view gives the simplest view of the nature of the proposition. Holding, then, that a Dicent does not assert, I naturally hold that an Argument need not actually be submitted or urged. I therefore define an argument as a sign which is represented in its signified interpretant not as a Sign of that interpretant (the conclusion) (for that would be to urge or submit it) but *as if* it were a Sign of the Interpretant or perhaps as if it were a Sign of the state of the universe to which it refers, in which the premises are taken for granted. I define a dicent as a sign represented in its signified interpretant *as if it were* in a Real Relation to its Object. (Or as being so, if it is asserted.) A rheme is defined as a sign which is represented in its signified interpretant as *if it were* a character or mark (or as being so).

According to my present view, a sign may appeal to its dynamic interpretant in three ways:

1st,    an argument only may be *submitted* to its interpretant, as something the reasonableness of which will be acknowledged.

2nd,   an argument or dicent may be *urged* upon the interpretant by an act of insistence.

3rd,    argument or dicent may be and a rheme can only be, presented to the interpretant for *contemplation.*

Finally, in its relation to its immediate interpretant, I would divide signs into three classes as follows:

1st,    those which are interpretable in thoughts or other signs of the same kind in infinite series,

2nd, those which are interpretable in actual experiences,

3rd, those which are interpretable in qualities of feelings or appearances. . . .

I use the word "*Sign*" in the widest sense for any medium for the communication or extension of a Form (or feature). Being medium, it is determined by something, called its Object, and determines something, called its Interpretant or Interpretand. But some distinctions have to be borne in mind in order rightly to understand what is meant by the Object and by the Interpretant. In order that a Form may be extended or communicated, it is necessary that it should have been really embodied in a Subject independently of the communication; and it is necessary that there should be another Subject in which the same Form is embodied only in consequence of the communication. The Form (and the Form is the Object of the Sign), as it really determines the former Subject, is quite independent of the sign; yet we may and indeed must say that the object of a sign can be nothing but what that sign represents it to be. Therefore, in order to reconcile these apparently conflicting truths, it is indispensable to distinguish the *immediate* object from the *dynamical* object.

The same form of distinction extends to the interpretant; but as applied to the interpretant, it is complicated by the circumstances that the sign not only determines the interpretant to represent (or to take the form of) the *object,* but also determines the interpretant to represent the sign. Indeed in what we may, from one point of view, regard as the principal kind of signs, there is one distinct part appropriated to representing the object, and another to representing how this very sign itself represents that object. The class of signs I refer to are the dicisigns. In "John is in love with Helen," the object signified is the pair, John and Helen. But the "is in love with" signifies the form this sign represents itself to represent John-and-Helen's Form to be. That this is so is shown by the precise equivalence between any verb in the indicative and the same made the object of

"I tell you": "Jesus wept" = "I tell you that Jesus wept."

There is the *Intentional* Interpretant, which is a determination of the mind of the utterer; the *Effectual* Interpretant, which is a determination of the mind of the interpreter; and the *Communicational* Interpretant, or say the *Cominterpretant,* which is a determination of that mind into which the minds of utterer and interpreter have to be fused in order that any communication should take place. This mind may be called the *commens.* It consists of all that is, and must be, well understood between utterer and interpreter, at the outset, in order that the sign in question should fulfill its function. This I proceed to explain.

No object can be denoted unless it be put into relation to the object of the *commens.* A man, tramping along a weary and solitary road, meets an individual of strange mien, who says, "There was a fire in Megara." If this should happen in the Middle United States, there might very likely be some village in the neighborhood called Megara. Or it may refer to one of the ancient cities of Megara, or to some romance. And the time is wholly indefinite. In short, nothing at all is conveyed, until the person addressed asks, "Where?"—"Oh about half a mile along there" pointing to whence he came. "And when?" "As I passed." Now an item of information has been conveyed, because it has been stated relatively to a well-understood common experience. Thus the Form conveyed is always a determination of the dynamical object of the *commind.* By the way, the dynamical object does not mean something out of the mind. It means something forced upon the mind in perception, but including more than perception reveals. It is an object of actual *Experience.*

I define a Sign as anything which is so determined by something else, called its Object, and so determines an effect upon a person, which effect I call its Interpretant, that the latter is thereby mediately determined by the former. My insertion of "upon a person" is a sop to Cerberus, because I despair of making my own broader conception understood. I recognize three Universes, which are distinguished by three Modalities of Being.

One of these Universes embraces whatever has its Being in itself alone, except that whatever is in this Universe must be present to one consciousness, or be capable of being so present in its entire Being. It follows that a member of this universe need not be subject to any law, not even to the principle of contradiction. I denominate the objects of this Universe *Ideas,* or *Possibles,* although the latter designation does not imply capability of actualization. On the contrary as a general rule, if not a universal one, an Idea is incapable of perfect actualization on account of its essential vagueness if for no other reason. For that which is not subject to the principle of contradiction is essentially vague. For example, geometrical figures belong to this Universe; now since every such figure involves lines which can only be *supposed* to exist as boundaries where three bodies come together, or to be the place common to three bodies, and since the boundary of a solid or liquid is merely the place at which its forces of cohesion are neither very great nor very small, which is essentially vague, it is plain that the idea is essentially vague or indefinite. Moreover, suppose the three bodies that come together at a line are wood, water, and air, then a whole space including this line is at every point either wood, water, or air; and neither wood and water, nor wood and air, nor water and air can together occupy any place. Then plainly the principle of contradiction, were it applicable, would be violated in the idea of a place where wood, water, and air come together. Similar antinomies affect all Ideas. We can only reason about them in respects which the antinomies do not affect, and often by arbitrarily assuming what upon closer examination is found to be absurd. There is this much truth in Hegel's doctrine, although he is frequently in error in applying the principle.

Another Universe is that of, first, Objects whose Being consists in their Brute reactions, and of, second, the Facts (reactions, events, qualities, etc.) concerning those Objects, all of which facts, in the last analysis, consist in their reactions. I call the Objects, Things, or more unambiguously, *Existents,* and the facts about them I call Facts. Every member of this Universe is either a Single Object subject, alike to the Principles of Contradiction and to that of Excluded Middle, or it is expressible by a proposition having such a singular subject.

The third Universe consists of the co-being of whatever is in its Nature *necessitant,* that is, is a Habit, a law, or something expressible in a universal proposition. Especially, *continua* are of this nature. I call objects of this universe *Necessitants.* It includes whatever we can know by logically valid reasoning. I note that the question you put on the first page of your letter as to whether a certain proposition is "thoroughly tested" and supports the test, or whether it is "logically proved," seems to indicate that you are in some danger of enlisting in that army of "cranks," who insist on calling a kind of reasoning "logical" which leads from true premises to false conclusions, thus putting themselves outside the pale of sanity. People, for example, who maintain that the reasoning of the "Achilles" (and the tortoise) is "logical," though they cannot state it in any sound syllogistic or other form acknowledged by sane reasoners. I knew a gentleman who had mind enough to be a crack chess-player, but who insisted that it was "logical" to reason

> It either rains or it doesn't rain,
> Now it rains;
> ∴ It doesn't rain.

This is on a perfect level with saying that [the] contemptible Achilles catch is "logical." The truth is that an inference is "logical," if, and only if, it is governed by a habit that would in the long run lead to the truth. I am confident you will assent to this. Then I trust you do not mean to lend any countenance to notions of logic that conflict with this. It is a part of our duty to frown sternly upon immoral *principles;* and logic is only an application of morality. Is it not?

A Sign may *itself* have a "possible" Mode of Being; e.g., a hexagon inscribed in or cir-

cumscribed about a conic. It is a Sign in that the collinearity of the intersections of opposite sides shows the curve to be a conic, if the hexagon is inscribed; but if it be circumscribed, the copunctuality of its three diameters (joining opposite vertices) [shows the curve to be a conic]. Its Mode of Being may be Actuality: as with any barometer. Or Necessitant: as the word "the" or any other in the dictionary. For a "possible" Sign I have no better designation than a *Tone,* though I am considering replacing this by "Mark." Can you suggest a really good name? An Actual sign I call a *Token;* a Necessitant Sign a *Type.*

It is usual and proper to distinguish two Objects of a Sign, the Mediate without, and the Immediate within the Sign. Its Interpretant is all that the Sign conveys: acquaintance with its Object must be gained by collateral experience. The Mediate Object is the Object outside of the Sign; I call it the *Dynamoid* Object. The Sign must indicate it by a hint; and this hint, or its substance, is the *Immediate* Object. Each of these two Objects may be said to be capable of either of the three Modalities, though in the case of the Immediate Object, this is not quite literally true. Accordingly, the Dynamoid Object may be a Possible,—when I term the Sign an *Abstractive,* such as the word Beauty; and it will be none the less an Abstractive if I speak of "the Beautiful," since it is the ultimate reference, and not the grammatical form, that makes the sign an *Abstractive.* When the Dynamoid Object is an Occurrence (Existent thing or Actual fact of past or future), I term the Sign a *Concretive;* any one barometer is an example, and so is a written narrative of any series of events. For a Sign whose Dynamoid Object is a Necessitant, I have at present no better designation than a *Collective,* which is not quite so bad a name as it sounds to be until one studies the matter: but for a person, like me, who thinks in quite a different system of symbols to words, it is so awkward and often puzzling to translate one's thought into words! If the Immediate Object is a Possible, that is, if the Dynamoid Object is indicated (always more or less vaguely) by means of its Qualities, etc., I call the Sign a

*Descriptive;* if the Immediate [Object is an Occurrence, I call the Sign a *Designative;* and if the Immediate Object is a Necessitant, I call the sign a *Copulant;* for in that case the Object has to be so identified by the Interpreter that the Sign may represent a necessitation. My name is certainly a temporary expedient.

It is evident that a Possible can determine nothing but a Possible; it is equally so that a Necessitant can be determined by nothing but a Necessitant. Hence it follows from the Definition of a Sign that since the Dynamoid Object determines the Immediate Object,

which determines the Sign itself,

which determines the Destinate Interpretant,

which determines the Effective Interpretant,

which determines the Explicit Interpretant,

the six trichotomies, instead of determining 729 classes of signs, as they would if they were independent, only yield 28 classes; and if, as I strongly opine (not to say almost prove) there are four other trichotomies of signs of the same order of importance, instead of making 59,049 classes, these will only come to 66. The additional four trichotomies are undoubtedly first,

| Icons | Indices | Symbols |

and then three referring to the Interpretants. One of these I am pretty confident is into:

| Suggestives | Imperatives | Indicatives |

where the Imperatives include Interrogatives. Of the other two I *think* that one must be into Signs assuring their Interpretants by

| Instinct | Experience | Form. |

The other I suppose to be what, in my *Monist* exposition of Existential Graphs, I called

| Semes | Phemes | Delomes. |

# What Pragmatism Is

The writer of this article has been led by much experience to believe that every physicist, and every chemist, and, in short, every master in any department of experimental science, has had his mind molded by his life in the laboratory to a degree that is little suspected. The experimentalist himself can hardly be fully aware of it, for the reason that the men whose intellects he really knows about are much like himself in this respect. With intellects of widely different training from his own, whose education has largely been a thing learned out of books, he will never become inwardly intimate, be he on ever so familiar terms with them; for he and they are as oil and water, and though they be shaken up together, it is remarkable how quickly they will go their several mental ways, without having gained more than a faint flavor from the association. Were those other men only to take skillful soundings of the experimentalist's mind—which is just what they are unqualified to do, for the most part—they would soon discover that, excepting perhaps upon topics where his mind is trammeled by personal feeling or by his bringing up, his disposition is to think of everything just as everything is thought of in the laboratory, that is, as a question of experimentation. Of course, no living man possesses in their fullness all the attributes characteristic of his type: it is not the typical doctor whom you will see every day driven in buggy or coupé, nor is it the typical pedagogue that will be met with in the first schoolroom you enter. But when you have found, or ideally constructed upon a basis of observation, the typical experimental-

From *The Monist,* vol. 15, 1905, pp. 161–181.

ist, you will find that whatever assertion you may make to him, he will either understand as meaning that if a given prescription for an experiment ever can be and ever is carried out in act, an experience of a given description will result, or else he will see no sense at all in what you say. If you talk to him as Mr. Balfour talked not long ago to the British Association[1] saying that "the physicist . . . seeks for something deeper than the laws connecting possible objects of experience," that "his object is physical reality" unrevealed in experiments, and that the existence of such non-experiential reality "is the unalterable faith of science," to all such ontological meaning, you will find the experimentalist mind to be color-blind. What adds to that confidence in this, which the writer owes to his conversations with experimentalists, is that he himself may almost be said to have inhabited a laboratory from the age of six until long past maturity; and having all his life associated mostly with experimentalists, it has always been with a confident sense of understanding them and of being understood by them.

That laboratory life did not prevent the writer (who here and in what follows simply exemplifies the experimentalist type) from becoming interested in methods of thinking; and when he came to read metaphysics, although much of it seemed to him loosely reasoned and determined by accidental prepossessions, yet in the writings of some philosophers, especially Kant, Berkeley, and Spinoza, he sometimes came upon strains of thought that recalled the ways of thinking of the laboratory, so that he felt he might trust to them; all of which has been true of other laboratory-men.

Endeavoring, as a man of that type naturally would, to formulate what he so approved, he framed the theory that a *conception, that is, the rational purport of a word or other expression, lies exclusively in its conceivable bearing upon the conduct of life; so that, since obviously nothing that might not result from experiment can have any direct bearing upon conduct, if one can define accurately all the conceivable experimental phenomena which the affirmation or denial of a concept could imply, one will have therein a complete definition of the concept, and there is absolutely nothing more in it.* For this doctrine he invented the name *pragmatism.* Some of his friends wished him to call it *practicism* or *practicalism* (perhaps on the ground that *praktikós* is better Greek than *pragmatikós*). But for one who had learned philosophy out of Kant, as the writer, along with nineteen out of every twenty experimentalists who have turned to philosophy, had done, and who still thought in Kantian terms most readily, *praktisch* and *pragmatisch* were as far apart as the two poles, the former belonging in a region of thought where no mind of the experimentalist type can ever make sure of solid ground under his feet, the latter expressing relation to some definite human purpose. Now quite the most striking feature of the new theory was its recognition of an inseparable connection between rational cognition and rational purpose; and that consideration it was which determined the preference for the name *pragmatism.*

Concerning the matter of philosophical nomenclature, there are a few plain considerations which the writer has for many years longed to submit to the deliberate judgment of those few fellow-students of philosophy who deplore the present state of that study, and who are intent upon rescuing it therefrom and bringing it to a condition like that of the natural sciences, where investigators, instead of condemning each the work of most of the others as misdirected from beginning to end, cooperate, stand upon one another's shoulders, and multiply incontestable results; where every observation is repeated, and isolated observations go for little; where every hypothesis that merits attention is subjected to severe but fair examination, and only after the predictions to which it leads have been remarkably borne out by experience is trusted at all, and even then only provisionally; where a radically false step is rarely taken, even the most faulty of those theories which gain wide credence being true in their main experiential predictions. To those students, it is submitted that no study can become scientific in the sense described until it provides itself with a suitable technical nomenclature, whose every term has a single definite meaning universally accepted among students of the subject, and whose vocables have no such sweetness or charms as might tempt loose writers to abuse them—which is a virtue of scientific nomenclature too little appreciated. It is submitted that the experience of those sciences which have conquered the greatest difficulties of terminology, which are unquestionably the taxonomic sciences, chemistry, mineralogy, botany, zoology, has conclusively shown that the one only way in which the requisite unanimity and requisite ruptures with individual habits and preferences can be brought about is so to shape the canons of terminology that they shall gain the support of *moral principle* and of every man's sense of decency; and that, in particular (under defined restrictions), the general feeling shall be that he who introduces a new conception into philosophy is under an obligation to invent acceptable terms to express it, and that when he has done so, the duty of his fellow–students is to accept those terms, and to resent any wresting of them from their original meanings, as not only a gross discourtesy to him to whom philosophy was indebted for each conception, but also as an injury to philosophy itself; and furthermore, that once a conception has been supplied with suitable and sufficient words for its expression, no other *technical* terms denoting the same things, considered in the same relations, should be countenanced. Should this suggestion find favor, it might be deemed needful that the philosophians in congress assembled should adopt, after due deliberation, convenient canons to limit the application of the principle. Thus, just as is done in chemistry, it might be wise to assign fixed meanings to certain prefixes and suffixes. For example, it might be agreed, perhaps, that the prefix *prope-* should mark a broad and rather indefinite extension of the meaning of the term to which it was prefixed; the name of a doctrine would naturally end in *-ism*, while *-icism* might mark a more strictly defined acception

of that doctrine, etc. Then again, just as in biology no account is taken of terms antedating Linnæus, so in philosophy it might be found best not to go back of the scholastic terminology. To illustrate another sort of limitation, it has probably never happened that any philosopher has attempted to give a general name to his own doctrine without that name's soon acquiring in common philosophical usage a signification much broader than was originally intended. Thus, special systems go by the names Kantianism, Benthamism, Comteanism, Spencerianism, etc., while transcendentalism, utilitarianism, positivism, evolutionism, synthetic philosophy, etc., have irrevocably and very conveniently been elevated to broader governments.

After awaiting in vain, for a good many years, some particularly opportune conjuncture of circumstances that might serve to recommend his notions of the ethics of terminology, the writer has now, at last, dragged them in over head and shoulders, on an occasion when he has no specific proposal to offer nor any feeling but satisfaction at the course usage has run without any canons or resolutions of a congress. His word "pragmatism" has gained general recognition in a generalized sense that seems to argue power of growth and vitality. The famed psychologist, James, first took it up,[2] seeing that his "radical empiricism" substantially answered to the writer's definition of pragmatism, albeit with a certain difference in the point of view. Next, the admirably clear and brilliant thinker, Mr. Ferdinand C. S. Schiller, casting about for a more attractive name for the "anthropomorphism" of his *Riddle of the Sphinx,* lit, in that most remarkable paper of his on "Axioms as Postulates,"[3] upon the same designation "pragmatism," which in its original sense was in generic agreement with his own doctrine, for which he has since found the more appropriate specification "humanism," while he still retains "pragmatism" in a somewhat wider sense. So far all went happily. But at present, the word begins to be met with occasionally in the literary journals, where it gets abused in the merciless way that words have to expect when they fall into literary clutches. Sometimes the manners of the British have effloresced in scolding at the word as ill-chosen—ill-chosen, that is, to express some meaning that it was rather designed to exclude. So then, the writer, finding his bantling "pragmatism" so promoted, feels that it is time to kiss his child good-by and relinquish it to its higher destiny; while to serve the precise purpose of expressing the original definition, he begs to announce the birth of the word "pragmaticism," which is ugly enough to be safe from kidnappers.[4]

Much as the writer has gained from the perusal of what other pragmatists have written, he still thinks there is a decisive advantage in his original conception of the doctrine. From this original form every truth that follows from any of the other forms can be deduced, while some errors can be avoided into which other pragmatists have fallen. The original view appears, too, to be a more compact and unitary conception than the others. But its capital merit, in the writer's eyes, is that it more readily connects itself with a critical proof of its truth. Quite in accord with the logical order of investigation, it usually happens that one first forms an hypothesis that seems more and more reasonable the further one examines into it, but that only a good deal later gets crowned with an adequate proof. The present writer, having had the pragmatist theory under consideration for many years longer than most of its adherents, would naturally have given more attention to the proof of it. At any rate, in endeavoring to explain pragmatism, he may be excused for confining himself to that form of it that he knows best. In the present article there will be space only to explain just what this doctrine (which, in such hands as it has now fallen into, may probably play a pretty prominent part in the philosophical discussions of the next coming years) really consists in. Should the exposition be found to interest readers of *The Monist,* they would certainly be much more interested in a second article which would give some samples of the manifold applications of pragmaticism (assuming it to be true) to the solution of problems of different kinds. After

that, readers might be prepared to take an interest in a proof that the doctrine is true—a proof which seems to the writer to leave no reasonable doubt on the subject, and to be the one contribution of value that he has to make to philosophy. For it would essentially involve the establishment of the truth of synechism. [The principle that continuity prevails in all thought, life, and society].

The bare definition of pragmaticism could convey no satisfactory comprehension of it to the most apprehensive of minds, but requires the commentary to be given below. Moreover, this definition takes no notice of one or two other doctrines without the previous acceptance (or virtual acceptance) of which pragmaticism itself would be a nullity. They are included as a part of the pragmatism of Schiller, but the present writer prefers not to mingle different propositions. The preliminary propositions had better be stated forthwith.

The difficulty in doing this is that no formal list of them has ever been made. They might all be included under the vague maxim, "Dismiss make-believes." Philosophers of very diverse stripes propose that philosophy shall take its start from one or another state of mind in which no man, least of all a beginner in philosophy, actually is. One proposes that you shall begin by doubting everything, and says that there is only one thing that you cannot doubt, as if doubting were "as easy as lying." Another proposes that we should begin by observing "the first impressions of sense," forgetting that our very percepts are the results of cognitive elaboration. But in truth, there is but one state of mind from which you can "set out," namely, the very state of mind in which you actually find yourself at the time you do "set out"—a state in which you are laden with an immense mass of cognition already formed, of which you cannot divest yourself if you would; and who knows whether, if you could, you would not have made all knowledge impossible to yourself? Do you call it *doubting* to write down on a piece of paper that you doubt? If so, doubt has nothing to do with any serious business. But do not make believe; if pedantry has not eaten all the reality out of you, recognize, as you must, that there is much that you do not doubt, in the least. Now that which you do not at all doubt, you must and do regard as infallible, absolute truth. Here breaks in Mr. Make Believe: "What! Do you mean to say that one is to believe what is not true, or that what a man does not doubt is *ipso facto* true?" No, but unless he can make a thing white and black at once, *he* has to regard what he does not doubt as absolutely true. Now you, *per hypothesiu,* are that man. "But you tell me there are scores of things I do not doubt. I really cannot persuade myself that there is not some one of them about which I am mistaken." You are adducing one of your make-believe facts, which, even if it were established, would only go to show that doubt has a *limen,* that is, is only called into being by a certain finite stimulus. You only puzzle yourself by talking of this metaphysical "truth" and metaphysical "falsity," that you know nothing about. All you have any dealings with are your doubts and beliefs,[5] with the course of life that forces new beliefs upon you and gives you power to doubt old beliefs. If your terms "truth" and "falsity" are taken in such senses as to be definable in terms of doubt and belief and the course of experience (as for example they would be if you were to define the "truth" as that to a belief in which belief would tend if it were to tend indefinitely toward absolute fixity), well and good: in that case, you are only talking about doubt and belief. But if by truth and falsity you mean something not definable in terms of doubt and belief in any way, then you are talking of entities of whose existence you can know nothing, and which Ockham's razor would clean shave off. Your problems would be greatly simplified if, instead of saying that you want to know the "Truth," you were simply to say that you want to attain a state of belief unassailable by doubt.

Belief is not a momentary mode of consciousness; it is a habit of mind essentially enduring for some time, and mostly (at least) unconscious; and like other habits, it is (until it meets with some surprise that begins its dis-

solution) perfectly self-satisfied. Doubt is of an altogether contrary genus. It is not a habit, but the privation of a habit. Now a privation of a habit, in order to be anything at all, must be a condition of erratic activity that in some way must get superseded by a habit.

Among the things which the reader, as a rational person, does not doubt is that he not merely has habits, but also can exert a measure of self-control over his future actions; which means, however, *not* that he can impart to them any arbitrarily assignable character, but, on the contrary, that a process of self-preparation will tend to impart to action (when the occasion for it shall arise) one fixed character, which is indicated and perhaps roughly measured by the absence (or slightness) of the feeling of self-reproach, which subsequent reflection will induce. Now, this subsequent reflection is part of the self-preparation for action on the next occasion. Consequently, there is a tendency, as action is repeated again and again, for the action to approximate indefinitely toward the perfection of that fixed character, which would be marked by entire absence of self-reproach. The more closely this is approached, the less room for self-control there will be; and where no self-control is possible there will be no self-reproach.

These phenomena seem to be the fundamental characteristics which distinguish a rational being. Blame, in every case, appears to be a modification, often accomplished by a transference, or "projection," of the primary feeling of self-reproach. Accordingly, we never blame anybody for what had been beyond his power of previous self-control. Now, thinking is a species of conduct which is largely subject to self-control. In all their features (which there is no room to describe here), logical self-control is a perfect mirror of ethical self-control—unless it be rather a species under that genus. In accordance with this, what you cannot in the least help believing is not, justly speaking, wrong belief. In other words, for you it is the absolute truth. True, it is conceivable that what you cannot help believing today, you might find you thoroughly disbelieve tomorrow. But then there is a certain distinction between things you "cannot" do, merely in the sense that nothing stimulates you to the great effort and endeavors that would be required, and things you cannot do because in their own nature they are insusceptible of being put into practice. In every stage of your excogitations, there is something of which you can only say, "I cannot think otherwise," and your experientially based hypothesis is that the impossibility is of the second kind.

There is no reason why "thought," in what has just been said, should be taken in that narrow sense in which silence and darkness are favorable to thought. It should rather be understood as covering all rational life, so that an experiment shall be an operation of thought. Of course, that ultimate state of habit to which the action of self-control ultimately tends, where no room is left for further self-control, is, in the case of thought, the state of fixed belief, or perfect knowledge.

Two things here are all-important to assure oneself of and to remember. The first is that a person is not absolutely an individual. His thoughts are what he is "saying to himself," that is, is saying to that other self that is just coming into life in the flow of time. When one reasons, it is that critical self that one is trying to persuade; and all thought whatsoever is a sign, and is mostly of the nature of language. The second thing to remember is that the man's circle of society (however widely or narrowly this phrase may be understood) is a sort of loosely compacted person, in some respects of higher rank than the person of an individual organism. It is these two things alone that render it possible for you—but only in the abstract, and in a Pickwickian sense— to distinguish between absolute truth and what you do not doubt.

Let us now hasten to the exposition of pragmaticism itself. Here it will be convenient to imagine that somebody to whom the doctrine is new, but of rather preternatural perspicacity, asks questions of a pragmaticist. Everything that might give a dramatic illusion must be stripped off, so that the result will be a sort of cross between a dialogue and a catechism, but a good deal more like the latter—something rather painfully reminiscent of Mangnall's *Historical Questions.*

*Questioner:* I am astounded at your definition of your pragmatism, because only last year I was assured by a person above all suspicion of warping the truth—himself a pragmatist—that your doctrine precisely was "that a conception is to be tested by its practical effects." You must surely, then, have entirely changed your definition very recently.

*Pragmatist:* If you will turn to Volumes VI and VII of the *Revue Philosophique,* or to the *Popular Science Monthly* for November 1877 and January 1878, you will be able to judge for yourself whether the interpretation you mention was not then clearly excluded. The exact wording of the English enunciation (changing only the first person into the second) was: "Consider what effects that might conceivably have practical bearing you conceive the object of your conception to have. Then your conception of those effects is the WHOLE of your conception of the object."

*Questioner:* Well, what reason have you for asserting that this is so?

*Pragmatist:* That is what I specially desire to tell you. But the question had better be postponed until you clearly understand what those reasons profess to prove.

*Questioner:* What, then, is the *raison d'être* of the doctrine? What advantage is expected from it?

*Pragmatist:* It will serve to show that almost every proposition of ontological metaphysics is either meaningless gibberish—one word being defined by other words, and they by still others, without any real conception ever being reached—or else is downright absurd; so that all such rubbish being swept away, what will remain of philosophy will be a series of problems capable of investigation by the observational methods of the true sciences—the truth about which can be reached without those interminable misunderstandings and disputes which have made the highest of the positive sciences a mere amusement for idle intellects, a sort of chess—idle pleasure its purpose, and reading out of a book its method. In this regard, pragmaticism is a species of prope-positivism. But what distinguishes it from other species is, first, its retention of a purified philosophy; secondly, its full acceptance of the main body of our instinctive beliefs; and thirdly, its strenuous insistence upon the truth of scholastic realism (or a close approximation to that, well stated by the late Dr. Francis Ellingwood Abbot in the Introduction to his *Scientific Theism*). So, instead of merely jeering at metaphysics, like other prope-positivists, whether by long-drawn-out parodies or otherwise, the pragmaticist extracts from it a precious essence, which will serve to give life and light to cosmology and physics. At the same time, the moral applications of the doctrine are positive and potent; and there are many other uses of it not easily classed. On another occasion, instances may be given to show that it really has these effects.

*Questioner:* I hardly need to be convinced that your doctrine would wipe out metaphysics. Is it not as obvious that it must wipe out every proposition of science and everything that bears on the conduct of life? For you say that the only meaning that, for you, any assertion bears is that a certain experiment has resulted in a certain way: nothing else but an experiment enters into the meaning. Tell me, then, how can an experiment, in itself, reveal anything more than that something once happened to an individual object and that subsequently some other individual event occurred?

*Pragmatist:* That question is, indeed, to the purpose—the purpose being to correct any misapprehensions of pragmaticism. You speak of an experiment in itself, emphasizing *in itself*. You evidently think of each experiment as isolated from every other. It has not, for example, occurred to you, one might venture to surmise, that every connected series of experiments constitutes a single collective experiment. What are the essential ingredients of an experiment? First, of course, an experimenter of flesh and blood. Secondly, a verifiable hypothesis. This is a proposition[6] relating to the universe environing the experimenter, or to some well-known part of it and affirming or denying of this only some experimental

possibility or impossibility. The third indispensable ingredient is a sincere doubt in the experimenter's mind as to the truth of that hypothesis.

Passing over several ingredients on which we need not dwell, the purpose, the plan, and the resolve, we come to the act of choice by which the experimenter singles out certain identifiable objects to be operated upon. The next is the external (or quasi-external) ACT by which he modifies those objects. Next, comes the subsequent *reaction* of the world upon the experimenter in a perception; and finally, his recognition of the teaching of the experiment. While the two chief parts of the event itself are the action and the reaction, yet the unity of essence of the experiment lies in its purpose and plan, the ingredients passed over in the enumeration.

Another thing: in representing the pragmaticist as making rational meaning to consist in an experiment (which you speak of as an event in the past), you strikingly fail to catch his attitude of mind. Indeed, it is not in an experiment, but in *experimental phenomena,* that rational meaning is said to consist. When an experimentalist speaks of a *phenomenon,* such as "Hall's phenomenon," "Zeemann's phenomenon" and its modification, "Michelson's phenomenon," or "the chessboard phenomenon," he does not mean any particular event that did happen to somebody in the dead past, but what *surely will* happen to everybody in the living future who shall fulfill certain conditions. The phenomenon consists in the fact that when an experimentalist shall come to *act* according to a certain scheme that he has in mind, then will something else happen, and shatter the doubts of skeptics, like the celestial fire upon the altar of Elijah.

And do not overlook the fact that the pragmaticist maxim says nothing of single experiments or of single experimental phenomena (for what is conditionally true in *future* can hardly be singular), but only speaks of *general kinds* of experimental phenomena. Its adherent does not shrink from speaking of general objects as real, since whatever is true represents a real. Now the laws of nature are true.

The rational meaning of every proposition lies in the future. How so? The meaning of a proposition is itself a proposition. Indeed, it is no other than the very proposition of which it is the meaning: it is a translation of it. But of the myriads of forms into which a proposition may be translated, what is that one which is to be called its very meaning? It is, according to the pragmaticist, that form in which the proposition becomes applicable to human conduct, not in these or those special circumstances, nor when one entertains this or that special design, but that form which is most directly applicable to self-control under every situation, and to every purpose. This is why he locates the meaning in future time; for future conduct is the only conduct that is subject to self-control. But in order that that form of the proposition which is to be taken as its meaning should be applicable to every situation and to every purpose upon which the proposition has any bearing, it must be simply the general description of all the experimental phenomena which the assertion of the proposition virtually predicts. For an experimental phenomenon is the fact asserted by the proposition that action of a certain description will have a certain kind of experimental result; and experimental results are the only results that can affect human conduct. No doubt, some unchanging idea may come to influence a man more than it had done; but only because some experience equivalent to an experiment has brought its truth home to him more intimately than before. Whenever a man acts purposively, he acts under a belief in some experimental phenomenon. Consequently, the sum of the experimental phenomena that a proposition implies makes up its entire bearing upon human conduct. Your question, then, of how a pragmaticist can attribute any meaning to any assertion other than that of a single occurrence is substantially answered.

*Questioner:* I see that pragmaticism is a thoroughgoing phenomenalism. Only why should you limit yourself to the phenomena of experimental science rather than embrace all observational science? Experiment, after all, is an uncommunicative informant. It never expiates: it only answers "yes" or "no"; or rather it usually snaps out "No!" or, at best, only utters an inarticulate grunt for the negation of its "no." The typical experimentalist is not much of an observer. It is the student of natural history to whom nature opens the treasury of her confidence, while she treats the cross-examining experimentalist with the reserve he merits. Why should your phenomenalism sound the meagre jew's-harp of experiment rather than the glorious organ of observation?

*Pragmaticist:* Because pragmaticism is not definable as "thoroughgoing phenomenalism," although the latter doctrine may be a kind of pragmatism. The *richness* of phenomena lies in their sensuous quality. Pragmaticism does not intend to define the phenomenal equivalents of words and general ideas, but, on the contrary, eliminates their sential element, and endeavors to define the rational purport, and this it finds in the purposive bearing of the word or proposition in question.

*Questioner:* Well, if you choose so to make Doing the Be-all and the End-all of human life, why do you not make meaning to consist simply in doing? Doing has to be done at a certain time upon a certain object. Individual objects and single events cover all reality, as everybody knows, and as a practicalist ought to be the first to insist. Yet, your meaning, as you have described it, is *general*. Thus, it is of the nature of a mere word and not a reality. You say yourself that your meaning of a proposition is only the same proposition in another dress. But a practical man's meaning is the very thing he means. What do you make to be the meaning of "George Washington"?

*Pragmaticist:* Forcibly put! A good half dozen of your points must certainly be admitted. It must be admitted, in the first place, that if pragmaticism really made Doing to be the Be-all and the End-all of life, that would be its death. For to say that we live for the mere sake of action, as action, regardless of the thought it carries out, would be to say that there is no such thing as rational purport. Secondly, it must be admitted that every proposition professes to be true of a certain real, individual object, often the environing universe. Thirdly, it must be admitted that pragmaticism fails to furnish any translation or meaning of a proper name, or other designation of an individual object. Fourthly, the pragmaticistic meaning is undoubtedly general; and it is equally indisputable that the general is of the nature of a word or sign. Fifthly, it must be admitted that individuals alone exist; and sixthly, it may be admitted that the very meaning of a word or significant object ought to be the very essence of reality of what it signifies. But when those admissions have been unreservedly made, if you find the pragmaticist still constrained most earnestly to deny the force of your objection, you ought to infer that there is some consideration that has escaped you. Putting the admissions together, you will perceive that the pragmaticist grants that a proper name (although it is not customary to say that it has a *meaning*) has a certain denotative function peculiar, in each case, to that name and its equivalents; and that he grants that every assertion contains such a denotative or pointing-out function. In its peculiar individuality, the pragmaticist excludes this from the rational purport of the assertion, although *the like* of it, being common to all assertions, and so, being general and not individual, may enter into the pragmaticistic purport. Whatever exists, *ex-sists*, that is, really acts upon other existents, so obtains a self-identity, and is definitely individual. As to the general, it will be a help to thought to notice that there are two ways of being general. A statue of a soldier on some village monument, in his overcoat and with his musket, is for each of a hundred families the image of its uncle, its sacrifice to the Union. That statue, then, though it is itself single, represents any one man of whom a certain predicate may be true. It is *objectively* general. The word "soldier," whether spoken or written, is general in the same way; while the name "George Washington" is not so. But each of these two terms remains one and the same noun, whether it be spoken or written, and whenever and wherever it be spoken or written. This noun is not an existent thing: it is a *type,* or *form,* to which

objects, both those that are externally existent and those which are imagined, may *conform,* but which none of them can exactly be. This is subjective generality. The pragmaticistic purport is general in both ways.

As to reality, one finds it defined in various ways; but if that principle of terminological ethics that was proposed be accepted, the equivocal language will soon disappear. For *realis* and *realitas* are not ancient words. They were invented to be terms of philosophy in the thirteenth century,[7] and the meaning they were intended to express is perfectly clear. That is *real* which has such and such characters, whether anybody thinks it to have those characters or not. At any rate, that is the sense in which the pragmaticist uses the word. Now, just as conduct controlled by ethical reason tends toward fixing certain habits of conduct, the nature of which (as, to illustrate the meaning, peaceable habits and not quarrelsome habits) does not depend upon any accidental circumstances, and *in that sense* may be said to be *destined;* so, thought, controlled by a rational experimental logic, tends to the fixation of certain opinions, equally destined, the nature of which will be the same in the end, however the perversity of thought of whole generations may cause the postponement of the ultimate fixation. If this be so, as every man of us virtually assumes that it is, in regard to each matter the truth of which he seriously discusses, then, according to the adopted definition of "real," the state of things which will be believed in that ultimate opinion is real. But, for the most part, such opinions will be general. Consequently, *some* general objects are real. (Of course, nobody ever thought that *all* generals were real; but the scholastics used to assume that generals were real when they had hardly any, or quite no, experiential evidence to support their assumption; and their fault lay just there, and not in holding that generals could be real.) One is struck with the inexactitude of thought even of analysts of power, when they touch upon modes of being. One will meet, for example, the virtual assumption that what is relative to thought cannot be real. But why not, exactly? *Red* is relative to sight, but the fact that this or that is in that relation to vision that we call being red is not *itself* relative to sight; it is a real fact.

Not only may generals be real, but they may also be *physically efficient,* not in every metaphysical sense, but in the common-sense acception in which human purposes are physically efficient. Aside from metaphysical nonsense, no sane man doubts that if I feel the air in my study to be stuffy, that thought may cause the window to be opened. My thought, be it granted, was an individual event. But what determined it to take the particular determination it did, was in part the general fact that stuffy air is unwholesome, and in part other *Forms,* concerning which Dr. Carus[8] has caused so many men to reflect to advantage— or rather, *by* which, and the general truth concerning which Dr. Carus's mind was determined to the forcible enunciation of so much truth. For truths, on the average, have a greater tendency to get believed than falsities have. Were it otherwise, considering that there are myriads of false hypotheses to account for any given phenomenon, against one sole true one (or if you will have it so, against every true one), the first step toward genuine knowledge must have been next door to a miracle. So, then, when my window was opened, because of the truth that stuffy air is *malsain,* a physical effort was brought into existence by the efficiency of a general and non-existent truth. This has a droll sound because it is unfamiliar; but exact analysis is with it and not against it; and it has besides, the immense advantage of not blinding us to great facts—such as that the ideas "justice" and "truth" are, notwithstanding the iniquity of the world, the mightiest of the forces that move it. Generality is, indeed, an indispensable ingredient of reality; for mere individual existence or actuality without any regularity whatever is a nullity. Chaos is pure nothing.

That which any true proposition asserts is *real,* in the sense of being as it is regardless of what you or I may think about it. Let this proposition be a general conditional proposition as to the future, and it is a real general such as is calculated really to influence human conduct; and such the pragmaticist holds to be the rational purport of every concept.

Accordingly, the pragmaticist does not make the *summum bonum* to consist in action, but makes it to consist in that process of evolution whereby the existent comes more and more to embody those generals which were just now said to be *destined,* which is what we strive to express in calling them *reasonable.* In its higher stages, evolution takes place more and more largely through self-control, and this gives the pragmaticist a sort of justification for making the rational purport to be general.

There is much more in elucidation of pragmaticism that might be said to advantage were it not for the dread of fatiguing the reader. It might, for example, have been well to show clearly that the pragmaticist does not attribute any different essential mode of being to an event in the future from that which he would attribute to a similar event in the past, but only that the practical attitude of the thinker toward the two is different. It would also have been well to show that the pragmaticist does not make Forms to be the *only* realities in the world, any more than he makes the reasonable purport of a word to be the only kind of meaning there is. These things are, however, implicitly involved in what has been said. There is only one remark concerning the pragmaticist's conception of the relation of his formula to the first principles of logic which need detain the reader.

Aristotle's definition of universal predication,[9] which is usually designated (like a papal bull or writ of court, from its opening words), as the *Dictum de omni* [said of all], may be translated as follows: "We call a predication (be it affirmative or negative), *universal,* when, and only when, there is nothing among the existent individuals to which the subject affirmatively belongs, but to which the predicate will not likewise be referred (affirmatively or negatively, according as the universal predication is affirmative or negative)." ... The important words "existent individuals" have been introduced into the translation (which English idiom would not here permit to be literal); but it is plain that "existent individuals" were what Aristotle meant. The other departures from literalness only serve to give modern English forms of expression. Now, it is well known that propositions in formal logic go in pairs, the two of one pair being convertible into another by the interchange of the ideas of antecedent and consequent, subject and predicate, etc. The parallelism extends so far that it is often assumed to be perfect; but it is not quite so. The proper mate of this sort to the *Dictum de omni* is the following definition of affirmative predication: We call a predication *affirmative* (be it universal or particular) when, and only when, there is nothing among the sensational effects that belong universally to the predicate which will not be (universally or particularly, according as the affirmative predication is universal or particular) said to belong to the subject. Now, this is substantially the essential proposition of pragmaticism. Of course, its parallelism to the *Dictum de omni* will only be admitted by a person who admits the truth of pragmaticism.

Suffer me to add one word more on this point. For if one cares at all to know what the pragmaticist theory consists in, one must understand that there is no other part of it to which the pragmaticist attaches quite as much importance as he does to the recognition in his doctrine of the utter inadequacy of action or volition or even of resolve or actual purpose, as materials out of which to construct a conditional purpose or the concept of conditional purpose. Had a purposed article concerning the principle of continuity and synthetizing the ideas of the other articles of a series in the early volumes of *The Monist* ever been written, it would have appeared how, with thorough consistency, that theory involved the recognition that continuity is an indispensable element of reality, and that continuity is simply what generality becomes in the logic of relatives, and thus, like generality, and more than generality, is an affair of thought, and is the essence of thought. Yet even in its truncated condition, an extra-intelligent reader might discern that the theory of those cosmological articles made reality to consist in

something more than feeling and action could supply, inasmuch as the primeval chaos, where those two elements were present, was explicitly shown to be pure nothing. Now, the motive for alluding to that theory just here is that in this way one can put in a strong light a position which the pragmaticist holds and must hold, whether that cosmological theory be ultimately sustained or exploded, namely, that the third category—the category of thought, representation, triadic relation, mediation, genuine thirdness, thirdness as such—is an essential ingredient of reality, yet does not by itself constitute reality, since this category (which in that cosmology appears as the element of habit) can have no concrete being without action, as a separate object on which to work its government, just as action cannot exist without the immediate being of feeling on which to act. The truth is that pragmaticism is closely allied to the Hegelian absolute idealism, from which, however, it is sundered by its vigorous denial that the third category (which Hegel degrades to a mere stage of thinking) suffices to make the world, or is even so much as self-sufficient. Had Hegel, instead of regarding the first two stages with his smile of contempt, held on to them as independent or distinct elements of the triune Reality, pragmaticists might have looked up to him as the great vindicator of their truth. (Of course, the external trappings of his doctrine are only here and there of much significance.) For pragmaticism belongs essentially to the triadic class of philosophical doctrines, and is much more essentially so than Hegelianism is. (Indeed, in one passage, at least, Hegel alludes to the triadic form of his exposition as to a mere fashion of dress.)

## Notes

1. *Reflections Suggested by the New Theory of Matter;* Presidential Address, British Association for the Advancement of Science, August 17, 1904.
2. See his *Pragmatism.*
3. In *Personal Idealism,* ed. by H. Sturt (1902), p. 63.
4. To show how recent the general use of the word "pragmatism" is, the writer may mention that, to

the best of his belief, he never used it in copy for the press before today, except by particular request, in *Baldwin's Dictionary*. Toward the end of 1890, when this part of the *Century Dictionary* appeared, he did not deem that the word had sufficient status to appear in that work. But he has used it continually in philosophical conversation since, perhaps, the mid-seventies.

5. It is necessary to say that "belief" is throughout used merely as the name of the contrary to doubt, without regard to grades of certainty or to the nature of the proposition held for true, i.e., "believed."

6. The writer, like most English logicians, invariably uses the word *proposition* not as the Germans define their equivalent, *Satz,* as the language-expression of a judgment (*Urtheil*), but as that which is related to any assertion, whether mental and self-addressed or outwardly expressed, just as any possibility is related to its actualization. The difficulty of the, at best, difficult problem of the essential nature of a Proposition has been increased, for the Germans, by their *Urtheil*, confounding, under one designation, the mental *assertion* with the *assertable.*

7. See Prantl, *Geschichte der Logik*, III, 91, Anm. 362.

8. "The Foundations of Geometry," by Paul Carus, *The Monist*, XIII, p. 370.

9. *Prior Analytics*, 24b, 28–30.

# Issues of Pragmaticism

Pragmaticism was originally enounced[1] in the form of a maxim, as follows: Consider what effects that might *conceivably* have practical bearings you *conceive* the objects of your *conception* to have. Then, your *conception* of those effects is the whole of your *conception* of the object.

I will restate this in other words, since ofttimes one can thus eliminate some unsuspected source of perplexity to the reader. This time it shall be in the indicative mood, as follows: The entire intellectual purport of any symbol consists in the total of all general modes of rational conduct which, conditionally upon all the possible different circumstances and desires, would ensue upon the acceptance of the symbol.

Two doctrines that were defended by the writer about nine years before the formulation of pragmaticism may be treated as consequences of the latter belief. One of these may be called Critical Common-sensism. It is a variety of the Philosophy of Common Sense, but is marked by six distinctive characters, which had better be enumerated at once.

*Character* I. Critical Common-sensism admits that there not only are indubitable propositions but also that there are indubitable inferences. In one sense, anything evident is indubitable; but the propositions and inferences which Critical Common-sensism holds to be original, in the sense one cannot "go behind" them (as the lawyers say), are indubitable in the sense of being acritical. The term "reasoning" ought to be confined to such fixation of one belief by another as is reasonable, deliberate, self-controlled. A reasoning must be conscious; and this consciousness is not mere "immediate consciousness," which (as I argued in 1868) is simple Feeling viewed from another side, but is in its ultimate nature (meaning in that characteristic element of it that is not reducible to anything simpler) a sense of taking a habit, or disposition to respond to a given kind of stimulus in a given kind of way. As to the nature of that, some *éclaircissements* [clarifying explanations] will appear below and again in my third paper, on the Basis of Pragmaticism.[2] But the secret of rational consciousness is not so much to be

From *The Monist,* vol. 15, 1905, pp. 481–499.

sought in the study of this one peculiar nucleolus, as in the review of the process of self-control in its entirety. The machinery of logical self-control works on the same plan as does moral self-control, in multiform detail. The greatest difference, perhaps, is that the latter serves to inhibit mad puttings forth of energy, while the former most characteristically insures us against the quandary of Buridan's ass. The formation of habits under imaginary action (see the paper ["How to Make Our Ideas Clear"] of January, 1878) is one of the most essential ingredients of both; but in the logical process the imagination takes far wider flights, proportioned to the generality of the field of inquiry, being bounded in pure mathematics solely by the limits of its own powers, while in the moral process we consider only situations that may be apprehended or anticipated. For in moral life we are chiefly solicitous about our conduct and its inner springs, and the approval of conscience, while in intellectual life there is a tendency to value existence as the vehicle of forms. Certain obvious features of the phenomena of self-control (and especially of habit) can be expressed compactly and without any hypothetical addition, except what we distinctly rate as imagery, by saying that we have an occult nature of which and of its contents we can only judge by the conduct that it determines, and by phenomena of that conduct. All will assent to that (or all but the extreme nominalist), but anti-synechistic thinkers wind themselves up in a factitious snarl by falsifying the phenomena in representing consciousness to be, as it were, a skin, a separate tissue, overlying an unconscious region of the occult nature, mind, soul, or physiological basis. It appears to me that in the present state of our knowledge a sound methodeutic prescribes that, in adhesion to the appearances, the difference is only relative and the demarcation not precise.

According to the maxim of Pragmaticism, to say that determination affects our occult nature is to say that it is capable of affecting deliberate conduct; and since we are conscious of what we do deliberately, we are conscious *habitualiter* of whatever hides in the depths of our nature; and it is presumable (and *only* presumable,[3] although curious instances are on record) that a sufficiently energetic effort of attention would bring it out. Consequently, to say that an operation of the mind is controlled is to say that it is, in a special sense, a conscious operation; and this no doubt is the consciousness of reasoning. For this theory requires that in reasoning we should be conscious, not only of the conclusion, and of our deliberate approval of it, but also of its being the result of the premiss from which it does result, and furthermore that the inference is one of a possible class of inferences which conform to one guiding principle. Now in fact we find a well-marked class of mental operations, clearly of a different nature from any others which do possess just these properties. They alone deserve to be called *reasonings;* and if the reasoner is conscious, even vaguely, of what his guiding principle is, his reasoning should be called a *logical argumentation.* There are, however, cases in which we are conscious that a belief has been determined by another given belief, but are not conscious that it proceeds on any general principle. Such is St. Augustine's *"cogito, ergo sum."* Such a process should be called, not a reasoning, but an *acritical inference.* Again, there are cases in which one belief is determined by another, without our being at all aware of it. These should be called *associational suggestions of belief.*

Now the theory of Pragmaticism was originally based, as anybody will see who examines the papers of November 1877 and January 1878, upon a study of that experience of the phenomena of self-control which is common to all grown men and women; and it seems evident that to some extent, at least, it must always be so based. For it is to conceptions of deliberate conduct that Pragmaticism would trace the intellectual purport of symbols; and deliberate conduct is self-controlled conduct. Now control may itself be controlled, criticism itself subjected to criticism; and ideally there is no obvious definite limit to the sequence. But if one seriously inquires whether it is possible that a completed series of actual efforts should have been endless or beginningless (I will spare the reader the discussion), I think he can only conclude that (with some vagueness as to what constitutes an effort) this must be regarded as impossible. It will be found to follow that there are, besides perceptual judgments, original (i.e., indubitable because uncriticized) beliefs of a general and recurrent kind, as well as indubitable acritical inferences.

It is important for the reader to satisfy himself that genuine doubt always has an external origin, usually from surprise; and that it is as impossible for a man to create in himself a genuine doubt by such an act of the will as would suffice to imagine the condition of a mathematical theorem, as it would be for him to give himself a genuine surprise by a simple act of the will.

I beg my reader also to believe that it would be impossible for me to put into these articles over two per cent of the pertinent thought which would be necessary in order to present the subject as I have worked it out. I can only make a small selection of what it seems most desirable to submit to his judgment. Not only must all steps be omitted which he can be expected to supply for himself, but unfortunately much more that may cause him difficulty.

*Character* II. I do not remember that any of the old Scotch philosophers ever undertook to draw up a complete list of the original beliefs, but they certainly thought it a feasible thing, and that the list would hold good for the minds of all men from Adam down. For in those days Adam was an undoubted historical personage. Before any waft of the air of evolution had reached those coasts how could they think otherwise? When I first wrote, we were hardly orientated in the new ideas, and my impression was that the indubitable propositions changed with a thinking man from year to year. I made some studies preparatory to an investigation of the rapidity of these changes, but the matter was neglected, and it has been only during the last two years [1903–1905] that I have completed a provisional inquiry

which shows me that the changes are so slight from generation to generation, though not imperceptible even in that short period, that I thought to own my adhesion, under inevitable modification, to the opinion of that subtle but well-balanced intellect, Thomas Reid, in the matter of Common Sense (as well as in regard to immediate perception, along with Kant).[4]

*Character* III. The Scotch philosophers recognized that the original beliefs, and the same thing is at least equally true of the acritical inferences, were of the general nature of instincts. But little as we know about instincts, even now, we are much better acquainted with them than were the men of the eighteenth century. We know, for example, that they can be somewhat modified in a very short time. The great facts have always been known; such as that instinct seldom errs, while reason goes wrong nearly half the time, if not more frequently. But one thing the Scotch failed to recognize is that the original beliefs only remain indubitable in their application to affairs that resemble those of a primitive mode of life. It is, for example, quite open to reasonable doubt whether the motions of electrons are confined to three dimensions, although it is good methodeutic to presume that they are until some evidence to the contrary is forthcoming. On the other hand, as soon as we find that a belief shows symptoms of being instinctive, although it may seem to be dubitable, we must suspect that experiment would show that it is not really so; for in our artificial life, especially in that of a student, no mistake is more likely than that of taking a paper-doubt for the genuine metal. Take, for example, the belief in the criminality of incest. Biology will doubtless testify that the practice is inadvisable; but surely nothing that it has to say could warrant the intensity of our sentiment about it. When, however, we consider the thrill of horror which the idea excites in us, we find reason in that to consider it to be an instinct; and from that we may infer that if some rationalistic brother and sister were to marry, they would find that the conviction of horrible guilt could not be shaken off.

In contrast to this may be placed the belief that suicide is to be classed as murder. There are two pretty sure signs that this is not an instinctive belief. One is that it is substantially confined to the Christian world. The other is that when it comes to the point of actual self-debate, this belief seems to be completely expunged and ex-sponged from the mind. In reply to these powerful arguments, the main points urged are the authority of the fathers of the church and the undoubtedly intense instinctive clinging to life. The latter phenomenon is, however, entirely irrelevant. For though it is a wrench to part with life, which has its charms at the very worst, just as it is to part with a tooth, yet there is no *moral* element in it whatever. As to the Christian tradition, it may be explained by the circumstances of the early Church. For Christianity, the most terribly earnest and most intolerant of religions (see *The Book of Revelations of St. John the Divine*)—and it remained so until diluted with civilization—recognized no morality as worthy of an instant's consideration except Christian morality. Now the early Church had need of martyrs, i.e., witnesses, and if any man had done with life, it was abominable infidelity to leave it otherwise than as a witness to its power. This belief, then, should be set down as dubitable; and it will no sooner have been pronounced dubitable, than Reason will stamp it as false.

The Scotch School appears to have no such distinction concerning the limitations of indubitability and the consequent limitations of the jurisdiction of original belief.

*Character* IV. By all odds, the most distinctive character of the Critical Common-sensist, in contrast to the old Scotch philosopher, lies in his insistence that the acritically indubitable is invariably vague.

Logicians have been at fault in giving Vagueness the go-by, so far as not even to analyze it. The present writer has done his best to work out the Stechiology (or Stoicheiology), Critic, and Methodeutic of the subject, but can here only give a definition or two with some proposals respecting terminology.

Accurate writers have apparently made a distinction between the *definite* and the *determinate*. A subject is *determinate* in respect to

any character which inheres in it or is (universally and affirmatively) predicated of it, as well as in respect to the negative of such character, these being the very same respect. In all other respects it is *indeterminate*. The *definite* shall be defined presently. A sign (under which designation I place every kind of thought, and not alone external signs) that is in any respect objectively indeterminate (i.e., whose object is undetermined by the sign itself) is objectively *general* in so far as it extends to the interpreter the privilege of carrying its determination further.[5] *Example:* "Man is mortal." To the question, What man? the reply is that the proposition explicitly leaves it to you to apply its assertion to what man or men you will. A sign that is objectively indeterminate in any respect is objectively *vague* in so far as it reserves further determination to be made in some other conceivable sign, or at least does not appoint the interpreter as its deputy in this office. *Example:* "A man whom I could mention seems to be a little conceited." The *suggestion* here is that the man in view is the person addressed; but the utterer does not authorize such an interpretation or *any* other application of what she says. She can still say, if she likes, that she does *not* mean the person addressed. Every utterance naturally leaves the right of further exposition in the utterer; and therefore, in so far as a sign is indeterminate, it is vague, unless it is expressly or by a well-understood convention rendered general. Usually an affirmative predication covers *generally* every essential character of the predicate, while a negative predication *vaguely* denies some essential character. In another sense, honest people, when not joking, intend to make the meaning of their words determinate, so that there shall be no latitude of interpretation at all. That is to say, the character of their meaning consists in the implications and non-implications of their words; and they intend to fix what is implied and what is not implied. They believe that they succeed in doing so, and if their chat is about the theory of numbers, perhaps they may. But the further their topics are from such presciss, or "abstract," subjects, the less possibility is there of such precision of speech. In so far as the implication is not determinate, it is usually left vague; but there are cases where an unwillingness to dwell on disagreeable subjects causes the utterer to leave the determination of the implication to the interpreter; as if one says, "That creature is filthy, in every sense of the term."

Perhaps a more scientific pair of definitions would be that anything is *general* in so far as the principle of excluded middle does not apply to it and is *vague* in so far as the principle of contradiction does not apply to it. Thus, although it is true that "Any proposition you please, *once you have determined its identity,* is either true or false"; yet *so long as it remains indeterminate and so without identity,* it need neither be true that any proposition you please is true, nor that any proposition you please is false. So likewise, while it is false that "A proposition *whose identity I have determined* is both true and false," yet until it is determinate, it may be true that a proposition is true and that a proposition is false.

In those respects in which a sign is not vague, it is said to be *definite,* and also with a slightly different mode of application, to be *precise,* a meaning probably due to *prœcisus* having been applied to curt denials and refusals. It has been the well-established, ordinary sense of *precise* since the Plantagenets; and it were much to be desired that this word, with its derivatives *precision, precisive,* etc., should, in the dialect of philosophy, be restricted to this sense. To express the act of *rendering precise* (though usually only in reference to numbers, dates, and the like), the French have the verb *préciser,* which, after the analogy of *décider,* should have been *précider.* Would it not be a useful addition to our English terminology of logic to adopt the verb *to precide,* to express the general sense, to render precise? Our older logicians with salutary boldness seem to have created for their service the verb to *prescind,* the corresponding Latin word meaning only to "cut off at the end," while the English word means to suppose without supposing some more or less determinately indicated accompaniment. In

geometry, for example, we "prescind" shape from color, which is precisely the same thing as to "abstract" color from shape, although very many writers employ the verb "to abstract" so as to make it the equivalent of "prescind." But whether it was the invention or the courage of our philosophical ancestors which exhausted itself in the manufacture of the verb "prescind," the curious fact is that instead of forming from it the noun *prescission,* they took pattern from the French logicians in putting the word *precision* to this second use. About the same time[6] (see Watts, *Logick,* 1725, I, vi, 9 *ad fin.*) the adjective *precisive* was introduced to signify what *prescissive* would have more unmistakably conveyed. If we desire to rescue the good ship Philosophy for the service of Science from the hands of lawless rovers of the sea of literature, we shall do well to keep prescind, presciss, prescission, and prescissive on the one hand, to refer to dissection in hypothesis, while precide, precise, precision, and precisive are used so as to refer exclusively to an expression of determination which is made either full or free for the interpreter. We shall thus do much to relieve the stem "abstract" from staggering under the double burden of conveying the idea of prescission as well as the unrelated and very important idea of the creation of *ens rationis* out of an *épos pteróen* [winged discourse]—to filch the phrase to furnish a name for an expression of non-substantive thought—an operation that has been treated as a subject of ridicule—this hypostatic abstraction—but which gives mathematics half its power.

The purely formal conception that the three affections of terms, *determination, generality,* and *vagueness,* form a group dividing a category of what Kant calls "functions of judgment" will be passed by as unimportant by those who have yet to learn how important a part purely formal conceptions may play in philosophy. Without stopping to discuss this, it may be pointed out that the "quantity" of propositions in logic, that is, the distribution of the *first* subject,[7] is either *singular* (that is, determinate, which renders it substantially negligible in formal logic), *or universal* (that is, general), or *particular* (as the mediæval logicians say, that is, vague or *indefinite*). It is a curious fact that in the logic of relations it is the first and last quantifiers of a proposition that are of chief importance. To affirm of anything that it is a horse is to yield to it *every* essential character of a horse; to deny of anything that it is a horse is vaguely to refuse to it *some* one or more of those essential characters of the horse. There are, however, predicates that are unanalyzable in a given state of intelligence and experience. These are, therefore, determinately affirmed or denied. Thus, this same group of concepts reappears. Affirmation and denial are in themselves unaffected by these concepts, but it is to be remarked that there are cases in which we can have an apparently definite idea of a border line between affirmation and negation. Thus, a point of a surface may be in a region of that surface, or out of it, or on its boundary. This gives us an indirect and vague conception of an intermediary between affirmation and denial in general, and consequently of an intermediate, or nascent state, between determination and indetermination. There must be a similar intermediacy between generality and vagueness. Indeed, in an article in the seventh volume of *The Monist* [Peirce, "The Logic of Relatives," *The Monist,* Vol. 7 (1897), pp. 161–217.] there lies just beneath the surface of what is explicitly said, the idea of an endless series of such *intermediacies*. We shall find below some application for these reflections.

*Character* V. The Critical Common-sensist will be further distinguished from the old Scotch philosopher by the great value he attaches to doubt, provided only that it be the weighty and noble metal itself, and no counterfeit nor paper substitute. He is not content to ask himself whether he does doubt, but he invents a plan for attaining to doubt, elaborates it in detail, and then puts it into practice, although this may involve a solid month of hard work; and it is only after having gone through such an examination that he will pronounce a belief to be indubitable. Moreover, he fully acknowledges that even then it may be

that some of his indubitable beliefs may be proved false.

The Critical Common-sensist holds that there is less danger to heuretic science in believing too little than in believing too much. Yet for all that, the consequences to heuretics of believing too little may be no less than disaster.

*Character* VI. Critical Common-sensism may fairly lay claim to this title for two sorts of reasons; namely, that on the one hand it subjects four opinions to rigid criticism: its own; that of the Scotch School; that of those who would base logic or metaphysics on psychology or any other special science, the least tenable of all the philosophical opinions that have any vogue; and that of Kant; while on the other hand it has besides some claim to be called Critical from the fact that it is but a modification of Kantism. The present writer was a pure Kantist until he was forced by successive steps into Pragmaticism. The Kantist has only to abjure from the bottom of his heart the proposition that a thing-in-itself can, however indirectly, be conceived; and then correct the details of Kant's doctrine accordingly, and he will find himself to have become a Critical Common-sensist.

Another doctrine which is involved in Pragmaticism as an essential consequence of it, but which the writer defended (*North American Review,* Vol. CXIII, pp. 449–472, 1871) before he had formulated, even in his own mind, the principle of pragmaticism, is the scholastic doctrine of realism. This is usually defined as the opinion that there are real objects that are general, among the number being the modes of determination of existent singulars, if, indeed, these be not the only such objects. But the belief in this can hardly escape being accompanied by the acknowledgment that there are, besides, real *vagues,* and especially real possibilities. For possibility being the denial of a necessity, which is a kind of generality, is vague like any other contradiction of a general. Indeed, it is the reality of some possibilities that pragmaticism is most concerned to insist upon. The article of

January 1878 ["How to Make Our Ideas Clear"] endeavored to gloze over this point as unsuited to the exoteric public addressed; or perhaps the writer wavered in his own mind. He said that if a diamond were to be formed in a bed of cotton-wool, and were to be consumed there without ever having been pressed upon by any hard edge or point, it would be merely a question of nomenclature whether that diamond should be said to have been hard or not. No doubt this is true, except for the abominable falsehood in the word "merely," implying that symbols are unreal. Nomenclature involves classification; and classification is true or false, and the generals to which it refers are either reals in the one case, or figments in the other. For if the reader will turn to the original maxim of pragmaticism at the beginning of this article, he will see that the question is, not what *did* happen, but whether it would have been well to engage in any line of conduct whose successful issue depended upon whether that diamond *would* resist an attempt to scratch it, or whether all other logical means of determining how it ought to be classed *would* lead to the conclusion which, to quote the very words of that article, would be "the belief which alone could be the result of investigation carried *sufficiently far.*" Pragmaticism makes the ultimate intellectual purport of what you please to consist in conceived conditional resolutions, or their substance; and therefore, the conditional propositions, with their hypothetical antecedents, in which such resolutions consist, being of the ultimate nature of meaning, must be capable of being true, that is, of expressing whatever there be which is such as the proposition expresses, independently of being thought to be so in any judgment, or being represented to be so in any other symbol of any man or men. But that amounts to saying that possibility is sometimes of a real kind.

Fully to understand this, it will be needful to analyze modality, and ascertain in what it consists. In the simplest case, the most subjective meaning, if a person does not know that a proposition is false, he calls it *possible.* If, however, he knows that it is *true,* it is much more than possible. Restricting the word to its characteristic applicability, a state of things has the Modality of the possible—that is, of the merely possible—only in case the contradictory state of things is likewise possible, which proves possibility to be the vague modality. One who knows that Harvard University has an office in State Street, Boston, and has impression that it is at No. 30, but yet suspects that 50 is the number, would say, "I think it is at No. 30, but it *may be* at No. 50," or "it *is possibly* at No. 50." Thereupon, another, who does not doubt his recollection, might chime in, "It *actually is* at No. 50," or simply "it *is* at No. 50," or "it *is* at No. 50, *de inesse.*" Thereupon, the person who had first asked what the number was might say, "Since you are so positive, it *must be* at No. 50," for "I know the first figure is 5. So, since you are both certain the second is a o, why 50 it *necessarily is.*" That is to say, in this most subjective kind of Modality, that which is known by direct recollection is in the Mode of *Actuality,* the determinate mode. But when knowledge is indeterminate among alternatives, either there is one state of things which alone accords with them all, when this is in the Mode of *Necessity,* or there is more than one state of things that no knowledge excludes, when each of these is in the Mode of *Possibility.*

Other kinds of subjective Modality refer to a Sign or Representamen which is assumed to be true, but which does not include the Utterer's (i.e., the speaker's, writer's, thinker's, or other symbolizer's) total knowledge, the different Modes being distinguished very much as above. There are other cases, however, in which, justifiably or not, we certainly think of Modality as objective. A man says, "I *can* go to the seashore if I like." Here is implied, to be sure, his ignorance of how he will decide to act. But this is not the point of the assertion. It is that the complete determination of conduct in the *act* not yet having taken place, the further determination of it belongs to the subject of the action regardless of external circumstances. If he had said, "I *must* go where my employers may send me," it would imply that the function of such further determination lay elsewhere. In

"You *may* do so and so," and "You *must* do so," the "may" has the same force as "can," except that in the one case freedom from particular circumstances is in question, and in the other freedom from a law or edict. Hence the phrase, "You *may* if you *can*." I must say that it is difficult for me to preserve my respect for the competence of a philosopher whose dull logic, not penetrating beneath the surface, leaves him to regard such phrases as misrepresentations of the truth. So an act of hypostatic abstraction which in itself is no violation of logic, however it may lend itself to a dress of superstition, may regard the collective tendencies to variableness in the world, under the name of Chance, as at one time having their way, and at another time overcome by the element of order; so that, for example, a superstitious cashier, impressed by a bad dream, may say to himself of a Monday morning, "*May be,* the bank has been robbed." No doubt, he recognizes his total ignorance in the matter. But besides that, he has in mind the absence of any particular cause which should protect his bank more than others that are robbed from time to time. He thinks of the variety in the universe as vaguely analogous to the indecision of a person, and borrows from that analogy the garb of his thought. At the other extreme stand those who declare as inspired (for they have no rational proof of what they allege) that an actuary's advice to an insurance company is based on nothing at all but ignorance.

There is another example of objective possibility: "A pair of intersecting rays, i.e., unlimited straight lines conceived as movable objects, *can* (or *may*) move, without ceasing to intersect, so that one and the same hyperboloid shall be completely covered by the track of each of them." How shall we interpret this, remembering that the object spoken of, the pair of rays, is a pure creation of the Utterer's imagination, although it is required (and, indeed, forced) to conform to the laws of space? Some minds will be better satisfied with a more subjective, or nominalistic, others with a more objective, realistic interpretation. But it must be confessed on all hands that whatever degree or kind of reality belongs to

pure space belongs to the substance of that proposition, which merely expresses a property of space.

Let us now take up the case of that diamond which, having been crystallized upon a cushion of jeweler's cotton, was accidentally consumed by fire before the crystal of corundum that had been sent for had had time to arrive, and indeed without being subjected to any other pressure than that of the atmosphere and its own weight. The question is, was that diamond *really* hard? It is certain that no discernible *actual* fact determined it to be so. But is its hardness not, nevertheless, a *real* fact? To say, as the article of January 1878 seems to intend, that it is just as an arbitrary "usage of speech" chooses to arrange its thoughts, is as much as to decide against the reality of the property, since the real is that which is such as it is regardless of how it is, at any time, thought to be. Remember that this diamond's condition is not an isolated fact. There is no such thing; and an isolated fact could hardly be real. It is an unsevered, though presciss part of the unitary fact of nature. Being a diamond, it was a mass of pure carbon, in the form of a more or less transparent crystal (brittle, and of facile octahedral cleavage, unless it was of an unheard-of variety), which, if not trimmed after one of the fashions in which diamonds may be trimmed, took the shape of an octahedron, apparently regular (I need not go into minutiæ), with grooved edges, and probably with some curved faces. Without being subjected to any considerable pressure, it could be found to be insoluble, very highly refractive, showing under radium rays (and perhaps under "dark light" and X-rays) a peculiar bluish phosphorescence, having as high a specific gravity as realgar or orpiment, and giving off during its combustion less heat than any other form of carbon would have done. From some of these properties hardness is believed to be inseparable. For like it they bespeak the high polemerization of the molecule. But however this may be, how can the hardness of all other diamonds fail to bespeak *some* real relation among the diamonds without which a piece of carbon would not be a diamond? Is it not a monstrous perversion of the word and concept *real* to say that the accident of the non-arrival of the corundum prevented the hardness of the diamond from having the *reality* which it otherwise, with little doubt, would have had?

At the same time, we must dismiss the idea that the occult state of things (be it a relation among atoms or something else), which constitutes the reality of a diamond's hardness, can possibly consist in anything but in the truth of a general conditional proposition. For to what else does the entire teaching of chemistry relate except to the "behavior" of different possible kinds of material substance? And in what does that behavior consist except that if a substance of a certain kind should be exposed to an agency of a certain kind, a certain kind of sensible result *would* ensue, according to our experiences hitherto. As for the pragmaticist, it is precisely his position that nothing else than this can be so much as *meant* by saying that an object possesses a character. He is therefore obliged to subscribe to the doctrine of a real Modality, including real Necessity and real Possibility.

A good question, for the purpose of illustrating the nature of Pragmaticism, is, What is Time? It is not proposed to attack those most difficult problems connected with the psychology, the epistemology, or the metaphysics of Time, although it will be taken for granted, as it must be according to what has been said, that Time is real. The reader is only invited to the humbler question of what we mean by Time, and not of every kind of meaning attached to Past, Present, and Future either. Certain peculiar feelings are associated with the three general determinations of Time; but those are to be sedulously put out of view. That the reference of events to Time is irresistible will be recognized; but as to how it may differ from other kinds of irresistibility is a question not here to be considered. The question to be considered is simply, What is the intellectual purport of the Past, Present, and Future? It can only be treated with the utmost brevity.

That Time is a particular variety of objective Modality is too obvious for argumentation. The Past consists of the sum of *faits*

*accomplis,* and this Accomplishment is the Existential Mode of Time. For the Past really acts upon us, and *that* it does, not at all in the way in which a Law or Principle influences us, but precisely as an Existent object acts. For instance, when a *Nova Stella* bursts out in the heavens, it acts upon one's eyes just as a light struck in the dark by one's own hands would; and yet it is an event which happened before the Pyramids were built. A neophyte may remark that its reaching the eyes, which is all we know, happens but a fraction of a second before we know it. But a moment's consideration will show him that he is losing sight of the question, which is not whether the distant Past can act upon us *immediately,* but whether it acts upon us just as any Existent does. The instance adduced (certainly a commonplace enough fact) proves conclusively that the mode of the Past is that of Actuality. Nothing of the sort is true of the Future, to compass the understanding of which it is indispensable that the reader should divest himself of his Necessitarianism—at best, but a scientific theory—and return to the Common-sense State of Nature. Do you never say to yourself, "I *can* do this or that as well tomorrow as today"? Your Necessitarianism is a theoretical pseudo-belief—a make-believe belief—that such a sentence does not express the real truth. That is only to stick to proclaiming the unreality of that Time, of which you are invited, be it reality or figment, to consider the meaning. You need not fear to compromise your darling theory by looking out at its windows. Be it true in theory or not, the unsophisticated conception is that everything in the Future is either *destined,* i.e., necessitated already, or is *undecided,* the contingent future of Aristotle. In other words, it is not Actual, since it does not act except through the idea of it, that is, as a law acts; but is either Necessary or Possible, which are of the same mode since (as remarked above) Negation being outside the category of modality cannot produce a variation in Modality. As for the Present instant, it is so inscrutable that I wonder whether no skeptic has ever attacked its reality. I can fancy one of them dipping his pen in his blackest ink to commence the assault, and then suddenly reflecting that his entire life is in the Present— the "living present," as we say, this instant when all hopes and fears concerning it come to their end, this Living Death in which we are born anew. It is plainly that Nascent State between the Determinate and the Indeterminate that was noticed above.

Pragmaticism consists in holding that the purport of any concept is its conceived bearing upon our conduct. How, then, does the Past bear upon conduct? The answer is self-evident: whenever we set out to do anything, we "go upon," we base our conduct on facts already known, and for these we can only draw upon our memory. It is true that we may institute a new investigation for the purpose; but its discoveries will only become applicable to conduct after they have been made and reduced to a memorial maxim. In short, the Past is the storehouse of all our knowledge.

When we say that we know that some state of things exists, we mean that it used to exist, whether just long enough for the news to reach the brain and be retransmitted to tongue or pen, or longer ago. Thus, from whatever point of view we contemplate the Past, it appears as the Existential Mode of Time.

How does the Future bear upon conduct? The answer is that future facts are the only facts that we can, in a measure, control; and whatever there may be in the Future that is not amenable to control are the things that we *shall* be able to infer, or *should* be able to infer, under favorable circumstances. There may be questions concerning which the pendulum of opinion never would cease to oscillate, however favorable circumstances may be. But if so, those questions are *ipso facto* not *real* questions, that is to say, are questions to which there is no true answer to be given. It is natural to use the future tense (and the conditional mood is but a mollified future) in drawing a conclusion or in stating a consequence. "If two unlimited straight lines in one plane and crossed by a third making the sum . . . then these straight lines *will* meet on the side, etc." It cannot be denied that acritical inferences may refer to the Past in its capacity as past; but

according to Pragmaticism, the conclusion of a Reasoning power must refer to the Future. For its meaning refers to conduct, and since it is a reasoned conclusion, must refer to deliberate conduct, which is controllable conduct. But the only controllable conduct is Future conduct. As for that part of the Past that lies beyond memory, the Pragmaticist doctrine is that the meaning of its being believed to be in connection with the Past consists in the acceptance as truth of the conception that we ought to conduct ourselves according to it (like the meaning of any other belief). Thus, a belief that Christopher Columbus discovered America really refers to the future. It is more difficult, it must be confessed, to account for beliefs that rest upon the double evidence of feeble but direct memory and upon rational inference. The difficulty does not seem insuperable; but it must be passed by.

What is the bearing of the Present instant upon conduct?

Introspection is wholly a matter of inference. One is immediately conscious of his Feelings, no doubt; but not that they are feelings of an *ego*. The *self* is only inferred. There is no time in the Present for any inference at all, least of all for inference concerning that very instant. Consequently, the present object must be an external object, if there be any objective reference in it. The attitude of the Present is either conative or perceptive. Supposing it to be perceptive, the perception must be immediately known as external—not indeed in the sense in which a hallucination is *not* external, but in the sense of being present regardless of the perceiver's will or wish. Now this kind of externality is conative externality. Consequently, the attitude of the present instant (according to the testimony of Common Sense, which is plainly adopted throughout) can only be a Conative attitude. The consciousness of the present is then that of a struggle over what shall be; and thus we emerge from the study with a confirmed belief that it is the Nascent State of the Actual.

But how is Temporal Modality distinguished from other Objective Modality? Not by any general character since Time is unique and *sui generis.* In other words, there is only one Time. Sufficient attention has hardly been called to the surpassing truth of this for Time as compared with its truth for Space. Time, therefore, can only be identified by brute compulsion. But we must not go further.

## Notes

1. *Popular Science Monthly,* Vol. 12 (Jan. 1878), p. 293. "How to Make Our Ideas Clear" An introductory article opens the volume, in the number for November 1877. "The Fixation of Belief,"
2. "Prolegomena to an Apology for Pragmaticism," *The Monist* Vol. 16 (Oct. 1906), pp. 492–546.
3. But see the experiments of J. Jastrow and me "On Slight Differences of Sensation" in the *Memoirs of the National Academy of Sciences,* Vol. III (1884), pp. 1–11.
4. I wish I might hope, after finishing some more difficult work, to be able to resume this study and to go to the bottom of the subject, which needs the qualities of age and does not call upon the powers of youth. A great range of reading is necessary; for it is the belief men *betray* and not that which they *parade* which has to be studied.
5. Hamilton and a few other logicians understood the subject of a universal proposition in the collective sense; but every person who is well-read in logic is familiar with many passages in which the leading logicians explain with an iteration that would be superfluous if all readers were intelligent, that such a subject is distributively, not collectively, general. A term denoting a collection is singular, and such a term is an "abstraction" or product of the operation of hypostatic abstraction as truly as is the name of the essence. "Mankind" is quite as much an abstraction and *ens rationis* as is "humanity." Indeed, every object of a conception is either a signate individual or some kind of indeterminate individual. Nouns in the plural are usually distributive and general; common nouns in the singular are usually indefinite.
6. But unfortunately it has not been in the writer's power to consult the *Oxford Dictionary* concerning these words; so that probably some of the statements in the text might be corrected with the aid of that work.
7. Thus returning to the writer's original nomenclature, in despite of *The Monist* VII, where an obviously defective argument was regarded as sufficient to determine a mere matter of terminology. But the Quality of propositions is there regarded from a point of view which seems extrinsic. I have not had time, however, to re-explore all the ramifications of this difficult question by the aid of existential graphs, and the statement in the text about the last quantifier may need modification.

---

# A Neglected Argument for the Reality of God

The word "God," so "capitalized" (as we Americans say), is *the* definable proper name, signifying *Ens necessarium* [necessary being]; in my belief Really creator of all three Universes of Experience.

Some words shall herein be capitalized when used, not as vernacular, but as terms defined. Thus an "idea" is the substance of an actual unitary thought or fancy; but "Idea," nearer Plato's idea of *idéa,* denotes anything whose Being consists in its mere capacity for getting fully represented, regardless of any person's faculty or impotence to represent it.

"Real" is a word invented in the thirteenth century to signify having Properties, i.e., characters sufficing to identify their subject, and possessing these whether they be anywise attributed to it by any single man or group of men, or not. Thus, the substance of a dream is not Real, since it was such as it was, merely in that a dreamer so dreamed it; but the fact of the dream is Real, if it was dreamed; since if so, its date, the name of the dreamer, etc., make up

---

From Hibbert Jovraar, vol. 7, 1908, pp. 90–112.

a set of circumstances sufficient to distinguish it from all other events; and these belong to it, i.e., would be true if predicated of it, whether *A*, *B*, or *C* Actually ascertains them or not. The "Actual" is that which is met with in the past, present, or future.

An "Experience" is a brutally produced conscious effect that contributes to a habit, self-controlled, yet so satisfying, on deliberation, as to be destructible by no positive exercise of internal vigor. I use the word "self-controlled" for "controlled by the thinker's self," and not for "uncontrolled" except in its own spontaneous, i.e., automatic, self-development, as Professor J. M. Baldwin[1] uses the word. Take for illustration the sensation undergone by a child that puts its forefinger into a flame with the acquisition of a habit of keeping all its members out of all flames. A compulsion is "Brute," whose immediate efficacy nowise consists in conformity to rule or reason.

Of the three Universes of Experience familiar to us all, the first comprises all mere Ideas, those airy nothings to which the mind of poet, pure mathematician, or another *might* give local habitation and a name within that mind. Their very airy-nothingness, the fact that their Being consists in mere capability of getting thought, not in anybody's Actually thinking them, saves their Reality. The second Universe is that of the Brute Actuality of things and facts. I am confident that their Being consists in reactions against Brute forces, notwithstanding objections redoubtable until they are closely and fairly examined. The third Universe comprises everything whose being consists in active power to establish connections between different objects, especially between objects in different Universes. Such is everything which is essentially a Sign—not the mere body of the Sign, which is not essentially such, but, so to speak, the Sign's Soul, which has its Being in its power of serving as intermediary between its Object and a Mind. Such, too, is a living consciousness, and such the life, the power of growth, of a plant. Such is a living constitution—a daily newspaper, a great fortune, a social "movement."

An "Argument" is any process of thought reasonably tending to produce a definite belief. An "Argumentation" is an Argument proceeding upon definitely formulated premisses.

If God Really be, and be benign, then, in view of the generally conceded truth that religion, were it but proved, would be a good outweighing all others, we should naturally expect that there would be some Argument for His Reality that should be obvious to all minds, high and low alike, that should earnestly strive to find the truth of the matter; and further, that this Argument should present its conclusion, not as a proposition of metaphysical theology, but in a form directly applicable to the conduct of life, and full of nutrition for man's highest growth. What I shall refer to as the N. A.—the Neglected Argument—seems to me best to fulfill this condition, and I should not wonder if the majority of those whose own reflections have harvested belief in God must bless the radiance of the N. A. for that wealth. Its persuasiveness is no less than extraordinary; while it is not unknown to anybody. Nevertheless, of all those theologians (within my little range of reading) who, with commendable assiduity, scrape together all the sound reasons they can find or concoct to prove the first proposition of theology, few mention this one, and they most briefly. They probably share those current notions of logic which recognize no other Arguments than Argumentations.

There is a certain agreeable occupation of mind which, from its having no distinctive name, I infer is not as commonly practiced as it deserves to be; for indulged in moderately— say through some five to six per cent of one's waking time, perhaps during a stroll—it is refreshing enough more than to repay the expenditure. Because it involves no purpose save that of casting aside all serious purpose, I have sometimes been half-inclined to call it reverie with some qualification; but for a frame of mind so antipodal to vacancy and dreaminess such a designation would be too excruciating a misfit. In fact, it is Pure Play. Now, Play, we all know, is a lively exercise of one's powers. Pure Play has no rules, except this very law of liberty. It bloweth where it listeth. It has no purpose, unless recreation. The particular occupation I mean—a *petite bouchée* [small mouthful] with the Universes—may take either the form of æsthetic contemplation, or that of distant castle-building (whether in Spain or within one's own moral training), or that of considering some wonder in one of the Universes, or some connection between two of the three, with speculation concerning its cause. It is this last kind—I will call it "Musement" on the whole—that I particularly recommend, because it will in time flower into the N. A. One who sits down with the purpose of becoming convinced of the truth of religion is plainly not inquiring in scientific singleness of heart, and must always suspect himself of reasoning unfairly. So he can never attain the entirety even of a physicist's belief in electrons, although this is avowedly but provisional. But let religious meditation be allowed to grow up spontaneously out of Pure Play without any breach of continuity, and the Muser will retain the perfect candor proper to Musement.

If one who had determined to make trial of Musement as a favorite recreation were to ask me for advice, I should reply as follows: The dawn and the gloaming most invite one to Musement; but I have found no watch of the nychthemeron that has not its own advantages for the pursuit. It begins passively enough with drinking in the impression of some nook in one of the three Universes. But impression soon passes into attentive observation, observation into musing, musing into a lively give and take of communion between self and self. If one's observations and reflections are allowed to specialize themselves too much, the Play will be converted into scientific study; and that cannot be pursued in odd half hours.

I should add: Adhere to the one ordinance of Play, the law of liberty. I can testify that the last half century, at least, has never lacked tribes of Sir Oracles, colporting brocards to bar off one or another roadway of inquiry; and a Rabelais would be needed to bring out all the fun that has been packed in their airs of infallibility. Auguste Comte, notwithstanding his having apparently produced some unquestionably genuine thinking, was long the chief of such a band. The vogue of each particular maxim of theirs was necessarily brief. For what distinction can be gained by repeating saws heard from all mouths? No bygone fashion seems more grotesque than a *panache* of obsolete wisdom. I remember the days when a pronouncement all the rage was that no science must borrow the methods of another; the geologist must not use a microscope, nor the astronomer a spectroscope. Optics must not meddle with electricity, nor logic with algebra. But twenty years later, if you aspired to pass for a commanding intellect, you would have to pull a long face and declare that "it is not the business of science to search for origins." This maxim was a masterpiece, since no timid soul, in dread of being thought naïve, would dare inquire what "origins" were, albeit the secret confessor within his breast compelled the awful self-acknowledgment of his having no idea into what else than "origins" of phenomena (in some sense of that indefinite word) man can inquire. That human reason can comprehend some causes is past denial, and once we are forced to recognize a given element in experience, it is reasonable to await positive evidence before we complicate our acknowledgment with qualifications. Otherwise, why venture beyond direct observation? Illustrations of this principle abound in physical science. Since, then, it is certain that man is able to understand the laws and the causes of some phenomena, it is reasonable to assume, in regard to any given problem, that it would get rightly solved by man, if a sufficiency of time and attention were devoted to it. Moreover, those problems that at first blush appear utterly insoluble receive, in that very circumstance, as Edgar Poe remarked[2] in his "The Murders in the Rue Morgue," their smoothly-fitting keys. This particularly adapts them to the Play of Musement.

Forty or fifty minutes of vigorous and unslackened analytic thought bestowed upon one of them usually suffices to educe from it all there is to educe, its general solution. There is no kind of reasoning that I should wish to discourage in Musement; and I should lament to find anybody confining it to a method of such moderate fertility as logical analysis. Only, the Player should bear in mind that the higher weapons in the arsenal of thought are not playthings but edge-tools. In any mere Play they can be used by way of exercise alone; while logical analysis can be put to its full efficiency in Musement. So, continuing the counsels that had been asked of me, I should say, "Enter your skiff of Musement, push off into the lake of thought, and leave the breath of heaven to swell your sail. With your eyes open, awake to what is about or within you, and open conversation with yourself; for such is all meditation." It is, however, not a conversation in words alone, but is illustrated, like a lecture, with diagrams and with experiments.

Different people have such wonderfully different ways of thinking that it would be far beyond my competence to say what courses Musements might not take; but a brain endowed with automatic control, as man's indirectly is, is so naturally and rightly interested in its own faculties that some psychological and semi-psychological questions would doubtless get touched; such, in the latter class, as this: Darwinians, with truly surprising ingenuity, have concocted, and with still more astonishing confidence have accepted as proved, one explanation for the diverse and delicate beauties of flowers, another for those of butterflies, and so on; but why is all nature—the forms of trees, the compositions of sunsets—suffused with such beauties throughout, and not nature only, but the other two Universes as well? Among more purely psychological questions, the nature of pleasure and pain will be likely to attract attention. Are they mere qualities of feeling, or are they rather motor instincts attracting us to some feelings and repelling others? Have pleasure and pain the same sort of constitution, or are they contrasted in this respect, pleasure arising upon the forming or strengthening of an association by resemblance, and

pain upon the weakening or disruption of such a habit or conception?

Psychological speculations will naturally lead on to musings upon metaphysical problems proper, good exercise for a mind with a turn for exact thought. It is here that one finds those questions that at first seem to offer no handle for reason's clutch, but which readily yield to logical analysis. But problems of metaphysics will inevitably present themselves that logical analysis will not suffice to solve. Some of the best will be motived by a desire to comprehend universe-wide aggregates of unformulated but partly experienced phenomena. I would suggest that the Muser be not too impatient to analyze these, lest some significant ingredient be lost in the process; but that he begin by pondering them from every point of view, until he seems to read some truth beneath the phenomena.

At this point a trained mind will demand that an examination be made of the truth of the interpretation; and the first step in such examination must be a logical analysis of the theory. But strict examination would be a task a little too serious for the Musement of hour fractions, and if it is postponed there will be ample remuneration even in the suggestions that there is not time to examine; especially since a few of them will appeal to reason as all but certain.

Let the Muser, for example, after well appreciating, in its breadth and depth, the unspeakable variety of each Universe, turn to those phenomena that are of the nature of homogeneities of connectedness in each; and what a spectacle will unroll itself! As a mere hint of them I may point out that every small part of space, however remote, is bounded by just such neighboring parts as every other, without a single exception throughout immensity. The matter of Nature is in every star of the same elementary kinds, and (except for variations of circumstance), what is more wonderful still, throughout the whole visible universe, about the same proportions of the different chemical elements prevail. Though the mere catalogue of known carbon-compounds alone would fill an unwieldy volume, and perhaps, if the truth were known, the number of amino-acids alone is greater, yet it is unlikely that there are in all more than about 600 elements, of which 500 dart through space too swiftly to be held down by the earth's gravitation, coronium being the slowest moving of these. This small number bespeaks comparative simplicity of structure. Yet no mathematician but will confess the present hopelessness of attempting to comprehend the constitution of the hydrogen-atom, the simplest of the elements that can be held to earth.

From speculations on the homogeneities of each Universe, the Muser will naturally pass to the consideration of homogeneities and connections between two different Universes, or all three. Especially in them all we find one type of occurrence, that of growth, itself consisting in the homogeneities of small parts. This is evident in the growth of motion into displacement, and the growth of force into motion. In growth, too, we find that the three Universes conspire; and a universal feature of it is provision for later stages in earlier ones. This is a specimen of certain lines of reflection which will inevitably suggest the hypothesis of God's Reality. It is not that such phenomena might not be capable of being accounted for, in one sense, by the action of chance with the smallest conceivable dose of a higher element; for if by God be meant the *Ens necessarium,* that very hypothesis requires that such should be the case. But the point is that that sort of explanation leaves a mental explanation just as needful as before. Tell me, upon sufficient authority, that all cerebration depends upon movements of neurites that strictly obey certain physical laws, and that thus all expressions of thought, both external and internal, receive a physical explanation, and I shall be ready to believe you. But if you go on to say that this explodes the theory that my neighbor and myself are governed by reason, and are thinking beings, I must frankly say that it will not give me a high opinion of your intelligence. But however that may be, in the Pure Play of Musement the idea of God's Reality will be sure sooner or later to be found an attractive fancy, which the Muser will develop

in various ways. The more he ponders it, the more it will find response in every part of his mind, for its beauty, for its supplying an ideal of life, and for its thoroughly satisfactory explanation of his whole threefold environment.

The hypothesis of God is a peculiar one, in that it supposes an infinitely incomprehensible object, although every hypothesis, as such, supposes its object to be truly conceived in the hypothesis. This leaves the hypothesis but one way of understanding itself; namely, as vague yet as true so far as it is definite, and as continually tending to define itself more and more, and without limit. The hypothesis, being thus itself inevitably subject to the law of growth, appears in its vagueness to represent God as so, albeit this is directly contradicted in the hypothesis from its very first phase. But this apparent attribution of growth to God, since it is ineradicable from the hypothesis, cannot, according to the hypothesis, be flatly false. Its implications concerning the Universes will be maintained in the hypothesis, while its implications concerning God will be partly disavowed, and yet held to be less false than their denial would be. Thus the hypothesis will lead to our thinking of features of each Universe as purposed; and this will stand or fall with the hypothesis. Yet a purpose essentially involves growth, and so cannot be attributed to God. Still it will, according to the hypothesis, be less false to speak so than to represent God as purposeless.

Assured as I am from my own personal experience that every man capable of so controlling his attention as to perform a little exact thinking will, if he examines Zeno's argument about Achilles and the tortoise, come to think, as I do, that it is nothing but a contemptible catch, I do not think that I either am or ought to be less assured, from what I know of the effects of Musement on myself and others, that any normal man who considers the three Universes in the light of the hypothesis of God's Reality, and pursues that line of reflection in scientific singleness of heart, will come to be stirred to the depths of his nature by the beauty of the idea and by its august practicality, even to the point of earnestly loving and adoring his strictly hypothetical God, and to that of desiring above all things to shape the whole conduct of life and all the springs of action into conformity with that hypothesis. Now to be deliberately and thoroughly prepared to shape one's conduct into conformity with a proposition is neither more nor less than the state of mind called Believing that proposition, however long the conscious classification of it under that head be postponed.

There is my poor sketch of the Neglected Argument, greatly cut down to bring it within the limits assigned to this article. Next should come the discussion of its logicality; but nothing readable at a sitting could possibly bring home to readers my full proof of the principal points of such an examination. I can only hope to make the residue of this paper a sort of table of contents, from which some may possibly guess what I have to say; or to lay down a series of plausible points through which the reader will have to construct the continuous line of reasoning for himself. In my own mind the proof is elaborated, and I am exerting my energies to getting it submitted to public censure. My present abstract will divide itself into three unequal parts. The first shall give the headings of the different steps of every well-conducted and complete inquiry, without noticing possible divergencies from the norm. I shall have to mention some steps which have nothing to do with the Neglected Argument in order to show that they add no jot nor tittle to the truth which is invariably brought just as the Neglected Argument brings it. The second part shall very briefly state, without argument (for which there is no room), just wherein lies the logical validity of the reasoning characteristic of each of the main stages of inquiry. The third part shall indicate the place of the Neglected Argument in a complete inquiry into the Reality of God, and shall show how well it would fill that place, and what its logical value is supposing the inquiry to be limited to this; and I shall add a few words to show how it might be supplemented.

Every inquiry whatsoever takes its rise in the observation, in one or another of the three Universes, of some surprising phenomenon, some experience which either disappoints an expectation, or breaks in upon some habit of expectation of the *inquisiturus* [person about to inquire or seek evidence]; and each apparent exception to this rule only confirms it. There are obvious distinctions between the objects of surprise in different cases; but throughout this slight sketch of inquiry such details will be unnoticed, especially since it is upon such that the logic-books descant. The inquiry begins with pondering these phenomena in all their aspects, in the search of some point of view whence the wonder shall be resolved. At length a conjecture arises that furnishes a possible Explanation, by which I mean a syllogism exhibiting the surprising fact as necessarily consequent upon the circumstances of its occurrence together with the truth of the credible conjecture, as premises. On account of this Explanation, the inquirer is led to regard his conjecture, or hypothesis, with favor. As I phrase it, he provisionally holds it to be "Plausible"; this acceptance ranges in different cases—and reasonably so—from a mere expression of it in the interrogative mood, as a question meriting attention and reply, up through all appraisals of Plausibility, to uncontrollable inclination to believe. The whole series of mental performances between the notice of the wonderful phenomenon and the acceptance of the hypothesis, during which the usually docile understanding seems to hold the bit between its teeth and to have us at its mercy, the search for pertinent circumstances and the laying hold of them, sometimes without our cognizance, the scrutiny of them, the dark laboring, the bursting out of the startling conjecture, the remarking of its smooth fitting to the anomaly, as it is turned back and forth like a key in a lock, and the final estimation of its Plausibility, I reckon as composing the First Stage of Inquiry. Its characteristic formula of reasoning I term Retroduction,[3] i.e., reasoning from consequent to antecedent. In one respect the designation seems inappropriate; for in most instances where conjecture mounts the high peaks of Plausibility—and is *really* most worthy of confidence—the inquirer is unable definitely to formulate just what the explained wonder is; or can only do so in the light of the hypothesis. In short, it is a form of Argument rather than of Argumentation.

Retroduction does not afford security. The hypothesis must be tested.

This testing, to be logically valid, must honestly start, not as Retroduction starts, with scrutiny of the phenomena, but with examination of the hypothesis, and a muster of all sorts of conditional experiential consequences which would follow from its truth. This constitutes the Second Stage of Inquiry. For its characteristic form of reasoning our language has, for two centuries, been happily provided with the name Deduction.

Deduction has two parts. For its first step must be by logical analysis to Explicate the hypothesis, i.e., to render it as perfectly distinct as possible. This process, like Retroduction, is Argument that is not Argumentation. But unlike Retroduction, it cannot go wrong from lack of experience, but so long as it proceeds rightly must reach a true conclusion. Explication is followed by Demonstration, or Deductive Argumentation. Its procedure is best learned from Book I of Euclid's *Elements,* a masterpiece which in real insight is far superior to Aristotle's *Analytics; and* its numerous fallacies render it all the more instructive to a close student. It invariably requires something of the nature of a diagram; that is, an "Icon," or Sign that represents its Object in resembling it. It usually, too, needs "Indices," or Signs that represent their Objects by being actually connected with them. But it is mainly composed of "Symbols," or Signs that represent their Objects essentially because they will be so interpreted. Demonstration should be *Corollarial* when it can. An accurate definition of Corollarial Demonstration would require a long explanation; but it will suffice to say that it limits itself to considerations already introduced or else involved in

the Explication of its conclusion; while *Theorematic* Demonstration resorts to a more complicated process of thought.

The purpose of Deduction, that of collecting consequents of the hypothesis, having been sufficiently carried out, the inquiry enters upon its Third Stage, that of ascertaining how far those consequents accord with Experience, and of judging accordingly whether the hypothesis is sensibly correct, or requires some inessential modification, or must be entirely rejected. Its characteristic way of reasoning is Induction. This stage has three parts. For it must begin with Classification, which is an Inductive Non-argumentational kind of Argument, by which general Ideas are attached to objects of Experience; or rather by which the latter are subordinated to the former. Following this will come the testing-argumentations, the Probations; and the whole inquiry will be wound up with the Sentential part of the Third Stage, which, by Inductive reasonings, appraises the different Probations singly, then their combinations, then makes self-appraisal of these very appraisals themselves, and passes final judgment on the whole result.

The Probations, or direct Inductive Argumentations, are of two kinds. The first is that which Bacon ill described as "*inductio illa quæ procedit per enumerationem simplicem*" [that induction which proceeds by simple enumeration]. So at least he has been understood. For an enumeration of instances is not essential to the argument that, for example, there are no such beings as fairies, or no such events as miracles. The point is that there is no well-established instance of such a thing. I call this Crude Induction. It is the only Induction which concludes a logically Universal Proposition. It is the weakest of arguments, being liable to be demolished in a moment, as happened toward the end of the eighteenth century to the opinion of the scientific world that no stones fall from the sky. The other kind is Gradual Induction, which makes a new estimate of the proportion of truth in the hypothesis with every new instance; and given any degree of error there will *sometime* be an estimate (or would be, if the probation were persisted in) which will be absolutely the last to be infected with so much falsity. Gradual Induction is either Qualitative or Quantitative and the latter either depends on measurements, or on statistics, or on countings.

Concerning the question of the nature of the logical validity possessed by Deduction, Induction, and Retroduction, which is still an arena of controversy, I shall confine myself to stating the opinions which I am prepared to defend by positive proofs. The validity of Deduction was correctly, if not very clearly, analyzed by Kant.[4] This kind of reasoning deals exclusively with Pure Ideas attaching primarily to Symbols and derivatively to other Signs of our own creation; and the fact that man has a power of Explicating his own meaning renders Deduction valid. Induction is a kind of reasoning that may lead us into error; but that it follows a method which, sufficiently persisted in, will be Inductively Certain (the sort of certainty we have that a perfect coin, pitched up often enough, will *sometime* turn up heads) to diminish the error below any predesignate degree, is assured by man's power of perceiving Inductive Certainty. In all this I am inviting the reader to peep through the big end of the telescope; there is a wealth of pertinent detail that must here be passed over.

Finally comes the bottom question of logical Critic, What sort of validity can be attributed to the First Stage of inquiry? Observe that neither Deduction nor Induction contributes the smallest positive item to the final conclusion of the inquiry. They render the indefinite definite; Deduction explicates; Induction evaluates; that is all. Over the chasm that yawns between the ultimate goal of science and such ideas of Man's environment as, coming over him during his primeval wanderings in the forest, while yet his very notion of error was of the vaguest, he managed to communicate to some fellow, we are building a cantilever bridge of induction, held together by scientific struts and ties. Yet every plank of its advance is first laid by Retroduction alone, that is to say, by the spontaneous conjectures of instinc-

tive reason; and neither Deduction nor Induction contributes a single new concept to the structure. Nor is this less true or less important for those inquiries that self-interest prompts.

The first answer we naturally give to this question is that we cannot help accepting the conjecture at such a valuation as that at which we do accept it; whether as a simple interrogation, or as more or less Plausible, or, occasionally, as an irresistible belief. But far from constituting, by itself, a logical justification such as it becomes a rational being to put forth, this pleading, that we *cannot help* yielding to the suggestion, amounts to nothing more than a confession of having failed to train ourselves to control our thoughts. It is more to the purpose, however, to urge that the strength of the impulse is a symptom of its being instinctive. Animals of all races rise far above the general level of their intelligence in those performances that are their proper function, such as flying and nest-building for ordinary birds; and what is man's proper function if it be not to embody general ideas in art-creations, in utilities, and above all in theoretical cognition? To give the lie to his own consciousness of divining the reasons of phenomena would be as silly in a man as it would be in a fledgling bird to refuse to trust to its wings and leave the nest, because the poor little thing had read Babinet,[5] and judged aerostation to be impossible on hydrodynamical grounds. Yes; it must be confessed that *if we knew* that the impulse to prefer one hypothesis to another really were analogous to the instincts of birds and wasps, it would be foolish not to give it play, within the bounds of reason; especially since we must entertain some hypothesis, or else forego all further knowledge than that which we have already gained by that very means. But is it a fact that man possesses this magical faculty? Not, I reply, to the extent of guessing right the first time, nor perhaps the second; but that the well-prepared mind has wonderfully soon guessed each secret of nature is historical truth. All the theories of science have been so obtained. But may they not have come fortuitously, or by some such modification of chance as the Darwinian sup-

poses? I answer that three or four independent methods of computation show that it would be ridiculous to suppose our science to have so come to pass. Nevertheless, suppose that it can be so "explained," just as that any purposed act of mine is supposed by materialistic necessitarians to have come about. Still, what of it? Does that materialistic explanation, supposing it granted, show that reason has nothing to do with my actions? Even the parallelists will admit that the one explanation leaves the same need of the other that there was before it was given; and this is certainly sound logic. There is a reason, an interpretation, a logic, in the course of scientific advance, and this indisputably proves to him who has perceptions of rational or significant relations, that man's mind must have been attuned to the truth of things in order to discover what he has discovered. It is the very bedrock of logical truth.

Modern science has been built after the model of Galileo, who founded it, on *il lume naturale*. That truly inspired prophet had said that, of two hypotheses, the *simpler* is to be preferred,[6] but I was formerly one of those who, in our dull self-conceit fancying ourselves more sly than he, twisted the maxim to mean the *logically* simpler, the one that adds the least to what has been observed, in spite of three obvious objections: first, that so there was no support for any hypothesis; secondly, that by the same token we ought to content ourselves with simply formulating the special observations actually made; and thirdly, that every advance of science that further opens the truth to our view discloses a world of unexpected complications. It was not until long experience forced me to realize that subsequent discoveries were every time showing I had been wrong, while those who understood the maxim as Galileo had done, early unlocked the secret, that the scales fell from my eyes and my mind awoke to the broad and flaming daylight that it is the simpler Hypothesis in the sense of the more facile and natural, the one that instinct suggests, that must be preferred; for the reason that, unless man have a natural bent in accordance with nature's, he has no chance of understanding nature at all.

Many tests of this principal and positive fact, relating as well to my own studies as to the researches of others, have confirmed me in this opinion; and when I shall come to set them forth in a book, their array will convince everybody. Oh, no! I am forgetting that armor, impenetrable by accurate thought, in which the rank and file of minds are clad! They may, for example, get the notion that my proposition involves a denial of the rigidity of the laws of association: it would be quite on a par with much that is current. I do not mean that logical simplicity is a consideration of no value at all, but only that its value is badly secondary to that of simplicity in the other sense.

If, however, the maxim is correct in Galileo's sense, whence it follows that man has, in some degree, a divinatory power, primary or derived, like that of a wasp or a bird, then instances swarm to show that a certain altogether peculiar confidence in a hypothesis, not to be confounded with rash cocksureness, has a very appreciable value as a sign of the truth of the hypothesis. I regret I cannot give an account of certain interesting and almost convincing cases. The N. A. excites this peculiar confidence in the very highest degree.

We have now to apply these principles to the evaluation of the N. A. Had I space I would put this into the shape of imagining how it is likely to be esteemed by three types of men: the first of small instruction with corresponding natural breadth, intimately acquainted with the N. A., but to whom logic is all Greek; the second, inflated with current notions of logic, but prodigiously informed about the N. A.; the third, a trained man of science who, in the modern spirit, has added to his specialty an exact theoretical and practical study of reasoning and the elements of thought, so that psychologists account him a sort of psychologist, and mathematicians a sort of mathematician.

I should, then, show how the first would have learned that nothing has any kind of value in itself—whether æsthetic, moral, or scientific—but only in its place in the whole production to which it appertains; and that an individual soul with its petty agitations and calamities is a zero except as filling its infinitesimal place, and accepting his little futility as his entire treasure. He will see that though his God would not *really* (in a certain sense) adapt means to ends, it is nevertheless quite true that there are relations among phenomena which finite intelligence must interpret, and truly interpret, as such adaptations; and he will macarize himself for his own bitterest griefs, and bless God for the law of growth with all the fighting it imposes upon him—Evil, i.e., what it is man's duty to fight, being one of the major perfections of the Universe. In that fight he will endeavor to perform just the duty laid upon him and no more. Though his desperate struggles should issue in the horrors of his rout, and he should see the innocents who are dearest to his heart exposed to torments, frenzy, and despair, destined to be smirched with filth, and stunted in their intelligence, still he may hope that it be best *for them,* will tell himself that in any case the secret design of God will be perfected through their agency, and even while still hot from the battle, will submit with adoration to His Holy will. He will not worry because the Universes were not constructed to suit the scheme of some silly scold.

The context of this I must leave the reader to imagine. I will only add that the third man, considering the complex process of self-control, will see that the hypothesis, irresistible though it be to first intention, yet needs Probation; and that though an infinite being is not tied down to any consistency, yet man, like any other animal, is gifted with power of understanding sufficient for the conduct of life. This brings him, for testing the hypothesis, to taking his stand upon Pragmaticism, which implies faith in common sense and in instinct, though only as they issue from the cupel-furnace of measured criticism. In short, he will say that the N. A. is the First Stage of a scientific inquiry, resulting in a hypothesis of the very highest Plausibility, whose ultimate test must lie in its value in the self-controlled growth of man's conduct of life.

Since I have employed the word *Pragmaticism,* and shall have occasion to use it once more, it may perhaps be well to explain it. About forty years ago, my studies of Berkeley, Kant, and others led me, after convincing myself that all thinking is performed in Signs, and that meditation takes the form of a dialogue, so that it is proper to speak of the "meaning" of a concept, to conclude that to acquire full mastery of that meaning it is requisite, in the first place, to learn to recognize the concept under every disguise, through extensive familiarity with instances of it. But this, after all, does not imply any true understanding of it; so that it is further requisite that we should make an abstract logical analysis of it into its ultimate elements, or as complete an analysis as we can compass. But, even so, we may still be without any living comprehension of it; and the only way to complete our knowledge of its nature is to discover and recognize just what general habits of conduct a belief in the truth of the concept (of any conceivable subject, and under any conceivable circumstances) would reasonably develop; that is to say, what habits would ultimately result from a sufficient consideration of such truth. It is necessary to understand the word "conduct," here, in the broadest sense. If, for example, the predication of a given concept were to lead to our admitting that a given form of reasoning concerning the subject of which it was affirmed was valid, when it would not otherwise be valid, the recognition of that effect in our reasoning would decidedly be a habit of conduct.

In 1871, in a Metaphysical Club in Cambridge, Massachusetts, I used to preach this principle as a sort of logical gospel, representing the unformulated method followed by Berkeley, and in conversation about it I called it "Pragmatism." In December [November] 1877 and January 1878 I set forth the doctrine in the *Popular Science Monthly;* and the two parts of my essay were printed in French in the *Revue Philosophique,* Volumes vi and vii. Of course, the doctrine attracted no particular attention, for, as I had remarked in my opening sentence, very few people care for logic. But in 1897 Professor James remodelled the matter, and transmogrified it into a doctrine of philosophy,[7] some parts of which I highly approved, while other and more prominent parts I regarded, and still regard, as opposed to sound logic. About the time Professor Papini[8] discovered, to the delight of the Pragmatist school, that this doctrine was incapable of definition, which would certainly seem to distinguish it from every other doctrine in whatever branch of science, I was coming to the conclusion that my poor little maxim should be called by another name; and accordingly, in April 1905 I renamed it *Pragmaticism.* I had never before dignified it by any name in print, except that, at Professor Baldwin's request, I wrote a definition of it for his *Dictionary of Psychology and Philosophy.* I did not insert the word in the *Century Dictionary,* though I had charge of the philosophical definitions of that work, for I have a perhaps exaggerated dislike of *réclame.*

It is that course of meditation upon the three Universes which gives birth to the hypothesis and ultimately to the belief that they, or at any rate two of the three, have a Creator independent of them, that I have throughout this article called the N. A., because I think the theologians ought to have recognized it as a line of thought reasonably productive of belief. This is the "humble" argument, the innermost of the nest. In the mind of a metaphysician it will have a metaphysical tinge; but that seems to me rather to detract from its force than to add anything to it. It is just as good an argument, if not better, in the form it takes in the mind of the clodhopper.

The theologians could not have *presented* the N. A., because that is a living course of thought of very various forms. But they might and ought to have *described* it, and should have defended it, too, as far as they could, without going into original logical researches, which could not be justly expected of them. They are accustomed to make use of the principle that that which convinces a normal man must be presumed to be sound reasoning; and therefore they ought to say whatever can truly be advanced to show that the N. A., if sufficiently developed, will convince any normal man.

Unfortunately, it happens that there is very little established fact to show that this is the case. I have not pretended to have any other ground for my belief that it is so than my assumption, which each one of us makes, that my own intellectual disposition is normal. I am forced to confess that no pessimist will agree with me. I do not admit that pessimists are, at the same time, thoroughly sane, and in addition are endowed in normal measure with intellectual vigor; and my reasons for thinking so are two. The first is, that the difference between a pessimistic and an optimistic mind is of such controlling importance in regard to every intellectual function, and especially for the conduct of life, that it is out of the question to admit that both are normal, and the great majority of mankind are naturally optimistic. Now, the majority of every race depart but little from the norm of that race. In order to present my other reason, I am obliged to recognize three types of pessimists. The first type is often found in exquisite and noble natures of great force of original intellect whose own lives are dreadful histories of torment due to some physical malady. Leopardi is a famous example. We cannot but believe, against their earnest protests, that if such men had had ordinary health, life would have worn for them the same color as for the rest of us. Meantime, one meets too few pessimists of this type to affect the present question. The second is the misanthropical type, the type that makes itself heard. It suffices to call to mind the conduct of the famous pessimists of this kind, Diogenes the Cynic, Schopenhauer, Carlyle, and their kin with Shakespeare's Timon of Athens, to recognize them as diseased minds. The third is the philanthropical type, people whose lively sympathies, easily excited, become roused to anger at what they consider the stupid injustices of life. Being easily interested in everything, without being overloaded with exact thought of any kind, they are excellent raw material for *littérateurs* [Literary men]: witness Voltaire. No individual remotely approaching the calibre of a Leibniz is to be found among them.

The third argument, enclosing and defending the other two, consists in the development of those principles of logic according to which the humble argument is the first stage of a scientific inquiry into the origin of the three Universes, but of an inquiry which produces, not merely scientific belief, which is always provisional, but also a living, practical belief, logically justified in crossing the Rubicon with all the freightage of eternity. The presentation of this argument would require the establishment of several principles of logic that the logicians have hardly dreamed of, and particularly a strict proof of the correctness of the maxim of Pragmaticism. My original essay, having been written for a popular monthly, assumes, for no better reason than that real inquiry cannot begin until a state of real doubt arises and ends as soon as Belief is attained, that "a settlement of Belief," or, in other words, a state of *satisfaction,* is all that Truth, or the aim of inquiry, consists in. The reason I gave for this was so flimsy, while the inference was so nearly the gist of Pragmaticism, that I must confess the argument of that essay might with some justice be said to beg the question. The first part of the essay, however, is occupied with showing that, if Truth consists in satisfaction, it cannot be any *actual* satisfaction, but must be the satisfaction which *would* ultimately be found if the inquiry were pushed to its ultimate and indefeasible issue. This, I beg to point out, is a very different position from that of Mr. Schiller and the pragmatists of today. I trust I shall be believed when I say that it is only a desire to avoid being misunderstood in consequence of my relations with pragmatism, and by no means as arrogating any superior immunity from error which I have too good reason to know that I do not enjoy, that leads me to express my personal sentiments about their tenets. Their avowedly undefinable position, if it be not capable of logical characterization, seems to me to be characterized by an angry hatred of strict logic, and even some disposition to rate any exact thought which interferes with their doctrines as all humbug. At the same time, it seems to me clear that their approximate acceptance of the Pragmaticist principle, and even that very casting aside of difficult distinctions (although I cannot

approve of it), has helped them to a mightily clear discernment of some fundamental truths that other philosophers have seen but through a mist, and most of them not at all. Among such truths—all of them old, of course, yet acknowledged by few—I reckon their denial of necessitarianism; their rejection of any "consciousness" different from a visceral or other external sensation; their acknowledgment that there are, in a Pragmatistical sense, Real habits (which Really *would* produce effects, under circumstances that may not happen to get actualized, and are thus Real generals); and their insistence upon interpreting all hypostatic abstractions in terms of what they *would* or *might* (not actually *will*) come to in the concrete. It seems to me a pity they should allow a philosophy so instinct with life to become infected with seeds of death in such notions as that of the unreality of all ideas of infinity[9] and that of the mutability of truth,[10] and in such confusions of thought as that of active willing (willing to control thought, to doubt, and to weigh reasons) with willing not to exert the will (willing to believe).[11]

## Notes

1. See his *Thought and Things* (London, 1906), p. 261.
2. "It appears to me that this mystery is considered insoluble for the very reason which should cause it to be regarded as easy of solution. I mean the *outré* [exaggerated] character of its features."
3. Or Abduction. [Peirce's logic of justifying hypotheses.]
4. *Kritik der Reinen Vernunft,* A154–158; B193–197.
5. Jacques Babinet (1794–1872), a popular writer on hydrodynamics and many other scientific subjects.
6. See "Dialogues Concerning the Two Great Systems of the World," in *Mathematical Collections and Translations* of Thomas Salisbury, Vol. 1, p. 301 (London, 1661).
7. See *The Will to Believe and Other Essays in Popular Philosophy* (1897).
8. See "What Pragmatism Is Like," *Popular Science Monthly,* Vol. 71 (1907), p. 351.
9. F. C. S. Schiller, *Humanism* (London, 1903), p. 314, note; *Studies in Humanism* (London, 1907), p. 295.
10. William James, *Pragmatism.*
11. William James, *The Will to Believe.*

# Suggestions for Further Reading

## Works by Peirce

*Writings of Charles S. Peirce: Chronological Edition,* ed. Peirce Edition Project (Bloomington: Indiana University Press, 1982–). The ongoing, definitive edition of the works of Peirce.

*Charles Sanders Peirce: Contributions to The Nation,* 3 volumes, eds. K. L. Ketner and J. E. Cook (Lubbock: Texas Tech University Press, 1975–79).

*Collected Papers of Charles Sanders Peirce,* 8 volumes, eds. C. Hartshorne and P. Weiss (vols. 1–6) and A. W. Burks (vols. 7–8) (Cambridge, Mass.: Belknap Press, Harvard University Press, 1935, 1958).

*The New Elements of Mathematics,* ed. C. Eisele (The Hague: Mouton, 1976).

*Pragmatism as a Principle and Method of Right Thinking:* The 1903 Harvard Lectures on Pragmatism, ed. P. A. Turrisi (Albany: State University of New York Press, 1997).

*Semiotic and Significs,* ed. C. S. Hardwick (Bloomington: Indiana University Press, 1977).

## Anthologies

*Chance, Love and Logic,* ed. M. Cohen (New York: Century, 1923, 1980).

*Charles S. Peirce: Selected Writings* (originally titled *Values in a Universe of Chance*), ed. P. P. Wiener (New York: Dover, 1961).

*The Essential Peirce: Selected Philosophical Writings,* 2 vols., eds. N. Houser and C. Kloesel (Bloomington: Indiana University Press, 1992 and 1998).

*Philosophical Writings of Peirce,* ed. J. Buchler (New York: Dover, 1940).

## Essential Works on Peirce

Douglas R. Anderson, *Strands of System: The Philosophy of Charles Peirce* (West Lafayette, Ind.: Purdue University Press, 1995).

Karl-Otto Apel, *Charles S. Peirce: From Pragmatism to Pragmaticism,* trans. J. M. Krois (Amherst, Mass.: University of Massachusetts Presss, 1981).

Justus Buchler, *Charles S. Peirce's Empiricism* (New York: Kegan Paul, 1939, 1966; reprinted by Octagon Books).

Vincent M. Colapietro, *Peirce's Approach to the Self* (Albany: State University of New York Press, 1989).

James K. Feibleman, *An Introduction to the Philosophy of Charles S. Peirce* (Cambridge, Mass.: MIT Press, 1969).

Thomas Goudge, *The Thought of C. S. Peirce* (New York: Dover, 1969).

Carl R. Hausman, *Charles S. Peirce's Evolutionary Philosophy* (Cambridge, UK: Cambridge University Press, 1993).

Kenneth Laine Ketner, *His Glassy Essence: An Autobiography of Charles S. Peirce* (Nashville: Vanderbilt University Press, 1998).

Christopher Hookway, *Peirce* (London: Routledge, 1985).

Murray Murphey, *The Development of Peirce's Philosophy* (Cambridge, Mass.: Harvard University Press, 1961; reprinted by Hackett Publishing Company).

Kelly Parker, *The Continuity of Peirce's Thought* (Nashville: Vanderbilt University Press, 1997).

Herman Parret, ed., *Peirce and Value Theory* (Amsterdam and Philadelphia: John Benjamins Publishing Co., 1994).

Vincent G. Potter, *Charles S. Peirce: Norms and Ideals* (New York: Fordham University Press, 1997).

Vincent G. Potter, *Peirce's Philosophical Perspectives* (New York: Fordham University Press, 1996).

Sandra B. Rosenthal, *Charles Peirce's Pragmatic Pluralism* (Albany: State University of New York Press, 1994).

Manley Thompson, *The Pragmatic Philosophy of C. S. Peirce* (Chicago: University of Chicago Press, 1953).

# WILLIAM JAMES

## Introduction by John J. McDermott

### James's Life: Cultural Context and Philosophical Background

The thought of William James is the vestibule to the speculative break-throughs of the twentieth century. He anticipates the directions of modern physics, psychoanalysis and depth psychology, modern art, and the emphasis on relations rather than on objects or substances. James is a process philosopher, by which we mean that he assesses the journey, the flow, to be more important than the outcome or the product.

A contemporary of Henri Bergson, whom he influenced, and a goad to the subsequent work of John Dewey and Alfred North Whitehead, James was also a decisive factor in the thought of Niels Bohr, Edmund Husserl, Miguel de Unamuno, Maria Montessori, and a countless host of lesser figures. Long an underground thinker, William James rivals Emerson as a writer who is read widely by nonprofessional philosophers. The appeal of the writings of William James transcends disciplinary boundaries, for commentators on science, psychology, art, politics, ethics, and religion find his works as stimulating as do philosophers. In fact, the work of William James is never subject to such artificial discipline boundaries as that found in a typical university curriculum. He wrote for reflective people, no matter their occupation or persuasion. As such, James is the thinker who most appeals to the average person seeking wisdom and depth in his or her own, personal experiences.

Nonetheless, James's thought is not without its technical virtuosity and requires more than a casual reading or scanning to reveal its profounder import. In this volume we have presented the major highlights of James's positions on psychology, ethics, metaphysics, and the theory of knowledge. The selections have been taken from the critical edition of *The Works of William James* published by Harvard University Press, texts that have been scrupulously edited and represent James's final thought on each issue. The limits of space do not allow us to present James's rich views on religion, psychical research, and his prescient commentary on European-American culture as found in his *Letters*.

Before detailing the major lineaments of James's thought, it will be helpful to our understanding if we discuss his cultural and family context. The biographical details of the life of a major thinker is always of some assistance in enabling us to grasp the issues, the responses, and the omissions found in the work. In the case of William James, the details are of paramount importance, for his life and his work were entwined in an unusually intimate way. Without attempting any psychobiography and without any speculation as to hidden meanings or hidden interpersonal relationships, we can still provide a portrait of James as an engaged, sometimes depressed and yet always alert person.[1]

William James was the son of Henry James, Sr., and Mary Robertson Walsh, both of Scottish-Irish Protestant lineage. William was the oldest of five children and felt the burden of making a career worthy of the expectations of his father, who, ironically, never had one himself. Having a comfortable inheritance and having had his leg amputated as a youth, Henry James,

Sr., concentrated on talking and writing imposing, verbose, and little-read theological books. He was a friend and confidant of the great literary figures in the American nineteenth century, for example, Margaret Fuller, Ralph Waldo Emerson, Bronson Alcott, Henry David Thoreau, James Russell Lowell, and Nathaniel Hawthorne. The family was inundated by ideas and was taken on frequent trips to Europe, where they received tutoring, especially in languages. The second son in the family was Henry James, Jr., the justly famous writer.[2] Two other sons, Garth Wilkinson and Robertson, lived star-crossed lives, mostly because of their experience in the American Civil War, a painful odyssey in which neither William nor Henry participated. The fifth child was Alice James, who suffered from neurasthenia until her death, from cancer, in 1892. She left behind a brilliant diary and many elegant letters. Trapped in a male-dominated family, her considerable literary talents found little room for public expression and she remained a victim throughout her life.[3]

Returning now to the life of William James, it is important to focus on his early years, from his birth in 1842 until 1870, when he reached an emotional crossroad at the age of twenty-eight. James was privately educated and in fact had no college degree, although he studied at Harvard College periodically. He did manage to sit for the examination required for a medical degree, which he received in 1869, while promising never to practice, for he regarded the state of nineteenth-century medicine as largely humbug. Nonetheless, he read widely and in several languages, especially French and German. In 1867, he began publishing unsigned reviews of some of the books he was reading. It was at this time, however, that James was under a cloud of depression and was suffering from deep feelings of insecurity and inadequacy.

Sometime toward the end of the decade, James underwent a frightening personal experience, called in nineteenth-century parlance a vastation. Taken from the work of the mystic-philosopher Emanuel Swedenborg, a vastation refers to the projecting of the inner self outward, usually in a grotesque form. Notably, this experience of William James was strikingly similar to one had by his father at approximately the same age in his own life. James records this experience surreptitiously, as though it came to him by an unknown French correspondent. We now know that it is an autobiographical report from William James and we offer it here in full.

> Whilst in this state of philosophic pessimism and general depression of spirits about my prospects, I went one evening into a dressing-room in the twilight to procure some article that was there; when suddenly there fell upon me without any warning, just as if it came out of the darkness, a horrible fear of my own existence. Simultaneously there arose in my mind the image of an epileptic patient whom I had seen in the asylum, a black-haired youth with greenish skin, entirely idiotic, who used to sit all day on one of the benches, or rather shelves against the wall, with his knees drawn up against his chin, and the coarse gray undershirt, which was his only garment, drawn over them inclosing his entire figure. He sat there like a sort of sculptured Egyptian cat or Peruvian mummy, moving nothing but his black eyes and looking absolutely non-human. This image and my fear entered into a species of combination with each other. *That shape am I,* I felt, potentially. Nothing that I possess can defend me against that fate, if the hour for it should strike for me as it struck for him. There was such a horror of him, and such a perception of my own merely momentary discrepancy from him, that it was as if something hitherto solid within my breast gave way entirely, and I became a mass of quivering fear. After this the universe was changed for me altogether. I awoke morning after morning with a horrible dread at the pit of my stomach, and with a sense of the insecurity of life that I never knew before, and that I have never felt since. It was like a revelation; and although the immediate feelings passed away, the experience has made me sympathetic with the morbid feelings of others ever since. It gradually faded, but for months I was unable to go out into the dark alone.
>
> In general I dreaded to be left alone. I remember wondering how other people could live, how I myself had ever lived, so unconscious of that pit of insecurity beneath the surface of life. My mother

in particular, a very cheerful person, seemed to me a perfect paradox in her unconsciousness of danger, which you may well believe I was very careful not to disturb by revelations of my own state of mind. I have always thought that this experience of melancholia of mine had a religious bearing. . . . I mean that the fear was so invasive and powerful that if I had not clung to scripture-texts like 'The eternal God is my refuge,' etc., 'Come unto me, all ye that labor and are heavy-laden,' etc., 'I am the resurrection and the life,' etc. I think I should have grown really insane.[4]

The key line here is "*That shape am I,* I felt, potentially," James, early on, became convinced of the diaphanous and utterly fragile character of the classically alleged, rock-bottom personal self. With exquisite originality James diagnoses the fabric of self-consciousness only to discover that it is neither a redoubt nor a bunker. He doubts the existence of the traditional "soul" and opts rather for a more free-flowing movement between the focus of one's own self and the fringe that we visit. These visits to the fringe turn up radically different versions of our own selves, for, it turns out, we are actually multiple selves. The fundamental question that nags James at this time has to do with whether we have any control over the making of our own self. In early 1870, James makes an entry in his diary that reveals his pervasive dubiety about his ability to transcend the jejune character of ordinary life, with its routine and often hypocritical demands. Although he does not admit his suicidal tendency until a subsequent entry, James in February of 1870, depressed by the death of his young and beautiful cousin Minny Temple, drew a tombstone in his diary and dallied with his own demise. The text reads as follows:

Feb. 1, 1870

. . . Today I about touched bottom, and perceive plainly that I must face the choice with open eyes: shall I frankly throw the moral business overboard, as one unsuited to my innate aptitudes, or shall I follow it, and it alone, making everything else merely stuff for it? I will give the latter alternative a fair trial. Who knows but the moral interest may become developed . . . Hitherto I have tried to fire myself with the moral interest, as an aid in the accomplishing of certain utilitarian ends.[5]

James hereby laments the bland nineteenth-century Protestant ethic that suffuses his life. Proper manners, career, and systemic hypocrisy are the constant accompaniments of his consciousness and his conscience. In that both his reading and the turbulence of his interior life taught him that there must be more, evermore, James casts a wistful glance at suicide but then, fortunately, begins to read the works of the philosopher Charles Renouvier, for whom the will is not so much an agent of approbation as it is an agent of change. In April of 1870, James makes a diary entry that is to be decisive for both his life and his thought.

April 30, 1870

I think that yesterday was a crisis in my life. I finished the first part of Renouvier's second "Essais" and see no reason why his definition of Free Will—"the sustaining of a thought *because I choose to* when I might have other thoughts"—need be the definition of an illusion. At any rate, I will assume for the present—until next year—that it is no illusion. My first act of free will shall be to believe in free will. For the remainder of the year, I will abstain from the mere speculation and contemplative *Grublei* in which my nature takes most delight, and voluntarily cultivate the feeling of moral freedom, by reading books favorable to it, as well as by acting. After the first of January, my callow skin being somewhat fledged, I may perhaps return to metaphysical study and skepticism without danger to my powers of action. For the present then remember: care little for speculation; much for the *form* of my action; recollect that only when habits of order are formed can we advance to really interesting fields of action—and consequently accumulate grain on grain of willful choice like a very miser; never forgetting how one link dropped undoes an indefinite number. *Principiis obsta*—Today has furnished the exceptionally passionate initiative which Bain posits as needful for the acquisition of habits. I will see to the sequel. Not in maxims, not in *Anschauungen,* but in accumulated *acts* of thought lies salvation. *Passer outre.* Hitherto, when I have felt like taking a free initiative, like daring to act originally, without carefully waiting for contemplation of the external world to determine all for me, suicide seemed the most manly form to put my daring into; now, I will go a step further with my will, not only act with it, but believe as well; believe in my individual reality and creative power. My belief, to be sure, *can't* be optimistic—but I will posit life (the real, the good) in the self-governing *resistance* of the ego to the world. Life shall [be built in] doing and suffering and creating.[6]

When one comes to know James's thought, this text reads like an early blueprint of all of his later intellectual concerns. We sort out only the major contention, namely, that the human will is cognitive. The first act of the will, with no rational guarantees provided, is to believe that the will is free. By this James does not mean free to assume that what we believe is necessarily true. Rather, the will is free to believe in possibilities underwent until the crush of empirical facticity rejects the belief. No optimism here, for James stresses the hazards of taking a chance, a risk, a gamble on the future of experience. Yet, were we to hang back, we would never know the possible paths extant, many of which are blocked from our view by the dominance of rote, habit, custom and ill-advised authority.

The concluding sentence of this diary entry is crucial to James's project, for he affirms the creative and constitutive activity of the self. He is aware of the presence of self-deception, setback, and foolhardy risk. Still, he reaches for the aggressive and chance-ridden character of moving out, moving into the unknown, for the personal alternative of acceptance of the religious, ethical, and social status quo is stultifying and depressing.

After his recovery, James began to plot his belated future. Throughout the 1870s he wrote book reviews, most of them also unsigned. The year 1878, however, was to be dramatically auspicious. In that year, he wrote and published his first detailed essays and he promised to deliver a textbook in psychology to the well-respected publisher Henry Holt. James had been teaching physiology and psychology at Harvard since 1873 and was now willing to structure his thoughts in a systematic way. Perhaps most important in his journey, James married Alice Howe Gibbens in 1878, thereby assuring him of both roots and sustenance away from the demands and carping of his paternal home. The next twelve years were to be very productive for James and they culminated in the publication of his magisterial two-volume work *The Principles of Psychology,* a book still regarded as the greatest work in the history of psychology and one of the classic written works in the history of the English language.

William James was to continue publishing until his death in 1910 at the age of sixty-eight. When finished, his collected works of published and unpublished writings will approximate twenty volumes. It would be impossible and improper for an introduction of this kind to probe all of the themes and arguments in such an extensive set of writings. All the more true is this in that an understanding of James's thought requires an acquaintance with his philosophical peers and his polemical opponents. His letters and writings bristle with praise, condemnation, and rhetorical questioning of the great minds of the European-American period from 1870 until 1910. Central to his concerns was the thought of Herbert Spencer, whom he loathed, Darwin, Shadworth Hodgson, Henri Bergson, and his friendly foil, colleague, and neighbor, Josiah Royce. Familiar to James was the thought of all the experimental psychologists and most of the philosophers of the nineteenth century. There were omissions, however, for he did not have a serious acquaintance with the work of Marx, Nietzsche, or Kierkegaard. Still, he was the first major thinker to realize the signal contribution and the rich intellectual future of the work of John Dewey and, long before any one else, James knew of the genius of Charles Sanders Peirce.

The bold and innovative thought of William James was not without its critics, primarily those of the incipient analytical philosophical persuasion, especially as found in the critiques of G. E. Moore and Bertrand Russell, both of which were dramatically wrong-headed and shallow.[7] James was not without responsibility for the rising tide of criticism directed to his work, for he often published his public lectures without recasting them with regard to the more critical and dubious philosophical reader. James was a flamboyant, witty, and brilliant lecturer whose prose style was often elegant at the expense of conceptual detail. Put differently, most of James's published works, especially those which are famous as, for example, *The Will to Believe, The Varieties of Religious Experience, Pragmatism,* and *A Pluralistic Universe,* are virtuoso performances in a prose that delights, tantalizes, and is often telescoped as to the assumptions and arguments at work behind the scene.

## Pragmatism, Radical Empiricism, and Pluralism

The present setting of this introduction does not have the girth sufficient to unravel all of James's assumptions active in his writing. Still, we can point to three texts that serve as mooring points for an understanding of his philosophical position, one which is demonstrated over and again in both his published work and in his unpublished papers. The first of these texts is from his early period as found in the essay "The Sentiment of Rationality," first published in 1879. The remaining two texts are to be found in his *Pragmatism,* published in 1907, although they represent cameo versions of two seemingly contradictory positions long at war in his thought throughout his reflective life.

The opening text reads as follows:

> If we survey the field of history and ask what feature all great periods of revival, of expansion of the human mind, display in common, we shall find, I think, simply this: that each and all of them have said to the human being, "The inmost nature of the reality is congenial to *powers* which you possess."[8]

This text shows James to be a pragmatic idealist, that is, a position which admits to the existence of the world in its sheer physicality but at the same time affirms the source of meaning for that world to be dependent on the creative imagination of the human mind. Reality is not a surd, having no internal coherence. The coherence, however, does not flash out as an obvious and intractable set of laws, as Aristotle would have it. Reality is not given, final, and complete to the human mind. Rather, it is "congenial" to our understanding and our principles of organization. Reality is not permanently opaque and unintelligible, as philosophical nihilism contends. To the contrary, the human mind and reality enter into a relationship in which the "powers" of human imagination and the "energies" of human activity act as a constituting source for meaning. Such meaning is never complete, for the "inmost nature of reality" is only "congenial" to our powers and, therefore, never fully explicated.

Following James, the history of human language and civilization is equivalent to the evolving meaning of reality. As with DNA, this process is open-ended and is laced with chance as a permanent strand in the relationship between the physical world and the human mind. James sees no possibility of reality ever being grasped whole and entire. He offers two reasons for this never-ending pluralism. First, nature itself is subject to multiple permutations that violate its own history and, second, each human perspective is precisely that, a perspective, and cannot be exactly dovetailed with the perspectives of other human beings. Consequently, James holds that the world is intelligible, but not in any final way. He describes reality as a pluriverse or a multiverse, riven with chance, mishap, and always denying any intellectual or conceptual closure.[9] In a notebook entry of 1903, James states his aversion to philosophical closure.

> What, on pragmatist terms, does 'nature itself' signify? To my mind it signifies the non-artificial; the artificial having certain definite aesthetic characteristics which I dislike, and can only apperceive in others as matters of personal taste,—to me bad taste. All neat schematisms with per-

manent and absolute distinctions, classifications with absolute pretensions, systems with pigeon-holes, etc., have this character. All 'classic,' clean, cut and dried, 'noble,' fixed, 'eternal,' *Weltan-schauungen* seem to me to violate the character with which life concretely comes and the expression which it bears of being, or at least of involving, a muddle and a struggle, with an 'ever not quite' to all our formulas, and novelty and possibility forever leaking in.[10]

William James's stress on "novelty," "possibility," and an "ever not quite" to all of our judgments has always irritated professional philosophers, known for their drive toward clarity and even closure. James is unquestionably an antifoundationalist philosopher, by which we mean that he opposes the effort, begun by René Descartes in the seventeenth century, to place philosophical inquiry on a footing that is absolutely secure, one that rivals the alleged certitude of mathematics. To be an antifoundationalist and an anti-Cartesian is now quite acceptable in contemporary philosophy, but it was the early pragmatists Chauncey Wright, Charles Sanders Peirce, and William James who were the first to challenge the arrogance of claims for absolute philosophical certitude. Yet, despite his proclivity for chance, novelty, and a permanent pluralism in our understanding of the world, James was not naive about the obduracy of nature and about the way in which nature has its own meaning, independent of the way in which we perceive it. In his *Pragmatism,* published in 1907, James issues a warning to those who fail to match conceptions with the way in which reality "concretely comes."

> *Woe to him whose beliefs*
> *play fast and loose with*
> *the order which realities*
> *follow in his experience;*
> *they will lead him nowhere*
> *or else make false connexions.*[11]

In order to explicate this text, some background information and analysis is essential. Before publishing *Pragmatism,* James had published a series of essays, in 1904–1905, subsequently collected posthumously in 1912 as *Essays in Radical Empiricism.* As early as 1897, in a preface to his *Will to Believe,* James had described his philosophical position as radical empiricism.

> Were I obliged to give a short name to the attitude in question, I should call it that of *radical empiricism.* . . . I say "empiricism" because it is contented to regard its most assured conclusions concerning matters of fact as hypotheses liable to modification in the course of future experience; and I say "radical," because it treats the doctrine of monism itself as an hypothesis. . . .
>
> He who takes for his hypothesis the notion that it [pluralism] is the permanent form of the world is what I call a radical empiricist. For him the crudity of experience remains an eternal element thereof. There is no possible point of view from which the world can appear an absolutely single fact.[12]

Again, in 1909, in another preface, James lays out the characteristics of radical empiricism.

> Radical empiricism consists first of a postulate, next of a statement of fact, and finally of a generalized conclusion.
>
> The postulate is that the only things that shall be debatable among philosophers shall be things definable in terms drawn from experience. [Things of an unexperienceable nature may exist *ad libitum,* but they form no part of the material for philosophic debate.]
>
> The statement of fact is that the relations between things, conjunctive as well as disjunctive, are just as much matters of direct particular experience, neither more so nor less so, than the things themselves.
>
> The generalized conclusion is that therefore the parts of experience hold together from next to next by relations that are themselves parts of experience. The directly apprehended universe needs,

in short, no extraneous transempirical connective support, but possesses in its own right a concatenated or continuous structure.[13]

Returning to the text from *Pragmatism* cited above, we can now see how James telescopes his deeper meanings, for nothing less than a grasp of his radical empiricism enables us to appreciate his warning. "Woe to him" (or her) refers to any attempt to forge or make relations that are in stark opposition to the way in which reality sets up.

Such an effort has the extremely baleful consequence of failing to "make connexions," that is, failing to hook into the flow of both consciousness and nature. James holds that objects are mock-ups, pockets, boxes of relations that are snipped and packaged for reasons of utility. Our task is to acknowledge these "substantive states," these "perches" in the stream, while yet regarding them as functional, placeholders, and pregnant with "connections" that transcend them. If we do not take these perches, these gatherings into consideration, then we may as well confuse water with stone and wood with cloth. On the other hand, if we allow ourselves only a literal reading of the flow, we become trapped as merely a definer, categorizer, and obsequious servant of the way in which the world has been passed down to us, in all of its obviousness, banality, and rigidity. Thus, the second text in *Pragmatism* states:

> In our cognitive as well as in our active life we are creative. We *add* both to the subject and to the predicate part of reality. The world stands really malleable, waiting to receive its final touches at our hand. Like the kingdom of heaven, it suffers violence willingly. Man *engenders* truths upon it.[14]

This text is extraordinary; especially given the warning by James, discussed above. Here we have in an unvarnished way James's doctrine of the Promethean self. The text itself is exquisite. Notice the emphasis on the "hands." Reality does not come readymade. It is true that for James, reality has its own relational network, its own obduracy. Yet, reality is malleable, pliant, awaiting our touch, our presence, our organization. The fabric known as the world results from the raw physicality of nature and the probing, constituting presence of the human imagination. Consequently, science is not final or absolute. Science functions more like a prose poem, gathering, relating, searching, and structuring, temporarily. It is the world which we come to know, more or less. It is the world with which we transact, for better or for worse. Yet, without human imagination, cognition, and construction, there would be no world, no relations, no metaphors, and, finally, no meaning.

This tension between the world as given, present, set up, in business, and our version of the world, splayed out over many disciplines, patterns, and charts, is precisely the center of James's philosophy. Human life cannot make a world out of whole cloth, *ab ovo*. Still, the world is meaningless without human articulation of its meaning, a meaning that is inseparable from how we came to mean the world. The problem, of course, is that the human version of the world is conflicted, for there is more than one of us. James was not sufficiently sophisticated about the social conditioning that pervades our personal world view. This sense of the social context for individual versions of experience was to be explored in depth by his successors, John Dewey and George Herbert Mead, as well as by his European counterparts, Karl Marx, Wilhelm Dilthey, and the twentieth-century founders of the sociology of knowledge, especially Karl Mannheim. Despite his comparative unawareness of the immediate social contexting of the individual self, James was aware of the pluralism of approaches to constructing a meaningful world, as witness his statement in *Pragmatism*:

> Ought not the existence of the various types of thinking which we have reviewed, each so splendid for certain purposes, yet all conflicting still, and neither one of them able to support a claim of absolute veracity, to awaken a presumption favorable to the pragmatistic view that all our theories are *instrumental,* are mental modes of *adaptation* to reality, rather than revelations or gnostic

answers to some divinely instituted world-enigma? . . . Certainly the restlessness of the actual theoretic situation, the value for some purposes of each thought-level, and the inability of either to
expel the others decisively, suggest this pragmatistic view.[15]

James's pluralistic approach to inquiry is distinctively American in that it allows everyone to
have his or her say before the inquiry is put to rest, and even a reopening of the discussion awaits
the slightest hint of new information, data, or perspective. For example in his essay "The Sentiment of Rationality," published in 1879, James stresses the role of temperament as crucial to
one's philosophical approach. In the absence of a full selection of this essay, I offer the reader
two long representative texts. First:

> . . . All those data that cannot be analytically identified with the attribute invoked as universal
> principle, remain as independent kinds or natures, associated empirically with the said attribute but
> devoid of rational kinship with it.
>
> Hence the unsatisfactoriness of all our speculations. On the one hand, so far as they retain any
> multiplicity in their terms, they fail to get us out of the empirical sand-heap world; on the other, so
> far as they eliminate multiplicity the practical man despises their empty barrenness. The most they
> can say is that the elements of the world are such and such, and that each is identical with itself
> wherever found; but the question Where is it found? the practical man is left to answer by his own
> wit. Which, of all the essences, shall here and now be held the essence of this concrete thing, the
> fundamental philosophy never attempts to decide. We are thus led to the conclusion that the simple
> classification of things is, on the one hand, the best possible theoretic philosophy, but is, on the
> other, a most miserable and inadequate substitute for the fulness of the truth. It is a monstrous
> abridgment of life, which, like all abridgments is got by the absolute loss and casting out of real mat-
> ter. This is why so few human beings truly care for philosophy. The particular determinations which
> she ignores are the real matter exciting needs, quite as potent and authoritative as hers. What does
> the moral enthusiast care for philosophical ethics? Why does the *Aesthetik* of every German philoso-
> pher appear to the artist as an abomination of desolation?

Second, the conclusion of the essay:

> To sum up: No philosophy will permanently be deemed rational by all men which (in addition
> to meeting logical demands) does not to some degree pretend to determine expectancy, and in a still
> greater degree make a direct appeal to all those powers of our nature which we hold in highest
> esteem. Faith, being one of these powers, will always remain a factor not to be banished from philo-
> sophic constructions, the more so since in many ways it brings forth its own verification. In these
> points, then, it is hopeless to look for literal agreement amongst mankind.
>
> The ultimate philosophy, we may therefore conclude, must not be too strait-laced in form, must
> not in all its parts divide heresy from orthodoxy by too sharp a line. There must be left over and
> above the propositions to be subscribed *ubique, semper, et ab omnibus,* another realm into which
> the stifled soul may escape from pedantic scruples and indulge its own faith at its own risks; and all
> that can here be done will be to mark out distinctly the questions which fall within faith's sphere.[16]

It is clear that for James, openness to experience, to novelty, to surprise is a cardinal tenet of
the philosophical enterprise. Inquiry which proceeds from narrow, a priori assumptions is anath-
ema in James's search for truth, meaning, and insight.

## Psychology, Metaphysics, Epistemology, and Ethics

The selections that follow illustrate James's basic philosophical, moral, and personal
approaches to the major questions that confront us as human beings. The order of these selec-

tions is not chronological but rather first introduces the reader to James's psychology, metaphysics, and pragmatic epistemology and then proceeds to the earlier moral writings. The rationale for this ordering is that the later thought of James is assumed by him in the earlier writings, which are only intelligible given the overall published agenda. Similarly, this discussion of the selections follows no chronology but rather seeks to help the reader obtain apertures into the seminal thought of William James.

Dividing the world into the "tough-minded" and the "tender-minded," as he does in *Pragmatism,* reveals James's thought as a mixture of both.

| THE TENDER-MINDED | THE TOUGH-MINDED |
|---|---|
| Rationalistic (going by 'principles'), | Empiricist (going by 'facts'), |
| Intellectualistic, | Sensationalistic, |
| Idealistic, | Materialistic, |
| Optimistic, | Pessimistic, |
| Religious, | Irreligious, |
| Free-willist, | Fatalistic, |
| Monistic, | Pluralistic, |
| Dogmatical. | Sceptical.[17] |

If we were to apply these tables to James, we would find that he is "tender-minded," to wit: Idealistic, Optimistic, Religious and Free-willist. We would find that he is also "tough-minded," to wit: Empiricist, Sensationalistic, and Pluralistic. To resolve this opposition, James invokes the sentiment of rationality, by which he means to stress the inordinate importance of how we "feel" about things, others, and the world as a factor in how we "think" about the same concerns.

The "Dilemma of Determinism" published in 1884, is a tour de force, one of James's most brilliant essays. The upshot of his position is that even if it turns out that all is determined, it would make no difference in any past experience, all of which were had under the guise of free will. Second, if all were to be determined from here on, there is considerable doubt as to whether we could or would live under such a rubric, leading James to conclude that, whatever the ultimate course may be, it is our decision *here* and *now* that "gives the palpitating reality to our moral life."

Another selection comes from James's classic chapter on "The Stream of Thought,"[18] from *The Principles of Psychology,* published in 1890. This chapter is a reworking of an important essay written by James in 1884, "On Some Omissions of Introspective Psychology."[19] At that time, James isolated two major approaches to epistemological certitude, that is, to a viable theory of knowledge. Both of these approaches were considered by James in a broad and nontechnical fashion, given that he was more interested in his resolution than in their proposals. In short, never trust a great, imaginative thinker to yield an accurate version of other great thinkers. That task is for the historians of ideas. Still, James is prescient when he cites the following problems at work in the Associationist and Idealist epistemologies, respectively.

First, James praises Associationism for its emphasis on particulars and on the role of the body in the knowing activity. Descended from Locke, the Associationists held that the mind was literally a responder to single bodily sensations and was able to associate a parallel set of ideas to the set of sensations had. James, however, denied that any such activity takes place in the human mind. In a chapter in the *Principles* entitled "The Methods and Snares of Psychology," James decries the naivete of the Associationist position.

> As each object may come and go, be forgotten and then thought of again, it is held that the thought of it has a precisely similar independence, self-identity, and mobility. The thought of the object's recurrent identity is regarded as the identity of its recurrent thought; and the perceptions of

multiplicity, of coexistence, of succession, are severally conceived to be brought about only through a multiplicity, a coexistence, a succession, of perceptions. The continuous flow of the mental stream is sacrificed, and in its place an atomism, a brickbat plan of construction, is preached, for the existence of which no good introspective grounds can be brought forward, and out of which presently grow all sorts of paradoxes and contradictions, the heritage of woe of students of the mind.

These words are meant to impeach the entire English psychology derived from Locke and Hume, and the entire German psychology derived from Herbart, as far as they both treat 'ideas' as separate subjective entities that come and go.[20]

James's basic critique of the Associationist doctrine is that it does not provide for any continuity in our experience, holding rather to a relationship of mere contiguity or next-by-next. The second position that James analyzes does provide continuity, for all experience is unintelligible unless it is grasped as an aspect of the Absolute Mind. Referring to this viewpoint as British Idealism, James criticizes its inability to account for particulars and the comparative absence of bodily sensations in the act of knowing. James waged a lifelong debate on the plausibility of the Idealist position with two of its most brilliant exponents, F. H. Bradley and Josiah Royce. The fundamental issue is whether one has to forgo experiential continuity in order to experience particulars or whether one has to forgo particulars in order to posit a general coherence in the way particular experiences hang together.

In his 1884 essay "On Some Omissions of Introspective Psychology" and again in his chapter "The Stream of Thought" in *The Principles of Psychology* of 1890, James rejects both positions in favor of a claim that we experience relations between objects as well as the objects themselves, thereby providing both the experience of particulars and the experience of continuity. He writes, "If there be such things as feelings at all, *then so surely as relations between objects exist* [in the nature of things], *so surely, and more surely, do feelings exist to which these relations are known.*" And, further, "we ought to say a feeling of *and,* a feeling of *if,* a feeling of *by,* quite as readily as we say a feeling of *blue* or a feeling of *cold.*"[21] James's contention that we have an affective grasp of relations leads him to diagnose the activity of consciousness as a flow, a stream, rather than as a container or a box. The selection below on "The Stream of Thought" provides a rich description of the activity of consciousness. A subsequent selection on "The World of Pure Experience" attempts to show that mind and body are not ultimately separate but only separate by name or by function. The flow of consciousness is whole and continuous, whereas our conceptual formulations tend to break it up into definitions, names, nouns, and other assorted categories.

It is true, of course, that to survive, human beings need placeholders, perches, moving points in the flow, which act as redoubts, way stations, and abodes. Were they not present, we would be carried in the stream as flotsam, rudderless. The task then is twofold: (1) forge those moorings that are most propitious and advantageous for our human needs and (2) avoid becoming trapped and mired such that we confuse our own temporary bunker with the entire fabric of possibility. The remaining three selections below address this issue head on. In "What Pragmatism Means," James stresses the importance of consequences as the source of evaluation of our acts and our beliefs. He urges us to liberate ourselves from a rote acceptance of dogmatic claims by opening ourselves to the call of experience, especially in its novel forms. In order for this to become a living attitude for us, we must forsake absolute certitude and beliefs that admit of no exception and generate intolerance rather than understanding for competing positions. In "The Moral Philosopher and the Moral Life," James stresses the importance of the strenuous mood, one which is forever seeking new possibilities, new vistas, and a wider range of choices.

The last selection to be considered is "The Will to Believe," James's best-known, most controversial, and most misunderstood essay. James is *not* saying that if one believes strongly enough, the belief will come true. He is saying that belief enables us to test hypotheses out of the range of our ordinary experience. If these hypotheses, when they unearth the data of new experience, prove to be inept, incomplete, or simply wrong, then they should be abandoned. We cannot know the worth of a belief until it is pressed forward into the crucible of new experience. James holds that the willingness to risk belief in possibilities that are often scoffed or mocked by common sense generates an energy that frequently leads to paths of insight otherwise closed off from us. This perpetual searching, this strenuous mood, pervades James's life and thought.

After the publication of *The Principles of Psychology,* James turned his attention to more directly philosophical works and he both lectured and published extensively until his death in 1910. His last book was entitled *A Pluralistic Universe,* in which he plumbed the reaches of extrasensory perception, the widest range of human consciousness, and wondered again about life after death. These were existentially appropriate themes at this time, for James was suffering from arteriosclerosis. In current terminology, he badly needed a heart bypass operation, obviously unavailable at the time. Instead, he went to Europe with his wife, Alice, and met his brother Henry while seeking some form of a cure through the mineral springs of the Continent or galvanic shock treatments. None of these nostrums worked and James returned home to die on Friday, August 26, 1910. Sixty-eight years of age, James nonetheless died prematurely. Had Kant or Dewey or Whitehead or Santayana died at that age, much of their work would have been undone. The autopsy revealed "acute enlargement of the heart,"[22] Despite the voluminous work that James had published, he was frustrated that he had not finished his major treatise on philosophy. On July 26, 1910, exactly one month before his death, James stated that this manuscript would not be finished. "Call it 'a beginning of an introduction to philosophy.' Say that I hope by it to round out my system, which is now too much like an arch built on only one side."[23] The manuscript was published posthumously as *Some Problems of Philosophy* and presented sufficient insight to make us greatly lament that he never finished this intended major work.

The selections in this volume reveal classical American philosophy at its best. The selections from James are especially rich in wisdom and beauty of prose style. The reader is encouraged to proceed on to a full reading of James's *Works,* now excellently edited and easily available. James is an unusual philosophical writer in that he reverses the usual response of the reader. Most philosophy, at first reading, is impenetrable and pockmarked with the jargon and technical phrasing of the period. Slowly, the reader becomes acquainted with these prose shortcuts and then sufficiently sophisticated to make his or her way through the text. On reading James, however, the first response is one of elation at the apparent simplicity and elegance of the literary style. It is only after several readings that the philosophical depth and complexity begin to emerge, much to the delight of the reader, who, first seduced, is now educated.

I leave the reader with two short texts from the writings of William James. The first is as follows: "It is, in short, the re-instatement of the vague and the inarticulate to its proper place in our mental life which I am so anxious to press on the attention."[24] The quest is clear: avoid a life lived by formulas, by definitions, and seek instead the fringe, the novel, the unspoken, the secret and the hidden recesses of being, which speak only to those who know how to listen.

The second text was written in 1876 and is found in a brief letter to *The Nation,* entitled "The Teaching of Philosophy in Our Colleges." At that time, James wrote: "one can never deny that philosophic study means the habit of always seeing an alternative, of not taking the usual for granted, of making conventionalities fluid again, of imagining foreign states of mind."[25] This request of James is not easy to fulfill. Each of us has our bedrock. Each of us is frightened of new ideas, new perspectives, new values, and new beliefs. The opponent to a liberal education praises the encrusted, the habitual, and the socially acceptable. Yet human life has moved forward by taking chances. We have no guarantee that the alternatives to our present beliefs, habits, and values are better. They may be injurious. But, then, they may be enriching. How do we know what to do unless we try? Seek, then, an alternative and test it against the penalty and possibility of experience. Such is the philosophical message of William James.

## Notes

1. The life of William James has received unusually close attention. In addition to his *Letters* and the works by Allen Feinstein Myers, Perry and Simon cited in the "Suggestions for Further Reading," see F. O. Matthiessen, *The James Family* (New York: Alfred A. Knopf, 1947).
2. Cf. Leon Edel, *Henry James,* 5 vols. (New York: J.B. Lippincott Company, 1953–1972). Also see *Henry James—Letters,* 4 vols., Leon Edel, ed. (Cambridge, Mass.: Harvard University Press, 1974–1984), and Ignas K. Skrupskelis and Elizabeth M. Berkeley, eds., *William and Henry James: Selected Letters,* introduction by John J. McDermott (Charlottesville and London: University of Virginia Press, 1997).
3. Cf. *The Diary of Alice James,* ed. by Leon Edel (New York: Dodd, Mead and Company, 1964). Jean Strouse, *Alice James—A Biography* (Boston: Houghton-Mifflin & Company, 1980). Ruth Bernard Yeazell, ed. *The Death and Letters of Alice James* (Boston: Exact Change, 1981, 1997).
4. *The Works of William James—The Varieties of Religious Experience,* pp. 134–135.
5. "Diary" in *The Writings of William James,* ed. John J. McDermott (Chicago: The University of Chicago Press, 1977), p. 7.
6. Ibid., pp. 7–8.
7. For the relevant texts in the ongoing critique of James's thought, especially his pragmatism, see *Pragmatic Philosophy,* ed. Amelie Rorty (New York: Doubleday and Company, 1966).
8. "The Sentiment of Rationality," in *The Works of William James—The Will to Believe,* p. 73.
9. *The Works of William James—A Pluralistic Universe,* passim.
10. Ralph Barton Perry, *The Thought and Character of William James,* 2 vols. (Boston: Little, Brown and Company, 1935), p. 700.
11. *The Works of William James—Pragmatism,* p. 99.
12. *The Works of Williams James—The Will to Believe,* pp. 5–6.
13. *The Works of William James—The Meaning of Truth,* pp. 6–7.
14. *The Works of William James—Pragmatism,* p. 123.
15. Ibid., p. 94.
16. "The Sentiment of Rationality," in *The Works of William James—The Will to Believe,* pp. 61, 89.
17. *The Works of William James—Pragmatism,* p. 13.
18. When James published his shorter version of *The Principles of Psychology* under the title of *Psychology: Briefer Course,* he renamed this chapter "The Stream of Consciousness," a title that has become tremendously famous as it has been allied with the literary work of Marcel Proust, James Joyce, and many other writers of the twentieth century.
19. "On Some Omissions of Introspective Psychology," in *The Works of William James—Essays in Psychology,* pp. 142–167.
20. *The Works of William James—The Principles of Psychology,* pp. 194–195.
21. Ibid., p. 238. (Also included in the selections in this volume; see below, pp. 116–117.)
22. For the record of James's wife, Alice, in her diary for these last days of his life, see Gay Wilson Allen, *William James: A Biography* (New York: The Viking Press, 1967), pp. 490–493.
23. Ibid., p. 469.
24. *The Works of William James—Psychology: Briefer Course,* p. 150.
25. "The Teaching of Philosophy," *The Works of William James—Essays in Philosophy,* p. 4.

# The Types of Philosophic Thinking

As these lectures are meant to be public, and so few, I have assumed all very special problems to be excluded, and some topic of general interest required. Fortunately, our age seems to be growing philosophical again—still in the ashes live the wonted fires. Oxford, long the seed-bed, for the English world, of the idealism inspired by Kant and Hegel, has recently

From *The Works of William James—A Pluralistic Universe,* ed. Frederick Burkhardt (Cambridge, Mass.: Harvard University Press, 1977 [1909]), pp. 7–23.

become the nursery of a very different way of thinking. Even non-philosophers have begun to take an interest in a controversy over what is known as pluralism or humanism. It looks a little as if the ancient English empiricism, so long put out of fashion here by nobler sounding germanic formulas, might be re-pluming itself and getting ready for a stronger flight than ever. It looks as if foundations were being sounded and examined afresh.

Individuality outruns all classification, yet we insist on classifying everyone we meet under some general head. As these heads usually suggest prejudicial associations to some hearer or other, the life of philosophy largely consists of resentments at the classing, and complaints of being misunderstood. But there are signs of clearing up, and, on the whole, less acrimony in discussion, for which both Oxford and Harvard are partly to be thanked. As I look back into the sixties, Mill, Bain and Hamilton were the only official philosophers in Britain. Spencer, Martineau and Hodgson were just beginning. In France, the pupils of Cousin were delving into history only, and Renouvier alone had an original system. In Germany, the hegelian impetus had spent itself, and, apart from historical scholarship, nothing but the materialistic controversy remained, with such men as Büchner and Ulrici as its champions. Lotze and Fechner were the sole original thinkers, and Fechner was not a professional philosopher at all.

The general impression made was of crude issues and oppositions, of small subtlety and of a widely spread ignorance. Amateurishness was rampant. Samuel Bailey's *Letters on the philosophy of the human mind,* published in 1855, are one of the ablest expressions of english associationism, and a book of real power. Yet hear how he writes of Kant: "No one, after reading the extracts, etc., can be surprised to hear of a declaration made by men of eminent abilities, that, after years of study, they had not succeeded in gathering one clear idea from the speculations of Kant. I should have been almost surprised if they had. In or about 1818, Lord Grenville, when visiting the lakes of England, observed to Professor Wil-

son, that after five years' study of Kant's philosophy, he had not gathered from it one clear idea. Wilberforce, about the same time, made the same confession to another friend of my own. 'I am endeavouring,' exclaims Sir James Mackintosh, in the irritation evidently of baffled efforts, 'to understand this accursed German Philosophy.' "

What Oxford thinker would dare to print such naif and provincial-sounding citations of authority to-day?

The torch of learning passes from land to land as the spirit bloweth the flame. The deepening of philosophic consciousness came to us english folk from Germany, as it will probably pass back ere long. Ferrier, J. H. Stirling, and, most of all, T. H. Green are to be thanked. If asked to tell in broad strokes what the main doctrinal change has been, I should call it a change from the crudity of the older english thinking, its ultra-simplicity of mind, both when it was religious and when it was antireligious, towards a rationalism derived in the first instance from Germany, but relieved from german technicality and shrillness, and content to suggest, and to remain vague, and to be, in the English fashion, devout.

By the time T. H. Green began at Oxford, the generation seemed to feel as if it had fed on the chopped straw of psychology and of associationism long enough, and as if a little vastness, even tho it went with vagueness, as of some moist wind from far away, reminding us of our pre-natal sublimity, would be welcome.

Green's great point of attack was the disconnectedness of the reigning English sensationalism. *Relating* was the great intellectual activity for him, and the key to this relating was believed by him to lodge itself at last in what most of you know as Kant's unity of apperception, transformed into a living spirit of the world.

Hence a monism of a devout kind. In some way we must be fallen angels, one with intelligence as such; and a great disdain for empiricism of the sensationalist sort has always characterized this school of thought, which, on the whole, has reigned supreme at Oxford and in the Scottish universities until the present day.

But now there are signs of its giving way to a wave of revised empiricism. I confess that I should be glad to see this latest wave prevail; so—the sooner I am frank about it the better—I hope to have my voice counted in its favor as one of the results of this lecture-course.

What do the terms empiricism and rationalism mean? Reduced to their most pregnant difference, *empiricism means the habit of explaining wholes by parts, and rationalism means the habit of explaining parts by wholes.* Rationalism thus preserves affinities with monism, since wholeness goes with union, while empiricism inclines to pluralistic views. No philosophy can ever be anything but a summary sketch, a picture of the world in abridgment, a foreshortened bird's-eye view of the perspective of events. And the first thing to notice is this, that the only material we have at our disposal for making a picture of the whole world is supplied by the various portions of that world of which we have already had experience. We can invent no new forms of conception, applicable to the whole exclusively, and not suggested originally by the parts. All philosophers, accordingly, have conceived of the whole world after the analogy of some particular feature of it which has particularly captivated their attention. Thus, the theists take their cue from manufacture, the pantheists from growth. For one man, the world is like a thought or a grammatical sentence in which a thought is expressed. For such a philosopher, the whole must logically be prior to the parts; for letters would never have been invented without syllables to spell, or syllables without words to utter.

Another man, struck by the disconnectedness and mutual accidentality of so many of the world's details, takes the universe as a whole to have been such a disconnectedness originally, and supposes order to have been superinduced upon it in the second instance, possibly by attrition and the gradual wearing away by internal friction of portions that originally interfered.

Another will conceive the order as only a statistical appearance, and the universe will be for him like a vast grab-bag with black and white balls in it, of which we guess the quantities only probably, by the frequency with which we experience their egress.

For another, again, there is no really inherent order, but it is we who project order into the world by selecting objects and tracing relations so as to gratify our intellectual interests. We *carve out* order by leaving the disorderly parts out; and the world is conceived thus after the analogy of a forest or a block of marble from which parks or statues may be produced by eliminating irrelevant trees or chips of stone.

Some thinkers follow suggestions from human life, and treat the universe as if it were essentially a place in which ideals are realized. Others are more struck by its lower features, and for them, brute necessities express its character better.

All follow one analogy or another; and all the analogies are with some one or other of the universe's subdivisions. Everyone is nevertheless prone to claim that his conclusions are the only logical ones, that they are necessities of universal reason, they being all the while, at bottom, accidents more or less of personal vision which had far better be avowed as such; for one man's vision may be much more valuable than another's, and our visions are usually not only our most interesting but our most respectable contributions to the world in which we play our part. What was reason given to men for, said some eighteenth-century writer, except to enable them to find reasons for what they want to think and do?—and I think the history of philosophy largely bears him out. "The aim of knowledge," says Hegel, "is to divest the objective world of its strangeness, and to make us more at home in it." Different men find their minds more at home in very different fragments of the world.

Let me make a few comments, here, on the curious antipathies which these partialities arouse. They are sovereignly unjust, for all the parties are human beings with the same essential interests, and no one of them is the wholly perverse demon which another often imagines him to be. Both are loyal to the world that bears them; neither wishes to spoil it; neither wishes to regard it as an insane incoherence; both want to keep it as a universe of some kind; and their differences are all secondary to this deep agreement. They may be only propensities to emphasize differently. Or one man may care for finality and security more than the other. Or their tastes in language may be different. One may like a universe that lends itself to lofty and exalted characterization. To another this may seem sentimental or rhetorical. One may wish for the right to use a clerical vocabulary, another a technical or professorial one. A certain old farmer of my acquaintance in America was called a rascal by one of his neighbors. He immediately smote the man, saying, "I won't stand none of your diminutive epithets." Empiricist minds, putting the parts before the whole, appear to rationalists, who start from the whole, and consequently enjoy magniloquent privileges, to use epithets offensively diminutive. But all such differences are minor matters which ought to be subordinated in view of the fact that, whether we be empiricists or rationalists, we are, ourselves, parts of the universe and share the same one deep concern in its destinies. We crave alike to feel more truly at home with it, and to contribute our mite to its amelioration. It would be pitiful if small aesthetic discords were to keep honest men asunder.

I shall myself have use for the diminutive epithets of empiricism. But if you look behind the words at the spirit, I am sure you will not find it matricidal. I am as good a son as any rationalist among you to our common mother.

What troubles me more than this misapprehension is the genuine abstruseness of many of the matters I shall be obliged to talk about, and the difficulty of making them intelligible at one hearing. But there are two pieces, 'zwei stücke,' as Kant would have said, in every philosophy—the final outlook, belief, or attitude to which it brings us, and the reasonings by which that attitude is reached and mediated. A philosophy, as James Ferrier used to tell us, must indeed be true, but that is the least of its requirements. One may be true without being a philosopher, true by guesswork or by revela-

tion. What distinguishes a philosopher's truth is that it is *reasoned*. Argument, not supposition, must have put it in his possession. Common men find themselves inheriting their beliefs, they know not how. They jump into them with both feet, and stand there. Philosophers must do more; they must first get reason's license for them; and to the professional philosophic mind the operation of procuring the license is usually a thing of much more pith and moment than any particular beliefs to which the license may give the rights of access. Suppose, for example, that a philosopher believes in what is called free-will. That a common man alongside of him should also share that belief, possessing it by a sort of inborn intuition, does not endear the man to the philosopher at all—he may even be ashamed to be associated with such a man. What interests the philosopher is the particular premises on which the free-will he believes in is established, the sense in which it is taken, the objections it eludes, the difficulties it takes account of, in short the whole form and temper and manner and technical apparatus that goes with the belief in question. A philosopher across the way who should use the same technical apparatus, making the same distinctions, etc., but drawing opposite conclusions and denying free-will entirely, would fascinate the first philosopher far more than would the naif co-believer. Their common technical interests would unite them more than their opposite conclusions separate them. Each would feel an essential consanguinity in the other, would think of him, write *at* him, care for his good opinion. The simple-minded believer in free-will would be disregarded by either. Neither as ally nor as opponent would his vote be counted.

In a measure this is doubtless as it should be, but like all professionalism it can go to abusive extremes. The end is after all more than the way, in most things human, and forms and methods may easily frustrate their own purpose. The abuse of technicality is seen in the infrequency with which, in philosophical literature, metaphysical questions are discussed directly and on their own merits.

Almost always they are handled as if through a heavy woolen curtain, the veil of previous philosophers' opinions. Alternatives are wrapped in proper names, as if it were indecent for a truth to go naked. The late Professor John Grote of Cambridge has some good remarks about this. "Thought," he says, "is not a professional matter—not something for so-called philosophers only or professed thinkers. The best philosopher is the man who can think most *simply*. . . . I wish that people would consider that thought—and philosophy is no more than good and methodical thought—is a matter *intimate* to them, a portion of their real selves . . . that they would *value* what they think, and be interested in it. . . . In my own opinion," he goes on, "there is something depressing in this weight of learning, with nothing that can come into one's mind, but one is told, Oh, that is the opinion of such and such a person long ago. . . . I can conceive nothing more noxious for students than to get into the habit of saying to themselves about their ordinary philosophical thought, 'Oh, somebody must have thought it all before.'" Yet this is the habit most encouraged at our seats of learning. You must tie your opinion to Aristotle's or Spinosa's; you must define it by its distance from Kant's; you must refute your rival's view by identifying it with Protagoras's. Thus does all spontaneity of thought, all freshness of conception, get destroyed. Everything you touch is shopworn. The over-technicality and consequent dreariness of the younger disciples at our american universities is appalling. It comes from too much following of german models and manners. Let me fervently express the hope that in this country you will hark back to the more humane english tradition. American students have to regain direct relations with our subject by painful individual effort in later life. Some of us have done so. Some of the younger ones, I fear, never will, so strong are the professional shop-habits already.

In a subject like philosophy it is really fatal to lose connexion with the open air of human nature, and to think in terms of shoptradition only. In Germany the forms are so profession-alized that anybody who has gained a teaching chair and written a book, however distorted and eccentric, has the legal right to figure forever in the history of the subject like a fly in amber. All later comers have the duty of quoting him and measuring their opinions with his opinion. Such are the rules of the professorial game—they think and write from each other and for each other and at each other exclusively. With this exclusion of the open air all true perspective gets lost, extremes and oddities count as much as sanities, and command the same attention; and if by chance anyone writes popularly and about results only, with his mind directly focussed on the subject, it is reckoned *oberflächliches zeug,* and *ganz unwissenschaftlich* [superficial stuff and entirely unscientific]. Professor Paulsen has recently written some feeling lines about this over-professionalism, from the reign of which in Germany his own writings, which sin by being 'literary,' have suffered loss of credit. Philosophy, he says, has long assumed in Germany the character of being an esoteric and occult science. There is a genuine fear of popularity. Simplicity of statement is deemed synonymous with hollowness and shallowness. He recalls an old professor saying to him once: "Yes, we philosophers, whenever we wish, can go so far that in a couple of sentences we can put ourselves where nobody can follow us." The professor said this with conscious pride, but he ought to have been ashamed of it. Great as technique is, results are greater. To teach philosophy so that the pupils' interest in technique exceeds that in results is surely a vicious aberration. It is bad form, not good form, in a discipline of such universal human interest. Moreover, technique for technique, doesn't David Hume's technique set, after all, the kind of pattern most difficult to follow? Isn't it the most admirable? The English mind, thank heaven, and the french mind, are still kept, by their aversion to crude technique and barbarism, closer to truth's natural probabilities. Their literatures show fewer obvious falsities and monstrosities than that of Germany. Think of the German literature of aesthetics, with the preposterousness of such an unaesthetic personage as Immanuel Kant enthroned in its centre! Think of German books on *religions-philosophie,* with the heart's battles translated into conceptual jargon and made dialectic. The most persistent setter of questions, feeler of objections, insister on satisfactions, is the religious life. Yet all its troubles can be treated with absurdly little technicality. The wonder is that, with their way of working philosophy, individual Germans should preserve any spontaneity of mind at all. That they still manifest freshness and originality in so eminent a degree, proves the indestructible richness of the German cerebral endowment.

Let me repeat once more that a man's vision is the great fact about him. Who cares for Carlyle's reasons, or Schopenhauer's, or Spencer's? A philosophy is the expression of a man's intimate character, and all definitions of the universe are but the deliberately adopted reactions of human characters upon it. In the recent book from which I quoted the words of Professor Paulsen, a book of successive chapters by various living German philosophers, we pass from one idiosyncratic personal atmosphere into another almost as if we were turning over a photograph album.

If we take the whole history of philosophy, the systems reduce themselves to a few main types which, under all the technical verbiage in which the ingenious intellect of man envelopes them, are just so many visions, modes of feeling the whole push, and seeing the whole drift of life, forced on one by one's total character and experience, and on the whole *preferred*—there is no other truthful word—as one's best working attitude. Cynical characters take one general attitude, sympathetic characters another. But no general attitude is possible towards the world as a whole, until the intellect has developed considerable generalizing power and learned to take pleasure in synthetic formulas. The thought of very primitive men has hardly any tincture of philosophy. Nature can have little unity for savages. It is a walpurgis-nacht procession, a checkered play of light and shadow, a medley of impish and elfish friendly and inimical powers. 'Close to nature' tho they live, they are anything but wordsworthians. If a bit of cosmic emotion ever thrills them, it is likely to be at midnight, when the camp smoke rises straight to the wicked full moon in the zenith, and the forest is all whispering with witchery and danger. The eeriness of the world, the mischief and the manyness, the littleness of the forces, the magical surprises, the unaccountability of every agent, these surely are the characters most impressive at that stage of culture, these communicate the thrills of curiosity and the earliest intellectual stirrings. Tempests and conflagrations, pestilences and earthquakes, reveal supramundane powers, and instigate religious terror rather than philosophy—Nature, more demonic than divine, is above all things *multifarious.* So many creatures that feed or threaten, that help or crush, so many beings to hate or love, to understand or start at—which is on top and which subordinate? Who can tell? They are co-ordinate, rather, and to adapt ourselves to them singly, to 'square' the dangerous powers and keep the others friendly, regardless of consistency or unity, is the chief problem. The symbol of nature at this stage, as Paulsen well says, is the sphinx, under whose nourishing breasts the tearing claws are visible.

But in due course of time the intellect awoke, with its passion for generalizing, simplifying and subordinating, and then began those divergences of conception which all later experience seems rather to have deepened than to have effaced, because objective nature has contributed to both sides impartially, and has let the thinkers emphasize different parts of her, and pile up opposite imaginary supplements.

Perhaps the most interesting opposition is that which results from the clash between what I lately called the sympathetic and the cynical temper. Materialistic and spiritualistic philosophies are the rival types that result: the former defining the world so as to leave man's soul upon it as a sort of outside passenger or alien, while the latter insists that the intimate and human must surround and underlie the brutal. This latter is the spiritual way of thinking.

Now there are two very distinct types or stages in spiritualistic philosophy, and my next purpose in this lecture is to make their contrast evident. Both types attain the sought-for intimacy of view, but the one attains it somewhat less successfully than the other.

The generic term spiritualism, which I began by using merely as the opposite of materialism, thus subdivides into two species, the more intimate one of which is monistic and the less intimate dualistic. The dualistic species is the *theism* that reached its elaboration in the scholastic philosophy, while the monistic species is the *pantheism* spoken of sometimes simply as idealism, and sometimes as 'post-Kantian' or 'absolute' idealism. Dualistic theism is professed as firmly as ever at all catholic seats of learning, whereas it has of late years tended to disappear at our British and American universities, and to be replaced by a monistic pantheism more or less open or disguised. I have an impression that ever since T. H. Green's time absolute idealism has been decidedly in the ascendent at Oxford. It is in the ascendent at my own university of Harvard.

Absolute idealism attains, I said, to the more intimate point of view; but the statement needs some explanation. So far as theism represents the world as God's world, and God as what Matthew Arnold called a magnified non-natural man, it would seem as if the inner quality of the world remained human, and as if our relations with it might be intimate enough—for what is best in ourselves appears then also outside of ourselves, and we and the universe are of the same spiritual species. So far, so good, then; and one might consequently ask, What more of intimacy do you require? To which the answer is that to be like a thing is not as intimate a relation as to be substantially fused into it, to form one continuous soul and body with it; and that pantheistic idealism, making us entitatively one with God, attains this higher reach of intimacy.

The theistic conception, picturing God and his creation as entities distinct from each other, still leaves the human subject outside of the deepest reality in the universe. God is from eternity complete, it says, and sufficient unto himself; he throws off the world by a free act and as an extraneous substance, and he throws off man as a third substance, extraneous to both the world and himself. Between them, God says 'one,' the world says 'two,' and man says 'three'—that is the orthodox theistic view. And orthodox theism has been so jealous of God's glory that it has taken pains to exaggerate everything in the notion of him that could make for isolation and separateness. Page upon page in scholastic books go to prove that God is in no sense implicated by his creative act, or involved in his creation. That his relation to the creatures he has made should make any difference to him, carry any consequence, or qualify his being, is repudiated as a pantheistic slur upon his self-sufficingness. I said a moment ago that theism treats us and God as of the same species, but from the orthodox point of view that was a slip of language. God and his creatures are *toto genere* distinct in the scholastic theology, they have absolutely *nothing* in common; nay, it degrades God to attribute to him any generic nature whatever; he can be classed with nothing. There is a sense, then, in which philosophic theism makes us outsiders and keeps us foreigners in relation to God, in which, at any rate, his connexion with us appears as unilateral and not reciprocal. His action can affect us, but he can never be affected by our reaction. Our relation, in short, is not a strictly social relation. Of course in common men's religion the relation is believed to be social, but that is only one of the many differences between religion and theology.

This essential dualism of the theistic view has all sorts of collateral consequences. Man being an outsider and a mere subject to God, not his intimate partner, a character of externality invades the field. God is not heart of our heart and reason of our reason, but our magistrate, rather; and mechanically to obey his commands, however strange they may be, remains our only moral duty. Conceptions of criminal law have in fact played a great part in defining our relations with him. Our relations with speculative truth show the same externality. One of our duties is to know truth, and rationalist thinkers have always assumed it to be our sovereign duty. But in scholastic theism we find truth already instituted and established without our help, complete apart from our knowing; and the most we can do is to acknowledge it passively and adhere to it, altho such adhesion as ours can make no jot of difference to what is adhered to. The situation here again is radically dualistic. It is not as if the world came to know itself, or God came to know himself, partly through us, as pantheistic idealists have maintained, but truth exists *per se* and absolutely, by God's grace and decree, no matter who of us knows it or is ignorant, and it would continue to exist unaltered, even tho we finite knowers were all annihilated.

It has to be confessed that this dualism and lack of intimacy has always operated as a drag and handicap on Christian thought. Orthodox theology has had to wage a steady fight within the schools against the various forms of pantheistic heresy which the mystical experiences of religious persons, on the one hand, and the formal or aesthetic superiorities of monism to dualism, on the other, kept producing. God as intimate soul and reason of the universe has always seemed to some people a more worthy conception than God as external creator. So conceived, he appeared to unify the world more perfectly, he made it less finite and mechanical, and in comparison with such a God an external creator seemed more like the product of a childish fancy. I have been told by Hindoos that the great obstacle to the spread of Christianity in their country is the puerility of our dogma of creation. It has not sweep and infinity enough to meet the requirements of even the illiterate natives of India.

Assuredly most members of this audience are ready to side with Hinduism in this matter. Those of us who are sexagenarians have witnessed in our own persons one of those gradual mutations of intellectual climate, due to innumerable influences, that make the thought of a past generation seem as foreign to its successor as if it were the expression of a different race of men. The theological machinery that spoke so livingly to our ancestors, with its finite age of the world, its creation out of noth-

ing, its juridical morality and eschatology, its relish for rewards and punishments, its treatment of God as an external contriver, an 'intelligent and moral governor,' sounds as odd to most of us as if it were some outlandish savage religion. The vaster vistas which scientific evolutionism has opened, and the rising tide of social democratic ideals, have changed the type of our imagination, and the older monarchical theism is obsolete or obsolescent. The place of the divine in the world must be more organic and intimate. An external creator and his institutions may still be verbally confessed at church in formulas that linger by their mere inertia, but the life is out of them, we avoid dwelling on them, the sincere heart of us is elsewhere.

I shall leave cynical materialism entirely out of our discussion as not calling for treatment before this present audience, and I shall ignore old-fashioned dualistic theism for the same reason. Our contemporary mind having once for all grasped the possibility of a more intimate *weltanschauung,* the only opinions quite worthy of arresting our attention will fall within the general scope of what may roughly be called the pantheistic field of vision, the vision of God as the indwelling divine rather than the external creator, and of human life as part and parcel of that deep reality.

As we have found that spiritualism in general breaks into a more intimate and a less intimate species, so the more intimate species itself breaks into two subspecies, of which the one is more monistic, the other more pluralistic in form. I say in form, for our vocabulary gets unmanageable if we don't distinguish between form and substance here. The inner life of things must be substantially akin anyhow to the tenderer parts of man's nature in any spiritualistic philosophy. The word 'intimacy' probably covers the essential difference. Materialism holds the foreign in things to be more primary and lasting, it sends us to a lonely corner with our intimacy. The brutal aspects overlap and outwear; refinement has the feebler and more ephemeral hold on reality.

From a pragmatic point of view the difference between living against a background of foreignness and one of intimacy means the difference between a general habit of wariness and one of trust. One might call it a social difference, for after all, the common *socius* of us all is the great universe whose children we are. If materialistic, we must be suspicious of this socius, cautious, tense, on guard. If spiritualistic, we may give way, embrace, and keep no ultimate fear.

The contrast is rough enough, and can be cut across by all sorts of other divisions, drawn from other points of view than that of foreignness and intimacy. We have so many different businesses with nature that no one of them yields us an all-embracing clasp. The philosophic attempt to define nature so that no one's business is left out, so that no one lies outside the door saying "Where do *I* come in?" is sure in advance to fail. The most a philosophy can hope for is not to lock out any interest forever. No matter what doors it closes, it must leave other doors open for the interests which it neglects. I have begun by shutting ourselves up to intimacy and foreignness because that makes so generally interesting a contrast, and because it will conveniently introduce a farther contrast to which I wish this hour to lead.

The majority of men are sympathetic. Comparatively few are cynics because they like cynicism, and most of our existing materialists are such because they think the evidence of facts impels them, or because they find the idealists they are in contact with too private and tender-minded; so, rather than join their company, they fly to the opposite extreme. I therefore propose to you to disregard materialists altogether for the present, and to consider the sympathetic party alone.

It is normal, I say, to be sympathetic in the sense in which I use the term. Not to demand intimate relations with the universe, and not to wish them satisfactory, should be accounted signs of something wrong. Accordingly when minds of this type reach the philosophic level, and seek some unification of their vision, they find themselves compelled to correct that aboriginal appearance of things by which savages are not troubled. That sphinx-like presence, with its breasts and claws, that first bald multifariousness, is too discrepant an object for philosophic contemplation. The intimacy and the foreignness cannot be written down as simply coexisting. An order must be made; and in that order the higher side of things must dominate. The philosophy of the absolute agrees with the pluralistic philosophy which I am going to contrast with it in these lectures, in that both identify human substance with the divine substance. But whereas absolutism thinks that the said substance becomes fully divine only in the form of totality, and is not its real self in any form but the *all*-form, the pluralistic view which I prefer to adopt is willing to believe that there may ultimately never be an all-form at all, that the substance of reality may never get totally collected, that some of it may remain outside of the largest combination of it ever made, and that a distributive form of reality, the *each*-form, is logically as acceptable and empirically as probable as the all-form commonly acquiesced in as so obviously the self-evident thing. The contrast between these two forms of a reality which we will agree to suppose substantially spiritual is practically the topic of this course of lectures. You see now what I mean by pantheism's two subspecies. If we give to the monistic subspecies the name of philosophy of the absolute, we may give that of radical empiricism to its pluralistic rival, and it may be well to distinguish them occasionally later by these names.

As a convenient way of entering into the study of their differences, I may refer to a recent article by Professor Jacks of Manchester College. Professor Jacks, in some brilliant pages in the *Hibbert Journal* for last October, studies the relation between the universe and the philosopher who describes and defines it for us. You may assume two cases, he says. Either what the philosopher tells us is extraneous to the universe he is accounting for, an indifferent parasitic outgrowth, so to speak; or the fact of his philosophizing is itself one of the things taken account of in the philosophy, and self-included in the description. In the former case the philosopher means by the universe everything *except* what his own presence brings; in the latter case his philosophy is itself an intimate part of the universe, and may be a part momentous enough to give a different turn to what the other parts signify. It may be a supreme reaction of the universe upon itself by which it rises to self-comprehension. It may handle itself differently in consequence of this event.

Now both empiricism and absolutism bring the philosopher inside and make man intimate, but the one being pluralistic and the other monistic, they do so in differing ways that need much explanation. Let me then contrast the one with the other way of representing the status of the human thinker.

For monism the world is no collection, but one great all-inclusive fact outside of which is nothing—nothing is its only alternative. When the monism is idealistic, this all-enveloping fact is represented as an absolute mind that makes the partial facts by thinking them, just as we make objects in a dream by dreaming them, or personages in a story by imagining them. To *be,* on this scheme, is, on the part of a finite thing, to be an object for the absolute; and on the part of the absolute it is to be the thinker of that assemblage of objects. If we use the word 'content' here, we see that the absolute and the world have an identical content. The absolute is nothing but the knowledge of those objects; the objects are nothing but what the absolute knows. The world and the all-thinker thus compenetrate and soak each other up without residuum. They are but two names for the same identical material, considered now from the subjective, and now from the objective point of view—gedanke and gedachtes [thoughts and things], as we would say if we were Germans.

We philosophers naturally form part of the material, on the monistic scheme. The absolute makes us by thinking us, and if we ourselves are enlightened enough to be believers in the absolute, one may then say that our philosophizing is one of the ways in which the absolute is conscious of itself. This is the full pantheistic scheme, the *identitätsphilosophie* [philosophy of identity], the immanence of God in his creation, a conception sublime from its tremendous unity. And yet that unity is incomplete, as a closer examination will show.

The absolute and the world are one fact, I said, when materially considered. Our philosophy, for example, is not numerically distinct from the absolute's own knowledge of itself, not a duplicate and copy of it, it is part of that very knowledge, is numerically identical with as much of it as our thought covers. The absolute just *is* our philosophy, along with everything else that is known, in an act of knowing which (to use the words of my gifted absolutist colleague Royce) forms in its wholeness one luminously transparent conscious moment.

But one as we are in this material sense with the absolute substance, that being only the whole of us, and we only the parts of it, yet in a formal sense something like a pluralism breaks out. When we speak of the absolute we *take* the one universal known material collectively or integrally; when we speak of its objects, of our finite selves, etc., we *take* that same identical material distributively and separately. But what is the use of a thing's *being* only once if it can be *taken* twice over, and if being taken in different ways makes different things true of it? As the absolute takes me, for example, I appear *with* everything else in its field of perfect knowledge. As I take myself, I appear *without* most other things in my field of relative ignorance. And practical differences result from its knowledge and my ignorance. Ignorance breeds mistake, curiosity, misfortune, pain, for me; I suffer those consequences. The absolute knows of those things, of course, for it knows me and my suffering, but it doesn't itself suffer. It can't be ignorant, for simultaneous with its knowledge of each question goes its knowledge of each answer. It can't be patient, for it has to wait for nothing, having everything at once in its possession. It can't be surprised; it can't be guilty. No attribute connected with succession can be applied to it, for it is all at once and wholly what it is, "with the unity of a single instant," and succession is not of it but in it, for we are continually told that it is 'timeless.'

Things true of the world in its finite aspects, then, are not true of it in its infinite capacity. *Quâ* finite and plural its accounts of itself to itself are different from what its account to itself *quâ* infinite and one must be.

With this radical discrepancy between the absolute and the relative points of view, it seems to me that almost as great a bar to intimacy between the divine and the human breaks out in pantheism as that which we found in monarchical theism, and hoped that pantheism might not show. We humans are incurably rooted in the temporal point of view.

The eternal's ways are utterly unlike our ways. "Let us imitate the All" said the original prospectus of that admirable Chicago quarterly called the *Monist*. As if we could, either in thought or conduct! We are invincibly parts, let us talk as we will, and must always apprehend the absolute as if it were a foreign being. If what I mean by this is not wholly clear to you at this point, it ought to grow clearer as my lectures proceed.

# The Stream of Thought

We now begin our study of the mind from within. Most books start with sensations, as the simplest mental facts, and proceed synthetically, constructing each higher stage from those below it. But this is abandoning the empirical method of investigation. No one ever had a simple sensation by itself. Consciousness, from our natal day, is of a teeming multiplicity of objects and relations, and what we call simple sensations are results of discriminative attention, pushed often to a very high degree. It is astonishing what havoc is wrought in psychology by admitting at the outset apparently innocent suppositions, that nevertheless contain a flaw. The bad consequences develop themselves later on, and are irremediable, being woven through the whole texture of the work. The notion that sensations, being the simplest things, are the first things to take up in psychology is one of these suppositions. The only thing which psychology has a right to postulate at the outset is the fact of thinking itself, and that must first be taken up and analyzed. If sensations then prove to be amongst the elements of the thinking, we shall be no worse off as respects them than if we had taken them for granted at the start.

*The first fact for us, then, as psychologists, is that thinking of some sort goes on.* I use the word thinking . . . for every form of consciousness indiscriminately. If we could say in English 'it thinks,' as we say 'it rains,' or 'it blows,' we should be stating the fact most simply and with the minimum of assumption. As we cannot, we must simply say that *thought goes on.*

## Five Characters in Thought

How does it go on? We notice immediately five important characters in the process, of which it shall be the duty of the present chapter to treat in a general way:

1) Every thought tends to be part of a personal consciousness.
2) Within each personal consciousness thought is always changing.
3) Within each personal consciousness thought is sensibly continuous.
4) It always appears to deal with objects independent of itself.

From *The Works of William James—The Principles of Psychology,* 3 vols., ed., Frederick Burkhardt, (Cambridge, Mass.: Harvard University Press, 1981 [1890]), pp. 219–240, 262–278.

5) It is interested in some parts of these objects to the exclusion of others, and welcomes or rejects—*chooses* from among them, in a word—all the while.

In considering these five points successively, we shall have to plunge *in medias res* as regards our vocabulary, and use psychological terms which can only be adequately defined in later chapters of the book. But everyone knows what the terms mean in a rough way; and it is only in a rough way that we are now to take them. This chapter is like a painter's first charcoal sketch upon his canvas, in which no niceties appear.

### 1)    Thought tends to Personal Form

When I say *every thought is part of a personal consciousness,* 'personal consciousness' is one of the terms in question. Its meaning we know so long as no one asks us to define it, but to give an accurate account of it is the most difficult of philosophic tasks. This task we must confront in the next chapter; here a preliminary word will suffice.

In this room—this lecture-room, say—there are a multitude of thoughts, yours and mine, some of which cohere mutually, and some not. They are as little each-for-itself and reciprocally independent as they are all-belonging-together. They are neither: no one of them is separate, but each belongs with certain others and with none beside. My thought belongs with my other thoughts, and your thought with your other thoughts. Whether anywhere in the room there be a mere thought, which is nobody's thought, we have no means of ascertaining, for we have no experience of its like. The only states of consciousness that we naturally deal with are found in personal consciousnesses, minds, selves, concrete particular I's and you's.

Each of these minds keeps its own thoughts to itself. There is no giving or bartering between them. No thought even comes into direct *sight* of a thought in another personal consciousness than its own. Absolute insulation, irreducible pluralism, is the law. It seems as if the elementary psychic fact were not

*thought* or *this thought* or *that thought,* but *my thought,* every thought being *owned.* Neither contemporaneity, nor proximity in space, nor similarity of quality and content are able to fuse thoughts together which are sundered by this barrier of belonging to different personal minds. The breaches between such thoughts are the most absolute breaches in nature. Everyone will recognize this to be true, so long as the existence of *something* corresponding to the term 'personal mind' is all that is insisted on, without any particular view of its nature being implied. On these terms the personal self rather than the thought might be treated as the immediate datum in psychology. The universal conscious fact is not 'feelings and thoughts exist,' but 'I think' and 'I feel.' No psychology, at any rate, can question the *existence* of personal selves. The worst a psychology can do is so to interpret the nature of these selves as to rob them of their worth. A French writer, speaking of our ideas, says somewhere in a fit of anti-spiritualistic excitement that, misled by certain peculiarities which they display, we 'end by personifying' the procession which they make,—such personification being regarded by him as a great philosophic blunder on our part. It could only be a blunder if the notion of personality meant something essentially different from anything to be found in the mental procession. But if that procession be itself the very 'original' of the notion of personality, to personify it cannot possibly be wrong. It is already personified. There are no marks of personality to be gathered *aliunde,* and then found lacking in the train of thought. It has them all already; so that to whatever farther analysis we may subject that form of personal selfhood under which thoughts appear, it is, and must remain, true that the thoughts which psychology studies do continually tend to appear as parts of personal selves.

I say 'tend to appear' rather than 'appear' on account of those facts of sub-conscious personality, automatic writing, etc., of which we studied a few in the last chapter. The buried feelings and thoughts proved now to exist in hysterical anæsthetics, in recipients of post-hypnotic suggestion, etc., themselves are parts of *secondary personal selves*. These selves are for the most part very stupid and contracted, and are cut off at ordinary times from communication with the regular and normal self of the individual; but still they form conscious unities, have continuous memories, speak, write, invent distinct names for themselves, or adopt names that are suggested; and, in short, are entirely worthy of that title of secondary personalities which is now commonly given them. According to M. Janet these secondary personalities are always abnormal, and result from the splitting of what ought to be a single complete self into two parts, of which one lurks in the background whilst the other appears on the surface as the only self the man or woman has. For our present purpose it is unimportant whether this account of the origin of secondary selves is applicable to all possible cases of them or not, for it certainly is true of a large number of them. Now although the *size* of a secondary self thus formed will depend on the number of thoughts that are thus split-off from the main consciousness, the *form* of it tends to personality, and the later thoughts pertaining to it remember the earlier ones and adopt them as their own. M. Janet caught the actual moment of inspissation (so to speak) of one of these secondary personalities in his anæsthetic somnambulist Lucie. He found that when this young woman's attention was absorbed in conversation with a third party, her anæsthetic hand would write simple answers to questions whispered to her by himself. "Do you hear?" he asked. *"No,"* was the unconsciously written reply. "But to answer you must hear." *"Yes, quite so."* "Then how do you manage?" *"I don't know."* "There must be someone who hears me." *"Yes."* "Who?" *"Someone other than Lucie."* "Ah! another person. Shall we give her a name?" *"No."* "Yes, it will be more convenient." *"Well, Adrienne, then."* "Once baptized, the subconscious personage," M. Janet continues, "grows more definitely outlined and displays better her psychological characters. In particular she shows us that she is conscious of the feelings excluded from the consciousness of the primary or normal personage. She it is who tells us that I am pinching the arm or touching the little finger in which Lucie for so long has had no tactile sensations."

In other cases the adoption of the name by the secondary self is more spontaneous. I have seen a number of incipient automatic writers and mediums as yet imperfectly 'developed,' who immediately and of their own accord write and speak in the name of departed spirits. These may be public characters, as Mozart, Faraday, or real persons formerly known to the subject, or altogether imaginary beings. Without prejudicing the question of real 'spirit-control' in the more developed sorts of trance-utterance, I incline to think that these (often deplorably unintelligent) rudimentary utterances are the work of an inferior fraction of the subject's own natural mind, set free from control by the rest, and working after a set pattern fixed by the prejudices of the social environment. In a spiritualistic community we get optimistic messages, whilst in an ignorant Catholic village the secondary personage calls itself by the name of a demon, and proffers blasphemies and obscenities, instead of telling us how happy it is in the summer-land.

Beneath these tracts of thought, which, however rudimentary, are still organized selves with a memory, habits, and sense of their own identity, M. Janet thinks that the facts of catalepsy in hysteric patients drive us to suppose that there are thoughts quite unorganized and impersonal. A patient in cataleptic trance (which can be produced artificially in certain hypnotized subjects) is without memory on waking, and seems insensible and unconscious as long as the cataleptic condition lasts. If, however, one raises the arm of such a subject it stays in that position, and the whole body can thus be moulded like wax under the hands of the operator, retaining for a considerable time whatever attitude he communicates to it. In hysterics whose arm, for example, is anæsthetic, the same thing may happen. The anæsthetic arm may remain passively in positions which it is made to assume; or if the hand be taken and made to hold a pencil and trace a certain letter, it will continue tracing that letter indefinitely on the paper. These acts, until recently, were supposed to be accompanied by no consciousness at all: they were physiological reflexes. M. Janet considers with much more plausibility that feeling escorts them. The feeling is probably merely that of the position or movement of the limb, and it produces no more than its natural effects when it discharges into the motor centres which keep the position maintained, or the movement incessantly renewed. Such thoughts as these, says M. Janet, "are known by *no one,* for disaggregated sensations reduced to a state of mental dust are not synthetized in any personality." He admits, however, that these very same unutterably stupid thoughts tend to develop memory,—the cataleptic ere long moves her arm at a bare hint; so that they form no important exception to the law that all thought tends to assume the form of personal consciousness.

## 2)   Thought is in Constant Change

I do not mean necessarily that no one state of mind has any duration—even if true, that would be hard to establish. The change which I have more particularly in view is that which takes place in sensible intervals of time; and the result on which I wish to lay stress is this, that *no state once gone can recur and be identical with what it was before.* Let us begin with Mr. Shadworth Hodgson's description:

> "I go straight to the facts, without saying I go to perception, or sensation, or thought, or any special mode at all. What I find, when I look at my consciousness at all, is, that what I cannot divest myself of, or not have in consciousness, if I have any consciousness at all, is a sequence of different feelings. I may shut my eyes and keep perfectly still, and try not to contribute anything of my own will; but whether I think, or do not think, whether I perceive external things or not, I always have a succession of different feelings. Anything else that I may have also, of a more special character, comes in as parts of this succession. Not to have the suc-

> cession of different feelings is not to be conscious at all. . . . The chain of consciousness is a sequence of *differents.*"

Such a description as this can awaken no possible protest from anyone. We all recognize as different great classes of our conscious states. Now we are seeing, now hearing; now reasoning, now willing; now recollecting, now expecting; now loving, now hating; and in a hundred other ways we know our minds to be alternately engaged. But all these are complex states. The aim of science is always to reduce complexity to simplicity; and in psychological science we have the celebrated 'theory of *ideas*' which, admitting the great difference among each other of what may be called concrete conditions of mind, seeks to show how this is all the resultant effect of variations in the *combination* of certain simple elements of consciousness that always remain the same. These mental atoms or molecules are what Locke called 'simple ideas.' Some of Locke's successors made out that the only simple ideas were the sensations strictly so called. Which ideas the simple ones may be does not, however, now concern us. It is enough that certain philosophers have thought they could see under the dissolving-view-appearance of the mind elementary facts of *any* sort that remained unchanged amid the flow.

And the view of these philosophers has been called little into question, for our common experience seems at first sight to corroborate it entirely. Are not the sensations we get from the same object, for example, always the same? Does not the same piano-key, struck with the same force, make us hear in the same way? Does not the same grass give us the same feeling of green, the same sky the same feeling of blue, and do we not get the same olfactory sensation no matter how many times we put our nose to the same flask of cologne? It seems a piece of metaphysical sophistry to suggest that we do not; and yet a close attention to the matter shows that *there is no proof that the same bodily sensation is ever got by us twice.*

*What is got twice is the same* OBJECT. We hear the same *note* over and over again; we see the same *quality* of green, or smell the same objective perfume, or experience the same *species* of pain. The realities, concrete and abstract, physical and ideal, whose permanent existence we believe in, seem to be constantly coming up again before our thought, and lead us, in our carelessness, to suppose that our 'ideas' of them are the same ideas. When we come, some time later, to the chapter on Perception, we shall see how inveterate is our habit of not attending to sensations as subjective facts, but of simply using them as stepping-stones to pass over to the recognition of the realities whose presence they reveal. The grass out of the window now looks to me of the same green in the sun as in the shade, and yet a painter would have to paint one part of it dark brown, another part bright yellow, to give its real sensational effect. We take no heed, as a rule, of the different way in which the same things look and sound and smell at different distances and under different circumstances. The sameness of the *things* is what we are concerned to ascertain; and any sensations that assure us of that will probably be considered in a rough way to be the same with each other. This is what makes off-hand testimony about the subjective identity of different sensations well-nigh worthless as a proof of the fact. The entire history of Sensation is a commentary on our inability to tell whether two sensations received apart are exactly alike. What appeals to our attention far more than the absolute quality or quantity of a given sensation is its *ratio* to whatever other sensations we may have at the same time. When everything is dark a somewhat less dark sensation makes us see an object white. Helmholtz calculates that the white marble painted in a picture representing an architectural view by moonlight is, when seen by daylight, from ten to twenty thousand times brighter than the real moonlit marble would be.

Such a difference as this could never have been *sensibly* learned; it had to be inferred from a series of indirect considerations. There are facts which make us believe that our sensibility is altering all the time, so that the same object cannot easily give us the same sensa-

tion over again. The eye's sensibility to light is at its maximum when the eye is first exposed, and blunts itself with surprising rapidity. A long night's sleep will make it see things twice as brightly on wakening, as simple rest by closure will make it see them later in the day. We feel things differently according as we are sleepy or awake, hungry or full, fresh or tired; differently at night and in the morning, differently in summer and in winter; and above all things differently in childhood, manhood, and old age. Yet we never doubt that our feelings reveal the same world, with the same sensible qualities and the same sensible things occupying it. The difference of the sensibility is shown best by the difference of our emotion about the things from one age to another, or when we are in different organic moods. What was bright and exciting becomes weary, flat, and unprofitable. The bird's song is tedious, the breeze is mournful, the sky is sad.

To these indirect presumptions that our sensations, following the mutations of our capacity for feeling, are always undergoing an essential change, must be added another presumption, based on what must happen in the brain. Every sensation corresponds to some cerebral action. For an identical sensation to recur it would have to occur the second time *in an unmodified brain*. But as this, strictly speaking, is a physiological impossibility, so is an unmodified feeling an impossibility; for to every brain-modification, however small, must correspond a change of equal amount in the feeling which the brain subserves.

All this would be true if even sensations came to us pure and single and not combined into 'things.' Even then we should have to confess that, however we might in ordinary conversation speak of getting the same sensation again, we never in strict theoretic accuracy could do so; and that whatever was true of the river of life, of the river of elementary feeling, it would certainly be true to say, like Heraclitus, that we never descend twice into the same stream.

But if the assumption of 'simple ideas of sensation' recurring in immutable shape is so easily shown to be baseless, how much more baseless is the assumption of immutability in the larger masses of our thought!

For there it is obvious and palpable that our state of mind is never precisely the same. Every thought we have of a given fact is, strictly speaking, unique, and only bears a resemblance of kind with our other thoughts of the same fact. When the identical fact recurs, we *must* think of it in a fresh manner, see it under a somewhat different angle, apprehend it in different relations from those in which it last appeared. And the thought by which we cognize it is the thought of it-in-those-relations, a thought suffused with the consciousness of all that dim context. Often we are ourselves struck at the strange differences in our successive views of the same thing. We wonder how we ever could have opined as we did last month about a certain matter. We have outgrown the possibility of that state of mind, we know not how. From one year to another we see things in new lights. What was unreal has grown real, and what was exciting is insipid. The friends we used to care the world for are shrunken to shadows; the women, once so divine, the stars, the woods, and the waters, how now so dull and common! the young girls that brought an aura of infinity, at present hardly distinguishable existences; the pictures so empty; and as for the books, what *was* there to find so mysteriously significant in Goethe, or in John Mill so full of weight? Instead of all this, more zestful than ever is the work, the work; and fuller and deeper the import of common duties and of common goods.

But what here strikes us so forcibly on the flagrant scale exists on every scale, down to the imperceptible transition from one hour's outlook to that of the next. Experience is remoulding us every moment, and our mental reaction on every given thing is really a resultant of our experience of the whole world up to that date. The analogies of brain-physiology must again be appealed to to corroborate our view.

Our earlier chapters have taught us to believe that, whilst we think, our brain changes, and that, like the aurora borealis, its whole internal equilibrium shifts with every pulse of change. The precise nature of the shifting at a given moment is a product of many factors. The accidental state of local nutrition or blood-supply may be among them. But just as one of them certainly is the influence of outward objects on the sense-organs during the moment, so is another certainly the very special susceptibility in which the organ has been left at that moment by all it has gone through in the past. Every brain-state is partly determined by the nature of this entire past succession. Alter the latter in any part, and the brain-state must be somewhat different. Each present brain-state is a record in which the eye of Omniscience might read all the foregone history of its owner. It is out of the question, then, that any total brain-state should identically recur. Something like it may recur; but to suppose *it* to recur would be equivalent to the absurd admission that all the states that had intervened between its two appearances had been pure nonentities, and that the organ after their passage was exactly as it was before. And (to consider shorter periods) just as, in the senses, an impression feels very differently according to what has preceded it; as one color succeeding another is modified by the contrast, silence sounds delicious after noise, and a note, when the scale is sung up, sounds unlike itself when the scale is sung down; as the presence of certain lines in a figure changes the apparent form of the other lines, and as in music the whole aesthetic effect comes from the manner in which one set of sounds alters our feeling of another; so, in thought, we must admit that those portions of the brain that have just been maximally excited retain a kind of soreness which is a condition of our present consciousness, a codeterminant of how and what we now shall feel.

Ever some tracts are waning in tension, some waxing, whilst others actively discharge. The states of tension have as positive an influence as any in determining the total condition, and in deciding what the *psychosis* shall be. All we know of submaximal nerve-irritations, and of the summation of apparently ineffective stimuli, tends to show that *no* changes in the brain are physiologically ineffective, and that presumably none are bare of psychological result. But as the brain-tension shifts from one relative state of equilibrium to another, like the gyrations of a kaleidoscope, now rapid and now slow, is it likely that its faithful psychic concomitant is heavier-footed than itself, and that it cannot match each one of the organ's irradiations by a shifting inward iridescence of its own? But if it can do this, its inward iridescences must be infinite, for the brain-redistributions are in infinite variety. If so coarse a thing as a telephone-plate can be made to thrill for years and never reduplicate its inward condition, how much more must this be the case with the infinitely delicate brain?

I am sure that this concrete and total manner of regarding the mind's changes is the only true manner, difficult as it may be to carry it out in detail. If anything seems obscure about it, it will grow clearer as we advance. Meanwhile, if it be true, it is certainly also true that no two 'ideas' are ever exactly the same, which is the proposition we started to prove. The proposition is more important theoretically than it at first sight seems. For it makes it already impossible for us to follow obediently in the footprints of either the Lockian or the Herbartian school, schools which have had almost unlimited influence in Germany and among ourselves. No doubt it is often *convenient* to formulate the mental facts in an atomistic sort of way, and to treat the higher states of consciousness as if they were all built out of unchanging simple ideas. It is convenient often to treat curves as if they were composed of small straight lines, and electricity and nerve-force as if they were fluids. But in the one case as in the other we must never forget that we are talking symbolically, and that there is nothing in nature to answer to our words. *A permanently existing 'idea' or 'Vorstellung' which makes its appearance before the footlights of consciousness at periodical intervals, is as mythological an entity as the Jack of Spades.*

What makes it convenient to use the mythological formulas is the whole organiza-

tion of speech, which, as was remarked a while ago, was not made by psychologists, but by men who were as a rule only interested in the facts their mental states revealed. They only spoke of their states as *ideas of this or of that thing.* What wonder, then, that the thought is most easily conceived under the law of the thing whose name it bears! If the thing is composed of parts, then we suppose that the thought of the thing must be composed of the thoughts of the parts. If one part of the thing have appeared in the same thing or in other things on former occasions, why then we must be having even now the very same 'idea' of that part which was there on those occasions. If the thing is simple, its thought is simple. If it is multitudinous, it must require a multitude of thoughts to think it. If a succession, only a succession of thoughts can know it. If permanent, its thought is permanent. And so on *ad libitum.* What after all is so natural as to assume that one object, called by one name, should be known by one affection of the mind? But, if language must thus influence us, the agglutinative languages, and even Greek and Latin with their declensions, would be the better guides. Names did not appear in them inalterable, but changed their shape to suit the context in which they lay. It must have been easier then than now to conceive of the same object as being thought of at different times in non-identical conscious states.

This, too, will grow clearer as we proceed. Meanwhile a necessary consequence of the belief in permanent self-identical psychic facts that absent themselves and recur periodically is the Humian doctrine that our thought is composed of separate independent parts and is not a sensibly continuous stream. That this doctrine entirely misrepresents the natural appearances is what I next shall try to show.

### 3) Within Each Personal Consciousness, Thought is Sensibly Continuous

I can only define 'continuous' as that which is without breach, crack, or division. I have already said that the breach from one mind to another is perhaps the greatest breach in nature. The only breaches that can well be conceived to occur within the limits of a single mind would either be *interruptions, time*-gaps during which the consciousness went out altogether to come into existence again at a later moment; or they would be breaks in the *quality,* or content, of the thought, so abrupt that the segment that followed had no connection whatever with the one that went before. The proposition that within each personal consciousness thought feels continuous means two things:

1. That even where there is a time-gap the consciousness after it feels as if it belonged together with the consciousness before it, as another part of the same self;
2. That the changes from one moment to another in the quality of the consciousness are never absolutely abrupt.

The case of the time-gaps, as the simplest, shall be taken first. And first of all, a word about time-gaps of which the consciousness may not itself be aware.

. . . we saw that such time-gaps existed, and that they might be more numerous than is usually supposed. If the consciousness is not aware of them, it cannot feel them as interruptions. In the unconsciousness produced by nitrous oxide and other anæsthetics, in that of epilepsy and fainting, the broken edges of the sentient life may meet and merge over the gap, much as the feelings of space of the opposite margins of the 'blind spot' meet and merge over that objective interruption to the sensitiveness of the eye. Such consciousness as this, whatever it be for the onlooking psychologist, is for itself unbroken. It *feels* unbroken; a waking day of it is sensibly a unit as long as that day lasts, in the sense in which the hours themselves are units, as having all their parts next each other, with no intrusive alien substance between. To expect the consciousness to feel the interruptions of its objective continuity as gaps, would be like expecting the eye to feel a gap of silence because it does not hear, or the ear to feel a gap of darkness because it does not see. So much for the gaps that are unfelt.

With the felt gaps the case is different. On waking from sleep, we usually know that we have been unconscious, and we often have an accurate judgment of how long. The judgment here is certainly an inference from sensible signs, and its ease is due to long practice in the particular field. The result of it, however, is that the consciousness is, *for itself,* not what it was in the former case, but interrupted and discontinuous, in the mere time-sense of the words. But in the other sense of continuity, the sense of the parts being inwardly connected and belonging together, because they are parts of a common whole, the consciousness remains sensibly continuous and one. What now is the common whole? The natural name for it is *myself, I,* or *me.*

When Paul and Peter wake up in the same bed, and recognize that they have been asleep, each one of them mentally reaches back and makes connection with but *one* of the two streams of thought which were broken by the sleeping hours. As the current of an electrode buried in the ground unerringly finds its way to its own similarly buried mate, across no matter how much intervening earth; so Peter's present instantly finds out Peter's past, and never by mistake knits itself on to that of Paul. Paul's thought in turn is as little liable to go astray. The past thought of Peter is appropriated by the present Peter alone. He may have a *knowledge,* and a correct one too, of what Paul's last drowsy states of mind were as he sank into sleep, but it is an entirely different sort of knowledge from that which he has of his own last states. He *remembers* his own states, whilst he only *conceives* Paul's. Remembrance is like direct feeling; its object is suffused with a warmth and intimacy to which no object of mere conception ever attains. This quality of warmth and intimacy and immediacy is what Peter's *present* thought also possesses for itself. So sure as this present is me, is mine, it says, so sure is anything else that comes with the same warmth and intimacy and immediacy, me and mine. What the qualities called warmth and intimacy may in themselves be will have to be matter for future consideration. But whatever past feelings appear with those qualities must be admitted to receive the greeting of the present mental state, to be owned by it, and accepted as belonging together with it in a common self. This community of self is what the time-gap cannot break in twain, and is why a present thought, although not ignorant of the time-gap, can still regard itself as continuous with certain chosen portions of the past.

Consciousness, then, does not appear to itself chopped up in bits. Such words as 'chain' or 'train' do not describe it fitly as it presents itself in the first instance. It is nothing jointed; it flows. A 'river' or a 'stream' are the metaphors by which it is most naturally described. *In talking of it hereafter, let us call it the stream of thought, of consciousness, or of subjective life.*

But now there appears, even within the limits of the same self, and between thoughts all of which alike have this same sense of belonging together, a kind of jointing and separateness among the parts, of which this statement seems to take no account. I refer to the breaks that are produced by sudden *contrasts in the quality* of the successive segments of the stream of thought. If the words 'chain' and 'train' had no natural fitness in them, how came such words to be used at all? Does not a loud explosion rend the consciousness upon which it abruptly breaks, in twain? Does not every sudden shock, appearance of a new object, or change in a sensation, create a real interruption, sensibly felt as such, which cuts the conscious stream across at the moment at which it appears? Do not such interruptions smite us every hour of our lives, and have we the right, in their presence, still to call our consciousness a continuous stream?

This objection is based partly on a confusion and partly on a superficial introspective view.

The confusion is between the thoughts themselves, taken as subjective facts, and the things of which they are aware. It is natural to make this confusion, but easy to avoid it when once put on one's guard. The things are discrete and discontinuous; they do pass before us in a train or chain, making often explosive appearances and rending each other in twain. But their comings and goings and contrasts no more break the flow of the thought that thinks them than they break the time and the space in which they lie. A silence may be broken by a thunder-clap, and we may be so stunned and confused for a moment by the shock as to give no instant account to ourselves of what has happened. But that very confusion is a mental state, and a state that passes us straight over from the silence to the sound. The transition between the thought of one object and the thought of another is no more a break in the *thought* than a joint in a bamboo is a break in the wood. It is a part of the *consciousness* as much as the joint is a part of the *bamboo*.

The superficial introspective view is the overlooking, even when the things are contrasted with each other most violently, of the large amount of affinity that may still remain between the thoughts by whose means they are cognized. Into the awareness of the thunder itself the awareness of the previous silence creeps and continues; for what we hear when the thunder crashes is not thunder *pure,* but thunder-breaking-upon-silence-and-contrasting-thunder-breaking-upon-silence-and-contrasting-with-it. Our feeling of the same objective thunder, coming in this way, is quite different from what it would be were the thunder a continuation of previous thunder. The thunder itself we believe to abolish and exclude the silence; but the *feeling* of the thunder is also a feeling of the silence as just gone; and it would be difficult to find in the actual concrete consciousness of man a feeling so limited to the present as not to have an inkling of anything that went before. Here, again, language works against our perception of the truth. We name our thoughts simply, each after its thing, as if each knew its own thing and nothing else. What each really knows is clearly the thing it is named for, with dimly perhaps a thousand other things. It ought to be named after all of them, but it never is. Some of them are always things known a moment ago more clearly; others are things to be known more clearly a moment hence. Our own bodily position, attitude, condition, is one of the things of which *some* awareness, however inattentive, invariably accompanies the knowledge of whatever else we know. We think; and as we think we feel our bodily selves as the seat of the thinking. If the thinking be *our* thinking, it must be suffused through all its parts with that peculiar warmth and intimacy that make it come as ours. Whether the warmth and intimacy be anything more than the feeling of the same old body always there, is a matter for the next chapter to decide. *Whatever* the content of the ego may be, it is habitually felt *with* everything else by us humans, and must form a *liaison* between all the things of which we become successively aware.

On this gradualness in the changes of our mental content the principles of nerve-action can throw some more light. When studying ... the summation of nervous activities, we saw that no state of the brain can be supposed instantly to die away. If a new state comes, the inertia of the old state will still be there and modify the result accordingly. Of course we cannot tell, in our ignorance, what in each instance the modifications ought to be. The commonest modifications in sense-perception are known as the phenomena of contrast. In æsthetics they are the feelings of delight or displeasure which certain particular orders in a series of impressions give. In thought, strictly and narrowly so called, they are unquestionably that consciousness of the *whence* and the *whither* that always accompanies its flows. If recently the brain-tract *a* was vividly excited, and then *b*, and now vividly *c*, the total present consciousness is not produced simply by *c*'s excitement, but also by the dying vibrations of *a* and *b* as well. If we want to represent the brain-process we must write it thus: *abc*—three different processes co-existing, and correlated with them a thought which is no one of the three thoughts which they would have produced had each of them occurred alone. But whatever this fourth thought may exactly be, it seems impossible that it should not be something *like* each of the three other thoughts whose tracts are concerned in its production, though in a fast-waning phase.

It all goes back to what we said in another connection. . . . As the total neurosis changes, so does the total psychosis change. But as the changes of neurosis are never absolutely discontinuous, so must the successive psychoses shade gradually into each other, although their *rate* of change may be much faster at one moment than at the next.

This difference in the rate of change lies at the basis of a difference of subjective states of which we ought immediately to speak. When the rate is slow we are aware of the object of our thought in a comparatively restful and stable way. When rapid, we are aware of a passage, a relation, a transition *from* it, or *between* it and something else. As we take, in fact, a general view of the wonderful stream of our consciousness, what strikes us first is this different pace of its parts. Like a bird's life, it seems to be made of an alternation of flights and perchings. The rhythm of language expresses this, where every thought is expressed in a sentence, and every sentence closed by a period. The resting-places are usually occupied by sensorial imaginations of some sort, whose peculiarity is that they can be held before the mind for an indefinite time, and contemplated without changing; the places of flight are filled with thoughts of relations, static or dynamic, that for the most part obtain between the matters contemplated in the periods of comparative rest.

*Let us call the resting-places the 'substantive parts,' and the places of flight the 'transitive parts,' of the stream of thought.* It then appears that the main end of our thinking is at all times the attainment of some other substantive part than the one from which we have just been dislodged. And we may say that the main use of the transitive parts is to lead us from one substantive conclusion to another.

Now it is very difficult, introspectively, to see the transitive parts for what they really are. If they are but flights to a conclusion, stopping them to look at them before the conclusion is reached is really annihilating them. Whilst if we wait till the conclusion *be* reached, it so exceeds them in vigor and stability that it quite eclipses and swallows them up in its glare. Let anyone try to cut a thought across in the middle and get a look at its section, and he will see how difficult the introspective observation of the transitive tracts is. The rush of the thought is so headlong that it almost always brings us up at the conclusion before we can arrest it. Or if our purpose is nimble enough and we do arrest it, it ceases forthwith to be itself. As a snowflake caught in the warm hand is no longer a flake but a drop, so, instead of catching the feeling of relation moving to its term, we find we have caught some substantive thing, usually the last word we were pronouncing, statically taken, and with its function, tendency, and particular meaning in the sentence quite evaporated. The attempt at introspective analysis in these cases is in fact like seizing a spinning top to catch its motion, or trying to turn up the gas quickly enough to see how the darkness looks. And the challenge to *produce* these psychoses, which is sure to be thrown by doubting psychologists at anyone who contends for their existence, is as unfair as Zeno's treatment of the advocates of motion, when, asking them to point out in what place an arrow *is* when it moves, he argues the falsity of their thesis from their inability to make to so preposterous a question an immediate reply.

The results of this introspective difficulty are baleful. If to hold fast and observe the transitive parts of thought's stream be so hard, then the great blunder to which all schools are liable must be the failure to register them, and the undue emphasizing of the more substantive parts of the stream. Were we not ourselves a moment since in danger of ignoring any feeling transitive between the silence and the thunder, and of treating their boundary as a sort of break in the mind? Now such ignoring as this has historically worked in two ways. One set of thinkers have been led by it to *Sensationalism.* Unable to lay their hands on any coarse feelings corresponding to the innumerable relations and forms of connection between the facts of the world, finding no *named* subjective modifications mirroring such relations, they have for the most part

denied that feelings of relation exist; and many of them, like Hume, have gone so far as to deny the reality of most relations *out* of the mind as well as in it. Substantive psychoses, sensations and their copies and derivatives, juxtaposed like dominoes in a game, but really separate, everything else verbal illusion,— such is the upshot of this view. The *Intellectualists,* on the other hand, unable to give up the reality of relations *extra mentem,* but equally unable to point to any distinct substantive feelings in which they were known, have made the same admission that the feelings do not exist. But they have drawn an opposite conclusion. The relations must be known, they say, in something that is no feeling, no mental modification continuous and consubstantial with the subjective tissue out of which sensations and other substantive states are made. They are known, these relations, by something that lies on an entirely different plane, by an *actus purus* of Thought, Intellect, or Reason, all written with capitals and considered to mean something unutterably superior to any fact of sensibility whatever.

But from our point of view both Intellectualists and Sensationalists are wrong. If there be such things as feelings at all, *then so surely as relations between objects exist in rerum natura, so surely, and more surely, do feelings exist to which these relations are known.* There is not a conjunction or a preposition, and hardly an adverbial phrase, syntactic form, or inflection of voice, in human speech, that does not express some shading or other of relation which we at some moment actually feel to exist between the larger objects of our thought. If we speak objectively, it is the real relations that appear revealed; if we speak subjectively, it is the stream of consciousness that matches each of them by an inward coloring of its own. In either case the relations are numberless, and no existing language is capable of doing justice to all their shades.

We ought to say a feeling of *and,* a feeling of *if,* a feeling of *but,* and a feeling of *by,* quite as readily as we say a feeling of *blue* or a feeling of *cold.* Yet we do not: so inveterate has our habit become of recognizing the existence of the substantive parts alone, that language almost refuses to lend itself to any other use. The Empiricists have always dwelt on its influence in making us suppose that where we have a separate name, a separate thing must needs be there to correspond with it; and they have rightly denied the existence of the mob of abstract entities, principles, and forces, in whose favor no other evidence than this could be brought up. But they have said nothing of that obverse error . . . of supposing that where there is *no* name no entity can exist. All *dumb* or anonymous psychic states have, owing to this error, been coolly suppressed; or, if recognized at all, have been named after the substantive perception they led to, as thoughts 'about' this object or 'about' that, the stolid word *about* engulfing all their delicate idiosyncrasies in its monotonous sound. Thus the greater and greater accentuation and isolation of the substantive parts have continually gone on.

Once more take a look at the brain. We believe the brain to be an organ whose internal equilibrium is always in a state of change— the change affecting every part. The pulses of change are doubtless more violent in one place than in another, their rhythm more rapid at this time than at that. As in a kaleidoscope revolving at a uniform rate, although the figures are always rearranging themselves, there are instants during which the transformation seems minute and interstitial and almost absent, followed by others when it shoots with magical rapidity, relatively stable forms thus alternating with forms we should not distinguish if seen again; so in the brain the perpetual rearrangement must result in some forms of tension lingering relatively long, whilst others simply come and pass. But if consciousness corresponds to the fact of rearrangement itself, why, if the rearrangement stop not, should the consciousness ever cease? And if a lingering rearrangement brings with it one kind of consciousness, why should not a swift rearrangement bring another kind of consciousness as peculiar as the rearrangement itself? The lingering consciousnesses, if of simple objects, we call 'sensations' or 'images,' according as they are vivid or faint; if of complex objects, we call them 'percepts' when vivid, 'concepts' or 'thoughts' when faint. For the swift consciousnesses we have only those names of 'transitive states,' or 'feelings of relation,' which we have used. As the brain-changes are continuous, so do all these consciousnesses melt into each other like dissolving views. Properly they are but one protracted consciousness, one unbroken stream.

### 4) Human Thought Appears to Deal with Objects Independent of Itself; that is, it is Cognitive, or Possesses the Function of Knowing

For Absolute Idealism, the infinite Thought and its objects are one. The Objects are, through being thought; the eternal Mind is, through thinking them. Were a human thought alone in the world there would be no reason for any other assumption regarding it. Whatever it might have before it would be its vision, would be there, in *its* 'there,' or then, in *its* 'then'; and the question would never arise whether an extra-mental duplicate of it existed or not. The reason why we all believe that the objects of our thoughts have a duplicate existence outside, is that there are *many* human thoughts, each with the *same* objects, as we cannot help supposing. The judgment that *my* thought has the same object as *his* thought is what makes the psychologist call my thought cognitive of an outer reality. The judgment that my own past thought and my own present thought are of the same object is what makes *me* take the object out of either and project it by a sort of triangulation into an independent position, from which it may *appear* to both. *Sameness* in a multiplicity of objective appearances is thus the basis of our belief in realities outside of thought. . . . we shall have to take up the judgment of sameness again.

To show that the question of reality being extra-mental or not is not likely to arise in the absence of repeated experiences of the *same,* take the example of an altogether unprecedented experience, such as a new taste in the throat. Is it a subjective quality of feeling, or an objective quality felt? You do not even ask the question at this point. It is simply *that taste.* But if a doctor hears you describe it, and says: "Ha! Now you know what *heartburn* is," then it becomes a quality already existent *extra mentem tuam,* which you in turn have come upon and learned. The first spaces, times, things, qualities, experienced by the child probably appear, like the first heartburn, in this absolute way, as simple *beings,* neither in nor out of thought. But later, by having other thoughts than this present one, and making repeated judgments of sameness among their objects, he corroborates in himself the notion of realities, past and distant as well as present, which realities no one single thought either possesses or engenders, but which all may contemplate and know. This, as was stated in the last chapter, is the *psychological* point of view, the relatively uncritical non-idealistic point of view of all natural science, beyond which this book cannot go. A mind which has become conscious of its own cognitive function, plays what we have called 'the psychologist' upon itself. It not only knows the things that appear before it; it knows that it knows them. This stage of reflective condition is, more or less explicitly, our habitual adult state of mind.

It cannot, however, be regarded as primitive. The consciousness of objects must come first. We seem to lapse into this primordial condition when consciousness is reduced to a minimum by the inhalation of anæsthetics or during a faint. Many persons testify that at a certain stage of the anæsthetic process objects are still cognized whilst the thought of self is lost. Professor Herzen says:

> During the syncope there is absolute psychic annihilation, the absence of all consciousness; then at the beginning of coming to, one has at a certain moment a vague, limitless, infinite feeling—a sense of *existence in general* without the least trace of distinction between the me and the not-me.

Dr. Shoemaker of Philadelphia describes during the deepest conscious stage of etherin-toxication a vision of

two endless parallel lines in swift longitudinal motion . . . on a uniform misty background . . . together with a constant sound or whirr, not loud but distinct . . . which seemed to be connected with the parallel lines. . . . These phenomena occupied the whole field. There were present no dreams or visions in any way connected with human affairs, no ideas or impressions akin to anything in past experience, no emotions, of course no idea of personality. There was no conception as to what being it was that was regarding the two lines, or that there existed any such thing as such a being; the lines and waves were all.

Similarly a friend of Mr. Herbert Spencer, quoted by him in *Mind* (vol. III, p. 556), speaks of "an undisturbed empty quiet everywhere, except that a stupid presence lay like a heavy intrusion *somewhere*—a blotch on the calm." This sense of objectivity and lapse of subjectivity, even when the object is almost indefinable, is, it seems to me, a somewhat familiar phase in chloroformization, though in my own case it is too deep a phase for any articulate after-memory to remain. I only know that as it vanishes I seem to wake to a sense of my own existence as something additional to what had previously been there.

Many philosophers, however, hold that the reflective consciousness of the self is essential to the cognitive function of thought. They hold that a thought, in order to know a thing at all, must expressly distinguish between the thing and its own self. This is a perfectly wanton assumption, and not the faintest shadow of reason exists for supposing it true. As well might I contend that I cannot dream without dreaming that I dream, swear without swearing that I swear, deny without denying that I deny, as maintain that I cannot know without knowing that I know. I may have either acquaintance-with, or knowledge-about, an object O without thinking about myself at all. It suffices for this that I think O, and that it exist. If, in addition to thinking O, I also think that I exist and that I know O, well and good; I then know one more thing, a fact about O, of which I previously was unmindful. That, however, does not prevent me from having already known O a good deal. O *per se,* or O *plus* P, are as good objects of knowledge as O *plus me* is. The philosophers in question simply substitute one particular object for all others, and call it *the* object *par excellence.* It is a case of the 'psychologist's fallacy'. *They* know the object to be one thing and the thought another; and they forthwith foist their own knowledge into that of the thought of which they pretend to give a true account. To conclude, then, *thought may, but need not, in knowing, discriminate between its object and itself.*

We have been using the word Object. *Something must now be said about the proper use of the term Object in Psychology.*

In popular parlance the word object is commonly taken without reference to the act of knowledge, and treated as synonymous with individual subject of existence. Thus if anyone ask what is the mind's object when you say 'Columbus discovered America in 1492,' most people will reply 'Columbus,' or 'America,' or, at most, 'the discovery of America.' They will name a substantive kernel or nucleus of the consciousness, and say the thought is 'about' that,—as indeed it is,—and they will call that your thought's 'object.' Really that is usually only the grammatical object, or more likely the grammatical subject, of your sentence. It is at most your 'fractional object'; or you may call it the 'topic' of your thought, or the 'subject of your discourse.' But the *Object* of your thought is really its entire content or deliverance, neither more nor less. It is a vicious use of speech to take out a substantive kernel from its content and call that its object; and it is an equally vicious use of speech to add a substantive kernel not articulately included in its content, and to call that its object. Yet either one of these two sins we commit, whenever we content ourselves with saying that a given thought is simply 'about' a certain topic, or that that topic is its 'object.' The object of my thought in the previous sentence, for example, is strictly speaking neither Columbus, nor America, nor its discovery. It is nothing short of the entire sentence, 'Columbus-discovered-America-in-

1492.' And if we wish to speak of it substantively, we must make a substantive of it by writing it out thus with hyphens between all its words. Nothing but this can possibly name its delicate idiosyncrasy. And if we wish to *feel* that idiosyncrasy we must reproduce the thought as it was uttered, with every word fringed and the whole sentence bathed in that original halo of obscure relations, which, like an horizon, then spread about its meaning.

Our psychological duty is to cling as closely as possible to the actual constitution of the thought we are studying. We may err as much by excess as by defect. If the kernel or 'topic,' Columbus, is in one way less than the thought's object, so in another way it may be more. That is, when named by the psychologist, it may mean much more than actually is present to the thought of which he is a reporter. Thus, for example, suppose you should go on to think: 'He was a daring genius!' An ordinary psychologist would not hesitate to say that the object of your thought was still 'Columbus.' True, your thought is *about* Columbus. It 'terminates' in Columbus, leads from and to the direct idea of Columbus. But for the moment it is not fully and immediately Columbus, it is only 'he,' or rather 'he-was-a-daring-genius'; which, though it may be an unimportant difference for conversational purposes, is, for introspective psychology, as great a difference as there can be.

The object of every thought, then, is neither more nor less than all that the thought thinks, exactly as the thought thinks it, however complicated the matter, and however symbolic the manner of the thinking may be. It is needless to say that memory can seldom accurately reproduce such an object, when once it has passed from before the mind. It either makes too little or too much of it. Its best plan is to repeat the verbal sentence, if there was one, in which the object was expressed. But for inarticulate thoughts there is not even this resource, and introspection must confess that the task exceeds her powers. The mass of our thinking vanishes for ever, beyond hope of recovery, and psychology only gathers up a few of the crumbs that fall from the feast.

The next point to make clear is that, *however complex the object may be, the thought of it is one undivided state of consciousness.* As Thomas Brown says:

I have already spoken too often to require again to caution you against a mistake, into which, I must confess, that the terms, which the poverty of our language obliges us to use, might, of themselves, very naturally lead you:—the mistake of supposing, that the most complex states of mind are not truly, in their very essence, as much one and indivisible, as those which we term simple—the complexity and seeming coexistence which they involve being relative to our feeling only, not to their own absolute nature. I trust I need not repeat to you, that, in itself, every notion, however seemingly complex, is, and must be, truly simple—being one state, or affection, of one simple substance, mind. Our conception of a whole army, for example, is as truly this one mind existing in this one state, as our conception of any of the individuals that compose an army: Our notion of the abstract numbers, eight, four, two, is as truly one feeling of the mind, as our notion of simple unity.

The ordinary associationist-psychology supposes, in contrast with this, that whenever an object of thought contains many elements, the thought itself must be made up of just as many ideas, one idea for each element, and all fused together in appearance, but really separate. The enemies of this psychology find (as we have already seen) little trouble in showing that such a bundle of separate ideas would never form one thought at all, and they contend that an Ego must be added to the bundle to give it unity, and bring the various ideas into relation with each other. We will not discuss the ego just yet, but it is obvious that if things are to be thought in relation, they must be thought together, and in one *something,* be that something ego, psychosis, state of consciousness, or whatever you please. If not thought with each other, things are not thought in relation at all. Now most believers in the

ego make the same mistake as the associationists and sensationists whom they oppose. Both agree that the elements of the subjective stream are discrete and separate and constitute what Kant calls a 'manifold.' But while the associationists think that a 'manifold' can form a single knowledge, the egoists deny this, and say that the knowledge comes only when the manifold is subjected to the synthetizing activity of an ego. Both make an identical hypothesis; but the egoist, finding it won't express the facts, adds another hypothesis to correct it. Now I do not wish just yet to 'commit myself' about the existence or nonexistence of the ego, but I do contend that we need not invoke it for this particular reason—namely, because the manifold of ideas has to be reduced to unity. *There is no manifold of coexisting ideas;* the notion of such a thing is a chimera. *Whatever things are thought in relation are thought from the outset in a unity, in a single pulse of subjectivity, a single psychosis, feeling, or state of mind.*

The reason why this fact is so strangely garbled in the books seems to be what . . . I called the psychologist's fallacy. We have the inveterate habit, whenever we try introspectively to describe one of our thoughts, of dropping the thought as it is in itself and talking of something else. We describe the things that appear to the thought, and we describe other thoughts *about* those things—as if these and the original thought were the same. If, for example, the thought be 'the pack of cards is on the table,' we say, "Well, isn't it a thought of the pack of cards? Isn't it of the cards as included in the pack? Isn't it of the table? And of the legs of the table as well? The table has legs—how can you think the table without virtually thinking its legs? Hasn't our thought then, all these parts—one part for the pack and another for the table? And within the pack-part a part for each card, as within the table-part a part for each leg? And isn't each of these parts an idea? And can our thought, then, be anything but an assemblage or pack of ideas, each answering to some element of what it knows?"

Now not one of these assumptions is true. The thought taken as an example is, in the first

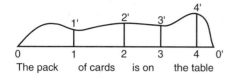

Fig. 1. The Stream of Consciousness.

place, not of 'a pack of cards.' It is of 'the-pack-of-cards-is-on-the-table,' an entirely different subjective phenomenon, whose Object implies the pack, and every one of the cards in it, but whose conscious constitution bears very little resemblance to that of the thought of the pack *per se.* What a thought *is,* and what it may be developed into, or explained to stand for, and be equivalent to, are two things, not one.

An analysis of what passes through the mind as we utter the phrase *the pack of cards is on the table* will, I hope, make this clear, and may at the same time condense into a concrete example a good deal of what has gone before.

It takes time to utter the phrase. Let the horizontal line in Fig. 1 represent time. Every part of it will then stand for a fraction, every point for an instant, of the time. Of course the thought has *time-parts.* The part 2–3 of it, though continuous with 1–2, is yet a different part from 1–2. Now I say of these time-parts that we cannot take any one of them so short that it will not after some fashion or other be a thought of the whole object 'the pack of cards is on the table.' They melt into each other like dissolving views, and no two of them feel the object just alike, but each feels the total object in a unitary undivided way. This is what I mean by denying that in the thought any parts can be found corresponding to the object's parts. Time-parts are not such parts.

Now let the vertical dimensions of the figure stand for the objects or contents of the thoughts. A line vertical to any point of the horizontal, as 1–1′, will then symbolize the object in the mind at the instant 1; a space above the horizontal, as 1–1′–2′–2, will symbolize all that passes through the mind during the time 1–2 whose line it covers. The entire diagram from 0 to 0′ represents a finite length of thought's stream.

Can we now define the psychic constitution of each vertical section of this segment? We can, though in a very rough way. Immediately after 0, even before we have opened our mouths to speak, the entire thought is present to our mind in the form of an intention to utter that sentence. This intention, though it has no simple name, and though it is a transitive state immediately displaced by the first word, is yet a perfectly determinate phase of thought, unlike anything else. . . . Again, immediately before 0′, after the last word of the sentence is spoken, all will admit that we again think its entire content as we inwardly realize its completed deliverance. All vertical sections made through any other parts of the diagram will be respectively filled with other ways of feeling the sentence's meaning. Through 2, for example, the cards will be the part of the object most emphatically present to the mind; through 4, the table. The stream is made higher in the drawing at its end than at its beginning, because the final way of feeling the content is fuller and richer than the initial way. As Joubert says, "we only know just what we meant to say, after we have said it." And as M. V. Egger remarks, "before speaking, one barely knows what one intends to say, but afterwards one is filled with admiration and surprise at having said and thought it so well."

This latter author seems to me to have kept at much closer quarters with the facts than any other analyst of consciousness. But even he does not quite hit the mark, for, as I understand him, he thinks that each word as it occupies the mind *displaces* the rest of the thought's content. He distinguishes the 'idea' (what I have called the total *object* or meaning) from the consciousness of the words, calling the former a very feeble state, and contrasting it with the liveliness of the words, even when these are only silently rehearsed. "The feeling," he says, "of the words makes ten or twenty times more noise in our consciousness than the sense of the phrase, which for consciousness is a very slight matter." And having distinguished these two things, he goes on to separate them in time, saying that the idea may either precede or follow the words, but that it is a 'pure illusion' to suppose them simultaneous. Now I believe that in all cases where the words are *understood,* the total idea may be and usually is present not only before and after the phase has been spoken, but also whilst each separate word is uttered. It is the overtone, halo, or fringe of the word, *as spoken in that sentence.* It is never absent; no word in an understood sentence comes to consciousness as a mere noise. We feel its meaning as it passes; and although our object differs from one moment to another as to its verbal kernel or nucleus, yet it is *similar* throughout the entire segment of the stream. The same object is known everywhere, now from the point of view, if we may so call it, of this word, now from the point of view of that. And in our feeling of each word there chimes an echo or foretaste of every other. The consciousness of the 'Idea' and that of the words are thus consubstantial. They are made of the same 'mind-stuff,' and form an unbroken stream. Annihilate a mind at any instant, cut its thought through whilst yet uncompleted, and examine the object present to the cross-section thus suddenly made; you will find, not the bald word in process of utterance, but that word suffused in verbal thought, will usually be some word. A series of sections 1–1′, taken at the moments 1, 2, 3, would then look like this:

The pack of cards
is on the table

Fig. 2. The Pack of Cards is on the Table.

The pack of cards
is on the table

Fig. 3. The Pack of Cards is on the Table.

The pack of cards
is on the table

Fig. 4. The Pack of Cards is on the Table.

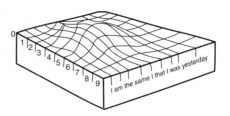

Fig. 5. I am the Same I that I was Yesterday.

The horizontal breadth stands for the entire object in each of the figures: the height of the curve above each part of that object marks the relative prominence of that part in the thought. At the moment symbolized by the first figure *pack* is the prominent part: in the third figure it is *table,* etc.

We can easily add all these plane sections together to make a solid, one of whose solid dimensions will represent time, whilst a cut across this at right angles will give the thought's content at the moment when the cut is made. Let it be the thought. 'I am the same I that I was yesterday.' If at the fourth moment of time we annihilate the thinker and examine how the last pulsation of his consciousness was made, we find that it was an awareness of the whole content with *same* most prominent, and the other parts of the thing known relatively less distinct. With each prolongation of the scheme in the time-direction, the summit of the curve of section would come further towards the end of the sentence. If we make a solid wooden frame with the sentence written on its front, and the time-scale on one of its sides, if we spread flatly a sheet of India rubber over its top, on which rectangular co-ordinates are painted, and slide a smooth ball under the rubber in the direction from 0 to 'yesterday,' the bulging of the membrane along this diagonal at successive moments will symbolize the changing of the thought's content in a way plain enough, after what has been said, to call for no more explanation. Or to express it in cerebral terms, it will show the relative intensities, at successive moments, of the several nerve-processes to which the various parts of the thought-object correspond.

The last peculiarity of consciousness to which attention is to be drawn in this first rough description of its stream is that

## 5) It is Always Interested More in one Part of its Object than in Another, and Welcomes and Rejects, or Chooses, all the While it Thinks

The phenomena of selective attention and of deliberative will are of course patent examples of this choosing activity. But few of us are aware how incessantly it is at work in operations not ordinarily called by these names. Accentuation and Emphasis are present in every perception we have. We find it quite impossible to disperse our attention impartially over a number of impressions. A monotonous succession of sonorous strokes is broken up into rhythms, now of one sort, now of another, by the different accent which we place on different strokes. The simplest of these rhythms is the double one, tick-tóck, tick-tóck, tick-tóck. Dots dispersed on a surface are perceived in rows and groups. Lines separate into diverse figures. The ubiquity of the distinctions, *this* and *that, here* and *there, now* and *then,* in our minds is the result of our laying the same selective emphasis on parts of place and time.

But we do far more than emphasize things, and unite some, and keep others apart. We actually *ignore* most of the things before us. Let me briefly show how this goes on.

To begin at the bottom, what are our very senses themselves but organs of selection? Out of the infinite chaos of movements, of which physics teaches us that the outer world consists, each sense-organ picks out those which fall within certain limits of velocity. To these it responds, but ignores the rest as completely as if they did not exist. It thus accentuates particular movements in a manner for which objectively there seems no valid ground; for, as Lange says, there is no reason whatever to think that the gap in Nature between the highest sound-waves and the lowest heat-waves is an abrupt break like that of our sensations; or that the difference between violet and ultra-

violet rays has anything like the objective importance subjectively represented by that between light and darkness. Out of what is in itself an undistinguishable, swarming *continuum,* devoid of distinction or emphasis, our senses make for us, by attending to this motion and ignoring that, a world full of contrasts, of sharp accents, of abrupt changes, of picturesque light and shade.

If the sensations we receive from a given organ have their causes thus picked out for us by the conformation of the organ's termination, Attention, on the other hand, out of all the sensations yielded, picks out certain ones as worthy of its notice and suppresses all the rest. Helmholtz's work on Optics is little more than a study of those visual sensations of which common men never become aware—blind spots, *muscæ volitantes,* after-images, irradiation, chromatic fringes, marginal changes of color, double images, astigmatism, movements of accommodation and convergence, retinal rivalry, and more besides. We do not even know without special training on which of our eyes an image falls. So habitually ignorant are most men of this that one may be blind for years of a single eye and never know the fact.

Helmholtz says that we notice only those sensations which are signs to us of *things.* But what are things? Nothing, as we shall abundantly see, but special groups of sensible qualities, which happen practically or æsthetically to interest us, to which we therefore give substantive names, and which we exalt to this exclusive status of independence and dignity. But in itself, apart from my interest, a particular dust-wreath on a windy day is just as much of an individual thing, and just as much or as little deserves an individual name, as my own body does.

And then, among the sensations we get from each separate thing, what happens? The mind selects again. It chooses certain of the sensations to represent the thing most *truly,* and considers the rest as its appearances, modified by the conditions of the moment. Thus my table-top is named *square,* after but one of an infinite number of retinal sensations which it yields, the rest of them being sensations of two acute and two obtuse angles; but I call the latter *perspective* views, and the four right angles the *true* form of the table, and erect the attribute squareness into the table's essence, for æsthetic reasons of my own. In like manner, the real form of the circle is deemed to be the sensation it gives when the line of vision is perpendicular to its centre—all its other sensations are signs of this sensation. The real sound of the cannon is the sensation it makes when the ear is close by. The real color of the brick is the sensation it gives when the eye looks squarely at it from a near point, out of the sunshine and yet not in the gloom; under other circumstances it gives us other color-sensations which are but signs of this—we then see it looks pinker or blacker than it really is. The reader knows no object which he does not represent to himself by preference as in some typical attitude, of some normal size, at some characteristic distance, of some standard tint, etc., etc. But all these essential characteristics, which together form for us the genuine objectivity of the thing and are contrasted with what we call the subjective sensations it may yield us at a given moment, are mere sensations like the latter. The mind chooses to suit itself, and decides what particular sensation shall be held more real and valid than all the rest.

Thus perception involves a twofold choice. Out of all present sensations, we notice mainly such as are significant of absent ones; and out of all the absent associates which these suggest, we again pick out a very few to stand for the objective reality *par excellence*. We could have no more exquisite example of selective industry.

That industry goes on to deal with the things thus given in perception. A man's empirical thought depends on the things he has experienced, but what these shall be is to a large extent determined by his habits of attention. A thing may be present to him a thousand times, but if he persistently fails to notice it, it cannot be said to enter into his experience. We are all seeing flies, moths, and beetles by the thousand, but to whom, save an entomologist,

do they say anything distinct? On the other hand, a thing met only once in a lifetime may leave an indelible experience in the memory. Let four men make a tour in Europe. One will bring home only picturesque impressions—costumes and colors, parks and views and works of architecture, pictures and statues. To another all this will be non-existent; and distances and prices, populations and drainage-arrangements, door- and window-fastenings, and other useful statistics will take their place. A third will give a rich account of the theatres, restaurants, and public balls, and naught beside; whilst the fourth will perhaps have been so wrapped in his own subjective broodings as to tell little more than a few names of places through which he passed. Each has selected, out of the same mass of presented objects, those which suited his private interest and has made his experience thereby.

If, now, leaving the empirical combination of objects, we ask how the mind proceeds *rationally* to connect them, we find selection again to be omnipotent. In a future chapter we shall see that all Reasoning depends on the ability of the mind to break up the totality of the phenomenon reasoned about, into parts, and to pick out from among these the particular one which, in our given emergency, may lead to the proper conclusion. Another predicament will need another conclusion, and require another element to be picked out. The man of genius is he who will always stick in his bill at the right point, and bring it out with the right element—'reason' if the emergency be theoretical, 'means' if it be practical—transfixed upon it. I here confine myself to this brief statement, but it may suffice to show that Reasoning is but another form of the selective activity of the mind.

If now we pass to its æsthetic department, our law is still more obvious. The artist notoriously selects his items, rejecting all tones, colors, shapes, which do not harmonize with each other and with the main purpose of his work. That unity, harmony, 'convergence of characters,' as M. Taine calls it, which gives to works of art their superiority over works of nature, is wholly due to *elimination*. Any natural subject will do, if the artist has wit enough to pounce upon some one feature of it as characteristic, and suppress all merely accidental items which do not harmonize with this.

Ascending still higher, we reach the plane of Ethics, where choice reigns notoriously supreme. An act has no ethical quality whatever unless it be chosen out of several all equally possible. To sustain the arguments for the good course and keep them ever before us, to stifle our longing for more flowery ways, to keep the foot unflinchingly on the arduous path, these are characteristic ethical energies. But more than these; for these but deal with the means of compassing interests already felt by the man to be supreme. The ethical energy *par excellence* has to go farther and choose which *interest* out of several, equally coercive, shall become supreme. The issue here is of the utmost pregnancy, for it decides a man's entire career. When he debates, Shall I commit this crime? choose that profession? accept that office, or marry this fortune?—his choice really lies between one of several equally possible future Characters. What he shall *become* is fixed by the conduct of this moment. Schopenhauer, who enforces his determinism by the argument that with a given fixed character only one reaction is possible under given circumstances, forgets that, in these critical ethical moments, what consciously *seems* to be in question is the complexion of the character itself. The problem with the man is less what act he shall now choose to do, than what being he shall now resolve to become.

Looking back, then, over this review, we see that the mind is at every stage a theatre of simultaneous possibilities. Consciousness consists in the comparison of these with each other, the selection of some, and the suppression of the rest by the reinforcing and inhibiting agency of attention. The highest and most elaborated mental products are filtered from the data chosen by the faculty next beneath, out of the mass offered by the faculty below that, which mass in turn was sifted from a still larger amount of yet simpler material, and so on. The mind, in short, works on the data it receives very much as a sculptor works on his block of stone. In a sense the statue stood there from eternity. But there were a thousand different ones beside it, and the sculptor alone is to thank for having extricated this one from the rest. Just so the world of each of us, howsoever different, our several views of it may be, all lay embedded in the primordial chaos of sensations, which gave the mere *matter* to the thought of all of us indifferently. We may, if we like, by our reasonings unwind things back to that black and jointless continuity of space and moving clouds of swarming atoms which science calls the only real world. But all the while the world *we* feel and live in will be that which our ancestors and we, by slowly cumulative strokes of choice, have extricated out of this, like sculptors, by simply rejecting certain portions of the given stuff. Other sculptors, other statues from the same stone! Other minds, other worlds from the same montonous and inexpressive chaos! My world is but one in a million alike embedded, alike real to those who may abstract them. How different must be the worlds in the consciousness of ant, cuttle-fish, or crab!

But in my mind and your mind the rejected portions and the selected portions of the original world-stuff are to a great extent the same. The human race as a whole largely agrees as to what it shall notice and name, and what not. And among the noticed parts we select in much the same way for accentuation and preference or subordination and dislike. There is, however, one entirely extraordinary case in which no two men ever are known to choose alike. One great splitting of the whole universe into two halves is made by each of us; and for each of us almost all of the interest attaches to one of the halves; but we all draw the line of division between them in a different place. When I say that we all call the two halves by the same names, and that those names are '*me*' and '*not-me*' respectively, it will at once be seen what I mean. The altogether unique kind of interest which each human mind feels in those parts of creation which it can call *me* or *mine* may be a moral riddle, but it is a fundamental psychological fact. No mind can take the same interest in his neighbor's *me* as in his own. The neighbor's me falls together with all the rest of things in one foreign mass, against which his own *me* stands out in startling relief. Even the trodden worm, as Lotze somewhere says, contrasts his own suffering self with the whole remaining universe, though he have no clear conception either of himself or of what the universe may be. He is for me a mere part of the world; for him it is I who am the mere part. Each of us dichotomizes the Kosmos in a different place.

# A World of Pure Experience

It is difficult not to notice a curious unrest in the philosophic atmosphere of the time, a loosening of old landmarks, a softening of oppositions, a mutual borrowing from one another on the part of systems anciently closed, and an interest in new suggestions, however vague, as if the one thing sure were the inadequacy of the extant school-solutions. The dissatisfaction with these seems due for the most part to a feeling that they are too abstract and academic. Life is confused and superabundant, and what the younger generation appears to crave is more of the temperament of life in its philosophy, even tho it were at some cost of logical rigor and of formal purity. Transcendental idealism is inclining to let the world wag incomprehensibly, in spite of its Absolute Subject and his unity of purpose. Berkeleyan idealism is abandoning the principle of parsimony and dabbling in panpsychic speculations. Empiricism flirts with teleology; and, strangest of all, natural realism, so long decently buried, raises its head above the turf, and finds glad hands outstretched from the most unlikely quarters to help it to its feet again. We are all biased by our personal feelings, I know, and I am personally discontented with extant solutions, so I seem to read the signs of a great unsettlement, as if the upheaval of more real conceptions and more fruitful methods were imminent, as if a true landscape might result, less clipped, straight-edged and artificial.

If philosophy be really on the eve of any considerable rearrangement, the time should be propitious for anyone who has suggestions of his own to bring forward. For many years past my mind has been growing into a certain type of *weltanschauung* [world view]. Rightly or wrongly, I have got to the point where I can hardly see things in any other pattern. I propose, therefore, to describe the pattern as clearly as I can consistently with great brevity, and to throw my description into the bubbling vat of publicity where, jostled by rivals and torn by critics, it will eventually either disappear from notice, or else, if better luck befall it, quietly subside to the profundities, and serve as a possible ferment of new growths or a nucleus of new crystallization.

## I.   Radical Empiricism

I give the name of 'radical empiricism' to my *weltanschauung* [world view]. Empiricism is known as the opposite of rationalism. Rationalism tends to emphasize universals and to make wholes prior to parts in the order of logic as well as in that of being. Empiricism, on the contrary, lays the explanatory stress upon the part, the element, the individual, and treats the whole as

From *The Works of William James—Essays in Radical Empiricism,* ed., Frederick Burkhardt (Cambridge, Mass.: Harvard University Press, 1976 [1904]), pp. 21–44.

a collection and the universal as an abstraction. My description of things, accordingly, starts with the parts and makes of the whole a being of the second order. It is essentially a mosaic philosophy, a philosophy of plural facts, like that of Hume and his descendants, who refer these facts neither to substances in which they inhere nor to an absolute mind that creates them as its objects. But it differs from the Humian type of empiricism in one particular which makes me add the epithet radical.

To be radical, an empiricism must neither admit into its constructions any element that is not directly experienced, nor exclude from them any element that is directly experienced. For such a philosophy, *the relations that connect experiences must themselves be experienced relations, and any kind of relation experienced must be accounted as 'real' as anything else in the system.* Elements may indeed be redistributed, the original placing of things getting corrected, but a real place must be found for every kind of thing experienced, whether term or relation, in the final philosophic arrangement.

Now, ordinary empiricism, in spite of the fact that conjunctive and disjunctive relations present themselves as being fully coordinate parts of experience, has always shown a tendency to do away with the connexions of things, and to insist most on the disjunctions. Berkeley's nominalism, Hume's statement that whatever things we distinguish are as "loose and separate" as if they had no manner of connexion, James Mill's denial that similars have anything 'really' in common, the resolution of the causal tie into habitual sequence, John Mill's account of both physical things and selves as composed of discontinuous possibilities, and the general pulverization of all experience by association and the mind-dust theory, are examples of what I mean.

The natural result of such a world-picture has been the efforts of rationalism to correct its incoherencies by the addition of trans-experiential agents of unification, substances, intellectual categories and powers, or selves; whereas, if empiricism had only been radical and taken everything that comes without disfa-

vor, conjunction as well as separation, each at its facevalue, the results would have called for no such artificial correction. *Radical empiricism,* as I understand it, *does full justice to conjunctive relations,* without, however, treating them as rationalism always tends to treat them, as being true in some supernal way, as if the unity of things and their variety belonged to different orders of truth, and vitality altogether.

## II.   Conjunctive Relations

Relations are of different degrees of intimacy. Merely to be 'with' one another in a universe of discourse is the most external relation that terms can have, and seems to involve nothing whatever as to farther consequences. Simultaneity and time-interval come next, and then space-adjacency and distance. After them, similarity and difference, carrying the possibility of many inferences. Then relations of activity, tying terms into series involving change, tendency, resistance, and the causal order generally. Finally, the relation experienced between terms that form states of mind, and are immediately conscious of continuing each other. The organization of the self as a system of memories, purposes, strivings, fulfilments or disappointments, is incidental to this most intimate of all relations, the terms of which seem in many cases actually to compenetrate and suffuse each other's being.

Philosophy has always turned on grammatical particles. With, near, next, like, from, towards, against, because, for, through, my— these words designate types of conjunctive relation arranged in a roughly ascending order of intimacy and inclusiveness. *A priori,* we can imagine a universe of withness but no nextness; or one of nextness but no likeness, or of likeness with no activity, or of activity with no purpose, or of purpose with no ego. These would be universes, each with its own grade of unity. The universe of human experience is, by one or another of its parts, of each and all these grades. Whether or not it possibly enjoys some still more absolute grade of union does not appear upon the surface.

Taken as it does appear, our universe is to a large extent chaotic. No one single type of connexion runs through all the experiences that compose it. If we take space-relations, they fail to connect minds into any regular system. Causes and purposes obtain only among special series of facts. The self-relation seems extremely limited and does not link two different selves together. *Prima facie,* if you should liken the universe of absolute idealism to an aquarium, a crystal globe in which goldfish are swimming, you would have to compare the empiricist universe to something more like one of those dried human heads with which the Dyaks of Borneo deck their lodges. The skull forms a solid nucleus; but innumerable feathers, leaves, strings, beads, and loose appendices of every description float and dangle from it, and save that they terminate in it, seem to have nothing to do with one another. Even so my experiences and yours float and dangle, terminating, it is true, in a nucleus of common perception, but for the most part out of sight and irrelevant and unimaginable to one another. This imperfect intimacy, this bare relation of *withness* between some parts of the sum total of experience and other parts, is the fact that ordinary empiricism over-emphasizes against rationalism, the latter always tending to ignore it unduly. Radical empiricism, on the contrary, is fair to both the unity and the disconnexion. It finds no reason for treating either as illusory. It allots to each its definite sphere of description, and agrees that there appear to be actual forces at work which tend, as time goes on, to make the unity greater.

The conjunctive relation that has given most trouble to philosophy is *the co-conscious transition,* so to call it, by which one experience passes into another when both belong to the same self. About the facts there is no question. My experiences and your experiences are 'with' each other in various external ways, but mine pass into mine, and yours pass into yours in a way in which yours and mine never pass into one another. Within each of our personal histories, subject, object, interest and purpose *are continuous or may be continuous.* Personal histories are processes of change in time, and *the change itself is one of the things immediately experienced.* 'Change' in this case means continuous as opposed to discontinuous transition. But continuous transition is one sort of a conjunctive relation; and to be a radical empiricist means to hold fast to this conjunctive relation of all others, for this is the strategic point, the position through which, if a hole be made, all the corruptions of dialectics and all the metaphysical fictions pour into our philosophy. The holding fast to this relation means taking it at its face-value, neither less nor more; and to take it at its face-value means first of all to take it just as we feel it and not to confuse ourselves with abstract talk *about* it, involving words that drive us to invent secondary conceptions in order to neutralize their suggestions and to make our actual experience again seem rationally possible.

What I do feel simply when a later moment of my experience succeeds an earlier one is that tho they are two moments, the transition from the one to the other is *continuous.* Continuity here is a definite sort of experience; just as definite as is the *discontinuity-experience* which I find it impossible to avoid when I seek to make the transition from an experience of my own to one of yours. In this latter case I have to get on and off again, to pass from a thing lived to another thing only conceived, and the break is positively experienced and noted. Tho the functions exerted by my experience and by yours may be the same (e.g., the same objects known and the same purposes followed), yet the sameness has in this case to be ascertained expressly (and often with difficulty and uncertainty) after the break has been felt; whereas in passing from one of my own moments to another the sameness of object and interest is unbroken, and both the earlier and the later experience are of things directly lived.

There is no other *nature,* no other whatness than this absence of break and this sense of continuity in that most intimate of all conjunctive relations, the passing of one experience into another when they belong to the same self. And this whatness is real empirical 'content' just as the whatness of separation and discontinuity is real content in the contrasted case.

Practically to experience one's personal continuum in this living way is to know the originals of the ideas of continuity and of sameness, to know what the words stand for concretely, to own all that they can ever mean. But all experiences have their conditions; and over-subtle intellects, thinking about the facts here, and asking how they are possible, have ended by substituting a lot of static objects of conception for the direct perceptual experiences. "Sameness," they have said, "must be a stark numerical identity; it can't run on from next to next. Continuity can't mean mere absence of gap; for if you say two things are in immediate contact, *at* the contact how can they be two? If, on the other hand, you put a relation of transition between them, that itself is a third thing, and needs to be related or hitched to its terms. An infinite series is involved," and so on. The result is that from difficulty to difficulty, the plain conjunctive experience has been discredited by both schools, the empiricists leaving things permanently disjoined, and the rationalists remedying the looseness by their absolutes or substances, or whatever other fictitious agencies of union they may have employed. From all which artificiality we can be saved by a couple of simple reflections: first, that conjunctions and separations are, at all events, coordinate phenomena which, if we take experiences at their face-value, must be accounted equally real; and second, that if we insist on treating things as really separate when they are given as continuously joined, invoking, when union is required, transcendental principles to overcome the separateness we have assumed, then we ought to stand ready to perform the converse act. We ought to invoke higher principles of *dis*union also, to make our merely experienced *dis*junctions more truly real. Failing thus, we ought to let the originally given continuities stand on their own bottom. We have no right to be lopsided or to blow capriciously hot and cold.

## III.   The Cognitive Relation

The first great pitfall from which such a radical standing by experience will save us is an artificial conception of the *relations between knower and known.* Throughout the history of philosophy the subject and its object have been treated as absolutely discontinuous entities; and thereupon the presence of the latter to the former, or the 'apprehension' by the former of the latter, has assumed a paradoxical character which all sorts of theories had to be invented to overcome. Representative theories put a mental 'representation,' 'image,' or 'content' into the gap, as a sort of intermediary. Commonsense theories left the gap untouched, declaring our mind able to clear it by a self-transcending leap. Transcendentalist theories left it impossible to traverse by finite knowers, and brought an absolute in to perform the saltatory act. All the while, in the very bosom of the finite experience, every conjunction required to make the relation intelligible is given in full. Either the knower and the known are:

(1)  the self-same piece of experience taken twice over in different contexts; or they are

(2)  two pieces of *actual* experience belonging to the same subject, with definite tracts of conjunctive transitional experience between them; or

(3)  the known is a *possible* experience either of that subject or another, to which the said conjunctive transitions *would* lead, if sufficiently prolonged.

To discuss all the ways in which one experience may function as the knower of another, would be incompatible with the limits of this essay. I have treated of type 1, the kind of knowledge called perception, in an article in the *Journal of Philosophy,* for September 1, 1904, called 'Does "consciousness" exist?' This is the type of case in which the mind enjoys direct 'acquaintance' with a present object. In the other types the mind has 'knowledge-about' an object not immediately there. Of type 2, the simplest sort of conceptual knowledge, I have given some account in two articles, published respectively in *Mind,* Vol. X., p. 27, 1885, and in the *Psychological Review,* Vol. II., p. 105, 1895. Type 3 can always formally and hypothetically be reduced to type 2, so that a brief description of that type will now put the present reader sufficiently at my point of view, and make him see what the actual meanings of the mysterious cognitive relation may be.

Suppose me to be sitting here in my library at Cambridge, at ten minutes' walk from 'Memorial Hall,' and to be thinking truly of the latter object. My mind may have before it only the name, or it may have a clear image, or it may have a very dim image of the hall, but such an intrinsic difference in the image makes no difference in its cognitive function. Certain *extrinsic* phenomena, special experiences of conjunction, are what impart to the image, be it what it may, its knowing office.

For instance, if you ask me what hall I mean by my image, and I can tell you nothing; or if I fail to point or lead you towards the Harvard Delta; or if, being led by you, I am uncertain whether the Hall I see be what I had in mind or not; you would rightly deny that I had 'meant' that particular hall at all, even tho my mental image might to some degree have resembled it. The resemblance would count in that case as coincidental merely, for all sorts of things of a kind resemble one another in this world without being held for that reason to take cognizance of one another.

On the other hand, if I can lead you to the hall, and tell you of its history and present uses; if in its presence I feel my idea, however imperfect it may have been, to have led hither and to be now *terminated;* if the associates of the image and of the felt hall run parallel, so that each term of the one context corresponds serially, as I walk, with an answering term of the other; why then my soul was prophetic, and my idea must be, and by common consent would be, called cognizant of reality. That percept was what I *meant,* for into it my idea has passed by conjunctive experiences of sameness and fulfilled intention. Nowhere is there jar, but every later moment continues and corroborates an earlier one.

In this continuing and corroborating, taken in no transcendental sense, but denoting definitely felt traditions, *lies all that the knowing of a percept by an idea can possibly contain or signify.* Wherever such transitions are felt, the first experience *knows* the last one. Where they do not, or where even as possibles they

cannot, intervene, there can be no pretence of knowing. In this latter case the extremes will be connected, if connected at all, by inferior relations—bare likeness or succession, or by 'withness' alone. Knowledge of sensible realities thus comes to life inside the tissue of experience. It is *made;* and made by relations that unroll themselves in time. Whenever certain intermediaries are given, such that, as they develope towards their terminus, there is experience from point to point of one direction followed, and finally of one process fulfilled, the result is that *their starting-point thereby becomes a knower and their terminus an object meant or known.* That is all that knowing (in the simple case considered) can be known-as, that is the whole of its nature, put into experiential terms, Whenever such is the sequence of our experiences we may freely say that we had the terminal object 'in mind' from the outset, even altho *at* the outset nothing was there in us but a flat piece of substantive experience like any other, with no self-transcendency about it, and no mystery save the mystery of coming into existence and of being gradually followed by other pieces of substantive experience, with conjunctively transitional experiences between. That is what we *mean* here by the object's being 'in mind.' Of any deeper more real way of its being in mind we have no positive conception, and we have no right to discredit our actual experience by talking of such a way at all.

I know that many a reader will rebel at this. "Mere intermediaries," he will say, "even tho they be feelings of continuously growing fulfilment, only *separate* the knower from the known, whereas what we have in knowledge is a kind of immediate touch of the one by the other, an 'apprehension' in the etymological sense of the word, a leaping of the chasm as by lightning, an act by which two terms are smitten into one over the head of their distinctness. All these dead intermediaries of yours are out of each other, and outside of their termini still."

But do not such dialectic difficulties remind us of the dog dropping his bone and snapping at its image in the water? If we knew any more real kind of union *aliunde,* we might be entitled to brand all our empirical unions as a sham. But unions by continuous transition are the only ones we know of, whether in this matter of a knowledge-about that terminates in an acquaintance, whether in personal identity, in logical predication through the copula 'is,' or elsewhere. If anywhere there were more absolute unions, they could only reveal themselves to us by just such conjunctive results. These are what the unions are *worth,* these are all that *we can ever practically mean* by union, by continuity. Is it not time to repeat what Lotze said of substances, that to *act like* one is to *be* one? Should we not say here that to be experienced as continuous is to be really continuous, in a world where experience and reality come to the same thing? In a picture gallery a painted hook will serve to hang a painted chain by, a painted cable will hold a painted ship. In a world where both the terms and their distinctions are affairs of experience, conjunctions that are experienced must be at least as real as anything else. They will be 'absolutely' real conjunctions, if we have no transphenomenal absolute ready, to derealize the whole experienced world by, at a stroke. If, on the other hand, we had such an absolute, not one of our opponents' theories of knowledge could remain standing any better than ours could; for the distinctions as well as the conjunctions of experience would impartially fall its prey. The whole question of how 'one' thing can know 'another' would cease to be a real one at all in a world where otherness itself was an illusion.

So much for the essentials of the cognitive relation where the knowledge is conceptual in type, or forms knowledge 'about' an object. It consists in intermediary experiences (possible, if not actual) of continuously developing progress, and finally, of fulfilment, when the sensible percept which is the object is reached. The percept here not only *verifies* the concept, proves its function of knowing that percept to be true, but the percept's existence as the terminus of the chain of intermediaries *creates* the function. Whatever terminates that chain was, because it now proves itself to be, what the concept 'had in mind.'

The towering importance for human life of this kind of knowing lies in the fact that an experience that knows another can figure as its *representative,* not in any quasi-miraculous 'epistemological' sense, but in the definite practical sense of being its *substitute* in various operations, sometimes physical and sometimes mental, which lead us to its associates and results. By experimenting on our ideas of reality, we may save ourselves the trouble of experimenting on the real experiences which they severally mean. The ideas form related systems, corresponding point for point to the systems which the realities form; and by letting an ideal term call up its associates systematically, we may be led to a terminus which the corresponding real term would have led to in case we had operated on the real world. This brings us to the general question of substitution, and some remarks on that subject seem to be the next thing in order.

## IV.   Substitution

In Taine's brilliant book on 'Intelligence,' substitution was for the first time named as a cardinal logical function, tho of course the facts had always been familiar enough. What, exactly, in a system of experiences, does the 'substitution' of one of them for another mean?

According to my view, experience as a whole is a process in time, whereby innumerable particular terms lapse and are superseded by others that follow upon them by transitions which, whether disjunctive or conjunctive in content, are themselves experiences, and must in general be accounted at least as real as the terms which they relate. What the nature of the event called 'superseding' signifies, depends altogether on the kind of transition that obtains. Some experiences simply abolish their predecessors without continuing them in any way. Others are felt to increase or to enlarge their meaning, to carry out their purpose, or to bring us nearer to their goal. They 'represent' them, and may fulfil their function better than they fulfilled it themselves. But to 'fulfil a function' in a world of pure experience can be conceived and defined in only one possible way. In such a world transitions and arrivals (or terminations) are the only events that happen, tho they happen by so many sorts of path. The only function that one experience can perform is to lead into another experience; and the only fulfilment we can speak of is the reaching of a certain experienced end. When one experience leads to (or can lead to) the same end as another, they agree in function. But the whole system of experiences as they are immediately given presents itself as a quasi-chaos through which one can pass out of an initial term in many directions and yet end in the same terminus, moving from next to next by a great many possible paths.

Either one of these paths might be a functional substitute for another, and to follow one rather than another might on occasion be an advantageous thing to do. As a matter of fact, and in a general way, the paths that run through conceptual experiences, that is, through 'thoughts' or 'ideas' that 'know' the things in which they terminate, are highly advantageous paths to follow. Not only do they yield inconceivably rapid transitions; but, owing to the 'universal' character which they frequently possess, and to their capacity for association with one another in great systems, they outstrip the tardy consecutions of the things themselves, and sweep us on towards our ultimate termini in a far more labor-saving way than the following of trains of sensible perception ever could. Wonderful are the new cuts and the short-circuits the thought-paths make. Most thought-paths, it is true, are substitutes for nothing actual; they end outside the real world altogether, in wayward fancies, utopias, fictions or mistakes. But where they do re-enter reality and terminate therein, we substitute them always; and with these substitutes we pass the greater number of our hours.

This notion of the purely substitutional or conceptual physical world brings us to the most critical of all the steps in the development of a philosophy of pure experience. The paradox of self-transcendency in knowledge comes back upon us here, but I think that our notions of pure experience and of substitution,

and our radically empirical view of conjunctive transitions, are *denkmittel* that will carry us safely through the pass.

## V. What Objective Reference is

Whosoever feels his experience to be something substitutional even while he has it, may be said to have an experience that reaches beyond itself. From inside of its own entity it says 'more,' and postulates reality existing elsewhere. For the transcendentalist, who holds knowing to consist in a *salto mortale* across an 'epistemological chasm,' such an idea presents no difficulty; but it seems at first sight as if it might be inconsistent with an empiricism like our own. Have we not explained that conceptual knowledge is made such wholly by the existence of things that fall outside of the knowing experience itself—by intermediary experiences and by a terminus that fulfills? Can the knowledge be there before these elements that constitute its being have come? And, if knowledge be not there, how can objective reference occur?

The key to this difficulty lies in the distinction between knowing as verified and completed, and the same knowing as in transit and on its way. To recur to the Memorial Hall example lately used, it is only when our idea of the Hall has actually terminated in the percept that we know 'for certain' that from the beginning it was truly cognitive of *that*. Until established by the end of the process, its quality of knowing that, or indeed of knowing anything, could still be doubted; and yet the knowing really was there, as the result now shows. We were *virtual* knowers of the Hall long before we were certified to have been its actual knowers, by the percept's retroactive validating power. Just so we are 'mortal' all the time, by reason of the virtuality of the inevitable event which will make us so when it shall have come.

Now the immensely greater part of all our knowing never gets beyond this virtual stage. It never is completed or nailed down. I speak not merely of our ideas of imperceptibles like ether-waves or dissociated 'ions,' or of 'ejects' like the contents of our neighbors' minds; I speak also of ideas which we might verify if we would take the trouble, but which we hold for true altho unterminated perceptually, because nothing says 'no' to us, and there is no contradicting truth in sight. *To continue thinking unchallenged is, ninety-nine times out of a hundred, our practical substitute for knowing in the completed sense.* As each experience runs by cognitive transition into the next one, and we nowhere feel a collision with what we elsewhere count as truth or fact, we commit ourselves to the current as if the port were sure. We live, as it were, upon the front edge of an advancing wave-crest, and our sense of a determinate direction in falling forward is all we cover of the future of our path. It is as if a differential quotient should be conscious and treat itself as an adequate substitute for a traced-out curve. Our experience, *inter alia,* is of variations of rate and of direction, and lives in these transitions more than in the journey's end. The experiences of tendency are sufficient to act upon—what more could we have *done* at those moments even if the later verification comes complete?

This is what, as a radical empiricist, I say to the charge that the objective reference which is so flagrant a character of our experiences involves a chasm and mortal leap. A positively conjunctive transition involves neither chasm nor leap. Being the very original of what we mean by continuity, it makes a continuum wherever it appears. I know full well that such brief words as these will leave the hardened transcendentalist unshaken. Conjunctive experiences *separate* their terms, he will still say: they are third things interposed, that have themselves to be conjoined by new links, and to invoke them makes our trouble infinitely worse. To 'feel' our motion forward is impossible. Motion implies terminus; and how can terminus be felt before we have arrived? The barest start and sally forwards, the barest tendency to leave the instant, involves the chasm and the leap. Conjunctive transitions are the most superficial of appearances, illusions of our sensibility which philosophical reflection pulverizes at a touch. Conception is our only trustworthy instrument, conception and the absolute working hand in hand. Conception disintegrates experience utterly, but its disjunctions are easily overcome again when the absolute takes up the task.

Such transcendentalists I must leave, provisionally at least, in full possession of their creed. I have no space for polemics in this essay, so I shall simply formulate the empiricist doctrine as my hypothesis, leaving it to work or not work as it may.

Objective reference, I say then, is an incident of the fact that so much of our experience comes as an insufficient and consists of process and transition. Our fields of experience have no more definite boundaries than have our fields of view. Both are fringed forever by a *more* that continuously developes, and that continuously supersedes them as life proceeds. The relations, generally speaking, are as real here as the terms are, and the only complaint of the transcendentalist's with which I could at all sympathize would be his charge that, by first making knowledge to consist in external relations as I have done, and by then confessing that nine-tenths of the time these are not actually but only virtually there, I have knocked the solid bottom out of the whole business, and palmed off a substitute of knowledge for the genuine thing. Only the admission, such a critic might say, that our ideas are self-transcendent and 'true' already, in advance of the experiences that are to terminate them, can bring solidity back to knowledge in a world like this, in which transitions and terminations are only by exception fulfilled.

This seems to me an excellent place for applying the pragmatic method. What would the self-transcendency affirmed to exist in advance of all experiential mediation or termination, be *known-as?* What would it practically result in for *us,* were it true?

It could only result in our orientation, in the turning of our expectations and practical tendencies into the right path; and the right path here, so long as we and the object are not yet face to face (or can never get face to face, as in the case of ejects), would be the path that led us into the object's nearest neighborhood. Where direct acquaintance is lacking, 'knowledge-about' is the next best thing, and an acquaintance with what actually lies about the object, and is most closely related to it, puts such knowledge within our grasp. Etherwaves and your anger, for example, are things in which my thoughts will never *perceptually* terminate, but my concepts of them lead me to their very brink, to the chromatic fringes and to the hurtful words and deeds which are their really next effects.

Even if our ideas did in themselves possess the postulated self-transcendency, it would still remain true that their putting us into possession of such effects *would be the sole cash-value of the self-transcendency for us.* And this cash-value, it is needless to say, is *verbatim et literatim* [word for word and letter for letter] what our empiricist account pays in. On pragmatist principles therefore, a dispute over self-transcendency is a pure logomachy. Call our concepts of ejective things self-transcendent or the reverse, it makes no difference, so long as we don't differ about the nature of that exalted virtue's fruits—fruits for us, of course, humanistic fruits.

If an absolute were proved to exist for other reasons, it might well appear that *his* knowledge is terminated in innumerable cases where ours is still incomplete. That, however, would be a fact indifferent to our knowledge. The latter would grow neither worse nor better, whether we acknowledged such an absolute or left him out.

So the notion of a knowledge still *in transitu* [in transit] and on its way joins hands here with that notion of a 'pure experience' which I tried to explain in my recent article entitled 'Does "consciousness" exist?' The instant field of the present is always experience in its 'pure' state, plain unqualified actuality, a simple *that,* as yet undifferentiated into thing and thought, and only virtually classifiable as objective fact or as someone's opinion about fact. This is as true when the field is conceptual as when it is perceptual. 'Memorial Hall' is 'there' in my idea as much as when I stand

before it. I proceed to act on its account in either case. Only in the later experience that supersedes the present one is this *naïf* immediacy retrospectively split into two parts, a 'consciousness' and its 'content,' and the content corrected or confirmed. While still pure, or present, any experience—mine, for example, of what I write about in these very lines—passes for 'truth.' The morrow may reduce it to 'opinion.' The transcendentalist in all his particular knowledges is as liable to this reduction as I am: his absolute does not save him. Why, then, need he quarrel with an account of knowledge that insists on naming this effect? Why not treat the working of the idea from next to next as the essence of its self-transcendency? Why insist that knowing is a static relation out of time when it practically seems so much a function of our active life? For a thing to be valid, says Lotze, is the same as to make itself valid. When the whole universe seems only to be making itself valid and to be still incomplete (else why its ceaseless changing?) why, of all things, should knowing be exempt? Why should it not be making itself valid like everything else? That some parts of it may be already valid or verified beyond dispute, the empirical philosopher, of course, like anyone else, may always hope.

## VI. The Conterminousness of Different Minds

With transition and prospect thus enthroned in pure experience, it is impossible to subscribe to the idealism of the English school. Radical empiricism has, in fact, more affinities with natural realism than with the views of Berkeley or of Mill, and this can be easily shown.

For the Berkeleyan school, ideas (the verbal equivalent of what I term experiences) are discontinuous. The content of each is wholly immanent, and there are no transitions with which they are consubstantial and through which their beings may unite. Your Memorial Hall and mine, even when both are percepts, are wholly out of connexion with each other.

Our lives are a congeries of solipsisms, out of which in strict logic only a God could compose a universe even of discourse. No dynamic currents run between my objects and your objects. Never can our minds meet in the *same*.

The incredibility of such a philosophy is flagrant. It is 'cold, strained, and unnatural' in a supreme degree; and it may be doubted whether even Berkeley himself, who took it so religiously, really believed, when walking through the streets of London, that his spirit and the spirits of his fellow wayfarers had absolutely different towns in view.

To me the decisive reason in favor of our minds meeting in *some* common objects at least is that, unless I make that supposition, I have no motive for assuming that your mind exists at all. Why do I postulate your mind? Because I see your body acting in a certain way. Its gestures, facial movements, words and conduct generally, are 'expressive,' so I deem it actuated as my own is, by an inner life like mine. This argument from analogy is my *reason,* whether an instinctive belief runs before it or not. But what is 'your body' here but a percept in *my* field? It is only as animating *that* object, *my* object, that I have any occasion to think of you at all. If the body that you actuate be not the very body that I see there, but some duplicate body of your own with which that has nothing to do, we belong to different universes, you and I, and for me to speak of you is folly. Myriads of such universes even now may coexist, irrelevant to one another; my concern is solely with the universe with which my own life is connected.

In that perceptual part of *my* universe which I call *your* body, your mind and my mind meet and may be called conterminous. Your mind actuates that body and mine sees it; my thoughts pass into it as into their harmonious cognitive fulfillment; your emotions and volitions pass into it as causes into their effects.

But that percept hangs together with all our other physical percepts. They are of one stuff with it; and if it be our common possession, they must be so likewise. For instance, your hand lays hold of one end of a rope and my hand lays hold of the other end. We pull against each other. Can our two hands be mutual objects in this experience, and the rope not be mutual also? What is true of the rope is true of any other percept. Your objects are over and over again the same as mine. If I ask you *where* some object of yours is, our old Memorial Hall, for example, you point to *my* Memorial Hall with *your* hand which *I* see. If you alter an object in your world, put out a candle, for example, when I am present, *my* candle *ipso facto* goes out. It is only as altering my objects that I guess you to exist. If your objects do not coalesce with my objects, if they be not identically where mine are, they must be proved to be positively somewhere else. But no other location can be assigned for them, so their place must be what it seems to be, the same.

Practically, then, our minds meet in a world of objects which they share in common, which would still be there, if one or several of the minds were destroyed. I can see no formal objection to this supposition's being literally true. On the principles which I am defending, a 'mind' or 'personal consciousness' is the name for a series of experiences run together by certain definite transitions, and an objective reality is a series of similar experiences knit by different transitions. If one and the same experience can figure twice, once in a mental and once in a physical context (as I have tried, in my article on 'Consciousness,' to show that it can), one does not see why it might not figure thrice, or four times, or any number of times, by running into as many different mental contexts, just as the same point, lying at their intersection, can be continued into many different lines. Abolishing any number of contexts would not destroy the experience itself or its other contexts, any more than abolishing some of the point's linear continuations would destroy the others, or destroy the point itself.

I well know the subtle dialectic which insists that a term taken in another relation must needs be an intrinsically different term. The crux is always the old Greek one, that the same man can't be tall in relation to one neighbor, and short in relation to another, for that would make him tall and short at once. In this essay I cannot stop to refute this dialectic, so I pass on, leaving my flank for the time exposed. But if my reader will only allow that the same '*now*' both ends his past and begins his future; or that, when he buys an acre of land from his neighbor, it is the same acre that successively figures in the two estates; or that when I pay him a dollar, the same dollar goes into his pocket that came out of mine; he will also in consistency have to allow that the same object may conceivably play a part in, as being related to the rest of, any number of otherwise entirely different minds. This is enough for my present point: the common-sense notion of minds sharing the same object offers no special logical or epistemological difficulties of its own; it stands or falls with the general possibility of things being in conjunctive relation with other things at all.

In principle, then, let natural realism pass for possible. Your mind and mine *may* terminate in the same percept, not merely against it, as if it were a third external thing, but by inserting themselves into it and coalescing with it, for such is the sort of conjunctive union that appears to be experienced when a perceptual terminus 'fulfills.' Even so, two hawsers may embrace the same pile, and yet neither one of them touch any other part, except that pile, of what the other hawser is attached to.

It is therefore not a formal question, but a question of empirical fact solely, whether, when you and I are said to know the 'same' Memorial Hall, our minds do terminate at or in a numerically identical percept. Obviously, as a plain matter of fact, they do *not*. Apart from color-blindness and such possibilities, we see the Hall in different perspectives. You may be on one side of it and I on another. The percept of each of us, as he sees the surface of the Hall, is moreover only his provisional terminus. The next thing beyond my percept is not your mind, but more percepts of my own into which my first percept developes, the interior of the Hall, for instance, or the inner structure of its bricks and mortar. If our minds were in a lit-

eral sense *con*terminous, neither could get beyond the percept which they had in common, it would be an ultimate barrier between them—unless indeed they flowed over it and became 'coconscious' over a still larger part of their content, which (thought-transference apart) is not supposed to be the case. In point of fact the ultimate common barrier can always be pushed, by both minds, farther than any actual percept of either, until at last it resolves itself into the mere notion of imperceptibles like atoms or ether, so that, where we do terminate in percepts, our knowledge is only speciously completed, being, in theoretic strictness, only a virtual knowledge of those remoter objects which conception carries out.

Is natural realism, permissible in logic, refuted then by empirical fact? Do our minds have no object in common after all?

Yes, they certainly have *space* in common. On pragmatic principles we are obliged to predicate sameness wherever we can predicate no assignable point of difference. If two named things have every quality and function indiscernible, and are at the same time in the same place, they must be written down as numerically one thing under two different names. But there is no test discoverable, so far as I know, by which it can be shown that the place occupied by your percept of Memorial Hall differs from the place occupied by mine. The percepts themselves may be shown to differ; but if each of us be asked to point out where his percept is, we point to an identical spot. All the relations, whether geometrical or causal, of the Hall originate or terminate in that spot wherein our hands meet, and where each of us begins to work if he wishes to make the Hall change before the other's eyes. Just so it is with our bodies. That body of yours which you actuate and feel from within must be in the same spot as the body of yours which I see or touch from without. 'There' for me means where I place my finger. If you do not feel my finger's contact to be 'there' in *my* sense, when I place it on your body, where then do you feel it? Your inner actuations of your body meet my finger *there;* it is *there* that you resist its push, or shrink back, or sweep the finger aside with your hand. Whatever farther knowledge either of us may acquire of the real constitution of the body which we thus feel, you from within and I from without, it is in that same place that the newly conceived or perceived constituents have to be located, and it is *through*that space that your and my mental intercourse with each other has always to be carried on, by the mediation of impressions which I convey thither, and of the reactions thence which those impressions may provoke from you.

In general terms, then, whatever differing contents our minds may eventually fill a place with, the place itself is a numerically identical content of the two minds, a piece of common property in which, through which, and over which they join. The receptacle of certain of our experiences being thus common, the experiences themselves might some day become common also. If that day ever did come, our thoughts would terminate in a complete empirical identity, there would be an end, so far as *those* experiences went, to our discussions about truth. No points of difference appearing, they would have to count as the same.

## VII.   Conclusion

With this we have the outlines of a philosophy of pure experience before us. At the outset of my essay, I called it a mosaic philosophy. In actual mosaics the pieces are held together by their bedding, for which bedding the substances, transcendental egos, or absolutes of other philosophies may be taken to stand. In radical empiricism there is no bedding; it is as if the pieces clung together by their edges, the transitions experienced between them forming their cement. Of course such a metaphor is misleading, for in actual experience the more substantive and the more transitive parts run into each other continuously, there is in general no separateness needing to be overcome by an external cement; and whatever separateness is actually experienced is not overcome, it stays and counts as separateness to the end.

But the metaphor serves to symbolize the fact that experience itself, taken at large, can grow by its edges. That one moment of it proliferates into the next by transitions which, whether conjunctive or disjunctive, continue the experiential tissue, cannot, I contend, be denied. Life is in the transitions as much as in the terms connected; often, indeed, it seems to be there more emphatically, as if our spurts and sallies forward were the real firing-line of the battle, were like the thin line of flame advancing across the dry autumnal field which the farmer proceeds to burn. In this line we live prospectively as well as retrospectively. It is 'of' the past, inasmuch as it comes expressly as the past's continuation; it is 'of' the future in so far as the future, when it comes, will have continued *it*.

These relations of continuous transition experienced are what make our experiences cognitive. In the simplest and completest cases the experiences are cognitive of one another. When one of them terminates a previous series of them with a sense of fulfilment, it, we say, is what those other experiences 'had in view.' The knowledge, in such a case, is verified, the truth is 'salted down.' Mainly, however, we live on speculative investments, or on our prospects only. But living on things *in posse* is as good as living in the actual, so long as our credit remains good. It is evident that for the most part it is good, and that the universe seldom protests our drafts.

In this sense we at every moment can continue to believe in an existing *beyond*. It is only in special cases that our confident rush forward gets rebuked. The beyond must of course always in our philosophy be itself of an experiential nature. If not a future experience of our own or a present one of our neighbor, it must be a thing in itself in Dr. Prince's and Professor Strong's sense of the term—that is, it must be an experience *for* itself whose relation to other things we translate into the action of molecules, ether-waves, or whatever else the physical symbols may be. This opens the chapter of the relations of radical empiricism to panpsychism, into which I cannot enter now.

The beyond can in any case exist simultaneously—for it can be experienced *to have existed* simultaneously—with the experience that practically postulates it by looking in its direction, or by turning or changing in the direction of which it is the goal. Pending that actuality of union, in the virtuality of which the 'truth,' even now, of the postulation consists, the beyond and its knower are entities split off from each other. The world is in so far forth a pluralism of which the unity is not fully experienced as yet. But, as fast as verifications come, trains of experience, once separate, run into one another; and that is why I said, earlier in my essay, that the unity of the world is on the whole undergoing increase. The universe continually grows in quantity by new experiences that graft themselves upon the older mass; but these very new experiences often help the mass to a more consolidated form.

These are the main features of a philosophy of pure experience. It has innumerable other aspects and arouses innumerable questions, but the points I have touched on seem enough to make an entering wedge. In my own mind such a philosophy harmonizes best with a radical pluralism, with novelty and indeterminism, moralism and theism, and with the 'humanism' lately sprung upon us by the Oxford and the Chicago schools. I cannot, however, be sure that all these doctrines are its necessary and indispensable allies. It presents so many points of difference, both from the common sense and from the idealism that have made our philosophic language, that it is almost as difficult to state it as it is to think it out clearly, and if it is ever to grow into a respectable system, it will have to be built up by the contributions of many co-operating minds. It seems to me, as I said at the outset of this essay, that many minds are, in point of fact, now turning in a direction that points toward radical empiricism. If they are carried farther by my words, and if then they add their stronger voices to my feebler one, the publication of this essay will have been worth while.

# What Pragmatism Means

Some years ago, being with a camping party in the mountains, I returned from a solitary ramble to find everyone engaged in a ferocious metaphysical dispute. The *corpus* of the dispute was a squirrel—a live squirrel supposed to be clinging to one side of a tree-trunk; while over against the tree's opposite side a human being was imagined to stand. This human witness tries to get sight of the squirrel by moving rapidly round the tree, but no matter how fast he goes, the squirrel moves as fast in the opposite direction, and always keeps the tree between himself and the man, so that never a glimpse of him is caught. The resultant metaphysical problem now is this: *Does the man go round the squirrel or not?* He goes round the tree, sure enough, and the squirrel is on the tree; but does he go round the squirrel? In the unlimited leisure of the wilderness, discussion had been worn threadbare. Everyone had taken sides, and was obstinate; and the numbers on both sides were even. Each side, when I appeared, therefore appealed to me to make it a majority. Mindful of the scholastic adage that whenever you meet a contradiction you must make a distinction, I immediately sought and found one, as follows: "Which party is right," I said, "depends on what you *practi-*

From *The Works of William James—Pragmatism,* ed. Frederick Burkhardt (Cambridge, Mass.: Harvard University Press, 1975 [1907]), pp. 27–44.

*cally mean* by 'going round' the squirrel. If you mean passing from the north of him to the east, then to the south, then to the west, and then to the north of him again, obviously the man does go around him, for he occupies these successive positions. But if on the contrary you mean being first in front of him, then on the right of him, then behind him, then on his left, and finally in front again, it is quite as obvious that the man fails to go round him, for by the compensating movements the squirrel makes, he keeps his belly turned towards the man all the time, and his back turned away. Make the distinction, and there is no occasion for any farther dispute. You are both right and both wrong according as you conceive the verb 'to go round' in one practical fashion or the other."

Altho one or two of the hotter disputants called my speech a shuffling evasion, saying they wanted no quibbling or scholastic hair-splitting, but meant just plain honest English 'round,' the majority seemed to think that the distinction had assuaged the dispute.

I tell this trivial anecdote because it is a peculiarly simple example of what I wish now to speak of as *the pragmatic method*. The pragmatic method is primarily a method of settling metaphysical disputes that otherwise might be interminable. Is the world one or many?—fated or free?—material or spiritual?—here are notions either of which may or may not hold good of the world; and disputes over such notions are unending. The pragmatic method in such cases is to try to interpret each notion by tracing its respective practical consequences. What difference would it practically make to anyone if this notion rather than that notion were true? If no practical difference whatever can be traced, then the alternatives mean practically the same thing, and all dispute is idle. Whenever a dispute is serious, we ought to be able to show some practical difference that must follow from one side or the other's being right.

A glance at the history of the idea will show you still better what pragmatism means. The term is derived from the same Greek word πρᾶγμα, meaning action, from which our words 'practice' and 'practical' come. It was first introduced into philosophy by Mr. Charles Peirce in 1878. In an article entitled 'How to Make Our Ideas Clear,' in the 'Popular Science Monthly' for January of that year, Mr. Peirce, after pointing out that our beliefs are really rules for action, said that, to develope a thought's meaning, we need only determine what conduct it is fitted to produce: that conduct is for us its sole significance. And the tangible fact at the root of all our thought-distinctions, however subtle, is that there is no one of them so fine as to consist in anything but a possible difference of practice. To attain perfect clearness in our thoughts of an object, then, we need only consider what conceivable effects of a practical kind the object may involve—what sensations we are to expect from it, and what reactions we must prepare. Our conception of these effects, whether immediate or remote, is then for us the whole of our conception of the object, so far as that conception has positive significance at all.

This is the principle of Peirce, the principle of pragmatism. It lay entirely unnoticed by anyone for twenty years, until I, in an address before Professor Howison's philosophical union at the university of California, brought it forward again and made a special application of it to religion. By that date (1898) the times seemed ripe for its reception. The word 'pragmatism' spread, and at present it fairly spots the pages of the philosophic journals. On all hands we find the 'pragmatic movement' spoken of, sometimes with respect, sometimes with contumely, seldom with clear understanding. It is evident that the term applies itself conveniently to a number of tendencies that hitherto have lacked a collective name, and that it has 'come to stay'.

To take in the importance of Peirce's principle, one must get accustomed to applying it to concrete cases. I found a few years ago that Ostwald, the illustrious Leipzig chemist, had been making perfectly distinct use of the principle of pragmatism in his lectures on the philosophy of science, tho he had not called it by that name.

"All realities influence our practice," he wrote me, "and that influence is their meaning for us. I am accustomed to put questions to my classes in this way: In what respects would the world be different if this alternative or that were true? If I can find nothing that would become different, then the alternative has no sense."

That is, the rival views mean practically the same thing, and meaning, other than practical, there is for us none. Ostwald in a published lecture gives this example of what he means. Chemists have long wrangled over the inner constitution of certain bodies called 'tautomerous.' Their properties seemed equally consistent with the notion that an instable hydrogen atom oscillates inside of them, or that they are instable mixtures of two bodies. Controversy raged; but never was decided. "It would never have begun," says Ostwald, "if the combatants had asked themselves what particular experimental fact could have been made different by one or the other view being correct. For it would then have appeared that no difference of fact could possible ensue; and the quarrel was as unreal as if, theorizing in primitive times about the raising of dough by yeast, one party should have invoked a 'brownie,' while another insisted on an 'elf' as the true cause of the phenomenon."

It is astonishing to see how many philosophical disputes collapse into insignificance the moment you subject them to this simple test of tracing a concrete consequence. There can *be* no difference anywhere that doesn't *make* a difference elsewhere—no difference in abstract truth that doesn't express itself in a difference in concrete fact and in conduct consequent upon that fact, imposed on somebody, somehow, somewhere and somewhen. The whole function of philosophy ought to be to find out what definite difference it will make to you and me, at definite instants of our life, if this world-formula or that world-formula be the true one.

There is absolutely nothing new in the pragmatic method. Socrates was an adept at it. Aristotle used it methodically. Locke, Berkeley and Hume made momentous contributions to truth by its means. Shadworth Hodgson keeps insisting that realities are only what they are 'known-as.' But these forerunners of pragmatism used it in fragments: they were preludes only. Not until in our time has it generalized itself, become conscious of a universal mission, pretended to a conquering destiny. I believe in that destiny, and I hope I may end by inspiring you with my belief.

Pragmatism represents a perfectly familiar attitude in philosophy, the empiricist attitude, but it represents it, as it seems to me, both in a more radical and in a less objectionable form than it has ever yet assumed. A pragmatist turns his back resolutely and once for all upon a lot of inveterate habits dear to professional philosophers. He turns away from abstraction and insufficiency, from verbal solutions, from bad *a priori* reasons, from fixed principles, closed systems, and pretended absolutes and origins. He turns towards concreteness and adequacy, towards facts, towards action, and towards power. That means the empiricist temper regnant, and the rationalist temper sincerely given up. It means the open air and possibilities of nature, as against dogma, artificiality and the pretence of finality in truth.

At the same time it does not stand for any special results. It is a method only. But the general triumph of that method would mean an enormous change in what I called in my last lecture the 'temperament' of philosophy. Teachers of the ultra-rationalistic type would be frozen out, much as the courtier type is frozen out in republics, as the ultramontane type of priest is frozen out in protestant lands. Science and metaphysics would come much nearer together, would in fact work absolutely hand in hand.

Metaphysics has usually followed a very primitive kind of quest. You know how men have always hankered after unlawful magic, and you know what a great part, in magic, *words* have always played. If you have his name, or the formula of incantation that binds him, you can control the spirit, genie, afrite, or whatever the power may be. Solomon knew the names of all the spirits, and having their names, he held them subject to his will. So the universe has always appeared to the natural mind as a kind of enigma, of which the key must be sought in the shape of some illuminating or powerbringing word or name. That word names the universe's *principle,* and to possess it is, after a fashion, to possess the universe itself. 'God,' 'Matter,' 'Reason,' 'the Absolute,' 'Energy,' are so many solving names. You can rest when you have them. You are at the end of your metaphysical quest.

But if you follow the pragmatic method, you cannot look on any such word as closing your quest. You must bring out of each word its practical cash-value, set it at work within the stream of your experience. It appears less as a solution, then, than as a program for more work, and more particularly as an indication of the ways in which existing realities may be *changed.*

*Theories thus become instruments, not answers to enigmas, in which we can rest.* We don't lie back upon them, we move forward, and, on occasion, make nature over again by their aid. Pragmatism unstiffens all our theories, limbers them up and sets each one at work. Being nothing essentially new, it harmonizes with many ancient philosophic tendencies. It agrees with nominalism for instance, in always appealing to particulars; with utilitarianism in emphasizing practical aspects; with positivism in its disdain for verbal solutions, useless questions, and metaphysical abstractions.

All these, you see, are *anti-intellectualist* tendencies. Against rationalism as a pretension and a method, pragmatism is fully armed and militant. But, at the outset, at least, it stands for no particular results. It has no dogmas, and no doctrines save its method. As the young Italian pragmatist Papini has well said, it lies in the midst of our theories, like a corridor in a hotel. Innumerable chambers open out of it. In one you may find a man writing an atheistic volume; in the next someone on his knees praying for faith and strength; in a third a chemist investigating a body's properties. In a fourth a system of idealistic metaphysics is being excogitated; in a fifth the impossibility of metaphysics is being shown. But they all

own the corridor, and all must pass through it if they want a practicable way of getting into or out of their respective rooms.

No particular results then, so far, but only an attitude of orientation, is what the pragmatic method means. *The attitude of looking away from first things, principles, 'categories,' supposed necessities; and of looking towards last things, fruits, consequences, facts.*

So much for the pragmatic method! You may say that I have been praising it rather than explaining it to you, but I shall presently explain it abundantly enough by showing how it works on some familiar problems. Meanwhile the word pragmatism has come to be used in a still wider sense, as meaning also a certain *theory of truth.* I mean to give a whole lecture to the statement of that theory, after first paving the way, so I can be very brief now. But brevity is hard to follow, so I ask for your redoubled attention for a quarter of an hour. If much remains obscure, I hope to make it clearer in the later lectures.

One of the most successfully cultivated branches of philosophy in our time is what is called inductive logic, the study of the conditions under which our sciences have evolved. Writers on this subject have begun to show a singular unanimity as to what the laws of nature and elements of fact mean, when formulated by mathematicians, physicists and chemists. When the first mathematical, logical and natural uniformities, the first *laws,* were discovered, men were so carried away by the clearness, beauty and simplification that resulted, that they believed themselves to have deciphered authentically the eternal thoughts of the Almighty. His mind also thundered and reverberated in syllogisms. He also thought in conic sections, squares and roots and ratios, and geometrized like Euclid. He made Kepler's laws for the planets to follow; he made velocity increase proportionally to the time in falling bodies; he made the law of the sines for light to obey when refracted; he established the classes, orders, families and genera of plants and animals, and fixed the distances between them. He thought the archetypes of all things, and devised their variations; and when we rediscover any one of these his wondrous institutions, we seize his mind in its very literal intention.

But as the sciences have developed farther, the notion has gained ground that most, perhaps all, of our laws are only approximations. The laws themselves, moreover, have grown so numerous that there is no counting them; and so many rival formulations are proposed in all the branches of science that investigators have become accustomed to the notion that no theory is absolutely a transcript of reality, but that any one of them may from some point of view be useful. Their great use is to summarize old facts and to lead to new ones. They are only a man-made language, a conceptual shorthand, as someone calls them, in which we write our reports of nature; and languages, as is well known, tolerate much choice of expression and many dialects.

Thus human arbitrariness has driven divine necessity from scientific logic. If I mention the names of Sigwart, Mach, Ostwald, Pearson, Milhaud, Poincaré, Duhem, Ruyssen, those of you who are students will easily identify the tendency I speak of, and will think of additional names.

Riding now on the front of this wave of scientific logic Messrs. Schiller and Dewey appear with their pragmatistic account of what truth everywhere signifies. Everywhere, these teachers say, 'truth' in our ideas and beliefs means the same thing that it means in science. It means, they say, nothing but this, *that ideas (which themselves are but parts of our experience) become true just in so far as they help us to get into satisfactory relation with other parts of our experience,* to summarize them and get about among them by conceptual short-cuts instead of following the interminable succession of particular phenomena. Any idea upon which we can ride, so to speak; any idea that will carry us prosperously from any one part of our experience to any other part, linking things satisfactorily, working securely, simplifying, saving labor; is true for just so much, true in so far forth, true *instrumentally.* This is the 'instrumental' view of truth taught so successfully at Chicago, the view that truth in our ideas

means their power to 'work,' promulgated so brilliantly at Oxford.

Messrs. Dewey, Schiller and their allies, in reaching this general conception of all truth, have only followed the example of geologists, biologists and philologists. In the establishment of these other sciences, the successful stroke was always to take some simple process actually observable in operation—as denudation by weather, say, or variation from parental type, or change of dialect by incorporation of new words and pronunciations—and then to generalize it, making it apply to all times, and produce great results by summating its effects through the ages.

The observable process which Schiller and Dewey particularly singled out for generalization is the familiar one by which any individual settles into *new opinions.* The process here is always the same. The individual has a stock of old opinions already, but he meets a new experience that puts them to a strain. Somebody contradicts them; or in a reflective moment he discovers that they contradict each other; or he hears of facts with which they are incompatible; or desires arise in him which they cease to satisfy. The result is an inward trouble to which his mind till then had been a stranger, and from which he seeks to escape by modifying his previous mass of opinions. He saves as much of it as he can, for in this matter of belief we are all extreme conservatives. So he tries to change first this opinion, and then that (for they resist change very variously), until at last some new idea comes up which he can graft upon the ancient stock with a minimum of disturbance of the latter, some idea that mediates between the stock and the new experience and runs them into one another most felicitously and expediently.

This new idea is then adopted as the true one. It preserves the older stock of truths with a minimum of modification, stretching them just enough to make them admit the novelty, but conceiving that in ways as familiar as the case leaves possible. An *outrée* [exaggerated] explanation, violating all our preconceptions, would never pass for a true account of a novelty. We should scratch round industriously till we found something less excentric. The most violent revolutions in an individual's beliefs leave most of his old order standing. Time and space, cause and effect, nature and history, and one's own biography remain untouched. New truth is always a go-between, a smoother-over of transitions. It marries old opinion to new fact so as ever to show a minimum of jolt, a maximum of continuity. We hold a theory true just in proportion to its success in solving this 'problem of maxima and minima.' But success in solving this problem is eminently a matter of approximation. We say this theory solves it on the whole more satisfactorily than that theory; but that means more satisfactorily to ourselves, and individuals will emphasize their points of satisfaction differently. To a certain degree, therefore, everything here is plastic.

The point I now urge you to observe particularly is the part played by the older truths. Failure to take account of it is the source of much of the unjust criticism leveled against pragmatism. Their influence is absolutely controlling. Loyalty to them is the first principle—in most cases it is the only principle; for by far the most usual way of handling phenomena so novel that they would make for a serious rearrangement of our preconceptions is to ignore them altogether, or to abuse those who bear witness for them.

You doubtless wish examples of this process of truth's growth, and the only trouble is their superabundance. The simplest case of new truth is of course the mere numerical addition of new kinds of facts, or of new single facts of old kinds, to our experience—an addition that involves no alteration in the old beliefs. Day follows day, and its contents are simply added. The new contents themselves are not true, they simply *come* and *are*. Truth is *what we say about* them, and when we say that they have come, truth is satisfied by the plain additive formula.

But often the day's contents oblige a rearrangement. If I should now utter piercing shrieks and act like a maniac on this platform, it would make many of you revise your ideas as to the probable worth of my philosophy.

'Radium' came the other day as part of the day's content, and seemed for a moment to contradict our ideas of the whole order of nature, that order having come to be identified with what is called the conservation of energy. The mere sight of radium paying heat away indefinitely out of its own pocket seemed to violate that conservation. What to think? If the radiations from it were nothing but an escape of unsuspected 'potential' energy, pre-existent inside of the atoms, the principle of conservation would be saved. The discovery of 'helium' as the radiation's outcome, opened a way to this belief. So Ramsay's view is generally held to be true, because, altho it extends our old ideas of energy, it causes a minimum of alteration in their nature.

I need not multiply instances. A new opinion counts as 'true' just in proportion as it gratifies the individual's desire to assimilate the novel in his experience to his beliefs in stock. It must both lean on old truth as grasp new fact; and its success (as I said a moment ago) in doing this, is a matter for the individual's appreciation. When old truth grows, then, by new truth's addition, it is for subjective reasons. We are in the process and obey the reasons. That new idea is truest which performs most felicitously its function of satisfying our double urgency. It makes itself true, gets itself classed as true, by the way it works; grafting itself then upon the ancient body of truth, which thus grows much as a tree grows by the activity of a new layer of cambium.

Now Dewey and Schiller proceed to generalize this observation and to apply it to the most ancient parts of truth. They also once were plastic. They also were called true for human reasons. They also mediated between still earlier truths and what in those days were novel observations. Purely objective truth, truth in whose establishment the function of giving human satisfaction in marrying previous parts of experience with newer parts played no role whatever, is nowhere to be found. The reasons why we call things true is the reason why they *are* true, for 'to be true' *means* only to perform this marriage-function.

The trail of the human serpent is thus over everything. Truth independent; truth that we *find* merely; truth no longer malleable to human need; truth incorrigible, in a word; such truth exists indeed superabundantly—or is supposed to exist by rationalistically minded thinkers; but then it means only the dead heart of the living tree, and its being there means only that truth also has its paleontology and its 'prescription,' and may grow stiff with years of veteran service and petrified in men's regard by sheer antiquity. But how plastic even the oldest truths nevertheless really are has been vividly shown in our day by the transformation of logical and mathematical ideas, a transformation which seems even to be invading physics. The ancient formulas are reinterpreted as special expressions of much wider principles, principles that our ancestors never got a glimpse of in their present shape and formulation.

Mr. Schiller still gives to all this view of truth the name of 'Humanism,' but, for this doctrine too, the name of pragmatism seems fairly to be in the ascendant, so I will treat it under the name of pragmatism in these lectures.

Such then would be the scope of pragmatism—first, a method; and second, a genetic theory of what is meant by truth. And these two things must be our future topics.

What I have said of the theory of truth will, I am sure, have appeared obscure and unsatisfactory to most of you by reason of its brevity. I shall make amends for that hereafter. In a lecture on 'common sense' I shall try to show what I mean by truths grown petrified by antiquity. In another lecture I shall expatiate on the idea that our thoughts become true in proportion as they successfully exert their go between function. In a third I shall show how hard it is to discriminate subjective from objective factors in Truth's development. You may not follow me wholly in these lectures; and if you do, you may not wholly agree with me. But you will, I know, regard me at least as serious, and treat my effort with respectful consideration.

You will probably be surprised to learn, then, that Messrs. Schiller's and Dewey's theories have suffered a hailstorm of contempt and ridicule. All rationalism has risen against them. In influential quarters Mr. Schiller, in particular, has been treated like an impudent school boy who deserves a spanking. I should not mention this, but for the fact that it throws so much sidelight upon that rationalistic temper to which I have opposed the temper of pragmatism. Pragmatism is uncomfortable away from facts. Rationalism is comfortable only in the presence of abstractions. This pragmatist talk about truths in the plural, about their utility and satisfactoriness, about the success with which they 'work,' etc., suggests to the typical intellectualist mind a sort of coarse lame second-rate make-shift article of truth. Such truths are not real truth. Such tests are merely subjective. As against this, objective truth must be something non-utilitarian, haughty, refined, remote, august, exalted. It must be an absolute correspondence of our thoughts with an equally absolute reality. It must be what we *ought* to think, unconditionally. The conditioned ways in which we *do* think are so much irrelevance and matter for psychology. Down with psychology, up with logic, in all this question!

See the exquisite contrast of the types of mind! The pragmatist clings to facts and concreteness, observes truth at its work in particular cases, and generalizes. Truth, for him, becomes a class-name for all sorts of definite working-values in experience. For the rationalist it remains a pure abstraction, to the bare name of which we must defer. When the pragmatist undertakes to show in detail just *why* we must defer, the rationalist is unable to recognize the concretes from which his own abstraction is taken. He accuses us of *denying* truth; whereas we have only sought to trace exactly why people follow it and always ought to follow it. Your typical ultra-abstractionist fairly shudders at concreteness: other things equal, he positively prefers the pale and spectral. If the two universes were offered, he would always choose the skinny outline rather than the rich thicket of reality. It is so much purer, clearer, nobler.

I hope that as these lectures go on, the concreteness and closeness to facts of the pragmatism which they advocate may be what approves itself to you as its most satisfactory peculiarity. It only follows here the example of the sister-sciences, interpreting the unobserved by the observed. It brings old and new harmoniously together. It converts the absolutely empty notion of a static relation of 'correspondence' (what that may mean we must ask later) between our minds and reality, into that of a rich and active commerce (that anyone may follow in detail and understand) between particular thoughts of ours, and the great universe of other experiences in which they play their parts and have their uses.

But enough of this at present? The justification of what I say must be postponed. I wish now to add a word in further explanation of the claim I made at our last meeting, that pragmatism may be a happy harmonizer of empiricist ways of thinking, with the more religious demands of human beings.

Men who are strongly of the fact-loving temperament, you may remember me to have said, are liable to be kept at a distance by the small sympathy with facts which that philosophy from the present-day fashion of idealism offers them. It is far too intellectualistic. Old fashioned theism was bad enough, with its notion of God as an exalted monarch, made up of a lot of unintelligible or preposterous 'attributes'; but, so long as it held strongly by the argument from design, it kept some touch with concrete realities. Since, however, darwinism has once for all displaced design from the minds of the 'scientific,' theism has lost that foothold; and some kind of an immanent or pantheistic deity working *in* things rather than above them is, if any, the kind recommended to our contemporary imagination. Aspirants to a philosophic religion turn, as a rule, more hopefully nowadays towards idealistic pantheism than towards the older dualistic theism, in spite of the fact that the latter still counts able defenders.

But, as I said in my first lecture, the brand of pantheism offered is hard for them to assimilate if they are lovers of facts, or empirically minded. It is the absolutistic brand, spurning the dust and reared upon pure logic. It keeps no connexion whatever with concreteness. Affirming the Absolute Mind, which is its substitute for God, to be the rational presupposition of all particulars of fact, whatever they

may be, it remains supremely indifferent to what the particular facts in our world actually are. Be they what they may, the Absolute will father them. Like the sick lion in Esop's fable, all footprints lead into his den, but *nulla vestigia retrorsum* [nothing earlier remains]. You cannot redescend into the world of particulars by the Absolute's aid, or deduce any necessary consequences of detail important for your life from your idea of his nature. He gives you indeed the assurance that all is well with *Him,* and for his eternal way of thinking; but thereupon he leaves you to be finitely saved by your own temporal devices.

Far be it from me to deny the majesty of this conception, or its capacity to yield religious comfort to a most respectable class of minds. But from the human point of view, no one can pretend that it doesn't suffer from the faults of remoteness and abstractness. It is eminently a product of what I have ventured to call the rationalistic temper. It disdains empiricism's needs. It substitutes a pallid outline for the real world's richness. It is dapper; it is noble in the bad sense, in the sense in which to be noble is to be inapt for humble service. In this real world of sweat and dirt, it seems to me that when a view of things is 'noble,' that ought to count as a presumption against its truth, and as a philosophic disqualification. The prince of darkness may be a gentleman, as we are told he is, but whatever the God of earth and heaven is, he can surely be no gentleman. His menial services are needed in the dust of our human trials, even more than his dignity is needed in the empyrean.

Now pragmatism, devoted tho she be to facts, has no such materialistic bias as ordinary empiricism labors under. Moreover, she has no objection whatever to the realizing of abstractions, so long as you get about among particulars with their aid and they actually carry you somewhere. Interested in no conclusions but those which our minds and our experiences work out together, she has no *a priori* prejudices against theology. *If theological ideas prove to have a value for concrete life, they will be true, for pragmatism, in the sense of being good for so much. For how much more they are true, will depend entirely on their relations to the other truths that also have to be acknowledged.*

What I said just now about the Absolute of transcendental idealism is a case in point. First, I called it majestic and said it yielded religious comfort to a class of minds, and then I accused it of remoteness and sterility. But so far as it affords such comfort, it surely is not sterile; it has that amount of value; it performs a concrete function. As a good pragmatist, I myself ought to call the Absolute true 'in so far forth,' then; and I unhesitatingly now do so.

But what does *true in so far forth* mean in this case? To answer, we need only apply the pragmatic method. What do believers in the Absolute mean by saying that their belief affords them comfort? They mean that since in the Absolute finite evil is 'overruled' already, we may, therefore, whenever we wish, treat the temporal as if it were potentially the eternal, be sure that we can trust its outcome, and, without sin, dismiss our fear and drop the worry of our finite responsibility. In short, they mean that we have a right ever and anon to take a moral holiday, to let the world wag in its own way, feeling that its issues are in better hands than ours and are none of our business.

The universe is a system of which the individual members may relax their anxieties occasionally, in which the don't-care method is also right for men, and moral holidays in order—that, if I mistake not, is part, at least, of what the Absolute is 'known-as,' that is the great difference in our particular experiences which his being true makes for us, that is part of his cash-value when he is pragmatically interpreted. Farther than that the ordinary lay-reader in philosophy who thinks favorably of absolute idealism does not venture to sharpen his conceptions. He can use the Absolute for so much, and so much is very precious. He is pained at hearing you speak incredulously of the Absolute, therefore, and disregards your criticisms because they deal with aspects of the conception that he fails to follow.

If the Absolute means this, and means no more than this, who can possibly deny the truth of it? To deny it would be to insist that men should never relax, and that holidays are never in order.

I am well aware how odd it must seem to some of you to hear me say that an idea is 'true' so long as to believe it is profitable to our lives. That it is *good,* for as much as it profits, you will gladly admit. If what we do by its aid is good, you will allow the idea itself to be good in so far forth, for we are the better for possessing it. But is it not a strange misuse of the word 'truth,' you will say, to call ideas also 'true' for this reason?

To answer this difficulty fully is impossible at this stage of my account. You touch here upon the very central point of Messrs. Schiller's, Dewey's and my own doctrine of truth, which I cannot discuss with detail until my sixth lecture. Let me now say only this, that truth is *one species of good,* and not, as is usually supposed, a category distinct from good, and co-ordinate with it. *The true is the name of whatever proves itself to be good in the way of belief, and good, too, for definite, assignable reasons.* Surely you must admit this, that if there were *no* good for life in true ideas, or if the knowledge of them were positively disadvantageous and false ideas the only useful ones, then the current notion that truth is divine and precious, and its pursuit a duty, could never have grown up or become a dogma. In a world like that, our duty would be to *shun* truth, rather. But in this world, just as certain foods are not only agreeable to our taste, but good for our teeth, our stomach and our tissues; so certain ideas are not only agreeable to think about, or agreeable as supporting other ideas that we are fond of, but they are also helpful in life's practical struggles. If there be any life that it is really better we should lead, and if there be any idea which, if believed in, would help us to lead that life, then it would be really *better for us* to believe in that idea, *unless, indeed, belief in it incidentally clashed with other greater vital benefits.*

'What would be better for us to believe'! This sounds very like a definition of truth. It comes very near to saying 'what we *ought* to believe': and in *that* definition none of you would find any oddity. Ought we ever not to believe what it is *better for us* to believe? And can we then keep the notion of what is better for us, and what is true for us, permanently apart?

Pragmatism says no, and I fully agree with her. Probably you also agree, so far as the abstract statement goes, but with a suspicion that if we practically did believe everything that made for good in our own personal lives, we should be found indulging all kinds of fancies about this world's affairs, and all kinds of sentimental superstitions about a world hereafter. Your suspicion here is undoubtedly well founded, and it is evident that something happens when you pass from the abstract to the concrete, that complicates the situation.

I said just now that what is better for us to believe is true *unless the belief incidentally clashes with some other vital benefit.* Now in real life what vital benefits is any particular belief of ours most liable to clash with? What indeed except the vital benefits yielded by *other beliefs* when these prove incompatible with the first ones? In other words, the greatest enemy of any one of our truths may be the rest of our truths. Truths have once for all this desperate instinct of self-preservation and of desire to extinguish whatever contradicts them. My belief in the Absolute, based on the good it does me, must run the gauntlet of all my other beliefs. Grant that it may be true in giving me a moral holiday. Nevertheless, as I conceive it,—and let me speak now confidentially, as it were, and merely in my own private person,—it clashes with other truths of mine whose benefits I hate to give up on its account. It happens to be associated with a kind of logic of which I am the enemy, I find that it entangles me in metaphysical paradoxes that are inacceptable, etc., etc. But as I have enough trouble in life already without adding the trouble of carrying these intellectual inconsistencies, I personally just give up the Absolute. I just *take* my moral holidays; or else as a professional philosopher, I try to justify them by some other principle.

If I could restrict my notion of the Absolute to its bare holiday-giving value, it wouldn't clash with my other truths. But we cannot easily thus restrict our hypotheses. They carry supernumerary features, and these it is that clash so. My disbelief in the Absolute means then disbelief in those other supernumerary features, for I fully believe in the legitimacy of taking moral holidays.

You see by this what I meant when I called pragmatism a mediator and reconciler and said, borrowing the word from Papini, that she 'unstiffens' our theories. She has in fact no prejudices whatever, no obstructive dogmas, no rigid canons of what shall count as proof. She is completely genial. She will entertain any hypothesis, she will consider any evidence. It follows that in the religious field she is at a great advantage both over positivistic empiricism, with its anti-theological bias, and over religious rationalism, with its exclusive interest in the remote, the noble, the simple, and the abstract in the way of conception.

In short, she widens the field of search for God. Rationalism sticks to logic and the empyrean. Empiricism sticks to the external senses. Pragmatism is willing to take anything, to follow either logic or the senses, and to count the humblest and most personal experiences. She will count mystical experiences if they have practical consequences. She will take a God who lives in the very dirt of private fact—if that should seem a likely place to find him.

Her only test of probable truth is what works best in the way of leading us, what fits every part of life best and combines with the collectivity of experience's demands, nothing being omitted. If theological ideas should do this, if the notion of God, in particular, should prove to do it, how could pragmatism possibly deny God's existence? She could see no meaning in treating as 'not true' a notion that was pragmatically so successful. What other kind of truth could there be, for her, than all this agreement with concrete reality?

In my last lecture I shall return again to the relations of pragmatism with religion. But you see already how democratic she is. Her manners are as various and flexible, her resources as rich and endless, and here conclusions as friendly as those of mother nature.

# The Moral Philosopher and the Moral Life

The main purpose of this paper is to show that there is no such thing possible as an ethical philosophy dogmatically made up in advance. We all help to determine the content of ethical philosophy so far as we contribute to the race's moral life. In other words, there can be no final truth in ethics any more than in physics, until the last man has had his experience and said his say. In the one case as in the other, however, the hypotheses which we now make while waiting, and the acts to which they prompt us, are among the indispensable conditions which determine what they "say" shall be.

First of all, what is the position of him who seeks an ethical philosophy? To begin with, he must be distinguished from all those who are satisfied to be ethical sceptics. He *will* not be a sceptic; therefore so far from ethical scepticism being one possible fruit of ethical philosophizing, it can only be regarded as that residual alternative to all philosophy which from the outset menaces every would-be philosopher who may give up the quest discouraged, and renounce his original aim. That aim is to find an account of the moral relations that obtain among things, which will weave them into the unity of a stable system, and make of the world what one may call a genuine universe from the ethical point of view. So far as the world resists reduction to the form of unity, so far as ethical propositions seem unstable, so far does the philosopher fail of his ideal. The subject-matter of his study is the ideals he finds existing in the world; the purpose which guides him is this ideal of his own, of getting them into a certain form. This ideal is thus a factor in ethical philosophy whose legitimate presence must never be overlooked; it is a positive contribution which the philosopher himself necessarily makes to the problem. But it is his only positive contribution. At the outset of his inquiry he ought to have no other ideals. Were he interested peculiarly in the triumph of any one kind of good, he would *protanto* cease to be a judicial investigator, and become an advocate for some limited element of the case.

There are three questions in ethics which must be kept apart. Let them be called respectively the *psychological* question, the *metaphysical* question, and the *casuistic* question. The psychological question asks after the historical *origin* of our moral ideas and judgments; the metaphysical question asks what the very *meaning* of the words "good," "ill," and "obligation" are; the casuistic question asks what is the *measure* of the various goods and ills which men recognize, so that the philosopher may settle the true order of human obligations.

## I

The psychological question is for most disputants the only question. When your ordinary doctor of divinity has proved to his own satisfaction that an altogether unique faculty called "conscience" must be postulated to tell us what is right and what is wrong; or when your popular-science enthusiast has proclaimed that "apriorism" is an exploded superstition, and that our moral judgments have gradually resulted from the teaching of the environment, each of these persons thinks that ethics is settled and nothing more is to be said. The familiar pair of names, Intuitionist and Evolutionist, so commonly used now to connote all possible differences in ethical opinion, really refer to the psychological question alone. The

From *The Works of William James—The Will to Believe*. Frederick Burkhardt, ed. (Cambridge, Mass: Harvard University Press, 1979 [1891]), pp. 141–162.

discussion of this question hinges so much upon particular details that it is impossible to enter upon it at all within the limits of this paper. I will therefore only express dogmatically my own belief, which is this—that the Benthams, the Mills, and the Bains have done a lasting service in taking so many of our human ideals and showing how they must have arisen from the association with acts of simple bodily pleasures and reliefs from pain. Association with many remote pleasures will unquestionably make a thing significant of goodness in our minds; and the more vaguely the goodness is conceived of, the more mysterious will its source appear to be. But it is surely impossible to explain all our sentiments and preferences in this simple way. The more minutely psychology studies human nature, the more clearly it finds there traces of secondary affections, relating the impressions of the environment with one another and with our impulses in quite different ways from those mere associations of coexistence and succession which are practically all that pure empiricism can admit. Take the love of drunkenness; take bashfulness, the terror of high places, the tendency to sea-sickness, to faint at the sight of blood, the susceptibility to musical sounds; take the emotion of the comical, the passion for poetry, for mathematics, or for metaphysics—no one of these things can be wholly explained by either association or utility. They *go with* other things that can be so explained, no doubt; and some of them are prophetic of future utilities, since there is nothing in us for which some use may not be found. But their origin is in incidental complications to our cerebral structure, a structure whose original features arose with no reference to the perception of such discords and harmonies as these.

Well, a vast number of our moral perceptions also are certainly of this secondary and brain-born kind. They deal with directly felt fitnesses between things, and often fly in the teeth of all the prepossessions of habit and presumptions of utility. The moment you get beyond the coarser and more commonplace moral maxims, the Decalogues and Poor

Richard's Almanacs, you fall into schemes and positions which to the eye of common-sense are fantastic and over-strained. The sense for abstract justice which some persons have is as excentric a variation, from the natural-history point of view, as is the passion for music or for the higher philosophical consistencies which consumes the soul of others. The feeling of the inward dignity of certain spiritual attitudes, as peace, serenity, simplicity, veracity; and of the essential vulgarity of others, as querulousness, anxiety, egoistic fussiness, etc.—are quite inexplicable except by an innate preference of the more ideal attitude for its own pure sake. The nobler thing *tastes* better, and that is all that we can say. "Experience" of consequences may truly teach us what things are *wicked,* but what have consequences to do with what is *mean* and *vulgar?* If a man has shot his wife's paramour, by reason of what subtle repugnancy in things is it that we are so disgusted when we hear that the wife and the husband have made it up and are living comfortably together again? Or if the hypothesis were offered us of a world in which Messrs. Fourier's and Bellamy's and Morris's utopias should all be outdone, and millions kept permanently happy on the one simple condition that a certain lost soul on the far-off edge of things should lead a life of lonely torture, what except a specifical and independent sort of emotion can it be which would make us immediately feel, even though an impulse arose within us to clutch at the happiness so offered, how hideous a thing would be its enjoyment when deliberately accepted as the fruit of such a bargain? To what, once more, but subtle brain-born feelings of discord can be due all these recent protests against the entire race-tradition of retributive justice?—I refer to Tolstoï with his ideas of non-resistance, to Mr. Bellamy with his substitution of oblivion for repentance (in his novel of Dr. Heidenhain's Process), to M. Guyau with his radical condemnation of the punitive ideal. All these subtleties of the moral sensibility go as much beyond what can be ciphered out from the "laws of association" as the delicacies of sentiment possible between a pair of young lovers go beyond such precepts of the "etiquette to be observed during engagement" as are printed in manuals of social form.

No! Purely inward forces are certainly at work here. All the higher, more penetrating ideals are revolutionary. They present themselves far less in the guise of effects of past experience than in that of probable causes of future experience, factors to which the environment and the lessons it has so far taught us must learn to bend.

This is all I can say of the psychological question now. In the last chapter of a recent work I have sought to prove in a general way the existence, in our thought, of relations which do not merely repeat the couplings of experience. Our ideals have certainly many sources. They are not all explicable as signifying corporeal pleasures to be gained, and pains to be escaped. And for having so constantly perceived this psychological fact, we must applaud the intuitionist school. Whether or not such applause must be extended to that school's other characteristics will appear as we take up the following questions.

The next one in order is the metaphysical question, of what we mean by the words "obligation," "good," and "ill."

# II

First of all, it appears that such words can have no application or relevancy in a world in which no sentient life exists. Imagine an absolutely material world, containing only physical and chemical facts, and existing from eternity without a God, without even an interested spectator: would there be any sense in saying of that world that one of its states is better than another? Or if there were two such worlds possible, would there be any rhyme or reason in calling one good and the other bad—good or bad positively, I mean, and apart from the fact that one might relate itself better to the other to the philosopher's private interests? But we must leave these private interests out of the account, for the philosopher is a mental fact, and we are asking whether goods and evils and obligations exist in physical facts *per se.* Surely there is no *status* for good and evil to exist in, in a purely insentient world. How can one physical fact, considered simply as a physical fact, be "better" than another? Betterness is not a physical relation. In its mere material capacity, a thing can no more be good or bad than it can be pleasant or painful. Good for what? Good for the production of another physical fact, do you say? But what in a purely physical universe demands the production of that other fact? Physical facts simply *are* or *are not;* and neither when present or absent, can they be supposed to make demands. If they do, they can only do so by having desires; and then they have ceased to be purely physical facts, and have become facts of conscious sensibility. Goodness, badness, and obligation must be *realized* somewhere in order really to exist; and the first step in ethical philosophy is to see that no merely inorganic "nature of things" can realize them. Neither moral relations nor the moral law can swing *in vacuo.* Their only habitat can be a mind which feels them; and no world composed of merely physical facts can possibly be a world to which ethical propositions apply.

The moment one sentient being, however, is made a part of the universe, there is a chance for goods and evils really to exist. Moral relations now have their *status,* in that being's consciousness. So far as he feels anything to be good, he *makes it good.* It *is* good, for him; and being good for him, is absolutely good, for he is the sole creator of values in that universe, and outside of his opinion things have no moral character at all.

In such a universe as that it would of course be absurd to raise the question of whether the solitary thinker's judgments of good and ill are true or not. Truth supposes a standard outside of the thinker to which he must conform; but here the thinker is a sort of divinity, subject to no higher judge. Let us call the supposed universe which he inhabits a *moral solitude.* In such a moral solitude it is clear that there can be no outward obligation, and that the only trouble the god-like thinker is liable to have will be over the consistency of his own several ideals with one another. Some of these will no doubt be more pungent and appealing than the rest, their goodness will have a profounder, more penetrating taste; they will return to haunt him with more obstinate regrets if violated. So the thinker will have to order his life with them as its chief determinants, or else remain inwardly discordant and unhappy. Into whatever equilibrium he may settle, though, and however he may straighten out his system, it will be a right system; for beyond the facts of his own subjectivity there is nothing moral in the world.

If now we introduce a second thinker with his likes and dislikes into the universe, the ethical situation becomes much more complex, and several possibilities are immediately seen to obtain.

One of these is that the thinkers may ignore each other's attitude about good and evil altogether, and each continue to indulge his own preferences, indifferent to what the other may feel or do. In such a case we have a world with twice as much of the ethical quality in it as our moral solitude, only it is without ethical unity. The same object is good or bad there, according as you measure it by the view which this one or that one of the thinkers takes. Nor can you find any possible ground in such a world for saying that one thinker's opinion is more correct than the other's, or that either has the truer moral sense. Such a world, in short, is not a moral universe but a moral dualism. Not only is there no single point of view within it from which the values of things can be unequivocally judged, but there is not even a demand for such a point of view, since the two thinkers are supposed to be indifferent to each other's thoughts and acts. Multiply the thinkers into a pluralism, and we find realized for us in the ethical sphere something like that world which the antique sceptics conceived of—in which individual minds are the measures of all things, and in which no one "objective" truth, but only a multitude of "subjective" opinions, can be found.

But this is the kind of world with which the philosopher, so long as he holds to the hope of a philosophy, will not put up. Among the various ideals represented, there must be, he thinks, some which have the more truth or authority; and to these the others *ought* to yield, so that system and subordination may reign. Here in the word "ought" the notion of *obligation* comes emphatically into view, and the next thing in order must be to make its meaning clear.

Since the outcome of the discussion so far has been to show us that nothing can be good or right except so far as some consciousness feels it to be good or thinks it to be right, we perceive on the very threshold that the real superiority and authority which are postulated by the philosopher to reside in some of the opinions, and the really inferior character which he supposes must belong to others, cannot be explained by any abstract moral "nature of things" existing antecedently to the concrete thinkers themselves with their ideals. Like the positive attributes good and bad, the comparative ones better and worse must be *realized* in order to be real. If one ideal judgment be objectively better than another, that betterness must be made flesh by being lodged concretely in someone's actual perception. It cannot float in the atmosphere, for it is not a sort of meteorological phenomenon, like the aurora borealis or the zodiacal light. Its *esse* is *percipi*, like the *esse* of the ideals themselves between which it obtains. The philosopher, therefore, who seeks to know which ideal ought to have supreme weight and which one ought to be subordinated, must trace the *ought* itself to the *de facto* constitution of some existing consciousness, behind which, as one of the data of the universe, he as a purely ethical philosopher is unable to go. This consciousness must make the one ideal right by feeling it to be right, the other wrong by feeling it to be wrong. But now what particular consciousness in the universe *can* enjoy this prerogative of obliging others to conform to a rule which it lays down?

If one of the thinkers were obviously divine, while all the rest were human, there would probably be no practical dispute about the matter. The divine thought would be the model, to which the others should conform.

But still the theoretic question would remain, What is the ground of the obligation, even here?

In our first essays at answering this question, there is an inevitable tendency to slip into an assumption which ordinary men follow when they are disputing with one another about questions of good and bad. They imagine an abstract moral order in which the objective truth resides; and each tries to prove that this pre-existing order is more accurately reflected in his own ideas than in those of his adversary. It is because one disputant is backed by this overarching abstract order that we think the other should submit. Even so, when it is a question no longer of two finite thinkers, but of God and ourselves—we follow our usual habit, and imagine a sort of *de jure* relation, which antedates and overarches the mere facts, and would make it right that we should conform our thoughts to God's thoughts, even though he made no claim to that effect, and though we preferred *de facto* to go on thinking for ourselves.

But the moment we take a steady look at the question, *we see not only that without a claim actually made by some concrete person there can be no obligation, but that there is some obligation wherever there is a claim.* Claim and obligation are, in fact, coextensive terms; they cover each other exactly. Our ordinary attitude of regarding ourselves as subject to an overarching system of moral relations, true "in themselves," is therefore either an out-and-out superstition, or else it must be treated as a merely provisional abstraction from that real Thinker in whose actual demand upon us to think as he does our obligation must be ultimately based. In a theistic-ethical philosophy that thinker in question is, of course, the Deity to whom the existence of the universe is due.

I know well how hard it is for those who are accustomed to what I have called the superstitious view, to realize that every *de facto* claim creates in so far forth an obligation. We inveterately think that something which we call the "validity" of the claim is what gives to it its obligatory character, and that this validity is something outside of the claim's mere existence as a matter of fact. It rains down upon the claim, we think, from some sublime dimension of being, which the moral law inhabits, much as upon the steel of the compass-needle the influence of the Pole rains down from out of the starry heavens. But again, how can such an inorganic abstract character of imperativeness, additional to the imperativeness which is in the concrete claim itself, *exist?* Take any demand, however slight, which any creature, however weak, may make. Ought it not, for its own sole sake, to be satisfied? If not, prove why not. The only possible kind of proof you could adduce would be the exhibition of another creature who should make a demand that ran the other way. The only possible reason there can be why any phenomenon ought to exist is that such a phenomenon actually is desired. Any desire is imperative to the extent of its amount; it *makes* itself valid by the fact that it exists at all. Some desires, truly enough, are small desires; they are put forward by insignificant persons, and we customarily make light of the obligations which they bring. But the fact that such personal demands as these impose small obligations does not keep the largest obligations from being personal demands.

If we must talk impersonally, to be sure we can say that "the universe" requires, exacts, or makes obligatory such or such an action, whenever it expresses itself through the desires of such or such a creature. But it is better not to talk about the universe in this personified way, unless we believe in a universal or divine consciousness which actually exists. If there be such a consciousness, then its demands carry the most of obligation simply because they are the greatest in amount. But it is even then not *abstractly* right that we should respect them. It is only *concretely* right—or right after the fact, and by virtue of the fact, that they are actually made. Suppose we do not respect them, as seems largely to be the case in this queer world. That ought not to be, we say; that is wrong. But in what way is this fact of wrongness made more acceptable or intelligible when we imagine it to consist rather in the laceration of an *à priori* ideal order than in the disappointment of a living personal God? Do we, perhaps, think that we cover God and protect him and make his impotence over us less ultimate, when we back him up with *à priori* blanket from which he may draw some warmth of further appeal? But the only force of appeal to *us,* which either a living God or an abstract ideal order can wield, is found in the "everlasting ruby vaults" of our own human hearts, as they happen to beat responsive and not irresponsive to the claim. So far as they do feel it when made by a living consciousness, it is life answering to life. A claim thus livingly acknowledged is acknowledged with a solidity and fulness which no thought of an "ideal" backing can render more complete; while if, on the other hand, the heart's response is withheld, the stubborn phenomenon is there of an impotence in the claims which the universe embodies, which no talk about an eternal nature of things can gloze over or dispel. An ineffective *à priori* order is as impotent a thing as an ineffective God; and in the eye of philosophy, it is as hard a thing to explain.

We may now consider that what we distinguished as the metaphysical question in ethical philosophy is sufficiently answered, and that we have learned what the words "good," "bad," and "obligation" severally mean. They mean no absolute natures, independent of personal support. They are objects of feeling and desire, which have no foothold or anchorage in Being, apart from the existence of actually living minds.

Whenever such minds exist, with judgments of goods and ill, and demands upon one another, there is an ethical world in its essential features. Were all other things, gods and men and starry heavens, blotted out from this universe, and were there left but one rock with two loving souls upon it, that rock would have as thoroughly moral a constitution as any possible world which the eternities and immensities could harbor. It would be a tragic constitution, because the rock's inhabitants would die. But while they lived, there would be real good things and real bad things in the universe; there would be obligations, claims, and expectations; obediences, refusals, and disappointments; compunctions and longings for harmony to come again, and inward peace of conscience when it was restored; there would, in short, be a moral life, whose active energy would have no limit but the intensity of interest in each other with which the hero and heroine might be endowed.

We, on this terrestrial globe, so far as the visible facts go, are just like the inhabitants of such a rock. Whether a God exist, or whether no God exist, in you blue heaven above us bent, we form at any rate an ethical republic here below. And the first reflection which this leads to is that ethics have as genuine and real a foothold in a universe where the highest consciousness is human, as in a universe where there is a God as well. "The religion of humanity" affords a basis for ethics as well as theism does. Whether the purely human system can gratify the philosopher's demand as well as the other is a different question, which we ourselves must answer ere we close.

### III

The last fundamental question in Ethics was, it will be remembered, the *casuistic* question. Here we are, in a world where the existence of a divine thinker has been and perhaps always will be doubted by some of the lookers-on, and where, in spite of the presence of a large number of ideals in which human beings agree, there are a mass of others about which no general consensus obtains. It is hardly necessary to present a literary picture of this, for the facts are too well known. The wars of the flesh and the spirit in each man, the concupiscences of different individuals pursuing the same unshareable material or social prizes, the ideals which contrast so according to races, circumstances, temperaments, philosophical beliefs, etc.—all form a maze of apparently inextricable confusion with no obvious Ariadne's thread to lead one out. Yet the philosopher, just because he is a philosopher, adds his own peculiar ideal to the confusion (with which if he were willing to be a sceptic he would be passably content), and insists that over all these individual opinions there is a *system of truth* which he can discover if he only takes sufficient pains.

We stand ourselves at present in the place of that philosopher, and must not fail to realize all the features that the situation comports. In the first place we will not be sceptics; we hold to it that there is a truth to be ascertained. But in the second place we have just gained the insight that that truth cannot be a self-proclaiming set of laws, or an abstract "moral reason," but can only exist in act, or in the shape of an opinion held by some thinker really to be found. There is, however, no visible thinker invested with authority. Shall we then simply proclaim our own ideals as the lawgiving ones? No; for if we are true philosophers we must throw our own spontaneous ideals, even the dearest, impartially in with that total mass of ideals which are fairly to be judged. But how then can we as philosophers ever find a test; how avoid complete moral scepticism on the one hand, and on the other escape bringing a wayward personal standard of our own along with us, on which we simply pin our faith?

The dilemma is a hard one, nor does it grow a bit more easy as we revolve it in our minds. The entire undertaking of the philosopher obliges him to seek an impartial test. That test, however, must be incarnated in the demand of some actually existent person; and how can he pick out the person save by an act in which his own sympathies and prepossessions are implied?

One method indeed presents itself, and has as a matter of history been taken by the more serious ethical schools. If the heap of things demanded proved on inspection less chaotic than at first they seemed, if they furnished their own relative test and measure, then the casuistic problem would be solved. If it were found that all goods *qua* goods contained a common essence, then the amount of this essence involved in any one good would show its rank in the scale of goodness, and order could be quickly made; for this essence would be *the* good upon which all thinkers were

agreed, the relatively objective and universal good that the philosopher seeks. Even his own private ideals would be measured by their share of it, and find their rightful place among the rest.

Various essences of good have thus been found and proposed as bases of the ethical system. Thus, to be a mean between two extremes; to be recognized by a special intuitive faculty; to make the agent happy for the moment; to make others as well as him happy in the long run; to add to his perfection or dignity; to harm no one; to follow from reason or flow from universal law; to be in accordance with the will of God; to promote the survival of the human species of this planet—are so many tests, each of which has been maintained by somebody to constitute the essence of all good things or actions so far as they are good.

No one of the measures that have been actually proposed has, however, given general satisfaction. Some are obviously not universally present in all cases—e.g., the character of harming no one, or that of following a universal law; for the best course is often cruel; and many acts are reckoned good on the sole condition that they be exceptions, and serve not as examples of a universal law. Other characters, such as following the will of God, are unascertainable and vague. Others again, like survival, are quite indeterminate in their consequences, and leave us in the lurch where we most need their help: a philosopher of the Sioux Nation, for example, will be certain to use the survival-criterion in a very different way from ourselves. The best, on the whole, of these marks and measures of goodness seems to be the capacity to bring happiness. But in order not to break down fatally, this test must be taken to cover innumerable acts and impulses that never *aim* at happiness; so that, after all, in seeking for a universal principle we inevitably are carried onward to the *most* universal principle—that *the essence of good is simply to satisfy demand.* The demand may be for anything under the sun. There is really no more ground for supposing that all our demands can be accounted for by one universal underlying kind of motive than there is ground for supposing that all physical phenomena are cases of a single law. The elementary forces in ethics are probably as plural as those of physics are. The various ideas have no common character apart from the fact that they are ideals. No single abstract principle can be so used as to yield to the philosopher anything like a scientifically accurate and genuinely useful casuistic scale.

A look at another peculiarity of the ethical universe, as we find it, will still farther show us the philosopher's perplexities. As a purely theoretic problem, namely, the casuistic question would hardly ever come up at all. If the ethical philosopher were only asking after the best *imaginable* system of goods he would indeed have an easy task; for all demands as such are *prima facie* respectable, and the best simply imaginary world would be one in which every demand was gratified as soon as made. Such a world would, however, have to have a physical constitution entirely different from that of the one which we inhabit. It would need not only a space, but a time, "of *n*—dimensions," to include all the acts and experiences incompatible with one another here below, which would then go on in conjunction—such as spending our money, yet growing rich; taking our holiday, yet getting ahead with our work; shooting and fishing, yet doing no hurt to the beasts; gaining no end of experience, yet keeping our youthful freshness of heart; and the like. There can be no question that such a system of things, however brought about, would be the absolutely ideal system; and that if a philosopher could create universe *à priori,* and provide all the mechanical conditions, that is the sort of universe which he should unhesitatingly create.

But this world of ours is made on an entirely different pattern, and the casuistic question here is most tragically practical. The actually possible in this world is vastly narrower than all that is demanded; and there is always a *pinch* between the ideal and the actual which can only be got through by leaving part of the ideal behind. There is hardly a

good which we can imagine except as competing for the possession of the same bit of space and time with some other imagined good. Every end of desire that presents itself appears exclusive of some other end of desire. Shall a man drink and smoke, *or* keep his nerves in condition?—he cannot do both. Shall he follow his fancy for Amelia, *or* for Henrietta?—both cannot be the choice of his heart. Shall he have the dear old Republican party, *or* a spirit of unsophistication in public affairs?—he cannot have both, etc. So that the ethical philosopher's demand for the right scale of subordination in ideals is the fruit of an altogether practical need. Some part of the ideal must be butchered, and he needs to know which part. It is a tragic situation, and no mere speculative conundrum, with which he has to deal.

Now *we* are blinded to the real difficulty of the philosopher's task by the fact that we are born into a society whose ideals are largely ordered already. If we follow the ideal which is conventionally highest, the others which we butcher either die and do not return to haunt us; or if they come back and accuse us of murder, everyone applauds us for turning to them a deaf ear. In other words, our environment encourages us not to be philosophers but partisans. The philosopher, however, cannot, so long as he clings to his own ideal of objectivity, rule out any ideal from being heard. He is confident, and rightly confident, that the simple taking counsel of his own intuitive preferences would be certain to end in a mutilation of the fulness of the truth. The poet Heine is said to have written "Bunsen" in the place of "Gott" in his copy of that author's work entitled "God in History," so as to make it read "Bunsen in der Geschichte." Now, with no disrespect to the good and learned Baron, is it not safe to say that any single philosopher, however wide his sympathies, must be just such a Bunsen in der Geschichte of the moral world, so soon as he attempts to put his own ideas of order into that howling mob of desires, each struggling to get breathing-room for the ideal to which it clings? The very best of men must not only be insensible, but be ludicrously and peculiarly insensible, to many goods. As a militant, fighting free-handed that the goods to which he *is* sensible may not be submerged and lost from out of life, the philosopher, like every other human being, is in a natural position. But think of Zeno and of Epicurus, think of Calvin and of Paley, think of Kant and Schopenhauer, of Herbert Spencer and John Henry Newman, no longer as one-sided champions of special ideals, but as schoolmasters deciding what all must think—and what more grotesque topic could a satirist wish for on which to exercise his pen? The fabled attempt of Mrs. Partington to arrest the rising tide of the North Atlantic with her broom was a reasonable spectacle compared with their effort to substitute the content of their clean-shaven systems for that exuberant mass of goods with which all human nature is in travail, and groaning to bring to the light of day. Think, furthermore, of such individual moralists, no longer as mere schoolmasters, but as pontiffs armed with the temporal power, and having authority in every concrete case of conflict to order which good shall be butchered and which shall be suffered to survive—all the notion really turns one pale. All one's slumbering revolutionary instincts waken at the thought of any single moralist wielding such powers of life and death. Better chaos forever than an order based on any closet-philosopher's rule, even though he were the most enlightened possible member of his tribe. No! if the philosopher is to keep his judicial position, he must never become one of the parties to the fray.

What can he do, then, it will now be asked, except to fall back on scepticism and give up the notion of being a philosopher at all? But do we not already see a perfectly definite path of escape which is open to him just because he is a philosopher, and not the champion of one particular ideal? Since everything which is demanded is by that fact a good, must not the guiding principle for ethical philosophy (since all demands conjointly cannot be satisfied in this poor world) be simply to satisfy at all times *as many demands as we can?* That act must be the best act, accordingly, which

makes for the *best whole,* in the sense of awakening the least sum of dissatisfactions. In the casuistic scale, therefore, those ideals must be written highest which *prevail at the least cost,* or by whose realization the least possible number of other ideals are destroyed. Since victory and defeat there must be, the victory to be philosophically prayed for is that of the more inclusive side—of the side which even in the hour of triumph will to some degree do justice to the ideals in which the vanquished party's interests lay. The course of history is nothing but the story of men's struggles from generation to generation to find the more and more inclusive order. *Invent some manner* of realizing your own ideals which will also satisfy the alien demands—that and that only is the path of peace! Following this path, society has shaken itself into one sort of relative equilibrium after another by a series of social discoveries quite analogous to those of science. Polyandry and polygamy and slavery, private warfare and liberty to kill, judicial torture and arbitrary royal power have slowly succumbed to actually aroused complaints; and though someone's ideals are unquestionably the worse off for each improvement, yet a vastly greater total number of them find shelter in our civilized society than in the older savage ways. So far then, and up to date, the casuistic scale is made for the philosopher already far better than he can ever make it for himself. An experiment of the most searching kind has proved that the laws and usages of the land are what yield the maximum of satisfaction to the thinkers taken all together. The presumption in cases of conflict must always be in favor of the conventionally recognized good. The philosopher must be a conservative, and in the construction of his casuistic scale must put the things most in accordance with the customs of the community on top.

And yet if he be a true philosopher he must see that there is nothing final in any actually given equilibrium of human ideals, but that, as our present laws and customs have fought and conquered other past ones, so they will in their turn be overthrown by any newly discovered order which will hush up the complaints that they still give rise to, without producing others louder still. "Rules are made for man, not man for rules"—that one sentence is enough to immortalize Green's *Prolegomena to Ethics.* And although a man always risks much when he breaks away from established rules and strives to realize a larger ideal whole than they permit, yet the philosopher must allow that it is at all times open to anyone to make the experiment, provided he fear not to stake his life and character upon the throw. The pinch is always here. Pent in under every system of moral rules are innumerable persons whom it weights upon, and goods which it represses; and these are always rumbling and grumbling in the background, and ready for any issue by which they may get free. See the abuses which the institution of private property covers, so that even to-day it is shamelessly asserted among us that one of the prime functions of the national government is to help the adroiter citizens to grow rich. See the unnamed and unnamable sorrows which the tyranny, on the whole so beneficent, of the marriage-institution brings to so many, both of the married and the unwed. See the wholesale loss of opportunity under our *régime* of so-called equality and industrialism, with the drummer and the counter-jumper in the saddle, for so many faculties and graces which could flourish in the feudal world. See our kindliness for the humble and the outcast, how it wars with that stern weeding-out which until now has been the condition of every perfection in the breed. See everywhere the struggle and the squeeze; and everlastingly the problem how to make them less. The anarchists, nihilists, and free-lovers; the free-silverites, socialists, and single-tax men; the free-traders and civil-service reformers; the prohibitionists and anti-vivisectionists; the radical darwinians with their idea of the suppression of the weak—these and all the conservative sentiments of society arrayed against them, are simply deciding through actual experiment by what sort of conduct the maximum amount of good can be gained and kept in this world. These experiments are to be judged, not *à priori,* but by actually finding, after the fact of their making, how much more

outcry or how much appeasement comes about. What closet-solutions can possibly anticipate the result of trials made on such a scale? Or what can any superficial theorist's judgment be worth, in a world where every one of hundreds of ideals has its special champion already provided in the shape of some genius expressly born to feel it, and to fight to death in its behalf? The pure philosopher can only follow the windings of the spectacle, confident that the line of least resistance will always be towards the richer and the more inclusive arrangement, and that by one tack after another some approach to the kingdom of heaven is incessantly made.

# IV

All this amounts to saying that, so far as the casuistic question goes, ethical science is just like physical science, and instead of being deducible all at once from abstract principles, must simply bide its time, and be ready to revise its conclusions from day to day. The presumption of course, in both sciences, always is that the vulgarly accepted opinions are true, and the right casuistic order that which public opinion believes in; and surely it would be folly quite as great, in most of us, to strike out independently and to aim at originality in ethics as in physics. Every now and then, however, someone is born with the right to be original, and his revolutionary thought or action may bear prosperous fruit. He may replace old "laws of nature" by better ones; he may, by breaking old moral rules in a certain place, bring in a total condition of things more ideal than would have followed had the rules been kept.

On the whole, then, we must conclude that no philosophy of ethics is possible in the old-fashioned absolute sense of the term. Everywhere the ethical philosopher must wait on facts. The thinkers who create the ideals come he knows not whence, their sensibilities are evolved he knows not how; and the question as to which of two conflicting ideals will give the best universe then and there, can be answered by him only through the aid of the experience of other men. I said some time ago, in treating of the "first" question, that the intuitional moralists deserve credit for keeping most clearly to the psychological facts. They do much to spoil this merit on the whole, however, by mixing with it that dogmatic temper which, by absolute distinctions and unconditional "thou shalt nots," changes a growing, elastic, and continuous life into a superstitious system of relics and dead bones. In point of fact, there are no absolute evils, and there are no non-moral goods; and the *highest* ethical life—however few may be called to bear its burdens—consists at all times in the breaking of rules which have grown too narrow for the actual case. There is but one unconditional commandment, which is that we should seek incessantly, with fear and trembling, so to vote and to act as to bring about the very largest total universe of good which we can see. Abstract rules indeed can help; but they help the less in proportion as our intuitions are more piercing, and our vocation is the stronger for the moral life. For every real dilemma is in literal strictness a unique situation; and the exact combination of ideals realized and ideals disappointed which each decision creates is always a universe without a precedent, and for which no adequate previous rule exists. The philosopher, then, *quâ* philosopher, is no better able to determine the best universe in the concrete emergency than other men. He sees, indeed, somewhat better than most men what the question always is—not a question of this good or that good simply taken, but of the two total universes with which these goods respectively belong. He knows that he must vote always for the richer universe, for the good which seems most organizable, most fit to enter to complex combinations, most apt to be a member of a more inclusive whole. But which particular universe this is he cannot know for certain in advance; he only knows that if he makes a bad mistake the cries of the wounded will soon inform him of the fact. In all this the philosopher is just like the rest of us non-philosophers; so far as we are just and sympathetic instinctively, and

so far as we are open to the voice of complaint. His function is in fact indistinguishable from that of the best kind of statesman at the present day. His books upon ethics, therefore, so far as they truly touch the moral life, must more and more ally themselves with a literature which is confessedly tentative and suggestive rather than dogmatic—I mean with novels and dramas of the deeper sort, with sermons, with books on statecraft and philanthropy and social and economical reform. Treated in this way ethical treatises may be voluminous and luminous as well; but they never can be *final,* except in their abstractest and vaguest features; and they must more and more abandon the old-fashioned, clear-cut, and would-be "scientific" form.

## V

The chief of all the reasons why concrete ethics cannot be final is that they have to wait on metaphysical and theological beliefs. I said some time back that real ethical relations existed in a purely human world. They would exist even in what we called a moral solitude if the thinker had various ideals which took hold of him in turn. His self of one day would make demands on his self of another; and some of the demands might be urgent and tyrannical, while others were gentle and easily put aside. We call the tyrannical demands *imperatives.* If we ignore these we do not hear the last of it. The good which we have wounded returns to plague us with interminable crops of consequential damages, compunctions, and regrets. Obligation can thus exist inside a single thinker's consciousness; and perfect peace can abide with him only so far as he lives according to some sort of a casuistic scale which keeps his more imperative goods on top. It is the nature of these goods to be cruel to their rivals. Nothing shall avail when weighed in the balance against them. They call out all the mercilessness in our disposition, and do not easily forgive us if we are so soft-hearted as to shrink from sacrifice in their behalf.

The deepest difference, practically, in the moral life of man is the difference between the easy-going and the strenuous mood. When in the easy-going mood the shrinking from present ill is our ruling consideration. The strenuous mood, on the contrary, makes us quite indifferent to present ill, if only the greater ideal be attained. The capacity for the strenuous mood probably lies slumbering in every man, but it has more difficulty in some than in others in waking up. It needs the wilder passions to arouse it, the big fears, loves, and indignations; or else the deeply penetrating appeal of some one of the higher fidelities, like justice, truth or freedom. Strong relief is a necessity of its vision; and a world where all the mountains are brought down and all the valleys are exalted is no congenial place for its habitation. This is why in a solitary thinker this mood might slumber on forever without waking. His various ideals, known to him to be mere preferences of his own, are too nearly of the same denominational value: he can play fast or loose with them at will. This too is why, in a merely human world without a God, the appeal to our moral energy falls short of its maximal stimulating power. Life, to be sure, is even in such a world a genuinely ethical symphony; but it is played in the compass of a couple of poor octaves, and the infinite scale of values fails to open up. Many of us, indeed—like Sir James Stephen in those eloquent *Essays by a Barrister*—would openly laugh at the very idea of the strenuous mood being awakened in us by those claims of remote posterity which constitute the last appeal of the religion of humanity. We do not love these men of the future keenly enough; and we love them perhaps the less the more we hear of their evolutionized perfection, their high average longevity and education, their freedom from war and crime, their relative immunity from pain and zymotic disease, and all their other negative superiorities. This is all too finite, we say; we see too well the vacuum beyond. It lacks the note of infinitude and mystery, and may all be dealt with in the don't-care mood. No need of agonizing ourselves or making others agonize for these good creatures just at present.

When, however, we believe that a God is there, and that he is one of the claimants, the infinite perspective opens out. The scale of the symphony is incalculably prolonged. The more imperative ideals now begin to speak with an altogether new objectivity and significance, and to utter the penetrating, shattering, tragically challenging note of appeal. They ring out like the call of Victor Hugo's alpine eagle, "qui parle au précipice et que le gouffre entend," and the strenuous mood awakens at the sound. It saith among the trumpets, ha, ha! it smelleth the battle afar off, the thunder of the captains and the shouting. Its blood is up; and cruelty to the lesser claims, so far from being a deterrent element, does but add to the stern joy with which it leaps to answer to the greater. All through history, in the periodical conflicts of puritanism with the don't-care temper, we see the antagonism of the strenuous and genial moods, and the contrast between the ethics of infinite and mysterious obligation from on high, and those of prudence and the satisfaction of merely finite need.

The capacity of the strenuous mood lies so deep down among our natural human possibilities that even if there were no metaphysical or traditional grounds for believing in a God, men would postulate one simply as a pretext for living hard, and getting out of the game of existence its keenest possibilities of zest. Our attitude towards concrete evils is entirely different in a world where we believe there are none but finite demanders, from what it is in one where we joyously face tragedy for an infinite demanders' sake. Every sort of energy and endurance, of courage and capacity for handling life's evils, is set free in those who have religious faith. For this reason the strenuous type of character will on the battle-field of human history always outwear the easy-going type, and religion will drive irreligion to the wall.

It would seem, too—and this is my final conclusion—that the stable and systematic moral universe for which the ethical philosopher asks is fully possible only in a world where there is a divine thinker with all-enveloping demands. If such a thinker existed, his way of subordinating the demands to one another would be the finally valid casuistic scale; his claims would be the most appealing; his ideal universe would be the most inclusive realizable whole. If he now exist, then actualized in his thought already must be that ethical philosophy which we seek as the pattern which our own must evermore approach. In the interest of our own ideal of systematically unified moral truth, therefore, we, as would-be philosophers, must postulate a divine thinker, and pray for the victory of the religious cause. Meanwhile, exactly what the thought of the infinite thinker may be is hidden from us even were we sure of his existence; so that our postulation of him after all serves only to let loose in us the strenuous mood. But this is what it does in all men, even those who have no inter-est in philosophy. The ethical philosopher, therefore, whenever he ventures to say which course of action is the best, is on no essentially different level from the common man. "See, I have set before thee this day life and good, and death and evil; therefore choose life that thou and thy seed may live"—when this challenge comes to us, it is simply our total character and personal genius that are on trial; and if we invoke any so-called philosophy, our choice and use of that also are but revelations of our personal aptitude or incapacity for moral life. From this unsparing practical ordeal no professor's lectures and no array of books can save us. The solving word, for the learned and the unlearned man alike, lies in the last resort in the dumb willingnesses and unwillingnesses of their interior characters, and nowhere else. It is not in heaven, neither is it beyond the sea; but the word is very nigh unto thee, in thy mouth and in thy heart, that thou mayest do it.

# The Dilemma of Determinism

A common opinion prevails that the juice has ages ago been pressed out of the free-will controversy, and that no new champion can do more than warm up stale arguments which everyone has heard. This is a radical mistake. I know of no subject less worn out, or in which inventive genius has a better chance of breaking open new ground—not, perhaps, of forcing a conclusion or of coercing assent, but of deepening our sense of what the issue between the two parties really is, of what the ideas of fate and to free-will imply. At our very side almost, in the past few years, we have seen falling in rapid succession from the press works that present the alternative in entirely novel lights. Not to speak of the English disciples of Hegel, such as Green and Bradley; not to speak of Hinton and Hodgson, nor of Hazard here—we see in the writings of Renouvier, Fouillé, and Delbœuf how completely changed and refreshed is the form of all the old disputes. I cannot pretend to vie in orginality with any of the old disputes. I cannot pretend to vie in originality with any of the masters I have named, and my ambition limits itself to just one little point. If I can make two of the necessarily implied corollaries of determinism clearer to you than they have been made before, I shall have made it possible for you to decide for or against that doctrine with a better understanding of what you are about. And if you prefer not to decide at all, but to

From *The Works of William James—The Will to Believe,* ed. Frederick Burkhardt (Cambridge, Mass.: Harvard University Press, 1979 [1884]), pp. 114–40.

remain doubters, you will at least see more plainly what the subject of your hesitation is. I thus disclaim openly on the threshold all pretension to prove to you that the freedom of the will is true. The most I hope is to induce some of you to follow my own example in assuming it true, and acting as if it were true. If it be true, it seems to me that this is involved in the strict logic of the case. Its truth ought not to be forced willy-nilly down our indifferent throats. It ought to be freely espoused by men who can equally well turn their backs upon it. In other words, our first act of freedom, if we are free, ought in all inward propriety to be to affirm that we are free. This should exclude, it seems to me, from the free-will side of the equation all hope of a coercive demonstration—a demonstration which I, for one, am perfectly contented to go without.

With thus much understood at the outset, we can advance. But not without one more point understood as well. The arguments I am about to urge all proceed on two suppositions: first, when we make theories about the world and discuss them with one another, we do so in order to attain a conception of things which shall give us subjective satisfaction; and, second, if there be two conceptions, and the one seems to us, on the whole, more rational than the other, we are entitled to suppose that the more rational one is the truer of the two. I hope that you are all willing to make these suppositions with me; for I am afraid that if there be any of you here who are not, they will find little edification in the rest of what I have to say. I cannot stop to argue the point; but I myself believe that all the magnificent achievements of mathematical and physical science—our doctrines of evolution, of uniformity of law, and the rest—proceed from our indomitable desire to cast the world into a more rational shape in our minds than the shape into which it is thrown there by the crude order of our experience. The world has shown itself, to a great extent, plastic to this demand of ours for rationality. How much farther it will show itself plastic no one can say. Our only means of finding out is to try; and I, for one, feel as free to try conceptions of moral as of mechanical or of

logical rationality. If a certain formula for expressing the nature of the world violates my moral demand, I shall feel as free to throw it overboard, or at least to doubt it, as if it disappointed my demand for uniformity of sequence, for example; the one demand being, so far as I can see, quite as subjective and emotional as the other is. The principle of causality, for example—what is it but a postulate, an empty name covering simply a demand that the sequence of events shall some day manifest a deeper kind of belonging of one thing with another than the mere arbitrary juxtaposition which now phenomenally appears? It is as much an altar to an unknown god as the one that Saint Paul found at Athens. All our scientific and philosophic ideals are altars to unknown gods. Uniformity is as much so as is free-will. If this be admitted, we can debate on even terms. But if anyone pretends that while freedom and variety are, in the first instance, subjective demands, necessity and uniformity are something altogether different, I do not see how we can debate at all.

To begin, then, I must suppose you acquainted with all the usual arguments on the subject. I cannot stop to take up the old proofs from causation, from statistics, from the certainty with which we can foretell one another's conduct, from the fixity of character, and all the rest. But there are two *words* which usually encumber these classical arguments, and which we must immediately dispose of if we are to make any progress. One is the eulogistic word *freedom*, and the other is the opprobrious word *chance*. The word "chance" I wish to keep, but I wish to get rid of the word "freedom." Its eulogistic associations have so far overshadowed all the rest of its meaning that both parties claim the sole right to use it, and determinists to-day insist that they alone are freedom's champions. Old-fashioned determinism was what we may call *hard* determinism. It did not shrink from such words as fatality, bondage of the will, necessitation, and the like. Nowadays, we have a *soft* determinism which abhors harsh words, and, repudiating fatality, necessity, and even predetermination, says that its real name is freedom; for freedom is only necessity understood, and bondage to the highest is identical with true freedom. Even a writer as little used to making capital out of soft words as Mr. Hodgson hesitates not to call himself a "free-will determinist."

Now, all that is a quagmire of evasion under which the real issue of fact has been entirely smothered. Freedom in all these senses presents simply no problem at all. No matter what the soft determinist mean by it—whether he mean the acting without external constraint, whether he mean the acting rightly, or whether he mean the acquiescing in the law of the whole—who cannot answer him that sometimes we are free and sometimes we are not? But there *is* a problem, an issue of fact and not of words, an issue of the most momentous importance, which is often decided without discussion in one sentence—nay, in one clause of a sentence—by those very writers who spin out whole chapters in their efforts to show what "true" freedom is; and that is the question of determinism, about which we are to talk to-night.

Fortunately, no ambiguities hang about this word or about its opposite, indeterminism. Both designate an outward way in which things may happen, and their cold and mathematical sound has no sentimental associations that can bribe our partiality either way in advance. Now, evidence of an external kind to decide between determinism and indeterminism is, as I intimated a while back, strictly impossible to find. Let us look at the difference between them and see for ourselves. What does determinism profess?

It professes that those parts of the universe already laid down absolute appoint and decree what the other parts shall be. The future has no ambiguous possibilities hidden in its womb: the part we call the present is compatible with only one totality. Any other future complement than the one fixed from eternity is impossible. The whole is in each and every part, and welds it with the rest into an absolute unity, an iron block, in which there can be no equivocation or shadow of turning.

"With Earth's first Clay They did the Last Man knead,
And there of the Last Harvest sow'd the Seed;
And the first Morning of Creation wrote
What the Last Dawn of Reckoning shall read."

Indeterminism, on the contrary, says that the parts have a certain amount of loose play on one another, so that the laying down of one of them does not necessarily determine what the other shall be. It admits that possibilities may be in excess of actualities, and that things not yet revealed to our knowledge may really in themselves be ambiguous. Of two alternative futures which we conceive, both may now be really possible; and the one become impossible only at the very moment when the other excludes it by becoming real itself. Indeterminism thus denies the world to be one unbending unit of fact. It says there is a certain ultimate pluralism in it; and, so saying, it corroborates our ordinary unsophisticated view of things. To that view, actualities seem to float in a wider sea of possibilities from out of which they are chosen; and, *somewhere,* indeterminism says, such possibilities exist, and form a part of truth.

Determinism, on the contrary, says they exist *nowhere,* and that necessity on the one hand and impossibility on the other are the sole categories of the real. Possibilities that fail to get realized are, for determinism, pure illusions: they never were possibilities at all. There is nothing inchoate, it says, about this universe of ours, all that was or is or shall be actual in it having been from eternity virtually there. The cloud of alternatives our minds escort this mass of actuality withal is a cloud of sheer deceptions, to which "impossibilities" is the only name that rightfully belongs.

The issue, it will be seen, is a perfectly sharp one, which no eulogistic terminology can smear over or wipe out. The truth *must* lie with one side or the other, and its lying with one side makes the other false.

The question relates solely to the existence of possibilities, in the strict sense of the term, as things that may, but need not, be. Both sides admit that a volition, for instance, has occurred. The indeterminists say another volition might have occurred in its place: the determinists swear that nothing could possibly have occurred in its place. Now can science be called in to tell us which of these two point-blank contradicters of each other is right? Science professes to draw no conclusions but such as are based on matters of fact, things that have actually happened; but how can any amount of assurance that something actually happened give us the least grain of information as to whether another thing might or might not have happened in its place? Only facts can be proved by other facts. With things that are possibilities and not facts, facts have no concern. If we have no other evidence than the evidence of existing facts, the possibility-question must remain a mystery never to be cleared up.

And the truth is that facts practically have hardly anything to do with making us either determinists or indeterminists. Sure enough, we make a flourish of quoting facts this way or that; and if we are determinists, we talk about the infallibility with which we can predict one another's conduct; while if we are indeterminists, we lay great stress on the fact that it is just because we cannot foretell one another's conduct, either in war or statecraft or in any of the great and small intrigues and businesses of men, that life is so intensely anxious and hazardous a game. But who does not see the wretched insufficiency of this so-called objective testimony on both sides? What fills up the gaps in our minds is something not objective, not external. What divides us into possibility men and anti-possibility men is different faiths or postulates—postulates of rationality. To this man the world seems more rational with possibilities in it—to that man more rational with possibilities excluded; and talk as we will about having to yield to evidence, what makes us monists or pluralists, determinists or indeterminists, is at bottom always some sentiment like this.

The stronghold of the deterministic sentiment is the antipathy to the idea of chance. As soon as we begin to talk indeterminism to our friends, we find a number of them shaking their heads. This notion of alternative possibility, they say, this admission that any one of several things may come to pass, is, after all, only a round-about name for chance; and chance is something the notion of which no sane mind can for an instant tolerate in the world. What is it, they ask, but barefaced crazy unreason, the negation of intelligibility and law? And if the slightest particle of it exist anywhere, what is to prevent the whole fabric from falling together, the stars from going out, and chaos from recommencing her topsy-turvy reign?

Remarks of this sort about chance will put an end to discussion as quickly as anything one can find. I have already told you that "chance" was a word I wished to keep and use. Let us then examine exactly what it means, and see whether it ought to be such a terrible bugbear to us. I fancy that squeezing the thistle boldly will rob it of its sting.

The sting of the word "chance" seems to lie in the assumption that it means something positive, and that if anything happens by chance, it must needs be something of an intrinsically irrational and preposterous sort. Now chance means nothing of the kind. It is a purely negative and relative term, giving us no information about that of which it is predicated, except that it happens to be disconnected with something else—not controlled, secured, or necessitated by other things in advance of its own actual presence. As this point is the most subtle one of the whole lecture, and at the same time the point on which all the rest hinges, I beg you to pay particular attention to it. What I say is that it tells us nothing about what a thing may be in itself to call it "chance." It may be a bad thing, it may be a good thing. It may be lucidity, transparency, fitness incarnate, matching the whole system of other things, when it has once befallen, in an unimaginably perfect way. All you mean by calling it "chance" is that this is not guaranteed, that it may also all out otherwise. For the system of other things has no positive hold on the chance-thing. Its origin is in a certain fashion negative; it escapes, and says, Hands off! coming, when it comes as a free gift, or not at all.

This negativeness, however, and this opacity of the chance-thing when thus considered *ab extra,* or from the point of view of previous things or distant things, do not preclude its having any amount of positiveness and luminosity from within, and at its own place and moment. All that its chance-character asserts about it is that there is something in it really of its own, something that is not the unconditional property of the whole. If the whole wants this property, the whole must wait till it can get it, if it be a matter of chance. That the universe may actually be a sort of joint-stock society of this sort, in which the sharers have both limited liabilities and limited powers, is of course a simple and conceivable notion.

Nevertheless, many persons talk as if the minutest dose of disconnectedness of one part with another, the smallest modicum of independence, the faintest tremor of ambiguity about the future, for example, would ruin everything, and turn this goodly universe into a sort of insane sand-heap or nulliverse, no universe at all. Since future human volitions are as a matter of fact the only ambiguous things we are tempted to believe in, let us stop for a moment to make ourselves sure whether their independent and accidental character need be fraught with such direful consequences to the universe as these.

What is meant by saying that my choice of which way to walk home after the lecture is ambiguous and matter of chance as far as the present moment is concerned? It means that both Divinity Avenue and Oxford Street are called; but that only one, and that one *either* one, shall be chosen. Now, I ask you seriously to support that this ambiguity of my choice is real; and then to make the impossible hypothesis that the choice is made twice over, and each time falls on a different street. In other words, imagine that I first walk through Divinity Avenue, and then imagine that the powers governing the universe annihilate ten minutes of time with all that it contained, and set me back at the door of this hall just as I was before the choice was made. Imagine then that, everything else being the same, I now make a different choice and traverse Oxford Street.

You, as passive spectators, look on and see the two alternative universes—one of them with me walking through Divinity Avenue in it, the other with the same me walking through Oxford Street. Now, if you are determinists you believe one of these universes to have been from eternity impossible: you believe it to have been impossible because of the intrinsic irrationality or accidentality somewhere involved in it. But looking outwardly at these universes, can you say which is the impossible and accidental one, and which the rational and necessary one? I doubt if the most iron-clad determinist among you could have the slightest glimmer of light on this point. In other words, either universe *after the fact* and once there would, to our means of observation and understanding, appear just as rational as the other. There would be absolutely no criterion by which we might judge one necessary and the other matter of chance. Suppose now we relieve the gods of their hypothetical task and assume my choice, once made, to be made forever. I go through Divinity Avenue for good and all. If, as good determinists, you now begin to affirm, what all good determinists punctually do affirm, that in the nature of things I *couldn't* have gone through Oxford Street—had I done so it would have been chance, irrationality, insanity, a horrid gap in nature—I simply call your attention to this, that your affirmation is what the Germans call a *Machtspruch,* a mere conception fulminated  as a dogma and based on no insight into details. Before my choice, either street seemed as natural to you as to me. Had I happened to take Oxford Street, Divinity Avenue would have figured in your philosophy as the gap in nature; and you would have so proclaimed it with the best deterministic conscience in the world.

But what a hollow outcry, then, is this against a chance which, if it were present to us, we could by no character whatever distinguish from a rational necessity! I have taken the most trivial of examples, but no possible example could lead to any different result. For what are the alternatives which, in point of fact, offer themselves to human volition?

What are those futures that now seem matters of chance? Are they not one and all like the Divinity Avenue and Oxford Street of our example? Are they not all of them *kinds* of things already here and based in the existing frame of nature? Is anyone ever tempted to produce an *absolute* accident, something utterly irrelevant to the rest of the world? Do not all the motives that assail us, all the futures that offer themselves to our choice, spring equally from the soil of the past; and would not either one of them, whether realized through chance or through necessity, the moment it was realized, seem to us to fit that past, and in the completest and most continuous manner to interdigitate with the phenomena already there?

The more one thinks of the matter, the more one wonders that so empty and gratuitous a hubbub as this outcry against chance should have found so great an echo in the hearts of men. It is a word which tells us absolutely nothing about what chances, or about the *modus operandi* of the chancing; and the use of it as a war-cry shows only a temper of intellectual absolutism, a demand that the world shall be a solid block, subject to one control—which temper, which demand, the world may not be bound to gratify at all. In every outwardly verifiable and practical respect, a world in which the alternatives that now actually distract *your* choice were decided by pure chance would be by *me* absolutely undistinguished from the world in which I now live. I am, therefore, entirely willing to call it, so far as your choices go, a world of chance for me. To *yourselves,* it is true, those very acts of choice, which to me are so blind, opaque, and external, are the opposites of this, for you are within them and effect them. To you they appear as decisions; and decisions, for him who makes them, are altogether peculiar psychic facts. Self-luminous and self-justifying at the living moment at which they occur, they appeal to no outside moment to put its stamp upon them or make them continuous with the rest of nature. Themselves it is rather who seem to make nature continuous; and in their strange and intense function of grating con-

sent to one possibility and withholding it from another, to transform an equivocal and double future into an inalterable and simple past.

But with the psychology of the matter we have no concern this evening. The quarrel which determinism has with chance fortunately has nothing to do with this or that psychological detail. It is a quarrel altogether metaphysical. Determinism denies the ambiguity of future volitions, because it affirms that nothing future can be ambiguous. But we have said enough to meet the issue. Indeterminate future volitions *do* mean chance. Let us not fear to shout it from the house-tops if need be; for we now know that the idea of chance is, at bottom, exactly the same thing as the idea of gift—the one simply being a disparaging, and the other a eulogistic, name for anything on which we have no effective *claim*. And whether the world be the better or the worse for having either chances or gifts in it will depend altogether on *what* these uncertain and unclaimable things turn out to be.

And this at last brings us within sight of our subject. We have seen what determinism means: we have seen that indeterminism is rightly described as meaning chance; and we have seen that chance, the very name of which we are urged to shrink from as from a metaphysical pestilence, means only the negative fact that no part of the world, however big, can claim to control absolutely the destinies of the whole. But although, in discussing the word "chance," I may at moments have seemed to be arguing for its real existence, I have not meant to do so yet. We have not yet ascertained whether this be a world of chance or no; at most, we have agreed that it seems so. And I now repeat what I said at the outset, that, from any strict theoretical point of view, the question is insoluble. To deepen our theoretic sense of the *difference* between a world of chances in it and a deterministic world is the most I can hope to do; and this I may now at last begin upon, after all our tedious clearing of the way.

I wish first of all to show you just what the notion that this is a deterministic world implies. The implications I call your attention to are all bound up with the fact that it is a world in which we constantly have to make what I shall, with your permission, call judgments of regret. Hardly an hour passes in which we do not wish that something might be otherwise; and happy indeed are those of us whose hearts have never echoed the wish of Omar Khayyam.

*"That we might catch ere closed the Book of Fate,*
*And make The Writer on a fairer leaf*
*Inscribe our names, or quite obliterate!*

*"Ah Love! could you and I with Fate conspire*
*To grasp this sorry Scheme of Things entire,*
*Would not we shatter it to bits—and then*
*Re-mould it nearer to the Heart's Desire!"*

Now, it is undeniable that most of these regrets are foolish, and quite on a par in point of philosophic value with the criticisms on the universe of that friend of our infancy, the hero of the fable "The Atheist and the Acorn,"

*"Fool! had that bough a pumpkin bore,*
*Thy whimsies would have worked no more," etc.*

Even from the point of view of our own ends, we should probably make a botch of remodelling the universe. How much more then from the point of view of ends we cannot see! Wise men therefore regret as little as they can. But still some regrets are pretty obstinate and hard to stifle—regrets for acts of wanton cruelty or treachery, for example, whether performed by others or by ourselves. Hardly anyone can remain *entirely* optimistic after reading the confession of the murderer at Brockton the other day: how, to get rid of the wife whose continued existence bored him, he inveigled her into a desert spot, shot her four times, and then, as she lay on the ground and said to him, "You didn't do it on purpose, did you, dear?" replied, "No, I didn't to it on purpose," as he raised a rock and smashed her skull. Such an occurrence, with the mild sentence and self-satisfaction of the prisoner, is a field for a crop of regrets, which one need not take up in detail. We feel that, although a perfect mechanical fit to the rest of the universe, it is a bad moral fit, and that something else would really have been better in its place.

But for the deterministic philosophy the murder, the sentence, and the prisoner's optimism were all necessary from eternity; and nothing else for a moment had a ghost of a chance of being put into their place. To admit such a chance, the determinists tell us, would be to make a suicide of reason; so we must steel our hearts against the thought. And here our plot thickens, for we see the first of those difficult implications of determinism and monism which it is my purpose to make you feel. If this Brockton murder was called for by the rest of the universe, if it had to come at its preappointed hour, and if nothing else would have been consistent with the sense of the whole, what are we to think of the universe? Are we stubbornly to stick to our judgment of regret, and say, though it *couldn't* be, yet it *would* have been a better universe with something different from this Brockton murder in it? That, of course, seems the natural and spontaneous thing for us to do; and yet it is nothing short of deliberately espousing a kind of pessimism. The judgment of regret calls the murder bad. Calling a thing bad means, if it means anything at all, that the thing ought not to be, that something else ought to be in its stead. Determinism, in denying that anything else can be in its stead, virtually defines the universe as a place in which what ought to be is impossible—in other words, as an organism whose constitution is afflicted with an incurable taint, an irremediable flaw. The pessimism of a Schopenhauer says no more than this—that the murder is a symptom; and that it is a vicious symptom because it belongs to a vicious whole, which can express its nature no otherwise than by bringing forth just such a symptom as that at this particular spot. Regret for the murder must transform itself, if we are determinists and wise, into a larger regret. It is absurd to regret the murder alone. Other things being what they are, *it* could not be different. What we should regret is that whole frame of things of which the murder is one member. I see no escape whatever from this pessimistic conclusion, if, being determinists, our judgment of regret is to be allowed to stand at all.

The only deterministic escape from pessimism is everywhere to abandon the judgment of regret. That this can be done, history shows to be not impossible. The devil, *quoad existentiam* [if existing] may be good. That is, although he be a *principle* of evil, yet the universe, with such a principle in it, may practically be a better universe than it could have been without. On every hand, in a small way, we find that a certain amount of evil is a condition by which a higher form of good is bought. There is nothing to prevent anybody from generalizing this view, and trusting that if we could but see things in the largest of all ways, even such matters as this Brockton murder would appear to be paid for by the uses that follow in their train. An optimism *quand même* [nevertheless], a systematic and infatuated optimism like that ridiculed by Voltaire in his *Candide,* is one of the possible ideal ways in which a man may train himself to look on life. Bereft of dogmatic hardness and lit up with the expression of a tender and pathetic hope, such an optimism has been the grace of some of the most religious characters that ever lived.

> *"Throb thine with Nature's throbbing breast,*
> *And all is clear from east to west."* *

Even cruelty and treachery may be among the absolutely blessed fruits of time, and to quarrel with any of their details may be blasphemy. The only real blasphemy, in short, may be that pessimistic temper of the soul which lets it give way to such things as regrets remorse, and grief.

Thus, our deterministic pessimism may become a deterministic optimism at the price of extinguishing our judgments of regret.

But does not this immediately bring us into a curious logical predicament? Our determinism leads us to call our judgments of regret wrong, because they are pessimistic in implying that what is impossible yet ought to be. But how then about the judgments of regret themselves? If they are wrong, other judg-

ments, judgments of approval presumably, ought to be in their place. But as they are necessitated, nothing else *can* be in their place; and the universe is just what it was before—namely, a place in which what ought to be appears impossible. We have got one foot out of the pessimistic bog, but the other one sinks all the deeper. We have rescued our actions from the bonds of evil, but our judgments are now held fast. When murders and treacheries cease to be sins, regrets are theoretic absurdities and errors. The theoretic and the active life thus play a kind of see-saw with each other on the ground of evil. The rise of either sends the other down. Murder and treachery cannot be good without regret being bad: regret cannot be good without treachery and murder being bad. Both, however, are supposed to have been foredoomed; so something must be fatally unreasonable, absurd, and wrong in the world. It must be a place of which either sin or error forms a necessary part. From this dilemma there seems at first sight no escape. Are we then so soon to fall back into the pessimism from which we thought we had emerged? And is there no possible way by which we may, with good intellectual consciences, call the cruelties and the treacheries, the reluctances and the regrets, *all* good together?

Certainly there is such a way, and you are probably most of you ready to formulate it yourselves. But, before doing so, remark how inevitably the question of determinism and indeterminism slides us into the question of optimism and pessimism, or, as our fathers called it, "the question of evil." The theological form of all these disputes is the simplest and the deepest, the form from which there is the least escape—not because, as some have sarcastically said, remorse and regret are clung to with a morbid fondness by the theologians as spiritual luxuries, but because they are existing facts of the world, and as such must be taken into account in the deterministic interpretation of all that is fated to be. If they are fated to be error, does not the bat's wing of irrationality still cast its shadow over the world?

The refuge from the quandary lies, as I said, not far off. The necessary acts we erroneously regret may be good, and yet our error in so regretting them may be also good, on one simple condition; and that condition is this: The world must not be regarded as a machine whose final purpose is the making real of any outward good, but rather as a contrivance for deepening the theoretic consciousness of what goodness and evil in their intrinsic natures are. Not the doing either of good or of evil is what nature cares for, but the knowing of them. Life is one long eating of the fruit of the tree of knowledge. I am in the habit, in thinking to myself, of calling this point of view the *gnostical* point of view. According to it, the world is neither an optimism nor a pessimism, but a *gnosticism*. But as this term may perhaps lead to some misunderstandings, I will use it as little as possible here, and speak rather of *subjectivism,* and the *subjectivistic* point of view.

Subjectivism has three great branches—we may call them scientificism, sentimentalism, and sensualism, respectively. They all agree essentially about the universe, in deeming that what happens there is subsidiary to what we think or feel about it. Crime justifies its criminality by awakening our intelligence of that criminality, and eventually our remorses and regrets; and the error included in remorse and regrets, the error of supposing that the past could have been different, justifies itself by its use. Its use is to quicken our sense of *what* the irretrievably lost is. When we think of it as that which might have been ("the saddest words of tongue or pen"), the quality of its worth speaks to us with a wilder sweetness; and, conversely, the dissatisfaction wherewith we think of what seems to have driven it from its natural place gives us the severer pang. Admirable artifice of nature! we might be tempted to exclaim—deceiving us in order the better to enlighten us, and leaving nothing undone to accentuate to our consciousness the yawning distance of those opposite poles of good and evil between which creation swings.

We have thus clearly revealed to our view what may be called the dilemma of determinism, so far as determinism pretends to think

things out at all. A merely mechanical determinism, it is true, rather rejoices in not thinking them out. It is very sure that the universe must satisfy its postulate of a physical continuity and coherence, but it smiles at anyone who comes forward with a postulate of moral coherence as well. I may suppose, however, that the number of purely mechanical or hard determinists among you this evening is small. The determinism to whose seductions you are most exposed is what I have called soft determinism—the determinism which allows considerations of good and bad to mingle with those of cause and effect in deciding what sort of a universe this may rationally be held to be. The dilemma of this determinism is one whose left horn is pessimism and whose right horn is subjectivism. In other words, if determinism is to escape pessimism, it must leave off looking at the goods and ills of life in a simple objective way, and regard them as materials, indifferent in themselves, for the production of consciousness, scientific and ethical, in us.

To escape pessimism is, as we all know, no easy task. Your own studies have sufficiently shown you the almost desperate difficulty of making the notion that there is a single principle of things, and that principle absolute perfection, rhyme together with our daily vision of the facts of life. If perfection be the principle, how comes there any imperfection here? If God be good, how came he to create—or, if he did not create, how comes he to permit—the devil? The evil facts must be explained as seeming: the devil must be whitewashed, the universe must be disinfected, if neither God's goodness nor his unity and power are to remain impugned. And of all the various ways of operating the disinfection, and making bad seem less bad, the way of subjectivism appears by far the best.

For, after all, is there not something rather absurd in our ordinary notion of external things being good or bad in themselves? Can murders and treacheries, considered as mere outward happenings, or motions of matter, be bad without anyone to feel their badness? And could paradise properly be good in the absence of a sentient principle by which the goodness was perceived? Outward goods and evils seem practically indistinguishable except in so far as they result in getting moral judgments made about them. But then the moral judgments seem the main thing, and the outward facts mere perishing instruments for their production. This is subjectivism. Everyone must at some time have wondered at that strange paradox of our moral nature, that, though the pursuit of outward good is the breath of its nostrils, the attainment of outward good would seem to be its suffocation and death. Why does the painting of any paradise or utopia, in heaven or on earth, awaken such yawnings for nirvana and escape? The white-robed harpplaying heaven of our sabbath-schools, and the ladylike tea-table elysium represented in Mr. Spencer's *Data of Ethics,* as the final consummation of progress, are exactly on a par in this respect—lubberlands, pure and simple, one and all. We look upon them from this delicious mess of insanities and realities, strivings and deadnesses, hopes and fears, agonies and exultations, which forms our present state, and *tedium vitæ* is the only sentiment they awaken in our breasts. To our crepuscular natures, born for the conflict, the Rembrandtesque moral chiaroscuro, the shifting struggle of the sunbeam in the gloom, such pictures of light upon light are vacuous and expressionless, and neither to be enjoyed nor understood. If *this* be the whole fruit of the victory, we say; if the generations of mankind suffered and laid down their lives; if prophets confessed and martyrs sang in the fire, and all the sacred tears were shed for no other end than that a race of creatures of such unexampled insipidity should succeed, and protract in *sæcula sæculorum* [Forever and Ever] their contented and inoffensives lives—why, at such a rate, better lose than win the battle, or at all events better ring down the curtain before the last act of the play, so that a business that began so importantly may be saved from so singularly flat a winding-up.

All this is what I should instantly say, were I called on to plead for gnosticism; and its real friends, of whom you will presently perceive I am not one, would say without difficulty a great deal more. Regarded as a stable finality, every outward good becomes a mere weariness to the flesh. It must be menaced, be occasionally lost, for its goodness to be fully felt as such. Nay, more than occasionally lost. No one knows the worth of innocence till he knows it is gone forever, and that money cannot buy it back. Not the saint, but the sinner that repenteth, is he to whom the full length and breadth, and height and depth, of life's meaning is revealed. Not the absence of vice, but vice there, and virtue holding her by the throat, seems the ideal human state. And there seems no reason to suppose it not a permanent human state. There is a deep truth in what the school of Schopenhauer insists on—the illusoriness of the notion of moral progress. The more brutal forms of evil that go are replaced by others more subtle and more poisonous. Our moral horizon moves with us as we move, and never do we draw nearer to the far-off line where the black waves and the azure meet. The final purpose of our creation seems most plausibly to be the greatest possible enrichment of our ethical consciousness, through the intensest play of contrasts and the widest diversity of characters. This of course obliges some of us to be vessels of wrath, whilst it calls others to be vessels of honor. But the subjectivist point of view reduces all these outward distinctions to a common denominator. The wretch languishing in the felon's cell may be drinking draughts of the wine of truth that will never pass the lips of the so-called favorite of fortune. And the peculiar consciousness of each of them is an indispensable note in the great ethical concert which the centuries as they roll are grinding out of the living heart of man.

So much for subjectivism! If the dilemma of determinism be to choose between it and pessimism, I see little room for hesitation from the strictly theoretical point of view. Subjectivism seems the more rational scheme. And the world may, possibly, for aught I know, be nothing else. When the healthy love of life is on one, and all its forms and its appetites seem so unutterably real; when the most brutal and the most spiritual things are lit by the same sun, and each is an integral part of the total richness—why, then it seems a grudging and sickly way of meeting so robust a universe to shrink from any of its facts and wish them not to be. Rather take the strictly dramatic point of view, and treat the whole thing as a great unending romance which the spirit of the universe, striving to realize its own content, is eternally thinking out and representing to itself.

No one, I hope, will accuse me, after I have said all this, of underrating the reasons in favor of subjectivism. And now that I proceed to say why those reasons, strong as they are, fail to convince my own mind, I trust the presumption may be that my objections are stronger still.

I frankly confess that they are of a practical order. If we practically take up subjectivism in a sincere and radical manner and follow its consequences, we meet with some that make us pause. Let a subjectivism begin in never so severe and intellectual a way, it is forced by the law of its nature to develop another side of itself and end with the corruptest curiosity. Once dismiss the notion that certain duties are good in themselves, and that we are here to do them, no matter how we feel about them; once consecrate the opposite notion that our performances and our violations of duty are for a common purpose, the attainment of subjective knowledge and feeling, and that the deepening of these is the chief end of our lives—and at what point on the downward slope are we to stop? In theology, subjectivism develops as its "left wing" antinomianism. In literature, its left wing is romanticism. And in practical life it is either a nerveless sentimentality or a sensualism without bounds.

Everywhere it fosters the fatalistic mood of mind. It makes those who are already too inert more passive still; it renders wholly reckless those whose energy is already in excess. All through history we find how subjectivism, as soon as it has a free career, exhausts itself in every sort of spiritual, moral, and practical license. Its optimism turns to an ethical indifference, which infallibly brings dissolution in its train. It is perfectly safe to say now that if the hegelian gnosticism, which has begun to show itself here and in Great Britain, were to become a popular philosophy, as it once was in Germany, it would certainly develop its left wing here as there, and produce a reaction of disgust. Already I have heard a graduate of this very school express in the pulpit his willingness to sin like David, if only he might repent like David. You may tell me he was only sowing his wild, or rather his tame, oats; and perhaps he was. But the point is that in the subjectivistic or gnostical philosophy oatsowing, wild or tame, becomes a systematic necessity and the chief function of life. After the pure and classic truths, the exciting and rancid ones must be experienced; and if the stupid virtues of the philistine herd do not then come in and save society from the influence of the children of light, a sort of inward putrefaction becomes its inevitable doom.

Look at the last runnings of the romantic school, as we see them in that strange contemporary Parisian literature, with which we of the less clever countries are so often driven to rinse out our minds after they have become clogged with the dullness and heaviness of our native pursuits. The romantic school began with the worship of subjective sensibility and the revolt against legality of which Rousseau was the first great prophet; and through various fluxes and refluxes, right wings and left wings, it stands to-day with two men of genius, M. Renan and M. Zola as its principal exponents—one speaking with its masculine, and the other with what might be called its feminine, voice. I prefer not to think now of less noble members of the school, and the Renan I have in mind is of course the Renan of latest dates. As I have used the term gnostic, both he and Zola are gnostics of the most pronounced sort. Both are athirst for the facts of life, and both think the facts of human sensibility to be of all facts the most worthy of attention. Both agree, moreover, that sensibility seems to be there for no higher purpose—certainly not, as the Philistines say, for the sake of bringing mere outward rights to pass and frustrating outward wrongs. One dwells on the sensibilities for their energy, the other for their sweetness; one speaks with a voice of bronze, the other with that of an Æolian harp; one ruggedly ignores the distinction of good and evil, the other plays the coquette between the craven unmanliness of his Philosophic Dialogues and the butterfly optimism of his *Souvenirs de jeunesse;* [memories of youth]. But under the pages of both there sounds incessantly the hoarse bass of *vanitas vanitatum, omnia vanitas,* [vanity of vanities, all is vanity], which the reader may hear, whenever he will, between the lines. No writer of this French romantic school has a word of rescue from the hour of satiety with the things of life—the hour in which we say, "I take no pleasure in them"—or from the hour of terror at the world's vast meaningless grinding, if perchance such hours should come. For terror and satiety are facts of sensibility like any others; and at their own hour they reign in their own right. The heart of the romantic utterances, whether poetical, critical, or historical, is this inward remedilessness, what Carlyle calls this far-off whimpering of wail and woe. And from this romantic state of mind there is absolutely no possible *theoretic* escape. Whether, like Renan, we look upon life in a more refined way, as a romance of the spirit; or whether, like the friends of Mr. Zola, we pique ourselves on our "scientific" and "analytic" character, and prefer to be cynical, and call the world a "roman experimental" [experimental novel] on an infinite scale—in either case the world appears to us potentially as what the same Carlyle once called it, a vast, gloomy, solitary Golgotha and mill of death.

The only escape is by the practical way. And since I have mentioned the nowadays much-reviled name of Carlyle, let me mention it once more, and say it is the way of his teaching. No matter for Carlyle's life, no matter for a great deal of his writing. What was the most important thing he said to us? He said: "Hang your sensibilities! Stop your snivelling complaints, and your equally snivelling raptures! Leave off your general emotional tomfoolery, and get to work like men!" But this means a complete

rupture with the subjectivist philosophy of things. It says conduct, and not sensibility, is the ultimate fact for our recognition. With the vision of certain works to be done, of certain outward changes to be wrought or resisted, it says our intellectual horizon terminates. No matter how we succeed in doing these outward duties, whether gladly and spontaneously, or heavily and unwillingly, do them we somehow must; for the leaving of them undone is perdition. No matter how we feel; if we are only faithful in the outward act and refuse to do wrong, the world will in so far be safe, and we quit of our debt towards it. Take, then, the yoke upon our shoulders; bend our neck beneath the heavy legality of its weight; regard something else than our feeling as our limit, our master, and our law; be willing to live and die in its service—and, at a stroke, we have passed from the subjective into the objective philosophy of things, much as one awakens from some feverish dream, full of bad lights and noises, to find one's self bathed in the sacred coolness and quiet of the air of the night.

But what is the essence of this philosophy of objective conduct, so old-fashioned and finite, but so chaste and sane and strong, when compared with its romantic rival? It is the recognition of limits, foreign and opaque to our understanding. It is the willingness, after bringing about some external good, to feel at peace; for our responsibility ends with the performance of that duty, and the burden of the rest we may lay on higher powers.

> *"Look to thyself, O Universe!*
> *Thou art better, and not worse,"*

we may say in that philosophy, the moment we have done our stroke of conduct, however small. For in the view of that philosophy the universe belongs to a plurality of semi-independent forces, each one of which may help or hinder, and be helped or hindered by, the operations of the rest.

But this brings us right back, after such a long détour, to the question of indeterminism and to the conclusion of all I came here to say to-night. For the only consistent way of representing a pluralism and a world whose parts may affect one another through their conduct being either good or bad is the indeterministic way. What interest, zest, or excitement can there be in achieving the right way, unless we are enabled to feel that the wrong way is also a possible and a natural way—nay, more, a menacing and an imminent way? And what sense can there be in condemning ourselves for taking the wrong way, unless we need have done nothing of the sort, unless the right way was open to us as well? I cannot understand the willingness to act, no matter how we feel, without the belief that acts are really good and bad. I cannot understand the belief that an act is bad, without regret at its happening. I cannot understand regret without the admission of real, genuine possibilities in the world. Only *then* is it other than a mockery to feel, after we have failed to do our best, that an irreparable opportunity is gone from the universe, the loss of which it must forever after mourn.

If you insist that this is all superstition, that possibility is in the eye of science and reason impossibility, and that if I act badly 'tis that the universe was foredoomed to suffer this defect, you fall right back into the dilemma, the labyrinth, of pessimism and subjectivism, from out of whose toils we have just wound our way.

Now, we are of course free to fall back, if we please. For my own part, though, whatever difficulties may beset the philosophy of objective right and wrong, and the indeterminism it seems to imply, determinism, with its alternative of pessimism or romanticism, contains difficulties that are greater still. But you will remember that I expressly repudiated awhile ago the pretension to offer any arguments which could be coercive in a so-called scientific fashion in this matter. And I consequently find myself, at the end of this long talk, obliged to state my conclusions in an altogether personal way. This personal method of appeal seems to be among the very conditions of the problem; and the most anyone can do is to confess as candidly as he can the grounds

for the faith that is in him, and leave his example to work on others as it may.

Let me, then, without circumlocution say just this. The world is enigmatical enough in all conscience, whatever theory we may take up towards it. The indeterminism I defend, the free-will theory of popular sense based on the judgment of regret, represents that world as vulnerable, and liable to be injured by certain of its parts if they act wrong. And it represents their acting wrong as a matter of possibility or accident, neither inevitable nor yet to be infallibly warded off. In all this, it is a theory devoid either of transparency or of stability. It gives us a pluralistic, restless universe, in which no single point of view can ever take in the whole scene; and to a mind possessed of the love of unity at any cost, it will, no doubt, remain forever inacceptable. A friend with such a mind once told me that the thought of my universe made him sick, like the sight of the horrible motion of a mass of maggots in their carrion bed.

But whilst I freely admit that the pluralism and the restlessness are repugnant and irrational in a certain way, I find that every alternative to them is irrational in a deeper way. The indeterminism with its maggots, if you please to speak so about it, offends only the native absolutism of my intellect—an absolutism which, after all, perhaps, deserves to be snubbed and kept in check. But the determinism with its necessary carrion, to continue the figure of speech, and with no possible maggots to eat the latter up, violates my sense of moral reality through and through. When, for example, I imagine such carrion as the Brockton murder, I cannot conceive it as an act by which the universe, as a whole, logically and necessarily expresses its nature without shrinking from complicity with such a whole. And I deliberately refuse to keep on terms of loyalty with the universe by saying blankly that the murder, since it does flow from the nature of the whole, is not carrion. There are *some* instinctive reactions which I, for one, will not tamper with. The only remaining alternative, the attitude of gnostical romanticism, wrenches my personal instincts in quite as violent a way. It falsifies the simple objectivity of their deliverance. It makes the goose-flesh the murder excites in me a sufficient reason for the perpetration of the crime. It transforms life from a tragic reality into an insincere melodramatic exhibition, as foul or as tawdry as anyone's diseased curiosity pleases to carry it out. And with its consecration of the "roman naturaliste" [naturalistic novel] state of mind, and its enthronement of the baser crew of Parisian *littérateurs* [authors] among the eternally indispensable organs by which the infinite spirit of things attains to that subjective illumination which is the task of its life, it leaves me in presence of a sort of subjective carrion considerably more noisome than the objective carrion I called it in to take away.

No! better a thousand times, than such systematic corruption of our moral sanity, the plainest pessimism, so that it be straightforward; but better far than that the world of chance. Make as great an uproar about chance as you please, I know that chance means pluralism and nothing more. If some of the members of the pluralism are bad, the philosophy of pluralism, whatever broad views with a clean breast of affection and an unsophisticated moral sense. And if I still wish to think of the world as a totality, it lets me feel that a world with a *chance* in it of being altogether good, even if the chance never come to pass, is better than a world with no such chance at all. That "chance" whose very notion I am exhorted and conjured to banish from my view of the future as the suicide of reason concerning it, that "chance" is—what? Just this—the chance that in moral respects the future may be other and better than the past has been. This is the only chance we have any motive for supposing to exist. Shame, rather, on its repudiation and its denial! For its presence is the vital air which lets the world live, the salt which keeps it sweet.

And here I might legitimately stop, having expressed all I care to see admitted by others to-night. But I know that if I do stop here, misapprehensions will remain in the minds of some of you, and keep all I have said from having its effect; so I judge it best to add a few more words.

In the first place, in spite of all my explanations, the word "chance" will still be giving trouble. Though you may yourselves be adverse to the deterministic doctrine, you wish a pleasanter word than "chance" to name the opposite doctrine by; and you very likely consider my preference for such a word a perverse sort of a partiality on my part. It certainly *is* a bad word to make converts with; and you wish I had not thrust it so butt-foremost at you—you wish to use a milder term.

Well, I admit there may be just a dash of perversity in its choice. The spectacle of the mere word-grabbing game played by the soft determinists has perhaps driven me too violently the other way; and, rather than be found wrangling with them for the good words, I am willing to take the first bad one which comes along, provided it be unequivocal. The question is of things, not of eulogistic names for them; and the best word is the one that enables men to know the quickest whether they disagree or not about the things. But the word "chance," with its singular negativity, is just the word for this purpose. Whoever uses it instead of "freedom," squarely and resolutely gives up all pretence to control the things he says are free. For *him,* he confesses that they are no better than mere chance would be. It is a word of *impotence,* and is therefore the only sincere word we can use, if, in granting freedom to certain things, we grant it honestly, and really risk the game. "Who chooses me must give me and forfeit all he hath." Any other word permits of quibbling, and lets us, after the fashion of the soft determinists, make a pretence of restoring the caged bird to liberty with one hand, whilst with the other we anxiously tie a string to its leg to make sure it does not get beyond our sight.

But now you will bring up your final doubt. Does not the admission of such an unguaranteed chance or freedom preclude utterly the notion of a Providence governing the world? Does it not leave the fate of the universe at the mercy of the chance-possibilities, and so far insecure? Does it not, in short, deny the craving of our nature for an ultimate peace behind all tempests, for a blue zenith above all clouds?

To this my answer must be very brief. The belief in free-will is not in the least incompatible with the belief in Providence, provided you do not restrict the Providence to fulminating nothing for *fatal* decrees. If you allow him to provide possibilities as well as actualities to the universe, and to carry on his own thinking in those two categories just as we do ours, chances may be there, uncontrolled even by him, and the course of the universe be really ambiguous; and yet the end of all things may be just what he intended it to be from all eternity.

An analogy will make the meaning of this clear. Suppose two men before a chessboard—the one a novice, the other an expert player of the game. The expert intends to beat. But he cannot foresee exactly what any one actual move of his adversary may be. He knows, however, all the *possible* moves of the latter; and he knows in advance how to meet each of them by a move of his own which leads in the direction of victory. And the victory infallibly arrives after no matter how devious a course, in the one predestined form of check-mate to the novice's king.

Let now the novice stand for us finite free agents, and the expert for the infinite mind in which the universe lies. Suppose the latter to be thinking out his universe before he actually creates it. Suppose him to say, I will lead things to a certain end, but I will not *now* decide on all the steps thereto. At various points, ambiguous possibilities shall be left open, *either* of which, at a given instant, may become actual. But whichever branch of these bifurcations become real, I know what I shall do at the *next* bifurcation to keep things from drifting away from the final result I intend.

The creator's plan of the universe would thus be left blank as to many of its actual details, but all possibilities would be marked down. The realization of some of these would be left absolutely to chance; that is, would only be determined when the moment of realization came. Other possibilities would be *contingently* determined; that is, their decision would have to wait till it was seen how the matters of absolute chance fell out. But the rest of the plan, including its final upshot, would be rigorously determined once for all. So the creator himself would not need to know *all* the details of actuality until they came; and at any time his own view of the world would be a view partly of facts and partly of possibilities, exactly as ours is now. Of one thing, however, he might be certain; and that is that his world was safe, and that no matter how much it might zigzag he could surely bring it home at last.

Now, it is entirely immaterial, in this scheme, whether the creator leave the absolute chance-possibilities to be decided by himself, each when its proper moment arrives, or whether, on the contrary, he alienate this power from himself, and leave the decision out and out to finite creatures such as we men are. The great point is that the possibilities are really *here*. Whether it be we who solve them, or he working through us, at those soul-trying moments when fate's scales seem to quiver, and good snatches the victory from evil or shrinks nerveless from the fight, is of small account, so long as we admit that the issue is decided nowhere else than *here* and *now*. That is what gives the palpitating reality to our moral life and makes it tingle, as Mr. Mallock says, with so strange and elaborate an excitement. This reality, this excitement, are what the determinisms, hard and soft alike, suppress by their denial that *anything* is decided here and now, and their dogma that all things were foredoomed and settled long ago. If it be so, may you and I have been foredoomed to the error of continuing to believe in liberty. It is fortunate for the winding up of controversy that in every discussion with determinism this *argumentum ad hominem* can be its adversary's last word.

# The Will to Believe

*Ha*

. . . I have brought with me to-night something like a sermon on justification by faith to read to you—I mean an essay in justification *of* faith, a defence of our right to adopt a believing attitude in religious matters, in spite of the fact that our merely logical intellect may not have been coerced. "The Will to Believe," accordingly, is the title of my paper.

I have long defended to my own students the lawfulness of voluntarily adopted faith; but as soon as they have got well imbued with the logical spirit, they have as a rule refused to admit my contention to be lawful philosophically, even though in point of fact they were personally all the time chock-full of some faith or other themselves. I am all the while, however, so profoundly convinced that my own position is correct, that your invitation has seemed to me a good occasion to make my statements more clear. Perhaps your minds will be more open than those with which I have hitherto had to deal. I will be as little technical as I can, though I must begin by setting up some technical distinctions that will help us in the end.

## I

Let us give the name of *hypothesis* to anything that may be proposed to our belief; and just as the electricians speak of live and dead wires, let us speak of any hypothesis as either *live* or *dead*. A live hypothesis is one which appeals as a real possibility to him whom it is proposed. If I ask you to believe in the Mahdi, the notion makes no electric connection with your nature—it refuses to scintillate with any credibility at all. As an hypothesis it is completely dead. To an Arab, however (even if he be not one of the Mahdi's followers), the hypothesis is among the mind's possibilities: it is alive. This shows that deadness and liveness in an hypothesis are not intrinsic properties, but relations to the individual thinker. They are measured by his willingness to act. The maximum of liveness in an hypothesis means willingness to act irrevocably. Practically, that means belief; but there is some believing tendency wherever there is willingness to act at all.

Next, let us call the decision between two hypotheses an *option*. Options may be of several kinds. They may be—1, *living* or *dead;* 2, *forced* or *avoidable;* 3, *momentous* or *trivial;* and for our purposes we may call an option a *genuine* option when it is of the forced, living and momentous kind.

1. A living option is one in which both hypotheses are live ones. If I say to you: "Be a theosophist or be a mahomedan," it is probably a dead option, because for you neither hypothesis is likely to be alive. But if I say "Be an agnostic or be a Christian," it is otherwise: trained as you are, each hypothesis makes some appeal, however small, to your belief.

2. Next, if I say to you: "Choose between going out with you umbrella or without it," I do not offer you a genuine option, for it is not forced. You can easily avoid it by not going out at all. Similarly, if I say "Either love me or hate me," "Either call my theory true or call it false," you option is avoidable. You may remain indifferent to me, neither loving nor hating, and you may decline to offer any judgment as to my theory. But if I say, "Either accept this truth or go without it," I put on you a forced option, for there is no standing place outside of the alternative. Every dilemma based on a complete logical disjunction, with no possibility of not choosing, is an option of this forced kind.

3. Finally, if I were Dr. Nansen and proposed to you to join my North Pole expedition, your option would be momentous; for this

From *The Works of William James—The Will to Believe,* ed. Frederick Burkhardt (Cambridge, Mass.: Harvard University Press, 1979 [1896]), pp. 13–33.

would probably be your only similar opportunity, and your choice now would either exclude you from the North Pole sort of immortality altogether or put at least the chance of it into your hands. He who refuses to embrace a unique opportunity loses the prize as surely as if he tried and failed. *Per contra,* the option is trivial when the opportunity is not unique, when the stake is insignificant, or when the decision is reversible if it later prove unwise. Such trivial options abound in the scientific life. A chemist finds an hypothesis live enough to spend a year in its verification: he believes in it to that extent. But if his experiments prove inconclusive either way, he is quit for his loss of time, no vital harm being done.

It will facilitate our discussion if we keep all these distinctions well in mind.

## II

The next matter to consider is the actual psychology of human opinion. When we look at certain facts, it seems as if our passional and volitional nature lay at the root of all our convictions. When we look at others, it seems as if they could do nothing when the intellect had once said its say. Let us take the latter facts up first.

Does it not seem preposterous on the very face of it to talk of our opinions being modifiable at will? Can our will either help or hinder our intellect in its perceptions of truth? Can we, by just willing it, believe that Abraham Lincoln's existence is a myth, and that the portraits of him in *McClure's Magazine* are all of someone else? Can we, by any effort of our will, or by any strength of wish that it were true, believe ourselves well and about when we are roaring with rheumatism in bed, or feel certain that the sum of the two one-dollar bills in our pocket must be a hundred dollars? We can *say* any of these things, but we are absolutely impotent to believe them, and of just such things is the whole fabric of the truths that we do believe in made up—matters of fact, immediate or remote, as Hume said, and relations between ideas, which are either

there or not there for us if we see them so, and which if not there cannot be put there by any action of our own.

In Pascal's *Thoughts* there is a celebrated passage known in literature as Pascal's wager. In it he tries to force us into Christianity by reasoning as if our concern with truth resembled our concern with the stakes in a game of chance. Translated freely his words are these: You must either believe or not believe that God is—which will you do? Your human reason cannot say. A game is going on between you and the nature of things which at the day of judgment will bring out either heads or tails. Weigh what your gains and your losses would be if you should stake all your have on heads, or God's existence: If you win in such case, you gain eternal beatitude; if you lose, you lose nothing at all. If there were an infinity of chances, and only one for God in this wager, still you ought to stake your all on God; for though you surely risk a finite loss by this procedure, any finite loss is reasonable, even a certain one is reasonable, if there is but the possibility of infinite gain. Go, then, and take holy water, and have masses said; belief will come and stupefy your scruples—*Cela vous fera croire et vous abêtira.* [that will make you believe and become stupid]. Why should you not? At bottom, what have you to lose?

You probably feel that when religious faith expresses itself thus, in the language of the gaming-table, it is put to its last trumps. Surely Pascal's own personal belief in masses and holy water had far other springs; and this celebrated page of his is but an argument for others, a last desperate snatch at a weapon against the hardness of the unbelieving heart. We feel that a faith in masses and holy water adopted wilfully after such a mechanical calculation would lack the inner soul of faith's reality; and if we were ourselves in the place of the Deity, we should probably take particular pleasure in cutting off believers of this pattern from their infinite reward. It is evident that unless there be some pre-existing tendency to believe in masses and holy water, the option offered to the will by Pascal is not a living option. Certainly no Turk ever took to masses and holy water on its account; and even to us Protestants these means of salvation seem such foregone possibilities that Pascal's logic, invoked for them specifically, leave us unmoved. As well might the Mahdi write to us, saying "I am the Expected One whom God has created in his effulgence. You shall be infinitely happy if you confess me; otherwise you shall be cut off from the light of the sun. Weigh, then, your infinite gain if I am genuine against your finite sacrifice if I am not!" His logic would be that of Pascal; but he would vainly use it on us, for the hypothesis he offers us is dead. No tendency to act on it exists in us to any degree.

The talk of believing by our volition seems, then, from one point of view, simply silly. From another point of view it is worse than silly, it is vile. When one turns to the magnificent edifice of the physical sciences, and sees how it was reared; what thousands of disinterested moral lives of men lie buried in its mere foundations; what patience and postponement, what choking down of preference, what submission to the icy laws of outer fact are wrought into its very stones and mortar; how absolutely impersonal it stands in its vast augustness—then how besotted and contemptible seems every little sentimentalist who comes blowing his voluntary smoke-wreaths, and pretending to decide things from out of his private dream! Can we wonder if those bred in the rugged and manly school of science should feel like spewing such subjectivism out of their mouths? The whole system of loyalties which grow up in the schools of science go dead against its toleration; so that it is only natural that those who have caught the scientific fever should pass over to the opposite extreme, and write sometimes as if the incorruptibly truthful intellect ought positively to prefer bitterness and unacceptableness to the heart in its cup.

> *"It fortifies my soul to know*
> *That, though I perish, Truth is so—"*

sings Clough, whilst Huxley exclaims: "My only consolation lies in the reflection that, however bad our posterity may become, so long as they hold by the plain rule of not pretending to believe what they have no reason to believe because it may be to their advantage so to pretend [the word 'pretend' is surely here redundant], they will not have reached the lowest depths of immorality." And that delicious *enfant terrible* Clifford writes: "Belief is desecrated when given to unproved and unquestioned statements, for the solace and private pleasure of the believer. . . . Whoso would deserve well of his fellows in this matter will guard the purity of his belief with a very fanaticism of jealous care, lest at any time it should rest on an unworthy object, and catch a stain which can never be wiped away. . . . If [a] belief has been accepted on insufficient evidence [even though the belief be true, as Clifford on the same page explains], the pleasure is a stolen one. . . . It is sinful, because it is stolen in defiance of our duty to mankind. That duty is to guard ourselves from such beliefs as from a pestilence, which may shortly master our own body and then spread to the rest of the town. . . . It is wrong always, everywhere, and for anyone, to believe anything upon insufficient evidence."

### III

All this strikes one as healthy, even when expressed, as by Clifford, with somewhat too much of robustious pathos in the voice. Free-will and simple wishing do seem, in the matter of our credences, to be only fifth wheels to the coach. Yet if anyone should thereupon assume that intellectual insight is what remains after wish and will and sentimental preference have taken wing, or that pure reason is what then settles our opinions, he would fly quite as directly in the teeth of the facts.

It is only our already dead hypotheses that our willing nature is unable to bring to life again. But what has made them dead for us is for the most part a previous action of our willing nature of an antagonistic kind. When I say "willing nature," I do not mean only such deliberate volitions as may have set up habits of belief that we cannot now escape from—I mean all such factors of belief as fear and hope, prejudice and passion, imitation and partisanship, the circumpressure of our caste and set. As a matter of fact we find ourselves believing, we hardly know how or why. Mr. Balfour gives the name of "authority" to all those influences, born of the intellectual climate, that make hypotheses possible or impossible for us, alive or dead. Here in this room, we all of us believe in molecules and the conservation of energy, in democracy and necessary progress, in Protestant Christianity and the duty of fighting for "the doctrine of the immortal Monroe," all for no reasons worthy of the name. We see into these matters with no more inner clearness, and probably with much less, than any disbeliever in them might possess. His unconventionality would probably have some grounds to show for its conclusions; but for us, not insight, but the *prestige* of the opinions, is what makes the spark shoot from them and light up in our sleeping magazines of faith. Our reason is quite satisfied, in nine hundred and ninety-nine cases out of every thousand of us, if it can find a few arguments that will do to recite in case our credulity is criticized by someone else. Our faith is faith in someone else's faith, and in the greatest matters this is most the case. Our belief in truth itself, for instance, that there is a truth, and that our minds and it are made for each other—what is it but a passionate affirmation of desire, in which our social system backs us up? We want to have a truth; we want to believe that our experiments and studies and discussions must put us in a continually better and better position towards it; and on this line we agree to fight out our thinking lives. But if a pyrrhonistic sceptic asks us *how we know* all this, can our logic find a reply? No! Certainly it cannot. It is just one volition against another—we willing to go in for life upon a trust or assumption which he, for his part, does not care to make.

As a rule we disbelieve all facts and theories for which we have no use. Clifford's cosmic emotions find no use for Christian feelings. Huxley belabors the bishops because there is no use for sacerdotalism in his scheme

of life. Newman, on the contrary, goes over to Romanism, and finds all sorts of reasons good for staying there, because a priestly system is for him an organic need and delight. Why do so few "scientists" even look at the evidence for telepathy, so called? Because they think, as a leading biologist, now dead, once said to me, that even if such a thing were true, scientists ought to band together to keep it suppressed and concealed. It would undo the uniformity of Nature and all sorts of other things without which scientists cannot carry on their pursuits. But if this very man had been showing something which as a scientist he might *do* with telepathy, he might not only have examined the evidence, but even have found it good enough. This very law which the logicians would impose upon us—if I may give the name of logicians to those who would rule out our willing nature here—is based on nothing but their own natural wish to exclude all elements for which they, in their professional quality of logicians, can find no use.

Evidently, then, our non-intellectual nature does influence our convictions. There are passional tendencies and volitions which run before and others which come after belief, and it is only the latter that are too late for the fair; and they are not too late when the previous passional work has been already in their own direction. Pascal's argument, instead of being powerless, then seems a regular clincher, and is the last stroke needed to make our faith in masses and holy water complete. The state of things is evidently far from simple; and pure insight and logic, whatever they might do ideally, are not the only things that really do produce our creeds.

## IV

Our next duty, having recognized this mixed-up state of affairs, is to ask whether it be simply reprehensible and pathological, or whether, on the contrary, we must treat it as a normal element in making up our minds. The thesis I defend is, briefly stated, this: *Our passional nature not only lawfully may, but must,*

*decide an option between propositions, when-
ever it is a genuine option that cannot by its
nature be decided on intellectual grounds; for
to say, under such circumstances, "Do not
decide, but leave the question open," is itself a
passional decision—just like deciding yes or
no—and is attended with the same risk of losing the truth.* The thesis thus abstractly
expressed will, I trust, soon become quite
clear. But I must first indulge in a bit more of
preliminary work.

## V

It will be observed that for the purposes of this
discussion we are on "dogmatic" ground—
ground, I mean, which leaves systematic
philosophical scepticism altogether out of
account. The postulate that there is truth, and
that it is the destiny of our minds to attain it,
we are deliberately resolving to make, though
the sceptic will not make it. We part company
with him, therefore, absolutely, at this point.
But the faith that truth exists, and that our
minds can find it, may be held in two ways. We
may talk of the *empiricist* way and of the
*absolutist* way of believing in truth. The absolutists in this matter say that we not only can
attain to knowing truth, but we can *know when*
we have attained to knowing it; whilst the
empiricists think that although we may attain
it, we cannot infallibly know when. To *know* is
one thing, and to know for certain *that* we
know is another. One may hold to the first
being possible without the second; hence the
empiricists and the absolutists, although neither of them is a sceptic in the usual philosophic sense of the term, show very different
degrees of dogmatism in their lives.

If we look at the history of opinions, we see
that the empiricist tendency has largely prevailed in science, whilst in philosophy the
absolutist tendency has had everything its own
way. The characteristic sort of happiness,
indeed, which philosophies yield has mainly
consisted in the conviction felt by each successive school or system that by it bottom-cer-
titude had been attained. "Other philosophies

are collections of opinions, mostly false; *my*
philosophy gives standing-ground forever"—
who does not recognize in this the key-note of
every system worthy of the name? A system,
to be a system at all, must come as a *closed*
system, reversible in this or that detail, perchance, but in its essential features never!

Scholastic orthodoxy, to which one must
always go when one wishes to find perfectly
clear statement, has beautifully elaborated this
absolutist conviction in a doctrine which it
calls that of "objective evidence." If, for example, I am unable to doubt that I now exist before
you, that two is less than three, or that if all men
are mortal then I am mortal too, it is because
these things illumine my intellect irresistibly.
The final ground of this objective evidence
possessed by certain propositions is the
*adæquatio intellectûs nostri cum rê* [intellect's
adequacy to the thing]. The certitude it brings
involves an *aptitudinem ad extorquendum cer-
tum assensum* [ability to obtain certain assent]
on the part of the truth envisaged, and on the
side of the subject, a *quietem in cognitione*
[thought at rest]. When once the object is mentally received, that leaves no possibility of
doubt behind; and in the whole transaction
nothing operates but the *entitas ipsa* [entity
itself] of the object and the *entitas ipsa* [entity
itself] of the mind. We slouchy modern
thinkers dislike to talk in Latin—indeed, we
dislike to talk in set terms at all; but at bottom
our own state of mind is very much like this
whenever we uncritically abandon ourselves:
You believe in objective evidence, and I do. Of
some things we feel that we are certain: we
know, and we know that we do know. There is
something that gives a click inside of us, a bell
that strikes twelve, when the hands of our mental clock have swept the dial and meet over the
meridian hour. The greatest empiricists among
us are only empiricists on reflection: when left
to their instincts, they dogmatize like infallible
popes. When the Cliffords tell us how sinful it
is to be Christians on such "insufficient evidence" insufficiency is really the last thing they
have in mind. For them the evidence is
absolutely sufficient, only it makes the other
way. They believe so completely in an anti-

christian order of the universe that there is no living option: Christianity is a dead hypothesis from the start.

## VI

But now, since we are all such absolutists by instinct, what in our quality of students of philosophy ought we to do about the fact? Shall we espouse and indorse it? Or shall we treat it as a weakness of our nature from which we must free ourselves, if we can?

I sincerely believe that the latter course is the only one we can follow as reflective men. Objective evidence and certitude are doubtless very fine ideals to play with, but where on this moonlit and dream-visited planet are they found? I am, therefore, myself a complete empiricist so far as my theory of human knowledge goes. I live, to be sure, by the practical faith that we must go on experiencing and thinking over our experience, for only thus can our opinions grow more true; but to hold any one of them—I absolutely do not care which—as if it never could be re-interpretable or corrigible, I believe to be a tremendously mistaken attitude, and I think that the whole history of philosophy will bear me out. There is but one indefectibly certain truth, and that is the truth that pyrrhonistic scepticism itself leaves standing—the truth that the present phenomenon of consciousness exists. That, however, is the bare starting-point of knowledge, the mere admission of a stuff to be philosophized about. The various philosophies are but so many attempts at expressing what this stuff really is. And if we repair to our libraries what disagreement do we discover! Where is a certainly true answer found? Apart from abstract propositions of comparison (such as two and two are the same as four), propositions which tell us nothing by themselves about concrete reality, we find no proposition ever regarded by anyone as evidently certain that has not either been called a falsehood, or at least had its truth sincerely questioned by someone else. The transcending of the axioms of geometry, not in play but in

earnest, by certain of our contemporaries (as Zöllner and Charles H. Hinton), and the rejection of the whole aristotelian logic by the Hegelians, are striking instances in point.

No concrete test of what is really true has ever been agreed upon. Some make the criterion external to the moment of perception, putting it either in revelation, the *consensus gentium,* the instincts of the heart, or the systematized experience of the race. Others make the perceptive moment its own test— Descartes, for instance, with his clear and distinct ideas guaranteed by the veracity of God; Reid with his "common-sense"; and Kant with his forms of synthetic judgment *a priori.* The inconceivability of the opposite; the capacity to be verified by sense; the possession of complete organic unity or self-relation, realized when a thing is its own other—are standards which, in turn, have been used. The much lauded objective evidence is never triumphantly there; it is a mere aspiration or *Grenzbegriff,* marking the infinitely remote ideal of our thinking life. To claim that certain truths now possess it, is simply to say that when you think them true and they *are* true, then their evidence is objective, otherwise it is not. But practically one's conviction that the evidence one goes by is of the real objective brand, is only one more subjective opinion added to the lot. For what a contradictory array of opinions have objective evidence and absolute certitude been claimed! The world is rational through and through—its existence is an ultimate brute fact; there is a personal God—a personal God is inconceivable; there is an extra-mental physical world immediately known—the mind can only know its own ideas; a moral imperative exists—obligation is only the resultant of desires; a permanent spiritual principle is in everyone—there are only shifting states of mind; there is an endless chain of causes—there is an absolute first cause; an eternal necessity—a freedom; a purpose—no purpose; a primal One—a primal Many; a universal continuity—an essential discontinuity in things; an infinity—no infinity. There is this—there is that; there is indeed nothing which someone has not thought absolutely true, whilst his neighbor deemed it absolutely false; and not an absolutist among them seems ever to have considered that the trouble may all the time be essential, and that the intellect, even with truth directly in its grasp, may have no infallible signal for knowing whether it be truth or no. When, indeed, one remembers that the most striking practical application to life of the doctrine of objective certitude has been the conscientious labors of the Holy Office of the Inquisition, one feels less tempted than ever to lend the doctrine a respectful ear.

But please observe, now, that when as empiricists we give up the doctrine of objective certitude, we do not thereby give up the quest or hope of truth itself. We still pin our faith on its existence, and still believe that we gain an ever better position towards it by systematically continuing to roll up experiences and think. Our great difference from the scholastic lies in the way we face. The strength of his system lies in the principles; the origin, the *terminus a quo* [beginning point] of his thought; for us the strength is in the outcome, the upshot, the *terminus ad quem* [destination point]. Not where it comes from but what it leads to is to decide. It matters not to an empiricist from what quarter an hypothesis may come to him: he may have acquired it by fair means or by foul; passion may have whispered or accident suggested it; but if the total drift of thinking continues to confirm it, that is what he means by its being true.

## VII

One more point, small but important, and our preliminaries are done. There are two ways of looking at our duty in the matter of opinion—ways entirely different, and yet ways about whose difference the theory of knowledge seems hitherto to have shown very little concern. *We must know the truth;* and *we must avoid error*—these are our first and great commandments as would-be knowers; but they are not two ways of stating an identical commandment, they are two separable laws. Although it may indeed happen that when we believe the

truth *A*, we escape as an incidental consequence from believing the falsehood *B*, it hardly ever happens that by merely disbelieving *B* we necessarily believe *A*. We may in escaping *B* fall into believing other falsehoods, *C* or *D*, just as bad as *B*; or we may escape *B* by not believing anything at all, not even *A*.

Believe truth! Shun error!—these, we see, are two materially different laws; and by choosing between them we may end by colouring differently our whole intellectual life. We may regard the chase for truth as paramount, and the avoidance of error as secondary; or we may, on the other hand, treat the avoidance of error as more imperative, and let truth take its chance. Clifford, in the instructive passage which I have quoted, exhorts us to the latter course. Believe nothing, he tells us, keep your mind in suspense forever, rather than by closing it on insufficient evidence incur the awful risk of believing lies. You, on the other hand, may think that the risk of being in error is a very small matter when compared with the blessings of real knowledge, and be ready to be duped many times in your investigation rather than postpone indefinitely the chance of guessing true. I myself find it impossible to go with Clifford. We must remember that these feelings of our duty about either truth or error are in any case only expressions of our passional life. Biologically considered, our minds are as ready to grind out falsehood as veracity, and he who says "Better go without belief forever than believe a lie!" merely shows his own preponderant private horror of becoming a dupe. He may be critical of many of his desires and fears, but this fear he slavishly obeys. He cannot imagine anyone questioning its binding force. For my own part, I have also a horror of being duped; but I can believe that worse things than being duped may happen to a man in this world: so Clifford's exhortation has to my ears a thoroughly fantastic sound. It is like a general informing his soldiers that it is better to keep out of battle forever than to risk a single wound. Not so are victories either over enemies or over nature gained. Our errors are surely not such awfully solemn things. In a world where we are so certain to incur them in spite of all our caution, a certain lightness of heart seems healthier than this excessive nervousness on their behalf. At any rate, it seems the fittest thing for the empiricist philosopher.

## VIII

And now, after all this introduction, let us go straight at our question. I have said, and now repeat it, that not only as a matter of fact do we find our passional nature influencing us in our opinions, but that there are some options between opinions in which this influence must be regarded both as an inevitable and as a lawful determinant of our choice.

　I fear here that some of you my hearers will begin to scent danger, and lend an inhospitable ear. Two first steps of passion you have indeed had to admit as necessary—we must think so as to avoid dupery, and we must think so as to gain truth; but the surest path to those ideal consummations, you will probably consider, is from now onwards to take no farther passional step.

　Well, of course I agree as far as the facts will allow. Wherever the option between losing truth and gaining it is not momentous, we can throw the chance of *gaining truth* away, and at any rate save ourselves from any chance of *believing falsehood,* by not making up our minds at all till objective evidence has come. In scientific questions, this is almost always the case; and even in human affairs in general, the need of acting is seldom so urgent that a false belief to act on is better than no belief at all. Law courts, indeed, have to decide on the best evidence attainable for the moment, because a judge's duty is to make law as well as to ascertain it, and (as a learned judge once said to me) few cases are worth spending much time over: the great thing is to have them decided on *any* acceptable principle, and got out of the way. But in our dealings with objective nature we obviously are recorders, not makers, of the truth; and decisions for the mere sake of deciding promptly and getting on to the next business would be wholly out of place. Throughout

the breadth of physical nature facts are what they are quite independently of us, and seldom is there any such hurry about them that the risks of being duped by believing a premature theory need be faced. The questions here are always trivial options, the hypotheses are hardly living (at any rate not living for us spectators), the choice between believing truth or falsehood is seldom forced. The attitude of sceptical balance is therefore the absolutely wise one if we would escape mistakes. What difference, indeed, does it make to most of us whether we have or have not a theory of the Röntgen rays, whether we believe or not in mind-stuff, or have a conviction about the causality of conscious states? It makes no difference. Such options are not forced on us. On every account it is better not to make them, but still keep weighing reasons *pro et contra* with an indifferent hand.

　I speak, of course, here of the purely judging mind. For purposes of discovery such indifference is to be less highly recommended, and science would be far less advanced than she is if the passionate desires of individuals to get their own faiths confirmed had been kept out of the game. See for example the sagacity which Spencer and Weismann now display. On the other hand, if you want an absolute duffer in an investigation, you must, after all, take the man who has no interest whatever in its results: he is the warranted incapable, the positive fool. The most useful investigator, because the most sensitive observer, is always he whose eager interest in one side of the question is balanced by an equally keen nervousness lest he become deceived. Science has organized this nervousness into a regular *technique,* her so-called method of verification; and she has fallen so deeply in love with the method that one may even say she has ceased to care for truth by itself at all. It is only truth as technically verified that interests her. The truth of truths might come in merely affirmative form, and she would decline to touch it. Such truth as that, she might repeat with Clifford, would be stolen in defiance of her duty to mankind. Human passions, however, are stronger than technical rules. "Le cœur a ses raisons," as Pascal says, "que la raison ne connaît point"; and however indifferent to all but the bare rules of the game the umpire, the abstract intellect, may be, the concrete players who furnish him the materials to judge of are usually, each one of them, in love with some pet "live hypothesis" of his own. Let us agree, however, that wherever there is no forced option, the dispassionately judicial intellect with no pet hypothesis, saving us, as it does, from dupery at any rate, ought to be our ideal.

The question next arises: Are there not somewhere forced options in our speculative questions, and can we (as men who may be interested at least as much in positively gaining truth as in merely escaping dupery) always wait with impunity till the coercive evidence shall have arrived? It seems *a priori* improbable that the truth should be so nicely adjusted to our needs and powers as that. In the great boarding-house of nature, the cakes and the butter and the syrup seldom come out so even and leave the plates so clean. Indeed, we should view them with scientific suspicion if they did.

## IX

*Moral questions* immediately present themselves as questions whose solution cannot wait for sensible proof. A moral question is a question not of what sensibly exists, but of what is good, or would be good if it did exist. Science can tell us what exists; but to compare the *worths,* both of what exists and of what does not exist, we must consult not science, but what Pascal calls our heart. Science herself consults her heart when she lays it down that the infinite ascertainment of fact and correction of false belief are the supreme goods for man. Challenge the statement and science can only repeat it oracularly, or else prove it by showing that such ascertainment and correction bring man all sorts of other goods which man's heart in turn declares. The question of having moral beliefs at all or not having them is decided by our will. Are our moral prefer-

ences true or false, or are they only odd biological phenomena, making things good or bad for *us,* but in themselves indifferent? How can your pure intellect decide? If your heart does not *want* a world of moral reality, your head will assuredly never make you believe in one. Mephistophelian scepticism, indeed, will satisfy the head's play-instincts much better than any rigorous idealism can. Some men (even at the student age) are so naturally cool-hearted that the moralistic hypothesis never has for them any pungent life, and in their supercilious presence the hot young moralist always feels strangely ill at ease. The appearance of knowingness is on their side, of *naiveté* and gullibility on his. Yet, in the inarticulate heart of him, he clings to it that he is not a dupe, and that there is a realm in which (as Emerson says) all their wit and intellectual superiority is no better than the cunning of a fox. Moral scepticism can no more be refuted or proved by logic than intellectual scepticism can. When we stick to it that there *is* truth (be it of either kind), we do so with our whole nature, and resolve to stand or fall by the results. The sceptic with his whole nature adopts the doubting attitude; but which of us is the wiser, Omniscience only knows.

Turn now from these wide questions of good to a certain class of questions of fact, questions concerning personal relations, states of mind between one man and another. *Do you like me or not?*—for example. Whether you do or not depends, in countless instances, on whether I meet you half-way, am willing to assume that you must like me, and show you trust and expectation. The previous faith on my part in your liking's existence is in such cases what makes your liking come. But if I stand aloof, and refuse to budge an inch until I have objective evidence, until you shall have done something apt, as the absolutists say, *ad extorquendum assensum meum,* ten to one your liking never comes. How many women's hearts are vanquished by the mere sanguine insistence of some man that they *must* love him! he will not consent to the hypothesis that they cannot. The desire for a certain kind of truth here brings about that special truth's existence; and so it is in innumerable cases of other sorts. Who gains promotions, boons, appointments, but the man in whose life they are seen to play the part of live hypotheses, who discounts them, sacrifices other things for their sake before they have come, and takes risks for them in advance? His faith acts on the powers above him as a claim, and creates its own verification.

A social organism of any sort whatever, large or small, is what it is because each member proceeds to his own duty with a trust that the other members will simultaneously do theirs. Wherever a desired result is achieved by the co-operation of many independent persons, its existence as a fact is a pure consequence of the precursive faith in one another of those immediately concerned. A government, an army, a commercial system, a ship, a college, an athletic team, all exist on this condition, without which not only is nothing achieved, but nothing is even attempted. A whole train of passengers (individually brave enough) will be looted by a few highwaymen, simply because the latter can count on one another, while each passenger fears that if he makes a movement of resistance, he will be shot before anyone else backs him up. If we believed that the whole car-full would rise at once with us, we should each severally rise, and train-robbing would never even be attempted. There are, then, cases where a fact cannot come at all unless a preliminary faith exists in its coming. *And where faith in a fact can help create the fact,* that would be an insane logic which should say that faith running ahead of scientific evidence is the "lowest kind of immorality" into which a thinking being can fall. Yet such is the logic by which our scientific absolutists pretend to regulate our lives!

## X

In truths dependent on our personal action, then, faith based on desire is certainly a lawful and possibly an indispensable thing.

But now, it will be said, these are childish human cases, and have nothing to do with great cosmical matters, like the question of religious faith. Let us then pass on to that. Religions differ so much in their accidents that in discussing the religious question we must make it very generic and broad. What then do we now mean by the religious hypothesis? Science says things are; morality says some things are better than other things; and religion says essentially two things.

First, she says that the best things are the more eternal things, the overlapping things, the things in the universe that throw the last stone, so to speak, and say the final word. "Perfection is eternal"—this phrase of Charles Secrétan seems a good way of putting this first affirmation of religion, an affirmation which obviously cannot yet be verified scientifically at all.

The second affirmation of religion is that we are better off even now if we believe her first affirmation to be true.

Now let us consider what the logical elements of this situation are *in case the religious hypothesis in both its branches be really true.* (Of course, we must admit that possibility at the outset. If we are to discuss the question at all, it must involve a living option. If for any of you religion be a hypothesis that cannot, by any living possibility be true, then you need go no farther. I speak to the "saving remnant" alone.) So proceeding, we see, first, that religion offers itself as a *momentous* option. We are supposed to gain, even now, by our belief, and to lose by our non-belief, a certain vital good. Secondly, religion is a *forced* option, so far as that good goes. We cannot escape the issue by remaining sceptical and waiting for more light, because, although we do avoid error in that way *if religion be untrue,* we lose the good, *if it be true,* just as certainly as if we positively chose to disbelieve. It is as if a man should hesitate indefinitely to ask a certain woman to marry him because he was not perfectly sure that she would prove an angel after he brought her home. Would he not cut himself off from that particular angel-possibility as decisively as if he went and married someone else? Scepticism, then, is not avoidance of option; it is option of a certain particular kind of risk. *Better risk loss of truth than chance of error*—that is your faith-vetoer's exact position. He is actively playing his stake as much as the believer is; he is backing the field against the religious hypothesis, just as the believer is backing the religious hypothesis against the field. To preach scepticism to us as a duty until "sufficient evidence" for religion be found, is tantamount therefore to telling us, when in presence of the religious hypothesis, that to yield to our fear of its being error is wiser and better than to yield to our hope that it may be true. It is not intellect against all passions, then; it is only intellect with one passion laying down its law. And by what, forsooth, is the supreme wisdom of this passion warranted? Dupery for dupery, what proof is there that dupery through hope is so much worse than dupery through fear? I, for one, can see no proof; and I simply refuse obedience to the scientist's command to imitate his kind of option, in a case where my own stake is important enough to give me the right to choose my own form of risk. If religion be true and the evidence for it be still insufficient, I do not wish, by putting your extinguisher upon my nature (which feels to me as if it had after all some business in this matter), to forfeit my sole chance in life of getting upon the winning side—that chance depending, of course, on my willingness to run the risk of acting as if my passional need of taking the world religiously might be prophetic and right.

All this is on the supposition that it really may be prophetic and right, and that, even to us who are discussing the matter, religion is a live hypothesis which may be true. Now to most of us religion comes in a still farther way that makes a veto on our active faith even more illogical. The more perfect and more eternal aspect of the universe is represented in our religions as having personal form. The universe is no longer a mere *It* to us, but a *Thou*, if we are religious; and any relation that may be possible from person to person might be possible here. For instance, although in one sense we are passive portions of the universe, in another we show a curious autonomy, as if we were small active centres on our own account. We feel, too, as if the appeal of religion to us

were made to our own active good-will, as if evidence might be forever withheld from us unless we met the hypothesis half-way. To take a trivial illustration: just as a man who in a company of gentlemen made no advances, asked a warrant for every concession, and believed no one's word without proof, would cut himself off by such churlishness from all the social rewards that a more trusting spirit would earn—so here, one who should shut himself up in snarling logicality and try to make the gods extort his recognition willy-nilly, or not get it at all, might cut himself off forever from his only opportunity of making the gods' acquaintance. This feeling, forced on us we know not whence, that by obstinately believing that there are gods (although not to do so would be so easy both for our logic and our life) we are doing the universe the deepest service we can, seems part of the living essence of the religious hypothesis. If the hypothesis *were* true in all its parts, including this one, then pure intellectualism, with its veto on our making willing advances, would be an absurdity; and some participation of our sympathetic nature would be logically required. I, therefore, for one, cannot see my way to accepting the agnostic rules for truth-seeking, or wilfully agree to keep my willing nature out of the game. I cannot do so for this plain reason, that *a rule of thinking which would absolutely prevent me from acknowledging certain kinds of truth if those kinds of truth were really there, would be an irrational rule.* That for me is the long and short of the formal logic of the situation, no matter what the kinds of truth might materially be.

I confess I do not see how this logic can be escaped. But sad experience makes me fear that some of you may still shrink from radically saying with me, *in abstracto,* that we have the right to believe at our own risk any hypothesis that is live enough to tempt our will. I suspect, however, that if this is so, it is because you have got away from the abstract logical point of view altogether, and are thinking (perhaps without realizing it) of some particular religious hypothesis which for you is dead. The freedom to "believe what we will" you apply to the case of some patent superstition; and the faith you think of is the faith defined by the schoolboy when he said, "Faith is when you believe something that you know ain't true." I can only repeat that this is misapprehension. *In concreto,* the freedom to believe can only cover living options which the intellect of the individual cannot by itself resolve; and living options never seem absurdities to him who has them to consider. When I look at the religious question as it really puts itself to concrete men, and when I think of all the possibilities which both practically and theoretically it involves, then this command that we shall put a stopper on our heart, instincts and courage, and *wait*—acting of course meanwhile more or less as if religion were *not* true—till doomsday, or till such time as our intellect and sense working together may have raked in evidence enough—this command, I say, seems to me the queerest idol ever manufactured in the philosophic cave. Were we scholastic absolutists, there might be more excuse. If we had an infallible intellect with its objective certitudes, we might feel ourselves disloyal to such a perfect organ of knowledge in not trusting to it exclusively, in not waiting for its releasing word. But if we are empiricists, if we believe that no bell in us tolls to let us know for certain when truth is in our grasp, then it seems a piece of idle fantasticality to preach so solemnly our duty of waiting for the bell. Indeed we *may* wait if we will—I hope you do not think that I am denying that—but if we do so, we do so at our peril as much as if we believed. In either case we *act,* taking our life in our hands. No one of us ought to issue vetoes to the other, nor should we bandy words of

abuse. We ought, on the contrary, delicately and profoundly to respect one another's mental freedom—then only shall we bring about the intellectual republic; then only shall we have that spirit of inner tolerance without which all our outer tolerance is soulless, and which is empiricism's glory; then only shall we live and let live in speculative as well as in practical things.

I began by a reference to Fitzjames Stephen; let me end by a quotation from him. "What do you think of yourself? What do you think of the world? . . . These are questions with which all must deal as it seems good to them. They are riddles of the Sphinx, and in some way or other we must deal with them. . . . In all important transactions of life we have to take a leap in the dark. . . . If we decide to leave the riddles unanswered, that is a choice. If we waver in our answer, that too is a choice; but whatever choice we make, we make it at our peril. If a man chooses to turn his back altogether on God and the future, no one can prevent him. No one can show beyond reasonable doubt that he is mistaken. If a man thinks otherwise, and acts as he thinks, I do not see how any one can prove that *he* is mistaken. Each must act as he thinks best, and if he is wrong so much the worse for him. We stand on a mountain pass in the midst of whirling snow and blinding mist, through which we get glimpses now and then of paths which may be deceptive. If we stand still, we shall be frozen to death. If we take the wrong road, we shall be dashed to pieces. We do not certainly know whether there is any right one. What must we do? 'Be strong and of a good courage.' Act for the best, hope for the best, and take what comes. . . .If death ends all, we cannot meet death better."

## *Suggestions for Further Reading*

**Works by James**

*The Works of William James.* Edited by Frederick Burkhardt. Cambridge: Harvard University Press, 1975–1988. This definitive edition of the writings of James consists of the following:

*Pragmatism.* Introduction by H. Standish Thayer. 1975.

*The Meaning of Truth.* Introduction by H. Standish Thayer 1975.

*Essays in Radical Empiricism.* Introduction by John J. McDermott. 1976.

*A Pluralistic Universe.* Introduction by Richard J. Bernstein. 1977.

*Essays in Philosophy.* Introduction by John J. McDermott. 1978.

*The Will to Believe.* Introduction by Edward H. Madden. 1979.

*Some Problems of Philosophy.* Introduction by Peter H. Hare. 1979.

*The Principles of Psychology. 3* Volumes. Introduction by Gerald E. Myers and Rand B. Evans. 1981.

*Essays in Religion and Morality.* Introduction by John J. McDermott. 1982.

*Talks to Teachers on Psychology.* Introduction by Gerald E. Myers. 1983.

*Essays in Psychology.* Introduction by William R. Woodward. 1983.

*Psychology: Briefer Course.* Introduction by Michael M. Sokal. 1984.

*The Varieties of Religious Experience.* Introduction by John E. Smith. 1985.

*Essays in Physical Research.* Introduction by Robert A. McDermott. 1986.

*Essays, Comments, and Reviews.* Introduction by Ignas A Skrupskelis. 1987.

*Manuscripts Essays and Notes.* Introduction by Ignas A. Skrupskelis. 1988.

*The Correspondence of William James.* Edited by Ignas K. Skrupskelis and Elizabeth M. Berkeley. Charlottesville, Vir.: University Press of Virginia, 1992—. The definitive edition of the correspondence of James.

### Anthologies

*William James: The Essential Writings,* ed. Bruce Wilshire. (Albany: State University of New York Press, 1984)

*The Writings of William James,* ed. John J. McDermott (Chicago: University of Chicago Press, 1977).

### Essential Works on James

Gay Wilson Allen, *William James: A Biography* (New York: Viking, 1967).

Jacques Barzun, *A Stroll with William James* (New York: Harper and Row, 1983).

George Cotkin, *William James: Public Philosopher* (Baltimore: Johns Hopkins University Press, 1990).

Patrick Kiaran Dooley, *Pragmatism as Humanism: The Philosophy of William James* (Chicago: Nelson Hall, 1974).

Howard M. Feinstein, *Becoming William James* (Ithaca, NY: Cornell University Press, 1984).

William J. Gavin, *William James and the Reinstatement of the Vague* (Philadelphia: Temple University Press, 1992).

Gerald E. Myers, *William James: His Thought and Life* (New Haven: Yale University Press, 1986).

Ralph Barton Perry, *The Thought and Character of William James,* 2 vols. (Boston: Little, Brown and Company, 1935).

Josiah Royce, *William James and Other Essays on the Philosophy of Life* (New York: Macmillan, 1911).

George Santayana, *Character and Opinion in the United States, with Remembrances of William James and Josiah Royce and Academic Life in America* (New York: Charles Scribner's Sons, 1920).

Charlene Haddock Seigfried, *Chaos and Context: A Study of William James* (Athens, Oh.: Ohio University Press, 1978).

Charlene Haddock Seigfried, *William James's Radical Reconstruction of Philosophy* (Albany: State University of New York Press, 1990).

Linda Simon, *Genuine Reality: A Life of William James* (New York: Harcourt Brace, 1998).

Ellen Kappy Suckiel, *Heaven's Champion: The Pragmatic Philosophy of William James* (Notre Dame, Ind.: University of Notre Dame Press, 1996).

Ellen Kappy Suckiel, *The Pragmatic Philosophy of William James* (Notre Dame, Ind.: University of Notre Dame Press, 1982).

John Wild, *The Radical Empiricism of William James* (New York: Doubleday, 1969).

Bruce Wilshire, *William James and Phenomenology: A Study of "The Principles of Psychology"* (Bloomington: Indiana University Press, 1968)

# JOSIAH ROYCE

## Introduction by Jacquelyn Ann Kegley

### Royce's Life: Cultural Context and Philosophical Background

To assess the lifework of Josiah Royce is no small task, for, like others before him, his work was not always appreciated in his time nor even properly labeled and understood by later thinkers. But even more, there were and are those who believe his system of thought to have been refuted by death and his words scattered to the winds of time.[1] But, for Royce, who in *The Problem of Christianity* affirmed a vision of reality as an unfolding process of interpretation, his very own words may be more prophetic and accurate than those estimates of his critics. He wrote:

> His [the philosopher's] immediate end may have been unattained, but a thousand years may not be long enough to develop for humanity the full significance of his reflective thought.[2]

Indeed, Royce is an enigmatic figure for many who reflect on American thought and life. He was a flaming-red-headed native Californian who grew up in a rugged mining town during the gold rush and became a Harvard professor who seemed to espouse what many of that time considered an anomaly, at least on the American scene. This puzzle was a philosophical position called idealism, a point of view that had dominated much of Western Europe in the last half of the nineteenth century. The puzzling aspect was its peculiar contrast to the pluralism and open-endedness of the growing, dominant American pragmatism of William James and the later naturalism of John Dewey. Further, it flew in the face of devastating criticisms from positivism and logical empiricism. Their emphases were antimetaphysical and thus contrary to any systematic philosophy, such as that of Royce. Finally, popular existentialist notions of absolute freedom and highly individualistic risk taking did not seem to fit with an idealism that emphasized the individual's place in the whole. It is thus no accident that Royce was viewed as outdated and outdone by the passage of time. In fact, the fruit of his mature philosophical development, *The Problem of Christianity,* was out of print for over fifty years.

It is indeed true that Royce struggled with a notion of a fully self-conscious Absolute Thought or God and, in one of his great works, *The World and the Individual,* presents a fully argued idealistic position on the nature of reality. He also wrote one of the finest interpretative works on idealism, *Lectures on Modern Idealism.*[3] But there is a breadth and depth of Royce's work that is ignored if one merely labels him an idealist. There was definite development in Royce's thought, though there was also continuity.[4] However, too many have focused narrowly on a few aspects of his work, to the neglect of others. Thus, for example, there are those who speak of Royce's religious philosophy, implying this is the totality of the matter, while neglecting the fact that he had a lifelong interest in science and the scientific method. This interest was expressed in early works such as *The Spirit of Modern Philosophy,* as well as in many of his later writings on philosophy of science and philosophy of mathematics.[5] In fact, among the students in his graduate seminar in 1913–14 were people like C. I. Lewis, Norbert Weiner, and T. S.

Eliot.[6] Lewis, for example, wrote in his autobiography that the "general tenor" of his thought—conceptual pragmatism—may have "taken shape" under the influence of Josiah Royce.[7]

Further, it is clearly the case that Royce's thought is not out of touch with the American pragmatic tradition, but fully in consonance with it in a number of places.[8] Indeed, in his *Lectures on Modern Idealism,* Royce himself declared:

> . . . I assert that personally I am both a pragmatist and an absolutist, that I believe each of these doctrines to involve the other and that therefore I regard them not only as reconcilable, but as truth reconciled.[9]

Royce's agreements with the pragmatism of Peirce, James, and Dewey will be evident as we proceed to outline some major themes and areas of his thought. It is especially appropriate to reexamine Royce's thought at this time in the philosophical scene in America. This is true because positions that have been dominant are being abandoned and many persons are searching for new visions of reality. In Royce's work are themes that are well worth contemplating in our search for new directions. Among these themes are: (1) his belief that one cannot ignore some sense of the absolute or eternal in dealing with truth and reality; (2) his understanding of science and scientific knowledge as interactive, communal, and socially grounded; (3) his strongly anti-Cartesian, social notions of self and self-knowledge; (4) his understanding of genuine community as an answer to the individualism-collectivism dilemma; and, (5) his analysis of religion and religious insight.

## The Absolute and the Eternal

It is in *The World and the Individual*[10] that Royce presented his fully developed argument for idealism, though he developed many of the central themes in previous works such as *The Religious Aspects of Philosophy and The Conception of God.*[11] In addition to this positive approach to idealism he also criticized other theories of reality that he found lacking in various ways, thus arguing that idealism remains as the only viable option.

Royce's central argument for the Absolute rests on his belief, which he shared with the pragmatists, that thought is purposive and that an idea is an expression of a purpose.[12] Essentially Royce's argument for Absolutist Thought and Will is as follows:

Thought is purposive and the aim of thought is self-possession or self-containment or complete fulfillment of purpose.[13] Thus, a person aims to sing a tune and he sings it. The song itself is the experienced datum and it completely embodies the original purpose.

This self-containment of thought is really the embodiment in some form of what Royce called the *internal* meanings of ideas. For, what an idea, say, of Mt. Everest, aims to find in its object, that which it is an idea *of,* which Royce called the *external* meaning of the idea, is nothing whatever but the idea's own conscious purpose of will (internal idea). An idea cannot represent something external either falsely or truly without an intention that brings idea and its representative function into existence.

Further, Royce held that the final embodiment of the internal meaning of an idea must be individual and determinate. It must be real. In his criticism of critical rationalism in *The World and the Individual,* Royce accepted and reaffirmed the basic thesis of this position, namely, that the real is the standard for ideas: "To be is precisely to fulfill or give warrant to ideas by making possible the experience that the ideas define."[14] Yet Royce felt that one must accept a further implication of this claim about the real, namely, that the real is determinate. Critical rationalism makes reality dependent on what is yet to be, namely, the experiences that would make a claim valid.

But, said Royce, this will not do because a merely possible experience could only answer some of our questions about an object whereas what is needed is the *full* answer. "For you are not put in the wrong by a reality to which you make no reference, and error is possible only concerning objects that we actually mean as our objects."[15] However vague my knowledge of an object may be, if my meaning has any significance, if the realm of validity is really valid, there must be a determinate object of my search such that when I know it or possess it fully I can say, "This is what I meant all along." There must be an identity between our initial purpose and our fulfilled purpose. The real, then, for Royce, is *"the complete embodiment, in individual form, and in final fulfillment, of the internal meaning of finite ideas."*[16]

Royce held that for truth and error to make sense, the purposes of thought must be fulfilled. This leads directly to Absolute Thought and Will, for this is what gives the final embodiment of internal meanings, which fulfills thought. The Absolute, as Individual, freely chooses its world and by its "idea" (internal meaning) determines the experience (external meaning) in which it finds perfect, rational fulfillment. "The Divine Will is simply *that aspect of the Absolute which is expressed in the concrete and differentiated* individuality of the World."[17]

Thus, we see that Royce agreed with pragmatism on some very fundamental issues, but disagreed at a crucial point. He was in full agreement with the pragmatists on the purposiveness of thought and also on its practical aspect. For Royce, our ideas counsel our behavior toward objects and they get verification in experience.[18] But Royce believed that pragmatism could not fully account either for the public nature of truth nor for its eternal and absolute aspect. Appeal to verification, argued Royce, is appeal to the consensus of human experience, and this takes one beyond verification. Further, Royce argued, of such a type of experience pragmatism could give no account:

> Pragmatism presupposes a certain unity of meaning and coherence of experience taken as a whole—a unity which can never at any one moment be tested by any human being. Unless the propositions which assert the existence and describe the nature of this presupposed unity are themselves true, Pragmatism has no meaning. But if they are true, Pragmatism presupposes a truth whereof it gives no adequate account.[19]

Royce liked to put the issue another way. Truth, argued Royce, is practical, but it is also decisive; it involves an imperative. It is because of this belief that Royce could not accept the pragmatic notion of "expected working," for in pragmatism, no decision seemed to be involved: *"What is needed for truth is an issue and a decisive counsel.* The word 'expectation' is too deliberately vague . . . truth and falsity are present only in case issues are sharply joined—yes or no."[20]

Royce found a perfect instance of what he means by absolute truth in an early essay by William James. James described the situation of the mountain climber who has reached a place where he could not retreat and a chasm that he can possibly jump if he resolutely decides that he can make it. But suppose, the climber is averse to believing without evidence. James concluded: He will "leave the matter undecided. I will not believe. . . . Whenever it becomes clear to me that I can leap I will leap. Till then, I decide nothing." But, notes Royce, it is here that James introduces an absolute truth, for "not to decide is itself a decision."[21]

Thus, we have an insight into what Royce called his Absolute Pragmatism. All thought is purposive, all truth is practical. However, Royce thought that the very practical nature of truth demanded its absoluteness. Further, Royce fully agreed with the pragmatists on the public nature of truth, namely, that truth is the ultimately agreed-upon belief, "the ideal limit of endless investigation." What is real establishes itself as the unanimous and "irresistable [*sic*] effect of inquiry," that is, in the confirmed beliefs of the scientific community. In fact, much is to be learned both about Royce's thought in general and particularly about those aspects of his thought worthy of further consideration when we examine his views on scientific knowledge. Thus, it is to these elements of the Roycean system we now turn.

## Scientific Knowledge as Public Communal Knowledge

As indicated earlier, Royce had a lifelong interest in the nature of our knowledge of the external world, the nature of science and scientific inquiry. Thus, in his early work *The Spirit of Modern Philosophy,* he delineated the World of Description, the world of science, the publicly describable world that manifests reproducibility and permanence and the ability to be categorized and to which such notion as permanence of substance, uniformity, and causation can be applied.[22] However, for Royce all knowledge of external reality, all knowledge of nature, is born out of a social context, a communal foundation, and is utterly dependent upon it.

First, community experience is that which distinguishes inner from outer, the outer world being the world whose presence can only be indicated to you by your definable communicable experience. Thus, it is social communication that accounts for the importance of spatial definiteness to externality:

> . . . Therefore, as only the definably localizable in space can be independently verified and agreed upon by a number of socially communicating beings, and as only what all can agree upon can stand the social test of externality, the principle that what is for all must, if in space at all, occupy a definite place of size and boundaries, becomes a relatively *a priori* principle for all the things of the verifiable world.[23]

The social grounding of physical knowledge, believed Royce, is also verified in the fact that more reliability is granted to the data of sight and touch than to the data of the other senses. These data and these qualities are those most open to social confirmation. I can see you touching and looking at an object. And if we hold or lift an object together, I can feel your grasp of the object just as surely as I feel the object. But in no similar way can I taste your tasting of the object, nor can I smell your smelling of the object.[24]

For Royce, then, our belief in the reality of nature and our knowledge of nature are inseparably bound up with our belief in the existence of our fellow beings. There is a fundamental relation between our being-with-others and our knowledge of nature. Royce wrote:

> Whatever the deeper reality behind Nature may turn out to be—*our* Nature, the realm of matter and of laws with which our science and our popular opinions have to do, is a realm which we conceive as *known* or *knowable to various men* in precisely the general sense in which we regard it as known or knowable to our private selves. Take away the social factor in our present view of Nature, and you would alter the most essential of the characters possessed for us by that physical realm in which we all believe.[25]

With this kind of understanding of external knowledge, it is no surprise that we should find that Royce, fully in the spirit of Thomas Kuhn's *The Structure of Scientific Revolutions,* recognized and pointed to the essentially social and historical nature of science itself. Royce argued that it is social needs of various kinds that guided the development of scientific knowledge, and particularly its drive to mathematize and quantify natural objects:

> Thus, in all stages of science, the social need of exact and quantitative agreement about commercially important matters has led men to look, amongst natural processes, for phenomena capable of exact description, subject to rigid law, and suitable for meeting the social need for exact description of commercially valuable objects. . . . In terms of this standard, man henceforth con-

ceives reality, so that in the end, after a long process of this discipline, he at last today believes it *a priori* necessary that real natural objects, in so far as they are real, should be subject to quantitatively exact laws.[26]

Much of Royce's later philosophical concerns were with the nature of scientific methodology. Again and again he affirmed the human and social character of science. Royce was well aware of what today we call the "theory-ladenness" of data, the human constructive aspect of scientific knowledge. Science works with certain leading ideas or guiding principles that are molded, but not predetermined in their details, by experience. We let facts speak, said Royce, but we also "talk back" to facts. We interpret as well as report. The theories of science are human as well as objective. Science is an effort, for Royce, to bring "internal meanings" into harmony with external verifications.[27] Thus, Royce declared, "Science does indeed primarily reveal to us not what the universe is apart from man, but *how man interprets his own experience.*"[28] Thus, Royce is in agreement with the pragmatists' emphasis on the social basis of concepts as well as with their belief that ideas, scientific or otherwise, are tools, instruments for dealing with reality and for predicting consequences of behavior. He is also in harmony with the emphasis in contemporary philosophy of science on the human and relative character of scientific concepts, emphasized by individuals like Kuhn or Feyerabend.

However, he would also be sympathetic to the new realism defended today by philosophers of science. Science is not purely relative nor a framework of prejudices. There is in scientific knowledge *both* coercive "thereness" and "meanings freely created." There is something of the object both immanent in, and transcendental to, human consciousness. Royce declared, "Neither God nor man faces any fact that has not something of the immediacy of a sense datum."[29]

However, Royce also attacked any notion of the merely given.[30] It is the function of the given always to point beyond itself to something not now presented.[31] There is in science both the empirical and the metaempirical:

> . . . Common sense transcends the given blindly; special science transcends the given systematically . . . all alike use the given, depend upon it, and are insofar empirical. And all alike transcend the humanly given, go beyond it, and are insofar relatively meta-empirical.[32]

Once again, Royce stressed the absolute as well as the relative nature of truth, the necessary as well as the contingent elements in knowledge. In fact, the clearest statement of Royce's "Absolute Pragmatism" occurs in his "Principles of Logic." Like Dewey, Royce stressed an instrumentalist approach to logic, namely, thought is constructive of reality, logic is logic of the will. Yet, what the "absolute truths" of mathematics and logic reveal to us is the absolute nature of will. Royce's argument is that the "logical constant," namely, the concepts of "relation" and of "class," unite "creation" and "discovery," an element of freedom and arbitrariness and an element of absoluteness. The empirical, or "found," aspect can be seen by observing that it is an empirical fact that a particular physical relation, such as that of father and child, should be present in the world. It is also a matter of experience that there are physical objects to classify, and, insofar as these classifications are arbitrary, they are "creations" or "constructions." The classifications may be suggested to us by physical processes, and if our perceptions followed no other routine, there would be no need for these classifications.

But, for Royce, the concepts of "relation" and "class" and the order system in which they are involved have an absolute nature. Such logical facts as the difference beween *yes* and *no* are not dependent on the contingent aspect of our sensations. The logician's world does have some necessary elements. Their "necessity depends upon the fact that without them no rational activity of any kind is possible."[33]

Thus, Royce is in full agreement with the pragmatic interpretation of the analytic-synthetic distinction: (1) that the term "analytic" is applicable to notions that are ultimate principles of our conceptual schematism and that gain this centrality because of their functional efficacy in unifying our knowledge; (2) that there are subjective, arbitrary elements involved in all theorizing; and, (3) that the process of inquiry, the search for truth, is an open one. However, although we can make no premature claims about the "truth" of our scientific theories, nor about what "necessary" truths or principles there are, nevertheless, absolute and necessary truths are to be found. Truth is useful, but it is also *true*. The community consensus is actual and real and the fulfillment of thought's purpose is guaranteed.

Royce thus stood fully in accord with the pragmatic notion of the interactive nature of knowledge, and it is an excellent corrective to the completely passive notion espoused by positivism and logical empiricism. However, with his emphasis on the 'absolute' and 'the necessary,' Royce also provided an interesting alternative to radical relativism. Indeed, Royce's views on self and community take us beyond all the worn-out dichotomies of absolute-relative, self-world, mind-body, spiritualism-materialism, freedom-determinism, egoism-altruism, to a refreshing new holistic view. It is to these views that I now turn.

## Royce on the Self

Like the pragmatists, Royce affirmed a strongly anti-Cartesian view of the self: "Whatever the self is it is not a thing. It is not, in Aristotle's sense, . . . a Substance."[34] Rather, the self is a process, having both a public, physical, and behavioral aspect and a private, inner aspect. Royce affirmed that one cannot speak of the self as independent of, and separate from, either body or nature. Genetic and physiological elements are important in the development of a self, and one must see the affinity of conscious human life with all of nature. Thus, "we have no right whatever to speak of really unconscious Nature but only of uncommunicative Nature."[35] Royce believed that unconscious and conscious nature share the following four features: "(1) irreversibility; (2) communication; (3) formation of habits; and (4) evolutionary growth."[36] Though there are difficulties with this view of affinities between human beings and nature, it is an insight related to the process philosophy of Alfred North Whitehead and the new physics of David Bohm, and one that has merit for recent discussions of mind-brain-body relations and of animal language, intelligence, and rights.

In addition to stressing the continuity of the human self with nature, Royce equally emphasized the fully public and empirical character of the self. "The concept of the human self, like the concept of Nature, comes to us, first, as an empirical concept, founded upon a certain class of experiences."[37] The self is a totality of facts, both public and private. Thus, among the public facts that both self and others may observe and comment on are the predominantly corporeal ones such as countenance, body, clothing, and physical actions.[38] And if these facts radically changed, Royce would argue, so would the self. Bodily continuity and the sense of body do function as one criterion, of self-identity, for Royce. "Always the contents which constitute the Ego . . . have been associated with relatively warm and enduring organic sensations viz. sensations coming from within our bodies."[39]

In addition to the public, corporeal facts of self, there is, for Royce, also a set of inner private facts equally important for the notion of an empirical self. There is the "equally empirical and phenomenal Self of the inner life, the series of states of consciousness, the feelings, thoughts, desires, memories, emotions, moods."[40] These, Royce argued, both I and others would acknowledge as belonging to me and going to make up what I am.

Royce, then, unlike some modern behaviorists, saw consciousness and states of consciousness as important aspects of the self. And, like James and Husserl, Royce, as can be seen from our discussion of "internal meanings" of ideas, stressed also the intentionality of consciousness.[41] Mental acts are always directed toward objects and also intend the object as having such-and-such meaning. Objects are also viewed in such-and-such way, that is, from specific perspectives. Thus, like James, Royce discusses the role of selective attention in all acts of consciousness. Attention selects only a few of the many impressions impinging on our sensibilities. Many such impressions slip away unretained; attention is thus a modifying, transforming process.[42] We see the world from a particular, often narrow point of view. This, Royce thought, demanded a need for transcendence of self and thus for checking things out with my fellow beings. Objectivity is intersubjectivity. External knowledge, for Royce, as we have already seen, is grounded in social interaction.

However, self-knowledge is equally so grounded. Royce argued that our very self-consciousness arises out of a social contrast between the self and the not-self, between what is mine and what is not mine: "I affirm that our empirical self-consciousness, from moment to moment depends upon a series of contrast effects, whose psychological origin lies in our literal social life. . . .[43] "Nobody amongst us men comes to self-consciousness, so far as I know except under the persistent influence of his social fellows."[44]

The social process by which self-consciousness develops is seen by Royce as a series of imitative acts. As the child imitates the acts of others, ideas about the meaning of these acts are acquired. Gradually, awareness develops of a basic contrast marking a boundary between two sets of mental contents, perceptions of others' deeds and meanings and perceptions of one's own deeds and meanings. The former appear as uncontrollable and belonging to another, while the latter have connected with them a sense of control. Ego is discovered in the awareness of self-control.

Thus, the self is developed out of a process of social interaction and further self is never known directly but only through interaction and interpretation. The self's continuity is born of community experience and dialogue, dialogue between self and others and dialogue with oneself. Self-reflection, for Royce, is interpretation of self to self. Suppose I remember a former promise. I am then interpreting this bit of my past self to my future self, and I may say to myself, "I am committed to do thus and so." "In brief," says Royce, "my idea of myself is an interpretation of my past—linked also with an interpretation of my hopes and intentions as to my future."[45] The self is a temporal, ongoing process, unified by continual communication. The self continually confers meaning on itself.

A self is also an expression of purpose. I am an intended future because I set goals and make value judgments about what is worth doing, thinking, seeking. Like Sartre, Royce saw self in terms of moral activity, but, unlike Sartre, not as an individualistic, anxiety-filled, forlorn decision maker. A self makes its decisions always in a social context contrasting its plan and ideal with those of others:

> By this meaning of my life plan, by this possession of an ideal, by this Intent always to remain another than my fellows despite my divinely planned unity with them—by this and not by possession of any Soul-Substance, I am defined and created a Self.[46]

In other words, my social and moral self is the result of a dialectic dialogue between self and others. This dialogic process has two important characteristics. First, both contact and separateness, similarity and contrast, imitation and creativity, accommodation and nonaccommodation are involved. The "other" allows me to create an external, social self by providing roles I can act out and imitate and by allowing me to internalize the objectified world of culture, to become socialized. I also must begin to have a distinct sense of my own self and action. I must carve out my own distinctive biography and develop my own individuality. If social conditions prohibit, or I fail to exercise my creativity, I may accommodate myself too much to others and become the "mass person" so dreaded by the existentialists.

Second, the interactive process of self and others is delicate and its product, an individual self, is a fragile thing. The formative power of the social situation is immensely strong. This is why we must stress equally the creative role of the individual in making of self *and* the obligation of the community to foster true individuals. Further, the interactive process can develop individuals who are too individualistic, too private, too unsocialized, too rebellious, too unsoftened by social sympathy. In other words, rampant individualism or stifling collectivism are two dangers to be avoided. Royce dealt with these dangers in *The Problem of Christianity,* where he developed his theory of community, to which we now turn.

## Royce's Theory of Community

In *The Problem of Christianity* Royce discusses the conditions for the existence of a genuine community. The first condition of community is "the power of the individual to extend his life, in ideal fashion, so as to regard it as including past and future events which lie far away in time, and which he does not now personally remember."[47] In other words, the community must have selves with chosen life plans who are also capable of extending the search for meaning beyond their personal plans. And they must be creative, truly individual selves, not mere conformers to the social will.

Communication among selves that involves attentive listening to the ideas and hopes of others is the second condition of true community. Community is, for Royce, a product of interpretation—a third form of mental activity, in addition to perception and cognition. It is triadic in nature and involves mediation between two minds. Thus, in interpreting Royce's thought to you, I, (1) the interpreter, who must both understand Royce and know something of my audience, make accessible (2) the object, Royce's thought to (3) a mind, you, to whom the interpretation is addressed. Three items, then, are brought into relationship by this interpretation. Further, the relationship is nonsymmetrical, that is, unevenly arranged with respect to all three of the terms. If the order were reversed, it would change the process.

Further, each of the terms of the relation corresponds to the three dimensions of time: past, present, and future. Thus, Royce's work, written in the past, I interpret to you now for your future interpretation. Thus, interpretation is a temporal process and is irreversible, partial, and ideally infinite. Once I have spoken or written, what has been said cannot be revoked. But neither is it the final word, for, unless arbitrarily stopped, there will be future interpretations of Royce and the process will continue.

Interpretation is also a process that creates community. It involves: (1) respect for selves as dynamos of ideas and purposes; (2) the will to interpret, which involves (a) a sense of dissatisfaction with partial meanings and the narrowness of one's own view of things and (b) the aim to unite; and (3) reciprocity and mutuality. Thus, in interpreting Royce to you, I had to be respectful of, and loyal to, Royce's thought, I had to be somewhat dissatisfied with my own views and ideas, and I had to put my ideas beside those of Royce so that they might interact. In so doing, I risked having my ideas changed and in conveying Royce's thought to you I now risk being told I am wrong and having the community of interpretation rectify my error. By attending to my interpretation of Royce, you chose to enter into the community of interpretation and you may risk having your ideas changed. If the attempt at interpretation is successful, a new meaning will come forth and a new unity of consciousness will be achieved. I will have united my mind and your mind with Royce's in a shared understanding.

Indeed, Royce's third condition for community is that unity actually be achieved. Each of the individuals involved must share a common past and/or a common future, that is, it becomes a community of memory and/or hope. As in the case of the self, community is the bringing forth of an embodied ideal. It involves the commitment of true selves to a higher goal they share. The community, like the self, is both one and many. Royce declared, "A community does not become one . . . by virtue of any reduction or melting of those various selves into a single merely present self or into a mass of passing experience."[48] In true community, there must be shared understanding and cooperation, genuine intersubjective interaction and sharing.

This is quite clear from the six subconditions for community which Royce outlined:[49] (1) each individual must direct his or her own deeds of cooperation; (2) each individual must encourage, stimulate, correct, and enjoy the deeds of others, just as do members of a really fine orchestra; (3) each member must appreciate the efforts of every member and understand that only by coordinating efforts can the community achieve its goals; (4) each must be aware of the future hopes of the community; (5) each self should identify his or her goals with those of the community; and (6) other selves in the community must concur in accepting each as a fellow member of the community.

These conditions and subconditions are presented by Royce as ideals to be aimed at or achieved. He is fully aware of the realities, dangers, and unwise provincialisms of real communal life. Royce provided a careful analysis of how highly cultivated societies train their members both in individualism and collectivism.[50] The individual gains self-consciousness by opposing his or her will to the social will, while the social will enflames self-will. The socially trained individual is taught not only to value his or her own will by opposition to the collective will, but also to respect the collective will. Collectivism, by training the individual to pride his or her own will, at the same time trains this self in collectivism. "*Individualism and collectivism are tendencies, each of which, as our social order grows, intensifies the other.*[51]

Royce further dealt with the interactive process of self and other and the difficulty of building community when, in his *War and Insurance,* he analyzed what he called "essentially dangerous community," namely, any social situation in which only two persons are involved. Royce argued for the need of a third party, an interpreter, to reconcile and mediate the interests of such dangerous pairs as borrower and lender and plaintiff and defendant.[52]

We recall that the work of interpretation asks us to transcend all stopping places, all dyadic relations, all dangerous dualisms that bind us to partial views, for example, materialism versus spiritualism and individualism versus collectivism. However, Royce was very much cognizant of what he identified as an aspect of man that worked against the development of genuine selves and communities, namely, original sin. Original sin expresses itself in the tendency to isolation and the proneness to betray one's ideals. Royce believed that the failure to sound to the depths the original sin of man, the social animal, and of the natural social order he creates leads to many social problems and to a misunderstanding of those conditions that make community possible. Thus, Royce tackled the nature of original sin and its overcoming.

## Religion, Original Sin, and the Beloved Community

To examine Royce's analysis of sin and guilt is especially appropriate for this time. This is so for at least three reasons. First, Royce recognized that sin expresses itself both individually and communally, and he thus drew our attention to the fact that an individual's sinful attitude and behavior and consequent redemption cannot be analyzed and understood in isolation from the individual's relations with others. Second, Royce's understanding of sin and moral development is quite contemporary. It bears resemblances not only to Freudian and existentialist ideas about guilt, but also to the moral development theories of psychologists Kohlberg and Erickson. However, Royce also had insights which go beyond these analyses in important ways. Finally, Royce delicately balanced stress on the depth of human sin and emphasis on human freedom and responsibility for sinful failings.

In all three of his major works on religion—*The Religious Aspects of Philosophy, The Sources of Religious Insight,* and *The Problem of Christianity*[53]—Royce argued that the essence of any religion is the postulate that man needs to be saved.[54] The need to be saved involves, for Royce, two central ideas: (1) that each individual has an ideal goal or standard in terms of which he estimates the meaning and value of his life; and, (2) that the conditions of human life work against the achievement of this goal and thus toward rendering one's life a senseless failure because of the falling short of one's true goal.[55]

One condition that works toward the failure to reach one's ideal goal is the very finitude of human consciousness. It rests on our propensity to narrow our focus of attention, to be overly selective. *"Our finitude means, then, an actual inattention—a lack of successful interest, at this conscious instant, in more than a very few details of the Universe."*[56] Royce was clear that this aspect of consciousness is not itself sinful, but rather provides the condition for sin. It is in human failure to seek to overcome this narrowness of view that sin resides.

Royce believed human sinfulness to involve two aspects. First, there is the sin of irresponsiveness. Because of our tendency toward narrowing our attention, in order fully to develop as human beings, we need deliberately to develop our powers of response to the universe around us. What is required is as much openness as possible. Sin occurs when we deliberately choose to narrow our focus or, more specifically, for Royce, choose to forget what we already know. It is in fact to deliberately disregard a goal of value which we have already identified and established for ourselves. "To sin is *consciously to choose to forget,* through a narrowing of the field of attention, an Ought that one already recognizes."[57]

The second aspect of sin, for Royce, is the sin of pride. Here what is involved is a lack of humility about our limited grasp of truth and reality. We stop the process of inquiry and assume that we have an absolute grasp of reality and truth. What is involved is an absolutizing of the finite. There is inordinate responsiveness to one's own present interests.[58]

In a sense, sin is the failure to recognize that reality and human nature have infinite dimensions. You will recall that, for Royce, the self is to be seen as an ethical category. One's task is to realize a life plan, to accomplish a unique task so that I am a self and a self who is nobody else. This possibility of aspiring to a goal outside of oneself is the possibility of a demand for self-transcendence.

But self-actualization and self-transcendence are closely related to the finitude of our consciousness. In order to achieve self-actualization, I need to seek self-knowledge. But in this quest, I fall prey to my narrowness of view and to sinful, deliberate self-forgetting:

> Nothing is more obvious about the natural course of our lives than is the *narrowness* of view to which we are usually subject. We are not only the victims of conflicting motives, but we are all too narrow to know that this is true. For we see our various interests, so to speak, one at a time. We forget one while living out another. And, so, we are prone to live many lives, seldom noting how ill harmonized they are. . . . We thus come to spend our days thwarting ourselves through the results of our fickleness, yet without knowing who it is that thwarts us. . . . The deeper tragedies of life thus result from this our narrowness of view.[59]

We have already discussed Royce's affirmation of the social grounding of self-consciousness. This belief becomes even more important in this context, for it was obvious to Royce that we need our fellows to help us gain insight into our self and to achieve self-transcendence. Social relations broaden our outlook because they require us to deal with other points of view:

> . . . Our social responsibilities tend to set limits to our fickleness. Social discipline removes some of our inner conflicts by teaching us not to indulge our caprices. Human companionship may calm,

may steady our vision, may bring us into intercourse with what is in general much better than a man's subliminal self, namely, his public, his humane, his greater social self, wherein he finds his soul and its interest writ large.[60]

Contact with our fellow human beings thus helps us expand our ideas, broaden our interests, and develop a more social self. Further, our fellow human beings help us judge and refine our behavior and therefore to have a more proper estimation of ourselves. "It is my knowledge of my fellows' doings, and of their behavior toward me—it is this which gives me the basis for the sort of comparison that I use whenever I succeed in more thoughtfully observing myself or estimating myself."[61]

This dependency on others for self-unification, self-knowledge, and self-transcendence, as already noted, has negative as well as positive aspects. The very social nature of our existence, in fact, also lays down the second condition for sin. And again, the social order can lead a person to sin in two specific ways. As indicated earlier, Royce saw clearly that in the development of social order, individualism and collectivism are two tendencies that feed on and intensify each other. The more the social will expresses itself, either individuals become more aware of their personal wants, choices, and ideals or individuals accommodate themselves more and more to the collective will.[62] Thus, the social order either constantly fosters that deeply rooted egoism by which an individual orients everything to himself or herself, or it encourages a person to give into the collective will and become a "they," a part of the crowd rather than a unique self.

The social order, then, tempts human beings into the sin of egoism or pride. "The social order, in training individuals, therefore breeds conscious sinners."[63] What is involved is an absolutizing of the self, a withdrawal into a world of self-sufficiency. It also is an attempt to mold the world and others according to one's own self-will. Royce wrote: "It is always abstractly possible, therefore, for the Self to conceive its search for self-expression as simply an undertaking not to obey, but to subdue, to its own present purpose, the world which is beyond."[64]

The other sin to which humans are tempted by the social order is that of self-forgetfulness and self-loss. One fails to achieve true self-actualization, to fulfill a life plan that marks one out as uniquely a self different from other selves. One refuses to take responsibility for one's existence. One loses oneself in the crowd. Thus, Royce wrote of guilt in terms of self-loss.

> Now, the sense of guilt, if deep and pervasive and passionate, involves at least a dim recognition that there is some central aim of life and that one has come hopelessly short of that aim . . . the true sense of guilt in its greatest manifestation involves a confession that the whole self is somehow tainted, the whole life, for the time being, wrecked.[65]

How, then, can one escape sin and guilt? For Royce, the answer is an act of loyalty and an act of grace. The act of loyalty is the individual's decision to love and be loyal to a community and thus to lead a life of devotion to that community. If the community is genuine as well as the loyalty, there will be a union of individual and social will, not a conformity of individual to social will, but a genuine blending. There will be genuine self-fulfillment, for the individual will achieve his or her own unique goal, and yet there will also be self-transcendence in that the individual genuinely chooses and loves the goal of the community:

> . . . even if the individual needs his social world as a means of grace and a gateway to salvation, the social order, in turn, needs individuals that are worth saving and can never be saved itself unless it expresses itself through the deeds and inner lives of souls deeply conscious of the dignity of selfhood, of the infinite worth of unique and intensely conscious personal life.[66]

Thus, while the individual must truly value and love the community and each of its members, equally the community must truly love the individual and value his or her uniqueness.

Here is where, for Royce, an act of grace is required. Such a community can only be created by a potent, loving, and loyal individual, who, acting as a leader, must declare that for him the community is real. In such a leader, and in his spirit, the community will begin its own life— that is, if the leader has the power to create what he loves. Royce believed that for Christianity, for example, there was such a leader in the person of Jesus Christ and that, therefore, the work of Jesus in establishing a genuine community provides the path to Christian salvation. Royce wrote:

> We know how Paul conceives the beginning of the new life wherein Christian salvation is to be found. This beginning he refers to the work of Christ. . . . He both knew and loved his community before it existed on earth. . . . On earth he called into this community its first members. He suffered and died that it might have life. Through his death and in his life the community lives. *He is now identical with the spirit of this community.*"[67]

The establishment of the Christian community and of any saving community rests, is achieved, through an act of grace. Grace involves a spiritual bond uniting many individuals into a genuine union, a spiritual bond established by the originating power of the individual creating the community and whose spirit still guides it. It also involves love, love of the community by all its members and love of each member by all other members of the community.[68] In other words, it is a genuine community as described by Royce, a community of shared past and common hope, a community of shared deeds, and a community of communication and interpretation. Royce called it the beloved community, and human salvation lies in loyalty and love of such a community.

However, Royce realized how deep was the human propensity to sin, and thus that is not all there is to say. There is another and even more tragic type of sin and that is betrayal or treason. After finding his cause, an individual may betray it. The traitor is one who has had an ideal and has loved it with all his heart, soul, mind, and strength, but has been deliberately false to his cause.

Such an act can only be overcome by an act of atonement. The sinner must be reconciled both to himself and to the community. Love must be restored, but "it will be the love for the member who *has been a traitor,* and the tragedy of the treason will permanently form part in and of this love."[69] How, then, is atonement to be accomplished?

The atonement must be accomplished by the community or, more likely, by an individual acting on behalf of the community as an incarnation, so to speak, of the spirit of the community. It involves a creative act that responds directly to the treasonous act but that also makes the world better than it was before the blow of treason fell on it. *"The world as transformed by this creative deed, is better than it would have been had all else remained the same, but had that deed of treason not been done at all."*[70]

Religion, then, for Royce, addresses the human being's need for salvation. It is to make one aware of the sins of narrowness of vision, pride, and betrayal. It also provides an answer to the overcoming of these sins, namely, love and loyalty and active deeds of atonement.

## Summary and Assessment

It is now time to assess briefly Royce's analysis of religion, sin, and salvation, and his views of community, self, science and scientific knowledge, and the absolute in truth and reality.

Royce's analysis of religion, and particularly of sin and salvation, I believe, provides us with useful insights. First, his view of sin captures the insight of Martin Luther's *"Simul vist us et peccator,"* simultaneously justified and sinner. Though I find my cause, my salvation, I can betray it and fall again into sin. In other words, conversion and salvation are ongoing processes, not a single event. Further, the call to loyalty is a call to critical faith and humble awareness that what we take to be worthy of our loyalty may be for this time and place, but not for all times and places and it may even be a mistaken loyalty. It is a continual call to openness and to constant guarding against narrowness of vision. To declare our goal as an absolute is a risk, and we must continually ask, is this providing true self-fulfillment. To have too narrow a vision of the absolute is idolatry, and thus we must follow the Roycean principle of loyalty and ask, Does my allegiance to this goal expand knowledge and community?

Second, Royce's view of sin and salvation as both personal and communal is a needed insight. Sin is sin against self, an act of self-betraying in not achieving one's fullest potential. It has consequences for me. But sin affects others; it has consequences for them. Personally to repent and achieve salvation is not enough. There must be attempts to heal the community. The sinner and others must move out in acts of love and atonement. If a lie is the act of betrayal, an act of truth and openness must occur that increases the sense of trust in the community and makes a sense of individual obligation higher and stronger. Further, it is the sense of community that allows the individual to reach out in love and action. Dietrich Bonhoffer states the issue well in his *Sanctorum Communio.*

> The man living in the fellowship of the I-Thou relationship is given the certainty that he is loved and through his faith in Christ receives the strength to be able to love in return.[71]
> . . . It is grace, nothing but grace that we are allowed to live in community with Christian brethren. . . . Communal life is again being recognized by Christians today as the grace that it is, as the extraordinary, the roses and lilies of the Christian life.[72]

Royce is insightful, I believe, in his stress on community as an important part of the religious message. And he calls upon us to be less complacent about the genuineness of community in Christian churches where saved individuals meet only once a week for worship. Indeed, he raises interesting questions for other religions where the emphasis seems much more on individual salvation than upon community and community action—except for Judaism, which has a long history of covenant relationship and consequent moral action.

What, then, about Royce's views on community? Certainly, Royce's views on both self and community provide a healthy corrective to the atomic individualism of the existentialists, who stress self-contained independent existence, the lonely, forlorn, anxiety-stricken self. For someone like Sartre, for example, togetherness with selves is accidental and external and even awful, for others always have "the book," the judgmental attitude, and "Hell is other people." For Royce, it is true that judgment by others plays a key role in self and moral development, but it is also true that it is others who help relieve our moral burden and even carry out acts of atonement for our treacherous deeds.

Further, our world is an ever increasingly interdependent world, and Royce's attempts to deal with dangerous conflicts via mediation and interpretation makes a great deal of sense. Royce's work on the characteristics of genuine community vis-aρ-vis false communities merits much attention. Neither individualism nor collectivism makes total sense in analyzing social relations, as many sociologists have recognized. Rather, a society is no mere aggregation of properties of its components, but rather involves additional characteristics derived from relationships among these components. The uniqueness of the individuals in relations as well as the uniqueness of their various relations must be recognized.

Before leaving Royce's views on community, however, it must be pointed out that his positive evaluation of community seems to neglect at times, though not always, the sins community can perpetuate on the individual, such as the infringements of freedom and dignity of a totalitarian state or even an overly paternalistic society that commits its mentally ill to institutionalization for "their own good and care."

Royce's holistic anti-Cartesian view of the self, so in concert with that of James and Dewey and other pragmatists, is a wholesome corrective to the current reductionism of behaviorists or identity-state materialists who would reduce self to a repertoire of behavior or collections of brain states. Royce fully recognizes both the role of genetic, physiological, and behavioral components of the self and the inner, conscious, intentional states recognized by humanistic psychology. Further, Royce affirms clearly the value dimension of human experience in his view that the self is essentially an ethical concept. In an age when science and technology are raising tremendous value questions for humankind, questions of rights and goals cannot be ignored. The whys of such technologies as genetic screening and engineering, of psychotechnology and computer-based artificial intelligence are extremely important, and recognition of the human being as a unique life plan worthy of consideration and respect is a valuable emphasis, both for the individual and the community.

This brings us directly to Royce's views on science. Long before Thomas Kuhn and a little before Husserl, Royce recognized that denial of the self-constructive features of human experience leads to a lack of critical reflection on science itself. The scientist-in-action is a creative knower, an interpreter and selector of ideas. Observation is a highly selective process, data collection is always guided by hypothesis and theory. We are well aware of these aspects of science today, and Royce fully recognized them, as did others like Peirce, James, and Dewey. However, Royce also recognized, as did Peirce, that emphasis on the interpretive nature of human consciousness and science as a human endeavor with certain guiding ideas and purposes had to be combined with the very real stubbornness of fact. Royce writes:

> Man is not merely made for science, but science is made for man. It expresses his deepest intellectual needs, as well as his careful observation. It is an effort to bring internal meanings into harmony with external verifications. It attempts to control as well as to submit, to conceive with rational unity as well as to accept data . . . the theories of science are human, as well as objective, internally rational as well as (when it is possible) subject to external tests.[73]

This, of course, is closely related to the transactional theory of knowledge of the pragmatists. But this leads also to Royce's continual belief in and stress on the absolute in thought, truth, and reality. Today, when an antimetaphysical stance is still part of the philosophical scene and when relativism—all views are equal in importance—is also much defended, Royce's views on the absolute become especially illuminative. One may or may not be persuaded by the logic of the matter. For example, why must thought fulfill itself or why must one be certain that truth is guaranteed? But a philosopher who can argue for both an affirmation of finality and a strong note of future seeking is at least worthy of deep consideration. Thus, Royce affirmed truth as decisive. It was a decision by Absolute Thought to affirm this world and other.

Yet Royce also continually wrote against any false dichotomizing of reality or any absolutizing of the finite, whether in religion or science. Both science and religion, as well as philosophy, are engaged in a common enterprise, namely, the endless task of inquiry, self, and community. Philosophy is, and science and religion should be, for Royce, communities of love for the truth, openness, and responsiveness to experience. "The very existence of science, then, is an illustration of our thesis that the universe is endlessly engaged in the spiritual task of interpreting its own life."[74] As for religion, Royce's message is clear: *"Look forward to the human and visible triumph of no form of the Christian Church."*[75]

## Notes

1. Thus, Morton White writes of Royce: "But, as the saying goes, the bigger they are, the harder they fall; and when the mighty Royce fell, it was as if the temple of American philosophy itself had collapsed." Morton

White, *Science and Sentiment: Philosophical Thought from Jonathan Edwards to John Dewey* (New York: Oxford University Press, 1972), p. 239.

2. *The Spirit of Modern Philosophy* (Boston: Houghton Mifflin & Company, 1892), p. 10.

3. *Lectures on Modern Idealism,* ed. J. Loewenberg (New Haven: Yale University Press, 1919).

4. Frank Oppenheim, "Josiah Royce's Intellectual Development: A Hypothesis," *Idealistic Studies* 6 (January 1976): 85–102; and *Royce's Voyage Down Under* (Lexington: University Press of Kentucky, 1980).

5. Daniel Robinson has provided us an excellent anthology of these works: *Royce's Logical Essays* (Dubuque: William C. Brown Company, 1951).

6. For a record of this seminar, see Harry T. Costello, *Josiah Royce's Seminar, 1913–1914,* ed. Grover Smith (New Brunswick, N.J.: Rutgers University Press, 1963).

7. See Fernando R. Molina, "Notes by C. I. Lewis on Royce's Theory of Categories," *Philosophical Research Archives* 1543, p. 183.

8. Mary Briody Mahowald, *An Idealistic Pragmatism* (The Hague: Martinus Nijhoff, 1971), pp. 175–176.

9. *Lectures on Modern Idealism,* p. 258.

10. *The World and the Individual,* 2 vols. (New York: Dover, 1959).

11. *The Religious Aspect of Philosophy* (Boston: Houghton Mifflin & Company, 1885) and *The Conception of God* (New York: The Macmillan Company, 1897).

12. Royce writes: "By the word 'Idea' . . . I shall mean in the end any state of consciousness, whether simple or complex, which, when present, is then and there viewed as at least the partial expression or embodiment of a single conscious purpose." *The World and the Individual,* Vol. 1, p. 22.

13. Royce had already argued this in "On Purpose in Thought," in *Fugitive Essays,* ed. J. Loewenberg (Cambridge, Mass.: Harvard University Press, 1920), pp. 216–219.

14. *The World and the Individual,* Vol. I, p. 203.

15. *The Conception of God,* p. 457.

16. *The World and the Individual,* Vol. I, p. 339. Italics are Royce's.

17. *The Conception of God,* p. 202.

18. Royce writes: *A judgement is true if it so guides or counsels our conduct through its interpretation of the object that the deed which it counsels meets our intent, i.e., fulfills as far as it goes the will that we have in mind when following this counsel we choose this.*" "Philadelphia Lectures," Unpublished Papers, Folio 83, No. 2, p. 13. Italics are Royce's.

19. "Error and Truth," in James Hastings, ed., *The Encyclopedia of Religion and Ethics* (New York: Charles Scribner's Sons, 1912), pp. 98–124. This was reprinted in *Royce's Logical Essays* and this quote appears on p. 118 of the reprint.

20. "Philadelphia Lectures," Unpublished Papers, Folio 83, No. 2, p. 13.

21. *Ibid.,* No. 3, p. 4.

22. *The Spirit of Modern Philosophy* (Boston: Houghton Mifflin & Company, 1896), pp. 392ff.

23. "The External World and Social Consciousness," *The Philosophical Review,* 3, 5 (September 1894): 520.

24. *Ibid.,* p. 519.

25. *The World and the Individual,* Vol. II, pp. 165–166. Italics are Royce's.

26. "The Social Factors of the Human Intellect," Unpublished Papers, Folio 68, No. 3 (1897), pp. 18–19.

27. Introduction to H. poincaré, *The Foundations of Science* (New York: The Science Press, 1913). Reprinted in *Royce's Logical Essays,* pp. 279–280.

28. "Richmond Lectures," Unpublished Papers, Folio 81 (1897), p. 34.

29. "A Critical Study of Reality," Unpublished Papers, Folio 81 (1897), p. 34.

30. "On Definitions and Debates," *The Journal of Philosophy* 9, (January 1912): 85–100.

31. "Columbia Lectures," Unpublished Papers, Folio 74, No. 5 (1910), pp. 52–53.

32. "A Critical Study of Reality," Unpublished Papers, Folio 81, (1897), pp. 34–35, 35a–b.

33. "The Principles of Logic," in *Royce's Logical Essays,* p. 363.

34. *The World and the Individual,* Vol. II, p. 268.

35. *Ibid.,* p. 225.

36. *Ibid.,* pp. 219–224.

37. *Ibid.,* p. 256.

38. *Ibid.,* p. 257.

39. *Ibid.,* p. 264.

40. *Ibid.,* p. 257.

41. For a discussion of some relationships between the thought of Royce and Husserl, see Jacquelyn Ann Kegley, "Royce and Husserl: Some Parallels and Food for Thought," *Transactions of the Charles S. Peirce Society* 14 (Summer 1978): 184–199.

42. *The Religious Aspect of Philosophy* (Boston: Houghton Mifflin & Company, 1885), p. 314. For a summary discussion of Jame's views on the nature of the consciousness, see Owen J. Flanagan, Jr., *The Science of the Mind* (Cambridge, Mass.: Bradford Books, 1984), pp. 23–53.
43. *The World and the Individual,* Vol. II, p. 200.
44. *Ibid.,* pp. 261–262.
45. *The Problem of Christianity,* Vol. II, p. 42.
46. *The World and the Individual,* Vol. II, p. 276. Italics are Royce's.
47. *The Problem of Christianity,* Vol. II, pp. 60–61.
48. *Ibid.,* p. 67.
49. Frank M. Oppenheim, "A Roycean Road to Community," *International Philosophical Quarterly* 10 (September 1970): 341–377.
50. *The Problem of Christianity,* Vol. I, pp. 127–155.
51. *Ibid.,* p. 152.
52. *War and Insurance* (New York: The Macmillan Company, 1914), pp. 30–35 and passim.
53. *The Religious Aspects of Philosophy* (Boston: Houghton Mifflin & Company, 1885); *The Sources of Religious Insight,* The Brass Lectures, Lake Forest College, 1911 (New York: Charles Scribner's Sons, 1912); and *The Problem of Christianity.*
54. *The Sources of Religious Insight,* pp. 8–9.
55. *Ibid.,* pp. 12, 28–29.
56. *The World and the Individual,* Vol. II, p. 59.
57. *Ibid.,* p. 359.
58. For an excellent analysis of Royce's understanding of sin, see Paul Ramsey, "The Idealistic View of Moral Evil," *Philosophy and Phenomenological Research* (June 1946): 554–589.
59. *The World and the Individual,* Vol. I, pp. 48–49.
60. *Ibid.,* p. 55.
61. *The Problem of Christianity,* pp. 130–131.
62. *Ibid.,* p. 145.
63. *Ibid.*
64. *The World and the Individual,* Vol. II, p. 349.
65. *The Sources of Religious Insight,* p. 66.
66. *Ibid.,* p. 60.
67. *The Problem of Christianity,* Vol. I, pp. 186–187.
68. *Ibid.,* p. 192.
69. *Ibid.,* p. 302.
70. *Ibid.,* p. 308. Italics are Royce's.
71. Dietrich Bonhoffer, *Sanctorum Communio: A Dogmatic Inquiry into the Sociology of the Church,* trans. R. Gregor Smith from the 3rd German ed., 1960 (London: Collins, 1963), p. 119.
72. Dietrich Bonhoffer, *Life Together* (New York: Harper & Row, 1954), p. 21.
73. *Royce's Logical Essays,* pp. 279–280.
74. *The Problem of Christianity,* pp. 429–430.
75. *Ibid.,* p. 430.

# The Temporal and the Eternal

The world of the facts that we ought to acknowledge is, in one of its aspects, present as the Object of Possible Attention, in every act of finite insight. Finitude means inatten-tion to the wealth and organization of the world's detail.

An obvious objection to this thesis is furnished by the nature of Time. How can Past and

From *The World and the Individual* (New York: Macmillan Company, 1899), pp. 111–151.

Future, which "do not exist," be in any sense "present," in the undistinguished unity of the facts which any finite thinker at any instant acknowledges?

In the Ninth Lecture of the First Series, we briefly considered the topic of temporal Being. We have to return to it here with more detail. There is an ancient distinction of the philosophers between the Temporal and the Eternal. It must be plain at this point, that we ascribe to the true world a certain eternal type of Being. Yet how shall we reconcile this with our equally obvious treatment of the world as existing in time? Plainly we have here a question that is of great importance for any understanding of the categories of experience. It belongs, then, in the context of these earlier discussions of our present series of lectures. Moreover, it is one that will constantly meet us later. The relation of Time to Nature will be of central concern to us. When we come to deal with the individual Self, we shall again have to face the question: In what sense has the Self of the individual a purely Temporal, and in what sense an Eternal type of reality? And before we can answer this question we must be more precise than we have yet been in defining the terms Time and Eternity. The issue here involved has a significance not only theoretical, but also intensely practical. It will need therefore a close and deliberate scrutiny. Time, as we shall soon see, is a concept of fundamentally practical meaning. The definition of the Eternal, on the other hand, has very close relations to the question as to the ultimate significance of all that is practical. Any rational decision as between a pessimistic and an optimistic view of the world, any account of the relations between God and Man, any view of the sense in which the evils and imperfections of the Universe can be comprehended or justified, any account of our ethical consciousness in terms reconcilable with our Idealism,—in brief, any philosophical reconciliation with religion and life, must turn in part upon a distinction between the Temporal and the Eternal, and upon an insight into their unity in the midst of their contrast. The problem at issue is one of the most delicate and, at

the same time, one of the simplest of the great issues of philosophy. I shall here have to deal with it at first in a purely theoretical fashion, and shall then proceed to its practical applications. For both aspects of the question we are now fully prepared.

# I

Time is known to us, both perceptually, as the psychologists would say, and conceptually. That is, we have a relatively direct experience of time at any moment, and we acknowledge the truth of a relatively indirect conception that we possess of the temporal order of the world. But our conception of time far outstrips in its development and in its organization anything that we are able directly to find in the time that is known to our perceptions. Much of the difficulty that appears in our metaphysical views about time is, however, due to lack of naïveté and directness in viewing the temporal aspects of reality. We first emphasize highly artificial aspects of our conception of time. Then we wonder how these various aspects can be brought into relation with the rest of the real world. Our efforts to solve our problem lead very easily to contradictions. We fail to observe how, in case of our more direct experience of time and of its meaning, various elements are woven into a certain wholeness,— the very elements which, when our artificial conception of time has sundered them, we are prone to view as irreconcilable with one another and with reality.

Our more direct perceptions of time form a complex sort of consciousness, wherein it is not difficult to distinguish several aspects. For the first, some Change is always occurring in our experience. This change may belong to the facts of any sense, or to our emotions, or to our ideas; but for us to be conscious is to be aware of change. Now this changing character of our experience is never the whole story of any of our clearer and more definite kinds of consciousness. The next aspect of the matter lies in the fact that our consciousness of change, wherever it is definite and wherever it accompanies definite successive acts of attention, goes along with the consciousness that for us something comes first, and something next, or that there is what we call a Succession of events. Of such successions, melodies, rhythms, and series of words or of other simple acts form familiar and typical examples. An elementary consciousness of change without such definite successions we can indeed have; but where we observe clearly what a particular change is, it is a change wherein one fact succeeds another.

A succession, as thus more directly experienced by us, involves a certain well-known relation amongst the events that make up the succession. Together these events form a temporal sequence or order. Each one of them is over and past when the next one comes. And this order of the experienced time-series has a determinate direction. The succession passes *from* each event *to* its successor, and not in the reverse direction; so that herein the observed time relations notoriously differ from what we view as space relations. For if in space *b* is next to *a*, we can read the relation equally well as a coexistence of *a* with *b* and as a coexistence of *b* with *a*. But in case *b* succeeds *a*, as one word succeeds another in a spoken sentence, then the relation is experienced as a passing from *a* to *b*, or as a passing over of *a* into *b*, in such wise that *a* is past, as an event, before *b* comes. This direction of the stream of time forms one of its most notable empirical characters. It is obviously related to that direction of the acts of the will whose logical aspect interested us in connection with the consideration of our discriminating consciousness.

But side by side with this aspect of the temporal order, as we experience this order, stands still another aspect, whose relation to the former has been persistently pointed out by many psychological writers, and as persistently, ignored by many of the metaphysical interpreters of the temporal aspect of the universe. When we more directly experience succession,—as, for instance, when we listen to a musical phrase or to a rhythmic series of drumbeats,—we not only observe that any antecedent member of the series is over and

past before the next number comes, but also, and without the least contradiction between these two aspects of our total experience, we observe that this whole succession, with both its former and later members, so far as with relative directness we apprehend the series of drum-beats or of other simple events, is present *at once* to our consciousness, in precisely the sense in which the unity of our knowing mental life always finds present at once many facts. It is, as I must insist, true that for my consciousness *b* is experienced as following *a*, and also that both *a* and *b* are *together* experienced as in this relation of sequence. To say this is no more contradictory than to say that while I experience two parts of a surface as, by virtue of their spatial position, mutually exclusive each of the other, I also may experience the fact that both these mutually exclusive parts go together to form one whole surface. The sense in which they form one surface is, of course, not the sense in which, as parts, they exclude each other, and form different surfaces. Well, just so, the sense in which *b*, as successor of *a*, is such, in the series of events in question, that *a* is over and gone when *b* comes, is not the sense in which *a* and *b* are together elements in the whole experienced succession. But that, in *both* of these senses, the relation of *b* to its predecessor *a* is an experienced fact, is a truth that any one can observe for himself. If I utter a line of verse, such as

*The curfew tolls the knell of parting day,*

the sound of the word *day* succeeds the sound of the word *parting,* and I unquestionably experience the fact that, for me, every earlier word of the line is over and past before the succeeding word or the last word, *day,* comes to be uttered or to be heard. Yet this is unquestionably not my whole consciousness about the succession. For I am certainly *also* aware that the *whole* line of poetry, as a succession of uttered sounds (or, at all events, a considerable portion of the line), is present to me at once, and as this one succession, when I speak the line. For only by virtue of experiencing this wholeness do I observe the rhythm, the music, and the meaning of the line. The sense in which the word *parting* is over before the word *day* comes, is like the sense in which one object in space is *where* any other object is *not,* so that the spatial *presence* of one object excludes the presence of another at that same part of space. Precisely so the presence of the word *day* excludes the presence of the word *parting* from its own place in the temporal succession. And, in our experience of succession, each element is *present* in a particular point of the series, in so far as, with reference to that point, other events of the series are either *past,* that is, over and done with, or are *future,* that is, are later in the series, or are *not yet when* this one point of the series is in *this* sense present. Every word of the uttered line of poetry, viewed in its reference to the other words, or to previous and later experiences, is *present* in its own place in the series, is *over and done with* before later events can come, or when they are present, and is *not yet* when the former events of the succession are present. And that all this is true, certainly is a matter of our experience of succession.

But the sense in which, nevertheless, the whole series of the uttered words of the line, or of some considerable portion of the line, is presented to our consciousness *at once,* is precisely the sense in which we apprehend this line as one line, and this succession as one succession. The whole series of words has for us its rhythmic unity, and forms an instance of conscious experience, whose unity we overlook at one glance. And unless we could thus overlook a succession and view at once its serially related and mutually exclusive events, we should never know anything whatever about the existence of succession, and should have no problem about time upon our hands.

This extremely simple and familiar character of our consciousness of succession,—this essentially double aspect of every experience of a present series of events,—this inevitably twofold sense in which the term *present* can be used in regard to our perception of temporal happenings,—this is a matter of the most fundamental importance for our whole conception of Time, and, as I may at once add, for our

conception of Eternity. Yet this is also a matter very frequently obscured, in discussion, by various devices often used to express the nature of the facts here in question. Sometimes, for the sake of a laudable attempt to define the term *present* in a wholly unambiguous way, those who are giving an account of our experience of time are led to assert that, since every part or element of any series of temporal events can be *present* only when all the other elements of the series are temporally non-existent, i.e. are either past or future, it must therefore be quite impossible for us to be conscious, *at once,* of a present succession involving a series of such elements. For how, they say, can I be conscious of the presence of all the successive words of the verse of poetry, when only one word is actually and temporally present at any one time? To comprehend how I can become in any sense aware of the series of successive words that constitutes the line of verse, such students of our problem are accustomed to say that when any one word as *passing,* or *day,* is present to my mind, the other words, even of the same line, can be present to consciousness *only* as coexistent memories or images of the former words, or as images of the expected coming words. From this point of view, I never really observe any sequence of conscious events as a sequence at all. I merely apprehend each element by itself; and I directly conclude from the images which in my experience are coexistent with this element, that there have been antecedent, and will be subsequent events in the series.

This interpretation of our consciousness of time is, however, directly counter to our time-experience, as any one may observe it for himself. For we do experience succession, and *at once* we do take note of facts that are in different times. For, I ask you, What word of mine is it that, as this single present word, you just *now* hear me speaking? If I pause a little, you perhaps dwell upon the last word that I utter before pausing, and call that the one present word. Otherwise, however, as I speak to you, you are conscious of series of successive words, of whole phrases, of word groups, of clauses. Within each one of these groups of words, you are indeed more or less clearly aware that every element has its own temporal place; and that, *in so far as* each element is taken by itself as present, the other elements either precede or succeed it, and in *this* sense are not in one time with it. But this very fact itself you know merely in so far as you actually experience series, each of which contains several successive words. These series come to you not merely by virtue of remembered facts, but also as experienced facts.

And in truth, were this not so, you could indeed have no experience of succession at all. You would then experience, at any one moment, merely the single word, or something less than any single word, together with the supposed coexistent and contemporaneous images of actually past or of coming words. But how, in that case, would your experience of time-sequences come to seem to you different from any experience whatever of coexistence? Nor is even this the only difficulty about the doctrine which supposes you to be unable to view a series of successive events as all at once presented to your consciousness. A still deeper difficulty results from such an effort to evade the double sense in which the facts of succession are known in your experience. If you can have present to you only *one* event at a time in a series of successive events, how long, or rather how short, must an event be to contain within itself no succession at all, or no difference between former and latter contents? In vain do you suppose that, at any time, you have directly present to your consciousness only one of the successive words that you hear me speak. Not thus do you escape our difficulty. For a spoken word is itself a series of temporally successive sounds. Can you hear at once the whole spoken word, or can you grasp at once this whole series? If so, my own foregoing account is in principle admitted. For then, in this presence of the facts of succession to your consciousness, there are our two former aspects, both of them, involved. *Each* element of the succession (namely, in this case, the elementary sounds that to your consciousness make up the word) is temporally present just when it occurs, but

*not* before or afterwards, in so far as it follows previous elements and succeeds later elements; and also *all* the elements are, in the other sense of the term, *present at once* to consciousness, as constituting this whole succession which you call the word. If, however, you deny that you actually hear, apart from memory or from imagery, any single whole word at once, I shall only the more continue to ask you, What is the least or the simplest element of succession that is such as to constitute a merely present experience, with *no* former or latter contents within it? What apart from any memory or any imagery, and wholly apart from ideas of the past or the future of your experience, is present to you, in an indivisible time instant, just *Now?* The question is obviously unanswerable, just because an absolutely indivisible instant of mathematical time, with no former and latter contained within it, neither constitutes nor contains any temporal event, nor presents to you any fact of temporal experience whatever, just as an indivisible point in space could contain no matter, nor itself ever become, in isolation, an object of spatial experience. On the other hand, an event such that in it you were unable to perceive any succession would help you in no whit to get the idea of time until you experienced it along with other events. What is now before you is a succession, within which are parts; and of these parts each, when and in so far as once your attention fixes it, and takes it in its time relations, is found as a present that in time both precedes and succeeds other facts, while these other facts are also just as truly before you as the observed element called the temporally present one is itself before you. And thus you cannot escape from our twofold interpretation of the experience of temporal succession. You are conscious of a series of successive states presented to you as a whole. You are also aware that each element of the succession excludes the others from its own place in time.

There is, to be sure, another frequent way of describing our consciousness of succession,— and a way that on the whole I find unsatisfactory. According to this view, events come to us in succession in our experience,—let us say the words of a spoken verse,—and *then* something often called the synthetic activity of the mind supervenes, and later binds together into unity, these successive facts, so that when this binding has taken place we *then* recognize the whole fagot of experience as a single succession. This account of the temporal facts, in terms of an activity called a synthesis, helps me, I must confess, no whit. What I find in consciousness is that a succession, such as a rhythm of drumbeats, a musical phrase, a verse of poetry, comes to me as one present whole, present in the sense that I know it all at once. And I also find that this succession is such that it has *within* it a temporal distinction, or order, of earlier and later elements. While these elements are at once known, they are *also* known as such that at the briefer instant *within* the succession when any one of them is to be temporally viewed as a present fact, none of the others are contemporaneous with that fact, but all are either *no longer* or *not yet* when, and in so far as, that element is taken as the present one. And I can not make this datum of experience any more definite by calling it a synthesis, or the mere result of a synthesis.

I have now characterized the more directly given features in our consciousness of succession. You see, as a result, that we men experience what Professor James, and others, have called our "specious present," as a serial whole, *within* which there are observed temporal differences of former and latter. And this our "specious present" has, when measured by a reference to time-keepers, a length which varies with circumstances, but which appears to be never any very small fraction of a second, and never more than a very few seconds in length. I have earlier referred to this length of our present moments as our characteristic "time-span" of consciousness, and have pointed out how arbitrary a feature and limitation of our consciousness it is. We shall return soon to the question regarding the possible metaphysical significance of this time-span of our own special kind of consciousness.

But it remains here to call closer attention to certain other equally important features of our more direct experience of time-succession. So far, we have spoken, in the main, as if succession were to us a mere matter of given facts, as colors and sounds are given. But all our experience also has relation to the interests whose play and whose success or defeat constitute the life of our will. Every serial succession of which we are conscious therefore has for us some sort of meaning. In it we find our success or our failure. In it our internal meanings are expressed, or hindered, thwarted or furthered. We are interested in life, even if it be, in idle moments, only the dreary interest of wondering what will happen next, or, in distressed moments, the interest in flying from our present fortune, or, in despairing moments, of wishing for the end; still more then if, in strenuous moments, our interest is in pursuing our ideal. And our interest in life means our conscious concern in passing on from any temporal present towards its richer fulfilment, or away from its relative insignificance. Now that Direction of temporal succession of which I before made mention, has the most intimate relations to this our interest in our experience. What is earlier in a given succession is related to what is later as being that *from* which we pass *towards* a desired fulfilment, or in search of a more complete expression of our purpose. We are never content in the temporal present in so far as we view it as temporal, that is, as an event in a series. For such a present has its meaning as a transition from its predecessors towards its successors.

Our temporal form of experience is thus peculiarly the form of the Will as such. Space often seems to spread out before us what we take to be the mere contents of our world; but time gives the form for the expression of all our meanings. Facts, in so far as, with an abstractly false Realism, we sunder them from their meanings, therefore tend to be viewed as merely in relations of coexistence; and the space-world is the favorite region of Realism. But ideas, when conscious, assume the consiously temporal form of inner existence, and appear to us as constructive processes. The visible world, when viewed as at rest, therefore interests us little in comparison with the same world when we take note of its movements, changes, successions. As the kitten ignores the dead leaves until the wind stirs them, but then chases them—so facts in general tend to appear to us all dead and indifferent when we disregard their processes. But in the movements of things lies for us, just as truly as in her small way for the kitten, all the glory and the tragedy, all the life and the meaning of our observed universe. This concern, this interest in the changing, binds us then to the lower animals, as it doubtless also binds us to beings of far higher than human grade. We watch the moving and tend to neglect the apparently changeless objects about us. And that is why narrative is so much more easily effective than description in the poetic arts; and why, if you want to win the attention of the child or of the general public, you must tell the story rather than portray coexistent truths, and must fill time with series of events, rather than merely crowd the space of experience or of imagination with manifold but undramatic details. For space furnishes indeed the stage and the scenery of the universe, but the world's play occurs in time.

Now all these familiar considerations remind us of certain of the most essential characters of our experience of time. Time, whatever else it is, is given to us as that within whose successions, in so far as for us they have a direct interest and meaning, every event, springing from, yet forsaking, its predecessors, aims on, towards its own fulfilment and extinction in the coming of its successors. Our experience of time is thus for us essentially an experience of longing, of pursuit, of restlessness. And this is the aspect which Schopenhauer and the Buddhists have found so intolerable about the very nature of our finite experience. Upon this dissatisfied aspect of finite consciousness we ourselves dwelt when, in the former series of lectures, we were first learning to view the world, for the moment, from the mystic's point of view. As for the higher justification of this aspect of our experience, that indeed belongs elsewhere. But as to the facts, every part of a succession is present in so far as when it is, that which is

*no longer* and that which is *not yet* both of them stand in essentially significant, or, if you will, in essentially practical relations to this present. It is true, of course, that when we view relatively indifferent time-series, such as the ticking of a watch or the dropping of rain upon the roof, we can disregard this more significant aspect of succession; and speak of the endless flight of time as an incomprehensible brute fact of experience, and as in so far seemingly meaningless. But no series of experiences upon which attention is fixed is wholly indifferent to us; and the temporal aspect of such series always involves some element of expectancy and some sense of something that no longer is; and both these conscious attitudes color our interest in the presented succession, and give the whole the meaning of life. Time is thus indeed the form of practical activity; and its whole character, and especially that direction of its succession of which we have spoken, are determined accordingly.

## II

I have dwelt long upon the time consciousness of our relatively direct experience, because here lies the basis for every deeper comprehension of the metaphysics both of time and of eternity. Our ordinary conception of time as an universal form of existence in the external world, is altogether founded upon a generalization, whose origin is in us men largely and obviously social, but whose materials are derived from our inner experience of the succession of significant events. The conceived relations of Past, Present, and Future in the real world of common-sense metaphysics, appear indeed at first sight, vastly to transcend anything that we ourselves have ever observed in our inner experience. The infinite and irrevocable past that no longer is, the expected infinite future that has as yet no existence, how remote these ideal constructions, supposed to be valid for all gods and men and things, seem at first sight from the brief and significant series of successive events that occur within the brief span of our actual human consciousness. Yet, as we saw in the ninth lecture of our former Series, common sense, as soon as questioned about special cases, actually conceives the Being of both the past and the future as so intimately related to the Being of the present that every definite conception of the real processes of the world, whether these processes are viewed as physical or as historical or explicitly as ethical, depends upon taking the past, the present, and the future as constituting a single whole, whose parts have no true Being except in their linkage. As a fact, moreover, the term *present,* when applied to characterize a moment or an event in the timestream of the real world, never means, in any significant application, the indivisible present of an ideal mathematical time. The present time, in case of the world at large, has an unity altogether similar to that of the present moment of our inner consciousness. We may speak of the present minute, hour, day, year, century. If we use the term *present* regarding any one of these divisions of time, but regard this time not as the experienced form of the inner succession of our own mental events, but as the time of the real world in which we ourselves form a part, then we indeed conceive that this present is world-embracing, and that suns move, light radiates between stars, that deeds of all men occur, and the minds of all men are conscious, in this same present time of which we thus make mention. Moreover, we usually view the world-time in question in terms of the conceptions of the World of Description, and so we conceive it as infinitely divisible, as measurable by various mathematical and physical devices, and as a continuous stream of occurrence. Yet in whatever sense we speak of the real present time of the world, this present, whether it is the present second, or the present century, or the present geological period, it is, for our conception, as truly a divisible and connected whole region of time, within which a succession of events takes place, as it is a world-embracing and connected time, within whose span the whole universe of present events is comprised. A mathematically indivisible present time, possessing no length, is simply no time at all. Whoever says, "In the universe at large only the present state of things is real, only the present movement of the stars, the present streamings of radiant light, the present deeds and thoughts of men are real; the whole past is dead; the whole future is not yet,"—any such reporter of the temporal existence of the universe may be invited to state how long his real present of the time-world is. If he replies, "The present moment is the absolutely indivisible and ideal boundary between present and future,"—then one may rejoin at once that in a mathematically indivisible instant, having no length, no event happens, nothing endures, no thought or deed takes place,—in brief, nothing whatever temporally exists,—and that, too, whatever conception you may have of Being. But if the real present is a divisible portion of time, then it contains within itself succession, precisely as the "specious present" of psychological time contains such internal succession. But in that case, within the real present of the time-world, there are already contained the distinctions that, in case of the time of experience, we have heretofore observed. If, in what you choose to call the present moment of the world's history, deeds are accomplished, suns actually move from place to place, light waves traverse the ether, and men's lives pass from stage to stage, then *within* what you thus call the present there are distinguishable and more elementary events, arranged in series, such that when any conceived element, or mere elementary portion of any series is taken in relation to its predecessors and successors, it is *not yet* when its antecedents are taken as temporally present, and is *past and gone* when its successors are viewed as present. The world's time is thus in all respects a generalized and extended image and correspondent of the observed time of our inner experience. In the time of our more direct experience, we find a twofold way in which we can significantly call a portion of time a present moment. The present, in our inner experience, means a whole series of events grasped by somebody as having some unity for his consciousness, and as having its own single internal meaning. This was what we meant by the present experience of this musical phrase, this spoken line of verse, this series of rhythmic beats. But, in the other sense of the world, an element within any such whole is present in so far as this element has antecedents and successors, so that they are *no longer* or *not yet* when it is temporally viewed as present, while in turn, in so far as any one of them is viewed as the present element, this element itself is either *not yet* or *no longer.* But precisely so, in the conceptual time of our real world, the Present means any section of the time-stream in so far as, with reference to anybody's consciousness, it is viewed as having relation to this unity of consciousness, and as in a single whole of meaning with this unity. Usually by "our time," or "the real time in which we now live," we mean no very long period of the conceived time-stream of the real world. But we never mean the indivisible *now* of an ideal mathematical time, because, in such an indivisible time-instant, nothing could happen, or endure, or genuinely exist. But within the present, if conceived as a section of the time-stream, there are internal differences of present, past, and future.

For, in a similar fashion, as the actual or supposed length of the "specious present" of our perceptual time is something arbitrary, determined by our peculiar human type of consciousness, so the length of the portion of conceptual time which we call the *present,* in the first sense of that term, namely, in the sense in which we speak of the "present age," is an arbitrary length, determined in this case, however, by our more freely chosen interest in some unity which gives relative wholeness and meaning to this present. If usually the "present age" is no very long time, still, at our pleasure, or in the service of some such unity of meaning as the history of civilization, or the study of geology, may suggest, we may conceive the present as extending over many centuries, or over a hundred thousand years. On the other hand, within the unity of this first present, any distinguishable event or element of an event is *present,* in the second, and more strictly temporal sense in so far as it has predecessors and successors, whereof the first are *no longer,* and the latter *not yet,* when this more elementary event is viewed as happening.

Nor does the parallelism between the perceptual and the conceptual time cease here. The perceptual time was the form in which meaning, and the practically significant aspects of consciousness, get their expression. The same is true of the conceptual time, when viewed in its relations to the real world. Not only is the time of human history, or of any explicitly teleological series of events, obviously the form in which the facts win their particular type of conceived meaning; but even the time of physical science gets its essential characters, as a conception, through considerations that can only be interpreted in terms of the Will, or of our interest in the meaning of the world's happenings.

For the conceived time-series, even when viewed in relation to the World of Description, still differs in constitution from the constitution of a line in space, or from the characters belonging to a mathematically describable physical movement of a body, in ways which can only be expressed in terms of significance. Notoriously, conceptual time has often been described as correspondent in structure to the structure of a line, or as correspondent again, in character, to the character of a uniformly flowing stream, or of some other uniform movement. But a line can be traversed in either direction, while conceptual time is supposed to permit but one way of passing from one instant to another in its course. An uniform flow, or other motion, has, like time, a fixed direction, but might be conceived as returning into itself without detriment to its uniformity. Thus an ideally regular watch "keeps time," as we say, by virtue of the uniformity of its motion; but its hands return ever again to the same places on the face; while the years of conceptual time return not again. And finally, if one supposed an ideally uniform physical flow or streaming in one rectilinear direction only, and in an infinite Euclidean space, the character of this movement might so far be supposed to correspond to that of an ideally conceived mathematical time; except for one thing. The uniformity and unchangeableness of the conceived physical flow would be a merely given character, dependent, perhaps, upon the fact that the physical movement in question was conceived as meeting with no obstacle or external hindrance; but the direction of the flow of time is a character essential to the very conception of time. And this direction of the flow of time can only be expressed in its true necessity by saying that in the case of the world's time, as in the case of the time of our inner experience, we conceive the past as leading towards, as aiming in the direction of the future, in such wise that the future depends for its meaning upon the past, and the past in its turn has its meaning as a process expectant of the future. In brief, only in terms of will, and only by virtue of the significant relations of the stages of a teleological process, has time, whether in our inner experience, or in the conceived world order as a whole, any meaning. Time is the form of the Will; and the real world is a temporal world in so far as, in various regions of that world, seeking differs from attainment, pursuit is external to its own goal, the imperfect tends towards its own perfection, or in brief, the internal meanings of finite life gradually win, in successive stages, their union with their own External Meaning. The general justification for this whole view of the time of the real world is furnished by our idealistic interpretation of Being. The special grounds for regarding the particular Being of time itself as in this special way teleological, are furnished by the foregoing analysis of our own experience of time, and by the fact that the conceptual time in terms of which we interpret the order of the world at large, is fashioned, so to speak, after the model of the time of our own experience.

### III

Having thus defined the way in which the conceptual time of the real world of common sense corresponds in its structure to the structure of the time known to our inner perception,

we are prepared to sketch our theory both of the sense in which the world of our idealistic doctrine appears to be capable of interpretation as a Temporal order, and of the sense in which, for this same theory, this world is to be viewed as an Eternal order. For, as a fact, in defining time we have already, and inevitably, defined eternity; and a temporal world must needs be, when viewed in its wholeness, an eternal world. We have only to review the structure of Reality in the light of the foregoing analysis in order to bring to our consciousness this result.

And so, first, the real world of our Idealism has to be viewed by us men as a temporal order. For it is a world where purposes are fulfilled, or where finite internal meanings reach their final expression, and attain unity with external meanings. Now in so far as any idea, as a finite Internal Meaning, still seeks its own Other, and consciously pursues that Other, in the way in which, as we have all along seen, every finite idea does pursue its Other, this Other is in part viewed as something beyond, *towards* which the striving is directed. But our human experience of temporal succession is, as we have seen, just such an experience of a pursuit directed towards a goal. And such pursuit demands, as an essential part or aspect of the striving in question, a consciousness that agrees in its most essential respect with our own experience of time. Hence, our only way of expressing the general structure of our idealistic realm of Being is to say that wherever an idea exists as a finite idea, still in pursuit of its goal, there appears to be some essentially temporal aspect belonging to the consciousness in question. To my mind, therefore, time, as the form of the will, is (in so far as we can undertake to define at all the detailed structure of finite reality) to be viewed as the most pervasive form of all finite experience, whether human or extrahuman. In pursuing its goals, the Self lives in time. And, to our view, every real being in the universe, in so far as it has not won union with the ideal, is pursuing that ideal; and, accordingly, so far as we can see, is living in time. Whoever, then, is finite, says, "not yet," and in part seeks his Other as involving what, to the seeker, is still future. For the finite world in general, then, as for us human beings, the distinction of past and future appears to be coextensive with life and meaning.

I have advisedly used, however, the phrase that the time-consciousness is a "part" or "aspect" of the striving. For from our point of view, the Other, the completion that our finite being seeks, is not *merely* something beyond the present, and is not merely a future experience, but is also inclusive of the very process of the striving itself. For the goal of every finite life is simply the totality whereof this life, in its finitude, is a fragment. When I seek my own goal, I am looking for the whole of myself. In so far as my aim is the absolute completion of my Selfhood, my goal is identical with the whole life of God. But, in so far as, by my whole individual Self, I mean my whole Self in contrast with the Selves of my fellows,—then the completion of my individual expression, in so far as I am this individual and no other,—i.e. my goal, as this Self, is still not any one point or experience in my life, nor any one stage of my life, but the totality of my individual life viewed as in contrast with the lives of other individuals. Consequently, while it is quite true that every incomplete being, every finite striving, regards itself as aiming towards a future, because its own goal is not yet attained; we have, nevertheless, to remember that the attainment of the goal involves more than any future moment, taken by itself, could ever furnish. For the Self in its entirety is the whole of a self-representative or recurrent process, and not the mere last moment or stage of that process. As we shall see, there is in fact no last moment. A life seeking its goal is, therefore, indeed, essentially temporal,—but it is so just as music is temporal,—except indeed that music is not only temporal, but temporally finite. For every work of musical art involves significant temporal series, wherein there is progression, and passage from chord to chord, from phrase to phrase, and from movement to movement. But just as any one musical composition has its value not only by virtue of its attainment of its final chord,

but also at every stage of the process that leads towards this conclusion; and just as the whole musical composition is, as a whole, an end in itself; so every finite Internal Meaning wins final expression, not merely through the last stage of its life (if it has a last stage), but through its whole embodiment. And, nevertheless, as the music attains wholeness only through succession; so every idea that is to win its complete expression, does so through temporal sequences.

Since, at all events, no other than such a temporal expression of meaning in life is in any wise definable for our consciousness, our Idealism can only express its view of the relation of finite and absolute life by viewing the whole world, and in particular the whole existence of any individual Self, as such a temporal process, wherein there is expressed, by means of a Well-Ordered Series of stages, a meaning that finally belongs to the whole life, but that at every temporal stage of the process in question appears to involve, in part, a beyond,—a something not yet won,—and so a distinction both of the past and the future of this Self from the content of any one stage of the process when that stage is viewed as the present one.

In the sense, therefore, our doctrine is obliged to conceive the entire world-life as including a temporal series of events. When considered with reference to any one of these events, the rest of the events that belong to the series of which any one finite Self takes account, are past and future, that is, they are *no longer* and *not yet;* just as, when viewed with reference to any one chord or phrase in the musical composition, all the other successive elements of the composition are either past or future.

The infinite divisibility of the time of our ordinary scientific conceptions is indeed due to that tendency of our own discriminating attention to an endless interpolation of intermediary stages,—a tendency which we studied in connection with our general account of the World of Description. We have, however, seen reasons, which, applied to time, would lead us to declare that an absolute insight would view the temporal order as a discrete series of facts ordered as any succession of facts expressing one purpose would be ordered, viz. like the whole numbers. On the other hand, we have no reason to suppose that our human consciousness distinctly observes intervals of time that in brevity anywhere nearly approach to the final truth about the temporal order. Within what is for us the least observable happening, a larger insight may indeed discriminate multitudes of events. In dealing with the concept of Nature, we shall see what significant use may be made of the hypothesis that there exists or may exist, finite consciousness for which the series of events that we regard as no longer distinguishable from merely elementary and indivisible happenings, are distinguished so minutely as to furnish content as rich as those which, from our point of view, occupy æons of the world's history. Our right to such hypotheses is incontestable, provided only that they help us to conceive the true unity of experience. Nevertheless, in the last analysis, the Absolute Will must be viewed as expressed in a well-ordered and discrete series of facts, which from our point of view may indeed appear, as we shall still further see, capable of discrimination *ad infinitum.*

But now secondly, and without the least conflict with the foregoing theses, I declare that this same temporal world is, when regarded in its wholeness, an Eternal order. And I mean by this assertion nothing whatever but that the whole real content of this temporal order, whether it is viewed from any one temporal instant as past or as present or as future, is *at once* known, i.e. is consciously experienced as a whole, by the Absolute. And I use this expression *at once* in the very sense in which we before used it when we pointd out that to your own consciousness, the whole musical phrase may be and often is known *at once, despite* the fact that each element of the musical succession, when taken as the temporally present one, excludes from its own temporal instant the other members of the sequence, so that they are either *no longer* or *not yet,* at the instant *when* this element is tem-

porally the present one. As we saw before, it is true that, in one sense, each one of the elements or partial events of a sequence excludes the former and the latter elements form being at the time *when* this particular element exists. But that, in another and equally obvious and empirical sense, *all* the members of an actually experienced succession are *at once* to any consciousness which observes the whole succession as a whole, is equally true. The term *present,* as we saw, is naturally used both to name the temporally present when it is opposed to whatever precedes or succeeds this present, and also to name the observed facts of a succession in so far as they are experienced as constituting one whole succession. In so far the term is indeed ambiguous. But even this ambiguity itself is due to the before-mentioned fact that, if you try to find an absolutely simple present temporal fact of consciousness, and still to view it as an event in time, you are still always led, in the World of Description, to observe or to conceive that this temporal fact is a complex event, having a true succession *within* itself. So that the *now* of temporal expression is never a *mere* now, unless indeed it be viewed either as the ideal mathematical instant within which *nothing* takes place, or else as one of the finally simple stages of the discrete series of facts which the absolute insight views as the expression of its Will.

As to the one hypothesis, an absolute instant in the mathematical sense is like a point, an ideal limit, and never appears as any isolated fact of temporal experience. Every *now* within which something happens is therefore *also* a succession; so that every temporal fact, every event, so far as we men can observe it, has to be viewed as present to experience in *both* the senses of the term present; since this fact *when* present may be contrasted with predecessors that are *no longer* and with successors that are *not yet,* while this same fact, when taken as an event occupying time, is viewed as a presented succession with former and latter members contained within it. As to the other hypothesis, it seems clear that we human beings observe no such ultimate and indivisible facts of experience just because, so far as we observe and discriminate facts, we are more or less under the bondage of the categories of the World of Description.

But, in view of the correspondence between the universal time of the world-order, as we conceive it, and the time of our internal experience, as we observe it, the temporal sequences must be viewed as having in the real world, and for the Absolute, the same twofold character that our temporal experiences have for ourselves. *Present,* in what we may call the inclusive sense of the term, is any portion of real time with all its included events, in so far as there is any reason to view it as a whole, and as known in this wholeness by a single experience. *Present,* in what we may by contrast call the exclusive sense, is any one temporal event, in so far as it is contrasted with antecedent and subsequent events, and in so far as it excludes them from coexistence with itself in the same portion of any succession. These two senses of the term *present* do not contradict each other in case of the world-order any more than they do in case of our own inner experience. Both senses express inevitably distinct and yet inseparable connected aspects of the significant life of the conscious will, whether in us, or in the universe at large. Our view declares that all the life of the world, and therefore all temporal sequences, are present at once to the Absolute. Our view also maintains that, without the least conflict with this sense in which the whole temporal order is known at once to the Absolute, there is another sense in which any portion of the temporal sequence of the world may be taken as present, when viewed with reference to the experience of any finite Self whose present it is, and when contrasted with what for this same point of view is the past and the future of the world. Now the events of the temporal order, when viewed in this latter way, are divided, with reference to the point of view of any finite Self, into what *now* is, and what *no longer* is, and what *is to be,* but is *not yet.* These same events, however, in so far as they are viewed at once by the Absolute, are for such view, all equally present. And this their presence is the presence of all time, as a *totum simul,* to the Absolute. And the presence in this sense, of all time at once to the Absolute, constitutes the Eternal order of the world,—eternal, since it is inclusive of all distinctions of temporal past and temporal future,—eternal, since, for this very reason, the totality of temporal events thus present at once to the Absolute has no events that precede, or that follow it, but contains all sequences within it,—eternal, finally, because this view of the world does not, like our partial glimpses of this or of that relative whole of sequence, pass away and give place to some other view, but includes an observation of every passing away, of every sequence, of every event and of whatever in time succeeds and follows that event, and includes all the views that are taken by the various finite Selves.

In order to conceive what, in general, such an eternal view of the temporal order involves, or to conceive in what sense the temporal order of the real world is also an eternal order, we have, therefore, but to remember the sense in which the melody, or other sequence, is known at once to our own consciousness, despite the fact that its elements when viewed merely in their temporal succession are, in so far, *not* at once. As we saw before, the brief span of our consciousness, the small range of succession, that we can grasp at once, constitutes a perfectly arbitrary limitation of our own special type of consciousness. But in principle a time-sequence, however brief, is already viewed in a way that is not *merely* temporal, when, despite its sequence, it is grasped at once, and is thus grasped not through mere memory, but by virtue of actual experience. A consciousness related to the whole of the world's events, and to the whole of time, precisely as our human consciousness is related to a single melody or rhythm, and to the brief but still extended interval of time which this melody or rhythm occupies,—such a consciousness, I say, is an Eternal Consciousness. In principle we already possess and are acquainted with the nature of such a consciousness, whenever we do experience any succession as one whole. The only thing

needed to complete our idea of what an actually eternal consciousness is, is the conceived
removal of that arbitrary limitation which permits us men to observe indeed at once a succession, but forbids us to observe a succession
at once in case it occupies more than a very
few seconds.

## IV

This definition of the relations of the Temporal and the Eternal accomplishes all the purposes that are usually in mind when we speak
of the divine knowledge as eternal. That eternity is a *totum simul* [totality at once], the
scholastics were well aware; and St. Thomas
develops our present concept with a clearness
that is only limited by the consequences of his
dualistic view of the relation of God and the
world. For after he has indeed well defined
and beautifully illustrated the inclusive eternity of the divine knowledge, he afterwards
conceives the temporal existence of the created world as sundered from the eternal life
which belongs to God. And hereby the advantages of an accurate definition of the eternal
are sacrificed for the sake of a special dogmatic interest.

Less subtle forms of speculation have led
to uses of the word *eternal,* whose meaning is
often felt to be far deeper than such usages can
render explicit. But as these subtle usages are
often stated, they are indeed open to the most
obvious objections. An eternal knowledge is
often spoken of as if it were one for which
there is *no* distinction whatever between past,
and present, and future. But such a definition
is as absurd as if one should speak of our
knowledge of a whole musical phrase or
rhythm, when we grasped such a whole at
once, as if the *at once* implied that there were
for us no temporal distinction between the first
and the last beat or note of the succession in
question. To observe the succession *at once* is
to have present with perfect clearness *all* the
time-elements of the rhythm or of the phrase
just as they are,—the succession, the tempo,
the intervals, the pauses,—and yet, without

losing any of their variety, to view them at
once as one present musical idea. Now for our
theory, that is precisely the way in which the
eternal consciousness views the temporal
order,—not ignoring one jot or tittle of its
sharp distinctions of past or of future, of succession or of duration,—but still viewing the
whole time-process as the expression of a single Internal Meaning. What we now call past
and future are not merely the *same* for God;
and, nevertheless, they are viewed *at once,*
precisely as the beginning and the end of the
rhythm are not the same for our experience,
but are yet at once seen as belonging to one
and the same whole succession.

Or again, an eternal knowledge is often
supposed to be one that abstracts from time, or
that takes no account of time; so that, for an
eternal point of view it is as if time were not at
all. But to say this is as if one were to speak of
observing at once the meaning or character of
the whole phrase or rhythm by simply failing
to take any note at all of the succession as
such. The meaning is the meaning of the succession; and is grasped only by observing this
succession as something that involves former
and latter elements, while these elements in
time exclude one another, and therefore follow, each one *after* its predecessor has temporally ceased, and *before* its successor temporally appears. Just so, we assert that the eternal
insight observes the whole of time, and all that
happens therein, and is eternal only by virtue
of the fact that it does know the whole of time.

Or again, some doctrines often speak of an
eternal insight as something wholly and inex-
plicably *different* from any temporal type of
consciousness, so that *how* God views His
truth as eternal truth, no man can say. But our
theory regards the essential relation of an eternal to a temporal type of consciousness as one
of the simplest of the relations that are of primal importance for the definition of the
Absolute. Listen to any musical phrase or
rhythm, and grasp it as a whole, and you
thereupon have present in you the image, so to
speak, of the divine knowledge of the temporal order. To view all the course of time just as
you then and there view the whole of that

sequence,—this is to be possessed of an eternal type of insight.

"But," so many hereupon object,—"it appears impossible to see how this sort of eternal insight is possible, since just now, in time, the infinite past,—including, say, the geological periods and the Persian invasion of Greece, is *no longer,* while the future is *not yet.* How then for God shall this difference of past and future be transcended, and all be seen at once?" I reply, In precisely the same sense all the notes of the melody except this note are not *when* this note sounds, but are either *no longer* or *not yet.* Yet you may know a series of these notes at once. Now precisely so God knows the whole time-sequence of the world at once. The difference is merely one of span. You now exemplify the eternal type of knowledge, even as you listen to any briefest sequence of my words. For you, too, know time even by sharing the image of the Eternal.

Or again, a common wonder appears regarding how the divine knowledge can be in such wise eternal as to suffer no change to occur in it. How God should be unchangeable, yet express His will in a changing world, is an ancient problem. Our doctrine answers the question at a stroke. The knowledge of all change is itself indeed unchangeable, just because any change that occurs or that can occur to any being is already included amongst the objectives known to the eternal point of view. The knowledge of this melody as one whole does not itself consist in an adding of other notes to the melody. The knowledge of all sequences does not itself follow as another sequence. Hence it is indeed not subject to the fate of sequence.

And finally, a mystery is very generally made of the fact that since time appears to us as inevitably infinite, and as therefore not, like the melody or the rhythm, capable of completion, an eternal knowledge, if it involves a knowledge of the whole of time, must be something that has to appear to us self-contradictory and impossible. Any complete answer to this objection involves, of course, a theory of the infinite. Such a theory I have set forth in the Supplementary Essay, published with the First Series of these lectures. The issue involved, that of the positive concept of an infinite whole, is indeed no simple one, and is not capable of any brief presentation. I can here only report that the considerations set forth in that Supplementary Essay have led me to the thesis that a Well-Ordered Infinite Series, under the sole condition that it embodies a single plan, may be rightly viewed as forming a totality, and as an individual whole, precisely as a musical theme or a rhythm is viewed by our experience as such a whole. That the universe itself is such an infinite series, I have endeavored, in that paper, to show in great detail. If you view the temporal order of the world as also forming such an endless whole, expressing a single plan and Will (as I think you have a right to do), then the argument of the Supplementary Essay in question will apply to our present problem. The whole of time will contain a single expression of the divine Will, and therefore, despite its endlessness, the time-world will be present as such a single whole to the Absolute whose Will this is, and whose life all this sequence embodies.

## V

In order to refer, as I close, to the practical interest which has guided me through all the abstract considerations even of this present lecture, I may be permitted to anticipate some of our later results about the Self, and, for the sake of illustration, to point out that from our point of view, as we shall later explain it more fully, your life, your Self, your will, your individuality, your deeds, can be and are present at once to the eternal insight of God; while, nevertheless, it is equally true that not only for you, but for God, your life is a genuine temporal sequence of deeds and strivings, whereof, when you view this life at the present temporal instant, the past is just now *no longer,* while the future is *not yet.* This twofold view of your nature, as a temporal process and as an eternal system of fact, is precisely as valid and as obvious as the twofold view of the melody or of the rhythm. Your temporal present looks back, as Will, upon your now irrevocable past. That past is irrevocable because it is the basis of your seeking for the future, and is the so far finished expression of your unique individual Will. Your future is the *not yet* temporally expressed region wherein you, as finite being, seek your own further expression. That future is still, in one aspect, as we shall see, causally undetermined, precisely in so far as therein something unique, that is yours and yours only, is to appear in the form of various individually designed expressions of your life-purpose,—various individual deeds. Therefore, as we shall be able to maintain, despite all your unquestionable causal and moral determinations, there will be an aspect of your future life that will be free, and yours, and such as no causation can predetermine, and such as even God possesses only in so far as your unique individuality furnishes it as a fact in His world.

And nevertheless, your future and your past, your aspect of individuality, and of freedom, and the various aspects wherein you are dependent upon the rest of the world, your whole life of deeds, and your attainment of your individual goal through your deeds,—all these manifold facts that are yours and that constitute you, are present at once to the Absolute,—as facts in the world, as temporal contents eternally viewed,—as a process eternally finished,—but eternally finished precisely by virtue of the temporal sequence of your deeds. And when you wonder how these aspects can be at once the aspects of your one life,—remember what is implied in the consciousness *at once* of the melody or the rhythm as a sequence,—and you will be in possession of the essential principle whereby the whole mystery is explained.

It is this view, once grasped in its various aspects, that will enable us to define in what sense man is one with God, and in what sense he is to be viewed as at present out of harmony with his own relation to God, and in that sense alienated from his true place in the eternal world. And so, in discussing this most elementary category, we are preparing the way

for a most significant result as to the whole life of any man.

The temporal man, viewed just now in time, appears, at first, to be sundered even from his own past and future, and still more from God. He is a seeker even for to-morrow's bread,—still more for his salvation. He knows not just at this instant even his own individuality; still less should he immediately observe his relation to the Absolute in his present deed and in his fleeting experience. Only when he laboriously reflects upon his inmost meaning, or by faith anticipates the result of such reflection, does he become aware of how intimately his life is bound up with an Absolute life. This our finite isolation is, however, especially and characteristically a *temporal* isolation. That inattention of which we spoke in the last lecture, is especially an inattention to all but this act, as it now appears to me. I am not one with my own eternal individuality, especially and peculiarly because this passing temporal instant is not the whole of time, and because the rest of time is *no longer* or else *not yet* *when* this instant passes. Herein lies my peculiarly insurmountable human limitation. This is my present form of consciousness. To be sure, I am not wholly thus bound in the chains of my finitude. Within my present form and span of consciousness there is already exemplified an eternal type of insight, whereby the *totum simul* is in many cases and in brief span won. But beyond this my span of presentation, time escapes me as a past and future that is at once real and still either no longer or else not yet. From the eternal point of view, however, just this my life is *at once* present, in its Individuality and its wholeness. And because of this fact, just in so far as I am the eternal or true Individual, I stand in the presence of God, with all my life open before Him, and its meaning revealed to Him and to me. Yet this my whole meaning, while one with His meaning, remains, in the eternal world, still this unique and individual meaning, which the life of no other individual Self possesses. So that in my eternal expression I lose not my individuality, but rather win my only genuine individual expression, even while I find my oneness with God.

Now, in time, I seek, as if it were far beyond me, that goal of my Selfhood, that complete expression of my will, which in God, and for God, my whole life at once possesses. I seek this goal as a far-off divine event,—as my future and success. I do well to seek. Seek and ye shall find. Yet the finding,— it does not occur merely as an event in time. It occurs as an eternal experience in this my whole striving. Every struggle, every tear, every misery, every failure, and repentance, and every rising again, every strenuous pursuit, every glimpse of God's truth,—all these are not mere incidents of the search for that which is beyond. They are all events in the life; they too are part of the fulfilment. In eternity all this is seen, and hereby,—even in and through these temporal failures, I win, in God's presence and by virtue of His fulfilment, the goal of life, which is the whole of life. What no temporal instance ever brings,— what all temporal efforts fail to win, that my true Self in its eternity, and in its oneness with the divine, possesses.

So much it has seemed that I might here venture to anticipate of later results, in order that the true significance of our elementary categories might be, however imperfectly, defined for us from the outset. For all the questions as to our deeper relations to the universe are bound up with this problem of Time and Eternity.

# The Body and the Members

We have repeatedly spoken of two levels of human life, the level of the individual and the level of the community.... We have also repeatedly emphasized the ethical and religious significance of loyalty; but our definition will help us throw clearer light upon the sources of this worth. And by thus sharpening the outlines of our picture of what a real community is, we shall be made ready to consider whether the concept of the community possesses a more than human significance....

## I

Our definition presupposes that there exist many individual selves. Suppose these selves to vary in their present experiences and purposes as widely as you will. Imagine them to be sundered from one another by such chasms of mutual mystery and independence as, in our natural social life, often seem hopelessly to divide and secrete the inner world of each of us from the direct knowledge and estimate of his fellows. But let these selves be able to look beyond their present chaos of fleeting ideas and of warring desires, far away into the past whence they came, and into the future wither their hopes lead them. As they thus look, let each one of them ideally enlarge his own individual life, extending himself into the past and future, so as to say of some far-off event, belonging, perhaps, to other generations of men, "I view that event as a part of my own life." "That former happening or achievement so predetermined the sense and the destiny which are now mine, that I am moved to regard it as belonging to my own past." Or again: "For that coming event I wait and hope as an event of my own future."

From *The Problem of Christianity* (Chicago: The University of Chicago Press, 1968 [1913]), pp. 251–271.

And further, let the various ideal extensions, forwards and backwards, include at least one common event, so that each of these selves regards that event as a part of his own life.

Then, *with reference to the ideal common past and future in question, I say that these selves constitute a community.* This is henceforth to be our definition of a community. The present variety of the selves who are the members of the spiritual body so defined, is not hereby either annulled or slighted. The motives which determine each of them thus ideally to extend his own life, may vary from self to self in the most manifold fashion.

Our definition will enable us, despite all these varieties of the members, to understand in what sense any such community as we have defined exists, and is one.

Into this form, which, when thus summarily described, seems so abstract and empty, life can and does pour the rich contents and ideals which make the communities of our human world so full of dramatic variety and significance.

## II

The *first* condition upon which the existence of a community, in our sense of the word, depends, is the power of an individual self to extend his life, an ideal fashion, so as to regard it as including past and future events which lie far away in time, and which he does not now personally remember. That this power exists, and that man has a self which is thus ideally extensible in time without any definable limit, we all know.

This power itself rests upon the principle that, however a man may come by his idea of himself, the self is no mere datum, but is in its essence a life which is interpreted, and which interprets itself, and which, apart from some sort of ideal interpretation, is a mere flight of ideas, or a meaningless flow of feelings, or a vision that sees nothing, or else a barren abstract conception. How deep the process of interpretation goes in determining the real nature of the self, we shall only later be able to estimate.

There is no doubt that what we usually call our personal memory does indeed give us assurances regarding our own past, so far as memory extends and is trustworthy. But our trust in our memories is itself an interpretation of their data. All of us regard as belonging, even to our recent past life, much that we cannot just now remember. And the future self shrinks and expands with our hopes and our energies. No one can merely, from without, set for us the limits of the life of the self, and say to us: "Thus far and no farther."

In my ideal extensions of the life of the self, I am indeed subject to some sort of control,— to what control we need not here attempt to formulate. I must be able to give myself some sort of reason, personal, or social, or moral, or religious, or metaphysical, for taking on or throwing off the burden, the joy, the grief, the guilt, the hope, the glory of past and of future deeds and experiences; but I must also myself personally share in this task of determining how much of the past and the future shall ideally enter into my life, and shall contribute to the value of that life.

And if I choose to say, "There is a sense in which *all* the tragedy and the attainment of an endless past and future of deeds and of fortunes enter into my own life," I say only what saints and sages of the most various creeds and experiences have found their several reasons for saying. The fact and the importance of such ideal extensions of the self must therefore be recognized. Here is the first basis for every clear idea of what constitutes a community.

The ideal extensions of the self may also include, as is well known, not only past and future events and deeds, but also physical things, whether now existent or not, and many other sorts of objects which are neither events nor deeds. The knight or the samurai regarded his sword as a part of himself. One's treasures and one's home, one's tools, and the things that one's hands have made, frequently come to be interpreted as part of the self. And any object in heaven or earth may be thus ideally appropriated by a given self. The ideal self of the Stoic or of the Mystic may, in various fashions, identify its will, or its very essence, with the whole universe. The Hindoo seer seeks to realize the words: "I am Brahm;" "That art thou."

In case such ideal extensions of the self are consciously bound up with deeds, or with other events, such as belong to the past or future life which the self regards as its own, our definition of the community warrants us in saying that many selves form one community when all are ideally extended so as to include the same object. But unless the ideal extensions of the self thus consciously involve past and future deeds and events that have to do with the objects in question, we shall not use these extensions to help us to define communities.

For our purposes, the community is a being that attempts to accomplish something in time and through the deeds of its members. These deeds belong to the life which each member regards as, in ideal, his own. It is in this way that both the real and the ideal Church are intended by the members to be communities in our sense. An analogous truth holds for such other communities as we shall need to consider. The concept of the community is thus, for our purposes, a practical conception. It involves the idea of deeds done, and ends sought or attained. Hence I shall define it in terms of members who themselves not only live in time, but conceive their own ideally extended personalities in terms of a time-process. In so far as these personalities possess a life that is for each of them his own, while it is, in some of its events, common to them all, they form a community.

Nothing important is lost, for our conception of the community, by this formal restriction, whereby common objects belong to a community only when these objects are bound up with the deeds of the community. For, when the warrior regards his sword as a part of himself, he does so because his sword is the instrument of his will, and because what he

does with his sword belongs to his literal or ideal life. Even the mystic accomplishes his identification of the self and the world only through acts of renunciation or of inward triumph. And these acts are the goal of his life. Until he attains to them, they form part of his ideal future self. Whenever he fully accomplishes these crowning acts of identification, the separate self no longer exists. When knights or mystics form a community, in our sense, they therefore do so because they conceive of deeds done, in common, with their swords, or of mystical attainments that all of them win together.

Thus then, while no authoritative limit can be placed upon the ideal extensions of the self in time, those extensions of the self which need be considered for the purposes of our theory of the community are indeed extensions in time, past or future; or at all events involve such extensions in time.

Memory and hope constantly incite us to the extensions of the self which play so large a part in our daily life. Social motives of endlessly diverse sort move us to consider "far and forgot" as if to us it were near, when we view ourselves in the vaster perspectives of time. It is, in fact, the ideally extended self, and not, in general, the momentary self, whose life is worth living, whose sense outlasts our fleeting days, and whose destiny may be worthy of the interest of beings who are above the level of human individuals. The present self, the fleeting individual of to-day, is a mere gesticulation of the self. The genuine person lives in the far-off past and future as well as in the present. It is, then, the ideally extended self that is worthy to belong to a significant community.

## III

The *second* condition upon which the existence of a community depends is the fact that there are in the social world a number of distinct selves capable of social communication, and, in general, engaged in communication.

The distinctness of the selves we have illustrated at length in our previous discussion. We need not here dwell upon the matter further, except to say, expressly, that a community does *not* become one, in the sense of my definition, by virtue of any reduction or melting of these various selves into a single merely present self, or into a mass of passing experience. That mystical phenomena may indeed form part of the life of a community, just as they may also form part of the life of an individual human being, I fully recognize.

About such mystical or quasi-mystical phenomena, occurring in their own community, the Corinthians consulted Paul. And Paul, whose implied theory of the community is one which my own definition closely follows, assured them in his reply that mystical phenomena are not essential to the existence of the community; and that it is on the whole better for the life of such a community as he was addressing, if the individual member, instead of losing himself "in a mystery," kept his own individuality, in order to contribute his own edifying gift to the common life. Wherein this common life consists we have yet further to see in what follows.

The *third* of the conditions for the existence of the community which my definition emphasizes consists in the fact that the ideally extended past and future selves of the members include at least some events which are, for all these selves, identical. This third condition is the one which furnishes both the most exact, the most widely variable, and the most important of the motives which warrant us in calling a community a real unit. The Pauline metaphor of the body and the members finds, in this third condition, its most significant basis,—a basis capable of exact description.

## IV

In addition to the instance which I cited at the last time, when I mentioned the New Zealanders and their legendary canoes, other and much more important illustrations may here serve to remind us how a single common past

or future event may be the central means of uniting many selves in one spiritual community. For the Pauline churches the ideal memory of their Lord's death and resurrection, defined in terms of the faith which the missionary apostle delivered to them in his teaching, was, for each believer, an acknowledged occurrence in his own past. For each one was taught the faith, "In that one event my individual salvation was accomplished."

This faith has informed ever since the ideal memory upon which Christian tradition has most of all depended for the establishment and the preservation of its own community. If we speak in terms of social psychology, we are obliged, I think, to regard this belief as the product of the life of the earliest Christian community itself. But once established, and then transmitted from generation to generation, this same belief has been ceaselessly recreative of the communities of each succeeding age. And the various forms of the Christian Church,—its hierarchical institutions, its schisms, its reformations, its sects, its heresies, have been varied, differentiated, or divided, or otherwise transformed, according as the individual believers who made up any group of followers of Christian tradition have conceived, each his own personal life as including and as determined by that one ideal event thus remembered, namely, his Lord's death and resurrection.

Since the early Church was aware of this dependence of its community upon its memory, it instinctively resisted every effort to deprive that memory of definiteness, to explain it away as the Gnostic heresies did, or to transform it from a memory into any sort of conscious allegory. The idealized memory, the backward looking faith of an individual believer, must relate to events that seem to him living and concrete. Hence the early Church insisted upon the words, "Suffered under Pontius Pilate." The religious instinct which thus insisted was true to its own needs. A very definite event must be viewed by each believer as part of the history of his own personal salvation. Otherwise his community would lose its coherence.

Paul himself, despite his determination to know Christ, not "after the flesh," but "after the Spirit," was unhesitating and uncompromising with regard to so much of the ideal Christian memory as he himself desired each believer to carry clearly in mind. Only by such common memories could the community be constituted. To be sure, the Apostle's Christology, on its more metaphysical side, cared little for such more precise technical formulations as later became historically important for the Church that formulated its creeds. But the events which Paul regarded as essential for salvation must be, as he held, plainly set down.

Since human memory is naturally sustained by commemorative acts, Paul laid the greatest possible stress upon the Lord's Supper, and made the proper ordering thereof an essential part of his ideal as a teacher. In this act of commemoration, wherein each member recalled the origin of his own salvation, the community maintained its united life.

## V

The early Church was, moreover, not only a community of memory, but a community of hope. Since, if the community was to exist, and to be vigorously alive, each believer must keep definite his own personal hope, while the event for which all hoped must be, for all, an identical event, something more was needed, in Paul's account of the coming end of the world, than the more dimly conceived common judgment had hitherto been in the minds of the Corinthians to whom Paul wrote. And therefore the great chapter on the resurrection emphasizes equally the common resurrection of all, and the very explicitly individual immortality of each man. Paul uses both the resurrection of Christ, and the doctrine of the spiritual body, to give the sharpest possible outlines to a picture which has ever since dominated not only the traditional Christian religious imagination, but the ideal of the united Church triumphant.

Nowhere better than in this very chapter can one find an example of the precise way in which the fully developed consciousness of a community solves its own problem of the one and the many, by clearly conceiving both the diversity of the members and the unity of the body in terms of the common hope for the same event.

The Apostle had to deal with the doctrine of the immortality of the individual man, and also with the corporate relations of humanity and of the Church to death and to the end of all things. The most pathetic private concerns and superstitions of men, the most conflicting ideas of matter, of spirit, and of human solidarity, had combined, in those days, to confuse the religious ideas which entered into the life of the early Church, when the words "death and resurrection" were in question. The Apostle himself was heir to a seemingly hopeless tangle of ancient and more or less primitive opinions regarding the human self and the cosmos, regarding the soul and the future.

A mystery-religion of Paul's own time might, and often did, assure the individual initiate of his own immortality. The older Messianic hope, or its successor in the early Christian consciousness, might be expressed, and was often expressed, in a picture wherein all mankind were together called before the judgment seat at the end. But minds whose ideas upon such topics came from various and bewildering sources,—minds such as those of Paul's Corinthians, might, and did, inquire: "What will personally happen to me? What will happen to all mankind?" The very contrast between these two questions was, at that time, novel. The growing sense of the significance of the individual self was struggling against various more or less mystical identifications of all mankind with Adam, or with some one divine or demonic power or spirit. Such a struggle still goes on to-day.

But Paul's task it was, in writing this chapter, to clarify his own religious consciousness, and to guide his readers through the mazes of human hope and fear to some precise view, both of human solidarity and individual destiny. His method consisted in a definition of his whole problem in terms of the relations between the individual, the community, and the divine being whom he conceived as the very life of this community. He undertook to emphasize the individual self, and yet to insist upon the unity of the Church and of its Lord. He made perfectly clear in each believer's mind the idea: "I myself, and not another, am to witness and to take part in this last great change." To this end Paul made use of the conception of the individual spiritual body of each man. But Paul also dwelt with equal decisiveness upon the thought, "The last event of the present world is to be, for all of us, *one* event; for we shall all together arise."

These two main thoughts of the great chapter are in the exposition clearly contrasted and united; and against this well-marked background Paul can then place statements about humanity viewed as one corporate entity,— monistic formulations, so to speak,—and can do this without fear of being misunderstood: "The first man Adam became a living soul. The last Adam became a quickening spirit. The first man is of the earth, earthy; the second man is the Lord from heaven." What these more monistic statements about mankind as one corporate entity are to mean, is made clear simply by teaching each believer to say, "I shall myself arise, with my own transformed and incorruptible body;" and also to say, "This event of the resurrection is one for all of us, for we shall arise together."

In such expressions Paul uses traditions whose sources were indeed obscure and whose meaning was, as one might have supposed, hopelessly ambiguous. The interpretations of these traditions on Paul's part might have been such as to lose sight of the destiny of the individual human being through a more or less mystical blending of the whole race. That would have been natural for a mind trained to think of Adam and of mankind as Paul was trained. Or, again, the interpretation might have taken the form of assuring the individual believer that he could win his own immortality, while leaving him no further ground for special interest in the community. Paul's religious genius aims straight at the central problem of clearing away this ambiguity, and of defining the immortal life, both of the individual and of the community. In the expected resurrection, as Paul pictures it, the individual finds his own life, and the community its common triumph over all the world-old powers of death. And the hope is referred back again to the memory. Was not Christ raised? By this synthesis Paul solves his religious problems, and defines sharply the relation of the individual and the community.

And therefore, whenever, upon the familiar solemn occasions, this chapter is read, not only is individual sorrow bidden to transform itself into an unearthly hope; but even upon earth the living and conscious community of the faithful celebrates the present oneness of spirit in which it triumphs. And the death over which it triumphs is the death of the lonely individual, whom faith beholds raised to the imperishable life in the spirit. This life in the spirit is also the life of the community. For the individual is saved, according to Paul, only in and through and with the community and its Lord.

## VI

Our present interest in these classic religious illustrations of the idea of the community is not directly due to their historical importance as parts of Christian tradition; but depends upon the help which they give us in seeing how a community, whether it be Christian or not, can really constitute a single entity, despite the multiplicity of its members. Our illustrations have brought before us the fact that hope and memory constitute, in communities, a basis for an unquestionable consciousness of unity, and that this common life in time does not annul the variety of the individual members at any one present moment.

We have still to see, however, the degree to which this consciousness of unity can find expression in an effectively united common life which not only contains common events, but also possesses common deeds and can arouse a common love—a love which passes the love wherewith individuals can love one another.

And here we reach that aspect of the conception of the community which is the most important, and also the most difficult aspect.

## VII

A great and essentially dramatic event, such as the imagined resurrection of the bodies of all men,—an event which interests us, and which fixes the attention by its miraculous apparition,—is well adapted to illustrate the union of the one and the many in the process of time. When Paul's genius seized upon this picture,—when, to use the well-known later scholastic phraseology, the spirits of men were thus "individuated by their bodies," even while the event of the resurrection fixed the eye of faith upon one final crisis through which all were to pass "in a moment, in the twinkling of an eye,"—when the Apostle thus instructed the faithful, a great lesson was also taught regarding the means whereby the ideal of a community and the harmonious union of the one and the many can be rendered brilliantly clear to the imagination, and decisively fascinating to the will.

But the lives of communities cannot consist of miraculous crises. A community, like an individual self, must learn to keep the consciousness of its unity through the vicissitudes of an endlessly shifting and often dreary fortune. The monotony of insignificant events, the chaos of lesser conflicts, the friction and the bickerings of the members, the individual failures and the mutual misunderstandings which make the members of a community forget the common past and future,—all these things work against the conscious unity of the life of a community. Memory and hope are alike clouded by multitudes of such passing events. The individual members cannot always recall the sense in which they identify their own lives and selves with what has been, or with what is yet to come.

And—hardest task of all—the members, if they are to conceive clearly of the common life, must somehow learn to bear in mind not merely those grandly simple events which, like great victories, or ancestral feats, or divine interferences, enter into the life of the community from without, and thus make their impression all at once.

No, the true common life of the community consists of deeds which are essentially of the nature of processes of coöperation. That is, the common life consists of deeds which many members perform together, as when the workmen in a factory labor side by side.

Now we all know that coöperation constantly occurs, and is necessary to every form and grade of society. We also know that commerce and industry and art and custom and language consist of vast complexes of coöperations. And in all such cases many men manage in combination to accomplish what no man, and no multitude of men working separately, could conceivably bring to pass. But what we now need to see is the way in which such coöperations can become part, not only of the life, but of the consciousness of a community.

## VIII

Every instance of a process of coöperation is an event, or a sequence of events. And our definition of a community requires that, if such coöperative activities are to be regarded as the deeds of a community, there must be individuals, each one of whom says: "That coöperation, in which many distinct individuals take part, and in which I also take part, is, or was, or will be, an event in my life." And many coöperating individuals must agree in saying this of the same process in which they all coöperate.

And all must extend such identifications of the self with these social activities far into the past, or into the future.

But it is notoriously hard—especially in our modern days of the dreary complexity of mechanical labor—for any individual man so to survey, and so to take interest in a vast coöperative activity that he says: "In my own ideally extended past and future that activity, its history, its future, its significance as an event or sequence of events, all have their ideally significant part. That activity, as the coöperation of many in one work, is also my life." To say such things and to think such thoughts grow daily harder for most of the coworkers of a modern social order.

Hence, as is now clear, the existence of a highly organized social life is by no means identical with the existence of what is, in our present and restricted sense, the life of a true community. On the contrary, and for the most obvious reasons, there is a strong mutual opposition between the social tendencies which secure coöperation on a vast scale, and the very conditions which so interest the individual in the common life of his community that it forms part of his own ideally extended life. We met with that opposition between the more or less mechanically coöperative social life,—the life of the social will on the one side, and the life of the true community on the other side,—when we were considering the Pauline doctrine of the law in an earlier lecture. In fact, it is the original sin of any highly developed civilization that it breeds coöperation at the expense of a loss of interest in the community.

The failure to see the reason why this opposition between the tendency to coöperation and the spirit of the community exists; the failure to sound to the depths the original sin of man the social animal, and of the natural social order which he creates;—such failure, I repeat, lies at the basis of countless misinterpretations, both of our modern social problems, and of the nature of a true community, and of the conditions which make possible any wider philosophical generalizations of the idea of the community.

## IX

Men do not form a community, in our present restricted sense of that word, merely in so far as the men coöperate. They form a community, in our present limited sense, when they not only coöperate, but accompany this coöperation with that ideal extension of the lives of individuals whereby each coöperating member says: "This activity which we per-

form together, this work of ours, its past, its future, its sequence, its order, its sense,—all these enter into my life, and are the life of my own self writ large."

Now coöperation results from conditions which a social psychology such as that of Wundt or of Tarde may analyze. Imitation and rivalry, greed and ingenuity, business and pleasure, war and industry, may all combine to make men so coöperate that very large groups of them behave, to an external observer, as if they were units. In the broader sense of the term "community," all social groups that behave as if they were units are regarded as communities. And we ourselves called all such groups communities in our earlier lectures before we came to our new definition.

But we have now been led to a narrower application of the term "community." It is an application to which we have restricted the term simply because of our special purpose in this inquiry. Using this restricted definition of the term "community," we see that groups which coöperate may be very far from constituting communities in our narrower sense. We also see how, in general, a group whose coöperative activities are very highly complex will require a correspondingly long period of time to acquire that sort of tradition and of common expectation which is needed to constitute a community in our sense,—that is, a community conscious of its own life.

Owing to the psychological conditions upon which social coöperation depends, such cooperation can very far outstrip, in the complexity of its processes, the power of any individual man's wit to understand its intricacies. In modern times, when social cooperation both uses and is so largely dominated by the industrial arts, the physical conditions of coöperative social life have combined with the psychological conditions to make any thorough understanding of the coöperative processes upon which we all depend simply hopeless for the individual, except within some narrow range. Experts become well acquainted with aspects of these forms of coöperation which their own callings involve. Less expert workers understand a less range of the coöperative processes in which they take part. Most individuals, in most of their work, have to coöperate as the cogs coöperate in the wheels of a mechanism. They work together; but few or none of them know how they coöperate, or what they must do.

But the true community, in our present restricted sense of the word, depends for its genuine common life upon such coöperative activities that the individuals who participate in these common activities understand enough to be able, first, to direct their own deeds of coöperation; secondly, to observe the deeds of their individual fellow workers, and thirdly to know that without just this combination, this order, this interaction of the coworking selves, just this deed could not be accomplished by the community. So, for instance, a chorus or an orchestra carries on its coöperative activities. In these cases coöperation is a conscious art. If hereupon these coöperative deeds, thus understood by the individual coworker, are viewed by him as linked, through an extended history with past and future deeds of the community, and if he then identifies his own life with this common life, and if his fellow members agree in this identification, then indeed the community both has a common life, and is aware of the fact. For then the individual coworker not only says: "This past and future fortune of the community belongs to my life;" but also declares: "This past and future deed of coöperation belongs to my life." "This, which none of us could have done alone,— this, which all of us together could not have accomplished unless we were ordered and linked in precisely this way,—this we together accomplished, or shall yet accomplish; and this deed of all of us belongs to my life."

A community thus constituted is essentially a community of those who are artists in some form of coöperation, and whose art constitutes, for each artist, his own ideally extended life. But the life of an artist depends upon his love for his art.

The community is made possible by the fact that each member includes in his own ideally extended life the deeds of coöperation which the members accomplish. When these deeds are hopelessly complex, how shall the individual member be able to regard them as genuinely belonging to his own ideally extended life? He can no longer understand them in any detail. He takes part in them, willingly or unwillingly. He does so because he is social, and because he must. He works in his factory, or has his share, whether greedily or honestly, in the world's commercial activities. And his coöperations may be skilful; and this fact also he may know. But his skill is largely due to external training, not to inner expansion of the ideals of the self. And the more complex the social order grows, the more all this coöperation must tend to appear to the individual as a mere process of nature, and not as his own work,—as a mechanism and not as an ideal extension of himself,—unless indeed love supplies what individual wit can no longer accomplish.

# X

If a social order, however complex it may be, actually wins and keeps the love of its members; so that,—however little they are able to understand the details of their present coöperative activities,—they still—with all their whole hearts and their minds and their souls, and their strength—desire, each for himself, that such coöperations should go on; and if each member, looking back to the past, rejoices in the ancestors and the heroes who have made the present life of this social group possible; and if he sees in these deeds of former generations the source and support of his present love; and if each member also looks forward with equal love to the future,—then indeed love furnishes that basis for the consciousness of the community which intelligence, without love, in a highly complex social realm, can no longer furnish. Such love—such loyalty—depends not upon losing sight of the variety of the callings of individuals, but upon seeing in the successful coöperation of all the members precisely that event which the individual member most eagerly loves as his own fulfilment.

When love of the community, nourished by common memories, and common hope, both exists and expresses itself in devoted individual lives, it can constantly tend, despite the complexity of the present social order, to keep the consciousness of the community alive. And when this takes place, the identification of the loyal individual self with the life of the community will tend, both in ideal and in feeling, to identify each self not only with the distant past and future of the community, but with the present activities of the whole social body.

Thus, for instance, when the complexities of business life, and the dreariness of the factory, have, to our minds, deprived our present social coöperations of all or of most of their common significance, the great communal or national festivity, bringing to memory the great events of past and future, not only makes us, for the moment, feel and think as a community with reference to those great past and future events, but in its turn, as a present event, reacts upon next day's ordinary labors. The festivity says to us: "We are one because of our common past and future, because of the national heroes and victories and hopes, and because we love all these common memories and hopes." Our next day's mood, consequent upon the festivity, bids us say: "Since we are thus possessed of this beloved common past and future, let this consciousness lead each of us even to-day to extend his ideal self so as to include the daily work of all his fellows, and to view his fellow members' life as his own."

Thus memory and hope tend to react upon the present self, which finds the brotherhood of present labor more significant, and the ideal identification of the present self with the self of the neighbor easier, because the ideal extension of the self into past and future has preceded.

And so, first, each of us learns to say: "This beloved past and future life, by virtue of the ideal extension, is my own life." Then, finding that our fellows have and love this past and future in common with us, we learn further to say: "In this respect we are all one loving and beloved community." Then we take a further step and say: "Since we are all members of

this community, therefore, despite our differences, and our mutual sunderings of inner life, each of us can, and will, ideally extend his present self so as to include the present life and deeds of his fellow."

So it is that, in the ideal church, each member not only looks backwards to the same history of salvation as does his fellow, but is even thereby led to an ideal identification of his present self with that of his fellow member that would not otherwise be possible. Thus, then, common memory and common hope, the central possessions of the community, tend, when enlivened by love, to mould the consciousness of the present, and to link each member to his community by ideal ties which belong to the moment as well as to the stream of past and future life.

## XI

Love, when it exists and triumphs over the complexities which obscure and confuse the common life, thus completes the consciousness of the community, in the forms which that consciousness can assume under human conditions. Such love, however, must be one that has the common deeds of the community as its primary object. No one understands either the nature of the loyal life, or the place of love in the constitution of the life of a real community, who conceives such love as merely a longing for the mystical blending of the selves or for their mutual interpenetration, and for that only. Love says to the individual: "So extend yourself, in ideal, that you aim, with all your heart and your soul and your mind and your strength, at *that* life of perfect definite deeds which never can come to pass unless all the members, despite their variety and their natural narrowness, are in perfect coöperation. Let this life be your art and also the art of all your fellow members. Let your community be as a chorus, and not as a company who forget themselves in a common trance."

Nevertheless, as Paul showed in the great chapter, such love of the self for the community can be and will be not without its own mystical element. For since we human beings are as narrow in our individual consciousness as we are, we cannot ideally extend ourselves through clearly understanding the complicated social activities in which the community is to take part. Therefore our ideal extensions of the self, when we love the community, and long to realize its life with intimacy, must needs take the form of *acting as if we could survey,* in some single unity of insight, that wealth and variety and connection which, as a fact, we cannot make present to our momentary view. Since true love is an emotion, and since emotions are present affections of the self, love, in longing for its own increase, and for its own fulfilment, inevitably longs to find what it loves as a fact of experience, and to be in the immediate presence of its beloved. Therefore, the love of a community (a love which, as we now see, is devoted to desiring the realization of an overwhelming vast variety and unity of coöperations), is, as an emotion, discontent with all the present sundering of the selves, and with all the present problems and mysteries of the social order. Such love, then, restless with the narrowness of our momentary view of our common life, desires this common life to be an immediate presence for all of us. Such an immediate presence of all the community to all the members would be indeed, if it could wholly and simply take place, a mere blending of the selves,—an interpenetration in which the individuals vanished, and in which, for that very reason, the real community would also be lost.

Love,—the love of Paul's great chapter,—the loyalty which stands at the center of the Christian consciousness,—is, as an emotion, a longing for such a mystical blending of the selves. This longing is present in Paul's account. It is in so far not the whole of charity. It is simply the mystical aspect of the love for the community.

But the Pauline charity is not merely an emotion. It is an interpretation. The ideal extension of the self gets a full and concrete meaning only by being actively expressed in the new deeds of each individual life. Unless each man knows how distinct he is from the whole community and from every member of it, he cannot render to the community what love demands,—namely, the devoted work. Love may be mystical, and work should be directed by clearly outlined intelligence; but the loyal spirit depends upon this union of a longing for unity with a will which needs its own expression in works of loyal art.

## XII

The doctrine of the two levels of human existence; the nature of a real community; the sense in which there can be, in individual human beings, despite their narrowness, their variety, and their sundered present lives, a genuine consciousness of the life of a community whereof they are members:—these matters we have now, within our limits, interpreted. The time-process, and the ideal extensions of the self in this time-process, lie at the basis of the whole theory of the community. The union and the contrast of the one and the many in the community, and the relation of the mystical element in our consciousness of the community to the active interpretation of the loyal life, these things have also been reviewed. Incidentally, so to speak, we have suggested further reasons why loyalty, whether in its distinctively Christian forms, or in any others, is a saving principle whenever it appears in an individual human life. For in the love of a community the individual obtains, for his ideally extended self, precisely the unity, the wealth, and the harmony of plan which his sundered natural existence never supplies.

Yet it must be not merely admitted, but emphasized, that all such analyses of the sort of life and of interpretation upon which communities and the loyalty of their members depend, does not and cannot explain the origin of loyalty, the true sources of grace, and the way in which communities of high level come into existence.

On the contrary, all the foregoing account of what a community is shows how the true spirit of loyalty, and the highest level of the consciousness of a human community, is at once so precious, and so difficult to create.

The individual man naturally, but capriciously, loves both himself and his fellow-man, according as passion, pity, memory, and hope move him. Social training tends to sharpen the contrasts between the self and the fellow-man; and higher cultivation, under these conditions of complicated social coöperation which we have just pointed out, indeed makes a man highly conscious that he depends upon his community, but also renders him equally conscious that, as an individual, he is much beset by the complexities of the social will, and does not always love his community, or any community. Neither the origin nor the essence of loyalty is explained by man's tendencies to love his individual fellow-man.

It is true that, within the limits of his power to understand his social order, the conditions which make a man conscious of his community also imply that the man should in some respects identify his life with that. But I may well know that the history, the future, the whole meaning of my community are bound up with my own life; and yet it is not necessary that on that account I should wholeheartedly love my own life. I may be a pessimist. Or I may be simply discontented. I may desire to escape from the life that I have. And I may be aware that my fellows, for the most part, also long to escape.

That the community is above my own individual level I shall readily recognize, since the community is indeed vastly more skilful and incomparably more powerful than I can ever become. But what is thus above me I need not on that account be ready wholly to love. To be sure, that man is indeed a sad victim of a misunderstood life who is himself able to be clearly aware of his community, to identify its history and its future, at least in part, with his own ideally extended life, and who is yet *wholly* unable ever to love the life which is thus linked with his own. Yet there remains the fate which Paul so emphasized, and which has determined the whole history of the Christian consciousness: Knowledge of the community is not love of the community. Love, when it comes, comes as from above.

Especially is this true of the love of the ideal community of all mankind. I can be genuinely in love with the community only in case I have somehow fallen in love with the universe. The problem of love is human. The solution of the problem, if it comes at all, will be, in its meaning, superhuman, and divine, if there be anything divine.

What our definition of the community enables us to add to our former views of the meaning of loyalty is simply this: If the universe proves to be, in any sense, of the nature of a community, then love for this community, and for God, will not mean merely love for losing the self, or for losing the many selves, in any interpenetration of selves. If one can find that all humanity, in the sense of our definition, constitutes a real community, or that the world itself is, in any genuine way, of the nature of a community such as we have defined; and *if* hereupon we can come to love this real community,—then the one and the many, the body and the members, our beloved and ourselves, will be joined in a life in which we shall be both preserved as individuals, and yet united to that which we love.

## XIII

Plainly a metaphysical study of the question whether the universe is a community will be as powerless as the foregoing analysis of the real nature of human communities to explain the origin of love, or to make any one fall in love with the universe. Yet something has been gained by our analysis of the problem which, from this point onwards, determines our metaphysical inquiry. If our results are in any way positive, they may enable us to view the problem of Christianity, that is, the problem of the religion of loyalty, in a larger perspective than that which human history, when considered alone, determines. The favorite methods of approaching the metaphysical problems of theology end by leaving the individual alone with God, in a realm which seems, to many minds, a realm of merely concepts, of intellectual abstractions, of barren theories. The ways which are just now in favor in the philosophy of religion seem to end in leaving the individual equally alone with his intuitions, his lurid experiences of sudden conversion, or his ineffable mysteries of saintly peace.

May we not hope to gain by a method which follows the plan now outlined? This method, first, encourages a man to interpret his own individual self in terms of the largest ideal extension of that self in time which his reasonable will can acknowledge as worthy of the aims of his life. Secondly, this method bids a man consider what right he has to interpret the life from which he springs, in the midst of which he now lives, as a life that in any universal sense coöperates with his own and ideally expresses its own meaning so as to meet with his own, and to have a history identical with his own. Thirdly, this method directs us to inquire how far, in the social order to which we unquestionably belong, there are features such as warrant in us hoping that, in the world's community, our highest love may yet find its warrant and its fulfilment.

Whatever the fortunes of the quest may be, we have now defined its plan, and have shown its perfectly definite relation to the historical problem of Christianity.

# The Will to Interpret

## I

. . . The metaphysical inquiry concerning the nature and the reality of the community is still our leading topic. To this topic whatever we shall have to say about interpretation is everywhere subordinate. But, since, if I am right, interpretation is indeed a fundamental cognitive process, we shall need still further to illustrate its nature and its principal forms. Every apparent digression from our main path will quickly lead us back to our central issues. Interpretation is, once for all, the main business of philosophy.

The present lecture will include two stages of movement towards our goal. First, we shall study the elementary psychology of the process of interpretation. Secondly, we shall portray the ideal that guides the truth-loving interpreter. The first of these inquiries will concern topics which are both familiar and neglected. The second part of our lecture will throw light upon the ethical problems with which our study of the Christian ideas has made us acquainted. At the close of the lecture our preparation for an outline of the metaphysics of interpretation will be completed.

## II

I have called interpretation an essentially social cognitive process; and such, in fact, it is. Man is an animal that interprets; and therefore man lives in communities, and depends upon them for insight and for salvation.

But the elementary psychological forms in which interpretation appears find a place in our lives whether or no we are in company; just as a child can sing when alone, although singing is, on the whole, a social activity. We shall need to consider how an interpreter con-

From *The Problem of Christianity* (Chicago: The University of Chicago Press, 1968 [1913]), pp. 297–319.

ducts his mental processes, even when he is taking no explicit account of other minds than his own.

In looking for the psychological foundations of interpretation, we shall be directed by Charles Peirce's formal definition of the mental functions which are involved. Wherever an interpretation takes place, however little it seems to be an explicit social undertaking, a triadic cognitive process can be observed. Let us look, then, for elementary instances of such triadic processes.

In the earliest of the logical essays to which, at the last time, I referred, Charles Peirce pointed out that every instance of conscious and explicit Comparison involves an elementary form of interpretation. This observation of Peirce's enables us to study interpretation in some of its simplest shapes, relieved of the complications which our social efforts to communicate with other minds usually involve.

Yet, even in this rudimentary form, interpretation involves the motives, which, upon higher levels, make its work so wealthy in results, and so significant in its contrasts with perception and conception.

## III

The most familiar instances of the mental process known as Comparison seem, at first sight, to consist of a consciousness of certain familiar dyadic relations,—relations of similarity and difference. Red contrasts with green; sound breaks in upon silence; one sensory quality collides, as it were, with another. The "shock of difference" awakens our attention. In other cases, an unexpected similarity of colors and tones attracts our interest. Or perhaps the odors of two flowers, or the flavors of two fruits, resemble one the other. Pairs of perceived objects are, in all these cases, in question. We express our observations in such judgments as: "A resembles B;" "D is unlike E."

Now Peirce's view of the nature of comparison depends upon noticing that familiar as such observations of similarity and dissimilarity may be, no one of them constitutes the whole of any complete act of comparison. Comparison, in the fuller sense of the word, takes place when one asks or answers the question: What constitutes the difference between A and B?" "*Wherein* does A resemble B?" "*Wherein* consists their distinction?" Let me first illustrate such a question in a case wherein the answer is easy.

If you write a word with your own hand, and hold it up before a mirror, your own handwriting becomes more or less unintelligible to you, unless you are already accustomed to read or to write mirror-script. Suppose, however, that instead of writing words yourself, you let someone else show you words already written. And suppose, further, that two words have been written side by side on the same sheet of paper, neither of them by your own hand. Suppose one of them to have been written upright, while the other is the counterpart of the first, except that it is the first turned upside down, or else is the first in mirror-script. If, without knowing how these words have been produced, you look at them, you can directly observe that the two written words differ in appearance, and that they also have a close resemblance. But, unless you were already familiar with the results of inverting a handwriting or of observing it in a mirror, you could not thus directly observe wherein consist the similarities and the differences of the two words which lie before you on the paper.

Since you are actually familiar with mirror-script, and with the results of turning a sheet of paper upside down, you will indeed no doubt be able to name the difference of the two supposed words. But in order to compare the two words thus presented side by side on the same sheet of paper, and to tell wherein they are similar and wherein they differ, you need what Peirce calls a mediating idea, or what he also calls "a third," which, as he phrases the matter, shall "represent" or "interpret" one of the two written words to, or in terms of, the other. You use such a "third" idea when you say, "This word is the mirror-script representative of that word." For now the difference is interpreted.

Thus a complete act of comparison involves such a "third," such a "mediating" image or idea,—such an "interpreter." By means of this "third" you so compare a "first" object with a "second" as to make clear to yourself wherein consists the similarity and the difference between the second and the first. Comparison must be triadic in order to be both explicit and complete. Likenesses and differences are the signs that a comparison is needed. But these signs are not their own interpretation.

. . . Still another familiar instance of comparison will show how needful it is to choose the right "third" in order to complete one's view of the matter. One may long have observed that a friend's face, when seen in a mirror, contrasts with the same face if seen apart from the mirror. . . . The idea of the vertical asymmetries is here the needed "third" which interprets the difference between the man's face when seen in the mirror and when seen out of the mirror.

A lady who had passed part of her life in Australia, and part in England, once told me that, for years, she had never been able to understand the difference which, to her eyes, existed between the full moon as seen in England and as observed by her during her years in Australia. At last she found the right mediating idea, when she came to notice how Orion also gradually became partially inverted during her journeys from English latitudes to those of the far southern seas. For the full moon, as she thus came to know, must be subject to similar apparent inversions; and this was the reason why the "man in the moon" had therefore been undiscoverable when she had heretofore looked for him in Australian skies.

## IV

When processes of comparison grow complicated, new "third" terms or "mediators" may be needed at each stage of one's undertaking. So it is when a literary parallel between two poets or two statesmen is in question. Now one and now another trait or event or fortune or deed may stand out as the mediating idea. But always, in such parallels, it is by means of the use of a "third" that each act of comparison is made possible,—whether the case in question be simple or complex. And the mediator plays each time the part which Peirce first formally defined.

Let there arise the problem of drawing a literary parallel between Shakespeare and Dante. The task appears hopelessly complex and indeterminate until, perhaps, the place which the sonnet occupied in the creative activity of each poet comes to our minds. Then indeed, although the undertaking is still vastly complicated, it is no longer quite so hopeless. If "with this key Shakespeare unlocked his heart," yet held fast its deepest mysteries; while Dante accompanied each of the sonnets of the *Vita Nuova* with a comment and an explanation, yet left unspoken what most fascinates us in the supernatural figure of his beloved,—then "the sonnet," viewed as an idea of a poetical form, mediates between our ideas of the two poets, and represents or interprets each of these ideas to the other.

This last example suggests an endless wealth of complexities. And the interpretation in question is also endlessly inadequate to our demands. But on its highest levels, as in its simplest instances, the process of explicit comparison is thus triadic, and to notice this fact is, for the purpose of our study of comparison, illuminating.

For when we merely set pairs of objects before us, and watch their resemblances and differences, we soon lose ourselves in mazes. Yet even when the mazes are indeed not to be penetrated by any skill, still a triadic comparison is much more readily guided towards the light. "How does A differ from C?" If you can reply to this question by saying that, by means of B, A can be altogether transformed into C, or can, at least, be brought into a close resemblance to C, then the comparison of A to C is made definite.

Let me choose still one more illustration of such a comparison. This time the illustration shall not come from the literary realm; yet it shall be more complex than is the instance of the comparison between a written word and its image in the mirror.

If you cut a strip of paper,—perhaps an inch wide and ten inches long,—you can bring the two ends together and fasten them with glue. The result will be a ring-strip of paper, whose form is of a type very familiar in the case of belts, finger-rings, and countless other objects. But this form can be varied in an interesting way. Before bringing the ends of the strip together, let one end of the paper be turned 180°. Holding the twisted end of the strip fast, glue it to the other. There now results an endless strip of paper having in it a single twist. Lay side by side an ordinary ring-strip that has no twist, and a ring-strip of paper that has been made in the way just indicated. The latter strip has a single twist in it. Hereupon ask a person who has not seen you make the two ring-strips, to compare them, and to tell you wherein they agree and wherein they differ.

To your question an ordinary observer, to whom this new form of ring-strip is unfamiliar, will readily answer that they obviously differ because one of them has no twist in it, while the other certainly has some kind of twist belonging to its structure. So far the one whom you question indeed makes use of a "third" idea. But this idea probably remains, so far, vague in his mind, and it will take your uninformed observer some time to make his comparison at all complete and explicit.

In order to aid him in his task, you may hereupon call his attention to the further fact that the ring-strip which contains the single twist has two extraordinary properties. It has, namely, but one side; and it also has but one edge. The mention of this fact will at first perplex the uninitiated observer. But when he has taken the trouble to study the new form, he will find that the idea of a "one-sided strip of paper" enables him to compare the new and the old form, and to interpret his idea of the new ring-form to his old idea of an ordinary ring such as has no twist, and possesses two sides.

## V

In all the cases of explicit comparison which we have just considered, what takes place has, despite the endless varieties of circumstance, an uniform character.

Whoever compares has before him what we have called two distinct ideas; perhaps his ideas of these two printed or written words; or again, his ideas of these two ring-strips of paper; or, in another instance, his ideas of Dante and of Shakespeare.

And the term "idea" is used, in the present discussion, in the sense which James and other representative pragmatists have made familiar in current discussion. Let us then hold clearly in mind this definition of the term "idea." For we shall even thereby be led to note facts which will lead us beyond what this definition emphasizes.

An idea, in this sense, is a more or less practical and active process, a "leading" as James calls it, whereby some set of conceptions and perceptions tend to be brought into desirable connections. An idea may consist mainly of some effort to characterize the data of perception through the use of fitting conceptions. Or, again, an idea may be a prediction of future perceptions. Or, an idea may be an active seeking for a way to translate conceptual "bank-notes" into perceptual cash. In any one idea, either the perceptual or the conceptual elements may, at any one moment, predominate. If the conceptual element is too marked for our purposes, the idea stands in need of perceptual fulfilment. If the perceptual element is too rich for our momentary interests, the idea needs further conceptual clarification. In any case, however, according to this view, the motives of an idea are practical, and the constituents of an idea are either the data of perception, or the conceptual processes whereby we characterize or predict or pursue such data.

But when, in Peirce's sense of the word, we have to make an explicit comparison, we have before us two distinct and contrasting ideas. It is their distinctness, it is their contrast, which determines our task. And these ideas involve, in general, not only different perceptual and different conceptual constituents, but also different and sometimes conflicting "leadings," different and sometimes mutually clashing interests, various and mutually estranged motives, activities, or constructions. These two ideas may contrast as do two forms of art. Or they may stand out the one over against the other as if they were two geometrical structures. They may collide as do two warring passions. They may first meet as simple strangers in our inner world. Their relations may resemble those of plaintiff and defendant in a suit at law. Or they may be as interestingly remote from one another as are the spiritual realms of two great poets. In such endlessly various fashions may the two ideas come before us.

The essential fact for our present study is that, in case of the comparisons which Peirce discusses, the problem, whether you call it a theoretical or a practical problem, is not that of linking percepts to their fitting concepts, nor that of paying the bank bills of conception in the gold of the corresponding perceptions. On the contrary, it is the problem either of arbitrating the conflicts; or of bringing to mutual understanding the estrangements; or of uniting in some community the separated lives of these two distinct ideas,—of ideas which, when left to themselves, decline to coalesce or to coöperate, or to enter into one life.

This problem, in the cases of comparison with which Peirce deals, is solved through a new act. For this act originality and sometimes even genius may be required. This new act consists in the invention or discovery of some third idea, distinct from both the ideas which are to be compared. This third idea, when once found, interprets one of the ideas which are the objects of the comparison, and interprets it to the other, or in the light of the other. What such interpretation means, the instances already considered have in part made clear. But the complexity and the significance of the processes involved require a further study. And this further study may here be centred about the question: What is gained by the sort of comparison which Peirce thus characterizes? And, since we have said that all such comparison involves an activity of interpreting one idea in the light of another, we may otherwise state our question thus: What, in these cases of comparison, is the innermost aim of the Will to Interpret which all these processes of comparison manifest?

## VI

The rhythm of the Hegelian dialect, wherein thesis, antithesis, and higher synthesis play their familiar parts, will here come to the minds of some who follow my words; and you may ask wherein Peirce's processes of comparison and interpretation differ from those dialectical movements through division into synthesis, which Hegel long since used as the basis of his philosophy. I reply at once that Peirce's theory of comparison, and of the mediating idea or "third" which interprets, is historically speaking, a theory not derived from Hegel, by whom at the time when he wrote these early logical papers, Peirce had been in no notable way influenced. I reply, further, that Peirce's concept of interpretation defines an extremely general process, of which the Hegelian dialectical triadic process is a very special case. Hegel's elementary illustrations of his own processes are ethical and historical. Peirce's theory of comparison is quite as well illustrated by purely mathematical as by explicitly social instances. There is no essential inconsistency between the logical and psychological motives which lie at the basis of Peirce's theory of the triad of interpretation, and the Hegelian interest in the play of thesis, antithesis, and higher synthesis. But Peirce's theory, with its explicitly empirical origin and its very exact logical working out, promises new light upon matters which Hegel left profoundly problematic.

Returning, however, to those illustrations of Peirce's theory of comparison which I have already placed before you, let us further consider the motives which make a comparison of distinct and contrasting ideas significant for the one who compares.

An idea, as I have said, is, in James's sense, a practical "leading." An idea, if, in James's sense, successful, and if successfully employed, leads through concepts to the desirable or to the corresponding percepts. But a comparison of ideas—that, too, is no doubt an active process. To what does it lead? It leads, as we have seen, to a new, to a third, to an interpreting idea. And what is this new idea? Is it "cash," or has it only "credit-value"? What does it present to our view? What does it bring to our treasury?

One must for the first answer this question in a very old-fashioned way. The new, the third, the interpreting idea, in these elementary cases of comparison, shows us, as far as it goes, ourselves, and also creates in us a new grade of clearness regarding what we are and what we mean. First, I repeat, the new or third idea shows us ourselves, as we are. Next, it also enriches our world of self-consciousness. It at once broadens our outlook and gives our mental realm definiteness and self-control. It teaches one of our ideas what another of our ideas means. It tells us how to know our right hand from the left; how to connect what comes to us in fragments; how to live as if life had some coherent aim. All this is indeed, thus far, very elementary information about what one gains by being able to hold three ideas at once in mind. But, in our own day, such information is important information. For our age, supposing that the contrast between perception and conception exhausts the possible types of cognitive processes, is accustomed to listen to those who teach us that self-knowledge also must be either intuitive (and, in that case, merely fluent and transient) or else conceptual (and, in that case, abstract and sterile).

But a dual antithesis between perceptual and conceptual knowledge is once for all inadequate to the wealth of the facts of life. When you accomplish an act of comparison, the knowledge which you attain is neither merely conceptual, nor merely perceptual, nor yet merely a practically active synthesis of perception and conception. It is a third type of knowledge. It interprets. It surveys from above. It is an attainment of a larger unity of consciousness. It is a conspectus. As the tragic artist looks down upon the many varying lives of his characters, and sees their various motives not interpenetrating, but coöperating, in the dramatic action which constitutes his

creation,—so any one who compares distinct ideas, and discovers the third or mediating idea which interprets the meaning of one in the light of the other, thereby discovers, or invents, a realm of conscious unity which constitutes the very essence of the life of reason.

Bergson, in his well-known portrayal, has glorified instinct in its contrast with the intellect. The intellect, as he holds, is a mere user of tools. Its tools are concepts. It uses them in its practical daily work to win useful percepts. It loves to be guided in its daily industries by rigid law. It is therefore most at home in the realm of mechanism and of death. Life escapes its devices. Its concepts are essentially inadequate. Instinct, on the contrary, so far as man still preserves that filmy cloud of luminous instinct and of intuition which, in Bergson's opinion, constitutes the most precious resource of genius, perceives, and sympathizes, and so comes in touch with reality.

That this account of the cognitive process is inadequate, both the artist and the prophets combine with the scientific observers of nature, with the mathematicians, and with the great constructive statesmen, to show us. Comparison is the instrument of what one may call, according to one's pleasure, either the observant reason, or the rational intuition whereby the world's leading minds have always been guided. And it is comparison, it is interpretation, which teaches us how to deal with the living, with the significant, and with the genuinely real.

Darwin, for instance, as a naturalist, saw, compared, and mediated. We all know how the leading ideas of Malthus furnished the mediating principle, the third, whereby Darwin first came to conceive how the contrasting ideas with which his hypotheses had to deal could be brought into unity. And that such comparison is peculiarly adapted to deal with the phenomena of life, let not only the genesis of Darwin's ideas, but the place of the process of comparison in the development of all the organic sciences, show.

If we turn to the other extreme of the world of human achievement, in order to learn what is the sovereign cognitive process, we shall find the same answer. For let us ask,—By means of what insight did Amos the prophet meet the religious problems of his own people and of his own day? He faced tragic contrasts, moral, religious, and political. Warring ideas were before him,—ideas, each of which sought its own percepts, through its own concepts of God, of worship, and of success. But Amos introduced into the controversies of his time the still tragic, but inspiring and mediating, idea of the God who, as he declared, delights not in sacrifices but in righteousness. And by this one stroke of religious genius the prophet directed the religious growth of the centuries that were to follow.

Think over the burial psalm, or the Pauline chapters on Charity and the Resurrection, if you would know what part comparison and mediation play in the greatest expressions of the religious consciousness. Remember Lear or the Iliad, if you wish to recall the functions of contrast and of mediation in poetry. Let the Sistine Madonna or Beethoven's Fifth Symphony illustrate the same process in other forms of the artistic consciousness.

If once you have considered a few such instances, then, summing up their familiar lessons, you may note that in none of these cases is it conception, in none of them is it bare perception, least of all is it inarticulate intuition, which has won for us the greatest discoveries, the incomparable treasures in science, in art, or in religion.

The really creative insight has come from those who first compared and then mediated, who could first see two great ideas at once, and then find the new third idea which mediated between them, and illumined.

We often use the word "vision" for this insight which looks down upon ideas as from above, and discovers the "third," thereby uniting what was formerly estranged. If by the word "intuition" one chooses to mean this grade of insight, then one may indeed say that creative mental prowess depends, in general, upon such intuition. But such intuition is no mere perception. It is certainly not conception. And the highest order of genius depends upon reaching the stage of Peirce's "third" type of

ideas. Comparison, leading to the discovery of that which mediates and solves, and to the vision of unity, is the psychological basis of poetry, as Shakespeare wrote, and of such prophecy as Paul praised when he estimated the spiritual gifts. Comparison, then, and interpretation constitute the cognitive function whereby we deal with life. Instinct and bare perception, left to themselves, can never reach this level.

# VII

When we consider the inner life of the individual man, the Will to Interpret appears, then, as the will to be self-possessed. One who compares his own ideas, views them as from above. He aims to pass from blind "leadings" to coherent insight and to resolute self-guidance. What one wins as the special object of one's insight depends, in such cases, upon countless varying psychological conditions, and upon one's success in finding or in inventing suitable mediators for the interpretation of one idea in the light of another. It may therefore appear as if in this realm of interior comparisons, where the objects compared are pairs of ideas, and where results of comparison consist in the invention of a third, there could be no question of attaining fixed or absolute truth. If anywhere pragmatism could be decisively victorious; if anywhere the purely relative and transient would seem in possession of the field,—one might suppose that comparison would constantly furnish us with instances of relative, shifting, and fluent truth.

As a fact, however, this is not the case. Comparison, which is so powerful an instrument in dealing with life, and with the fluent and the personal, is also perfectly capable of bringing us into the presence of the exact and of the necessary. All depends upon what ideas are compared, and upon the purpose for which they are compared, and upon the skill with which the vision of unity is attained.

Let the comparison of the two ring-strips of paper show what I here have in mind. The difference between a ring-strip which contains as single twist, and another which is constructed in the usual way, seems at first sight to be both insignificant and inexact. A closer study shows that the geometry of surfaces that possess but a single side can be developed into as exact a branch of pure mathematics as you can mention. The development in question would depend upon assuming, quite hypothetically, a few simple principles which are suggested, although not indeed capable of being proved, by experience of the type which recent pragmatism has well analyzed. The branch of pure mathematics in question would consist of deductions from these few single principles. The deductions would interpret these principles, viewed in some sort of unity and compared together.

But recent pragmatism has not well analyzed the process whereby, in pure mathematics, the consequences which follow from a set of exactly stated hypotheses are determined. This process, the genuine process of deduction, depends upon a series of ideal experiments. These experiments are performed by means of putting together ideas, two and two, by comparing the ideas that are thus brought together, by discovering mediators, and by reading the results of the combination. This process may lead to perfectly exact results which are absolutely true.

I know of no writer who has better or more exactly analyzed the way in which such ideal experiments can lead to novel and precise results than Peirce has done. His analysis of the deductive process was first made a good while since, and anticipated results which Mr. Bertrand Russell and others have since reached by other modes of procedure.

Peirce has shown that, when you interpret your combinations of ideas through ideal experiments, using, for instance, diagrams and symbols as aids, the outcome may be a truth as exact as the ideas compared are themselves exact. It may also be in your own experience as novel a result as your ideal experiment is novel. It may also be an absolute and immutable truth.

What you discover, in a case of deduction, is not that certain conclusions are, in themselves, considered true, but that they follow from, that they are implied by, certain hypothetically assumed premises. But a discovery that certain premises imply a certain conclusion, is the discovery of a fact. This fact may be found, not by perception, nor by conception, but by interpretation. None the less, it is a fact and it may be momentous.

It is customary to imagine that such a deductive process can get out of given premises nothing novel, but only (as people often say)—only what was already present in the premises. This customary view of deduction is incorrect. As Peirce repeatedly pointed out (long before any other writer had explicitly dealt with the matter), you can write out upon a very few sheets of paper all the principles which are actually used as the fundamental hypotheses that lie at the basis of those branches of pure mathematics which have thus far been developed. Yet the logical consequences which follow from these few mathematical hypotheses are so numerous that every year a large octavo volume in fine print is needed to contain merely the titles, and very brief abstracts, of the technical papers containing novel results which have been, during that year, published as researches in pure mathematics.

The mathematical papers in question embody, in general, consequences already implied by the few fundamental hypotheses which I have just mentioned. An infinite wealth of still unknown consequences of the same principles remains yet to be explored and stated. All of these consequences can be won, in pure mathematics, by a purely deductive procedure.

Thus endlessly wealthy, thus possessed of an inexhaustible fecundity, is the genuine deductive process. Peirce long ago showed why. And while the mathematical procedure which is in question cannot here be further discussed, it is enough for our present purpose to indicate why this fecundity of deduction exists.

## VIII

Deduction, in the real life of the exact sciences, is a process that recent pragmatism has no means of describing, simply because recent pragmatism is the prey of the dual classification of the cognitive processes, and views what it calls the "workings" of ideas merely in terms of the relations between conceptions and perceptions,—between "credit-values" and "cash-values."

Pragmatism, as James defined it, regards an idea as a "leading," whereby one pursues or seeks particulars; and whereby one sometimes obtains, and sometimes fails to obtain, the "cash-values" which one aims to get. Such a doctrine has no place for the understanding of what happens when, looking down as it were from above, one compares two ideas, and looks for a mediating idea. But just this is what happens in all cases of explicit comparison.

Now in the individual case, an interpretation, a mediating idea, may come to mind through almost any play of association, or as the result of almost any degree of skill in invention, or as the outcome either of serious or of playful combinations. In consequence, an interpretation may prove to be, in the single case, of purely relative and momentary truth and value.

But this, on the other hand, need not be the fortune of interpretation. The results of a comparison may express absolute truths,—truths which once seen can never be reversed. This absoluteness itself may be due to either one of two reasons.

In pure mathematics, a deduction, if correct at all, leads to an absolutely correct and irrevocably true discovery of a relation of implication between exactly stated premises and some conclusion. Deduction does this because deduction results from a comparison, and because the ideas compared may be, and in pure mathematics are, exact enough to suggest, at some moment, to the observant reasoner, an interpretation which, if it applies at all, applies universally to every pair of ideas identical in meaning with the pair of ideas here compared.

The act of comparison may be momentary, and may even be as an event, an accident. The inventive watcher of his own ideas may have been led to his deduction by whatever motive you please. But the interpretation, once discovered, may nevertheless represent a truth which is absolute precisely *because* it is hypothetical. For the assertion: "P implies Q," or "If P, then Q," is an assertion about a matter of fact. And this assertion, if true at all, is always and irrevocably true about the same pair of ideas or propositions: P and Q.

Or again, the result of an interpretation may be absolutely true, because, for whatever reason, the interpretation in question counsels the one who makes the interpretation to do some determinate and individual deed. This deed may be such as to accomplish at the moment when it is done, some ideally valuable result. But deeds once done are irrevocable. If, by interpreting your ideas in a certain way, at a certain moment, you have been led to do a worthy deed,—then the interpretation remains as irrevocably true as the good deed remains irrevocably done.

The principle, then, relating to the value and to the truth of one's acts of interior and conscious comparison, is that they express an insight which surveys, as from above, an unity wherein are combined various ideas. These ideas, as they first come, are pragmatic leadings which may be mutually estranged, or mutually hostile, or widely contrasted, or intimately interconnected. But, whatever the ideas may have been before they were compared,—as a result of the comparison of the two ideas, one of them is interpreted in the light of the other. The interpretation may possess all the exactness of mathematics, or all the transiency of a chance observation of the play of one's inner life. It may result in Paul's vision of the charity that never faileth, ruling supreme over the contrasts and the bickerings of passing passion; or it may solve a problem of comparative natural history or of comparative philology. Whatever the varieties of the cases in question, comparison can occur, and can reach truth, simply because we are wider than any of our ideas, and can win a vision which shall look down upon our own inner warfare, and upon our own former self-estrangements, as well as upon our own inner contrasts of exact definition. This vision observes not data of sense and not mere abstract concepts. Nor does it consist simply in our pragmatic leadings, and in their successes and failures. It observes what may interpret ideas to other ideas; as prophets and poets interpret to us what otherwise would remain, in seeming, hopelessly various and bewilderingly strange. It is not more intuition that we want. It is such interpretation which alone can enlighten and guide and significantly inspire. Upon the comparisons which thus interpret, our spiritual triumphs depend. Such triumphs are not merely the pragmatic successes of single ideas. They are the attainment of mastery over life.

## IX

Our lengthy study of comparison and interpretation, as they are present in the inner life of the individual man, has prepared us for a new view of the social meaning of the Will to Interpret. Here I must once more take a temporary leave of Peirce's guidance, and trust to my own resources.

One who compares a pair of his own ideas may attain, if he is successful, that vision of unity, that grade of self-possession, which we have now illustrated. But one who undertakes to interpret his neighbor's ideas is in a different position.

In general as we have seen, an interpreter, in his social relations with other men, deals with two different minds, neither of which he identifies with his own. His interpretation is a "third" or mediating idea. This "third" is aroused in the interpreter's mind through signs which come to him from the mind that he interprets. He addresses this "third" to the mind to which he interprets the first. The psychology of the process of social interpretation, so far as that process goes on in the interpreter's individual mind, is identical with that psychology of comparison which we have now outlined. Nobody can interpret, unless the idea which he interprets has become more or less clearly and explicitly one of his own ideas, and unless he compares it with another idea which is, in some sense, his own.

But, from the point of view of the interpreter, the essential difference between the case where he is interpreting the mind of one of his neighbors to the mind of another neighbor, and the case wherein he is comparing two ideas of his own, is a difference in the clearness of vision which is, under human conditions, attainable.

When I compare two ideas of my own, the luminous self-possession which then, for a time, may come to be mine, forms for me an ideal of success in interpretation. This ideal I can attain only at moments. But these moments set a model for all my interpretations to follow.

When I endeavor to interpret my neighbor's mind, my interpretation has to remain remote from its goal. The luminous vision of the results of comparison comes to me, at best, only partially and with uncertainty. My neighbor's ideas I indeed in a measure grasp, and compare with other ideas, and interpret; but, as I do this, I see through a glass darkly. Only those ideas whose comparisons with other ideas, and whose resulting triadic interpretations I can view face to face, can appear to me to have become in a more intimate and complete sense my own individual ideas. When I possess certain ideas sufficiently to enable me to seek for their interpretation, but so that, try as I will, I can never clearly survey, as from above, the success of any of my attempted interpretations,—then these ideas remain, from my own point of view, ideas that never become wholly my own. Therefore these relatively alien ideas can be interpreted at all only by using the familiar hypothesis that they belong to the self of some one else. Under ordinary social conditions this other mind is viewed as the mind of my neighbor. Neither of my neighbor nor of myself have I any direct intuition. But of my own ideas I can hope to win the knowledge which the most successful comparisons exemplify. Of my neighbor's ideas I can never win, under human conditions, any interpretation but one which remains hypothetical, and which is never observed, under these human conditions, as face to face with its own object, or with the idea of the other neighbors to whom the interpretation is addressed.

The Will to Interpret is, in our social relations, guided by a purpose which we are now ready to bring into close relations with the most significant of all the ethical ideals which, in our foregoing lectures, we have portrayed.

The interpreter, the mind to which he addresses his interpretation, the mind which he undertakes to interpret,—all these appear, in our explicitly human and social world, as three distinct selves,—sundered by chasms which, under human conditions, we never cross, and contrasting in their inner lives in whatever way the motives of men at any moment chance to contrast.

The Will to Interpret undertakes to make of these three selves a Community. In every case of ideally serious and loyal effort truly to interpret this is the simplest, but, in its deepest motives, the most purely spiritual of possible communities. Let us view that simple and ideal community as the interpreter himself views it, precisely in so far as he is sincere and truth-loving in his purpose as interpreter.

# X

I, the interpreter, regard you, my neighbor, as a realm of ideas, of "leadings," of meanings, of pursuits, of purposes. This realm is not wholly strange and incomprehensible to me. For at any moment, in my life as interpreter, I am dependent upon the results of countless previous efforts to interpret. The whole past history of civilization has resulted in that form and degree of interpretation of you and of my other fellow-men which I already possess, at any instant when I begin afresh the task of interpreting your life or your ideas. You are to me, then, a realm of ideas which lie outside of the centre which my will to interpret can momentarily illumine with the clearest grade of vision. But I am discontent with my narrowness and with your estrangement. I seek unity with you. And since the same will to interpret you is also expressive of my analogous interests in all my other neighbors, what I here and now specifically aim to do is this: I mean to interpret you to somebody else, to some other neighbor, who is neither yourself nor myself. Three of us, then, I seek to bring into the desired unity of interpretation.

Now if I could succeed in interpreting you to another man as fully as, in my clearest moments, I interpret one of my ideas to another, my process of interpretation would simply reduce to a conscious comparison of ideas. I should then attain, as I succeeded in my interpretation, a luminous vision of your ideas, of my own, and of the ideas of the one to whom I interpret you. This vision would look down, as it were, from above. In the light of it, we, the selves now sundered by the chasms of the social world, should indeed not interpenetrate. For our functions as the mind interpreted, the mind to whom the other is interpreted, and the interpreter, would remain as distinct as now they are. There would be no melting together, no blending, no mystic blur, and no lapse into mere intuition. But for me the vision of the successful interpretation would simply be the attainment of my own goal as interpreter. This attainment would as little confound our persons as it would divide our substance. We should remain, for me, many, even when viewed in this unity.

Yet this vision, if I could win it, would constitute an event wherein your will to be interpreted would also be fulfilled. For if you are indeed ready to accept my service as interpreter, you even now possess this will to be interpreted. And if there exists the one to whom I can interpret you, that other also wills that you should be interpreted to him, and that I should be the interpreter.

If, then, I am worthy to be an interpreter at all, we three,—you, my neighbor, whose mind I would fain interpret,—you, my kindly listener, to whom I am to address my interpretation,—we three constitute a Community. Let us give to this sort of community a technical name. Let us call it a Community of Interpretation.

The form of such a community is determinate.

One goal lies before us all, one event towards which we all direct our efforts when we take part in this interpretation. This ideal event is a goal, unattainable under human social conditions, but definable, as an ideal, in terms of the perfectly familiar experience which every successful comparison of ideas involves. It is a goal towards which we all may work together: you, when you give me the signs that I am to interpret; our neighbor, when he listens to my interpretation; I, when I devote myself to the task.

This goal:—Our individual experience of our successful comparisons of our own ideas shows us wherein it consists, and that it is no goal which an abstract conception can define in terms of credit-values, and that it is also no goal which a possible perception can render to me in the cash of any set of sensory data. Yet it is a goal which each of us can accept as his own. I can at present aim to approach that goal through plans, through hypotheses regarding you which can be inductively tested. I can view that goal as a common future event. We can agree upon that goal. And herewith I interpret not only you as the being whom I am to interpret, but also myself as in ideal the interpreter who aims to approach the vision of the unity of precisely this community. And you, and my other neighbor to whom I address my interpretation, can also interpret yourselves accordingly.

The conditions of the definition of our community will thus be perfectly satisfied. We shall be many selves with a common ideal future event at which we aim. Without essentially altering the nature of our community, our respective offices can be, at our pleasure, interchanged. You, or my other neighbor, can at any moment assume the function of interpreter; while I can pass to a new position in the new community. And yet, we three shall constitute as clearly as before a Community of Interpretation. The new community will be in a perfectly definite relation to the former one; and may grow out of it by a process as definite as is every form of conscious interpretation.

Thus there can arise, in our community, no problem regarding the one and the many, the quest and the goal, the individual who approaches the goal by one path or by another,—no question to which the definition of the community of interpretation will not at once furnish a perfectly precise answer.

Such an answer will be based upon the perfectly fundamental triadic relation which is essential to every process of interpretation, whether such process takes place within the inner life of an individual human being, or goes on in the world of ordinary social intercourse.

## XI

Thus, then, if I assume for the moment the rôle of an interpreter, I can define my office, my Community of Interpretation, and my place in that community.

It will be observed that the sort of truth which, as interpreter, I seek, cannot be stated in terms as simple as those with which the current pragmatism is satisfied. My interpretation, if I offer to our common neighbor any interpretation of your mind, will of course be an idea of my own,—namely, precisely that "third" idea which I contribute to our community as my interpretation of you. And no doubt I shall desire to make as sure as I can that this idea of mine "works." But no data of my individual perception can ever present to me the "workings" which I seek.

For I want my interpretation of you to our neighbor to be such as you would accept and also such as our neighbor would comprehend, were each of us already in the position of the ideal observer from above, whose vision of the luminous unity of my interpretation and its goal I am trying to imitate whenever I try to interpret your mind.

Thus, from the outset, the idea which I offer as my interpretation of your mind, is offered not for the sake of, or in the pursuit of, any individual or private perception of my own, either present or expected or possible. I am not looking for workings that could conceivably be rendered in my perceptual terms. I am ideally aiming at an ideal event,—the spiritual unity of our community. I can define that unity in perfectly empirical terms; because I have compared pairs of ideas which were my own, and have discovered their mediating third idea. But I do not expect to perceive that unity as any occurrence in my own individual life, or as any working of one of my own personal ideas. In brief, I have to define the truth of my interpretation of you in terms of what the ideal observer of all of us would view as the unity which he observed. This truth cannot be defined in merely pragmatic terms.

In a community thus defined, the interpreter obviously assumes, in a highly significant sense, the chief place. For the community is one of interpretation. Its goal is the ideal unity of insight which the interpreter would possess were these who are now his neighbors transformed into ideas of his own which he compared; that is, were they ideas between which his own interpretation successfully mediated. The interpreter appears, then, as the one of the three who is most of all the spirit of the community, dominating the ideal relations of all three members.

But the one who is, in ideal, this chief, is so because he is first of all servant. His office it is to conform to the mind which he interprets, and to the comprehension of the mind to which he addresses his interpretation. And his own ideas can "work" only if his self-surrender, and his conformity to ideas which are not his own, is actually a successful conformity; and only if his approach to a goal which, as a member of a human community of interpretation, he can never reach, is a real approach.

## XII

Such are the relationships which constitute a Community of Interpretation. I beg you to observe, as we close, the ethical and religious significance which the structure of such a community makes possible. In case our interpretations actually approach success, a community of interpretation possesses such ethical and religious significance, with increasing definiteness and beauty as the evolution of such a community passes from simpler to higher stages.

Upon interpretation, as we have already seen, every ideal good that we mortals win

together, under our human social conditions, depends. Whatever else men need, they need their communities of interpretation.

It is indeed true that such communities can exist, at any time, in the most various grades of development, of self-consciousness, and of ideality. The communities of interpretation which exist in the market-places of the present social world, or that lie at the basis of the diplomatic intercourse of modern nations, are communities whose ideal goal is seldom present to the minds of their members; and it is not love which often seems to be their consciously ruling motive.

Yet, on the whole, it is not perception, and it is not conception; while it certainly is interpretation which is the great humanizing factor in our cognitive processes and which makes the purest forms of love for communities possible. Loyalty to a community of interpretation enters into all the other forms of true loyalty. No one who loves mankind can find a worthier and more significant way to express his love than by increasing and expressing among men the Will to Interpret. This will inspires every student of the humanities; and is present wherever charity enters into life. When Christianity teaches us to hope for the community of all mankind, we can readily see that the Beloved Community, whatever else it is, will be, when it comes, a Community of Interpretation. When we consider the ideal form and the goal of such a community, we see that in no other form, and with no other ideal, can we better express the constitution of the ideal Church, be that conceived as the Church on earth, or as the Church triumphant in some ideal realm of super-human and all seeing insight, where I shall know even as I am known.

And, if, in ideal, we aim to conceive the divine nature, how better can we conceive it than in the form of the Community of Interpretation, and above all in the form of the Interpreter, who interprets all to all, and each individual to the world, and the world of spirits to each individual.

In such an interpreter, and in his community, the problem of the One and the Many would find its ideally complete expression and solution. The abstract conceptions and the mystical intuitions would be at once transcended, and illumined, and yet retained and kept clear and distinct, in and through the life of one who, as interpreter, was at once servant to all and chief among all, expressing his will through all, yet, in his interpretations, regarding and loving the will of the least of these brethren. In him the Community, the Individual, and the Absolute would be completely expressed, reconciled, and distinguished.

This, to be sure, is, at this point of our discussion, still merely the expression of an ideal, and not the assertion of a metaphysical proposition. But in the Will to Interpret, the divine and the human seem to be in closest touch with each other.

The mere form of interpretation may be indeed momentarily misused for whatever purpose of passing human folly you will. But if the ideal of interpretation is first grasped; and if then the Community of Interpretation is conceived as inclusive of all individuals; and as unified by the common hope of the far-off event of complete mutual understanding; and, finally, if love for this community is awakened,—then indeed this love is able to grasp, in ideal, the meaning of the Church Universal, of the Communion of Saints, and of God the Interpreter.

Merely to define such ideals is not to solve the problems of metaphysics. But it is to remove many obstacles from the path that leads towards insight.

These ideals, however, are grasped and loved whenever one first learns fully to comprehend what Paul meant when he said: "Wherefore let him that speaketh with tongues pray that he may interpret." This word is but a small part of Paul's advice. But in germ it contains the whole meaning of the office, both of philosophy and of religion.

# Loyalty to Loyalty, Truth, and Reality

We have deliberately declined, so far, to consider what the causes are to which men ought to be loyal. To turn to this task is the next step in our philosophy of loyalty. . . .

Now, it is obvious that nobody can be equally and directly loyal to all of the countless actual social causes that exist. It is obvious also that many causes which conform to our general definition of a possible cause may appear to any given person to be hateful and evil causes, to which he is justly opposed. A robber band, a family engaged in a murderous feud, a pirate crew, a savage tribe, a Highland robber clan of the old days—these might constitute causes to which somebody has been, or is, profoundly loyal. Men have loved such cases devotedly, have served them for a lifetime. Yet most of us would easily agree in thinking such causes unworthy of anybody's loyalty. Moreover, different loyalties may obviously stand in mutual conflict, whenever their causes are opposed. Family feuds are embittered by the very strength of the loyalty of both sides. My country, if I am the patriot inflamed by the warspirit, seems an absolutely worthy cause; but my enemy's country usually seems hateful to me just because of my own loyalty; and therefore even my individual enemy may be hated because of the supposed baseness of his cause. War-songs call the individual enemy evil names just because he possesses the very personal qualities that, in our own loyal fellow-countrymen, we most admire. "No refuge could save the hireling and

From *The Philosophy of Loyalty* (New York: Macmillan Company, 1908), pp. 107–146, 307–348.

slave." Our enemy, as you see, is a slave, because he serves his cause so obediently. Yet just such service we call, in our own country's heroes, the worthiest devotion.

Meanwhile, in the foregoing account of loyalty as a spiritual good to the loyal man, we have insisted that true loyalty, being a willing devotion of the self to its cause, involves some element of autonomous choice. Tradition has usually held that a man ought to be loyal to just that cause which his social station determines for him. Common sense generally says, that if you were born in your country, and still live there, you ought to be loyal to that country, and to that country only, hating the enemies across the border whenever a declaration of war requires you to hate them. But we have declared that true loyalty includes some element of free choice. Hence our own account seems still further to have complicated the theory of loyalty. For in answering in our last lecture the ethical individualists who objected to loyalty, we have ourselves deliberately given to loyalty an individualistic coloring. And if our view be right, and if tradition be wrong, so much the more difficult appears to be the task of defining wherein consists that which makes a cause worthy of loyalty for a given man, since tradition alone is for us an insufficient guide. . . .

. . . If loyalty is a supreme good, the mutually destructive conflict of loyalties is in general a supreme evil. If loyalty is a good for all sorts and conditions of men, the war of man against man has been especially mischievous, not so much because it has hurt, maimed, impoverished, or slain men, as because it has so often robbed the defeated of their causes, of their opportunities to be loyal, and sometimes of their very spirit of loyalty.

If, then, we look over the field of human life to see where good and evil have most clustered, we see that the best in human life is its loyalty; while the worst is whatever has tended to make loyalty impossible, or to destroy it when present, or to rob it of its own while it still survives. And of all things that thus have warred with loyalty, the bitterest woe of humanity has been that so often it is the loyal themselves who have thus blindly and eagerly gone about to wound and to slay the loyalty of their brethren. The spirit of loyalty has been misused to make men commit sin against this very spirit, holy as it is. For such a sin is precisely what any wanton conflict of loyalties means. Where such a conflict occurs, the best, namely, loyalty, is used as an instrument in order to compass the worst, namely, the destruction of loyalty.

It is true, then, that some causes are good, while some are evil. But the test of good and evil in the causes to which men are loyal is now definable in terms which we can greatly simplify in view of the foregoing considerations.

If, namely, I find a cause, and this cause fascinates me, and I give myself over to its service, I in so far attain what, for me, if my loyalty is complete, is a supreme good. But my cause, by our own definition, is a social cause, which binds many into the unity of one service. My cause, therefore, gives me, of necessity, fellow-servants, who with me share this loyalty, and to whom this loyalty, if complete, is also a supreme good. So far, then, being loyal myself, I not only get but give good; for I help to sustain, in each of my fellow-servants, his own loyalty, and so I help him to secure his own supreme good. In so far, then, my loyalty to my cause is also a loyalty to my fellows' loyalty. But now suppose that my cause, like the family in a feud, or like the pirate ship, or like the aggressively warlike nation, lives by the destruction of the loyalty of other families, or of its own community, or of other communities. Then, indeed, I get a good for myself and for my fellow-servants by our common loyalty; but I war against this very spirit of loyalty as it appears in our opponent's loyalty to his own cause.

And so, a cause is good, not only for me, but for mankind, in so far as it is essentially a *loyalty to loyalty,* that is, is an aid and a furtherance of loyalty in my fellows. It is an evil cause in so far as, despite the loyalty that it arouses in me, it is destructive of loyalty in the world of my fellows. My cause is, indeed, always such as to involve some loyalty to loyalty, because, if I am loyal to any cause at all, I have fellow-servants whose loyalty mine supports. But in so far as my cause is a predatory cause, which lives by overthrowing the loyalties of others, it is an evil cause, because it involves disloyalty to the very cause of loyalty itself.

. . . since my loyalty is never my mere fate, but is always also my choice, I can of course determine my loyalty, at least to some extent, by the consideration of the actual good and ill which my proposed cause does to mankind. And since I now have the main criterion of the good and ill of causes before me, I can define a principle of choice which may so guide me that my loyalty shall become a good, not merely to myself, but to mankind.

This principle is now obvious. I may state it thus: In so far as it lies in your power, so choose your cause and so serve it, that, by reason of your choice and of your service, there shall be more loyalty in the world rather than less. And, in fact, so choose and so serve your individual cause as to secure thereby the greatest possible increase of loyalty among men. More briefly: *In choosing and in serving the cause to which you are to be loyal, be, in any case, loyal to loyalty.*

This precept, I say, will express how one should guide his choice of a cause, in so far as he considers not merely his own supreme good, but that of mankind. That such autonomous choice is possible, tends, as we now see, not to complicate, but to simplify our moral situation. For if you regard men's loyalty as their fate, if you think that a man must be loyal simply to the cause which tradition sets before him, without any power to direct his own moral attention, then indeed the conflict of loyalties seems an insoluble problem; so that, if men find themselves loyally involved in feuds, there is no way out. But if, indeed, choice plays a part,—a genuine even if limited part, in directing the individual's choice of the cause to which he is to be loyal, then indeed this choice may be so directed that loyalty to the universal loyalty of all mankind

shall be furthered by the actual choices which each enlightened loyal person makes when he selects his cause. . . .

. . . Here would be for me not only an unity of inner and outer, but an unity with the unity of all human life. What I sought for myself I should then be explicitly seeking for my whole world. All men would be my fellow-servants of my cause. In principle I should be opposed to no man's loyalty. I should be opposed only to men's blindness in their loyalty. I should contend only against that tragic disloyalty to loyalty which the feuds of humanity now exemplify. I should preach to all others, I should strive to practise myself, that active mutual furtherance of universal loyalty which is what humanity obviously most needs, if indeed loyalty, just as the willing devotion of a self to a cause, is a supreme good.

And since all who are human are as capable of loyalty as they are of reason, since the plainest and the humblest can be as true-hearted as the great, I should nowhere miss the human material for my task. I should know, meanwhile, that if indeed loyalty, unlike the "mercy" of Portia's speech, is not always mightiest in the mightiest, it certainly, like mercy, becomes the throned monarch better than his crown. So that I should be sure of this good of loyalty as something worthy to be carried, so far as I could carry it, to everybody, lofty or humble.

Thus surely it would be humane and reasonable for me to define my cause to myself,—if only I could be assured that there is indeed some practical way of making loyalty to loyalty the actual cause of my life. Our question therefore becomes this: Is there a practical way of serving the universal human cause of loyalty to loyalty? And if there is such a way, what is it? Can we see how personally so to act that we bring loyalty on earth to a fuller fruition, to a wider range of efficacy, to a more effective sovereignty over the lives of men? If so, then indeed we can see how to work for the cause of the genuine kingdom of heaven.

Yet I fear that as you have listened to this sketch of a possible and reasonable cause, such as could be a proper object of our loyalty, you will all the while have objected: This may be a definition of a possible cause, but it is an unpractical definition. For what is there that one can do to further the loyalty of mankind in general? Humanitarian efforts are an old story. They constantly are limited in their effectiveness both by the narrowness of our powers, and by the complexity of the human nature which we try to improve. And if any lesson in philanthropy is well known, it is this, that whoever tries simply to help mankind as a whole, loses his labor, so long as he does not first undertake to help those nearest to him. Loyalty to the cause of universal loyalty— how, then, shall it constitute any practical working scheme of life?

I answer at once that the individual man, with his limited powers can indeed serve the cause of universal loyalty only by limiting his undertakings to some decidedly definite personal range. He must have his own special and personal cause. But this cause of his can indeed be chosen and determined so as to constitute a deliberate effort to further universal loyalty. When I begin to show you how this may be, I shall at once pass from what may have seemed to you a very unpractical scheme of life, to a realm of familiar and commonplace virtuous activities. The only worth of my general scheme will then lie in the fact that, in the light of this scheme, we can, as it were, see the commonplace virtues transfigured and glorified by their relation to the one highest cause of all. My thesis is *that all the commonplace virtues, in so far as they are indeed defensible and effective, are special forms of loyalty to loyalty, and are to be justified, centralized, inspired, by the one supreme effort to do good, namely, the effort to make loyalty triumphant in the lives of all men.*

The first consideration which I shall here insist upon is this: Loyalty, as we have all along seen, depends upon a very characteristic and subtle union of natural interest, and of free choice. Nobody who merely follows his natural impulses as they come is loyal. Yet nobody can be loyal without depending upon and using his natural impulses. If I am to be loyal, my cause must from moment to moment fascinate me, awaken my muscular vigor, stir me with some eagerness for work, even if this be painful work. I cannot be loyal to barren abstractions. I can only be loyal to what my life can interpret in bodily deeds. Loyalty has its elemental appeal to my whole organism. My cause must become one with my human life. Yet all this must occur not without my willing choice. I must control my devotion. It will possess me, but not without my voluntary complicity; for I shall accept the possession. It is, then, with the cause to which you personally are loyal, as it was with divine grace in an older theology. The cause must control you, as divine grace took saving control of the sinner; but only your own will can accept this control, and a grace that merely compels can never save.

Now that such an union of choice with natural interest is possible, is a fact of human nature, which every act of your own, in your daily calling, may be used to exemplify. You cannot do steady work without natural interest; but whoever is the mere prey of this passing interest does no steady work. Loyalty is a perfect synthesis of certain natural desires, of some range of social conformity, and of your own deliberate choice.

In order to be loyal, then, to loyalty, I must indeed first choose forms of loyal conduct which appeal to my own nature. This means that, upon one side of my life, I shall have to behave much as the most unenlightened of the loyal do. I shall serve causes such as my natural temperament and my social opportunities suggest to me. I shall choose friends whom I like. My family, my community, my country, will be served partly because I find it interesting to be loyal to them.

Nevertheless, upon another side, all these my more natural and, so to speak, accidental loyalties, will be controlled and unified by a deliberate use of the principle that, whatever my cause, it ought to be such as to further, so far as in me lies, the cause of universal loyalty. Hence I shall not permit my choice of my special causes to remain a mere chance. My causes must form a system. They must constitute in their entirety a single cause, my life of loyalty. When apparent conflicts arise amongst the causes in which I am interested, I shall deliberately undertake, by devices which we shall hereafter study in these lectures, to reduce the conflict to the greatest possible harmony. Thus, for instance, I may say, to one of the causes in which I am naturally bound up:—

> *I could not love thee, dear, so much,*
> *Loved I not honour more.*

And in this familiar spirit my loyalty will aim to be, even within the limits of my own personal life, an united, harmonious devotion, not to various conflicting causes, but to one system of causes, and so to one cause.

Since this one cause is my choice, the cause of my life, my social station will indeed suggest it to me. My natural powers and preferences will make it fascinating to me, and yet I will never let mere social routine, or mere social tradition, or mere private caprice, impose it upon me. I will be individualistic in my loyalty, carefully insisting, however, that whatever else I am, I shall be in all my practical activity, a loyal individual, and, so far as in me lies, one who chooses his personal causes for the sake of the spread of universal loyalty. Moreover, my loyalty will be a growing loyalty. Without giving up old loyalties I shall annex new ones. There will be evolution in my loyalty.

The choice of my cause will in consequence be such as to avoid unnecessary conflict with the causes of others. So far I shall indeed negatively show loyalty to loyalty. It shall not be my cause to destroy other men's loyalty. Yet since my cause, thus chosen and thus organized, still confines me to my narrow personal range, and since I can do so little directly for mankind, you may still ask whether, by such a control of my natural interests, I am indeed able to do much to serve the cause of universal loyalty.

Well, it is no part of the plan of this discourse to encourage illusions about the range of influence that any one poor mortal can exert. But that by the mere force of my practical and personal loyalty, if I am indeed loyal, I am doing something for the cause of universal loyalty, however narrow my range of deeds, this a very little experience of the lives of other people tends to teach me. For who, after all, most encourages and incites me to loyalty? I answer, any loyal human being, whatever his cause, so long as his cause does not arouse my hatred, and does not directly injure my chance to be loyal. My fellow's special and personal cause need not be directly mine. Indirectly he inspires me by the very contagion of his loyalty. He sets me the example. By his loyalty he shows me the worth of loyalty. Those humble and obscure folk of whom I have before spoken, how precious they are to us all as inspiring examples, because of their loyalty to their own.

From what men, then, have I gained the best aid in discovering how to be myself loyal? From the men whose personal cause is directly and consciously one with my own? That is indeed sometimes the case. But others, whose personal causes were apparently remote in very many ways from mine, have helped me to some of my truest glimpses of loyalty.

. . . Loyalty, then, is contagious. It infects not only the fellow-servant of your own special cause, but also all who know of this act. Loyalty is a good that spreads. Live it and you thereby cultivate it in other men. Be faithful, then, so one may say, to the loyal man; be faithful over your few things, for the spirit of loyalty, secretly passing from you to many to whom you are a stranger, may even thereby make you unconsciously ruler over many things. Loyalty to loyalty is then no unpractical cause. And you serve it not by becoming a mere citizen of the world, but by serving your own personal cause. We set before you, then, no unpractical rule when we repeat our moral formula in this form: Find your own cause, your interesting, fascinating, personally engrossing cause; serve it with all your might and soul and strength; but so choose your cause, and so serve it, that thereby you show forth your loyalty to loyalty, so that because of your choice and service of your cause, there is a maximum of increase of loyalty amongst your fellow-men.

. . . Herewith we approach a thesis which is central in my whole philosophy of loyalty. I announced that thesis in other words in the opening lecture. My thesis is that *all those duties which we have learned to recognize as the fundamental duties of the civilized man, the duties that every man owes to every man, are to be rightly interpreted as special instances of loyalty to loyalty.* In other words, all the recognized virtues can be defined in terms of our concept of loyalty. And this is why I assert that, when rightly interpreted, loyalty is the whole duty of man.

For consider the best-known facts as to the indirect influence of certain forms of loyal conduct. When I speak the truth, my act is directly an act of loyalty to the personal tie which then and there binds me to the man to whom I consent to speak. My special cause is, in such a case, constituted by this tie. My fellow and I are linked in a certain unity,—the unity of some transaction which involves our speech one to another. To be ready to speak the truth to my fellow is to have, just then, no eye to see and no tongue to speak save as this willingly accepted tie demands. In so far, then, speaking the truth is a special instance of loyalty. But whoever speaks the truth, thereby does what he then can do to help everybody to speak the truth. For he acts so as to further the general confidence of man in man. How far such indirect influence can extend, no man can predict.

Precisely so, in the commercial world, honesty in business is a service, not merely and not mainly to the others who are parties to the single transaction in which at any one time this faithfulness is shown. The single act of business fidelity is an act of loyalty to that general confidence of man in man upon which the whole fabric of business rests. On the contrary, the unfaithful financier whose disloyalty is the final deed that lets loose the avalanche of a panic, has done far more harm to general public confidence than he could possibly do to those whom his act directly assails. Honesty, then, is owed not merely and not even mainly to those with whom we directly deal when we do honest acts; it is owed to mankind at large, and it benefits the community and the general cause of commercial loyalty.

Such a remark is in itself a commonplace; but it serves to make concrete my general thesis that every form of dutiful action is a case of loyalty to loyalty. For what holds thus of truthfulness and of commercial honesty holds, I assert, of every form of dutiful action. Each such form is a special means for being, by a concrete deed, loyal to loyalty.

We have sought for the worthy cause; and we have found it. This simplest possible of considerations serves to turn the chaotic mass of separate precepts of which our ordinary conventional moral code consists into a system unified by the one spirit of universal loyalty. By your individual deed you indeed cannot save the world, but you can at any moment do what in you lies to further the cause which both for you and for the human world constitutes the supreme good, namely, the cause of universal loyalty. Herein consists your entire duty.

Review in the light of this simple consideration, the usually recognized range of human duties. How easily they group themselves about the one principle: *Be loyal to loyalty.*

Have I, for instance, duties to myself? Yes, precisely in so far as I have the duty to be actively loyal at all. For loyalty needs not only a willing, but also an effective servant. My duty to myself is, then, the duty to provide my cause with one who is strong enough and skilful enough to be effective according to my own natural powers. The care of health, self-cultivation, self-control, spiritual power—these are all to be morally estimated with reference to the one principle that, since I have no eyes to see or tongue to speak save as the cause commands, I will be as worthy an instrument of the cause as can be made, by my own efforts, out of the poor material which my scrap of human nature provides. The highest personal cultivation for which I have time is thus required by our principle. But self-cultivation which is not related to loyalty is worthless.

Have I private and personal rights, which I ought to assert? Yes, precisely in so far as my private powers and possessions are held in trust for the cause, and are, upon occasion, to be defended for the sake of the cause. My rights are morally the outcome of my loyalty. It is my right to protect my service, to maintain my office, and to keep my own merely in order that I may use my own as the cause commands. But rights which are not determined by my loyalty are vain pretence.

As to my duties to my neighbors, these are defined by a well-known tradition in terms of two principles, justice and benevolence. These two principles are mere aspects of our one principle. Justice means, in general, fidelity to human ties in so far as they are ties. Justice thus concerns itself with what may be called the mere forms in which loyalty expresses itself. Justice, therefore, is simply one aspect of loyalty—the more formal and abstract side of loyal life. If you are just, you are decisive in your choice of your personal cause, you are faithful to the loyal decision once made, you keep your promise, you speak the truth, you respect the loyal ties of all other men, and you contend with other men only in so far as the defence of your own cause, in the interest of loyalty to the universal cause of loyalty, makes such contest against aggression unavoidable. All these types of activity, within the limits that loyalty determines, are demanded if you are to be loyal to loyalty. Our principle thus at once requires them, and enables us to define their range of application. But justice, without loyalty, is a vicious formalism.

Benevolence, on the other hand, is that aspect of loyalty which directly concerns itself with your influence upon the inner life of human beings who enjoy, who suffer, and whose private good is to be affected by your deeds. Since no personal good that your fellow can possess is superior to his own loyalty, your own loyalty to loyalty is itself a supremely benevolent type of activity. And since your fellow-man is an instrument for the furtherance of the cause of universal loyalty,

his welfare also concerns you, in so far as, if you help him to a more efficient life, you make him better able to be loyal. Thus benevolence is an inevitable attendant of loyalty. And the spirit of loyalty to loyalty enables us to define wherein consists a wise benevolence. Benevolence without loyalty is a dangerous sentimentalism. Thus viewed, then, loyalty to universal loyalty is indeed the fulfilment of the whole law.

What must be true about the universe if even loyalty itself is a genuine good, and not a merely inevitable human illusion?

Well, loyalty is a service of causes. A cause, if it really is what our definition requires, links various human lives to the unity of one life. Therefore, if loyalty has any basis in truth, human lives can be linked in some genuine spiritual unity. Is such unity a fact, or is our belief in our causes a mere point of view, a pathetic fallacy? Surely, if any man, however loyal, discovers that his cause is a dream, and that men remain as a fact sundered beings, not really linked by genuine spiritual ties, how can that man remain loyal? Perhaps his supreme good indeed lies in believing that such unities are real. But if this belief turns out to be an illusion, and if a man detects the illusion, can he any longer get the good out of loyalty?

. . . How paradoxical a world, then, must the real world be, if the faith of the loyal is indeed well founded! A spiritual unity of life, which transcends the individual experience of any man, must be real. For loyalty, as we have seen, is a service of causes that, from the human point of view, appear superpersonal. Loyalty holds these unities to be good. If loyalty is right, the real goodness of these causes is never completely manifested to any one man, or to any mere collection of men. Such goodness, then, if completely experienced at all, must be experienced upon some higher level of consciousness than any one human being ever reaches. If loyalty is right, social causes, social organizations, friendships, families, countries, yes, humanity, as you see, must have the sort of unity of consciousness which individual human persons fragmentarily get, but must have this unity upon a higher level than that of our ordinary human individuality.

Some such view, I say, must be held if we are to regard loyalty as in the end anything more than a convenient illusion. Loyalty has its metaphysical aspect. It is an effort to conceive human life in an essentially superhuman way, to view our social organizations as actual personal unities of consciousness, unities wherein there exists an actual experience of that good which, in our loyalty, we only partially apprehend. If the loyalty of the lovers is indeed well founded in fact, then, they, as separate individuals, do not constitute the whole truth. Their spiritual union also has a personal, a conscious existence, upon a higher than human level. An analogous unity of consciousness, an unity superhuman in grade, but intimately bound up with, and inclusive of, our apparently separate personalities, must exist, if loyalty is well founded, wherever a real cause wins the true devotion of ourselves. Grant such an hypothesis, and then loyalty becomes no pathetic serving of a myth. The good which our causes possess, then, also becomes a concrete fact for an experience of a higher than human level. That union of self-sacrifice with self-assertion which loyalty expresses becomes a consciousness of our genuine relations to a higher social unity of consciousness in which we all have our being. For from this point of view we are, and we have our worth, by virtue of our relation to a consciousness of a type superior to the human type. And meanwhile the good of our loyalty is itself a perfectly concrete good, a good which is present to that higher experience, wherein our cause is viewed in its truth, as a genuine unity of life. And because of this fact we can straightforwardly say: We are loyal not for the sake of the good that we privately get out of loyalty, but for the sake of the good that the cause—this higher unity of experience—gets out of this loyalty. Yet our loyalty gives us what is, after all, our supreme good, for it defines our true position in the world of that social will wherein we live and move and have our being.

I doubt not that such a view of human life,—such an assertion that the social will is a concrete entity, just as real as we are, and of still a higher grade of reality than ourselves,—will seem to many of you mythical enough. Yet thus to view the unity of human life is, after all, a common tendency of the loyal. The fact I have illustrated in every lecture in this course. That such a view need not be mythical, that truth and reality can be conceived only in such terms as these, that our philosophy of loyalty is a rational part of a philosophy which must view the whole world as one unity of consciousness, wherein countless lesser unities are synthesized,—this is a general philosophical thesis which I must next briefly expound to you.

My exposition, as you see, must be, in any case, an attempt to show that the inevitable faith of the loyal—their faith in their causes, and in the real goodness of their causes—has truth, and since I must thus, in any case, discourse of truth, I propose briefly to show you that whoever talks of any sort of truth whatever, be that truth moral or scientific, the truth of a common sense or the truth of a philosophy, inevitably implies, in all his assertions about truth, that the world of truth of which he speaks is a world possessing a rational and spiritual unity, is a conscious world of experience, whose type of consciousness is higher in its level than is the type of our human minds, but whose life is such that our life belongs as part to this living whole. This world of truth is the one that you must define, so I insist, if you are to regard any proposition whatever as true, and are then to tell, in a reasonable way, what you mean by the truth of that proposition.

The world of truth is therefore essentially a world such as that in whose reality the loyal believe when they believe their cause to be real. Moreover, this truth world has a goodness about it, essentially like that which the loyal attribute to their causes. Truth seeking and loyalty are therefore essentially the same process of life merely viewed in two different aspects. Whoever is loyal serves what he takes to be a truth, namely, his cause. On the other hand, whoever seeks truth for its own sake fails of his own business if he seeks it merely as a barren abstraction, that has no life in it. If a truth seeker knows his business, he is, then, in the sense of our definition, serving a cause which unifies our human life upon some higher level of spiritual being than the present human level. He is therefore essentially loyal. Truth seeking is a moral activity; and on the other hand, morality is wholly inadequate unless the light of eternal truth shines upon it.

This, I say, will be my thesis. Some of you will call it very mystical, or at least a very fantastic thesis. It is not so. It ought to be viewed as a matter of plain sense. It is, I admit, a thesis which many of the most distinguished amongst my colleagues, who are philosophers, nowadays view sometimes with amusement, and sometimes with a notable impatience. This way of regarding the world of truth, which I have just defined as mine, is especially and most vivaciously attacked by my good friends, the pragmatists,—a group of philosophers who have of late been disposed to take truth under their especial protection, as if she were in danger from the tendency of some people who take her too seriously.

When I mention pragmatism, I inevitably bring to your minds the name of one whom we all honor,—the philosopher who last year so persuasively stated, before the audience of this Institute, the pragmatist theory of philosophical method, and of the nature of truth. It is impossible for me to do any justice, within my limits, to the exposition which Professor James gave of his own theory of truth. Yet since the antithesis between his views and those which I have now to indicate to you may be in itself an aid to my own exposition, I beg you to allow me to use, for the moment, some of his assertions about the nature of truth as a means of showing, by contrast, how I find myself obliged to interpret the same problem. The contrast is accompanied, after all, by so much of deeper agreement that I can well hope that my sketch of the current situation in the philosophical controversies about truth may not seem to you merely a dreary report of differences of opinion.

Professor James, in discussing the nature of truth, in his recent book on pragmatism, begins, as some of you will remember, by accepting the classic definition of truth as the agreement of our ideas with reality. Whoever knows or possesses a truth has, then, in his mind, an idea, an opinion, a judgment, or some complex of such states of mind. If his views are true, then these his ideas or opinions are in agreement with something called reality. Thus, for instance, if a loyal man believes his cause, say, his friendship or his club or his nation, to be a reality, and if his belief is true, his loyal opinion is in agreement with the real world. So far, of course, all of you will accept the definition of truth here in question.

Professor James now goes on to point out that, in some cases, our ideas agree with what we call real things by copying those things. So, if, with shut eyes, you think of the clock on the wall, your image of the clock is a copy of its dial. But, as my colleague continues, our power to copy real objects by ideas of our own is obviously a very limited power. You believe that you have at least some true ideas about many objects which are far too complex or too mysterious for you to copy them. Your power to become sure that your ideas do copy the constitution of anything whatever which exists outside of you is also very limited, because, after all, you never get outside of your own experience to see what the real things would be if taken wholly in themselves. hence, on the whole, one cannot say that the agreement of our ideas with reality which constitutes their truth is essentially such as to demand that our ideas should be copies. For we believe that we have true ideas even when we do not believe them to be copies.

Moreover (and herewith we approach a consideration which is, for my colleague's theory of truth, very essential), not only does truth not consist merely in copying facts; but also truth cannot be defined in terms of any other static or fixed relation between ideas and facts. The only way to conceive that agreement between ideas and facts which constitutes truth is to think of the "practical consequences" which follow from possessing true ideas. "True ideas," in Professor Jame's words, "lead us, namely, through the acts and other ideas which they instigate, into or up to or towards other parts of experience with which we feel all the while that the original ideas remain in agreement. The connections and transitions come to us, from point to point, as being progressive, harmonious, satisfactory. This function of agreeable leading is what we mean by an idea's verification." So far my colleague's words. He goes on, in his account, to mention many illustrations of the way in which the truth of ideas is tested, both in the world of common sense, and in the world of science, by the usefulness, by the success, which attaches to the following out of true ideas to their actual empirical consequences. The wanderer lost in the woods gets true ideas about his whereabouts whenever he hits upon experiences and ideas which set him following the path which actually leads him home. In science, hypotheses are tested as to their truth, by considering what experiences they lead us to anticipate, and by then seeing whether these anticipations can be fulfilled in a satisfactory way. "True," says Professor James, "is the name for whatever idea starts the verification process." For instance, then, the verifiable scientific hypothesis, if once tested by the success of its results in experience, is in so far declared true. And similarly, the idea of following a given path in the woods in order to get home is declared true, if you follow the path and get home.

In consequence, every true idea is such in so far as it is useful in enabling you to anticipate the sort of experience that you want; and every idea that is useful as a guide of life is in so far true. The personal tests of usefulness, as of truth, are for every one of us personal and empirical. My own direct tests of truth are of course thus limited to my own experience. I find my own ideas true just in so far as I find them guiding me to the experience that I want to get. But of course, as my colleague constantly insists, we give credit, as social beings, to one another's verifications. Hence I regard as true many ideas that I personally have not followed out to any adequately experienced

consequences. The "overwhelmingly large" number of the ideas by which we live, "we let pass for true without attempting to verify." We do this, says Professor James, "because it *works* to do so, everything we know conspiring with the belief, and nothing interfering." That is, we regard as true those ideas which we personally find it convenient, successful, expedient to treat as verifiable, even though we never verify them. The warrant of these unverifiable truths is, however, once more, the empirical usefulness of living as if they were verifiable. "Truth lives," says Professor James, "for the most part on a credit system. . . . But this all points to direct face-to-face verification somewhere, without which the fabric of truth collapses like a financial system with no cash basis whatever. You accept my verification of one thing, I yours of another. We trade on each other's truth. But beliefs verified concretely by *somebody* are the posts of the whole superstructure." The indirectly verifiable ideas, that is, the ideas which somebody else verifies, or even those which nobody yet verifies, but which agree sufficiently with verified ideas, we accept because it is advantageous to accept them. It is the same thing, then, to say that an idea is true because it is useful and to say that it is useful because it is true.

Agreement with reality thus turns out, as my colleague insists, "to be an affair of leading,—leading that is useful because it is into quarters that contain objects that are important." And my colleague's account of truth culminates in these notable expressions: "'The true,' to put it very briefly, is only the expedient in the way of our thinking, just as 'the right' is only the expedient in the way of our behaving." "Pragmatism faces forward towards the future." That is, an idea is true by virtue of its expedient outcome. "It pays for our ideas to be validated, verified. Our obligation to seek truth is part of our general obligation to do what pays. The payment true ideas bring are the sole why of our duty to follow them."

The sum and substance of this theory of truth, as you see, is that the truth of an idea is determined by its "success" in yielding what my colleague frequently calls "the cash values in terms of experience," which appear as consequences of holding this idea. These values may either take the form of direct verifications in terms of sensible facts, as when one finds one's way out of the woods and sees one's home; or else the form of practically satisfying and expedient beliefs, which clash with no sensible experience, and which are personally acceptable to those who hold them. It is "expedient" to connect the latter beliefs with sensible cash values when you can. If you cannot turn them into such cash, you are at liberty to hold them, but with the conviction that, after all, the personally expedient is the true.

In any case, as you see, whatever else truth is, it is nothing static. It changes with the expediencies of your experience. And therefore those who conceive the realm of truth as essentially eternal are the objects of my colleague's most charming philosophical fury.

We have, then, an authoritative exposition of pragmatism before us. You must see that this doctrine, whether it be true doctrine, or whether it be indeed simply for some people an expedient doctrine, is certainly one that concerns our philosophy of loyalty, now that indeed we have reached the place where the relation between loyalty and truth has become, for us, a critically important relation. May we venture to ask ourselves, then: Is this pragmatism a fair expression of what we mean by truth?

In reply let me at once point out the extent to which I personally agree with my colleague, and accept his theory of truth. I fully agree with him that whenever a man asserts a truth, his assertion is a deed,—a practical attitude, an active acknowledgment of some fact. I fully agree that the effort to verify this acknowledgment by one's own personal experience, and the attempt to find truth in the form of a practical congruity between our assertions and our attained empirical results, is an effort which in our individual lives inevitably accompanies and sustains our every undertaking in the cause of truth seeking. Modern pragmatism is not indeed as original

as it seems to suppose itself to be in emphasizing such views. The whole history of modern idealism is full of such assertions. I myself, as a teacher of philosophy, have for years insisted upon viewing truth in this practical way. I must joyously confess to you that I was first taught to view the nature of truth in this way when I was a young student of philosophy; and I was taught this by several great masters of modern thought. These masters were Kant, Fichte, Hegel, and Professor James himself, whose lectures, as I heard them in my youth at the Johns Hopkins University, and whose beautiful conversations and letters in later years, inspired me with an insight that helped me, rather against his own advice, to read my German idealists aright, and to see what is, after all, the eternal truth beneath all this pragmatism. For Professor James's pragmatism, despite its entertaining expressions of horror of the eternal, actually does state one aspect of eternal truth. It is, namely, eternally true that all search for truth is a practical activity, with an ethical purpose, and that a purely theoretical truth, such as should guide no significant active process, is a barren absurdity. This, however, is so far precisely what Fichte spent his life in teaching. Professor James taught me, as a student, much the same lesson; and I equally prize and honor all of my masters for that lesson; and I have been trying to live up to it ever since I first began to study the nature of truth.

So far, then, I am a pragmatist. And I also fully agree that, if we ever get truth, the attainment of truth means a living and practical success in those active undertakings in terms of which we have been trying to assert and to verify our truth. I doubt not that to say, "This is true," is the same as to say: "The ideas by means of which I define this truth are the practically and genuinely successful ideas, the ideas such that, when I follow them, I really fulfil my deepest needs." All this I not only admit; but I earnestly insist that truth is an ethical concept; and I thank from my heart the great pragmatist who so fascinated his audience last year in this place; I thank him that he taught them what, in my youth, he helped to teach me, namely, that winning the truth means winning the success which we need, and for which the whole practical nature of our common humanity continually groans and travails together in pain until now.

And yet, and yet all this still leaves open one great question. When we seek truth, we indeed seek successful ideas. But what, in Heaven's name, constitutes success? Truth-seeking is indeed a practical endeavor. But what, in the name of all the loyal, is the goal of human endeavor? Truth is a living thing. We want leading and guidance. "Lead, kindly light,"—thus we address the truth. We are lost in the woods of time. We want the way, the truth, and the life. For nothing else does all our science and our common sense strive. But what is it to have genuine abundance of life? For what do we live?

Here our entire philosophy of loyalty, so far as it has yet been developed, comes to our aid. The loyal, as we have said, are the only human beings who can have any reasonable hope of genuine success. If they do not succeed, then nobody succeeds. And of course the loyal do indeed live with a constant, although not with an exclusive, reference to their own personal experience and to that of other individual men. They feel their present fascination for their cause. It thrills through them. Their loyalty has, even for them, in their individual capacity what Professor James calls a cash value. And of course they like to have their friends share such cash values. Yet I ask you: Are the loyal seeking *only* the mere collection of their private experiences of their personal thrills of fascination? If you hear loyal men say: "We are in this business just for what we as individuals—we and our individual fellows—can get out of it," do you regard that way of speech as an adequate expression of their really loyal spirit? When Arnold von Winkelried rushed on the Austrian spears, did he naturally say: "Look you, my friends, I seek, in experiential terms, the cash value of my devotion; see me draw the cash." My colleague would of course retort that the hero in question, according to the legend, said, as he died: "Make way for

liberty." He therefore wanted liberty, as one may insist, to get these cash values. Yes, but liberty was no individual man, and no mere heap of individual men. Liberty was a cause, a certain superhuman unity of the ideal life of a free community. It was indeed expedient that one man should die for the people. But the people also was an *unio mystica* of many in one. For that cause the hero died. And no man has ever yet experienced, in his private and individual life, the whole true cash value of that higher unity. Nor will all the individual Swiss patriots, past, present, or future, viewed as a mere collection of creatures of a day, ever draw the cash in question. If the cause exists, the treasure exists, and is indeed a cash value upon a level higher than that of our passing human life. But loyalty does not live by selling its goods for present cash in the temple of its cause. Such pragmatism it drives out of the temple. It serves, and worships, and says to the cause: "Be thine the glory."

Loyalty, then, seeks success and from moment to moment indeed thrills with a purely fragmentary and temporary joy in its love of its service. But the joy depends on a belief in a distinctly superhuman type of unity of life. And so you indeed cannot express the value of your loyalty by pointing at the mere heap of the joyous thrills of the various loyal individuals. The loyal serve a real whole of life, an experiential value too rich for any expression in merely momentary terms.

Now, is it not very much so with our love of any kind of truth? Of course, we mortals seek for whatever verification of our truths we can get in the form of present success. But can you express our human definition of truth in terms of any collection of our human experiences of personal expediency?

Well, as to our concept of truth, let us consider a test case by way of helping ourselves to answer this question. Let us suppose that a witness appears, upon some witness-stand, and objects to taking the ordinary oath, because he has conscientious scruples, due to the fact that he is a recent pragmatist, who has a fine new definition of truth, in terms of which alone he can be sworn. Let us suppose him, hereupon, to be granted entire liberty to express his oath in his own way. Let him accordingly say, using, with technical scrupulosity, my colleague's definition of truth: "I promise to tell whatever is expedient and nothing but what is expedient, so help me future experience." I ask you: Do you think that this witness has expressed, with adequacy, that view of the nature of truth that you really wish a witness to have in mind? Of course, if he were a typical pragmatist, you would indeed be delighted to hear his testimony on the witness-stand or anywhere else. But would you accept his formula?

But let me be more precise as to the topic of this witness's possible testimony. I will use for the purpose Kant's famous case. Somebody, now dead, let us suppose, has actually left with the witness a sum of money as a wholly secret deposit to be some time returned. No written record was made of the transaction. No evidence exists that can in future be used to refute the witness if he denies the transaction and keeps the money. The questions to be asked the witness relate, amongst other things, to whatever it may be that he believes himself to know about the estate of the deceased. I now ask, not what his duty is, but simply what it is that he rationally means to do in case he really intends to tell the truth about that deposit. Does he take merely the "forward-looking" attitude of my colleague's pragmatism? Does he mean merely to predict, as expedient, certain consequences which he expects to result either to him or to the heirs of the estate? Of course his testimony will have consequences. But is it these which he is trying to predict? Are they his true object? Or does the truth of his statement mean the same as the expediency, either to himself or to the heirs, of any consequence whatever which may follow from his statement? Does the truth of his statement about the deposit even mean the merely present empirical fact that he now feels a belief in this statement or that he finds it just now congruent with the empirical sequences of his present memories? No, for the witness is not trying merely to tell how he feels. He is trying to tell the truth about the

deposit. And the witness's belief is not the truth of his belief. Even his memory is not the truth to which he means to be a witness. And the future consequences of his making a true statement are for the witness irrelevant, since they are for the law and the heirs to determine. Yet one means something perfectly definite by the truth of the testimony of that witness. And that truth is simply inexpressible in such terms as those which my colleague employs. Yet the truth here in question is a simple truth about the witness's own personal past experience.

Now, such a case is only one of countless cases where we are trying to tell the truth about something which we all regard as being, in itself, a matter of genuine and concrete experience, while nevertheless we do not mean, "It is expedient just now for me to think this," nor yet, "I predict such and such consequences for my own personal experience, or for the future experience of some individual man; and these predicted consequences constitute the truth of my present assertion." I say there are countless such cases where the truth that we mean is empirical indeed, but transcends all such expediencies and personal consequences. The very assertion, "Human experience, taken as a totality of facts, exists," is a momentous example of just such an assertion. We all believe that assertion. If that assertion is not actually true, then our whole frame of natural science, founded as it is on the common experience of many observers, crumbles into dust, our common sense world is nothing, business and society are alike illusions, loyalty to causes is meaningless. Now that assertion, "Human experience, that is, the totality of the experiences of many men, really exists," is an assertion which you and I regard as perfectly true. Yet no individual man has ever verified, or ever will verify, that assertion. For no man, taken as this individual man, experiences the experience of anybody but himself. Yet we all regard that assertion as true.

My colleague, of course, would say, as in fact he has often said, that his assertion is one of the numerous instances of that process of trading on credit which he so freely illustrates.

We do not verify this assertion. But we accept it on credit as verifiable. However, the credit simile is a dangerous one here, so long as one conceives that the verification which would pay the cash would be a payment in the form of such human experience as you and I possess. For the assertion, "The experience of many men exists," is an assertion that is essentially unverifiable by any one man. If the "cash value" of the assertion means, then, its verifiability by any man, then the credit in question is one that simply cannot be turned into such cash by any conceivable process, occurring in our individual lives, since the very idea of the real existence of the experience of many men excludes, by its definition, the direct presence of this experience of various men within the experience of any one of these men. The credit value in question would thus be a *mere* fiat value, so long as the only cash values are those of the experiences of individual men, and the truth of our assertion would mean simply that we find it expedient to treat as verifiable what we know cannot be verified. Hereupon, of course, we should simply be trading upon currency that has no cash value. Whoever does verify the fact that the experience of many men exists, if such a verifier there be, is a superhuman being, an union of the empirical lives of many men in the complex of a single experience. And if our credit of the assertion that many men exist is convertible into cash at all, that cash is not laid up where the moth and rust of our private human experience doth from moment to moment corrupt the very data that we see; but is laid up in a realm where our experiences, past, present, future, are the object of a conspectus that is not merely temporal and transient. Now all the natural sciences make use of the persuasion that the experiences of various men exist, and that there is a unity of such experiences. This thesis, then, is no invention of philosophers.

My colleague, in answer, would of course insist that as a fact you and I are now believing that many men exist, and that human experience in its entirety exists, *merely* because, in the long run, we find that this belief is indeed congruous with our current and purely personal experience, and is therefore an expedient idea of ours. But I, in answer, insist that common sense well feels this belief to be indeed from moment to moment expedient, and yet clearly distinguishes between that expediency and the truth which common sense all the while attributes to the belief. The distinction is precisely the one which my fancied illustration of the pragmatist on the witness-stand has suggested. It is a perfectly universal distinction and a commonplace one. Tell me, "This opinion is true," and whatever you are talking about I may agree or disagree or doubt; yet in any case you have stated a momentous issue. But tell me, "I just now find this belief expedient, it feels to me congruous" and you have explicitly given me just a scrap of your personal biography, and have told me no other truth whatever than a truth about the present state of your feelings.

If, however, you emphasize my colleague's wording to the effect that a truth is such because it proves to be an idea that is expedient "in the long run," I once more ask you: *When* does a man experience the whole of the real facts about the "long run"? At the beginning of the long run, when the end is not yet, or at the end, when, perhaps, he forgets, like many older men, what were once the expediencies of his youth? What decides the truth about the long run? My exalted moments, when anything that I like seems true, or my disappointed moments, when I declare that I have always had bad luck? To appeal to the genuinely real "long run" is only to appeal in still another form to a certain ideally fair conspectus of my own whole life,—a conspectus which I, in my private human experience, never get. Whoever gets the conspectus of my whole life, to see what, in the long run, is indeed for me expedient,—whoever, I say, gets that conspectus, if such a being there indeed is,—is essentially superhuman in his type of consciousness. For he sees what I only get in the form of an idea; namely, the true sense and meaning of my life.

In vain, then, does one try adequately to define the whole of what we mean by truth either in terms of our human feelings of expediency or in terms of our instantaneous thrills of joy in success, or in terms of any other verifications that crumble as the instant flies. All such verifications we use, just as we use whatever perishes. Any such object is a fragment, but we want the whole. Truth is itself a cause, and is largely as one must admit, for us mortals, just now, what we called, in our last lecture, a lost cause—else how should these pragmatists be able thus to imagine a vain thing, and call that truth which is but the crumbling expediency of the moment? Our search for truth is indeed a practical process. The attainment of truth means success. Our verifications, so far as we ever get them, are momentary fragments of that success. But the genuine success that we demand is an ethical success, of precisely the type which all the loyal seek, when they rejoice in giving all for their cause.

But you will now all the more eagerly demand in what sense we can ever get any warrant for saying that we know any truth whatever. In seeking truth we do not seek the mere crumbling successes of the passing instants of human life. We seek a city out of sight. What we get of success within our passing experience is rationally as precious to us as it is, just because we believe that attainment to be a fragment of an essentially superhuman success, which is won in the form of a higher experience than ours,—a conspectus wherein our human experiences are unified. But what warrant have we for this belief?

I will tell you how I view the case. We need unity of life. In recognizing that need my own pragmatism consists. Now, we never find unity present to our human experience in more than a fragmentary shape. We get hints of higher unity. But only the fragmentary unity is won at any moment of our lives. We therefore form ideas—very fallible ideas—of some unity of experience, at unity such as our idea of any science or any art or any united people or of any community or of any other cause, any other union of many human experiences in one, defines. Now, if our ideas are in any case indeed true, then such an unity is as a fact successfully experienced upon some higher

level than ours, and is experienced in some conspectus of life which wins what we need, which approves our loyalty, which fulfils our rational will, and which has in its wholeness what we seek. And then we ourselves with all our ideas and strivings are in and of this higher unity of life. Our loyalty to truth is a hint of this unity. Our transient successes are fragments of the true success. But suppose our ideas about the structure of this higher unity to be false in any of their details. Suppose, namely, any of our causes to be wrongly viewed by us. Then there is still real that state of facts, whatever it is, which, if just now known to us, would show us this falsity of our various special ideas. Now, only an experience, a consciousness of some system of contents, could show the falsity of any idea. Hence this real state of facts, this constitution of the genuine universe, whatever it is, must again be a reality precisely in so far as it is also a conspectus of facts of experience.

We therefore already possess at least one true idea, precisely in so far as we say: "The facts of the world are what they are; the real universe exposes our errors and makes them errors." And when we say this, we once more appeal to a conspectus of experience in which ours is included. For I am in error only in case my present ideas about the true facts of the whole world of experience are out of concord with the very meaning that I myself actively try to assign to these ideas. My ideas are in any detail false, only if the very experience to which I mean to appeal, contains in its conspectus contents which I just now imperfectly conceive. In any case, then, the truth is possessed by precisely that whole of experience which I never get, but to which my colleague also inevitably appeals when he talks of the "long run," or of the experiences of humanity in general.

Whatever the truth, then, or the falsity of any of my special convictions about this or that fact may be, the real world, which refutes my false present ideas in so far as they clash with its wholeness, and which confirms them just in so far as they succeed in having significant relations to its unity,—this real world, I say, is a conspectus of the whole of experience. And this whole of experience is in the closest real relation to my practical life, precisely in so far as, for me, the purpose of my life is to get into unity with the whole universe, and precisely in so far as the universe itself is just that conspectus of experience that we all mean to define and to serve whatever we do, or whatever we say.

But the real whole conspectus of experience, the real view of the totality of life, the real expression of that will to live in and for the whole, which every assertion of truth and every loyal deed expresses—well, it must be a conspectus that includes whatever facts are indeed facts, be they past, present, or future. I call this whole of experience an eternal truth. I do not thereby mean, as my colleague seems to imagine, that the eternal first exists, and that then our life in time comes and copies that eternal order. I mean simply that the whole of experience includes all temporal happenings, contains within itself all changes, and, since it is the one whole that we all want and need, succeeds in so far as it supplements all failures, accepts all, even the blindest of services, and wins what we seek. Thus winning it is practically good and worthy.

But if one insists, How do you know all this? I reply: I know simply that to try to deny the reality of this whole of truth is simply to reaffirm it. Any special idea of mine may be wrong, even as any loyal deed may fail, or as any cause may become, to human vision, a lost cause. But to deny that there is truth, or that there is a real world, is simply to say that the whole truth is that there is no whole truth, and that the real fact is that there is no fact real at all. Such assertions are plain self-contradictions. And on the other hand, by the term "real world," defined as it is for us by our ideal needs, we mean simply that whole of experience in which we live, and in unity with which we alone succeed.

Loyalty, then, has its own metaphysic. This metaphysic is expressed in a view of things which conceives our experience as bound up in a real unity with all experience,—a unity which is essentially good, and in which all our ideas possess their real fulfilment and success. Such a view is true, simply because if you deny its truth you reaffirm that very truth under a new form.

Truth, meanwhile, means, as pragmatism asserts, the fulfilment of a need. But we all need the superhuman, the city out of sight, the union with all life,—the essentially eternal. This need is no invention of the philosophers. It is the need which all the loyal feel, whether they know it or not, and whether they call themselves pragmatists or not. To define this need as pragmatism in its recent forms has done, to reduce truth to expediency, is to go about everything *cash, cash,* in a realm where there is no cash of the sort that loyalty demands, that every scientific inquiry presupposes, and that only the unity of the experiences of many in one furnishes.

If we must, then, conceive recent pragmatism under the figure of a business enterprise,—a metaphor which my colleague's phraseology so insistently invites,—I am constrained therefore to sum up its position thus: First, with a winning clearness, and with a most honorable frankness it confesses bankruptcy, so far as the actually needed cash payments of significant truth are concerned. Secondly, it nevertheless declines to go into the hands of any real receiver, for it is not fond of anything that appears too absolute. And thirdly, it proposes simply and openly to go on doing business under the old style and title of the truth. "After all," it says, "are we not, every one of us, fond of credit values?"

But I cannot conceive the position of the loyal to be, in fact, so hopelessly embarrassed as this. The recent pragmatists themselves are, in fact, practically considered very loyal lovers of genuine truth. They simply have mistaken the true state of their accounts. We all know, indeed, little enough. But the loyal man, I think, whether he imagines himself to be a recent pragmatist or not, has a rational right to say this: My cause partakes of the nature of the only truth and reality that there is. My life is an effort to manifest such eternal truth, as well as I can, in a series of temporal deeds. I may serve my cause ill. I may conceive it erroneously. I may lose it in the thicket of this world of transient experience. My every human deed may involve a blunder. My mortal life may seem one long series of failures. But I know that my cause liveth. My true life is hid with the cause and belongs to the eternal.

# Loyalty and Religion

## I

. . . We have called this realm of true life, and of genuine and united experience,—this realm which, if our argument at the last time was sound, includes our lives in that very whole which constitutes the real universe,—we have called this realm, I say, an eternal world,—eternal, simply because, according to our theory, it includes all temporal happenings and strivings in the conspectus of a single consciousness and fulfils all our rational purposes together, and is all that we seek to be. For, as we argued, this realm of reality is conscious, is united, is self-possessed, and is perfected through the very wealth of the ideal sacrifices and of the loyal devotion which are united so as to constitute its fulness of being. In view of the philosophy that was thus sketched, I now propose a new definition of loyalty; and I say that this definition results from all of our previous study: *Loyalty is the will to manifest, so far as is possible, the Eternal, that is, the conscious and superhuman unity of life, in the form of the acts of an individual Self.* Or, if you prefer to take the point of view of an individual human self, if you persist in looking at the world just as we find it in our ordinary experience, and if you regard the metaphysical doctrine just sketched merely as an ideal theory of life, and *not* as a demonstrable philosophy, I can still hold to my definition of loyalty by borrowing a famous phrase from the dear friend and colleague some of whose views I at the last time opposed. I can, then, simply state my new definition of loyalty in plainer and more directly obvious terms thus: *Loyalty is the Will to Believe in something eternal, and to express that belief in the practical life of a human being.*

This, I say, is my new definition of loyalty, and in its metaphysical form, it is my final definition. Let me expound it further, and let me show a little more in detail how it results from the whole course of our inquiry.

## II

. . . Now, whatever may be said of wonders, or of mystical revelations, our philosophy of loyalty is naturally interested in pointing out a road to the spiritual world, if, indeed, there be such a world,—a road, I say, which has a plain relation to our everyday moral life. And it seems to me, both that there is a genuinely spiritual world, and that there is a path of inquiry which can lead from such a practical faith in the higher world as loyalty embodies in its deeds, to a rational insight into the general constitution of this higher realm. I do not offer my opinions upon this subject as having any authority. I can see no farther through stone walls than can my fellow, and I enjoy no special revelations from any super-human realm. But I ask you, as thoughtful people, to consider what your ordinary life, as rational beings, implies as its basis and as its truth.

From *The Philosophy of Loyalty* (New York: Macmillan Company, 1908), pp. 356–398.

What I was expounding at the close of my last lecture was a view of things which seems to me to be implied in any attempt to express, in a reasonable way, where we stand in our universe.

We all of us have to admit, I think, that our daily life depends upon believing in realities which are, in any case, just as truly beyond the scope of our ordinary individual experience as any spiritual realm could possibly be. We live by believing in one another's minds as realities. We give credit to countless reports, documents, and other evidences of present and past facts; and we do all this, knowing that such credit cannot be adequately verified by any experience such as an individual man can obtain. Now, the usual traditional account of all these beliefs of ours is that they are forced upon us, by some reality which is, as people say, wholly independent of our knowledge, which exists by itself apart from our experience, and which may be, therefore, entirely alien in its nature to any of our human interests and ideals.

But modern philosophy,—a philosophy in whose historical course of development our recent pragmatism is only a passing incident,—that philosophy which turns upon analyzing the bases of our knowledge, and upon reflectively considering what our human beliefs and ideas are intended to mean and to accomplish, has taught us to see that we can never deal with any wholly independent reality. The recent pragmatists, as I understand them, are here in full and conscious agreement with my own opinion. We can deal with no world which is out of relation to our experience. On the contrary, the real world is known to us in terms of *our* experience, is defined for us by *our* ideas, and is the object of *our* practical endeavors. Meanwhile, to declare anything real is to assert that it has its place in some realm of experience, be this experience human or superhuman. To declare that anything whatever is a fact, is simply to assert that some proposition, which you or I or some other thinking being can express in the form of intelligible ideas, is a true proposition. And the truth of the propositions itself is nothing

dead, is nothing independent of ideas and of experience, but is simply the successful fulfilment of some demand,—a demand which you can express in the form of an assertion, and which is fulfilled in so far, and only in so far, as some region of live experience contains what meets that demand. Meanwhile, every proposition, every assertion that anybody can make, is a deed; and every rational deed involves, in effect, an assertion of a fact. If the prodigal son says, "I will arise and go to my father," he even thereby asserts something to be true about himself, his father, and his father's house. If an astronomer or a chemist or a statistician or a man of business reports "this or that is a fact," he even thereby performs a deed,—an act having an ideal meaning, and embodying a live purpose; and he further declares that the constitution of experience is such as to make this deed essentially reasonable, successful, and worthy to be accepted by every man.

The real world is therefore *not* something independent of us. It is a world whose stuff, so to speak,—whose content,—is of the nature of experience, whose structure meets, validates, and gives warrant to our active deeds, and whose whole nature is such that it can be interpreted in terms of ideas, propositions, and conscious meanings, while in turn it gives to our fragmentary ideas and to our conscious life whatever connected meaning they possess. Whenever I have purposes and fail, so far, to carry them out, that is because I have not yet found the true way of expressing my own relation to reality. On the other hand, precisely in so far as I have understood some whole of reality, I have carried out successfully some purpose of mine.

There is, then, no merely theoretical truth, and there is no reality foreign, in its nature, to experience. Whoever actually lives the whole conscious life such as *can* be lived out with a definitely reasonable meaning,—such a being, obviously superhuman in his grade of consciousness, not only knows the real world, but *is* the real world. Whoever is conscious of the whole content of experience possesses all reality. And our search for reality is simply an effort to discover what the whole fabric of experience is into which our human experience is woven, what the system of truth is in which our partial truths have their place, what the ideally significant life is for the sake of which every deed of ours is undertaken. When we try to find out what the real world is, we are simply trying to discover the sense of our own individual lives. And we can define that sense of our lives only in terms of a conscious life in which ours is included, in which our ideas get their full meaning expressed, and in which what we fail to carry out to the full is carried out to the full.

### III

Otherwise stated, when I think of the whole world of facts,—the "real world,"—I inevitably think of something that is *my own* world, precisely in so far as that world is an object of any reasonable idea of mine. It is true, of course, that, in forming an idea of my world of facts, I do not thereby give myself, at this instant, the least right to spin out of my inner consciousness any adequate present ideas of the detail of the contents of my real world. In thinking of the real world, I am indeed thinking of the whole of that very system of experience in which my experience is bound up, and in which I, as an individual, have my very limited and narrow place. But just now I am not in possession of that whole. I have to work for it and wait for it, and faithfully to be true to it. As a creature living along, from moment to moment, in time, I therefore indeed have to wait ignorantly enough for coming experience. I have to use as I can my fallible memory in trying to find out about my own past experience. I have no way of verifying what your experience is, except by using tests—and again the extremely fallible tests—which we all employ in our social life. I need the methods of the sciences of experience to guide me in the study of whatever facts fall within their scope. I use those practical and momentary successes upon which recent pragmatism insists, whenever I try to get a concrete verification of my opinions. And so far I stand, and must rightly stand, exactly where any man of common sense, any student of a science, any plain man, or any learned man stands. I am a fallible mortal, simply trying to find my way as I can in the thickets of experience.

And yet all this my daily life, my poor efforts to remember and to predict, my fragmentary inquiries into this or that matter of science or of business, my practical acknowledgment of your presence as real facts in the real world of experience, my personal definition of the causes to which I devote myself,—these are all undertakings that are overruled, and that are rendered significant, simply in so far as they are reasonable parts of one all-embracing enterprise. This enterprise is my active attempt to find out my true place in the real world. But now I can only define my real world by conceiving it in terms of experience. I can find my place in the world only by discovering where I stand in the whole system of experience. For what I mean by a fact is something that somebody finds. Even a merely possible fact is something only in so far as somebody actually *could* find it. And the sense in which it *is* an actual fact that somebody *could* find in his experience a determinate fact, is a sense which again can only be defined in terms of concrete, living, and not merely possible, and in terms of some will or purpose expressed in a conscious life. Even possible facts, then, are *really* possible only in so far as something is actually experienced, or is found by somebody. Whatever is real, then, be it distant or near, past or future, present to your mind or to mine, a physical fact or a moral fact, a fact of our possible human experience, or a fact of a superhuman type of experience, a purpose, a desire, a natural object or an ideal object, a mechanical system or a value,—whatever, I say, is real, *is real as a content present to some conscious being.* Therefore, when I inquire about the real world, I am simply asking what contents of experience, human or superhuman, are actually and consciously found by somebody. My inquiries regarding facts, of whatever grade the facts may be, are therefore inevitably an effort to find out *what the world's experience is.* In all my common sense, then, in all my science, in all my social life, I am trying to discover what the universal conscious life which constitutes the world contains as its contents, and views as its own.

But even this is not the entire story of my place in the real world. For I cannot inquire about facts without forming my own ideas of these facts. In so far as my ideas are true, my own personal ideas are therefore active processes that go on within the conscious life of the world. If my ideas are true, they succeed in agreeing with the very world consciousness that they define. But this agreement, this success, if itself it is a fact at all, is once more a fact of experience,—yet not merely of my private experience, since I myself never personally find, within the limits of my own individual experience, the success that every act of truth seeking demands. If I get the truth, then, at any point of my life, my success is real only in so far as some conscious life, which includes my ideas and my efforts, and which also includes the very facts of the world whereof I am thinking, actually observes my success, in the form of a conspectus of the world's facts, and of my own efforts to find and to define them.

In so far, then, as I get the truth about the world, I myself am a fragmentary conscious life that is included within the conscious conspectus of the world's experience, and that is in one self-conscious unity with that world consciousness. And it is in this unity with the world consciousness that I get my success, and am in concord with the truth.

But of course any particular idea of mine, regarding the world, or regarding any fact in the world, may be false. However, this possibility of my error is itself a real situation of mine, and involves essentially the same relation between the world and myself which obtains in case I have true ideas. For I can be in error about an object only in case I really mean to agree with that object, and to agree with it in a way which only my own purposes, in seeking this agreement, can possibly define. It is only by virtue of my own undertakings that I can fail in my undertakings. It is only because, after all, I am loyal to the world's whole truth that I can so express myself in fallible ideas, and in fragmentary opinions that, as a fact, I may, at any moment, undertake too much for my own momentary success to be assured, so that I can indeed in any one of my assertions fail justly to accord with that world consciousness which I am all the while trying to interpret in my own transient way. But when I thus fail, I momentarily fail *to interpret my place in the very world consciousness whose life I am trying to define.* But my failure, when and in so far as it occurs, is once more a fact,—and therefore a fact for the world's consciousness. If I blunder, but am sincere, if I think myself right, but am not right, then my error is a fact for a consciousness which includes my fallible attempts to be loyal to the truth, but which sees how they just now lose present touch with their true cause. Seeing this my momentary defeat, the world consciousness sees, however, my loyalty, and in its conspectus assigns, even to my fragmentary attempts at truth, their genuine place in the single unity of the world's consciousness. My very failure, then, like every loyal failure, is still a sort of success. It is an effort to define my place in the unity of the world's conspectus of all conscious life. I cannot fall out of that unity. I cannot flee from its presence. And I err only as the loyal may give up their life for their cause. Whether I get truth, then, or whether I err in detail, *my loyal search for truth insures the fact that I am in a significant unity with the world's conscious life.*

The thesis that the world is one whole and a significant whole of conscious life is, for these reasons, a thesis which can only be viewed as an error, by reinstating this very assertion under a new form. For any error of mine concerning the world is possible only in so far as I really mean to assert the truth about the world; and this real meaning of mine can exist only as a fact within the conspectus of consciousness for which the real whole world exists, and within which I myself live.

This, then, in brief, is my own theory of truth. This is why I hold this theory to be no fantastic guess about what may be true, but a logically inevitable conclusion about how every one of us, wise or ignorant, is actually defining his own relation to truth, whether he knows the fact or not. I expressed my theory at the last time in terms of a polemic against the recent pragmatists; but as a fact of their view, in its genuine and deeper meaning, is no more opposed to mine than my young Russian's vehement protest against loyalty, quoted in my second lecture, was, in its true spirit, opposed to my own view. My young Russian, you may remember, hated what he took to be loyalty, just because he was so loyal. And even so my friends, the recent pragmatists, reassert my theory of truth even in their every attempt to deny it. For, amongst other things, they assert that their own theory of truth is actually true. And that assertion implies just such a conspectus of all truth in one view,—just such a conspectus as I too assert.

## IV

We first came in sight of this theory of truth, in these discussions, for a purely practical reason. Abstract and coldly intellectual as the doctrine, when stated as I have just stated it, may appear, we had our need to ask what truth is, because we wanted to know whether the loyal are right in supposing, as they inevitably do suppose, that their personal causes, and that their cause of causes, namely, universal loyalty, that any such causes, I say, possess genuine foundation in truth. Loyalty, as we found, is a practical service of superhuman objects. For our causes transcend expression in terms of our single lives. If the cause lives, then all conscious moral life—even our poor human life—is in unity with a superhuman conscious life, in which we ourselves dwell; and in this unity we win, in so far as we are loyal servants of our cause, a success which no transient human experience of ours, no joyous thrill of the flying moment, no bitterness of private defeat and loss, can do more or less than to illustrate, to illumine, or to idealize.

We asked: Is this faith of the loyal in their causes a pathetic fallacy? Our theory of truth

has given us a general answer to this intensely practical question. The loyal try to live in the spirit. But, if thereupon they merely open their eyes to the nature of the reasonable truth, they see that it is in the spirit only that they do or can live. They would be living in this truth, as mere passing fragments of conscious life, as mere blind series of mental processes, even if they were not loyal. For all life, however, dark and fragmentary, is either a blind striving for conscious unity with the universal life of which it is a fragment, or else, like the life of the loyal, is a deliberate effort to express such a striving in the form of a service of a superhuman cause. *And all lesser loyalties, and all serving of imperfect or of evil causes, are but fragmentary forms of the service of the cause of universal loyalty.* To serve universal loyalty is, however, to view the interests of all conscious life as one; and to do this is to regard all conscious life as constituting just such an unity as our theory of truth requires. Meanwhile, since truth seeking is indeed itself a practical activity, what we have stated in our theory of truth is itself but an aspect of the very life that the loyal are leading. Whoever seeks any truth is loyal, for he is determining his life by reference to a life which transcends his own. And he is loyal to loyalty; for whatever truth you try to discover is, if true, valid for everybody, and is therefore worthy of everybody's loyal recognition. The loyal, then, are truth seekers; and the truth seekers are loyal. And all of them live for the sake of the unity of all life. And this unity includes us all, but is superhuman.

Our view of truth, therefore, meets at once an ethical and a logical need. The real world is precisely that world in which the loyal are at home. Their loyalty is no pathetic fallacy. Their causes are real facts in the universe. The universe as a whole possesses that unity which loyalty to loyalty seeks to express in its service of the whole of life.

Herewith, however, it occurs to us to ask one final question. Is not this real world, whose true unity the loyal acknowledge by their every deed, and whose conscious unity every process of truth seeking presupposes,—

is not this also the world which religion recognizes? If so, what is the relation of loyalty to religion?

The materials for answering this question are now in our hands. We have been so deliberate in preparing them for our present purpose, just for the sake of making our answer the simpler when it comes.

## V

We have now defined loyalty as the will to manifest the eternal in and through the deeds of individual selves. As for religion,—in its highest historical forms (which here alone concern us),—religion, as I think, may be defined as follows. Religion (in these its highest forms) *is the interpretation both of the eternal and of the spirit of loyalty through emotion, and through a fitting activity of the imagination.*

Religion, in any form, has always been an effort to interpret and to make use of some superhuman world. The history, the genesis, the earlier and simpler forms of religion, the relations of religion and morality in the primitive life of mankind, do not here concern us. It is enough to say that, in history, there has often been a serious tension between the interests of religion and those of morality. For the higher powers have very generally seemed to man to be either nonmoral or immoral. This very tension, only too frequently, still exists for many people to-day. One of the greatest and hardest discoveries of the human mind has been the discovery of how to reconcile, not religion and science, but religion and morality. Whoever knows even a small portion of the history of the cults of mankind is aware of the difficulties to which I refer. The superhuman has been conceived by men in terms that were often far enough from those which loyalty requires. Whoever will read over the recorded works of a writer nowadays too much neglected, the rugged and magnificently loyal Old Testament prophet Amos, can see for himself how bravely the difficulty of conceiving the superhuman as the righteous, was faced by

one of the first who ever viewed the relation of religion and morality as our best teachers have since taught us to view them. And yet such a reader can also see how hard this very task of the prophet was. When we remember also that so great a mind as that of the originator of Buddhism, after all the long previous toil of Hindoo thought upon this great problem, could see no way to reconcile religion and morality, except by bringing them both to the shores of the mysterious and soundless ocean of Nirvana, and sinking them together in its depths (an undertaking which Buddha regarded as the salvation of the world), we get a further view of the nature of the problem. When we remember that St. Paul, after many years of lonely spiritual struggle, attempted in his teaching to reconcile morality and religion by an interpretation of Christianity which has ever since kept the Christian world in a most inspiring ferment of theological controversy and of practical conflict, we are again instructed as to the seriousness of the issue. But as a fact, the experience of the civilized man has gradually led him to see how to reconcile the moral life and the religious spirit. Since this reconciliation is one which our theory of truth, and of the constitution of the real world, substantially justifies, we are now ready for a brief review of the entire situation.

People often say that mere morality is something very remote from true religion. Sometimes people say this in the interests of religion, meaning to point out that mere morality can at best make you a more or less tolerable citizen, while only religion can reconcile you, as such people say, to that superhuman world whose existence and whose support alone make human life worth living. But sometimes almost the same assertion is made in the interest of pure morality, viewed as something independent of religion. Some people tell you, namely, that since, as they say, religion is a collection of doubtful beliefs, of superstitions, and of more or less exalted emotions, morality is all the better for keeping aloof from religion. Suffering man needs your help; your friends need as much happiness as you can give them; conventional morality is, on the whole, a good thing. Learn righteousness, therefore, say they, and leave religion to the fantastic-minded who love to believe. The human is what we need. Let the superhuman alone.

Now, our philosophy of loyalty, aiming at something much larger and richer than the mere sum of human happiness in individual men, has taught us that there is no such sharp dividing line between the human and the superhuman as these attempts to sunder the provinces of religion and morality would imply. The loyal serve something more than individual lives. Even Nietzsche, individualist and ethical naturalist though he was, illustrates our present thesis. He began the later period of his teaching by asserting that "God is dead"; and (lest one might regard this as a mere attack upon monotheism, and might suppose Nietzsche to be an old-fashioned heathen polytheist) he added the famous remark that, in case any gods whatever existed, he could not possibly endure being himself no god. "*Therefore,*" so he reasoned, "*there are no gods.*" All this seems to leave man very much to his own devices. Yet Nietzsche at once set up the cult of the ideal future being called the *Uebermensch* or Superman. And the *Uebermensch* is just as much of a god as anybody who ever throned upon Olympus or dwelt in the sky. And if the doctrine of the "Eternal Recurrence," as Nietzsche defined it, is true, the *Uebermensch* belongs not only to the ideal future, but has existed an endless number of times already.

If our philosophy of loyalty is right, Nietzsche was not wrong in this appeal to the superhuman. The superhuman we indeed have always with us. Life has no sense without it. But the superhuman need not be the magical. It need not be the object of superstition. And if we are desirous of unifying the interests of morality and religion, it is well indeed to begin, as rugged old Amos began, by first appreciating what righteousness is, and then by interpreting righteousness, in a perfectly reasonable and non-superstitious way, in superhuman terms. Then we shall be ready to appreciate what religion, whose roots are indeed by no means wholly in our moral nature, nevertheless has to offer us as a supplement to our morality.

## VI

Loyalty is a service of causes. But, as we saw, we do not, we cannot, wait until somebody clearly shows us how good the causes are in themselves, before we set about serving them. We first practically learn of the goodness of our causes through the very act of serving them. Loyalty begins, then, in all of us, in elemental forms. A cause fascinates us—we at first know not clearly why. We give ourselves willingly to that cause. Herewith our true life begins. The cause may indeed be a bad one. But at worst it is our way of interpreting the true cause. If we let our loyalty develop, it tends to turn into the service of the universal cause. Hence I deliberately declined, in this discussion, to *base* my theory of loyalty upon that metaphysical doctrine which I postponed to my latest lectures. It is a very imperfect view of the real world which most youth get before them before they begin to be loyal. Hosts of the loyal actually manifest the eternal in their deeds, and know not that they do so. They only know that they are given over to their cause. The first good of loyalty lies, then, in the fact which we emphasized in our earlier lectures. Reverberating all through you, stirring you to your depths, loyalty first unifies your plan of life, and thereby gives you what nothing else can give,—your self as a life lived in accordance with a plan, your conscience as your plan interpreted for you through your ideal, your cause expressed as your personal purpose in living.

In so far, then, one can indeed be loyal without being consciously and explicitly religious. One's cause, in its first intention, appears to him human, concrete, practical. It is *also* an ideal. It is *also* a superhuman entity. It also really *means* the service of the eternal. But this fact may be, to the hard-working, and especially to the unimaginative, and, in a worldly sense, fairly successful man, a latent fact. He then, to be sure, gradually idealizes his cause as he goes; but this idealizing in so far becomes no very explicitly emphasized process in his life, although, as we have seen, some tendency to deify the cause is inevitable.

Meanwhile, such an imperfectly developed but loyal man may also accept, upon traditional grounds, a religion. This religion will then tell him about a superhuman world. But in so far the religion need not be, to his mind, an essential factor in his practical loyalty. He may be superstitious; or he may be a religious formalist; or he may accept his creed and his church simply because of their social respectability and usefulness; or, finally, he may even have a rich and genuine religious experience, which still may remain rather a mysticism than a morality, or an æsthetic comfort rather than a love of his cause.

In such cases, loyalty and religion may long keep apart. But the fact remains that loyalty, if sincere, involves at least a latent belief in the superhuman reality of the cause, and means at least an unconscious devotion to the one and eternal cause. But such a belief is also a latent union of morality and religion. Such a service is an unconscious piety. The time may come, then, when the morality will consciously need this union with the religious creed of the individual whose growth we are portraying.

This union must begin to become an explicit union whenever that process which, in our sixth lecture, we called the idealizing of the cause, reaches its higher levels. We saw that those higher levels are reached in the presence of what seems to be, to human vision, a lost cause. If we believe in the lost cause, we become directly aware that we are indeed seeking a city out of sight. If such a cause is real, it belongs to a superhuman world. Now, every cause worthy, as we said, of lifelong service, and capable of unifying our life plans, shows sooner or later that it is a cause *which we cannot successfully express in any set of human experiences of transient joys and of crumbling successes.* Human life taken merely as it flows, viewed merely as it passes by in time and is gone, is indeed a lost river of experience that plunges down the mountains of youth and sinks in the deserts of age. Its significance comes solely through its relations to the air and the ocean and the great deeps of universal experience. For by such poor figures I may, in passing, symbolize that really rational relation of our personal experience to universal conscious experience,—that relation to which I have devoted these last two lectures.

Everybody ought to serve the universal cause in his own individual way. For this, as we have seen, is what loyalty, when it comes to know its own mind, really means. But whoever thus serves inevitably *loses* his cause in our poor world of human sense-experience, because his cause is too good for this present temporal world to express it. And that is, after all, what the old theology meant when it called you and me, as we now naturally are, lost beings. Our deepest loyalty lies in devoting ourselves to causes that are just now lost to our poor human nature. One can express this, of course, by saying that the true cause is indeed real enough, in the higher world, while it is our poor human nature which is lost. Both ways of viewing the case have their truth. Loyalty means a transformation of our nature.

Lost causes, then, we must serve. But as we have seen, in our sixth lecture, loyalty to a lost cause has two companions, grief and imagination. Now, these two are the parents of all the higher forms of genuinely ethical religion. If you doubt the fact, read the scriptures of any of the great ethical faiths. Consult the psalter, the hymns, the devotional books, or the prayers of the church. Such religion interprets the superhuman in forms that our longing, our grief, and our imagination invent, but also in terms that are intended to meet the demands of our highest loyalty. For we are loyal to that unity of life which, as our truer moral consciousness learns to believe, owns the whole real world, and constitutes the cause of causes. In being loyal to universal loyalty, we are serving the unity of life.

This true unity of the world-life, however, is at once very near to us and very far from us. Very near it is; for we have our being in it, and depend upon it for whatever worth we have. Apart from it we are but the gurgling stream soon to be lost in the desert. In union with it we have individual significance in and for the whole. But we are very far from it also, because our human experience throws such fragmentary light upon the details of our relation to its activities. Hence in order to feel our relations to it as vital relations, we have to bring it near to our feelings and to our imaginations. And we long and suffer the loneliness of this life as we do so. But because we know of the details of the world only through our empirical sciences, while these give us rather materials for a rational life than a view of the unity of life, we are indeed left to our imagination to assuage grief and to help in the training of loyalty. For here, that is, precisely as to the *details* of the system of facts whereby our life is linked to the eternal, our science forsakes us. We can know *that* we are thus linked. *How* we are linked, our sciences do not make manifest to us.

Hence the actual content of the higher ethical religions is endlessly rich in legend and in other symbolic portrayal. This portrayal is rich in emotional meaning and in vivid detail. What this portrayal attempts to characterize is, in its general outline, an absolute truth. This truth consists in the following facts: *First, the rational unity and goodness of the world-life; next, its true but invisible nearness to us, despite our ignorance; further, its fulness of meaning despite our barrenness of present experience; and yet more, its interest in our personal destiny as moral beings; and finally, the certainty that, through our actual human loyalty, we come, like Moses, face to face with the true will of the world, as a man speaks to his friend.* In recognizing these facts, we have before us what may be called the creed of the Absolute Religion.

You may well ask, of course, whether our theory of truth, as heretofore expounded, gives any warrant to such religious convictions. I hold that it does give warrant to them. The symbols in which these truths are expressed by one or another religion are indeed due to all sorts of historical accidents, and to the most varied play of the imaginations both of the peoples and of the religious geniuses of our race. But that our relations to the world-life are relations wherein we are consciously met, from the other side, by a superhuman and yet strictly personal conscious life, in which our own personalities are themselves bound up, but which also is not only richer but is more concrete and definitely conscious and real than we are,—this seems to me to be an inevitable corollary of my theory of truth.

## VII

And now, finally, to sum up our whole doctrine of loyalty and religion. Two things belonging to the world-life we know—two at least, if my theory is true: *it is defined in terms of our own needs; and it includes and completes our experience.* Hence, in any case, it is precisely as live and elemental and concrete as we are; and there is not a need of ours which is not its own. If you ask why I call it good— well, the very arguments which recent pragmatism has used are, as you remember, here my warrant. A truth cannot be a merely theoretical truth. True is that which successfully fulfils an idea. Whoever, again, is not succeeding, or is facing an evil, or is dissatisfied, is inevitably demanding and defining facts that are far beyond him, and that are not yet consciously his own. A knower of the totality of truth is therefore, of necessity, in possession of the fulfilment of all rational purposes. If, however, you ask why this world-life permits any evil whatever, or any finitude, or any imperfections, I must indeed reply that here is no place for a general discussion of the whole problem of evil, which I have repeatedly and wearisomely considered in other discussions of mine. But this observation does belong here. Our theory of evil is indeed no "shallow optimism," but is founded upon the deepest, the bitterest, and the dearest moral experience of the human race. The *loyal,* and they alone, know the one great good of suffering, of ignorance, of finitude, of loss, of defeat—*and that is just the good of loyalty,* so long as the cause itself can only be viewed as indeed a living whole. Spiritual peace is surely no easy thing. We win that peace only through stress and suffering and loss and labor. But when we find the preciousness of the idealized cause emphasized through grief, we see that, whatever evil is, it at least *may* have its place in an ideal order. What would be the universe without loyalty; and what would loyalty be without trial? And when we remember that, from this point of view, our own griefs are the griefs of the very world consciousness itself, in so far as this world-life is expressed in our lives, it may well occur to us that the life of loyalty with all its griefs and burdens and cares may be the very foundation of the attainment of that spiritual triumph which we must conceive as realized by the world spirit.

Perhaps, however, one weakly says: "If the world will attains in its wholeness what we seek, why need we seek that good at all?" I answer at once that our whole philosophy of loyalty instantly shows the vanity of such speech. Of course, the world-life does *not* obtain the individual good that is involved in my willing loyalty unless indeed *I am loyal.* The cause may in some way triumph without me, but not as *my* cause. We have never defined our theory as meaning that the world-life is *first* eternally complete, but *then* asks us, in an indifferent way, to copy its perfections. Our view is that each of us who is loyal is doing his unique deed in that whole of life which we have called the eternal simply because it is the conspectus of the totality of life, past, present, and future. If my deed were not done, the world-life would miss my deed. Each of us can say that. The very basis of our theory of truth, which we found upon the deeds, the ideas, the practical needs, of each of us, gives every individual his unique place in the world order—his deed that nobody else can do, his will which is his own. "Our wills are ours to make them thine." The unity of the world is *not* an ocean in which we are lost, but a life which is and which needs all our lives in one. Our loyalty defines that unity for us as a living, active unity. We have come to the unity through the understanding of our loyalty. It is

an eternal unity only in so far as it includes all time and change and life and deeds. And therefore, when we reach this view, since the view simply fulfils what loyalty demands, our loyalty remains as precious to us, and as practical, and as genuinely a service of a cause, as it was before. It is no sort of "moral holiday" that this whole world-life suggests to us. It is precisely as a whole life of ideal strivings in which we have our places as individual selves and are such selves only in so far as we strive to do our part in the whole,—it is thus, and thus only, that our philosophy of loyalty regards the universe.

Religion, therefore, precisely in so far as it attempts to conceive the universe as a conscious and personal life of superhuman meaning, and as a life that is in close touch with our own meaning, is eternally true. But now it is just this *general* view of the universe as a rational order that is indeed open to our rational knowledge. No part of such a doctrine gives us, however, the present right as human beings to determine with any certainty the details of the world-life, except in so far as they come within the scope of our scientific and of our social inquiries. Hence, when religion, in the service of loyalty, interprets the world-life to us with symbolic detail, it gives us indeed merely symbols of the eternal truth. That this truth is indeed eternal, that our loyalty brings us into personal relations with a personal world-life, which values our every loyal deed, and needs that deed, all this is true and rational. And just this is what religion rightly illustrates. But the parables, the symbols, the historical incidents that the religious imagination uses in its portrayals,—these are the more or less sacred and transient *accidents* in which the "real presence" of the divine at once shows itself to us, and hides the detail of its inner life from us. These accidents of the religious imagination endure through many ages; but they also vary from place to place and from one nation or race of men to another, and they ought to do so. Whoever sees the living truth of the person and conscious and ethical unity of the world *through* these symbols is possessed of the absolute religion, whatever be his nominal creed or church. Whoever overemphasizes the empirical details of these symbols, and then asks us to accept these details as literally true, commits an error which seems to me simply to invert that error whereof, at the last time, I ventured to accuse my pragmatist friends. Such a literalist, who reads his symbols as revelations of the detailed structure of the divine life, seems to me, namely, to look for the eternal *within* the realm of the mere data of human sense and imagination. To do this, I think, is indeed to seek the risen Lord in the open sepulchre.

Concerning the living truth of the whole conscious universe, one can well say, as one observes the special facts of human sense and imagination: "He is not here; he is arisen." Yet equally from the whole circle of the heaven of that entire self-conscious life which *is* the truth, there comes always, and to all the loyal, the word: "Lo, I am with you always, even unto the end of the world."

# Provincialism

I propose, in this address, to define certain issues which, as I think, the present state of the world's civilization, and of our own national life, make both prominent and critical.

## I

The world "provincialism," which I have used as my title, has been chosen because it is the best single word that I have been able to find to suggest the group of social tendencies to which I want to call your especial attention. I intend to use this word in a somewhat elastic sense, which I may at once indicate. When we employ the word "provincialism" as a concrete term, speaking of "a provincialism," we mean, I suppose, any social disposition, or custom, or form of speech or of civilization, which is especially characteristic of a province. In this sense one speaks of the provincialisms of the local dialect of any English shire, or of any German country district. This use of the term in relation to the dialects of any language is very common. But one may also apply the term to name, not only the peculiarities of a local dialect, but the fashions, the manners, and customs of a given restricted region of any country. One also often employs the word "provincialism" as an abstract term, to name not only the customs or social tendencies themselves, but that fondness for them, that pride in them, which may make the inhabitants of a province indisposed to conform to the ways of those who come from without, and anxious to follow persistently their own local traditions. Thus the word "provincialism" applies both to the social habits of a given region, and to the mental interest which inspires and maintains these habits. But both uses of the term imply, of course, that one first knows what is to be meant by the word "province." This word, however, is one of an especially elastic usage. Sometimes, by a province, we mean a region as restricted as a single English county, or as the smallest of the old German principalities. Sometimes, however, one speaks of the whole of New England, or even of the Southern states of our Union, as constituting one province; and I know of no easy way of defining how large a province may be. For the term,

From *Race Questions, Provincialism, and Other American Problems* (New York: MacMillan, 1908) pp. 57–108.

in this looser sense, stands for no determinate political or legal division of a country. Meanwhile we all, in our minds, oppose the term "province" to the term "nation," as the part is opposed to the whole. Yet we also often oppose the terms "provincial" and "metropolitan," conceiving that the country districts and the smaller towns and cities belong even to the province, while the very great cities belong rather to the whole country, or even to the world in general. Yet here the distinction that we make is not the same as the former distinction between the part of a country and the whole country. Nevertheless, the ground for such an identification of the provincial with that which pertains to country districts and to smaller cities can only lie in the supposed tendency of the great city to represent better the interests of the larger whole than do the lesser communities. This supposition, however, is certainly not altogether well founded. In the sense of possessing local interests and customs, and of being limited to ideas of their own, many great cities are almost as distinctly provincial as are certain less populous regions. The plain people of London or of Berlin have their local dialect; and it seems fair to speak of the peculiarities of such dialects as provincialisms. And almost the same holds true of the other social traditions peculiar to individual great cities. It is possible to find, even amongst the highly cultivated classes of ancient cities, ideas and fashions of behavior as characteristically local, as exclusive in their indifference to the ways of outsiders, as are the similarly characteristic ways and opinions of the country districts of the same nationality. And so the opposition of the provincial to the metropolitan, in manners and in beliefs, seems to me much less important than the other opposition of the province, as the more or less restricted part of the nation as the whole. It is this latter opposition that I shall therefore emphasize in the present discussion. But I shall not attempt to define how large or how well organized, politically, a province must be. For my present purpose a county, a state, or even a large section of the country, such as New England, might constitute a province.

For me, then, a province shall mean any one part of a national domain, which is, geographically and socially, sufficiently unified to have a true consciousness of its own unity, to feel a pride in its own ideals and customs, and to possess a sense of its distinction from other parts of the country. And by the term "provincialism" I shall mean, first, the tendency of such a province to possess its own customs and ideals; secondly, the totality of these customs and ideals themselves; and thirdly, the love and pride which leads the inhabitants of a province to cherish as their own these traditions, beliefs, and aspirations.

## II

I have defined the term used as my title. But now, in what sense do I propose to make provincialism our topic? You will foresee that I intend to discuss the worth of provincialism, i.e., to consider, to some extent, whether it constitutes a good or an evil element in civilization. You will properly expect me, therefore, to compare provincialism with other social tendencies; such tendencies as patriotism, the larger love of humanity, and the ideals of higher cultivation. Precisely these will constitute, in fact, the special topics of my address. But all that I have to say will group itself about a single thesis, which I shall forthwith announce. My thesis is that, in the present state of the world's civilization, and of the life of our own country, the time has come to emphasize, with a new meaning and intensity, the positive value, the absolute necessity for our welfare, of a wholesome provincialism, as a saving power to which the world in the near future will need more and more to appeal.

The time was (and not very long since), when, in our own country, we had to contend against very grave evils due to false forms of provincialism. What has been called sectionalism long threatened our national unity. Our Civil War was fought to overcome the ills due to such influences. There was, therefore, a time when the virtue of true patriotism had to be founded upon a vigorous condemnation of certain powerful forms of provincialism. And our national education at that time depended both upon our learning common federal ideals, and upon our looking to foreign lands for the spiritual guidance of older civilizations. Furthermore, not only have these things been so in the past, but similar needs will, of course, be felt in the future. We shall always be required to take counsel of the other nations in company with whom we are at work upon the tasks of civilization. Nor have we outgrown our spiritual dependence upon older forms of civilization. In fact we shall never outgrow a certain inevitable degree of such dependence. Our national unity, moreover, will always require of us a devotion that will transcend in some directions the limits of all our provincial ideas. A common sympathy between the different sections of our country will, in future, need a constantly fresh cultivation. Against the evil forms of sectionalism we shall always have to contend. All this I well know, and these things I need not in your presence emphasize. But what I am to emphasize is this: The present state of civilization, both in the world at large, and with us, in America, is such as to define a new social mission which the province alone, but not the nation, is able to fulfil. False sectionalism, which disunites, will indeed always remain as great an evil as ever it was. But the modern world has reached a point where it needs, more than ever before, the vigorous development of a highly organized provincial life. Such a life, if wisely guided, will not mean disloyalty to the nation; and it need not mean narrowness of spirit, nor yet the further development of jealousies between various communities. What it will mean, or at least may mean,—this, so far as I have time, I wish to set forth in the following discussion. My main intention is to define the right form and the true office of provincialism,—to portray what, if you please, we may well call the Higher Provincialism,—to portray it, and then to defend it, to extol it, and to counsel you to further just such provincialism.

Since this is my purpose, let me at once say that I address myself, in the most explicit terms, to men and women who, as I hope and presuppose, are and wish to be, in the wholesome sense, provincial. Every one, as I maintain, ought, ideally speaking, to be provincial,—and that no matter how cultivated, or humanitarian, or universal in purpose or in experience he may be or may become. If in our own country, where often so many people are still comparative strangers to the communities in which they have come to live, there are some of us who, like myself, have changed our provinces during our adult years, and who have so been unable to become and to remain in the sense of European countries provincial; and if, moreover, the life of our American provinces everywhere has still too brief a tradition,—all that is our misfortune, and not our advantage. As our country grows in social organization, there will be, in absolute measure, more and not less provincialism amongst our people. To be sure, as I hope, there will also be, in absolute measure, more and not less patriotism, closer and not looser national ties, less and not more mutual sectional misunderstanding. But the two tendencies, the tendency toward national unity and that toward local independence of spirit, must henceforth grow together. They cannot prosper apart. The national unity must not kill out, nor yet hinder, the provincial self-consciousness. The loyalty to the Republic must not lessen the love and the local pride of the individual community. The man of the future must love his province more than he does to-day. His provincial customs and ideals must be more and not less highly developed, more and not less self-conscious, well-established, and earnest. And therefore, I say, I appeal to you as to a company of people who are, and who mean to be, provincial as well as patriotic,—servants and lovers of your own community and of its ways, as well as citizens of the world. I hope and believe that you all intend to have your community live its own life, and not the life of any other community, nor yet the life of a mere abstraction called humanity in general. I hope that you are fully aware how provincialism, like monogamy, is an essential basis of true civilization. And it is with this presupposition that I undertake to suggest something toward a definition and defence of the higher provincialism and of its office in civilization.

## III

With this programme in mind, let me first tell you what seem to me to be in our modern world, and, in particular, in our American world, the principal evils which are to be corrected by a further development of a true provincial spirit, and which cannot be corrected without such a development.

The first of these evils I have already mentioned. It is a defect incidental, partly to the newness of our own country, but partly also to those world-wide conditions of modern life which make travel, and even a change of home, both attractive and easy to dwellers in the most various parts of the globe. In nearly every one of our American communities, at least in the northern and in the western regions of our country, there is a rather large proportion of people who either have not grown up where they were born, or who have changed their dwelling-place in adult years. I can speak all the more freely regarding this class of our communities, because, in my own community, I myself, as a native of California, now resident in New England, belong to such a class. Such classes, even in modern New England, are too large. The stranger, the sojourner, the newcomer, is an inevitable factor in the life of most American communities. To make him welcome is one of the most gracious of the tasks in which our people have become expert. To give him his fair chance is the rule of our national life. But it is not on the whole well when the affairs of a community remain too largely under the influence of those who mainly feel either the wanderer's or the new resident's interest in the region where they are now dwelling. To offset the social tendencies due to such frequent changes of dwelling-place we need the further development and the intensification of the community spirit. The sooner the new resident learns to share this spirit, the better for him and for his community. A sound instinct, therefore, guides even our newer communities, in the more fortunate cases, to a rapid development of such a local sentiment as makes the stranger feel that he must in due measure conform if he would be permanently welcome, and must accept the local spirit if he is to enjoy the advantages of his community. As a Californian I have been interested to see both the evidences and the nature of this rapid evolution of the genuine provincial spirit in my own state. How swiftly, in that country, the Californians of the early days seized upon every suggestion that could give a sense of the unique importance of their new provincial life. The associations that soon clustered about the tales of the life of Spanish missionaries and Mexican colonists in the years before 1846,—these our American Californians cherished from the outset. This, to us often half-legendary past, gave us a history of our own. The wondrous events of the early mining life,—how earnestly the pioneers later loved to rehearse that story; and how proud every young Californian soon became of the fact that his father had had his part therein. Even the Californian's well-known and largely justified glorification of his climate was, in his own mind, part of the same expression of his tendency to idealize whatever tended to make his community, and all its affairs, seem unique, beloved, and deeply founded upon some significant natural basis. Such a foundation was, indeed, actually there; nature had, indeed, richly blessed his land; but the real interest that made one emphasize and idealize all these things, often so boastfully, was the interest of the loyal citizen in finding his community an object of pride. Now you, who know well your own local history, will be able to observe the growth amongst you of this tendency to idealize your past, to glorify the bounties that nature has showered upon you, all in such wise as to give the present life of your community more dignity, more honor, more value in the eyes of yourselves and of strangers. In fact, that we all do thus glorify our various provinces, we well know; and with what feelings we accompany the process, we can all observe for ourselves. But it is well to remember that the special office, the principal use, the social justification, of such mental tendencies in ourselves lies in the aid that they give us in becoming loyal to our community, and in assimilating to our own social order the strangers that are within our gates. It is the especial art of the colonizing peoples, such as we are, and such as the English are, to be able by devices of this sort rapidly to build up in their own minds a provincial loyalty in a new environment. The French, who are not a colonizing people, seem to possess much less of this tendency. The Chinese seem to lack it almost altogether. Our own success as possessors of new lands depends upon this one skill in making the new lands where we came to dwell soon seem to us glorious and unique. I was much impressed, some years ago, during a visit to Australia and New Zealand, with the parallel developments in the Australasian colonies. They too have already their glorious past history, their unique fortunes, their romances of the heroic days,—and, in consequence, their provincial loyalty and their power to assimilate their newcomers. So learn to view your new community that every stranger who enters it shall at once feel the dignity of its past, and the unique privilege that is offered to him when he is permitted to belong to its company of citizens,—this is the first rule of the people of every colonizing nation when they found a new province.

Thus, then, I have pointed out the first evil with which our provincialism has to deal—the evil due to the presence of a considerable number of not yet assimilated newcomers in most of our communities. The newcomers themselves are often a boon and welcome indeed. But their failure to be assimilated constitutes, so long as it endures, a source of social danger, because the community needs well-knit organization. We meet this danger by the development of a strong provincial spirit amongst those who already constitute the centralized portion of the community. For thus a dignity is given to the social order which makes the newcomer long to share in its honors by deserving its confidence. But this aspect of provincialism, this usefulness of local pride, is indeed the best known aspect of my topic. I pass at once to the less frequently recognized uses of the provincial spirit, by mentioning the second of the evils with which a wise provincialism is destined to contend.

## IV

This second modern evil arises from, and constitutes, one aspect of the levelling tendency of recent civilization. That such a levelling tendency exists, most of us recognize. That it is the office of the province to contend against some of the attendant evils of this tendency, we less often observe. By the levelling tendency in question I mean that aspect of modern civilization which is most obviously suggested by the fact that, because of the ease of communication amongst distant places, because of the spread of popular education, and because of the consolidation and of the centralization of industries and of social authorities, we tend all over the nation, and, in some degree, even throughout the civilized world, to read the same daily news, to share the same general ideas, to submit to the same overmastering social forces, to live in the same external fashions, to discourage individuality, and to approach a dead level of harassed mediocrity. One of the most marked of all social tendencies is in any age that toward the mutual assimilation of men in so far as they are in social relations with one another. One of the strongest human predispositions is that toward imitation. But our modern conditions have greatly favored the increase of the numbers of people who read the same books and newspapers, who repeat the same phrases, who follow the same social fashions, and who thus, in general, imitate one another in constantly more and more ways. The result is a tendency to crush the individual. Furthermore there are modern economic and industrial developments, too well known to all of you to need any detailed mention here, which lead toward similar results. The independence of the small trader or manufacturer becomes lost in the great commercial or industrial combination. The vast corporation succeeds and displaces the individual. Ingenuity and initiative become subordinated to the discipline of an impersonal social order. And each man, becoming, like his fellow, the servant of masters too powerful for him to resist, and too complex in their undertakings for him to understand, is, in so far, disposed unobtrusively to conform to the ways of his innumerable fellow-servants, and to lose all sense of his unique moral destiny as an individual.

I speak here merely of tendencies. As you know, they are nowhere unopposed tendencies. Nor do I for an instant pretend to call even these levelling tendencies wholly, or principally, evil. But for the moment I call attention to what are obviously questionable, and in some degree are plainly evil, aspects of these modern tendencies. Imitation is a good thing. All civilization depends upon it. But there may be a limit to the number of people who ought to imitate precisely the same body of ideas and customs. For imitation is not man's whole business. There ought to be some room left for variety. Modern conditions have often increased too much what one might call the purely mechanical carrying-power of certain ruling social influences. There are certain metropolitan newspapers, for instance, which have far too many readers for the good of the social order in which they circulate. These newspapers need not always be very mischievous ones. But when read by too vast multitudes, they tend to produce a certain monotonously uniform triviality of mind in a large proportion of our city and suburban population. It would be better if the same readers were divided into smaller sections, which read different newspapers, even if these papers were of no higher level. For then there would at least be a greater variety in the sorts of triviality which from day to day occupied their minds. And variety is the beginning of individual independence of insght and of conviction. As for the masses of people who are under the domination of the great corporations that employ them, I am here not in the least dwelling upon their economic difficulties. I am pointing out that the lack of initiative in their lives tends to make their spiritual range

narrower. They are too little disposed to create their own world. Now every man who gets into a vital relation to God's truth becomes, in his own way, a creator. And if you deprive a man of all incentive to create, you in so far tend to cut him off from God's truth. Or, in more common language, independence of spirit flourishes only when a man at least believes that he has a chance to change his fortunes if he persistently wills to do so. But the servant of some modern forms of impersonal social organization tends to lose this belief that he has a chance. Hence he tends to lose independence of spirit.

Well, this is the second of the evils of the modern world which, as I have said, provincialism may tend to counteract. Local spirit, local pride, provincial independence, influence the individual man precisely because they appeal to his imitative tendencies. But thereby they act so as to render him more or less immune in presence of the more trivial of the influences that, coming from without his community, would otherwise be likely to reduce him to the dead level of the customs of the whole nation. A country district may seem to a stranger unduly crude in its ways; but it does not become wiser in case, under the influence of city newspapers and of summer boarders, it begins to follow city fashions merely for the sake of imitating. Other things being equal, it is better in proportion as it remains self-possessed,—proud of its own traditions, not unwilling indeed to learn, but also quite ready to teach the stranger its own wisdom. And in similar fashion provincial pride helps the individual man to keep his self-respect even when the vast forces that work toward industrial consolidation, and toward the effacement of individual initiative, are besetting his life at every turn. For a man is in large measure what his social consciousness makes him. Give him the local community that he loves and cherishes, that he is proud to honor and to serve,—make his ideal of that community lofty,—give him faith in the dignity of his province,—and you have given him a power to counteract the levelling tendencies of modern civilization.

## V

The third of the evils with which a wise provincialism must contend is closely connected with the second. I have spoken of the constant tendency of modern life to the mutual assimilation of various parts of the social order. Now this assimilation may occur slowly and steadily, as in great measure it normally does; or, on the other hand, it may take more sudden and striking forms, at moments when the popular mind is excited, when great emotions affect the social order. At such times of emotional disturbance, society is subject to tendencies which have recently received a good deal of psychological study. They are the tendencies to constitute what has often been called the spirit of the crowd or of the mob. Modern readers of the well-known book of Le Bon's on "The Crowd" well know what the tendencies to which I refer may accomplish. It is true that the results of Le Bon are by no means wholly acceptable. It is true that the psychology of large social masses is still insufficiently understood, and that a great many hasty statements have been made about the fatal tendency of great companies of people to go wrong. Yet in the complex world of social processes there can be no doubt that there exist such processes as the ones which Le Bon characterizes. The mob-spirit is a genuine psychological fact which occasionally becomes important in the life of all numerous communities. Moreover, the mob-spirit is no new thing. It has existed in some measure from the very beginning of social life. But there are certain modern conditions which tend to give the mob-spirit new form and power, and to lead to new social dangers that are consequent upon the presence of this spirit.

I use the term "mob-spirit" as an abbreviation for a very large range of phenomena, phenomena which may indeed be classed with all the rest of the imitative phenomena as belonging to one genus. But the mob-phenomena are distinguished from the other imitative phenomena by certain characteristic emotional tendencies which belong to excited crowds of people, and which do not belong to the more strictly normal social activities. Man, as an imitative animal, naturally tends, as we have seen, to do whatever his companions do, so long as he is not somehow aroused to independence and to individuality. Accordingly, he easily shares the beliefs and temperaments of those who are near enough to him to influence him. But now suppose a condition of things such as may readily occur in any large group of people who have somehow come to feel strong sympathy with one another, and who are for any reason in a relatively passive and impressible state of mind. In such a company of people let any idea which has a strong emotional coloring come to be suggested, by the words of the leader, by the singing of a song, by the beginning of any social activity that does not involve clear thinking, that does not call upon a man to assert his own independence. Such an idea forthwith tends to take possession in an extraordinarily strong degree of every member of the social group in question. As a consequence, the individual may come to be, as it were, hypnotized by his social group. He may reach a stage where he not merely lacks a disposition to individual initiative, but becomes for the time simply unable to assert himself, to think his own thoughts, or even to remember his ordinary habits and principles of conduct. His judgment for the time becomes one with that of the mass. He may not himself observe this fact. Like the hypnotized subject, the member of the excited mob may feel as if he were very independently expressing himself. He may say: "This idea is my own idea," when as a fact the ruling idea is suggested by the leaders of the mob, or even by the accident of the momentary situation. The individual may be led to acts of which he says: "These things are my duty, my sacred privilege, my right," when as a fact the acts in question are forced upon him by the suggestions of the social mass of which at the instant he is merely a helpless member. As the hypnotized subject, again, thinks his will free when an observer can see that he is obliged to follow the suggestions of the hypnotizer, so the member of the mob may feel all the sense of pure initiative, although as a fact he is in bondage to the will of another, to the motives of the moment.

All such phenomena are due to very deep-seated and common human tendencies. It is no individual reproach to any one of us that, under certain conditions, he would lose his individuality and become the temporary prey of the mob-spirit. Moreover, by the word "mob" itself, or by the equivalent word "crowd," I here mean no term that reflects upon the personal characters or upon the private intelligence of the individuals who chance to compose any given mob. In former ages when the defenders of aristocratic or of monarchical institutions used to speak with contempt of the mob, and oppose to the mob the enlightened portion of the community, the wise who ought to rule, or the people whom birth and social position secured against the defects of the mob, the term was used without a true understanding of the reason why crowds of people are upon occasion disposed to do things that are less intelligent than the acts of normal and thoughtful people would be. For the modern student of the psychology of crowds, a crowd or a mob means not in any wise a company of wicked, of debased, or even of ignorant persons. The term means merely a company of people who, by reason of their sympathies, have for the time being resigned their individual judgment. A mob might be a mob of saints or of cutthroats, of peasants or of men of science. If it were a mob it would lack due social wisdom whatever its membership might be. For the members of the mob are sympathizing rather than criticising. Their ruling ideas then, therefore, are what Le Bon calls atavistic ideas; ideas such as belong to earlier and cruder periods of civilization. Opposed to the mob in which the good sense of individuals is lost in a blur of emotion, and in a helpless suggestibility,—opposed to the mob, I say, is the small company of thoughtful individuals who are taking counsel together. Now our modern life, with its vast unions of people, with its high development of popular sentiments, with its passive and sympathetic love for knowing and feeling whatever other

men know and feel, is subject to the disorders of larger crowds, of more dangerous mobs, than have ever before been brought into sympathetic union. One great problem of our time, then, is how to carry on popular government without being at the mercy of the mob-spirit. It is easy to give this mob-spirit noble names. Often you hear of it as "grand popular enthusiasm." Often it is highly praised as a loyal party spirit or as patriotism. But psychologically it is the mob-spirit whenever it is the spirit of a large company of people who are no longer either taking calm counsel together in small groups, or obeying an already established law or custom, but who are merely sympathizing with one another, listening to the words of leaders, and believing the large print headings of their newspapers. Every such company of people is, in so far, a mob. Though they spoke with the tongues of men and of angels, you could not then trust them. Wisdom is not in them nor in their mood. However highly trained they may be as individuals, their mental processes, as a mob, are degraded. Their suffrages, as a mob, ought not to count. Their deeds come of evil. The next mob may undo their work. Accident may render their enthusiasm relatively harmless. But, as a mere crowd, they cannot be wise. They cannot be safe rulers. Who, then, are the men who wisely think and rightly guide? They are, I repeat, the men who take counsel together in small groups, who respect one another's individuality, who meanwhile criticise one another constantly, and earnestly, and who suspect whatever the crowd teaches. In such men there need be no lack of wise sympathy, but there is much besides sympathy. There is individuality, and there is a willingness to doubt both one another and themselves. To such men, and to such groups, popular government ought to be intrusted.

Now these principles are responsible for the explanation of the well-known contrast between those social phenomena which illustrate the wisdom of the enlightened social order, and the phenomena which, on the contrary, often seem such as to make us despair for the moment of the permanent success of popular government. In the rightly constituted social group where every member feels his own responsibility for his part of the social enterprise which is in hand, the result of the interaction of individuals is that the social group may show itself wiser than any of its individuals. In the mere crowd, on the other hand, the social group may be, and generally is, more stupid than any of its individual members. Compare a really successful town meeting in a comparatively small community with the accidental and sometimes dangerous social phenomena of a street mob or of a great political convention. In the one case every individual may gain wisdom from his contact with the social group. In the other case every man concerned, if ever he comes again to himself, may feel ashamed of the absurdity of which the whole company was guilty. Social phenomena of the type that may result from the higher social group, the group in which individuality is respected, even while social loyalty is demanded,—these phenomena may lead to permanent social results which as tradition gives them a fixed character may gradually lead to the formation of permanent institutions, in which a wisdom much higher than that of any individual man may get embodied. A classic instance of social phenomena of this type, and of the results of such social activities as constantly make use of individual skill, we find in language. However human language originated, it is certain that it was never the product of the mob-spirit. Language has been formed through the efforts of individuals to communicate with other individuals. Human speech is, therefore, in its structure, in its devices, in its thoughtfulness, essentially the product of the social activities of comparatively small groups of persons whose ingenuity was constantly aroused by the desire of making some form of social coöperation definite, and some form of communication amongst individuals effective. The consequence is that the language of an uncultivated people, who have as yet no grammarians to guide them and no literature to transmit the express wisdom of individual guides from generation to generation, may, nevertheless,

be on the whole much more intelligent than is any individual that speaks the language.

Other classic instances of social processes wherein the group appears wiser than the individual are furnished to us by the processes that resulted through centuries of development in the production of the system of Roman law or of the British constitution. Such institutions embody more wisdom than any individual who has taken part in the production of these institutions has ever possessed. Now the common characteristic of all such social products seems to me to be due to the fact that the social groups in which they originated were always such as encouraged and as in fact necessitated an emphasis upon the contrasts between various individuals. In such groups what Tarde has called "the universal opposition" has always been an effective motive. The group has depended upon the variety and not the uniformity of its members. On the other hand, the other sort of social group, the mob, has depended upon the emotional agreement, the sympathy, of its members. It has been powerful only in so far as they forgot who they individually were, and gave themselves up to the suggestions of the moment.

It follows that if we are to look for the source of the greatest dangers of popular government, we must expect to find them in the influence of the mob spirit. Le Bon is right when he says that the problem of the future will become more and more the problem how to escape from the domination of the crowd. Now I do not share Le Bon's pessimism when he holds, as he seems to do, that all popular government necessarily involves the tendency to the prevalence of the mob-spirit. So far as I can see Le Bon and most of the other writers who in recent times have laid so much stress upon the dangers of the mob, have ignored, or at least have greatly neglected, that other social tendency, that tendency to the formation of smaller social groups, which makes use of the contrasts of individuals, and which leads to a collective wisdom greater than any individual wisdom. But why I do insist upon this is that the problem of the future for popular government must involve the higher development, the better organization, the more potent influence, of the social groups of the wiser type, and the neutralization through their influence of the power of the mob-spirit. Now the modern forms of the mob-spirit have become so portentous because of a tendency that is in itself very good, even as may be the results to which it often leads. This tendency is that toward a very wide and inclusive human sympathy, a sympathy which may be as undiscriminating as it often is kindly. Sympathy, however, as one must recollect, is not necessarily even a kindly tendency. For one may sympathize with any emotion,—for instance, with the emotions of a cruelly ferocious mob. Sympathy itself is a sort of neutral basis for more rational mental development. The noblest structures may be reared upon its soil. The basest absurdities may, upon occasion, seem to be justified, because an undiscriminating sympathy makes them plausible. Now modern conditions have certainly tended, as I have said, to the spread of sympathy. Consider modern literature with its disposition to portray any form of human life, however ignoble or worthless, or on the other hand, however lofty or inspiring,—to portray it not because of its intrinsic worth but because of the mere fact that it exists. All sorts and conditions of men,—yes, all sorts and conditions of emotion, however irrational, have their hearing in the world of art to-day, win their expression, charm their audience, get, as we say, their recognition. Never were men so busy as now with the mere eagerness to sympathize with, to feel whatever is the lot of any portion of humanity. Now, as I have said, this spread of human sympathy, furthered as it is by all the means at the disposal of modern science, so far as that science deals with humanity, is a good thing just in so far as it is a basis upon which a rational philanthropy and a more intelligent social organization can be founded. But this habit of sympathy disposes us more and more to the influence of the mob. When the time of popular excitement comes, it finds us expert in sharing the emotions of the crowd, but often enervated by too frequent indulgence in just such emotion. The result is that modern mobs are much vaster, and in some respects more excitable than ever they were before. The psychological conditions of the mob no longer need include the physical presence of a crowd of people in a given place. It is enough if the newspapers, if the theatre, if the other means of social communication, serve to transmit the waves of emotional enthusiasm. A nation composed of many millions of people may fall rapidly under the hypnotic influence of a few leaders, of a few fatal phrases. And thus, as our third evil, we have not only the general levelling tendency of modern social life, but the particular tendency to emotional excitability which tends to make the social order, under certain conditions, not only monotonous and unideal, but actively dangerous.

Yet, as we have seen, this evil is not, as Le Bon and the pessimists would have it, inherent in the very fact of the existence of a social order. There are social groups that are not subject to the mob-spirit. And now if you ask how such social groups are nowadays to be fostered, to be trained, to be kept alive for the service of the nation, I answer that the place for fostering such groups is the province, for such groups flourish under conditions that arouse local pride, the loyalty to one's own community, the willingness to remember one's own ways and ideals, even at the moment when the nation is carried away by some levelling emotion. The lesson would then be: Keep the province awake, that the nation may be saved from the disastrous hypnotic slumber so characteristic of excited masses of mankind.

## VI

I have now reviewed three types of evils against which I think it is the office of provincialism to contend. As I review these evils, I am reminded somewhat of the famous words of Schiller in his "Greeting to the New Century," which he composed at the outset of the nineteenth century. In his age, which in some respects was so analogous to our own, despite certain vast differences, Schiller found himself overwhelmed as he contemplated the social problem of the moment by the vast national conflict, and the overwhelming forces which seemed to him to be crushing the more ideal life of his nation, and of humanity. With a poetic despair that we need indeed no longer share, Schiller counsels his reader, in certain famous lines, to flee from the stress of life into the still recesses of the heart, for, as he says, beauty lives only in song, and freedom has departed into the realm of dreams. Now Schiller spoke in the romantic period. We no longer intend to flee from our social ills to any realm of dreams. And as to the recesses of the heart, we now remember that out of the heart are the issues of life. But so much my own thesis and my own counsel would share in common with Schiller's words. I should say to-day that our national unities have grown so vast, our forces of social consolidation have become so paramount, the resulting problems, conflicts, evils, have been so intensified, that we, too, must flee in the pursuit of the ideal to a new realm. Only this realm is, to my mind, so long as we are speaking of social problems, a realm of real life. It is the realm of the province. There must we flee from the stress of the now too vast and problematic life of the nation as a whole. There we must flee, I mean, not in the sense of a cowardly and permanent retirement, but in the sense of a search for renewed strength, for a social inspiration, for the salvation of the individual from the overwhelming forces of consolidation. Freedom, I should say, dwells now in the small social group, and has its securest home in the provincial life. The nation by itself, apart from the influence of the province, is in danger of becoming an incomprehensible monster, in whose presence the individual loses his right, his self-consciousness, and his dignity. The province must save the individual.

But, you may ask, in what way do I conceive that the wise provincialism of which I speak ought to undertake and carry on its task? How is it to meet the evils of which I have been speaking? In what way is its influence to be exerted against them? And how can the province cultivate its self-consciousness without tending to fall back again into the ancient narrowness from which small communities were so long struggling to escape? How can we keep broad humanity and yet cultivate provincialism? How can we be loyally patriotic, and yet preserve our consciousness of the peculiar and unique dignity of our own community? In what form are our wholesome provincial activities to be carried on?

I answer, of course, in general terms, that the problem of the wholesome provincial consciousness is closely allied to the problem of any individual form of activity. An individual tends to become narrow when he is what we call self-centred. But, on the other hand, philanthropy that is not founded upon a personal loyalty of the individual to his own family and to his own personal duties is notoriously a worthless abstraction. We love the world better when we cherish our own friends the more faithfully. We do not grow in grace by forgetting individual duties in behalf of remote social enterprises. Precisely so, the province will not serve the nation best by forgetting itself, but by loyally emphasizing its own duty to the nation and therefore its right to attain and to cultivate its own unique wisdom. Now all this is indeed obvious enough, but this is precisely what in our days of vast social consolidation we are some of us tending to forget.

Now as to the more concrete means whereby the wholesome provincialism is to be cultivated and encouraged, let me appeal directly to the loyal member of any provincial community, be it the community of a small town, or of a great city, or of a country district. Let me point out what kind of work is needed in order to cultivate that wise provincialism which, as you see, I wish to have grow not in opposition to the interests of the nation, but for the very sake of saving the nation from the modern evil tendencies of which I have spoken.

First, then, I should say a wholesome provincialism is founded upon the thought that while local pride is indeed a praiseworthy accompaniment of every form of social activity, our province, like our own individuality, ought to be to all of us rather an ideal than a mere boast. And here, as I think, is a matter which is too often forgotten. Everything valuable is, in our present human life, known to us as an ideal before it becomes an attainment, and in view of our human imperfections, remains to the end of our short lives much more a hope and an inspiration than it becomes a present achievement. Just because the true issues of human life are brought to a finish not in time but in eternity, it is necessary that in our temporal existence what is most worthy should appear to us as an ideal, as an Ought, rather than as something that is already in our hands. The old saying about the bird in the hand being worth two in the bush does not rightly apply to the ideal goods of a moral agent working under human limitations. For him the very value of life includes the fact that its goal as something infinite can never at any one instant be attained. In this fact the moral agent glories, for it means that he has something to do. Hence the ideal in the bush, so to speak, is always worth infinitely more to him than the food or the plaything of time that happens to be just now in his hands. The difference between vanity and self-respect depends largely upon this emphasizing of ideals in the case of the higher forms of self-consciousness, as opposed to the emphasis upon transient temporal attainments in the case of the lower forms. Now what holds true of individual self-consciousness ought to hold true of the self-consciousness of the community. Boasting is often indeed harmless and may prove a stimulus to good work. It is therefore to be indulged as a tribute to our human weakness. But the better aspect of our provincial consciousness is always its longing for the improvement of the community.

And now, in the second place, a wise provincialism remembers that it is one thing to seek to make ideal values in some unique sense our own, and it is quite another thing to believe that if they are our own, other people cannot possess such ideal values in their own equally unique fashion. A realm of genuinely spiritual individuality is one where each individual has his own unique significance, so that none could take another's place. But for just that very reason all the unique individuals of the truly spiritual order stand in relation to the same universal light, to the same divine whole in relation to

which they win their individuality. Hence all the individuals of the true spiritual order have ideal goods in common, as the very means whereby they can win each his individual place with reference to the possession and the employment of these common goods. Well, it is with provinces as with individuals. The way to win independence is by learning freely from abroad, but by then insisting upon our own interpretation of the common good. A generation ago the Japanese seemed to most European observers to be entering upon a career of total self-surrender. They seemed to be adopting without stint European customs and ideals. They seemed to be abandoning their own national independence of spirit. They appeared to be purely imitative in their main purposes. They asked other nations where the skill of modern sciences lay, and how the new powers were to be gained by them. They seemed to accept with the utmost docility every lesson, and to abandon with unexampled submissiveness, their purpose to remain themselves. Yet those of us who have watched them since, or who have become acquainted with representative Japanese students, know how utterly superficial and illusory that old impression of ours was regarding the dependence, or the extreme imitativeness, or the helpless docility, of the modern Japanese. He has now taught us quite another lesson. With a curious and on the whole not unjust spiritual wiliness, he has learned indeed our lesson, but he has given it his own interpretation. You always feel in intercourse with a Japanese how unconquerable the spirit of his nation is, how inaccessible the recesses of his spirit have remained after all these years of free intercourse with Europeans. In your presence the Japanese always remains the courteous and respectful learner so long as he has reason to think that you have anything to teach him. But he remains as absolutely his own master with regard to the interpretation, the use, the possession of all spiritual gifts, as if he were the master and you the learner. He accepts the gifts, but their place in his national and individual life is his own. And we now begin to see that the feature of the Japanese nationality as a member of the civilized company of nations is to be something quite unique and independent. Well, let the Japanese give us a lesson in the spirit of true provincialism. Provincialism does not mean a lack of plasticity, an unteachable spirit; it means a determination to use the spiritual gifts that come to us from abroad in our own way and with reference to the ideals of our own social order.

And therefore, thirdly, I say in developing your provincial spirit, be quite willing to encourage your young men to have relations with other communities. But on the other hand, encourage them also to make use of what they thus acquire for the furtherance of the life of their own community. Let them win aid from abroad, but let them also have, so far as possible, an opportunity to use this which they acquire in the service of their home. Of course economic conditions rather than deliberate choice commonly determine how far the youth of a province are able to remain for their lifetime in a place where they grow up. But so far as a provincial spirit is concerned, it is well to avoid each of two extremes in the treatment of the young men of the community,—extremes that I have too often seen exemplified. The one extreme consists in maintaining that if young men mean to be loyal to their own province, to their own state, to their own home, they ought to show their loyalty by an unwillingness to seek guidance from foreign literature, from foreign lands, in the patronizing of foreign or distant institutions, or in the acceptance of the customs and ideas of other communities than their own. Against this extreme let the Japanese be our typical instance. They have wandered far. They have studied abroad. They have assimilated the lore of other communities. And they have only gained in local consciousness, in independence of spirit, by the ordeal. The other extreme is the one expressed in that tendency to wander and to encourage wandering, which has led so many of our communities to drive away the best and most active young men. We want more of the determination to find, if possible, a place for our youth in their own communities.

Finally, let the province more and more seek its own adornment. Here I speak of a matter that in all our American communities has been until recently far too much neglected. Local pride ought above all to centre, so far as its material objects are concerned, about the determination to give the surroundings of the community nobility, dignity, beauty. We Americans spend far too much of our early strength and time in our newer communities upon injuring our landscapes, and far too little upon endeavoring to beautify our towns and cities. We have begun to change all that, and while I have no right to speak as an æsthetic judge concerning the growth of the love of the beautiful in our country, I can strongly insist that no community can think any creation of genuine beauty and dignity in its public buildings or in the surroundings of its towns and cities too good a thing for its own deserts. For we deserve what in such realms we can learn how to create or to enjoy, or to make sacrifices for. And no provincialism will become dangerously narrow so long as it is constantly accompanied by a willingness to sacrifice much in order to put in the form of great institutions, of noble architecture, and of beautiful surroundings an expression of the worth that the community attaches to its own ideals.

## Suggestions for Further Reading

**Works by Royce**

*The Conception of Immortality* (Boston: Houghton Mifflin and Company, 1900).

*The Feud at Oak Creek: A Novel of California Life* (Boston: Houghton Mifflin & Company, 1887).

*Fugitive Essays by Josiah Royce,* ed. J. Loewenberg (Cambridge, Mass.: Harvard University Press, 1920).

*The Hope of the Great Community* (New York: Macmillan, 1916).

*Lectures on Modern Idealism,* ed. J. Loewenberg (New Haven: Yale University Press, 1919).

*The Letters of Josiah Royce,* ed. J. Clendenning (Chicago: University of Chicago Press, 1970).

*Outlines of Psychology* (New York: Macmillan, 1903).

*The Philosophy of Loyalty* (New York: Macmillan, 1908; reprinted with an introduction by John J. McDermott by Vanderbilt University Press, 1995).

*The Problem of Christianity,* 2 vols. (New York: Macmillan, 1913; reprinted in a single volume by University of Chicago Press, 1968).

*Race Questions, Provincialism, and Other American Problems* (New York: Macmillan, 1908).

*The Religious Aspect of Philosophy* (Boston: Houghton Mifflin & Company, 1885).

*Royce's Logical Essays,* ed. D. S. Robinson (Dubuque, Ia.: William C. Brown Co., 1951).

*The Sources of Religious Insight* (New York: Charles Scribner's Sons, 1912).

*The Spirit of Modern Philosophy* (Boston: Houghton Mifflin & Company, 1892).

*Studies of Good and Evil* (New York: D. Appleton, 1898).

*War and Insurance* (New York: Macmillan, 1914).

*William James and Other Essays on the Philosophy of Life* (New York: Macmillan, 1911).

*The World and the Individual,* 2 vols. (New York: Macmillan, 1899; reprinted by Dover, 1959, and by Peter Smith, 1976).

### Anthologies

*The Basic Writings of Josiah Royce,* 2 vols., ed. John J. McDermott (Chicago: University of Chicago Press, 1990).

*The Philosophy of Josiah Royce,* ed. J. K. Roth (New York: Thomas Y. Crowell Co., 1971).

### Essential Works on Royce

John Clendenning, *The Life and Thought of Josiah Royce* (Madison, Wisc.: University of Wisconsin Press, 1985).

James Harry Cotton, *Royce on the Human Self* (Cambridge, Mass.: Harvard University Press, 1954).

Peter Fuss, *The Moral Philosophy of Josiah Royce* (Cambridge, Mass.: Harvard University Press, 1965).

Jacquelyn Ann K. Kegley, *Genuine Individuals and Genuine Communities: A Roycean Public Philosophy* (Nashville: Vanderbilt University Press, 1997).

Bruce Kuklick, *Josiah Royce: An Intellectual Biography* (Indianapolis, Ind.: Bobbs-Merrill, 1972).

Mary Brody Mahowald, *An Idealistic Pragmatist* (The Hague: Martinus Nijhoff, 1972).

Gabriel Marcel, *Royce's Metaphysics* (Chicago: Henry Regnery Company, 1956).

Frank M. Oppenheim, *Royce's Voyage Down Under: A Journey of the Mind* (Lexington, Ken.: University Press of Kentucky, 1980).

Frank M. Oppenheim, *Royce's Mature Ethics* (Notre Dame, Ind.: University of Notre Dame Press, 1993).

Frank M. Oppenheim, *Royce's Mature Philosophy of Religion* (Notre Dame, Ind.: University of Notre Dame Press, 1987).

John E. Smith, *Royce's Social Infinite* (New York: The Liberal Arts Press, 1950).

Griffin Trotter, *The Loyal Physician: Roycean Ethics and the Practice of Medicine* (Nashville: Vanderbilt University Press, 1997).

# GEORGE SANTAYANA

## Introduction by John Lachs

### Santayana's Life: Cultural Context and Philosophical Background

George Santayana was born in Madrid, Spain, on December 16, 1863. His mother brought him to the United States when he was nine years old, and he received his education at Boston Latin School and Harvard University. Although he lived through two world wars, his life was uneventful. He remained a bachelor, teaching philosophy at Harvard from 1889 to 1912, when he quit his job to devote himself to writing and travel. He went to Europe but established no permanent home anywhere: for forty years, he journeyed between Spain, Italy, France, and England. He died in Rome in 1952 and is buried there.

Santayana's philosophical ideas crystallized in opposition to the largely Hegelian idealisms current at the time he was a student. He resolutely rejected mind and will as world-creative forces; in his view, there are no minds beyond those connected to individual persons. He was skeptical of our ability to detect grand schemes of progress in history and came close to positivism in maintaining that values are relational accretions that must be distinguished from the physical world of facts. His vision of our condition is naturalistic, in that he sees humans as animals trying to make their way in a world fraught with danger, but also tragic because he thinks conflicts are difficult to avoid and our momentary flowering is followed by inevitable fall.

Santayana was a student, and later a colleague, of James and Royce. He read Peirce and profited from his elaborate studies of symbolism. The Library of Living Philosophers volume on Dewey contains an important philosophical exchange between him and Santayana. In it, these major American thinkers pay little heed to the significant similarities between their views and focus on their disagreements. But in spite of significant American influences on his thought, the most important of which is William James' *The Principles of Psychology,* Santayana's great teachers are Plato and especially Aristotle. The categories he uses, such as essence, matter, and substance, are traditional, if not scholastic. His views of morality and of the spiritual life invite comparison with those of Schopenhauer. Santayana's brilliant grasp of the history of philosophy enabled him to draw extensively on a wide variety of sources. His most remarkable achievement is to have forged a unified and novel system out of such disparate elements.

From before the time he enrolled as an undergraduate at Harvard, Santayana wrote almost without interruption until a few weeks before his death. *The Sense of Beauty,* his first book, appeared in 1896. His literary output includes more than twenty volumes of splendidly written philosophy, literary essays, translations, poetry, autobiography, and even a best-selling novel entitled *The Last Puritan.* Various libraries in the United States still hold unpublished manuscripts of his. A definitive edition of his works is in the process of being published by MIT Press.

In spite of a long writing career, Santayana's opinions changed little over the years. The earlier work, especially the five volumes of *The Life of Reason,* attempted to develop a naturalistic theory of the human condition by means of an analysis of historically situated thought, institutions, and activities. The humanistic tone of these books made them the admired and influential staple of American liberals for many years after the turn of the century. The later work, especially the four volumes of *The Realms of Being,* repeat many of the same points in more accessible, ontological language. Surprisingly, the clearer books gained little acceptance and it is only now that Santayana's star is on the rise again.

## Santayana's System

The selections in this volume (except for his influential observations on "the Genteel Tradition" in American thought and culture) are all from Santayana's ontological period, which commenced after his resignation from Harvard and reached full maturity with the publication, in 1923, of *Scepticism and Animal Faith.* This book is unquestionably the most important and best of Santayana's philosophical works. It presents a fully developed and original system of thought. The conceptual framework it advances offers a persuasive answer to the modern problem of accommodating the results of science without losing the spiritual and moral dimensions of human existence.

The aim of the system is to purify and defend the time-tested beliefs of common sense. But Santayana's skeptical disposition protected him from the naivete of supposing that we have direct access to common sense through ordinary language or the beliefs that seem natural or intuitively right. Instead, he set as his starting point the primary reality of action. To disentangle the tenets of common sense or "animal faith," we must examine what general beliefs the physical actions necessary for life embody.

Eating, for instance, is overt expression of our trust in the independent existence of things and in their power to nourish us. Playing football indicates the conviction that bodies share a common space in which they can, from time to time, touch one another. Waiting for the bus is indication of our tacit commitment that the contents of space are unevenly distributed, while kicking a vicious dog reveals the view that objects in space can have a significant and sustained effect on one another. The philosophy of animal faith consists in the systematic development of the important general beliefs implicated in action. Its justification is that we affirm these beliefs every time we act; though philosophers can deny them in their private thoughts, they give their denial the lie with each movement and every written word.

Although the system of animal faith could be developed without preliminaries as an inventive approach to dealing with the problems of philosophy, Santayana thinks that we must first dispose of traditional views. It would indeed be best if, in accord with the hopes and efforts of many important thinkers, we could find a philosophical method to guarantee the truth and certainty of our opinions. But the power of skepticism makes futile such search for indubitability. It is the possibility of skepticism that destroys traditional epistemology and leaves the field open for animal faith.

The scrutiny to which Santayana subjects our cherished beliefs is unparalleled in the history of skepticism. He begins by questioning our most tenuous opinions, such as those about God, the distant past, and the general structure of the world. It is obvious that these cannot stand up to the rigorous standard of absolute certainty. What about our perceptions? Do they give us incontrovertible information about the world? Santayana notes that sensory consciousness is a combination of some immediately present quality or relation and a collection of beliefs about it and about what it reveals. The quality before the mind is past dispute, but it means nothing and can contribute nothing to knowledge without an account of how it relates to things and other sensations. Any such account, however, is only a matter of opinion, and opinion is always open to doubt.

The same analysis destroys assurance in the veracity of memory. When I remember that I had bacon and eggs for breakfast this morning, I might have a picture before me of what the eggs looked like, some sense of how my hands moved, and a pleasant notion of how the bacon tasted. But these data of consciousness do not constitute a memory; I can call them up in anticipation of eating or in idle revery. They become memory only if I (correctly) believe that they match what happened or what I experienced at an earlier time. And such beliefs are on occasion false and remain ever open to question.

Doubts about memory remove the possibility of knowing persons or selves. Such beings have to enjoy self-identity through a period of time, and no evidence we could adduce for this amounts to proof. Even mathematics fails to yield certain knowledge because it requires memory: the operations of addition and substraction are impossible unless we remember the first number when we focus on the second we wish to relate to it. Finally, Santayana argues that the recognition of an event as a change involves memory of an earlier state and therefore falls short of the dignity of certain information.

We are thus left with nothing but the immediate datum of consciousness. Of this we can be sure when we possess it, but we can know nothing about it and nothing by means of it. The moment we think or say anything concerning it, we lose our right to assurance. The certainty, therefore, is not that of knowing it but of having it, that is, of the simple presence of an unmeaning object before consciousness. The object is neither physical nor mental; it is a changeless, self-identical feature in the contemplation of which we can be absorbed, but which does not characterize anything beyond itself. Certainty can thus be achieved only at the cost of significance. All we can *know,* in the most demanding sense of this term, is the self-identity of whatever may be presented, and this yields no information about either self or world.

The unanswerable force of skepticism yields two important discoveries. The first is recognition that the skeptic shares with the bulk of the philosophical tradition a disastrous criterion of knowledge. According to this standard, knowledge must be unchanging and absolutely certain. The skeptic's success shows not that knowledge is impossible, but only that the rationalist standard by which we measure it is ill-conceived. The demand for total assurance is never imposed in science or in daily life; it is a speculative invention of philosophers. For generations, thinkers have established an ideal beyond our reach and, measuring ordinary cognitive attainments by it, have denounced everything everyone has always believed as worthless, uncertified opinion.

The result is that by setting unreasonable requirements, philosophy distances itself from the concerns of living. In sharp contrast with this, Santayana announces his intention to develop an honest philosophy. He means by this simply the refusal to believe in his reflective moments what he would not or cannot express in his actions. The philosopher is not a detached mind contemplating the world and announcing the standards to which it must aspire.

The second discovery made possible by the skeptical reduction is of neutral objects or essences. These essences are forms or structures that can serve as themes of consciousness. Some of them can be embodied in the material world: as such, they give nature to the things we encounter or eat. Every quality and relation is an essence intrinsically. Each number is an essence or contemplatable form, as is every quality of taste and every human shape from the thin to the obese.

Essences are not restricted to what is important or noble or interesting to us. Every conceivable wickedness and ugliness and boredom has its own special form that renders it just what it is. In fact, even events have a characteristic structure or collection of properties: Santayana calls such forms "tropes." The entirety of *Hamlet* can be seen as a single, immensely complex pattern, and, if we think of it that way, each performance of *Hamlet* becomes simply a separate occasion on which a given essence is embodied in an extended event.

The totality of all forms Santayana names "the realm of essence." We must not think of this "realm" as taking up space, as being located somewhere in the physical universe, or as requiring resources to sustain it. Essences are not physical objects and, if the notion of existence is restricted to items that operate in time and space, they do not exist. This does not mean that they lack reality. On the contrary, they are very real indeed, if only we do not mistakenly suppose that reality must mean the possession of physical or causal power. For they are ever ready to be conceived or embodied if the requisite organ is available to focus on them or to imprint them on the material world.

Essences are eternal in the sense that time makes no difference to their self-identity. Only the physical world has a history; the number 2 is forever without reference to someone who thinks of it and when it is thought. Essences thus do not undergo change. On the contrary, they make alteration possible by providing the features from which and to which existing things can change. But this eternity of forms does not endow them with any moral or metaphysical prerogatives. All essences are on a par in terms of value: none has any intrinsic worth. Whatever good they might be arises from their relation to sentient creatures, and such relations are always external and irrelevant to their nature. This implies that, Plato's views notwithstanding, essences are not intrinsically ideals to which we naturally aspire. Some essence or other may be chosen as a goal by some living being, but even this elevation to a special dignity is alien to their cool and neutral self-identity.

Forms could not serve as ideals, moreover, because there are too many of them. In fact, Santayana maintains that there is an infinite number of essences, each a little or a lot different from all the rest. It is not difficult to think of this infinity if we begin by noting that there is an infinite number of numbers, each a self-identical essence. Each possible shape is an essence also, as is every possible event. The movements that occur on the court in a basketball game, if they are viewed as a totality, constitute a vastly complex essence. If we change one of these motions in the minutest way, we have a slightly different whole and thus another essence. By the permutations and combinations of the motions and by changing the identity, shape, and clothes of the players, we can think of an indefinitely large number of basketball-game essences.

Is there a perfect game? Yes, if we mean the one in which our team prevails. But clearly no, if we look for the pattern all games approximate but never quite attain. All essences are exactly what they are, and even the most boring contest embodies perfectly one of the infinite number of these perfectly self-identical forms. Which one gets embodied is of concern to us but not to the forms; they are passively available for existence but never seek it.

No essence is dependent for its own reality on embodiment in the material world or envisagement by a mind. If anything, the dependence relation goes the other way: without forms, there could be no structured physical objects, and minds would have nothing to think about. Essences, therefore, are absolutely necessary for the existence of anything, even though they themselves do not exist in space and time. Santayana likens them to the garments existence wears or could conceivably wear, and the whole realm of essence to the costumer's gallery that features an inexhaustible supply of garbs.

Much as essences are necessary for there to be a changing material world, they cannot by themselves constitute it. Existence features external, contingent and shifting relations, none of which can be accounted for by essences alone. The material world is always in flux; things in it are constantly coming into being and passing away. Such instability is radically alien to the eternal and placid forms. There must be a force that wrenches a few essences out of the infinity available and endows them with momentary existence. Traditionally, this force was conceived as the creative power of God, who selects the best possible world for actualization. But Santayana sees little reason to suppose that the world in which we live is the best in any sense and thinks that attributing intelligence and good will to the force of existence is an expression of unwarranted optimism.

Accordingly, he names the power that renders essences existent "matter," not in deference to science and its conception of the physical world but as an expression of his convictions that it is not intelligent and that it is at best indifferent to human welfare. This means that there is no ultimate reason why matter selects one set of essences for instantiation rather than any of the others from an infinity of alternatives. The fact that existence falls into habits and tends to repeat the same patterns (tropes) does not remove the arbitrariness of what takes place: the hundredth occurrence of an event is as groundless, though not as surprising, as the first. Matter, therefore, is unintelligible; it is a surd present everywhere but not reducible to a rational principle.

Santayana calls existence "an insane emphasis" and likens matter to a whirlwind that whips essences, as though they were grains of sand, into the vortex of existence. The total inexplicability of existence is seen best by reflecting on the remarkable fact that even its essence is inadequate to give us an insight into its power. For the essence of existence (or of matter) is but another essence, and no essence can be responsible for calling anything into changing, spatio-temporal being. Matter in its creative role thus has no essence at all; it is the faceless other, the natureless counterpart of form. Since our minds can take in only the lucid essences of things, their matter remains to be encountered and dealt with by our bodies.

Following Aristotle, Santayana maintains that all existing things are compounds of matter and form. The entire world of existence he names "substance" or "the field of action." Both of these designations must be stressed. To say that the world is substance amounts to asserting that it exists independently of us and that it is an enduring cosmos rich in potentialities. Adding that it is a field of action cautions us to think of it as a changing, dynamic reality with which we constantly interact. The stability of substance and the changeability of process are in this way united by Santayana as twin features of a universe to which our primary relation is always that of action.

Change in nature consists of the substitution of one essence for another. This interplay of matter and essence defines Santayana's third realm, the realm of truth. Truth is the permanent fact that some essence did, does, or will at some time characterize a portion of the flux of nature. Ideas, judgments, or propositions are true only because they repeat some part of this truth or, in other words, recapture in mind the essence that was embodied. The truth, therefore, always consists of forms, and the realm of truth is simply that segment of the realm of essence that contains all the forms that will have been actualized in the world's history.

This account of truth establishes it as objective and free of any personal, social, or historical influences. There are, of course, personal, social, and historical truths. But these also are objective and unchanging; new perspectives rooted in novel situations and structured by special interests and purposes can make no difference to them. On the contrary, eternally self-identical truths serve as the standard that the historical diversity of views—inquiry itself—must approximate. This is what Santayana means when he says that the truth about anything is the standard comprehensive description of it; he thinks it is an ideal we aim at, it is complete, and it is a permanent record preserved in eternal forms.

Santayana's remarkable affirmation of the objectivity of truth does not compel him to embrace the "eternal verities" of prior philosophical systems. For his objective truths are all humble facts about the world of space and time and about what minds think; they are not grand generalizations or intuitively apprehended principles concerning the nature of reality. Moreover, the presence of truth as a silent witness of whatever occurs neither lessens the labor nor eliminates the tenuousness of human inquiry. We may well capture the truth about some fact without knowing that we did so: the essences constituting the realm of truth are intrinsically no differ-

ent from those destined never to be embodied. Consequently, truth does not shine by its own light, and to identify an essence as a truth requires the hard work of empirical investigation.

Apprehending the literal truth about objects by means of perception is extremely unlikely. Our senses operate on a scale radically different from the subatomic and even the molecular processes that affect us. Accordingly, it is improbable that the essences characterizing nature at those levels could ever be replicated in sensory consciousness. Santayana does not think that this matters much: all knowledge is symbolic cognition and, as such, requires no similarity between the sign in consciousness and what it signifies in the external world.

If there were such a resemblance or identity, we could never know it, and if there is none, we shall never miss it so long as appropriate symbolism is available to do the work of meaning for the mind. Objective truth exerts, therefore, no direct formative influence on the conduct of inquiry; it serves merely as the passive and distant ideal we aim to attain. But our approach to it is gradual at best and, since we must employ the abstract and simplified symbols native to consciousness, it would be a rare and surprising accident if we ever reached it.

Discussion of knowledge brings Santayana's fourth realm of being to the center of attention. The realm of spirit is conditioned in its existence: the consciousnesses that constitute it are produced by matter when it reaches a high level of organization. But spirit is not simply matter shaped by complex tropes. As the cognitive awareness without which knowledge and feeling would be impossible, it is a novel, irreducibly different, emergent form of being. Values themselves require the work of spirit. If there were no consciousness, creation and destruction within the material world would go on unabated, but none of it would be either good or bad.

Santayana's choice of the word "spirit" for awareness reflects his desire to call attention to the spiritual perfection of which humans are capable. In order to understand spirituality, however, we must first get a clear picture of the nature of consciousness. It comes in units called "intuitions," each of which is a moment of cognitive awareness.

Intuition is an act of consciousness, directed at an object. The skeptical reduction convinced Santayana that the object directly before the mind is always an essence. Consciousness apprehends the essence, but such immediate grasp does not constitute knowledge in any significant sense. To make it yield information about existing things, it must be related to them. The relating is accomplished by what Santayana calls "intent," the expression in the sphere of mind of the momentum of animal life. Intent takes the presented essence for a sign of the existence and nature of the physical object we confront, and in doing so it converts immediate awareness into knowledge.

Ordinary cognition consists, in this way, of a presentational and a belief element. An essence or group of essences is presented; as hungry animals, we cannot take them at face value and enjoy them as a picture show. We embrace the conviction, instead, that such essences reveal something about existence. Skeptics can suspend this belief, as can artists when they deal with the pure forms of shapes and sounds. Mathematicians, in contemplating the relation between theorems or numbers irrespective of what these might tell us about the world, also observe the pure play of essences. And all of us can break the hold of belief over us by simply enjoying the sensory appearances or ideas or daydreams we have without taking an interest in whether they are false or true.

When we banish belief from consciousness, intuition is pure. Given the animal basis of mind, such absorption in the immediate is difficult to sustain. But for however short a time we can enjoy it, it opens a life free from the concerns of daily existence and the partiality of the animal in us. This readiness to behold and to take delight in whatever may be presented is the very essence of mind: although consciousness depends on the human organism—the "psyche"—for its existence, its nature is to look past the changing world at eternal essences.

That mind in its purity should take no interest in the battles of the material world is particularly appropriate because it can gain no satisfaction there. Since it consists only of cognitive acts directed on essences, it can exercise no physical power. The psyche is adequate to deal with the vicissitudes of material life; consciousness neither can nor needs to help. And since it can only look on, its attention to the psyche's work fills its days with frustration and worry.

Pure intuition liberates mind to do what is unique to it. The perfection of consciousness is to be the unattached spectator of all time and existence and the contemplator of every possibility. Such transcendence in thought of the physical is what we normally mean by spirituality; and this is precisely the excellence and fulfillment of which calling consciousness "spirit" reminds us. Absorption in pure intuition, even if temporary, constitutes the spiritual life—for Santayana. It is the only escape from the endless toil and dissatisfaction of animal existence. As the ready contemplation of whatever essence happens our way, the spiritual life is free of values and empty of striving.

We have, of course, no release from the fate of animals: we are destined to struggle and to die. Santayana does not believe that there is a God or a life to come. In a posthumously published fragment he wryly remarks that although he has been called many names, no one has ever called him an optimist. Accordingly, the spiritual life represents only intellectual dominion and ideal escape; physically we continue as vulnerable beasts. Since consciousness is individual, the survival of the community provides no comfort for Santayana. Life has only the meaning we find in it before we die. The distant future of humankind is by no means assured; but even if it were, it would be of no significance to those living today.

If there is no God to distinguish right from wrong and if the world consists of embodied essences that constitute a collection of facts without intrinsic value, there can be no good that is either universal or objective. In fact, Santayana makes a point of dissociating values from any changeless or holy sphere. They are simply expressions of the impulses and interests of needy animals. Nothing, therefore, is good in and of itself, irrespective of our organic strivings and the actual context of the flux of life.

Values arise when organism, environment, and consciousness stand in suitable relations to one another. The specific material constitution of the individual forms the basis of selectivity: to someone with my nature, certain objects in the world are food, others poison. The psyche has a definite structure and identifiable needs, desiring things and pursuing its interests relentlessly. Such cravings and seekings are organic, and that means material, facts.

In the process of living, the psyche generates an awareness of its efforts, and this consciousness sees what the organism seeks as suffused with goodness. Goodness is an essence that can be intuited but not embodied. Its organic equivalent is impulse on the part of the psyche; when all goes well, the objects sought are experienced as satisfactory. To call something valuable, therefore, is to say that, as a result of the psyche's interest in it, spirit bathes it in a favorable light or experiences it as characterized by the essence good.

This remarkable theory escapes the usual objections to naturalistic views of the ground of value. In a way reminiscent of James' "The Moral Philosopher and the Moral Life," it regards morality as firmly tied to the desires and predicaments of living beings and refuses to reduce goodness to any one or collection of physical qualities. Moreover, it sets new standards for pluralism and toleration in moral theory, maintaining that one's good depends on one's nature and that natures are always individual.

The view that our fulfillment is not to be measured by how closely we approximate some general human ideal is grounded not only in the sympathetic observation of our diversity, but also in Santayana's conception of the realm of essence. The infinity of forms eliminates their normative force: instead of all members of a species having to share a generic essence that prescribes what they ought to be, each can embody in a full and perfect way its own form or pattern of existence. Since perfection is omnimodal, we can display our varied natures with innocent delight. Given the contingencies of society and the physical world, some of these patterns of life may, of course, not yield good results. But this judgment derives not from social standards or rules laid down by God, but from their incompatibility with existing facts.

The spiritual life gives us reprieve from the world of organically based values. In pure intuition, aesthetic enjoyment of the immediate takes the place of desire and animal striving. Morality, in the sense of self-realization or of discharging all that is latent in us, constitutes the perfection of the psyche. Spirituality, on the other hand, is the excellence of consciousness or mind. The contrast is reminiscent of Aristotle's distinction between moral and intellectual virtue, but Santayana, characteristically, refuses to accept the Aristotelian claim that contemplation is superior.

Values can be compared only in the private imagination, and the validity of the comparison never reaches beyond the individual. It may indeed be true that, for some people, spirituality is better than action in the world. But there is no legitimate way to generalize this judgment: others, given their different natures, can rightly claim that the peace of contemplating essences is death itself. Since all values are relative to the natures of the persons who hold them, there can be no moral agreement without shared psychic constitution.

## Santayana, America, and Europe

Although Santayana's philosophy has been called eclectic, its diverse elements compose a remarkably unified whole. Some commentators maintain that his thought is European, perhaps even scholastic, in character and hence cannot be American in any proper sense. But this judgment presupposes too sharp a contrast between European and American modes of thought, when in fact the continuity between them is obvious and pervasive. Santayana himself has a tendency to resist labeling thoughts by their national origin, and strives to formulate a framework of ideas that comes close to articulating the universal human condition.

In spite of this, however, Santayana's philosophy is undeniably a product of its author's age and social milieu. It shares with the thought of James and Dewey a dogged empiricism and distrust of speculation, a sympathy for varied perfections, and the all-important insistence on the primacy of action. All three great philosophers agree in viewing human beings as natural organisms and nature as an autonomous system. They are at one in their respect for the richness and immediacy of experience and in grounding the good in the needs and desires of human beings.

Santayana shows much less sympathy for the work of Royce, whom he criticizes in detail, and the speculations of Peirce, whom he steadfastly disregards. Both suffer, in his view, from the romanticizing optimism that sees purposiveness or God's purposes everywhere. They think that the good is destined to prevail and that there is no irretrievable loss in the cruel march of events. Belief in progress and in ceaseless self-improvement strikes Santayana as a pernicious obstacle to achieving the finite, even small, perfection open to us. He rejects the infinite striving at the base of such systems and laments the inability of moralists to see the animal heat behind their moral fervor.

Throughout his life, Santayana was fascinated by the American experience. He diagnosed intellectual life in this country as suffering from the insecurity and effeminacy of the "genteel tradition," a cast of mind that looks to Europe to define its standards of propriety. He saw the power of America in its self-confident industry and unreflective drive to create something new and perfect after its kind. He shares this admiration for the process of life with Dewey and, though he often attacked what he saw as the excesses of pragmatism, there is little doubt that he agrees with many of its central tenets.

There are significant philosophical differences between Santayana on the one hand, and Dewey and James on the other. But they are sufficiently close on enough fundamental issues to warrant calling Santayana an American philosopher. In fact, in one respect Santayana is closer to the American grain than most of those native thinkers, such as Peirce, Dewey, and Mead, who are thought to define the tradition. For, remembering Hegel, they tend to stress the formative and nurturing primacy of the community. Santayana, by contrast, celebrates the individual as the fountainhead of all value and the center of the moral world.

At a time when pragmatism is in the midst of a great revival and naturalistic theories are stronger than ever, Santayana's views deserve close study. His honesty as a thinker, his insistence that action form the foundation of philosophy, his appreciation for the diversity of human goods and his sensitivity to the spiritual side of life make his system a serious contender for belief.

His views sit at the crossroads of the philosophical world: they have persuasive similarities not only with the ideas of Dewey and the existentialists but, surprisingly, also with the work of such thinkers as Wittgenstein. They combine the clarity characteristic of analytic philosophy with the moral concerns that dominate Continental and American thought. The goal of uniting the findings of science with the positive insights of religion has eluded many a great philosopher. Santayana comes as close as any in the twentieth century to blending the two in a humane and satisfying edifice of thought.

# The Genteel Tradition in American Philosophy

Ladies and gentlemen,—The privilege of addressing you to-day is very welcome to me, not merely for the honour of it, which is great, nor for the pleasures of travel, which are many, when it is California that one is visiting for the first time, but also because there is something I have long wanted to say which this occasion seems particularly favourable for saying. America is still a young country, and this part of it is especially so; and it would have been nothing extraordinary if, in this young country, material preoccupations had altogether absorbed people's minds, and they had been too much engrossed in living to reflect upon life, or to have any philosophy. The opposite, however, is the case. Not only have you already found time to philosophise in California, as your society proves, but the eastern colonists from the very beginning were a sophisticated race. As much as in clearing the land and fighting the Indians they were occupied, as they expressed it, in wrestling with the Lord. The country was new, but the race was tried, chastened, and full of solemn memories. It was an old wine in new bottles; and America did not have to wait for its present universities, with their departments of academic philosophy, in order to possess a living philosophy—to have a distinct vision of the universe and definite convictions about human destiny.

Now this situation is a singular and remarkable one, and has many consequences, not all

From *Winds of Doctrine Studies in Contemporary Opinion* (New York: Charles Scribner's Sons, 1913), pp. 186–215. Originally delivered to the Philosophical Union of the University of California, August 25, 1911.

of which are equally fortunate. America is a young country with an old mentality: it has enjoyed the advantages of a child carefully brought up and thoroughly indoctrinated; it has been a wise child. But a wise child, an old head on young shoulders, always has a comic and an unpromising side. The wisdom is a little thin and verbal, not aware of its full meaning and grounds; and physical and emotional growth may be stunted by it, or even deranged. Or when the child is too vigorous for that, he will develop a fresh mentality of his own, out of his observations and actual instincts; and this fresh mentality will interfere with the traditional mentality, and tend to reduce it to something perfunctory, conventional, and perhaps secretly despised. A philosophy is not genuine unless it inspires and expresses the life of those who cherish it. I do not think the hereditary philosophy of America has done much to atrophy the natural activities of the inhabitants; the wise child has not missed the joys of youth or of manhood; but what has happened is that the hereditary philosophy has grown stale, and that the academic philosophy afterwards developed has caught the stale odour from it. America is not simply, as I said a moment ago, a young country with an old mentality: it is a country with two mentalities, one a survival of the beliefs and standards of the fathers, the other an expression of the instincts, practice, and discoveries of the younger generations. In all the higher things of the mind—in religion, in literature, in the moral emotions—it is the hereditary spirit that still prevails, so much so that Mr. Bernard Shaw finds that America is a hundred years behind the times. The truth is that one-half of the American mind, that not occupied intensely in practical affairs, has remained, I will not say high-and-dry, but slightly becalmed; it has floated gently in the backwater, while, alongside, in invention and industry and social organisation, the other half of the mind was leaping down a sort of Niagara Rapids. This division may be found symbolised in American architecture: a neat reproduction of the colonial mansion—with some modern comforts introduced surreptitiously—

stands beside the sky-scraper. The American Will inhabits the sky-scraper; the American Intellect inhabits the colonial mansion. The one is the sphere of the American man; the other, at least predominantly, of the American woman. The one is all aggressive enterprise; the other is all genteel tradition.

Now, with your permission, I should like to analyse more fully how this interesting situation has arisen, how it is qualified, and whither it tends. And in the first place we should remember what, precisely, that philosophy was which the first settlers brought with them into the country. In strictness there was more than one; but we may confine our attention to what I will call Calvinism, since it is on this that the current academic philosophy has been grafted. I do not mean exactly the Calvinism of Calvin, or even of Jonathan Edwards; for in their systems there was much that was not pure philosophy, but rather faith in the externals and history of revelation. Jewish and Christian revelation was interpreted by these men, however, in the spirit of a particular philosophy, which might have arisen under any sky, and been associated with any other religion as well as with Protestant Christianity. In fact, the philosophical principle of Calvinism appears also in the Koran, in Spinoza, and in Cardinal Newman; and persons with no very distinctive Christian belief, like Carlyle or like Professor Royce, may be nevertheless, philosophically, perfect Calvinists. Calvinism, taken in this sense, is an expression of the agonised conscience. It is a view of the world which an agonised conscience readily embraces, if it takes itself seriously, as, being agonised, of course it must. Calvinism, essentially, asserts three things: that sin exists, that sin is punished, and that it is beautiful that sin should exist to be punished. The heart of the Calvinist is therefore divided between tragic concern at his own miserable condition, and tragic exultation about the universe at large. He oscillates between a profound abasement and a paradoxical elation of the spirit. To be a Calvinist philosophically is to feel a fierce pleasure in the existence of misery, especially of one's own, in that this misery seems to manifest the fact that the Absolute is irresponsible or infinite or holy. Human nature, it feels, is totally depraved: to have the instincts and motives that we necessarily have is a great scandal, and we must suffer for it; but that scandal is requisite, since otherwise the serious importance of being as we ought to be would not have been vindicated.

To those of us who have not an agonised conscience this system may seem fantastic and even unintelligible; yet it is logically and intently thought out from its emotional premises. It can take permanent possession of a deep mind here and there, and under certain conditions it can become epidemic. Imagine, for instance, a small nation with an intense vitality, but on the verge of ruin, ecstatic and distressful, having a strict and minute code of laws, that paints life in sharp and violent chiaroscuro, all pure righteousness and black abominations, and exaggerating the consequences of both perhaps to infinity. Such a people were the Jews after the exile, and again the early Protestants. If such a people is philosophical at all, it will not improbably be Calvinistic. Even in the early American communities many of these conditions were fulfilled. The nation was small and isolated; it lived under pressure and constant trial; it was acquainted with but a small range of goods and evils. Vigilance over conduct and an absolute demand for personal integrity were not merely traditional things, but things that practical sages, like Franklin and Washington, recommended to their countrymen, because they were virtues that justified themselves visibly by their fruits. But soon these happy results themselves helped to relax the pressure of external circumstances, and indirectly the pressure of the agonised conscience within. The nation became numerous; it ceased to be either ecstatic or distressful; the high social morality which on the whole it preserved took another colour; people remained honest and helpful out of good sense and good will rather than out of scrupulous adherence to any fixed principles. They retained their instinct for order, and often created order with surprising quickness; but the sanctity of law, to be

obeyed for its own sake, began to escape them; it seemed too unpractical a notion, and not quite serious. In fact, the second and native-born American mentality began to take shape. The sense of sin totally evaporated. Nature, in the words of Emerson, was all beauty and commodity; and while operating on it laboriously, and drawing quick returns, the American began to drink in inspiration from it æsthetically. At the same time, in so broad a continent, he had elbow-room. His neighbours helped more than they hindered him; he wished their number to increase. Good will became the great American virtue; and a passion arose for counting heads, and square miles, and cubic feet, and minutes saved—as if there had been anything to save them for. How strange to the American now that saying of Jonathan Edwards, that men are naturally God's enemies! Yet that is an axiom to any intelligent Calvinist, though the words he uses may be different. If you told the modern American that he is totally depraved, he would think you were joking, as he himself usually is. He is convinced that he always has been, and always will be, victorious and blameless.

Calvinism thus lost its basis in American life. Some emotional natures, indeed, reverted in their religious revivals or private searchings of heart to the sources of the tradition; for any of the radical points of view in philosophy may cease to be prevalent, but none can cease to be possible. Other natures, more sensitive to the moral and literary influences of the world, preferred to abandon parts of their philosophy, hoping thus to reduce the distance which should separate the remainder from real life.

Meantime, if anybody arose with a special sensibility or a technical genius, he was in great straits; not being fed sufficiently by the world, he was driven in upon his own resources. The three American writers whose personal endowment was perhaps the finest— Poe, Hawthorne, and Emerson—had all a certain starved and abstract quality. They could not retail the genteel tradition; they were too keen, too perceptive, and too independent for that. But life offered them little digestible material, nor were they naturally voracious.

They were fastidious, and under the circumstances they were starved. Emerson, to be sure, fed on books. There was a great catholicity in his reading; and he showed a fine tact in his comments, and in his way of appropriating what he read. But he read transcendentally, not historically, to learn what he himself felt, not what others might have felt before him. And to feed on books, for a philosopher or a poet, is still to starve. Books can help him to acquire form, or to avoid pitfalls; they cannot supply him with substance, if he is to have any. Therefore the genius of Poe and Hawthorne, and even of Emerson, was employed on a sort of inner play, or digestion of vacancy. It was a refined labour, but it was in danger of being morbid, or tinkling, or self-indulgent. It was a play of intra-mental rhymes. Their mind was like an old music-box, full of tender echoes and quaint fancies. These fancies expressed their personal genius sincerely, as dreams may; but they were arbitrary fancies in comparison with what a real observer would have said in the premises. Their manner, in a word, was subjective. In their own persons they escaped the mediocrity of the genteel tradition, but they supplied nothing to supplant it in other minds.

The churches, likewise, although they modified their spirit, had no philosophy to offer save a new emphasis on parts of what Calvinism contained. The theology of Calvin, we must remember, had much in it besides philosophical Calvinism. A Christian tenderness, and a hope of grace for the individual, came to mitigate its sardonic optimism; and it was these evangelical elements that the Calvinistic churches now emphasised, seldom and with blushes referring to hell-fire or infant damnation. Yet philosophic Calvinism, with a theory of life that would perfectly justify hell-fire and infant damnation if they happened to exist, still dominates the traditional metaphysics. It is an ingredient, and the decisive ingredient, in what calls itself idealism. But in order to see just what part Calvinism plays in current idealism, it will be necessary to distinguish the other chief element in that complex system, namely, transcendentalism.

Transcendentalism is the philosophy which the romantic era produced in Germany, and independently, I believe, in America also. Transcendentalism proper, like romanticism, is not any particular set of dogmas about what things exist; it is not a system of the universe regarded as a fact, or as a collection of facts. It is a method, a point of view, from which any world, no matter what it might contain, could be approached by a self-conscious observer. Transcendentalism is systematic subjectivism. It studies the perspectives of knowledge as they radiate from the self; it is a plan of those avenues of inference by which our ideas of things must be reached, if they are to afford any systematic or distant vistas. In other words, transcendentalism is the critical logic of science. Knowledge, it says, has a station, as in a watch-tower; it is always seated here and now, in the self of the moment. The past and the future, things inferred and things conceived, lie around it, painted as upon a panorama. They cannot be lighted up save by some centrifugal ray of attention and present interest, by some active operation of the mind.

This is hardly the occasion for developing or explaining this delicate insight; suffice it to say, lest you should think later that I disparage transcendentalism, that as a method I regard it as correct and, when once suggested, unforgettable. I regard it as the chief contribution made in modern times to speculation. But it is a method only, an attitude we may always assume if we like and that will always be legitimate. It is no answer, and involves no particular answer, to the question: What exists; in what order is what exists produced; what is to exist in the future? This question must be answered by observing the object, and tracing humbly the movement of the object. It cannot be answered at all by harping on the fact that this object, if discovered, must be discovered by somebody, and by somebody who has an interest in discovering it. Yet the Germans who first gained the full transcendental insight were romantic people; they were more or less frankly poets; they were colossal egotists, and wished to make not only their own knowledge but the whole universe centre about themselves. And full as they were of their romantic isolation and romantic liberty, it occurred to them to imagine that all reality might be a transcendental self and a romantic dreamer like themselves; nay, that it might be just their own transcendental self and their own romantic dreams extended indefinitely. Transcendental logic, the method of discovery for the mind, was to become also the method of evolution in nature and history. Transcendental method, so abused, produced transcendental myth. A conscientious critique of knowledge was turned into a sham system of nature. We must therefore distinguish sharply the transcendental grammar of the intellect, which is significant and potentially correct, from the various transcendental systems of the universe, which are chimeras.

In both its parts, however, transcendentalism had much to recommend it to American philosophers, for the transcendental method appealed to the individualistic and revolutionary temper of their youth, while transcendental myths enabled them to find a new status for their inherited theology, and to give what parts of it they cared to preserve some semblance of philosophical backing. This last was the use to which the transcendental method was put by Kant himself, who first brought it into vogue, before the terrible weapon had got out of hand, and become the instrument of pure romanticism. Kant came, he himself said, to remove knowledge in order to make room for faith, which in his case meant faith in Calvinism. In other words, he applied the transcendental method to matters of fact, reducing them thereby to human ideas, in order to give to the Calvinistic postulates of conscience a metaphysical validity. For Kant had a genteel tradition of his own, which he wished to remove to a place of safety, feeling that the empirical world had become too hot for it; and this place of safety was the region of transcendental myth. I need hardly say how perfectly this expedient suited the needs of philosophers in America, and it is no accident if the influence of Kant soon became dominant here. To embrace this philosophy was regarded as a sign of profound metaphysical insight, although the

most mediocre minds found no difficulty in embracing it. In truth it was a sign of having been brought up in the genteel tradition, of feeling it weak, and of wishing to save it.

But the transcendental method, in its way, was also sympathetic to the American mind. It embodied, in a radical form, the spirit of Protestantism as distinguished from its inherited doctrines; it was autonomous, undismayed, calmly revolutionary; it felt that Will was deeper than Intellect; it focussed everything here and now, and asked all things to show their credentials at the bar of the young self, and to prove their value for this latest born moment. These things are truly American; they would be characteristic of any young society with a keen and discursive intelligence, and they are strikingly exemplified in the thought and in the person of Emerson. They constitute what he called self-trust. Self-trust, like other transcendental attitudes, may be expressed in metaphysical fables. The romantic spirit may imagine itself to be an absolute force, evoking and moulding the plastic world to express its varying moods. But for a pioneer who is actually a world-builder this metaphysical illusion has a partial warrant in historical fact; far more warrant than it could boast of in the fixed and articulated society of Europe, among the moon-struck rebels and sulking poets of the romantic era. Emerson was a shrewd Yankee, by instinct on the winning side; he was a cheery, child-like soul, impervious to the evidence of evil, as of everything that it did not suit his transcendental individuality to appreciate or to notice. More, perhaps, than anybody that has ever lived, he practised the transcendental method in all its purity. He had no system. He opened his eyes on the world every morning with a fresh sincerity, marking how things seemed to him then, or what they suggested to his spontaneous fancy. This fancy, for being spontaneous, was not always novel; it was guided by the habits and training of his mind, which were those of a preacher. Yet he never insisted on his notions so as to turn them into settled dogmas; he felt in his bones that they were myths. Sometimes, indeed, the bad example of other transcendentalists, less true than he to their method, or the pressing questions of unintelligent people, or the instinct we all have to think our ideas final, led him to the very verge of system-making; but he stopped short. Had he made a system out of his notion of compensation, or the over-soul, or spiritual laws, the result would have been as thin and forced as it is in other transcendental systems. But he covered truth; and he returned to experience, to history, to poetry, to the natural science of his day, for new starting-points and hints toward fresh transcendental musings.

To covet truth is a very distinguished passion. Every philosopher says he is pursuing the truth, but this is seldom the case. As Mr. Bertrand Russell has observed, one reason why philosophers often fail to reach the truth is that often they do not desire to reach it. Those who are genuinely concerned in discovering what happens to be true are rather the men of science, the naturalists, the historians; and ordinarily they discover it, according to their lights. The truths they find are never complete, and are not always important; but they are integral parts of the truth, facts and circumstances that help to fill in the picture, and that no later interpretation can invalidate or afford to contradict. But professional philosophers are usually only apologists: that is, they are absorbed in defending some vested illusion or some eloquent idea. Like lawyers or detectives, they study the case for which they are retained, to see how much evidence or semblance of evidence they can gather for the defence, and how much prejudice they can raise against the witnesses for the prosecution; for they know they are defending prisoners suspected by the world, and perhaps by their own good sense, of falsification. They do not covet truth, but victory and the dispelling of their own doubts. What they defend is some system, that is, some view about the totality of things, of which men are actually ignorant. No system would have ever been framed if people had been simply interested in knowing what is true, whatever it may be. What produces systems is the interest in maintaining against all comers that some favourite or inherited idea of ours is sufficient and right.

A system may contain an account of many things which, in detail, are true enough; but as a system, covering infinite possibilities that neither our experience nor our logic can prejudge, it must be a work of imagination and a piece of human soliloquy. It may be expressive of human experience, it may be poetical; but how should any one who really coveted truth suppose that it was true?

Emerson had no system; and his coveting truth had another exceptional consequence: he was detached, unworldly, contemplative. When he came out of the conventicle or the reform meeting, or out of the rapturous close atmosphere of the lecture-room, he heard Nature whispering to him: "Why so hot, little sir?" No doubt the spirit or energy of the world is what is acting in us, as the sea is what rises in every little wave; but it passes through us, and cry out as we may, it will move on. Our privilege is to have perceived it as it moves. Our dignity is not in what we do, but in what we understand. The whole world is doing things. We are turning in that vortex; yet within us is silent observation, the speculative eye before which all passes, which bridges the distances and compares the combatants. On this side of his genius Emerson broke away from all conditions of age or country and represented nothing except intelligence itself.

There was another element in Emerson, curiously combined with transcendentalism, namely, his love and respect for Nature. Nature, for the transcendentalist, is precious because it is his own work, a mirror in which he looks at himself and says (like a poet relishing his own verses), "What a genius I am! Who would have thought there was such stuff in me?" And the philosophical egotist finds in his doctrine a ready explanation of whatever beauty and commodity nature actually has. No wonder, he says to himself, that nature is sympathetic, since I made it. And such a view, one-sided and even fatuous as it may be, undoubtedly sharpens the vision of a poet and a moralist to all that is inspiriting and symbolic in the natural world. Emerson was particularly ingenious and clear-sighted in feeling the spiritual uses of fellowship with the elements.

This is something in which all Teutonic poetry is rich and which forms, I think, the most genuine and spontaneous part of modern taste, and especially of American taste. Just as some people are naturally enthralled and refreshed by music, so others are by landscape. Music and landscape make up the spiritual resources of those who cannot or dare not express their unfulfilled ideals in words. Serious poetry, profound religion (Calvinism, for instance), are the joys of an unhappiness that confesses itself; but when a genteel tradition forbids people to confess that they are unhappy, serious poetry and profound religion are closed to them by that; and since human life, in its depths, cannot then express itself openly, imagination is driven for comfort into abstract arts, where human circumstances are lost sight of, and human problems dissolve in a purer medium. The pressure of care is thus relieved, without its quietus being found in intelligence. To understand oneself is the classic form of consolation; to elude oneself is the romantic. In the presence of music or landscape human experience eludes itself; and thus romanticism is the bond between transcendental and naturalistic sentiment. The winds and clouds come to minister to the solitary ego.

Have there been, we may ask, any successful efforts to escape from the genteel tradition, and to express something worth expressing behind its back? This might well not have occurred as yet; but America is so precocious, it has been trained by the genteel tradition to be so wise for its years, that some indications of a truly native philosophy and poetry are already to be found. I might mention the humorists, of whom you here in California have had your share. The humorists, however, only half escape the genteel tradition; their humour would lose its savour if they had wholly escaped it. They point to what contradicts it in the facts; but not in order to abandon the genteel tradition, for they have nothing solid to put in its place. When they point out how ill many facts fit into it, they do not clearly conceive that this militates against the standard, but think it a funny perversity in the facts. Of course, did they earnestly respect the genteel tradition, such an incongruity would seem to them sad, rather than ludicrous. Perhaps the prevalence of humour in America, in and out of season, may be taken as one more evidence that the genteel tradition is present pervasively, but everywhere weak. Similarly in Italy, during the Renaissance, the Catholic tradition could not be banished from the intellect, since there was nothing articulate to take its place; yet its hold on the heart was singularly relaxed. The consequence was that humorists could regale themselves with the foibles of monks and of cardinals, with the credulity of fools, and the bogus miracles of the saints; not intending to deny the theory of the church, but caring for it so little at heart that they could find it infinitely amusing that it should be contradicted in men's lives and that no harm should come of it. So when Mark Twain says, "I was born of poor but dishonest parents," the humour depends on the parody of the genteel Anglo-Saxon convention that it is disreputable to be poor; but to hint at the hollowness of it would not be amusing if it did not remain at bottom one's habitual conviction.

The one American writer who has left the genteel tradition entirely behind is perhaps Walt Whitman. For this reason educated Americans find him rather an unpalatable person, who they sincerely protest ought not to be taken for a representative of their culture; and he certainly should not, because their culture is so genteel and traditional. But the foreigner may sometimes think otherwise, since he is looking for what may have arisen in America to express, not the polite and conventional American mind, but the spirit and the inarticulate principles that animate the community, on which its own genteel mentality seems to sit rather lightly. When the foreigner opens the pages of Walt Whitman, he thinks that he has come at last upon something representative and original. In Walt Whitman democracy is carried into psychology and morals. The various sights, moods, and emotions are given each one vote; they are declared to be all free and equal, and the innumerable commonplace moments of life are suffered to speak like the others. Those moments formerly reputed great are not excluded, but they are made to march in the ranks with their companions—plain foot-soldiers and servants of the hour. Nor does the refusal to discriminate stop there; we must carry our principle further down, to the animals, to inanimate nature, to the cosmos as a whole. Whitman became a pantheist; but his pantheism, unlike that of the Stoics and of Spinoza, was unintellectual, lazy, and self-indulgent; for he simply felt jovially that everything real was good enough, and that he was good enough himself. In him Bohemia rebelled against the genteel tradition; but the reconstruction that alone can justify revolution did not ensue. His attitude, in principle, was utterly disintegrating; his poetic genius fell back to the lowest level, perhaps, to which it is possible for poetic genius to fall. He reduced his imagination to a passive sensorium for the registering of impressions. No element of construction remained in it, and therefore no element of penetration. But his scope was wide; and his lazy, desultory apprehension was poetical. His work, for the very reason that it is so rudimentary, contains a beginning, or rather many beginnings, that might possibly grow into a noble moral imagination, a worthy filling for the human mind. An American in the nineteenth century who completely disregarded the genteel tradition could hardly have done more.

But there is another distinguished man, lately lost to this country, who has given some rude shocks to this tradition and who, as much as Whitman, may be regarded as representing the genuine, the long silent American mind—I mean William James. He and his brother Henry were as tightly swaddled in the genteel tradition as any infant geniuses could be, for they were born before 1850, and in a Swedenborgian household. Yet they burst those bands almost entirely. The ways in which the two brothers freed themselves, however, are interestingly different. Mr. Henry James has done it by adopting the point of view of the outer world, and by turning the genteel American tradition, as he turns everything else, into a subject-matter for analysis. For him it is a curious habit of mind, intimately comprehended, to be compared with other habits of mind, also well known to him. Thus he has overcome the genteel tradition in the classic way, by understanding it. With William James too this infusion of worldly insight and European sympathies was a potent influence, especially in his earlier days; but the chief source of his liberty was another. It was his personal spontaneity, similar to that of Emerson, and his personal vitality, similar to that of nobody else. Convictions and ideas came to him, so to speak, from the subsoil. He had a prophetic sympathy with the dawning sentiments of the age, with the moods of the dumb majority. His scattered words caught fire in many parts of the world. His way of thinking and feeling represented the true America, and represented in a measure the whole ultra-modern, radical world. Thus he eluded the genteel tradition in the romantic way, by continuing it into its opposite. The romantic mind, glorified in Hegel's dialectic (which is not dialectic at all, but a sort of tragi-comic history of experience), is always rendering its thoughts unrecognisable through the infusion of new insights, and through the insensible transformation of the moral feeling that accompanies them, till at last it has completely reversed its old judgments under cover of expanding them. Thus the genteel tradition was led a merry dance when it fell again into the hands of a genuine and vigorous romanticist like William James. He restored their revolutionary force to its neutralised elements, by picking them out afresh, and emphasising them separately, according to his personal predilections.

For one thing, William James kept his mind and heart wide open to all that might seem, to polite minds, odd, personal, or visionary in religion and philosophy. He gave a sincerely respectful hearing to sentimentalists, mystics, spiritualists, wizards, cranks, quacks, and impostors—for it is hard to draw the line, and James was not willing to draw it prematurely. He thought, with his usual modesty, that any of these might have something to teach him. The lame, the halt, the blind, and those speaking with tongues could come to him with the certainty of finding sympathy; and if they were not healed, at least they were comforted, that a famous professor should take them so seriously; and they began to feel that after all to have only one leg, or one hand, or one eye, or to have three, might be in itself no less beauteous than to have just two, like the stolid majority. Thus William James became the friend and helper of those groping, nervous, half-educated, spiritually disinherited, passionately hungry individuals of which America is full. He became, at the same time, their spokesman and representative before the learned world; and he made it a chief part of his vocation to recast what the learned world has to offer, so that as far as possible it might serve the needs and interests of these people.

Yet the normal practical masculine American, too, had a friend in William James. There is a feeling abroad now, to which biology and Darwinism lend some colour, that theory is simply an instrument for practice, and intelligence merely a help toward material survival. Bears, it is said, have fur and claws, but poor naked man is condemned to be intelligent, or he will perish. This feeling William James embodied in that theory of thought and of truth which he called pragmatism. Intelligence, he thought, is no miraculous, idle faculty, by which we mirror passively any or everything that happens to be true, reduplicating the real world to no purpose. Intelligence has its roots and its issue in the context of events; it is one kind of practical adjustment, an experimental act, a form of vital tension. It does not essentially serve to picture other parts of reality, but to connect them. This view was not worked out by William James in its psychological and historical details; unfortunately he developed it chiefly in controversy against its opposite, which he called intellectualism, and which he hated with all the hatred of which his kind heart was capable. Intellectualism, as he conceived it, was pure pedantry; it impoverished and verbalised everything, and tied up nature in red tape. Ideas and rules that may have been occasionally useful it put in the place of the full-blooded irrational movement of life which had called them into being; and these abstractions, so soon obsolete, it strove to fix and to worship for ever. Thus all creeds and theories and all formal precepts sink in the estimation of the pragmatist to a local and temporary grammar of action; a grammar that must be changed slowly by time, and may be changed quickly

by genius. To know things as a whole, or as they are eternally, if there is anything eternal in them, is not only beyond our powers, but would prove worthless, and perhaps even fatal to our lives. Ideas are not mirrors, they are weapons; their function is to prepare us to meet events, as future experience may unroll them. Those ideas that disappoint us are false ideas; those to which events are true are true themselves.

This may seem a very utilitarian view of the mind; and I confess I think it a partial one, since the logical force of beliefs and ideas, their truth or falsehood as assertions, has been overlooked altogether, or confused with the vital force of the material processes which these ideas express. It is an external view only, which marks the place and conditions of the mind in nature, but neglects its specific essence; as if a jewel were defined as a round hole in a ring. Nevertheless, the more materialistic the pragmatist's theory of the mind is, the more vitalistic his theory of nature will have to become. If the intellect is a device produced in organic bodies to expedite their processes, these organic bodies must have interests and a chosen direction in their life; otherwise their life could not be expedited, nor could anything be useful to it. In other words—and this is a third point at which the philosophy of William James has played havoc with the genteel tradition, while ostensibly defending it—nature must be conceived anthropomorphically and in psychological terms. Its purposes are not to be static harmonies, self-unfolding destinies, the logic of spirit, the spirit of logic, or any other formal method and abstract law; its purposes are to be concrete endeavours, finite efforts of souls living in an environment which they transform and by which they, too, are affected. A spirit, the divine spirit as much as the human, as this new animism conceives it, is a romantic adventurer. Its future is undetermined. Its scope, its duration, and the quality of its life are all contingent. This spirit grows; it buds and sends forth feelers, sounding the depths around for such other centres of force or life as may exist there. It has a vital momentum, but no predetermined goal. It uses its past as a stepping-stone, or rather as a diving-board, but has an absolutely fresh will at each moment to plunge this way or that into the unknown. The universe is an experiment; it is unfinished. It has no ultimate or total nature, because it has no end. It embodies no formula or statable law; any formula is at best a poor abstraction, describing what, in some region and for some time, may be the most striking characteristic of existence; the law is a description *a posteriori* of the habit things have chosen to acquire, and which they may possibly throw off altogether. What a day may bring forth is uncertain; uncertain even to God. Omniscience is impossible; time is real; what had been omniscience hitherto might discover something more to-day. "There shall be news," William James was fond of saying with rapture, quoting from the unpublished poem of an obscure friend, "there shall be news in heaven!" There is almost certainly, he thought, a God now; there may be several gods, who might exist together, or one after the other. We might, by our conspiring sympathies, help to make a new one. Much in us is doubtless immortal; we survive death for some time in a recognisable form; but what our career and transformations may be in the sequel we cannot tell, although we may help to determine them by our daily choices. Observation must be continual if our ideas are to remain true. Eternal vigilance is the price of knowledge; perpetual hazard, perpetual experiment keep quick the edge of life.

This is, so far as I know, a new philosophical vista: it is a conception never before presented, although implied, perhaps, in various quarters, as in Norse and even Greek mythology. It is a vision radically empirical and radically romantic; and as William James himself used to say, the visions and not the arguments of a philosopher are the interesting and influential things about him. William James, rather too generously, attributed this vision to M. Bergson, and regarded him in consequence as a philosopher of the first rank, whose thought was to be one of the turning-points in history. M. Bergson had killed intellectualism. It was his book on creative evolution, said James with humorous emphasis, that had come at last to "*écraser l'infâme* [crush the infamous and base]." We may suspect, notwithstanding, that intellectualism, infamous and crushed, will

survive the blow; and if the author of the Book of Ecclesiastes were now alive, and heard that there shall be news in heaven, he would doubtless say that there may possibly be news there, but that under the sun there is nothing new— not even radical empiricism or radical romanticism, which from the beginning of the world has been the philosophy of those who as yet had had little experience; for to the blinking little child it is not merely something in the world that is new daily, but everything is new all day.

I am not concerned with the rights and wrongs of that controversy; my point is only that William James, in this genial evolutionary view of the world, has given a rude shock to the genteel tradition. What! The world a gradual improvisation? Creation unpremeditated? God a sort of young poet or struggling artist? William James is an advocate of theism; pragmatism adds one to the evidences of religion; that is excellent. But is not the cool abstract piety of the genteel getting more than it asks for? This empirical naturalistic God is too crude and positive a force; he will work miracles, he will answer prayers, he may inhabit distinct places, and have distinct conditions under which alone he can operate; he is a neighbouring being, whom we can act upon, and rely upon for specific aids, as upon a personal friend, or a physician, or an insurance company. How disconcerting! Is not this new theology a little like superstition? And yet how interesting, how exciting, if it should happen to be true! I am far from wishing to suggest that such a view seems to me more probable than conventional idealism or than Christian orthodoxy. All three are in the region of dramatic system-making and myth to which probabilities are irrelevant. If one man says the moon is sister to the sun, and another that she is his daughter, the question is not which notion is more probable, but whether either of them is at all expressive. The so-called evidences are devised afterwards, when faith and imagination have prejudged the issue. The force of William James's new theology, or romantic cosmology, lies only in this: that it has broken the spell of the genteel tradition, and enticed faith in a new direction, which on second thoughts may prove no less alluring than the old. The important fact is not that the new fancy might possibly be true—who shall know that?—but that it has entered the heart of a leading American to conceive and to cherish it. The genteel tradition cannot be dislodged by these insurrections; there are circles to which it is still congenial, and where it will be preserved. But it has been challenged and (what is perhaps more insidious) it has been discovered. No one need be browbeaten any longer into accepting it. No one need be afraid, for instance, that his fate is sealed because some young prig may call him a dualist; the pint would call the quart a dualist, if you tried to pour the quart into him. We need not be afraid of being less profound, for being direct and sincere. The intellectual world may be traversed in many directions; the whole has not been surveyed; there is a great career in it open to talent. That is a sort of knell, that tolls the passing of the genteel tradition. Something else is now in the field; something else can appeal to the imagination, and be a thousand times more idealistic than academic idealism, which is often simply a way of white-washing and adoring things as they are. The illegitimate monopoly which the genteel tradition had established over what ought to be assumed and what ought to be hoped for has been broken down by the first-born of the family, by the genius of the race. Henceforth there can hardly be the same peace and the same pleasure in hugging the old proprieties. Hegel will be to the next generation what Sir William Hamilton was to the last. Nothing will have been disproved, but everything will have been abandoned. An honest man has spoken, and the cant of the genteel tradition has become harder for young lips to repeat.

With this I have finished such a sketch as I am here able to offer you of the genteel tradition in American philosophy. The subject is complex, and calls for many an excursus and qualifying footnote; yet I think the main outlines are clear enough. The chief fountains of this tradition were Calvinism and transcendentalism. Both were living fountains; but to keep them alive they required, one an agonised conscience, and the other a radical subjective criticism of knowledge. When these rare meta-

physical preoccupations disappeared—and the American atmosphere is not favourable to either of them—the two systems ceased to be inwardly understood; they subsisted as sacred mysteries only; and the combination of the two in some transcendental system of the universe (a contradiction in principle) was doubly artificial. Besides, it could hardly be held with a single mind. Natural science, history, the beliefs implied in labour and invention, could not be disregarded altogether; so that the transcendental philosopher was condemned to a double allegiance, and to not letting his left hand know the bluff that his right hand was making. Nevertheless, the difficulty in bringing practical inarticulate convictions to expression is very great, and the genteel tradition has subsisted in the academic mind for want of anything equally academic to take its place.

The academic mind, however, has had its flanks turned. On the one side came the revolt of the Bohemian temperament, with its poetry of crude naturalism; on the other side came an impassioned empiricism, welcoming popular religious witnesses to the unseen, reducing science to an instrument of success in action, and declaring the universe to be wild and young, and not to be harnessed by the logic of any school.

This revolution, I should think, might well find an echo among you, who live in a thriving society, and in the presence of a virgin and prodigious world. When you transform nature to your uses, when you experiment with her forces, and reduce them to industrial agents, you cannot feel that nature was made by you or for you, for then these adjustments would have been pre-established. Much less can you feel it when she destroys your labour of years in a momentary spasm. You must feel, rather, that you are an offshoot of her life; one brave little force among her immense forces. When you escape, as you love to do, to your forests and your sierras, I am sure again that you do not feel you made them, or that they were made for you. They have grown, as you have grown, only more massively and more slowly. In their non-human beauty and peace they stir the sub-human depths and the superhuman possibilities of your own spirit. It is no transcendental logic that they teach; and they give no sign of any deliberate morality seated in the world. It is rather the vanity and superficiality of all logic, the needlessness of argument, the relativity of morals, the strength of time, the fertility of matter, the variety, the unspeakable variety, of possible life. Everything is measurable and conditioned, indefinitely repeated, yet, in repetition, twisted somewhat from its old form. Everywhere is beauty and nowhere permanence, everywhere an incipient harmony, nowhere an intention, nor a responsibility, nor a plan. It is the irresistible suasion of this daily spectacle, it is the daily discipline of contact with things, so different from the verbal discipline of the schools, that will, I trust, inspire the philosophy of your children. A Californian whom I had recently the pleasure of meeting observed that, if the philosophers had lived among your mountains their systems would have been different from what they are. Certainly, I should say, very different from what those systems are which the European genteel tradition has handed down since Socrates; for these systems are egotistical; directly or indirectly they are anthropocentric, and inspired by the conceited notion that man, or human reason, or the human distinction between good and evil, is the centre and pivot of the universe. That is what the mountains and the woods should make you at last ashamed to assert. From what, indeed, does the society of nature liberate you, that you find it so sweet? It is hardly (is it?) that you wish to forget your past, or your friends, or that you have any secret contempt for your present ambitions. You respect these, you respect them perhaps too much; you are not suffered by the genteel tradition to criticise or to reform them at all radically. No; it is the yoke of this genteel tradition itself that these primeval solitudes lift from your shoulders. They suspend your forced sense of your own importance not merely as individuals, but even as men. They allow you, in one happy moment, at once to play and to worship, to take yourselves simply, humbly, for what you are, and to salute the wild, indifferent, non-censorious infinity of nature. You are admonished that what you can do avails little materially, and in the end nothing. At the same time, through wonder and pleasure, you are taught speculation. You learn what you are really fitted to do, and where lie your natural dignity and joy, namely, in representing many things, without being them, and in letting your imagination, through sympathy, celebrate and echo their life. Because the peculiarity of man is that his machinery for reaction on external things has involved an imaginative transcript of these things, which is preserved and suspended in his fancy; and the interest and beauty of this inward landscape, rather than any fortunes that may await his body in the outer world, constitute his proper happiness. By their mind, its scope, quality, and temper, we estimate men, for by the mind only do we exist as men, and are more than so many storage-batteries for material energy. Let us therefore be frankly human. Let us be content to live in the mind.

# Some Meanings of the Word "Is"

*Language is Loose because Significant.*— Words, as Bacon said, are wise men's counters, they mark some gain or some wager of thought. If they prejudice philosophy, they contain philosophy. The articulation of language, however, can never be the articulation

From *Obiter Scripta: Lectures, Essays and Reviews,* eds. Justus Buchler and Benjamin Schwartz (New York: Charles Scribner's Sons, 1936), pp. 189–212.

of things. Language is a by-product of animal life which may eventually serve as a record or as an instrument; it helps to summarize, classify, and analyze man's contact with the world, reducing things to human perspectives on a human scale. Nor can language preserve the scope or movement even of thought, since it marks only certain terms or *termini*—boundary stones like statues at the end of vistas—on which attention is sharply arrested; the approach, the atmosphere, and the setting remain unnamed. A word cannot be adequate if it has a meaning at all; only whistling is adequate. Significant speech is a lasso thrown into the air, lucky if it catches some living thing by a leg or by a horn. It would be idle as well as ungrateful to quarrel with words when one must use them; but in venturing upon a long discourse it may be prudent to notice the degree to which some important term abbreviates the facts it stands for, or puts them under an alien category; and since I am about to distinguish various realms of being, I will begin with some consideration of the word "*is*," for this little word has many meanings.

*First meaning of the word "is": Identity.*—Of these meanings the most radical and proper is that in which I may say of any thing that it is what it is. This asseveration does not commit me to any description of the object nor to any assertion of its existence. I merely note its idiosyncrasy as a particular counter in the pile, something which, whatever it may be, is that object and no other. Its qualitative identity enables me to distinguish it, to study it, and to hold it fast in thought, so that I may eventually frame a definition of it, and perhaps assert or deny its existence. The copula properly denotes this singular and exclusive identity of each term with itself; not only in the abstract case of *A* is *A*, but also when the term (e.g., the triangle) is specifically determined up to a certain degree of articulation (e.g., as a plane enclosed by three straight lines); an articulation which the verb "*to be*" (when I say, Let *a*, *b*, *c* be a triangle) registers and posits, so as to permit me to identify the object in question; for if an object had no specific character, it would be meaningless to say that *it* was before me or was the theme of my discourse.

That what I see, I see, or what I am, I am, may seem a vain assertion; practical minds are not interested in any thing except for the sake of something else. They are camp-followers or heralds of the flux of nature, without self-possession. Yet if that which is actual and obvious at the moment never had a satisfying character, no satisfaction would ever be possible, and life would be what a romantic philosophy would make it—a wild-goose chase. In reality, to a simple or to a recollected spirit, the obvious often is enough. Its identity may have a deep charm, like that of a jewel. I may long ruminate upon it, and impress it upon myself by repetitions, as when, fixing my mind's eye on some essence ideally determinate, I say to myself "No, no," or "Business is business." The repetition serves to detach and to render indubitable the essence meant, so that my judgment may recognize it to the exclusion of circumstances, which do not alter essences.

*Identity the principle of essence.*—This being the most radical intimate meaning of the word "*is*," I have felt justified in usurping the term "*essence*," derived from the same root, to designate any ideal or formal nature, any thing always necessarily identical with itself. Essence so understood much more truly *is* than any substance or any experience or any event: for a substance, event, or experience may change its form or may exist only by changing it, so that all sorts of things that are proper to it in one phase will be absent from it in another. It will not be a unit at all, save by external delimitation. Perhaps some abstract constancy in quantity, energy, or continuity may be discovered to run through it, but this constant element will never be the actual experience, event, or substance in its living totality at any moment. Or perhaps all the phases of such an existence may be viewed together and synthesized into one historical picture; but this picture would again not be the existent substance, experience, or event unrolling itself in act. It would be only a description of that portion of the flux seen under the form of eternity; in other words, it would be an essence and not an existence. Essence is just that character which any existence wears in so far as it remains identical with itself and so long as it does so; the very character which it throws overboard by changing, and loses altogether when it becomes something else. To be able to become something else, to suffer change and yet endure, is the privilege of existence, be it in a substance, an event, or an experience; whereas essences can be exchanged, but not changed. Existence at every step casts off one essence and picks up another: we call it the same existence when we are able to trace its continuity in change, by virtue of its locus and proportions; but often we are constrained to give up the count, and to speak of a new event, a new thing, or a new experience. The essences or forms traversed in mutation render this mutation possible and describable: without their eternal distinctness no part of the flux could differ in any respect from any other part, and the whole world would collapse into a lump without order or quality. So much more profound is the eternal being of the essences traversed in change, than that of the matter or attention or discourse which plays with those essences at touch and go.

*Notion of the Realm of Essence.*—Nothing, then, more truly *is* than character. Without this wedding garment no guest is admitted to the feast of existence: whereas the unbidden essences do not require that invitation (with which very low characters are sometimes honoured) in order to preserve their proud identity out in the cold. There those few privileged revellers will soon have to rejoin them, not a whit fatter for their brief surfeit of being. After things lose their existence, as before they attain it, although it is true of them that they have existed or will exist, they have no internal being except their essences, quite as if they had never broached Existence at all: yet the identity of each essence with itself and difference from every other essence suffices to distinguish and define them all in eternity, where they form the Realm of Essence. True and false assertions may be made about any one of them, such, for instance, as that it does not exist; or that it includes or excludes some other essence, or is included or excluded by it.

*Transition to Looser Meanings: Posited or Problematical Identities.*—Nevertheless, the hypnotic charm of identity, or the dialectic pattern of essences, soon wearies a restive animal and seems to him idiotic. Having once observed and established the identity of every essence with itself, I may well turn to something else and put the word "*is*" to more pregnant uses. Identity itself will interest me more when, being that of a thing and not of an essence, it becomes problematical. I shall then be intent, not on some term directly present to intuition, but on some ulterior term signified by one or more different symbols themselves given immediately. The identity of things and persons is regularly masked in this way by their various names or appearances, so that their identity may be denied by the sceptic, and the assertion of it, far from being trivial, may be instructive, surprising or tragic. Thus pointing to a stranger in rags I may say: "This is Odysseus, the King"; or I may discover that XI is eleven, or that 11 is 7 + 4. Evidently such identifications do not intend to identify the two terms in their immediacy: the present aspect of Odysseus is not that of a king, those two Roman letters are not the English word "eleven," nor is one of those arithmetical symbols actually the other. So when I say "This is John," it would not be a very penetrating criticism of my poor human logic to argue that I was confusing a man with a sound, and pronouncing them identical. The identity is that of John with himself, an intended and existing object. The sound of his name and his image to sight are converging symbols, both signifying the same living person, with his ancestry and continuity in the material world. This term, posited as identical with itself, is removed from immediacy and belongs to a plane of being believed in by me, which if my animal faith misleads me need not exist at all: yet even in that case, I should be setting up a fixed theme of discourse, to which ulterior ideas might also be relevant; as when I point to a picture and say: "This is not Saint George but the Archangel Michael, because he has wings." I am content if the hints of sense, fused in the heat of recognition, lead me to some staunch ideal identity.

*Second Meaning: Equivalence.*—I may, however, be less concerned with the ulterior essence or thing through which two different symbols are identified than in the diversity of the symbols themselves. It is silly to urge that water is water, but interesting to note that *aqua* is *eau*. Where the native word carries the mind straight to the object, the foreign words interpose their own idiosyncrasy, and I not only notice their presence, but the fact that they have no resemblance whatever to the object they signify. They lead a life of their own, the life of sense or of language, in which touch may be sharpened into smell or sight, and a Latin word may become a French one which retains none of the original sounds, yet has exactly the same meaning. I thus learn that words and sensations may signify the same thing in endlessly different ways; and when some monoglot idiot balks at this wealth of synonyms (like Pierrot willing to touch a "dead man" but not a "corpse"), I can rebuke him by saying, "But it's the same thing!" The thing is indeed the same, but not the æsthetic essences that symbolize it to the fancy. So when Walt Whitman exclaims, "Alabama, Minnesota, Maryland, Vermont!" if his inspiration had not faltered and he had completed the list, the poetic essence of that catalogue would not be identical with the single cry, "The United States!" Attention forms individuals. When the parts are taken separately, each is at the centre of the world, and stops at its own boundary: when they are taken together, no boundaries are visible and many a feature found in one part may form a unit, like a river or a road, with a feature continuing it in another part. Sometimes, too, when two very different expressions are alleged to be equivalent, the identification of their objects seems doubtful or even shocking: as if instead of six square yards of carpet I am offered 7776 square inches of it, or a vote instead of freedom, or the most real of beings instead of God.

Equivalent terms coupled by the word "*is*" are, accordingly, far from identical; and even if the identity of the object meant to be granted, the substitution of one term for the other may make an important difference to the lover of form, thought, or language. Even in matters of business, there is a choice of methods and manners; if you pay a bill in gold or in coppers, by cheque or in bank-notes, the sum may be the same, but the action and the experience are different. The medium in such a transaction may seem irrelevant, but some medium is indispensable, and the interest in the choice of that medium is ineradicable: because the immediate is always with us.

Now in philosophy there is a medium which plays a great part, namely, thought. Thought is an outsider in respect to the things, facts, events, and essences which it considers; for although thought is itself an event and has an essence, it cannot at the time consider that fact. Even that which it considers it cannot exhaust. It identifies, connects, and describes its objects not according to their intrinsic natures but according to their names or images in discourse, and to the dialectical relations of these names or images.

*Third Meaning: Definition.*—Hence the importance which some philosophers give to definition. They are always asking you to tell them *what* some natural object is—man, matter, time, God—as if any definition whatever which you might offer of such deep-lying realities would be likely to come nearer to the thing as it is than do current names, sundry indications, or even the sum total of your discourse on that subject. Man, they say, *is* a rational animal: a circle *is* a plane figure bounded by a curve every part of which is equally distant from a point within the centre. These definitions may be correct; but if I had no independent knowledge of what a man or a circle was, I could not judge whether they were correct or not. Pure discourse likes to take the bit in its teeth; and a geometer might tell me that he need have no notion whatever of the circle save that which the definition gives him, and that all his deductions would follow just as well from that premise; indeed, it is only from that premise that they must follow if they are to be valid mathematically. The definition of the circle *is* the circle for the geometer. It would therefore be better, and worthier of the purity of deductive science, to drop such terms as circle, which suggests wheels, round eyes, and other vulgar objects, and to invent a symbol or formula to express the definition only, without any images borrowed from sense.

I believe this is the right method of dialectic; and if it is rigorously employed, it keeps discourse revolving about essences alone, and only about such essences as it has explicitly selected. But then, let it be remembered, these essences are not alleged to be the essences of anything existing. What follows from the algebraic formula for the circle is not alleged to hold good of hoops or rose-windows or the course of the planets. So that when any material, visible, or imagined circle is said to *be* a circle in the mathematical sense, the assertion is worse than false: it is irrelevant. Nothing can *be* the definition of it: at best the definition may be true of it. No definition, and no dialectic proceeding from the definition, can vouch for this natural truth. Only animal faith, trust in appearances, or experience in practical arts can justify such a presumption, or can even propose it. Definition is therefore perfectly useless for natural knowledge; but it is, when strictly adhered to, a fountain of deductions which are unimpeachable in themselves, although their relevance to matters of fact is problematical, and can only be asserted by one who knows those facts independently.

Definitions are complex names and they have the same function as names. They cannot repeat the essence of a thing, because its essence is its whole texture and character. An adequate definition of any existing thing would be as complicated as the thing itself, and true only of that individual, or of such others, if any, as were indistinguishable from it internally. Nevertheless, like names, definitions are sometimes useful. If I asked a man, "Who are you?" he might not unreasonably think the question impertinent, seeing that I was in his presence, and he might reply "I am myself." So when I ask of a thing, "What is that?" if the thing could overhear me, it might justly retort, "I am that I am." If, however, the man I challenged was of a mild and affable temper, and explained that he was Jenkins, that name might not be unmeaning to me. I might instantly conclude that I had not heard of him before, and should probably not hear of him again. So if I learned that the tone before me was a work of poetry, although poetry is proverbially difficult to define, I should know that all further consideration of it on my part was optional. Definitions may inform me of the place in which conventional discourse puts the object before me, and if I trust the wisdom of the definer, I shall have a useful hint concerning the ways of that object. A card may suffice to tell me the sex, rank, and nationality of the person whose name it bears, and may even enable me to guess whether he comes to pay his compliments or to solicit a subscription. Though a name seems to report who a man is, and a definition what a thing is, yet the thing no more is its definition than the man is his name.

*Fourth Meaning: Predication.*—Most often, perhaps, in common speech, the word "*is*" marks some property in what presumably has other properties as well, as in the formula A is B. Such a formula would be self-contradictory if being always meant identity. Wine is wine, and red is red, but red is not wine nor (in the sense of identity) can wine be red. Yet this is the constant assertion made by the word "*is*" when it attributes qualities to substances or predicates adjectives of nouns.

How an adjective can belong to a substantive is best seen when the adjective is a mere epithet and grammatically redundant, as when Homer speaks of the wine-coloured sea. Predication is supplementary definition, and as definition is never adequate to facts, further definition of them is always possible. The word "sea" and the images it may call up are one complex symbol for that element on which Homer had so often been tossed; the essence "purple," now emerging in the same context, is an added symbol for the same object. Predication is an elaborate naming under pressure of sensation or shifts of thought: it is poetry. Intuition here mixes its pigments and lays them on, stroke by stroke. The whole composition, at each stage, will no doubt be imputed to some substance, as if it formed its essence; but the very multiplication of epithets shows how inexhaustible and external that substance is in its truth; the poet is enduring and celebrating a divine power, and singing its many names. His whole discourse is the modulation of one vast epithet. It does not transgress the sphere of essence, but touches in turn and brings to the focus of attention now one manifestation of the god and now another. In study, whether artistic or scientific, the originality of mind is by no means laid aside; study merely carries out with a greater volume and force the primary poetry of the senses, by which intuition arises in the beginning, when each organ, stimulated by the unimaginable currents of its substance, chooses the essences which shall symbolize that stimulus to consciousness. The essence which any particular organ or any particular poet shall evoke depends, of course, on the material conditions which, in creating intuition at all, create its language, according to the "genius" of that poet or of that organ. Every quality possibly found in any thing, or predicated of it, is a fundamental and separate essence evoked on that occasion. The circumstance that some essences are used as subjects in discourse and some as attributes is itself only rhetorical; but it corresponds to the fact that in nature some formal units are more constant than others; as, for instance, the mass of a body is more constant than its position; therefore, in discourse we call the mass the substance and the position the accident. In the realm of essence, however, all elements are simply juxtaposed, and the trick of predicating one essence of another is only a means of carrying attention from some whole to a feature included in it, or to some larger whole in which it is a feature; in other words a means of analysis or synthesis. The resulting term in both cases is simply an essence, all surface; and there is no meaning in calling an essence the substance or the attribute of any other. Animal faith, with the intent which expresses it intellectually, may use any or all essences as predicates of a substance posited beyond them; but these predicates are poetic epithets for that substance, not constituents of it. They vary with the senses and genius of the observer. A stained-glass window, after I have studied it for a moment, offers a vastly different essence to my intuition from that contained in my first glimpse of it; and the simplest natural object is far more complicated than any Gothic design.

*Fifth Meaning: Existence.*—When I assume that there is a substance perhaps without pretending to know what it is, save that I have this local and temporal encounter with it, I am using the word "*is*" in an entirely different sense in which it means existence. This assertion of existence is imposed on me antecedently by the actions or expectations in the midst of which intuition arises, and without which it would never arise; and to this underlying faith is due the habit of predication itself, and the function of giving names. Essences present to intuition would never be predicated of one another, or understood to signify anything but what they obviously are, were they not projected into a common place and time, the seat of a presumed substance, by confusion with which the given essences (in reality only terms for intuition) are reputed to exist too. I do not need to believe in what I actually see; if I could limit myself to seeing, such a belief would be superfluous and unmeaning; but I am compelled to believe in the butt of my actions or the objects of my fears or memories, substances on which my efforts converge, or from which influences radiate upon me. The vague light, without outline or colour, which may first come to me from the church window is certainly not the composition which I afterwards discover there, yet I call them perceptions of the same thing, because I am convinced *a priori,* by the persevering attitude of my body and other converging circumstances, that a common source existed for both images, namely, a single material window fixed in its place, designed by its particular architect and built by his particular masons and glaziers. If no such natural object existed, that vague light and that precise composition would have nothing to do with each other; and unless I surreptitiously assign a natural existence to myself and give dates to those intuitions in my personal history, the light and the composition would have no temporal or spatial relations, and would not belong to one world, or exist at all. For the realm of existence (as I understand the word) is that arena of action, conveniently called nature, of which animals are parts and to which they are addressed before they have intuitions, if they ever have them; and the meaning of intuitions, when they come, is to mark the salient points of this world of nature, in so far as the sensitive animal can cope with it or is affected by it. The terms of intuition, the given essences, come to him as signals; and they are names to him for what exists about him, long before he notices their æsthetic quality. It is a great misfortune, at least for philosophy, that the word "*is,*" which denotes the qualitative idiosyncrasy of any essence whatsoever, should also have been used to denote existence, something peculiar to the flux of nature, and only as actually flowing.[1]

*Existence means being in external relations.*—When the word "*is*" designates existence, it claims for the object of intent a place in this flux; an object of intent (such as I have when on being startled I cry, "what's that?") is sufficiently identified by the external relations through which I approach it. I may completely ignore or mistake its true nature—an error or indifference which would be impossible if that object were not distinguished already as the object I mean to regard. It is whatever is there now, in such a context, creating such a disturbance. Its hidden nature, whatever it may be, is embodied in existence, and turned from an eternal essence into a fact when it is caught somewhere in the net of time, space, evolution, derivation, and association. Lying myself in the same context, I can turn to it by groping; and on coming into material contact with it, I may have rapid and varied intuitions supplying me with various notes, in the terms of my personal senses and emotions, which are my comment on it; perhaps it appears to be something small, black, rapidly moving, and unpleasant. These miscellaneous characteristics, the essences present to my intuition, are its names in my discourse; of course they are not the essence of that object itself, which for all my description reveals might as well be a mouse as a mosquito; nor do I seriously sup-

pose they form its essence, since I remain still curious and apprehensive of what that essence may secretly be; whether, for instance, it may be such as to render the thing poisonous. But since I have only my chance intuitions by which to describe that object, I am tempted to assign existence, for the nonce to this accidental description, as if it were the true essence of the thing; the radical and perpetual occasion of human illusion, dogmatism, and error.

Whether the claim to existence made on behalf of any object is just or not is a question that can never be decided by analyzing the given description of what is said to exist, but only by exploring the flux of nature, by experience or testimony, until the region in which the existing thing is alleged to lie (for if it exists it must lie somewhere) is thoroughly explored, and I can judge whether my original description, granting my terms and my circumstances, was a fair description of what actually lies there. If it was a fair description, I may conclude that what I had in mind really existed; if not, I must admit that I was mistaken, since what really existed was something not fairly describable in that way, nor properly called by that name. A very inadequate designation of the object—for example, in the case of the existence of God—may be perfectly correct and sufficient for human purposes; but the places and times (say the miracles or revelations or eschatological events) in which the existence of such an object would be unmistakably manifested must be definitely fixed; otherwise the *existence* of the object, the very point in question, would not be broached at all; for it is idle to say that a thing exists or does not exist; if I do not say when or where it is to be met with in the world of action.

*Sixth Meaning: Actuality.*—To this natural sphere the word "existence" may be confined with advantage; for even a living intuition, or bit of actual discourse, is generated at some particular point of space and time and expresses a material predicament of some animal. Had intuition no such root and status in nature, it could not be said to exist. Inwardly considered, each intuition is invisible, being the act of seeing something else; and it cannot run up against itself or find itself in any part of the landscape which it views, and to which it lends a specious unity and actuality. Moreover, if an intuition were not posited from the outside, as the thought of some particular person at some particular time, even its spiritual synthetic function would vanish; for it would be indistinguishable from the unity of the essence discerned—an eternal and non-existential object. A living intuition is, accordingly, a phase of animal life; and apart from such heats of nature the light of thought would never shine and no essence would ever appear. Nevertheless, considered in itself, an intuition is autonomous; it knows nothing of its organs or conditions, but single-mindedly greets whatever essence may appear, or borne onwards by animal faith, idolatrously regards that essence as a whole world, or as a chief part of a world, existing absolutely. Here, surely, is a very vivid and notable event, an existence possessing such unity, scope, and concentration as no other existence possesses; indeed scope, concentration, and unity have no other principle than intuition. Yet in this superlative existence proper to intuition there is something ironical. While it exists so positively that some philosophers admit no other reality, it is indiscoverable in the context of nature where existence must lie. Moreover, a chief characteristic of existence is flux, even conventionally static things, like houses, being composed by external and therefore reversible relations; but intuition (though externally considered it has a date and duration) is a synthesis, and therefore no flux. A flux which was all flux could never appear; in becoming a specious flux, it is caught in a unitary vista. Intuition is not a divisible event, like all events in nature. The separation and temporal order of its terms, like these terms themselves, are specious, an idea of succession and not a succession of facts; and there is no possibility whatever of placing various intuitions, apart from their organs and objects, in any relation of contiguity or succession.

Intuitions are therefore not existences in the same sense as natural things, nor events after the fashion of natural events; and yet we must say of them preeminently that they exist and arise, unless we are willing to banish spirit from nature altogether and to forget, when we do so, that spirit in us is then engaged in discovering nature and in banishing spirit. Why should philosophers wish to impoverish the world in order to describe it more curtly? Its exuberance will make it easier to describe, if they adapt their logic to its constitution. Intuition is an emanation of life, an intellectual response of the animal to his vicissitudes; it is an actualization or hypostasis of formal facts in nature, not an added existence on the same plane as its organ. If either the substance or the intuition were a phenomenon (which neither is), the relation of intuition to substance might be called epiphenomenal; for the two are not collateral, but the intuition is as completely dependent on the body for arising, as the body and nature at large are dependent on intuition for being imagined, loved, or described. This spiritual hypostasis of life into intuition is therefore less and more than natural existence and deserves a different name. I will call it actuality. *Is,* applied to spirit or to any of its modes, accordingly means is actual; in other words, exists not by virtue of inclusion in the dynamic, incessant, and infinitely divisible flux of nature, but by its intrinsic incandescence, which brings essences to light and creates the world of appearances.

*Seventh Meaning: Derivation.*—Belief in existence leads to still another use of the word *"is,"* the most misleading of all, by which one thing is said to be another because it is derived from it, or has the same substance. Suppose intuition presents me with a point of light; taking that essence instinctively for the sign of some existence, I may say to myself, "There is a spark." But in the world of nature, to which I am now addressed, a spark is not isolated fact; it has some origin, some substance, some consequences, and these probably interest me much more than my bare intuition of a point of light. But what origin, what substance, what consequences? It is conventionally known to me that a point of light may mean a spark from a horse's hoof, a burning cinder, a rocket, a distant lamp-post, a motor on the road, a revolving light-house, a ship at sea, or a blow in the eye. Nevertheless, ignoring those familiar possibilities, I may say to myself, "This spark is a firefly and not a star." I have thus travelled in search of explanation very far indeed from my datum. Instead of saying, "A point is a point," I first said, "A spark exists"; and then I said, "This spark is an insect." The word "*is*" has become a synonym of "*comes from*"; it attributes to an alleged fact a source in another alleged fact, asserting that the two are continuous genetically, however different they may be in character.

If this license in the use of the word "*is*" be allowed (and it would be pedantic to forbid it), I may still ask which of various suggested things a particular thing is; and I may find myself traversing the whole flux of nature in search for the being of the simplest object. This search becomes more confusing, and at the same time more urgent, when a psychological world is interposed, or substituted for the world of matter; one school of philosophers will then maintain that everything physical is really mental, and another school that everything mental is really physical. A capital instance of this habit is found in the phrase, dear to critical philosophers, that something "is nothing but" something else. Thus we hear that a word is nothing but a *flatus vocis,* that a house is nothing but bricks and mortar, that a mind is nothing but a bundle of perceptions, that God is nothing but a tendency not ourselves that makes for righteousness, or that matter is nothing but a permanent possibility of sensation. The phrase "nothing but" claims adequacy for the definition that follows: but a definition can define adequately an essence only, it cannot pretend to exhaust a fact; therefore, if such assertions are taken strictly, they themselves become "nothing but" definitions of fresh terms, and not discoveries. If on the contrary we take them loosely, as indicating the partial origin of certain facts or ideas, they may be correct; every fact and idea has antecedents which might be discovered if our knowledge of nature and of dreams were sufficiently profound. But in practice this sort of naturalistic analysis is seldom thorough; in none of the five examples given above, for instance, is the origin of the facts or ideas in question assigned correctly. One element in their composition may be specified: but the radical phrase "nothing but," in excluding all other elements (not to speak of the resulting unities of form), turns a shrewd observation into a cheap error. Even if the derivation of any fact could be assigned adequately, that fact would not be identical with what brought it about; and to say that things *are* what they are made of is to use the verb "to be" in a confused and confusing way, although the poverty of language may render such speech inevitable.

Here are seven distinct meanings of the word "*is,*" which it will be well to distinguish if I wish to know what I am saying. In practice the ambiguities of language are neutralized by looseness and good sense in the interpretation of it; but a philosopher leads himself into foolish difficulties and more foolish dogmas if he assumes that words have fixed meanings to which single facts in nature must correspond. He ought, therefore, to use language more freely than the public rather than more strictly, since he professes to have a clearer view of things. My purpose is not to limit the uses of the word "*is,*" but to become and remain aware that these uses are various, and that no argument in which they figure has the least cogency, even within the sphere of dialectic, until these uses are discriminated.

## Notes

1. The Spanish language is comparatively discriminating in this matter, having three verbs for "to be" which cannot be used interchangeably. "To be or not to be" must be rendered by *existir;* "That is the question" requires *ser;* "There's the rub" demands *estar.* Existence, essence, and condition or position are thus distinguished instinctively; but idiom profits more by this nicety than does philosophy, and I must say despairingly "*Sea lo que Dios quiera,*" "Be it [i.e., let it happen] as God will." Fortunately events have some English verbs to themselves—"occur," "happen," "arise"—and we need not say stupidly that they simply are. The phrase "there is" (like the German *ist da, es giebt, ist vorhanden*) also helps to distinguish existence from pure being.

# Scepticism

Scepticism is not sleep, and in casting a doubt on any belief, or proving the absurdity of any idea, the sceptic is by no means losing his sense of what is proposed. He is merely doubting or denying the *existence* of any such object. In scepticism, therefore, everything turns on the meaning of the word existence, and it will be worth while to stop a moment here to consider it further.

I have already indicated roughly how I am using the word existence, namely, to designate such being as is in flux, determined by external relations, and jostled by irrelevant events. Of course this is no definition. The term existence is only a name. In using it I am merely pointing out to the reader, as if by a gesture, what this word designates in my habits of speech, as if in saying Cæsar I pointed to my dog, lest some one should suppose I meant the Roman emperor. The Roman emperor, the dog, and the sound Cæsar are all indefinable; but they might be described more particularly, by using other indicative and indefinable names, to mark their characteristics or the events in which they figured. So the whole realm of being which I point to when I say existence might be described more fully; the description of it would be physics or perhaps psychology; but the exploration of that realm, which is open only to animal faith, would not concern the sceptic.

The sceptic turns from such indefinite confusing objects to the immediate, to the datum; and perhaps for a moment he may fancy he has found true existence there; but if he is a good sceptic he will soon be undeceived. Certainly in the immediate he will find freedom from the struggle of assertion and counter-assertion: no report there, no hypothesis, no ghostly reduplication of the obvious, no ghostly imminence of the not-given. Is not the obvious, he might ask, the truly existent? Yet the obvious is only the apparent; and this in both senses of

this ambiguous word. The datum is apparent in the sense of being self-evident and luminous; and it is apparent also in the sense of merely appearing and being unsubstantial. In this latter sense, the apparent threatens to become the non-existent. Does not the existent profess to be more than apparent: to be not so much the self-evident as that which I am seeking evidence for, in the sense of testimony? Is not the existent, then (which from its own point of view, or physically, is more than the apparent), cognitively and from my point of view less than the apparent? Does it not need witnesses to bear testimony to its being? And what can recommend those witnesses to me except their intrinsic eloquence? I shall prove no sceptic if I do not immediately transfer all my trust from the existence reported to the appearance reporting it, and substitute the evidence of my senses for all lawyer's evidence. I shall forget the murders and embroglios talked about in the court, and gaze at the judge in his scarlet and ermine, with the pale features of an old fox under his grey wig; at the jury in their stolidity; at the witness stammering; at the counsel, officially insolent, not thinking of what he is saying mechanically, but whispering something that really interests him in an aside, almost yawning, and looking at the clock to see if it is time for luncheon; and at the flood of hazy light falling aslant on the whole scene from the high windows. Is not the floating picture, in my waking trance, the actual reality, and the whole world of existence and business but a perpetual fable, which this trance sustains?

The theory that the universe is nothing but a flux of appearances is plausible to the sceptic; he thinks he is not believing much in believing it. Yet the residuum of dogma is very remarkable in this view; and the question at once will assail him how many appearances he shall

---

From *Scepticism and Animal Faith* (New York: Charles Scribners Sons, 1923) pp. 42–48.

assert to exist, of what sort, and in what order, if in any, he shall assert them to arise; and the various hypotheses that may be suggested concerning the character and distribution of appearances will become fresh data in his thought; and he will find it impossible to decide whether any such appearances, beyond the one now passing before him, are ever actual, or whether any of the suggested systems of appearances actually exists. Thus existence will loom again before him, as something problematical, at a distance from that immediacy into which he thought he had fled.

Existence thus seems to re-establish itself in the very world of appearances, so soon as these are regarded as facts and events occurring side by side or one after the other. In each datum taken separately there would be no occasion to speak of existence. It would be an obvious appearance; whatever appeared there would be simply and wholly apparent, and the fact that it appeared (which would be the only fact involved) would not appear in it at all. This fact, the existence of the intuition, would not be asserted until the appearance ceased to be actual, and was viewed from the outside, as something that presumably had occurred, or would occur, or was occurring elsewhere. In such an external view there might be truth or error; not so in each appearance taken in itself, because in itself and as a whole each is a pure appearance and bears witness to nothing further. Nevertheless, when some term within this given appearance comes to be regarded as a sign of some other appearance not now given, the question is pertinent whether that other appearance exists or not. Thus existence and nonexistence seem to be relevant to appearances in so far as they are problematical and posited from outside, not in so far as they are certain and given.

Hence an important conclusion which at first seems paradoxical but which reflection will support; namely, that the notion that the datum exists is unmeaning, and if insisted upon is false. That which exists is the fact that the datum is given at that particular moment and crisis in the universe; the intuition, not the datum, is the fact which occurs; and this fact, if known at all, must be asserted at some other moment by an adventurous belief which may be true or false. That which is certain and given, on the contrary, is something of which existence cannot be predicated, and which, until it is used as a description of something else, cannot be either false or true.

I see here how halting is the scepticism of those modern philosophers who have supposed that to exist is to be an idea in the mind, or an object of consciousness, or a fact of experience, if by these phrases no more is meant than to be a datum of intuition. If there is any existence at all, presence to consciousness is neither necessary nor sufficient to render it an existence. Imagine a novelist whose entire life was spent in conceiving a novel, or a deity whose only function was to think a world. That world would not exist, any more than the novel would comprise the feelings and actions of existing persons. If that novelist, in the heat of invention, believed his personages real, he would be deceived: and so would that deity if he supposed his world to exist merely because he thought of it. Before the creation could be actual, or the novel historical, it would have to be enacted elsewhere than in the mind of its author. And if it was so enacted, it would evidently not be requisite to its existence that any imaginative person, falsely conceiving himself to be its author, should form an image of it in his mind. If he did so, that remarkable clairvoyance would be a fact requiring explanation; but it would be an added harmony in the world, not the ground of its existence.

If for the sake of argument I accept the notion that presence to intuition is existence, I may easily disprove it by a *reductio ad absurdum*. If nothing not given in intuition can exist, then all those beliefs in existing facts beyond my intuition, by which thought is diversified when it is intelligent, would be necessarily false, and all intelligence would be illusion. This implication might be welcome to me, if I wished not to entertain any opinions which might conceivably be wrong. But the next implication is more disconcerting, namely, that the intuitions in which such illusion appears can have no existence themselves: for being instances of intuition they could not be data for any intuition. At one moment I may *believe* that there are or have been or will be other moments; but evidently they would not be *other* moments, if they were data to me now, and nothing more. If presence to intuition were necessary to existence, intuition itself would not exist; that is, no other intuition would be right in positing it; and as this absence of transcendence would be mutual, nothing would exist at all. And yet, since presence to intuition would be sufficient for existence, everything mentionable would exist without question, the non-existent could never be thought of, to deny anything (if I knew what I was denying) would be impossible, and there would be no such thing as fancy, hallucination, illusion, or error.

I think it is evidently necessary to revise a vocabulary which lends itself to such equivocation, and if I keep the words existence and intuition at all, to lend them meanings which can apply to something possible and credible. I therefore propose to use the word existence (in a way consonant, on the whole, with ordinary usage) to designate not data of intuition but facts or events believed to occur in nature. These facts or events will include, *first,* intuitions themselves, or instances of consciousness, like pains and pleasures and all remembered experiences and mental discourse; and *second,* physical things and events, having a transcendent relation to the data of intuition which, in belief, may be used as signs for them; the same transcendent relation which objects of desire have to desire, or objects of pursuit to pursuit; for example, such a relation as the fact of my birth (which I cannot even remember) has to my present persuasion that I was once born, or the event of my death (which I conceive only abstractly) to my present expectation of some day dying. If an angel visits me, I may intelligibly debate the question whether he exists or not. On the one hand, I may affirm that he came in through the door, that is, that he existed before I saw him; and I may continue in perception, memory, theory, and expectation to assert that he was a fact of nature: in that case I believe in his existence. On the other hand, I may suspect that he was only an event in me, called a dream; an event not at all included in the angel as I saw him, nor at all like an angel in the conditions of its existence; and in this case I disbelieve in my vision: for visiting angels cannot honestly be said to exist if I entertain them only in idea.

Existences, then, from the point of view of knowledge, are facts or events affirmed, not images seen or topics merely entertained. Existence is accordingly not only doubtful to the sceptic, but odious to the logician. To him it seems a truly monstrous excrescence and superfluity in being, since anything existent is more than the description of it, having suffered an unintelligible emphasis or materialisation to fall upon it, which is logically inane and morally comic. At the same time, existence suffers from defect of being and obscuration; any ideal nature, such as might be exhaustively given in intuition, when it is materialised loses the intangibility and eternity proper to it in its own sphere; so that existence doubly injures the forms of being it embodies, by ravishing them first and betraying them afterwards.

Such is existence as approached by belief and affirmed in animal experience; but I shall find in the sequel that considered physically, as it is unrolled amidst the other realms of being, existence is a conjunction of natures in adventitious and variable relations. According to this definition, it is evident that existence can never be given in intuition; since no matter how complex a datum may be, and no matter how many specious changes it may picture, its specious order and unity are just what they are: they can neither suffer mutation nor acquire new relations: which is another way of saying that they cannot exist. If this whole evolving world were merely given in idea, and were not an external object posited in belief and in action, it could not exist nor evolve. In order to exist it must enact itself ignorantly and successively, and carry down all ideas of it in its own current.

# Essence

## I. Various Approaches to Essence

The modern or romantic man is an adventurer; he is less interested in what there may be to find than in the lure of the search and in his hopes, guesses, or experiences in searching. Essence is perfectly indifferent to being discovered and unaffected by the avenue through which any discoverer may approach it; and for that very reason the explorer ignores it, and asks what it can possibly be. Now the subjective attitude in philosophy is not only prevalent in these times, but always legitimate; because a mind capable of self-consciousness is always free to reduce all things to its own view of them. Before considering the realm of essence in itself, therefore, I will indicate some paths by which even the most rambling reflection may be led to it. Essence is indeed everywhere at hand; and a scrupulous scepticism, falling back on immediate appearance, is itself a chief means of discovering the pervasive presence of essences.

In a volume on *Scepticism and Animal Faith,* to which the present work is a sequel, I have described in detail the approach to essence through scepticism. Knowledge such as animal life requires is something transitive, a form of belief in things absent or eventual or somehow more than the state of the animal knowing them. It needs to be information. Otherwise the animal mind would be the prisoner of its dreams, and no better informed than a stone about its environment, its past, or its destiny.

It follows that such transitive knowledge will always be open to doubt. It is a claim or presumption arising in a responsive organism; yet in spite of this biological status, it ventures upon assertions concerning facts elsewhere. This boldness exposes it to all sorts of errors; for opinion will vary with its organ and, on that irrelevant ground, will make varying assertions about its outlying objects. Nor is it to be presumed that initially the terms in which objects are conceived are their intrinsic qualities; the terms may be, in quality as in existence, generated in the organ of sense, as are words or optical perspectives. Knowledge of nature or of absent experience is accordingly no less questionable in its texture than in its scope. Its validity is only presumptive and its terms are merely symbols.

The sceptic once on this scent will soon trace essence to its lair. He will drop, as dubious and unwarranted, the belief in a past, an environment, or a destiny. He will dismiss all thought of any truth to be discovered or any mind engaged in that egregious chase; and he will honestly confine himself to noting the features of the passing apparition. At first he may still assume that he can survey the passage and transformation of his dreams; but soon, if he is truly sceptical and candid, he will confess that this alleged order of appearances and this extended experience are themselves only dreamt of, like the future or the remoter past or the material environment—those discarded idols of his dogmatic days. Nothing will remain but some appearance now; and that which appears, when all gratuitous implications of a world beyond or of a self here are discarded, will be an *essence.* Nor will his own spirit, or spirit absolute (which grammar may still seem to insert, under the form of the pronoun I, as a prior agent in this intuition of essence) be anything but another name for the absolute phantom, the unmeaning presence, into which knowledge will have collapsed.

This approach to essence through scepticism is by no means the only one possible, even for a critic of knowledge. Scepticism can impugn only such knowledge as is a form of faith, and posits a removed object; but the

From *Realms of Being* (New York: Charles Scribner's Sons, 1942 [1937]), pp. 1–25.

dialectician ignores this sort of knowledge as much as he can, and by his initial attitude plants himself in the realm of essence, and wishes to confine himself to it. What is dialectic? Precisely an analysis or construction of ideal forms which abstracts from such animal faith as might be stimulated by their presence, and traces instead the inherent patterns or logical relations of these forms as intuition reveals them. To the dialectician animal faith seems wanton and superfluous, and in his overt reasoning, if not in his secret assumptions, he neither posits any objects of natural knowledge nor seeks to describe them. Such preoccupation with dark external facts and hidden events seems to him but a grovelling instinct; and the persuasion that one's ideas describe natural objects, though inevitable perhaps in sniffing one's way through this nether world, he laughs at as a vain presumption, unworthy of the name of science. In practice, as a man amongst men, the dialectician may have mixed views. If he is an enthusiast or a naturalist in disguise, using dialectic for some ulterior purpose, he will probably embrace his conclusions not merely as implications of his premises, but as objects of hot animal faith; and he may even think he has discovered a metaphysical world, when in truth he has merely elaborated a system of essences, altogether imaginary, and in no way more deeply rooted in reality than any system of essences which a poet or a musician might compose. This eventual mystification, however, by which dialectic is represented as revealing facts, does not destroy its native competence to describe essences; in its purity it will be free from error, because free from any pretence to define ulterior existences. Now this very purity, this identity of the object envisaged with the definition given to it in thought, seems to the dialectician the perfection of science, because it is the last refuge of certitude. But certitude and dialectical cogency are far removed from animal faith, and unnecessary to it; and animal faith, when it describes in suitable symbols (of which a dialectical system may be one) the objects encountered in action, is what I call knowl-edge. The question of titles and preferences does not concern me here; in any case the dialectician, whether his art be called knowledge or not, has discovered the realm of essence (or some province in it) and has devoted himself to exploring it.

This acquaintance with essence I call intuition, whether it be passive, æsthetic, and mystical, or on the contrary analytical and selective, as in reasoned discourse; because at every point demonstration or inference depends for its force on intuition of the intrinsic relation between the given terms. So in planning a series of moves in chess, as in originally inventing that game, the mind *sees* the consequences implied at each stage by the rules of procedure: these rules are mere essences, but their implications are precise in any hypothetical position of the pieces. If chess were not a well-established game and if material chess-boards and chess-men had never existed, a day-dream in which particular imaginary matches were traced out, could hardly be called knowledge: but every possibility and every consequence involved at each juncture would be equally definite, and the science of chess—even if chess never had existed in the world—would be an exact science. Evidently an exact science is not without an object, ideal as this object may be: indeed, the ideal definition of that object, the absence of all ambiguity as to what it is, renders exact science of it possible. Such definable non-existent objects of exact science have being in an eminent degree; their nature and their eternal intrinsic relations to other comparable natures are perfectly determinate. They are what they are; and of all the meanings of the word *is*—existence, substance, equivalence, definition, etc., the most radical and proper is that in which I may say of anything that it is what it is. This asseveration does not commit me to any classification of the object or to any assertion of its existence. I merely note its idiosyncrasy, its qualitative identity, which enables me to distinguish it, study it, and hold it fast in my intent, so that I may eventually frame a definition of it, and perhaps assert or deny its existence. If any object had no such specific character, there would be no truth in saying that *it* was before me, or could ever again be the theme of memory or discourse. Essences, by being eternally what they are, enable existence to pass from one phase to another, and enable the mind to note and describe the change.

That what I see, I see, or what I am, I am, may seem a vain assertion: practical minds are not interested in anything except for the sake of something else. They are camp-followers or heralds of events, without self-possession. Yet if that which is actual and possessed at the moment never had a satisfying character, no satisfaction would ever be possible; the mind could never dip twice into the same subject or know its friends from its enemies, and life would be what a romantic philosophy would make it—an idle escape from one error into another. Radical flux is indeed characteristic of existence, where it is innocent, since there can be no mistake or regret where there is no purpose: but the mind, even if describing only the series of its own illusions, attempts to describe it with truth: and it could not so much as fail in this attempt unless that series of illusions and each of its terms had a precise inexpungible character. Then the question whether in some ulterior sense those phases were illusions or not, becomes a subsidiary question. In any case, internally, they were what they were; and to a simple and recollected spirit the obvious often is enough. Its identity may have a deep charm, like that of a jewel. I may long ruminate upon it and impress it upon myself by repetitions, which to a lover never seem vain. Even in the midst of distractions, if I say to myself "No, no," or "Business is business," the repetition serves to detach and to render indubitable the essence meant; it raises that material accident to the intellectual level, where my judgement henceforth may recognise it to the exclusion of circumstances, which do not alter essences, but only cases.

Sometimes sense itself, without any dialectical analysis, distinguishes essences from facts, and recognises them in their ideal sphere. This happens for a very simple reason. The stimulus that calls animal attention to some external fact, in provoking an act of the body, also presents some image to the mind. Moreover this labour of perception may be more or less welcome, pleasant, or life-enhancing, apart from its ulterior uses; and sometimes this incidental emotion is so strong that it overpowers the interest which I may have had originally in the external facts; and, I may suspend my action or continue it automatically, while my thought is absorbed in the image and arrested there. As I was jogging to market in my village cart, beauty has burst upon me and the reins have dropped from my hands. I am transported, in a certain measure, into a state of trance. I see with extraordinary clearness, yet what I see seems strange and wonderful, because I no longer look in order to understand, but only in order to see. I have lost my preoccupation with fact, and am contemplating an essence.

This experience, in modern times, is called æsthetic; but it has no exclusive connection with the arts or with the beautiful. It is really intellectual, and the high Platonic road. That the clearest and purest reality should be formal or ideal, and something on which no animal instinct could possibly be directed, may seem a paradox; it may be denied by cynics—often very dull people; it may be used by metaphysicians as an argument for the supernatural origin and destiny of the soul. It is important at once to discard any such inferences, not only because they are in themselves mistaken, thin, and superstitious, but particularly, at this point in my argument, because they encumber the notion of essence with a moral significance quite extraneous to it, and may distort and discredit it altogether. When a thing is beautiful, I stop to look at it; and in this way its beauty helps me to drink in the actual appearance, and to be satisfied with that ethereal draught. But if the thing were ugly or uninteresting, it would have an absolute appearance just as much, and would present an essence to intuition; only that in that case I should have no motive—no vital animal motive—for dwelling upon that essence, or noticing it at all. If the thing is beautiful, this is not because it manifests an essence, but because the essence which it manifests is one to which my nature is attuned, so that the intuition of it is a delightful exercise to my senses and to my soul. This pleasure and refreshment welling up in me, I courteously thank the object for, and call its intrinsic charm: but an intrinsic charm is a contradiction in terms, and all that the object possesses is affinity to my life, and power over it, without which it would be impossible for me to observe it or to think it beautiful.

The beautiful is itself an essence, an indefinable quality felt in many things which, however disparate they may be otherwise, receive this name by virtue of a special emotion, half wonder, half love, which is felt in their presence. The essence of the beautiful, when made an object of contemplation by itself, is rather misleading: like the good and like pure Being, it requires much dialectical and spiritual training to discern it in its purity and in its fullness. At first the impetuous philosopher, seeing the world in so many places flowering into beauty, may confuse his physics with a subjective or teleological reference to the beautiful, thereby turning this essence, which marks a spiritual consummation, into a material power: or, if he is not an enthusiast, he may dwell so much on the instinctive and pleasant bonds which attach men to what they call beautiful, that he may bury the essence of the beautiful altogether under heavy descriptions of the occasions on which perhaps it appears. I will not stop to discuss these complications: however apt to become entangled itself, the beautiful is a great liberator of other essences. The most material thing, in so far as it is felt to be beautiful, is instantly immaterialised, raised above external personal relations, concentrated and deepened in its proper being, in a word, sublimated into an essence: while on the other hand, many unnoticed Platonic ideas, relations, or unsubstantial aspects of things, when the thrill of beauty runs through them, are suddenly revealed, as in poetry the secret harmonies of feelings and of words. In this way innumerable natural themes of happiness, which no one could possibly mistake for things, become members of the human family,

and in turn restore the prodigal mind, perhaps long wasted on facts, to its home circle of essence.

This native affinity of the mind to essence rather than to fact is mind itself, the very nature of spirit or intellectual light. The sort of intelligence which adapts one natural being to another, and may be found in the conduct of animals, or even in the structure of their bodies, does not consist in thinking; it is an adaptation of life to its conditions, a form of behaviour in matter, which must exist and flourish before thinking or even feeling can arise at all. Intuition would be impossible without an underlying animal life, a psyche; for how should the sheer light of intuition actualise itself, or choose the essence on which it should fall? A psyche, the hereditary organisation and movement of life in an animal, must first exist and sustain itself by its "intelligent" adaptations to the ambient world: but these adaptations are not conscious until, by virtue of their existence, intuition arises; and intuition arises when the inner life of the animal, or its contact with external things, is expressed in some actual appearance, in some essence given in feeling or thought. The psyche and the material circumstances, by their special character and movement, determine the choice and succession of themes on which intuition shall be employed in some particular person; in so far as spirit is kindled there at all, it will have raised those themes to the plane of essence; the whole movement of nature and of human affairs, which imposes those themes, becomes itself only another theme for contemplation, if present to the mind at all. This contemplation does not require a man to shut his eyes or to fix them exclusively on the stars; it does not require him to stop living or acting. Often the most contemplative minds are the most worldly-wise, and the most capable of directing business. But though they may survey or foresee action, they do not live in action, because they see it in its wholeness and in its results; as a spectator who sees the plot of a play understands the emotions of the characters; but does not succumb to them; or as a writer, very busy with his pen and conveying much ink from inkstand to paper, may be thinking of his subject; and the words will probably come most aptly when, as words, they come unconsciously, and when the truth which they express absorbs the whole mind. The same thing happens in a game of ball, or in the game of politics, when the player is good; the quick adjustment of his faculties and organs, being automatic, kindles in his mind a graphic image and a pure emotion, to be the signs of his achievement to his inner man.

The natural and the spiritual fruits of life are not opposed, but they are different. Its natural fruits are more life, persisting through readjustments and an incessant generation of new forms, so that youth may fill the place of age and attain an equal, though not identical, perfection. It is in these perfections, or in approaches which partly anticipate them, that the spiritual fruits are found. As we have seen, they may ripen early, and may be gathered at all seasons, when any phase of life is perfected in action; but the spiritual fruits are internal or tangential to this action, not consequent upon it, like the natural fruits: they may be omnipresent in existence, but only by everywhere transmuting existence into essence. Spirit is life looking out of the window; the work of the household must have been done first, and is best done by machinery. Moral triumphs are not æsthetic, because they have other occasions, but they are equally intellectual when realised in the spirit; they lie in the joy of having done *this:* they are a passage into essence. Finality, though it is not felt as beauty, marks the great moments of passion satisfied or purposes achieved. Into some scene, into some phrase, into some gesture in itself trivial, the whole burden of a long experience may then be cast, and happiness may be centred and realised in some simple event or in some silent moment.

I should need but to enlarge this canvas in order to paint the whole happiness possible to man. In what should it lie? In going on, and simply not stopping? In passing to some better experience? But in what would it be better? In being fuller or longer? I think the longer and the fuller a bad life is, the worse it is. How,

then, should it be made better? Only surely, by bringing all its activities, as far as possible, to intrinsic perfection and mutual harmony, so that at each step, and in every high moment of synthesis and reflection, intuition may fall on an essence beyond which it need not look, finding in it peace, liberation, and a sufficient token that fate, so far as that expression of spirit is concerned, has lost its terrors. Without such vision realised at each of its stages, life would be a mere fatality, automatism at odds with itself, a procession of failures. Spirit would have been called into being by a false promise; its only hope would be that by sleep supervening, or by distraction so extreme as to destroy the organic harmonies on which intuition depends, that mistake should be corrected and forgotten.

This possible conflict between matter and spirit is a family quarrel; it is not a shock between independent forces brought together by accident, since spirit cannot exist except in matter, and matter cannot become interested in its formations and fortunes save by creating a spirit that may observe and celebrate them. How happily spirit and matter may lead their common life together appears in play at the beginning, and in contemplation at the end. It is only in the middle when animal faculties are inwardly perfect and keen enough to be conscious, but are outwardly ill-adjusted and ignorant, that trouble arises; because the mind sees and wants one thing, and circumstances impose something different, requiring a disposition and a form of imagination in the animal to which his play-life is not adapted. Spirit— the voice of the inner nature in so far as it is already formed and definite—accordingly suffers continual defeats, by the defeat of those animal impulses which it expresses; and if these impulses become confused or exhausted, it sinks with them into vice or discouragement. It would soon perish altogether, and annul the moral problem which its existence creates, unless in some way a harmony could be re-established between the individual and the world. This may be done in society at large by some firm political and moral regimen; or it may be done religiously by the discipline of the inner man, so that a part of him is weaned from the passions and interests which distract the world and is centred upon purely intellectual or spiritual aspiration. Religion is hard for external events to defeat, since ill-fortune stimulates it as much at least as good fortune. Thus within strict limits, and in a soberer garb, the play-life of childhood is restored to the soul.

Hence that happy quarrel of philosophers—happy because both parties are right— as to whether wisdom is a meditation on life or on death. But in the midst of one we are in the other, not only in that existence is transition, but far more remarkably, in that life triumphant is life transmuted into something which is not life—into union with essence, with so much of the eternal as is then manifested in the transitory. This manifestation, with all the approaches to it, is life itself; and death is the fading of that vision, the passing of that essence back into its native heaven, depriving us by its obscuration of a part of ourselves, so that existence in us must lapse into some different phase, or into total darkness. Life, if by this word we understand the process of mutation, is itself death; to be fed is to kill, to advance is to reject and abandon. The truly creative movement is only upward, and life, in so far as it means light and accomplishment, is only some predestined intuition achieved, some wished-for essence made manifest. Existence itself is a momentary victory of essence: a victory over matter, in that matter, which might have taken any other form, takes this particular one and keeps circling about it, as if fascinated; not that there is really any magic here, but that matter, which has to have some form or other, is willing enough to be true to the one it has, and (so indifferent is it to form) to renounce for an indefinite time its native right to inconstancy: as a hardened traveller, not caring what inn he stays at, may remain good-naturedly at the one in which he happens to be lodged. Essence is victorious also over spirit, and no less amiably victorious; since it is in essence that spirit aspires to lose itself and to find its quietus, as it was from essence that matter managed to

borrow some character and some beauty. What Spinoza meant by meditation on life was, I take it, the effort to wrest the truth of nature out of empirical confusion, so that all the vicissitudes of things might appear under the form of eternity; and what Socrates and Plato meant by meditation on death was almost the same thing. Only the Greeks, by distinguishing many gods and many divine ideas, could humanise and make friends with at least some of them; and in sympathy with those beautiful immortals they could survey and dismiss earthly existence with a touch of disdain; whereas the piety of thrifty and moralising nations, when enlightened, issues only in a scrupulous natural philosophy. Being overawed by the facts, and eager for existence and prosperity, they miss the liberal life; they prefer perpetual servitude, if well fed, to emancipation, such as interest in pure essences affords; and often (though not in Spinoza) they substitute a troubled hope in some fabulous resurrection for the present union with the eternal which is natural to spirit.

Thus scepticism, dialectic, contemplation, and spiritual discipline, all lead to the discrimination of essence; and anyone who has trodden any of these paths to the end will not need to be told what essence means, or that it is a most real and interesting realm of being. But it is not the whole of being: on the contrary, were there nothing but essence, not one of these approaches to it would be open: there would be no possible movement, no events, no life, and no preference. Considered in itself, essence is certainly the deepest, the only inevitable, form of reality; but I am here speaking of approaches to it, that is, of considerations drawn from human experience that may enable us to discern that primary reality and to recognise it to be such in contrast to our own form of being. We stand, then, on another plane, the plane of scattered experience, brute fact, contingent existence; if we did not, the discernment of essence would have no novelty for us, it would reveal no night-firmament behind our day, it would not liberate us from ourselves or from the incubus of accidental things. If we were prompted, then, by our new insight to cry that our old life was all illusion, we might be turning this insight into a new folly. Enlightenment itself would be impossible if chance experiences had not preceded, perfectly real in their own way; indeed existence (something that has no foothold whatever in the realm of essence) is presupposed and contained in any assertion or denial, and in the intuition of essence itself. The existence and distribution of enlightenment, as of any other fact, places us to begin with in another realm, the realm of matter, which must be begged separately: without it there could be no manifestation of essence, whether in nature or in discourse.

The priority of the realm of essence is therefore not temporal or dynamic. It is an infinite field for selection; evidently it cannot select or emphasise any part of itself. When the selection takes place, we accordingly refer it to a different principle, which we may call chance, fact, or matter: but this principle would be a mere word, a term without indicative force, if it did not select some feature of the realm of essence to be its chosen form: in other words, if this brute accident were not some accident in particular, contrasted with the infinity of other forms which it has not chosen. To appeal to fact, to thump existence with empirical conviction, is accordingly but to emphasise some essence, like a virtuous bridegroom renouncing all others: the exclusion is opportune, but the bride after all is only one of a million, and the mind has simply wedded an essence. The principle of constancy, or perhaps of inconstancy—the selective principle—is matter; yet whatever way it may turn, it must embrace one essence or another.

The approaches to essence are therefore as various as those predispositions in matter which determine the poses of life. Or we may say that for the mind there is a single avenue to essence, namely, attention. Awaken attention, intensify it, purify it into white flame, and the actual and unsubstantial object of intuition will stand before you in all its living immediacy and innocent nakedness. But notice: this attention, discovering nothing but essence, is itself an animal faculty: it is called forth by material stress, or by passion. The passions, in so far as they are impulses to action, entangle us materially in the flux of substance, being intent on seizing, transforming, or destroying something that exists: but at the same time, in so far as they quicken the mind, they are favourable to the discernment of essence; and it is only a passionate soul that can be truly contemplative. The reward of the lover, which also chastens him, is to discover that in thinking he loved anything of this world he was profoundly mistaken. Everybody strives for possession; that is the animal instinct on which everything hangs; but possession leaves the true lover unsatisfied: his joy is in the character of the thing loved, in the essence it reveals, whether it be here or there, now or then, his or another's. This essence, which for action was only a signal letting loose a generic animal impulse, to contemplation is the whole object of love, and the sole gain in loving. Naturally essences seem thin abstractions to those absorbed in action, whose heart is set on the eventual, and to whom the actual is never anything: the actual in experience is never more than an echo or supplement to deeper facts, a shimmer on the surface of the great sea labouring beneath; yet the actual in experience is never an abstraction from experience itself; it is the whole fruit of that hidden labour, the entire reality for the spirit. It is therefore not as a quality attributed to external things that essence is best distinguished; for the colour or the shape of an apple may be supposed to exist in it, and when drawn out and imagined existing alone they may seem ghostly; neither the roundness nor the redness of the apple would be edible. To a greedy child they would be miserable cheats; but not so to the painter or the geometer. The child might be better initiated into the nature of essence (which is not far from the innocent mind) if he chose as an instance the pleasure of eating the apple, or of snatching it from another boy's hand; essences which he would distinguish easily from their opposites, and which he would not be tempted to incorporate into apples. A little experience would convince him that these intangible pleasures gave importance to apples, and not apples to them; and he would join the painter of still life, and the geometer, in finding that things are mere instruments, and that only essences are essential. Interest, in marking the differences and precise characters of things, which are all that the mind can take from them, is the great revealer of essence. Herein appears the thoroughly intellectual or poetical virtue of spirit. The more intense and dominating it is, the less it dwells on the machinery which may control its existence, and the more exclusively it addresses itself to the true or the beautiful, that is, to the essences which experience would manifest if it were pure and perfect.

## II.   The Being Proper to Essences

The principle of essence, we have seen, is identity: the being of each essence is entirely exhausted by its definition; I do not mean its definition in words, but the character which distinguishes it from any other essence. Every essence is perfectly individual. There can be no question in the realm of essence of mistaken identity, vagueness, shiftiness, or self-contradiction. These doubts arise in respect to natural existences or the meanings or purposes of living minds: but in every doubt or equivocation both alternatives are genuine essences; and in groping and making up my mind I merely hesitate between essences, not knowing on which to arrest my attention. There is no possibility of flux or ambiguity within any of the alternatives which might be chosen at each step.

This inalienable individuality of each essence renders it a universal; for being perfectly self-contained and real only by virtue of its intrinsic character, it contains no reference to any setting in space or time, and stands in no adventitious relations to anything. Therefore without forfeiting its absolute identity it may be repeated or reviewed any number of times. Such embodiments or views of it, like the copies of a book or the acts of reading of it, will be facts or events in nature (which is a net of external relations); but the copies would not be copies of the same book, nor the readings of it, unless (and in so far as) the same essence reappeared in them all. Physical obstacles to exact repetitions or reproductions do not affect the essential universality of every essence, even if by chance it occurs only once, or never occurs at all; because, in virtue of its perfect identity and individuality, it cannot fall out of the catalogue of essences, where it fills its particular place. If I try to delete it, I reinstate it, since in deleting *that* I have recognised and defined it anew, bearing witness to its possessing the whole being which it can claim as an essence. There accordingly it stands, waiting to be embodied or noticed, if nature or attention ever choose to halt at that point or to traverse it. Every essence in its own realm is just as central, just as normal, and just as complete as any other: it is therefore always just as open to exemplification or to thought, without the addition or subtraction of one iota of its being. Time and space may claim and repeat it as often or as seldom as they will: that is their own affair. The flux is free to have such plasticity as it has, and to miss all that it misses; and it is free to be as monotonous as it likes, if it finds it easier to fall again and again into the same form, rather than to run away into perpetual and unreturning novelties. The realm of essence is the scale of measurement, the continuum of variation, on which these repetitions or these novelties may be plotted and compared. Re-embodiments or re-surveys of an essence (if they occur) bind the parts of the flux together ideally, and render it amenable to description. The essential universality of these forms makes any fact, in so far as it exhibits them, distinct and knowable: the universal and the individual being so far from contrary that they are identical. I am not myself unless I re-enact now the essence of myself, which I may re-enact at all times and places.

Since essences are universals not needing to figure in any particular place or time, but fit to figure in any, it is not possible to investigate the realm of essence by empirical exploration. You cannot go in search of that which is nowhere. Some essences will appear or occur to you, since whatever intuition life may awaken in you must light up some essence or other; but what further essences, if any, there may be is not discoverable by simply waiting for them to turn up. Nature is indeed very rich in forms, compared with the inertia and monotony of experience in home-keeping animals, revolving in their private circle of habits and ideas; but nature too is built on a single plan—all nuclei and planets, all life and death—and as much a slave of routine as any of her creatures. The unexemplified is not exemplified there, the unthought of is not thought of: not because in itself it resists being created or described, but because nature and thought happen not to bloom in any way but that in which they have taken to blooming. In part, indeed, this restriction may be due to local prejudice and ignorance in the observer, who draws the periphery of nature with his compass. Another man, a different animal, a spirit native to another world may even now be greeting the essences which it has not entered into my heart to conceive. Evidently my limitations cannot forbid them to rejoice in their different experience; nor can the limitations of any actual experience forbid the essences it leaves out to be just those which are absent. An essence is an inert theme, something which cannot bring itself forward, but must be chosen, if chosen, by some external agent; and evidently the choice made by this agent, contingent as it is and wholly arbitrary, cannot render unavailable the other inert themes which other agents, or itself in a different moment of its flux, might choose instead. The very contingency of existence, the very blindness of life, throw the doors wide open towards the infinity of being. Even if some philosopher or some god thought himself omniscient, surprises might be in store for him, and thoughts new to his thought; nay, even supposing that his whole experience and the entire history of his world lay synthesised before him under the form of eternity, and that he was not a victim of sheer egotism in asserting that nothing more could ever exist, still the wanton idiosyncrasy of that total fact the enormity of that accident, could not be blustered away. Existence is irrational for a deeper and more intrin-sic reason than because one part of it may not be deducible from another: any part, and all its parts together, are irrational in merely existing, and in being otherwise than as essences are, that is, identical with themselves and endowed with that formal being which it is impossible that anything, whatever it be, should not possess. Not that essence can resist or resent this irrational selection which existence makes of its riches: on the contrary, essence is a sort of invitation to the dance; it tempts nature with openings in every direction; and in so doing it manifests its own inexhaustible variety. Its very being is to set no limits to the forms of being. The multitude of essences is absolutely infinite.

This assertion has an audacious sound, and I should not venture upon it, had it not a counterpart or corollary which takes away all its venom, namely, that essences do not *exist*. If I were in pursuit of substance, I should distrust any description of it not purely tentative, empirical, and scrupulously modest: but the bold definition which Spinoza gives of what he calls substance that it is Being absolutely infinite, seems to me a perfect and self-justifying definition of the realm of essence: because in conceiving and defining such an object we prove it to possess the only being which we mean to ascribe to it. Denying it to be infinite, or denying that any supposed element in it existed, we should be designating these missing elements and that absent infinity: whereby we should be instituting them ideally, and recognising them to be essences. The realm of essence is comparable to an infinite Koran—or the Logos that was in the beginning—written in invisible but indelible ink, prophesying all that Being could ever be or contain: and the flux of existence is the magical reagent, travelling over it in a thin stream, like a reader's eye, and bringing here one snatch of it and there another to the light for a passing moment. Each reader may be satisfied with his own verse, and think it the whole of Scripture: but the mere assertion of this limit, or suspicion that other readers might find other texts, is enough to show that the non-existent cannot be limited, since the limits of the existent might always be changed. To deny the being of essence, because it may happen to be unrealised, is self-contradictory: for if it is not realised, it must have a quality, distinguishing it from realised forms. Unrealised forms may not interest a sluggish mind: an arithmetician who was happy in the thought of whole numbers, might deprecate all mention of vulgar fractions or repeating decimals, and might swear to die without them, lest his safe and honest arithmetic should be complicated with unrealities. But unrealities of that sort nevertheless envelop his realities on every side; and it is his arrest at his realities that, if you like, is unreal; there is no reason in it, and no permanence; whereas the unrealities are unchangeable, inevitable, and always standing behind the door. Even if the whole realm of essence (as Spinoza assumed) were realised somewhere at some time in the life of nature, essence would remain a different and a non-existent realm: because the realisation of each part could be only local and temporary, and for all the rest of time and in all the worlds that excluded it, each fact would fade into the corresponding essence, and would remain certain and inevitable as an essence only, and as a fact merely presumptive.

Essence so understood much more truly *is* than any substance or any experience or any event: for a substance, event, or experience may change its form or may exist only by changing it, so that all sorts of things that are proper to it in one phase will be absent from it in another. It will not be a unit at all, save by external delimitation. Perhaps some abstract constancy in quantity, energy, or continuity may be discovered to run through it, but this constant element will never be the actual experience, event, or substance in its living totality at any moment. Or perhaps all the phases of such an existence may be viewed together and synthesised into one historical picture; but this picture would again not be the existent substance, experience, or event unrolling itself in act. It would be only a description of that portion of the flux seen under the form of eternity; in other words, it would be an essence and not an existence. Essence is just that character which any existence wears in so far as it remains identical with itself and so long as it does so; the very character which it throws overboard by changing, and loses altogether when it becomes something else. To be able to become something else, to suffer change and yet endure, is the privilege of existence, be it in a substance, an event, or an experience; whereas essences can be exchanged, but not changed. Existence at every step casts off one essence and picks up another: we call it the same existence when we are able to trace its continuity in change, by virtue of its locus and proportions; but often we are constrained to give up the count, and to speak of a new event, a new thing, or a new experience. The essences or forms traversed in mutation render this mutation possible and describable: without their eternal distinctness no part of the flux could differ in any respect from any other part, and the whole would collapse into a lump without order or quality. So much more profound is the eternal being of the essences traversed in change, than that of the matter or attention or discourse which plays with those essences at touch and go.

Nothing, then, more truly *is* than character. Without this wedding garment no guest is admitted to the feast of existence: whereas the unbidden essences do not require that invitation (with which very low characters are sometimes honoured) in order to preserve their proud identity out in the cold. There those few privileged revellers will soon have to rejoin them, not a whit fatter for their brief surfeit of being. After things lose their existence, as before they attain it, although it is true of them that they have existed or will exist, they have no internal being except their essences, quite as if they had never broached Existence at all: yet the identity of each essence with itself and difference from every other essence suffices to distinguish and define them all in eternity, where they form the Realm of Essence. True and false assertions may be made about any one of them, such, for instance, as that it does not exist; or that it includes or excludes some other essence, or is included or excluded by it.

Here is a further character inseparable from essence: all essences are eternal. No hyperbole or rhetorical afflatus is contained in this assertion, as if some prophet pronounced some law or some city to be everlasting. That any existing thing should be everlasting, though not impossible, is incongruous with the contingency of existence. God or matter, if they are everlasting, are so by a sort of *iterated contingency* and perpetual reproduction; for it is in the nature of existence to be here and perhaps not there, now and perhaps not then; it must be explored to discover how far it may stretch; it must wait and see how long it shall last. The assumption that it lasts or stretches for ever can be made only impetuously, by animal enthusi-asm, when the feeling of readiness and omnipotence makes some living creature defy all threats of disaster. Yet so long as we live in time, the ghost of the murdered past will always fill the present with a profound uneasiness. If the eternity of essence were conceived after that fashion, it would indeed be a rash boast; no essence has an essential lien on existence anywhere, much less everywhere and always. Its eternity has nothing to do with such mortal hazards. It is merely the self-identity proper to each of the forms which existence may put on or off, illustrate somewhere or perhaps illustrate always, or very likely never illustrate at all.

# Substance

1. Since substance is posited, and not given in intuition, as essences may be given, *substance is external to the thought which posits it.*

2. Since it is posited in action, or in readiness for action, the substance posited is external not merely to the positing thought (as a different thought would be) but is external to the physical agent which is the organ of that action, as well as of that thought. In other words, *Substance has parts and constitutes a physical space.* Conversely, the substantial agent in action and thought is external to the surrounding portions of substance with which it can interact. *All the parts of substance are external to one another.*

3. Since substance is engaged in action, and action involves change, *substance is in flux and constitutes a physical time.* Changes are perpetually occurring in the relations of its parts, if not also in their intrinsic characters.

4. Since the agents in action and reaction are distinct in position and variable in character, and since they induce changes in one another, *substance is unequally distributed.* It diversifies the field of action, or physical time and space.

5. Since there is no occasion for positing any substance save as an agent in the field of action, all recognisable substance must lie in the same field in which the organism of the observer occupies a relative centre. Therefore, wherever it works and solicits recognition, *substance composes a relative cosmos.*

A mutual externality, or *Auseinander-sein*—an alternation of centres such as moment and moment, thing and thing, place and place, person and person—is characteristic of existence. Each centre is equally actual and equally central, yet each is dependent on its neighbours for its position and on its predecessors for its genesis. The

From "Indispensable Properties of Substance." From *Realms of Being* (New York: Charles Scribner's Sons, 1942 [1937]), pp. 202–217.

existential interval from one centre to another is bridged naturally by generation or motion—by a transition actually taking place from one moment, place, or character to another, in such a manner that the former moment, place, or character is abandoned and lost. The same interval may still be bridged cognitively by faith or intent, cognition being a substitute for a transition which cannot be executed materially, because the remote term of it is past or not next in the order of genesis or transformation. But this interval can never be bridged by synthesis in intuition. Synthesis in intuition destroys the existential status of the terms which it unites, since it excludes any alternation or derivation between them. It unites at best the essences of some natural things into an ideal picture. On the other hand the conjunction of existences in nature must always remain successive, external, and unsynthesised. Nature shows no absolute limits and no privileged partitions; whereas the richest intuition, the most divine omniscience, is imprisoned in the essence which it beholds. It cannot break through into existence unless it loses itself and submits to transition; and the foretaste or aftertaste of such transition, present in feeling, must posit something eventual, something absent from intuition, if even the sense or idea of existence is to arise at all. Then the mind engaged in action may begin to live by faith in the outlying conditions of life, and by an instinctive tension towards obscure events.

It might seem that memory eludes this necessity, and actually encloses some parts of the past in the present, and brings the movement of events bodily within the circle of intuition. But this is an illusion founded on the fact that memory contains both imagery and knowledge: the imagery is all present, but that of which it gives knowledge, when memory is true, is past and gone. Even if, by a rare favour, the original aspect of the past experience should be reproduced exactly, it will not be the past event, nor even the present one, that will be given in intuition, but the dateless essence common to both.

The cognitive value of this apparition will hang on the ulterior fact that such an apparition, or the event which it reports, occurred before, at a point of time which was its own centre, and not a marginal feature in the present perspective. Memory, then, in so far as it is, or even claims to be, knowledge, is faith in the absent, and bridges external relations by intent only, not by synthesis in intuition.

A mutual externality is also requisite among the instances of spirit, that is, among thoughts that are to be regarded as existences and events. This at first sight might seem contrary to the apparent self-existence and self-evidence of conscious being, and to the transcendental status of spirit, which, because it is a logical counterpart to any datum, might be alleged to be an omnipresent fact, existing absolutely. But this, although it may pass for criticism, is the sophistry of reflection, which can readily take its verbal terms for existences or substances, and ignore the natural springs of feeling and of reflection itself. An instance of spirit, a pure feeling or intuition, if it had no date or place in nature, would not be an event or existence at all, but only another name, and a mythical name, for the essence conceived to be present there. The life of thought, in its conscious intensity, lies in the syntheses which it is perpetually making among its changing materials. These acts of synthesis, these glances and insights, are historical facts; they arise and are distinguishable on the level of experience from their material conditions; but they are not substances. Their substance is their organ in its movement and in its changing tensions: it is the psyche. The case is like that of a collision between two vehicles, or checkmate in a game of chess. The collision is a new fact, on the plane of human affairs, as is the checkmate which ends the game; so, too, are the chagrin or the severe pain which these events may occasion. But the pain or the chagrin could no more arise, or come into existence, without the living persons who endure them—persons moving in the realm of matter—than the checkmate could occur without the match, or the collision without the vehicles. If a feeling or thought is to be actual, and not a metaphorical name for some eternal essence, it must therefore arise out of material events, and in the midst of them: it must stand in external relations.

Thus the first indispensable condition for the being of substance is indispensable also to any form of existence, mental or historical as well as physical. Existence, like substance, is essentially diffuse and many-centred. One fact can be reached cognitively from another fact only by faith, and materially only by transition; and the cognitive or the initial fact itself can exist only by virtue of its position or action in a natural system extending beyond it.

It follows that substance is in flux, virtual, if not actual. External relations are such as are due to the position, not to the inherent character, of the terms. They are, therefore, always variable, and existence, although it may endure by accident for any length of time, is inherently mortal and transitory, being adventitious to the essences which figure in it. When Hamlet says, *To be or not to be,* he is pondering the alternative between existence and non-existence, and feeling the contingency of both. The question is not whether he shall be or not be Hamlet: death might cause him to forget his essence, but could not abolish it or transform it into another essence. In the realm of essence all these essences are eternally present and no alternative arises: which is perhaps the ultimate truth conveyed by the doctrine of eternal salvation or punishment. But the accidents of death, or dreams, or oblivion continually confront this life, and existence is an optional form of being. Shall this beloved or detested essence presently lose it? And on what other essence shall it fall next? To this pressing question the realm of essence supplies no answer, and the contemplative mind is hopelessly puzzled by it. *Solvitur ambulando:* the event, the propulsive currents of substance merging and rushing into new forms, will precipitate a solution without ever considering alternatives; and it is perhaps because they never stop to think before they act, that they are able to act at all.

Something not essence, then, actualises and limits the manifestation of every essence that figures in nature or appears before the mind. To this dark principle of existence we give the name of substance; so that substance, by definition, is the soil, the medium, and the creative force which secretly determines any option like that of Hamlet. Every such option is momentary and local; for although substance is external to essence and to thought, and its parts are external to one another, yet substance is internal to the things which it forms by occupying those contrasted places and assuming these various qualities. It is *their* substance, the principle of their existence, the ground of all the spontaneous changes which they undergo. It is indefinitely, perhaps infinitely, deep and inhuman; but whatever else its intrinsic essence may be, it is certainly complex, local, and temporal. Its secret flux involves at least as many contrasts and variations as the course of nature shows on the surface. Otherwise the ultimate core of existence would not exist, and the causes of variation would not vary. But how shall that which puts on this specious essence here and not there, be in the same inner condition in both places? Or how shall that which explodes now, have been equally active before? Substance, if it is to fulfil the function in virtue of which it is recognised and posited, must accordingly be for ever changing its own inner condition. It must be in flux.

Undoubtedly the word substance suggests permanence rather than change, because the substances best known to man (like the milk and the wet sand of the young architect) evidently pass from place to place and from form to form while retaining their continuity and quantity. Such permanence is not contrary to flux, but a condition of flux. The degree of permanence which substance may have in any particular process, and the name which should be given to this permanent factor, are questions for scientific discussion. They may not, and need not, receive any ultimate answer. But that *some* permanence, not the casual persistence of this or that image, is interwoven with the flux of things, follows from the reality of this flux itself. If change were total at any point, there transformation and existence would come to an end. The next, completely new, fact would not be next; it would be the centre, or the beginning, of a separate world. In other words, events, if they are to be successive or contiguous, must be pervaded by a common medium, in which they may assume relations external to their respective essences; for the internal or logical relations between these essences will never establish any succession or continuity among them, nor transport them at all into the sphere of existence. The critics of empiricism who have insisted that a series of sensations is not the sensation of a series, might well have added that the sensation of a series is no more than an isolated term on its own account, unless there is a background common to those terms and to this synthetic idea—a background in relation to which they may respectively take such places as shall render them contiguous or successive, although there is nothing within any of them to indicate such a position. This background, for human perception, is the field of vision symbolising the field of action; in this specious field the position of objects is distinguished before the objects are clearly specified or posited; but this unity of perspective, relative to the momentary station and thought of the observer, cannot embrace the existential flux itself, in which the events reported and the observer, with his thought, are incidental features. For the continuity and successiveness of this existing series, synthesis in apprehension is useless: it merely creates one more item—a living thought—to be ranged among its neighbours in the flux of existence. That which is requisite is the *natural derivation* of one phase in this flux from another, or a *natural tension* between them, determining their respective characters and positions. Such derivation and such tension, essential to action, involve a substance within or between events. There may be very much more in substance than that; but this is enough to disclose the existence of a substance, and to begin the human description of it by its functions.

Permanence, therefore, need not be set down separately among the radical properties attributed to substance: it is sufficiently expressed in the possibility of change, of continuity, of succession, and of the inclusion of actual events in a natural series, which shall not be a mere perspective in imagination.

Action and animal faith look in some specific direction; the butt of action, which is what I call substance, must be particular, local, and circumscribed. It must be capable of varying its position or its condition; for otherwise I could neither affect it by my action, nor await and observe its operation. In battle, in the chase, or in labour, attention is turned to a particular quarter, to something substantial there: it would defeat all action and art if all quarters were alike, and if I couldn't face a fact without turning my back on exactly the same fact in the rear; and the price of bread would be indifferent, if one substance being everywhere present I could find the same substance in the air. Action evidently would be objectless in an infinite vacuum or a homogeneous plenum; and even the notion or possibility of action would vanish if I, the agent, had not distinguishable parts, so that at least I might swim forward rather than backward in that dense vacuity.

A field of action must, then, be diversified substantially, not pictorially only; that which is at work in it here must not be equally at work in it there; the opportunities which it opens to me now must not be the same which it opened and will open always. Any conception of substance which represents it as undivided and homogeneous is accordingly not a conception of nature or of existence: and if such an object is ever called substance, it must be in a metaphysical sense which I do not attach to the word. One test of such evasions into the realm of essence is ability, or ambition, to give a precise definition of what substance is. *Materia prima* may be defined—Plotinus has an admirable exposition of it, like the Athanasian creed—because it is avowedly something incapable of existence, and at best one of those ideal terms which serve to translate nature into the language of thought. *Materia prima* is a grammatical essence, comparable to the transcendental ego, the "I think," which according to Kant must accompany all experience. The discrimination of such essences distinguishes one logic from another, and leaves everything in nature, except human language, just as it was. The existing substance of things, on the contrary, is that which renders them dynamic; it is wherever dynamic things are, not where they are not; it determines their aspects and powers; and we may learn, since it exists in us also, to play with it and to let it play on us, in specific ways. But it would be frivolous to attempt to define it, as if a set of words, or of blinking ideas, could penetrate to the heart of existence and determine how, from all eternity, it must have been put together. What we may discover of it is not its essence but its place, its motion, its aspects, its effects. Were it an essence given in intuition, a visionary presence to sense or to language, it would forfeit those very functions which compel us to posit it, and which attest its formidable reality. Chief of these functions is a perpetual and determinate revolution in the heavens, and fertility and decay upon earth. In this flux there is a relative permanence and continuity; but substance is not for that reason less agitated than the familiar face of nature, or nearer to the impassibility of an eternal essence. Far otherwise. Investigation rather shows that this substance (which may be traced experimentally in many of its shifts) is in a continual silent ferment, by which gross visible objects are always being undermined and transformed: so much so that science often loses its way amid those subtle currents of the elements, and stops breathless at some too human image.

There are certain celebrated doctrines which, in their forms of expression, are excluded at once from natural philosophy by these considerations. I may not say, for instance, with Parmenides that Being is and Not-Being is not, if what I am seeking to describe is the substance of nature. If for dialectical reasons, which are not directly relevant to physics, I wished to regard pure Being as the essence of matter, I should be compelled to distribute this pure Being unequally in a void: a result which would contradict my premise that Not-Being is not, since this void would not only exist but would be the only true theatre of existence, because it would be

the only seat of change. The pure Being or matter distributed in it, by hypothesis, is impassible and everywhere identical. Nature and life would therefore be due to the redistribution in the bosom of Not-Being of a pure Being in itself immutable. We should thus be led to the system of Democritus: a possible and even a model system of physics, although, in its expression, too Eleatic, and borrowing from that dialectical school a false air of necessity.

Similarly, at the threshold of natural philosophy, the Vedanta system must yield to the Samkhya: and this the Indians seem to have admitted by regarding the two systems as orthodox and compatible. It might be well if in the West we could take a hint from this comprehensiveness. The unity and simplicity of pure Being is not incompatible with the infinite variety of essences implied in it; and many things are true in the realm of essence which, if taken to describe existence, would be unmeaning or contrary to fact. It would suffice to distinguish the two spheres more carefully, for the legitimacy of systems, verbally most unlike, to become equal: although certainly those which were drawn from insight into essence would be more profound and unshakable than those drawn from observation of nature, since nature might as well have offered quite a different spectacle. On the other hand, it is the order and ground of this spectacle that interests the natural philosopher; and to him that more inward and more sublime intuition of essential Being is a waste of time, or a rhetorical danger.

One more illustration: the language of Spinoza about substance ought to yield, in physics, to that of Aristotle, in spite of the fact that a follower of Descartes could not help being more enlightened in mechanical matters than a follower of Socrates. Nevertheless it was Aristotle who gave the name of substance to compound natural things actually existing, and Spinoza who bestowed it on an ambiguous metaphysical object, now pure Being, now the universe in its infinity—in either case an ideal unity and an essence incapable of realisation all at once, if at all, in any natural locus. No discrimination of infinite Being into infinitely numerous attributes would ever generate existence, since all would remain eternal; and no enumeration of the possible modes of each attribute would turn them into particular things or into living minds, since each mode would imply all the others, and all would be equally rooted everywhere. In Aristotle, on the contrary, the name of substance is given where the office of substance is performed, and where one fact here asserts itself against another fact there; so that substance is the principle of individuation and exclusion, the condition of existence, succession, and rivalry amongst natural things. Even if these things, as conceived by Aristotle, have too much of an animate unity, and are mysteriously fixed in their genera and species, and redolent of moral suggestions, all this is but the initial dramatic rendering of their human uses, and the poetry of good prose. It does not prevent a more disinterested analysis, a microscopic and telescopic science, from disclosing in time the deeper mechanisms and analogies of nature, and its finer substance: just as the static zoology and the political psychology of Aristotle do not prevent us from peeping into the seething elementary passions beneath those classical masks. Things have not ceased to wear the sensuous and moral forms which interested the Greeks; but we may discover how those shells were generated, and what currents of universal substance have cast them up.

Finally, the practical intellect, in positing substance, imposes on it a certain relevance to the agent, who is to be in dynamic relations with it. The objects which art and sanity compel me to recognise as substantial, must affect me together, even if in very different ways. They must all impinge, directly or indirectly, on my action now; and it is by this test that I distinguish fact from fiction and true memory from fancy. Facts are dynamically connected with that which I now posit as substantial, and objects of fancy are not so connected. The field of animal faith spreads out from a living centre; observation cannot abandon its base, but from this vital station it may extend its perspectives over everything to which it can assign existence. Among these accredited things there may be other centres of observation, actual or eventual; but if the original organ and station, and these other stations and organs accredited by it, were not parts of one and the same substantial world, no means would remain of identifying the objects observed from one centre with those observed from another. I can acknowledge the existence of other moral centres in the world which I posit, but only if these centres are agencies, earthly or celestial, at work in my field of action, and dynamically connected with my own existence. All credible animation, of ascertainable character, must animate substances found in the same world with myself, and collateral with my own substance.

Perhaps this argument has some analogy to Spinoza's proof of the unity of substance. He tells us that substance is one, because if there were two or more substances they could bear no relation to one another. In other words, there can be but one universe, since anything outside, by being outside, would be related to it and collateral, and so after all would form a part of it. Yet if one universe, or one substance, can exist absolutely, and out of all relation to anything else, why should not any number of them exist, each centred in itself? The necessity of lying in external relations in order to exist, far from proving that only one system of facts is possible, proves that any closed circle of facts, in interplay with one another and with nothing else, will form a complete universe. Each part of this system will exist by virtue of its active position there, and may be discovered by any members of it who are sufficiently intelligent and adventurous; but from no part of that universe will anything beyond that universe be discoverable. Does this fact preclude the being of a different system, a separate universe, possessing the same sort of inward life and reality? I cannot think so. Transcendental necessities are relative to particular centres of experience; they have no jurisdiction beyond. Those other universes, to us, would be undiscoverable; but ours, too, would be undiscoverable to them; and yet we exist here without their leave. Might they not exist without ours?

What logic enables us to assert, therefore, is not that there is only one universe, but that each universe must be one, by virtue of a domestic economy determining the relative position and character of the events which compose it. Anything beyond this dynamic field is beyond the field of posited existence and possible knowledge. If there are other centres and active substances moving in other spheres, the relation of these disconnected spheres is not a physical relation: no journey and no transformation can bridge it: it lies in the realm of truth. Each of these worlds will exemplify its chosen essence; and the internal and unchangeable relations between these essences will be the only relations between those worlds. One will not exist before the other, nor will they be simultaneous; nor will either lie in any direction from the other, or at any distance. No force or influence will pass between them of any traceable physical or historical kind. If omniscience should see any harmony, contrast, or mutual fulfilment between their natures, that spiritual bond would be of the sort which links essences together by a logical necessity, and which a contemplative spirit may stop to disentangle and admire if it can and will.

Indeed, we may go further and say even of a single universe taken as a whole that its status is that of a truth rather than of an existence. Each part of it will exist, and if animate may truly feel its internal tension and life, and may truly assert the existence of the other parts also; yet the whole system—perhaps endless in its time and space—never exists at once or in any assignable quarter. Its existence is only posited from within its limits: externally its only status is that of a truth. Its essence was not condemned to be a closet-tragedy; living actors have been found to play it and a shifting stage to exhibit for a moment those convincing scenes. This essence has therefore the eternal dignity of a truth: it is the complete description of an event. Yet this event, taken as a whole, being unapproachable from outside, dateless, and nowhere, is in a sense a supernatural event. Those scenes are undiscoverable, save to those who play them, and that tumult is an ancient secret in the bosom of truth.

Indeed, good sense might suffice to convince anyone that no arguments or definitions can prevent things from being as numerous and as separate as they may chance to be. There is an infinite diversity of essences: what shall dissuade the fatality of existence, which must be groundless, from composing such changeful systems as it likes, on planes of being utterly incommensurable and incommunicable? The most a man can say for himself, or for any other element from which exploration may start, is that whatever is to enter his field of action must belong to the same dynamic system with himself. In experience and art, as in the nebular hypothesis, this dynamic oneness of the world is primitive. It is not put together by conjoining elements found existing separately, but is the locus in which they are found; for if they were not found there, they would be essences only and not facts. In mature human perception the essences given are doubtless distinct and the objects which they suggest are clearly discriminated: here is the dog, there the sun, the past nowhere, and the night coming. But beneath all this definition of images and attitudes of expectancy, there is always a voluminous feeble sensibility in the vegetative soul. Even this sensibility posits existence; the contemplation of pure Being might supervene only after all alarms, groupings, and beliefs had been suspended—something it takes all the discipline of Indian sages to begin to do. The vegetative soul enjoys an easier and more Christian blessedness: it sees not, yet it believes. But believes in what? In whatever it may be that envelopes it; in what we, in our human language, call space, earth, sunlight, and motion; in the throbbing possibility of putting forth something which we call leaves, for which that patient soul has no name and no image. The unknown total environment is what every intellect posits at birth; whatever may be attempted in action or discovered in nature will be a fresh feature in that field. Everything relevant to mortal anxiety lies within that immensity, be it an object of earthly fear or pursuit or of religious hope. Animal faith and material destiny move in a relative cosmos.

# Teleology and Psyche

## I.  Teleology

We have already seen that explanation by habit or law is a reduction of events to their rhythms or repetitions; we gain no insight into why or how a thing happens by saying that it has often happened before. Did we really wish to understand, we should inquire into the inner elements of such a mutation in any one of its instances: because a thing must happen each time by a concourse of motions there, and not because the same thing happens also in other places; although naturally it will happen again if the conditions which produced it here are repeated. Now a different form of mock explanation appears in what is called teleology, when the ground of things is sought in their excellence, in their harmony with their surroundings, or in the adaptation of organs to their functions and of actions to their intentions.

Such correspondences exist: teleology, if it be only a name for them, is a patent and prevalent fact in nature. Indeed the adaptation of things to one another is involved in their coexistence: a thing can arise only by finding and taking its place where other things make room for it. Everything in the moving equilibrium of nature is necessarily cooperative. But the question becomes interesting (and unanswerable) when we ask why, at any point, this so singular thing should have found such a singular set of conditions as to permit or compel it to exist there. A wider view, exploring antecedents and consequents, and discovering analogies, may enlarge the prospect, and, as happens in the books of naturalists, may so pleasantly occupy the mind with pictures and stories, that we may stop asking for reasons. And to invoke adaptation itself, as if this were a cause of adaptation, would be to halt at a word, adding perhaps to it, as an element of power, the bated breath with which we pronounce it.

Yet this human scale and these human emotions, which we impose so fatuously on the universe, bear witness, on the plane of thought, to the existence of organisms and of life on the plane of matter; for we should have no emotions and no scale to impose on other things if our own being were not definite, animate, and self-assertive.

In human society teleology takes a special and conscious form: it becomes art. Not only do tropes—which here we call methods—everywhere dominate the scene, but very often the method is explicitly adopted or modified, and the action planned; foresight and intention occupy the first moment of it, and execution of that prevision occupies the second moment. Here the preformation of events and the preadaptation of instruments to their uses is a simple fact of history. Knowing how our passions and purposes watchfully realise their avowed ends, may we not reasonably assimilate obscure events to these deliberate actions, the causes of which seem clear to us and intimately confessed? As we do things when we wish, must not all nature, or God working through nature, wish everything when they do it? Must not some idea, seen under the form of the good, guide and attract every movement in nature?

Yes: that is the normal way of speaking, the rhetorical or poetical way of describing nature in human terms from the human point of view. But moral sentiment, poetry, and theology are forms of literature, not of science; they are not wrong in their own sphere, and their rightness becomes intelligible, and takes its place in natural history, when we see its relativity to human experience, and its psychic seat. There,

From *Realms of Being* (New York: Charles Scribner's Sons, 1942 [1937]), pp. 310–327; and from *Physical Order and Moral Liberty,* eds. John and Shirley Lachs (Nashville: Vanderbilt University Press, 1969) pp. 197–201.

in literature, a sceptic should be the last to quarrel with the use of moral analogies in describing nature: poetry does not contradict science, because in daring to be poetry, it avows a complete ignorance and disdain of the prose of things. Poetry is poetry, and opens up a legitimate vista within its own world, but only to a poetic spirit; in its material existence it is a flood of verbiage incidental to human passions and their rhetorical automatisms. In its biological capacity poetry can be described only in prose; and all its insights reappear as incidents and as subjective creations bred in the realm of matter.

Before indicating, in the tentative way which alone is possible, the material basis of teleology, it may be well to examine the logic of it in the imagination; for the contrast between poetry and prose is by no means absolute, and any scrupulous study of moral philosophy compels us to restore that subject, and ourselves who pursue it, to our place in nature. The clearness of moral life after all is only a verbal clearness; a sort of facility and acceleration by which our acts and feelings come to a climax and fulfil their natural tropes. We are left in the dark concerning the manner of this fulfilment. We are even more in the dark as to the ground of the ideas and wishes which, as we say, guide our conduct; when all goes well, we need not stop to question them, but presently when they clash with one another and fail of fulfilment, the easy miracle of their power begins to seem dubious, and subterranean bonds between them and the world of action become visible in a new, a biological, direction.

Consider first the existential presence of human wishes and ideas. Is it conceivably an original fact and unconditioned? Why should any wish or idea arise at all here and now? Is the mid-void peopled with them, as with little winged heads of cherubs, without bodies and without support? Surely if anything ever had a cause and was evidently secondary, it is human will and fancy; to take them for absolute beings, or original powers, would be to allow theoretical sophistries to blind us to the plainest facts. If I want water, it is because my throat is parched; if I dream of love, it is because sex is ripening within me. Nature has fixed the character, and circumstances have fixed the occasion, for this ferment of desire and conception. Conscious will is a symptom, not a cause; its roots as well as its consequences are invisible to it, material, and often incongruous and astonishing.

But suppose that the mind, like some morose tyrant, determines to shut all doors and windows against the outer world, and to see only by the lamp of self-consciousness. What will be the stuff of its meditations? Nothing but animal wishes and barn-yard ideas; demands for food, air, liberty of motion; dreams of wild things to be chased, eaten, played with, or hidden; or perhaps of fame to be won, empires conquered, friendship and love and praise. How comes absolute free-will or a groundless moral energy to choose these singular objects? Could it not have employed its inviolable leisure and its infinite invention in conceiving something better than such a very humble, cruel, and nasty animal world? And could not its sentiment have been less sentimental, less unctuous and constrained, less tainted by terror and desperate delusion? Why are human love and religion so tormented, if they are masters of the world? If they command miraculously and matter obeys, is it not because matter had first created them and dictated the commands which they were to issue?

Evidence of this, if it were needed, might also be found in the loose character of ideas and wishes compared with their fulfilments, even when they are materially fulfilled. These ideas and wishes are personal, confused, and incomplete. When a law-giver designs a constitution or an architect an edifice, a thousand contrary principles and suggestions assault his mind. Unless he is very precipitate, or an absolute slave of habit, the plan will take shape in his mind to his own surprise; it will be a sudden concretion of subtle currents and accidents within him, the harmony and relevance of which, if any, we call his genius or his ability. Even when these are greatest, and most seasoned by experience, their prophetic virtue will be only abstract and partial; the event will be a new surprise, as was the idea. For it is hardly possible that the edifice when complete, or the constitution when in actual operation, should produce the same impression on the mind as the plan conceived there originally. The plan arose by a synthesis of acquired impulses within one body: the work arises by a concourse of actions which, even if still those of the same person only, and obedient to the same vital impulses as the idea (as happens in singing, speaking, or making a gesture) yet occur now in the outer world, in a comparatively foreign material, and with a greater admixture of accidental concomitants. Therefore a man's actions and works seem to him less a part of himself than his intentions, but to others seem more so: because to others he is a personage and to himself he is a mind.

Ideas and wishes, then, are mental echoes of movements proper to bodily life; were they not, they could have no application and no relevance to the world. The more accurately they prefigure events and seem to control them by prescribing their tropes, the better they prove their own fidelity to the ruling impulses of matter. Clear ideas are evidences of clean arts; a firm and victorious will bears witness to a strong and opportune economy in the organism. Indeed, for a scientific psychology behaviour is the only conceivable seat of mind, and intelligence simply a certain plasticity in organisms which enables them to execute tropes in subtle harmony with their material opportunities. True, mind and intelligence are something more in fact. This we perceive when, in reflection, we gather up sensuous images, memories, lyric effusions, and dramatic myths into a literary psychology, which may be remarkably convincing but remains purely literary; for it cannot follow the flux of its subject-matter by observation and measurement, but must recreate it in imagination, and leave it at that. Similarly, the history which interweaves intentions with events and ideas with motions may give a capital description of moral perspectives, but it is simply literature.

Total events in nature are never wholly mental, and it is on their material side, through their substance and physical tensions, that they are derived from previous events and help to shape the events which follow. But this doctrine is based on far-reaching considerations which may often be ignored; and when only the mental side of an event is discovered, the material and substantial side of it may be denied, and states of mind, in their purity, may be regarded as total natural events. It will then seem plausible to regard them as links in the chain of natural causes, for are they not moments in experience, as memory or dramatic reconstruction may survey it? But this amphibious psycho-physics, even if we admitted it, would not be teleological. Each mental event would transmit existence and energy to its successor in proportion to its own intensity and quality, just as if it were a form of matter. It would not thereby exercise any magical moral control over its consequences. Thus intense thought might make the head ache, fear might cause paralysis, amusement laughter, or love a want of appetite and early death. The teleological virtue of wishes and ideas is accordingly something quite distinct from their alleged physical influence; indeed it is only when we disregard this incongruous mechanical efficacy attributed to them that we begin to understand what their teleological virtue would mean: it would mean a miraculous preestablished harmony between the commands or wishes of the spirit and events in the world. It would mean the exercise of divine power, which a well-advised human being could never attribute to himself, but only to the grace of God, perhaps passing through him.

Teleology then retreats into a theology, or into a cosmological idealism, fraught with curious alternatives: for a divine mind, if conscious and omniscient as high theology would make it, would not be an event; it would be a decree, a commandment, or an eternal glory relative to all events, but on a different plane from any of them. If, on the contrary, the divine will was immanent in the world and intermingled with all natural events, it would evidently not be separate or self-conscious; indeed, it would be only a poetic synonym for the actual fertility of matter, and for the tropes exhibited in its evolution. In either case, after making our bow to this divine will, out of deference to antiquity and to human rhetoric, we should be reduced to studying as far as possible the crawling processes of nature. These will be the seat of such teleology as surely exists, and as a critical philosophy may record without falling into rhetorical ambiguities. Organic life is a circular trope which at each repetition touches or approaches a point which we regard as its culmination, and call maturity. In man, maturity involves feelings, intentions, and spiritual light: but it is idle to regard the whole trope as governed by these top moments in it, which are more highly conditioned, volatile, and immaterial than are their organs, their occasions, or their fruits.

Nature is full of coiled springs and predestined rhythms; of mechanisms so wound up that, as soon as circumstances permit, they unroll themselves through a definite series of phases. A seed, if suitable sown and watered, will grow into one particular sort of plant, and into no other. At the inception of such a trope the predestined movement is said to be "potential"; there is a "predisposition" in matter at that point to execute the whole movement. What is this predisposition? Examination of a seed would probably never disclose in it a perfect model of the future flower, any more than examination of a young man's passions, or of his body, would disclose there the poems which these passions might ultimately inspire. Potentiality seems to be an imputed burden, a nominal virtue attributed to the first term of a trope because of the character of the rest of it. Yet, sometimes, as in a seed, the imputed burden is genuine, and potentiality is pregnancy. A true beginning and sufficient cause of what ensues is really found there; but this initial reality need not at all resemble that which it will become. Its nature is internal, hidden, perhaps inexpressible in the terms of human observation at all; so far is it from being an image cast into that well from the outside, or a reflex name given to it in view of the future. The tropes which mark the obvious metres of nature tell nothing of the inspiration, the secret labour, or the mechanism which brings them forth.

Heredity is an obvious case of repetition; but its temporal scale is so large in respect to an observer of his own species that individualities may seem to him more striking and self-grounded than uniformities. Yet from a little distance, or in an alien species, heredity recedes into a monotonous succession of waves and a multitudinous repetition of objects. Both impressions are just, and nature, here seen at close quarters, reveals the complexity of her endless pulsations. There is a curious involution of the organism in the seed. The seed is not merely the first state of the organism in the offspring but was also a part of a similar organism in the parent. This notable trope is apt to blind us to the mechanism requisite for its repetition. We are solicited by the magic rhyme of it to rest content with explaining the beginning of life by the end, the part by the whole, the actual by the ideal, the existent by the non-existent. Abandoning physics altogether as incapable of solving the mystery, we may wonderingly record the reappearance, by the will of God, of new generations of every species, each after its kind. But as in the Christian sacraments, so here in natural reproduction, the grace of God does not operate without physical continuity in its channels; and it would be by tracing that continuity, and the accidents which often cause it to deviate from its course, that reproduction might be seen in its natural setting. The multitude of successes would not then blind us to the far greater number of failures. To arise in this world and to become something specific is in each instance a fresh and doubtful undertaking.

Prodigious complexity is something to which nature is not averse, like a human artist, but on the contrary is positively prone; and in animals the attainment of such prodigious complexity is made possible by the fact that a special environment is at hand, in the body of the parent, enabling the young organism to run through its earlier and fundamental phases safely, surely, and quickly. So unerring is this development that the animal is often born complete; yet there is enough wavering, with false starts in directions once taken by the species and since abandoned, to show that the core of the seed need contain no prefigurement of the whole result, but that this result is reached tentatively in reproduction, as it was originally in evolution; only that the ovum is a far better locus for a perfect development of the psyche than was the bleak outer world.

Nevertheless the manner of this quick and spontaneous growth is little understood, and only the total trope remains to furnish our imagination. Seeing its dramatic unity, we feel that the first term must be pregnant with the ultimate issue, as the first act of a good play—assuming human nature and the ways of the world—is pregnant with the last. We forget that poetic genius itself must have natural sources and reason external guides; and we attribute the perpetual attainment of some natural perfection to the miraculous power of the trope realised in it, or to the divine will contemplating that trope and, as if fascinated by its magic beauty, commanding matter to reproduce it for ever and ever.

Final causes certainly exist in the conduct of human beings, yet they are always inadequate to describe the events in which they are manifested, since such events always presuppose a natural occasion and a mechanical impulse; and these cannot flow from the purpose or choice which they make possible and pertinent. The whole operation of final causes therefore requires, beneath and within it, a deeper flow of natural forces which we may darkly assign to fate or matter or chance or the unfathomable will of God. Yet, since without this irrational occasion or afflatus those purposes and choices could never have taken shape, it ought to suffice for our reasonable satisfaction if, in some measure, the natural perfections of things are manifested in them, and if there is some degree of harmony between the world and the spirit. Moral tropes have their proper status and dignity if they are actually found in the human aspect of events; they are not rendered false or nugatory merely because the material existence presupposed in them has a different method of progression. Medicine and psychology are now disclosing a truth which men of experience have perceived in all ages, that virtues and vices are equally phases of a controllable physical life: a fact which takes nothing away from their beauty or horror. They are the moral qualities of a natural being.

Mechanical tropes in their turn are incompetent to describe or measure spiritual realities, such as excellence or happiness or spirit itself; nor is it reasonable to require them to do so. They will be amply authenticated if they can serve to trace the whole material backing and occasions of those moral harmonies or spiritual lights. These, in order to arise do not require a different mechanism of their own, or a different occasion; the material mechanism and the material occasion fully suffice to introduce and to justify them. The physical terror of murder has made murder criminal; the animal warmth and transport of love have made love tender and deep. Of course, a deepening of apprehension is required, founded itself on a changed habit, a finer involution of responses in the organism; so that the same things which were done and regarded brutally may be done and regarded with a far-reaching sense of all that they involve. This new sense sees light and glow in the fire, of which the blinder senses could feel only the heat. Hence if either the naturalist or the moralist is a man of a single sense he must be left to grope in his professional half-light. Nature in his children will probably redress the balance.

The fact that natural organisms are far more closely purposeful than works of art, may itself serve to reveal the true superposition of art upon nature. Art is a human, marginal, not indispensable extension of natural teleology. The essential organic tropes, passions, and powers of man must have been first firmly rooted in the race, before anyone could conceive a project, or be able to execute it as conceived. Even highly civilised humanity forms its plans only dreamfully, and is cheated by its own impotence, or by contrary currents, in the execution of them. Often the most fixed purposes and the most vehement efforts are wasted; indeed, they are always wasted in some measure, because no designer can foresee all the circumstances of his work, or its ulterior uses. Any work, when it exists, is a part of the realm of matter, and has its fortunes there, far from all control or intention. The saintly Henry the Sixth founded Eton and King's College for the salvation of souls; they have served admirably together with the playing-fields to form the pensive but quite earthly ethos of the modern Englishman. In the works of nature there is not this division, nor this irony; the uses are not forecast in any purpose, consciously prophetic; they are simply the uses which the thing finds or develops, as it changes under the control of the changing circumstances. Thus the precision of adjustment between organs and functions, far from being a miracle,is in one sense a logical necessity or tautology; since nothing has any functions but those which it has come to have, when plasticity here with stimulus and opportunity there have conspired to establish them.

An organism is a concretion in matter which can feed, defend, and reproduce itself. Its initial form of expansion finds a natural limit, beyond which circumstances do not suffer it to go: then, unless it perishes altogether, it reproduces itself: that is, it breaks up into parts, some of which repeat the original form of expansion, while the others dissolve into their elements and die. Expansion thus becomes rhythmical, repeating a constant trope; except that, if the force of concretion and accretion is powerful at that centre, and if the circumstances are favourable, that trope may become internally more complex: in other words, the organism may acquire fresh organs. These will reappear in each generation in their due place and season, if the environment continues to give them play; and in this way a race and a species will be established, individual and recognisable, yet subject to private variations and also to generic shifts, by the atrophy of some organs and the development of others.

If, then, we understood genesis we should understand heredity; for an organ cannot arise, either the first time or the last, except spontaneously, and as if it had never existed before. But how can it arise at all? By what genetic impulse does some nucleus of matter modify its parts, and complicate their sympathetic movements, without losing its unity of action

in respect to external things? It is for the naturalists to reply, in so far as observation or experiment enables them to trace the actual genesis of bodies; for as to the verbal explanations which they may offer, they are not likely to be on the scale or in the terms proper to the flux or to the concretions of matter at a depth so far below that of human language. Let matter take shape as it will: all that concerns me here is the nature of the teleology present in the result. Organs must arise before they can exercise what we call their function, and this function must be one which the circumstances usually render possible and self-maintaining. Is the philosopher reduced to impressions on the human scale? Must he blankly confess that nature is mysteriously inspired, and that matter gathers itself into organisms as if it were magically guided by the love of that life and those achievements of which such organisms will be capable?

Not quite. Moralistic physics is wiser than natural science in not ignoring eventual spiritual issues; but these issues are no factors in generation. On the contrary, they are themselves uncertain, conditioned, and precarious; so that if we reach any depth or honesty in our reflection we cannot attribute the movement of nature to the antecedent influence of the future good which she might realise. Instead, we must attribute the pursuit of this good, and its eventual realisation, to her previous blind disposition, fortified by the fact that circumstances were favourable to that development: and this last fact is no accident, since (as we have just seen) the adaptation of the parts of nature to one another is necessary to their existence, and nature could not retain any disposition for which circumstances did not make room, at least for the moment. In a word, the teleology present in the world must be distinguished from final causes. The latter are mythical and created by a sort of literary illusion. The germination, definition, and prevalence of any good must be grounded in nature herself, not in human eloquence.

The conditions of existence, as I conceive it, involve change and involve adaptation: perhaps if we ponder these necessities we shall gain some insight into the origin of organisms and the secret of life. Each natural moment has a forward tension, it is a moment of transition. Its present quality was determined by the force of lateral tensions guiding the previous dynamic stress of its substance; and the issue, as this moment passes into the next, will be determined by the lateral tensions to which its inner or forward tension is now subject. Is it not then native and proper to existence in its primary elements to congregate and to roll itself together into shells fashioned by its seeds, and into seeds fostered by its climate? And will not this initial concretion at any point go on swallowing what it can, destroying what it must, and harmonising its own complexity, until some contrary wind or some inner exhaustion disperses its elements? May not this disruption itself become less frequent with the extension of any cosmos, and the better co-ordination of the motions within it? A natural moment may be prolonged or reiterated; it may be caught up in a trope itself indefinitely recurrent, so that associated moments, duly spaced and controlled by their mutual tensions, may for a long time reappear in a fixed order. Any trope will recur if within its substance, or near by, there is generated a fresh natural moment, like the original one, and under similar conditions. Nothing more is required for a swarming or a hereditary life to cover the face of nature.

Every natural moment, in which matter at any point holds some essence unchanged, is fit to be the seed of all creatures and the centre of all thought. Some sequels might be reached only by a great and prosperous development from that moment outward; others might require the dissolution of this complex, and a fresh beginning, in some other direction, from one of its radical elements. But forwards or backwards, everything might be arranged round any nucleus, without the least violence or suppression of its original life, if only it were planted in the requisite soil. This profound naturalness of the greatest complications becomes clear to us in health, when we move spontaneously and think smoothly; it is only in disease that we tremble at our own incredible complexity, and that harmony becomes a prob-

lem. In fact harmony in itself is neither more difficult nor rarer than disorder: that which demands a rare concourse of circumstances is harmony *of this sort, here;* and yet, in the special circumstances in which anything arises, harmony with that thing is presupposed, otherwise that particular thing would not have arisen. When our own ready-made being and action are the facts in the foreground, we instinctively and justifiably take it for granted that surrounding nature is in harmony with them and will give them suitable play; they are not unconditioned or omnipotent, but they are co-operative with their world. It is only when a different harmony, not native to us, is suggested, that it seems to us impossibly difficult of attainment and, if actual, miraculous. Before we could adapt our presumptions and impulses to that alien order we should need to retrace our steps and follow that other path of development. Everything that is, except where it is, would be infinitely improbable.

Thus the very fluidity of the flux, in its moving equilibrium, causes every concretion that can arise to arise, and every organism to maintain itself which can maintain itself. Such is the feeble yet ineradicable sympathy in the poor heart of matter towards the whole realm of essence. With many a false start, with a momentum and an organic memory often disastrous, with an inertia always trustfully blind, existence passes inevitably and in many streams from what it is to what it can be; it changes in the very act of continuing, and undermines its condition in surrounding it with developments and supports. Then, when any of these concretions collapses, as they must all collapse in turn, it returns to the charge, perhaps in the same direction, like Sisyphus, or like Proteus, in quite another. In the first case we speak of reproduction, in the second of evolution: but these words do not stand for different forces or principles but only for different results. In reproduction the flux repeats the same trope, in evolution it changes that trope for one more complex or appropriate, imposed by a new balance of forces.

That collapse is inevitable follows from the fact that existence is essentially chaotic. Its parts, perhaps infinite in multitude, will be always readjusting their mutual tensions, so that, ultimately, the ground gives way under any edifice. And the catastrophe may ruin more than that confident system; it may radically transmute the elements which composed it, since every essence which matter may wear is arbitrary and, if occasion offers, may be exchanged for some other. Moreover, any trope has limits. The matter which executes or reproduces it, having done so, falls back into the relative chaos which remains the background of everything; so that death, in every instance, is the end of life; and in nature at large death can be only temporarily and imperfectly circumvented by fertility. I speak of fertility in a particular species and within one moral world: for of new creations there is presumably no end, and one perfection can neither remember nor desire another.

I confess that the life of the spider, or my own life, is not one which, if I look at it as a whole, seems to me worth realising; and to say that God's ways are not our ways, and that human tastes and scruples are impertinent, is simply to perceive that moral values cannot preside over nature, and that what arises is not the good, in any prior or absolute sense, but only the possible at that juncture: a natural growth which as it takes form becomes a good in its own eyes, or in the eyes of a sympathetic poet. Then this good realised endows with a relative and retrospective excellence all the conditions favourable to its being, as if with prophetic kindness and parental devotion they had conspired to produce it. The spider is a marvel of pertinacity, and I am not without affection for my own arts and ideas; we both of us heartily welcome the occasions for our natural activities; but when those occasions and activities have passed away, they will not be missed.

## II.   Psyche or Tropes

The most remarkable and solid unit in the moral world is the individual person: nor are any beginning or endings in nature more unmistakable than birth and death. Neither, indeed, is absolute: a life is a trope; a substance runs through it which pre-existed and which survives: while the recognisable trope itself does not disappear with the disappearance of each of its instances, but defines them one after the other. Yet by falling into this recognisable human form, modified in each case by circumstances, that flowing substance generates a man. How? A seed, a fostering environment, food, and time are required for birth. The elements absorbed would be impotent of themselves to compose such a being; the seed must contain a material nucleus of order—I will call it a psyche—by which the requisite elements are selected, arranged, and kept for a time (which we call a life) in organic circulation; else they form sediments, or are exuded, until the organising force of the psyche proves too weak for its many commitments, so that the circulation ceases, and death ensues. There is no psyche in the residuum: yet the human trope does not become in consequence suddenly obsolete; it continues to develop out of the seed which the dead man, or his contemporaries, had shed in their prime, and is reproduced with slight variations in their offspring and descendants for indefinite ages.

Such, in the rough, is the most notable instance of genesis which a philosopher can observe; and he can observe it from within as well as from without, a fact which may compensate in a measure for the rough view, all out of scale with the presumable texture of nature, which the outside presents to his senses, or even to his biological science. Generation is a miracle to his mind, but to his instincts it is a destiny, even more irresistibly insidious when not understood than when foreseen and desired. The inner human cycle of hunger, playfulness, hunting, love, and paternity proves to experience that genesis and the ordering of human life are perfectly spontaneous and blind inwardly, however familiar or mechanical they may come to seem when surveyed from a distance.

A philosopher whose reflection remains on the level of humanism might be content to say that there exists a miraculous supermaterial power, the idea of man in God, perpetually renewing its operation in nature. This expresses the broad facts, though without accounting for the occasions on which they arise, or the variations which they show. If a divine idea operates, it operates only under conditions, the chief of which are that the psyche be transmitted by sexual fertilisation, and that its growth be fostered by a suitable environment. Moreover, the most rapid glance at the world will show that the human psyche is only one among many; all animals and plants are generated and preserved in a similar fashion; they all go through the cycle of birth, propagation and death. Indeed, the analogy runs deeper. The seasons, the weather, the rise and fall of human institutions, even celestial and chemical motions obey some such vital rhythm, yet with this notable difference, that in inanimate processes genesis is from the end of one trope to the beginning of the next, whereas in living beings the propagation is from the middle of each trope. After its fertile prime, individual life has a waste end, a decline in which it is addressed to death, not to reproduction. Some animals, however, go through metamorphoses; they seem to change their species without surrendering their individuality; the whole grub passes into the butterfly, wholly unlike itself and yet not another. The psyche here has several forms of life in store, to be developed alternatively or in succession, producing bodies of different aspect and scale, which nevertheless are bodies of the same soul, or the thoughts and the acts dictated by the same passion may carry out a single impulse in entirely different transcripts and expressions. This is presumably the native method of nature, the sequel being a precipitate, not a copy, of the previous fact, and transformation rather than persistence of form being the very condition of existence and life. And it is not insects only that pass through dissimilar phases of growth, in which a superficial observer would not recognise the same animal: all seeds are strangely dissimilar from the full grown plant or animal from which they come and into which they develop; and even in

man there is much transformation from birth to old age, both in aspect and powers, with a succession of different instincts, long latent and perhaps never actually exhibited. The notion that like comes from like, and that it would be miraculous if any thing arose that had not preexisted, is a shallow empirical impression: never justified strictly, since things are never just as they were, and justified roughly only by projecting generic images, words, and other convenient essences upon the substance of things, and supposing that they exhaust the reality; when in fact they serve merely to name or to transcribe it. Sensibility itself, the latest begotten and most original child of nature, this empiricism thinks, must also be like its parent, or else inexplicable and spurious; whereas, even on its material side, it is a wholly new trope, involving subtle suspended reactions and cross-associations in the nervous system; the mental transcript of which, when by a lyrical impulse the psyche transcribes it mentally, must be doubly and trebly original. As intuition is the most living form of life, the keenest edge of existence, so it is naturally the most novel and variable, playing like light reflected from summit to summit in the waves of animal effort and readjustment which from that keenness and agitation sink again, normally into a calm, to sleep the pregnant sleep of universal matter. If there were an eye that could trace this matter in all its shifts and collocations, it might perceive the individual necessity of every new form and sudden insecure embodiment of essence, and of every repetition, itself conditioned and unstable; the fairest things being on the whole rare, yet occasionally and in certain fields frequent like wild flowers; and the large issue of events always unprecedented, an unintended continual culmination continually breaking down, and yielding to some fresh posture of affairs. In this flux the tropes which such an eye would recognise and name would be multitudinous and of all sorts and lengths; their appearance would be always a result, never a cause, and their monotony, when they were monotonous, would itself be local and temporary.

The human eye, however, cannot trace the flux of matter in its true texture and complexity: it can note only here one trope and there another, within the range of its own vision and on its own scale. And when these tropes cross and are superposed, as in human experience occurs inevitably (some perceptible tropes being mechanical others moral, some vital and others literary) reflection becomes sadly confused; for all these units are superficial and precarious, none of them belongs to the inmost, efficacious texture of substance, and yet the human mind is tempted to make them the measure of things, as if the meter of nature created the words and was all their burden. But nature is not such a bad poet; the numbers bubble unbidden up from her heart, and she does not know the style in which she babbles. Hence a comic predicament for the acrobatic philosopher of nature—serious human philosophy being that of spirit: that none of the phenomena or laws or measures which he may note are true parts of the object which he wishes to study. They are tropes, and the flux of nature is not a collection of tropes, but a pervasive flux of substance in which the tropes are only resulting figures, as the tropes of rhetoric are in living speech. Science is therefore but a mask for nature, as the senses and their perspectives are other masks; and I must be content to play with her in these assumed characters, in so far as her part and mine are rôles which I can study and learn, and a visible pageant; although meantime both she and I are living our true lives, even in acting that comedy and wearing those masks, as actors and actresses are silently and sadly toiling in their private persons, and growing old in the real world, even when still bravely playing their same young parts upon the stage.

# Hypostatic Ethics

If Mr. Russell, in his essay on "The Elements of Ethics," had wished to propitiate the unregenerate naturalist, before trying to convert him, he could not have chosen a more skilful procedure; for he begins by telling us that "what is called good conduct is conduct which is a means to other things which are good on their own account; and hence . . . the study of what is good or bad on its own account must be included in ethics." Two consequences are involved in this: first, that ethics is concerned with the economy of all values, and not with "moral" goods only, or with duty; and second, that values may and do inhere in a great variety of things and relations, all of which it is the part of wisdom to respect, and if possible to establish. In this matter, according to our author, the general philosopher is prone to one error and the professed moralist to another. "The philosopher, bent on the construction of a system, is inclined to simplify the facts unduly . . . and to twist them into a form in which they can all be deduced from one or two general principles. The moralist, on the other hand, being primarily concerned with conduct, tends to become absorbed in means, to value the actions men ought to perform more than the ends which such actions serve. . . . Hence most of what they value in this world would have to be omitted by many moralists from any imagined heaven, because there such things as self-denial and effort and courage and pity could find no place. . . . Kant has the bad eminence of combining both errors in the highest possible degree, since he holds that there is nothing good except the virtuous will—a view which

From *Winds of Doctrine* (Gloucester, Mass.: Peter Smith, 1971 [1913]), pp. 138–154.

simplifies the good as much as any philosopher could wish, and mistakes means for ends as completely as any moralist could enjoin."

Those of us who are what Mr. Russell would call ethical sceptics will be delighted at this way of clearing the ground; it opens before us the prospect of a moral philosophy that should estimate the various values of things known and of things imaginable, showing what combinations of goods are possible in any one rational system, and (if fancy could stretch so far) what different rational systems would be possible in places and times remote enough from one another not to come into physical conflict. Such ethics, since it would express in reflection the dumb but actual interests of men, might have both influence and authority over them; two things which an alien and dogmatic ethics necessarily lacks. The joy of the ethical sceptic in Mr. Russell is destined, however, to be short-lived. Before proceeding to the expression of concrete ideals, he thinks it necessary to ask a preliminary and quite abstract question, to which his essay is chiefly devoted; namely, what is the right definition of the predicate "good," which we hope to apply in the sequel to such a variety of things? And he answers at once: The predicate "good" is indefinable. This answer he shows to be unavoidable, and so evidently unavoidable that we might perhaps have been absolved from asking the question; for, as he says, the so-called definitions of "good"—that it is pleasure, the desired, and so forth—are not definitions of the predicate "good," but designations of the things to which this predicate is applied by different persons. Pleasure, and its rivals, are not synonyms for the abstract quality "good," but names for classes of concrete facts that are supposed to possess that quality. From this correct, if somewhat trifling, observation, however, Mr. Russell, like Mr. Moore before him, evokes a portentous dogma. Not being able to define good, he hypostasises it. "Good and bad," he says, "are qualities which belong to objects independently of our opinions, just as much as round and square do; and when two people differ as to whether a thing is good, only one of them

can be right, though it may be very hard to know which is right." "We cannot maintain that for me a thing ought to exist on its own account, while for you it ought not; that would merely mean that one of us is mistaken, since in fact everything either ought to exist, or ought not." Thus we are asked to believe that good attaches to things for no reason or cause, and according to no principles of distribution; that it must be found there by a sort of receptive exploration in each separate case; in other words, that it is an absolute, not a relative thing, a primary and not a secondary quality.

That the quality "good" is indefinable is one assertion, and obvious; but that the presence of this quality is unconditioned is another, and astonishing. My logic, I am well aware, is not very accurate or subtle; and I wish Mr. Russell had not left it to me to discover the connection between these two propositions. Green is an indefinable predicate, and the specific quality of it can be given only in intuition; but it is a quality that things acquire under certain conditions, so much so that the same bit of grass, at the same moment, may have it from one point of view and not from another. Right and left are indefinable; the difference could not be explained without being invoked in the explanation; yet everything that is to the right is not to the right on no condition, but obviously on the condition that some one is looking in a certain direction; and if some one else at the same time is looking in the opposite direction, what is truly to the right will be truly to the left also. If Mr. Russell thinks this is a contradiction, I understand why the universe does not please him. The contradiction would be real, undoubtedly, if we suggested that the *idea* of good was at any time or in any relation the *idea* of evil, or the *intuition* of right that of left, or the *quality* of green that of yellow; these disembodied essences are fixed by the intent that selects them, and in that ideal realm they can never have any relations except the dialectical ones implied in their nature, and these relations they must always retain. But the contradiction disappears when, instead of considering the qualities in themselves, we consider the things of which those qualities are aspects; for the qualities of things are not compacted by implication, but are conjoined irrationally by nature, as she will; and the same thing may be, and is, at once yellow and green, to the left and to the right, good and evil, many and one, large and small; and whatever verbal paradox there may be in this way of speaking (for from the point of view of nature it is natural enough) had been thoroughly explained and talked out by the time of Plato, who complained that people should still raise a difficulty so trite and exploded. Indeed, while square is always square, and round round, a thing that is round may actually be square also, if we allow it to have a little body, and to be a cylinder.

But perhaps what suggests this hypostasis of good is rather the fact that what others find good, or what we ourselves have found good in moods with which we retain no sympathy, is sometimes pronounced by us to be bad; and far from inferring from this diversity of experience that the present good, like the others, corresponds to a particular attitude or interest of ours, and is dependent upon it, Mr. Russell and Mr. Moore infer instead that the presence of the good must be independent of all interests, attitudes, and opinions. They imagine that the truth of a proposition attributing a certain relative quality to an object contradicts the truth of another proposition, attributing to the same object an opposite relative quality. Thus if a man here and another man at the antipodes call opposite directions up, "only one of them can be right, though it may be very hard to know which is right."

To protect the belated innocence of this state of mind, Mr. Russell, so far as I can see, has only one argument, and one analogy. The argument is that "if this were not the case, we could not reason with a man as to what is right." "We do in fact hold that when one man approves of a certain act, while another disapproves, one of them is mistaken, which would not be the case with a mere emotion. If one man likes oysters and another dislikes them, we do not say that either of them is mistaken." In other words, we are to maintain our preju-

dices, however absurd, lest it should become unnecessary to quarrel about them! Truly the debating society has its idols, no less than the cave and the theatre. The analogy that comes to buttress somewhat this singular argument is the analogy between ethical propriety and physical or logical truth. An ethical proposition may be correct or incorrect, in a sense justifying argument, when it touches what is good as a means, that is, when it is not intrinsically ethical, but deals with causes and effects, or with matters of fact or necessity. But to speak of the truth of an ultimate good would be a false collocation of terms; an ultimate good is chosen, found, or aimed at; it is not opined. The ultimate intuitions on which ethics rests are not debatable, for they are not opinions we hazard but preferences we feel; and it can be neither correct nor incorrect to feel them. We may assert these preferences fiercely or with sweet reasonableness, and we may be more or less incapable of sympathising with the different preferences of others; about oysters we may be tolerant, like Mr. Russell, and about character intolerant; but that is already a great advance in enlightenment, since the majority of mankind have regarded as hateful in the highest degree any one who indulged in pork, or beans, or frogs' legs, or who had a weakness for anything called "unnatural"; for it is the things that offend their animal instincts that intense natures have always found to be, intrinsically and *par excellence,* abominations.

I am not sure whether Mr. Russell thinks he has disposed of this view where he discusses the proposition that the good is the desired and refutes it on the ground that "it is commonly admitted that there are bad desires; and when people speak of bad desires, they seem to mean desires for what is bad." Most people undoubtedly call desires bad when they are generically contrary to their own desires, and call objects that disgust them bad, even when other people covet them. This human weakness is not, however, a very high authority for a logician to appeal to, being too like the attitude of the German lady who said that Englishmen called a certain object *bread,* and Frenchmen called it *pain,* but that it really was *Brod.* Scholastic philosophy is inclined to this way of asserting itself; and Mr. Russell, though he candidly admits that there are ultimate differences of opinion about good and evil, would gladly minimise these differences, and thinks he triumphs when he feels that the prejudices of his readers will agree with his own; as if the constitutional unanimity of all human animals, supposing it existed, could tend to show that the good they agreed to recognise was independent of their constitution.

In a somewhat worthier sense, however, we may admit that there are desires for what is bad, since desire and will, in the proper psychological sense of these words, are incidental phases of consciousness, expressing but not constituting those natural relations that make one thing good for another. At the same time the words desire and will are often used, in a mythical or transcendental sense, for those material dispositions and instincts by which vital and moral units are constituted. It is in reference to such constitutional interests that things are "really" good or bad; interests which may not be fairly represented by any incidental conscious desire. No doubt any desire, however capricious, represents some momentary and partial interest, which lends to its objects a certain real and inalienable value; yet when we consider, as we do in human society, the interests of men, whom reflection and settled purposes have raised more or less to the ideal dignity of individuals then passing fancies and passions may indeed have bad objects, and be bad themselves, in that they thwart the more comprehensive interests of the soul that entertains them. Food and poison are such only relatively, and in view of particular bodies, and the same material thing may be food and poison at once; the child, and even the doctor, may easily mistake one for the other. For the human system whiskey is truly more intoxicating than coffee, and the contrary opinion would be an error; but what a strange way of vindicating this real, though relative, distinction, to insist that whiskey is more intoxicating in itself, without reference to any animal; that it is pervaded, as it were, by

an inherent intoxication, and stands dead drunk in its bottle! Yet just in this way Mr. Russell and Mr. Moore conceive things to be dead good and dead bad. It is such a view, rather than the naturalistic one, that renders reasoning and self-criticism impossible in morals; for wrong desires, and false opinions as to value, are conceivable only because a point of reference or criterion is available to prove them such. If no point of reference and no criterion were admitted to be relevant, nothing but physical stress could give to one assertion of value greater force than to another. The shouting moralist no doubt has his place, but not in philosophy.

That good is not an intrinsic or primary quality, but relative and adventitious, is clearly betrayed by Mr. Russell's own way of arguing, whenever he approaches some concrete ethical question. For instance, to show that the good is not pleasure, he can avowedly do nothing but appeal "to ethical judgments with which almost every one would agree." He repeats, in effect, Plato's argument about the life of the oyster, having pleasure with no knowledge. Imagine such mindless pleasure, as intense and prolonged as you please, and would you choose it? Is it your good? Here the British reader, like the blushing Greek youth, is expected to answer instinctively, No! It is an *argumentum ad hominem* (and there can be no other kind of argument in ethics); but the man who gives the required answer does so not because the answer is self-evident, which it is not, but because he is the required sort of man. He is shocked at the idea of resembling an oyster. Yet changeless pleasure, without memory or reflection, without the wearisome intermixture of arbitrary images, is just what the mystic, the voluptuary, and perhaps the oyster find to be good. Ideas, in their origin, are probably signals of alarm; and the distress which they marked in the beginning always clings to them in some measure, and causes many a soul, far more profound than that of the young Protarchus or of the British reader, to long for them to cease altogether. Such a radical hedonism is indeed inhuman; it undermines all conventional ambitions, and is not a possible foundation for political or artistic life. But that is all we can say against it. Our humanity cannot annul the incommensurable sorts of good that may be pursued in the world, though it cannot itself pursue them. The impossibility which people labour under of being satisfied with pure pleasure as a goal is due to their want of imagination, or rather to their being dominated by an imagination which is exclusively human.

The author's estrangement from reality reappears in his treatment of egoism, and most of all in his "Free Man's Religion." Egoism, he thinks, is untenable because "if I am right in thinking that my good is the only good, then every one else is mistaken unless he admits that my good, not his, is the only good." "Most people . . . would admit that it is better two people's desires should be satisfied than only one person's. . . . Then what is good is not good *for me* or *for you,* but is simply good." "It is, indeed, so evident that it is better to secure a greater good for *A* than a lesser good for *B,* that it is hard to find any still more evident principle by which to prove this. And if *A* happens to be some one else, and *B* to be myself, that cannot affect the question, since it is irrelevant to the general question who *A* and *B* may be." To the question, as the logician states it after transforming men into letters, it is certainly irrelevant; but it is not irrelevant to the case as it arises in nature. If two goods are somehow rightly pronounced to be equally good, no circumstance can render one better than the other. And if the locus in which the good is to arise is somehow pronounced to be indifferent, it will certainly be indifferent whether that good arises in me or in you. But how shall these two pronouncements be made? In practice, values cannot be compared save as represented or enacted in the private imagination of somebody: for we could not conceive that an alien good *was* a good (as Mr. Russell cannot conceive that the life of an ecstatic oyster is a good) unless we could sympathise with it in some way in our own persons; and on the warmth which we felt in so representing the alien good would hang our conviction that it was truly valuable, and had

worth in comparison with our own good. The voice of reason, bidding us prefer the greater good, no matter who is to enjoy it, is also nothing but the force of sympathy, bringing a remote existence before us vividly *sub specie boni.* Capacity for such sympathy measures the capacity to recognise duty and therefore, in a moral sense, to have it. Doubtless it is conceivable that all wills should become co-operative, and that nature should be ruled magically by an exact and universal sympathy; but this situation must be actually attained in part, before it can be conceived or judged to be an authoritative ideal. The tigers cannot regard it as such, for it would suppress the tragic good called ferocity, which makes, in their eyes, the chief glory of the universe. Therefore the inertia of nature, the ferocity of beasts, the optimism of mystics, and the selfishness of men and nations must all be accepted as conditions for the peculiar goods, essentially incommensurable, which they can generate severally. It is misplaced vehemence to call them intrinsically detestable, because they do not (as they cannot) generate or recognise the goods we prize.

In the real world, persons are not abstract egos, like *A* and *B,* so that to benefit one is clearly as good as to benefit another. Indeed, abstract egos could not be benefited, for they could not be modified at all, even if somehow they could be distinguished. It would be the qualities or objects distributed among them that would carry, wherever they went, each its inalienable cargo of value, like ships sailing from sea to sea. But it is quite vain and artificial to imagine different goods charged with such absolute and comparable weights; and actual egoism is not the thin and refutable thing that Mr. Russell makes of it. What it really holds is that a given man, oneself, and those akin to him, are qualitatively better than other beings; that the things they prize are intrinsically better than the things prized by others; and that therefore there is no injustice in treating these chosen interests as supreme. The injustice, it is felt, would lie rather in not treating things so unequal unequally. This feeling may, in many cases, amuse the impartial observer, or make him indignant; yet it may, in every case, according to Mr. Russell, be absolutely just. The refutation he gives of egoism would not dissuade any fanatic from exterminating all his enemies with a good conscience; it would merely encourage him to assert that what he was ruthlessly establishing was the absolute good. Doubtless such conscientious tyrants would be wretched themselves, and compelled to make sacrifices which would cost them dear; but that would only extend, as it were, the pernicious egoism of that part of their being which they had allowed to usurp a universal empire. The twang of intolerance and of self-mutilation is not absent from the ethics of Mr. Russell and Mr. Moore, even as it stands; and one trembles to think what it may become in the mouths of their disciples. Intolerance itself is a form of egoism, and to condemn egoism intolerantly is to share it.

I cannot help thinking that a consciousness of the relativity of values, if it became prevalent, would tend to render people more truly social than would a belief that things have intrinsic and unchangeable values, no matter what the attitude of any one to them may be. If we said that goods, including the right distribution of goods, are relative to specific natures, moral warfare would continue, but not with poisoned arrows. Our private sense of justice itself would be acknowledged to have but a relative authority, and while we could not have a higher duty than to follow it, we should seek to meet those whose aims were incompatible with it as we meet things physically inconvenient, without insulting them as if they were morally vile or logically contemptible. Real unselfishness consists in sharing the interests of others. Beyond the pale of actual unanimity the only possible unselfishness is chivalry—a recognition of the inward right and justification of our enemies fighting against us. This chivalry has long been practised in the battle-field without abolishing the causes of war; and it might conceivably be extended to all the conflicts of men with one another, and of the warring elements within each breast. Policy, hypnotisation, and even

surgery may be practised without exorcisms or anathemas. When a man has decided on a course of action, it is a vain indulgence in expletives to declare that he is sure that course is absolutely right. His moral dogma expresses its natural origin all the more clearly the more hotly it is proclaimed; and ethical absolutism, being a mental grimace of passion, refutes what it says by what it is. Sweeter and more profound, to my sense, is the philosophy of Homer, whose every line seems to breathe the conviction that what is beautiful or precious has not thereby any right to existence; nothing has such a right; nor is it given us to condemn absolutely any force—god or man—that destroys what is beautiful or precious, for it has doubtless something beautiful or precious of its own to achieve.

The consequences of a hypostasis of the good are no less interesting than its causes. If the good were independent of nature, it might still be conceived as relevant to nature, by being its creator or mover; but Mr. Russell is not a theist after the manner of Socrates; his good is not a power. Nor would representing it to be such long help his case; for an ideal hypostasised into a cause achieves only a mythical independence. The least criticism discloses that it is natural laws, zoological species, and human ideals, that have been projected into the empyrean; and it is no marvel that the good should attract the world where the good, by definition, is whatever the world is aiming at. The hypostasis accomplished by Mr. Russell is more serious, and therefore more paradoxical. If I understand it, it may be expressed as follows: In the realm of eternal essences, before anything exists, there are certain essences that have this remarkable property, that they ought to exist, or at least that, if anything exists, it ought to conform to them. What exists, however, is deaf to this moral emphasis in the eternal; nature exists for no reason; and, indeed, why should she have subordinated her own arbitrariness to a good that is no less arbitrary? This good, however, is somehow good notwithstanding; so that there is an abysmal wrong in its not being obeyed. The world is, in principle, totally depraved;

but as the good is not a power, there is no one to redeem the world. The saints are those who, imitating the impotent dogmatism on high, and despising their sinful natural propensities, keep asserting that certain things are in themselves good and others bad, and declaring to be detestable any other saint who dogmatises differently. In this system the Calvinistic God has lost his creative and punitive functions, but continues to decree groundlessly what is good and what evil, and to love the one and hate the other with an infinite love or hatred. Meanwhile the reprobate need not fear hell in the next world, but the elect are sure to find it here.

What shall we say of this strangely unreal and strangely personal religion? Is it a ghost of Calvinism, returned with none of its old force but with its old aspect of rigidity? Perhaps: but then, in losing its force, in abandoning its myths, and threats, and rhetoric, this religion has lost its deceptive sanctimony and hypocrisy; and in retaining its rigidity it has kept what made it noble and pathetic; for it is a clear dramatic expression of that human spirit—in this case a most pure and heroic spirit—which it strives so hard to dethrone. After all, the hypostasis of the good is only an unfortunate incident in a great accomplishment, which is the discernment of the good. I have dwelt chiefly on this incident, because in academic circles it is the abuses incidental to true philosophy that create controversy and form schools. Artificial systems, even when they prevail, after a while fatigue their adherents, without ever having convinced or refuted their opponents, and they fade out of existence not by being refuted in their turn, but simply by a tacit agreement to ignore their claims: so that the true insight they were based on is too often buried under them. The hypostasis of philosophical terms is an abuse incidental to the forthright, unchecked use of the intellect; it substitutes for things the limits and distinctions that divide them. So physics is corrupted by logic; but the logic that corrupts physics is perhaps correct, and when it is moral dialectic, it is more important than physics itself. Mr. Russell's ethics *is* ethics. When we mortals have once assumed the moral attitude, it is certain that an indefinable value accrues to some things as opposed to others, that these things are many, that combinations of them have values not belonging to their parts, and that these valuable things are far more specific than abstract pleasure, and far more diffused than one's personal life. What a pity if this pure morality, in detaching itself impetuously from the earth, whose bright satellite it might be, should fly into the abyss at a tangent, and leave us as much in the dark as before!

## The Implied Being of Truth

From the beginning of discourse there is a subtle reality posited which is not a thing: I mean the truth. If intuition of essence exists anywhere without discourse, the being of truth need not be posited there, because intuition of itself is intransitive, and having no object other than the datum, can be neither true nor false. Every essence picked up by intuition is equally real in its own sphere; and every degree of articulation reached in intuition defines one of a series of essences, each contained in or containing its neighbour, and each equally central in that infinite progression. The central one, for apprehension, is the one that happens to appear at that moment. Therefore in pure intuition there is no fear of pick-

From *Scepticism and Animal Faith* (New York: Charles Scribner's Sons, 1923) pp. 262–271.

ing up the wrong thing, as if the object were a designated existence in the natural world; and therefore the being of truth is not broached in pure intuition.

Truth is not broached even in pure dialectic, which is only the apprehension of a system of essences so complex and finely articulated, perhaps, as to tax human attention, or outrun it if unaided by some artifice of notation, but essentially only an essence like any other. Truth, therefore, is as irrelevant to dialectic as to merely æsthetic intuition. Logic and mathematics are not true inherently, however cogent or extensive. They are ideal constructions based on ideal axioms; and the question of truth or falsity does not arise in respect to them unless the dialectic is asserted to apply to the natural world, or perhaps when a dispute comes up as to the precise essence signified by some word, such as, for instance, infinity.

When men first invented language and other symbols, or fixed in reflection the master-images of their dreams and thoughts, it seemed to them that they were discovering parts of nature, and that even in those developments they must be either right or wrong. There was a *true* name for every object, a part of its nature. There was a *true* logic, and a *true* ethics, and a *true* religion. Certainly in so far as these mixed disciplines were assertions about alleged facts, they were either right or wrong; but in so far as they were systems of essences, woven together in fancy to express the instincts of the mind, they were only more or less expressive and fortunate and harmonious, but not at all true or false. Dialectic, though so fine-spun and sustained, is really a more primitive, a more dream-like, exercise of intuition than are animal faith and natural science. It is more spontaneous and less responsible, less controlled by secondary considerations, as poetry is in contrast with prose. If only the animals had a language, or some other fixed symbols to develop in thought, I should be inclined to believe them the greatest of dialecticians and the greatest of poets. But as they seem not to speak, and there is no ground for supposing that they rehearse their feelings reflectively in discourse, I will suppose them to be very empty-headed when they

are not very busy; but I may be doing them an injustice. In any case their dreams would not suggest to them the being of truth; and even their external experience may hardly do so.

It might seem, perhaps, that truth must be envisaged even by the animals in action, when things are posited; especially as uncertainty and change of tactics and purpose are often visible in their attitudes. Certainly truth is there, if the thing pursued is such as the animal presumes it to be; and in searching for it in the right quarter and finding it, he enacts a true belief and a true perception, even if he does not realise them spiritually. What he realises spiritually, I suppose, is the pressure of the situation in which he finds himself, and the changes in his object; but that his belief from moment to moment was right or wrong he probably never notices. Truth would then not come within his purview, nor be distinguished amongst his interests. He would want to be successful, not to be right.

So in a man, intent experience, when not reflective, need not disclose the being of truth. Sometimes, in a vivid dream, objects suffer a transformation to which I eagerly adapt myself, changing my feelings and actions with complete confidence in the new facts; and I never ask myself which view was true, and which action appropriate. I live on in perfect faith, never questioning the present circumstances as they appear, nor do I follow my present policy with less assurance than I did the opposite policy a moment before. This happens to me in dreams; but politicians do the same thing in real life, when the lives of nations are at stake. In general I think that the impulse of action is translated into a belief in changed things long before it reproaches itself with having made any error about them. The recognition of a truth to be discerned may thus be avoided; because although a belief in things must actually be either true or false, it is directed upon the present existence and character of these things, not upon its own truth. The active object posited alone interests the man of action; if he were interested in the rightness of the action, he would not be a man of action but a philosopher. So long as things continue to be perceived in one form or another, and can be posited accordingly, the active impulse is released, and the machine runs on prosperously until some hitch comes, or some catastrophe. It is then always the things that are supposed to have changed, not the forms of folly. Even the most pungent disappointment, as when a man loses a bet, is not regarded otherwise than as a misfortune. It is all the fault of the dice; they might and ought to have turned up differently. This, I say to myself, is an empirical world; all is novelty in it, and it is luck and free will that are to blame. My bet was really right when I made it; there was no error about the future then, for I acted according to the future my fancy painted, which was the only future there was. My act was a creative act of vitality and courage; but afterwards things accountably went wrong, and betrayed their own promise.

I am confirmed in this surmise about the psychology of action by the reasoning of empirical and romantic philosophers, who cling to this instinctive attitude and deny the being of truth. No substance exists, according to their view, but only things as they seem from moment to moment; so that it is idle to contrast opinion with truth, seeing that there is nothing, not even things, except in opinion. They can easily extend this view to the future of opinion or of experience, and maintain that the future does not exist except in expectation; and at a pinch, although the flesh may rebel against such heroic subjectivism, they may say that the past, too, exists only in memory, and that no other past can be thought of or talked about; so that there is no truth, other than current opinion, even about the past. If an opinion about the past, they say, seems problematical when it stands alone, we need but corroborate it by another opinion about the past in order to make it true. In other words, though the word truth is familiar to these philosophers, the idea of it is unintelligible to them, and absent altogether from their apprehension of the world.

The experience which perhaps makes even the empiricist awake to the being of truth, and brings it home to any energetic man, is the experience of other people lying. When I am falsely accused, or when I am represented as thinking what I do not think, I rebel against that contradiction to my evident self-knowledge; and as the other man asserts that the liar is myself, and a third person might very well entertain that hypothesis and decide against me, I learn that a report may fly in the face of the facts. There is, I then see clearly, a comprehensive standard description for every fact, which those who report it as it happened repeat in part, whereas on the contrary liars contradict it in some particular. And a little further reflection may convince me that even the liar must recognise the fact to some extent, else it would not be *that* fact that he was misrepresenting; and also that honest memory and belief, even when most unimpeachable, are not exhaustive and not themselves the standard for belief or for memory, since they are now clearer and now vaguer, and subject to error and correction. That standard comprehensive description of any fact which neither I nor any man can ever wholly repeat, is the truth about it.

The being of truth thus seems to be first clearly posited in disputation; and a consequence of this accident (for it is an accident from the point of view of the truth itself under what circumstances men most easily acknowledge its authority)—a consequence is that truth is often felt to be somehow inseparable from rival opinions; so that people say that if there was no mind and consequently no error there could be no truth. They mean, I suppose, that nothing can be correct or incorrect except some proposition or judgement regarding some specific fact; and that the same constitution of the fact which renders one description correct, renders any contradictory description erroneous. "Truth" is often used in this abstract sense for correctness, or the quality which all correct judgements have in common; and another word, perhaps "fact" or "reality," would then have to be used for that standard comprehensive description of the object to which correct judgements conform. But a fact is not a description of itself; and as to the word "reality," if it is understood to mean existence, it too cannot designate a description, which is an essence only. Facts are transitory, and any part of existence to which a definite judgement is addressed is transitory too; and when they have lapsed, it is only their essence that subsists and that, being partially recovered and assigned to them in a retrospective judgement, can render this judgement true. Opinions are true or false by repeating or contradicting some part of the truth about the facts which they envisage; and this truth about the facts is the standard comprehensive description of them—something in the realm of essence, but more than the essence of any fact present within the limits of time and space which that fact occupies; for a comprehensive description includes also all the radiations of that fact—I mean, all that perspective of the world of facts and of the realm of essence which is obtained by taking this fact as a centre and viewing everything else only in relation with it. The truth about any fact is therefore infinitely extended, although it grows thinner, so to speak, as you travel from it to further and further facts, or to less and less relevant ideas. It is the splash any fact makes, or the penumbra it spreads, by dropping through the realm of essence. Evidently no opinion can embrace it all, or identify itself with it; nor can it be identified with the facts to which it relates, since they are in flux, and it is eternal.

The word truth ought, I think, to be reserved for what everybody spontaneously means by it: the standard comprehensive description of any fact in all its relations. Truth is not an opinion, even an ideally true one; because besides the limitation in scope which human opinions, at least, can never escape, even the most complete and accurate opinion would give precedence to some terms, and have a direction of survey; and this direction might be changed or reversed without lapsing into error; so that the truth is the field which various true opinions traverse in various directions, and no opinion itself. An even more impressive difference between truth and any true discourse is that discourse is an event; it has a date not that of its subject-matter, even if the subject-matter be existential and roughly contemporary; and in human beings it is conversant almost entirely with the past only, whereas truth is dateless and absolutely identical whether the opinions which seek to reproduce it arise before or after the event which the truth describes.

The eternity of truth is inherent in it: all truths—not a few grand ones—are equally eternal. I am sorry that the word eternal should necessarily have an unction which prejudices dry minds against it, and leads fools to use it without understanding. This unction is not rhetorical, because the nature of truth is really sublime, and its name ought to mark its sublimity. Truth is one of the realities covered in the eclectic religion of our fathers by the idea of God. Awe very properly hangs about it, since it is the immovable standard and silent witness of all our memories and assertions; and the past and the future, which in our anxious life are so differently interesting and so differently dark, are one seamless garment for the truth, shining like the sun. It is not necessary to offer any evidence for this eternity of truth, because truth is not an existence that asks to be believed in, and that may be denied. It is an essence involved in positing any fact, in remembering, expecting, or asserting anything; and while no truth need be acknowledged if no existence is believed in, and none would obtain if there was no existence in fact, yet on the hypothesis that anything exists, truth has appeared, since this existence must have one character rather than another, so that only one description of it in terms of essence will be complete; and this complete description, covering all its relations, will be the truth about it. No one who understands what is meant by this eternal being of truth can possibly deny it; so that no argument is required to support it, but only enough intensity of attention to express what we already believe.

Inspired people, who are too hot to think, often identify the truth with their own tenets, to signify by a bold hyperbole how certain they feel in their faith; but the effect is rather that they lead foolish people, who may see that this faith may be false, to suppose that therefore the truth may be false also. Eternal truths, in the mouth of both parties, are then tenets which the remotest ancestors of man are reputed to have held, and which his remotest descendants are forbidden to abandon. Of course there are no eternal tenets: neither the opinions of men, nor mankind, nor anything existent can be eternal; eternity is a property of essences only.

Even if all the spirits in heaven and earth had been so far unanimous on any point of doctrine, there is no reason, except the monotony and inertia of nature, why their logic or religion or morals should not change to-morrow from top to bottom, if they all suddenly grew wiser or differently foolish.

At the risk of being scholastic I will suggest the uses to which the word eternal and the terms akin to it might be confined if they were made exact.

A thing that occupied but one point of physical time would be *instantaneous*. No essence is instantaneous, because none occupies any part of physical time or space; and I doubt whether any existence is instantaneous either; for if the mathematicians decide that the continuous or extended must be composed of an infinite number of inextended and non-contiguous units, in bowing to their authority I should retain a suspicion that nothing actual is confined to any of these units, but that the smallest event has duration and contains an infinite number of such units; so that one event (though not one instant) can be contiguous to another.

A given essence containing no specious temporal progression or perspective between its parts would be *timeless*. Colour, for instance, or number, is timeless. The timeless often requires to be abstracted from the total datum, because round any essence as actually given there is an atmosphere of duration and persistence, suggesting the existential flux of nature behind the essence. Colour seems to shine, that is, to vibrate. Number seems to

mount, and to be built up. The timeless is therefore better illustrated in objects like laws or equations or definitions, which though intent on things in time, select relations amongst them which are not temporal.

A being that should have no external temporal relations and no locus in physical time would be *dateless*. Thus every given essence and every specious present is dateless, internally considered, and taken transcendentally, that is, as a station for viewing other things or a unit framing them in. Though dateless, the specious present is not timeless, and an instant, though timeless, is not dateless.

Whatsoever, having once arisen, never perishes, would be *immortal*. I believe there is nothing immortal.

Whatsoever exists through a time infinite in both directions is *everlasting*. Matter, time, the life of God, souls as Plato conceived them, and the laws of nature are commonly believed to be everlasting. In the nature of the case this can be only a presumption.

That which without existing is contemporary with all times is *eternal*. Truth is dateless and eternal, but not timeless, because, being descriptive of existence, it is a picture of change. It is frozen history. As Plato said that time was a moving image of eternity, we might say that eternity was a synthetic image of time. But it is much more than that, because, besides the description of all temporal things in their temporal relations, it contains everything that is not temporal at all; in other words, the whole realm of essence, as well as the whole realm of truth.

# The Nature of Spirit

Everything that exists is confined to a specific character at a particular place and time; if it escaped from those bonds it would cease to be itself. Such an escape occurs continually in the realm of matter, where everything gradually lapses into something different; and this con-

From *Realms of Being* (New York: Charles Scribner's Sons, 1942 [1937]), pp. 555–572.

tinuous flux, with its various tempos, composes the great symphony of nature. In living substance, plasticity and fertility are a virtue: matter might say, with Shelley's cloud, *I change but I never die.* That which dies at every turn is only the negligible cloud-rack of the moment, easily replaced or even improved upon. To lament that individuals or even species should vanish would be natural only to some elegiac poet who clung to lost occasions and to remembered forms, not being ready for the next, and lagging sentimentally behind the glorious march of time, always buoyant with victory and strewn with wreckage.

The case is otherwise when we come to the realm of spirit, as we do in that melancholy poet. Not that spirit is less mobile or elastic than matter. In its ideal vocation, as we shall find, it is infinitely more so. Even in its existence it is as evanescent as any cloud. But the inevitable concentration of existence at each point into something specific rises in the moral world to a higher power. Individuation from being passive and imputed here becomes positive and self-assured. Spirit, in its briefest and feeblest flash, sets up a moral centre for the universe.

Contingence and partiality, in one direction, embitter spiritual life. Why should "I" (that is, spirit in me) be condemned to lodge in this particular body, with these parents and nationality and education and ridiculous fate? Why choose this grotesque centre from which to view the universe? You may say that other people exist in plenty, viewing the universe from their several positions, so that in giving this involuntary pre-eminence to myself I am perhaps not more grotesque than the average man, or even than the most intelligent. But that only makes matters worse, if isolation, partiality, error, and conceit are multiplied indefinitely, and inevitably attached to conscious existence.

In another direction, however, the imprisoned spirit escapes from its cage as no physical fact can escape. Without quitting its accidental station it can look about; it can *imagine* all sorts of things unlike itself; it can take long views over the times and spaces surrounding its temporary home, it can even view itself quizzically from the outside, as in a mirror, and laugh at the odd figure that it cuts. Intelligence is in a humorous position: confinement galls it, it rebels against contingency; yet it sees that without some accidental centre and some specific interests and specific organs, it could neither exist nor have the means of surveying anything. It had better be reconciled to incarnation, if it is at all attached to existence or even to knowledge.

This is the force of intelligence, marvellous if we try to conceive it on the analogy of material being, but perfectly natural and obvious if we look at it congruously and from within. Spirit in each of its instances assumes a transcendental station, and looks out from there on all the world. Wherever it is, is here; whenever it is, is now. Yet *here* and *now,* for intelligence, are not what they are for physical being, or for external indication, a particular, accidental, dead position. For intelligence *here* and *now* are movable essences, to be found wherever spirit may wander; and they name no particular material point, but the centre found, at each point, for all distances and directions. So that the bitterness of confinement is mitigated by a continual change of prisons, and the accident of place by the inevitable vastness of the prospect.

A consequence of this intellectual nature of spirit marks it particularly, or even defines it in popular philosophy. Spirit is invisible, intangible, unapproachable from the outside. The materialist might like to deny its existence; but that is not the inclination of mankind at large. Only, being necessarily familiar with material things, and having shaped language and expectation in conformity with physical happenings, people find it impossible not to materialize the spirit of which they are vividly conscious; so that critical philosophy sometimes, in clearing up the notion of spirit, and removing superstitious and physical analogies, seems to have nothing left. But that comes of being, like the primitive mind, preoccupied with matter, and disinclined to conceive spirit in spiritual terms. This disinclination is not confined to scoffers: religious philosophers also love to materialize spirit, in order to make it seem more solid and important, the pure air of a truly spiritual sphere being far too thin and cold for their lusty constitution.

Let me consider the various ways in which the notion of spirit is apt to be materialized. The sequel will then be less exposed to gross misunderstanding.

Spirits, in folklore, legend, and dreams, are often ghosts; that is, they are visible but intangible spectres of dead, absent, or supernatural persons. Such apparitions, for a critical psychologist, might not be physical facts, since the images have their basis in the observer's brain, and are falsely incorporated into outer space: an error that the waking dreamer himself discovers when he attempts to embrace a ghost and finds nothing but air. Genuine believers in the survival and return of the dead, like doubting Thomas and modern Spiritualists, require their spirits to be tangible as well as visible, to come and go and preserve a continuous physical existence, to eat and especially to talk. Their bodies may be called "spiritual," but are conceived as extracts or magical restitutions of the human body, ethereal, astral, but not immaterial. They move about in another world or in the margins of this world, and are not pure intelligences but complete natural individuals, having a body and a soul.

The native land of ghosts is memory, memory transforming sensations, or drowsily confusing, recasting, or exaggerating old impressions into dreams. Imagination is fertile; and the old maxim that there is nothing in the mind which was not first in the senses seems to me far from accurate. There is never anything in the mind that *at that time* is not given in a kind of sensation, that is, given directly: but these images are not old images or fragments of old images surviving and recombined, as the fragments of an ancient temple might be built into a modern wall. Images, considered in themselves and objectively, are essences and perfectly immaterial. That which is immaterial has no substance, no persistence, and no effects: it offers no possibility of being stored, divided, redistributed, or recombined. Ideas

are not animals that may breed other animals. They may recur, wholly or in part, but only when a living psyche inwardly reverts to much the same movement as on some former occasion. The given essence will then be the same or nearly the same as formerly. But it must be evoked afresh, and unless evoked it has no existence whatever. It is truly a ghost, belief in it is illusion, and its apparition or specious presence depends entirely on the dreaming psyche that weaves it together.

Dreams, and all the sensuous garments that fancy bestows on nature, are made of stuff much more spiritual than any "spirits" supposed to be persisting and active persons, stealthily revisiting the earth, or sending messages to it from some neighbouring region. The primitive idea that when the body sleeps the spirit may travel to distant places, and receive monitions concerning secret or future things, though poetical, is true in this sense: that in dreams the contribution that the psyche makes to experience predominates over the contribution ordinarily made by external things. This predominance of the psychic we call *inspiration;* the existence and the rush of it are spirit itself. When this predominance is excessive and persists in waking hours, we go mad; any strong passion, in its recklessness and self-assurance, has madness in it. Yet the same inspiration permeates sensibility and desire, perception and thought, all experience being but a dream controlled, and all reason but fancy domesticated and harnessed to human labours. In dreams, when the spirit seems to travel, it merely smoulders like a fire no longer fanned by the wind: and in that withdrawal and concentration, together with much fragmentary nonsense, it may develop and fancifully express its absolute impulses, building the world nearer to the heart's desire. Hence dreams may be morally prophetic: or a more voluminous inspiration, from the same source, may combine with waking intelligence and art to produce some work of genius. The notion that spirit can escape from the psyche, or comes into us originally, as Aristotle says, from beyond the gates, merely inverts mythologically a natural truth: namely that the spirit is immaterial and transcendental. It issues from the psyche like the genie from Sinbad's bottle, and becomes, in understanding and in judgment, an authority over its source, and a transcendental centre for making a survey of everything.

That the wildest imaginations are, in their origin, native to matter appears clearly in this, that they are produced by drugs. Nor is this incompatible with their æsthetic or prophetic or intellectual value. The priestess at Delphi inhaled the vapours of her cave before uttering her oracles; other ritual practices have an intentionally hypnotic or narcotic influence; wine and music, martial or religious, notoriously rouse the spirit to boldness and to conviction. Nor is this a scandal, as if pure reason could move either the heart or the world. Pure reason is an ideal brought to light in the spirit by the organization of forces all originally irrational and wild: and this organization in turn is a product of long friction and forced adjustments. So much so, that in human life inspiration and reason come to seem holiday marvels, appearing when some suppressed strain or forbidden harmony is allowed to assert itself, in fancy only, during some lull in action. Prophecy is the swan-song of lost causes. The action that accompanies it has no tendency to fulfil it. If it survives like Hebrew prophecy in later Judaism and in Christianity, it becomes a purely spiritual discipline, mystic where it was martial, and ascetic where it was political. The communism of Plato's Republic could be realized only in the cloister.

Spirit is thus, in a certain sense, the native land of ghosts, of ideas, of phenomena; but it is not at all a visible ghost or phenomenon in its own being. Its own essence is an invisible stress; the vital, intellectual, and moral actuality of each moment.

Another way in which spirit may be materialized is by confusion with the psyche and with those cosmic currents by which the psyche is fed. Wind and breath have given their name to spirit, and most aptly. The air is invisible, yet the winds are a terrible reality, and though they may soon be stilled, the calm supervening is no longer deceptive. I have learned that what seemed vacancy was a reservoir of power, that air, ether, and energy filled that apparent void. I discover that innumerable atoms are floating there, ready to make fresh havoc in the world, or to be breathed in and renew life in my breast. What is this life in me but vital oxygen drawn into my lungs; what is this warm breath exhaled but my very spirit and will? Invisible as it is, does it not quicken my body and inspire all my action? Is it not one with the spirit of the winds howling in the storm or ruffling the sea or carrying seeds far and wide over the fertile earth? Is not the world, then, full of spirits? And is not spirit perhaps the one universal power astir in all things, as it stirs in me?

Such poetic confusions are spontaneous in a candid mind. They may be corrected by science and by logical analysis; but it would be a foolish philosophy that should ignore the continuities and analogies that run through the universe and that at once impress the attentive poet. The principle of life is not exactly wind or air. Life began in the sea and a great seclusion and darkness are requisite for seeds to germinate and for organic patterns to take shape undisturbed. Storms and struggles come afterwards on occasion; a normal order and distribution of elements, or distinct self-defending organisms, must have arisen first. Yet the currents within and without such organisms or such elements remain continuous. A psyche, the organic order and potentiality in a living body, depends upon ambient forces and reacts upon them; and the sense of this dependence and of this reaction is the spirit.

This spirit is something ontologically altogether incongruous with air, ether, energy, motion, or substance. Spirit is the *witness* of the cosmic dance; in respect to that agitation it is transcendental and epiphenomenal; yet it crowns some impulse, raises it to actual unity and totality, and being the fruition of it, could not arise until that organ had matured. An immense concretion of elements to make a habitat and of tropisms to make an animal must have preceded. Being fetched from such depths, spirit feels a profound kinship with its mothering elements. It suffers with the body and it speaks for the heart. Even if it dreams that it travels to distant spheres, it merely reports in a fable the scope of physical sensibility and the depths from which messages are received. In its station, in its interests, in its language, it always remains at home. To say that it travels, or witnesses the distant, is as if we said that the radio conveyed us to the concert which it conveys to us. The travelling, the waves, the transmissions are all physical. How should they be anything else? Instruments are material; even the composer, when he first conceived those accords, was listening to a spontaneous music bred in his psyche out of theoretically traceable impressions, tensions and outbursts of potential energy within him. The chain of these motions is materially uninterrupted, else the composer's imagined music would never have reached our ears; and spiritual union, both in perception and in passion, depends upon physical concordance. The number of spirits that may have lived through the measures of that melody helps me not at all to hear it now; the physical source must be tapped afresh in each case, and the physical receiver must be capable of vibrating afresh to the message.

Spiritualists and mystics are often more perceptive than rationalists; but they are not for that reason perceptive of spiritual things. They are, more probably, supersensitive materially. They feel influences vibrating through the universe to which the din of vulgar affairs has deafened most of us: and they dream of physical survivals and renewals, of physical Elysiums, with endless vistas of warm physical love or physical peace. They hover, they glide, they wallow; and they think themselves spirits. But there is nothing less spiritual than the shallows of indistinction and of torpid oneness. The universe is perforce one, and its parts easily break down and are lost in one another; but such collapse destroys the very possibility of spirit, which is not an ether or a fluid coursing through space, but a moral focus of recollection, discrimination and judgment.

Language in these subjects is particularly ambiguous and charged with emotion; it serves less to discriminate one thing from another than to attribute to one thing, miraculously, the powers and dignities of something else. So the power of nature is often attributed to spirit or identified with it: with a curious result. For if spirit be only the laws or tendencies discoverable in nature, it is only a form to be found in matter, and not an immaterial invisible inward intensity of being. And there is malice in this abuse of language: for we are expected to conceive that laws or tendencies are thoughts (essences being confused with the intuition of essences) and that nature being describable in those intelligible terms is secretly governed by intelligence: so that we may attribute power also to our own wishes and imaginations, and depute ourselves to be co-rulers of the universe.

Now our *selves,* our organisms or persons, undoubtedly play a more or less efficacious part in physical events. It would be a miracle if our bodies, with so much stored and redistributable energy as they contain, did not redirect by their action all sorts of other motions in the environment. A man habitually identifies himself as much with his body as with his spirit: and since both are called "I," it is no wonder if what happens in each is felt to be also the work of the other. And the connection is radical and intimate in reality; the problem not being how the two happen to be united but in what respects we may justly distinguish them. The difference between myself as a transcendental centre or spirit and myself as a fact in the world is, in one sense, unbridgeable; but not because they are two facts incongruously or miraculously juxtaposed in the same field, but because they are realizations of the same fact in two incomparable realms of being. There is only one fact, more or less complex and extended, an incident in the flux of existence; and this fact lying in the realm of matter by virtue of its origin, place, time, and consequences, contains a transcendental apprehension of all things, in moral terms and in violent perspective, taken from itself as centre. Such sensibility is proper to the natural fact, when this fact is a living animal; but you can no more pass, at the same level, from sensation to matter, than you can pass from extension to duration, from colour to sound, from sound to meaning, or from logic to love. The organization of matter is something logically incomparable with its mere persistence or energy, yet can only exist with the latter; so spirit is logically incomparable with body, yet is a moral integration and dignity accruing to body when body develops a certain degree of organization and of responsiveness to distant things. Nor does spirit, in its new language, discourse about anything save that very world, with all its radiations, in which it has arisen.

Perhaps it is not logically impossible that spirit should exist without a body: but in that case how should spirit come upon any particular images, interests, or categories? If occupied with nothing, it would not be a conscious being; and if occupied with everything possible, that is, with the whole realm of essence at once, it would not be the consciousness of a living soul, having a particular moral destiny, but only a hypostasis of intelligence, abstracted from all particular occasions. But can intelligence be abstracted from particular occasions and from problems set by contingent facts? Logic and mathematics would surely never have taken shape if nature had not compelled attention to dwell on certain forms of objects or of language, and rewarded in practice the elaboration of those forms in thought. Indeed spirit, once abstracted from animal life and independent of all facts, would have forfeited that intensity, trepidation, and movement, that capacity for inquiry and description, which make spirit a focus of knowledge. It would have evaporated into identity with the realm of essence. Even divine spirits, as conceived in human poetry and religion, are thinking, loving, and planning minds, functions which all belong to animal life, and presuppose it.

In some speculative myths spirit is represented as a self-existent potentiality pregnant with the seeds of a particular development; so that spirit, as in a dream, gradually creates world upon world, and the experience of them, out of its magic bosom. There is sometimes poetic truth in such myths, but they describe, from some local point of view, a perspective in the realm of matter, not at all the history of spirit. Spirit is not a seed, it is not a potentiality, it is not a power. It is not even—though this touches more nearly its actual character—a grammar of though or divine Logos, predetermining the structure of creation and its destiny. That, if found anywhere, would be found in the realm of truth; but we may doubt that any alleged Logos, or any psychological system of categories or forms of intuition, prescribes limits to the truth. It prescribes at best one type of logic, one set of senses, in which a particular existent world might be apprehended by its inhabitants.

Yet these myths, as often happens, have a real foothold in the nature of the facts. They catch some transcendental privilege or predicament proper to spirit and transfer it, together with the name of spirit, to the spheres of matter or truth. Spirit has an initial vagueness; it awakes, it looks, it waits, it oscillates between universal curiosity and primeval sleep. Certainly the feelings and images arising are specific; and spirit has no *a priori* notion of any different feelings or images to contrast with the given ones. Yet it is in no way predisposed or limited to these; it is not essentially, like the psyche, even a slave of habit, so as to think the given necessary and the not given impossible. Spirit is infinitely open. And this is no ontological marvel or mystic affinity of spirit to the absolute. It is merely the natural indistinction of primitive wakefulness, of innocent attention. Spirit is like a child with eyes wide open, heart simple, faith ready, intellect pure. It does not suspect the trouble the world is going to give it. It little knows the contortions, the struggles, the disasters which the world imposes on itself. There is a horrid confusion in attributing to spirit the dogged conservatism and catastrophic evolution of the natural world.

To the primitive blankness of spirit corresponds its eventual hospitality to all sorts of things. But this hospitality is not connivance, not complicity. It is an intellectual hospitality open to all truth, even to all fiction and to all essence, as these things may present themselves. It is not an equal pleasure in them all. Spirit is a product of the psyche; the psyche makes for a specific order and direction of life; spirit congenitally shares in this vitality and this specific impulse. The psyche needs to prepare for all things that may chance in its life: it needs to be universally vigilant, universally retentive. In satisfying this need it forms the spirit, which therefore initially tends to look, to remember, to understand. But the psyche takes this step, so impartial and unprejudiced officially, for a perfectly selfish domestic reason, namely, to prepare the home defences and enlarge the home dominion. The spirit, therefore, is like Goethe's Watchman, who was born to gaze, and possessed all the world in idea, yet was set on that watch-tower for an urgent purpose, with a specific duty to be vigilant. Hence the storms and forest-fires, the invasions or rebellions that he might observe, would not leave him cold, but would distress him in his fidelity, disturb his power of vision, and perhaps bring him and his tower to the ground. Not that spirit trembles for its own being. It is the most volatile of things, and the most evanescent, a flame blown or extinguished by any wind: but no extinction here can prevent it from blazing up there, and its resurrection is as perpetual as its death. What torments it is no selfish fear but a vicarious sympathy with its native psyche and her native world, which it cannot bear to feel dragged hither and thither in tragic confusion, but craves to see everywhere well-ordered and beautiful, *so that it may be better seen and understood.* This is the specific function of spirit, which it lives by fulfilling, and dies if it cannot somehow fulfil. But as it is unresisting yet indomitable in its existence, so it is resourceful in its art, and ultimately victorious; because the worst horrors and absurdities in the world, when they are past or distant, so that life here is not physically disturbed by them, can be raised in the spirit to the level of reflection, becoming mere pictures of hell and marvellous in that capacity. Thus a constant suggestion and echo of sorrow, which cannot but suffuse existence, adds strange dignity to the tragedy and renders the spirit freer from

the world and surer in its own intrinsic possessions.

It is not in respect to large cosmic fatalities, such as war and death, that spirit is most perplexed. Love, self-sacrifice, and martyrdom are capable of turning those fatalities into occasions for lyrical joy and tragic liberation. The worst entanglements, from the spirit's point of view, arise within the psyche, in what in religious parlance is called sin. This strangles spirit at its source, because the psyche is primarily directed upon all sorts of ambitions irrelevant to spirit, producing stagnation, inflation, self-contradiction, and hatred of the truth. It is with difficulty that spirit can make itself heard in such a tumult. Spirit is no random blast, no irresponsible free demand, but speaks for a soul reduced to harmony and for the sane mind. This sanity implies not only integrity within, but also adjustment to the outer universe. So that whilst spirit is physically the voice of the soul crying in the wilderness, it becomes vicariously and morally the voice of the wilderness admonishing the soul.

Let me tabulate, as briefly as possible, the principal words and ideas that mark the differences, the bonds, and the confusions that exist between matter and spirit. Such a glossary may help the reader to criticize his favourite modes of expression and to be patient with those of other people.

BODY. Ancient usage identifies a man with his body, as Homer in the first lines of the Iliad:[1] and in English we still speak of *nobody* and *everybody*. This places man quite correctly in the realm of matter amongst other bodies, but it treats him and them summarily and externally as gross units and dead weights, ignoring their immaterial properties and their subtle physical substance and relations.

ORGANISM. This word still designates the body, since the organization of an organism must exist somewhere and on a particular scale, if it is to exist at all. But a body is an organism only by virtue of its vital power of nutrition and reproduction. By these functions bodily life becomes continuous with the ambient forces on which it feeds and theoretically with the whole dynamic universe. Thus an organism is both a closed system of vital tropes and a nucleus in the general cosmic process.

PSYCHE. The forms of inorganic matter, though distinct from matter logically, are clearly passive: matter may fall into them innumerable times, yet if anywhere disturbed, they show no tendency to reinstate themselves. This tendency defines an organism: its actual form hides a power to maintain or restore that form. This power or potentiality, often concentrated in a seed, dwells in the matter of the organism, but is mysterious; so that for observation the form itself seems to be a power (when locked in that sort of substance or seed) and to work towards its own manifestation. The self-maintaining and reproducing pattern or structure of an organism, conceived as a power, is called a psyche. The psyche, in its moral unity, is a poetic or mythological notion, but needed to mark the hereditary vehement movement in organisms towards specific forms and functions.

ANIMAL. All natural organisms have psyches, and are at the same time in dynamic relations to the whole physical world. When the organism waits for favourable opportunities to unfold itself, the psyche is vegetative; when it goes to seek favourable opportunities, it is animal.

This is an important step in laying the ground for spirit. The unity of the organism subtends the moral unity of the spirit, which raises that unity to an actual and intense existence; the impulse of the psyche, making for a specific perfection of form and action, underlies the spiritual distinction between good and evil; and the power of locomotion gives the spirit occasion for perception and knowledge. Will is no doubt deeper than intelligence in the spirit, as it is in the animal; yet will without intelligence would not be spirit, since it would not distinguish what it willed or what it suffered. So that the passage from vegetation to action seems to produce the passage from a dark physical excitability to the *qui vive* of consciousness.

SOUL. The same thing that looked at from the outside or biologically is called the psyche, looked at morally from within is called the soul. This change of aspect so transforms the object that it might be mistaken for two separate things, one a kind of physical organization and the other a pure spirit. And spirit is in fact involved in feeling and knowing life from the inside: not that spirit is then *self*-conscious, or sees nothing save its own states, but that it is then the medium and focus for apprehension, and imposes on its objects categories and qualities of its own. A psyche, when spirit awakes in it, is turned into a soul. Not only can the career of that psyche now be reviewed in memory, or conceived in prophecy, but many a private impulse or thought never exhibited to the world can now be added to one's history; so that oneself is now not merely the body, its power, and its experience, but also an invisible guest, the soul, dwelling in that body and having motions and hopes of its own. This soul can be conceived to issue out of the body, to pass into a different body, or to remain thinking and talking to itself without a body at all. This, for the psyche, would have been inconceivable; for, as Aristotle shows, the psyche, or specific form of organization and movement, in an elephant, can no more pass into the body of a fly, than the faculty of cutting can pass from an axe into a lyre, or the faculty of making music from the lyre into the axe. The soul, however, having an apparently independent discoursing and desiring faculty, and a power to imagine all sorts of non-existent things, may easily be conceived to pass from one body to another, as by a change of domicile, and to have had forgotten incarnations, with an endless future.

SELF OR PERSON. If memory, dreams, and silent musings seem to detach the soul from bodily life, social relations and moral qualities may re-attach the soul to the world, not now biologically but politically. Politically a man cannot be separated from his body; but it is not by his bodily faculties that he chiefly holds his own in society, or conceives his individuality. He is a person, a self, a character; he has a judicial and economic status; he lives in his ambitions, affections, and repute. All this again, as in the notion of the soul, cannot come about without the secret intervention of spirit: yet these ideas, although spirit must be there to entertain them, are not spiritual ideas; the interests chiefly concerned are those of animal or social bodies. Even moral worth or immortal life are ideals borrowed from animal impulses and animal conditions. In a different biological setting, or in a realm of pure spirits, those social duties and services would be impossible: and the will to live forever is nothing but the animal will to go on living expressed reflectively and transferred, somewhat incongruously, to the social self or historical person.

SPIRIT. Psyches, we have said, take on the character of souls when spirit awakes in them. Spirit is an awareness natural to animals, revealing the world and themselves in it. Other names for spirit are consciousness, attention, feeling, thought, or any word that marks the total *inner* difference between being awake or asleep, alive or dead. This difference is morally absolute; but physically the birth of spirit caps a long growth during which excitability and potentiality of various kinds are concentrated in organisms and become transmissible. The *outer* difference between sleeping and waking, life and death, is not absolute; and we may trace certain divergences between the path of transmission for the psyche and the basis of distribution for the spirit. Life follows the seed, through long periods of unconsciousness and moral nonexistence; whereas spirit lives in the quick interplay of each sensitive individual and the world, and often is at its height when, after keen experience, the brain digests the event at leisure, and the body is sexually quiescent or reduced by old age to a mere husk. In the spirit, by definition, there is nothing persistent or potential. It is pure light and perpetual actuality. Yet the intensity and scope of this moral illumination, as well as the choice of characters lighted up, the order of the scenes and how long each shall last, all hang on the preparations nature may have made for this free entertainment.

## Note

1. The wrath of Achilles cast many souls of heroes to Hades and *themselves* to dogs and vultures.

# Liberation

From what does distraction distract the spirit? If the flesh, the world, and the devil impede the proper movement of life, they must impinge upon something deeper than themselves or degrade something better. But what is this deeper or better thing? Those who regard spirit as a separate substance, and spiritual life as essentially another life in another world, seem to solve the problem clearly; but I fear they would find it still on their hands if they actually passed into that other world. The moral adventure of existence would simply have been extended; and if that life were really life and that world really a world, the spirit would find itself there as much entangled and beset, if not as much tormented, as it ever was in the human body. So too if we suppose spirit to have first inhabited some celestial sphere, according to the Platonic myth. Evidently even in that sphere, if we take the myth literally, the spirit must have been subject to distraction. How else were its incarnations determined, or how else was it tempted to quit heaven at all? From the beginning those two ill-matched horses gave the charioteer no end of trouble. And if we choose a milder fable,

From *Realms of Being* (New York: Charles Scribner's Sons, 1942 [1937]), pp. 736–767.

and conceive a Garden of Eden where all was health, safety, and abundance, we invoke only an animal placidity, into which spiritual joy might break perhaps at rare intervals and (I should think) wistfully; because animal peace, to spirit, is half cloying, half pathetic, except as some fleeting posture or aspect of it may be caught up and turned into a lyric note or a charming picture.

And why are such pictures or notes momentarily satisfying to the spirit, when the life from which they are drawn, in its monotony and decay, seems so gross and melancholy? Because spirit is essentially a culmination, and perfect happiness a quality to be attained occasionally by natural life, not another nonnatural life existing beyond. To say that we are distracted here because we belong by nature to a different region is simply contrary to fact. Nothing could bloom more naturally or tremble and sing more congruously than spirit does on earth; and the myths about a paradise, past or future, are transparent parables, expressing the rare, transporting, ecstatic quality that distinguishes the culminating moments of natural life from its endless difficulties, hardships, and embroiled hopes. These moments are sometimes the gift of a happy change in circumstances, as when agony ends and lovers are reunited; but sometimes, more spiritually, the supreme moment liberates us from circumstances altogether, and we feel withdrawn into an inner citadel of insight and exaltation. Let us consider how this can be.

Apocalypses and Last Judgments and cosmological wonders interest our moral or political passions: they give us a foretaste—conceivably not false—of catastrophes and triumphs awaiting the human race. They need not be inspired by a narrow partisanship, but may contain spontaneous insights into the genesis and fate of life in a thousand nonhuman or superhuman forms: dreams of angels and Titans, of Gods and devils. Like inspiration of any kind, such revelations may bring to light and may fortify the rebellion of the psyche against oppression and hopeless routine. So far, the thunders of prophecy, political or cosmic, will give voice to the spirit, and may promise to emancipate it. They may awaken it when perhaps it was sleeping; but they are not needed and not satisfying. Not needed, because clear and varied notes enough of the spiritual gamut are struck spontaneously at every turn in daily life, even if drowned in the hubbub; and not satisfying, because those lurid transformations of the scene into hells and heavens, or into marches and counter-marches of reforming hosts, only redouble the pressure of circumstances upon the spirit, and browbeat it into being joyful or revengeful. All this may involve fevers and nightmares of singular violence, but shortlived: nothing can be more dead than dead prophecies. The shouts of triumph in one camp cannot render the spirit, which is universal, deaf to the groans of the other; and by the indefinite prospect of fresh revolutions and fresh catastrophes, far from being redeemed, the spirit is tied more excruciatingly than ever to the wheel of fortune.

The Indians, who gave themselves time to unravel this question without private prejudices, saw that salvation could come only by *not* being born again: not because another life was not possible and might not be more splendid, but because, being life, it would be subject to accident, confusion, and responsibility. It would be essentially distracted. But not being born again is a negative solution, and personal. The very notion of being born again confuses the psyche with the spirit; for the spirit is inevitably born again so long as there is consciousness anywhere, whereas the psyche might perhaps be restored to life by the resurrection or re-creation of a corresponding body, but would lose its identity in proportion to the transformations suffered by this body and by its habitat. If the moral heritage or Will of any soul were extinguished by discipline and penance, so much of the transmissible energy or burden of existence would be destroyed and the universe would continue to live somewhat diminished in volume. I have not read anywhere that the universe was at last to be totally extinguished by this process, the last man being a saint by whose salvation existence came to an end altogether; nor would such a prospect make any difference in the moral issue. Under the form of eternity that finished history would remain a fact, with all the beauties and horrors that it may have contained; and the spirit said to have quitted it would still be faced by that fact, and be condemned to digest it for ever, if by poetic licence we conceive the spirit to survive disembodied. Salvation, then, must not be the beginning of a new life, which would make salvation again urgent; nor can it be existence without life, which except for dead matter would be a contradiction in terms.

When each sage reaches Nirvana or reverts to perfect identity with Brahma, who then is it that is saved? Certainly not the man, for he has abandoned and disallowed his personal being, even to the extreme of assuring us that *he* never existed at all, but that there was never anything but Brahma existing in him. Not the world; for this, even if with some diminution of potency or debt, continues to wag. And surely not Brahma, or the trance of Nirvana itself, for this has never been and never can be troubled. How then is spirit ever liberated, when in its proper nature it was always free, and in every phase of vital illusion it is still captive?

I think the Indians themselves give us the key to this enigma when they tell us that, in reality, the departed or finite being never existed, but only the One or the Absolute existed in him. This assertion, taken historically or physically, is indeed self-contradictory and contrary to fact: for only the finite and transitory property *exists*. But two genuine insights are conveyed by that mystic formula. In the first place, there is one plane, that of matter, or physical energy, on which the universe forms a single dynamic system and is presumably of one substance; so that all other realities, not being possessed of any substance, force, or permanence of their own, are called unrealities by the impulsive realist. On this analogy, mind in its turn may be reduced to an alleged spiritual substance. As the dissolution of bodies or worlds turns them all into water or ether or electricity or dust, so the dis-

solution of ideas and emotions is conceived to leave pure spirit, deep sleep, Brahma or Nirvana standing. Thus as matter was, in a dynamic sense, the only "reality" in this variegated world, so pure and calm spirit may seem to have been the only lasting "reality" in our distracted consciousness.

Modern philosophy has enabled us to dismiss this notion of an underlying substantial spirit. There is something substantial underlying our feelings and thoughts, but it is the psyche, or the organic life of the body, the substance of which, in its turn, is the common matter of the whole universe. Spirit is as far as possible from being a substance: it is at the other end of the scale, the very flower of appearance, actuality, light and evanescence.

But in the second place the Indians, in telling us that Brahma was always the only reality in our lives, summon us to turn from that physical problem about the one substance in the cosmos to the moral problem of finding the quintessence of peace and joy in ourselves. Their philosophy here takes the same turn that Greek philosophy took in Socrates, and substitutes morals for physics. Now, morally considered, the only "reality" is the good. To say that Brahma is the only reality in our souls will then amount to saying that the only *good* in our thoughts and feelings, and in our whole existence, comes of pure spirit being alive in us. In fact spirit in our thoughts and feelings is terribly distracted; but it can be more or less so; and the nearer we come, at any moment, to spontaneous, disinterested, pure intuition, so much more nearly has spirit within us been freed from ourselves, and so much more completely have we become, in that act, identical with Brahma. There was something in us always, since consciousness awoke, that saw our persons as part of the world. From the beginning there was a moral ambiguity in our souls. We might identify ourselves with the self which we found existing and at work; we might adopt its passions and limits; we might almost forget that there might be other selves or other passions morally as real as our own. Yet such egotism is naturally unstable and perverse, because in seeing our persons as part of the world and at work there, spirit in us cannot help assimilating our action and fate to that of the other creatures visible in the same world; and sincerity then compels us either to admit the other wills as equally important and legitimate with our own (which would undermine our fighting morality) or else to detach our genuine allegiance from ourselves also, regard our passions as follies, our views as illusions, and identify ourselves not with ourselves, but with the spirit within us. This spirit will be qualitatively the same as exists, or may exist, in other creatures also: not in so far as each accepts and pursues his animal or political impulses, but only in so far as, like spirit in us, he detaches himself from those impulses, regards them as pathetic accidents, and equates them with our contrasting impulses, and those of all other creatures.

Physically, existentially, historically, nothing will be changed by this second insight; but morally the whole natural world, with our own persons in it, will be removed to a distance. It will have become foreign. It will touch us, and exist morally for us, only as the scene of our strange exile, and as being the darkness, the cravings, the confusion in which the spirit finds itself plunged, and from which, with infinite difficulty and uncertainty, it hopes to be delivered.

Thus when the Indians tell us that only ignorance makes us suppose that a world exists or that we have a natural self living in that world, I would understand them to speak of *moral* ignorance only; for they themselves heartily believe, for instance, in the transmigration of souls or (what is morally the same thing) in Karma. Spirit therefore has a long variegated experience of this ignorance, which is at the same time knowledge of the world, and of the path to salvation; and the created selves that obscure and distract spirit in this process are parts of the vast realm of genesis, with all its earths and heavens. It is not scientific or natural ignorance to discover and understand this too real machinery; but it is ignorance in the heart, ignorance of its spiritual vocation, to attach itself absolutely to anything relative. Those sufferings and triumphs weigh upon

spirit only because they arouse spirit; otherwise they would be indifferent and morally null; and they are good rather than evil, true monitors rather than false, only in so far as they liberate spirit and pass into it, as oil shines only when consumed and turned into flame. Once lighted, this flame turns back upon all that it illuminates and upon its own fuel, as upon alien if not hostile facts. Being light, it thinks it shines of itself; but this is only the most inward and subtlest form of its distraction, when it torments itself about its own existence, perpetuity, and prerogatives, instead of simply shining upon all that there may be to shine upon, and consuming all its gross substance in that spiritual office. It is from the fumes of untoward matter obscuring the flame that liberation is needed, not from the fit occasion of this burning. The burning forms the flame that is to be saved; to be saved from its own impurities, from its obstructions and vacillations, so that it may neither suffer in shining nor fear not to shine.

That it should cease to shine here, upon these circumstances from this odd animal centre, follows from the natural instability of existence, and of the world in which spirit is kindled. To have lighted those things once is enough, if not too much. In any case they cannot lapse from the purview of spirit, which is addressed to all truth; they cannot lose their pertinence to that spiritual life which they once diversified; much less can their passing prevent other occasions and other objects from arousing spirit afresh. Frankly, this irrepressible vitality of that fire which by its very essence is continually consuming itself and ceasing to be, devours rather than sustains the animal soul; and those elegiac sentiments which gather round death, loss, old age, and mutation are not in the least modified by the assurance that truth is eternal and that life and beauty may be perpetually renewed in other shapes. On the contrary, both the eternity of truth and the vitality of nature merely perpetuate the reign of death and of sorrow; and far from promising an escape from destruction; they overwhelm the natural soul with a sense of how thorough that destruction is, how pervasive, minute, and hopeless. To be told that spirit may be inwardly emancipated from fortune, and that in innumerable other creatures it may live through endless adventures, sounds like bitter mockery to the poor wight mourning the loss of all his treasures, and shuddering horribly before his open grave. The soul so much concerned about its immortality is not spirit, but is an animal psyche, a principle of natural impulsive life. As thunderbolts, floods, famines and wars, sickness and blindness fill this human soul with horror, and as social obloquy torments it morally, so when by a sudden ray of intuition it foresees its own end, it is appalled and sometimes the thought of resurrection in the flesh, sometimes that of immortality for the soul only, arises in reflection to mitigate that despair.

Both these thoughts spring from the same intelligence that brought the knowledge of death. Life is a perpetual resurrection; and spirit too is continually being born again. In essence it is incapable of growing old or weary or embarrassed by past errors. Wherever there is existence there is youth; and death at every stroke by intercepting memory restores spontaneity. In another direction all that perishes in time is in truth and for spirit raised to immortality. Life moves on, but the achievement of life remains undeniable, even if forgotten. Here are two honest counterparts to death, not adventitious hopes or hypotheses, but implications inherent in the fact of death from the first. Resurrection is involved naturally, though not logically, in death, because life is a self-repeating trope, a rhythm in which death is the cæsura; and ideal immortality is implied logically in the truth of any finished life, which death rounds and frames in its wholeness. The Phœnix that continually rises again, however, is no individual psyche, but mere spirit: not impersonal, since it can exist only in some person, yet not the past personality of any dead man; only the same rational light breaking out anew in some fresh creature. Such a resurrection of the spirit does not liberate it: on the contrary, in this new incarnation it must begin its redemption again, or at least continue it, if by a moral heredity the new psyche takes up the task where the old psyche left off. This is not only the Indian and Platonic doctrine but in principle also the Christian. The number of incarnations is reduced to two (or to three, if we admit Purgatory), but spirit awakes in the second life with that degree of moral virtue which it had achieved in the first. This rank it now retains in each soul for ever, either in hell or in heaven; or else, according to Origen and some modern Protestants, it continues its moral adventures in circumstances perhaps more favourable than those it lived in on earth. We are not told whether the test of progress in either case would be an approach to liberation from existence altogether, as the Indians and other mystics aver. Probably not: the picture is rather that of an endless process, monotonous or varied, but essentially quite empirical and naturalistic.

Resurrection is the good old Hebraic hope. Such a prophecy satisfies the moral or political enthusiasm of the prophets and promises relief and compensation to Job. It does not profess to disengage the spirit from accidental bonds. Suppose the prophecy came true and we began to live in the Millennium or in the New Jerusalem. As we walked those golden streets and gazed at those crowned and white-robed phantoms that discoursed music in eternal peace, the still solitary spirit within us might well ask whether all this was not a dream, whether the heart was not deceived and disappointed by it, and whether reality possessed no other dimensions. Spirit would still need to do what it does on earth, what it is the nature of spirit to do everywhere, namely by its own intellectual insight to introduce us into the spheres of truth or of essence, detaching us from each thing with humility and humour, and attaching us to all things with justice, charity and pure joy. Is this what, after all, we should understand by heaven? In that case the heavenly kingdom is already come, and exists potentially within us; and there would be no occasion for spiritual pride to turn its back on heaven, since heaven would open wherever spiritual humility happened to look.

No dramatic eschatology would be involved in such inward salvation. We should simply return to innocence as before nature in us was distracted; or we should achieve natural perfection in some particular faculty, for the moment predominant, say in poetic intuition or in universal sympathy. It is an error to identify spirit with cold intelligence, or to think even intelligence primarily cold; however impartial our inspection of truth might become—and it never is wholly impartial—that very impartiality and scope, that very perception of contrary movements crossing or ignoring one another, and all issuing in the least expected or desired of destinies, would excite a tremendous and exhilarating emotion in the heart. Spirit has its lyric triumphs in childhood and in the simple life: wedding-days and moonlight nights and victories in war and soft music and pious trust. It breaks out momentarily in the shabbiest surroundings, in laughter, understanding, and small surrenders of folly to reason. Such moments are far from permanently lifting the soul they visit into a high spiritual sphere; often they come to ne'er-do-wells, poets, actors, or rakes. The spark dies in the burnt paper; yet it had the quality of a flame or a star. All the saint or the sage can add is constancy to that light, so that it colours all their thoughts and actions, turning the material circumstances into almost indifferent occasions. Yet the least disciplined or integrated of us sometimes feel something within us rising above ourselves, a culmination, a release, a transport beyond distraction. It was but summer lightning, and the sultriness continues unabated; yet that flash has given us a taste of liberty.

This is a spiritual gift, a gift of grace; it is not an earthly or even a moral benefit. Against circumstances and vices there are natural correctives; to apply them is the task of war, medicine, and labour; but easier circumstances or healthier passions will not liberate the spirit from oppression by things not spiritual. Prosperity might even deaden and misguide it more completely than ever misfortune could. For instance, that erotic passion which moralists think of when the flesh is mentioned is a conspicuous source of inspiration and spiritual courage; before it entangles us in sordid complications, it liberates us from the drab world, where everything suddenly seems foreign and worthless. The snares and slavery that love prepares for mankind are like venereal diseases; surprises for the young lover, shocks to his confident emotions, emotions in which nature and spirit seemed at last to have flowed together into an intense harmony.

It is then the flesh as a power that liberates us from the flesh as an obsession. That which is liberated is still love. It may ignore the flesh that breeds it; it may turn its rays away from their source upon the most remote or ethereal objects; it may even consume its substance and exhaust its organ. But that would be the end, not merely of all possible relapses into fleshliness, but of love itself and the blessing of its ultimate visions. Love presupposes a creature addressed to objects naturally harmonious with its deepest needs: otherwise love (if it could be imagined still to subsist) would be a blind unsatisfiable longing, incapable of fixing upon any true object, or even distinguishing the predestined beauty for which it longed.

We find, then, that it was not the flesh in its simple animal functions that imprisoned the spirit, but the world and the mind, complicating those impulses or compelling them to hide, that overwhelmed the young Eros with all manner of extraneous reproaches, jealousies, sorrows, and cares. We should liberate the spirit quite enough from the flesh if we could liberate the flesh from all that, as flesh, distorts, starves, and degrades it.

Nor is it liberation for the spirit to be removed from the world. This, too, is physically impossible: but even in the sense in which a hermit or a lover of nature may flee from the world of men, liberation is problematical. It will not ensue if the hermit or poet still takes thought for what he shall eat or drink, what people will think of him, or how he may persuade them to reform their ways. As the flesh is the necessary organ of spirit, so the world is its inevitable environment, and its appointed theme when spirit is intelligent. Perhaps a purely sensuous, musical, or conceptual life might never discern a material or social world beyond the sphere of linked images; but when images are acted upon and understood, when objects, events, possibilities and certainties loom before the mind, then spirit, by becoming intelligent, becomes a conscious and absorbed inhabitant of nature. It lives by finding itself in the world, by seeing how the world wags, by tracing with emotion the tragedies of history. The greater the range or deeper the insight of spirit the more inextricably will it live the life of the world, though not as the world lives it. Ignorance is not liberation; and for that reason the world is such a slave to itself, not in the least understanding its own mechanism or foreseeing its destiny. But spirit, in the measure in which, by attentive study and sympathy, it may have understood the world, will be liberated from it, that is, from distraction by it.

And as for the devil—all that mesh of deceit, which language, imagination, reasoning and self-consciousness weave round the spirit out of its own creations—the devil needs indeed to be exorcised, but cannot be destroyed so long as spirit endures, because in their substance the two are one. We have seen how the distraction of the spirit by the devil reaches its height in insanity and suicide: on the way to which there are many stages and devious paths of sophistication, obsession, delusion, and fanatical pride. We need only follow the thread backward through that diabolical labyrinth to find the gate to freedom: not always, or perhaps often, a gate by which we entered or which we recognize as opening upon fields native to our souls; because we are born in original sin, hatched within the labyrinth, and accustomed from childhood to be little spitfires and little devils rather than innocent clear minds. Yet, though probably never experienced, perfect health and simple knowledge would have awakened and filled full within any animal a spirit free from distraction, and so attuned to its successive intuitions as to find the devil's whisperings inane and utterly repulsive. To this innocence, armed with the strength of unclouded spiritual wisdom, we may penitentially return; but only a long discipline can avail in most cases to smooth out all sophistry and banish all pride, so that undisturbed by the

devil, spirit may deploy all its notes and all its tints in a new springtime of inspiration.

Health and knowledge: essentially nothing more is requisite for liberation from distraction by the flesh, the world, and the devil. Negatively we may observe this liberation in placid sleep. A sleeping child is not distracted, yet he is alive. Nature has given him health; fortune has not yet taxed his powers unduly; and while consciousness is in abeyance, the feelings and images ready to appear, and forming his latent store of knowledge, will serve perfectly to express his simple contacts with the world. But spirit in the sleeping child is in what Aristotle would call its first entelechy: it is ready, it is perfect, but not employed. It must awake before all that brimming potentiality can pass into action. And then, after a first phase of confidence and eager experiment, trouble will begin. Foreseeing this, must we say with the Indians that liberation can come only by reverting to that deep sleep in which all things are alike and nothing ever happens? It would be foolish to deny both the physical and the moral insight enveloped in this doctrine, but discrimination is needed. There is, let us allow, a universal substance to which we all return and which was always the real force and agent within us; and a worshipper of mere force, permanence, or existence may see in all that is evanescent (that is, in all that is in any honest sense *spiritual*) a vain delusion from which it is blessed to relapse into unconsciousness. This unconsciousness will not be death, because unconscious substance retains all its energy and potentiality, and will still breed, very likely, endless worlds out of itself. But in a spiritual sense is this liberation? Is it even liberation from life, if you are tired of thinking, loving, hating, and hoping, and wish for eternal rest? It would be death indeed to *you,* if that is what you long for: but the unconsciousness of universal substance is immensely alive (else we should not be here, with our troubled phenomenal world) and the end of spiritual troubles in you will not dry up the fountain of spirit or of endless distraction in the universe. The liberation, if you call death a liberation, will therefore be personal only, material and unspiritual. The spirit will not have learned how to live; and to speak of freedom where there is no life, of freedom in non-existence, would surely be an abuse of language.

No: liberation cannot be liberation from spirit itself; and therefore not from those natural circumstances which make spirit possible. On the other hand, these circumstances plunge the spirit, as we have seen, into all sorts of distraction, since the organ of spirit, not by chance but essentially, forms a particular and specific nucleus in the organization of nature. Were not the psyche a special nucleus, subject to external interference and needing external support, it could never have become the organ of spirit, that is, of an intellectual and moral self-transcendence. Living suspended upon circumstances the psyche felt this suspense, reached and covered those circumstances by its concern, and thereby became spirit. Individual life must subsist, with a station from which to survey the world, a set of organs and interests to canalize that survey, to render it graphic, lyrical, tragic, and moral, if ever spirit is to arise or to endure or if in any positive sense it is to be liberated. Yet how shall it be liberated if it must continue, while it exists, to face a world of circumstances not only alien in themselves but often inimical? Between extinction on the one hand, and endless distraction on the other, it might seem that for spirit there were no salvation at all.

Perhaps a surer and more positive idea of liberation may be drawn from observing what spiritual men are than by discussing what they say. They are not all alike. Some are initially spiritual and free, not needing liberation, but birdlike and gay like children, or bovine and steady like peasants. Others who are more sophisticated represent all degrees of regeneration, from comfortable worldly wisdom to the extreme of asceticism. Even frankly mundane sages, like Goethe, while blandly smiling on the world, the flesh and the devil, seem to disinfect those influences by the breadth of their knowledge and sympathy, being too mature to run amok with any one folly. But such equilibrium seems rather the gift of a sound temperament than of a renovating philosophy. Nature at a certain distance and on a large scale looks sublimely calm, as if God lived there; but all is strain, torment, and disaster in the parts, if we take them on the scale of their inner effort and animation. So an Olympian naturalism lives at peace with all the vices, and is more selfish than sympathetic, thinking that inevitableness and beauty justify nature as they justify woman, no matter how much she may entangle or how much she may suffer.

In such pantheistic allegiance and respect for nature as a whole, spirit may be philosophical, absorbed in curiosity and wonder, impressed by the size, force, complexity, and harmony of the universe; the eyes are open, but the mind is still in leading strings. So it should be in natural science; so it was in that happy childhood of philosophy represented by the Ionian cosmologers. Yet at two points the existence of spirit, with its transcendental rights, is bound to assert itself. The naturalist, being a man, must also be a moralist; and he must find himself dividing this seamless garment of nature, by a sort of optical iridescence, into the shifting colours of good and evil; and he will probably turn his reflection from pure science to giving counsel to his soul and to his country about the wiser way of life. At the same time, within his natural philosophy, he must ultimately notice the existence of sensation and emotion in animals, with his own moral philosophy crowning that immaterial and invisible experience; he must discover the witnessing and judging spirit. This is the adolescence of philosophy, and has its sentimental dangers. Only in the most home-keeping, industrious, unheroic souls will spirit be content, when self-conscious, to accept reality uncritically, and to run every errand of instinct or opportunity with the alacrity of a trained dog. Either overwhelmed by the disproportion between outer and inner forces, they will turn against themselves in the hope of suppressing all moral distinction or rebellion; or they will reserve the moral sphere as a private retreat, a humorous or sarcastic or poetical oasis for the spirit in the environing desert.

This last was, at heart, the path chosen by Socrates and his less metaphysical followers, who were not also followers of Plato. Cynics and Cyrenaics, like Confucians and sceptics elsewhere, summoned the spirit to live on its own resources, in studious or domestic peace, dominating the world only intellectually, describing it sometimes scientifically, sometimes satirically, and cultivating abstention from passion and war, and from excessive confidence in fortune or in human virtue. The spirit, as these men saw, was invulnerable in its idyllic modesty, and far more divine than the thundering gods; yet the authority of this spirit over the rest of the human soul remained precarious, and philosophy when honest had to be composed in a minor key. Minor, that is, in its philosophical pretensions, yet often merry and running into *scherzo;* for in fact this homely strain in Socratic wisdom has flowed ever since through all the pleasant fields of literature and worldly wisdom, while religion and science, not always more spiritually, frowned from the heights. For can it be regarded as a triumph of spirit to live, artificially exalted, on its own illusions? The zeal, the trembling anxiety, the fanaticism with which these illusions are sometimes defended betray their non-spiritual source. They represent psychic and political forces struggling to maintain a particular form of life, and dragging the spirit into their vortex, which is by no means identical with the free and natural organ of spirit.

No doubt the metaphysical side of Socratic philosophy, the hypostasis of language and morals into cosmic powers, expressed spiritual enthusiasm, and seemed to support it; yet in the end we find that it contaminated and betrayed the spirit. Earthly warfare against the world is an earthly and worldly business; it impoverishes its own side by condemning too large a part of nature and of human nature, which might also have served the spirit; and it constrains such spirit as it fosters into a false alliance with particular opinions and moralities. Spirit soon has to cry aloud to be saved from such salvation. Plato, who had the soul of a poet, knew perfectly how much he was

sacrificing to the desperate enterprise of maintaining an impregnable and incorruptible city on earth; and the Church afterwards acknowledged that on earth it was but a Church militant; triumph, liberation, happiness could come only in heaven. Mankind were to remain an enlisted army, heavily armed, narrowly hedged, covered with blood and mire; spirit was to visit them only in the weariness of the twilight, and to rise heavenward in the smoke of their camp-fires.

A dogged allegiance to a particular temperament or country or religion, though it be an animal virtue, is heroic; it keys the whole man up to sacrifice and to integrity; so that persons devoted to such a specific allegiance attain a high degree of spirituality more often, perhaps, than sceptics or original philosophers. Yet pantheism, or joyful allegiance to nature as a whole, also has its saints; it too, in one sense, is a special allegiance, since it excludes every irreconcilable passion. Indeed what essential difference can it make to the liberation of spirit from what world or what passions it is liberated? To be liberated, let me repeat, is not to lose or destroy the positive possessions to which the spirit was attached. It is merely to disinfect them, to view them as accidents, to enjoy them without claiming them, to transcend without despising them. So we find the pantheists, when they are spiritual, retreating from this infinitely deployed universe into an inner silence and simplicity that holds infinity, as it were, in suspense; and we also find the disciples of particular religions interpreting their tenets as symbols or occasions for an inward revelation that renders those tenets indifferent.

When St. John of the Cross, for instance, who knew that the accepted facts of religion did not prevent the spirit from passing into the darkest night, tells us that the one guide out of that darkness must be *faith,* what does he understand by this word? The dogmas of the Catholic Church? But those he never seems to have questioned or lost sight of. Any partial heresy seemed to him perverse, and he had no intellectual or historical lights to show him the whole system of Christianity from the outside, as one figment of imagination among many. Faith in that system, as a materially true account of the facts, had not prevented his spiritual desolation. How should it save him from it? The faith to invoke would seem to be rather faith in salvation itself, allegiance to the whole enterprise of the religious life, *Fides caritate formata,* trust that beyond that blank negation and inner death which utter self-surrender involved there would come in the end a positive liberty, a clear vision, a living flame of love. And it could come, it did come; although even the most exquisite poetic inspiration could not avail to express its nature in adequate images. The verses of St. John of the Cross have the lyric brevity, simplicity, and passion that anonymous popular ditties in Spain borrow, perhaps, from the East; there is something so entire, frank and ultimate about such effusions, that they are not unspiritual even when merely amorous or witty. The man who sings them, and perhaps improvises them, sees himself and his feelings from above, as did Catullus when he wrote: *Odi et amo.* Here is a torment that, in seeing how animal it is, has become spiritual. At least it has become awareness of a double life; you are perishing in the sea of fortune and passion, and you are making a philosophy or a poem out of your shipwreck. Or while the whole world is asleep you are slipping out invisibly into the night on the secret errands of your love.

It was a godsend to Christian mystics that the Song of Solomon was canonical. It countenanced allegories that otherwise might have seemed scandalous. The flesh as we have seen is naturally a breeder of spirit; even vulgar infatuation often touches ultimate insights, defiance of the world, self-surrender. And spontaneous sublimations here may well be used as types of sublimation for all the passions. Yet I find two defects in erotic symbolism, even in the delicate hands of St. John of the Cross, in which it was comparatively safe; because he seems to have had a less erotic temperament, or a more manly control over it, than many other mystics. One defect is that (as in the Song of Solomon itself) the images

overpower the thought, if indeed the thought ever existed; and we are charmed by a lascivious picture or a poetic sigh, when we ought to be transported into a perfectly spiritual, entirely sacrificial bliss. The Indians, with their metaphysical intensity, are better guides here. The other defect is that lovers asleep in each other's arms on a bed of roses represent a pleasant death rather than a sublime life. Appeasement of a sensual instinct makes a bad symbol for attainment of intellectual light. The true spiritual sublimation of love is charity, not inebriation, or blind transports, or happy sleep. So that if in its imagery I find erotic mysticism less instructive than Indian concentration on pure spirit, in their issue I find both schools alike too negative, too drowsy, too unintellectual. Blank ecstasy is a form of intoxication, not of disintoxication. Instead of cleansing the lamp, it puts out the light.

St. John of the Cross is now in great favour even among the merely curious in spiritual matters, because he is the most poetical and psychologically expert of mystics; but neither in speculation nor in heroism was his genius of the first order. What the essence of liberation is might be more readily gathered from St. Francis of Assisi, or from Buddha: one would teach us the cheeriness of utter renunciation, and the other its infinite peace. But I am not writing a history, and will jump at once to the supreme instance obvious to all natives of Christendom. Obvious to believers, because where could spirit be freer or less tainted than in God made man? Obvious also to unbelievers, if they have any discernment; because at the moment when ancient civilization touched the summit of its greatness and of its misery the Hellenized Jews were exiles in the midst of that world; they learned from it without loving it, and were weaned from their own national ambition and bigotry, sublimating these into a purely religious zeal, still filled with prophetic grandeur and fire: and, to be the heart of this new religion, they composed the legend and maxims of Christ. Christ was supreme spirit incarnate in a human creature, suffering and dying guiltlessly in that creature, and immediately rising again and carrying with him into eternity his earthly body strangely transfigured, and thus opening the way of salvation for the spirit in all flesh.

What is this salvation, not as the Christian myth describes it (we have settled our accounts with myth) but as the adored person of Christ exhibits it, and as his followers would experience it if they shared his passion and his resurrection?

Christ in the Gospels continually tells us that he is subject to "the Father," who has "sent" him into this world. Liberation, as a Christian should desire it, cannot be liberation from fortune or domination over it. Spirit is *sent*-into this world: it does not command this world, much less create it. It may work miracles here, when it feels the silent consent or monition of the Father prompting it to invoke them; but they are secondary, and the fuss the world makes about them is disheartening. "The Father" represents the realm of matter, where the sun shines on the just and the unjust, where to him that hath shall be given, where the lilies of the field flourish and the sparrows fall, where the house built on a rock will stand (for a season), where the poor are always with us, and where there shall be weeping and gnashing of teeth. Miracles belong to that natural sphere, and manifest the hidden sympathies and harmonies between its parts. The spirit notes them, but does not dwell upon them, or value them except as evidences of the unfathomable fatherly power on which spirit itself depends.

Jewish tradition unhesitatingly identified this universal power with Jehovah, conceived at once as a national patron and as the divine vindicator prophetically invoked by an aggressive conscience; but these strains are separable and not spiritual. "The Father" we hear of in the Gospels bears a more intimate and a more universal relation to the spirit. He generates and inspires it, and at the same time subjects it to the chances and cruelties of an impartial natural economy. To this economy the spirit submits painfully yet gladly; because the beauty and terror of that impartiality liberate the spirit itself from its accidental bonds. Family, race,

religion, human conceit, human hypocrisy are transfixed by the clear spirit in Christ with a terrible detachment; but where love is refused, this is not because it does not exist; it exists overpoweringly for everything that the Father has created, that is simple, that is young, that suffers and is mangled in the hideous madhouse of this world.

Thus we see by the example of Christ that spirit, even when conceived to have been originally disembodied and voluntarily incarnate, is neither contaminated by its descent nor made proud by its intrinsic elevation. In Christ spirit did not need to be saved, it was free initially; yet it was inspired to love and willing to suffer; neither tempted, like the gods of Greece, to become an accomplice to human passions, nor like Lucifer to shut itself up in solitary pride. It was humble towards universal power, wisely respectful towards the realm of matter. Salvation could not consist in pretending to be independent, that is, in becoming mad. It could not consist in correcting the divine economy, and becoming creative, that is, in becoming guilty. Humility, piety, is a prerequisite to spirituality. It is much more than a prudential virtue, good for those who wish to prosper in the world. It enables spirit to recognize the truth and to be inwardly steady, clear, fearless, and without reproach.

Spirit is not the whole of life, only a child of the family. The others, the uninspired, cry out even more urgently and need to be helped first. The good Samaritan is more spiritual than the Pharisee. Learning and science and art scarcely deserve to be mentioned, or only ironically, in that they refute and stultify themselves. Spirit, being at once vital and disinterested, cannot but be merciful. Wounds, weakness, conflicts are the immediate evils; when these are healed, we may turn to higher things. Nor is this last possible or necessary to everybody; the parting word rather is: "Sin no more." Enough, to strike at the source of each grief, to staunch this wound, stop this pain, banish this care. Why force anybody to be greater than he naturally is? There is nothing enlightened in moral snobbery; and spirit feels more at home amid simple things, if they are perfect, than in ambitious minds. Its own perfection consists in charity, in the perception and love of possible perfections in all other things.

Thus the innate humility of spirit is turned not only towards the realm of matter, the universal power on which spirit depends, but also towards the realm of spirit itself, towards all the lives, languages, and loves into which spirit can enter. To corporal works of mercy Christ adds spiritual charities: patience, forgiveness, understanding, defence of the heart against cant, hypocrisy, isolation, and the insanities of conscience. Spirit, that suffers distraction by the disorder of its instruments, rejoices in the salvation and perfectness of all creatures and all aspirations, as in so many preludes or approaches to its own happiness. It is not spirit that sins, but the terrible cross-pressure of a thousand motions in nature that stifle and confuse it, when they allow it to open its lips at all.

St. Paul tells us that Christ liberates us from the law, and therefore from sin, saving us by faith and an infusion of the spirit. This might be (and has been) interpreted so as to countenance moral licence; as the charity of Jesus in the Gospels has been interpreted by sentimental or romantic moderns as an invitation to indulge all their corrupt inclinations. But health and morality are not based on spirit, spirit is based on them; and no spiritual insight can abolish or weaken the difference between what nature allows and rewards and what she punishes and condemns to everlasting torments. The point is that spirit, caught in this vice, suffers guiltlessly for that natural disease and corruption; and to rescue that guiltlessness, to extricate spirit from inner madness as well as from outward oppression, is the double work of mercy proper to Christian charity. The moral economy of the universe is not destroyed or suspended: rewards and punishments, saving miraculous exemptions, take their natural course; but sins are forgiven because they *ought* to be forgiven, because the suffering they bring to the spirit, *the spirit* never deserved.

Is it too bold an interpretation of Christian dogma to say that this inevitable innocence of the spirit, in all it suffers, is symbolized by the passion and death of Christ, and by his resurrection? The possible liberation of the spirit is not a liberation from suffering or death, but through suffering and death. This suffering and death need not be bloody; often some silent spirit is overwhelmed like a modest brook grown brackish and lost in a tidal river. Suffering and death come from the contrariety of motions in nature and, among these, from the way in which life rises into spirit and sinks away from it. Yet this spirit, however cruelly circumstances may play with it, remains congenitally positive, self-justified, heroic; it has been sent into the world by the very power by which the world was created; and it aspires to live, and to find a good and beautiful world to live in. It loves, and although it suffers only because it loves, it wills to love and to suffer. Our sufferings will chasten and transfigure our attachment to the circumstances and passions that caused those sufferings. Death will soon annual the ignominy that confined spirit in us to our private views and private interests. Even now, by accepting that death in advance, we may identify ourselves dramatically with the spirit in us that endures and surmounts those accidents and laugh at that death, since apart from those accidents spirit in us is identical with spirit everywhere, a divine witness, a divine sufferer, immortal, and only temporarily and involuntarily incarnate in a myriad distracted lives.

So the Cross is a symbol for the true liberation, the ultimate dominion, possible to the spirit in man. Salvation comes by shifting the centre of appreciation from the human psyche to the divine spirit. It is a shift within the psyche, otherwise it would not enter at all into our lives; but in each human soul some spark of divine spirit cohabits with the animal nature of the rest; and shifting the living centre from some other faculty to this spark, which is the focus of intellect, by no means abolishes the remaining faculties; these merely become, for appreciation, peripheral. This means a change of heart, a conversion, momentarily real, but relapsing and becoming more or less nominal and merely intended as life goes on. For genetically and substantially those nonspiritual faculties were not peripheral but primary, and the nucleus from which intelligence and spirit were put forth. So that man is irremediably a human person assuming and adopting a divine nature, and not, like the Christ of theology, a divine person assuming a human nature added to and subordinate to his native divinity. This religious image is formed in worship, it expresses an unattainable limit of aspiration, it is hyperbolic. It represents as a descent from heaven that inward darkness which is in fact a presupposition to the idea of heaven. It would be heaven to shed all these backsliding inclinations and distracting cares, and to live only in the spirit; but spirit would have nothing to live with and nothing to live for, if it had begun and ended by being a spirit. For us to wish to become divine persons like Christ would be chimerical and, for the pious Christian, blasphemous; but Christ may come and dwell within us, transfusing our human nature with divine light, so that our natural functions, while continuing to be performed, and performed perhaps more healthily and beautifully than before, will now be performed with detachment and humility and an eye seeing what lies beyond.

The fact that spirit is grafted on the animal psyche and is a continual hypostasis of natural life prevents the sacrifices imposed by spirit from being unrewarded, and the spiritual life from being merely negative. Calvary is not the end: there is the Resurrection. And this postmortal life has two stages, or two dimensions. One is a rebirth by expansion and re-incarnation in all those phases of spirit in which the spirit is free, and therefore self-forgetful. Selflessness can see no difference in value between what is enjoyed here and what is enjoyed there, by one man or by another. Envy is abolished; the very limits of sense and imagination seem virtually to break down; you feel all you have not felt, know all you have not known, live in every one who has ever lived. Yet with a happy partiality; because the endless evils and sufferings which fill actual lives fill them precisely because the will in those creatures has not been liberated. There the spirit cares for what does not concern it, wills things contrary to itself and to one another, and in a word is subject to distraction. This we are now supposed to have overcome: and surely the passions and illusions that are dead in ourselves are not to be replaced in us by adopting the passions and illusions alive in others. Only the clear spirit in each can be identified with the clear spirit in all the rest. The distracted spirit in the world will be succoured with charity, and not hated even in its madness; but only the liberated spirit will be embraced with joy. For this reason hell does not poison heaven. The modern sentiment that heaven could not help being poisoned by the mere existence of such an eternal contradiction to its bliss, though generous, is not intelligent. As all truths fall together into the truth and are perfectly welcome to the intellect, all errors being understood and rejected, so all sane joys add themselves together uncontaminated in the heart, when the heart is pure; while the sorrows and hatreds, though perceived, cannot be shared. Pain is itself a kind of hatred, and however intense it may be elsewhere, it cannot find its way into a free spirit. But this very freedom lifts the spirit, in its outlook and virtual attainment, into the presence of all good, wherever this good may be realized; so that it now clings to the earth, and to its native soil, only by the hidden roots of which it is unconscious, while its head flowers out and drinks the light from every quarter of the heavens. Self, so turned into a mere pedestal, ceases to intercept intuition, yet continues to make intuition a possible temporal and local fact, and determines its point of view, language, and perspectives. Spirit continues to live, and to inhabit persons; but it feels no drag in this attachment, can carry away and transform its body as it will, and rise into any heaven to which it has a natural bent.

This I seem to see symbolized in the risen Christ appearing unannounced, unrecognized, in various disguises; a real body, yet not as it was; the same person, and yet escaped from his trammels, having finished his mission, transmitting his work, without regret or anxiety, into other hands. There remain a few relics of the man, but the spirit has passed untraceably into new mansions. If we come sorrowfully at dawn to the grave where we thought he was laid yesterday, we behold young men, strangers, sitting by the stone that has been rolled away, and saying: "He is not here, he is risen. Why seek ye the living among the dead? He goeth before you into Galilee. There shall ye see him."

Such is the escape or migration, or resurrection of spirit horizontally, in the direction of further instances and developments. But there is also, and simultaneously, a possible liberation ideally, in the vertical direction, when at any moment, or habitually, the spirit in a man recalls its universality, its merely momentary lodgment here, or preoccupation with this trouble, and expands intuitively into the equilibrium of all moments, and the convergence of all insights, under the intense firmament of truth. Here there is no longer any pang of loss, any dubiousness in re-union, any groping in the twilight of birth and death. Birth and death have become integral to life, like the outburst and the close of a phrase in music: there are no winding-sheets or sepulchres or embalmings; we have been initiated into the mystery of the divinity of Christ. In Adam, in the human psyche, the spirit is secondary, dependent, intermittent, only a point of view occasionally taken histrionically, by transcending animal egotism only the better to serve it; but in Christ, in the spirit that then enters into us, the opposite happens. There the centre is divine, and what is put on like a garment or a dramatic mask is human nature. And though this assumption of humanity be voluntary, the very fact that it is voluntary makes it incomplete. The humanity that can coexist with divinity in the same person must be a singularly chastened, subordinated humanity. Such in fact is the humanity depicted in Christ and admitted by Christians into their ideal of life.

A divine person coming down into the world to redeem it could not adopt its errors or its vices. He could not even adopt its passions, however legitimate or inevitable in the natural man. He could not marry and have a family claiming his special affection in contrast to mankind at large. He could not possess a home or a country that should tether his heart and compel him to defend them. He could not

become a national hero, like Joshua or Solomon or Ezra. He might speak figuratively, and with great pity in his heart, of the kingdom to come: but it was not one in which his disciples should sit on thrones, like Cæsar, judging the nations. The first condition was that they should leave their nets by the seashore, take up their cross, and follow him. Nor was this a temporary repentance, because the end of the world was at hand, and it was not worth while making earthly provision. The end of the world is always at hand. The world is transitory, not only because our lives in it are short, but because it is unstable and contradictory and self-devouring essentially. In the true kingdom to come, in the soul transformed into spirit, there would be no anxiety about place or person, no marriage or giving in marriage, no pride of knowledge or power, no rebellion against suffering. These things are in the order of nature. The Father has ordained them. There can be no thought of abolishing them in their sphere. Christ himself came eating and drinking, living with the poor, and even feasting with the rich. Why not, when these things were profoundly indifferent in themselves, and the spirit could strengthen itself and pray in the midst of them whatever they might be?

Christianity was thus a fundamentally new religion, a religion of the spirit. It completely reversed the inspiration of the Jews in their frank original hopes, and rather resembled Neo-Platonism and Buddhism. The Jews did well, from their point of view, to reject it, and the Protestants, from theirs, to reform it so as to revert to the cultus of marriage, thrift, science, and nationality. Nevertheless a religion or philosophy without repentance, without disillusion or asceticism, reckons without its host. The Jews themselves produced Christianity, and the Greeks helped them to do it. After all, it is the spirit that makes human nature human; and in the confused, tormented, corrupt life of Christendom, not only do we find many a bright focus of mercy, sanctity, poetry, speculation, and love, but even the tone and habit of the common mind seem shot through with more wit and insight, more merriment and kindness, than in ages and nations that have never asked to be saved. Salvation is demanded, and in one sense is possible, because by virtue of his intelligence man already has one foot in eternity. Each passion, each period of life, each political enterprise, after its heats are over (or even in the midst of them, when spirit shines through) enacts a tragedy which though vain materially need not be vain morally. Error and suffering, by the very change of heart that they provoke, may be offered up as a holocaust; affections lost as joys may be preserved as allegiances; and all experience may be accepted for the insights which it brings. Brings, that is, to the spirit and for the spirit; because if after stumbling we merely plodded on, and if after dying we were merely made flesh again, the wheel of nature would go on grinding brutally for ever, no music would be heard in those spheres, and the soul would have sinned and suffered only to go on sinning and suffering unredeemed.

## Suggestions for Further Reading

**Works by Santayana**

*The Works of George Santayana,* eds. Herman J. Saatkamp, Jr. and William G. Holzberger (Cambridge, Mass.: The MIT Press, 1986–). The ongoing, definitive edition of the works of Santayana.

*Character and Opinion in the United States* (New York: Charles Scribner's Sons, 1921).
*Dialogues in Limbo* (New York: Charles Scribner's Sons, 1926).
*Dominations and Powers* (New York: Charles Scribner's Sons, 1950).
*The Idea of Christ in the Gospels* (New York: Charles Scribner's Sons, 1946).
*Interpretations of Poetry and Religion* (New York: Charles Scribner's Sons, 1900).
*The Last Puritan: A Memoir in the Form of a Novel* (New York: Charles Scribner's Sons, 1936).
*Letters,* ed. Daniel Cory (New York: Scribner, 1955).
*The Life of Reason,* 4 vols. (New York: Charles Scribner's Sons, 1905).
*Lotze's System of Philosophy,* ed. Paul G. Kuntz (Bloomington, Ind.: Indiana University Press, 1971 [1889]).
*Obiter Scripta* (New York: Charles Scribner's Sons, 1936).
*Persons and Places; The Middle Span;* and, *My Host the World* (New York: Charles Scribner's Sons, 1944, 1945, 1953; reprinted in one volume in *The Works of George Santayana.*)
*Physical Order and Moral Liberty,* ed. John and Shirley Lachs (Nashville: Vanderbilt University Press, 1969).
*Platonism and the Spiritual Life* (New York: Charles Scribner's Sons, 1927).
*Poems of George Santayana* (New York: Dover, 1970 [1896]).
*The Realms of Being,* 4 vols. (New York: Charles Scribner's Sons, 1927, 1930, 1938, 1940).
*Scepticism and Animal Faith* (New York: Charles Scribner's Sons, 1923).
*The Sense of Beauty* (New York: Charles Scribner's Sons, 1896).
*Soliloquies in England and Later Soliloquies* (New York: Charles Scribner's Sons, 1922).
*Some Turns of Thought in Modern Philosophy* (New York: Charles Scribner's Sons, 1933).
*Winds of Doctrine* (New York: Charles Scribner's Sons, 1926).

**Essential Works on Santayana**

Herman J. Saatkamp, Jr. and John Jones, *George Santayana: A Bibliographical Checklist, 1880–1980* (Bowling Green, Ken.: Philosophy Documentation Center, 1982). This bibliography is updated annually in *Overheard in Seville: Bulletin of the Santayana Society,* eds. Herman J. Saatkamp, Jr. and Angus Kerr-Lawson, and distributed by the Department of Philosophy, Texas A & M University.

Willard E. Arnett, *George Santayana* (New York: Washington Square Press, 1968).

John Lachs, *George Santayana* (Boston: Twayne Publishers, 1988).

Corliss Lamont, *Dialogue on George Santayana* (New York: Horizon Press, 1959).

Henry S. Levinson, *Santayana, Pragmatism, and the Spiritual Life* (Chapel Hill, N.C.: University of North Carolina Press, 1992).

John McCormick, *George Santayana: A Biography* (New York: Knopf, 1987).

Paul A. Schilpp, ed., *The Philosophy of George Santayana: Library of Living Philosophers* (Evanston, Ill.: Northwestern University Press, 1940).

Beth Singer, *The Rational Society: A Critical Study of Santayana's Social Thought* (Cleveland: Press of Case Western Reserve University, 1970).

Irving Singer, *Santayana's Aesthetics: A Critical Introduction* (Cambridge, Mass.: Harvard University Press, 1957).

Timothy L. S. Sprigge, *George Santayana: An Examination of His Philosophy* (Boston: Routledge and Kegan Paul, 1974).

# JOHN DEWEY

## Introduction by John J. Stuhr

### Dewey's Life: Cultural Context and Philosophical Background

. . . it is important, even necessary to appreciate what phases of historical thought—past and present—enter deeply into determination of the thinking of any philosopher.[1]

. . . I seem to be unstable, chameleon-like, yielding one after another to many diverse and even incompatible influences; struggling to assimilate something from each and yet striving to carry it forward in a way that is logically consistent with what has been learned from its predecessors. Upon the whole, the forces that have influenced me have come from persons and from situations more than from books—not that I have not, I hope, learned a great deal from philosophical writings, but that what I have learned from them has been technical in comparison with what I have been forced to think upon and about because of some experience in which I found myself entangled.[2]

. . . I shall never cease to be grateful that I was born at a time and a place where the earlier ideal of liberty and the self-governing community of citizens still sufficiently prevailed so that I unconsciously imbibed a sense of its meaning. In Vermont, perhaps even more than elsewhere, there was embodied in the spirit of the people the conviction that governments were like the houses we live in, made to contribute to our welfare, and that those who lived in them were as free to change and extend the one as they were the other when developing needs of the human family called for such alterations and modifications.[3]

In sketching Dewey's personal and intellectual development, it may be instructive at the outset to recall briefly the context of his extraordinarily vigorous and long life (1859–1952). Dewey's ninety-two years spanned the American Civil War, the Spanish-American War, the Russian Revolution, World War I, the Great Depression, World War II, and Auschwitz. Born in the year in which Darwin's *Origin of Species* appeared, Dewey witnessed the development of relativity theory and quantum mechanics, and the creation and use of the atom bomb. The electric light, telephone, television, automobile, and airplane were invented during his life. In short, Dewey's lifetime was a period of unprecedented and far-reaching change in America and the world.

John Dewey was born in Burlington, Vermont, in 1859, the third of the four sons of Archibald and Lucina Rich Dewey. His parents were third-generation Vermonters, and each had been born and raised on a family farm before moving to Burlington, where John's father became a grocer. With the exception of a winter spent in war-torn northern Virginia, where his father was a quartermaster of a Vermont cavalry regiment, Dewey's childhood was spent in Vermont. There he boated on Lake Champlain and hiked in the Adirondacks, delivered newspapers and tallied lumber, joined the First Congregational Church at age eleven (at his mother's urging), and did well in public school, though he found it routine and dull. Dewey began high school in 1872, and completed in three years the four-college preparatory course in Latin, Greek, French, English grammar and literature, and mathematics.

At the age of fifteen, Dewey entered the University of Vermont, from which he graduated with seventeen classmates in 1879. In addition to continuing his classical education, Dewey studied evolutionary thought and the philosophies of the German idealists, the Scottish realists, and the intuitionalists. He was also, indeed mainly, stimulated by his extracurricular reading of contemporary English periodicals and their discussions of evolution and the relation of science to traditional values. Following graduation with honors, Dewey taught high school for two years in Oil City, Pennsylvania, developing his lifelong interest in schools and the educational process, and committing himself to further study of philosophy. Dewey spent the following year teaching in a village school near Burlington and studying philosophy on a tutorial basis. At this time he sent an essay, "The Metaphysical Assumptions of Materialism," to W. T. Harris, editor of *Speculative Philosophy*. Harris accepted the article (and, later, two others) and, in response to Dewey's questions, encouraged him to pursue a career in philosophy. Dewey decided on the new graduate school at Johns Hopkins University: he applied for a fellowship, which he did not receive, then applied for a smaller scholarship, which again he did not receive, and, after borrowing $500 from an aunt, finally began the graduate program without aid.

At Johns Hopkins, Dewey studied history and political science (which he found insufficiently philosophical) in addition to philosophy and psychology. He studied logic under Charles Peirce, but had little interest *at this time* in Peirce's important work. He was greatly stimulated, on the other hand, by his work with George S. Morris, whose personality deeply influenced and impressed Dewey, and whose positions Dewey came to adopt at this time. Dewey's early Congregational evangelicalism and undergraduate intuitionalism were rapidly replaced by neo-Hegelian idealism, by a view of reality as an organic unity, and by Morris's mixture of Hegelian and Aristotelian logic (which he called "real" as opposed to "formal" logic). The influence of Morris, according to Dewey, was reenforced both by the general movement of philosophy in this direction (and away from atomistic individualism and sensationalistic empiricism) and by Dewey's own emotional makeup. Terming his earlier study of philosophy a mere "intellectual gymnastic," Dewey described Hegel's synthesis as an "immense release" and a "liberation": ". . . it supplied a demand for unification that was doubtless an intense emotional craving, and yet was a hunger that only an intellectualized subject could easily satisfy."[4] Long after he had abandoned Hegelian idealism for a more naturalistic, experiential view of existence and a more pragmatic, instrumental account of logic and inquiry, Dewey wrote that "acquaintance with Hegel has left a permanent deposit in my thinking."[5] Morris, impressed by Dewey, proved influential in other ways as well: he helped Dewey secure teaching experience and, at last, a fellowship; following Dewey's receipt of the Ph.D. in 1884, Morris was influential in obtaining for Dewey an instructorship at the University of Michigan.

With the exception of a year at the University of Minnesota, Dewey spent the next ten years at the University of Michigan. During this time, Dewey published his *Psychology*, an attempt to combine empirical physiological psychology with philosophical idealism, as well as a study of the philosophy of Leibniz and many articles on idealism, ethics, and education. Here too Dewey began his long friendships and collaboration with James Tufts and George Herbert Mead (whose large influence on his thinking Dewey frequently acknowledged). Dewey married Alice Chipman in 1886; three children were born to them in Michigan, and three more were born following the family move to Chicago.

In 1894, Dewey moved to the University of Chicago to accept a professorship in philosophy and the chairmanship of the Department of Philosophy, Psychology, and Education. Dewey's ten years in Chicago were productive, eventful, and important. The gradual shift begun at Michigan from idealism to pragmatism and instrumentalism became complete during his Chicago years, galvanized by his study of William James's *Principles of Psychology* (which had appeared in 1890). Dewey clearly acknowledged the importance of James's work both in the development of his thinking and in the development of American pragmatism more generally. Referring to James's *Principles* as "the great exception to what was said about no very fundamental vital influence issuing from books," Dewey writes: "The objective biological approach of the Jamesian psychology led straight to the perception of the importance of distinctive social categories, especially communication and participation. It is my conviction that a great deal of our philosophizing needs to be done over again from this point of view, and that there will ultimately result an integrated synthesis in a philosophy congruous with modern science and related to actual needs in education, morals, and religion."[6] Following James, Dewey claims in "The Development of American Pragmatism" that the fundamental categories of perception and conception are sustained by and in their value in application to concrete experiences: "It is therefore not the origin of a concept, it is its application which becomes the criterion of its value; and here we have the whole of pragmatism in embryo."[7]

Dewey's publications during his Chicago years reflect James's influence, make evident his shift from an idealistic psychology to one increasingly behavioristic and social, mark the further development of his pragmatism and instrumentalism, and attest to his continuing interest in educational and social problems. Dewey's work and philosophical orientation dovetailed with that of other important thinkers (including Mead, Tufts, Addison Moore, and Edward Scribner Ames) in a variety of disciplines at Chicago. The publication in 1903 of *Studies in Logical Theory,* with essays by Dewey and others at Chicago, led William James to speak of the "Chicago School" (with Dewey its acknowledged leader) and of the ascendancy of pragmatism in American philosophy.

Dewey's work at Chicago also included his founding of an elementary school, sponsored and supervised by the Department of Philosophy and known as the "laboratory school" or, popularly, the "Dewey school." More than a laboratory for teaching methods, the world-famous school was a vehicle for and focus of cultural inquiry. The theory and aims of the education at this school are generalized in Dewey's *The School and Society* (1900) and *The Child and the Curriculum* (1902). Dewey also worked with supervisors of the Chicago public schools and with Jane Addams at the well-known Hull House, a settlement house seeking to ameliorate the urban problems facing America's immigrants. Despite his many successes and accomplishments, the Chicago years were not without tragedy for Dewey: his third child died in 1895 at the age of two, and his fourth child died at the age of eight in 1904 (after which the Deweys adopted an orphaned boy in Italy). Furthermore, personal, financial, and political problems within the university culminated in an unpleasant end to the laboratory school and Alice Dewey's work there: it was merged with the Chicago Institute, directed by the University School of Education. Following this, Dewey resigned at once and shortly thereafter accepted a professorship of philosophy at Columbia University in New York City.

Dewey taught at Columbia University and its Teachers College from 1904 until his retirement in 1930, continuing to make New York City his home until his death in 1952. His activities and accomplishments during this time are staggering. His participation in civic, national, and international affairs greatly increased. His work at Teachers College helped spread progressive education throughout the United States, and his writings, lectures, and travels spurred educational changes in many foreign countries, including Japan, China, Turkey, Mexico, and the U.S.S.R Concerned for academic autonomy and freedom of inquiry, he founded the American Association of University Professors, was involved in the founding of the teacher union movement in New York City, and was a charter member of the New York Teacher's Guild of the American Federation of Teachers. In 1937, at age seventy-eight, Dewey served impressively in Mexico as chairman of the Commission of Inquiry into the Charges Made Against Leon Trotsky in the Moscow Trials. Throughout these years, Dewey wrote voluminously on public affairs and current issues for popular magazines and journals such as *The New Republic*. Despite these activities, Dewey found time for his most important philosophical lecturing and writing during this period. A mere listing of this work[8] demonstrates the depth, scope, and sheer volume of Dewey's philosophical output (which continued past supposed "farewell celebrations" in 1929, 1939, and 1949). Almost all of the selections below are drawn from these writings.

Alice Dewey died in 1927 of arteriosclerosis, having perhaps never fully recovered from the death of her two children and the loss of her involvement and position at the Chicago laboratory school. In 1946, Dewey married Roberta Grant, whose family came from Oil City and had known Dewey for many years. Two children were adopted during John's marriage with Roberta. Dewey enjoyed good health and remained active into his nineties, as his correspondence and publications indicate. He suffered a broken hip while playing with his children in the late autumn of 1951, following his ninety-second birthday; while recovering, he became ill with pneumonia on May 31, 1952, and died the next day.

## The Nature and Aims of Philosophy

... philosophy is inherently criticism, having its distinctive position among various modes of criticism in its generality; a criticism of criticism, as it were. Criticism is discriminating judgment, careful appraisal, and judgment is appropriately termed criticism wherever the subject-matter of discrimination concerns goods or values.

... philosophy is and can be nothing but this critical operation and function become aware of itself and its implications, pursued deliberately and systematically. It starts from actual situations of belief, conduct and appreciative perception which are characterized by immediate qualities of good and bad, and from the modes of critical judgment current at any given time in all the regions of value; these are its data, its subject-matter. These values, criticisms, and critical methods, it subjects to further criticism as comprehensive and consistent as possible. The function is to regulate the further appreciation of goods and bads; to give greater freedom and security in those acts of direct selection, appropriation, identification and of rejection, elimination, destruction which enstate and which exclude objects of belief, conduct and contemplation.[9]

The social and moral effects of the separation of theory and practice have been merely hinted at. They are so manifold and so pervasive that an adequate consideration of them would involve nothing less than a survey of the whole field of morals, economics and politics. It cannot be justly stated that these effects are in fact direct consequences of the quest for certainty by thought and knowledge isolated from action. For, as we have seen, this quest was itself a reflex product of actual conditions. But it may be truly asserted that this quest, undertaken in religion and philosophy, has had results which have reinforced the conditions which originally brought it about. Moreover, search for safety and consolation amid the perils of life by means other than intelligent action, by feeling and thought alone, began when actual means of control were lacking, when arts were undeveloped. It had then a relative historic justification that is now lacking. The primary problem for thinking which lays claim to be philosophic in its breadth and depth is to assist in bringing about a reconstruction of all beliefs rooted in a basic separation of knowledge and action; to develop a system of operative ideas congruous with present knowledge and with present facilities of control over natural events and energies.[10]

The sort of thing the philosophers of an earlier period did is now done; in substance it is no longer called for. Persistence in repetition of a work that has little or no significance in the life-conditions (including those of physical science) that now exist is as sure a way as could be found for promoting the remoteness of philosophy from human concerns which is already tending to alienate popular regard and esteem by reducing philosophy to a kind of highly professionalized busy-work. In the meantime, there is a kind of intellectual work to be done which it is of utmost importance to mankind to have done, but which from the general human point of view does not need to be done in the name of philosophy provided only that it be done. From the standpoint of philosophy, that is philosophers, it may not be a matter of life or death but it is a matter of self-respect as well as of popular esteem.[11]

Dewey's work constitutes a sweeping reconstruction of philosophy itself. As a result, any attempt to grasp his thought must include an understanding of his view of the nature of philosophy. What is philosophy, according to Dewey? To begin, Dewey emphasizes that philosophy—

like the arts, scientific experimentation, politics, business, sports, and sex—is a human activity: it is an undertaking, a "doing," something that we engage in and undergo. As a reflective activity, moreover, it is purposeful, and thus intrinsically connected to the situation that called forth the reflection. A philosophy thus is situated in experience, and experience in turn supplies the criteria for its evaluation. While this may seem obvious, this view is anything but common in the history of philosophy. As a meaningful, purposeful human activity, philosophy is essentially temporal and spatial: it is historically and culturally located, and this location constitutes and is intrinsic to it. So, the problems, terminology, methods, arguments, and positions of previous philosophers were shaped by and in turn shaped the cultural conditions and problems of the day. Philosophers at present, Dewey insists, also function in intrinsic connection to and through contemporary situations, events, difficulties, and values. These connections, for Dewey, are not bonds that must be broken so as to build a philosophy more true, pure, or eternal. Rather, they define and constitute the context in and through which philosophies as definite historical, cultural occurrences have meaning and mark change.

The implications of this view are profound and far-reaching. Stated negatively, philosophy, for Dewey, is not the achievement of, or even the quest for, certainty. It cannot and does not begin in total doubt or some presuppositionless state and it issues in no absolute knowledge or eternal truths. It does not provide knowledge of supposed final causes or some ultimate, transcendent reality. It concerns no special, self-contained, disciplinary subject matter, problems that are philosophical rather than, for example, psychological, social, economic, biological. It is not a form of disinterested contemplation, a passive mirroring of reality, a spectator sport or form of intellectual voyeurism uninvolved intrinsically with experienced problems and efforts to ameliorate them.

Stated positively, Dewey understands philosophy as follows. First, the ultimate *subject matter* of philosophy is experience and its problems. "Reference to the primacy and ultimacy of the material of ordinary experience protects us," Dewey writes, "from creating artificial problems which deflect the energy and attention of philosophers from the real problems that arise out of actual subject-matter."[12] It is in this spirit that Dewey praises Ralph Waldo Emerson for judging every philosophy by its reference to the immediacies of life[13] and reminds us that philosophy must not be a study of philosophy, but a study, by means of philosophy, of life-experience and our beliefs about and in this experience.[14] This point is made forcefully in *Reconstruction in Philosophy:*

> Instead of the disputes of rivals about the nature of reality, we have the scene of human clash of social purpose and aspirations. Instead of impossible attempts to transcend experience, we have the significant record of the efforts of men to formulate the things of experience to which they are most deeply and passionately attached. Instead of impersonal and purely speculative endeavors to contemplate as remote beholders the nature of absolute things-in-themselves, we have a living picture of the choice of thoughtful men about what they would have life to be, and to what ends they would have men shape their intelligent activities.
>
> . . . When it is acknowledged that under disguise of dealing with ultimate reality, philosophy has been occupied with the precious values embedded in social traditions, that it has sprung from a clash of social ends and from a conflict of inherited institutions with incompatible contemporary tendencies, it will be seen that the task of future philosophy is to clarify men's ideas as to the social and moral strifes of their own day. Its aim is to become so far as is humanly possible an organ for dealing with these conflicts.[15]

Second, the *method* of philosophy, accordingly, is empirical and critical. It is the systematic attempt to intelligently assess experienced values (evident in perception belief, and action), judgments about these values, and methods of making such judgments. Dewey writes:

> . . . the business of philosophy is *criticism of belief* . . . so widely current socially as to be dominant factors in culture. Methods of critical inquiry mark . . . a philosopher, but the subject-matter

with which he deals is not his own. The beliefs themselves are social products, social facts and social forces.[16]

This critical method, for Dewey, is experimental and scientific in the sense in which " 'scientific' means regular methods of controlling the formation of judgments regarding some subject-matter."[17] Dewey contrasts this notion of philosophy as method with the earlier view of philosophy as system: philosophy is primarily method, and system only as method establishes an arrangement of problems and ideas as conducive to further inquiry and critical understanding of concrete problems.[18]

Third, the *orientation* of philosophy is thus pragmatic: it is called forth by and in experienced problems, and its consequences in action directed at these problems are the measure of its success and its truth. As such, philosophy is instrumental rather than final:[19]

> The experimental method of modern science, its erection into the ultimate mode of verification, is simply this fact obtaining recognition. Only action can reconcile the old, the general, and the permanent with the changing, the individual, and the new. It is action as progress, as development, making over the wealth of the past into capital with which to do an enlarging and freer business, which alone can find its way out of the cul-de-sac of the theory of knowledge. . . . Then the dominating interest becomes the *use* of knowledge; the conditions under which and ways in which it may be most organically and effectively employed to direct conduct.[20]

> When the practice of knowledge ceased to be dialectical and became experimental, knowing became preoccupied with changes and the test of knowledge became the ability to bring about certain changes. Knowing, for experimental sciences, means a certain kind of intelligently conducted doing; it ceases to be contemplative and becomes in a true sense practical. Now this implies that philosophy, unless it is to undergo a complete break with the authorized spirit of science, must also alter its nature. It must assume a practical nature; it must become operative and experimental.[21]

Action, then, not only yields or establishes truth, but is central to the very meaning of truth:

> Just as to say an idea was true all the time is a way of saying *in retrospect* that it has come out in a certain fashion, so to say that an idea is "eternally true" is to indicate *prospective* modes of application which are indefinitely anticipated. Its meaning, therefore, is strictly pragmatic. It does not indicate a property inherent in the idea as intellectualized existence, but denotes a property of use and employment. Always at hand when needed is a good enough eternal for reasonably minded persons.[22]

Fourth, philosophy, understood as the *result* of this critical method in action, is intrinsically connected to the cultural context in which this method operates. Dewey writes:

> Even in considering the nature of a philosophy we cannot get away from the biological idea of human activity as a response to an environment, in this case a reflective response to a social environment. We cannot understand an act, whether overt or reflective, unless we understand the medium in which it occurs and to which it is a response.[23]

The cultural context of a philosophy—be it an elucidation of meaning, an analysis of concepts, an interpretation of other thinkers, or a recommendation of policies—is an intrinsic aspect of that philosophy. Contexts vary, but some context always exists (even if ignored). Accordingly, the task of philosophy is the critical transformation of the context in which it is called forth, and not the denial of this context in the name of eternal truth, presuppositionless thought, or acultural analysis. It is this spirit that Dewey suggested that *Reconstruction in Philosophy* should be renamed *Reconstruction of Philosophy:* ". . . the distinctive office, problems, and subjectmatter of philosophy grow out of stresses and strains in the community life in which a given form of philosophy arises, and . . . its specific problems vary with the changes in human life that are always going on. . . ."[24]

# A Philosophy of Experience

Two things have rendered possible a new conception of experience and a new conception of the relation of reason to experience, or, more accurately, of the place of reason *in* experience. The primary factor is the change that has taken place in the actual nature of experience, its contents and methods, as it is actually lived. The other is the development of a psychology based upon biology which makes possible a new scientific formulation of the nature of experience.[25]

Thus the value of the notion of experience for philosophic reflection is that it denotes both the field, the sun and clouds and rain, seeds, and harvest, and the man who labors, who plans, invents, uses, suffers, and enjoys. Experience denotes what is experienced, the world of events and persons; and it denotes that world caught up into experiencing, the career and destiny of mankind. Nature's place in man is no less significant than man's place in nature. Man in nature is man subjected; nature in man, recognized and used, is intelligence and art.[26]

In short, the requirement is that we shall think things as they are themselves, not make them into objects constructed by thinking.[27]

Given the above understanding of the nature and tasks of philosophy, perhaps it is not surprising that Dewey's view of experience stands at the center of his philosophy and informs his writings on issues in education, politics, economics, society, morals, art, and religion. At the outset, it is vital to distinguish Dewey's theory of experience and his "empiricism" from the philosophical traditions and theories which he seeks to overcome and abandon. Dewey's major criticisms of traditional empiricism are neatly summarized in "The Need for a Recovery of Philosophy" (included in the selections below). Here Dewey rejects the traditional view of experience as something subjective and psychical, as "particularistic" or composed of discrete sense data assembled by the understanding, as primarily an affair of knowing, as directed primarily at the past, and as something separate from and opposed to thought.

How, then, does Dewey positively characterize experience? In beginning to understand his view, it cannot be overemphasized that Dewey is not using the word "experience" in its conventional sense. For Dewey, experience is not to be understood in terms of the experienc*ing* subject, or as the interaction of a subject and object that exist separate from their interaction. Instead, Dewey's view is radically empirical:[28] experience is an activity in which subject and object are unified and *constituted* as partial features and relations within this ongoing, unanalyzed unity. Dewey warns us not to misconstrue aspects of this unified experience-activity: distinctions made in reflection do not refer to things that exist as separate substances prior to and outside of that reflection. If we do confuse them, we invent the philosophical problem of how to get them together:

What has been completely divided in philosophical discourse into man *and* world, inner *and* outer, self *and* not-self, subject *and* object, individual *and* social, private *and* public, etc., are in actuality parties in life-transactions. The philosophical 'problem' of trying to get them together is artificial. On the basis of fact, it needs to be replaced by consideration of the conditions under which they occur as *distinctions,* and of the special uses served by the distinctions.[29]

The error of materialist and idealist alike—the error of conferring existential status upon the products of reflection—is the result of neglect of the context of reflection on experience. Philosophers frequently have ignored or overextended this context:

The trouble is not with analysis, but with the philosopher who ignores the context in which and for the sake of which the analysis occurs. In this sense, a characteristic defect of philosophy *is* connected with analysis. There are a multitude of ways of commiting the analytic fallacy. It is found whenever the distinctions or elements that are discriminated are treated as if they were final and self-sufficient.[30]

. . . every generalization occurs under limiting conditions set by the contextual situation. When this fact is passed over . . . a principle valid under specifiable conditions is perforce extended without limit. . . . All statements about the universe as a whole, reality as an unconditioned unity, involve the same fallacy. There is genuine meaning in the act of inquiry into the reality of a given situation. . . . Within the limits of context found in any valid inquiry, "reality" thus means the confirmed outcome, actual or potential, or the inquiry that is undertaken. . . . When "reality" is sought for at large, it is without intellectual import. . . . Results of inquiry are in these philosophers *ipso facto* converted into a sweeping metaphysical doctrine.[31]

The context of reflection on experience includes, for Dewey, at least those aspects he terms "background" and "selective interest." Background constitutes the tacit framework, the setting, the taken-for-granted in any reflection. (Of course, this "given" may become problematic and thus be the subject matter of some other reflection.) Reflection—indeed, all experience—is saturated with the results of past reflection; reflection is never presuppositionless, and experience is always "funded." Selective interest, the concerns or attitude of a subject, is not the subject matter of reflection but rather determines or selects the actual subject matter of reflection. Thus, Dewey writes that the subject, while implicated in all thinking, cannot entirely be made an explicit object of thought, but, since it affects all thought, must be seen as an aspect of context.[32] Selective interest, when acknowledged, does not lead to the impossibility of scientific inquiry or some sort of philosophical subjectivism: "To be objective," Dewey writes, "is to have a certain sort of selective interest operative."[33] Philosophy, then, is not an attempt to transcend or escape all selective interest, but instead to adopt that standpoint which enables us to deal with our problems. Similarly, an account or philosophy of experience arises from within experience itself, from selective interests within a background.

When reflection recognizes this, the primary unity of experience is evident:

> An organism does not live *in* an environment; it lives by means of an environment. . . . The processes of living are enacted by the environment as truly as by the organism; for they *are* an integration.[34]

> . . . natural operations like breathing and digesting, acquired ones like speech and honesty, are functions of the surroundings as truly as of a person. They are the things done by the environment by means of organic structures or acquired dispositions.[35]

> "Environment" is not something around and about human activities in an external sense; it is their *medium,* or *milieu,* in the sense in which a *medium* is *inter*-mediate in the execution or carrying out of human activities, as well as being the channel *through* which they move and the *vehicle by* which they go on.[36]

Dewey stressed this point throughout his work. It is evident in his early writings, such as his famous essay "The Reflex Arc Concept in Psychology:" ". . . the reflex arc idea, as commonly employed, is defective in that is assumes sensory stimulus and motor response as distinct psychical existences, while in reality they are always inside a co-ordination and have their significance purely from the part played in. . . .the co-ordination."[37] It is evident in his last book, *Knowing and the Known,* wherein he terms experience "transactional" rather than "interactional" in an effort to emphasize the unity of subject and object in experience: "Our position is that the traditional language . . . shatters the subject-matter into fragments in advance of inquiry and thus destroys instead of furthering comprehensive observation of it."[38] And it is evident in his 1951 Introduction for a reissue of *Experience and Nature:*

> Were I to write (or rewrite) *Experience and Nature* today I would entitle the book *Culture and Nature* . . . because of my growing realization that the historical obstacles which prevented understanding of my use of "experience" are, for all practical purposes, insurmountable. I would substitute the term "culture" . . . to designate the inclusive subject-matter which characteristically "mod-

ern" (post-medieval) philosophy breaks up into dualisms of subject and object, mind and the world, psychological and physical. . . .

It is a prime philosophical consideration that "culture" includes the material and the ideal in their reciprocal interrelationships and (in marked contrast with the prevailing use of "experience") "culture" designates, also in their reciprocal interconnections, that immense diversity of human affairs, interests, concerns, values which compartmentalists pigeonhole under "religion" "aesthetics" "politics" "economics" etc., etc.[39]

In this light, Dewey characterizes experience and its pervasive, generic traits. Dewey develops these points in great detail, and I shall do little more than list them here. First, experience is eventful, active, precarious, and hazardous. Even that which is stable and fixed is merely stable relative to specifiable changes, and is not absolutely stable. Traditional philosophies have denied this in their quests for certainty, their attempts to make stability of meanings and values prevail over the instability of actual experience by converting valued characteristics to be made good in that experience into a metaphysics of an antecedently sure and fixed existence. In longing for a perfect or safe world, that is, philosophers have claimed ultimate reality for their values and have turned the goals of experience into the antecedently existing causal conditions of that experience. Despite this, experience—the unity of experienc*ing* subject and experienc*ed* object—is undeniably precarious, changing, unsettled.

Second, experience is continuous. Experience not only is eventful, it undergoes change itself. That is, experience is not simply a succession of events; rather, these events have a temporal connection and relation. Experience is connected, conjoining and disjoining, resisting and yielding, modifying and being influenced, organized and confused, planned and surprising. Connections, changes, continuities, relations, changing-in-the-direction-of and being-in-transition-toward are pervasive, experienced features of experience. Events interact and transform one another.

Third, experience is not merely changing and continuous; it is historical. Experience, that is, is not an undifferentiated flow; rather, Dewey says, it consists of experiences, affairs with beginnings and endings, initiations and consummations. As such, there are no final ends *for* experience (as traditional teleological philosophies and religions hold), but only ends-in-view (and means to them) *within* experience. Nor is there fate (as mechanists hold), but only orders within historical events—orders that we can control so as to achieve particular ends.

Fourth, experience is qualitative: within each experience there is an immediate, individual, brute quality, a quality that renders an experience *that* particular experience—*that* meal, *that* snowstorm, *that* philosophy lecture, and so on. This qualitative aspect of experience is not an object of knowledge; indeed, Dewey says that qualitative dimension of experience cannot be known or communicated, since the objects of knowledge are mediate rather than immediate, concern the relations among experiences and not the immediate quality of an experience. This qualitative character of experience is not something subjective, for experience is not something subjective: qualities belong as much to the things experienced as to the experiencing subject.[40] So, a particular experience, as it occurs, simply is; that particular experience, as it is connected by reflection to things beyond itself, becomes a sign and refers.

Fifth, this leads to a further characterization of experience: it is experimental and practical. Reflection may make an experience its object, and this attention to the experience as it is related to and indicative of something else makes possible the control of experience. We may, for instance, focus not on the painfulness of a situation as immediate quality, but on the pain as an indication of the presence of certain other conditions, which we may then alter so as to end the pain. It is in this sense that Dewey defines inquiry as the transformation of a situation, identifies the subject matter of inquiry as the conditions upon which the occurrence of (qualitative) experience depends, characterizes knowing as instrumental, and explains that truth is simply the process of verification taken as a product. In this sense, truth is consequential and "made," rather than fixed, and reality (for Dewey as for Peirce) is that which reflective inquiry is forced to reach rather than something given antecedent to it.

Sixth, implicit in the above is the claim that experience is meaningful: communication pervades experience, events become objects with meaning, experience is "funded." The relations and consequences of an object, as determined in inquiry, can become the very meaning (both referential and immanent) of the thing itself. Inquiry may show, for example, that a creaking sound indicates—referentially means—a splitting mast. But this relation may also enter into the nature—the immanent or "had" meaning—of the sound itself, as the sound comes to be heard as the sound of the mast splitting. For Dewey, these transformations are due to language: it is "(1) the agency by which other institutions and acquired habits are *transmitted*," "(2) it *permeates* both the forms and the contents of all other cultural activities," and "(3) it has its own distinctive structure which is capable of abstraction as form."[41] And language, Dewey stresses, operates in and through the behavior or action of a social group or community.

Seventh, in this sense experience is social. Dewey's point here is not simply that one lives with others. In addition, he is claiming that social meanings, conditions, and forms of life enter into and constitute the individual; individual and environment are constituted in and by the inclusive unity of experience or culture. We are creatures of habit, Dewey asserts, and habits, as results of social conditions and demands for certain kinds of activity, constitute the self.[42] Ironically, this fundamental social character of the self is overlooked or denied by much social philosophy:

> The underlying philosophy and psychology of earlier liberalism led to a conception of individuality as something ready-made, already possessed, and needing only the removal of certain legal restrictions to come into full play. It was not conceived as a moving thing, something that is attained only by continuous growth. Because of this failure, the dependence in fact of individuals upon social conditions was made little of . . . social arrangements and institutions were thought of as things that operate from without, not entering in any significant way into the internal make-up of individuals.[43]

The individual mind, however, is not "individual" but social: its observations, beliefs, meanings, and values are formed by and exist in and through social processes. Thus, Dewey claims in *Philosophy and Civilization* that the social is *the* inclusive philosophic idea: the physical, organic, mental, and individual are distinctions that fall within it and function "only where association is manifested in the form of participation and communication."[44]

## The Reconstruction of Culture

> American philosophy must be born out of and must repond to the demands of democracy, as democracy strives to voice and to achieve itself on a vaster scale, and in a more thorough and final way than history has previously witnessed. And, democracy is something at once too subtle and too complex and too aspiring to be caught in the meshes of a single philosophical school or sect.
>
> It is, then, to the needs of democracy in America that we turn to find the fundamental problems of philosophy; and to its tendencies, its working forces, that we look for the points of view and the terms in which philosophy will envisage and solve these problems.[45]

> The beginning of a culture stripped of egoistic illusions is the perception that we have as yet no culture; that our culture is something to achieve, to create. . . .
>
> To set up as protector of a shrinking classicism requires only the accidents of a learned education, the possession of leisure and a reasonably apt memory for some phrases, and a facile pen for others. To transmute a society built on an industry which is not yet humanized into a society which wields its knowledge and its industrial power in behalf of a democratic culture requires the courage of an inspired imagination.[46]

We have the physical tools of communication as never before. The thoughts and aspirations congruous with them are not communicated, and hence are not common. Without such communication the public will remain shadowy and formless, seeking spasmodically for itself, but seizing and holding its shadow rather than its substance. Till the Great Society is converted into a Great Community, the Public will remain in eclipse. Communication can alone create a great community. Our Babel is not one of tongues but of the signs and symbols without which shared experience is impossible.[47]

Dewey's important writings on education, ethics, politics, art, and religion are rooted in the view and method of experience outlined above and constitute a *reconstruction,* a reconstruction of both our thinking and our society. Dewey is critically rethinking our dominant beliefs and institutions, arguing that they are founded on faulty conceptions of experience, and are obsolete, irrelevant, and detrimental in light of changes in the actual conditions of contemporary life. These two kinds of arguments run throughout Dewey's work. He constantly faults *theorists* who have invented problems by converting interrelated aspects in experience (and distinguished by reflection) into opposed entitites with separate existence (prior to reflection). Thus, for example, Dewey rejects educational policies that begin with a fixed opposition between child and curriculum, school and society, and education and life. He rejects ethical theories erected on the opposition between means and ends, and criticizes political philosophies and programs rooted in a metaphysical separation of individual and society, and private and public interest. He criticizes the split between aesthetic experience and ordinary life, between art and everyday objects, and between creation and appreciation. And, he rejects the identification of the religious with the supernatural and its underlying dichotomy of natural and divine realms. These dualisms are without basis in actual experience. As such, they give rise to artificial problems that divert our energies; they should be abandoned.

Dewey also constantly faults *institutions* and *practices* that fail to acknowledge and adapt to the changing cultural situation in and through which they exist and operate, and so present themselves as embodying eternal, ahistorical truths. As conditions change—and Dewey thinks they have changed rapidly—these ways of life become outdated, disintegrated with actual life conditions, and detrimental to achievement of shared human purposes. Thus, Dewey rejects and seeks to reconstruct, for example, traditional notions of education, individualism, community, liberalism, the free market, democracy, God, and the religious and aesthetic dimensions of experience.

These general lines of argument are evident in Dewey's writings. These writings are extensive, and I shall simply highlight some of the major instances of these arguments and their conclusions. To begin, Dewey's notion of growth is central to his influential work in education, and his views on education are central to his writings on democracy, community, and the nature of philosophy itself. Dewey defines growth as the cumulative movement of action toward a later result, and stresses that, as such, growth does not *have* an end but rather *is* an end. Accordingly, the educational process is one of continual reconstruction and self-transformation directed at no end beyond itself. (Here it is important to differentiate education in general from the schooling process or formal education.) Since growth, for Dewey, is one with life-experience (and not the end of life), growth is the criterion for assessing cultural practices: Dewey directs us to examine to what extent habits, relationships, practices, associations, institutions, and traditions promote growth and the desire for further growth, renew the meanings of experience, and harmoniously adjust individual and environment. The social environment, Dewey writes, "is truly educative in its effect in the degree in which an individual shares or participates in some conjoint activity" and becomes a "directive guardian" of this shared activity.[48] This makes clear the connection between democracy and education:

A society which makes provision for participation in its good of all its members on equal terms and which secures flexible readjustment of its institutions through interaction of the different forms of associated life is in so far democratic. Such a society must have a type of education which gives individuals a personal interest in social relationships and control, and the habits of mind which secure social changes without introducing disorder.[49]

Dewey's social and political writings focus on this task of creating a genuinely democratic society, a society in which individualism and community flourish. Individual and community, the private and the public do not stand in necessary opposition; instead, they require one another, and any opposition between them marks not a metaphysical fact but a historical social problem that demands conceptual and political reconstruction. This reconstruction is needed, Dewey argues, because rapid cultural change has submerged the individual by overturning the traditional loyalties and attachments that constitute the basis of real individuality. This reconstructive action has been paralyzed by traditional conceptions of individuality as something "ready-made" and in need only of being unrestricted, and so served by laissez-faire economic policies and traditional political liberalism. These traditional conceptions, blind to their own historical relativity and the developmental character of individuality, once may have served the goals of individuality, liberty, and intelligence, but now, under new conditions, effectively hinder the realization of these goals as they have actual meaning in these new conditions. Thus, Dewey writes:

> Above all, in identifying the extension of liberty in all of its modes with extension of their particular brand of economic liberty, they completely failed to anticipate the bearing of private control of the means of production and distribution upon the effective liberty of the masses in industry as well as in cultural goods.[50]

By contrast, liberty today, Dewey claims, must signify liberation, through the controlled use of science and technology, from material insecurity and economic coercion that prevent many from participating in the resources of our culture, that effectively inhibit genuine growth, and block the transition from a formal democracy to a genuine community.[51] The development of a new individualism, then, requires the creation of a community—what Dewey calls "the Great Community"—and this in turn requires the development and application of critical methods of scientific inquiry for dealing with complex, often technical, social problems.

Efforts to establish a community of and in experience are attempts to liberate experience, to create and extend the shared consummatory values and meanings in our lives. Dewey's writings on the aesthetic and religious dimensions of experience are two particularly rich instances of this. In *Art as Experience,* Dewey identifies art with experience that has a certain purposeful, consummatory, integrated, unified quality. This provides a basis for recovering the continuity between objects of art and everyday objects, and between aesthetic experience and daily living. The philosophic task, then, is pragmatic: it does not consist in efforts to compartmentalize experience or its objects, but in describing the aesthetic and the conditions upon which it depends. Dewey writes:

> A conception of fine art that sets out from its connection with discovered qualities of ordinary experience will be able to indicate the factors and forces that favor the normal development of common human activities into matters of artistic growth. It will also be able to point out those conditions that arrest its normal growth.[52]

In linking aesthetic experience with growth, Dewey connects it with the evaluation of society:

> Esthetic experience is always more than esthetic. In it a body of matters and meanings, not in themselves esthetic, *become* esthetic as they enter into an ordered rhythmic movement toward consummation. . . . The material of esthetic experience in being human—human in connection with the nature of which it is a part—is social. Esthetic experience is a manifestation, a record and celebra-

tion of the life of a civilization, a means of promoting its development, and is also the ultimate judgment upon the quality of a civilization.[53]

It is in the same spirit that Dewey carefully distinguishes between religion (as an institutionally organized body of beliefs and practices, often concerned with a supernatural power) and the religious quality of experience (as any "activity pursued in behalf of an ideal end against obstacles and in spite of threats of personal loss because of conviction of its general and enduring value"[54]). Again, this provides a basis for reconstructing continuities between the religious character of experience and everyday life, and for enlarging the latter by means of the former. The religious thus acquires a "human abode" and can be understood in a manner consistent with actual experience and methods of inquiry:

> I have said those things because of a firm belief that the claim on the part of religions to possess a monopoly of ideals and of the supernatural means by which alone, it is alleged, they can be furthered, stands in the way of realization of distinctively religious values inherent in natural experience.[55]

> Ours is the responsibility of conserving, transmitting, rectifying and expanding the heritage of values we have received that those who come after us may receive it more solid and secure, more widely accessible and more generously shared than we received it. Here are all the elements for a religious faith that shall not be confined to sect, class, or race. Such a faith has always been implicitly the common faith of mankind. It remains to make it explicit and militant.[56]

In large part, Dewey's views on cultural reconstruction still wait on our understanding and, above all, our action. Their ultimate and eventual importance, at least in Dewey's own view, must lie in their promotion and justification of this undertaking. Their ultimate value and truth must lie in this practice. The time is ripe, Dewey tells us, for this endeavor.

## Notes

References below are to the definitive edition of the works of John Dewey, and are abbreviated as follows: *EW* for *John Dewey: The Early Works, 1882–1885,* 5 vols. (Carbondale and Edwardsville: Southern Illinois University Press, 1969–1972); *MW* for *John Dewey: The Middle Works, 1899–1924,* 15 vols. (Carbondale and Edwardsville: Southern Illinois University Press, 1976–1983); *LW* for *John Dewey: The Later Works, 1925–1953,* 17 vols. (Carbondale and Edwardsville: Southern Illinois University Press, 1981–1990).

1. "Experience, Knowledge and Value: A Rejoinder," in *The Philosophy of John Dewey,* ed. Paul Arthur Schilpp (LaSalle, Ill.: Open Court, 1971), p. 521.
2. "From Absolutism to Experimentalism," LW 5: 155.
3. "James Marsh and American Philosophy," LW 5: 194.
4. "From Absolutism to Experimentalism," LW 5: 153.
5. Ibid., p. 154. See also the discussion of this period in Dewey's life in George Dykhuizen's *The Life and Mind of John Dewey* (Carbondale and Edwardsville: Southern Illinois University Press, 1973).
6. "From Absolutism to Experimentalism," LW 5: 159.
7. "The Development of American Pragmatism," LW 2: 16.
8. As a partial list: *How We Think* and *The Influence of Darwin and Other Essays on Contemporary Thought* in 1910; *Essays in Experimental Logic* and *Democracy and Education* in 1916; *Reconstruction in Philosophy* in 1920; *Human Nature and Conduct* in 1922; *Experience and Nature* in 1925, when Dewey was 65; *The Public and its Problems* in 1927; *The Quest for Certainty* in 1929; *Individualism: Old and New* in 1930; *Philosophy and Civilization* in 1931; the revised edition of *Ethics* with James Tufts in 1932; *Art as Experience* and *A Common Faith* in 1934; *Liberalism and Social Action* in 1935; *Logic: The Theory of Inquiry* and *Experience and Education* in 1938; *Freedom and Culture* and *Theory of Valuation* in 1939; *Problems of Men* in 1946; and, with Arthur Bentley, *Knowing and the Known* in 1949.
9. "Existence, Value and Criticism," in *Experience and Nature,* LW 1: 298, 302.

10. "The Construction of Good," in *The Quest for Certainty,* LW 4: 226.

11. Manuscript page in the John Dewey Papers housed in the Special Collections of Morris Library, Southern Illinois University at Carbondale, 102/58/10.

12. "Experience and Philosophic Method," in *Experience and Nature,* LW 1: 26. Included in the selections below, pp. 460–471.

13. "Emerson—the Philosopher of Democracy," *MW,* Vol. 3, p. 188. *MW 3: 188.*

14. "Experience and Philosophic Method," LW 1: 40. Included in the selections below, pp. 460–471.

15. "Changing Conceptions of Philosophy," in *Reconstruction in Philosophy,* MW 12: 94.

16. "Philosophy," LW 5: 164.

17. "Logical Conditions of a Scientific Treatment of Morality," MW 3: 3.

18. "Philosophy and American National Life," MW 3: 76–77. See also "The Significance of the Problem of Knowledge, EW 5: 22; and "The Pragmatism of Peirce," MW 10: 77.

19. "Philosophy and American National Life," MW 3: 76–77.

20. "The Significance of the Problem of Knowledge," EW 5: 21–22.

21. "Changed Conceptions of the Ideal and the Real," in *Reconstruction in Philosophy,* MW 12: 149.

22. "The Intellectual Criterion for Truth," MW 4: 71. See also "What Pragmatism Means by Practical," *MW* 4: 109.

23. "Philosophy," *LW* 5:163.

24. "Introduction: Reconstruction as Seen Twenty-Five Years Later," MW 12: 256. See also the discussion in "Philosophy and American National Life": ". . . a philosophy has to be conceived and stated in terms of conditions and factors that are moving generally in non-philosophic life" MW 3:73.

25. "Changed Conceptions of Experience and Reason," in *Reconstruction in Philosophy,* MW 12: 127–128. See also Dewey's discussion of Whitehead's substitution of the idea of organism for the idea of mechanism: "The Changing Intellectual Climate," LW 2: 233.

26. "Appendix 2: Experience and Philosophic Method," LW 1: 384.

27. Introduction to *Essays in Experimental Logic,* MW 10: 337.

28. See the discussions of radical empiricism above, pp. 4, 144, 181, and 234.

29. *Knowing and the Known* LW 16: 248.

30. "Context and Thought," LW 6: 6–7.

31. Ibid., LW 6: 8–9.

32. LW 6: 14 FF.

33. Ibid.

34. "The Existential Matrix of Inquiry: Biological," in *Logic: The Theory of Inquiry,* LW 12: 32.

35. "Habits as Social Functions," in *Human Nature and Conduct,* MW 14: 15.

36. *Knowing and the Known,* LW 16: 244.

37. "The Reflex Arc Concept in Psychology," *EW* 5: 99.

38. *Knowing and the Known,* LW 16: 67.

39. "Appendix I: The Unfinished Introduction" to *Experience and Nature,* pp. 361–363.

40. "Nature, Life and Body-Mind," in *Experience and Nature,* pp. 198ff.

41. "The Existential Matrix of Inquiry: Cultural," in *Logic: The Theory of Inquiry;* LW 12: 48–65. See also the discussion of communication in *Democracy and Education.* Dewey writes: "Society not only continues to exist *by* transmission, *by* communication, but it may fairly be said to exist *in* transmission, *in* communication" MW 9: 7.

42. See "The Place of Habit in Conduct," in *Human Nature and Conduct.*

43. *Liberalism and Social Action* (New York: Capricorn Books/G.P. Putnam's, 1935, 1963), p. 39 LW 11: 30.

44. See "The Inclusive Philosophic Idea," LW 3: 41–54.

45. "Philosophy and American National Life," MW 3: 73–74.

46. "American Education and Culture," MW 10: 198.

47. "The Eclipse of the Public," in *The Public and its Problems,* LW 2: 323–324.

48. *Democracy and Education,* MW 9: 26, 332.

49. Ibid., p. 105.

50. *Liberalism and Social Action,* pp. 35–36. LW 11: 25.

51. LW 11: 36. See also "Towards a New Individualism," in *Individualism: Old and New, LW* 5: 85–86.

52. *Art as Experience* LW 10: 17.

53. Ibid., p. 326. LW 10: 329.

54. *A Common Faith* LW 9: 19.

55. Ibid., pp. 27–28. LW 9: 19–20.

56. Ibid., p. 87. LW 9: 57–58.

# The Need for a Recovery of Philosophy

Intellectual advance occurs in two ways. At times increase of knowledge is organized about old conceptions, while these are expanded, elaborated and refined, but not seriously revised, much less abandoned. At other times, the increase of knowledge demands qualitative rather than quantitative change; alteration, not addition. Men's minds grow cold to their former intellectual concerns; ideas that were burning fade; interests that were urgent seem remote. Men face in another direction; their older perplexities are unreal; considerations passed over as negligible loom up. Former problems may not have been solved, but they no longer press for solution.

Philosophy is no exception to the rule. But it is unusually conservative—not, necessarily, in proffering solutions, but in clinging to problems. It has been so allied with theology and theological morals as representatives of men's chief interests, that radical alteration has been shocking. Men's activities took a decidedly new turn, for example, in the seventeenth century, and it seemed as if philosophy, under the lead of thinkers like Bacon and Descartes, was to execute an about-face. But, in spite of the ferment, it turned out that many of the older problems were but translated form Latin into the vernacular or into the new terminology furnished by science.

The association of philosophy with academic teaching has reinforced this intrinsic conservatism. Scholastic philosophy persisted in universities after men's thoughts outside of the walls of colleges had moved in other directions. In the last hundred years intellectual advances of science and politics have in like fashion been crystallized into material of instruction and now resist further change. I would not say that the spirit of teaching is hostile to that of liberal inquiry, but a philosophy which exists largely as something to be taught rather than wholly as something to be reflected upon is conducive to discussion of views held by others rather than to immediate response. Philosophy when taught inevitably magnifies the history of past thought, and leads professional philosophers to approach their subject-matter through its formulation in received systems. It tends, also, to emphasize points upon which men have divided into schools, for these lend themselves to retrospective definition and elaboration. Consequently, philosophical discussion is likely to be a dressing out of antithetical traditions, where criticism of one view is thought to afford proof of the truth of its opposite (as if formulation of views guaranteed logical exclusives). Direct preoccupation with contemporary difficulties is left to literature and politics.

If changing conduct and expanding knowledge ever required a willingness to surrender not merely old solutions but old problems it is now. I do not mean that we can turn abruptly away from all traditional issues. This is impossible; it would be the undoing of the one who attempted it. Irrespective of the professionalizing of philosophy, the ideas philosophers discuss are still those in which Western civilization has been bred. They are in the backs of the heads of educated people. But what serious-minded men not engaged in the professional business of philosophy most want to know is what modifications and abandonments of intellectual inheritance are required by the newer industrial, political, and scientific movements. They want to know what these newer movements mean when translated into general ideas. Unless professional philosophy can mobilize itself sufficiently to assist

From "The Need for a Recovery of Philosophy" in *John Dewey: The Middle Works, 1899–1924*, Vol. 10, Ed. Jo Ann Boydston (Carbondale and Edwardsville: Southern Illinois University, 1980 [1917]), pp. 3–11, 22–24, 37–48.

in this clarification and redirection of men's thoughts, it is likely to get more and more sidetracked from the main currents of contemporary life.

This essay may, then, be looked upon as an attempt to forward the emancipation of philosophy form too intimate and exclusive attachment to traditional problems. It is not in intent a criticism of various solutions that have been offered, but raises a question *as to the genuineness, under the present conditions of science and social life, of the problems.*

The limited object of my discussion will, doubtless, give an exaggerated impression of my conviction as to the artificiality of much recent philosophizing. Not that I have wilfully exaggerated in what I have said, but that the limitations of my purpose have led me not to say many things pertinent to a broader purpose. A discussion less restricted would strive to enforce the genuineness, in their own context, of questions now discussed mainly because they have been discussed rather than because contemporary conditions of life suggest them. It would also be a grateful task to dwell upon the precious contributions made by philosophic systems which as a whole are impossible. In the course of the development of unreal premises and the discussion of artificial problems, points of view have emerged which are indispensable possessions of culture. The horizon has been widened; ideas of great fecundity struck out; imagination quickened; a sense of the meaning of things created. It may even be asked whether these accompaniments of classic systems have not often been treated as a kind of guarantee of the systems themselves. But while it is a sign of an illiberal mind to throw away the fertile and ample ideas of a Spinoza, a Kant, or a Hegel, because their setting is not logically adequate, it is surely a sign of an undisciplined one to treat their contributions to culture as confirmations of premises with which they have no necessary connection.

———◦∞◦———

A criticism of current philosophizing from the standpoint of the traditional quality of its problems must begin somewhere, and the choice of a beginning is arbitrary. It has appeared to me that the notion of experience implied in the questions most actively discussed gives a natural point of departure. For, if I mistake not, it is just the inherited view of experience common to the empirical school and its opponents which keeps alive many discussions even of matters that on their face are quite remote from it, while it is also this view which is most untenable in the light of existing science and social practice. Accordingly I set out with a brief statement of some of the chief contrasts between the orthodox description of experience and that congenial to present conditions.

(i) In the orthodox view, experience is regarded primarily as a knowledge-affair. But to eyes not looking through ancient spectacles, it assuredly appears as an affair of the intercourse of a living being with its physical and social environment. (ii) According to tradition experience is (at least primarily) a psychical thing, infected throughout by "subjectivity." What experience suggests about itself is a genuinely objective world which enters into the actions and sufferings of men and undergoes modifications through their responses. (iii) So far as anything beyond a bare present is recognized by the established doctrine, the past exclusively counts. Registration of what has taken place, reference to precedent, is believed to be the essence of experience. Empiricism is conceived of as tied up to what has been, or is, "given." But experience in its vital form is experimental, an effort to change the given; it is characterized by projection, by reaching forward into the unknown; connexion with a future is its salient trait. (iv) The empirical tradition is committed to particularism. Connexions and continuities are supposed to be foreign to experience, to be by-products of dubious validity. An experience that is an undergoing of an environment and a striving for its control in new directions is pregnant with connexions. (v) In the traditional notion experience and thought are antithetical terms. Inference, so far as it is other than a revival of what has been given in the past, goes beyond experience; hence it is either invalid, or else a measure of desperation by which, using experience as a springboard, we jump out to a world of stable things and other selves. But experience, taken free of the restrictions imposed by the older concept, is full of inference. There is, apparently, no conscious experience without inference; reflection is native and constant.

These contrasts, with a consideration of the effect of substituting the account of experience relevant to modern life for the inherited account, afford the subject-matter of the following discussion.

Suppose we take seriously the contribution made to our idea of experience by biology,—not that recent biological science discovered the facts, but that it has so emphasized them that there is no longer an excuse for ignoring them or treating them as negligible. Any account of experience must now fit into the consideration that experiencing means living; and that living goes on in and because of an environing medium, not in a vacuum. Where there is experience, there is a living being. Where there is life, there is a double connexion maintained with the environment. In part, environmental energies constitute organic functions; they enter into them. Life is not possible without such direct support by the environment. But while all organic changes depend upon the natural energies of the environment for their origination and occurrence, the natural energies sometimes carry the organic functions prosperously forward, and sometimes act counter to their continuance. Growth and decay, health and disease, are alike continuous with activities of the natural surroundings. The difference lies in the bearing of what happens upon future life-activity. From the standpoint of this future reference environmental incidents fall into groups: those favorable to life-activities, and those hostile.

The successful activities of the organism, those within which environmental assistance is incorporated, react upon the environment to bring about modifications favorable to their own future. The human being has upon his hands the problem of responding to what is going on around him so that these changes will take one turn rather than another, namely,

that required by its own further functioning. While backed in part by the environment, its life is anything but a peaceful exhalation of environment. It is obliged to struggle—that is to say, to employ the direct support given by the environment in order indirectly to effect changes that would not otherwise occur. In this sense, life goes on by means of controlling the environment. Its activities must change the changes going on around it; they must neutralize hostile occurrences; they must transform neutral events into cooperative factors or into an efflorescence of new features.

Dialectic developments of the notion of self-preservation, of the *conatus essendi,* often ignore all the important facts of the actual process. They argue as if self-control, self-development, went on directly as a sort of unrolling push from within. But life endures only in virtue of the support of the environment. And since the environment is only incompletely enlisted in our behalf, self-preservation—or self-realization or whatever—is always indirect—always an affair of the way in which our present activities affect the direction taken by independent changes in the surroundings. Hindrances must be turned into means.

We are also given to playing loose with the conception of adjustment, as if that meant something fixed—a kind of accommodation once for all (ideally at least) of the organism *to* an environment. But as life requires the fitness of the environment to the organic functions, adjustment to the environment means not passive acceptance of the latter, but acting so that the environing changes take a certain turn. The "higher" the type of live, the more adjustment takes the form of an adjusting of the factors of the environment to one another in the interest of life; the less the significance of living, the more it becomes an adjustment to a given environment till at the lower end of the scale the differences between living and the non-living disappear.

These statements are of an external kind. They are about the conditions of experience, rather than about experiencing itself. But assuredly experience as it concretely takes place bears out the statements. Experience is primarily a process of undergoing: a process of standing something; of suffering and passion, of affection, in the literal sense of these words. The organism has to endure, to undergo, the consequences of its own actions. Experience is no slipping along in a path fixed by inner consciousness. Private consciousness is an incidental outcome of experience of a vital objective sort; it is not its source. Undergoing, however, is never mere passivity. The most patient patient is more than a receptor. He is also an agent—a reactor, one trying experiments, one concerned with undergoing in a way which may influence what is still to happen. Sheer endurance, side-steeping evasions, are, after all, ways of treating the environment with a view to what such treatment will accomplish. Even if we shut ourselves up in the most clam-like fashion, we are doing something; our passivity is an active attitude, not an extinction of response. Just as there is no assertive action, no aggressive attack upon things as they are, which is all action, so there is no undergoing which is not on our part also a going on and a going through.

Experience, in other words, is a matter of *simultaneous* doings and sufferings. Our undergoings are experiments in varying the course of events; our active tryings are trials and tests of ourselves. This duplicity of experience shows itself in our happiness and misery, our successes and failures. Triumphs are dangerous when dwelt upon or lived off from; successes use themselves up. Any achieved equilibrium of adjustment with the environment is precarious because we cannot evenly keep pace with changes in the environment. These are so opposed in direction that we must choose. We must take the risk of casting in our lot with one movement or the other. Nothing can eliminate all risk, all adventure; the one thing doomed to failure is to try to keep even with the whole environment at once—that is to say, to maintain the happy moment when all things go our way.

The obstacles which confront us are stimuli to variation, to novel response, and hence are occasions of progress. If a favor done us by the environment conceals a threat, so its disfavor is a potential means of hitherto unexperienced modes of success. To treat misery as anything but misery, as for example a blessing in disguise or a necessary factor in good, is disingenuous apologetics. But to say that the progress of the race has been stimulated by ills undergone, and that men have been moved by what they suffer to search out new and better courses of action is to speak veraciously.

The preoccupation of experience with things which are coming (are now coming, not just to come) is obvious to any one whose interest in experience is empirical. Since we live forward; since we live in a world where changes are going on whose issue means our weal or woe; since every act of ours modifies these changes and hence is fraught with promise, or charged with hostile energies—what should experience be but a future implicated in a present! Adjustment is no timeless state; it is a continuing process. To say that a change takes time may be to say something about the event which is external and uninstructive. But adjustment of organism to environment takes time in the pregnant sense; every step in the process is conditioned by reference to further changes which it effects. What is going on in the environment is the concern of the organism; not what is already "there" in accomplished and finished form. In so far as the issue of what is going on may be affected by intervention of the organism, the moving event is a challenge which stretches the agent-patient to meet what is coming. Experiencing exhibits things in their unterminated aspect moving toward determinate conclusions. The finished and done with is of import as affecting the future, not on its own account: in short, because it is not, really, done with.

Anticipation is therefore more primary than recollection; projection than summoning of the past; the prospective than the retrospective. Given a world like that in which we live, a world in which environing changes are partly favorable and partly callously indifferent, and experience is bound to be prospective in import; for any control attainable by the living creature depends upon what is done to alter the state of things. Success and failure are the primary "categories" of life; achieving of good and averting of ill are its supreme interests; hope and anxiety (which are not self-enclosed states of feeling, but active attitudes of welcome and wariness) are dominant qualities of experience. Imaginative forecast of the future is this forerunning quality of behavior rendered available for guidance in the present. Day-dreaming and castle-building and esthetic realization of what is not practically achieved are offshoots of this practical trait, or else practical intelligence is a chastened fantasy. It makes little difference. Imaginative recovery of the bygone is indispensable to successful invasion of the future, but its status is that of an instrument. To ignore its import is the sign of an undisciplined agent; but to isolate the past, dwelling upon it for its own sake and giving it to the eulogistic name of knowledge, is to substitute the reminiscence of old-age for effective intelligence. The movement of the agent-patient to meet the future is partial and passionate; yet detached and impartial study of the past is the only alternative to luck in assuring success to passion.

———

This description of experience would be but a rhapsodic celebration of the commonplace were it not in marked contrast to orthodox philosophical accounts. The contrast indicates that traditional accounts have not beem empirical, but have been deductions, from unnamed premises, of what experience *must* be. Historic empiricism has been empirical in a technical and controversial sense. It has said, Lord, Lord, Experience, Experience; but in practice it has served ideas *forced into* experience, not *gathered from* it. . . .

. . . The description of experience has been forced into conformity with this prior conception; it has been primarily a deduction from it, actual empirical facts being poured into the molds of the deductions. The characteristic feature of this prior notion is the assumption that experience centres in, or gathers about, or proceeds from a centre or subject which is outside the course of natural existence, and set over against it:—it being of no importance, for present purposes, whether this antithetical subject is termed soul, or spirit, or mind, or ego, or consciousness, or just knower or knowing subject. . . .

The problem of knowledge as conceived in the industry of epistemology is the problem of knowledge *in general*—of the possibility, extent, and validity of knowledge in general. What does this "in general" mean? In ordinary life there are problems a-plenty of knowledge in particular; every conclusion we try to reach, theoretical or practical, affords such a problem. But there is no problem of knowledge in general. I do not mean, of course, that general statements cannot be made about knowledge, or that the problem of attaining these general statements is not a genuine one. On the contrary, specific instances of success and failure in inquiry exist, and are of such a character that one can discover the conditions conducing to success and failure. Statement of these conditions constitutes logic, and is capable of being an important aid in proper guidance of further attempts at knowing. But this logical problem of knowledge is at the opposite pole from the epistemological. Specific problems are about right conclusions to be reached— which means, in effect, right ways of going about the business of inquiry. They imply a difference between knowledge and error consequent upon right and wrong methods of inquiry and testing; not a difference between experience and the world. The problem of knowledge *überhaupt* exits because it is assumed that there is a knower in general, who is outside of the world to be known, and who is defined in terms antithetical to the traits of the world. With analogous assumptions, we could invent and discuss a problem of digestion in general. All that would be required would be to conceive the stomach and food-material as inhabiting different worlds. Such an assumption would leave on our hands the question of the possibility, extent, nature, and genuineness of any transaction between stomach and food. . . .

What are the bearings of our discussion upon the conception of the present scope and office of philosophy? What do our conclusions indicate and demand with reference to philosophy itself? For the philosophy which reaches such conclusions regarding knowledge and mind must apply them, sincerely and whole-heartedly, to its idea of its own nature. For philosophy claims to be one form or mode of knowing. If, then, the conclusion is reached that knowing is a way of employing empirical occurrences with respect to increasing power to direct the consequences which flow from things, the application of the conclusion must be made to philosophy itself. It, too, becomes not a contemplative survey of existence nor an analysis of what is past and done with, but an outlook upon future possibilities with reference to attaining the better and averting the worse. Philosophy must take, with good grace, its own medicine.

It is easier to state the negative results of the changed idea of philosophy than the positive ones. The point that occurs to mind most readily is that philosophy will have to surrender all pretension to be peculiarly concerned with ultimate reality, or with reality as a complete (i.e., completed) whole: with *the* real object. The surrender is not easy of achievement. The philosophic tradition that comes to us from classic Greek thought and that was reinforced by Christian philosophy in the Middle Ages discriminates philosophical knowing from other modes of knowing by means of an alleged peculiarly intimate concern with supreme, ultimate, true reality. To deny his trait to philosophy seems to many to be the suicide of philosophy; to be a systematic adoption of skepticism or agnostic positivism. . . .

It is often said that pragmatism, unless it is content to be a contribution to mere methodology, must develop a theory of Reality. But the chief characteristic trait of the pragmatic notion of reality is precisely that no theory of Reality in general, *überhaupt,* is possible or needed. It occupies the position of an emancipated empiricism or a thoroughgoing naïve realism. It finds that "reality" is a *denotative* term, a word used to designate indifferently everything that happens. Lies, dreams, insanities, deceptions, myths, theories are all of them just the events which they specifically are. Pragmatism is content to take its stand with science; for science finds all such events to be subject-matter of description and inquiry—just like stars and fossils, mosquitoes and malaria, circulation and vision. It also takes its stand with daily life, which finds that such things really have to be reckoned with as they occur interwoven in the texture of events.

The only way in which the term reality can ever become more than a blanket denotative term is through recourse to specific events in all their diversity and thatness. Speaking summarily, I find that the retention by philosophy of the notion of a Reality fedually superior to the events of everyday occurrence is the chief source of the increasing isolation of philosophy from common sense and science. For the latter do not operate in any such region. As with them of old, philosophy in dealing with real difficulties finds itself still hampered by reference to realities more real, more ultimate, than those which directly happen.

I have said that identifying the cause of philosophy with the notion of superior reality is the cause of an *increasing* isolation from science and practical life. The phrase reminds us that there was a time when the enterprise of science and the moral interests of men both moved in a universe invidiously distinguished from that of ordinary occurrence. While all that happens is equally real—since it really happens—happenings are not of equal worth. Their respective consequences, their import, varies tremendously. Counterfeit money, although real (or rather *because* real), is really different from valid circulatory medium, just as disease is really different from health; different in specific structure and so different in consequences. In occidental thought, the Greeks were the first to draw the distinction between the genuine and the spurious in a generalized fashion and to formulate and enforce its tremendous significance for the conduct of life. But since they had at command no technique of experimental analysis and no adequate technique of mathematical analysis, they were compelled to treat the difference of the true and the false, the dependable and the deceptive, as signifying two kinds of existence, the truly real and the apparently real.

Two points can hardly be asserted with too much emphasis. The Greeks were wholly right in the feeling that questions of good and ill, as far as they fall within human control, are bound up with discrimination of the genuine from the spurious, of "being" from what only pretends to be. But because they lacked adequate instrumentalies for coping with this difference in specific situations, they were forced to treat the difference as a wholesale and rigid one. Science was concerned with vision of ultimate and true reality; opinion was concerned with getting along with apparent realities. Each had its appropriate region permanently marked off. Matters of opinion could never become matters of science; their intrinsic nature forbade. When the practice of science went on under such conditions, science and philosophy were one and the same thing. Both had to do with ultimate reality in its rigid and insuperable difference from ordinary occurrences.

We have only to refer to the way in which medieval life wrought the philosophy of an ultimate and supreme reality into the context of practical life to realize that for centuries political and moral interests were bound up with the distinction between the absolutely real and the relatively real. The difference was no matter of a remote technical philosophy, but one which controlled life from the cradle to the grave, from the grave to the endless life after death. By means of a vast institution, which in effect was state as well as church, the claims of ultimate reality were enforced; means of access to it were provided. Acknowledgment of The Reality brought security in this world and salvation in the next. It is not necessary to report the story of the change which has since taken place. It is enough for our purposes to note that none of the modern philosophies of a superior reality, or *the* real object, idealistic or realistic, holds that its insight makes a difference like that between sin and holiness, eternal condemnation and eternal bliss. While in its own context the philosophy of ultimate reality entered into the vital concerns of men, it now tends to be an ingenious dialectic exercised in professorial corners by a few who have retained ancient premises while rejecting their application to the conduct of life.

The increased isolation from science of any philosophy identified with the problem of *the* real is equally marked. For the growth of science has consisted precisely in the invention of an equipment, a technique of appliances and procedures, which, accepting all occurrences as homogeneously real, proceeds to distinguish the authenticated from the spurious, the true from the false, by specific modes of treatment in specific situations. The procedures of the trained engineer, of the competent physician, of the laboratory expert, have turned out to be the only ways of discriminating the counterfeit from the valid. And they have revealed that the difference is not one of antecedent fixity of existence, but one of mode of treatment and of the consequences thereon attendant. After mankind has learned to put its trust in specific procedures in order to make its discriminations between the false and the true, philosophy arrogates to itself the enforcement of the distinction at its own cost.

More than once, this essay has intimated that the counterpart of the idea of invidiously real reality is the spectator notion of knowledge. If the knower, however defined, is set over against the world to be known, knowing consists in possessing a transcript, more or less accurate but otiose, of real things. Whether this transcript is presentative in character (as realists say) or whether it is by means of states of consciousness which represent things (as subjectivists say), is a matter of great importance in its own context. But, in another regard, this difference is negligible in comparison with the point in which both agree. Knowing is viewing from outside. But it it be true that the self or subject of experience is part and parcel of the course of events, it follows that the self *becomes* a knower. It becomes a mind in virtue of a distinctive way of partaking in the course of events. The significant distinction is no longer between the knower *and* the world; it is between different ways of being in and of the movement of things; between a brute physical way and a purposive, intelligent way.

There is no call to repeat in detail the statements which have been advanced. Their net purport is that the directive presence of future possibilities in dealing with existent conditions is what is meant by knowing; that the self becomes a knower or mind when anticipation of future consequences operates as its stimulus. What we are now concerned with is the effect of this conception upon the nature of philosophic knowing.

As far as I can judge, popular response to pragmatic philosophy was moved by two quite different considerations. By some it was thought to provide a new species of sanctions, a new mode of apologetics, for certain religious ideas whose standing had been threatened. By others, it was welcomed because it was taken as a sign that philosophy was about to surrender its otiose and speculative remoteness; that philosophers were beginning to recognize that philosophy is of account only if, like everyday knowing and like science, it affords guidance to action and thereby makes a difference in the event. It was welcomed as a sign that philosophers were willing to have the worth of their philosophizing measured by responsible tests.

I have not seen this point of view emphasized, or hardly recognized, by professional critics. The difference of attitude can probably be easily explained. The epistemological universe of discourse is so highly technical that only those who have been trained in the history of thought think in terms of it. It did not occur, accordingly, to non-technical readers to interpret the doctrine that the meaning and validity of thought are fixed by differences made in consequences and in satisfactoriness to mean consequences in personal feelings. Those who were professionally trained, how-

ever, took the statement to mean that consciousness or mind in the mere act of looking at things modifies them. It understood the doctrine of test of validity by consequences to mean that apprehensions and conceptions are true if the modifications effected by them were of an emotionally desirable tone.

Prior discussion should have made it reasonably clear that the source of this misunderstanding lies in the neglect of temporal considerations. The change made in things by the self in knowing is not immediate and, so to say, cross-sectional. It is longitudinal—in the redirection given to changes already going on. Its analogue is found in the changes which take place in the development of, say, iron ore into a watch-spring, not in those of the miracle of transubstantiation. For the static, cross-sectional, non-temporal relation of subject and object, the pragmatic hypothesis substitutes apprehension of a thing in terms of the results in other things which it is tending to effect. For the unique epistemological relation, it substitutes a practical relation of a familiar type:— responsive behavior which changes in time the subject-matter to which it applies. The unique thing about the responsive behavior which constitutes knowing is the specific difference which marks it off from other modes of response, namely, the part played in it by anticipation and prediction. Knowing is the act, stimulated by this foresight, of securing and averting consequences. The success of the achievement measures the standing of the foresight by which response is directed. The popular impression that pragmatic philosophy means that philosophy shall develop ideas relevant to the actual crisis of life, ideas influential in dealing with them and tested by the assistance they afford, is correct.

Reference to practical response suggests, however, another misapprehension. Many critics have jumped at the obvious association of the word pragmatic with practical. They have assumed that the intent is to limit all knowledge, philosophic included, to promoting "action," understanding by action either just any bodily movement, or those bodily movements which conduce to the preservation and grosser well-being of the body. James's statement that general conceptions must "cash in" has been taken (especially by European critics) to mean that the end and measure of intelligence lies in the narrow and coarse utilities which it produces. Even an acute American thinker, after first criticizing pragmatism as a kind of idealistic epistemology, goes on to treat it as a doctrine which regards intelligence as a lubricating oil facilitating the workings of the body.

One source of the misunderstanding is suggested by the fact that "cashing in" to James meant that a general idea must always be capable of verification in specific existential cases. The notion of "cashing in" says nothing about the breadth or depth of the specific consequences. As an empirical doctrine, it could not say anything about them in general; the specific cases must speak for themselves. If one conception is verified in terms of eating beefsteak, and another in terms of a favorable credit balance in the bank, that is not because of anything in the theory, but because of the specific nature of the conceptions in question, and because there exist particular events like hunger and trade. If there are also existences in which the most liberal esthetic ideas and the most generous moral conceptions can be verified by specific embodiment, assuredly so much the better. The fact that a strictly empirical philosophy was taken by so many critics to imply an *a priori* dogma about the kind of consequences capable of existence is evidence. I think, of the inability of many philosophers to think in concretely empirical terms. Since the critics were themselves accustomed to get results by manipulating the concepts of "consequences" and of "practice," they assumed that even a would-be empiricist must be doing the same sort of thing. It will, I suppose, remain for a long time incredible to some that a philosopher should really intend to go to specific experiences to determine of what scope and depth practice admits, and what sort of consequences the world permits to come into being. Concepts are so clear; it takes so little time to develop their implications; experiences are so confused, and it

requires so much time and energy to lay hold of them. And yet these same critics charge pragmatism with adopting subjective and emotional standards!

As a matter of fact, the pragmatic theory of intelligence means that the function of mind is to project new and more complex ends—to free experience from routine and from caprice. Not the use of thought to accomplish purposes already given either in the mechanism of the body or in that of the existent state of society, but the use of intelligence to liberate and liberalize action, is the pragmatic lesson. Action restricted to given and fixed ends may attain great technical efficiency; but efficiency is the only quality to which it can lay claim. Such action is mechanical (or becomes so), no matter what the scope of the pre-formed end, be it the Will of God or *Kultur.* But the doctrine that intelligence develops within the sphere of action for the sake of possibilities not yet given is the opposite of a doctrine of mechanical efficiency. Intelligence *as* intelligence is inherently forward-looking; only by ignoring its primary function does it become a mere means for an end already given. The latter *is* servile, even when the end is labeled moral, religious, or esthetic. But action directed to ends to which the agent has not previously been attached inevitably carries with it a quickened and enlarged spirit. A pragmatic intelligence is a creative intelligence, not a routine mechanic.

All this may read like a defense of pragmatism by one concerned to make out for it the best case possible. Such is not, however, the intention. The purpose is to indicate the extent to which intelligence frees action from a mechanically instrumental character. Intelligence is, indeed, instrumental *through* action to the determination of the qualities of future experience. But the very fact that the concern of intelligence is with the future, with the as-yet-unrealized (and with the given and the established only as conditions of the realization of possibilities), makes the action in which it takes effect generous and liberal; free of spirit. Just that action which extends and approves intelligence has an intrinsic value of its own in being instrumental:—the intrinsic value of being informed with intelligence in behalf of the enrichment of life. By the same stroke, intelligence becomes truly liberal: knowing is a human undertaking, not an esthetic appreciation carried on by a refined class or a capitalistic possession of a few learned specialists, whether men of science or of philosophy.

More emphasis has been put upon what philosophy is not than upon what it may become. But it is not necessary, it is not even desirable, to set forth philosophy as a scheduled program. There are human difficulties of an urgent, deep-seated kind which may be clarified by trained reflection, and whose solution may be forwarded by the careful development of hypotheses. When it is understood that philosophic thinking is caught up in the actual course of events, having the office of guiding them towards a prosperous issue, problems will abundantly present themselves. Philosophy will not solve these problems; philosophy is vision, imagination, reflection— and these functions, apart from action, modify nothing and hence resolve nothing. But in a complicated and perverse world, action which is not informed with vision, imagination, and reflection, is more likely to increase confusion and conflict than to straighten things out. It is not easy for generous and sustained reflection to become a guiding and illuminating method in action. Until it frees itself from identification with problems which are supposed to depend upon Reality as such, or its distinction from a world of Appearance, or its relation to a Knower as such, the hands of philosophy are tied. Having no chance to link its fortunes with a responsible career by suggesting things to be tried, it cannot identify itself with questions which actually arise in the vicissitudes of life. Philosophy recovers itself when it ceases to be a device for dealing with the problems of philosophers and becomes a method, cultivated by philosophers, for dealing with the problems of men.

Emphasis must vary with the stress and special impact of the troubles which perplex men. Each age knows its own ills, and seeks its own remedies. One does not have to forecast a particular program to note that the central need of any program at the present day is an adequate conception of the nature of intelligence and its place in action. Philosophy cannot disavow responsibility for many misconceptions of the nature of intelligence which now hamper its efficacious operation. It has at least a negative task imposed upon it. It must take away the burdens which it has laid upon the intelligence of the common man in struggling with his difficulties. It must deny and eject that intelligence which is naught but a distant eye, registering in a remote and alien medium the spectacle of nature and life. To enforce the fact that the emergence of imagination and thought is relative to the connexion of the sufferings of men with their doings is of itself to illuminate those sufferings and to instruct those doings. To catch mind in its connexion with the entrance of the novel into the course of the world is to be on the road to see that intelligence is itself the most promising of all novelties, the revelation of the meaning of that transformation of past into future which is the reality of every present. To reveal intelligence as the organ for the guidance of this transformation, the sole director of its quality, is to make a declaration of present untold significance for action. To elaborate these convictions of the connexion of intelligence with what men undergo because of their doings and with the emergence and direction of the creative, the novel, in the world is of itself a program which will keep philosophers busy until something more worth while is forced upon them. For the elaboration has to be made through application to all the disciplines which have an intimate connexion with human conduct:—to logic, ethics, esthetics, economics, and the procedure of the sciences formal and natural.

I also believe that there is a genuine sense in which the enforcement of the pivotal position of intelligence in the world and thereby in control of human fortunes (so far as they are manageable) is the peculiar problem in the problems of life which come home most closely to ourselves—to ourselves living not merely in the early twentieth century but in the

United States. It is easy to be foolish about the connexion of thought with national life. But I do not see how any one can question the distinctively national color of English, or French, or German philosophies. And if of late the history of thought has come under the domination of the German dogma of an inner evolution of ideas, it requires but a little inquiry to convince oneself that the dogma itself testifies to a particularly nationalistic need and origin. I believe that philosophy in America will be lost between chewing a historic cud long since reduced to woody fibre, or an apologetics for lost causes (lost to natural science), or a scholastic, schematic formalism, unless it can somehow bring to consciousness America's own needs and its own implicit principle of successful action.

This need and principle, I am convinced, is the necessity of a deliberate control of policies by the method of intelligence, an intelligence which is not the faculty of intellect honored in text-books and neglected elsewhere, but which is the sum-total of impulses, habits, emotions, records and discoveries which forecast what is desirable and undesirable in future possibilities, and which contrive ingeniously in behalf of imagined good. Our life has no background of sanctified categories upon which we may fall back; we rely upon precedent as authority only to our own undoing—for with us there is such a continuously novel situation that final reliance upon precedent

entails some class interest guiding us by the nose whither it will. British empiricism, with its appeal to what has been in the past, is, after all, only a kind of *a priorism*. For it lays down a fixed rule for future intelligence to follow; and only the immersion of philosophy in technical learning prevents our seeing that this is the essence of *a priorism*.

We pride ourselves upon being realistic, desiring a hard-headed cognizance of facts, and devoted to mastering the means of life. We pride ourselves upon a practical idealism, a lively and easily moved faith in possibilities as yet unrealized, in willingness to make sacrifice for their realization. Idealism easily becomes a sanction of waste and carelessness, and realism a sanction of legal formalism in behalf of things as they are—the rights of the possessor. We thus tend to combine a loose and ineffective optimism with assent to the doctrine of take who take can: a deification of power. All peoples at all times have been narrowly realistic in practice and have then employed idealization to cover up in sentiment and theory their brutalities. But never, perhaps, has the tendency been so dangerous and so tempting as with ourselves. Faith in the power of intelligence to imagine a future which is the projection of the desirable in the present, and to invent the instrumentalities of its realization, is our salvation. And it is a faith which must be nurtured and made articulate: surely a sufficiently large task for our philosophy.

# The Postulate of Immediate Empiricism

Immediate empiricism postulates that things—anything, everything, in the ordinary or non-technical use of the term "thing"—are

what they are experienced as. Hence, if one wishes to describe anything truly, his task is to tell what it is experienced as being. If it is a

From, "The Postulate of Immediate Empiricism" in *John Dewey: The Middle Works, 1899–1924,* Vol. 3, Ed. Jo Ann Boydston (Carbondale and Edwardsville: Southern Illinois University Press, 1977 [1905]), pp. 158–166.

horse that is to be described, or the *equus* that is to be defined, then must the horse-trader, or the jockey, or the timid family man who wants a "safe driver," or the zoologist or the paleontologist tell us what the horse is which is experienced. If these accounts turn out different in some respects, as well as congruous in others, this is not reason for assuming the content of one to be exclusively "real," and that of others to be "phenomenal"; for each account of what is experienced will manifest that it is the account *of* the horse-dealer, or *of* the zoologist, and hence will give the conditions requisite for understanding the differences as well as the agreements of the various accounts. And the principle varies not a whit if we bring in the psychologist's horse, the logician's horse or the metaphysician's horse.

In each case, the nub of the question is, *what sort of experience* is denoted or indicated: a concrete and determinate experience, varying, when it varies, in specific real elements, and agreeing, when it agrees, in specific real elements, so that we have a contrast, not between a Reality, and various approximations to, or phenomenal representations of Reality, but between different reals of experience. And the reader is begged to bear in mind that from this standpoint, when "an experience" or "some sort of experience" is referred to, "some thing" or "some sort of thing" is always meant.

Now, this statement that things are what they are experienced to be is usually translated into the statement that things (or, ultimately, Reality, Being) *are* only and just what they are *known* to be or that things are, or Reality *is,* what it is for a conscious knower—whether the knower be conceived primarily as a perceiver or as a thinker being a further and secondary question. This is the root-paralogism of all idealisms, whether subjective or objective, pyschological or epistemological. By our postulate, things are what they are experienced to be; and, unless knowing is the sole and only genuine mode of experiencing, it is fallacious to say that Reality is just and exclusively what it is or would be to an all-competent all-knower; or even that it *is,* relatively and piecemeal, what it is to a finite and partial

knower. Or, put more positively, knowing is one mode of experiencing, and the primary philosophic demand (from the standpoint of immediatism) is to find out *what* sort of an experience knowing is—or, concretely how things are experienced when they are experienced *as* known things.[1] By concretely is meant, obviously enough (among other things), such an account of the experience of things as known that will bring out the characteristic traits and distinctions they possess as things of a knowing experience, as compared with things experienced aesthetically, or morally, or economically, or technologically. To assume that, because from the *standpoint of the knowledge experience* things *are* what they are known to be, therefore, metaphysically, absolutely, without qualification, everything in its reality (as distinct from its "appearance," or phenomenol occurrence) is what a knower would find it to be, is, from the immediatist's standpoint, if not the root of all philosophic evil, at least one of its main roots. For this leaves out of account what the knowledge standpoint is itself *experienced as.*

I start and am flustered by a noise heard. Empirically, that noise *is* fearsome; it *really* is, not merely phenomenally or subjectively so. That is *what* it is experienced as being. But, when I experience the noise as a *known* thing, I find it to be innocent of harm. It is the tapping of a shade against the window, owing to movements of the wind. The experience has changed; that is, the thing experienced has changed—not that an unreality has given place to a reality, nor that some transcendental (unexperienced) Reality has changed,[2] not that truth has changed, but just and only the concrete reality experienced has changed. I now feel ashamed of my fright; and the noise as fearsome is changed to noise as a wind-curtain fact, and hence practically indifferent to my welfare. This is a change of experienced, existence effected through the medium of cognition. The content of the latter experience cognitively regarded is doubtless *truer* than the content of the earlier; but it is in no sense more real. To call it truer, moreover must, from the empirical standpoint, mean a concrete *difference* in actual things experienced.[3] Again, in many cases, only in retrospect is the prior experience cognitionally regarded at all. In such cases, it is only in regard to contrasted content *in* a subsequent experience that the determination "truer" has force.

Perhaps some reader may now object that as matter of fact the entire experience *is* cognitive, but that the earlier parts of it are only imperfectly so, resulting in a phenomenon that is not real; while the latter part, being a more complete cognition, results in what is relatively, at least, more real.[4] In short, a critic may say that, when I was frightened by the noise, I *knew* I was frightened; otherwise there would have been no experience at all. At this point, it is necessary to make a distinction so simple and yet so all-fundamental that I am afraid the reader will be inclined to pooh-pooh it away as a mere verbal distinction. But to see that to the empiricist this distinction is not verbal, but genuine, is the precondition of any understanding of him. The immediatist must, by his postulate, ask what is the fright experienced *as*. Is what is actually experienced, I-know-I-am-frightened, or I-*am*-frightened? I see absolutely no reason for claiming that the experience *must* be described by the former phrase. In all probability (and all the empiricist logically needs is just one case of this sort) the experience is simply and just of fright-at-the-noise. Later one may (or may not) have an experience describable *as* I-know-I-am- (or-was) and improperly or properly, frightened. But this is a different experience—that is, a different *thing*. And if the critic goes on to urge that the person "*really*" must have known that he was frightened, I can only point out that the critic is shifting the venue. He may be right, but, if so, it is only because the "really" is something not concretely experienced (whose nature accordingly is the critic's business); and this is to depart from the empiricist's point of view, to attribute to him a postulate he expressly repudiates.

The material point may come out more clearly if I say that we must make a distinction between a thing as *cognitive,* and one as *cognized.*[5] I should define a cognitive experience as one that has certain bearings or implications which induce and fulfill themselves in a subsequent experience in which the relevant thing is experienced *as* cognized, *as* a known object, and is thereby transformed, or reorganized. The fright-at-the-noise in the case cited is obviously *cognitive,* in this sense. By description, it induces an investigation or inquiry in which both noise and fright are objectively stated or presented—the noise as a shade-wind fact, the fright as an organic reaction to a sudden acoustic stimulus, a reaction that under the given circumstances was useless or even detrimental, a maladaptation. Now, pretty much all of experience is of this sort (the "is" meaning, of course, is experienced *as*), and the empiricist is false to his principle if he does not duly note this fact.[6] But he is equally false to his principle if he permits himself to be confused as to the concrete differences in the two things experienced.

There are two little words through explication of which the empiricist's position may be brought out—"*as*" and "*that.*" We may express his presupposition by saying that things are what they are experienced *as* being; or that to give a just account of anything is to tell what *that* thing is experienced to be. By these words I want to indicate the absolute, final, irreducible and inexpugnable concrete *quale* which everything experienced not so much *has* as *is*. To grasp this aspect of empiricism is to see what the empiricist means by objectivity, by the element of control. Suppose we take, as a crucial case for the empiricist, an out and out illusion, say of Zöllner's lines. These are experienced as convergent; they are "truly" parallel. If things are what the are experienced as being, how can the distinction be drawn between illusion and the true state of the case? There is no answer to this question except by sticking to the fact that the experience of the lines as divergent is a concrete qualitative thing or *that*. It is *that* experience which it is, and no other. And if the reader rebels at the iteration of such obvious tautology, I can only reiterate that the realization of the *meaning* of this tautology is the key to the whole question of the objectivity of experience, as that stands to the empiricist. The lines of *that* experience *are* divergent: not merely *seem* so. The question of truth is not as to whether Being or Non-Being, Reality or mere Appearance, is experienced, but as to the *worth* of a certain concretely experienced thing. The only way of passing upon this question is by sticking in the most uncompromising fashion to *that* experience as real. *That* experience is that two lines with certain cross-hatchings are apprehended as convergent; only by taking that experience as real and as fully real, is there any basis for or way of going to an experienced knowledge that the lines are parallel. It is in the concrete thing *as experienced* that all the grounds and clues to its own intellectual or logical rectification are contained. It is because this thing, afterwards adjudged false, is a concrete *that,* that it develops into a corrected experience (that is, experience of a corrected thing—we reform things just as we reform ourselves or a bad boy) whose full content is not a whit more real, but which is true or truer.[7]

If *any* experience, then a *determinate* experience; and this determinateness is the only, and is the adequate, principle of control, or "objectivity." The experience may be of the vaguest sort. I may not see any thing which I can identify as a familiar object—a table, a chair, etc. It may be dark; I may have only the vaguest impression that there is something which looks like a table. Or I may be completely befogged and confused, as when one rises quickly from sleep in a pitch-dark room. But this vagueness, this doubtfulness, this confusion is the thing experienced, and, *qua* real, is as "good" a reality as the self-luminous vision of an Absolute. It is not just vagueness, doubtfulness, confusion, at large or in general. It is *this* vagueness, and no other; absolutely unique, absolutely what *it* is.[8] Whatever gain in clearness, in fullness, in trueness of content is experienced must grow out of some element in the experience of *this* experienced *as* what it is. To return to the illusion: If the experience of the lines as convergent is illusory, it is because of some elements in the thing as experienced, not because of something defined in terms of externality to this particular experi-

ence. If the illusoriness can be detected, it is because the thing experienced is real, having within its experienced reality elements whose *own mutual* tension effects its reconstruction. Taken concretely, the experience of convergent lines contains within itself the elements of the transformation of its own content. It is *this* thing, and not some separate truth, that clamors for its own reform. There is, then, from the empiricist's point of view, no need to search for some aboriginal *that* to which all successive experiences are attached, and which is somehow thereby undergoing continuous change. Experience is always of *thats;* and the most comprehensive and inclusive experience of the universe that the philosopher himself can obtain is the experience of a characteristic *that.* From the empiricist's point of view, this is as true of the exhaustive and complete insight of a hypothetical all-knower as of the vague, blind experience of the awakened sleeper. As reals, they stand on the same level. As trues, the latter has by definition the better of it; but if this insight is in any way the truth of the blind awakening, it is because the latter has, in its *own* determinate *quale,* elements of real continuity with the former; it is, *ex hypothesi,* transformable through a series of experienced reals without break of continuity, into the absolute thought-experience. There is no need of logical manipulation to effect the transformation, nor *could* any logical consideration effect it. If effected at all it is just by immediate experiences, each of which is just as real (no more, no less) as either of the terms between which they lie. Such, at least, is the meaning of the empiricist's contention. So, when he talks of experience, he does not mean some grandiose, remote affair that is cast like a net around a succession of fleeting experiences; he does not mean an indefinite total, comprehensive experience which somehow engirdles an endless flux, he means that *things* are what they are experienced to be, and that every experience is *some* thing.

From the postulate of empiricism, then (or, what is the same thing, from a *general* consideration of the concept of experience), nothing can be deduced, not a single philosophical proposition.[9] The reader may hence conclude that all this just comes to the truism that experience is experience, or is what it is. If one attempts to draw conclusions from the bare concept of experience, the reader is quite right. But the real significance of the principle is that of a method of philosophical analysis—a method identical in kind (but differing in problem and hence in operation) with that of the scientist. If you wish to find out what subjective, objective, physical, mental, cosmic, psychic, cause, substance, purpose, activity, evil, being, quality—any philosophic term, in short—means, go to experience and see what the thing is experienced *as.*

Such a method is not spectacular; it permits of no off-hand demonstrations of God, freedom, immortality, nor of the exclusive reality of matter, or ideas, or consciousness, etc. But it supplies a way of telling what all these terms mean. It may seem insignificant, or chillingly disappointing, but only upon condition that it be not worked. Philosophic conceptions have, I believe, outlived their usefulness considered as stimulants to emotion, or as a species of sanctions; and a larger, more fruitful and more valuable career awaits them considered as specifically experienced meanings. . . .

## Notes

1. I hope the reader will not therefore assume that from the empiricist's standpoint knowledge is of small worth or import. On the contrary, from the empiricist's standpoint it has *all* the worth which it is concretely experienced as possessing—which is simply tremendous. But the exact *nature* of this worth is a thing to be found out in describing what we mean by experiencing objects as known—the actual differences made or found in experience.

2. Since the non-empiricist believes in things-in-themselves (which he may term "atoms," sensations," transcendental unities, *a priori* concepts, an absolute experience, or whatever), and since he finds that the empiricist makes much of change (as he must, since change is continuously experienced) he assumes that the empiricist means *his own* non-empirical Realities are in continual flux, and he naturally shudders at having his divinities so violently treated. But, once recognize that the empiricist doesn't have any such Realities at all, and the entire problem of the relation of change to reality takes a very different aspect.

3. It would lead us aside from the point to try to tell just what is the nature of the experienced difference we call truth. Professor James's recent articles may well be consulted. The point to bear in mind here is just what sort of a thing the empiricist must mean by true, or truer (the noun Truth is, of course, a generic name for all cases of "Trues"). The adequacy of any particular account is not a matter to be settled by general reasoning, but by finding out what sort of an experience the truth-experience actually is.

4. I say "relatively," because the transcendalist still holds that finally the cognition is imperfect, giving us only some symbol or phenomenon of Reality (which *is* only in the Absolute or in some Thing-in-Itself)—otherwise the curtain-wind fact would have as much ontological reality as the existence of the Absolute itself: a conclusion at which the non-empiricist perhorresces, for no reason obvious to me—save that it would put an end to his transcendentalism.

5. In general, I think the distinction between *-ive* and *-ed* one of the most fundamental of philosophic distinctions, and one of the most neglected. The same holds of *-tion* and *-ing*.

6. What is criticized, now as "geneticism" (if I may coin the word) and now as "pragmatism" is, in its truth, just the fact that the empiricist does take account of the experienced "drift, occasion and contexture" of things experienced—to use Hobbes's phrase.

7. Perhaps the point would be clearer if expressed in this way: Except as subsequent estimates of *worth* are introduced, "real" means only existent. The eulogistic connotation that makes the term Reality equivalent to *true* or *genuine* being has great pragmatic significance, but its confusion with reality as existence is the point aimed at in the above paragraph.

8. One does not so easily escape medieval Realism as one thinks. Either every experienced thing has its own determinateness, its own unsubstitutable, unredeemable reality, or else "generals" *are* separate existences after all.

9. Excepting, of course, some negative ones. One could say that certain views are certainly *not* true, because, by hypothesis, they refer to nonentities, i.e., non-empiricals. But even here the empricist must go slowly. From his own standpoint, even the most professedly transcendental statements are, after all, real as experiences, and hence negotiate some transaction with facts. For this reason, he cannot, in theory, reject them *in toto*, but has to show concretely how they arose and how they are to be corrected. In a word, his logical relationship to statements that profess to relate to things-in-themselves, unknowables, inexperienced substances, etc., is precisely that of the psychologist to the Zöllner lines.

# Experience and Philosophic Method

The title, Experience and Nature, is intended to signify that the philosophy here presented may be termed either empirical naturalism or naturalistic empiricism, or, taking "experience" in its usual signification, naturalistic humanism.

To many the associating of the two words will seem like talking of a round square, so engrained is the notion of the separation of man and experience from nature. Experience, they say, is important for those beings who have it, but is too causal and sporadic in its occurrence to carry with it any important implications regarding the nature of Nature. Nature, on the other hand, is said to be complete apart from experience. Indeed, according to some thinkers the case is even in worse plight: Experience to them is not only something extraneous which is occasionally superimposed upon nature, but it forms a veil or screen which shuts us off from nature, unless in some way it can be "transcended." So something non-natural by way of reason or intuition is introduced, something supra-empirical. According to an opposite school experience fares as badly, nature being thought to signify something wholly material and mechanistic; to frame a theory of experience in naturalistic terms is, accordingly, to degrade and deny the noble and ideal values that characterize experience.

I know of no route by which dialectical argument can answer such objections. They arise from associations with words and cannot be dealt with argumentatively. One can only hope in the course of the whole discussion to disclose the meanings which are attached to "experience" and "nature," and thus insensibly produce, if one is fortunate, a change in the significations previously attached to them. This process of change may be hastened by calling attention to another context in which nature and experience get on harmoniously together—wherein experience presents itself as the method, and the only method, for getting at nature, penetrating its secrets, and wherein nature empirically disclosed (by the use of empirical method in natural science) deepens, enriches and directs the further development of experience.

In the natural sciences there is a union of experience and nature which is not greeted as a monstrosity; on the contrary, the inquirer must use empirical method if his findings are to be treated as genuinely scientific. The investigator assumes as a matter of course that experience, controlled in specifiable ways, is the avenue that leads to the facts and laws of nature. He uses reason and calculation freely; he could not get along without them. But he sees to it that ventures of this theoretical sort start from and terminate in directly experienced subject-matter. Theory may intervene in a long course of reasoning, many portions of which are remote from what is directly experienced. But the vine of pendant theory is attached at both ends to the pillars of observed subjectmatter. And this experienced material is the same for the scientific man and the man in the street. The latter cannot follow the intervening reasoning without special preparation. But stars, rocks, trees, and creeping things are the same material of experience for both.

These commonplaces take on significance when the relation of experience to the formation of a philosophic theory of nature is in question. They indicate that experience, if scientific inquiry is justified, is no infinitesimally thin layer or foreground of nature, but that it penetrates into it, reaching down into its depths, and in such a way that its grasp is capable of expansion; it tunnels in all directions and

From "Experience and Philosophic Method," in *Experience and Nature, John Dewey: The Later Works, 1925–1953,* Vol. 1, Ed. Jo Ann Boydston (Carbondale and Edwardsville: Southern Illinois University Press, 1981 [1925]), pp. 10–14, 16–21, 26–28, 30–31, 33–41.

in so doing brings to the surface things at first hidden—as miners pile high on the surface of the earth treasures brought from below. Unless we are prepared to deny all validity to scientific inquiry, these facts have a value that cannot be ignored for the general theory of the relation of nature and experience.

It is sometimes contended, for example, that since experience is a late comer in the history of our solar system and plant, and since these occupy a trivial place in the wide areas of celestial space, experience is at most a slight and insignificant incident in nature. No one with an honest respect for scientific conclusions can deny that experience as an existence is something that occurs only under highly specialized conditions, such as are found in a highly organized creature which in turn requires a specialized environment. There is no evidence that experience occurs everywhere and everywhen. But candid regard for scientific inquiry also compels the recognition that when experience does occur, no matter at what limited portion of time and space, it enters into possession of some portion of nature and in such a manner as to render other of its precincts accessible.

A geologist living in 1928 tells us about events that happened not only before he was born but millions of years before any human being came into existence on this earth. He does so by starting from things that are now the material of experience. Lyell revolutionized geology by perceiving that the sort of thing that can be experienced now in the operations of fire, water, pressure, is the sort of thing by which the earth took on its present structural forms. Visiting a natural history museum, one beholds a mass of rock and, reading a label, finds that it comes from a tree that grew, so it is affirmed, five million years ago. The geologist did not leap from the thing he can see and touch to some event in by-gone ages; he collated this observed thing with many others, of different kinds, found all over the globe; the results of his comparisons he than compared with data of other experiences, say, the astronomer's. He translates, that is, observed coexistences into non-observed,

inferred sequences. Finally he dates his object, placing it in an order of events. By the same sort of method he predicts that at certain places some things not yet experienced will be observed, and then he takes pains to bring them within the scope of experience. The scientific conscience is, moreover, so sensitive with respect to the necessity of experience that when it reconstructs the past it is not fully satisfied with inferences drawn from even a large and cumulative mass of uncontradicted evidence; it sets to work to institute conditions of heat and pressure and moisture, etc., so as actually to reproduce in experiment that which he has inferred.

These commonplaces prove that experience is *of* as well as *in* nature. It is not experience which is experienced, but nature—stones, plants, animals, diseases, health, temperature, electricity, and so on. Things interacting in certain ways *are* experience; they are what is experienced. Linked in certain other ways with another natural object—the human organism—they are *how* things are experienced as well. Experience thus reaches down into nature; it has depth. It also has breadth and to an indefinitely elastic extent. It stretches. That stretch constitutes inference.

Dialectical difficulties, perplexities due to definitions given to the concepts that enter into the discussion, may be raised. It is said to be absurd that what is only a tiny part of nature should be competent to incorporate vast reaches of nature within itself. But even were it logically absurd one would be bound to cleave to it as a fact. Logic, however, is not put under a strain. The fact that something is an occurrence does not decide what kind of an occurrence it is; that can be found out only by examination. To argue from an experience "being an experience" to what it is of and about is warranted by no logic, even though modern thought has attempted it a thousand times. A bare event is no event at all; *something* happens. What that something is, is found out by actual study. This applies to seeing a flash of lightning and holds of the longer event called experience. The very existence of science is evidence that experience is such an occurrence that it penetrates into nature and expands without limit through it.

These remarks are not supposed to prove anything about experience and nature for philosophical doctrine; they are not supposed to settle anything about the worth of empirical naturalism. But they do show that in the case of natural science we habitually treat experience as starting point, and as method for dealing with nature, and as the goal in which nature is disclosed for what it is. To realize this fact is at least to weaken those verbal associations which stand in the way of apprehending the force of empirical method in philosophy.

The same considerations apply to the other objection that was suggested: namely, that to view experience naturalistically is to reduce it to something materialistic, depriving it of all ideal significance. If experience actually presents esthetic and moral traits, then these traits may also be supposed to reach down into nature, and to testify to something that belongs to nature as truly as does the mechanical structure attributed to it in physical science. To rule out that possibility by some general reasoning is to forget that the very meaning and purport of empirical method is that things are to be studied on their own account, so as to find out what is revealed when they are experienced. The traits possessed by the subject-matters of experience are as genuine as the characteristics of sun and electron. They are *found,* experienced, and are not to be shoved out of being by some trick of logic. When found, their ideal qualities are as relevant to the philosophic theory of nature as are the traits found by physical inquiry.

To discover some of these general features of experienced things and to interpret their significance for a philosophic theory of the universe in which we live is the aim of this volume. From the point of view adopted, the theory of empirical method in philosophy does for experienced subject-matter on a liberal scale what it does for special sciences on a technical scale. It is this aspect of method with which we are especially concerned in the present chapter. . . .

This empirical method I shall call the *denotative* method. That philosophy is a mode of reflection, often of a subtle and penetrating sort, goes without saying. The charge that is brought against the non-empirical method of philosophizing is not that it depends upon theorizing, but that it fails to use refined, secondary products as a path pointing and leading back to something in primary experience. The resulting failure is three-fold.

First, there is no verification, no effort even to test and check. What is even worse, secondly, is that the things of ordinary experience do not get enlargement and enrichment of meaning as they do when approached through the medium of scientific principles and reasonings. This lack of function reacts, in the third place, back upon the philosophic subject-matter in itself. Not tested by being employed to see what it leads to in ordinary experience and what new meanings it contributes, this subject-matter becomes arbitrary, aloof—what is called "abstract" when that word is used in a bad sense to designate something which exclusively occupies a realm of its own without contact with the things of ordinary experience.

As the net outcome of these three evils, we find that extraordinary phenomenon which accounts for the revulsion of many cultivated persons from any form of philosophy. The objects of reflection in philosophy, being reached by methods that seem to those who employ them rationally mandatory, are taken to be "real" in and of themselves—and supremely real. Then it becomes an insoluble problem why the things of gross, primary experience, should be what they are, or indeed why they should be at all. The refined objects of reflection in the natural sciences, however, never end by rendering the subject-matter from which they are derived a problem; rather, when used to describe a path by which some goal in primary experience is designated or denoted, they solve perplexities to which that crude material gives rise but which it cannot resolve of itself. They become means of control, of enlarged use and enjoyment of ordinary things. They may generate new problems, but these are problems of the same sort, to be dealt with by further use of the same methods of inquiry and experimentation. The problems to which empirical method gives rise afford, in a word, opportunities for more investigations yielding fruit in new and enriched experiences. But the problems to which non-empirical method gives rise in philosophy are blocks to inquiry, blind alleys; they are puzzles rather than problems, solved only by calling the original material of primary experience, "phenomenal," mere appearance, mere impressions, or by some other disparaging name.

Thus there is here supplied, I think, a first-rate test of the value of any philosophy which is offered us: Does it end in conclusions which, when they are referred back to ordinary life-experiences and their predicaments, render them more significant, more luminous to us, and make our dealings with them more fruitful? Or does it terminate in rendering the things of ordinary experience more opaque than they were before, and in depriving them of having in "reality" even the significance they had previously seemed to have? Does it yield the enrichment and increase of power of ordinary things which the results of physical science afford when applied in every-day affairs? Or does it become a mystery that these ordinary things should be what they are; and are philosophic concepts left to dwell in separation in some technical realm of their own? It is the fact, I repeat, that so many philosophies terminate in conclusions that make it necessary to disparge and condemn primary experience, leading those who hold them to measure the sublimity of their "realities" as philosophically defined by remoteness from the concerns of daily life, which leads cultivated common sense to look askance at philosophy.

These general statements must be made more definite. We must illustrate the meaning of empirical method by seeing some of its results in contrast with those to which non-empirical philosophies conduct us. We begin by nothing that "experience" is what James called a double-barreled word.[1] Like its congeners, life and history, it includes *what* men do and suffer, *what* they strive for, love believe and endure, and also *how* men act and are acted upon, the ways in which they do and suffer, desire and enjoy, see, believe, imagine— in short, processes of *experiencing*. "Experi-ence" denotes the planted field, the sowed seeds, the reaped harvests, the changes of night and day, spring and autumn, wet and dry, heat and cold, that are observed, feared, longed for; it also denotes the one who plants and reaps, who works and rejoices, hopes, fears, plans, invokes magic or chemistry to aid him, who is downcast or triumphant. It is "double-barreled" in that it recognizes in its primary integrity no division between act and material, subject and object, but contains them both in an unanalyzed totality. "Thing" and "thought," as James says in the same connection, are single-barreled; they refer to products discriminated by reflection-out of primary experience.[2]

It is significant that "life" and "history" have the same fullness of undivided meaning. Life denotes a function, a comprehensive activity, in which organism and environment are included. Only upon reflective analysis does it break up into external conditions—air breathed, food taken, ground walked upon— and internal structures—lungs respiring, stomach digesting, legs walking. The scope of "history" is notorious: it is the deeds enacted, the tragedies undergone; and it is the human comment, record, and interpretation that inevitable follow. Objectively, history takes in rivers, mountains, fields and forests, laws and institutions; subjectively it includes the purposes and plans, the desires and emotions, through which these things are administered and transformed.

Now empirical method is the only method which can do justice to this inclusive integrity of "experience." It alone takes this integrated unity as the starting point for philosophic thought. Other methods begin with results of a reflection that has already torn in two the subject-matter experienced and the operations and states of experiencing. The problem is then to get together again what has been sundered—which is as if the king's men started with the fragments of the egg and tried to construct the whole egg out of them. For empirical method the problem is nothing so impossible of solution. Its problem is to note how and why the whole is distinguished into subject and object, nature and mental operations.

Having done this, it is in a position to see *to what effect* the distinction is made: how the distinguished factors function in the further control and enrichment of the subject-matters of crude but total experience. Non-empirical method starts with a reflective product as if it were primary, as if it were the originally "given." To non-empirical method, therefore, object and subject, mind and matter (or whatever words an ideas are used) are separate and independent. Therefore it has upon its hands the problem of how it is possible to know at all; how an outer world can affect an inner mind; how the acts of mind can reach out and lay hold of objects defined in antithesis to them. Naturally it is at a loss for an answer, since its premises make the fact of knowledge both unnatural and unempirical. One thinker turns metaphysical materialist and denies reality to the mental; another turns psychological idealist, and holds that matter and force are merely disguised psychical events. Solutions are given up as a hopeless task, or else different schools pile one intellectual complication on another only to arrive by a long and tortuous course at that which naïve experience already has in its own possession.

The first and perhaps the greatest difference made in philosophy by adoption respectively of empirical or non-empirical method is, thus, the difference made in what is selected as original material. To a truly naturalistic empiricism, the moot problem of the relation of subject and object is the problem of what consequences follow in and for primary experience from the distinction of the physical and the psychological or mental from each other. The answer is not far to seek. To distinguish in reflection the physical and to hold it in temporary detachment is to be set upon the road that conducts to tools and technologies, to construction of mechanisms, to the arts that ensue in the wake of the sciences. That these constructions make possible a better regulation of the affairs of primary experience is evident. Engineering and medicine, all the utilities that make for expansion of life, are the answer. There is better administration of old familiar things, and there is invention of new objects and satisfactions. Along with this added ability in regulation goes enriched meaning and value in things, clarification, increased depth and continuity—a result even more precious than is the added power of control.

The history of the development of the physical sciences is the story of the enlarging possession by mankind of more efficacious instrumentalities for dealing with the conditions of life and action. But when one neglects the connection of these scientific objects with the affairs of primary experience, the result is a picture of a world of things indifferent to human interests because it is wholly apart from experience. It is more than merely isolated, for it is set in opposition. Hence when it is viewed as fixed and final in itself it is a source of oppression to the heart and paralysis to imagination. Since this picture of the physical universe and philosophy of the character of physical objects is contradicted by every engineering project and every intelligent measure of public hygiene, it would seem to be time to examine the foundations upon which it rests, and find out how and why such conclusions are come to.

When objects are isolated from the experience through which they are reached and in which they function, experience itself becomes reduced to the mere process of experiencing, and experiencing is therefore treated as if it were also complete in itself. We get the absurdity of an experiencing which experiences only itself, states and processes of consciousness, instead of the things of nature. Since the seventeenth century this conception of experience as the equivalent of subjective private consciousness set over against nature, which consists wholly of physical objects, has wrought havoc in philosophy. It is responsible for the feeling mentioned at the outset that "nature" and "experience" are names for things which have nothing to do with each other.

Let us inquire how the matter stands when these mental and physical objects are looked at in their connection with experience in its primary and vital modes. As has been suggested, these objects are not original, isolated and self-sufficient. They represent the discriminated analysis of the process of experiencing from subject-matter experienced. Although breathing is in fact a function that includes both air and the operations of the lungs, we may detach the latter for study, even though we cannot separate it in fact. So while we always know, love, act for and against *things,* instead of experiencing ideas, emotions and mental intents, the attitudes themselves may be made a special object of attention, and thus come to form a distinctive subject-matter of reflective, although not of primary, experience.

We primarily observe things, not observations. But the *act* of observation may be inquired into and form a subject of study and become thereby a refined object; so many the acts of thinking, desire, purposing, the state of affection, reverie, etc. Now just as long as these attitudes are not distinguished and abstracted, they are incorporated into subject-matter. It is a notorious fact that the one who hates finds the one hated an obnoxious and despicable character; to the lover his adored one is full of intrinsically delightful and wonderful qualities. The connection between such facts and the fact of animism is direct. . . .

There is another important result for philosophy of the use of empirical method which, when it is developed, introduces our next topic. Philosophy, like all forms of reflective analysis, takes us away, for the time being, from the things had in primary experience as they directly act and are acted upon, used and enjoyed. Now the standing temptation of philosophy, as its course abundantly demonstrates, is to regard the results of reflection as having, in and of themselves, a reality superior to that of the material of any other mode of experience. The commonest assumption of philosophies, common even to philosophies very different from one another, is the assumption of the identity of objects of knowledge and ultimately real objects. The assumption is so deep that it is usually not expressed; it is taken for granted as something so fundamental that it does not need to be stated. A technical example of the view is found in the contention of the Cartesian school—including

Spinoza—that emotion as well as sense is but confused thought which when it becomes clear and definite or reaches its goal is *cognition.* That esthetic and moral experience reveal traits of real things as truly as does intellectual experience, that poetry may have a metaphysical import as well as science, is rarely affirmed, and when it is asserted, the statement is likely to be meant in some mystical or esoteric sense rather than in a straightforward everyday sense.

Suppose however that we start with no presuppositions save that what is experienced, since it is a manifestation of nature, may, and indeed, must be used as testimony of the characteristics of natural events. Upon this basis, reverie and desire are pertitnent for a philosophic theory of the true nature of things; the possibilities present in imagination that are not found in observation, are something to be taken into account. The features of objects reached by scientific or reflective experiencing are important, but so are all the phenomena of magic, myth, politics, painting and penitentiaries. The phenomena of social life are as relevant to the problem of the relation of the individual and universal as are those of logic; the existence in political organization of boundaries and barriers, of centralization, of interaction across boundaries, of expansion and absorption, will be quite as important for metaphysical theories of the discrete and the continuous as is anything derived from chemical analysis. The existence of ignorance as well as of wisdom, of error and even insanity as well as of truth will be taken into account.

That is to say, nature is construed in such a way that all these things, since they are actual, are naturally possible; they are not explained away into mere "appearance" in contrast with reality. Illusions are illusions, but the occurrence of illusions is not an illusion, but a genuine reality. What is really "in" experience extends much further than that which at any time is *known.* From the standpoint of knowledge, objects must be distinct; their traits must be explicit; the vague and unrevealed is a limitation. Hence whenever the habit of identifying reality with the object of knowledge as such prevails, the obscure and vague are explained away. It is important for philosophic theory to be aware that the distinct and evident are prized and why they are. But it is equally important to note that the dark and twilight abound. For in any object of primary experience there are always potentialities which are not explicit; any object that is overt is charged with possible consequences that are hidden; the most overt act has factors which are not explicit. Strain thought as far as we may and not all consequences can be foreseen or made an express or known part of reflection and decision. In the face of such empirical facts, the assumption that nature in itself is all of the same kind, all distinct, explicit and evident, having no hidden possibilities, no novelties or obscurities, is possible only on the basis of a philosophy which at some point draws an arbitrary line between nature and experience.

In the assertion (implied here) that the great vice of philosophy is an arbitrary "intellectualism," there is no slight cast upon intelligence and reason. By "intellectualism" as an indictment is meant the theory that all experiencing is a mode of knowing, and that all subject-matter, all nature, is, in principle, to be reduced and transformed till it is defined in terms identical with the characteristics presented by refined objects of science as such. The assumption of "intellectualism" goes contrary to the facts of what is primarily experienced. For things are objects to be treated, used, acted upon and with, enjoyed and endured, even more than things to be known. They are things *had* before they are things cognized.

The isolation of traits characteristic of objects known, and then defined as the sole ultimate realities, accounts for the denial to nature of the characters which make things lovable and contemptible, beautiful and ugly, adorable and awful. It accounts for the belief that nature is an indifferent, dead mechanism; it explains why characteristics that are the valuable and valued traits of objects in actual experience are thought to create a fundamentally troublesome philosophical problem. Recognition of their genuine and primary real-

ity does not signify that no thought and knowledge enter in when things are loved, desired and striven for; it signifies that the former are subordinate, so that the genuine problem is how and why, to what effect, things thus experienced are transformed into objects in which cognized traits are supreme and affectional and volitional traits incidental and subsidiary. . . .

We have spoken of the difference which acceptance of empirical method in philosophy makes in the problem of subject-object and in that of the alleged all-inclusiveness of cognitive experience.[3] There is an intimate connection between these two problems. When real objects are identified, point for point, with knowledge-objects, all affectional and volitional objects are inevitably excluded from the "real" world, and are compelled to find refuge in the privacy of an experiencing subject or mind. Thus the notion of the ubiquity of all comprehensive cognitive experience results by a necessary logic in setting up a hard and fast wall between the experiencing subject and that nature which is experienced. The self becomes not merely a pilgrim but an unnaturalized and unnaturalizable alien in the world. The only way to avoid a sharp separation between the mind which is the centre of the processes of experiencing and the natural world which is experienced is to acknowledge that all modes of experiencing are ways in which some genuine traits of nature come to manifest realization.

The favoring of cognitive objects and their characteristics at the expense of traits that excite desire, command action and produce passion, is a special instance of a principle of selective emphasis which introduces partiality and partisanship into philosophy. Selective emphasis, with accompanying omission and rejection, is the heart-beat of mental life. To object to the operation is to discard all thinking. But in ordinary matters and in scientific inquiries, we always retain the sense that the material chosen is selected for a purpose; there is no idea of denying what is left out, for what is omitted is merely that which is not relevant to the particular problem and purpose in hand.

But in philosophies, this limiting condition is often wholly ignored. It is not noted and remembered that the favored subject-matter is chosen for a purpose and that what is left out is just as real and important in its own characteristic context. It tends to be assumed that because qualities that figure in poetical discourse and those that are central in friendship do not figure in scientific inquiry, they have no reality, at least not the kind of unquestionable reality attributed to the mathematical, mechanical or magneto-electric properties that constitute matter. It is natural to men to take that which is of chief value to them at the time as *the* real. Reality and superior value are equated. In ordinary experience this fact does no particular harm; it is at once compensated for by turning to other things which since they also present value are equally real. But philosophy often exhibits a cataleptic rigidity in attachment to that phase of the total objects of experience which has become especially dear to a philosopher. *It* is real at all hazards and only it; other things are real only in some secondary and Pickwickian sense. . . .

This bias toward treating objects selected because of their value in some special context as the "real," in a superior and invidious sense, testifies to an empirical fact of importance. Philosophical simplifications are due to choice, and choice marks an interest *moral* in the broad sense of concern for what is good. Our constant and unescapable concern is with prosperity and adversity, success and failure, achievement and frustration, good and bad. Since we are creatures with lives to live, and find ourselves within an uncertain environment, we are constructed to note and judge in terms of bearing upon weal and woe—upon value. Acknowledgment of this fact is a very different thing, however, from the transformation effected by philosophers of the traits they find good (simplicity, certainty, nobility, permanence, etc.) into fixed traits of real Being. The former presents something *to be accomplished,* to be brought about by the *actions* in which choice is manifested and made genuine. The latter ignores the need of action to effect the better and to prove the honesty of choice;

it converts what is desired into antecedent and final features of a reality which is supposed to need only logical warrant in order to be contemplatively enjoyed as true Being.

For reflection the eventual is always better or worse than the given. But since it would also be better if the eventual good were now given, the philosopher, belonging by status to a leisure class relieved from the urgent necessity of dealing with conditions, converts the eventual into some kind of Being, something which *is,* even if it does not *exist.* Permanence, real essence, totality, order, unity, rationality, the *unum, verum et bonum* of the classic tradition, are eulogistic predicates. When we find such terms used to describe the foundations and proper conclusions of a philosophic system, there is ground for suspecting that an artificial simplification of existence has been performed. Reflection determining preference for an eventual good has dialectically wrought a miracle of transubstantiation. . . .

Honest empirical method will state when and where and why the act of selection took place, and thus enable others to repeat it and test its worth. Selective choice, denoted as an empirical event, reveals the basis and bearing of intellectual simplifications; they then cease to be of such a self-enclosed nature as to be affairs only of opinion and argument, admitting no alternatives save complete acceptance or rejection. Choice that is disguised or denied is the source of those astounding differences of philosophic belief that startle the beginner and that become the plaything of the expert. Choice that is avowed is an experiment to be tried on its merits and tested by its results. Under all the captions that are called immediate knowledge, or self-sufficient certitude of belief, whether logical, esthetic or epistemological, there is something selected for a purpose, and hence not simple, not self-evident and not intrinsically eulogizable. State the purpose so that it may be re-experienced, and its value and the pertinency of selection undertaken in its behalf may be tested. The purport of thinking, scientific and philosophic, is not to eliminate choice but to render it less arbitrary and more significant. It loses its arbitrary character when its quality and consequences are such as to commend themselves to the reflection of others after they have betaken themselves to the situations indicated; it becomes significant when reason for the choice is found to be weighty and its consequences momentous. When choice is avowed, others can repeat the course of the experience; it is an experiment to be tried, not an automatic safety device. . . .

This discussion of empirical method has had a double content. On one hand, it has tried to make clear, from the analogy of empirical method in scientific inquiry, what the method signifies (and does *not* signify) for philosophy. Such a discussion would, however, have little definite import unless the *difference* that is made in philosophy by the adoption of empirical method is pointed out. For that reason, we have considered some typical ways and important places in which traditional philosophies have gone astray through failure to connect their reflective results with the affairs of everyday primary experience. Three sources of large fallacies have been mentioned, each containing within itself many more sub-varieties than have been hinted at. The three are the complete separation of subject and object, (of *what* is experienced from *how* it is experienced); the exaggeration of the features of known objects at the expense of the qualities of objects of enjoyment and trouble, friendship and human association, art and industry; and the exclusive isolation of the results of various types of selective simplification which are undertaken for diverse unavowed purposes.

It does not follow that the products of these philosophies which have taken the wrong, because non-empirical, method are of no value or little worth for a philosophy that pursues a strictly empirical method. The contrary is the case, for no philosopher can get away from experience even it he wants to. The most fantastic views ever entertained by superstitious people had some basis in experienced fact; they can be explained by one who knows enough about them and about the conditions under which they were formed. And philosophers have been not more but less superstitious than their fellows; they have been, as a class, unusually reflective and inquiring. If some of their products have been fantasies, it was not because they did not, even unwittingly, start from empirical method; it was not wholly because they substituted unchecked imagination for thought. No, the trouble has been that they have failed to note the empirical needs that generate their problems, and have failed to return the refined products back to the context of actual experience, there to receive their check, inherit their full content of meaning, and give illumination and guidance in the immediate perplexities which originally occasioned reflection.

The chapters which follow make no pretence, accordingly, of starting to philosophize afresh as if there were no philosophies already in existence, or as if their conclusions were empirically worthless. Rather the subsequent discussions rely, perhaps excessively so, upon the main results of great philosophic systems, endeavoring to point out their elements of strength and of weakness when their conclusions are employed (as the refined objects of all reflection must be employed) as guides back to the subject-matter of crude, everyday experience.

Our primary experience as it comes is of little value for purposes of analysis and control, crammed as it is with things that need analysis and control. The very existence of reflection is proof of its deficiencies. Just as ancient astronomy and physics were of little scientific worth, because, owing to the lack of apparatus and techniques of experimental analysis, they had to take the things of primary observation at their face value, so "common-sense" philosophy usually repeats current conventionalities. What is averred to be implicit reliance upon what is given in common experience is likely to be merely an appeal to prejudice to gain support for some fanaticism or defence for some relic of conservative tradition which is beginning to be questioned.

The trouble, then, with the conclusions of philosophy is not in the least that they are results of reflection and theorizing. It is rather that philosophers have borrowed from various sources the conclusions of special analyses, particularly of some ruling science of the day, and imported them direct into philosophy, with no check by either the empirical objects from which they arose or those to which the conclusions in question point. Thus Plato trafficked with the Pythagoreans and imported mathematical concepts; Descartes and Spinoza took over the presuppositions of geometrical reasoning; Locke imported into the theory of mind the Newtonian physical corpuscles, converting them into given "simple ideas"; Hegel borrowed and generalized without limit the rising historical method of his day; contemporary English philosophy has imported from mathematics the notion of primitive indefinable propositions, and given them a content from Locke's simple ideas, which had in the meantime become part of the stock in trade of psychological science.

Well, why not, as long as what is borrowed has a sound scientific status? Because in scientific inquiry, refined methods justify themselves by opening up new fields of subject-matter for exploration; they create new techniques of observation and experimentation. Thus when the Michelson-Morley experiment disclosed, as a matter of gross experience, facts which did not agree with the results of accepted physical laws, physicists did not think for a moment of denying the validity of what was found in that experience, even though it rendered questionable an elaborate intellectual apparatus and system. The coincidence of the bands of the interferometer was accepted as its face value in spite of its incompatibility with Newtonian physics. Because scientific inquirers accepted it at its face value they at once set to work to reconstruct their theories; they questioned their reflective premises, not the full "reality" of what they saw. This task of re-adjustment compelled not only new reasonings and calculations in the development of a more comprehensive theory, but opened up new ways of inquiry into experienced subject-matter. Not for a moment did

they think of explaining away the features of an object in gross experience because it was not in logical harmony with theory—as philosophers have so often done. Had they done so, they would have stultified science and shut themselves off from new problems and new findings in subject-matter. In short, the material of refined scientific method is continuous with that of the actual world as it is concretely experienced.

But when philosophers transfer into their theories bodily and as finalities the refined conclusions they borrow from the sciences, whether logic, mathematics or physics, these results are not employed to reveal new subject-matters and illuminate old ones of gross experience; they are employed to cast discredit on the latter and to generate new and artificial problems regarding the reality and validity of the things of gross experience. Thus the discoveries of psychologists taken out of their own empirical context are in philosophy employed to cast doubt upon the reality of things external to mind and to selves, things and properties that are perhaps the most salient characteristics of ordinary experience. Similarly, the discoveries and methods of physical science, the concepts of mass, space, motion, have been adopted wholesale in isolation by philosophers in such a way as to make dubious and even incredible the reality of the affections, purposes and enjoyments of concrete experience. The objects of mathematics, symbols of relations having no explicit reference to actual existence, efficacious in the territory to which mathematical technique applies, have been employed in philosophy to determine the priority of essences to existence, and to create the insoluble problem of why pure essence ever descends into the tangles and tortuosities of existence.

What empirical method exacts of philosophy is two things: First, that refined methods and products be traced back to their origin in primary experience, in all its heterogeneity and fullness; so that the needs and problems out of which they arise and which they have to satisfy be acknowledged. Secondly, that the secondary schools methods and conclusions be brought back to the things of ordinary experience, in all their coarseness and crudity, for verification. In this way, the methods of analytic reflection yield material which form the ingredients of a method of designation, denotation, in philosophy. A scientific work in physics or astronomy gives a record of calculations and deductions that were derived from past observations and experiments. But it is more than a record; it is also an indication, an assignment, of further observations and experiments to be performed. No scientific report would get a hearing if it did not describe the apparatus by means of which experiments were carried on and results obtained; not that apparatus is worshipped, but because this procedure tells other inquirers how they are to go to work to get results which will agree or disagree in their experience with those previously arrived at, and thus confirm, modify and rectify the latter. The recorded scientific result is in effect a *designation* of a method to be followed and a *prediction* of what will be found when specified observations are set on foot. That is all a philosophy can be or do. In the chapters that follow I have undertaken a revision and reconstruction of the conclusions, the reports, a number of historic philosophic systems, in order that they may be usable methods by which one may go to his own experience, and, discerning what is found by use of the method, come to understand better what is already within the common experience of mankind.

There is a special service which the study of philosophy may render. Empirically pursued it will not be a study of philosophy but a study, by means of philosophy, of life-experience. But this experience is already overlaid and saturated with the products of the reflection of past generations and by-gone ages. It is filled with interpretations, classifications, due to sophisticated thought, which have become incorporated into what seems to be fresh naïve empirical material. It would take more wisdom than is possessed by the wisest historic scholar to track all of these absorbed borrowings to their original sources. If we may for the moment call these materials prejudices (even

if they are true, as long as their source and authority is unknown), then philosophy is a critique of prejudices. These incorporated results of past reflection, welded into the genuine materials of first-hand experience, may become organs of enrichment if they are detected and reflected upon. If they are not detected, they often obfuscate and distort. Clarification and emancipation follow when they are detected and cast out; and one great object of philosophy is to accomplish this task.

An empirical philosophy is in any case a kind of intellectual disrobing. We cannot permanently divest ourselves of the intellectual habits we take on and wear when we assimilate the culture of our own time and place. But intelligent furthering of culture demands that we take some of them off, that we inspect them critically to see what they are made of and what wearing them does to us. We cannot achieve recovery of primitive naïveté. But there is attainable a cultivated naïveté of eye, ear and thought, one that can be acquired only through the discipline of severe thought. If the chapters which follow contribute to an artful innocence and simplicity they will have served their purpose.

I am loath to conclude without reference to the larger liberal humane value of philosophy when pursued with empirical method. The most serious indictment to be brought against non-empirical philosophies is that they have cast a cloud over the things of ordinary experience. They have not been content to rectify them. They have discredited them at large. In casting aspersion upon the things of everyday experience, the things of action and affection and social intercourse, they have done something worse than fail to give these affairs the intelligent direction they so much need. It would not matter much if philosophy had been reserved as a luxury of only a few thinkers. We endure many luxuries. The serious matter is that philosophies have denied that common experience is capable of developing from within itself methods which will secure direction for itself and will create inherent standards of judgment and value. No one knows how many of the evils and deficiencies that are pointed to as reasons for flight from experience are themselves due to the disregard of experience shown by those peculiarly reflective. To waste of time and energy, to disillusionment with life that attends every deviation from concrete experience must be added the tragic failure to realize the value that intelligent search could reveal and mature among the things of ordinary experience. I cannot calculate how much of current cynicism, indifference and pessimism is due to these causes in the deflection of intelligence they have brought about. It has even become in many circles a sign of lack of sophistication to imagine that life is or can be a fountain of cheer and happiness. Philosophies no more than religions can be acquitted of responsibility for bringing this result to pass. The transcendental philosopher has probably done more than the professed sensualist and materialist to obscure the potentialities of daily experience for joy and for self-regulation. If what is written in these pages has no other result than creating and promoting a respect for concrete human experience and its potentialities, I shall be content.

## Notes

1. *Essays in Radical Empiricism,* p. 10.
2. It is not intended, however, to attribute to James precisely the interpretation given in the text.
3. To avoid misapprehension, it may be well to add a statement on the latter point. It is not denied that any experienced subject-matter whatever may *become* an object of reflection and cognitive inspection. But the emphasis is upon "become"; the cognitive never *is* all-inclusive: that is, when the material of a prior non-cognitive experience is the object of knowledge, it and the act of knowing are themselves included within a new and wider non-cognitive experience—and *this* situation can never be transcended. It is only when the temporal character of experienced things is forgotten that the idea of the total "transcendence" of knowledge is asserted.

# Existence as Precarious and Stable

We have substituted sophistication for superstition, at least measurably so. But the sophistication is often as irrational and as much at the mercy of words as the superstition it replaces. Our magical safeguard against the uncertain character of the world is to deny the existence of chance, to mumble universal and necessary law, the ubiquity of cause and effect, the uniformity of nature, universal progress, and the inherent rationality of the universe. These magic formulae borrow their potency from conditions that are not magical. Through science we have secured a degree of power of prediction and of control; through tools, machinery and an accompanying technique we have made the world more conformable to our needs, a more secure abode. We have heaped up riches and means of comfort between ourselves and the risks of the world. We have professionalized amusement as an agency of escape and forgetfulness. But when all is said and done, the fundamentally hazardous character of the world is not seriously modified, much less eliminated. Such an incident as the last war and preparations for a future war remind us that it is easy to overlook the extent to which, after all, our attainments are only devices for blurring the disagreeable

From "Existence as Precarious and Stable," in *Experience and Nature, John Dewey: The Later Works, 1925–1953,* Vol. 1, Ed. Jo Ann Boydston, (Carbondale and Edwardsville: Southern Illinois University, 1981, [1925]), pp. 45–47, 51–52. 57–58, 61–63.

recognition of a fact, instead of means of altering the fact itself.

What has been said sounds pessimistic. But the concern is not with morals but with metaphysics, with, that is to say, the nature of the existential world in which we live. It would have been as easy and more comfortable to emphasize good luck, grace, unexpected and unwon joys, those unsought for happenings which we so significantly call happiness. We might have appealed to good fortune as evidence of this important trait of hazard in nature. Comedy is as genuine as tragedy. But it is traditional that comedy strikes a more superficial note than tragedy. And there is an even better reason for appealing to misfortunes and mistakes as evidence of the precarious nature of the world. The problem of evil is a well-recognized problem, while we rarely or never hear of a problem of good. Goods we take for granted; they are as they should be; they are natural and proper. The good is a recognition of our deserts. When we pull out a plum we treat it as evidence of the *real* order of cause and effect in the world. For this reason it is difficult for the goods of existence to furnish as convincing evidence of the uncertain character of nature as do evils. It is the latter we term accidents, not the former, even when their adventitious character is as certain.

What of it all, it may be asked? In the sense in which an assertion is true that uncontolled distribution of good and evil is evidence of the precarious, uncertain nature of existence, it is a truism, and no problem is forwarded by its reiteration. But it is submitted that just this predicament of the inextricable mixture of stability and uncertainty gives rise to philosophy, and that it is reflected all its recurrent problems and issues. If classic philosophy says so much about unity and so little about unreconciled diversity, so much about the eternal and permanent, and so little about change (save as something to be resolved into combinations of the permanent), so much about necessity and so little about contingency, so much about the comprehending universal and so little about the recalcitrant particular, it may well be because the ambiguousness and ambivalence

of reality are actually so pervasive. Since these things form the problem, solution is more apparent (although not more actual), in the degree in which whatever of stability and assurance the world presents is fastened upon and asserted.

Upon their surface, the reports of the world which form our different philosophies are various to the point of stark contrariness. They range from spiritualism to materialism, from absolutism to relativistic phenomenalism, from transcendentalism to positivism, from rationalism to sensationalism, from idealism to realism, from subjectivism to bald objectivism, from Platonic realism to nominalism. The array of contradictions is so imposing as to suggest to sceptics that the mind of man had tackled an impossible job, or that philosophers have abandoned themselves to vagary. These radical oppositions in philosophers suggest however another consideration. They suggest that all their different philosophies have a common premise, and that their diversity is due to acceptance of a common premise. Variant philosophies may be looked at as different ways of supplying recipes for denying to the universe the character of contingency which it possesses so integrally that its denial leaves the reflecting mind without a clew, and puts subsequent philosophising at the mercy of temperament, interest and local surroundings.

Quarrels among conflicting types of philosophy are thus family quarrels. They go on within the limits of a too domestic circle, and can be settled only by venturing further afield, and out of doors. Concerned with imputing complete, finished and sure character to the world of real existence, even if things have to be broken into two disconnected pieces in order to accomplish the result, the character desiderated can plausibly be found in reason or in mechanism; in rational conceptions like those of mathematics, or brute things like sensory data; in atoms or in essences; in consciousness or in a physical externality which forces and overrides consciousness.

As against this common identification of reality with what is sure, regular and finished, experience in unsophisticated forms gives evidence of a different world and points to a different metaphysics. We live in a world which is an impressive and irresistible mixture of sufficiencies, tight completenesses, order, recurrences which make possible prediction and control, and singularities, ambiguities, uncertain possibilities, processes going on to consequences as yet indeterminate. They are mixed not mechanically but vitally like the wheat and tares of the parable. We may recognize them separately but we cannot divide them, for unlike wheat and tares they grow from the same root. Qualities have defects as necessary conditions of their excellencies; the instrumentalities of truth are the causes of error; change gives meaning to permanence and recurrence makes novelty possible. A world that was wholly risky would be a world in which adventure is impossible, and only a living world can include death. Such facts have been celebrated by thinkers like Heracleitus and Lao-tze; they have been greeted by theologians as furnishing occasions for exercise of divine grace; they have been elaborately formulated by various schools under a principle of relativity, so defined as to become itself final and absolute. They have rarely been frankly recognized as fundamentally significant for the formation of a naturalistic metaphysics. . . .

Since thinkers claim to be concerned with knowledge of existence, rather than with imagination, they have to make good the pretention to knowledge. Hence they transmute the imaginative perception of the stably good object into a definition and description of true reality in contrast with lower and specious existence, which, being precarious and incomplete, along involves us in the necessity of choice and active struggle. Thus they remove from actual existence the very traits which generate philosophic reflection and which give point and bearing to its conclusions. In briefest formula, "reality" becomes what we wish existence to be, after we have analyzed its defects and decided upon what would remove them; "reality" is what existence would be if our reasonably justified preferences were so completely established in

nature as to exhaust and define its entire being and thereby render search and struggle unnecessary. What is left over, (and since trouble, struggle, conflict, and error still empirically exist, something *is* left over) being excluded by definition from full reality is assigned to a grade or order of being which is asserted to be metaphysically inferior; an order variously called appearance, illusion, mortal mind, or the merely empirical, against what really and truly is. Then the problem of metaphysics alters: instead of being a detection and description of the generic traits of existence, it becomes an endeavor to adjust or reconcile to each other two separate realms of being. Empirically we have just what we started with: the mixture of the precarious and problematic with the assured and complete. But a classificatory device, based on desire and elaborated in reflective imagination, has been introduced by which the two traits are torn apart, one of them being labelled reality, and the other appearance. The genuinely moral problem of mitigating and regulating the troublesome factor by active employment of the stable factor then drops out of sight. The dialectic problem of logical reconciliation of two notions has taken its place. . . .

The union of the hazardous and the stable, of the incomplete and the recurrent, is the condition of all experienced satisfaction as truly as of our predicaments and problems. While it is the source of ignorance, error and failure of expectation, it is the source of the delight which fulfillments bring. For if there were nothing in the way, if there were no deviations and resistances, fulfillment would be at once, and in so being would fulfill nothing, but merely be. It would not be in connection with desire or satisfaction. Moreover when a fulfillment comes and is pronounced good, it is *judged* good, distinguished and asserted, simply because it is in jeopardy, because it occurs amid indifferent and divergent things. Because of this mixture of the regular and that which cuts across stability, a good object once experienced acquires ideal quality and attracts demand and effort to itself. A particular ideal may be an illusion, but having ideals is no illusion. It embodies features of existence. Although imagination is often fantastic it is also an organ of nature; for it is the appropriate phase of indeterminate events moving toward eventualities that are now but possibilities. A purely stable world permits of no illusions, but neither is it clothed with ideals. It just exists. To be good is to be better than; and there can be no better except where there is shock and discord combined with enough assured order to make attainment of harmony possible. Better objects when brought into existence are existent not ideal; they retain ideal quality only retrospectively as commemorative of issue from prior conflict and prospectively, in contrast with forces which make for their destruction. Water that slakes thirst, or a conclusion that solves a problem have ideal character as long as thirst or problem persists in a way which qualifies the result. But water that is not a satisfaction of need has no more ideal quality than water running through pipes into a reservoir; a solution ceases to be a solution and becomes a bare incident of existence when its antecedent generating conditions of doubt, ambiguity and search are lost from its context. While the precarious nature of existence is indeed the source of all trouble, it is also an indispensable condition of ideality, becoming a sufficient condition when conjoined with the regular and assured.

We long, amid a troubled world, for perfect being. We forget that what gives meaning to the notion of perfection is the events that create longing, and that, apart from them, a "perfect" world would mean just an unchanging brute existential thing. The ideal significance of esthetic objects is no exception to this principle. Their satisfying quality, their power to compose while they arouse, is not dependent upon definite prior desire and effort as is the case with the ideally satisfying quality of practical and scientific objects. It is part of their peculiar satisfying quality to be gratuitous, not purchased by endeavor. The contrast to other things of this detachment from toil and labor in a world where most realizations have to be bought, as well as the contrast to trouble

and uncertainty, give esthetic objects their peculiar traits. If all things came to us in the way our esthetic objects do, none of them would be a source of esthetic delight. . . .

A philosophy which accepts the denotative or empirical method accepts at full value the fact that reflective thinking transforms confusion, ambiguity and discrepancy into illumination, definiteness and consistency. But it also points to the contextual situation in which thinking occurs. It notes that the starting point is the actually *problematic,* and that the problematic phase resides in some actual and specifiable situation.

It notes that the means of converting the dubious into the assured, and the incomplete into the determinate, is use of assured and established things, which are just as empirical and as indicative of the nature of experienced things as is the uncertain. It thus notes that thinking is no different in kind from the use of natural materials and energies, say fire and tools, to refine, reorder, and shape other natural materials, say ore. In both cases, there are matters which as they stand are unsatisfactory and there are also adequate agencies for dealing with them and connecting them. At no point of place is there any jump outside empirical, natural objects and their relations. Thought and reason are not specific powers. They consist of the procedures intentionally employed in the application to each other of the unsatisfactorily confused and indeterminate on one side and the regular and stable on the other. Generalizing from such observations, empirical philosophy perceives that thinking is a continuous process of temporal reorganization within one and the same world of experienced things, not a jump from the latter world into one of objects constituted once for all by thought. It discovers thereby the empirical basis of rational idealism, and the point at which it empirically goes astray. Idealism fails to take into account the specified or concrete character of the uncertain situation in which thought occurs; it fails to note the empirically concrete nature of the subject-matter, acts, and tools by which determination and consistency are reached; it fails to note that the conclusive eventual objects having the latter properties are themselves as many as the situations dealt with. The conversion of the logic of reflection into an ontology of rational being is thus due to arbitrary conversion of an eventual natural function of unification into a causal antecedent reality; this in turn is due to the tendency of the imagination working under the influence of emotion to carry unification from an actual, objective and experimental enterprise, limited to particular situations where it is needed, into an unrestricted, wholesale movement which ends in an all-absorbing dream.

The occurrence of reflection is crucial for dualistic metaphysics as well as for idealistic ontologies. Reflection occurs only in situations qualified by uncertainty, alternatives, questioning, search, hypotheses, tentative trials or experiments which test the worth of thinking. A naturalistic metaphysics is bound to consider reflection as itself a natural event occurring *within* nature because of traits of the latter. It is bound to inference from the empirical traits of thinking in precisely the same way as the sciences make inferences from the happening of suns, radioactivity, thunderstorms or any other natural event. Traits of reflection are as truly indicative or evidential of the traits of *other* things as are the traits of these events. A theory of the nature of the occurrence and career of a sun reached by denial of the obvious traits of the sun, or by denial that these traits are so connected with the traits of other natural events that they can be used as evidence concerning the nature of these other things, would hardly possess scientific standing. Yet philosophers, and strangely enough philosophers who call themselves realists, have constantly held that the traits which are characteristic of thinking, namely, uncertainty, ambiguity, alternatives, inquiring, search, selection, experimental reshaping of external conditions, do not possess the same existential character as do the objects of valid knowledge. They have denied that these traits are evidential of the character of the world within which thinking occurs. They have not, as realists, asserted that these traits are mere appearances; but they have

often asserted and implied that such things are only personal or psychological in contrast with a world of objective nature. But the interests of empirical and denotative method and of naturalistic metaphysics wholly coincide. The world must actually be such as to generate ignorance and inquiry; doubt and hypothesis, trial and temporal conclusions; the latter being such that they develop out of existences which while wholly "real" are not as satisfactory, as good, or as significant, as those into which they are eventually re-organized. The ultimate evidence of genuine hazard, contingency, irregularity and indeterminateness in nature is thus found in the occurrence of thinking. The traits of natural existence which generate the fears and adorations of superstitious barbarians generate the scientific procedures of disciplined civilization. The superiority of the latter does not consist in the fact that they are based on "real" existence, while the former depend wholly upon a human nature different from nature in general. It consists in the fact that scientific inquiries reach *objects* which are better, because reached by method which controls them and which adds greater control to life itself, method which mitigates accident, turns contingency to account, and releases thought and other forms of endeavor.

The conjunction of problematic and determinate characters in nature renders every existence, as well as every idea and human act, an experiment in fact, even though not in design. To be intelligently experimental is but to be conscious of this intersection of natural conditions so as to profit by it instead of being at its mercy. The Christian idea of this world and this life as a probation is a kind of distorted recognition of the situation; distorted because it applied wholesale to one stretch of existence in contrast with another, regarded as original and final. But in truth anything which can exist at any place and at any time occurs subject to tests imposed upon it by surroundings, which are only in part compatible and reinforcing. These surroundings test its strength and measure its endurance. As we can discourse of change only in terms of velocity and acceleration which involve relations to other things, so assertion of the permanent and enduring is comparative. The stablest thing we can speak of is not free from conditions set to it by other things. That even the solid earth mountains, the emblems of constancy, appear and disappear like the clouds is an old theme of moralists and poets. The fixed and unchanged being of the Democritean atom is now reported by inquirers to possess some of the traits of his nonbeing, and to embody a temporary equilibrium in the economy of nature's compromises and adjustments. A thing may endure *secula seculorum* and yet not be everlasting; it will crumble before the gnawing tooth of time, as it exceeds a certain measure. Every existence is an event. . . .

# Nature, Communication and Meaning

Of all affairs, communication is the most wonderful. That things should be able to pass from the plane of external pushing and pulling to that of revealing themselves to man, and thereby to themselves; and that the fruit of communication should be participation, sharing, is a wonder by the side of which transubstantiation pales. When communication occurs, all natural events are subject-to reconsideration and revision; they are re-adapted to meet the requirements of conversation, whether it be public discourse or that preliminary discourse termed thinking. Events turn into objects, things with a meaning. They may be referred to when they do not exist, and thus be operative among things distant in space and time, through vicarious presence in a new medium. Brute efficiencies and inarticulate consummations as soon as they can be spoken of are liberated from local and accidental contexts, and are eager for naturalization in any non-insulated, communicating, part of the world. Events when once they are named lead an independent and double life. In addition to their original existence, they are subject to ideal experimentation: their meanings may be infinitely combined and re-arranged in imagination, and the outcome of this inner experimentation—which is thought—may issue forth in interaction with crude or raw events. Meanings having been deflected from the rapid and roaring stream of events into a calm and traversable canal, rejoin the main stream, and, color, temper and compose its course. Where communication exists, things in acquiring meaning, thereby acquire representatives, surrogates, signs and implicates, which are infinitely more amenable to management, more permanent and more accommodating, than events in their first estate.

By this fashion, qualitative immediacies cease to be dumbly rapturous, a possession that is obsessive and an incorporation that involves submergence: conditions found in sensations and passions. They become capable of survey, contemplation, and ideal or logical elaboration; when something can be said of qualities they are purveyors of instruction. Learning and teaching come into being, and there is no event which may not yield information. A directly enjoyed thing adds to itself meaning, and enjoyment is thereby idealized. Even the dumb pang of an ache achieves a significant existence which it can be designated and descanted upon; it ceases to be merely oppressive and becomes important; it gains

From "Nature, Communication and Meaning," in *Experience and Nature, John Dewey: The Later Works, 1925–1953,* Vol. 1, Ed. Jo Ann Boydston (Carbondale and Edwardsville: Southern Illinois University Press. 1981 [1925]). pp. 132–133, 138, 141–142, 145–151, 158–161.

importance, because it becomes representative; it has the dignity of an office.

In view of these increments and transformations, it is not suprising that meanings, under the name of forms and essences, have often been hailed as modes of Being beyond and above spatial and temporal existence, invulnerable to vicissitude; nor that thought as their possession has been treated as a non-natural spiritual energy, disjoined from all that is empirical. Yet there is a natural bridge that joins the gap between existence and essence; namely communication, language, discourse. Failure to acknowledge the presence and operation of natural interaction in the form of communication creates the gulf between existence and essence, and that gulf is factitious and gratuitous. . . .

When events have communicable meaning, they have marks, notations, and are capable of con-notation and de-notation. They are more than mere occurrences; they have implications. Hence inference and reasoning are possible; these operations are reading the message of things, which things utter because they are involved in human associations. When Aristotle drew a distinction between sensible things that are more noted—known—to us and rational things that are more noted—known—in themselves, he was actually drawing a distinction between things that operate in a local, restricted universe of discourse, and things whose marks are such that they readily enter into indefinitely extensive and varied discourse.

The interaction of human beings, namely, association, is not different in origin from other modes of interaction. There is a peculiar absurdity in the question of how individuals become social, if the question is taken literally. Human beings illustrate the same traits of both immediate uniqueness and connection, relationship, as do other things. No more in their case than in that of atoms and physical masses is immediacy the whole of existence and therefore an obstacle to being acted upon by and affecting other things. Everything that exists in as far as it is known and knowable is in interaction with other things. It is associ-

ated, as well as solitary, single. The catching up of human individuals into association is thus no new and unprecedented fact; it is a manifestation of a commonplace of existence. Significance resides not in the bare fact of association, therefore, but in the consequences that flow from the distinctive patterns of human association. There is, again, nothing new or unprecedented in the fact that assemblage of things confers upon the assembly and its constituents, new properties by means of unlocking energies hitherto pent in. The significant consideration is that assemblage of organic human beings transforms sequence and coexistence into participation. . . .

The heart of language is not "expression" of something antecedent, much less expression of antecedent thought. It is communication; the establishment of cooperation in an activity in which there are partners, and in which the activity of each is modified and regulated by partnership. To fail to understand is to fail to come into agreement in action; to misunderstand is to set up action at cross purposes. Take speech as behavioristically as you will, including the elimination of all private mental states, and it remains true that it is markedly distinguished from the signaling acts of animals. Meaning is not indeed a psychic existence; it is primarily a property of behavior, and secondarily a property of objects. But the behavior of which it is a quality is a distinctive behavior; cooperative, in that response to another's act involves contemporaneous response to a thing as entering into the other's behavior, and this upon both sides. It is difficult to state the exact physiological mechanism which is involved. But about the fact there is no doubt. It constitutes the intelligibility of acts and things. Possession of the capacity to engage in such activity is intelligence. Intelligence and meaning are natural consequences of the peculiar form which interaction sometimes assumes in the case of human beings. . . .

Language is specifically a mode of interaction of at least two beings, a speaker and a hearer; it presupposes an organized group to which these creatures belong, and from whom they have acquired their habits of speech. It is therefore a relationship, not a particularity. This consideration alone condemns traditional nominalism. The meaning of signs moreover always includes something common as between persons and an object. When we attribute meaning to the speaker as *his* intent, we take for granted another person who is to share in the execution of the intent, and also something, independent of the persons concerned, through which the intent is to be realized. Persons and thing must alike serve as means in a common, shared consequence. This community of partaking is meaning.

The invention and use of tools have played a large part in consolidating meanings, because a tool is a thing used as means to consequences, instead of being taken directly and physically. It is intrinsically relational, anticipatory, predictive. Without reference to the absent, or "transcendence," nothing is a tool. The most convincing evidence that animals do not "think" is found in the fact that they have no tools, but depend upon their own relatively-fixed bodily structures to effect results. Because of such dependence they have no way of distinguishing the immediate existence of anything from its potential efficiencies; no way of projecting its consequences to define a nature or essence. Anything whatever used as a tool exhibits distinction and identification. Fire existentially burns; while fire which is employed in order to cook and keep warm, especially after other things, like rubbing sticks together, are used as means to generate it, is an existence having meaning and potential essence. The presence of inflammation and terror or discomfort is no longer the whole story; an occurrence is now an object; and while it is absurd to hold (as idealism virtually does) that the meaning of an existence is the real substance of the existence, it is equally absurd not to recognize the full transformative import of what has happened.

As to be a tool, or to be used as means for consequences, is to have and to endow with meaning, language, being the tool of tools, is the cherishing mother of all significance. For other instrumentalities and agencies, the things usually thought of as appliances, agencies and furnishings, can originate and develop only in social groups made possible by language. Things become tools ceremonially and institutionally. The notoriously conventionalized and traditional character of primitive utensils and their attendant symbolizations demonstrate this fact. Moreover, tools and artifices of agency are always found in connection with some division of labor which depends upon some device of communication. The statement can be proved in a more theoretical way. Immediacy as such is transient to the point of evanescence, and its flux has to be fixed by some easily recoverable and recurrent act within control of the organism, like gesture and spoken sounds, before things can be intentionally utilized. A creature might accidentally warm itself by a fire or use a stick to stir the ground in a way which furthered the growth of food-plants. But the effect of comfort ceases with the fire, existentially; a stick even though once used as a lever would revert to the status of being just a stick, unless the *relationship* between it and its consequence were distinguished and retained. Only language, or some form of artificial signs, serves to register the relationship and make it fruitful in other contexts of particular existence. Spears, urns, baskets, snares may have originated accidentally in some consummatory consequence of natural events. But only repetition through concerted action accounts for their becoming institutionalized as tools, and this concert of action depends upon the use of memoranda and communication. To make another aware of the possibility of a use or objective relationship is to perpetuate what is otherwise an incident as an agency; communication is a condition of consciousness.

Thus every meaning is generic or universal. It is something common between speaker, hearer and the things to which speech refers. It is universal also as a means of generalization. For a meaning is a method of action, a way of using things as means to a shared consummation, and method is general, though the things to which it is applied are peculiar. The meaning, for example, or portability is something in which two persons and an object share. But portability after it is once apprehended becomes a way of treating other things; it is extended widely. Whenever there is a chance, it is applied; application ceases only when a thing refuses to be treated in this way. And even then refusal may be only a challenge to develop the meaning of portability until the thing can be transported. Meanings are rules for using and interpreting things; interpretation being always an imputation of potentiality for some consequence.

It would be difficult to imagine any doctrine more absurd than the theory that general ideas or meanings arise by the comparison of a number of particulars, eventuating in the recognition of something common to them all. Such a comparison may be employed to check a suggested widened application of a rule. But generalization is carried spontaneously as far as it will plausibly go; usually much further than it will actually go. A newly acquired meaning is forced upon everything that does not obviously resist its application, as a child uses a new word whenever he gets a chance or as he plays with a new toy. Meanings are self-moving to new cases. In the end, conditions force a chastening of this spontaneous tendency. The scope and limits of application are ascertained experimentally in the process of application. The history of science, to say nothing of popular beliefs, is sufficient indication of the difficulty found in submitting this irrational generalizing tendency to the discipline of experience. To call it *a priori* is to express a fact; but to impute the *a priori* character of the generalizing force of meanings to *reason* is to invert the facts. Rationality is acquired when the tendency becomes circumspect, based upon observation and tested by deliberate experiment.

Meaning is objective as well as universal. Originating as a concerted or combined method of using or enjoying things, it indicates a possible interaction, not a thing in separate singleness. A meaning may not of course have the particular objectivity which is imputed to it, as whistling does not actually portend wind, nor the ceremonial sprinkling of water indicate rain. But such magical impu-

tations of external reference testify to the objectivity of meaning as such. Meanings are naturally the meaning of something or other; difficulty lies in discriminating the right thing. It requires the discipline of ordered and deliberate experimentation to teach us that some meanings delightful or horrendous as they are, are meanings communally developed in the process of communal festivity and control, and do not represent the polities, and ways and means of nature apart from social arts. Scientific meanings were superadded to esthetic and affectional meanings when objects instead of being defined in terms of their consequences in social interactions and discussion were defined in terms of their consequences with respect to one another. This discrimination permitted esthetic and affective objects to be freed from magical imputations, which were due to attributing to them *in rerum natura* the consequences they had in the transmitted culture of the group.

Yet the truth of classic philosophy in assigning objectivity to meanings, essences, ideas remains unassailable. It is heresy to conceive meanings to be private, a property of ghostly psychic existences. Berkeley with all his nominalism, saw that "ideas," though particular in existence, are general in function and office. His attribution of the ideas which are efficacious in conduct to an order established by God, while evincing lack of perception of their naturalistic origin in communication or communal interaction, manifests a sounder sense of the objectivity of meanings than has been shown by those who eliminated his theology while retaining his psychology. The inconsistency of the sensationalists who, stopping short of extreme scepticism, postulate that some associations of ideas correspond to conjunctions among things is also reluctantly extorted evidence of how intimation of the objectivity of ideas haunts the mind in spite of theory to the contrary.

Meanings are objective because they are modes of natural interaction; such an interaction; although primarily between organic beings, as includes things and energies external to living creatures. The regulative force of legal meanings affords a convenient illustration. A traffic policemen holds up his hand or blows a whistle. His act operates as a signal to direct movements. But it is more than an episodic stimulus. It embodies a rule of social action. Its proximate meaning is its near-by consequences in coordination of movements of persons and vehicles; its ulterior and permanent meaning—essence—is its consequence in the way of security of social movements. Failure to observe the signal subjects a person to arrest, fine or imprisonment. The essence embodied in the policeman's whistle is not an occult reality superimposed upon a sensuous or physical flux and imparting form to it; a mysterious subsistence somehow housed within a psychical event. Its essence is the rule, comprehensive and persisting, the standardized habit, of social interaction, and for the sake of which the whistle is used. The pattern, archetype, that forms the essence of the whistle as a particular noise is an orderly arrangement of the movements of persons and vehicles established by social agreement as its consequence. This meaning is independent of the psychical landscape, the sensations and imagery, of the policeman and others concerned. But it is not on that account a timeless spiritual ghost nor pale logical subsistence divorced from events.

The case is the same with the essence of any non-human event, like gravity, or virtue, or vertebrate. Some consequences of the interaction of things concern us; the consequences are not *merely* physical; they enter finally into human action and destiny. Fire burns and the burning is of moment. It enters experience; it is fascinating to watch swirling flames; it is important to avoid its dangers and to utilize its beneficial potencies. When we name an event, calling it fire, we speak proleptically; we do not name an immediate event; that is impossible. We employ a term of discourse; we invoke a meaning, namely, the potential consequences of the existence. The ultimate meaning of the noise made by the traffic officer is the total consequent system of social behavior, in which individuals are subjected, by means of noise, to social coordination; its proximate meaning is a

coordination of the movements of persons and vehicles in the neighborhood and directly affected. Similarly the ultimate meaning, or essence, denominated fire, is the consequences of certain natural events within the scheme of human activities, in the experience of social intercourse, the hearth and domestic alter, shared comfort, working of metals, rapid transit, and other such affairs. "Scientifically," we ignore these ulterior meanings. And quite properly; for when a sequential order of changes is determined, the final meaning in immediate enjoyments and appreciations is capable of control.

While classic thought, and its survival in later idealisms, assumed that the ulterior human meanings, meanings of direct association in discourse, are forms of nature apart from their place in discourse, modern thought is given to making a sharp separation between meanings determined in terms of the causal relationship of things and meanings in terms of human association. Consequently, it treats the latter as negligible or as purely private, not the meanings of natural events at all. It identifies the proximate meanings with the only valid meanings, and abstract relations become an idol. To pass over in science the human meanings of the consequences of natural interactions is legitimate; indeed it is indispensable. To ascertin and state meanings in abstraction from social or shared situations is the only way in which the latter can be intelligently modified, extended and varied. Mathematical symbols have least connection with distinctively human situations and consequences; and the finding of such terms, free from esthetic and moral significance, is a necessary part of the technique. Indeed, such elimination of ulterior meanings supplies perhaps the best possible empirical definition of mathemtical relations. They are meanings without direct reference to human behavior. Thus an essence becomes wholly "intellectual" or scientific, devoid of consummatory implication; it expresses the purely instrumental without reference to the objects to which the events in question are instrumental. It then becomes the starting point of reflection that may terminate in ends or consequences in human suffering and enjoyment not previously experienced. Abstraction from any particular consequence (which is the same thing as taking instrumentality generally), opens the way to new uses and consequences. . . .

If scientific discourse is instrumental in function, it also is capable of becoming an enjoyed object to those concerned in it. Upon the whole, human history shows that thinking in being abstract, remote and technical has been laborious; or at least that the process of attaining such thinking has been rendered painful to most by social circumstances. In view of the importance of such activity and its objects, it is a priceless gain when it becomes an intrinsic delight. Few would philosophize if philosophic discourse did not have its own inhering fascination. Yet it is not the satisfactoriness of the activity which defines science or philosophy; the definition comes from the structure and function of subject-matter. To say that knowledge as the fruit of intellectual discourse is an end in itself is to say what is esthetically and morally true for some persons, but it conveys nothing about the structure of knowledge; and it does not even hint that its objects are not instrumental. These are questions that can be decided only by an examination of the things in question. Impartial and disinterested thinking, discourse in terms of scrutinized, tested, and related meanings, is a fine art. But it is an art as yet open to comparatively few. Letters, poetry, song, the drama, fiction, history, biography, engaging in rites and ceremonies hallowed by time and rich with the sense of the countless multitudes that share in them, are also modes of discourse that, detached from immediate instrumental consequences of assistance and cooperative action, are ends for most persons. In them discourse is both instrumental and final. No person remains unchanged and has the same future efficiencies, who shares in situations made possible by communication. Subsequent consequences may be good or bad, but they are there. The part of wisdom is not to deny the causal fact because of the intrinsic value of the immediate experience. It is to make the immediately satisfactory object the object which will also be most fertile.

The saying of Matthew Arnold that poetry is a criticism of life sounds harsh to the ears of some persons of strong esthetic bent; it seems to give poetry a moral and instrumental function. But while poetry is not a criticism of life in intent, it is in effect, and so is all art. For art fixes those standards of enjoyment and appreciation with which other things are compared; it selects the objects of future desires; it stimulates effort. This is true of the objects in which a particular person finds his immediate or esthetic values, and it is true of collective man. The level and style of the arts of literature, poetry, ceremony, amusement, and recreation which obtain in a community, furnishing the staple objects of enjoyment in that community, do more than all else to determine the current direction of ideas and endeavors in the community. They supply the meanings in terms of which life is judged, esteemed, and criticized. For an outside spectator, they supply material for a critical evaluation of the life led by that community.

Communication is uniquely instrumental and uniquely final. It is instrumental as liberating us from the otherwise overwhelming pressure of events and enabling us to live in a world of things that have meaning. It is final as a sharing in the objects and arts precious to a community, a sharing whereby meanings are enhanced, deepened and solidified in the sense of communion. Because of its characteristic agency and finality, communication and its congenial objects are objects ultimately worthy of awe, admiration, and loyal appreciation. They are worthy as means, because they are the only means that make life rich and varied in meanings. They are worthy as ends, because in such ends man is lifted from his immediate isolation and shares in a communion of meanings. Here, as in so many other things, the great evil lies in separating instrumental and final functions. Intelligence is partial and specialized, because communication and participation are limited, sectarian, provincial, confined to class, party, professional group. By the same token, our enjoyment of ends is luxurious and corrupting for some; brutal, trivial, harsh for others; exclusion from the life of free and full communication excluding both alike from full possession of meanings of the things that enter experience. When the instrumental and final functions of communication live together in experience, there exists an intelligence which is the method and reward of the common life, and a society worthy to command affection, admiration, and loyalty.

# The Pattern of Inquiry

The existence of inquiries is not a matter of doubt. They enter into every area of life and into every aspect of every area. In everyday living, men examine; they turn things over intellectually; they infer and judge as "naturally" as they reap and sow, produce and exchange commodities. As a mode of conduct, inquiry is as accessible to objective study as are these other modes of behavior. Because of the intimate and decisive way in which inquiry and its conclusions enter into the management of all affairs of life, no study of the latter is adequate save as it is noted how they are affected by the methods and instruments of inquiry that currently obtain. Quite apart, then, from the particular hypothesis about logical forms that is put forth, study of the objective facts of inquiry is a matter of tremendous import, practically and intellectually. These materials provide the theory of logical forms with a subject-matter that is not only objective but is objective in a fashion that enables logic to avoid the three mistakes most characteristic of its history.

1. In virtue of its concern with objectively observable subject-matter by reference to which reflective conclusions can be tried and tested, dependence upon subjective and "mentalistic" states and processes is eliminated.

2. The distinctive existence and nature of forms is acknowledged. Logic is not compelled, as historic "empirical" logic felt compelled to do, to reduce logical forms to mere transcripts of the empirical materials that antecede the existence of the former. Just as art-forms and legal forms are capable of independent discussion and development, so are logical forms, even though the "independence" in question is intermediate, not final and complete. As in the case of these other forms, they originate *out of* experiential material, and when constituted introduce new ways of operating with prior materials, which ways modify the material out of which they develop.

3. Logical theory is liberated from the unobservable, transcendental and "intuitional."

When methods and results of inquiry are studied as objective data, the distinction that has often been drawn between noting and reporting the ways in which men *do* think, and prescribing the ways in which they *ought* to think, takes on a very different interpretation from that usually given. The usual interpretation is in terms of the difference between the psychological and the logical, the latter consisting of "norms" provided from some source wholly outside of and independent of "experience."

The way in which men *do* "think" denotes, as it is *here* interpreted, simply the ways in which men at a given time carry on their inquiries. So far as it is used to register a difference from the ways in which they *ought* to

From "The Pattern of Inquiry," in *Logic: The Theory of Inquiry, John Dewey: The Later Works, 1925–1953*, Vol. 12, Ed. Jo Ann Boydston (Carbondale and Edwardsville: Southern Illinois University Press, 1986 [1938]), pp. 106–122.

think, it denotes a difference like that between good and bad farming or good and bad medical practice. Men think in ways they should not when they follow methods of inquiry that experience of past inquiries shows are not competent to reach the intended end of the inquiries in question.

Everybody knows that today there are in vogue methods of farming generally followed in the past which compare very unfavorably in their results with those obtained by practices that have already been introduced and tested. When an expert tells a farmer he *should* do thus and so, he is not setting up for a bad farmer an ideal drawn from the blue. He is instructing him in methods that have been tried and that have proved successful in procuring results. In a similar way we are able to contrast various kinds of inquiry that are in use or that have been used in respect to their economy and efficiency in reaching warranted conclusions. We know that some methods of inquiry are better than others in just the same way in which we know that some methods of surgery, farming, road-making, navigating or what-not are better than others. It does not follow in any of these cases that the "better" methods are ideally perfect, or that they are regulative or "normative" because of conformity to some absolute form. They are the methods which experience up to the present time shows to be the best methods available for achieving certain results, while abstraction of these methods does supply a (relative) norm or standard for further undertakings.

The search for the pattern of inquiry is, accordingly, not one instituted in the dark or at large. It is checked and controlled by knowledge of the kinds of inquiry that have and that have not worked; methods which, as was pointed out earlier, can be so compared as to yield reasoned or rational conclusions. For, through comparison-contrast, we ascertain *how* and *why* certain means and agencies have provided warrantably assertible conclusions, while others have not and *cannot* do so in the sense in which "cannot" expresses an intrinsic incompatibility between means used and consequences attained.

We may now ask: What is the *definition* of Inquiry? That is, what is the most highly generalized conception of inquiry which can be justifiably formulated? The definition that will be expanded, directly in the present chapter and indirectly in the following chapters, is as follows: *Inquiry is the controlled or directed transformation of an indeterminate situation into one that is so determinate in its constituent distinctions and relations as to convert the elements of the original situation into a unified whole.*

The original indeterminate situation is not only "open" to inquiry, but it is open in the sense that its constituents do not hang together. The determinate situation on the other hand, *qua* outcome of inquiry, is a closed and, as it were, finished situation or "universe of experience." "Controlled or directed" in the above formula refers to the fact that inquiry is competent in any given case in the degree in which the operations involved in it actually do terminate in the establishment of an objectively unified existential situation. In the intermediate course of transition and transformation of the indeterminate situation, *dis*course through use of symbols is employed as means. In received logical terminology, propositions, or terms and the relations between them, are intrinsically involved.

I. *The Antecedent Conditions of Inquiry: The Indeterminate Situation.* Inquiry and questioning, up to a certain point, are synonymous terms. We inquire when we question; and we inquire when we seek for whatever will provide an answer to a question asked. Thus it is of the very nature of the indeterminate situation which evokes inquiry to be *questionable;* or, in terms of actuality instead of potentiality, to be uncertain, unsettled, disturbed. The peculiar quality of what pervades the given materials, constituting them a situation, is not just uncertainty at large; it is a unique doubtfulness which makes that situation to be just and only the situation it is. It is this unique quality that not only evokes the particular inquiry engaged in but that exercises control over its special procedures. Otherwise, one procedure in inquiry would be as likely to occur and to be effective as any other. Unless a situation is uniquely qualified in its very indeterminateness, there is a condition of complete panic; response to it takes the form of blind and wild overt activities. Stating the matter from the personal side, we have "lost our heads." A variety of names serves to characterize indeterminate situations. They are disturbed, troubled, ambiguous, confused, full of conflicting tendencies, obscure, etc.

It is the *situation* that has these traits. *We* are doubtful because the situation is inherently doubtful. Personal states of doubt that are not evoked by and are not relative to some existential situation are pathological; when they are extreme they constitute the mania of doubting. Consequently, situations that are disturbed and troubled, confused or obscure, cannot be straightened out, cleared up and put in order, by manipulation of our personal states of mind. The attempt to settle them by such manipulations involves what psychiatrists call "withdrawal from reality." Such an attempt is pathological as far as it goes, and when it goes far it is the source of some form of actual insanity. The habit of disposing of the doubtful as if it belonged only to *us* rather than to the existential situation in which we are caught and implicated is an inheritance from subjectivistic psychology. The biological antecedent conditions of an unsettled situation are involved in that state of imbalance in organic-environmental interactions which has already been described. Restoration of integration can be effected, in one case as in the other, only by operations which actually modify existing conditions, not by merely "mental" processes.

It is, accordingly, a mistake to suppose that a situation is doubtful only in a "subjective" sense. The notion that in actual existence everything is completely determinate has been rendered questionable by the progress of physical science itself. Even if it had not been, complete determination would not hold of existences as an *environment*. For Nature is an environment only as it is involved in interaction with an organism, or self, or whatever name be used.[1]

Every such interaction is a temporal process, not a momentary cross-sectional occurrence. The situation in which it occurs is indeterminate, therefore, with respect to its *issue*. If we call it *confused,* then it is meant that its outcome cannot be anticipated. It is called *obscure* when its course of movement permits of final consequences that cannot be clearly made out. It is called *conflicting* when it tends to evoke discordant responses. Even were existential conditions unqualifiedly determinate in and of themselves, they are indeterminate in *significance:* that is, in what they import and portend in their interaction with the organism. The organic responses that enter into the production of the state of affairs that is temporally later and sequential are just as existential as are environing conditions.

The immediate *locus* of the problem concerns, then, what kind of responses the organism shall make. It concerns the interaction of organic responses and environing conditions in their movement toward an existential issue. It is a commonplace that in any troubled state of affair *things* will come out differently according to what is done. The farmer won't get grain unless he plants and tills; the general will win or lose the battle according to the way he conducts it, and so on. Neither the grain nor the tilling, neither the outcome of the battle nor the conduct of it, are "mental" events. Organic interaction becomes inquiry when existential consequences are anticipated; when environing conditions are examined with reference to their potentialities; and when responsive activities are selected and ordered with reference to actualization of some of the potentialities, rather than others, in a final existential situation. Resolution of the indeterminate situation is active and operational. If the inquiry is adequately directed, the final issue is the unified situation that has been mentioned.

II. *Institution of a Problem.* The unsettled or indeterminate situation might have been called a *problematic* situation. This name would have been, however, proleptic and anticipatory. The indeterminate situation becomes problematic in the very process of being subjected to inquiry. The indeterminate situation comes into existence from existential causes, just as does, say, the organic imbalance of hunger. There is nothing intellectual or cognitive in the existence of such situations, although they are the necessary condition of cognitive operations or inquiry. In themselves they are precognitive. The first result of evocation of inquiry is that the situation is taken, adjudged, to be problematic. To see what a situation requires inquiry is the initial step in inquiry.[2]

Qualification of a situation as problematic does not, however, carry inquiry far. It is but an initial step in institution of a problem. A problem is not a task to be performed which a person puts upon himself or that is placed upon him by others—like a so-called arithmetical "problem" in school work. A problem represents the partial transformation by inquiry of a problematic situation into a determinate situation. It is a familiar and significant saying that a problem well put is half-solved. To find out *what* the problem and problems are which a problematic situation presents to be inquired into, is to be well along in inquiry. To mis-take the problem involved is to cause subsequent inquiry to be irrelevant or to go astray. Without a problem, there is blind groping in the dark. The way in which the problem is conceived decides what specific suggestions are entertained and which are dismissed; what data are selected and which rejected; it is the criterion for relevancy and irrelevancy of hypotheses and conceptual structures. On the other hand, to set up a problem that does not grow out of an actual situation is to start on a course of dead work, nonetheless dead because the work is "busy work." Problems that are self-set are mere excuses for seeming to do something intellectual, something that has the semblance but not the substance of scientific activity.

III. *The Determination of a Problem-Solution.* Statement of a problematic situation in terms of a problem has no meaning save as the problem instituted has, in the very terms of its statement, reference to a possible solution. Just because a problem well stated is on its way to solution, the determining of a genuine problem is a *progressive* inquiry; the cases in which a problem and its probable solution flash upon an inquirer are cases where much prior ingestion and digestion have occurred. If we assume, prematurely, that the problem involved is definite and clear, subsequent inquiry proceeds on the wrong track. Hence the question arises: How is the formation of a genuine problem so controlled that further inquiries will move toward a solution?

The first step in answering this question is to recognize that no situation which is *completely* indeterminate can possibly be converted into a problem having definite constituents. The first step then is to search out the *constituents* of a given situation which, as constituents, are settled. When an alarm of fire is sounded in a crowded assembly hall, there is much that is indeterminate as regards the activities that may produce a favorable issue. One may get out safely or one may be trampled and burned. The fire is characterized, however, by some settled traits. It is, for example, located *somewhere*. Then the aisles and exits are at fixed places. Since they are settled or determinate in *existence*, the first step in institution of a problem is to settle them in *observation*. There are other factors which, while they are not as temporally and spatially fixed, are yet observable constituents; for example, the behavior and movements of other members of the audience. All of these observed conditions taken together constitute "the facts of the case." They constitute the terms of the problem, because they are conditions that must be reckoned with or taken account of in any relevant solution that is proposed.

A *possible* relevant solution is then suggested by the determination of factual conditions which are secured by observation. The possible solution presents itself, therefore, as an *idea*, just as the terms of the problem (which are facts) are instituted by observation. Ideas are anticipated consequences (forecasts) of what will happen when certain operations are executed under and with respect to observed conditions.[3] Observation of facts and suggested meanings or ideas arise and develop in correspondence with each other. The more the facts of the case come to light in consequence of being subjected to observation, the clearer and more pertinent become the conceptions of the way the problem constituted by these facts is to be dealt with. On the other side, the clearer the idea, the more definite, as a truism, become the operations of observation and of execution that must be performed in order to resolve the situation.

An idea is first of all an anticipation of something that may happen; it marks a *possibility.* When it is said, as it sometimes is, that science is *prediction,* the anticipation that constitutes every idea an idea is grounded in a set of controlled observations and of regulated conceptual ways of interpreting them. Because inquiry is a progressive determination of a problem and its possible solution, ideas differ in grade according to the stage of inquiry reached. At first, save in highly familiar matters, they are vague. They occur at first simply as suggestions; suggestions just spring up, flash upon us, occur to us. They may then become stimuli to direct an overt activity but they have as yet no logical status. Every idea originates as a suggestion, but not every suggestion is an idea. The suggestion becomes an idea when it is examined with reference to its functional fitness; its capacity as a means of resolving the given situation.

This examination takes the form of reasoning, as a result of which we are able to appraise better than we were at the outset, the pertinency and weight of the meaning now entertained with respect to its functional capacity. But the final test of its possession of these properties is determined when it actually functions—that is, when it is put into operation so as to institute by means of observation facts not previously observed, and is then used to organize them with other facts into a coherent whole.

Because suggestions and ideas are of that which is not present in given existence, the meanings which they involve must be embodied in some symbol. Without some kind of symbol no idea; a meaning that is completely disembodied can not be entertained or used.

Since an existence (which *is* an existence) is the support and vehicle of a meaning and is a symbol instead of a merely physical existence only in this respect, embodied meanings or ideas are capable of objective survey and development. To "look at an idea" is not a mere literary figure of speech.

"Suggestions" have received scant courtesy in logical theory. It is true that when they just "pop into our heads," because of the workings of the psycho-physical organism, they are not logical. But they are both the conditions and the primary stuff of logical ideas. The traditional empiristic theory reduced them, as has already been pointed out, to mental copies of physical things and assumed that they were *per se* identical with ideas. Consequently it ignored the function of ideas in directing observation and in ascertaining relevant facts. The rationalistic school, on the other hand, saw clearly that "facts" apart from ideas are trivial, that they acquire import and significance only in relation to ideas. But at the same time it failed to attend to the operative and functional nature of the latter. Hence, it treated ideas as equivalent to the ultimate structure of "Reality." The Kantian formula that apart from each other "perceptions are blind and conceptions empty" marks a profound logical insight. The insight, however, was radically distorted because perceptual and conceptual contents were supposed to originate from different sources and thus required a third activity, that of synthetic understanding, to bring them together. In logical fact, perceptual and conceptual materials are instituted in functional correlativity with each other, in such a manner that the former locates and describes the problem while the latter represents a possible method of solution. Both are determinations in and by inquiry of the original problematic situation whose pervasive quality controls their institution and their contents. Both are finally checked by their capacity to work together to introduce a resolved unified situation. As distinctions they represent logical divisions of labor.

IV. *Reasoning.* The necessity of developing the meaning-contents of ideas in their relations to one another has been incidentally noted. This process, operating with symbols (constituting propositions) is reasoning in the sense of ratiocination or rational discourse.[4] When a suggested meaning is immediately accepted, inquiry is cut short. Hence the conclusion reached is not grounded, even if it happens to be correct. The check upon immediate acceptance is the examination of the meaning as a meaning. This examination consists in noting what the meaning in question implies in relation to other meanings in the system of which it is a member, the formulated relation constituting a proposition. If such and such a relation of meanings is accepted, then we are committed to such and such other relations of meanings because of their membership in the same system. Through a series of intermediate meanings, a meaning is finally reached which is more clearly *relevant* to the problem in hand than the originally suggested idea. It indicates operations which can be performed to test its applicability, whereas the original idea is usually too vague to determine crucial operations. In other words, the idea or meaning when developed in discourse directs the activities which, when executed, provide needed evidential material.

The point made can be most readily appreciated in connection with scientific reasoning. An hypothesis, once suggested and entertained, is developed in relation to other conceptual structures until it receives a form in which it can instigate and direct an experiment that will disclose precisely those conditions which have the maximum possible force in determining whether the hypothesis should be accepted or rejected. Or it may be that the experiment will indicate what modifications are required in the hypothesis so that it may be applicable, i.e., suited to interpret and organize the facts of the case. In many familiar situations, the meaning that is most relevant has been settled because of the eventuations of experiments in prior cases so that it is applicable almost immediately upon its occurrence. But, indirectly, if not directly, an idea or suggestion that is not developed in terms of the constellation of meanings to which it belongs can lead only to overt response. Since the latter terminates inquiry, there is then no adequate inquiry into the meaning that is used to settle the given situation, and the conclusion is in so far logically ungrounded.

V. *The Operational Character of Facts-Meanings.* It was stated that the observed facts of the case and the ideational contents expressed in ideas are related to each other, as, respectively, a clarification of the problem involved and the proposal of some possible solution; that they are, accordingly, functional divisions in the work of inquiry. Observed facts in their office of locating and describing the problem are existential; ideational subject-matter is non-existential. How, then, do they cooperate with each other in the resolution of an existential situation? The problem is insoluble save as it is recognized that both observed facts and entertained ideas are operational. Ideas are operational in that they instigate and direct further operations of observation; they are proposals and plans for acting upon existing conditions to bring new facts to light and to organize all the selected facts into a coherent whole.

What is meant by calling facts operational? Upon the negative side what is meant is that they are not self-sufficient and complete in themselves. They are selected and described, as we have seen, for a purpose, namely statement of the problem involved in such a way that its material both indicates a meaning relevant to resolution of the difficulty and serves to test its worth and validity. In regulated inquiry facts are selected and arranged with the express intent of fulfilling this office. They are not merely *results* of operations of observation which are executed with the aid of bodily organs and auxiliary instruments of art, but they are the particular facts and kinds of facts that will link up with one another in the definite ways that are required to produce a definite end. Those not found to connect with others in furtherance of this end are dropped and others are sought for. Being functional, they are necessarily operational. Their function is to serve as evidence and their evidential quality is judged on the basis of their capacity to form an ordered whole in response to operations prescribed by the ideas they occasion and support. If "the facts of the case" were final and complete in themselves, if they did not have a special operative force in resolution of the problematic situation, they could not serve as evidence.

The operative force of facts is apparent when we consider that no fact in isolation has evidential potency. Facts are evidential and are tests of an idea in so far as they are capable of being organized with one another. The organization can be achieved only as they *interact* with one another. When the problematic situation is such as to require extensive inquiries to effect its resolution, a series of interactions intervenes. Some observed facts point to an idea that stands for a possible solution. This idea evokes more observations. Some of the newly observed facts link up with those previously observed and are such as to rule out other observed things with respect to their evidential function. The new order of facts suggests a modified idea (or hypothesis) which occasions new observations whose result again determines a new order of facts, and so on until the existing order is both unified and complete. In the course of this serial process, the ideas that represent possible solutions are tested or "proved."

Meantime, the order of facts, which present themselves in consequence of the experimental observations the ideas call out and direct, are *trial* facts. They are provisional. They are "facts" if they are observed by sound organs and techniques. But they are not on that account the *facts of the case.* They are tested or "proved" with respect to their evidential function just as much as ideas (hypotheses) are tested with reference to their power to exercise the function of resolution. The operative force of both ideas and facts is thus practically recognized in the degree in which they are connected with *experiment.* Naming them "operational" is but a theoretical recognition of what is involved when inquiry satisfies the conditions imposed by the necessity for experiment.

I recur, in this connection, to what has been said about the necessity for symbols in inquiry. It is obvious, on the face of matters, that a possible mode of solution must be carried in symbolic form since it is a possibility, not an assured present existence. Observed facts, on the other hand, are existentially present. It might seem therefore, that symbols are not required for referring to them. But if they are not carried and treated by means of symbols, they lose their provisional character, and in losing this character they are categorically asserted and inquiry comes to an end. The carrying on of inquiry requires that the facts be taken as *re*presentative and not just as *pre*sented. This demand is met by formulating them in propositions—that is, by means of symbols. Unless they are so represented they relapse into the total qualitative situation.

VI. *Common Sense and Scientific Inquiry.* The discussion up to this point has proceeded in general terms which recognized no distinction between common sense and scientific inquiry. We have now reached a point where the community of pattern in these two distinctive modes of inquiry should receive explicit attention. It was said in earlier chapters that the difference between them resides in their respective subject-matters, not in their basic logical forms and relations; that the difference in subject-matters is due to the difference in the problems respectively involved; and, finally, that this difference sets up a difference in the ends or objective consequences they are concerned to achieve. Because common sense problems and inquiries have to do with the interactions into which living creatures enter in connection with environing conditions in order to establish objects of use and enjoyment, the symbols employed are those which have been determined in the habitual culture of a group. They form a system but the system is practical rather than intellectual. It is constituted by the traditions, occupations, techniques, interests, and established institutions of the group. The meanings that compose it are carried in the common everyday language of communication between members of the group. The meanings involved in this common language system determine what individuals of the group may and may not do in relation to physical objects and in relations to one another. They regulate *what* can be used and enjoyed and *how* use and enjoyment shall occur.

Because the symbol-meaning systems involved are connected directly with cultural life-activities and are related to each other in virtue of this connection, the specific meanings which are present have reference to the specific and limited environing conditions under which the group lives. Only those things of the environment that are taken, according to custom and tradition, as having connection with and bearing upon this life, enter into the meaning system. There is no such thing as disinterested intellectual concern with either physical or social matters. For, until the rise of science, there were no problems of common sense that called for such inquiry. Disinterestedness existed practically in the demand that group interests and concerns be put above private needs and interests. But there was no intellectual disinterestedness beyond the activities, interests and concerns of the group. In other words, there was no science as such, although, as was earlier pointed out, there did exist information and techniques which were available for the purposes of scientific inquiry and out of which the latter subsequently grew.

In scientific inquiry, then, meanings are related to one another on the ground of their character *as* meanings, freed from direct reference to the concerns of a limited group. Their intellectual abstractness is a product of this liberation, just as the "concrete" is practically identified by directness of connection with environmental interactions. Consequently a new language, a new system of symbols related together on a new basis, comes into existence, and in this new language semantic coherence, as such, is the controlling consideration. To repeat what has already been said, connection with problems of use and enjoyment is the source of the dominant role of qualities, sensible and moral, and of ends in common sense.

In science, since meanings are determined on the ground of their relation as meanings to one another, *relations* become the objects of

inquiry and qualities are relegated to a secondary status, playing a part only as far as they assist in institution of relations. They are subordinate because they have an instrumental office, instead of being themselves, as in prescientific common sense, the matters of final importance. The enduring hold of common sense is testified to historically by the long time it took before it was seen that scientific objects are strictly relational. First tertiary qualities were eliminated; it was recognized that moral qualities are not agencies in determining the structure of nature. Then secondary qualities, the wet-dry, hot-cold, light-heavy, which were the explanatory principles of physical phenomena in Greek science, were ejected. But so-called primary qualities took their place, as with Newton and the Lockeian formulation of Newtonian existential postulates. It was not until the threshold of our time was reached that scientific inquirers perceived that their own problems and methods required an interpretation of "primary qualities" in terms of relations, such as position, motion and temporal span. In the structure of distinctively scientific objects these relations are indifferent to qualities.

The foregoing is intended to indicate that the different objectives of common sense and of scientific inquiry demand different subject-matters and that this difference in subject-matters is not incompatible with the existence of a common pattern in both types. There are, of course, secondary logical forms which reflect the distinction of properties involved in the change from qualitative and teleological subject-matter to non-qualitative and non-teleological relations. But they occur and operate within the described community of pattern. They are explicable, and explicable only, on the ground of the distinctive problems generated by scientific subject-matter. The independence of scientific objects from limited and fairly direct reference to the environment as a factor in activities of use and enjoyment, is equivalent, as has already been intimated, to their *abstract* character. It is also equivalent to their *general* character in the sense in which the generalizations of science are different from the generalizations with which common sense is familiar. The generality of *all* scientific subject-matter as such means that it is freed from restriction to conditions which present themselves at particular times and places. Their reference is to *any* set of time and place conditions—a statement which is not to be confused with the doctrine that they have no reference to actual existential occasions. Reference to time-place of existence is necessarily involved, but it is reference to whatever set of existences fulfills the general relations laid down in and by the constitution of the scientific object.[5]

*Summary.* Since a number of points have been discussed, it will be well to round up conclusions reached about them in a summary statement of the structure of the common pattern of inquiry. Inquiry is the directed or controlled transformation of an indeterminate situation into a determinately unified one. The transition is achieved by means of operations of two kinds which are in functional correspondence with each other. One kind of operations deals with ideational or conceptual subject-matter. This subject-matter stands for possible ways and ends of resolution. It anticipates a solution, and is marked off from fancy because, or, in so far as, it becomes operative in instigation and direction of new observations yielding new factual material. The other kind of operations is made up of activities involving the techniques and organs of observation. Since these operations are existential they modify the prior existential situation, bring into high relief conditions previously obscure, and relegate to the background other aspects that were at the outset conspicuous. The ground and criterion of the execution of this work of emphasis, selection and arrangement is to delimit the problem in such a way that existential material may be provided with which to test the ideas that represent possible modes of solution. Symbols, defining terms and propositions, are necessarily required in order to retain and carry forward both ideational and existential subject-matters in order that they may serve their proper functions in the control of inquiry. Otherwise the

problem is taken to be closed and inquiry ceases.

One fundamentally important phase of the transformation of the situation which constitutes inquiry is central in the treatment of judgment and its functions. The transformation is existential and hence temporal. The pre-cognitive unsettled situation can be settled only by modification of its constituents. Experimental operations change existing conditions. Reasoning, as such, can provide means for effecting the change of conditions but by itself cannot effect it. Only execution of existential operations directed by an idea in which ratiocination terminates can bring about the re-ordering of environing conditions required to produce a settled and unified situation. Since this principle also applies to the meanings that are elaborated in science, the experimental production and re-arrangement of physical conditions involved in natural science is further evidence of the unity of the pattern of inquiry. The temporal quality of inquiry means, then, something quite other than the process of inquiry takes time. It means that the objective subject-matter of inquiry undergoes temporal modification. . . .

## Notes

1. Except of course a purely mentalistic name, like *consciousness.* The alleged problem of "interactionism" versus automatism, parallelism, etc., is a problem (and an insoluble one) because of the assumption involved in its statement—the assumption, namely, that the interaction in question is with something mental instead of with biological-cultural human beings.

2. If by "two-valued logic" is meant a logic that regards "true and false" as the sole logical values, then such a logic is necessarily so truncated that clearness and consistency in logical doctrine are impossible. Being the matter of a problem is a primary logical property.

3. The theory of *ideas* that has been held in psychology and epistemology since the time of Locke's successors is completely irrelevant and obstructive in logical theory. For in treating them as copies of perceptions or "impressions," it ignores the prospective and anticipatory character that defines *being* an idea. Failure to define ideas func-

tionally, in the reference they have to a solution of a problem, is one reason they have been treated as merely "mental." The notion, on the other hand, that ideas are fantasies is a derivative. Fantasies arise when the function an idea performs is ruled out when it is entertained and developed.

4. "Reasoning" is sometimes used to designate *inference* as well as ratiocination. When so used in logic the tendency is to identify inference and implication and thereby seriously to confuse logical theory.

5. The consequences that follow are directly related to the statement. . . . that the elimination of qualities and ends is intermediate; that, in fact, the construction of purely relational objects has enormously liberated and expanded common sense uses and enjoyments by conferring control over production of qualities, by enabling new ends to be realistically instituted, and by providing competent means for achieving them.

# Education as Growth

1. *The Conditions of Growth*—In directing the activities of the young, society determines its own future in determining that of the young. Since the young at a given time will at some later date compose the society of that period, the latter's nature will largely turn upon the direction children's activities were given at an earlier period. This cumulative movement of action toward a later result is what is meant by growth.

The primary condition of growth is immaturity. This may seem to be a mere truism—saying that a being can develop only in some point in which he is undeveloped. But the prefix "im" of the word immaturity means something positive, not a mere void or lack. It is noteworthy that the terms "capacity" and "potentiality" have a double meaning, one sense being negative, the other positive. Capacity may denote mere receptivity, like the capacity of a quart measure. We may mean by potentiality a merely dormant or quiescent state—a capacity to become something different under external influences. But we also mean by capacity an ability, a power; and by potentiality potency, force. Now when we say that immaturity means the possibility of growth, we are not referring to absence of

powers which may exist at a later time; we express a force positively present—the *ability* to develop.

Our tendency to take immaturity as mere lack, and growth as something which fills up the gap between the immature and the mature is due to regarding childhood *comparatively*, instead of intrinsically. We treat it simply as a privation because we are measuring it by adulthood as a fixed standard. This fixes attention upon what the child has not, and will not have till he becomes a man. This comparative standpoint is legitimate enough for some purposes, but if we make it final, the question arises whether we are not guilty of an overweening presumption. Children, if they could express themselves articulately and sincerely, would tell a different tale; and there is excellent adult authority for the conviction that for certain moral and intellectual purposes adults must become as little children.

The seriousness of the assumption of the negative quality of the possibilities of immaturity is apparent when we reflect that it sets up as an ideal and standard a static end. The fulfillment of growing is taken to mean an *accomplished* growth: that is to say, an Ungrowth, something which is no longer

From "Education as Growth," in *Democracy and Education, John Dewey: The Middle Works, 1899–1924,* Vol. 9, Ed. Jo Ann Boydston, (Carbondale and Edwardsville: Southern Illinois University Press, 1980 [1916]), pp. 46–58.

growing. The futility of the assumption is seen in the fact that every adult resents the imputation of having no further possibilities of growth; and so far as he finds that they are closed to him mourns the fact as evidence of loss, instead of falling back on the achieved as adequate manifestation of power. Why an unequal measure for child and man?

Taken absolutely, instead of comparatively, immaturity designates a positive force or ability,—the *power* to grow. We do not have to draw out or educe positive activities from a child, as some educational doctrines would have it. Where there is life, there are already eager and impassioned activities. Growth is not something done to them; it is something they do. The positive and constructive aspect of possibility gives the key to understanding the two chief traits of immaturity, dependence and plasticity. (1) It sounds absurd to hear dependence spoken of as something positive, still more absurd as a power. Yet if helplessness were all there were in dependence, no development could ever take place. A merely impotent being has to be carried, forever, by others. The fact that dependence is accompanied by growth in ability, not by an ever increasing lapse into parasitism, suggests that it is already something constructive. Being merely sheltered by others would not promote growth. For (2) it would only build a wall around impotence. With reference to the physical world, the child is helpless. He lacks at birth and for a long time thereafter power to make his way physically, to make his own living. If he had to do that by himself, he would hardly survive an hour. On this side his helplessness is almost complete. The young of the brutes are immeasurably his superiors. He is physically weak and not able to turn the strength which he possesses to coping with the physical environment.

1. The thoroughgoing character of this helplessness suggests, however, some compensating power. The relative ability of the young of brute animals to adapt themselves fairly well to physical conditions from an early period suggests the fact that their life is not intimately bound up with the life of those about them. They are compelled, so to speak, to have physical gifts because they are lacking in social gifts. Human infants, on the other hand, can get along with physical incapacity just because of their social capacity. We sometimes talk and think as if they simply happened to be *physically* in a social environment; as if social forces exclusively existed in the adults who take care of them, they being passive recipients. If it were said that children are themselves marvelously endowed with *power* to enlist the cooperative attention of others, this would be thought to be a backhanded way of saying that others are marvelously attentive to the needs of children. But observation shows that children are gifted with an equipment of the first order for social intercourse. Few grown-up persons retain all of the flexible and sensitive ability of children to vibrate sympathetically with the attitudes and doings of those about them. Inattention to physical things (going with incapacity to control them) is accompanied by a corresponding intensification of interest and attention as to the doings of people. The native mechanism of the child and his impulses all tend to facile social responsiveness. The statement that children, before adolescence, are egotistically self-centered, even if it were true, would not contradict the truth of this statement. It would simply indicate that their social responsiveness is employed on their own behalf, not that it does not exist. But the statement is not true as matter of fact. The facts which are cited in support of the alleged pure egoism of children really show the intensity and directness with which they go to their mark. If the ends which form the mark seem narrow and selfish to adults, it is only because adults (by means of a similar engrossment in their day) have mastered these ends, which have consequently ceased to interest them. Most of the remainder of children's alleged native egoism is simply an egoism which runs counter to an adult's egoism. To a grown-up person who is too absorbed in his own affairs to take an interest in children's affairs, children doubtless seem unreasonably engrossed in *their* own affairs.

From a social standpoint, dependence denotes a power rather than a weakness; it involves interdependence. There is always a danger that increased personal independence will decrease the social capacity of an individual. In making him more self-reliant, it may make him more self-sufficient; it may lead to aloofness and indifference. It often makes an individual so insensitive in his relations to others as to develop an illusion of being really able to stand and act alone—an unnamed form of insanity which is responsible for a large part of the remediable suffering of the world.

2. The specific adaptability of an immature creature for growth constitutes his *plasticity*. This is something quite different from the plasticity of putty or wax. It is not a capacity to take on change of form in accord with external pressure. It lies near the pliable elasticity by which some persons take on the color of their surroundings while retaining their own bent. But it is something deeper than this. It is essentially the ability to learn from experience; the power to retain from one experience something which is of avail in coping with the difficulties of a later situation. This means power to modify actions on the basis of the results of prior experiences, the power to *develop dispositions*. Without it, the acquisition of habits is impossible.

It is a familiar fact that the young of the higher animals, and especially the human young, have to *learn* to utilize their instinctive reactions. The human being is born with a greater number of instinctive tendencies than other animals. But the instincts of the lower animals perfect themselves for appropriate action at an early period after birth, while most of those of the human infant are of little account just as they stand. An original specialized power of adjustment secures immediate efficiency, but, like a railway ticket, it is good for one route only. A being who, in order to use his eyes, ears, hands, and legs, has to experiment in making varied combinations of their reactions, achieves a control that is flexible and varied. A chick, for example, pecks accurately at a bit of food in a few hours after hatching. This means that definite coordina-

tions of activities of the eyes in seeing and of the body and head in striking are perfected in a few trials. An infant requires about six months to be able to gauge with approximate accuracy the action in reaching which will coordinate with his visual activities; to be able, that is, to tell whether he can reach a seen object and just how to execute the reaching. As a result, the chick is limited by the relative perfection of its original endowment. The infant has the advantage of the *multitude* of instinctive tentative reactions and of the experiences that accompany them, even though he is at a temporary disadvantage because they cross one another. In learning an action, instead of having it given ready-made, one of necessity learns to vary its factors, to make varied combinations of them, according to change of circumstances. A possibility of continuing progress is opened up by the fact that in learning one act, methods are developed good for use in other situations. Still more important is the fact that the human being acquires a habit of learning. He learns to learn.

The importance for human life of the two facts of dependence and variable control has been summed up in the doctrine of the significance of prolonged infancy.[1] This prolongation is significant from the standpoint of the adult members of the group as well as from that of the young. The presence of dependent and learning beings is a stimulus to nurture and affection. The need for constant continued care was probably a chief means in transforming temporary cohabitations into permanent unions. It certainly was a chief influence informing habits of affectionate and sympathetic watchfulness; that constructive interest in the well-being of others which is essential to associated life. Intellectually, this moral development meant the introduction of many new objects of attention; it stimulated foresight and planning for the future. Thus there is a reciprocal influence. Increasing complexity of social life requires a longer period of infancy in which to acquire the needed powers; this prolongation of dependence means prolongation of plasticity, or power of acquiring variable and novel modes of control.

Hence it provides a further push to social progress.

2. *Habits as Expressions of Growth*—We have already noted that plasticity is the capacity to retain and carry over from prior experience factors which modify subsequent activities. This signifies the capacity to acquire habits, or develop definite dispositions. We have now to consider the salient features of habits. In the first place, a habit is a form of executive skill, of efficiency in doing. A habit means an ability to use natural conditions as means to ends. It is an active control of the environment through control of the organs of action. We are perhaps apt to emphasize the control of the body at the expense of control of the environment. We think of walking, talking, playing the piano, the specialized skills characteristic of the etcher, the surgeon, the bridge-builder, as if they were simply ease, deftness, and accuracy on the part of the organism. They are that, of course; but the measure of the value of these qualities lies in the economical and effective control of the environment which they secure. To be able to walk is to have certain properties of nature at our disposal—and so with all other habits.

Education is not infrequently defined as consisting in the acquisition of those habits that effect an adjustment of an individual and his environment. The definition expresses an essential phase of growth. But it is essential that adjustment be understood in its active sense of *control* of means for achieving ends. If we think of a habit simply as a change wrought in the organism, ignoring the fact that this change consists in ability to effect subsequent changes in the environment, we shall be led to think of "adjustment" as a conformity to environment as wax conforms to the seal which impresses it. The environment is thought of as something fixed, providing in its fixity the end and standard of changes taking place in the organism; adjustment is just fitting ourselves to this fixity of external conditions.[2] Habit as *habituation* is indeed something *relatively* passive; we get used to our surroundings—to our clothing, our shoes, and gloves; to the atmosphere as long as it is fairly equable; to our daily associates, etc. Conformity to the environment, a change wrought in the organism without reference to ability to modify surroundings, is a marked trait of such habituations. Aside from the fact that we are not entitled to carry over the traits of such adjustments (which might well be called *accommodations,* to mark them off from active adjustments) into habits of active use of our surroundings, two features of habituations are worth notice. In the first place, we get used to things by *first* using them.

Consider getting used to a strange city. At first, there is excessive stimulation and excessive and ill-adapted response. Gradually certain stimuli are selected because of the relevancy, and others are degraded. We can say either that we do not respond to them any longer, or more truly that we have effected a persistent response to them—an equilibrium of adjustment. This means, in the second place, that this enduring adjustment supplies the background upon which are made specific adjustments, as occasion arises. We are never interested in changing the *whole* environment; there is much that we take for granted and accent just as it already is. Upon this background our activities focus at certain points in an endeavor to introduce needed changes. Habituation is thus our adjustment to an environment which at the time we are not concerned with modifying, and which supplies a leverage to our active habits.

Adaptation, in fine, is quite as much adaptation *of* the environment to our own activities as of our activities *to* the environment. A savage tribe manages to live on a desert plain. It adapts itself. But its adaptation involves a maximum of accepting, tolerating, putting up with things as they are, a maximum of passive acquiescence, and a minimum of active control, of subjection to use. A civilized people enters upon the scene. It also adapts itself. It introduces irrigation; it searches the world for plants and animals that will flourish under such conditions; it improves, by careful selection, those which are growing there. As a consequence, the wilderness blossoms as a rose. The savage is merely habituated; the civilized man has habits which transform the environment.

The significance of habit is not exhausted, however, in its executive and motor phase. It means formation of intellectual and emotional disposition as well as an increase in ease, economy, and efficiency of action. Any habit marks an *inclination*—an active preference and choice for the conditions involved in its exercise. A habit does not wait, Micawberlike, for a stimulus to turn up so that it may get busy; it actively seeks for occasions to pass into full operation. If its expression is unduly blocked, inclination shows itself in uneasiness and intense craving. A habit also marks an intellectual disposition. Where there is a habit, there is acquaintance with the materials and equipment to which action is applied. There is a definite way of understanding the situations in which the habit operates. Modes of thought, of observation and reflection, enter as forms of skill and of desire into the habits that make a man an engineer, an architect, a physician, or a merchant. In unskilled forms of labor, the intellectual factors are at minimum precisely because the habits involved are not of a high grade. But there are habits of judging and reasoning as truly as of handling a tool, painting a picture, or conducting an experiment.

Such statements are, however, understatements. The habits of mind involved in habits of the eye and hand supply the latter with their significance. Above all, the intellectual element in a habit fixes the relation of the habit to varied and elastic use, and hence to continued growth. We speak of *fixed* habits. Well, the phrase may mean powers so well established that their possessor always has them as resources when needed. But the phrase is also used to mean ruts, routine ways, with loss of freshness, open-mindedness, and originality. Fixity of habit may mean that something has a fixed hold upon us, instead of our having a free hold upon things. This fact explains two points in a common notion about habits: their identification with mechanical and external modes of action to the neglect of mental and moral attitudes, and the tendency to give them a bad meaning, an identification with "bad habits."

Many a person would feel surprised to have his aptitude in his chosen profession called a habit, and would naturally think of his use of tobacco, liquor, or profane language as typical of the meaning of habit. A habit is to him something which has a hold on him, something not easily thrown off even though judgment condemn it.

Habits reduce themselves to routine ways of acting, or degenerate into ways of action to which we are enslaved just in the degree in which intelligence is disconnected from them. Routine habits are unthinking habits; "bad" habits are habits so severed from reason that they are opposed to the conclusions of conscious deliberation and decision. As we have seen, the acquiring of habits is due to an original plasticity of our natures: to our ability to vary responses till we find an appropriate and efficient way of acting. Routine habits, and habits that possess us instead of our possessing them, are habits which put an end to plasticity. They mark the close of power to vary. There can be no doubt of the tendency of organic plasticity, of the physiological basis, to lessen with growing years. The instinctively mobile and eagerly varying action of childhood, the love of new stimuli and new developments, too easily passes into a "settling down," which means aversion to change and a resting on past achievements. Only an environment which secures the full use of intelligence in the process of forming habits can counteract this tendency. Of course, the same hardening of the organic conditions affects the physiological structures which are involved in thinking. But this fact only indicates the need of persistent care to see to it that the function of intelligence is invoked to its maximum possibility. The short-sighted method which falls back on mechanical routine and repetition to secure external efficiency of habit, motor skill without accompanying thought, marks a deliberate closing in of surroundings upon growth.

3. *The Educational Bearings of the Conception of Development*—We have had so far but little to say in this chapter about education. We have been occupied with the conditions

and implications of growth. If our conclusions are justified, they carry with them, however, definite educational consequences. When it is said that education is development, everything depends upon *how* development is conceived. Our net conclusion is that life is development, and that developing, growing, is life. Translated into its educational equivalents, this means (i) that the educational process has no end beyond itself; it is its own end; and that (*ii*) the educational process in one of continual reorganizing, reconstructing, transforming.

1. Development when it is interpeted in *comparative* terms, that is, with respect to the special traits of child and adult life, means the direction of power into special channels: the formation of habits involving executive skill, definiteness of interest, and specific objects of observation and thought. But the comparative view is not final. The child has specific powers; to ignore that fact is to stunt or distort the organs upon which his growth depends. The adult uses his powers to transform his environment, thereby occasioning new stimuli which redirect his powers and keep them developing. Ignoring this fact means arrested development, a passive accommodation. Normal child and normal adult alike, in other words, are engaged in growing. The difference between them is not the difference between growth and no growth, but between the modes of growth appropriate to different conditions. With respect to the development of powers devoted to coping with specific scientific and economic problems we may say the child should be growing in manhood. With respect to sympathetic curiosity, unbiased responsiveness, and openness of mind, we may say that the adult should be growing in childlikeness. One statement is as true as the other.

Three ideas which have been criticized, namely, the merely privative nature of immaturity, static adjustment to a fixed environment, and rigidity of habit, are all connected with a false idea of growth or development,—that it is a movement toward a fixed goal. Growth is regarded as *having* an end, instead of *being* an

end. The educational counterparts of the three fallacious ideas are first, failure to take account of the instinctive or native powers of the young; secondly, failure to develop initiative in coping with novel situations; thirdly, an undue emphasis upon drill and other devices which secure automatic skill at the expense of personal perception. In all cases, the adult environment is accepted as a standard for the child. He is to be brought up *to* it.

Natural instincts are either disregarded or treated as nuisances—as obnoxious traits to be suppressed, or at all events to be brought into conformity with external standards. Since conformity is the aim, what is distinctively individual in a young person is brushed aside, or regarded as a source of mischief or anarchy. Conformity is made equivalent to uniformity. Consequently, there are induced lack of interest in the novel, aversion to progress, and dread of the uncertain and the unknown. Since the end of growth is outside of and beyond the process of growing, external agents have to be resorted to to induce movements towards it. Whenever a method of education is stigmatized as mechanical, we may be sure that external pressure is brough to bear to reach an external end.

2. Since in reality there is nothing to which growth is relative save more growth, there is nothing to which education is subordinate save more education. It is a commonplace to say that education should not cease when one leaves school. The point of this commonplace is that the purpose of school education is to insure the continuance of education by organizing the powers that insure growth. The inclination to learn from life itself and to make the conditions of life such that all will learn in the process of living is the finest product of schooling.

When we abandon the attempt to define immaturity by means of fixed comparison with adult accomplishments, we are compelled to give up thinking of it as denoting lack of desired traits. Abandoning this notion, we are also forced to surrender our habit of thinking of instruction as a method of supplying this lack by pouring knowledge into a mental and moral hole which awaits filling. Since life means growth, a living creature lives as truly and positively at one stage as at another, with the same intrinsic fullness and the same absolute claims. Hence education means the enterprise of supplying the conditions which insure growth, or adequacy of life, irrespective of age. We first look with impatience upon immaturity, regarding it as something to be got over as rapidly as possible. Then the adult formed by such educative methods looks back with impatient regret upon childhood and youth as a scene of lost opportunities and wasted powers. This ironical situation will endure till it is recognized that living has its own intrinsic quality and that the business of education is with that quality.

Realization that life is growth protects us from that so-called idealizing of childhood which in effect is nothing but lazy indulgence. Life is not to be identified with every superficial act and interest. Even though it is not always easy to tell whether what appears to be mere surface fooling is a sign of some nascent as yet untrained power, we must remember that manifestations are no to be accepted as ends in themselves. They are signs of possible growth. They are to be turned into means of development, of carrying power forward, not indulged or cultivated for their own sake. Excessive attention to surface phenomena (even in the way of rebuke as well as of encouragement) may lead to their fixation and thus to arrested development. What impulses are moving toward, not what they have been, is the important thing for parent and teacher. The true principle of respect for immaturity cannot be better put than in the words of Emerson: "Respect the child. Be not too much his parent. Trespass not on his solitude. But I hear the outcry which replies to this suggestion: Would you verily throw up the reins of public and private discipline; would you leave the young child to the mad career of his own passions and whimsies, and call this anarchy a respect for the child's nature? I answer,— Respect the child, respect him to the end, but

also respect yourself. . . . The two points in a boy's training are, to keep his *naturel* and train off all but that; to keep his *naturel,* but stop off his uproar, fooling, and horse-play; keep his nature *and arm it with knowledge in the very direction in which it points.*" And as Emerson goes on to show this reverence for childhood and youth instead of opening up an easy and easy-going path to the instructors, "involves at once immense claims on the time, the thought, on the life of the teacher. It requires time, use, insight, event, all the great lessons and assistances of God; and only to think of using it implies character and profoundness."

*Summary*—Power to grow depends upon needs for others and plasticity. Both of these conditions are at their height in childhood and youth. Plasticity or the power to learn from experience means the formation of habits. Habits give control over the environment, power to utilize it for human purposes. Habits take the form both of habituation, or a general and persistent balance of organic activities with the surroundings, and of active capacities to readjust activity to meet new conditions. The former furnishes the background of growth; the latter constitute growing. Active habits involve thought, invention, and initiative in applying capacities to new aims. They are opposed to routine which marks an arrest of growth. Since growth is the characteristic of life, education is all one with growing; it has no end beyond itself. The criterion of the value of school education is the extent in which it creates a desire for continued growth and supplies means for making the desire effective in fact.

## Notes

1. Intimations of its significance are found in a number of writers, but John Fiske, in his *Excursions of an Evolutionist,* is accredited with its first systematic exposition.
2. This conception is, of course, a logical correlate of the conceptions of the external relation of stimulus and response, considered in the last chapter, and of the negative conceptions of immaturity and plasticity noted in this chapter.

# The Lost Individual

The development of a civilization that is outwardly corporate—or rapidly becoming so—has been accompanied by a submergence of the individual. Just how far this is true of the individual's opportunities in action, how far initiative and choice in what an individual does are restricted by the economic forces that make for consolidation, I shall not attempt to say. It is arguable that there has been a diminution of the range of decision and activity for the many along with exaggeration of opportunity of personal expression for the few. It may be contended that no one class in the past has the power now possessed by an industrial oligarchy. On the other hand, it may be held that this power of the few is, with respect to genuine individuality, specious; that those outwardly in control are in reality as much carried by forces external to themselves as are the many; that in fact these forces impel them into a common mold to such an extent that individuality is suppressed.

What is here meant by "the lost individual" is, however, so irrelevant to this question that it is not necessary to decide between the two views. For by it is meant a moral and intellectual fact which is independent of any manifestation of power in action. The significant thing is that the loyalties which once held individuals, which gave them support, direction and unity of outlook on life, have well-nigh disappeared. In consequence, individuals are confused and bewildered. It would be difficult to find in history an epoch as lacking in solid and assured objects of belief and approved ends of action as is the present. Stability of individuality is dependent upon stable objects to which allegiance firmly attaches itself. There are, of course, those who are still militantly fundamentalist in religious and social creed. But their very clamor is evidence that the tide is

set against them. For the others, traditional objects of loyalty have become hollow or are openly repudiated, and they drift without sure anchorage. Individuals vibrate between a past that is intellectually too empty to give stability and a present that is too diversely crowded and chaotic to afford balance or direction to ideas and emotion.

Assured and integrated individuality is the product of definite social relationships and publicly acknowledged functions. Judged by this standard, even those who seem to be in control, and to carry the expression of their special individual abilities to a high pitch, are submerged. They may be captains of finance and industry, but until there is some consensus of belief as to the meaning of finance and industry in civilization as a whole, they cannot be captains of their own souls—their beliefs and aims. They exercise leadership surreptitiously and, as it were, absent-mindedly. They lead, but it is under cover of impersonal and socially undirected economic forces. Their reward is found not in what they do, in their social office and function, but in a deflection of social consequences to private gain. They receive the acclaim and command the envy and admiration of the crowd, but the crowd is also composed of private individuals who are equally lost to a sense of social bearings and uses.

The explanation is found in the fact that while the actions promote corporate and collective results, these results are outside their intent and irrelevant to that reward of satisfaction which comes from a sense of social fulfillment. To themselves and to others, their business is private and its outcome is private profit. No complete satisfaction is possible where such a split exists. Hence the absence of a sense of social value is made up for by an

From "The Lost Individual," in *Individualism, Old and New, John Dewey: The Later Works, 1925–1953*, Vol. 5, Ed. Jo Ann Boydston (Carbondale and Edwardsville: Southern Illinois University Press, 1984 [1930]), pp. 66–76.

exacerbated acceleration of the activities that increase private advantage and power. One cannot look into the inner consciousness of his fellows, but if there is any general degree of inner contentment on the part of those who form our pecuniary oligarchy, the evidence is sadly lacking. As for the many, they are impelled hither and yon by forces beyond their control.

The most marked trait of present life, economically speaking, is insecurity. It is tragic that millions of men desirous of working should be recurrently out of employment; aside from cyclical depressions there is a standing army at all times who have no regular work. We have not any adequate information as to the number of these persons. But the ignorance even as to the numbers is slight compared with our inability to grasp the psychological and moral consequences of the precarious condition in which vast multitudes live. Insecurity cuts deeper and extends more widely than bare unemployment. Fear of loss of work, dread of the oncoming of old age, create anxiety and eat into self-respect in a way that impairs personal dignity. Where fears abound, courageous and robust individuality is undermined. The vast development of technological resources that might bring security in its train has actually brought a new mode of insecurity, as mechanization displaces labor. The mergers and consolidations that mark a corporate age are beginning to bring uncertainty into the economic lives of the higher salaried class, and that tendency is only just in its early stage. Realization that honest and industrious pursuit of a calling or business will not guarantee any stable level of life lessens respect for work and stirs large numbers to take a chance of some adventitious way of getting the wealth that will make security possible: witness the orgies of the stock-market in recent days.

The unrest, impatience, irritation and hurry that are so marked in American life are inevitable accompaniments of a situation in which individuals do not find support and contentment in the fact that they are sustaining and sustained members of a social whole.

They are evidence, psychologically, of abnormality, and it is as idle to seek for their explanation within the deliberate intent of individuals as it is futile to think that they can be got rid of by hortatory moral appeal. Only an acute maladjustment between individuals and the social conditions under which they live can account for such widespread pathological phenomena. Feverish love of anything as long as it is a change which is distracting, impatience, unsettlement, nervous discontentment, and desire for excitement, are not native to human nature. They are so abnormal as to demand explanation in some deep-seated cause.

I should explain a seeming hypocrisy on the same ground. We are not consciously insincere in our professions of devotion to ideals of "service"; they mean something. Neither the Rotarian nor the big business enterprise uses the term merely as a cloak for "putting something over" which makes for pecuniary gain. But the lady doth protest too much. The wide currency of such professions testifies to a sense of a social function of business which is expressed in words because it is so lacking in fact, and yet which is felt to be rightfully there. If our external combinations in industrial activity were reflected in organic integrations of the desires, purposes and satisfactions of individuals, the verbal protestations would disappear, because social utility would be a matter of course.

Some persons hold that a genuine mental counterpart of the outward social scheme is actually forming. Our prevailing mentality, our "ideology," is said to be that of the "business mind" which has become so deplorably pervasive. Are not the prevailing standards of value those derived from pecuniary success and economic prosperity? Were the answer unqualifiedly in the affirmative, we should have to admit that our outer civilization is attaining an inner culture which corresponds to it, however much we might disesteem the quality of that culture. The objection that such a condition is impossible, since man cannot live by bread, by material prosperity alone, is tempting, but it may be said to beg the question. The conclusive answer is that the business mind is not itself unified. It is divided within itself and must remain so as long as the results of industry as the determining force in life are corporate and collective while its animating motives and compensations are so unmitigatedly private. A unified mind, even of the business type, can come into being only when conscious intent and consummation are in harmony with consequences actually effected. This statement expresses conditions so psychologically assured that it may be termed a law of mental integrity. Proof of the existence of the split is found in the fact that while there is much planning of future development with a view to dividends within large business corporations, there is no corresponding coordinated planning of social development.

The growth of corporateness is arbitrarily restricted. Hence it operates to limit individuality, to put burdens on it, to confuse and submerge it. It crowds more out than it incorporates in an ordered and secure life. It has made rural districts stagnant while bringing excess and restless movement to the city. The restriction of corporateness lies in the fact that it remains on the cash level. Men are brought together on the one side by investment in the same joint stock company, and on the other hand by the fact that the machine compels mass production in order that investors may get their profits. The results affect all society in all its phases. But they are as inorganic as the ultimate human motives that operate are private and egoistic. An economic individualism of motives and aims underlies our present corporate mechanisms, and undoes the individual.

The loss of individuality is conspicuous in the economic region because our civilization is so predominantly a business civilization. But the fact is even more obvious when we turn to the political scene. It would be a waste of words to expatiate on the meaninglessness of present political platforms, parties and issues. The old-time slogans are still reiterated, and to a few these words still seem to have a real meaning. But it is too evident to need argument that on the whole our politics,

as far as they are not covertly manipulated in behalf of the pecuniary advantage of groups, are in a state of confusion; issues are improvised from week to week with a constant shift of allegiance. It is impossible for individuals to find themselves politically with surety and efficiency under such conditions. Political apathy broken by recurrent sensations and spasms is the natural outcome.

The lack of secure objects of allegiance, without which individuals are lost, is especially striking in the case of the liberal. The liberalism of the past was characterized by the possession of a definite intellectual creed and program; that was its distinction from conservative parties which needed no formulated outlook beyond defense of things as they were. In contrast, liberals operated on the basis of a thought-out social philosophy, a theory of politics sufficiently definite and coherent to be easily translated into a program of policies to be pursued. Liberalism today is hardly more than a temper of mind, vaguely called forward-looking, but quite uncertain as to where to look and what to look forward to. For many individuals, as well as in its social results, this fact is hardly less than a tragedy. The tragedy may be unconscious for the mass, but they show its reality in their aimless drift, while the more thoughtful are consciously disturbed. For human nature is self-possessed only as it has objects to which it can attach itself.

I do not think it is fantastic to connect our excited and rapacious nationalism with the situation in which corporateness has gone so far as to detach individuals from their old local ties and allegiances but not far enough to give them a new centre and order of life. The most militaristic of nations secures the loyalty of its subjects not by physical force but through the power of ideas and emotions. It cultivates ideals of loyalty, of solidarity, and common devotion to a common cause. Modern industry, technology and commerce have created modern nations in their external form. Armies and navies exist to protect commerce, to make secure the control of raw materials, and to command markets. Men would not sacrifice their lives for the purpose of securing economic gain for a few if the conditions presented themselves to their minds in this bald fashion. But the balked demand for genuine cooperativeness and reciprocal solidarity in daily life finds an outlet in nationalistic sentiment. Men have a pathetic instinct toward the adventure of living and struggling together; if the daily community does not feed this impulse, the romantic imagination pictures a grandiose nation in which all are one. If the simple duties of peace do not establish a common life, the emotions are mobilized in the service of a war that will supply its temporary stimulation.

I have thus far made no reference to what many persons would consider the most serious and the most overtly evident of all the modes of loss of secure objects of loyalty—religion. It is probably easy to exaggerate the extent of the decadence of religion in an outward sense, church membership, church-going and so on. But it is hardly possible to overstate its decline as a vitally integrative and directive force in men's thought and sentiments. Whether even in the ages of the past that are called religious, religion was itself the actively central force that it is sometimes said to have been may be doubted. But it cannot be doubted that it was the symbol of the existence of conditions and forces that gave unity and a centre to men's views of life. It at least gathered together in weighty and shared symbols a sense of the objects to which men were so attached as to have support and stay in their outlook on life.

Religion does not now effect this result. The divorce of church and state has been followed by that of religion and society. Wherever religion has not become a merely private indulgence, it has become at best a matter of sects and denominations divided from one another by doctrinal differences, and united internally by tenets that have a merely historical origin, and a purely metaphysical or else ritualistic meaning. There is no such bond of social unity as once united Greeks, Romans, Hebrews, and Catholic medieval Europe. There are those who realize what is portended by the loss of religion as an integrating bond.

Many of them despair of its recovery through the development of social values to which the imagination and sentiments of individuals can attach themselves with intensity. They wish to reverse the operation and to form the social bond of unity and of allegiance by regeneration of the isolated individual soul.

Aside from the fact that there is no consensus as to what a new religious attitude is to centre itself about, the injunction puts the cart before the horse. Religion is not so much a root of unity as it is its flower or fruit. The very attempt to secure integration for the individual, and through him for society, by means of a deliberate and conscious cultivation of religion, is itself proof of how far the individual has become lost through detachment from acknowledged social values. It is no wonder that when the appeal does not take the form of dogmatic fundamentalism, it tends to terminate in either some form of esoteric occultism or private estheticism. The sense of wholeness which is urged as the essence of religion can be built up and sustained only through membership in a society which has attained a degree of unity. The attempt to cultivate it first in individuals and then extend it to form an organically unified society is fantasy. Indulgence in this fantasy infects such interpretations of American life as are found, to take one signal example, in Waldo Frank's *The Rediscovery of America*.[1] It marks a manner of yearning and not a principle of construction.

For the idea that the outward scene is chaotic because of the machine, which is a principle of chaos, and that it will remain so until individuals reinstitute wholeness within themselves, simply reverses the true state of things. The outward scene, if not fully organized, is relatively so in the corporateness which the machine and its technology have produced; the inner man is the jungle which can be subdued to order only as the forces of organization at work in externals are reflected in corresponding patterns of thought, imagination and emotion. The sick cannot heal themselves by means of their disease, and disintegrated individuals can achieve unity only as the dominant energies of community life are incorporated to form their minds. If these energies were, in reality, mere strivings for private pecuniary gain, the case would indeed be hopeless. But they are constituted by a collective art of technology, which individuals merely deflect to their private ends. There are the beginnings of an objective order through which individuals may get their bearings.

Conspicuous signs of the disintegration of individuality due to failure to reconstruct the self so as to meet the realities of present social life have not been mentioned. In a census that was taken among leaders of opinion concerning the urgency of present social problems, the state of law, the courts, lawlessness and criminality stood at the head of the list, and by a considerable distance. We are even more emphatically than when Kipling wrote the words, the people that make "the laws they flout, and flout the laws they make." We combine an ardor unparalleled in history for "passing" laws with a casual and deliberate disregard for them when they are on the statute books. We believe—to judge by our legislative actions—that we can create morals by law (witness the prohibition amendment for an instance on a large scale) and neglect the fact that all laws except those which regulate technical procedures are registrations of existing social customs and their attendant moral habits and purposes. I can, however, only think of this phenomenon as a symptom, not as a cause. It is a natural expression of a period in which changes in the structure of society have dissolved old bonds and allegiances. We attempt to make good this social relaxation and dissolution by legal enactments, while the actual disintegration discloses itself in the lawlessness which reveals the artificial character of this method of securing social integrity.

Volumes could be formed by collecting articles and editorials written about relaxation of traditional moral codes. A movement has caught public attention, which, having for some obscure reason assumed the name "humanism," proposes restraint and modera-

tion, exercised in and by the higher volition of individuals, as the solution of our ills. It finds that naturalism as practiced by artists and mechanism as taught by philosophers who take their clew from natural science, have broken down the inner laws and imperatives which can alone bring order and loyalty. I should be glad to be able to believe that artists and intellectuals have any power in their hands; if they had, after using it to bring evil to society, they might change face and bring healing to it. But a sense of fact, together with a sense of humor, forbids the acceptance of any such belief. Literary persons and academic thinkers are now, more than ever, effects, not causes. They reflect and voice the disintegration which new modes of living, produced by new forms of industry and commerce, have introduced. They give witness to the unreality that has overtaken traditional codes in the face of the impact of new forces; indirectly, they proclaim the need of some new synthesis. But this synthesis can be humanistic only as the new conditions are themselves taken into account and are converted into the instrumentalities of a free and humane life. I see no way to "restrain" or turn back the industrial revolution and its consequences. In the absence of such a restraint (which would be efficacious if only it could occur), the urging of some inner restraint through the exercise of the higher personal will, whatever that may be, is itself only a futile echo of just the old individualism that has so completely broken down.

There are many phases of life which illustrate to anyone who chooses to think in terms of realities instead of words the utter irrelevance of the proposed remedy to actual conditions. One might take the present estate of amusements, of the movies, the radio, and organized vicarious sport, and ask just how this powerful eruption in which the resources of technology are employed for economic profit is to be met by the application of the inner *frein* or brake. Perhaps the most striking instance is found in the disintegration due to changes in family life and sex morale. It was not deliberate human intention that undermined the traditional household as the centre of industry and education and as the focus of moral training; that sapped the older institution of enduring marriage. To ask the individuals who suffer the consequences of the general undermining and sapping to put an end to the consequences by acts of personal volition is merely to profess faith in moral magic. Recovery of individuals capable of stable and effective self-control can be had only as there is first a humbler exercise of will to observe existing social realities and to direct them according to their own potentialities.

Instances of the flux in which individuals are loosened from the ties that once gave order and support to their lives are glaring. They are indeed so glaring that they blind our eyes to the causes which produce them. Individuals are groping their way through situations which they do not direct and which do not give them direction. The beliefs and ideals that are uppermost in their consciousness are not relevant to the society in which they outwardly act and which constantly reacts upon them. Their conscious ideas and standards are inherited from an age that has passed away; their minds, as far as consciously entertained principles and methods of interpretation are concerned, are at odds with actual conditions. This profound split is the cause of distraction and bewilderment.

Individuals will refind themselves only as their ideas and ideals are brought into harmony with the realities of the age in which they act. The task of attaining this harmony is not an easy one. But it is more negative than it seems. If we could inhibit the principles and standards that are merely traditional, if we could slough off the opinions that have no living relationship to the situations in which we live, the unavowed forces that now work upon us unconsciously but unremittingly would have a chance to build minds after their own pattern, and individuals might, in consequence, find themselves in possession of objects to which imagination and emotion would stably attach themselves.

I do not mean, however, that the process of rebuilding can go on automatically. Discrimination is required in order to detect the beliefs and institutions that dominate merely because of custom and inertia, and in order to discover the moving realities of the present. Intelligence must distinguish, for example, the tendencies of the technology which produce the new corporateness from those inheritances proceeding out of the individualism of an earlier epoch which arrest and divide the operation of the new dynamics. It is difficult for us to conceive of individualism except in terms of stereotypes derived from former centuries. Individualism has been identified with ideas of initiative and invention that are bound up with private and exclusive economic gain. As long as this conception possesses our minds, the ideal of harmonizing our thought and desire with the realities of present social conditions will be interpreted to mean accommodation and surrender. It will even be understood to signify rationalization of the evils of existing society. A stable recovery of individuality waits upon an elimination of the older economic and political individualism, an elimination which will liberate imagination and endeavor for the task of making corporate society contribute to the free culture of its members. Only by economic revision can the sound element in the older individualism—equality of opportunity—be made a reality.

It is the part of wisdom to note the double meaning of such ideas as "acceptance." There is an acceptance that is of the intellect; it signifies facing facts for what they are. There is another acceptance that is of the emotions and will; that involves commitment of desire and effort. So far are the two from being identical that acceptance in the first sense is the precondition of all intelligent refusal of acceptance in the second sense. There is a prophetic aspect to all observation; we can perceive the meaning of what exists only as we forecast the consequences it entails. When a situation is as confused and divided within itself as is the present social estate, choice is implicated in observation. As one perceives different tendencies and different possible consequences, preference inevitably goes out to one or the other. Because acknowledgment in thought brings with it intelligent discrimination and choice, it is the first step out of confusion, the first step in forming those objects of significant allegiance out of which stable and efficacious individuality may grow. It might even perform the miracle of rendering conservatism relevant and thoughtful. It certainly is the prerequisite of an anchored liberalism.

**Note**

1. After a brilliant exposition of the dissolution of the European synthesis, he goes on to say "man's need of order and his making of order are his science, his art, his religion; and these are all to be referred to the initial sense of order called the self," quite oblivious of the fact that this doctrine of the primacy of the self is precisely a reaction of the romantic and subjective age to the dissolution he has depicted, having its meaning only in that dissolution.

# Search for The Great Community

. . . That government exists to serve its community, and that this purpose cannot be achieved unless the community itself shares in selecting its governors and determining their policies, are a deposit of fact left, as far as we can see, permanently in the wake of doctrines and forms, however transitory the latter. They are not the whole of the democratic idea, but they express it in its political phase. Belief in this political aspect is not a mystic faith as if in some overruling providence that cares for children, drunkards and others unable to help themselves. It marks a well-attested conclusion from historic facts. We have every reason to think that whatever changes may take place in existing democratic machinery, they will be of a sort to make the interest of the public a more supreme guide and criterion of governmental activity, and to enable the public to form and manifest its purposes still more authoritatively. In this sense the cure for the ailments of democracy is more democracy. The prime difficulty, as we have seen, is that of discovering the means by which a scattered, mobile and manifold public may so recognize

itself as to define and express its interests. This discovery is necessarily precedent to any fundamental change in the machinery. We are not concerned therefore to set forth counsels as to advisable improvements in the political forms of democracy. Many have been suggested. It is no derogation of their relative worth to say that consideration of these changes is not at present an affair of primary importance. The problem lies deeper; it is in the first instance an intellectual problem: the search for conditions under which the Great Society may become the Great Community. When these conditions are brought into being they will make their own forms. Until they have come about, it is somewhat futile to consider what political machinery will suit them.

In a search for the conditions under which the inchoate public now extant may function democratically, we may proceed from a statement of the nature of the democratic idea in its generic social sense.[1] From the standpoint of the individual, it consists in having a responsible share according to capacity in forming and directing the activities of the groups to which

From "Search for The Great Community," in *The Public and Its Problems, John Dewey: The Later Works 1925–1953.* Vol. 2, Ed. Jo Ann Boydston (Carbondale and Edwardsville: Southern Illinois University Press, 1984 [1927]), pp. 327–350.

one belongs and in participating according to need in the values which the groups sustain. From the standpoint of the groups, it demands liberation of the potentialities of members of a group in harmony with the interests and goods which are common. Since every individual is a member of many groups, this specification cannot be fulfilled except when different groups interact flexibly and fully in connection with other groups. A member of a robber band may express his powers in a way consonant with belonging to that group and be directed by the interest common to its members. But he does so only at the cost of repression of those of his potentialities which can be realized only through membership in other groups. The robber band cannot interact flexibly with other groups; it can act only through isolating itself. It must prevent the operation of all interests save those which circumscribe it in its separateness. But a good citizen finds his conduct as a member of a political group enriching and enriched by his participation in family life, industry, scientific and artistic associations. There is a free give-and-take: fullness of integrated personality is therefore possible of achievement, since the pulls and responses of different groups reenforce one another and their values accord.

Regarded as an idea, democracy is not an alternative to other principles of associated life. It is the idea of community life itself. It is an ideal in the only intelligible sense of an ideal: namely, the tendency and movement of some thing which exists carried to its final limit, viewed as completed, perfected. Since things do not attain such fulfillment but are in actuality distracted and interfered with, democracy in this sense is not a fact and never will be. But neither in this sense is there or has there ever been anything which is a community in its full measure, a community unalloyed by alien elements. The idea or ideal of a community presents, however, actual phases of associated life as they are freed from restrictive and disturbing elements, and are contemplated as having attained their limit of development. Wherever there is conjoint activity whose consequences are appreciated as good by all singular persons who take part in it, and where the realization of the good is such as to effect an energetic desire and effort to sustain it in being just because it is a good shared by all, there is in so far a community. The clear consciousness of a communal life, in all its implications, constitutes the idea of democracy.

Only when we start from a community as a fact, grasp the fact in thought so as to clarify and enhance its constituent elements, can we reach an idea of democracy which is not utopian. The conceptions and shibboleths which are traditionally associated with the idea of democracy take on a veridical and directive meaning only when they are construed as marks and traits of an association which realizes the defining characteristics of a community. Fraternity, liberty and equality isolated from communal life are hopeless abstractions. Their separate assertion leads to mushy sentimentalism or else to extravagant and fanatical violence which in the end defeats its own aims. Equality then becomes a creed of mechanical identity which is false to facts and impossible of realization. Effort to attain it is divisive of the vital bonds which hold men together; as far as it puts forth issue, the outcome is a mediocrity in which good is common only in the sense of being average and vulgar. Liberty is then thought of as independence of social ties, and ends in dissolution and anarchy. It is more difficult to sever the idea of brotherhood from that of a community, and hence it is either practically ignored in the movements which identify democracy with Individualism, or else it is a sentimentally appended tag. In its just connection with communal experience, fraternity is another name for the consciously appreciated goods which accrue from an association in which all share, and which give direction to the conduct of each. Liberty is that secure release and fulfillment of personal potentialities which take place only in rich and manifold association with others: the power to be an individualized self making a distinctive contribution and enjoying in its own way the fruits of association. Equality denotes the unhampered share which each individual member of the community has in the consequences of associated action. It is equitable because it is measured only be need and capacity to utilize, not by extraneous factors which deprive one in order that another may take and have. A baby in the family is equal with others, not because of some antecedent and structural quality which is the same as that of others, but in so far as his needs for care and development are attended to without being sacrificed to the superior strength, possessions and matured abilities of others. Equality does not signify that kind of mathematical or physical equivalence in virtue of which any one element may be substituted for another. It denotes effective regard for whatever is distinctive and unique in each, irrespective of physical and psychological inequalities. It is not a natural possession but is a fruit of the community when its action is directed by its character as a community.

Associated or joint activity is a condition of the creation of a community. But association itself is physical and organic, while community life is moral, that is emotionally, intellectually, consciously sustained. Human beings combine in behavior as directly and unconsciously as do atoms, stellar masses and cells; as directly and unknowingly as they divide and repel. They do so in virtue of their own structure, as man and woman unite, as the baby seeks the breast and the breast is there to supply its need. They do so from external circumstances, pressure from without, as atoms combine or separate in presence of an electric charge, or as sheep huddle together from the cold. Associated activity needs no explanation; things are made that way. But no amount of aggregated collective action of itself constitutes a community. For beings who observe and think, and whose ideas are absorbed by impulses and become sentiments and interests, "we" is as inevitable as "I." But "we" and "our" exist only when the consequences of combined action are perceived and become an object of desire and effort, just as "I" and "mine" appear on the scene only when a distinctive share in mutual action is consciously asserted or claimed. Human associations may be ever so organic in origin and firm in operation, but they develop into societies in a human sense only as their consequences, being known, are esteemed and sought for. Even if "society" were as much an organism as some writers have held, it would not on that account be society. Interactions, transactions, occur *de facto* and the results of interdependence follow. But participation in activities and sharing in results are additive concerns. They demand *communication* as a prerequisite.

Combined activity happens among human beings; but when nothing else happens it passes as inevitably into some other mode of interconnected activity as does the interplay of iron and the oxygen of water. What takes place is wholly describable in terms of energy, or, as we say in the case of human interactions, of force. Only when there exist *signs* or *symbols* of activities and of their outcome can the flux be viewed as from without, be arrested for consideration and esteem, and be regulated. Lightning strikes and rives a tree or rock, and the resulting fragments take up and continue the process of interaction, and so on and on. But when phases of the process are represented by signs a new medium is interposed. As symbols are related to one another, the important relations of a course of events are recorded and are preserved as meanings. Recollection and foresight are possible; the new medium facilitates calculation, planning, and a new kind of action which intervenes in what happens to direct its course in the interest of what is foreseen and desired.

Symbols in turn depend upon and promote communication. The results of conjoint experience are considered and transmitted. Events cannot be passed from one to another, but meanings may be shared by means of signs. Wants and impulses are then attached to common meanings. They are thereby transformed into desires and purposes, which, since they implicate a common or mutually understood meaning, present new ties, converting a conjoint activity into a community of interest and endeavor. Thus there is generated what, metaphorically, may be termed a general will and social consciousness: desire and choice on the part of individuals in behalf of activities that, by means of symbols, are communicable and shared by all concerned. A community thus presents an order of energies transmuted into one of meanings which are appreciated and mutually referred by each to every other on the part of those engaged in combined action. "Force" is not eliminated but is transformed in use and direction by ideas and sentiments made possible by means of symbols.

The work of conversion of the physical and organic phase of associated behavior into a community of action saturated and regulated by mutual interest in shared meanings, consequences which are translated into ideas and desired objects by means of symbols, does not occur all at once nor completely. At any given time, it sets a problem rather than marks a settled achievement. We are born organic beings associated with others, but we are not born members of a community. The young have to be brought within the traditions, outlook and interests which characterize a community by means of education: by unremitting instruction and by learning in connection with the phenomena of overt association. Everything which is distinctively human is learned, not native, even though it could not be learned without native structures which mark man off from other animals. To learn in a human way and to human effect is not just to acquire added skill through refinement of original capacities.

To learn to be human is to develop through the give-and-take of communication an effective sense of being an individually distinctive member of a community; one who understands and appreciates its beliefs, desires and methods, and who contributes to a further conversion of organic powers into human resources and values. But this translation is never finished. The old Adam, the unregenerate element in human nature, persists. It shows itself wherever the method obtains of attaining results by use of force instead of by the method of communication and enlightenment. It manifests itself more subtly, pervasively and effectually when knowledge and the instrumentalities of skill which are the product of

communal life are employed in the service of wants and impulses which have not themselves been modified by reference to a shared interest. To the doctrine of "natural" economy which held that commercial exchange would bring about such an interdependence that harmony would automatically result, Rousseau gave an adequate answer in advance. He pointed out that interdependence provides just the situation which makes it possible and worth while for the stronger and abler to exploit others for their own ends, to keep others in a state of subjection where they can be utilized as animated tools. The remedy he suggested, a return to a condition of independence based on isolation, was hardly seriously meant. But its desperateness is evidence of the urgency of the problem. Its negative character was equivalent to surrender of any hope of solution. By contrast it indicates the nature of the only possible solution: the perfecting of the means and ways of communication of meanings so that genuinely shared interest in the consequences of interdependent activities may inform desire and effort and thereby direct action.

This is the meaning of the statement that the problem is a moral one dependent upon intelligence and education. We have in our prior account sufficiently emphasized the role of technological and industrial factors in creating the Great Society. What was said may even have seemed to imply acceptance of the deterministic version of an economic interpretation of history and institutions. It is silly and futile to ignore and deny economic facts. They do not cease to operate because we refuse to note them, or because we smear them over with sentimental idealizations. As we have also noted, they generate as their result overt and external conditions of action and these are known with various degrees of adequacy. What actually happens in consequence of industrial forces is dependent upon the presence or absence of perception and communication of consequences, upon foresight and its effect upon desire and endeavor. Economic agencies produce one result when they are left to work themselves out on the merely physical level, or on that level modified only as the knowledge, skill and technique which the community has accumulated are transmitted to its members unequally and by chance. They have a different outcome in the degree in which knowledge of consequences is equitably distributed, and action is animated by an informed and lively sense of a shared interest. The doctrine of economic interpretation as usually stated ignores the transformation which meanings may effect; it passes over the new medium which communication may interpose between industry and its eventual consequences. It is obsessed by the illusion which vitiated the "natural economy": an illusion due to failure to note the difference made in action by perception and publication of its consequences, actual and possible. It thinks in terms of antecedents, not of the eventual; of origins, not fruits.

We have returned, through this apparent excursion, to the question in which our earlier discussion culminated: What are the conditions under which it is possible for the Great Society to approach more closely and vitally the status of a Great Community, and thus take form in genuinely democratic societies and state? What are the conditions under which we may reasonably picture the Public emerging from its eclipse?

The study will be an intellectual or hypothetical one. There will be no attempt to state how the required conditions might come into existence, nor to prophesy that they will occur. The object of the analysis will be to show that *unless* ascertained specifications are realized, the Community cannot be organized as a democratically effective Public. It is not claimed that the conditions which will be noted will suffice, but only that at least they are indispensable. In other words, we shall endeavor to frame a hypothesis regarding the democratic state to stand in contrast with the earlier doctrine which has been nullified by the course of events.

Two essential constituents in that older theory, as will be recalled, were the notions that each individual is of himself equipped with the intelligence needed, under the operation of

self-interest, to engage in political affairs; and that general suffrage, frequent elections of officials and majority rule are sufficient to ensure the responsibility of elected rulers to the desires and interests of the public. As we shall see, the second conception is logically bound up with the first and stands or falls with it. At the basis of the scheme lies what Lippmann has well called the idea of the "omnicompetent" individual: competent to frame policies, to judge their results; competent to know in all situations demanding political action what is for his own good, and competent to enforce his idea of good and the will to effect it against contrary forces. Subsequent history has proved that the assumption involved illusion. Had it not been for the misleading influence of a false psychology, the illusion might have been detected in advance. But current philosophy held that ideas and knowledge were functions of a mind or consciousness which originated in individuals by means of isolated contact with objects. But in fact, knowledge is a function of association and communication; it depends upon tradition, upon tools and methods socially transmitted, developed and sanctioned. Faculties of effectual observation, reflection and desire are habits acquired under the influence of the culture and institutions of society, not readymade inherent powers. The fact that man acts from crudely intelligized emotion and from habit rather than from rational consideration, is now so familiar that it is not easy to appreciate that the other idea was taken seriously as the basis of economic and political philosophy. The measure of truth which it contains was derived from observation of a relatively small group of shrewd business men who regulated their enterprises by calculation and accounting, and of citizens of small and stable local communities who were so intimately acquainted with the persons and affairs of their locality that they could pass competent judgment upon the bearing of proposed measures upon their own concerns.

Habit is the mainspring of human action, and habits are formed for the most part under the influence of the customs of a group. The organic structure of man entails the formation of habit, for, whether we wish it or not, whether we are aware of it or not, every act effects a modification of attitude and set which directs future behavior. The dependence of habit-forming upon those habits of a group which constitute customs and institutions is a natural consequence of the helplessness of infancy. The social consequences of habit have been stated once for all by James: "Habit is the enormous fly-wheel of society, its most precious conservative influence. It alone is what keeps us within the bounds of ordinance, and saves the children of fortune from the uprisings of the poor. It alone prevents the hardest and most repulsive walks of life from being deserted by those brought up to tread therein. It keeps the fisherman and the deck-hand at sea through the winter; it holds the miner in his darkness, and nails the country-man to his log-cabin and his lonely farm through all the months of snow; it protects us from invasion by the natives of the desert and the frozen zone. It dooms us all to fight out the battle of life upon the lines of our nurture or our early choice, and to make the best of a pursuit that disagrees, because there is no other for which we are fitted and it is too late to begin again. It keeps different social strata from mixing."

The influence of habit is decisive because all distinctively human action has to be learned, and the very heart, blood and sinews of learning is creation of habitudes. Habits bind us to orderly and established ways of action because they generate ease, skill and interest in things to which we have grown used and because they instigate fear to walk in different ways, and because they leave us incapacitated for the trial of them. Habit does not preclude the use of thought, but it determines the channels within which it operates. Thinking is secreted in the interstices of habits. The sailor, miner, fisherman and farmer think, but their thoughts fall within the framework of accustomed occupations and relationships. We dream beyond the limits of use and wont, but only rarely does revery become a source of acts which break bounds; so rarely that we

name those in whom it happens demonic geniuses and marvel at the spectacle. Thinking itself becomes habitual along certain lines; a specialized occupation. Scientific men, philosophers, literary persons, are not men and women who have so broken the bonds of habits that pure reason and emotion undefiled by use and wont speak through them. They are persons of a specialized infrequent habit. Hence the idea that men are moved by an intelligent and calculated regard for their own good is pure mythology. Even if the principle of self-love actuated behavior, it would still be true that the *objects* in which men find their love manifested, the objects which they take as constituting their peculiar interests, are set by habits reflecting social customs.

These facts explain why the social doctrinaires of the new industrial movement had so little prescience of what was to follow in consequence of it. These facts explain why the more things changed, the more they were the same; they account, that is, for the fact that instead of the sweeping revolution which was expected to result from democratic political machinery, there was in the main but a transfer of vested power from one class to another. A few men, whether or not they were good judges of their own true interest and good, were competent judges of the conduct of business for pecuniary profit, and of how the new governmental machinery could be made to serve their ends. It would have taken a new race of human beings to escape, in the use made of political forms, from the influence of deeply engrained habits, of old institutions and customary social status, with their inwrought limitations of expectation, desire and demand. And such a race, unless of disembodied angelic constitution, would simply have taken up the task where human beings assumed it upon emergence from the condition of anthropoid apes. It spite of sudden and catastrophic revolutions, the essential continuity of history is doubly guaranteed. Not only are personal desire and belief functions of habit and custom, but the objective conditions which provide the resources and tools of actions, together with its limitations, obstructions and traps, are precipitates of the past, perpetuating, willy-nilly, its hold and power. The creation of a *tabula rasa* in order to permit the creation of a new order is so impossible as to set at naught both the hope of buoyant revolutionaries and the timidity of scared conservatives.

Nevertheless, changes take place and are cumulative in character. Observation of them in the light of their recognized consequences arouses reflection, discovery, invention, experimentation. When a certain state of accumulated knowledge, of techniques and instrumentalities is attained, the process of change is so accelerated, that, as to-day, it appears externally to be the dominant trait. But there is a marked lag in any corresponding change of ideas and desires. Habits of opinion are the toughest of all habits; when they have become second nature, and are supposedly thrown out of the door, they creep in again as stealthily and surely as does first nature. And as they are modified, the alteration first shows itself negatively, in the disintegration of old beliefs, to be replaced by floating, volatile and accidentally snatched up opinions. Of course there has been an enormous increase in the amount of knowledge possessed by mankind, but it does not equal, probably, the increase in the amount of errors and half-truths which have got into circulation. In social and human matters, especially, the development of a critical sense and methods of discriminating judgment has not kept pace with the growth of careless reports and of motives for positive misrepresentation.

What is more important, however, is that so much of knowledge is not knowledge in the ordinary sense of the word, but is "science." The quotation marks are not used disrespectfully, but to suggest the technical character of scientific material. The layman takes certain conclusions which get into circulation to be science. But the scientific inquirer knows that they constitute science only in connection with the methods by which they are reached. Even when true, they are not science in virtue of their correctness, but by reason of the apparatus which is employed in reaching them. This apparatus is so highly specialized that it requires more labor to acquire ability to use and understand it than to get skill in any other instrumentalities possessed by man. Science, in other words, is a highly specialized language, more difficult to learn than any natural language. It is an artificial language, not in the sense of being factitious, but in that of being a work of intricate art, devoted to a particular purpose and not capable of being acquired nor understood in the way in which the mother tongue is learned. It is, indeed, conceivable that sometime methods of instruction will be devised which will enable laymen to read and hear scientific material with comprehension, even when they do not themselves use the apparatus which is science. The latter may then become for large numbers what students of language call a passive, if not an active, vocabulary. But that time is in the future.

For most men, save the scientific workers, science is a mystery in the hands of initiates, who have becomes adepts in virtue of following ritualistic ceremonies from which the profane herd is excluded. They are fortunate who get as far as a sympathetic appreciation of the methods which give pattern to the complicated apparatus: methods of analytic, experimental observation, mathematical formulation and deduction, constant and elaborate check and test. For most persons, the reality of the apparatus is found only in its embodiments in practical affairs, in mechanical devices and in techniques which touch life as it is lived. For them, electricity is *known* by means of the telephones, bells and lights they use, by the generators and magnetos in the automobiles they drive, by the trolley cars in which they ride. The physiology and biology they are acquainted with is that they have learned in taking precautions against germs and from the physicians they depend upon for health. The science of what might be supposed to be closest to them, of human nature, was for them an esoteric mystery until it was applied in advertising, salesmanship and personnel selection and management, and until, through psychiatry, it spilled over into life and popular consciousness, through its bearings upon "nerves," the morbidities and common forms of crankiness which make it difficult for persons to get along with one another and with themselves. Even now, popular psychology is a mass of cant, of slush and of superstition worthy of the most flourishing days of the medicine man.

Meanwhile the technological application of the complex apparatus which is science has revolutionized the conditions under which associated life goes on. This may be known as a fact which is stated in a proposition and assented to. But it is not known in the sense that men understand it. They do not know it as they know some machine which they operate, or as they know electric light and steam locomotives. They do not understand *how* the change has gone on nor *how* it affects their conduct. Not understanding its "how," they cannot use and control its manifestations. They undergo the consequences, they are affected by them. They cannot manage them, though some are fortunate enough—what is commonly called good fortune—to be able to exploit some phase of the process for their own personal profit. But even the most shrewd and successful man does not in any analytic and systematic way—in a way worthy to compare with the knowledge which he has won in lesser affairs by means of the stress of experience—know the system within which he operates. Skill and ability work within a framework which we have not created and do not comprehend. Some occupy strategic positions which give them advance information of forces that affect the market; and by training and an innate turn that way they have acquired a special technique which enables them to use the vast impersonal tide to turn their own wheels. They can dam the current here and release it there. The current itself is as much beyond them as was ever the river by the side of which some ingenious mechanic, exploying a knowledge which was transmitted to him, erected his sawmill to make boards of trees which he had not grown. That within limits those successful in affairs have knowledge and skill is not to be doubted. But such knowledge goes relatively but little further than that of the competent skilled operator who manages a machine. It suffices to employ the conditions which are before him. Skill enables him to turn the flux of events this way or that in his own neighborhood. It gives him no control of the flux.

Why should the public and its officers, even if the latter are termed statesmen, be wiser and more effective? The prime condition of a democratically organized public is a kind of knowledge and insight which does not yet exist. In its absence, it would be the height of absurdity to try to tell what it would be like if it existed. But some of the conditions which must be fulfilled if it is to exist can be indicated. We can borrow that much from the spirit and method of science even if we are ignorant of it as a specialized apparatus. An obvious requirement is freedom of social inquiry and of distribution of its conclusions. The notion that men may be free in their thought even when they are not in its expression and dissemination has been sedulously propagated. It had its origin in the idea of a mind complete in itself, apart from action and from objects. Such a consciousness presents in fact the spectacle of mind deprived of its normal functioning, because it is baffled by the actualities in connection with which alone it is truly mind, and is driven back into secluded and impotent revery.

There can be no public without full publicity in respect to all consequences which concern it. Whatever obstructs and restricts publicity, limits and distorts public opinion and checks and distorts thinking on social affairs. Without freedom of expression, not even methods of social inquiry can be developed. For tools can be evolved and perfected only in operation; in application to observing, reporting and organizing actual subject-matter; and this application cannot occur save through free and systematic communication. The early history of physical knowledge, of Greek conceptions of natural phenomena, proves how inept become the conceptions of the best endowed minds when those ideas are elaborated apart from the closest contact with the events which they purport to state and explain. The ruling ideas and methods of the human sciences are in much the same condition to-day. They are also evolved on the basis of past gross observation, remote from constant use in regulation of the material of new observations.

The belief that thought and its communication are now free simply because legal restrictions which once obtained have been done away with is absurd. Its currency perpetuates the infantile state of social knowledge. For it blurs recognition of our central need to possess conceptions which are used as tools of directed inquiry and which are tested, rectified and caused to grow in actual use. No man and no mind was ever emancipated merely by being left alone. Removal of formal limitations is but a negative condition; positive freedom is not a state but an act which involves methods and instrumentalities for control of conditions. Experience shows that sometimes the sense of external oppression, as by censorship, acts as a challenge and arouses intellectual energy and excites courage. But a belief in intellectual freedom where it does not exist contributes only to complacency in virtual enslavement, to sloppiness, superficility and recourse to sensations as a substitute for ideas: marked traits of our present estate with respect to social knowledge. On one hand, thinking deprived of its normal course takes refuge in academic specialism, comparable in its way to what is called scholasticism. On the other hand, the physical agencies of publicity which exist in such abundance are utilized in ways which constitute a large part of the present meaning of publicity: advertising, propaganda, invasion of private life, the "featuring" of passing incidents in a way which violates all the moving logic of continuity, and which leaves us with those isolated intrusions and shocks which are the essence of "sensations."

It would be a mistake to identify the conditions which limit free communication and circulation of facts and ideas, and which thereby arrest and pervert social thought or inquiry, merely with overt forces which are obstructive. It is true that those who have ability to manipulate social relations for their own advantage have to be reckoned with. They have an uncanny instinct for detecting what-

ever intellectual tendencies even remotely threaten to encroach upon their control. They have developed an extraordinary facility in enlisting upon their side the inertia, prejudices and emotional partisanship of the masses by use of a technique which impedes free inquiry and expression. We seem to be approaching a state of government by hired promoters of opinion called publicity agents. But the more serious enemy is deeply concealed in hidden entrenchments.

Emotional habituations and intellectual habitudes on the part of the mass of men create the conditions of which the exploiters of sentiment and opinion only take advantage. Men have got used to an experimental method in physical and technical matters. They are still afraid of it in human concerns. The fear is the more efficacious because like all deep-lying fears it is covered up and disguised by all kinds of rationalizations. One of its commonest forms is a truly religious idealization of, and reverence for, established institutions; for example in our own politics, the Constitution, the Supreme Court, private property, free contract and so on. The words "scared" and "sanctity" come readily to our lips when such things come under discussion. They testify to the religious aureole which protects the institutions. If "holy" means that which is not to be approached nor touched, save with ceremonial precautions and by specially anointed officials, then such things are holy in contemporary political life. As supernatural matters have progressively been left high and dry upon a secluded beach, the actuality of religious taboos has more and more gathered about secular institutions, especially those connected with the nationalistic state.[2] Psychiatrists have discovered that one of the commonest causes of mental disturbance is an underlying fear of which the subject is not aware, but which leads to withdrawal from reality and to unwillingness to think things through. There is a social pathology which works powerfully against effective inquiry into social institutions and conditions. It manifests itself in a thousand ways; in querulousness, in impotent drifting, in uneasy snatching at distractions, in idealization of the long established, in a facile optimism assumed as a cloak, in riotous glorification of things "as they are," in intimidation of all dissenters—ways which depress and dissipate thought all the more effectually because they operate with subtle and unconscious pervasiveness.

The backwardness of social knowledge is marked in its division into independent and insulated branches of learning. Anthropology, history, sociology, morals, economics, political science, go their own ways without constant and systematized fruitful interaction. Only in appearance is there a similar division in physical knowledge. There is continuous cross-fertilization between astronomy, physics, chemistry and the biological sciences. Discoveries and improved methods are so recorded and organized that constant exchange and intercommunication take place. The isolation of the humane subjects from one another is connected with their aloofness from physical knowledge. The mind still draws a sharp separation between the world in which man lives and the life of man in and by that world, a cleft reflected in the separation of man himself into a body and a mind, which, it is currently supposed, can be known and dealt with apart. That for the past three centuries energy should have gone chiefly into physical inquiry, beginning with the things most remote from man such as heavenly bodies, was to have been expected. The history of the physical sciences reveals a certain order in which they developed. Mathematical tools had to be employed before a new astronomy could be constructed. Physics advanced when ideas worked out in connection with the solar system were used to describe happenings on the earth. Chemistry waited on the advance of physics; the sciences of living things required the material and methods of physics and chemistry in order to make headway. Human psychology ceased to be chiefly speculative opinion only when biological and physiological conclusions were available. All this is natural and seemingly inevitable. Things which had the most outlying and indirect connection with human interests had to be mastered in

some degree before inquiries could competently converge upon man himself.

Nevertheless the course of development has left us of this age in a plight. When we say that a subject of science is technically specialized, or that it is highly "abstract," what we practically mean is that it is not conceived in terms of its bearing upon human life. All *merely* physical knowledge is technical, couched in a technical vocabulary communicable only to the few. Even physical knowledge which does affect human conduct, which does modify what we do and undergo, is also technical and remote in the degree in which its bearings are not understood and used. The sunlight, rain, air and soil have always entered in visible ways into human experience; atoms and molecules and cells and most other things with which the sciences are occupied affect us, but not visibly. Because they enter life and modify experience in imperceptible ways, and their consequences are not realized, speech about them is technical; communication is by means of peculiar symbols. One would think, then, that a fundamental and ever-operating aim would be to translate knowledge of the subject-matter of physical conditions into terms which are generally understood, into signs denoting human consequences of services and disservices rendered. For ultimately all consequences which enter human life depend upon physical conditions; they can be understood and mastered only as the latter are taken into account. One would think, then, that any state of affairs which tends to render the things of the environment unknown and incommunicable by human beings in terms of their own activities and sufferings would be deplored as a disaster; that it would be felt to be intolerable, and to be put up with only as far as it is, at any given time, inevitable.

But the facts are to the contrary. Matter and the material are words which in the minds of many convey a note of disparagement. They are taken to be foes of whatever is of ideal value in life, instead of as conditions of its manifestation and sustained being. In consequence of this division, they do become in fact enemies, for whatever is consistently kept apart from human values depresses thought and renders values sparse and precarious in fact. There are even some who regard the materialism and dominance of commercialism of modern life as fruits of undue devotion to physical science, not seeing that the split between man and nature, artifically made by a tradition which originated before there was understanding of the physical conditions that are the medium of human activities, is the benumbing factor. The most influential form of the divorce is separation between pure and applied science. Since "application" signifies recognized bearing upon human experience and well-being, honor of what is "pure" and contempt for what is "applied" has for its outcome a science which is remote and technical, communicable only to specialists, and a conduct of human affairs which is haphazard, biased, unfair in distribution of values. What is applied and employed as the alternative to knowledge in regulation of society is ignorance, prejudice, class-interest and accident. Science is converted into knowledge in its honorable and emphatic sense *only* in application. Otherwise it is truncated, blind, distorted. When it is then applied, it is in ways which explain the unfavorable sense so often attached to "application" and the "utilitarian": namely, use for pecuniary ends to the profit of a few.

At present, the application of physical science is rather *to* human concerns than *in* them. That is, it is external, made in the interests of its consequences for a possessing and acquisitive class. Application *in* life would signify that science was absorbed and distributed; that it was the instrumentality of that common understanding and thorough communication which is the precondition of the existence of a genuine and effective public. The use of science to regulate industry and trade has gone on steadily. The scientific revolution of the seventeenth century was the precursor of the industrial revolution of the eighteenth and nineteenth. In consequence, man has suffered the impact of an enormously enlarged control of physical energies without any corresponding ability to control himself and his own affairs. Knowledge divided against itself, a

science to whose incompleteness is added in artificial split, has played its part in generating enslavement of men, women and children in factories in which they are animated machines to tend inanimate machines. It has maintained sordid slums, flurried and discontented careers, grinding poverty and luxurious wealth, brutal exploitation of nature and man in times of peace and high explosives and noxious gases in time of war. Man, a child in understanding of himself, has placed in his hands physical tools of incalculable power. He plays with them like a child, and whether they work harm or good is largely a matter of accident. The instrumentality becomes a master and works fatally as if possessed of a will of its own—not because it has a will but because man has not.

The glorification of "pure" science under such conditions is a rationalization of an escape; it marks a construction of an asylum of refuge, a shirking of responsibility. The true purity of knowledge exists not when it is uncontaminated by contact with use and service. It is wholly a moral matter, an affair of honesty, impartiality and generous breadth of intent in search and communication. The adulteration of knowledge is due not to its use, but to vested bias and prejudice, to one-sidedness of outlook, to vanity, to conceit of possession and authority, to contempt or disregard of human concern in its use. Humanity is not, as was once thought, the end for which all things were formed; it is but a slight and feeble thing, perhaps an episodic one, in the vast stretch of the universe. But for man, man is the centre of interest and the measure of importance. The magnifying of the physical realm at the cost of man is but an abdication and a flight. To make physical science a rival of human interests is bad enough, for it forms a diversion of energy which can ill be afforded. But the evil does not stop there. The ultimate harm is that the understanding by man of his own affairs and his ability to direct them are sapped at their root when knowledge of nature is disconnected from its human function.

It has been implied throughout that knowledge is communication as well as understanding. I well remember the saying of a man, uneducated from the standpoint of the schools, in speaking of certain matters: "Sometime they will be found out and not only found out, but they will be known." The schools may suppose that a thing is known when it is found out. My old friend was aware that a thing is fully known only when it is published, shared, socially accessible. Record and communication are indispensable to knowledge. Knowledge cooped up in a private consciousness is a myth, and knowledge of social phenomena is peculiarly dependent upon dissemination, for only by distribution can such knowledge be either obtained or tested. A fact of community life which is not spread abroad so as to be a common possession is a contradiction in terms. Dissemination is something other than scattering at large. Seeds are sown, not by virtue of being thrown out at random, but by being so distributed as to take root and have a chance of growth. Communication of the results of social inquiry is the same thing as the formation of public opinion. This marks one of the first ideas framed in the growth of political democracy as it will be one of the last to be fulfilled. For public opinion is judgment which is formed and entertained by those who constitute the public and is about public affairs. Each of the two phases imposes for its realization conditions hard to meet.

Opinions and beliefs concerning the public presuppose effective and organized inquiry. Unless there are methods for detecting the energies which are at work and tracing them through an intricate network of interactions to their consequences, what passes as public opinion will be "opinion" in its derogatory sense rather than truly public, no matter how widespread the opinion is. The number who share error as to fact and who partake of a false belief measures power for harm. Opinion casually formed and formed under the direction of those who have something at stake in having a lie believed can be *public* opinion only in name. Calling it by this name, acceptance of the name as a kind of warrant, magnifies its capacity to lead action estray. The more who share it, the more injurious its influence.

Public opinion, even if it happens to be correct, is intermittent when it is not the product of methods of investigation and reporting constantly at work. It appears only in crises. Hence its "rightness" concerns only an immediate emergency. Its lack of continuity makes it wrong from the standpoint of the course of events. It is as if a physician were able to deal for the moment with an emergency in disease but could not adapt his treatment of it to the underlying conditions which brought it about. He may then "cure" the disease—that is, cause its present alarming symptoms to subside—but he does not modify its causes; his treatment may even effect them for the worse. Only continuous inquiry, continuous in the sense of being connected as well as persistent, can provide the material of enduring opinion about public matters.

There is a sense in which "opinion" rather than knowledge, even under the most favorable circumstances, is the proper term to use—namely, in the sense of judgment, estimate. For in its strict sense, knowledge can refer only to what *has* happened and been done. What is still *to be* done involves a forecast of a future still contingent, and cannot escape the liability to error in judgment involved in all anticipation of probabilities. There may well be honest divergence as to policies to be pursued, even when plans spring from knowledge of the same facts. But genuinely public policy cannot be generated unless it be informed by knowledge, and this knowledge does not exist except when there is systematic, thorough, and well-equipped search and record.

Moreover, inquiry must be as nearly contemporaneous as possible; otherwise it is only of antiquarian interest. Knowledge of history is evidently necessary for connectedness of knowledge. But history which is not brought down close to the actual scene of events leaves a gap and exercises influence upon the formation of judgments about the public interest only by guess-work about intervening events. Here, only too conspicuously, is a limitation of the existing social sciences. Their material comes too late, too far after the event, to enter effectively into the formation of public opinion about the immediate public concern and what is to be done about it.

A glance at the situation shows that the physical and external means of collecting information in regard to what is happening in the world have far outrun the intellectual phase of inquiry and organization of its results. Telegraph, telephone, and now the radio, cheap and quick mails, the printing press, capable of swift reduplication of material at low cost, have attained a remarkable development. But when we ask what sort of material is recorded and how it is organized, when we ask about the intellectual form in which the material is presented, the tale to be told is very different. "News" signifies something which has just happened, and which is new just because it deviates from the old and regular. But its *meaning* depends upon relation to what it imports, to what its social consequences are. This important cannot be determined unless the new is placed in relation to the old, to what has happened and been integrated into the course of events. Without coordination and consecutiveness, events are not events, but mere occurrences, intrusions; an event implies that out of which a happening proceeds. Hence even if we discount the influence of private interests in procuring suppression, secrecy and misrepresentation, we have here an explanation of the triviality and "sensational" quality of so much of what passes as news. The catastrophic, namely, crime, accident, family rows, personal clashes and conflicts, are the most obvious forms of breaches of continuity; they supply the element of shock which is the strictest meaning of sensation; they are the *new* par excellence, even though only the date of the newspaper could inform us whether they happened last year or this, so completely are they isolated from their connections.

So accustomed are we to this method of collecting, recording and presenting social changes, that it may well sound ridiculous to say that a genuine social science would manifest its reality in the daily press, while learned books and articles supply and polish tools of inquiry. But the inquiry which alone can furnish knowledge as a precondition of public judgments must be contemporary and quotidian. Even if social sciences as a specialized apparatus of inquiry were more advanced than they are, they would be comparatively impotent in the office of directing opinion on matters of concern to the public as long as they are remote from application in the daily and unremitting assembly and interpretation of "news." On the other hand, the tools of social inquiry will be clumsy as long as they are forged in places and under conditions remote from contemporary events.

What has been said about the formation of ideas and judgments concerning the public apply as well to the distribution of the knowledge which makes it an effective possession of the members of the public. Any separation between the two sides of the problem is artificial. The discussion of propaganda and propagandism would alone, however, demand a volume, and could be written only by one much more experienced than the present writer. Propaganda can accordingly only be mentioned, with the remark that the present situation is one unprecedented in history. The political forms of democracy and quasi-democratic habits of thought on social matters have compelled a certain amount of public discussion and at least the simulation of general consultation in arriving at political decisions. Representative government must at least seem to be founded on public interests as they are revealed to public belief. The days are past when government can be carried on without any pretense of ascertaining the wishes of the governed. In theory, their assent must be secured. Under the older forms, there was no need to muddy the sources of opinion on political matters. No current of energy flowed from them. To-day the judgments popularly formed on political matters are so important, in spite of all factors to the contrary, that there is an enormous premium upon all methods which affect their formation.

The smoothest road to control of political conduct is by control of opinion. As long as interests of pecuniary profit are powerful, and a public has not located and identified itself, those who have this interest will have an unresisted motive for tampering with the springs of political action in all that affects them. Just as in the conduct of industry and exchange generally the technological factor is obscured, deflected and defeated by "business," so specifically in the management of publicity. The gathering and sale of subject-matter having a public import is part of the existing pecuniary system. Just as industry conducted by engineers on a factual technological basis would be a very different thing from what it actually is, so the assembling and reporting of news would be a very different thing if the genuine interests of reporters were permitted to work freely.

One aspect of the matter concerns particularly the side of dissemination. It is often said, and with a great appearance of truth, that the freeing and perfecting of inquiry would not have any especial effect. For, it is argued, the mass of the reading public is not interested in learning and assimilating the results of accurate investigation. Unless these are read, they cannot seriously affect the thought and action of members of the public; they remain in secluded library alcoves, and are studied and understood only by a few intellectuals. The objection is well taken save as the potency of art is taken into account. A technical highbrow presentation would appeal only to those technically high-brow; it would not be news to the masses. Presentation is fundamentally important, and presentation is a question of art. A newspaper which was only a daily edition of a quarterly journal of sociology or political science would undoubtedly possess a limited circulation and a narrow influence. Even at that, however, the mere existence and accessibility of such material would have some regulative effect. But we can look much further than that. The material would have such an enormous and widespread human bearing that its bare existence would be an irresistible invitation to a presentation of it which would have a direct popular appeal. The freeing of the artist in literary presentation, in other words, is as much a precondition of the desirable creation of adequate opinion on public matters as is the freeing of social inquiry. Men's conscious life of opinion and judgement often proceeds on a superficial and trivial plane. But their lives reach a deeper level. The function of art has always been to break through the crust of conventionalized and routine consciousness. Common things, a flower, a gleam of moonlight, the song of a bird, not things rare and remote, are means with which the deeper levels of life are touched so that they spring up as desire and thought. This process is art. Poetry, the drama, the novel, are proofs that the problem of presentation is not insoluble. Artists have always been the real purveyors of news, for it is not the outward happening in itself which is new, but the kindling by it of emotion, perception and appreciation.

We have but touched lightly and in passing upon the conditions which must be fulfilled if the Great Society is to become a Great Community; a society in which the ever-expanding and intricately ramifying consequences of associated activities shall be known in the full sense of that word, so that an organized, articulate Public comes into being. The highest and most difficult kind of inquiry and a subtle, delicate, vivid and responsive art of communication must take possession of the physical machinery of transmission and circulation and breathe life into it. When the machine age has thus perfected its machinery it will be a means of life and not its despotic master. Democracy will come into its own, for democracy is a name for a life of free and enriching communion. It had its seer in Walt Whitman. It will have its consummation when free social inquiry is indissolubly wedded to the art of full and moving communication.

## Notes

1. The most adequate discussion of this ideal with which I am acquainted is T. V. Smith's *The Democratic Way of Life.*
2. The religious character of nationalism has been forcibly brought out by Carlton Hayes, in his *Essays on Nationalism,* especially Chap. 4.

# The Live Creature and Aesthetic Experience

## The Live Creature

By one of the ironic perversities that often attend the course of affairs, the existence of the works of art upon which formation of an esthetic theory depends has become an obstruction to theory about them. For one reason, these works are products that exist externally and physically. In common conception, the work of art is often identified with the building, book, painting, or statue in its existence apart from human experience. Since the actual work of art is what the product does with and in experience, the result is not favorable to understanding. In addition, the very perfection of some of these products, the prestige they possess because of a long history of unquestioned admiration, creates conventions that get in the way of fresh insight. When an art product once attains classic status, it somehow becomes isolated from the human conditions under which it was brought into being and from the human consequences it engenders in actual life-experience.

When artistic objects are separated from both conditions of origin and operation in experience, a wall is built around them that renders almost opaque their general significance, with which esthetic theory deals. Art is remitted to a separate realm, where it is cut off from that association with the materials and aims of every other form of human effort, undergoing, and achievement. A primary task is thus imposed upon one who undertakes to write upon the philosophy of the fine arts. This task is to restore continuity between the refined and intensified forms of experience that are works of art and the everyday events, doings, and sufferings that are universally recognized to constitute experience. Mountain peaks do not float unsupported; they do not even just rest upon the earth. They *are* the earth in one of its manifest operations. It is the business of those who are concerned with the theory of the earth, geographers and geologists, to make this fact evident in its various implications. The theorist who would deal philosophically with fine art has a like task to accomplish. . . .

In order to *understand* the esthetic in its ultimate and approved forms, one must begin with it in the raw; in the events and scenes that hold the attentive eye and ear of man, arousing his interest and affording him enjoyment as he looks and listens: the sights that hold the crowd—the fire-engine rushing by; the machines excavating enormous holes in the earth; the human-fly climbing the steepleside; the men perched high in air on girders, throwing and catching red-hot bolts. The sources of art in human experience will be learned by him who sees how the tense grace of the ball-player infects the onlooking crowd; who notes the delight of the housewife in tending her plants, and the intent interest of her goodman in tending the patch of green in front of the house; the zest of the spectator in poking the wood burning on the hearth and in watching the darting flames and crumbling coals. These people, if questioned as to the reason for their actions, would doubtless return reasonable answers. The man who poked the sticks of burning wood would say he did it to make the fire burn better; but he is none the less fascinated by the colorful drama of change enacted before his eyes and imaginatively partakes in it. He does not remain a cold spectator. What Coleridge said of the reader of poetry is true in its way of all who are happily absorbed in their activities of mind and body: "The reader should be carried forward, not merely or chiefly by the mechanical

From "The Live Creature" and "Having an Experience," in *Art as Experience, John Dewey: The Later Works, 1925–1953,* Vol. 10, Ed. Jo Ann Boydston (Carbondale and Edwardsville, Ill,: Southern Illinois University Press, 1987 [1934]), pp. 9–12, 42–45, 46–49, 50–52, 53–63.

impulse of curiosity, not by a restless desire to arrive at the final solution, but by the pleasurable activity of the journey itself."

The intelligent mechanic engaged in his job, interested in doing well and finding satisfaction in his handiwork, caring for his materials and tools with genuine affection, is artistically engaged. The difference between such a worker and the inept and careless bungler is as great in the shop as it is in the studio. Oftentimes the product may not appeal to the esthetic sense of those who use the product. The fault, however, is oftentimes not so much the worker as with the conditions of the market for which his product is designed. Were conditions and opportunities different, things as significant to the eye as those produced by earlier craftsmen would be made.

So extensive and subtly pervasive are the ideas that set Art upon a remote pedestal, that many a person would be repelled rather than pleased if told that he enjoyed his casual recreations, in part at least, because of their esthetic quality. The arts which today have most vitality for the average person are things he does not take to be arts: for instance, the movie, jazzed music, the comic strip, and, too frequently, newspaper accounts of love-nests, murders, and exploits of bandits. For, when what he knows as art is relegated to the museum and gallery, the unconquerable impulse towards experiences enjoyable in themselves finds such outlet as the daily environment provides. Many a person who protests against the museum conception of art, still shares the fallacy from which that conception springs. For the popular notion comes from a separation of art from the objects and scenes of ordinary experience that many theorists and critics pride themselves upon holding and even elaborating. The time when select and distinguished objects are closely connected with the products of usual vocations are the times when appreciation of the former is most rife and most keen. When, because of their remoteness, the objects acknowledged by the cultivated to be works of fine art seem anemic to the mass of people, esthetic hunger is likely to seek the cheap and the vulgar. . . .

## Having an Experience

Experience occurs continuously, because the interaction of live creature and environing conditions is involved in the very process of living. Under conditions of resistance and conflict, aspects and elements of the self and the world that are implicated in this interaction qualify experience with emotions and ideas so that conscious intent emerges. Oftentimes, however, the experience had is inchoate. Things are experienced but not in such a way that they are composed into *an* experience. There is distraction and dispersion; what we observe and what we think, what we desire and what we get, are at odds with each other. We put our hands to the plow and turn back; we start and then we stop, not because the experience has reached the end for the sake of which it was initiated but because of extraneous interruptions or of inner lethargy.

In contrast with such experience, we have *an* experience when the material experienced runs its course to fulfillment. Then and then only is it integrated within and demarcated in the general stream of experience from other experiences. A piece of work is finished in a way that is satisfactory; a problem receives its solution; a game is played through; a situation, whether that of eating a meal, playing a game of chess, carrying on a conversation, writing a book, or taking part in a political campaign, is so rounded out that its close is a consummation and not a cessation. Such an experience is a whole and carries with it its own individualizing quality and self-sufficiency. It is *an* experience.

Philosophers, even empirical philosophers, have spoken for the most part of experience at large. Idiomatic speech, however, refers to experiences each of which is singular, having its own beginning and end. For life is no uniform uninterrupted march or flow. It is a thing of histories, each with its own plot, its own inception and movement toward its close, each having its own particular rhythmic movement; each with its own unrepeated quality pervading it throughout. A flight of stairs, mechanical as it is, proceeds by individualized steps, not by undifferentiated progression, and an inclined plane is at least marked off from other things by abrupt discreteness.

Experience in this vital sense is defined by those situations and episodes that we spontaneously refer to as being "real experiences"; those things of which we say in recalling them, "that *was* an experience." It may have been something of tremendous importance— a quarrel with one who was once an intimate, a catastrophe finally averted by a hair's breadth. Or it may have been something that in comparison was slight—and which perhaps because of its very slightness illustrates all the better what is to be an experience. There is that meal in a Paris restaurant of which one says "that *was* an experience." It stands out as an enduring memorial of what food may be. Then there is that storm one went through in crossing the Atlantic—the storm that seemed in its fury, as it was experienced, to sum up in itself all that a storm can be, complete in itself, standing out because marked out from what went before and what came after.

In such experiences, every successive part flows freely without seam and without unfilled blanks, into what ensues. At the same time there is no sacrifice of the self-identity of the parts. A river, as distinct from a pond, flows. But its flow gives a definiteness and interest to its successive portions greater than exist in the homogenous portions of a pond. In an experience, flow is from something to something. As one part leads into another and as one part carries on what went before, each gains distinctness in itself. The enduring whole is diversified by successive phases that are emphases of its varied colors.

Because of continuous merging, there are no holes, mechanical junctions, and dead centers when we have *an* experience. There are pauses, places of rest, but they punctuate and define the quality of movement. They sum up what has been undergone and prevent its dissipation and idle evaporation. Continued acceleration is breathless and prevents parts from gaining distinction. In a work of art, different acts, episodes, occurrences melt and fuse into unity, and yet do not disappear and lose their own character as they do so—just as in a genial conversation there is a continuous interchange and blending, and yet each speaker not only retains his own character but manifests it more clearly than in his wont.

An experience has a unity that gives it its name, *that* meal, that storm, that rupture of friendship. The existence of this unity is constituted by a single *quality* that pervades the entire experience in spite of the variation of its constituent parts. This unity is neither emotional, practical, nor intellectual, for these terms name distinctions that reflection can make within it. In discourse *about* an experience, we must make use of these adjectives of interpretation. In going over an experience in mind *after* its occurence, we may find that one property rather than another was sufficiently dominant so that it characterizes the experience as a whole. There are absorbing inquiries and speculations which a scientific man and philosopher will recall as "experiences" in the emphatic sense. In final import they are intellectual. But in their actual occurrence they were emotional as well; they were purposive and volitional. Yet the experience was not a sum of these different characters; they were lost in it as distinctive traits. No thinker can ply his occupation save as he is lured and rewarded by total integral experiences that are intrinsically worth while. Without them he would never know what it is really to think and would be completely at a loss in distinguishing real thought from the spurious article. Thinking goes on in trains of ideas, but the ideas form a train only because they are much more than what an analytic psychology calls ideas. They are phases, emotionally and practically distinguished, of a developing underlying quality; they are its moving variations, not separate and independent like Locke's and Hume's so-called ideas and impressions, but are subtle shadings of a pervading and developing hue.

We say of an experience of thinking that we reach or draw a conclusion. Theoretical formulation of the process is often made in such terms as to conceal effectually the similarity of "conclusion" to the consummating phase of every developing integral experience. These formulations apparently take their cue from the separate propositions that are premises and the proposition that is the conclusion as they appear on the printed page. The impression is derived that there are first two independent and ready-made entities that are then manipulated so as to give rise to a third. In fact, in an experience of thinking, premisses emerge only as a conclusion becomes manifest. The experience, like that of watching a storm reach its height and gradually subside, is one of continuous movement of subject-matters. Like the ocean in the storm, there are a series of waves; suggestions reaching out and being broken in a clash, or being carried onwards by a coöperative wave. If a conclusion is reached, it is that of a movement of anticipation and cumulation, one that finally comes to completion. A "conclusion" is no separate and independent thing; it is the consummation of a movement.

Hence *an* experience of thinking has its own esthetic quality. It differs from those experiences that are acknowledged to be esthetic, but only in its materials. The material of the fine arts consists of qualities; that of experience having intellectual conclusion are signs or symbols having no intrinsic quality of their own, but standing for things that may in another experience be qualitatively experienced. The difference is enormous. It is one reason why the strictly intellectual art will never be popular as music is popular. Nevertheless, the experience itself has a satisfying emotional quality because it possesses internal integration and fulfillment reached through ordered and organized movement. This artistic structure may be immediately felt. In so far, it is esthetic. What is even more important is that not only is this quality a significant motive in undertaking intellectual inquiry and in keeping it honest, but that no intellectual activity is an integral event (is *an* experience), unless it is rounded out with this quality. Without it, thinking is inconclusive. In short, esthetic cannot be sharply marked off from intellectual experience since the latter must bear an esthetic stamp to be itself complete.

The same statement holds good of a course of action that is dominantly practical, that is, one that consists of overt doings. It is possible to be efficient in action and yet not have a conscious experience. The activity is too automatic to permit of a sense of what it is about and where it is going. It comes to an end but not to a close or consummation in consciousness. Obstacles are overcome by shrewd skill, but they do not feed experience ... For in much of our experience we are not concerned with the connection of one incident with what went before and what comes after. There is no interest that controls attentive rejection or selection of what shall be organized into the developing experience. Things happen, but they are neither definitely included nor decisively excluded; we drift. We yield according to external pressure, or evade and compromise. There are beginnings and cessations, but no genuine initiations and concludings. One thing replaces another, but does not absorb it and carry it on. There is experience, but so slack and discursive that it is not *an* experience. Needless to say, such experiences are anesthetic.

Thus the non-esthetic lies within two limits. At one pole is the loose succession that does not begin at any particular place and that ends—in the sense of ceasing—at no particular place. At the other pole is arrest, constriction, proceeding from parts having only a mechanical connection with one another. There exists so much of one and the other of these two kinds of experience that unconsciously they come to be taken as norms of all experience. Then, when the esthetic appears, it so sharply contrasts with the picture that has been formed of experience, that it is impossible to combine its special qualities with the features of the picture and the esthetic is given an outside place and status. The account that has been given of experience dominantly intellectual and practical is intended to show that there is no such contrast involved in having an experience; that, on the contrary, no experience of whatever sort is a unity unless it has esthetic quality.

The enemies of the esthetic are neither the practical nor the intellectual. They are the humdrum; slackness of loose ends; submission to convention in practice and intellectual procedure. Rigid abstinence, coerced submission, tightness on one side and dissipation, incoherence and aimless indulgence on the other, are deviations in opposite directions from the unity of an experience. Some such considerations perhaps induced Aristotle to invoke the "mean proportional" as the proper designation of what is distinctive of both virtue and the esthetic. He was formally correct. "Mean" and "proportion" are, however, not self-explanatory, nor to be taken over in a prior mathematical sense, but are properties belonging to an experience that has a developing movement toward its own consummation.

I have emphasized the fact that every integral experience moves toward a close, an ending, since it ceases only when the energies active in it have done their proper work. This closure of a circuit of energy is the opposite of arrest, of *stasis*. Maturation and fixation are polar opposite. Struggle and conflict may be themselves enjoyed, although they are painful, when they are experienced as means of developing an experience; members in that they carry it forward, not just because they are there. There is, as will appear later, an element of undergoing, of suffering in its large sense, in every experience. Otherwise there would be no taking in of what preceded. For "taking in" in any vital experience is something more than placing some*thing* on the top of consciousness over what was previously known. It involves reconstruction which may be painful. Whether the necessary undergoing phase is by itself pleasurable or painful is a matter of particular conditions. It is indifferent to the total esthetic quality, save that there are few intense esthetic experiences that are wholly gleeful. They are certainly not to be characterized as amusing, and as they bear down upon us they involve a suffering that is none the less consistent with, indeed a part of, the complete perception that is enjoyed.

I have spoken of the esthetic quality that rounds out an experience into completeness and unity as emotional. The reference may cause difficulty. We are given to thinking of emotions as things as simple and compact as are the words by which we name them. Joy, sorrow, hope, fear, anger, curiosity, are treated as if each in itself were a sort of entity that enters full-made upon the scene, an entity that may last a long time or a short time, but whose duration, whose growth and career, is irrelevant to its nature. In fact emotions are qualities, when they are significant, of a complex experience that moves and changes. I say, when they are *significant,* for otherwise they are but the outbreaks and eruptions of a disturbed infant. All emotions are qualifications of a drama and they change as the drama develops. Persons are sometimes said to fall in love at first sight. But what they fall into is not a thing of that instant. What would love be were it compressed into a moment in which there is no room for cherishing and for solicitude? The intimate nature of emotion is manifested in the experience of one watching a play on the stage or reading a novel. It attends the development of a plot; and a plot requires a stage, a space, wherein to develop and time in which to unfold. Experience is emotional but there are not separate things called emotions in it.

By the same token, emotions are attached to events and objects in their movement. They are not, save in pathological instances, private. And even an "objectless" emotion demands something beyond itself to which to attach itself, and thus it soon generates a delusion in lack of something real. Emotion belongs of a certainty to the self. But it belongs to the self that is concerned in the movement of events toward an issue that is desired or disliked. We jump instantaneously when we are scared, as we blush on the instant when we are ashamed. But fright and shamed modesty are not in this case emotional states. Of themselves they are but automatic reflexes. In order to become emotional they must become parts of an inclusive and enduring situation that involves concern for objects and their issues. The jump of fright becomes emotional fear when there is found or thought to exist a threatening object that must be dealt with or escaped from. The blush becomes the emotion of shame when a person connects, in thought, an action he has performed with an unfavorable reaction to himself of some other person.

Physical things from far ends of the earth are physically transported and physically caused to act and react upon one another in the construction of a new object. The miracle of mind is that something similar takes place in experience without physical transport and assembling. Emotion is the moving and cementing force. It selects what is congruous and dyes what is selected with its color, thereby giving qualitative unity to materials externally disparate and dissimilar. It thus provides unity in and through the varied parts of an experience. When the unity is of the sort already described, the experience has esthetic character even though it is not, dominantly, an esthetic experience. . . .

There are, therefore, common patterns in various experiences, no matter how unlike they are to one another in the details of their subject matter. There are conditions to be met without which an experience cannot come to be. The outline of the common pattern is set by the fact that every experience is the result of interaction between a live creature and some aspect of the world in which he lives. A man does something; he lifts, let us say, a stone. In consequence he undergoes, suffers, something: the weight, strain, texture of the surface of the thing lifted. The properties thus undergone determine further doing. The stone is too heavy or too angular, not solid enough; or else the properties undergone show it is fit for the use for which it is intended. The process continues until a mutual adaptation of the self and the object emerges and that particular experience comes to a close. What is true of this simple instance is true, as to form, of every experience. The creature operating may be a thinker in his study and the environment with which he interacts may consist of ideas instead of a stone. But interaction of the two constitutes the total experience that is had, and the close which completes it is the institution of a felt harmony.

An experience has pattern and structure, because it is not just doing and undergoing in alternation, but consists of them in relationship. To put one's hand in the fire that consumes it is not necessarily to have an experience. The action and its consequence must be joined in perception. This relationship is what gives meaning; to grasp it is the objective of all intelligence. The scope and content of the relations measure the significant content of an experience. A child's experience may be intense, but, because of lack of background from past experience, relations between undergoing and doing are slightly grasped, and the experience does not have great depth or breadth. No one ever arrives at such maturity that he perceives all the connections that are involved. There was once written (by Mr. Hinton) a romance called "The Unlearner." It portrayed the whole endless duration of life after death as a living over of the incidents that happened in a short life on earth, in continued discovery of the relationships involved among them.

Experience is limited by all the causes which interfere with perception of the relations between undergoing and doing. There may be interference because of excess on the side of doing or of excess on the side of receptivity, of undergoing. Unbalance on either side blurs the perception of relations and leaves the experience partial and distorted, with scant or false meaning. Zeal for doing, lust for action, leaves many a person, especially in this hurried and impatient human environment in which we live, with experience of an almost incredible paucity, all on the surface. No one experience has a chance to complete itself because something else is entered upon so speedily. What is called experience becomes so dispersed and miscellaneous as hardly to deserve the name. Resistance is treated as an obstruction to be beaten down, not as an invitation to reflection. An individual comes to seek, unconsciously even more than by deliberate choice, situations in which he can do the most things in the shortest time.

Experiences are also cut short from maturing by excess of receptivity. What is prized is then the mere undergoing of this and that, irrespective of perception of any meaning. The crowding together of as many impressions as possible is thought to be "life," even though no one of them is more than a flitting and a sipping. The sentimentalist and the day-dreamer may have more fancies and impressions pass through their consciousness than has the man who is animated by lust for action. But his experience is equally distorted, because nothing takes root in mind when there is no balance between doing and receiving. Some decisive action is needed to order to establish contact with the realities of the world and in order that impressions may be so related to facts that their value is tested and organized.

Because perception of relationship between what is done and what is undergone constitutes the work of intelligence, and because the artist is controlled in the process of his work by his grasp of the connection between what he has already done and what he is to do next, the idea that the artist does not think as intently and penetratingly as a scientific inquirer is absurd. A painter must consciously undergo the effect of his every brush stroke or he will not be aware of what he is doing and where his work is going. Moreover, he has to see each particular connection of doing and undergoing in relation to the whole that he desires to produce. To apprehend such relations is to think, and is one of the most exacting modes of thought. The difference between the picture of different painters is due quite as much to differences of capacity to carry on this thought as it is to differences of sensitivity to bare color and to differences in dexterity of execution. As respects the basic quality of pictures, difference depends, indeed, more upon the quality of intelligence brought to bear upon perception of relations than upon anything else—though of course intelligence cannot be separated from direct sensitivity and is connected, though in a more external manner, with skill.

Any idea that ignores the necessary rôle of intelligence in production of works of art is based upon identification of thinking with use of one special kind of material, verbal signs and words. To think effectively in terms of relations of qualities is as severe a demand upon thought as to think in terms of symbols, verbal and mathematical. Indeed, since words are easily manipulated in mechanical ways, the production of a work of genuine art prob-

ably demands more intelligence than does most of the so-called thinking that goes on among those who pride themselves on being "intellectuals." . . .

Art denotes a process of doing or making. This is as true of fine as of technological art. Art involves molding of clay, chipping of marble, casting of bronze, laying on of pigments, construction of buildings, singing of songs, playing of instruments, enacting rôles on the stage, going through rhythmic movements in the dance. Every art does something with some physical material, the body or something outside the body, with or without the use of intervening tools, and with a view to production of something visible, audible, or tangible. So marked is the active or "doing" phase of art, that the dictionaries usually define it in terms of skilled action, ability in execution. The Oxford Dictionary illustrates by a quotation from John Stuart Mill: "Art is an endeavor after perfection in execution" while Matthew Arnold calls it "pure and flawless workmanship."

The word "esthetic" refers, as we have already noted, to experience as appreciative, perceiving, and enjoying. It denotes the consumer's rather than the producer's standpoint. It is Gusto, taste; and, as with cooking, overt skillful action is on the side of the cook who prepares, while taste is on the side of the consumer, as in gardening there is a distinction between the gardener who plants and tills and the householder who enjoys the finished product.

These very illustrations, however, as well as the relation that exists in having an experience between doing and undergoing, indicate that the distinction between esthetic and artistic cannot be pressed so far as to become a separation. Perfection in execution cannot be measured or defined in terms of execution; it implies those who perceive and enjoy the product that is executed. The cook prepares food for the consumer and the measure of the value of what is prepared is found in consumption. Mere perfection in execution, judged in its own terms in isolation, can probably be attained better by a machine than by human art. By itself, it is at most technique, and there are great artists who are not in the first ranks as technicians (witness Cézanne), just as there are great performers on the piano who are not great esthetically, and as Sargent is not a great painter.

Craftsmanship to be artistic in the final sense must be "loving"; it must care deeply for the subject matter upon which skill is exercised. A sculptor comes to mind whose busts are marvelously exact. It might be difficult to tell in the presence of a photograph of one of them and of a photograph of the original which was of the person himself. For virtuosity they are remarkable. But one doubts whether the maker of the busts had an experience of his own that he was concerned to have those share who look at his products. To be truly artistic, a work must also be esthetic—that is, framed for enjoyed receptive perception. Constant observation is, of course, necessary for the maker while he is producing. But if his perception is not also esthetic in nature, it is a colorless and cold recognition of what has been done, used as a stimulus to the next step in a process that is essentially mechanical.

In short, art, in its form, unites the very same relation of doing and undergoing, outgoing and incoming energy, that makes an experience to be an experience. Because of elimination of all that does not contribute to mutual organization of the factors of both action and reception into one another, and because of selection of just the aspects and traits that contribute to their interpenetration of each other, the product is a work of esthetic art. Man whittles, carves, sings, dances, gestures, molds, draws and paints. The doing or making is artistic when the perceived result is of such a nature that *its* qualities *as perceived* have controlled the question of production. The act of producing that is directed by intent to produce something that is enjoyed in the immediate experience of perceiving his qualities that a spontaneous or uncontrolled activity does not have. The artist embodies in himself the attitude of the perceiver while he works.

Suppose, for the sake of illustration, that a finely wrought object, one whose texture and proportions are highly pleasing in perception, has been believed to be a product of some primitive people. Then there is discovered evidence that proves it to be an accidental natural product. As an external thing, it is now precisely what it was before. Yet at once it ceases to be a work of art and becomes a natural "curiosity." It now belongs in a museum of natural history, not in a museum of art. And the extraordinary thing is that the difference that is thus made is not one of just intellectual classification. A difference is made in appreciative perception and in a direct way. The esthetic experience—in its limited sense—is thus seen to be inherently connected with the experience of making.

The sensory satisfaction of eye and ear, when esthetic, is so because it does not stand by itself but is linked to the activity of which it is the consequence. Even the pleasures of the plate are different in quality to an epicure than in one who merely "likes" his food as he eats it. The difference is not of mere intensity. The epicure is conscious of much more than the taste of the food. Rather, there enter into the taste, as directly experienced, qualities that depend upon reference to its source and its manner of production in connection with criteria of excellence. As production must absorb into itself qualities of the product as perceived and be regulated by them, so, on the other side, seeing, hearing, tasting, become esthetic when relation to a distinct manner of activity qualifies what is perceived.

There is an element of passion in all esthetic perception. Yet when we are overwhelmed by passion, as in extreme rage, fear, jealousy, the experience is definitely nonesthetic. There is no relationship felt to the qualities of the activity that has generated the passion. Consequently, the material of the experience lacks elements of balance and proportion. For these can be present only when, as in the conduct that has grace or dignity, the act is controlled by an exquisite sense of the relations which the act sustains—its fitness to the occasion and to the situation.

The process of art in production is related to the esthetic in perception organically—as the Lord God in creation surveyed his work and found it good. Until the artist is satisfied in perception with what he is doing, he continues shaping and reshaping. The making comes to an end when its result is experienced as good—and that experience comes not by mere intellectual and outside judgment but in direct perception. An artist, in comparison with his fellows, is one who is not only especially gifted in powers of execution but in unusual sensitivity to the qualities of things. This sensitivity also directs his doing and makings.

As we manipulate, we touch and feel, as we look, we see; as we listen, we hear. The hand moves with etching needle or with brush. The eye attends and reports the consequence of what is done. Because of this intimate connection, subsequent doing is cumulative and not a matter of caprice nor yet of routine. In an emphatic artistic-esthetic experience, the relation is so close that it controls simultaneously both the doing and the perception. Such vital intimacy of connection cannot be had if only hand and eye are engaged. When they do not, both of them, act as organs of the whole being, there is but a mechanical sequence of sense and movement, as in walking that is automatic. Hand and eye, when the experience is esthetic, are but instruments through which the entire live creature, moved and active throughout, operates. Hence the expression is emotional and guided by purpose.

Because of the relation between what is done and what is undergone, there is an immediate sense of things in perception as belonging together or as jarring; as reinforcing or as interfering. The consequences of the act of making as reported in sense show whether what is done carries forward the idea being executed or marks a deviation and break. In as far as the development of an experience is *controlled* through reference to these immediately felt relations of order and fulfillment, that experience becomes dominantly esthetic in nature. The urge to action becomes an urge to that kind of action which will result in an object satisfying in direct perception. The pot-

ter shapes his clay to make a bowl useful for holding grain; but he makes it in a way so regulated by the series of perceptions that sum up the serial acts of making, that the bowl is marked by enduring grace and charm. The general situation remains the same in painting a picture or molding a bust. Moreover, at each stage there is anticipation of what is to come. This anticipation is the connecting link between the next doing and its outcome for sense. What is done and what is undergone are thus reciprocally, cumulatively, and continuously instrumental to each other.

The doing may be energetic, and the undergoing may be acute and intense. But unless they are related to each other to form a whole in perception, the thing done is not fully esthetic. The making for example may be a display of technical virtuosity, and the undergoing a gush of sentiment or a revery. If the artist does not perfect a new vision in his process of doing, he acts mechanically and repeats some old model fixed like a blue print in his mind. An incredible amount of observation and of the kind of intelligence that is exercised in perception of qualitative relations characterizes creative work in art. The relations must be noted not only with respect to one another, two by two, but in connection with the whole under construction; they are exercised in imagination as well as in observation. Irrelevancies arise that are tempting distractions; digressions suggest themselves in the guise of enrichments. There are occasions when the grasp of the dominant idea grows faint, and then the artist is moved unconsciously to fill in until his thought grows strong again. The real work of an artist is to build up an experience that is coherent in perception while moving with constant change in its development.

When an author puts on paper ideas that are already clearly conceived and consistently ordered, the real work has been previously done. Or, he may depend upon the greater perceptibility induced by the activity and its sensible report to direct his completion of the work. The mere act of transcription is esthetically irrelevant save as it enters integrally into the formation of an experience moving to completeness. Even the composition conceived in the head and, therefore, physically private, is public in its significant content, since it is conceived with reference to execution in a product that is perceptible and hence belongs to the common world. Otherwise it would be an aberration or a passing dream. The urge to express through painting the perceived qualities of a landscape is continuous with demand for pencil or brush. Without external embodiment, an experience remains incomplete; physiologically and functionally, sense organs are motor organs and are connected, by means of distribution of energies in the human body and not merely anatomically, with other motor organs. It is no linguistic accident that "building," "construction," "work," designate both a process and its finished product. Without the meaning of the verb that of the noun remains blank.

Writer, composer of music, sculptor, or painter can retrace, during the process of production, what they have previously done. When it is not satisfactory in the undergoing or perceptual phase of experience, they can to some degree start afresh. This retracing is not readily accomplished in the case of architecture—which is perhaps one reason why there are so many ugly buildings. Architects are obliged to complete their idea before its translation into a complete object of perception takes place. Inability to build up simultaneously the idea and its objective embodiment imposes a handicap. Nevertheless, they too are obliged to think out their ideas in terms of the medium of embodiment and the object of ultimate perception unless they work mechanically and by rote. Probably the esthetic quality of medieval cathedrals is due in some measure to the fact that their constructions were not so much controlled by plans and specifications made in advance as is now the case. Plans grew as the building grew. But even a Minerva-like product, if it is artistic, presupposes a prior period of gestation in which doings and perceptions projected in imagination interact and mutually modify one another. Every work of art follows the plan of, and pattern of, a complete experience, rendering it more intensely and concentratedly felt.

It is not so easy in the case of the perceiver and appreciator to understand the intimate union of doing and undergoing as it is in the case of the maker. We are given to supposing that the former merely takes in what is there in finished form, instead of realizing that this taking in involves activities that are comparable to those of the creator. But receptivity is not passivity. It, too, is a process consisting of a series of responsive acts that accumulate toward objective fulfillment. Otherwise, there is not perception but recognition. The difference between the two is immense. Recognition is perception arrested before it has a chance to develop freely. In recognition there is a beginning of an act of perception. But this beginning is not allowed to serve the development of a full perception of the thing recognized. It is arrested at the point where it will serve some *other* purpose, as we recognize a man on the street in order to greet or to avoid him, not so as to see him for the sake of seeing what is there.

In recognition we fall back, as upon a stereotype, upon some previously formed scheme. Some detail or arrangement of details serves as cue for bare identification. It suffices in recognition to apply this bare outline as a stencil to the present object. Sometimes in contact with a human being we are struck with traits, perhaps of only physical characteristics, of which we were not previously aware. We realize that we never knew the person before; we had not seen him in any pregnant sense. We now begin to study and to "take in." Perception replaces bare recognition. There is an act of reconstructive doing, and consciousness becomes fresh and alive. *This* act of seeing involves the cooperation of motor elements even though they remain implicit and do not become overt, as well as coöperation of all funded ideas that may serve to complete the new picture that is forming. Recognition is too easy to arouse vivid consciousness. There is not enough resistance between new and old to secure consciousness of the experience that is had. Even a dog that barks and wags his tail joyously on seeing his master return is more fully alive in his reception of his friend than is a human being who is content with mere recognition.

Bare recognition is satisfied when a proper tag or label is attached, "proper" signifying one that serves a purpose outside the act of recognition—as a salesman identifies wares by a sample. It involves no stir of the organism, no inner commotion. But an act of perception proceeds by waves that extend serially throughout the entire organism. There is, therefore, no such thing in perception as seeing or hearing *plus* emotion. The perceived object or scene is emotionally pervaded throughout. When an aroused emotion does not permeate the material that is perceived or thought of, it is either preliminary or pathological.

The esthetic or undergoing phase of experience is receptive. It involves surrender. But adequate yielding of the self is possible only through a controlled activity that may well be intense. In much of our intercourse with our surroundings we withdraw; sometimes from fear, if only of expending unduly our store of energy; sometimes from preoccupation with other matters, as in the case of recognition. Perception is an act of the going-out of energy in order to receive, not a withholding of energy. To steep ourselves in a subject-matter we have first to plunge into it. When we are only passive to a scene, it overwhelm us and, for lack of answering activity, we do not perceive that which bears us down. We must summon energy and pitch it at a responsive key in order to *take* in.

Every one knows that it requires apprenticeship to see through a microscope or telescope, and to see a landscape as the geologist sees it. The idea that esthetic perception is an affair for odd moments is one reason for the backwardness of the arts among us. The eye and the visual apparatus may be intact; the object may be physically there, the cathedral of Notre Dame, or Rembrandt's portrait of Hendrik Stoeffel. In some bald sense, the latter may be "seen." They may be looked at, possibly recognized, and have their correct names

attached. But for lack of continuous interaction between the total organism and the objects, they are not perceived, certainly not esthetically. A crowd of visitors steered through a picture-gallery by a guide, with attention called here and there to some high point, does not perceive; only by accident is there even interest in seeing a picture for the sake of subject matter vividly realized.

For to perceive, a beholder must *create* his own experience. And his creation must include relations comparable to those which the original producer underwent. They are not the same in any literal sense. But with the perceiver, as with the artist, there must be an ordering of the elements of the whole that is in form, although not in details, the same as the process of organization the creator of the work consciously experienced. Without an act of recreation the object is not perceived as a work of art. The artist selected, simplified, clarified, abridged and condensed according to his interest. The beholder must go through these operations according to his point of view and interest. In both, an act of abstraction, that is of extraction of what is significant, takes place. In both, there is comprehension in its literal signification—that is, a gathering together of details and particulars physically scattered into an experienced whole. There is work done on the part of the percipient as there is on the part of the artist. The one who is too lazy, idle, or indurated in convention to perform this work will not see or hear. His "appreciation" will be a mixture of scraps of learning with conformity to norms of conventional admiration and with a confused, even if genuine, emotional excitation.

The considerations that have been presented imply both the community and the unlikeness, because of specific emphasis, of *an* experience, in its pregnant sense, and esthetic experience. The former has esthetic quality; otherwise its materials would not be rounded out into a single coherent experience. It is not possible to divide in a vital experience the practical, emotional, and intellectual from one another and to set the properties of one over against the characteristics of the others. The emotional phase binds parts together into a single whole; "intellectual" simply names the fact that the experience has meaning; "practical" indicates that the organism is interacting with events and objects which surround it. The most elaborate philosophic or scientific inquiry and the most ambitious industrial or political enterprise has, when its different ingredients constitute an integral experience, esthetic quality. For then its varied parts are linked to one another, and do not merely succeed one another. And the parts through their experienced linkage move toward a consummation and close, not merely to cessation in time. This consummation, moreover, does not wait in consciousness for the whole undertaking to be finished. It is anticipated throughout and is recurrently savored with special intensity.

Nevertheless, the experiences in question are dominantly intellectual or practical, rather than *distinctively* esthetic, because of the interest and purpose that initiate and control them. In an intellectual experience, the conclusion has value on its own account. It can be extracted as a formula or as a "truth," and can be used in its independent entirety as factor and guide in other inquiries. In a work of art there is no such single self-sufficient deposit. The end, the terminus, is significant not by itself but as the integration of the parts. It has no other existence. A drama or novel is not the final sentence, even if the characters are disposed of as living happily ever after. In a distinctively esthetic experience, characteristics that are subdued in other experiences are dominant; those that are subordinate are controlling—namely, the characteristics in virtue of which the experience is an integrated complete experience on its own account.

In every integral experience there is form because there is dynamic organization. I call the organization dynamic because it takes time to complete it, because it is a growth. There is inception, development, fulfillment. Material is ingested and digested through interaction with that vital organization of the results of prior experience that constitutes the mind of the worker. Incubation goes on until

what is conceived is brought forth and is rendered perceptible as part of the common world. An esthetic experience can be crowded into a moment only in the sense that a climax of prior long enduring processes may arrive in an outstanding movement which so sweeps everything else into it that all else is forgotten. That which distinguishes an experience as esthetic is conversion of resistance and tensions, of excitations that in themselves are temptations to diversion, into a movement toward an inclusive and fulfilling close.

Experiencing like breathing is a rhythm of intakings and outgivings. Their succession is punctuated and made a rhythm by the existence of intervals, periods in which one phase is ceasing and the other is inchoate and preparing. William James aptly compared the course of a conscious experience to the alternate flights and perchings of a bird. The flights and perchings are intimately connected with one another; they are not so many unrelated lightings succeeded by a number of equally unrelated hoppings. Each resting place in experience is an undergoing in which is absorbed and taken home the consequences of prior doing, and, unless the doing is that of utter caprice or sheer routine, each doing carries in itself meaning that has been extracted and conserved. As with the advance of an army, all gains from what has been already effected are periodically consolidated, and always with a view to what is to be done next. If we move too rapidly, we get away from the base of supplies—of accrued meanings—and the experience is flustered, thin, and confused. If we dawdle too long after having extracted a net value, experience perishes of inanition.

The *form* of the whole is therefore present in every member. Fulfilling, consummating, are continuous functions, not mere ends, located at one place only. An engraver, painter, or writer is in process of completing at every stage of his work. He must at each point retain and sum up what has gone before as a whole and with reference to a whole to come. Otherwise there is no consistency and no security in his successive acts. The series of doings in the rhythm of experience give variety and movement; they save the work from monotony and useless repetitions. The undergoings are the corresponding elements in the rhythm, and they supply unity; they save the work from the aimlessness of a mere succession of excitations. An object is peculiarly and dominantly esthetic, yielding the enjoyment characteristic of esthetic perception, when the factors that determine anything which can be called *an* experience are lifted high above the threshold of perception and are made manifest for their own sake.

# Faith and Its Object

All religions, as I pointed out in the preceding chapter, involve specific intellectual beliefs, and they attach—some greater, some less—importance to assent to these doctrines as true, true in the intellectual sense. They have literatures held especially sacred, containing historical material with which the validity of the religions is connected. They have developed a doctrinal apparatus it is incumbent upon "believers" (with varying degrees of strictness in different religions) to accept. They also insist that there is some special and isolated channel of access to the truths they hold.

No one will deny, I suppose, that the present crisis in religion is intimately bound up with these claims. The skepticism and agnosticism that are rife and that from the standpoint of the religionist are fatal to the religious spirit are directly bound up with the intellectual contents, historical, cosmological, ethical, and theological, asserted to be indispensable in everything religious. There is no need for me here to go with any minuteness into the causes that have generated doubt and disbelief, uncertainty and rejection, as to these contents. It is enough to point out that all the beliefs and ideas in question, whether having to do with historical and literary matters, or with astronomy, geology and biology, or with the creation and structure of the world and man, are connected with the supernatural, and that this connection is the factor that has brought doubt upon them; the factor that from the standpoint of historic and institutional religions is sapping the religious life itself.

The obvious and simple facts of the case are that some views about the origin and constitution of the world and man, some views about the course of human history and personages and incidents in that history, have become so interwoven with religion as to be identified with it. On the other hand, the growth of knowledge and of its methods and tests has been such as to make acceptance of these beliefs increasingly onerous and even impossible for large numbers of cultivated men and women. With such persons, the result is that the more these ideas are used as the basis and justification of a religion, the more dubious that religion becomes . . .

The significant bearing for my purpose of all this is that new methods of inquiry and reflection have become for the educated man today the final arbiter of all questions of fact, existence, and intellectual assent. Nothing less than a revolution in the "seat of intellectual authority" has taken place. This revolution, rather than any particular aspect of its impact upon this and that religious belief, is the central thing. In this revolution, every defeat is a

From "Faith and Its Object," in *A Common Faith, John Dewey: The Later Works,* 1934, pp. 29–35, 37–54, 56–57. 1925–1953 vol. 9, Ed. Jo Ann Boydston (Carbondale and Edwardsville, Ill.: Southern Illinois University Press, 1986 [1934]), pp. 21–25, 26–36, 38–39.

stimulus to renewed inquiry; every victory won is the open door to more discoveries, and every discovery is a new seed planted in the soil of intelligence, from which grow fresh plants with new fruits. The mind of man is being habituated to a new method and ideal: There is but one sure road of access to truth—the road of patient, cooperative inquiry operating by means of observation, experiment, record and controlled reflection. . . .

The positive lesson is that religious qualities and values if they are real at all are not bound up with any single item of intellectual assent, not even that of the existence of the God of theism; and that, under existing conditions, the religious function in experience can be emancipated only through surrender of the whole notion of special truths that are religious by their own nature, together with the idea of peculiar avenues of access to such truths. For were we to admit that there is but one method for ascertaining fact and truth—that conveyed by the word "scientific" in its most general and generous sense—no discovery in any branch of knowledge and inquiry could then disturb the faith that is religious. I should describe this faith as the unification of the self through allegiance to inclusive ideal ends, which imagination presents to us and to which the human will responds as worthy of controlling our desires and choices.

It is probably impossible to imagine the amount of intellectual energy that has been diverted from normal processes of arriving at intellectual conclusions because it has gone into rationalization of the doctrines entertained by historic religions. The set that has thus been given the general mind is much more harmful, to my mind, than are the consequences of any one particular item of belief, serious as have been those flowing from acceptance of some of them. The modern liberal version of the intellectual content of Christianity seems to the modern mind to be more rational than some of the earlier doctrines that have been reated against. Such is not the case in fact. The theological philosophers of the Middle Ages had no greater difficulty in giving rational form to all the doctrines of the Roman church than has the liberal theologian of today in formulating and justifying intellectually the doctrines he entertains. This statement is as applicable to the doctrine of continuing miracles, penance, indulgences, saints and angels, etc., as to the trinity, incarnation, atonement, and the sacraments. The fundamental question, I repeat, is not of this and that article of intellectual belief but of intellectual habit, method and criterion.

One method of swerving aside the impact of changed knowledge and method upon the intellectual content of religion is the method of division of territory and jurisdiction into two parts. Formerly these were called the realm of nature and the realm of grace. They are now often known as those of revelation and natural knowledge. Modern religious liberalism has no definite names for them, save, perhaps, the division, referred to in the last chapter, between scientific and religious experience. The implication is that in one territory the supremacy of scientific knowledge must be acknowledged, while there is another region, not very precisely defined, of intimate personal experience wherein other methods and criteria hold sway.

This method of justifying the peculiar and legitimate claim of certain elements of belief is always open to the objection that a positive conclusion is drawn from a negative fact. Existing ignorance or backwardness is employed to assert the existence of a division in the nature of the subject-matter dealt with. Yet the gap may only reflect, at most, a limitation now existing but in the future to be done away with. The argument that because some province or aspect of experience has not yet been "invaded" by scientific methods, it is not subject to them, is as old as it is dangerous. Time and time again, in some particular reserved field, it has been invalidated. Psychology is still in its infancy. He is bold to the point of rashness who asserts that intimate personal experience will never come within the ken of natural knowledge.

It is more to the present point, however, to consider the region that is claimed by religionists as a special reserve. It is mystical experience. The difference, however, between mystic experience and the theory about it that is offered to us must be noted. The experience is a fact to be inquired into. The theory, like any theory, is an interpretation of the fact. The idea that by its very nature the experience is a veridical realization of the direct presence of God does not rest so much upon examination of the facts as it does upon importing into their interpretation a conception that is formed outside them. In its dependence upon a prior conception of the supernatural, which is the thing to be proved, it begs the question. . . .

There is no reason for denying the existence of experiences that are called mystical. On the contrary, there is every reason to suppose that, in some degree of intensity, they occur so frequently that they may be regarded as normal manifestations that take place at certain rhythmic points in the movement of experience. The assumption that denial of a particular interpretation of their objective content proves that those who make the denial do not have the experience in question, so that if they had it they would be equally persuaded of its objective source in the presence of God, has no foundation in fact. As with every empirical phenomenon, the occurrence of the state called mystical is simply an occasion for inquiry into its mode of causation. There is no more reason for converting the experience itself into an immediate knowledge of its cause than in the case of an experience of lightning or any other natural occurrence.

My purpose, then, in this brief reference to mysticism is not to throw doubt upon the existence of particular experiences called mystical. Nor is it to propound any theory to account for them. I have referred to the matter merely as an illustration of the general tendency to mark off two distinct realms in one of which science has jurisdiction, while in the other, special modes of immediate knowledge of religious objects have authority. This dualism as it operates in contemporary interpretation of mystic experience in order to validate certain beliefs is but a reinstatement of the old dualism between the natural and the supernatural, in terms better adapted to the cultural conditions of the present time. Since it is the conception of the supernatural that science calls in question, the circular nature of this type of reasoning is obvious.

Apologists for a religion often point to the shift that goes on in scientific ideas and materials as evidence of the unreliability of science as a mode of knowledge. They often seem peculiarly elated by the great, almost revolutionary, change in fundamental physical conceptions that has taken place in science during the present generation. Even if the alleged unreliability were as great as they assume (or even greater), the question would remain: Have we any other recourse for knowledge? But in fact they miss the point. Science is not constituted by any particular body of subject-matter. It is constituted by a method, a method of changing beliefs by means of tested inquiry as well as of arriving at them. It is its glory, not its condemnation, that its subject-matter develops as the method is improved. There is no special subject-matter of belief that is sacrosanct. The identification of science with a particular set of beliefs and ideas is itself a hold-over of ancient and still current dogmatic habits of thought which are opposed to science in its actuality and which science is undermining.

For scientific method is adverse not only to dogma but to doctrine as well, provided we take "doctrine" in its usual meaning—a body of definite beliefs that need only to be taught and learned as true. This negative attitude of science to doctrine does not indicate indifference to truth. It signifies supreme loyalty to the method by which truth is attained. The scientific-religious conflict ultimately is a conflict between allegiance to this method and allegiance to even an irreducible minimum of belief so fixed in advance that it can never be modified.

The method of intelligence is open and public. The doctrinal method is limited and private. This limitation persists even when knowledge of the truth that is religious is said to be arrived at by a special mode of experience, that termed "religious." For the latter is assumed to be a very special kind of experience. To be sure it is asserted to be open to all who obey certain conditions. Yet the mystic experience yields, as we have seen, various results in the way of belief to different persons, depending upon the surrounding culture of those who undergo it. As a method, it lacks the public character belonging to the method of intelligence. Moreover, when the experience in question does not yield consciousness of the presence of God, in the sense that is alleged to exist, the retort is always at hand that it is not a genuine religious experience. For by definition, only that experience *is* religious which arrives at this particular result. The argument is circular. The traditional position is that some hardness or corruption of heart prevents one from having the experience. Liberal religionists are now more humane. But their logic does not differ.

It is sometimes held that beliefs about religious matters are symbolic, like rites and ceremonies. This view may be an advance upon that which holds to their literal objective validity. But as usually put forward it suffers from an ambiguity. Of what are the beliefs symbols? Are they symbols of things experienced in other modes than those set apart as religious, so that the things symbolized have an independent standing? Or are they symbols in the sense of standing for some transcendental reality—transcendental because not being the subject-matter of experience generally? Even the fundamentalist admits a certain quality and degree of symbolism in the latter sense in objects of religious belief. For he holds that the objects of these beliefs are so far beyond finite human capacity that our beliefs must be couched in more or less metaphorical terms. The conception that faith is the best available substitute for knowledge in our present estate still attaches to the notion of the symbolic character of the materials of faith; unless by ascribing to them a symbolic nature we mean that these materials stand for something that is verifiable in general and public experience.

Were we to adopt the latter point of view, it would be evident not only that the intellectual articles of a creed must be understood to be symbolic of moral and other ideal values, but the facts taken to be historic and used as concrete evidence of the intellectual articles are themselves symbolic. These articles of a creed present events and persons that have been made over by the idealizing imagination in the interest, at their best, of moral ideals. Historic personages in their divine attributes are materializations of the ends that enlist devotion and inspire endeavor. They are symbolic of the reality of ends moving us in many forms of experience. The ideal values that are thus symbolized also marked human experience in science and art and the various modes of human association: they mark almost everything in life that rises from the level of manipulation of conditions as they exist. It is admitted that the objects of religion are ideal in contrast with our present state. What would be lost if it were also admitted that they have authoritative claim upon conduct just because they are ideal? The assumption that these objects of religion exist already in some realm of Being seems to add nothing to their force, while it weakens their claim over us as ideals, in so far as it bases that claim upon matters that are intellectually dubious. The question narrows itself to this: Are the ideals that move us genuinely ideal or are they ideal only in contrast with our present estate?

The import of the question extends far. It determines the meaning given to the word "God." On one score, the word can mean only a particular Being. On the other score, it denotes the unity of all ideal ends arousing us to desire and actions. Does the unification have a claim upon our attitude and conduct because it is already, apart from us, in realized existence, or because of its own inherent meaning and value? Suppose for the moment that the word "God" means the ideal ends that at a given time and place one acknowledges as having authority over his volition and emotion, the values to which one is supremely devoted, as far as these ends, through imagination, take on unity. If we make this supposition, the issue will stand out clearly in contrast with the doctrine of religions that "God" designates some kind of Being having prior and therefore non-ideal existence.

The word "non-ideal" is to be taken literally in regard to some religions that have historically existed, to all of them as far as they are neglectful of moral qualities in their divine beings. It does not apply in the same *literal* way to Judaism and Christianity. For they have asserted that the Supreme Being has moral and spiritual attributes. But it applies to them none the less in that these moral and spiritual characters are thought of as properties of a particular existence and are thought to be of religious value for us because of this embodiment in such an existence. Here, as far as I can see, is the ultimate issue as to the difference between a religion and the religious as a function of experience.

The idea that "God" represents a unification of ideal values that is essentially imaginative in origin when the imagination supervenes in conduct is attended with verbal difficulties owing to our frequent use of the word "imagination" to denote fantasy and doubtful reality. But the reality of ideal ends as ideals is vouched for by their undeniable power in action. An ideal is not at illusion because imagination is the organ through which it is apprehended. For *all* possibilities reach us through the imagination. In a definite sense the only meaning that can be assigned the term "imagination" is that things unrealized in fact come home to use and have power to stir us. The unification effected through imagination is not fanciful, for it is the reflex of the unification of practical and emotional attitudes. The unity signifies not a single Being, but the unity of loyalty and effort evoked by the fact that many ends are one in the power of their ideal, or imaginative, quality to stir and hold us.

We may well ask whether the power and significance in life of the traditional conceptions of God are not due to the ideal qualities referred to by them, the hypostatization of them into an existence being due to a conflux of tendencies in human nature that converts the object of desire into an antecedent reality (as was mentioned in the previous chapter) with beliefs that have prevailed in the cultures of the past. For in the older cultures the idea of the supernatural was "natural," in the sense in which "natural" signifies something customary and familiar. It seems more credible that religious persons have been supported and consoled by the reality with which ideal values appeal to them than that they have been up-borne by sheer matter of fact existence. That, when once men are inured to the idea of the union of the ideal and the physical, the two should be so bound together in emotion that it is difficult to institute a separation, agrees with all we know of human psychology.

The benefits that will accrue, however, from making the separation are evident. The dislocation frees the religious values of experience once for all from matters that are continually becoming more dubious. With that release there comes emancipation from the necessity of resort to apologetics. The reality of ideal ends and values in their authority over us is an undoubted fact. The validity of justice, affection, and that intellectual correspondence of our ideas with realities that we call truth, is so assured in its hold upon humanity that it is unnecessary for the religious attitude to encumber itself with the apparatus of dogma and doctrine. Any other conception of the religious attitude, when it is adequately analyzed, means that those who hold it care more for force than for ideal values—since all that an Existence can add is force to establish, to punish, and to reward. There are, indeed, some persons who frankly say that their own faith does not require any guarantee that moral values are backed up by physical force, but who hold that the masses are so backward that ideal values will not affect their conduct unless in the popular belief these values have the sanction of a power that can enforce them and can execute justice upon those who fail to comply.

There are some persons, deserving of more respect, who say: "We agree that the beginning must be made with the primacy of the ideal. But why stop at this point? Why not search with the utmost eagerness and vigor for all the evidence we can find, such as is supplied by history, by presence of design in nature, which may lead on to the belief that the ideal is already extant in a Personality having objective existence?"

One answer to the question is that we are involved by this search in all the problems of the existence of evil that have haunted theology in the past and that the most ingenious apologists have not faced, much less met. If these apologists had not identified the existence of ideal goods with that of a Person supposed to originate and support them—a Being, moreover, to whom omnipotent power is attributed—the problem of the occurrence of evil would be gratuitous. The significance of ideal ends and meanings is, indeed, closely connected with the fact that there are in life all sorts of things that are evil to us because we would have them otherwise. Were existing conditions wholly good, the notion of possibilities to be realized would never emerge.

But the more basic answer is that while if the search is conducted upon a strictly empirical basis there is no reason why it should not take place, as a matter of fact it is always undertaken in the interest of the supernatural. Thus it diverts attention and energy from ideal values and from the exploration of actual conditions by means of which they may be promoted. History is testimony to this fact. Men have never fully used the powers they possess to advance the good in life, because they have waited upon some power external to themselves and to nature to do the work they are responsible for doing. Dependence upon an external power is the counterpart of surrender of human endeavor. Nor is emphasis on exercising our own powers for good an egoistical or a sentimentally optimistic recourse. It is not the first, for it does not isolate man, either individually or collectively, from nature. It is not the second, because it makes no assumption beyond that of the need and responsibility for human endeavor, and beyond the conviction that, if human desire and endeavor were enlisted in behalf of natural ends, conditions would be bettered. It involves no expectation of a millennium of good.

Belief in the supernatural as a necessary power for apprehension of the ideal and for practical attachment to it has for its counterpart a pessimistic belief in the corruption and impotency of natural means. That is axiomatic in Christian dogma. But this apparent pessimism has a way of suddenly changing into an exaggerated optimism. For according to the terms of the doctrine, if the faith in the supernatural is of the required order, regeneration at once takes place. Goodness, in all essentials, is thereby established; if not, there is proof that the established relation to the supernatural has been vitiated. This romantic optimism is one cause for the excessive attention to individual salvation characteristic of traditional Christianity. Belief in a sudden and complete transmutation through conversion and in the objective efficacy of prayer, is too easy a way out of difficulties. It leaves matters in general just about as they were before; that is, sufficiently bad so that there is additional support for the idea that only supernatural aid can better them. The position of natural intelligence is that there exists a *mixture* of good and evil, and that reconstruction in the direction of the good which is indicated by ideal ends, must take place, if at all, through continued cooperative effort. There is at least enough impulse toward justice, kindliness, and order so that if it were mobilized for action, not expecting abrupt and complete transformation to occur, the disorder, cruelty, and oppression that exist would be reduced.

The discussion has arrived at a point where a more fundamental objection to the position I am taking needs consideration. The misunderstanding upon which this objection rests should be pointed out. The view I have advanced is sometimes treated as if the identification of the divine with ideal ends left the ideal wholly without roots in existence and without support from existence. The objection implies that my view commits one to such a separation of the ideal and the existent that the ideal has no chance to find lodgment even as a seed that might grow and bear fruit. On the contrary, what I have been criticizing is the *identification* of the ideal with a particular Being, especially when that identification makes necessary the conclusion that this Being is outside of nature, and what I have tried to show is that the ideal itself has its roots in natural conditions; it emerges when the imagination idealizes existence by laying hold of the possibilities offered to thought and action. There are values, goods, actually realized upon a natural basis—the goods of human association, of art and knowledge. The idealizing imagination seizes upon the most precious things found in the climacteric moments of experience and projects them. We need no external criterion and guarantee for their goodness. They are had, they exist as good, and out of them we frame our ideal ends.

Moreover, the ends that result from our projection of experienced goods into objects of thought, desire and effort exist, only they exist *as* ends. Ends, purposes, exercise determining power in human conduct. The aims of philanthropists, of Florence Nightingale, of Howard, of Wilberforce, of Peabody, have not been idle dreams. They have modified institutions. Aims, ideals, do not exist simply in "mind"; they exist in character, in personality and action. One might call the roll of artists, intellectual inquirers, parents, friends, citizens who are neighbors, to show that purposes exist in an *operative* way. What I have been objecting to, I repeat, is not the idea that ideals are linked with existence and that they themselves exist, through human embodiment, as forces, but the idea that their authority and value depend upon some prior complete embodiment—as if the efforts of human beings in behalf of justice, or knowledge or beauty, depended for their effectiveness and validity upon assurance that there already existed in some supernal region a place where criminals are humanely treated, where there is no serfdom or slavery, where all facts and truths are already discovered and possessed, and all beauty is eternally displayed in actualized form.

The aims and ideals that move us are generated through imagination. But they are not made out of imaginary stuff. They are made out of the hard stuff of the world of physical and social experience. The locomotive did not exist before Stevenson, nor the telegraph before the time of Morse. But the conditions for their existence were there in physical material and energies and in human capacity. Imagination seized hold upon the idea of a rearrangement of existing things that would evolve new objects. The same thing is true of a painter, a musician, a poet, a philanthropist, a moral prophet. The new vision does not arise out of nothing, but emerges through seeing, in terms of possibilities, that is, of imagination, old things in new relations serving a new end which the new end aids in creating.

Moreover the process of creation is experimental and continuous. The artist, scientific man, or good citizen, depends upon what others have done before him and are doing around him. The sense of new values that become ends to be realized arises first in dim and uncertain form. As the values are dwelt upon and carried forward in action they grow in definiteness and coherence. Interaction between aim and existent conditions improves and tests the ideal; and conditions are at the same time modified. Ideals change as they are applied in existent conditions. The process endures and advances with the life of humanity. What one person and one group accomplish becomes the standing ground and starting point of those who succeed them. When the vital factors in this natural process are generally acknowledged in emotion, thought and action, the process will be both accelerated and purified through elimination of that irrelevant element that culminates in the idea of the supernatural. When the vital factors attain the religious force that has been drafted into supernatural religions, the resulting reinforcement will be incalculable.

These considerations may be applied to the idea of God, or, to avoid misleading conceptions, to the idea of the divine. This idea is, as I have said, one of ideal possibilities unified through imaginative realization and projection. But this idea of God, or of the divine, is also connected with all the natural forces and conditions—including man and human association—that promote the growth of the ideal and that further its realization. We are in the presence neither of ideals completely embodied in existence nor yet of ideals that are mere rootless ideals, fantasies, utopias. For there are forces in nature and society that generate and support the ideals. They are further unified by the action that gives them coherence and solidity. It is this *active* relation between ideal and actual to which I would give the name "God." I would not insist that the name *must* be given. There are those who hold that the associations of the term with the supernatural are so numerous and close that any use of the word "God" is sure to give rise to misconception and be taken as a concession to traditional ideas.

They may be correct in this view. But the facts to which I have referred are there, and they need to be brought out with all possible clearness and force. There exist concretely and experimentally goods—the values of art in all its forms, of knowledge, of effort and of rest after striving, of education and fellowship, of friendship and love, of growth in mind and body. These goods are there and yet they are relatively embryonic. Many persons are shut out from generous participation in them; there are forces at work that threaten and sap existent goods as well as prevent their expansion. A clear and intense conception of a union of ideal ends with actual conditions is capable of arousing steady emotion. It may be fed by every experience, no matter what its material.

In a distracted age, the need for such an idea is urgent. It can unify interests and energies now dispersed; it can direct action and generate the heat of emotion and the light of intelligence. Whether one gives the name "God" to this union, operative in thought and action, is a matter for individual decision. But the *function* of such a working union of the ideal and actual seems to me to be identical with the force that has in fact been attached to the conception of God in all the religions that have a spiritual content; and a clear idea of that function seems to me urgently needed at the present time.

The sense of this union may, with some persons, be furthered by mystical experiences, using the term "mystical" in its broadest sense. That result depends largely upon temperament. But there is a marked difference between the union associated with mysticism and the union which I had in mind. There is

nothing mystical about the latter; it is natural and moral. Nor is there anything mystical about the perception or consciousness of such union. Imagination of ideal ends pertinent to actual conditions represents the fruition of a disciplined mind. There is, indeed, even danger that resort to mystical experiences will be an escape, and that its result will be the passive feeling that the union of actual and ideal is already accomplished. But in fact this union is active and practical; it is a *uniting,* not something given.

One reason why personally I think it fitting to use the word "God" to denote that uniting of the ideal and actual which has been spoken of, lies in the fact that aggressive atheism seems to me to have something in common with traditional supernaturalism. I do not mean merely that the former is mainly so negative that it fails to give positive direction to thought, though that fact is pertinent. What I have in mind especially is the exclusive preoccupation of both militant atheism and supernaturalism with man in isolation. For in spite of supernaturalism's reference to something beyond nature, it conceives of this earth as the moral center of the universe and of man as the apex of the whole scheme of things. It regards the drama of sin and redemption enacted within the isolated and lonely soul of man as the one thing of ultimate importance. Apart from man, nature is held either accursed or negligible. Militant atheism is also affected by lack of natural piety. The ties binding man to nature that poets have always celebrated are passed over lightly. The attitude taken is often that of man living in an indifferent and hostile world and issuing blasts of defiance. A religious attitude, however, needs the sense of a connection of man, in the way of both dependence and support, with the enveloping world that the imagination feels is a universe. Use of the words "God" or "divine" to convey the union of actual with ideal may protect man from a sense of isolation and from consequent despair or defiance.

In any case, whatever the name, the meaning is selective. For it involves no miscellaneous worship of everything in general. It selects those factors in existence that generate and support our idea of good as an end to be striven for. It excludes a multitude of forces that at any given time are irrelevant to this function. Nature produces whatever gives reinforcement and direction but also what occasions discord and confusion. The "divine" is thus a term of human choice and aspiration. A humanistic religion, if it excludes our relation to nature, is pale and thin, as it is presumptuous, when it takes humanity as an object of worship. . . .

For, I would remind readers in conclusion, it is the intellectual side of the religious attitude that I have been considering. I have suggested that the religious element in life has been hampered by conceptions of the supernatural that were imbedded in those cultures wherein man had little control over outer nature and little in the way of sure method of inquiry and test. The crisis today as to the intellectual content of religious belief has been caused by the change in the intellectual climate due to the increase of our knowledge and our means of understanding. I have tried to show that this change is not fatal to the religious values in our common experience, however adverse its impact may be upon historic religions. Rather, provided that the methods and results of intelligence at work are frankly adopted, the change is liberating.

It clarifies our ideals, rendering them less subject to illusion and fantasy. It relieves us of the incubus of thinking of them as fixed, as without power of growth. It discloses that they develop in coherence and pertinency with increase of natural intelligence. The change gives aspiration for natural knowledge a definitely religious character, since growth in understanding of nature is seen to be organically related to the formation of ideal ends. The same change enables man to select those elements in natural conditions that may be organized to support and extend the sway of ideals. All purpose is selective, and all intelligent action includes deliberate choice. In the degree in which we cease to depend upon belief in the supernatural, selection is enlightened and choice can be made in behalf of ideals whose inherent relations to conditions and consequences are understood. Were the naturalistic foundations and bearings of religion grasped, the religious element in life would emerge from the throes of the crisis in religion. Religion would then be found to have its natural place in every aspect of human experience that is concerned with estimate of possibilities, with emotional stir by possibilities as yet unrealized, and with all action in behalf of their realization. All that is significant in human experience falls within this frame.

## Suggestions for Further Reading

**Works by Dewey**

*John Dewey: The Early Works, 1882–1898,* 5 vols., ed. Jo Ann Boydston (Carbondale and Edwardsville, Ill.: Southern Illinois University Press, 1969–1972).

*John Dewey: The Middle Works, 1899–1924,* 15 vols., ed. Jo Ann Boydston (Carbondale and Edwardsville, Ill.: Southern Illinois University Press, 1976–1983).

*John Dewey: The Later Works, 1925–1953,* 17 vols., ed. Jo Ann Boydston (Carbondale and Edwardsville, Ill.: Southern Illinois University Press, 1981–1990).

*John Dewey: The Collected Works, 1882–1953, Index,* ed. Jo Ann Boydston (Carbondale and Edwardsville, Ill.: Southern Illinois University Press, 1991).

These volumes constitute the definitive edition of the works of Dewey.

**Anthologies**

*The Essential Dewey,* 2 vols., ed. Larry Hickman and Thomas Alexander (Bloomington, Ind.: Indiana University Press, 1998).

*Intelligence in the Modern World,* ed. Joseph Ratner (New York: Random House, 1939).
*The Philosophy of John Dewey,* ed. John J. McDermott (Chicago: University of Chicago Press, 1981).

**Essential Works on Dewey**

Thomas M. Alexander, *John Dewey's Theory of Art, Experience, and Nature: The Horizons of Feeling* (Albany: State University of New York Press, 1987).

Richard J. Bernstein, *John Dewey* (New York: Washington Square Press, 1967; reprinted by Ridgeview, 1981).

Raymond D. Boisvert, *Dewey's Metaphysics* (New York: Fordham University Press, 1988).

Raymond D. Boisvert, *John Dewey: Rethinking Our Time* (Albany: State University of New York Press, 1998).

James Campbell, *Understanding John Dewey* (Chicago: Open Court, 1995).

Michael Eldridge, *Transforming Experience: John Dewey's Cultural Instrumentalism* (Nashville: Vanderbilt University Press, 1998).

James Gouinlock, *John Dewey's Philosophy of Value* (New York: Humanities Press, 1972).

Larry A. Hickman, *John Dewey's Pragmatic Technology* (Bloomington, Ind.: Indiana University Press, 1990).

Larry A. Hickman, ed., *Reading Dewey* (Bloomington, Ind.: Indiana University Press, 1998).

Victor Kestenbaum, *The Phenomenological Sense of John Dewey: Habit and Meaning* (Atlantic Highlands, N.J.: Humanities Press, 1997).

Alan Ryan, *John Dewey and the High Tide of American Liberalism* (New York: Norton, 1995).

Paul A. Schilpp, ed., *The Philosophy of John Dewey, Library of Living Philosophers* (LaSalle, Ill.: Open Court, 1939).

Ralph W. Sleeper, *The Necessity of Pragmatism: John Dewey's Conception of Philosophy* (New Haven, Conn.: Yale University Press, 1986).

John J. Stuhr, *Experience and Criticism: John Dewey's Reconstruction of Philosophy* (Nashville: Vanderbilt University Press, 2000).

John J. Stuhr, *John Dewey* (Nashville: Carmichael and Carmichael, 1991).

John J. Stuhr, ed., *Philosophy and the Reconstruction of Culture: Pragmatic Essays After Dewey* (Albany: State University of New York Press, 1993).

J.E. Tiles, ed., *John Dewey: Critical Assessments,* 4 vols. (New York: Routledge, 1992).

Jennifer Welchman, *Dewey's Ethical Thought* (Ithaca, N.Y.: Cornell University Press, 1995).

Robert B. Westbrook, *John Dewey and American Democracy* (Ithaca, N.Y.: Cornell University Press, 1991).

# GEORGE HERBERT MEAD

## Introduction by James Campbell

### Mead's Life: Cultural Context and Philosophical Background

George Herbert Mead was born on February 27, 1863, in the midst of the Civil War, between Lincoln's Emancipation Proclamation and his Gettysburg Address. Though he was born in New England, in the small town of South Hadley, Massachusetts, he moved with his family to Ohio while still a child. The family relocated so his father, Hiram Mead, a Protestant minister, could assume the chair in homiletics at the Oberlin Theological Seminary. After his father's death in 1881, Mead's mother, Elizabeth Storrs Billings Mead, briefly taught at Oberlin College. (She later served as the president of Mount Holyoke College from 1890 to 1900.) Mead thus grew to self-consciousness in an educational atmosphere, amidst the late nineteenth-century conflicts between science and religion over the primacy of efficient or final explanations. His own description of this situation conveys a sense of the difficulties felt by one who recognized values on either side: "We wished to be free to follow our individual thinking and feeling into an intelligent and sympathetic world without having to bow before incomprehensible dogma or to anticipate the shipwreck of our individual ends and values. We wanted full intellectual freedom and yet the conservation of the values for which had stood Church, State, Science, and Art."[1] This theme of the preservation and reconciliation of values, later developed in a philosophy of social reconstruction, remained a vital part of mead's thought throughout his life.

Mead graduated from Oberlin College in 1883, after studying the classics and literature, in addition to philosophy. He taught primary school in Ohio for a year, and then worked for a few years as a tutor and a railroad surveyor in Wisconsin and Minnesota. In the fall of 1887, Mead went to Harvard for a year of further study with William James and Josiah Royce. The next year he went to Leipzig, and then in 1889 on to Berlin for doctoral study in philosophy and physiological psychology. He married Helen Castle in 1891 and returned with her to the United States, without completing work on his doctorate, to take up a teaching position in philosophy at the University of Michigan. In 1894, he moved to the recently opened University of Chicago, where he taught for the rest of his career. He died in Chicago in April, 1931.[2]

As a young man, Mead intended to follow his father into the pulpit. Later he was inclined toward running a reformist newspaper. Neither of these professions, however, seemed likely to provide him with sufficient intellectual challenge; and he finally settled on an academic career as a teacher of philosophy. This career enabled him to integrate his desire for social service with a highly intellectual life. Throughout his long teaching career at the University of Chicago, and without losing his identity as a professional philosopher, Mead was a tireless worker in many of the city's reform efforts: education, labor questions, women's suffrage, the Hull House, the University's Settlement House and its Experimental School, the City Club, the Immigrants' Protective League, and others.[3]

John Dewey, Mead's close personal and professional friend, wrote that he was unwilling to speculate about what his own thought might have been like were it not for "the seminal ideas" that he derived from Mead. Still, Mead's influence among his contemporaries was less than it might have been because, as Dewey noted elsewhere, Mead "published but little, and that little was of a comparatively scattered and almost fragmentary character."[4] Many of these published pieces have since been gathered together by Andrew J. Reck in *Selected Writings: George Herbert Mead* [SW][5]; the collective impacts of this volume suggests that Mead's published writings only appeared to be fragmentary. Once re-articulated, they can be seen to comprise the skeleton of a powerful philosophic view.

Still, Dewey's point remains valid in the sense that, compared to the living colleague that he knew, the published Mead was little more than a skeleton. Dewey further observed that Mead's "intellectual influence upon associates and the students in his classes was so profound as to be revolutionary." Mead was a powerful extemporaneous lecturer, a professor to whose classroom students often returned year after year to hear the most recent reformulations of his ideas on philosophic topics of vital human concern. Regrettably, he published few of these ideas. Mead was, Dewey tells us, "always dissatisfied with what he had done; always outgrowing his former expressions," and consequently he was "reluctant to fix his ideas in the printed word . . ."[6] Fortunately for us, however, in his later years the powerful impact of these lectures inspired some of Mead's students to have stenographic reports taken. After his death, this same impact further inspired some of his colleagues and students to cooperate with family members to see a number of volumes of his ideas into print.

First to appear, in 1932, was *The Philosophy of the Present* [PP], edited by Arthur E. Murphy, drawn from the text of Mead's 1930 Carus Lectures on the role of temporality, and especially on the role of the present, in any understanding of existence. The lectures remained unrevised at the time of Mead's death,[7] but they are supplemented in this volume by some manuscript materials and by two previously published essays. *Mind, Self, and Society from the Standpoint of a Social Behaviorist* [MSS], edited by Charles W. Morris, was published two years later. This volume presents Mead's views on social psychology as compiled from stenographic copies of two different sets of lectures on the topic, supplemented occasionally by other related notes and manuscript materials. In 1936, Mead's ideas on the flow of philosophic thought in the previous century, again drawn primarily from stenographic lecture notes, was published under the title of *Movements of Thought in the Nineteenth Century* [MT], edited by Merritt H. Moore. Two years later, *The Philosophy of the Act* [PA], edited by Morris and others, appeared. It contained unpublished manuscripts derived mostly from the last decade or so of Mead's life that explore a wide range of topics central to human action and thought. Finally in 1982, *The Individual and the Social Self* [ISS], edited by David L. Miller, was published. This volume, also drawn primarily from stenographic notes, contains material similar to that found in *Mind, Self and Society* and *The Philosophy of the Act,* but presented in a different way. The original materials for these volumes, as well as other stenographic notes, manuscripts, and some correspondence remain at the University of Chicago.[8]

These volumes flesh out the skeleton of Mead's thought presented in his published works. They are edited volumes, however, and it is always necessary to keep in mind that we are not dealing directly with Mead's ideas. These volumes come to us through the filter of students, stenographers, and editors. The manuscripts and the stenographic records are of different levels of completeness. There are factual errors in the stenographic records—names and titles of books, for example, were misreported—and, if these simple factual matters are occasionally wrong, we must assume that some of Mead's complex philosophic ideas did not come across exactly as he intended them. Further, keeping in mind what Dewey called Mead's reluctance "to fix his ideas in the printed word," Mead would certainly have wanted to make changes of greater or lesser degree had he seen his lectures and drafts thus `fixed.' Still, I think it is legitimate to consider these volumes as representing Mead's thought, especially if we remain guided by the skeleton provided by his published essays and reviews and focus on the themes to which he returned again and again.

## An Overview of Mead's thought

Mead is a thinker for whom process and evolution were central issues; and it is consequently not hard to find strong philosophic roots in his work that lead to Hegel and Darwin. In Hegel's work, Mead found the recognition "that the world evolves, that reality itself is in a process of evolution" (MT 154). With each new synthesis, something fundamentally new emerges: "new forms arise out of conflicts of old forms" (MT 145). The achievement of Darwin, as Mead sees it, was to have worked out the mechanism for the resolution of these conflicts, at least on the biological level. Darwin saw, Mead notes, "a life-process, that may take now one, and now another, form" (MT 161), depending on its response to the environmental situation. Evolution throughout the range of living things is thus, in Mead's words, "the process of meeting and solving problems" (MT 143). Humans, with their highly developed cultures, address their problems of living through the many institutions that have arisen "in the social process" (MT 148). Hegel's influence can be found returning here, Mead continues, for it was Hegel who insisted that "it is not the human animal as an individual" that "gets control over his environment." Rather, "it is society" (MT 168).

In many ways Mead's work complements that of his more famous colleague, John Dewey. Both write within a framework of emergent evolution. Both attempt to understand the importance of human existence while at the same time demonstrating, by means of a purely naturalistic world-view, our rootedness in nature. Both explore the nature of our social existence and the processes by which a society develops and reconstructs. And although their perspectives remain generally parallel throughout, each elaborates freely his own point of view. One clear distinction is to be found in the different ways in which they explore human attempts to solve problems. Dewey's efforts are directed toward questions of the method by which the process of problem-solving is carried out: what the pattern of inquiry is, how many steps this process contains, what the distinct traits of these steps are, what the order of their occurrence is, how problem-solving can be improved, etc.[9] Mead's discussions of problem-solving, on the other hand, focus on the model of human life that stands behind this reconstructive activity, examining the human factors and traits that make us intelligent problem-solvers. A second instance of how Mead's and Dewey's generally parallel views are distinguishable can be found in their presentations of social psychology. Here Dewey's focus is upon the roles played in human life by habits, impulses, and intelligence,[10] whereas Mead's focus is on understanding the development and nature of self-consciousness, particularly as it reflects the larger society in which individuals develop. For him, the goal of social psychology is to understand "experience from the standpoint of society" and "minds and selves" as "essentially social products, products or phenomena of the social side of human experience . . ." (MSS 1).

With some general sense of Mead's philosophic context, we can turn now to an exclusive consideration of his work. We see immediately that he offers us an understanding of reality that places humans firmly within nature. He sees human experiencing as "a natural process" like eating or reproducing, and leaves no room for "otherworldliness" in his thought (PA 517, 515). Mead thus aims to offer a metaphysics that is "descriptive of the world so far as it comes within the range of our thought," so that we can discover "the essential characters of the world as they enter into our experience . . ." (PA 626).

For Mead, one of the primary characteristics of the experienced world is that it consists of enduring physical objects. Mead intends here no simple-minded realism; but throughout his work he remains committed to the standpoint of the scientist rather than that of the epistemologist. Unlike the latter, whom Mead sees as attempting "to reach a world outside of the individual's experience" as a means of testing that very experience, the scientist is attempting to solve "a problem that lies within an unquestioned world of observation and experiment" (PP 108).[11] Mead writes further that "[t]he attitude of the scientist never contemplates or could contemplate the possibility of a world in which there would be no reality by which to test his hypothetical solution of the problem that arises" (SW 205). In the world in which we humans live with one another, problems arise and are addressed. For Mead, these are the problems of the scientist, not those of the epistemologist.

Central to this agreement with the scientist is Mead's repeated emphasis on the importance of human manipulation, on direct manual contact with the things of nature, for our understanding of the world. We have what he calls "distance" experiences with our eyes, ears, and noses; but their "promise" is fulfilled only in touching (PA 142, 103). "The reality of what we see," he tells us, "is what we can handle . . ." (PA 105). By manipulating the things of the world with our hands, we are able to avoid any wholesale epistemological problems, Mead believes, because "[t]he ultimate experience of contact is not subject to the divergencies of distance experience" (PA 281).[12] In a fashion similar to this defense of physical objects, Mead is able to recognize the validity of relativity physics without surrendering to it our legitimate experiential, manipulatory realm: "For the vast majority of experiences the Newtonian definition of the object that is there in terms of absolute space, time, and mass is adequate" (PA 251).

While Mead's understanding of nature is rooted in the methods of the scientist and concerned to take seriously the reality of temporal processes, it emphasizes as well our need to recognize the emergence of novelty. Although this emergence is often narrowly construed, Mead maintains that it "belongs not only to the experience of human social organisms" but is found also "in a nature which science and the philosophy that has followed it have separated from human nature" (PP 14). As an example, Mead asks us to consider a chemical compound: "When things get together, there then arises something that was not there before, and that character is something that cannot be stated in terms of the elements which go to make up the combination" (PA 641). The compound water, for instance, has properties that are different from those of the hydrogen and oxygen atoms that comprise it. More generally, emergence is a category that allows us to account for temporal continuity in nature without being forced into the straitjacket of determinism.[13]

Mead believes that we have difficulty understanding the concept of emergence because we have such a poor understanding of the present. We often assume a sort of 'knife-edge' instantaneous 'now' that we should recognize to be specious.[14] The present is rather, he maintains, a fuzzy-ended segment of the stream of thought that includes some 'past' and 'future,' and in which we can experience causality and time and motion. In the flow of experience there is a strong component of continuity. "There is direction," he writes. "There is dependence or conditioning. What is taking place flows out of that which is taking place" (SW 346). Experience is not all continuity, however; and, while its flow contains a strong component of continuity, we recognize as well "a tang of novelty in each moment of experience." Experience carries both sameness and change as it flows along: "as present passes into present there is always some break in the continuity . . ." (SW 350). The flow of time in nature is a kind of passage "within which what is taking place conditions that which is arising," but these conditions "do not determine in its full reality that which emerges" (PP 16).

In addition, for Mead, the present plays an additional role because the past is always grounded in some current situation; it is the past of some present. "The past as it appears," he writes, "is in terms of representations of various sorts, typically in memory images, which are themselves present" (SW 345). Further, he continues, "our assurances concerning the past are never attained by a congruence between the constructed past and a real past independent of this construction" since "this accepted past lies in a present and is subject, itself, to possible reconstruction" (PP 29–30). As a result, Mead maintains, even the past is unpredictable: "We are continually reconstructing the world from our own standpoint. And that reconstruction holds just as really with the so-called 'irrevocable' past as with reference to a future. The past is just as uncertain as the future is" (MT 417).

We reconstruct these pasts hypothetically as they become inadequate to the problems of our new present. As Mead puts it, "the estimate and import of all histories lies in the interpretation and control of the present . . ." (PP 28); and, as presents change, new pasts will be required. Our reconstructions of the past, he notes, "never contemplate the finality of their findings. They are always subject to conceivable reformulations, on the discovery of later evidence, and this reformulation may be complete" (PP 29). Such complete, or near complete, reconstructions are found in our own experience that, as Mead puts is, "[e]very generation re-writes its history" (MT 291). He writes further: "The histories that we have transcribed would have been as impossible to the pens of our fathers as the world we live in would have been inaccessible to their eyes and to their minds . . ." (SW 335). With regard to the future, this hypothetical stance holds true as well. We cannot know where or when problems will arise and reconstruction will be necessary. All that we can be sure of is that whatever emerges will be fitted in. As Mead continues, "the emergent has no sooner appeared than we set about rationalizing it, that is, we undertake to show that it, or at least the conditions that determine its appearance, can be found in the past that lay behind it" (PP 14). Upon rethinking, we are able to understand more clearly how nature and we reached our present situation. One of his formulations is that "new things continually arise, the novelty of whose occurrence is worn down into the reliability of that which becomes familiar" (PP 36–37). This later familiarity should not blind us, however, to the real novelty of that which has emerged.

Emergence is possible because of another fundamental trait of existence, which Mead calls "sociality." By this term he means "the capacity of being several things at once" (PP 49). If there is to be continuity without rigid determinism, there must be within nature the ability of the various pieces to participate contemporaneously in multiple systems. These systems, which he elsewhere calls "perspectives," have "objective existence" (PA 114). A stone, for example, is simultaneously in chemical, thermal, gravitational, and perhaps visual and architectural systems. Mead explains this principle of sociality further as follows: "in the present within which emergent change takes place the emergent object belongs to different systems in its passage from the old to the new because of its systematic relationship with other structures, and possesses the characters it has because of its membership in these different systems" (PP 65). Mead is careful to emphasize here too that sociality is more than just a human trait. As he puts it, the appearance of human minds capable of occupying their own systems as well as those of others is "only the culmination of that sociality which is found throughout the universe . . ." (PP 86).

Before we turn to Mead's understanding of human nature, it is important to re-emphasize that his understandings of nature and human nature are intimately related, and that his claims about aspects of the former are often based on his claims about aspects of the latter. We humans are, for Mead, truly rooted in nature; and far too often dualistic philosophies have hampered our understanding of ourselves and of our place in nature by portraying properties that are actually found more generally in existence as just human or 'subjective.' Sociality is found in the fact that our lives participate in the lives of others, and also in the fact that nature is a set of systems or perspectives. Emergence is found in the free action of humans, and also in the other processes of nature.

## Human Nature as Social

With this continuity of nature and human nature in mind, we can begin to consider Mead's understanding of human nature. In doing so, we will see that he offers us a carefully elaborated and compelling picture of humanity as wholly naturalized—developing and living within the natural world—and a reinterpretation of our basic ideas and institutions to accommodate this understanding of human nature. For Mead's analysis, two aspects of human nature are central: we humans are, first of all, social in our innermost being, emergents from and thrivers within the social process; and, secondly, we humans are live, active creatures who attempt to meet and solve the problems of living. I will explore Mead's discussion of the problem-solving aspect of human nature in the next section; in this section, the topic will be his view on the social aspect of human nature.

For Mead, the human self is fundamentally social. I can hope to do only minimal justice to the full implications of his analysis in this brief introduction. While I cannot delineate fully the discussion of the evolutionary emergence of self-consciousness that he offers primarily in *Mind, Self, and Society,* I can summarize his presentation of the arising of gesture, significant symbols, the vocal gesture, and language in the particularly highly developed human creature. Following Wilhelm Wundt, Mead describes the gesture as "that part of the social act which serves as a stimulus to other forms involved in the same social act" (MSS 42). The social act could be, for example, the encounter between a dog and a stranger, in which the gesture might be the bristling of the dog's fur, or the interaction between a customer and a cashier, in which the gesture might be the extending of money from the customer's hand. These gestures often call out responding gestures from others involved in the same social act. While avoiding any necessary attribution of intention in such a "conversation" of gestures (MSS 43), Mead maintains that gestures do have meaning: "The response of one organism to the gesture of another in any given social act is the meaning of that gesture . . ." (MSS 78). When such meaningful gestures have the same meaning for the different symbols," he notes, "when they implicitly arouse in an individual making them the same responses which they explicitly arouse, or are supposed to arouse, in other individuals" (MSS 47). In the instance of the interaction between the customer and the cashier, each shares the meaning of the gesture of offering money in exchange for goods. Vocal gestures play a special role. "In the case of the vocal gesture," Mead tells us, "the form hears its own stimulus just as when this is used by other forms, so it tends to respond also to its own stimulus as it responds to the stimulus of other forms. That is, birds tend to sing to themselves, babies to talk to themselves" (MSS 65). As these vocal gestures begin to take on meaning for the growing child, that child begins to listen to what he or she is saying. The centrality of language as the use of meaningful vocal gestures remains throughout our lives: "we can hear ourselves talking, and the import of what we say is the same to ourselves that it is to others" (MSS 62). Moreover, language itself (as we shall see shortly) is essential to Mead's understanding of the development of a self.

We can now consider, again briefly, some of the factors of Mead's overall understanding of the social aspect of the human self. The first point to make clear about his perspective is that he views the human self as ever in process. While he values increasing human individuality as essential, his sense of individuality is not a ballistic one. In other words, he does not offer a sense of individuality in which one's 'true' course is 'internal' and purely one's own, and in which all influence from 'without' is 'interference' that 'deflects' the individual from his or her 'proper' goal. For Mead, there is no specifiable target state of human fulfillment, either individually or as a group; there is no ultimate state of being 'finally' or 'completely' fulfilled that is safe from setback or relapse. As human individuals, we remain in process as long as we live. We continue to develop and change, to expand and to contract.[15]

If we go beyond this point that the self is in process to an analysis of the sort of process that Mead believes the self is engaged in, two factors come to our attention: the self is emergent and indirect. Beginning with the former, the emerging self develops in the ongoing course of experience. His point can be made both phylogenetically and ontogenetically. On the former level of the history of the human race, Mead believes that there would be no humans today had our minds and selves "not arisen within or emerged out of the human social process in its lower stages of development . . ." (MSS 227). This emergence of human self-consciousness was not according to some preordained plan nor required of simple natural necessity. In a fundamental sense, he maintains, it just happened. Similarly, on the individual level, a person's self is not a preformed thing that becomes actualized at a certain age. When Mead says that the self emerges, that "it is not initially there, at birth, but arises" (MSS 135), he means this in the strong sense that the person literally comes into being in the process of living.

The self, moreover, emerges indirectly or reflexively. It "arises in the process of social experience and activity"; it develops "within the social process, within the empirical matrix of social interactions" (MSS 135, 133). The individual does not develop a self prior to taking his or her place within society. Rather, the individual develops his or her self by degree and under the influence of the society. It is thus true both that it is "impossible to conceive of a self arising outside of social experience" (MSS 140), and that in the long run we continue to need others. "Selves," he notes, "can only exist in definite relationships to other selves" (MSS 164).

Let us consider the reflexive nature of the self further. The individual, Mead tells us, "enters his own experience as a self or individual, not directly or immediately, not by becoming a subject to himself, but only in so far as he first becomes an object to himself just as other individuals are objects to him or in his experience . . ." (MSS 138). That is, before becoming self-conscious, a person must first assume a place within a social group: "only in so far as he takes the attitudes of the organized social group to which he belongs toward the organized, co-operative social activity or set of such activities in which that group as such is engaged, does he develop a complete self or possess the sort of complete self he has developed" (MSS 155). This growth can be demonstrated in the movement of a child from one level of social action to another. At the level of play, Mead writes, "the child is acquiring the roles of those who belong to his society." The child is trying out various social roles with which he or she is familiar. He continues that in play "the child is continually acting as a parent, a teacher, a preacher, a grocery man, a policeman, a pirate, or an Indian." While the child develops to the level of games, however, there is more than the free interaction of roles that is found in play: "in a game there is a regulated procedure, and rules. The child must not only take the role of the other, as he does in the play, but he must assume the various roles of all the participants in the game, and govern his action accordingly" (SW 284–285). The child must be able "to take the attitude of everyone else involved in that game" and to maintain these different roles in "a definite relationship to each other" (MSS 151). When involved in a game, Mead writes, the child "sees himself in terms of the group or the gang and speaks with a passion for rules and standards. Its social advantage and even necessity makes this approach to himself imperative. He must see himself as the whole group sees him" (SW 246). It is at this point, when the child is able to evaluate his or her ideas and conduct from the 'outside' through the eyes of a "generalized other," that we can talk comfortably of a self. As Mead puts it, "it is this generalized other in his experience which provides him with a self" (SW 285). Thus the game, Mead continues, "represents the passage in the life of the child from taking the role of others in play to the organized part that is essential to self-consciousness in the full sense of the term" (MSS 152). A child who can participate in a complex, multi-roled game is also able to participate in other organized, cooperative social activities.

The role of language as the form of reflexive communication is essential to the emerging self. As Mead writes, it is impossible that "consciousness of a self as an object would ever have arisen in man if he had not had the mechanism of talking to himself . . ." (SW 140). The reason for this is that "the individual can hear what he says and in hearing what he says is tending to respond as the other person responds" (MSS 69–70). It is in this responding to himself or herself that self-consciousness emerges. "It is in addressing himself in the role of an other that his self arises in experience" (PP 168).[16]

With this brief glimpse at Mead's view of the self as a process of reflexive emergence, we are now ready to explore the heart of his understanding of the social self: its duality of "I" and "me."

Mead intends here neither a dichotomy of distinct halves within the self nor a rigid balance maintaining itself throughout life. Rather, he intends a functional distinction between these two "phases" of the self (MSS 192), both of which are "essential to the self in its full expression," and a fluid mutuality in which "[t]he relative values of the 'me' and the 'I' depend very much on the situation" (MSS 199).

The "me" is that phase of the self that contains the values and traditions of one's society. "We are individuals born into a certain nationality, located at a certain spot geographically, with such and such family relations, and such and such political relations," Mead explains. "All of these represent a certain situation which constitutes the 'me' . . ." (MSS 182). The "me" is the "conventional" and "habitual" phase of the self. The "me" thus "has to have those habits, those responses which everybody has; otherwise the individual could not be a member of the community" (MSS 197). The "me" is "essentially a member of a social group . . . Its values are the values that belong to society" (MSS 214). In fact, Mead maintains, we are usually so well integrated into society that "[n]o hard-and-fast line can be drawn between our own selves and the selves of others, since our own selves exist and enter as such into our experience only in so far as the selves of others exist and enter as such into our experience also" (MSS 164). It is the "me" that gives the self its "form" or stability (MSS 209). This means, in part, that the "me" must itself demonstrate some sort of unity: "the 'me' is the organized set of attitudes of others which one himself assumes" (MSS 175). Of course, there remains a certain amount of diversity in the "me": it continues to change with the processive development of the self and it includes inconsistent strands within it, especially in the modern world full of the frequently conflicting values inherent in our multiple roles as citizens, workers, and family members. Mead's emphasis in his consideration of the "me" is primarily upon unity, however, and especially that unity that underlies a self-conscious community. "The very organization of the self-conscious community is dependent upon individuals taking the attitude of the other individuals," Mead tells us; and our accomplishing this in the larger social group "is dependent upon getting the attitude of the group as distinct from that of a separate individual—getting what I have termed a 'generalized other'" (MSS 256). It is at this point that, for Mead, intelligence or rationality becomes possible. "A human organism does not become a rational being until he has achieved such an organized other in his field of social response," because only then can the individual carry on "that conversation with himself which we call thought" (PP 87) and bring this attitude to bear in his dealings with "the social problems of various kinds which confront that group or community at any given time . . ." (MSS 156).

Mead tells us that the "I" phase of the human self, on the other hand, "is the response of the organism to the attitudes of the others . . . The attitudes of the others constitute the organized 'me,' and then one reacts toward that as an 'I'" (MSS 175). In another formulation, he puts it this way: "The 'I' is the response of the individual to the attitude of the community as this appears in his own experience" (MSS 196). These passages may imply a certain temporal primacy of the "me," but the two phases of the self actually develop together. Ontologically, the two phases are co-equal. As Mead explains, "there would not be a 'me' without a response in the form of the 'I'" any more than there would be "an 'I' in the sense in which we use that term if there were not a 'me' . . ." (MSS 182). The importance of the "I" is a result of the fact that this phase of the self introduces novelty into our actions. To the extent that an individual were simply a "me," that person would be, as we have seen, habitual and conventional; but the response of the "I" offers "something that is more or less uncertain" (MSS 176), "something that is never entirely calculable" (MSS 178). The "I" is thus the phase of the self that gives us freedom and initiative and openness to change. It is the "I" that enables us to break free of our group's set way of thinking, to recognize problems, and to suggest possibilities of change. In this way, Mead continues, the "I" is responsible for the "reconstruction of the society, and so of the 'me' which belongs to that society" (MSS 214). It is, he emphasizes, in the "reactions of the individual, the 'I,' over against the situation in which the 'I' finds itself, that important social changes take place" (MSS 217).

Mead was conscious of the necessity that we take account of these two phases of the self in our educational endeavors. While we recognize that it is not the job of education to *make* the self social, since it is social already, still we can set up our educational goals and procedures to foster social growth. We can do this in part by attempting to develop "the unique characteristic of the human individual—that he can place himself in different perspectives" (PA 182). Instead of attempting to cram the child full of information, it is better to try to expand his or her "me" by helping the child enter into the perspectives of others. Literature and the social sciences, for example, are essential to our coming to understand the traditions and beliefs of peoples other than ourselves. Similarly, we should not attempt to teach natural science without teaching the history of science: the traditions and the personalities, with their problems, their struggles, and their successes, etc. (cf. SW 66–68). We can also attempt to develop the student's "I," and thereby to enhance his or her sense of the need to become an evaluator rather than just a repeater, by attempting to convert instruction into "an interchange of experience" or a "conversation" between the instructor and the student, and among the students themselves (SW 118–119).

We have now taken an initial look at Mead's understanding of the social aspect of the self as a duality that grows out of a reflexive and emergent process and at the educational implications of this view. I would like to turn at this point to a consideration of some of the other consequences of his view, and close this examination of Mead's understanding of the social aspect of human nature with a glimpse at some of the implications of this view for the moral life. Mead was explicitly attempting to construct his ethical theory on a social basis, in terms of his social theory of "the origin, development, nature, and structure of the self" (MSS 379). There are two primary implications of this project. The first is the importance of fostering the duality of the "I" and the "me"; the second, the recognition of our need to choose our "me." We can consider these implications in turn.

First, it is important to continue to foster the duality of the "I" and the "me." We have seen that Mead maintains that both phases of the self are essential and go hand-in-hand. He also recognizes, however, that the balance between the two changes from situation to situation. Hence, we recognize the importance of the self's striving to remain dual. The "me" contains the person's set of socially derived values; the "I" is the reaction to them. It is consequently necessary to be part of the group, but necessary as well to attempt to maintain some critical 'distance.' This is because there are situations, primarily those of a religious or patriotic nature, in which the "I" and the "me" can, as Mead puts it, "fuse" (MSS 273) and make "the good of the community the supreme good of the individual" (SW 355). These fusion situations, as we all know, are emotionally very satisfying. In Mead's words, they give rise to a "peculiar sense of exaltation" (MSS 273). When this fusion occurs, when people weld themselves completely to their group and its traditions, they abandon their own individual critical distance and become social automata—a dangerous stance for moral agents.[17]

One way to maintain our critical distance from the group is to recall that we have some responsibility in the choice of the "me." This is the second of the primary ethical implications of Mead's understanding of the social aspect of the self. Although far too often we equate "custom" with "morality" (MSS 168), we must recognize that as individuals in modern pluralistic societies we have at our fingertips a rich supply of value options resulting from our experiences and our studies. We thus have a great wealth of possible choices from which to select our moral frames-of-reference. Mead recognizes, of course, that these value options are not equally available to all members of society, and that not all individuals are equally able to make use of what is available. It is for these reasons that Mead puts emphasis on the social importance of education. While we cannot ignore the challenges offered to Mead's belief in the high degree of freedom of the "I" when faced with contemporary forms of thought 'management,'[18] we must remember that for him the claim is primarily a moral one. We *should* see our "me" as chosen, Mead tells us. We have a duty to ourselves and to our communities to evaluate our moral frames-of-reference, not simply to accept them. We can adopt as our moral frame-of-reference the community of scholars and its values, or the community of racists and its values. We can draw our standards from contemporary advertising, from ancient ideals, or from anticipated future needs. We can claim that our present community has perfect moral values and strive only to embody them, or we can challenge our community by reference to other values that we consider to be superior.

Mead discusses this point in terms of the ethical breadth of the "generalized other." He tells us that in moving away from what he calls "a community of a narrow diameter" (MSS 265), a sub-community like a gang or clique, or in overcoming any of "the prejudices of the community," the reformer "expresses the principles of the community more completely" (MSS 217) than those who stay behind. In this way, the individual, through his or her "I," has chosen from within the diversity of the "me" certain ideal values and challenged other persons in the community to abandon their present actions and to live up to these ideals in their social practice. In a still broader sense, we are able to move from what we conceive to be "a narrow and restricted community to a larger one" (MSS 199) by rejecting the values that are currently functioning within our own community and by adopting the ideals of some other community that we believe to be superior. In this way, the individual reformer can oppose his or her present community from the point of view of a better one, "from the point of view of what he considers a higher and better society than that which exists" (MSS 389).

It is at this level that the individual is most fully social, in both the descriptive and the moral sense of that term. He or she functions as a social critic, fully integrated within the life of the community but calling on its members to live up to its ideal values, or perhaps even calling on them to abandon their society's limited ideals for better ones. The ethical life, this life of social criticism, thus requires the maintenance of the duality of the "I" and the "me" and a commitment to the advance of the group and of the human community. "All the things worth while are shared experiences," Mead tells us (MSS 385)[19]; and, for him, the ideal of democracy is the continued growth of pluralism and co-operative participation in society such that shared experience can be attained. Ultimately, what he holds out as our moral goal is developing an integrated and enriching community. As he puts is, "the attainment of that functional differentiation and social participation in the full degree is a sort of ideal which lies before the human community" (MSS 326). This is a severe standard of morality, no doubt; but it is one rooted in his understanding of human nature as fundamentally social. And, as we shall see, it is the highest standard possible for people whose lives consist in overcoming problems.

## Human Nature as Pragmatic

The second major aspect of human nature in Mead's understanding is that humans are pragmatic creatures. They are problem-solvers. The human animal lives her or his life, most of the time, in what he calls "the attitude of immediate experience" (PA 14). We live ordinarily "in a world that is simply there and to which we are so adjusted that no thinking is involved . . ." (MSS 135).[20] Numerous actions—walking, chewing, climbing stairs, greeting of passers-by, automobile driving—are usually carried on automatically, without deliberate plan or self-conscious involvement. Of course, this is not always the case; and, in the process of our lives, things do go wrong. "The life in which the human community finds itself inevitably presents a set of problems," Mead writes (PA 79). Specific problems develop and jolt us from this habitual realm of immediate experience into the attitude of "reflective analysis" (PA 14). As Mead tells us, "reasoning conduct appears where impulsive conduct breaks down" (MSS 348). Conflicts inevitably give rise to reflection; and, he continues, the proper purpose of thinking is problem-solving. "Reflection is a process of solving problems . . . We seek a hypothesis which will set free the processes that have been stopped in the situation that we call problematic" (MT 135, 359).

These problems are solved through reconstruction, through the reassessment and reordering of the problematic situations. In our ability to reconstruct, Mead sees us as continuous with the rest of nature. Nature's own evolutionary process proceeds "by reconstruction in the presence of conflicts . . ." (PP 174), because each plant and animal variation results from such a reconstruction in nature. Actions too are reconstructions; and in the behavior of animals, and often in that of people, problems are solved by reconstruction that involves no thought.[21] Mead remains, however, more centrally concerned with reflective human reconstruction: that is, with attempts on the part of an individual or individuals, on recognizing the existence of a particular problem, to deliberate and experiment until it is possible to effect situational changes sufficient to ameliorate or eliminate it.

In Mead's analysis, the key to reflective human reconstruction is our ability to slow down our responses to allow for deliberate experimentation. "The achievement of the human animal, or rather of human social conduct," he notes, "is the arrest of passage, and the establishment of a 'now'" (PA 161). It is in this created 'now'—between our recognition of the problem and our hypothetically grounded attempt at its resolution—that we "manipulate," a term that he uses to demonstrate (as we saw previously) his recognition of the importance of the human hand. For Mead, "man's manual contacts, intermediate between the beginnings and the ends of his acts, provide a multitude of different stimuli to a multitude of different ways of doing things, and thus invite alternative impulses to express themselves in the accomplishment of his acts . . ." Moreover, when we are able to manipulate such "elaborations and extensions" of our hands (MSS 363) as books and computers, we can give rise to far more new possibilities.[22] The ability to fashion these alternate possibilities through manual contacts would not have been greatly beneficial to humans, however, if they did not have a central nervous system that could make use of such possibilities; and ours offers us both a memory and "the field and the mechanism for selection with reference to distant futures . . ." (PP 66).

It is in this collapsing of past and future into the 'now,' in this conscious interrelation of what has happened and what is to come, that Mead again discusses intelligence. "It is the possibility of delayed response," he notes, "which principally differentiates reflective conduct from nonreflective conduct in which the response is always immediate" (MSS 117). In addition to having the internal dialogue made possible by the "I" and the "me," the intelligent person now has something—the felt problem and the fruits of manipulation—about which to converse with himself or herself. As a result of this "inner conversation" (MSS 141), individuals are able to act more intelligently. "Intelligence," he continues, "is essentially the ability to solve the problems of present behavior in terms of its possible future consequences as implicated on the basis of past experience . . ." (MSS 100).

As with the social aspect of human nature, Mead recognizes that the problem-solving aspect of human nature has educational implications. Because humans can improve their abilities as problem-solvers, it is important that our educational institutions adopt such improvements as one of their deliberate goals. This means, he writes, a turning away from an emphasis on the acquisition of "mere information"—that is, "[w]hatever is stored up, without immediate need, for some later occasion, for display or to pass examinations"—and a turn toward "knowledge"—whatever "helps anyone to understand better a question he is trying to answer, a problem he is trying to solve" (SW 69). A good education thus focuses on the solving of problems; and he believes, moreover, that students can become better at problem-solving only by becoming more skilled in the use of the scientific method. By this, Mead, like the other pragmatists, means nothing particularly esoteric. For him, using the scientific method to solve problems or answer questions simply means rejecting other methods of arriving at conclusions such as tenaciously holding beliefs without question, relying on authorities and group discipline to produce unity of belief, and accepting those beliefs that appear self-evidently true. In place of such inadequate methods of solving problems and answering questions, Mead would have us develop our students' skills for the long-term cooperative addressing of problems.[23]

This emphasis on problem-solving as a fundamental aspect of human nature draws us toward an examination of Mead's understanding of the role of thought in human life. We can consider three related strands of his view in turn. One major strand is the rootedness of intelligence in action. Our ability to think is not decorative but functional. We are reconstructors—good or poor reconstructors. We are better or worse, more or less intelligent, depending on the level and quality of our thought. When problems arise, we seldom face an easy selection between a clear good and a clear evil. Rather, we are normally called on to evaluate: to deliberate and then choose from a number of conflicting possible courses of action the one that appears best. "All of our impulses are possible sources of happiness," Mead tells us. We thus recognize the importance of being able to evaluate and choose among alternatives. We do this by examining the likely future consequences of each option: "there are some impulses which lead simply to disintegration . . . There are certain of our impulses which find their expression, for example, in cruelty . . . they are not desirable because the results which they bring are narrowing, depressing, and deprive us of social relations. They also lead, so far as others are concerned, to injury to other individuals" (MSS 383–384). It is in these attempts to foster through careful evaluation favorable consequences for ourselves and for others that we find Mead's emphasis on the importance of agents keeping their thought rooted in practical concerns.

Another strand of Mead's analysis of the role of thought in human life is that it is largely through the problems we face and our responses to them that we construct our explicit image of human nature. We can consider this point in the context of our claims about fundamental human rights. What our rights are, and more importantly what these rights mean in a specific rather than a vague sense, are only discoverable, he writes, in the addressing of problems. "The contents" of these rights "have always been formulated negatively, with reference to restrictions to be overcome" (SW 159). Each particular restatement of a right thus remains only "a *working* conception" (SW 154) of the ideal. Thus it is in our responses to the particular social problems we face that we discover what we mean *practically* by our claims that people are 'equal' and 'free.' We must discover, in the context of our present problematic situations, what we mean specifically by our claims that, for example, a satisfactory human life requires having an effective say in the political, economic, religious, medical, and other aspects of one's life or that a certain punishment is 'cruel and unusual.' It is in these ongoing attempts to reconceive our social ideals to make them appropriate to new problematic situations that we formulate our explicit understanding of human nature.

A third strand of Mead's emphasis on problem-solving as a fundamental aspect of human life has to do with how large a role it plays in satisfactory living. "Life is a process of continued reconstruction," Mead tells us (MT 292). At times, he goes still further, as when he maintains that "[i]t is the realization of the problem and its solution that is the whole zest of living . . ." (PA 511). Living, for Mead, *is* problem-solving: preserving our architectural heritage and preparing dinners, making marriages work and paying our bills, phrasing apologies and performing concertos, finding our keys and formulating an adequate metaphysics. Each of these is an instance of problem-solving, some heroic and some mundane; but all of them are illustrations of his view that living is addressing problems. This is not to say, however, that for Mead solving problems has no value beyond being rid of the specific difficulties. He notes that "the solution of each problem brings with it a deeper meaning and a richer value in living" (PA 511). Each solution brings a clearer understanding and appreciation of the complexity and interrelations of living, and of the reasons for and costs of failure. Thus, each solution also brings a commitment to further efforts in the future. This is why Mead maintains that we should find "the meaning of life in marshaling all the values that are involved in the problems of conduct and interpretation, and seeking such a reconstruction of them as will motivate conduct that recognizes all the interests that are involved" (PA 512).

Surely Mead's analysis of our situation is a severe one. Even if we understand our problems in a rich and variegated way such that, for example, our place in the universe is conceived of as a problem, some will find his view degrading and deflating. There is in Mead's view no sheltered role for intellectual contemplation, since even "entirely disinterested knowledge" has a job to do in his analysis: "Knowledge for its own sake is the slogan of freedom, for it alone makes possible the continual reconstruction and enlargement of the ends of conduct" (SW 210). There is in Mead's view no privileged role for relaxation either, because we have never done enough. Faced with the ongoing reality of our social ills, we could always do a bit more, we could always pursue an alternative line of response, we could always try harder.[24] We are ever called to address our problems, to take an active role in community decision-making. The benefit that Mead sees here is that we realize through our attempts to solve our problems higher levels of meaning and self-discovery as members of a cooperative community.[25]

## Pragmatism and Philosophy

In the two prior sections, we examined Mead's social and pragmatic understanding of human nature. We human beings, all of us, are fundamentally members of communities and fundamentally solvers of problems. In this section, I want to explore briefly the relationship between his pragmatic understanding of our human nature and philosophy. What is the meaning or the importance of philosophy for such people? What care should such people—we—have for philosophy? The simplest answer, although clearly the wrong one, is 'none.' Although philosophy in some senses would surely be without value to such pragmatic individuals, philosophy understood in a particular way is of central importance. This importance, and the sense of philosophy that will satisfy it, will take some time to characterize.

Beginning negatively, for Mead philosophy does not have any importance simply because historically it has been seen as important or as something with which the 'educated' person is familiar. Nor is philosophy important if it simply makes us happy or helps us to feel good about living. The importance of philosophy to people like us, Mead maintains, is: first, that we are ever on the frontier of new and serious problems and we need all the help we can get to solve them; and, second, that philosophy can function as an aid in the clarification, evaluation, and solution of these problems.

My introduction of the term 'frontier' here is deliberate. Mead himself makes use of the frontier metaphor with great effect in a 1930 essay entitled "The Philosophies of Royce, James, and Dewey in Their American Setting" (SW 371–391), and in a companion piece, "The Philosophy of John Dewey," published posthumously.[26] Mead writes that "[t]he most illuminating conception that has been found for the interpretation of the history of the American community has been that of Professor Turner,[27] that of the Pioneer." What distinguished the pioneer, the settler of the frontier, Mead writes, was that "[h]e traveled light, and what he carried with him had to be useful enough to justify its transportation."[28] He sees this frontier analysis as offering an explanation for the development in these Western towns and cities of a life within which "the directive forces in the community" (SW 376), the economic and political forces, operated without a highly intellectualized culture. The America of the pioneers "abandoned European culture as a vital part of its living."[29] On the frontier, such culture could not justify itself.

Although the actual open frontier about which Mead was writing was declared closed more than one hundred years ago, still in his day, and even in our own, the pragmatist sees great value in this frontier analogy. The pioneer is not just the lonesome soul of our past, and the frontier is more than the fringe of unsettled land; the pioneer is us and the frontier, ever dangerous, is here and now. We simply cannot afford to lug around philosophic baggage that we are not using to deal with our social problems. It is important to recognize, however, that this proscription is not of a particular philosopher or school of philosophy, but of a mentality. What Mead wants to proscribe is a mentality that sees philosophy as a kind of intellectual decoration and humans as having time for such fancies.

It would be a mistake to think, however, that because of this position Mead has no place for aesthetics. The aesthetic, he writes, is a phase of experience that is able "to catch the enjoyment that belongs to the consummation, the outcome, of an undertaking . . ." (SW 296). Tied as it is to the consummation of actions, however, to the solution of problems, aesthetic enjoyment must be earned. The aesthetic "accompanies, inspires, and dedicates common action . . ." (SW 298). In our world of hunger and illiteracy, of unexamined customs and intellectual bankruptcy, the pragmatist has made a decision on moral grounds to forgo philosophy as decoration for philosophy as a tool in the clarification, evaluation, and solution of problems.

Mead offers us another phrasing of this same distinction when he considers the difference between the roles played by philosophy when our culture is merely "an adornment of life" and when it functions as "an interpretation of life."[30] For example, Mead suggests that in his teaching and writing Josiah Royce offered his students a philosophy that functioned only within a culture that was second-hand, imported, "foreign" to their situation (SW 380). Royce's students, and Mead was one of them, "found in his luminous expositions another cathedral window through which to receive the culture of Europe but no method of living."[31] Royce's philosophy was a segment in a culture that functioned as "part of the escape from the crudity of American life," Mead contended, "not an interpretation of it" (SW 383).[32] Dewey, on the other hand, he wrote, offered "thought as a method of life"[33]; and it is fair to say that Mead attempted to do the same himself. For both of them, and for other pragmatists of their day and ours, the role of philosophy in life is to foster thinking about and focus attention on fundamental problems, to attempt to understand and thereby to facilitate the amelioration of our shared difficulties. Only then will we have a philosophy that functions as "an interpretation of life" rather than as an "adornment."

Mead's position here has implications for our study of the history of philosophy. If we explore the importance of the history of philosophy, or of history in general, to present-day living, we find in Mead's work, as we might expect, a central emphasis on the role that history plays. Mead cares not at all for the accumulation of "mere information" (SW 69). He cares, as we have seen above, for how history *functions*. "History serves a community in the same way as the memory does the individual," he maintains. We use the past "so as to make our present situation intelligible" (PA 80–81). Consequently, Mead continues, "the estimate and import of all histories lies in the interpretation and control of the present . . ." (PP 28). Thus the evaluation of the history of past philosophy must lie in terms of "the interpretation and control of the present." So, we must ask ourselves, what is there in the history of philosophy that will do this?

Simply put, what our study of the history of philosophy offers us is a broadening of self-consciousness—it offers us "a larger self" (MSS 386)—with which to address our problems. The study of the history of philosophy enables us to explore other aspects of our problems and to consider other possible solutions. Among our gains from the study of the philosophic visions of Kant and Edwards, of Emerson and Bradley, of Wittgenstein and Hartshorne, are alternative categorical schemes and new challenges to our accepted views. All of this results in a larger self with which to face our problems. But, for Mead, this larger self should not—again, this is a moral claim—be allowed to function as a decoration or simply a means to personal happiness. It must participate in the creation of "a larger social whole in terms of which the social conflicts that necessitate the reconstruction of the given society are harmonized or reconciled, and by reference to which, accordingly, these conflicts can be solved or eliminated" (MSS 308–309). It is also important to keep in mind that since our social problems are not purely philosophic problems, we cannot hope to effect adequate social reconstruction through the study of philosophy alone.

## Notes

1. Mead, "Josiah Royce—A Personal Impression," *International Journal of Ethics,* XXVII (1917), 168.
2. Additional biographical material on Mead and his family can be found in David L. Miller, *George Herbert Mead: Self, Language, and the World* (Chicago: University of Chicago Press, 1980), xi–xxxviii; Neil Coughlan, *Young John Dewey* (Chicago: University of Chicago Press, 1975), 113–150; and Gary A. Cook, *George Herbert Mead: The Making of a Social Pragmatist* (Urbana: University of Illinois Press), 1–36, 183–194.
3. For a further discussion of Mead's work as a social reformer, see: Darnell Rucker, *The Chicago Pragmatists* (Minneapolis: University of Minnesota Press, 1969), 20–22; Mary Jo Deegan and John S. Burger, "George Herbert Mead and Social Reform: His Work and Writings," *Journal of the History of the Behavioral Sciences,* XIV (1978), 362–373; Cook, *George Herbert Mead,* 99–114.
4. Dewey, "George Herbert Mead as I Knew Him" (1931), *Later Works of John Dewey,* ed. Jo Ann Boydston, 17 volumes (Carbondale: Southern Illinois University Press, 1981–1990), 6:24; "The Work of George Mead" (1936), *Later Works of John Dewey,* 11:450.
5. *Selected Writings: George Herbert Mead* [SW], ed. Andrew J. Reck, (Chicago: University of Chicago Press, [1964] 1981). A briefer selection of Mead's writings was edited by John W. Petras and published under the title, *George Herbert Mead: Essays on His Social Philosophy* (New York: Teachers College Press, 1968). The best available bibliography of the published works of Mead has been compiled by Gary Cook and can be found in *George Herbert Mead,* 215–220.
6. Dewey, "The Work of George Mead," *Later Works,* 11:450; "George Herbert Mead as I Knew Him," *Later Works,* 6:25.
7. Dewey writes that Mead "was planning to expand them to three of four times their present length, an expansion which would have clarified the thought and not merely swelled the number of words" ("Prefatory Remarks" to PP, xl).
8. *The Philosophy of the Present* [PP], ed. Arthur E. Murphy, (Chicago: University of Chicago Press, [1932] 1980); *Mind, Self, and Society from the Standpoint of a Social Behaviorist* [MSS], ed. Charles W. Morris, (Chicago: University of Chicago Press, 1934); *Movements of Thought in the Nineteenth Century* [MT], ed. Merritt H. Moore, (Chicago: University of Chicago Press, 1936); *The Philosophy of the Act* [PA], ed. Charles W. Morris, et al., (Chicago: University of Chicago Press, 1938); *The Individual and the Social Self* [ISS], ed. David L. Miller, (Chicago: University of Chicago Press, 1982). The Mead Papers are housed in the Special Collections Division of the Joseph Regenstein Library at the University of Chicago.
9. See Dewey, *How We Think* (1933), *Later Works of John Dewey,* 8:199–209; *Logic, The Theory of Inquiry* (1938), *Later Works of John Dewey,* 12:105–122.
10. See Dewey, *Human Nature and Conduct: An Introduction to Social Psychology* (1922), *Middle Works of John Dewey,* ed. Jo Ann Boydston, 15 volumes, (Carbondale: Southern Illinois University Press, 1976–1983), vol. 14.
11. Elsewhere, Mead continues: "It has long been a subject of comment, both within and without philosophic circles, that epistemology, the problem of knowledge, has excited not the slightest interest among scientists, whose profession is that of discovering what has been unknown" (PA 26; cf. 280; PP 140–141).
12. Cf. SW 77-9, 135; MSS 184–185, 237, 248, 362–363; PP 60.
13. Dewey writes: "His interest in the concept of emergence is, for example, a reflex of that factor of his own intellectual experience by which new insights were constantly budding and having then to be joined to what he had thought previously, instead of merely displacing old ideas. He felt within himself both the emergence of the new and the inevitable continuity of the new with the old" ("Prefatory Remarks" to PP, xxxix).
14. Cf. William James: "the practically cognized present is no knife-edge, but a saddle-back, with a certain breadth of its own on which we sit perched, and from which we look in two directions into time" (*The Principles of Psychology* [Cambridge: Harvard University Press, (1890) 1981], 3 vol., 1:574).
15. Cf. John Dewey: "To learn to be human is to develop through the give-and-take of communication an effective sense of being an individually distinctive member of a community . . ." (*The Public and Its Problems* [1927] *Later Works* 2: 332).
16. Mead continues elsewhere: "We can talk to ourselves, and this we do in the inner forum of what we call thought. We are in possession of selves just insofar as we can and do take the attitudes of others toward ourselves and respond to those attitudes. We approve of ourselves and condemn ourselves. We pat ourselves on

the back and in blind fury attack ourselves. We assume the generalized attitude of the group . . ." (SW 288; cf. MSS 68–69, 171, 194).

17. I have explored this question of social fusion elsewhere: "George Herbert Mead on Social Fusion and the Social Critic," *Frontiers in American Philosophy,* ed. Robert W. Burch and Herman J. Saatkamp, Jr., vol. 1 (College Station: Texas A&M University Press, 1992), 243–252; and "Community without Fusion: Dewey, Mead, Tufts," *Pragmatism: From Progressivism to Postmodernism,* ed. Robert Hollinger and David Depew, (Westport, CT: Praeger, 1995), 56–71.

18. See, for example, C. Wright Mills, *The Sociological Imagination* (New York: Grove Press, 1961), 165–176.

19. Compare this comment with Dewey's: "Shared experience is the greatest of human goods" (*Experience and Nature* [1929], *Later Works of John Dewey,* 1:157).

20. Cf. MSS 102–103, 212–3; PA 368–369.

21. Cf. MSS 92–93; MT 344–346; PA 79, 504; ISS 42–43.

22. Cf. PA 16–23; ISS 119–120, 173–175.

23. See Charles S. Peirce, "The Fixation of Belief" (1877), *Collected Papers of Charles Sanders Peirce,* ed. Charles Hartshorne, Paul Weiss and Arthur W. Burks, 8 vol. (Cambridge: Harvard University Press, 1931–1956), 5.358–5.387.

24. As Dewey writes in this regard, "the better is too often the enemy of the still better" (*Liberalism and Social Action* [1935], *Later Works of John Dewey,* 11:50).

25. For more on Mead's understanding of pragmatism, the pragmatic theory of meaning, the pragmatic theory of truth, etc., see MT 344–359; PA 360–364; SW 320–344.

26. Mead, "The Philosophy of John Dewey," *International Journal of Ethics,* XLVI (1935), 64–81.

27. Mead is referring here to Frederick Jackson Turner (1861–1932), author of *The Frontier in American History* (New York: Holt, 1920).

28. "The Philosophy of John Dewey," 64.

29. Ibid., 67.

30. Ibid., 66.

31. Ibid., 72; cf. "Josiah Royce—A Personal Impression," 168–170; Gary A. Cook, "George Herbert Mead: An Unpublished Essay on Royce and James," *Transactions of the Charles S. Peirce Society,* XXVIII/3 (Summer 1992), 588–590.

32. It must be recalled here that Mead is writing from the standpoint of the impact that Royce had on him when he was a student at Harvard in 1887–88. Whether Mead's evaluation should be seen as adequate for an understanding of Royce's whole thought is doubtful, especially if we keep in mind Royce's later work and his 1915 self-evaluation: "my deepest motives and problems have centred about the Idea of the Community, although this idea has only come gradually to my clear consciousness" ("Words of Prof. Royce at the Walton Hotel at Philadelphia, December 29, 1915," *The Basic Writings of Josiah Royce,* ed. John J. McDermott, 2 vol. [Chicago: University of Chicago Press, 1969], 1:34).

33. Mead, "The Philosophy of John Dewey," 72; cf. SW 390–391.

# The Vocal Gesture and the Significant Symbol

The concept of imitation has been used very widely in the field of the vocal gesture. There we do seem to have a tendency on the part of certain organisms to reproduce sounds which are heard. Human beings and the talking birds provide illustrations. But even here "imitation" is hardly an immediate tendency, since it takes quite a while to get one bird to reproduce the song, or for the child to take over the phonetic gesture of the human form. The vocal gesture is a stimulus to some sort of response; it is not simply a stimulus to the calling out of the sound which the animal hears. Of course, the bird can be put into a situation where it

From *Mind, Self, and Society from the Standpoint of a Social Behaviorist,* Ed. Charles W. Morris, (Chicago: Univ. of Chicago Press, 1934), pp. 61–68.

may reach the mere repetition of that which it hears. If we assume that one sound that the bird makes calls out another sound, when the bird hears this first sound it responds by the second. If one asked why one note answers to another, one would have to go to some process where the vocal gesture would have a different physiological significance. An illustration is the cooing process of pigeons. There one note calls out another note in the other form. It is a conversation of gestures, where a certain attitude expressing itself in a certain note calls out another attitude with its corresponding note. If the form is to call out in itself the same note that it calls out in the other, it must act as the other acts, and use the note that the other makes use of in order to reproduce the particular note in question. So you find, if you put the sparrow and the canary together in neighboring cages, where the call of one calls out a series of notes in the other, that if the sparrow finds itself uttering a note such as a canary does, the vocal gesture here must be more or less of the same type. Where that situation exists, the sparrow in its own process of vocalization makes use of such notes as those which the canary makes use of. The sparrow is influencing not only the canary, but also in hearing itself it is influencing itself. The note that it is making use of, if it is identical with the note of the canary, calls out a response in itself that the canary's note would call out in itself. Those are the situations that have become emphasized and maintained where one has what we term "imitation." Where the sparrow is actually making use of a phonetic vocal gesture of the canary through a common note in the repertoire of both of them, then the sparrow would be tending to bring out in itself the same response that would be brought out by the note of the canary. That, then, would give an added weight in the experience of the sparrow to that particular response.

If the vocal gesture which the sparrow makes is identical with that which it hears when the canary makes use of the same note, then it is seen that its own response will be in that case identical with the response to the canary's note. It is this which gives such peculiar importance to the vocal gesture: it is one of those social stimuli which affect the form that makes it in the same fashion that it affects the form when made by another. That is, we can hear ourselves talking, and the import of what we say is the same to ourselves that it is to others. If the sparrow makes use of a canary's note it is calling out in itself the response that the canary's note calls out. In so far, then, as the sparrow does make use of the same note that the canary makes use of, it will emphasize the vocal responses to this note because they will be present not only when the canary makes use of it but also when the sparrow makes use of it. In such a case it is presupposed that the particular stimulus is present in the form itself, that is, that the vocal stimulus which calls out the particular note which is learned is present in the repertoire of the sparrow as well as in that of the canary. If one recognizes that, then one can see that those particular notes answering to this stimulus will be, so to speak, written in, underlined. They will become habitual. We are supposing that one note calls out another, a stimulus calls out a response. If this note which calls out this response is used not only by the canary but also by the sparrow, then whenever the sparrow hears the canary it makes use of that particular note, and if it has the same note in its own repertoire then there is a double tendency to bring about this particular response, so that it becomes more frequently made use of and becomes more definitely a part of the singing of the sparrow than otherwise. Such are the situations in which the sparrow does take the rôle of the canary in so far as there are certain notes to which it tends to react just as the canary does. There is a double weight, so to speak, upon this particular note or series of notes. It is in such a fashion that we can understand the learning by the sparrow of the canary's song. One has to assume a like tendency in the two forms if one is going to get any mechanism for imitation at all.

To illustrate this further let us go back to the conversation of gestures in the dog-fight. There the stimulus which one dog gets from the other is to a response which is different from the response of the stimulating form. One dog is attacking the other, and is ready to spring at the other dog's throat; the reply on the part of the second dog is to change its position, perhaps to spring at the throat of the first dog. There is a conversation of gestures, a reciprocal shifting of the dogs' positions and attitudes. In such a process there would be no mechanism for imitation. One dog does not imitate the other. The second dog assumes a different attitude to avoid the spring of the first dog. The stimulus in the attitude of one dog is not to call out the response in itself that it calls out in the other. The first dog is influenced by its own attitude, but it is simply carrying out the process of a prepared spring, so that the influence on the dog is simply in reinforcing the process which is going on. It is not a stimulus to the dog to take the attitude of the other dog.

When, however, one is making use of the vocal gesture, if we assume that one vocal element is a stimulus to a certain reply, then when the animal that makes use of that vocal gesture hears the resulting sound he will have aroused in himself at least a tendency to respond in the same way as the other animal responds. It may be a very slight tendency—the lion does not appreciably frighten itself by its roar. The roar has an effect of frightening the animal he is attacking, and it has also the character of a challenge under certain conditions. But when we come to such elaborate processes of vocalization as those of the song of birds, there one vocal gesture calls out another vocal gesture. These, of course, have their function in the intercourse of the birds, but the gestures themselves become of peculiar importance. The vocalization plays a very large part in such a process as wooing, and one call tends to call out another note. In the case of the lion's roar the response is not so much a vocal sound as it is a flight, or, if you like, a fight. The response is not primarily a vocal response. It is rather the action of the form itself. But in the song of birds, where vocalization is carried out in an elaborate fashion, the stimulus does definitely call out a certain response so that the bird when singing is influenced by its own stimulus to a response which will be like that which is produced in another form. That response which is produced in itself, since it is also produced by the influence of others, gets twice the emphasis that it would have if it were just called out by the note of others. It is called out more frequently than the response to other sounds. It is this that gives the seeming evidence of imitation in the case of sounds or vocal gestures.[1] The stimulus that calls out a particular sound may be found not only in the other forms of the group but also in the repertoire of the particular bird which uses the vocal gesture. This stimulus $A$ calls out the response $B$. Now if this stimulus $A$ is not like $B$, and if we assume that $A$ calls out $B$, then if $A$ is used by other forms these forms will respond in the fashion $B$. If this form also uses the vocal gesture $A$, it will be calling out in itself the response $B$, so that the response $B$ will be emphasized over against other responses because it is called out not only by the vocal gestures of other forms but also by the form itself. This would never take place unless there were an identity represented by $A$, in this case an identity of stimuli.

In the case of the vocal gesture the form hears its own stimulus just as when this is used by other forms, so it tends to respond also to its own stimulus as it responds to the stimulus of other forms. That is, birds tend to sing to themselves, babies to talk to themselves. The sounds they make are stimuli to make other sounds. Where there is a specific sound that calls out a specific response, then if this sound is made by other forms it calls out this response in the form in question. If the sparrow makes use of this particular sound then the response to that sound will be one which will be heard more frequently than another response. In that way there will be selected out of the sparrow's repertoire those elements which are found in the song of the canary, and gradually such selection would build up in the song of the sparrow those elements which are common to both, without assuming a particular tendency of imitation. There is here a selective process by which is picked out what is common. "Imitation" depends upon the individual influencing himself as others influence him, so that he is under the influence not only of the other but also of himself in so far as he uses the same vocal gesture.

The vocal gesture, then, has an importance which no other gesture has. We cannot see ourselves when our face assumes a certain expression. If we hear ourselves speak we are more apt to pay attention. One hears himself when he is irritated using a tone that is of an irritable quality, and so catches himself. But in the facial expression of irritation the stimulus is not one that calls out an expression in the individual which it calls out in the other. One is more apt to catch himself up and control himself in the vocal gesture than in the expression of the countenance.

It is only the actor who uses bodily expressions as a means of looking as he wants others to feel. He gets a response which reveals to him how he looks by continually using a mirror. He registers anger, he registers love, he registers this, that, or the other attitude, and he examines himself in a glass to see how he does so. When he later makes use of the gesture it is present as a mental image. He realizes that that particular expression does call out fright. If we exclude vocal gestures, it is only by the use of the mirror that one could reach the position where he responds to his own gestures as other people respond. But the vocal gesture is one which does give one this capacity for answering to one's own stimulus as another would answer.

If there is any truth in the old axiom that the bully is always the coward, it will be found to rest on the fact that one arouses in himself that attitude of fear which his bullying attitude arouses in another, so that when put into a particular situation which calls his bluff, his own attitude is found to be that of the others. If one's own attitude of giving way to the bullying attitude of others is one that arouses the bullying attitude, he has in that degree aroused the attitude of bullying in himself. There is a certain amount of truth in this when we come back to the effect upon one's self of the gesture of which he makes use. In so far as one calls out the attitude in himself that one calls out in others, the response is picked out and strengthened. That is the only basis for what we call imitation. It is not imitation in the sense of simply doing what one sees another person doing. The mechanism is that of an individual calling out in himself the response which he calls out in another, consequently giving greater weight to those responses than to the other responses, and gradually building up those sets of responses into a dominant whole. That may be done, as we say, unconsciously. The sparrow does not know it is imitating the canary. It is just a gradual picking up of the notes which are common to both of them. And that is true wherever there is imitation.

So far as exclamatory sounds are concerned (and they would answer in our own vocal gestures to what is found in those of animals), the response to these does not enter into immediate conversation, and the influence of these responses on the individual are comparatively slight. It seems to be difficult to bring them into relationship with significant speech. We are not consciously frightened when we speak angrily to someone else, but the meaning of what we say is always present to us when we speak. The response in the individual to an exclamatory cry which is of the same sort as that in the other does not play any important part in the conduct of the form. The response of the lion to its roar is of very little importance in the response of the form itself, but our response to the meaning of what we say is constantly attached to our conversation. We must be constantly responding to the gesture we make if we are to carry on successful vocal conversation. The meaning of what we are saying is the tendency to respond to it. You ask somebody to bring a visitor a chair. You arouse the tendency to get the chair in the other, but if he is slow to act you get the chair yourself. The response to the vocal gesture is the doing of a certain thing, and you arouse that same tendency in yourself. You are always replying to yourself, just as other people reply. You assume that in some degree there must be identity in the reply. It is action on a common basis.

I have contrasted two situations to show what a long road speech or communication has to travel from the situation where there is nothing but vocal cries over to the situation in which significant symbols are utilized. What is peculiar to the latter is that the individual responds to his own stimulus in the same way as other people respond. Then the stimulus becomes significant; then one is saying something. As far as a parrot is concerned, its "speech" means nothing, but where one significantly says something with his own vocal process he is saying it to himself as well as to everybody else within reach of his voice. It is only the vocal gesture that is fitted for this sort of communication, because it is only the vocal gesture to which one responds or tends to respond as another person tends to respond to it. It is true that the language of the hands is of the same character. One sees one's self using the gestures which those who are deaf make use of. They influence one the same way as they influence others. Of course, the same is true of any form of script. But such symbols

have all been developed out of the specific vocal gesture, for that is the basic gesture which does influence the individual as it influences others. Where it does not become significant is in the vocalization of the two birds. Nevertheless, the same type of process is present, the stimulus of the one bird tending to call out the response in another bird which it tends to call out, however slightly, in the bird itself.

## Notes

1. An attempt was made by James Mark Baldwin to carry back imitation to a fundamental biological process—a tendency on the part of the organism to reinstate a pleasurable sensation. . . . . In the process of mastication the very process of chewing reinstates the stimulus, brings back the flavor. Baldwin would call this self-imitation. This process, if it takes place at all, does not by any means meet the situation with which we are dealing (1912).

# Thought, Communication, and the Significant Symbol

We have contended that there is no particular faculty of imitation in the sense that the sound or the sight of another's response is itself a stimulus to carry out the same reaction, but rather that if there is already present in the individual an action like the action of another, then there is a situation which makes imitation possible. What is necessary now to carry through that imitation is that the conduct and the gesture of the individual which calls out a response in the other should also tend to call out the same response in himself. In the dog-fight this is not present: the attitude in the one dog does not tend to call out the same attitude in the other. In some respects that actually may

occur in the case of two boxers. The man who makes a feint is calling out a certain blow from his opponent, and that act of his own does have that meaning to him, that is, he has in some sense initiated the same act in himself. It does not go clear through, but he has stirred up the centers in his central nervous system which would lead to his making the same blow that his opponent is led to make, so that he calls out in himself, or tends to call out, the same response which he calls out in the other. There you have the basis for so-called imitation. Such is the process which is so widely recognized at present in manners of speech, of dress, and of attitudes.

From *Mind, Self, and Society from the Standpoint of a Social-Behaviorist* Ed. Charles W. Morris. (Chicago: Univ. of Chicago Press, 1934) pp. 68–75.

We are more or less unconsciously seeing ourselves as others see us. We are unconsciously addressing ourselves as others address us; in the same way as the sparrow takes up the note of the canary we pick up the dialects about us. Of course, there must be these particular responses in our own mechanism. We are calling out in the other person something we are calling out in ourselves, so that unconsciously we take over these attitudes. We are unconsciously putting ourselves in the place of others and acting as others act. I want simply to isolate the general mechanism here, because it is of very fundamental importance in the development of what we call self-consciousness and the appearance of the self. We are, especially through the use of the vocal gestures, continually arousing in ourselves those responses which we call out in other persons, so that we are taking the attitudes of the other persons into our own conduct. The critical importance of language in the development of human experience lies in this fact that the stimulus is one that can react upon the speaking individual as it reacts upon the other.

A behaviorist, such as Watson, holds that all of our thinking is vocalization. In thinking we are simply starting to use certain words. That is in a sense true. However, Watson does not take into account all that is involved here, namely, that these stimuli are the essential elements in elaborate social processes and carry with them the value of those social processes. The vocal process as such has this great importance, and it is fair to assume that the vocal process, together with the intelligence and thought that go with it, is not simply a playing of particular vocal elements against each other. Such a view neglects the social context of language.[1]

The importance, then, of the vocal stimulus lies in this fact that the individual can hear what he says and in hearing what he says is tending to respond as the other person responds. When we speak now of this response on the part of the individual to the others we come back to the situation of asking some person to do something. We ordinarily express that by saying that one knows what he is asking you to do. Take the illustration of asking someone to do something, and then doing it one's self. Perhaps the person addressed does not hear you or acts slowly, and then you carry the action out yourself. You find in yourself, in this way, the same tendency which you are asking the other individual to carry out. Your request stirred up in you that same response which you stirred up in the other individual. How difficult it is to show someone else how to do something which you know how to do yourself! The slowness of the response makes it hard to restrain yourself from doing what you are teaching. You have aroused the same response in yourself as you arouse in the other individual.

In seeking for an explanation of this, we ordinarily assume a certain group of centers in the nervous system which are connected with each other, and which express themselves in the action. If we try to find in a central nervous system something that answers to our word "chair," what we should find would be presumably simply an organization of a whole group of possible reactions so connected that if one starts in one direction one will carry out one process, if in another direction one will carry out another process. The chair is primarily what one sits down in. It is a physical object at a distance. One may move toward an object at a distance and then enter upon the process of sitting down when one reaches it. There is a stimulus which excites certain paths which cause the individual to go toward that object and to sit down. Those centers are in some degree physical. There is, it is to be noted, an influence of the later act on the earlier act. The later process which is to go on has already been initiated and that later process has its influence on the earlier process (the one that takes place before this process, already initiated, can be completed). Now, such an organization of a great group of nervous elements as will lead to conduct with reference to the objects about us is what one would find in the central nervous system answering to what we call an object. The complications are very great, but the central nervous system has an almost infinite number of elements in it, and they can be organized not only in spatial connection with each other, but also from a temporal standpoint. In virtue of this last fact, our conduct is made up of a series of steps which follow each other, and the later steps may be already started and influence the earlier ones. The thing we are going to do is playing back on what we are doing now. That organization in the neural elements in reference to what we call a physical object would be what we call a conceptual object stated in terms of the central nervous system.

In rough fashion it is the initiation of such a set of organized sets of responses that answers to what we call the idea or concept of a thing. If one asked what the idea of a dog is, and tried to find that idea in the central nervous system, one would find a whole group of responses which are more or less connected together by definite paths so that when one uses the term "dog" he does tend to call out this group of responses. A dog is a possible playmate, a possible enemy, one's own property or somebody else's. There is a whole series of possible responses. There are certain types of these responses which are in all of us, and there are others which vary with the individuals, but there is always an organization of the responses which can be called out by the term "dog." So if one is speaking of a dog to another person he is arousing in himself this set of responses which he is arousing in the other individual.

It is, of course, the relationship of this symbol, this vocal gesture, to such a set of responses in the individual himself as well as in the other that makes of that vocal gesture what I call a significant symbol. A symbol does tend to call out in the individual a group of reactions such as it calls out in the other, but there is something further that is involved in its being a significant symbol: this response within one's self to such a word as "chair," or "dog," is one which is a stimulus to the individual as well as a response. This is what, of course, is involved in what we term the meaning of a thing, or its significance.[2] We often act with reference to objects in what we call an intelligent fashion, although we can act without the meaning of the object being present in our experience. One can start to dress for dinner, as they tell of the absent-minded college professor, and find himself in his pajamas in bed. A certain process of undressing was started and carried out mechanically; he did not recognize the meaning of what he was doing. He intended to go to dinner and found he had gone to bed. The meaning involved in his action was not present. The steps in this case were all intelligent steps which controlled his conduct with reference to later action, but he did not think about what he was doing. The later action was not a stimulus to his response, but just carried itself out when it was once started.

When we speak of the meaning of what we are doing we are making the response itself that we are on the point of carrying out a stimulus to our action. It becomes a stimulus to a later stage of action which is to take place from the point of view of this particular response. In the case of the boxer the blow that he is starting to direct toward his opponent is to call out a certain response which will open up the guard of his opponent so that he can strike. The meaning is a stimulus for the preparation of the real blow he expects to deliver. The response which he calls out in himself (the guarding reaction) is the stimulus to him to strike where an opening is given. This action which he has initiated already in himself thus becomes a stimulus for his later response. He knows what his opponent is going to do, since the guarding movement is one which is already aroused, and becomes a stimulus to strike where the opening is given. The meaning would not have been present in his conduct unless it became a stimulus to strike where the favorable opening appears.

Such is the difference between intelligent conduct on the part of animals and what we call a reflective individual.[3] We say the animal does not think. He does not put himself in a position for which he is responsible; he does not put himself in the place of the other person and say, in effect, "He will act in such a way and I will act in this way." If the individual can act in this way, and the attitude which he calls out in himself can become a stimulus to him for another act, we have meaningful conduct. Where the response of the other person is called out and becomes a stimulus to control his action, then he has the meaning of the other person's act in his own experience. That is the general mechanism of what we term "thought," for in order that thought may exist there must be symbols, vocal gestures generally, which arouse in the individual himself the response which he is calling out in the other, and such that from the point of view of that response he is able to direct his later conduct. It involves not only communication in the sense in which birds and animals communicate with each other, but also an arousal in the individual himself of the response which he is calling out in the other individual, a taking of the rôle of the other, a tendency to act as the other person acts. One participates in the same process the other person is carrying out and controls his action with reference to that participation. It is that which constitutes the meaning of an object, namely, the common response in one's self as well as in the other person, which becomes, in turn, a stimulus to one's self.

If you conceive of the mind as just a sort of conscious substance in which there are certain impressions and states, and hold that one of those states is a universal, then a word becomes purely arbitrary—it is just a symbol.[4] You can then take words and pronounce them backwards, as children do; there seems to be absolute freedom of arrangement and language seems to be an entirely mechanical thing that lies outside of the process of intelligence. If you recognize that language is, however, just a part of a co-operative process, that part which does lead to an adjustment to the response of the other so that the whole activity can go on, then language has only a limited range of arbitrariness. If you are talking to another person you are, perhaps, able to scent the change in his attitude by something that would not strike a third person at all. You may know his mannerism, and that becomes a gesture to you, a part of the response of the individual. There is a certain range possible within the gesture as to what is to serve as the sym-

bol. We may say that a whole set of separate symbols with one meaning are acceptable; but they always are gestures, that is, they are always parts of the act of the individual which reveal what he is going to do to the other person so that when the person utilizes the clue he calls out in himself the attitude of the other. Language is not ever arbitrary in the sense of simply denoting a bare state of consciousness by a word. What particular part of one's act will serve to direct co-operative activity is more or less arbitrary. Different phases of the act may do it. What seems unimportant in itself may be highly important in revealing what the attitude is. In that sense one can speak of the gesture itself as unimportant, but it is of great importance as to what the gesture is going to reveal. This is seen in the difference between the purely intellectual character of the symbol and its emotional character. A poet depends upon the latter; for him language is rich and full of values which we, perhaps, utterly ignore. In trying to express a message in something less than ten words, we merely want to convey a certain meaning, while the poet is dealing with what is really living tissue, the emotional throb in the expression itself. There is, then, a great range in our use of language; but whatever phase of this range is used is a part of a social process, and it is always that part by means of which we affect ourselves as we affect others and mediate the social situation through this understanding of what we are saying. That is fundamental for any language; if it is going to be language one has to understand what he is saying, has to affect himself as he affects others.

## Notes

1. Gestures, if carried back to the matrix from which they spring, are always found to inhere in or involve a larger social act of which they are phases. In dealing with communication we have first to recognize its earliest origins in the unconscious conversation of gestures. Conscious communication—conscious conversation of gestures—arises when gestures become signs, that is, when they come to carry for the individuals mak-

ing them and the individuals responding to them, definite meanings or significations in terms of the subsequent behavior of the individuals making them; so that, by serving as prior indications, to the individuals responding to them, of the subsequent behavior of the individuals making them, they make possible the mutual adjustment of the various individual components of the social act to one another, and also, by calling forth in the individuals making them the same responses implicitly that they call forth explicitly in the individuals to whom they are made, they render possible the rise of self-consciousness in connection with this mutual adjustment.

2. The inclusion of the matrix or complex of attitudes and responses constituting any given social situation or act, within the experience of any one of the individuals implicated in that situation or act (the inclusion within his experience of his attitudes toward other individuals, of their responses to his attitudes toward them, of their attitudes toward him, and of his responses to these attitudes) is all that an *idea* amounts to; or at any rate is the only basis for its occurrence or existence "in the mind" of the given individual.

In the case of the unconscious conversation of gestures, or in the case of the process of communication carried on by means of it, none of the individuals participating in it is conscious of the meaning of the conversation—that meaning does not appear in the experience of any one of the separate individuals involved in the conversation or carrying it on; whereas, in the case of the conscious conversation of gestures, or in the case of the process of communication carried on by

means of it, each of the individuals participating in it is conscious of the meaning of the conversation, precisely because that meaning does appear in his experience, and because such appearance is what consciousness of that meaning implies.

3. [For the nature of animal conduct see "Concerning Animal Perception," *Psychological Review,* XIV (1907), SW 73–81 383 ff.]

4. Müller attempts to put the values of thought into language; but this attempt is fallacious, because language has those values only as the most effective mechanism of thought merely because it carries the conscious or significant conversation of gestures to its highest and most perfect development. There must be some sort of an implicit attitude (that is, a response which is initiated without being fully carried out) in the organism making the gesture—an attitude which answers to the overt response to the gesture on the part of another individual, and which corresponds to the attitude called forth or aroused in this other organism by the gesture—if thought is to develop in the organism making the gesture. And it is the central nervous system which provides the mechanism for such implicit attitudes or responses.

The identification of language with reason is in one sense an absurdity, but in another sense it is valid. It is valid, namely, in the sense that the process of language brings the total social act into the experience of the given individual as himself involved in the act, and thus makes the process of reason possible. But though the process of reason is and must be carried on in terms of the process of language—in terms, that is, of words—it is not simply constituted by the latter.

# Meaning[1]

We are particularly concerned with intelligence on the human level, that is, with the adjustment to one another of the acts of different human individuals within the human social process; an adjustment which takes place through communication: by gestures on the lower planes of human evolution, and by significant symbols (gestures which possess

meanings and are hence more than mere substitute stimuli) on the higher planes of human evolution.

The central factor in such adjustment is "meaning." Meaning arises and lies within the field of the relation between the gesture of a given human organism and the subsequent behavior of this organism as indicated to

From *Mind, Self, and Society from the Standpoint of a Social Behaviorist,* Ed. Charles W. Morris. (Chicago: Univ. of Chicago Press, 1934) pp. 75–82.

another human organism by that gesture. If that gesture does so indicate to another organism the subsequent (or resultant) behavior of the given organism, then it has meaning. In other words, the relationship between a given stimulus—as a gesture—and the later phases of the social act of which it is an early (if not the initial) phase constitutes the field within which meaning originates and exists. Meaning is thus a development of something objectively there as a relation between certain phases of the social act; it is not a psychical addition to that act and it is not an "idea" as traditionally conceived. A gesture by one organism, the resultant of the social act in which the gesture is an early phase, and the response of another organism to the gesture, are the relata in a triple or threefold relationship of gesture to first organism, of gesture to second organism, and of gesture to subsequent phases of the given social act; and this threefold relationship constitutes the matrix within which meaning arises, or which develops into the field of meaning. The gesture stands for a certain resultant of the social act, a resultant to which there is a definite response on the part of the individuals involved therein; so that meaning is given or stated in terms of response. Meaning is implicit—if not always explicit—in the relationship among the various phases of the social act to which it refers, and out of which it develops. And its development takes place in terms of symbolization at the human evolutionary level.

We have been concerning ourselves, in general, with the social process of experience and behavior as it appears in the calling out by the act of one organism of an adjustment to that act in the responsive act of another organism. We have seen that the nature of meaning is intimately associated with the social process as it thus appears, that meaning involves this three-fold relation among phases of the social act as the context in which it arises and develops: this relation of the gesture of one organism to the adjustive response of another organism (also implicated in the given act), and to the completion of the given act—a relation such that the second organism responds to the gesture of the first as indicating or referring to the completion of the given act. For example, the chick's response to the cluck of the mother hen is a response to the meaning of the cluck; the cluck refers to danger or to food, as the case may be, and has this meaning or connotation for the chick.

The social process, as involving communication, is in a sense responsible for the appearance of new objects in the field of experience of the individual organisms implicated in that process. Organic processes or responses in a sense constitute the objects to which they are responses; that is to say, any given biological organism is in a way responsible for the existence (in the sense of the meanings they have for it) of the objects to which it physiologically and chemically responds. There would, for example, be no food—no edible objects—if there were no organisms which could digest it. And similarly, the social process in a sense constitutes the objects to which it responds, or to which it is an adjustment. That is to say, objects are constituted in terms of meanings within the social process of experience and behavior through the mutual adjustment to one another of the responses or actions of the various individual organisms involved in that process, an adjustment made possible by means of a communication which takes the form of a conversation of gestures in the earlier evolutionary stages of that process, and of language in its later stages.

Awareness or consciousness is not necessary to the presence of meaning in the process of social experience. A gesture on the part of one organism in any given social act calls out a response on the part of another organism which is directly related to the action of the first organism and its outcome; and a gesture is a symbol of the result of the given social act of one organism (the organism making it) in so far as it is responded to by another organism (thereby also involved in that act) as indicating that result. The mechanism of meaning is thus present in the social act before the emergence of consciousness or awareness of meaning occurs. The act or adjustive response of the second organism gives to the gesture of the first organism the meaning which it has.

Symbolization constitutes objects not constituted before, objects which would not exist except for the context of social relationships wherein symbolization occurs. Language does not simply symbolize a situation or object which is already there in advance; it makes possible the existence or the appearance of that situation or object, for it is a part of the mechanism whereby that situation or object is created. The social process relates the responses of one individual to the gestures of another, as the meanings of the latter, and is thus responsible for the rise and existence of new objects in the social situation, objects dependent upon or constituted by these meanings. Meaning is thus not to be conceived, fundamentally, as a state of consciousness, or as a set of organized relations existing or subsisting mentally outside the field of experience into which they enter; on the contrary, it should be conceived objectively, as having its existence entirely within this field itself.[2] The response of one organism to the gesture of another in any given social act is the meaning of that gesture, and also is in a sense responsible for the appearance or coming into being of the new object— or new content of an old object—to which that gesture refers through the outcome of the given social act in which it is an early phase. For, to repeat, objects are in a genuine sense constituted within the social process of experience, by the communication and mutual adjustment of behavior among the individual organisms which are involved in that process and which carry it on. Just as in fencing the parry is an interpretation of the thrust, so, in the social act, the adjustive response of one organism to the gesture of another is the interpretation of that gesture by that organism—it is the meaning of that gesture.

At the level of self-consciousness such a gesture becomes a symbol, a significant symbol. But the interpretation of gestures is not, basically, a process going on in a mind as such, or one necessarily involving a mind; it is an external, overt, physical, or physiological process going on in the actual field of social experience. Meaning can be described, accounted for, or stated in terms of symbols or

language at its highest and most complex stage of development (the stage it reaches in human experience), but language simply lifts out of the social process a situation which is logically or implicitly there already. The language symbol is simply a significant or conscious gesture.

Two main points are being made here: (1) that the social process, through the communication which it makes possible among the individuals implicated in it, is responsible for the appearance of a whole set of new objects in nature, which exist in relation to it (objects, namely, of "common sense"); and (2) that the gesture of one organism and the adjustive response of another organism to that gesture within any given social act bring out the relationship that exists between the gesture as the beginning of the given act and the completion or resultant of the given act, to which the gesture refers. These are the two basic and complementary logical aspects of the social process.

The result of any given social act is definitely separated from the gesture indicating it by the response of another organism to that gesture, a response which points to the result of that act as indicated by that gesture. This situation is all there—is completely given—on the non-mental, non-conscious level, before the analysis of it on the mental or conscious level. Dewey says that meaning arises through communication.[3] It is to the content to which the social process gives rise that this statement refers; not to bare ideas or printed words as such, but to the social process which has been so largely responsible for the objects constituting the daily environment in which we live: a process in which communication plays the main part. That process can give rise to these new objects in nature only in so far as it makes possible communication among the individual organisms involved in it. And the sense in which it is responsible for their existence— indeed for the existence of the whole world of common-sense objects—is the sense in which it determines, conditions, and makes possible their abstraction from the total structure of events, as identities which are relevant for everyday social behavior; and in that sense, or as having that meaning, they are existent only relative to that behavior. In the same way, at a later, more advanced stage of its development, communication is responsible for the existence of the whole realm of scientific objects as well as identities abstracted from the total structure of events by virtue of their relevance for scientific purposes.

The logical structure of meaning, we have seen, is to be found in the threefold relationship of gesture to adjustive response and to the resultant of the given social act. Response on the part of the second organism to the gesture of the first is the interpretation—and brings out the meaning—of that gesture, as indicating the resultant of the social act which it initiates, and in which both organisms are thus involved. This threefold or triadic relation between gesture, adjustive response, and resultant of the social act which the gesture initiates is the basis of meaning; for the existence of meaning depends upon the fact that the adjustive response of the second organism is directed toward the resultant of the given social act as initiated and indicated by the gesture of the first organism. The basis of meaning is thus objectively there in social conduct, or in nature in its relation to such conduct. Meaning is a content of an object which is dependent upon the relation of an organism or group of organisms to it. It is not essentially or primarily a psychical content (a content of mind or consciousness), for it need not be conscious at all, and is not in fact until significant symbols are evolved in the process of human social experience. Only when it becomes identified with such symbols does meaning become conscious. The meaning of a gesture on the part of one organism is the adjustive response of another organism to it, as indicating the resultant of the social act it initiates, the adjustive response of the second organism being itself directed toward or related to the completion of that act. In other words, meaning involves a reference of the gesture of one organism to the resultant of the social act it indicates or initiates, as adjustively responded to in this reference by another organism; and the adjustive

response of the other organism is the meaning of the gesture.

Gestures may be either conscious (significant) or unconscious (non-significant). The conversation of gestures is not significant below the human level, because it is not conscious, that is, not *self*-conscious (though it is conscious in the sense of involving feelings or sensations). An animal as opposed to a human form, in indicating something to, or bringing out a meaning for, another form, is not at the same time indicating or bringing out the same thing or meaning to or for himself; for he has no mind, no thought, and hence there is no meaning here in the significant or self-conscious sense. A gesture is not significant when the response of another organism to it does not indicate to the organism making it what the other organism is responding to.[4]

Much subtlety has been wasted on the problem of the meaning of meaning. It is not necessary, in attempting to solve this problem, to have recourse to psychical states, for the nature of meaning, as we have seen, is found to be implicit in the structure of the social act, implicit in the relations among its three basic individual components: namely, in the triadic relation of a gesture of one individual, a response to that gesture by a second individual, and completion of the given social act initiated by the gesture of the first individual. And the fact that the nature of meaning is thus found to be implicit in the structure of the social act provides additional emphasis upon the necessity, in social psychology, of starting off with the initial assumption of an ongoing social process of experience and behavior in which any given group of human individuals is involved, and upon which the existence and development of their minds, selves, and self-consciousness depend.

### Notes

1. [See also "Social Consciousness and the Consciousness of Meaning," *Psychological Bulletin,* VII (1910) SW 123–134; 397 ff.; "The Mechanism of Social Consciousness," *Journal of Philosophy,* IX (1912), SW 134–141 401 ff.]

2. Nature has meaning and implication but not indication by symbols. The symbol is distinguishable from the meaning it refers to. Meanings are in nature, but symbols are the heritage of man (1924).
3. [See John Dewey, *Experience and Nature*, chap. v.]
4. There are two characters which belong to that which we term "meanings," one is participation and the other is communicability. Meaning can arise only in so far as some phase of the act which the individual is arousing in the other can be aroused in himself. There is always to this extent participation. And the result of this participation is communicability, i.e., the individual can indicate to himself what he indicates to others. There is communication without significance where the gesture of the individual calls out the response in the other without calling out or tending to call out the same response in the individual himself. Significance from the standpoint of the observer may be said to be present in the gesture which calls out the appropriate response in the other or others within a co-operative act, but it does not become significant to the individuals who are involved in the act unless the tendency to the act is aroused within the individual who makes it, and unless the individual who is directly affected by the gesture puts himself in the attitude of the individual who makes the gesture (MS).

# The Nature of Reflective Intelligence

In the type of temporary inhibition of action which signifies thinking, or in which reflection arises, we have presented in the experience of the individual, tentatively and in advance and for his selection among them, the different possibilities or alternatives of future action open to him within the given social situation—the different or alternative ways of completing the given social act wherein he is implicated, or which he has already initiated. Reflection or reflective behavior arises only under the conditions of self-consciousness, and makes possible the purposive control and organization by the individual organism of its conduct, with reference to its social and physical environment, i.e., with reference to the various social and physical situations in which it becomes involved and to which it reacts. The organization of the self is simply the organization, by the individual organism, of the set of attitudes toward its social environment—and toward itself from the standpoint of that environment, or as a functioning element in the process of social experience and behavior constituting that environment—which it is able to take. It is essential that such reflective intelligence be dealt with from the point of view of social behaviorism.

I said a moment ago that there is something involved in our statement of the meaning of an object which is more than the mere response, however complex that may be. We may respond to a musical phrase and there may be nothing in the experience beyond the response; we may not be able to say why we respond or what it is we respond to. Our attitude may simply be that we like some music and do not like other music. Most of our recognitions are of this sort. We pick out the book we want but could not say what the character of the book is. We probably could give a more detailed account of the countenance of a man we meet for the first time than of our most intimate friends. With our friends we are ready to start our conversation the moment they are there; we do not have to make sure who they are. But if we try to pick out a man who has been described to us we narrowly examine the person to make sure he answers to the account that is given to us. With a person with whom we are

From *Mind, Self, and Society from the Standpoint of a Social Behaviorist*, Ed. Charles W. Morris, (Chicago: Univ. of Chicago Press, 1934). pp. 90–100.

familiar we carry on our conversation without thinking of these things. Most of our processes of recognition do not involve this identification of the characters which enable us to identify the objects. We may have to describe a person and we find we cannot do it—we know him too well. We may have to pick those details out, and then if we are taking a critical attitude we have to find out what it is in the object that calls out this complex response. When we are doing that we are getting a statement of what the nature of the object is, or if you like, its meaning. We have to indicate to ourselves what it is that calls out this particular response. We recognize a person, say, because of the character of his physique. If one should come into the room greatly changed by a long attack of sickness, or by exposure to the tropical sun, one's friends would not be able to recognize him immediately. There are certain elements which enable us to recognize a friend. We may have to pick out the characters which make recognition successful, to indicate those characters to somebody or to ourselves. We may have to determine what the stimuli are that call out a response of this complex character. That is often a very difficult thing to do, as is evidenced by musical criticism. A whole audience may be swept away by a composition and perhaps not a person there will be able to state what it is in the production that calls out this particular response, or to tell what the various reactions are in these individuals. It is an unusual gift which can analyze that sort of an object and pick out what the stimulus is for so complex an action.

What I want to call attention to is the process by which there is an indication of those characters which do call out the response. Animals of a type lower than man respond to certain characters with a nicety that is beyond human capacity, such as odor in the case of a dog. But it would be beyond the capacity of a dog to indicate to another dog what the odor was. Another dog could not be sent out by the first dog to pick out this odor. A man may tell how to identify another man. He can indicate what the characters are that will bring about a certain response. That ability absolutely distin-

guishes the intelligence of such a reflective being as man from that of the lower animals, however intelligent they may be. We generally say that man is a rational animal and lower animals are not. What I wanted to show, at least in terms of behavioristic psychology, is that what we have in mind in this distinction is the indication of those characters which lead to the sort of response which we give to an object. Pointing out the characters which lead to the response is precisely that which distinguishes a detective office that sends out a man, from a bloodhound which runs down a man. Here are two types of intelligence, each one specialized; the detective could not do what the bloodhound does and the bloodhound could not do what the detective does. Now, the intelligence of the detective over against the intelligence of the bloodhound lies in this capacity to indicate what the particular characters are which will call out his response of taking the man.[1]

Such would be a behaviorist's account of what is involved in reason. When you are reasoning you are indicating to yourself the characters that call out certain responses—and that is all you are doing. If you have the angle and a side you can determine the area of a triangle; given certain characters there are certain responses indicated. There are other processes, not exactly rational, out of which you can build up new responses from old ones. You may pick out responses which are there in other reactions and put them together. A book of directions may provide a set of stimuli which lead to a certain set of responses, and you pick them out of your other complex responses, perhaps as they have not been picked out before. When you write on a typewriter you may be instructed as to the way in which to use it. You can build up a fairly good technique to start with, but even that is a process which still involves the indication of the stimuli to call out the various responses. You unite stimuli which have not been united in the past, and then these stimuli take with them the compound responses. It may be a crude response at first, and must be freed from the responses had in the past. The way in which you react toward the doubling of letters when you write is different from the way you react in writing the letters on a typewriter. You make mistakes because the responses you utilize have been different, have been connected with a whole set of other responses. A drawing teacher will sometimes have pupils draw with the left hand rather than the right, because the habits of the right hand are very difficult to get rid of. This is what you are doing when you act in a rational fashion: you are indicating to yourself what the stimuli are that will call out a complex response, and by the order of the stimuli you are determining what the whole of the response will be. Now, to be able to indicate those stimuli to other persons or to yourself is what we call rational conduct as distinct from the unreasoning intelligence of the lower animals, and from a good deal of our own conduct.

Man is distinguished by that power of analysis of the field of stimulation which enables him to pick out one stimulus rather than another and so to hold on to the response that belongs to that stimulus, picking it out from others, and recombining it with others. You cannot get a lock to work. You notice certain elements, each of which brings out a certain sort of response; and what you are doing is holding on to these processes of response by giving attention to the stimuli. Man can combine not only the responses already there, which is the thing an animal lower than man can do, but the human individual can get into his activities and break them up, giving attention to specific elements, holding the responses that answer to these particular stimuli, and then combining them to build up another act. That is what we mean by learning or by teaching a person to do a thing. You indicate to him certain specific phases or characters of the object which call out certain sorts of responses. We state that generally by saying consciousness accompanies only the sensory process and not the motor process. We can directly control the sensory but not the motor processes; we can give our attention to a particular element in the field and by giving such attention and so holding on to the stimulus we can get control of the response. That is the way we get control of our action; we do not directly control our response through the motor paths themselves.

There is no capacity in the lower forms to give attention to some analyzed element in the field of stimulation which would enable them to control the response. But one can say to a person "Look at this, just see this thing" and he can fasten his attention on the specific object. He can direct attention and so isolate the particular response that answers to it. That is the way in which we break up our complex activities and thereby make learning possible. What takes place is an analysis of the process by giving attention to the specific stimuli that call out a particular act, and this analysis makes possible a reconstruction of the act. An animal makes combinations, as we say, only by trial and error, and the combination that is successful simply maintains itself.

The gesture as worked out in the conduct of the human group serves definitely to indicate just these elements and thus to bring them within the field of voluntary attention. There is, of course, a fundamental likeness between voluntary attention and involuntary attention. A bright light, a peculiar odor, may be something which takes complete control of the organism and in so far inhibits other activity. A voluntary action, however, is dependent upon the indication of a certain character, pointing it out, holding on to it, and so holding on to the response that belongs to it. That sort of an analysis is essential to what we call human intelligence, and it is made possible by language.

The psychology of attention ousted the psychology of association. An indefinite number of associations were found which lie in our experience with reference to anything that comes before us, but associational psychology never explained why one association rather than another was the dominant one. It laid down rules that if a certain association had been intense, recent, and frequent it would be dominant, but often there are in fact situations in which what seems to be the weakest element in the situation occupies the mind. It was not until the psychologist took up the analysis of attention that he was able to deal with such situations, and to realize that voluntary attention is dependent upon indication of some character in the field of stimulation. Such indication makes possible the isolation and recombination of responses.

In the case of the vocal gesture there is a tendency to call out the response in one form that is called out in the other, so that the child plays the part of parent, of teacher, or preacher. The gesture under those conditions calls out certain responses in the individual which it calls out in the other person, and carrying it out in the individual isolates that particular character of the stimulus. The response of the other is there in the individual isolating the stimulus. If one calls out quickly to a person in danger, he himself is in the attitude of jumping away, though the act is not performed. He is not in danger, but he has those particular elements of the response in himself, and we speak of them as meanings. Stated in terms of the central nervous system, this means that he has stirred up its upper tracts which would lead to the actual jumping away. A person picks out the different responses involved in escape when he enters the theater and notices the signs on the program cautioning him to choose the nearest exit in case of fire. He has all the different responses, so to speak, listed before him, and he prepares what he is going to do by picking out the different elements and putting them together in the way required. The efficiency engineer comes in to pick out this, that, or the other thing, and chooses the order in which they should be carried out. One is doing the same himself in so far as he is self-conscious. Where we have to determine what will be the order of a set of responses, we are putting them together in a certain fashion, and we can do this because we can indicate the order of the stimuli which are going to act upon us. That is what is involved in the human intelligence as distinguished from the intelligence type of the lower forms. We cannot tell an elephant that he is to take hold of the other elephant's tail; the stimulus will not indicate the same thing to the elephant as to ourselves. We can create a situation which is a stimulus to the elephant but we cannot get the elephant to indicate to itself what

this stimulus is so that he has the response to it in his own system.

The gesture provides a process by means of which one does arouse in himself the reaction that might be aroused in another, and this is not a part of his immediate reaction in so far as his immediate physical environment is concerned. When we tell a person to do something the response we have is not the doing of the actual thing, but the beginning of it. Communication gives to us those elements of response which can be held in the mental field. We do not carry them out, but they are there constituting the meanings of these objects which we indicate. Language is a process of indicating certain stimuli and changing the response to them in the system of behavior. Language as a social process has made it possible for us to pick out responses and hold them in the organism of the individual, so that they are there in relation to that which we indicate. The actual gesture is, within limits, arbitrary. Whether one points with his finger, or points with the glance of the eye, or motion of the head, or the attitude of the body, or by means of a vocal gesture in one language or another, is indifferent, provided it does call out the response that belongs to that thing which is indicated. That is the essential part of language. The gesture must be one that calls out the response in the individual, or tends to call out the response in the individual, which its utilization will bring out in another's response. Such is the material with which the mind works. However slight, there must be some sort of gesture. To have the response isolated without an indication of a stimulus is almost a contradiction in terms. I have been trying to point out what this process of communication does in the way of providing us with the material that exists in our mind. It does this by furnishing those gestures which in affecting us as they affect others call out the attitude which the other takes, and that we take in so far as we assume his rôle. We get the attitude, the meaning, within the field of our own control, and that control consists in combining all these various possible responses to furnish the newly constructed act demanded by the problem. In such a way we can state rational conduct in terms of a behavioristic psychology.

I wish to add one further factor to our account: the relation of the temporal character of the nervous system to foresight and choice.

The central nervous system makes possible the implicit initiation of a number of possible alternative responses with reference to any given object or objects for the completion of any already initiated act, in advance of the actual completion of that act; and thus makes possible the exercise of intelligent or reflective choice in the acceptance of that one among these possible alternative responses which is to be carried into overt effect.[2]

Human intelligence, by means of the physiological mechanism of the human central nervous system, deliberately selects one from among the several alternative responses which are possible in the given problematic environmental situation; and if the given response which it selects is complex—i.e., is a set or chain or group or succession of simple responses—it can organize this set or chain of simple responses in such a way as to make possible the most adequate and harmonious solution by the individual of the given environmental problem.

It is the entrance of the alternative possibilities of future response into the determination of present conduct in any given environmental situation, and their operation, through the mechanism of the central nervous system, as part of the factors or conditions determining present behavior, which decisively contrasts intelligent conduct or behavior with reflex, instinctive, and habitual conduct or behavior—delayed reaction with immediate reaction. That which takes place in present organic behavior is always in some sense an emergent from the past, and never could have been precisely predicted in advance—never could have been predicted on the basis of a knowledge, however complete, of the past, and of the conditions in the past which are relevant to its emergence; and in the case of organic behavior which is intelligently controlled, this element of spontaneity is especially prominent by virtue of the present influence exercised over such behavior by the possible future results or consequences which it may have. Our ideas of or about future conduct are our tendencies to act in several alternative ways in the presence of a given environmental situation—tendencies or attitudes which can appear, or be implicitly aroused, in the structure of the central nervous system in advance of the overt response or reaction to that situation, and which thus can enter as determining factors into the control or selection of this overt response. Ideas, as distinct from acts, or as failing to issue in overt behavior, are simply what we do not do; they are possibilities of overt responses which we test out implicitly in the central nervous system and then reject in favor of those which we do in fact act upon or carry into effect. The process of intelligent conduct is essentially a process of selection from among various alternatives; intelligence is largely a matter of selectivity.

Delayed reaction is necessary to intelligent conduct. The organization, implicit testing, and final selection by the individual of his overt responses or reactions to the social situations which confront him and which present him with problems of adjustment, would be impossible if his overt responses or reactions could not in such situations be delayed until this process of organizing, implicitly testing, and finally selecting is carried out; that is, would be impossible if some overt response or other to the given environmental stimuli had to be immediate. Without delayed reaction, or except in terms of it, no conscious or intelligent control over behavior could be exercised; for it is through this process of selective reaction—which can be selective only because it is delayed—that intelligence operates in the determination of behavior. Indeed, it is this process which constitutes intelligence. The central nervous system provides not only the necessary physiological mechanism for this process, but also the necessary physiological condition of delayed reaction which this process presupposes. Intelligence is essentially the ability to solve the problems of present behavior in terms of its possible future consequences as implicated on the basis of past experience—the ability, that is, to solve the problems of present behavior in the light of, or by reference to, both the past and the future; it involves both memory and foresight. And the process of exercising intelligence is the process of delaying, organizing, and selecting a response or reaction to the stimuli of the given environmental situation. The process is made possible by the mechanism of the central nervous system, which permits the individual's taking of the attitude of the other toward himself, and thus becoming an object to himself. This is the most effective means of adjustment to the social environment, and indeed to the environment in general, that the individual has at his disposal.

An attitude of any sort represents the beginning, or potential initiation, of some composite act or other, a social act in which, along with other individuals, the individual taking the given attitude is involved or implicated. The traditional supposition has been that the purposive element in behavior must ultimately be an idea, a conscious motive, and hence must imply or depend upon the presence of a mind. But the study of the nature of the central nervous system shows that in the form of physio-logical attitudes (expressed in specific physio-logical sets) different possible completions to the given act are there in advance of its actual completion, and that through them the earlier parts of the given act are affected or influenced (in present conduct) by its later phases; so that the purposive element in behavior has a physi-ological seat, a behavioristic basis, and is not fundamentally nor necessarily conscious or psychical.

## Notes

1. Intelligence and knowledge are inside the process of conduct. Thinking is an elaborate process of. . . . presenting the world so that it will be favorable for conduct, so that the ends of the life of the form may be reached (MS).

   Thinking is pointing out—to think about a thing is to point it out before acting (1924).
2. It is an advantage to have these responses ready before we get to the object. If our world were right on top of us, in contact with us, we would have no time for deliberation. There would be only one way of responding to that world.

   Through his distance organs and his capacity for delayed responses the individual lives in the future with the possibility of planning his life with reference to that future (1931).

# The Nature of Scientific Knowledge

We have reached certain points in the implications of the method of experimental science which may be summarily restated. In the first place, the scientist's knowing is a search for the unknown, a discovery, but it is a search for what has disappeared in the conflicts of conduct, that is, for objects which will remove the antagonism—it is a search for the solution of a problem. This dissipates the Platonic puzzle of how we can seek to know what is unknown. It is interesting to note that Plato's solution of the puzzle is found in the form of ignorance as a problem, that of recollecting what has been forgotten. Unfortunately this theory could not apply to the discovery of new types of objects which were foreign to the world of past experience.

In the second place, experimental science implies a real world uninfected by the problem, which can be used to test the discoveries

From *The Philosophy of the Act,* Ed. Charles W. Morris, et al., (Chicago: Univ. of Chicago Press, 1938), pp. 45–62.

which science makes. If knowledge is discovery of the unknown, this world is not known—it is simply there.

In the third place, as the world that is there is not known and may not therefore as non-known have ascribed to it the sort of logical necessity that does obtain in the logical structure of hypotheses, experimental science finds nothing contradictory in the later appearance of a problem in any portion of the world which has been used to test the solution of a former problem. That a contradiction should appear in the hypothesis is proof of its faulty and, in that sense, unreal, character, but that the sun ceases to be an object revolving about the earth in no way invalidates the world by which we test the hypothesis of the revolution of the earth on its axis by the shifting of the path of the pendulum's swing. Logical necessity obtains in the field of reflective thinking. To transfer it to the world that is there, and within which thought is occupied in the solution of problems, would be to dismiss experimental science as a meaningless and pernicious discipline and to return to the science of dogma.

In the fourth place, in observation and in experiment, science finds a field that belongs both to the world that is there and to the reflective thought of discovery, that is, of knowledge. The problem does not exist *in vacuo*. It is in the world that is there, but a certain portion of the world that is there has disappeared. The disease that is conveyed by contact disappears in the evidence of sporadic cases, notwithstanding its epidemic character. But the scourge is all the more tragically there. The instances of the disease are now observed and recorded by physicians and health officers who are seeking to discover the mechanism of the spread of the infection. These data embodied in various hypotheses exist in the minds of the investigators. As the observations of competent investigators of the actual epidemic, they are there as parts of the experiences of these individuals, and the records of them are parts of their biographies. The test case of the heroic scientist, who has remained immune to the fever after wearing the clothes of those who were sick of it and sleeping in their beds, who succumbs to it when stung by the mosquito, begins in the field of scientific data and personal biographies and ends in the impersonal world to which belongs the two-chaptered history of the yellow-fever parasite. In so far as these data are imbedded in the lives of these individuals, they are personal but hard facts. So long as they are tentatively suggestive of objects that would harmonize conflicting ways of cataloguing and treating the disease, they are in the minds of men as part of the structure of their ideas.

We must distinguish here between what belongs to the experience of the individual qua individual and what is in his mind and may be termed "subjective." In the former sense the observation may be called private because the investigator alone observes it. Indeed it may be such an instance that he alone can observe it, if, for example, it is his own ache or pain, or if no one else has seen it, and it is an instance that is not repeated. This circumstance does not abstract it from the world that is there, since these men are there in that world together with the events that take place in their lives. But, in so far as the experience suggests what is known of the relation of the mosquito to malaria and a possible parasitic organism that may be the cause of yellow fever, we are in the presence of an idea and of what we will call "subjective." Such an object is not as yet there and may never be there. It is an ideal object. Such objects, as before remarked, have the same locus as erroneous objects after the error has been detected and are not to be confused, because they are placed in individuals' minds, with individuals' experiences, which are peculiar to them, but are objects in the world that is there. I am not, of course, ignoring the problems involved in this distinction. I am for the time being merely insisting that experimental science never takes the position so common in philosophy, which confuses the two. To the experimental scientist the data of observation and experiment never lose the actuality of the unquestioned world because they can happen for the time being only in the lives of particular individuals, or because they are fitted to serve in the mental processes of discovery. They are solid realities that can bridge the gaps between discredited theories and the discoveries of science.

It is the position of the positivist that what is observed is, as a fact of experience, there in a sense in which it never can be false. He recognizes that there may be false inferences drawn from the observation or the experiment, but as a fact of immediate experience it simply is and therefore is not open to possible question. This assumption does not answer to the procedure of science, for whatever may be the theory of sensation, the scientist's observation always carries a content or character in what is observed that may conceivably be shown under other conditions to be erroneous, though the probability of this be very slight. In psychological terms, an observation is never a mere determination of a sensation (if there is any such thing in adult experience) but is a perception, and, whether all perceptions involve judgments or not, they are frequently illusory, as, for example, in the perceptions of mirrored objects, and can never be free from the possibility of analogous errors.

What gives to the observation or experiment its validity is its position in the world that is there, that is not questioned. It is indeed carefully isolated from what has fallen into question, and this meticulous cleansing from all implications of the abandoned doctrine, and all as yet hypothetical interpretations, creates the impression of an experience which may not be subjected to any further question; but, as we know, there is no part or portion of the world that may not conceivably be the field of a scientific problem.

In the so-called exact sciences we seem to approach an object which is nearly free from all possibility of contingency—the physical particles. These particles are approximations to that which is unextended in space and time, but they carry a character—that of mass or of electrical energy—which does not approach zero, however minute it may become, and it is a character which is reached from numberless observations and not a little speculative theory. Furthermore, the procedures in our laboratories and observatories by which these

characters are reached involve perceptual objects of the most complex nature, subject under other conditions to all sorts of conceivable questions. In other words, while the methods of mathematical analysis and extensive abstraction constitute a body of doctrines which in themselves are necessary, as long as the terms carry the same references, their applications are dependent upon their functioning within the problematic situations which arise in research science and appeal for their validity in practice to the court of observation and experiment.

The scientist's attitude is that of a man in a going concern which requires at various points readjustments and reconstructions. The success of the readjustments and reconstructions is found in the triumph over the difficulty, as evidenced by the fact that the concern continues to operate. He finds his tests in the parts of the whole which still operate. This does not imply that readjustments may not be called for later at these very points to which he now appeals for confirmation of the success of his solutions of the immediate problems before him. Surrounding the most profound analysis of the structure of matter, and the widest survey of the galaxies of the heavens, lies the field of things within which experiment and observation take place without question, and which gives its validity to cosmologies and electronic theories of matter. It may seem a misnomer to speak of the world within which lie the observation and experiment as surrounding such hypothetical constructions as the electrical theory of matter, or the galactic form of the universe, since these hypothetical constructions so far transcend, in the subatomic world or in the indefinite stretches of the heavens, all the world of objects which includes our observations and experiments. We seem rather to be islanded in a very minute region occupied by perceptual objects that are in their constitution vague, indeterminate, and incurably contingent, surrounded from within and from without by a universe, which science presents, that is occupied by objects that approximate exactness of definition and necessity in their forms and changes. And yet the scientist, when he times microscopic oil drops as they move toward or away from charged plates, or when he measures the distances of photographed stars from one another before and during an eclipse, has not at all the attitude of a man perched insecurely upon obscure and adventitious data. The world that is there has taken up into itself all the order, definition, and necessity of earlier scientific advance. It is not there as hypothesis, in so far as the hypotheses have justified themselves in experiment, nor is it there as analyzed relations, events, and particles. These characters have passed into things, and for the time being at any rate, they are there unanalyzed, with the same authority as that of the so-called sensible experience. It is only necessary to emphasize again the distinction of the data as parts of the mental process of anticipating hypothetical objects, and as imbedded in the world of unquestioned reality in the experience of the individuals to whom the problem has come and who are trying to solve it, as well as in the impersonal world within which these individuals exist.

What renders such a statement of the world (not as known but as there) somewhat bizarre is that we enter the world of the scientist by the process of learning. In schools and institutions of higher learning we are taught the doctrines of modern science. Most of us take no part in the work of discovering what is there found out, but we acquire it by a process of learning, in which we may retrace some of the steps which research has followed, while in the main we accept it largely on faith in the men and their methods, especially faith in the checking-up of the results of certain individuals by all the others in the field. Scientific journalism as well as the daily press keeps us informed of the latest advances, and, having learned these facts, we say that we now know them. The world that stretches so far beyond our experience seems in this sense a world of knowledge.

It is true that all acquirement of information, in so far as it is more than a mere parrot-like facility in repeating what is read or heard, is a reflective process in which a problematic situation is met with discovery, though the hypotheses and their tests are those of others. Our own hypotheses and tests have to do largely with the competence of the sources upon which we draw. Admitting, however, all the criticism that the layman can bring to his education, this world of knowledge is evidently of quite a different character from the world that is there, the world that is seen and felt, whose reality is the touchstone of our discoveries and inventions, and very different from the discoveries and inventions themselves, which are the knowledge par excellence of research science.

It is in the acquirement of information that the copy theory finds its explanation. There, what is known must answer feature for feature to its prototype. This field of so-called knowledge is that of the assimilation of the experience of others to one's own experience. There may be involved in it the discovery of these other experiences by the individual, and it is in so far knowledge, but the content of that which is said to be learned is not discovered in the sense in which the other has discovered it.

In its simplest form what takes place here is the indication to one individual by another of an object which is of moment in their co-operative activity. This gesture becomes symbolic when it arouses in the individuals the attitudes which reaction to the objects involves, together, generally, with some imagery of the result of that action. It becomes communication when the individual indicating the object takes also the attitude of the individual to whom he is indicating it plus that of his response, while the individual to whom the object is indicated takes the attitude of him who is indicating it. We call this taking of one anothers' attitudes consciousness of what we are doing and of what the other is doing, and we incorrectly apply the term "knowledge" to this. The mechanism and import of this social procedure will be discussed later. What I wish to point out at present is that this process in itself does not involve discovery, any more than does that of perception. When doubt and discrepancies arise in the process of communication, as they continually do arise, the necessity of establishing agreement between the symbols mutually used, and that which they symbolize and the results of the conduct they imply, calls for a one to one correspondence between the symbols and those things and characters symbolized in the experiences of the different individuals, and this gives rise to the theory of knowledge as an agreement between the state of mind and that which is known. Such a determination of mutual agreement in co-operative conduct is indeed essential not only to this conduct but to what is called "thinking" in the individual, but it is not a discovery of that which needs to be known. It is at most a part of the technique by which the discovery is made. When the discrepancy arises, we must discover what the import of the symbols is, and here real knowledge takes place. We find out what the other person is referring to—in common parlance, what he means—but the process can go on without discrepancies. The other indicates to us what is there, and our so-called consciousness of this need not introduce any reflective attitude in our conduct. To call the correspondence between the attitudes involved in pointing out a savage dog and the conduct which takes place "knowledge," whether one points it out to one's self or to another, is to give to "knowledge" an entirely different value from that involved in discovery.

In any education that is worthy of the name, what is acquired does go toward the solution of the problems that we all carry with us, and is the subject of reflection, and leads to the fashioning of new hypotheses and the appearance of new objects; but this takes place after the communication which is the mutual indication of objects and characters by the use of gestures which are common symbols, that is, symbols with identical references. The correspondence theory of knowledge has grown up around the recognition of the relation between that which the symbol refers to in the object and the attitudes of response in others and in ourselves. There is here a one to one correspondence, but the relation of these objects and their characters to what we can infer from them in the discovery of the novel

element which meets our problematic situations is of an entirely different sort.

In this "meeting of minds" which takes place in conversation, learning, reading, and thinking, there are generally present problematic situations and discovery, though this is by no means always the case. If someone informs us that an expected acquaintance has arrived, there is no more of a problem, or discovery in the sense of a solution, than would be involved in the friend's appearing around the corner. The varied landscape and hurry of events that sweep us along in books of travel and adventure embrace no more of reflection than the travel and adventure in which we are involved. A great deal of learning is a direct following of indications, or a gradual taking-over of the form and technique of others that goes on without inference. A good deal of thinking even, notably much of reverie and also straight-away ordering of conduct in an unquestioned situation, may be free from dubitation and ratiocination. A field of concentrated inferential thought does include the common reference of symbols in conversation, writing, and thinking—in other words, that part of logic which has to do with the technique of communication either with others or with one's self—together with the epistemologies and metaphysics which have sprung from this and obscured it with their tangled and forest growth. Here lie the problems of successful reference to identical objects and characters through identical symbols mutually employed by different selves, and these problems are of peculiar interest and importance to those involved in the exact and mathematical sciences. These problems demand theories of definition and implication, in so far as this does not depend upon the concrete content of that to which reference is made.

The environment of living organisms is constantly changing, is constantly invaded with other and different things. The assimilation of what occurs and that which recurs with what is elapsing and what has elapsed is called "experience." Without anticipating a later discussion of the social nature of the self and of thinking, I shall claim that the analysis of experimental science, including experimental psychology, never operates in a mind or an experience that is not social, and by the term "social" I imply that in the thought of the scientist the supposition of his mind and his self always involves other minds and selves as presuppositions and as standing upon the same level of existence and evidence. It may be that the scientist, in a self-centered moment, might think away all else but his self and its thinking, but even if in imagination he succeeded in annihilating all save the dot on the *i*, its having any thoughts at all would depend entirely upon its preserving its previous habits of conversing with others and so with himself; and, as this precious hoard of past experience wore away under incessant use and decay, the dot would follow the *i* into nonentity. The dividend that I wish to see declared on this social nature of mind and the self is the equal immediacy that may attach to the assimilation of others' experience with that of our own. We so inevitably utilize the attitude of the other, which is involved in addressing ourselves and in attending to him, that we give the same logical validity to what he relates of his experience as that which we give to what we relate to ourselves of our own past experience, unless on other grounds we are occupying the seat of the critic. It has, of course, only the validity that attaches to a relation, and is one remove from the assurance that attaches to the so-called memory image. But this validity at this remove is all that we can claim for most of our memory. Memory images constitute but a minute part of the past that stretches out behind us. For most of it we depend upon records, which come back to one form or another of language, and we refresh our memory as really in inquiring of a companion what took place on a certain occasion as in questioning ourselves. His testimony may not be as trustworthy as our own because of difference of interest and possible prejudice, but on other occasions for the same reason his testimony may outrank our own in reliability. While the actual image of the event has an evidential character that is peculiar, not infrequently it may be shown by the testimony of others to

have been the product of imagination or to have been shifted from its proper place in the record. But still more fundamentally, the building-up of a memory record involves, in the first place, a social world as definitely as the physical world, within which the events took place, and involves, in the second place, experience which was actually or potentially social in its nature to the extent that whatever happens or has happened to us has its character over against actual or possible audiences or observers whose selves are essential to the existence of our own selves, the mechanism of whose conversation is not only as immediate as our replies but, when imported into the inner forum, constitutes the mechanism of our own thought.

I am anticipating the detailed presentation of this doctrine of mind to make clear my distinction between information and knowledge as discovery through inference. Information is the experience arising from the direction of attention through the gestures of others to objects and their characters, and cannot be called "knowledge" if that term is denied to perception as immediate experience under the direction of the attention springing from the organic interest of the individual. Perception is not itself to be distinguished from information, in so far as one uses a social mechanism in pointing out objects and characters to himself as another. The perceptions of a self may be already in the form of information. Logically stated they exist in a universe of discourse. Knowledge, on the other hand, deliberately fashions hypothetical objects whose reality it tests by observation and experiment. The justification for this is found in the actual disappearance of objects and their characters in the problems that arise in conduct.

Actually so much both of perception and of information is shot through with reflective construction and reconstruction that it is difficult to disentangle them from each other. It is, however, a part of scientific technique to accomplish this disentanglement. Observations and experiments are always in the form of information, even while they are being made, but they are scrupulously teased out from the web of inference and hypothesis. From this purity depart in varying degrees our perceptions as well as our information. It is a commonplace that one may be very well informed and do very little thinking, indeed be quite helpless over against a situation in which the information must be used to suggest or test hypotheses. The reliability itself of the observation or information, however, does call for a certain sort of verification, that of its repetition, either in the experience of the individual or in the mouths of other witnesses, and here, as above remarked, we find the source of the copy or correspondence theories of knowledge. Indeed, if information is knowledge, the copy theory of knowledge is entirely legitimate.

In presenting the world that is there as in some sense surrounding what is problematic, it was stated that what had in the past been approved by experiment and observation was taken up into this world and resided there as organized objects, things behaving toward one another in expected manners. Over against these unquestioned things lie the elements and relations of the working hypotheses of science. These are in a peculiar degree the objects of our knowledge. They are still lacking in complete verification. They are received only provisionally, and the objects which we constitute by means of them are complex hypotheses anticipating further tests in the use which we make of them. While they work, they pass as objects, but always with a proviso attached, which keeps the scientist's attention alive to possible departures from the result which the hypothesis implies. He is looking for such departures and eager to find them. In such far-reaching speculations as those regarding the structure of matter this field of knowledge is enormously extended, though it does not actually include the world within which the observation and experiment themselves take place, though the analysis which the investigation involves extends into the world of unquestioned things. For the purposes of our calculations we state the apparatus of our laboratories, for example, in the same terms which we use in our hypothetical constructions and thus seem to bring them within the scope of the investigation. But

the scientist is in no doubt in regard to the distinction between the finding of fact and the hypothetical form in which he has stated things which are there, irrespective of the validity of the expressions into which they have been translated. Such translations may be perhaps called "objects of knowledge," though with the recognition that the success or failure of the hypothesis, into the terms of which we have translated these unquestioned things and their processes, does not affect their reality in the observation or experiment. In this sense there is no limit to the field of knowledge, for we may state the whole universe in terms of such working hypotheses, if we only remember the limits of this formulation. But it is also necessary to recognize that the *raison d'être* for translation is found in the function of the apparatus of experimental science and not in the revelation of reality. What reveals this latter fact is the ineradicable difference between the immediate concrete event to which appeal is made in experiment and observation, and any formulation of this in terms of a current working hypothesis. The actual position of the spectral line, or of the photographic image on the plate, is the brute fact by which the hypothesis is tested, and there is no methodological relation between the exactly determined position of these and a resolution of them into, say, electrons. It is conceivable that this should be done. It would vastly confuse and delay the attainment of any knowledge from the measurement and would have no conceivable connection with getting that knowledge. To call such a translation "knowledge" is to depart from the significance which the term "knowledge" has in an experimental science.

The world, then, in which science operates has, at its core and in a certain sense surrounding its findings and speculations, the environment of immediate experience. At the point of its problems the immediate things are so analyzed that they may pass into the formulations of the scientist's hypothesis, while the finding of observation and experiment remains immediate experience, that is, is located in the surrounding borderland. It is these two aspects of the world of immediate experience that call for especial attention. From the standpoint of the discovery of the new, from the standpoint of research, the world of immediate experience is a core and seems to be reduced to the island of vague, indeterminate, and contingent data that are contrasted with the clear-cut, sharply defined, and necessary elements and events of scientific theory; an apparently incongruous situation, for the acceptance of the clear-cut, sharply defined, and necessary world is dependent upon the findings in the island of vague, indeterminate, and contingent data, the field of observation and experiment. It is an apparent incongruity that has given birth to much philosophic speculation.

That the incongruity is only apparent is fairly evident, since the scientist, out of whose method and its achievements it has arisen, is not aware of it. If it were presented to him in the terms just used, he would presumably reply that one cannot both have his cake and eat it; that, if one is in search of definition and certainty at a point in experience at which they have disappeared, it is but natural that the definition of the problem should exhibit this fact of their disappearance and that the very data which will serve in the verification of a hypothetical order of defined and necessary things must be themselves infected with indeterminateness and contingency; that the home of experimental medicine is in the hospital; that the gospel of science summons not the logically righteous but sinners to repentance. He would likely add, however, that because, before the discovery of the germ of yellow fever, the clinical picture of the disease was indeterminate and its incidence contingent, there would have been no justification in ascribing the same indeterminateness and contingency to the clinical picture of diphtheria—in other words, that the form in which the data appear in any one problem is pertinent to that problem alone.

But while the statement of the problem, together with the observation and experiment that are involved in verification, constitutes a core of immediate experience whose analyzed elements are indeterminate and contingent as compared with defined elements and necessary relations in a hypothetical scientific theory, these data do belong to objects in an immediate world that is a going concern, and as such is unquestioned. Such a world may be said to contain the problem within itself, and so to surround the problem. It has taken up into itself the solutions of past problems successfully solved. There is involved in it also a considerable apparatus of working hypothesis, which is not always distinguished from the world that is there. The distinction lies in the fact that back of the working hypothesis there is always a question mark, and in the back of the scientist's mind in using the working hypothesis lies the problem implied in its being only a working hypothesis. The world that is there is the common world within which the intelligent community lives and moves and has its being. In physical diameter it may be a small world as compared with the scope of physical hypotheses which in a logical sense it surrounds. Its logical compass of the hypothesis is shown in the data of observation and experiment that must be brought to bear upon the hypothesis before it can be established.

This compass of the problem, and the hypothetical solution of it, is logical in so far as the analysis involved in the problem, the inference involved in the formation of the hypothesis, and the sufficiency of evidence involved in observation and experiment all rest upon a world of things that is there, not as known but as containing conditions of knowledge. But the world that is there includes and surrounds the problem in the sense that the problem is also there within the field of conduct, for, as has been indicated, the problem arises in the conduct of individuals and out of the conflict of acts which inhibit one another because the same object calls out mutually antagonistic responses. When these problems pass into the field of reflection, they are so formulated that they would occur in any experience, that is, they take on a universal form. Such a formulation is essential to the reflective process of their solution. Their actual occurrence, however, in the world that is there awaits the advent of the conflict of responses in the experience of some individual; and the solution as well, inasmuch as it departs from the common or universal habits of the community, must be an individual achievement before it can become the attitude of all and be thus universalized. So located in its historical setting, the problem is evidently as completely surrounded by the world that is there as the hole left by a name that has been forgotten is surrounded by all the other names and things and happenings by which one attempts its recall. But while occurrence of the problem and of its solution must be in the field of conduct of some one individual, the things and events that constitute its border are matters of common and undisputed validity. The problem must happen to an individual, it can have no other locus than in his biography, but the terms in which he defines it and seeks its solution must be universal, that is, have common import.

This location of the problem in the experience of the individual in its historical setting dates not only the problem but also the world within which that problem arises. For a world within which an essential scientific problem has arisen is a different world from that within which this problem does not exist, that is, different from the world that is there when this problem has been solved. The world of Daltonian atoms and electricity (which was considered a form of motion), within which appeared the problem of the ion in electrolysis and the breakup of the atom in radioactive substances, is a different world from that whose ultimate elements are particles of electricity. Such worlds dated by the problems upon whose solutions they have appeared are social in the sense that they belong to the history of the human community, since reflective thought is a social undertaking, and since the individual in whose experience both the problem and its solution must arise presupposes the community out of which he springs.

It is the double aspect of these worlds that has been the occasion of so much philosophic speculation. On the one hand, they have provided the tests of reality for experimental science, and, on the other, they have successively lost their validity and have passed away into the realm of ideas. I have already indicated the scientist's rejoinder to this apparent assault upon his method. His method implies not that there has been, is, or will be any one authentic world that constitutes the core and envelope of his problems, but that there always have been, and are, and will be facts, or data, which, stated in terms of these different worlds by the individuals in whose experience they have appeared, can be recognized as identical; and that every world in which problems appear and are attacked by the experimental method is in such a sense a going concern that it can test hypothetical solutions. I have further insisted that as a scientist his goal in the pursuit of knowledge is not a final world but the solution of his problem in the world that is there.

There have existed two different attitudes toward these so-called facts or data. Because it has been assumed that the observations of the old watchers of the heavens in the valley of Mesopotamia, and of Hipparchus, and of Tycho Brahe, and present astronomers possessed a certain identity, there has arisen a picture of the world made up of that which can be regarded as common to all, a picture made of abstractions. It is a picture through which we can look before and after, and determine the date of Thales when he predicted an eclipse, and what eclipses will take place a thousand years hence. If we assign a metaphysical reality to these facts, we reach a universe which has been the subject matter of popular and technical philosophies. If, on the other hand, we restrict ourselves to the determinations of experimental science, we have nothing but the common indication of things and characters in a world that is there, an indication that abstracts from all but that which is there when a problematic situation has robbed it of some object and concentrates attention upon those characters and things which are the stimuli to mutually inhibiting responses. As I have already insisted, it is only in the experience of the individual, at some moment in that experience, that such a conflict can take place. Non-problematic things are there for everyone. But while these observations took place in individual experiences, in the experiences of those individuals for whom these problems arose, it is the assumption of experimental science that a like experience would have arisen for any other individual whose experience had been infected with the same problem and that, in so far as successive problems have involved identical problematic elements, it is possible to identify the same observation in the experience of different individuals.

The Mesopotamian soothsayer who had hit upon the succession of the eclipses and enshrined it in the Great Saros, and the Greek astronomer who by a scientific explanation of the eclipses had worked out the same succession, and the modern Copernican astronomer who substitutes the motion of the earth in its orbit for that of the sun about the earth and dates these eclipses still more accurately, were all observing the same phenomenon. For each there was a different world that was there, but in these worlds there were actual or identical observations of individuals which connect these worlds with one another and enable the later thinker to take up into his own the worlds that have preceded his. The common content of these observations, by means of which different worlds are strung together in human history, depends upon the assumption that different individuals have had or would have the same experiences. So far as there is any universality in these contents, it goes back to an actual or implied indication of the same things and characters by different individuals, in the same or like situations, that is, it goes back to implications in regard to social behavior in inferential processes, especially to the social nature of the knowledge or evidential import of observation.

However, the experimental scientist, apart from some philosophic bias, is not a positivist. He has no inclination to build up a universe out of such scientific data, which in their abstraction can be identified as parts of many different worlds. The reference of his data is always to the solution of problems in the world that is there about him, the world that tests the validity of his hypothetical reconstructions. Nothing would more completely squeeze the interest out of his world than the resolution of it into the data of observation.

# Play, the Game, and the Generalized Other

Another set of background factors in the genesis of the self is represented in the activities of play and the game.

Among primitive people, as I have said, the necessity of distinguishing the self and the organism was recognized in what we term the "double": the individual has a thing-like self that is affected by the individual as it affects other people and which is distinguished from the immediate organism in that it can leave the body and come back to it. This is the basis for the concept of the soul as a separate entity.

We find in children something that answers to this double, namely, the invisible, imaginary companions which a good many children produce in their own experience. They organize in this way the responses which they call out in other persons and call out also in themselves. Of course, this playing with an imaginary companion is only a peculiarly interesting phase of ordinary play. Play in this sense, especially the stage which precedes the organized games, is a play at something. A child plays at being a mother, at being a teacher, at

From *Mind, Self, and Society from the Standpoint of a Social Behaviorist,* Ed. Charles W. Morris (Chicago: Univ. of Chicago Press, 1934) pp. 149–164.

being a policeman; that is, it is taking different rôles, as we say. We have something that suggests this in what we call the play of animals: a cat will play with her kittens, and dogs play with each other. Two dogs playing with each other will attack and defend, in a process which if carried through would amount to an actual fight. There is a combination of responses which checks the depth of the bite. But we do not have in such a situation the dogs taking a definite rôle in the sense that a child deliberately takes the rôle of another. This tendency on the part of the children is what we are working with in the kindergarten where the rôles which the children assume are made the basis for training. When a child does assume a rôle he has in himself the stimuli which call out that particular response or group of responses. He may, of course, run away when he is chased, as the dog does, or he may turn around and strike back just as the dog does in his play. But that is not the same as playing at something. Children get together to "play Indian." This means that the child has a certain set of stimuli which call out in itself the responses that they would call out in others, and which answer to an Indian. In the play period the child utilizes his own responses to these stimuli which he makes use of in building a self. The response which he has a tendency to make to these stimuli organizes them. He plays that he is, for instance, offering himself something, and he buys it; he gives a letter to himself and takes it away; he addresses himself as a parent, as a teacher; he arrests himself as a policeman. He has a set of stimuli which call out in himself the sort of responses they call out in others. He takes this group of responses and organizes them into a certain whole. Such is the simplest form of being another to one's self. It involves a temporal situation. The child says something in one character and responds in another character, and then his responding in another character is a stimulus to himself in the first character, and so the conversation goes on. A certain organized structure arises in him and in his other which replies to it, and these carry on the conversation of gestures between themselves.

If we contrast play with the situation in an organized game, we note the essential difference that the child who plays in a game must be ready to take the attitude of everyone else involved in that game, and that these different rôles must have a definite relationship to each other. Taking a very simple game such as hide-and-seek, everyone with the exception of the one who is hiding is a person who is hunting. A child does not require more than the person who is hunted and the one who is hunting. If a child is playing in the first sense he just goes on playing, but there is no basic organization gained. In that early stage he passes from one rôle to another just as a whim takes him. But in a game where a number of individuals are involved, then the child taking one rôle must be ready to take the rôle of everyone else. If he gets in a ball nine he must have the responses of each position involved in his own position. He must know what everyone else is going to do in order to carry out his own play. He has to take all of these rôles. They do not all have to be present in consciousness at the same time, but at some moments he has to have three or four individuals present in his own attitude, such as the one who is going to throw the ball, the one who is going to catch it, and so on. These responses must be, in some degree, present in his own make-up. In the game, then, there is a set of responses of such others so organized that the attitude of one calls out the appropriate attitudes of the other.

This organization is put in the form of the rules of the game. Children take a great interest in rules. They make rules on the spot in order to help themselves out of difficulties. Part of the enjoyment of the game is to get these rules. Now, the rules are the set of responses which a particular attitude calls out. You can demand a certain response in others if you take a certain attitude. These responses are all in yourself as well. There you get an organized set of such responses as that to which I have referred, which is something more elaborate than the rôles found in play. Here there is just a set of responses that follow on each other indefinitely. At such a stage we speak of a child as not yet having a fully developed self. The child responds in a fairly intelligent fashion to the immediate stimuli that come to him, but they are not organized. He does not organize his life as we would like to have him do, namely, as a whole. There is just a set of responses of the type of play. The child reacts to a certain stimulus, and the reaction is in himself that is called out in others, but he is not a whole self. In his game he has to have an organization of these rôles; otherwise he cannot play the game. The game represents the passage in the life of the child from taking the rôle of others in play to the organized part that is essential to self-consciousness in the full sense of the term.

We were speaking of the social conditions under which the self arises as an object. In addition to language we found two illustrations, one in play and the other in the game, and I wish to summarize and expand my account on these points. I have spoken of these from the point of view of children. We can, of course, refer also to the attitudes of more primitive people out of which our civilization has arisen. A striking illustration of play as distinct from the game is found in the myths and various of the plays which primitive people carry out, especially in religious pageants. The pure play attitude which we find in the case of little children may not be found here, since the participants are adults, and undoubtedly the relationship of these play processes to that which they interpret is more or less in the minds of even the most primitive people. In the process of interpretation of such rituals, there is an organization of play which perhaps might be compared to that which is taking place in the kindergarten in dealing with the plays of little children, where these are made into a set that will have a definite structure or relationship. At least something of the same sort is found in the play of primitive people. This type of activity belongs, of course, not to the everyday life of the people in their dealing with the objects about them—there we have a more or less definitely developed self-consciousness—but in their attitudes toward the forces about them, the nature upon which they depend; in their attitude toward this nature which is vague and uncertain, there we have a much more primitive response; and that response finds its expression in taking the rôle of the other, playing at the expression of their gods and their heroes, going through certain rites which are the representation of what these individuals are supposed to be doing. The process is one which develops, to be sure, into a more or less definite technique and is controlled; and yet we can say that it has arisen out of situations similar to those in which little children play at being a parent, at being a teacher—vague personalities that are about them and which affect them and on which they depend. These are personalities which they take, rôles they play, and in so far control the development of their own personality. This outcome is just what the kindergarten works toward. It takes the characters of these various vague beings and gets them into such an organized social relationship to each other that they build up the character of the little child.[1] The very introduction of organization from outside supposes a lack of organization at this period in the child's experience. Over against such a situation of the little child and primitive people, we have the game as such.

The fundamental difference between the game and play is that in the [former] the child must have the attitude of all the others involved in that game. The attitudes of the other players which the participant assumes organize into a sort of unit, and it is that organization which controls the response of the individual. The illustration used was of a person playing baseball. Each one of his own acts is determined by his assumption of the action of the others who are playing the game. What he does is controlled by his being everyone else on that team, at least in so far as those attitudes affect his own particular response. We get then an "other" which is an organization of the attitudes of those involved in the same process.

The organized community or social group which gives to the individual his unity of self may be called "the generalized other." The attitude of the generalized other is the attitude of the whole community.[2] Thus, for example, in the case of such a social group as a ball team, the team is the generalized other in so far as it enters—as an organized process or social activity—into the experience of any one of the individual members of it.

If the given human individual is to develop a self in the fullest sense, it is not sufficient for him merely to take the attitudes of other human individuals toward himself and toward one another within the human social process, and to bring that social process as a whole into his individual experience merely in these terms: he must also, in the same way that he takes the attitudes of other individuals toward himself and toward one another, take their attitudes toward the various phases or aspects of the common social activity or set of social undertakings in which, as members of an organized society or social group, they are all engaged; and he must then, by generalizing these individual attitudes of that organized society or social group itself, as a whole, act toward different social projects which at any given time it is carrying out, or toward the various larger phases of the general social process which constitutes its life and of which these projects are specific manifestations. This getting of the broad activities of any given social whole or organized society as such within the experiential field of any one of the individuals involved or included in that whole is, in other words, the essential basis and prerequisite of the fullest development of that individual's self: only in so far as he takes the attitudes of the organized social group to which he belongs toward the organized, co-operative social activity or set of such activities in which that group as such is engaged, does he develop a complete self or possess the sort of complete self he has developed. And on the other hand, the complex co-operative processes and activities and institutional functionings of organized human society are also possible only in so far as every individual involved in them or belonging to that society can take the general attitudes of all other such individuals with reference to these processes and activities and institutional functionings, and to the organized social whole of experiential relations and interactions thereby constituted—and can direct his own behavior accordingly.

It is in the form of the generalized other that the social process influences the behavior of the individuals involved in it and carrying it on, i.e., that the community exercises control over the conduct of its individual members; for it is in this form that the social process or community enters as a determining factor into the individual's thinking. In abstract thought the individual takes the attitude of the generalized other[3] toward himself, without reference to its expression in any particular other individuals; and in concrete thought he takes that attitude in so far as it is expressed in the attitudes toward his behavior of those other individuals with whom he is involved in the given social situation or act. But only by taking the attitude of the generalized other toward himself, in one or another of these ways, can he think at all; for only thus can thinking—or the internalized conversation of gestures which constitutes thinking—occur. And only through the taking by individuals of the attitude or attitudes of the generalized other toward themselves is the existence of a universe of discourse, as that system of common or social meanings which thinking presupposes at its context, rendered possible.

The self-conscious human individual, then, takes or assumes the organized social attitudes of the given social group or community (or of some one section thereof) to which he belongs, toward the social problems of various kinds which confront that group or community at any given time, and which arise in connection with the correspondingly different social projects or organized co-operative enterprises in which that group or community as such is engaged; and as an individual participant in these social projects or co-operative enterprises, he governs his own conduct accordingly. In politics, for example, the individual identifies himself with an entire political party and takes the organized attitudes of that entire party toward the rest of the given social community and toward the problems which confront the party within the given social situation; and he consequently reacts or responds in terms of the organized attitudes of the party as a whole. He thus enters into a special set of social relations with all the other individuals who belong to that political party; and in the same way he enters into various other special sets of social relations, with various other classes of individuals respectively, the individuals of each of these classes being the other members of some one of the particular organized subgroups (determined in socially functional terms) of which he himself is a member within the entire given society or social community. In the most highly developed, organized, and complicated human social communities—those evolved by civilized man—these various socially functional classes or subgroups of individuals to which any given individual belongs (and with the other individual members of which he thus enters into a special set of social relations) are of two kinds. Some of them are concrete social classes or subgroups, such as political parties, clubs, corporations, which are all actually functional social units, in terms of which their individual members are directly related to one another. The others are abstract social classes or subgroups, such as the class of debtors and the class of creditors, in terms of which their individual members are related to one another only more or less indirectly, and which only more or less indirectly function as social units, but which afford or represent unlimited possibilities for the widening and ramifying and enriching of the social relations among all the individual members of the given society as an organized and unified whole. The given individual's membership in several of these abstract social classes or subgroups makes possible his entrance into definite social relations (however indirect) with an almost infinite number of other individuals who also belong to or are included within one or another of these abstract social classes or subgroups cutting across functional lines of demarcation which divide different human social communities from one another, and including individual members from several (in some cases from all) such communities. Of these abstract social classes or subgroups of human individuals the one which is most inclusive and extensive is, of course, the one defined by the logical universe of discourse (or system of universally signifi-

cant symbols) determined by the participation and communicative interaction of individuals; for of all such classes or subgroups, it is the one which claims the largest number of individual members, and which enables the largest conceivable number of human individuals to enter into some sort of social relation, however indirect or abstract it may be, with one another—a relation arising from the universal functioning of gestures as significant symbols in the general human social process of communication.

I have pointed out, then, that there are two general stages in the full development of the self. At the first of these stages, the individual's self is constituted simply by an organization of the particular attitudes of other individuals toward himself and toward one another in the specific social acts in which he participates with them. But at the second stage in the full development of the individual's self that self is constituted not only by an organization of these particular individual attitudes, but also by an organization of the social attitudes of the generalized other or the social group as a whole to which he belongs. These social or group attitudes are brought within the individual's field of direct experience, and are included as elements in the structure or constitution of his self, in the same way that the attitudes of particular other individuals are; and the individual arrives at them, or succeeds in taking them, by means of further organizing, and then generalizing, the attitudes of particular other individuals in terms of their organized social bearings and implications. So the self reaches its full development by organizing these individual attitudes of others into the organized social or group attitudes, and by thus becoming an individual reflection of the general systematic pattern of social or group behavior in which it and the others are all involved—a pattern which enters as a whole into the individual's experience in terms of these organized group attitudes which, through the mechanism of his central nervous system, he takes toward himself, just as he takes the individual attitudes of others.

The game has a logic, so that such an organization of the self is rendered possible:

there is a definite end to be obtained; the actions of the different individuals are all related to each other with reference to that end so that they do not conflict; one is not in conflict with himself in the attitude of another man on the team. If one has the attitude of the person throwing the ball he can also have the response of catching the ball. The two are related so that they further the purpose of the game itself. They are interrelated in a unitary, organic fashion. There is a definite unity, then, which is introduced into the organization of other selves when we reach such a stage as that of the game, as over against the situation of play where there is a simple succession of one rôle after another, a situation which is, of course, characteristic of the child's own personality. The child is one thing at one time and another at another, and what he is at one moment does not determine what he is at another. That is both the charm of childhood as well as its inadequacy. You cannot count on the child; you cannot assume that all the things he does are going to determine what he will do at any moment. He is not organized into a whole. The child has no definite character, no definite personality.

The game is then an illustration of the situation out of which an organized personality arises. In so far as the child does take the attitude of the other and allows that attitude of the other to determine the thing he is going to do with reference to a common end, he is becoming an organic member of society. He is taking over the morale of that society and is becoming an essential member of it. He belongs to it in so far as he does allow the attitude of the other that he takes to control his own immediate expression. What is involved here is some sort of an organized process. That which is expressed in terms of the game is, of course, being continually expressed in the social life of the child, but this wider process goes beyond the immediate experience of the child himself. The importance of the game is that it lies entirely inside of the child's own experience, and the importance of our modern type of education is that it is brought as far as possible within this realm. The different attitudes

that a child assumes are so organized that they exercise a definite control over his response, as the attitudes in a game control his own immediate response. In the game we get an organized other, a generalized other, which is found in the nature of the child itself, and finds its expression in the immediate experience of the child. And it is that organized activity in the child's own nature controlling the particular response which gives unity, and which builds up his own self.

What goes on in the game goes on in the life of the child all the time. He is continually taking the attitudes of those about him, especially the rôles of those who in some sense control him and on whom he depends. He gets the function of the process in an abstract sort of a way at first. It goes over from the play into the game in a real sense. He has to play the game. The morale of the game takes hold of the child more than the larger morale of the whole community. The child passes into the game and the game expresses a social situation in which he can completely enter; its morale may have a greater hold on him than that of the family to which he belongs or the community in which he lives. There are all sorts of social organizations, some of which are fairly lasting, some temporary, into which the child is entering, and he is playing a sort of social game in them. It is a period in which he likes "to belong," and he gets into organizations which come into existence and pass out of existence. He becomes a something which can function in the organized whole, and thus tends to determine himself in his relationship with the group to which he belongs. That process is one which is a striking stage in the development of the child's morale. It constitutes him a self-conscious member of the community to which he belongs.

Such is the process by which a personality arises. I have spoken of this as a process in which a child takes the rôle of the other, and said that it takes place essentially through the use of language. Language is predominantly based on the vocal gesture by means of which co-operative activities in a community are carried out. Language in its significant sense is that vocal gesture which tends to arouse in the individual the attitude which it arouses in others, and it is this perfecting of the self by the gesture which mediates the social activities that gives rise to the process of taking the rôle of the other. The latter phrase is a little unfortunate because it suggests an actor's attitude which is actually more sophisticated than that which is involved in our own experience. To this degree it does not correctly describe that which I have in mind. We see the process most definitely in a primitive form in those situations where the child's play takes different rôles. Here the very fact that he is ready to pay out money, for instance, arouses the attitude of the person who receives money; the very process is calling out in him the corresponding activities of the other person involved. The individual stimulates himself to the response which he is calling out in the other person, and then acts in some degree in response to that situation. In play the child does definitely act out the rôle which he himself has aroused in himself. It is that which gives, as I have said, a definite content in the individual which answers to the stimulus that affects him as it affects somebody else. The content of the other that enters into one personality is the response in the individual which his gesture calls out in the other.

We may illustrate our basic concept by a reference to the notion of property. If we say "This is my property, I shall control it," that affirmation calls out a certain set of responses which must be the same in any community in which property exists. It involves an organized attitude with reference to property which is common to all the members of the community. One must have a definite attitude of control of his own property and respect for the property of others. Those attitudes (as organized sets of responses) must be there on the part of all, so that when one says such a thing he calls out in himself the response of the others. He is calling out the response of what I have called a generalized other. That which makes society possible is such common responses, such organized attitudes, with reference to what we term property, the cults of religion, the process

of education, and the relations of the family. Of course, the wider the society the more definitely universal these objects must be. In any case there must be a definite set of responses, which we may speak of as abstract, and which can belong to a very large group. Property is in itself a very abstract concept. It is that which the individual himself can control and nobody else can control. The attitude is different from that of a dog toward a bone. A dog will fight any other dog trying to take the bone. The dog is not taking the attitude of the other dog. A man who says "This is my property" is taking an attitude of the other person. The man is appealing to his rights because he is able to take the attitude which everybody else in the group has with reference to property, thus arousing in himself the attitude of others.

What goes to make up the organized self is the organization of the attitudes which are common to the group. A person is a personality because he belongs to a community, because he takes over the institutions of that community into his own conduct. He takes its language as a medium by which he gets his personality, and then through a process of taking the different rôles that all the others furnish he comes to get the attitude of the members of the community. Such, in a certain sense, is the structure of a man's personality. There are certain common responses which each individual has toward certain common things, and in so far as those common responses are awakened in the individual when he is affecting other persons he arouses his own self. The structure, then, on which the self is built is this response which is common to all, for one has to be a member of a community to be a self. Such responses are abstract attitudes, but they constitute just what we term a man's character. They give him what we term his principles, the acknowledged attitudes of all members of the community toward what are the values of that community. He is putting himself in the place of the generalized other, which represents the organized responses of all the members of the group. It is that which guides conduct controlled by principles, and a person who has such an organized group of responses is a man whom we say has character, in the moral sense.

It is a structure of attitudes, then, which goes to make up a self, as distinct from a group of habits. We all of us have, for example, certain groups of habits, such as the particular intonations which a person uses in his speech. This is a set of habits of vocal expression which one has but which one does not know about. The sets of habits which we have of that sort mean nothing to us; we do not hear the intonations of our speech that others hear unless we are paying particular attention to them. The habits of emotional expression which belong to our speech are of the same sort. We may know that we have expressed ourselves in a joyous fashion but the detailed process is one which does not come back to our conscious selves. There are whole bundles of such habits which do not enter into a conscious self, but which help to make up what is termed the unconscious self.

After all, what we mean by self-consciousness is an awakening in ourselves of the group of attitudes which we are arousing in others, especially when it is an important set of responses which go to make up the members of the community. It is unfortunate to fuse or mix up consciousness, as we ordinarily use that term, and self-consciousness. Consciousness, as frequently used, simply has reference to the field of experience, but self-consciousness refers to the ability to call out in ourselves a set of definite responses which belong to the others of the group. Consciousness and self-consciousness are not on the same level. A man alone has, fortunately or unfortunately, access to his own toothache, but that is not what we mean by self-consciousness.

I have so far emphasized what I have called the structures upon which the self is constructed, the framework of the self, as it were. Of course we are not only what is common to all: each one of the selves is different from everyone else; but there has to be such a common structure as I have sketched in order that we may be members of a community at all. We cannot be ourselves unless we are also members in whom there is a community of attitudes which control the attitudes of all. We cannot have rights unless we have common attitudes. That which we have acquired as self-conscious persons makes us such members of society and gives us selves. Selves can only exist in definite relationships to other selves. No hard-and-fast line can be drawn between our own selves and the selves of others, since our own selves exist and enter as such into our experience only in so far as the selves of others exist and enter as such into our experience also. The individual possesses a self only in relation to the selves of the other members of his social group; and the structure of his self expresses or reflects the general behavior pattern of this social group to which he belongs, just as does the structure of the self of every other individual belonging to this social group.

## Notes

1. "The Relation of Play to Education," *University of Chicago Record,* I (1896–97), 141–145.
2. It is possible for inanimate objects, no less than for other human organisms, to form parts of the generalized and organized—the completely socialized—other for any given human individual, in so far as he responds to such objects socially or in a social fashion (by means of the mechanism of thought, the internalized conversation of gestures). Any thing—any object or set of objects, whether animate or inanimate, human or animal, or merely physical—toward which he acts, or to which he responds, socially, is an element in what for him is the generalized other; by taking the attitudes of which toward himself he becomes conscious of himself as an object or individual, and thus develops a self or personality. Thus, for example, the cult, in its primitive form, is merely the social embodiment of the relation between the given social group or community and its physical environment—an organized social means, adopted by the individual members of that group or community, of entering into social relations with that environment, or (in a sense) of carrying on conversations with it; and in this way that environment becomes part of the total generalized other for each of the individual members of the given social group or community.

3. We have said that the internal conversation of the individual with himself in terms of words or significant gestures—the conversation which constitutes the process or activity of thinking—is carried on by the individual from the standpoint of the "generalized other." And the more abstract that conversation is, the more abstract thinking happens to be, the further removed is the generalized other from any connection with particular individuals. It is especially in abstract thinking, that is to say, that the conversation involved is carried on by the individual wi.h the generalized other, rather than with any particular individuals. Thus it is, for example, that abstract concepts are concepts stated in terms of the attitudes of the entire social group or community; they are stated on the basis of the individual's consciousness of the attitudes of the generalized other toward them, as a result of his taking these attitudes of the generalized other and then responding to them. And thus it is also that abstract propositions are stated in a form which anyone—any other intelligent individual—will accept.

# The "I" and the "Me"

We have discussed at length the social foundations of the self, and hinted that the self does not consist simply in the bare organization of social attitudes. We may now explicitly raise the question as to the nature of the "I" which is aware of the social "me." I do not mean to raise the metaphysical question of how a person can be both "I" and "me," but to ask for the significance of this distinction from the point of view of conduct itself. Where in conduct does the "I" come in as over against the "me?" If one determines what his position is in society and feels himself as having a certain function and privilege, these are all defined with reference to an "I," but the "I" is not a "me" and cannot become a "me." We may have a better self and a worse self, but that again is not the "I" as over against the "me," because they are both selves. We approve of one and disapprove of the other, but when we bring up one or the other they are there for such approval as "me's." The "I" does not get into the limelight; we talk to ourselves, but do not see ourselves. The "I" reacts to the self which arises through the taking of the attitudes of others. Through taking those attitudes we have introduced the "me" and we react to it as an "I."

The simplest way of handling the problem would be in terms of memory. I talk to myself, and I remember what I said and perhaps the emotional content that went with it. The "I" of this moment is present in the "me" of the next moment. There again I cannot turn around quick enough to catch myself. I become a "me" in so far as I remember what I said. The "I" can be given, however, this functional relationship. It is because of the "I" that we say that we are never fully aware of what we are, that we surprise ourselves by our own action. It is as we act that we are aware of ourselves. It is in memory that the "I" is constantly present in experience. We can go back directly a few moments in our experience, and then we are dependent upon memory images for the rest. So that the "I" in memory is there as the spokesman of the self of the second, or minute, or day ago. As given, it is a "me," but it is a "me" which was the "I" at the earlier time. If you ask, then, where directly in your own experience the "I" comes in, the answer is that it comes in as a historical figure. It is what you were a second ago that is the "I" of the "me." It is another "me" that has to take that rôle. You cannot get the immediate response of

From *Mind, Self, and Society from the Standpoint of a Social Behaviorist,* Ed. Charles W. Morris, (Chicago: Univ. of Chicago Press, 1934), pp. 173–178.

the "I" in the process.[1] The "I" is in a certain sense that with which we do identify ourselves. The getting of it into experience constitutes one of the problems of most of our conscious experience; it is not directly given in experience.

The "I" is the response of the organism to the attitudes of the others; the "me" is the organized set of attitudes of others which one himself assumes. The attitudes of the others constitute the organized "me," and then one reacts toward that as an "I." I now wish to examine these concepts in greater detail.

There is neither "I" nor "me" in the conversation of gestures; the whole act is not yet carried out, but the preparation takes place in this field of gesture. Now, in so far as the individual arouses in himself the attitudes of the others, there arises an organized group of responses. And it is due to the individual's ability to take the attitudes of these others in so far as they can be organized that he gets self-consciousness. The taking of all of those organized sets of attitudes gives him his "me"; that is the self he is aware of. He can throw the ball to some other member because of the demand made upon him from other members of the team. That is the self that immediately exists for him in his consciousness. He has their attitudes, knows what they want and what the consequence of any act of his will be, and he has assumed responsibility for the situation. Now, it is the presence of those organized sets of attitudes that constitutes that "me" to which he as an "I" is responding. But what that response will be he does not know and nobody else knows. Perhaps he will make a brilliant play or an error. The response to that situation as it appears in his immediate experience is uncertain, and it is that which constitutes the "I."

The "I" is his action over against that social situation within his own conduct, and it gets into his experience only after he has carried out the act. Then he is aware of it. He had to do such a thing and he did it. He fulfils his duty and he may look with pride at the throw which he made. The "me" arises to do that duty— that is the way in which it arises in his experi-

ence. He had in him all the attitudes of others, calling for a certain response; that was the "me" of that situation, and his response is the "I."

I want to call attention particularly to the fact that this response of the "I" is something that is more or less uncertain. The attitudes of others which one assumes as affecting his own conduct constitute the "me," and that is something that is there, but the response to it is as yet not given. When one sits down to think anything out, he has certain data that are there. Suppose that it is a social situation which he has to straighten out. He sees himself from the point of view of one individual or another in the group. These individuals, related all together, give him a certain self. Well, what is he going to do? He does not know and nobody else knows. He can get the situation into his experience because he can assume the attitudes of the various individuals involved in it. He knows how they feel about it by the assumption of their attitudes. He says, in effect, "I have done certain things that seem to commit me to a certain course of conduct." Perhaps if he does so act it will place him in a false position with another group. The "I" as a response to this situation, in contrast to the "me" which is involved in the attitudes which he takes, is uncertain. And when the response takes place, then it appears in the field of experience largely as a memory image.

Our specious present as such is very short. We do, however, experience passing events; part of the process of the passage of events is directly there in our experience, including some of the past and some of the future. We see a ball falling as it passes, and as it does pass part of the ball is covered and part is being uncovered. We remember where the ball was a moment ago and we anticipate where it will be beyond what is given in our experience. So of ourselves; we are doing something, but to look back and see what we are doing involves getting memory images. So the "I" really appears experientially as a part of a "me." But on the basis of this experience we distinguish that individual who is doing something from the "me" who puts the problem up to him. The response enters into his experience only when it takes place. If he says he knows what he is going to do, even there he may be mistaken. He starts out to do something and something happens to interfere. The resulting action is always a little different from anything which he could anticipate. This is true even if he is simply carrying out the process of walking. The very taking of his expected steps puts him in a certain situation which has a slightly different aspect from what is expected, which is in a certain sense novel. That movement into the future is the step, so to speak, of the ego, of the "I." It is something that is not given in the "me."

Take the situation of a scientist solving a problem, where he has certain data which call for certain responses. Some of this set of data call for his applying such and such a law, while others call for another law. Data are there with their implications. He knows what such and such coloration means, and when he has these data before him they stand for certain responses on his part; but now they are in conflict with each other. If he makes one response he cannot make another. What he is going to do he does not know, nor does anybody else. The action of the self is in response to these conflicting sets of data in the form of a problem, with conflicting demands upon him as a scientist. He has to look at it in different ways. That action of the "I" is something the nature of which we cannot tell in advance.

The "I," then, in this relation of the "I" and the "me," is something that is, so to speak, responding to a social situation which is within the experience of the individual. It is the answer which the individual makes to the attitude which others take toward him when he assumes an attitude toward them. Now, the attitudes he is taking toward them are present in his own experience, but his response to them will contain a novel element. The "I" gives the sense of freedom, of initiative. The situation is there for us to act in a self-conscious fashion. We are aware of ourselves, and of what the situation is, but exactly how we

will act never gets into experience until after the action takes place.

Such is the basis for the fact that the "I" does not appear in the same sense in experience as does the "me." The "me" represents a definite organization of the community there in our own attitudes, and calling for a response, but the response that takes place is something that just happens. There is no certainty in regard to it. There is a moral necessity but no mechanical necessity for the act. When it does take place then we find what has been done. The above account gives us, I think, the relative position of the "I" and "me" in the situation, and the grounds for the separation of the two in behavior. The two are separated in the process but they belong together in the sense of being parts of a whole. They are separated and yet they belong together. The separation of the "I" and the "me" is not fictitious. They are not identical, for, as I have said, the "I" is something that is never entirely calculable. The "me" does call for a certain sort of an "I" in so far as we meet the obligations that are given in conduct itself, but the "I" is always something different from what the situation itself calls for. So there is always that distinction, if you like, between the "I" and the "me." The "I" both calls out the "me" and responds to it. Taken together they constitute a personality as it appears in social experience. The self is essentially a social process going on with these two distinguishable phases. If it did not have these two phases there could not be conscious responsibility, and there would be nothing novel in experience.

## Notes

1. The sensitivity of the organism brings parts of itself into the environment. It does not, however, bring the life-process itself into the environment, and the complete imaginative presentation of the organism is unable to present the living of the organism. It can conceivably present the conditions under which living takes place but not the unitary life-process. The physical organism in the environment always remains a thing (MS).

# The Philosophical Basis of Ethics

The evolutionary point of view has had more than one important result for philosophical thought. Not the least important among these has been the conception of the evolution of evolution. Not only can we trace in the history of thought the evolution of the conception of evolution, but we find ourselves with a consciousness which we conceive of as evolved; the contents and the forms of these contents can be looked upon as the products of development. Among these contents and forms are found the temporal and spatial qualities of things, of the world. The very time process as well as the space of the universe lies in experience which is itself presented as the result of an evolution that arises in and through spatial conditions, which is first and foremost a temporal process.

The peculiarity of this situation lies in the fact that the evolution appears in the immediate findings of science. Our geological and biological sciences unhesitatingly present epochs antedating man in terms of man's consciousness, and biology and scientific psychology as unhesitatingly present that consciousness as an evolution within which all the distinctions must be explained by the same general laws as those which are appealed to to account for animal organs and functions. It is true that occasionally a scientist such as Poincaré[1] recognizes that even the number system, as well as Euclidean space, is but a construction which has arisen and maintained itself because of its practical advantages, though we can draw no conclusions from these practical advantages to their metaphysical reality. If this position be generalized, there results the conception of an evolution within which the environment—that which our science has presented as a fixed datum in its physical nature—has been evolved as well as the form which has adapted itself to that environment; that the space within which evolution has

taken place has arisen by the same laws; that the very time which makes an evolution presentable has arisen in like manner. Now, to a certain extent the conception of an evolution of environment as well as of the form has domesticated itself within our biological science. It has become evident that an environment can exist for a form only insofar as the environment answers to the susceptibilities of the organism; that the organism determines thus its own environment; that the effect of every adaptation is a new environment which must change with that which responds to it. The full recognition, however, that form and environment must be phases that answer to each other, character for character, appears in ethical theory.

In a certain sense this is found in the statement which genetic psychology makes of the development of the consciousness of the individual. Here there can be no evolution of the intelligence except insofar as the child's world answers to increased powers of conscious control. The world and the individual must keep pace with each other in the life history of the individual. But the child comes into a world which receives him as a child. The world of the adult, from the point of view of descriptive psychology, is an independent environment within which the child and his world evolve. Within the field of ethics, on the other hand, the moral individual and his world cannot consistently be presented as themselves lying inside another moral field. The growth of moral consciousness must be coterminous with that of the moral situation. The moral life lies in the interaction of these two; the situation rises up in accusation of the moral personality which is unequal to it, and the personality rises to the situation only by a process which reconstructs the situation as profoundly as it reconstructs the self. No man has found moral power within himself except

From *Selected Writings*, Ed Andrew J. Reck, (Chicago: Univ. of Chicago Press, 1981 [1908].) pp. 82–93.

insofar as he has found a meaning in his world that answered to the new-found power, or discovered a deeper ethical meaning in his environment that did not reveal new capacities for activities within himself. Moral evolution takes place then as does that of the child; the moral personality and its world must arise *pari passu* [simultaneously], but, unlike the psychologist's statement of the development of the child, it does not lie inside a larger determining environment.

I am not ignorant of evolutionary ethics, nor that every type of ethical theory in these days has felt itself bound to interpret the development of moral consciousness in terms of custom and institutions. Thus we seem to postulate not only a community moral consciousness, a moral world which determines the growth of the moral consciousness of the individual, but also we imply that this determining moral environment goes back into a past that antedates moral consciousness itself. From this point of view, morality, i.e., control by community habit, has determined the development of individual moral consciousness as tyrannically as the intellectual world has controlled the growth of intelligence in the members of society. But this paradox disappears when we recognize that this control by the community over its members provides indeed the material out of which reflective moral consciousness builds up its own situation, but cannot exist as a situation until the moral consciousness of the individual constructs it.

It is another statement of the same thing that moral consciousness is the most concrete consciousness—the most inclusive statement which can be given of immediate experience. There is no phase of activity, intellectual or physical, no type of inner experience, no presentation of outer reality, which does not find its place within the moral judgment. There is nothing which may not be a condition or an element of conduct, and moral consciousness reaches its climax in the estimation of every possible content of the individual and his situation. There is no other type of consciousness which must not abstract from other phases to assure its own existence. One cannot carry out an acute analysis and respond to the beauty of the object of analysis, one cannot swell with emotion and dispassionately observe. But we place every phase of our experience within the sweep of conscience; there is no one of these phases of consciousness which has not its legitimate function within the activity when viewed as moral. It is but a step further to claim that the abstractions of science and the expressions of the emotion and the direction of attention in perception and inference must find their functions, and hence their reason for existence, in the act; and that morality inheres in the act alone, but in none of these functions of the act (if I may be allowed two meanings of function in the same sentence).

It is, of course, possible to make this a metaphysical doctrine. If one finds reality in immediate experience and admits that the various intellectual, aesthetic, and perceptual processes exist only as parts and functions of an act which is the ultimate form of immediate experience, then the recognition of the ethical statement of this act as its fullest statement would found metaphysics upon ethics. The presentation of such a doctrine, however, would demand first of all a discussion of the meaning of the terms "immediate experience," of "reality," and the "cognitive state" that answers to it. I have no wish to enter this debatable field, that is loosely defined by the term "pragmatism."

There are, however, certain implications of modern ethical doctrine which fall within the lines which I have indicated above; that are of interest quite apart from their relation to metaphysical and logical speculations. The implications to which I refer are those that flow from evolutionary doctrine on the one side and from the identification of purposive activity with moral activity, and the recognition that our intelligence is through and through purposive. The first implication that flows from this position is that the fundamental necessity of moral action is simply the necessity of action at all; or stated in other terms, that the motive does not arise from the relations of antecedently given ends of activities, but rather that the motive is the recognition of the end as it arises in consciousness. The other implication is that the moral interpretation of our experience must be found within the experience itself.[2]

We are familiar with three ethical standpoints, that which finds in conscious control over action only the further development of conduct which has already unconsciously been determined by ends, that which finds conduct only where reflective thought is able to present a transcendental end, and that which recognizes conduct only where the individual and the environment—the situation—mutually determine each other. In the first case, moral necessity in conduct, for the conscious individual, is quite relative. It depends upon the degree of recognition which he reaches of the forces operating through him. Furthermore, the motive to act with reference to the end of the fullest life of the species is one which is primarily quite narrowly individualistic, and depends for a social interpretation upon the community of which the individual is a member. Moral necessity in conduct from this point of view is quite independent of the activity itself. So far from being the most fundamental reality it is a derivative by which, through what it is hard not to call a hocus-pocus, the individual acts, for what is only indirectly his own—a distant end, through a social *Dressur*.[3] It is, of course, natural that this point of view should mediate the process of training by which men are to be led unwittingly to socially worthy action, rather than the immediate conduct of the individual who finds himself face to face with a moral problem. It is the standpoint of the publicist and the reformer of social institutions.

But if we admit that the evolutionary process consists in a mutual determination of the individual and his environment—not the determination of the individual by his environment, moral necessity in conduct is found in the very evolutionary situation. The possibility of intelligent action waits upon the determination of the conditions under which that action is to take place. The statement of these conditions becomes the end, when it is recognized that the statement is in terms of the

activities that make up the personality of the individual. The content of the end is the mutuality of statement of personality, i.e., the tendencies to activity, in terms of the personalities who make up the environment, i.e., the conditions of the expression of the activities. It is because the man must recognize the public good in the exercise of his powers, and state the public good in terms of his own outgoing activities that his ends are moral. But it is not the public good which comes in from outside himself and lays a moral necessity upon him, nor is it a selfish propensity that drives him on to conduct.

It is inconceivable that such an outside end should have any but an extraneous position. It could never come into a personality except by the door of its own interest. The end could not be a social end. Nor could a purely individual propensity through the agency of community training become social. The moral necessity lies not in the end acting from without, nor in the push of inclination from within, but in the relation of the conditions of action to the impulses to action. The motive is neither a purely rational, external end, nor a private inclination, but the impulse presented in terms of its consequences over against the consequences of the other impulses. The impulse so conditioned, so interpreted, becomes a motive to conduct. The moral necessity is that all activity which appears as impulse and environment should enter into the situation, and there is nothing which ensures this completeness of expression except the full interrelationship of the self and the situation. That one fully recognized the conflict which the impulse involves in its consequences with the consequences of all the other social processes that go to make him up, is the moral dictum. From the reconstructions that this recognition involves the immediate statement of the end appears. To enforce this dictum is simply to live as fully and consciously and as determinedly as possible.

The moral necessity for education is not an ideal of intelligence that lies before us of the clear refulgence of the intellect. It is the necessity of knowledge to do what is trying to be done, the dependence of the uninformed impulse upon means, method, and interpretation. The necessity of uprightness in public affairs does not rest upon a transcendental ideal of perfection of the self, nor upon the attainment of the possible sum of human happiness, but upon the economy and effectiveness, and consistency demanded in the industrial, commercial, social, and aesthetic activities of those that make up the community. To push reform is to give expression to all these impulses and present them in their consequences over against those of all the other social impulses out of which an organism of personalities arises.

There is abroad a feeling of lack of moral force; we look before and after—to our ancestors, our posterity—for incentive to right conduct, when in fact there is no moral necessity which is not involved in the impulses to conduct themselves. To correct one abuse we must emphasize the interests it jeopardizes. There is no reservoir of moral power, except that which lies in the impulses behind these interests. To correct the sin of the individual is to awaken through the consequences of the sin the normal activities which are inhibited by the excess. It is this healthful, aggressive, moral attitude, which it seems to me is encouraged by the recognition that moral consciousness is the most concrete, the most inclusive of all. Here we must abstract from nothing, and here we cannot appeal from ourselves to a power without ourselves that makes for righteousness. In the fullness of immediate experience, with the consciousness that out of the struggle to act must arise all power to mediate action, lies salvation. In like manner evolution in moral conduct can appeal to no environment without to stamp itself upon the individual; nor to him to adapt himself to a fixed order of the universe, but environment as well as individual appears in immediate experience; the one coterminous with the other, and moral endeavor appears in the mutual determination of one by the other.

Nowhere is this point of view more needed than in the struggles which fill our industrial and commercial life. The individual is treated as if he were quite separable from his environment; and still more is the environment conceived as if it were quite independent of the individual. Both laborer and the society which employs him are exhorted to recognize their obligations to each other, while each continues to operate within its own narrow radius; and because the employer regards the labor union as a fixed external environment of his activity, and would have all the relations between laborer and employer determined by the method in which he bargains and does business, he becomes a narrow individualist; and because the laborer would determine these same relations by the methods which he has used in building up this union, he becomes a socialist. What will take that and other allied problems out of the vicious circles in which they are at present found, is the recognition that it is the incompleteness with which the different social interests are present that is responsible for the inadequacy of the moral judgments. If the community educated and housed its members properly, and protected machinery, food, market, and thoroughfares adequately, the problems at present vexing the industrial world would largely disappear. We resent the introduction of the standard of life into the question of the wages; and yet if the social activities involved in the conception of the standard of life were given full expression, the wage question would be nearly answered. Every such problem is the inevitable indication of what has been left undone, of impulses checked, or interest overlooked. We turn back to history and talk about the evolution of man as if his environment were not the projection of himself in the conditions of conduct, as if the fulfillment of the Law and the Prophets were not the realization of all that is in us. The sources of power lie in that which has been overlooked. Again and again we are surprised to find that the moral advance has not been along the straight line of the moral struggles in which a sin seemed to be faced by righteous effort, but by the appearance of a novel interest which has changed the whole nature of the problem. If we were willing to recognize that the environment which surrounds the moral self is but the statement of the conditions under which his different conflicting impulses may get their expression, we would perceive that the reorganization must come from a new point of view which comes to consciousness through the conflict. The environment must change *pari passu* with the consciousness. Moral advance consists not in adapting individual natures to the fixed realities of a moral universe, but in constantly reconstructing and recreating the world as the individuals evolve.

The second implication to which reference has been made, is that we must find the interpretation of moral consciousness within the act. The appeal to a moral order which transcends either metaphysically or temporally the moral situation; the besetting assumption of the moralist that a moral reconstruction can be made intelligible only by a perfect moral order from which we have departed, or toward which we are moving, have very grave practical consequences which it becomes us to consider. In the first place these assumptions rob our moral consciousness of the intellectual interest which belongs to them of right. If morality connotes merely conformity to a given order, our intellectual reaction is confined to the recognition of agreement and disagreement, beyond that the moral reaction can be only emotional and instinctive. There may be, indeed, intellectual processes involved in stating this moral order, but such statement is confined, in the nature of the case, to apologetic and speculative thought, to thought which cannot be a part of the immediate moral consciousness.

A moral order to which we must conform can never be built up in thought in the presence of an exigency. There are only two types of reaction in a practical situation. One may respond to well-recognized cues by well-formed habits, or one may adapt and reconstruct his habits by new interpretation of the situation. In the first instance we have habitual conduct, in the second that type of reaction which has been most explicitly worked out by the natural sciences. Most of our action, of course, falls within the first category, and involves no moral struggle. The second type, on the other hand, is that in which practically all our moral issues arise. If a practical scientific problem arises, such as the engineering problems in constructing railroads or driving tunnels, we recognize that the intellectual process by which the problem is solved cannot be a mere reference to a perfect model of conduct already in existence. On the contrary, just because the engineer is face to face with a real problem he must find in the physical situation facts of which he is at present ignorant, and at the same time readjust his habits; in fact, it is the possible readjustment of the habit that directs his attention in investigating the situation, and, on the other hand, what is discovered serves to mediate the formation of the new habit. In a word, there is the typical play of attention back and forth between perception and response. In any such process the criterion which governs the whole and its two phases—three phases if we distinguish between perception of the new data and the formation of the hypothesis by which they are interpreted and mediated in the response—can never be external to the process. There exists as yet no plan of procedure which the engineer discovers or receives as a vision in the mount. The control is found in the relation of the different phases of the act which have been sketched above. It is the possibility of reaction to a stimulus that holds the reaction in the field of investigation and it is the continued investigation of the field of stimulus which keeps the reaction continuous and pertinent. The control is then that which was earlier referred to as the process of evolution in which individual and environment mutually determine each other. It is the criterion of action, which uses working hypotheses, but which cannot possibly be identified with an external ideal. This process, whether met in the field of mechanical invention, or the range of engineering, or that of scientific research, is recognized as the most absorbing, most interesting, most fascinating intellectually with which the mind of man can occupy itself, and this interest belongs legitimately to the solution of every moral problem, for the procedure is identical intellectually.

Yet we succeed in robbing our reflective moral consciousness of a great part of this interest. For there is and can be no interest in merely identifying certain types of conduct with those found in a given theory. For example, there is no intellectual interest involved in merely identifying the control exercised by a financier over an industry with the concept of property, and justifying him in doing what he will, within the limits of the law, with his own. There may be a very vigorous emotional reaction against the suggestion that he be interfered with in these vested rights; or, on the other hand, against an institution of property which permits such individualistic exploitation of social values, but there is no intellectual interest except that which is either apologetic or purely speculative. It does not come into the moral reaction to the situation. And yet the enormous content of interest which does attach to these moral questions is attested by the social sciences which have sprung up and expanded in every college and university.

It is interesting to compare the intellectual treatment which such problems receive at the hands of the scientific investigator and the pulpit. In the latter there is at present no apparatus for investigation. The pulpit is committed to a right and wrong which are unquestioned, and from its point of view unquestionable. Its function then is not the intellectual one of finding out what in the new situation is right, but in inspiring to a right conduct which is supposed to be so plain that he who runs may read. The result has been that in the great moral issues of recent industrial history, such as the child labor, woman's labor, protection of machinery, and a multitude more, the pulpit has been necessarily silent. It had not the means nor the technique for finding out what was the right thing to do. The science of hygiene threatens the universal issue of temperance, while we can look forward to the time when investigation may enable us to approach understandingly the prostitute and her trade, and change the social conditions which have made her possible instead of merely scourging an abstract sin.

The loss to the community from the elimination of the intellectual phase of moral conduct it would be difficult to overestimate and this loss is unavoidable as long as the interpretation of conduct lies outside the immediate experience, as long as we must refer to a moral order without, to intellectually present the morality of conduct.

In conclusion may I refer to another loss which moral conduct dependent upon an external ideal involves. The interpretation of sin and wrong with reference to a moral order external to the conduct fails to identify the moral defect with the situation out of which it springs and by whose reconstruction it may be eliminated. An illustration will at once indicate, I think, what I have in mind. The responsibility for death and accident upon our railroads cannot be laid at the doors of the system and those that work it, if an abstract doctrine of property and contract is used to judge the conduct of railroad managers and directors. The imperative necessity of the situation is that responsibility should be tested by the consequences of an act; that the moral judgment should find its criterion in the mutual determination of the individual and the situation. As it is, men who would risk their own lives to save a drowning man, regard themselves as justified in slaughtering others by the thousand to save money. Abstract valuations take the place of concrete valuations, and as the abstract external valuations are always the precipitations of earlier conduct, they are pretty uniformly inadequate.

But not only does an external moral ideal rob immediate moral conduct of its most important values, but it robs human nature of the most profound solace which can come to those who suffer—the knowledge that the loss and the suffering, with its subjective poignancy, has served to evaluate conduct, to determine what is and what is not worthwhile.

## Notes

1. [Henri Poincare (1854–1912), French mathematician and philosopher of science, author of *Science et méthode* (1905; English translation, 1914) and *La science et l'hypothèse* (1902; English translation, 1905).

2. The full analysis of the position assumed here has been given by Prof. John Dewey in his article, "The Logical Conditions of a Scientific Treatment of Morality," (1903) in *The Middle Works John*

*Dewey:* Ed. Jo Ann Boydston, (Carbondale: Southern Illinois Univ. Press, 1976–83), Fifteen Volumes, 3: 3–39.

3. ["Training" or "breaking in."]

# Realism, Pragmatism, and Science

Philosophy has in this as well as in other centuries occupied itself with the interpretation of what science has accomplished. In modern times science and philosophy are separated from each other. Science reaches certain results. It tests them. We can act upon them. Philosophy has been occupied with the question of meanings. Some philosophers feel that philosophy goes further and can criticize the propositions, the presuppositions of science. But as a general rule it can be said that what philosophy has been doing, especially since the time of the Renaissance, is to interpret the results of science. Well, now, mathematics has been going ahead at a frightful rate during this last century, and the realists represent an attempt to interpret it from the point of view of its own technique. You get very strange results looking at this development of mathematics from our empirical point of view.

Alongside of this realistic philosophy we find another—pragmatism—which has developed out of a different aspect of the scientific movements of the period. This doctrine has two outstanding figures: one of them is William James, the other, John Dewey. There are differences in the formulation of pragmatism on the part of these two men. That of James is to be found in his volume entitled *Pragmatism;* that of Dewey, in his earlier statements in his *Essays in Experimental Logic,* and in a more elaborate statement in his more recent book, *Experience and Nature.* Back of the work of both lies the common

assumption of the testing of the truth of an idea, of a hypothesis, by its actual working.

Our problem now is to put this statement in relationship to the doctrines which we discussed earlier. In them the test of truth lies in the coherence, the orderliness of ideas, the way in which ideas fit into a general logical structure as it arises in the mind, a mind which is not only a mind but also a creator of the world, all minds being simply phases of a more general, an Absolute, mind. From this standpoint the world was the result of the thought process of the Absolute. Our thinking is but one of the finite and imperfect elements of this process—imperfect because a mere phase. It would be impossible for us to think of the world in a true fashion because of our finite character. But in proportion as our thinking is coherent, to that degree we can assume that our mind approaches truth.

The point that needs particularly to be recognized in an approach to the pragmatic doctrine is the relationship of thinking to conduct. The undertaking of the Romantic idealists and the rationalists was to present thought as that which discovered the world. It had the distinct business of finding out what the nature of things is. That is, cognition is a process which arose, so to speak, for its own sake. One is curious, one wants to know the world; and knowledge is a simple getting of the nature of the world. Its tests lie, from that standpoint, in the product or in the nature of what is known. This is a copy theory of knowledge; one has in

From "Science Raises Problems for Philosophy—Realism and Pragmatism," *Movements of Thought in the Nineteenth Century* (Chicago: University of Chicago Press, 1936) pp. 343–359.

his mind the impression of that which exists outside; or one may have a coherence theory such as that to which I have referred above, that which fits into a structure which lies outside. The function of knowledge in either case is to give as close a resemblance as possible to something which lies outside the mind.

If we approach the world from the standpoint of the sort of experience with which the psychology we have been presuming deals, we can see that intelligence in its simplest phase, and also in a later phase, really lies inside of a process of conduct. The animal, even the plant, has to seek out what is essential to its life. It has to avoid that which is dangerous for it in its life-process. A plant shows its intelligence by driving down its roots, in its adjustment to the climate. When you get into the animal kingdom, you find much more adjustment and an environment which involves more dangers, in which the getting of food, the avoiding of enemies, the carrying-on of the process of reproduction, take on the form of an adventure. Intelligence consists in the stimulation of those elements which are of importance to the form itself, the selection of both positive and negative elements, getting what is desirable, avoiding what is dangerous. These are the ways in which intelligence shows itself.

For example, the intelligence of the human form is one which has arisen through its ability to analyze this world by discrimination, and, through significant symbols, to indicate to other forms with which it works and to the form itself what the elements are that are of importance to it. It is able to set up such a structure of symbols, images, which stand for the object that it needs. Thinking is an elaborate process of selecting, an elaborate process of presenting the world so that it will be favorable for conduct. Whatever is its later function—it has one of knowledge, which is for its own sake—in its earlier phases we have intelligence, and then thought, as lying inside of conduct. That is, the test of intelligence is found in action. The test of the object is found in conduct itself. What the animal needs is its food, freedom from its enemy. If it responds to the right stimuli, it reaches that food, that

safety. The animal has no other test as to whether it has made such a proper selection except in the result attained. You can test your stimulus only by the result of your conduct which is in answer to it. You see, that takes the research method over into life. The animal, for example, faces a problem. It has to adjust itself to a new situation. The way in which it is going brings danger or offers some unexpected possibility of getting food. It acts upon this and thus gets a new object; and if its response to that object is successful, it may be said to be the true object for that stimulus. It is true in the sense that it brings about a result which the conduct of the animal calls for. If we look upon the conduct of the animal form as a continual meeting and solving of problems, we can find in this intelligence, even in its lowest expression, an instance of what we call "scientific method" when this has been developed into the technique of the most elaborate science. The animal is doing the same thing the scientist is doing. It is facing a problem, selecting some element in the situation which may enable it to carry its act through to completion. There is inhibition there. It tends to go in one direction, then another direction; it tends to seek this thing and avoid that. These different tendencies are in conflict; and until they can be reconstructed, the action cannot go on. The only test the animal can bring to such a reconstruction of its habits is the ongoing of its activity. This is the experimental test; can it continue in action? And that is exactly the situation found also in science.

Take such a problem, for example, as that of the radiation of the sun or of the stars. It is assumed that that radiation is due to the compression which comes with attraction. Then, knowing what the mass of the star is, what the direction of attraction is, and the compression that follows from it, one can figure out how much heat the star can radiate. On that basis it was figured out some forty years ago that the sun has not been in its present condition for a period of more than twenty million years and that it might be perhaps seventeen million years before it became dark and cold, so far as the earth is concerned. Geologists, on the other hand, were turning back the pages of the history of the earth and working out its history. In this process they got various tests as to what the time periods had been. And all these tests called for far longer periods than the astrophysicist was willing to grant. The former dealt in terms of a hundred million years. In recent research we have discovered a new test which is perhaps the most accurate of all; that is the radiation of radioactive bodies. We know, for example, that bodies of this type are continually breaking down. We can see them doing it. In the dark we can see the sparkling which represents a continual discharge of energy, the breaking-down of higher atomic structures into lower. At first this process seemed to be indefinite; but when it was worked out, it was found that such a process in radium might last for several hundred years. The rate of disintegration could be figured out. We know something about the elements, the parts of the earth, that are radioactive; and in that way we can determine what the rate is at which certain minerals which result from such a disintegration as this could have formed, how long a time would be necessary to build them up. Taking this and all the other tests, the scientists set up their theory of the history of the world—the geologist writing his history on one time schedule, and the physicist writing his on the basis of another. We get a clash here. One calls for a period of several hundred million years; the other denies any period longer than twenty million years. There you get a typical scientific problem.

What I want to point out is that it stops the scientist in his process of reconstructing the past. You are reconstructing it on one doctrine or the other. You cannot use both of them. And yet there are facts which lie behind each of them. What is the source of the energy of the sun? It is not burning up coal. It undoubtedly produces heat by the very compression that follows from attraction. That is the only source of heat which can be found. On that basis the age of the earth is twenty million years. And yet, here we have a history which the geologist and the archeological zoölogist and the botanist have been writing on the basis

of other data. And the two stop each other. The process of writing the history of the earth cannot be continued, because the two theories are in conflict with each other. You have these exceptional situations arising over against each other. What is taking place is the recognition that there is another source of energy which has not been attacked, so to speak, in the doctrine of the scientists themselves. This very energy, which is found in the process of radiation which we make use of in our radium watches and clocks, represents a source of energy which the suns may themselves be drawing upon. In its process of radiation, the sun is actually turning our more than four million tons of energy per square yard every few minutes. It is using itself up. Its mass is passing over into the form of radiation. We know that light has weight. Of course, that weight represents just so much mass. Mass must come from the radiation of the sun. The sun is breaking down its own atoms and getting the energy that is in them. We do not know just what the exact process is by which this takes place, whether it is due simply to the immense crushing power of such a great mass as that at the center; but we know that there is much energy in an atom. If you could explode an atom, I think it is said that you could carry the S.S. Leviathan across the ocean on the amount of atomic energy found in a drop of oil—perhaps it is two or three drops if you like, I have forgotten the figures—but there is an enormous amount of energy shut up in the structure of the atoms themselves.

Given such a problem as that, what does the scientist do? He proceeds to start to write his history of the stars as he finds them, the giant and the dwarf stars, the white and blue and red stars, in their different stages of evolution. He starts to write of them on the basis of the hypothesis that these suns have been continually expending the energy involved in their atomic structure in the form of radiation. And that is brought, of course, into its relationship with the geological and biological history of the earth. Could one go on writing the history of the stars and of the surface of the earth so that they do not come into conflict with each other? It was found that there is plenty of time provided under the now recognized form of expenditure of the energy of the sun—a hundred million years or so, instead of twenty million years. So the process of interpreting the world, working out the scientific statement by means of the new hypothesis, could be continued.

Now, what constitutes the test of the hypothesis? The test of it is that you can continue the sort of conduct that was going on. It is the same sort of test which the animal finds. If it finds itself in a difficult situation and sees escape, it rushes off in that direction and gets away. That is a fair test, for it, of what we call a hypothesis. It did not present ideas to itself in terms of significant symbols, but it was a good working hypothesis. It could continue its action of living that way, where it could not have continued it otherwise.

Well, in the same fashion, from a logical standpoint, the scientist is engaged in stating the past history of the world, and he comes up against this blank wall of insufficient time. Now, when he collates the history of the surface and the history of the radiation of the sun, he gets a clue—a hole, so to speak—which will let him escape from that difficulty. That constitutes the test of the truth of his hypothesis. It means that he can continue the process of stating the history of the world within which he is living. And, of course, the process of stating the world, stating our past, is a process of getting control over that world, getting its meaning for future conduct.

That is the importance of the pragmatic doctrine. It finds its test of the so-called "true" in hypotheses and in the working of these hypotheses. And when you ask what is meant by the "working of the hypotheses," we mean that a process which has been inhibited by a problem can, from this standpoint, start working again and going on. Just as the animal no longer stands there, dodging this way and that to avoid its enemy, but can shoot away and get out of danger, so the scientist does not simply have to stand before a history which allows him only twenty million years and a history of two or three hundred million years. He can now

continue the process of giving the history of the world, having this conception of the source of energy which had not been recognized before. Putting it into behavioristic terms, what we mean by the test of the truth is the ability to continue a process which had been inhibited.

A certain statement of the pragmatic doctrine implied that a thing was true if it satisfied desire. And the critics of the doctrine thought that this satisfaction meant the pleasure one could get out of it. That is, if a hypothesis was pleasing to an individual, then it was true. What I have just stated is, however, what is implied in this doctrine—that the test of truth lies in the continued working of the very processes that have been checked in the problem. It is a pleasant thing to get going again after we have been caught and shut in. It is a pleasant thing to have a new planet swim into our ken. But it is not pleasure which constitutes the test, but the ability to keep going, to keep on doing things which we have been trying to do but which we had to stop. That is one phase of the pragmatic doctrine—the testing of a hypothesis by its working.

The other phase I have touched on earlier. You see the attitude of which I have been speaking brings the process of knowing inside of conduct. Here, again, you have a relationship between pragmatic doctrine and the behavioristic type of psychology. Knowing is a process of adjustment; it lies within this process. Cognition is simply a development of the selective attitude of an organism toward its environment and the readjustment that follows upon such a selection. This selection we ordinarily connect with what we call "discrimination," the pointing-out of things and the analysis in this pointing. This is a process of labeling the elements so that you can refer to each under its proper tag, whether that tag is a pointing of the finger, a vocal gesture, or a written word. The thinking process is to enable you to reconstruct your environment so that you can act in a different fashion, so that your knowledge lies inside of the process and is not a separate affair. It does not belong to a world of spirit by itself. Knowledge is power; it is a part of conduct that brings out the other phase that is connected with pragmatism, especially in Dewey's statement.

This phase is its instrumentalism. What selection, and its development into reflective thought, gives us is the tools we need, the instruments we need to keep up our process of living in the largest sense. Knowledge is a process of getting the tools, the instruments. Go back to the illustration I have used above of the atoms as a source of energy. This concept becomes a tool by means of which the length of the life of the stars can be estimated. And when you have that, you can relate it to the age of life on the surface of the earth.

Perhaps the best statement to bring out the importance of this instrumentalism is the term "scientific apparatus." We think of that generally as the actual tools of the scientist; but we know that the term "apparatus" is also used for the ideas, the units, the relations, the equations. When we speak of a scientist's apparatus we are thinking of the very ideas of which he can make use, just as he can use the things which he has in his laboratory. An idea of a certain type, such as that of the energy of an atom, becomes a tool by means of which one is able to construct the picture of a star as a source of energy. There, you see, the object as such is a means which enables one to carry on a process of reconstruction such as is given in scientific doctrine.

Well then, the sources of the pragmatic doctrine are these: one is behavioristic psychology, which enables one to put intelligence in its proper place within the conduct of the form, and to state that intelligence in terms of the activity of the form itself; the other is the research process, the scientific technique, which comes back to the testing of a hypothesis by its working. Now, if we connect these two by recognizing that the testing in its working-out means the setting-free of inhibited acts and processes, we can see that both of them lead up to such a doctrine as the one I have just indicated, and that perhaps the most important phase of it is this: that the process of knowing lies inside of the process of conduct. For this reason pragmatism has been spoken of as a practical sort of philosophy, a sort of bread-and-butter philosophy. It brings the process of thought, of knowledge, inside of conduct.

Because pragmatism has these two aspects, it will be well to spend a little more time in their consideration. The first phase is that of the motor psychology. We have referred to its development into behaviorism. The other phase of the problem is that of the scientific method. The rationalistic philosophies assumed a certain structure of the object as being given in the nature of the object itself, a certain structure of knowledge which the object has and which also lies in the mind—as some thought an innate idea, others a something which the mind could directly perceive. The psychological approach of the empiricists translated this structure of the object over into the relations of states of consciousness to each other. Substance and attribute, cause and effect, and the other so-called "categories" were stated in terms of the mere association of different states of consciousness with each other. If they happened to be associated in a certain way, certain structures arose; if associated otherwise, other structures would have arisen. But they were not structures directly, not objects as such. They were mental structures, subject to mental laws. It was generally assumed that there were structures of things that answered to these mental structures, that lie behind them, as illustrated in the so-called "causal theory of perception," the theory that our mind is causally affected by things and that these things impress themselves on the mind and that with these impressions come not only the sense qualities but also the relations of these qualitative elements to each other. That is the structure of the object. Both rationalism and empiricism assumed that there are certain structures in the object which the mind gets hold of, and that it is through these structures that one can know the laws of causation, the laws of the relationship of qualities to substances, and so on. Particularly, however, it was in the law of causation that science and philosophy found the reality of things. What were the uniform successions of events to each other in a causal series? Everything, as far as possible, was carried back to causal laws or uniformities.

The history of science since the Renaissance is really a history of the research process. At first this research was conceived of, and still is largely conceived of, as a simple discovery of something which is out there. Discoveries followed each other closely, so that one statement of the object was rapidly succeeded by another statement. This seemed only natural, because men were finding out more about the world through the scientific method. And this new scientific method carried with it another criterion than that which belonged to the older period, the criterion of experiment, of experimental tests, of experimentation that included observation. Exceptions arose, we have seen, and a problem was formulated, and then a hypothesis for the solution of the problem was presented, and then this solution had to be tested. That is, one had to see whether or not this new hypothesis would work. If it did, then the hypothesis became an accepted theory; if it did not, a new one was substituted for it and subjected to the same test.

This test or experiment—the research method—in some sense took the place of the mathematical method in which one proceeded seemingly by demonstration, by deduction. At least the assumption of the latter was that, if one had all the ultimate elements of things, one could deduce from their mathematical relations what the structure of the world is. This was essentially the position of Descartes. He assumed that he could conceive of the world as made up of ultimate spatial elements which were moving with reference to each other, and, given this motion and the spatial elements, could work out what the structure of things must be. He identified matter with space itself and assumed a great whirl of this, with the consequent movement of all the different particles in relation to each other; and he undertook to show how the world arose out of such simple motions. He undertook to do this by means of the mathematical laws of physics. Leibnitz also assumed that, if one could only get hold of

these ultimate laws, it was conceivable that one could work out the nature of things from them. In fine, the rationalist went on the assumption that there were certain structures of things of which the mind got hold.

The practice of research science, which I have described at some length above, was continually to approach, continually to seek for, new problems, and with these new problems to find new hypotheses. And these new hypotheses brought with them new worlds which took the place of the old worlds. The test of them was one which lay in the experience of man. It was to be found in the actual process of cognition as it lay in experience itself. The test became the ultimate test, and from this standpoint the mathematical theory simply presented an apparatus for working out hypotheses, for determining what the situation must be within which the test could take place. But the assurance in regard to new hypotheses, with their new structure of the world, rested upon the test of experience itself. It is this scientific method, which finds the test of the truth of a hypothesis in its working, that has got its philosophic expression in the pragmatic doctrine.

This doctrine is nothing but an expression of the scientific method, which is an experimental method. It has advanced by the positing of hypotheses. It has advanced from problems toward their solution, and these problems have called for analysis. And in the case of changes that we have been describing, this analysis is of the type mentioned above. But, besides these analyses, it is necessary that the scientist should present some hypothesis as a solution to the problem. The hypothesis is not simply a statement of the ultimate elements and the relations between them. If that were the case, one's thinking would be mere deduction, mere demonstration. Given the elements and their relations, we can see that possible combinations can be made and conclusions deduced. That leads to the curious situation that Poincaré has pointed out, that in mathematical science we seem to advance simply by drawing the necessary conclusions from the premises. In that case there should be nothing in the conclusion which was not in the premises; and yet these sciences have advanced from one achievement to another, discovering that which is new, reaching results which are foreign to the positions from which thinking started. Mathematical science has not been simply a recording of the necessary results which can be drawn from a set of given premises. It has been an achievement such as that found in the physical sciences. For example, within mathematics itself we have seen the development of so-called "transcendental numbers." How shall we explain this: that we get, by a purely deductive process, results not found in the premises? Actually, the conclusion that we have to reach is that we are not using simply a deductive process. For, after stating our problem by means of the most penetrating analysis, we reach a point at which a reconstruction of thought takes place. The scientist, including the mathematician, presents a hypothesis and then tests it. In mathematics this testing of the hypothesis is generally hidden, covered up. The way in which the mathematician or mathematical scientist justifies himself is by giving a necessary line of reasoning, and one loses the point at which the hypothesis is made.

Put it in this way: If you should take any other view of the world than our own—such as that expressed by the Ptolemaic theory, the geocentric theory of the world—on the basis of that account you could state the positions of all the different planetary bodies; you could tell where they would all be, could predict eclipses, and other relations. Up to some time in the eighteenth century you could have covered the whole field of astronomy by a Ptolemaic account of the world. But, by working out that doctrine with all its implications, you could not have deduced from it the Copernican, the heliocentric, theory. By the most complete set of deductions possible you could not have reached the latter theory as a necessary result of the former. When one has accepted the statement of the Copernican theory that the sun is the center, then you can show why the conclusions that you drew from the Ptolemaic theory were accurate. You can show why it is that,

when the sun seems to revolve about the earth, you can get the same statement of the relative positions of sun and earth and the other planets whether you regard the earth as revolving on its axis or the sun as revolving about the earth. You can take the geocentric theory with the heavens revolving about the earth, or the heliocentric with the earth as revolving about the sun, and show that in either case you get the same relative positions of the different bodies. That is, you can deduce the results of the Ptolemaic theory from the results of the Copernican theory. But you could not move in the opposite direction at the time when the Copernican theory took the place of the Ptolemaic. To put it in a more general form, later hypotheses which you present and accept must be able to take up into themselves all the facts gathered before, all the results which have been attained; and they must be able to show how these results were reached. But you cannot advance by a mere process of deduction from an earlier to a later hypothesis. Of course, if your later hypothesis is merely a correcting of errors, you can. If a statement of your bank account is not right, you can go back and find the mistake. But you cannot deduce later theories from earlier ones. You cannot deduce the theory of electromagnetism from a theory of solid atoms. But, given the theory as it is being worked out, we can state mass in terms of electromagnetism. From the standpoint of mathematical science, we seem always to have only a process of deduction; and the point at which the new hypothesis comes in is one which is very apt to be completely hidden. It is not realized that this has taken place in the mind of the scientist who has a new idea, for, just as soon as he has a new idea, he states the whole in terms of a set of equations where the results follow necessarily from the premises. And in this way he covers up the hypothesis that he has fashioned. Actually, the hypothetical method is essential to development even inside the field of exact mathematics.

Mathematical technique has shown itself peculiarly powerful in dealing with problems which science has approached. It succeeded, for example, in dealing with the problem of change. That problem was never attacked by the ancient world, that is, the problem of change while it is occurring. The ancient world considered change in terms of qualitative elaboration, in terms of degeneration and decay, but always from the point of view of the result being attained. Motion, in particular, was studied in terms of spaces which were in the past, in times which had elapsed. The ancient thinkers never undertook to deal with each change while it was going on.

Now, that is just the problem that presented itself in dealing with what in modern mathematics are called "acceleration" and "deceleration," that is, increase and decrease in velocity. How can you estimate the change that is uniformly taking place within change itself? You have a body moving toward the earth. You can measure the length of the fall and the time of the fall. But this fall is not one in which velocity has been constant. On the contrary, its velocity has been uniformly increasing. That seemed to mean that the ratio between the distance passed over and the time elapsed is itself continually changing. And yet this ratio always means a certain distance passed over in a certain elapsed time. That is, you have to take a certain distance and a certain time as uniform. We say that a body has fallen so far in a half or in a thousandth of a second, and that its velocity is such and such. That means it has passed over this fixed portion of its path in this fixed time. Then the next portion may represent a ration which gives a greater time or a greater space. But each portion of it has to be treated as if it were fixed. The problem of the falling body is the problem of a process in which the velocity is uniformly increased. It is that problem that the "infinitesimal calculus," as Leibnitz termed it, or "fluxions," as Newton called it—terms which refer to identical methods at bottom—was invented to solve. These are the methods which mathematics has used for dealing with a seemingly insoluble problem. What Leibnitz and Newton did was to find a way of stating numbers in terms of infinitesimals, of distances that are so slight, times so short, that they can be neglected. A more accurate statement was one in which these dis-

tances were stated in terms of the law of change. A still more satisfactory treatment was a statement in terms of limits. That is, it was found out that as one approached a certain limit a certain law was indicated. And it was assumed, then, that this law must be true of the limit itself. What was true of the different situations as you approached this limit, so to speak, must be true of the limit itself.

There are different ways of stating a mathematical procedure by means of which, as I have said, the scientist was able to deal with the law of change while that change itself was occurring—of getting at the law of the change of a change. It is this that has enabled science to get inside of, and to deal with, a process that is going on. The method is one of analysis which goes farther and farther and discovers laws by means of this continued analysis. It was the effectiveness of this analysis which gave prestige to mathematics. It was no longer simply a static science of Euclidean geometry, no longer a mere statement of equations between static quantities; it was a method by means of which one could get inside the processes which were themselves going on, and get the laws of those changes which were occurring.

As I have said, the realistic philosophy has been a generalization, in some sense, of this mathematical method which has been so remarkable in its achievements. It has enabled the scientist to enter all sorts of fields—those of the changes of air, of fluids of all sorts; those of the changes with which physics and chemistry have to deal; those of the changes of heat, for example. It was a method which, by its analysis, was able to get back to ultimate elements—ultimate at least for the time being—and get relations existing between these elements even when the relations were changing. Knowledge, then, seemed to consist in getting hold of ultimate elements and the relations between them and also the study, as I have said, of the relations of relations, the changes of changes. It seemed to consist in getting hold of the ultimate elements and relata and the relations between them. That has been the goal of realistic thought.

This movement and the pragmatic are the two which are peculiarly characteristic of the modern period, for both of them grow out of phases of the scientific process: the one arises out of the mathematical technique which has been greatly generalized, so that it goes into the field of pure logic in which mathematics and philosophy are brought together; the other is a development of the technique of experimental science and the recognition that the test of a hypothesis lies in the successful solution of a problem and that human advance consists in the solution of problems, solutions that have to be stated in terms of the processes that have been stopped by the problem. Progress is not toward a known goal. We cannot tell what the goal is toward which we are moving, and we do not test our movements or direct them according to any fixed goal that we can set up. What we do do, in the face of difficulties or problems, is to seek solutions. We seek a hypothesis which will set free the processes that have been stopped in the situation that we call problematic.

# The Present as the Locus of Reality

The subject of this lecture is found in the proposition that reality exists in a present. The present of course implies a past and a future, and to these both we deny existence. Whitehead's suggestion that, as specious presents vary in temporal spread, one present can be conceived which could take in the whole of temporal reality, would seemingly leave to us passage but would eliminate the past and the future. Whatever else it would be it would not be a present, for that out of which it had passed would not have ceased to exist, and that which is to exist would already be in that inclusive present. Whether this would still leave the character of passage might be doubted, but in any case the essential nature of the present and of existence would have disappeared. For that which marks a present is its becoming and its disappearing. While the flash of the meteor is passing in our own specious presents it is all there if only for a fraction of a minute. To extend this fraction of a minute into the whole process of which it is a fragment, giving to it the same solidity of existence which the flash possesses in experience, would be to wipe out its nature as an event. Such a conspectus of existence would not be an eternal present, for it would not be a present at all. Nor would it be an existence. For a Parmenidean reality does not exist. Existence involves non-existence; it does take place. The world is a world of events.

There is little purpose or profit in setting up antinomies and overthrowing the one by the other, or in relegating permanence to a subsistent, timeless world while the event, in which there is nothing but passage, is made the substantial element in existent things. The permanent character that we are interested in is one that abides in existence, and over against which change exists as well. There is, that is, the past which is expressed in irrevocability, though there has never been present in experience a past which has not changed with the passing generations. The pasts that we are involved in are both irrevocable and revocable. It is idle, at least for the purposes of experience, to have recourse to a "real" past within which we are making constant discoveries; for that past must be set over against a present

From *The Philosophy of the Present*, Ed. Arthur E. Murphy, (Chicago: Univ. of Chicago Press, 1980 [1932]), pp. 1–31.

within which the emergent appears, and the past, which must then be looked at from the standpoint of the emergent, becomes a different past. The emergent when it appears is always found to follow from the past, but before it appears it does not, by definition, follow from the past. It is idle to insist upon universal or eternal characters by which past events may be identified irrespective of any emergent, for these are either beyond our formulation or they become so empty that they serve no purpose in identification. The import of the infinite in ancient and modern mathematical thought illustrates this impotence.

The possibility remains of pushing the whole of real reality into a world of events in a Minkowski space-time that transcends our frames of reference, and the characters of events into a world of subsistent entities. How far such a conception of reality can be logically thought out I will not undertake to discuss. What seems to me of interest is the import which such a concept as that of irrevocability has in experience.

I will not spend time or rhetoric in presenting the moving picture of the histories that have succeeded each other from the myths of primitive ages up to Eddington's or Jeans' account of "The Universe about Us." It is only of interest to note that the rapidity with which these pasts succeed each other has steadily increased with the increase in critical exactitude in the study of the past. There is an entire absence of finality in such presentations. It is of course the implication of our research method that the historian in any field of science will be able to reconstruct what has been, as an authenticated account of the past. Yet we look forward with vivid interest to the reconstruction, in the world that will be, of the world that has been, for we realize that the world that will be cannot differ from the world that is without rewriting the past to which we now look back.

And yet the character of irrevocability is never lost. That which has happened is gone beyond recall and, whatever it was, its slipping into the past seems to take it beyond the influence of emergent events in our own conduct or in nature. It is the "what it was" that changes, and this seemingly empty title of irrevocability attaches to it whatever it may come to be. The importance of its being irrevocable attaches to the "what it was," and the "what it was" is what is not irrevocable. There is a finality that goes with the passing of every event. To every account of that event this finality is added, but the whole import of this finality belongs to the same world in experience to which this account belongs.

Now over against this evident incidence of finality to a present stands a customary assumption that the past that determines us is *there.* The truth is that the past is there, in its certainty or probability, in the same sense that the setting of our problems is there. I am proceeding upon the assumption that cognition, and thought as a part of the cognitive process, is reconstructive, because reconstruction is essential to the conduct of an intelligent being in the universe.[1] This is but part of the more general proposition that changes are going on in the universe, and that as a consequence of these changes the universe is becoming a different universe. Intelligence is but one aspect of this change. It is a change that is part of an ongoing living process that tends to maintain itself. What is peculiar to intelligence is that it is a change that involves a mutual reorganization, an adjustment in the organism and a reconstitution of the environment; for at its lowest terms any change in the organism carries with it a difference of sensitivity and response and a corresponding difference in the environment. It is within this process that so-called conscious intelligence arises, for consciousness is both the difference which arises in the environment because of its relation to the organism in its organic process of adjustment, and also the difference in the organism because of the change which has taken place in the environment. We refer to the first as meaning, and to the second as ideation. The reflection of the organism in the environment and the reflection of environment in the organism are essential phases in the maintenance of the life process that constitutes conscious intelligence.

I will consider the import of consciousness in a later lecture. At present my interest is only to locate that activity to which cognition belongs and of which thought is an expression. I am distinguishing in particular that existence of the world for the individual and social organism which answers to the more general usage of the term consciousness from that situation which answers to the term "consciousness of." It is the latter which, to my mind, connotes cognition. The distinction between the two falls in with that which I have suggested between the problem and its setting. The setting within which adjustment takes place is essential to the adjustment and falls within what belongs to the "field of consciousness," as that term is generally used—especially when we recognize the implications of that which is more definitely in the field of consciousness. The term "field of awareness" is at times used in the same sense, but it is more apt to carry with it the value of "awareness of" than is the term "consciousness." In other words, in knowledge there is always the presupposition of a world that is there and that provides the basis for the inferential and ideational process of cognition. This of course restricts cognition or "consciousness of" to that which has within it an inferential strain.

Now the world which is there in its relationship to the organism, and which sets the conditions for the adjustment of the organism and the consequent change in and of that world, includes its past. We approach every question of a historical character with a certain apparatus, which may be nicely defined, and this more technically defined material of documents, oral testimony, and historical remains subtends a given past which extends backward from the memories of yesterday and today, and which we do not question. We use the apparatus to answer hypothetically the historical questions which press upon us, and to test our hypotheses when they have been elaborated. It is of course understood that any part of this apparatus and of the past within which it is embedded may itself fall under doubt, but even the most heroic skepticism in its very enunciation cannot get away from the memory of the words and ideas which formulate the skeptical doctrine.

Some such given past is involved in questions bearing upon the past. And this given past extends the specious present. It is true that the ultimate agreement between the meanings of two documents may lie in experience in a specious present, but only upon the supposition of the comparison we have previously made of the documents. This comparison stretches back of us and remains unquestioned until someone points out an error therein and thus brings it into question, but then only upon the basis of his and others' past. Take the ingenious suggestion, of Gosse's father, I believe, that God had created the world with its fossils and other evidences of a distant past to try men's faith; and bring the suggestion up to a half an hour ago. Suppose that the world came into existence, with its exact present structure, including the so-called contents of our minds, thirty minutes ago, and that we had some ulterior evidence analogous to Mr. Gosse's fundamentalist views, that this had taken place. We could examine the hypothesis only in the light of some past that was there, however meager it had become. And this past extends indefinitely, there being nothing to stop it, since any moment of it, being represented, has its past, and so on.

What do we mean, now, by the statement that there has been some real past with all its events, in independence of any present, whose contents we are slowly and imperfectly deciphering? We come back of course to the very corrections which we make in our historical research, and to the higher degree of evidence of that which has been discovered over that which can be offered for the discarded account. Higher degrees of probability and added evidence imply that there is or has been some reality there which we are bringing to light. There is thus a palpable reference to the unquestioned past by means of whose evidence we investigate and solve the problems that arise. And the very fact to which I have referred, that any accepted account of the past, though not now in question, may be conceivably thrown into doubt, seems to imply some unquestionable past which would be the background for the solution of all conceivable problems. Let us admit this for the time being, and ask the further question whether this past independent of any present does enter at all into our investigations—I mean as a presupposition that plays any part in our thinking? If we should take away this presupposition would our apparatus and the operation of it in historical research be in any way affected? Certainly not, if we concern ourselves only with the problems with which historians in social or scientific history are concerned. Here the reference is always and solely to the given past out of which a problem has arisen; and the outlines of the problem and the tests to which presented hypotheses are subjected, are found in the given past. As we have seen, this given past may itself at a later date be affected with doubt and brought under discussion. And yet the possible dubiety of the given past in no way affects the undertaking. This is another way of saying that the dubiety of all possible pasts never enters into the historian's thinking. The only approach to such entrance is the demand that all past pasts should be accounted for and taken up into the latest statement. And every past past, in so far as it is reconstructed, is in so far shown to be incorrect. In the implications of our method we seem to approach a limiting statement, even if at infinity, which would fill out all gaps and correct all errors. But if we are making corrections there must seemingly be some account that is correct, and even if we contemplate an indefinite future of research science which will be engaged in the undertaking we never escape from this implication.

There is another way of saying this, and that is that our research work is that of discovery, and we can only discover what is there whether we discover it or not. I think however that this last statement is in error, if it is supposed to imply that there is or has been a past which is independent of all presents, for there may be and beyond doubt is in any present with its own past a vast deal which we do not discover, and yet this which we do or do not discover will take on different meaning and be

different in its structure as an event when viewed from some later standpoint. Is there a similar error in the conception of correction of the past error and in the suggestion that it implies the absolutely correct, even if it never reaches it? I am referring to the "in-itself" correctness of an account of events, implied in a correction which a later historian makes. I think that the absolute correctness which lies back in the historian's mind would be found to be the complete presentation of the given past, if all its implications were worked out. If we could know everything implied in our memories, our documents and our monuments, and were able to control all this knowledge, the historian would assume that he had what was absolutely correct. But a historian of the time of Aristotle, extending thus his known past, would have reached a correct past which would be at utter variance with the known world of modern science, and there are only degrees of variance between such a comparison and those which changes due to research are bringing out in our pasts from year to year. If we are referring to any other "in-itself" correctness it must be either to that of a reality which by definition could never get into our experience, or to that of a goal at infinity in which the type of experience in which we find ourselves ceases. It is of course possible to assume that the experience within which we find ourselves is included in some world or experience that transcends it. My only point is that such an assumption plays no part in our judgments of the correctness of the past. We may have other reasons, theological or metaphysical, for assuming a real past that could be given in a presentation independent of any present, but that assumption does not enter into the postulations or technique of any sort of historical research.

While the conception of an "in-itself" irrevocable past is perhaps the common background of thinking, it is interesting to recur to the statement that I made earlier that the research scientist looks forward not only with equanimity but also with excited interest to the fundamental changes which later research will bring into the most exact determinations which we can make today. The picture which this offers is that of presents sliding into each other, each with a past which is referable to itself, each past taking up into itself those back of it, and in some degree reconstructing them from its own standpoint. The moment that we take these earlier presents as existences apart from the presentation of them as pasts they cease to have meaning to us and lose any value they may have in interpreting our own present and determining our futures. They may be located in the geometry of Minkowski space-time, but even under that assumption they can reach us only through our own frames of reference or perspectives; and the same would be true under the assumptions of any other metaphysics which located the reality of the past in pasts independent of any present.

It would probably be stated that the irrevocability of the past is located in such a metaphysical order, and that is the point which I wish to discuss. The historian does not doubt that something has happened. He is in doubt as to what has happened. He also proceeds upon the assumption that if he could have all the facts or data, he could determine what it was that happened. That is, his idea of irrevocability attaches, as I have already stated, to the "what" that has happened as well as to the passing of the event. But if there is emergence, the reflection of this into the past at once takes place. There is a new past, for from every new rise the landscape that stretches behind us becomes a different landscape. The analogy is faulty, because the heights are there, and the aspects of the landscapes which they reveal are also there and could be reconstructed from the present of the wayfarer if he had all the implications of his present before him; whereas the emergent is not there in advance, and by definition could not be brought within even the fullest presentation of the present. The metaphysical reality suggested by Eddington's phrase that our experience is an adventuring of the mind into the ordered geometry of space-time[2] would, however, correspond to a preëxistent landscape.

There is of course the alternative doctrine of Whitehead that perspectives exist in nature as intersecting time systems, thus yielding not only different presents but also different pasts that correspond to them. I cannot, however, see how Whitehead with the fixed geometry of space-time which he accepts can escape from a fixed order of events, even though the "what" of these events depends upon the ingression of eternal objects arising through the action of God, thus giving rise to emergence.[3] The point at issue is whether the necessity with which the scientist deals is one that determines the present out of a past which is independent of that or any present. An ordered space-time involves such a metaphysical necessity. From this standpoint the different pasts of experience are subjective reinterpretations, and the physicist is not interested in making them a part of the whole scheme of events. Whitehead's philosophy is a valiant attempt to harmonize this sort of geometric necessity with emergence and the differences of varying perspectives. I do not believe that this can be accomplished, but I am more interested in the answer to the question, whether the necessity which is involved in the relations of the present and the past derives from such a metaphysical necessity, that is, from one that is independent of any present.

I revert here to my original proposition that a reality that transcends the present must exhibit itself in the present. This alternative is that found in the attitude of the research scientist, whether he confesses it in his doctrine or not. It is that there is and always will be a necessary relation of the past and the present but that the present in which the emergent appears accepts that which is novel as an essential part of the universe, and from that standpoint rewrites its past. The emergent then ceases to be an emergent and follows from the past which has replaced the former past. We speak of life and consciousness as emergents but our rationalistic natures will never be satisfied until we have conceived a universe within which they arise inevitably out of that which preceded them. We cannot make the emergent a part of the thought relation of past and present, and even when we have seemingly accepted it we push biochemistry and behavioristic psychology as far as we can in the effort to reduce emergence to a disappearing point. But granting the research scientist a complete victory—a wholly rationalized universe within which there is determined order—he will still look forward to the appearance of new problems that will emerge in new presents to be rationalized again with another past which will take up the old past harmoniously into itself.

Confessedly, the complete rationality of the universe is based upon an induction, and what the induction is based upon is a moot point in philosophic doctrine. Granted any justifiable reason for believing it, all our correlations greatly strengthen it. But is there such a reason? At this crucial point there is the greatest uncertainty. Evidently the scientist's procedure ignores this. It is not a moot question with him. It is not a question in his procedure at all. He is simply occupied in finding rational order and stretching this back, that he may previse the future. It is here that his given world functions. If he can fit his hypothesis into this world and if it anticipates that which occurs, it then becomes the account of what has happened. If it breaks down, another hypothesis replaces it and another past replaces that which the first hypothesis implied.

The long and short of it is that the past (or the meaningful structure of the past) is as hypothetical as the future. Jeans' account of what has been taking place inside of Aldebaran or Sirius Minor during the past millions of years is vastly more hypothetical than the astronomer's catalogue of what eclipses will take place during the next century and where they will be visible. And the metaphysical assumption that there has been a definite past of events neither adds to nor subtracts from the security of any hypothesis which illuminates our present. It does indeed offer the empty form into which we extend any hypothesis and develop its implications, but it has not even the fixity which Kant found in his forms of intuition. The paradoxes of relativity, what Whitehead terms the different meanings of time in different time systems, reveal the hypothetical nature of the ruled schedules of the past into which we are to fit the events which our phys-

ical theories unroll behind us. We may have recourse to the absolute space-time with its coincidences of events and intervals between them, but even here it is open to argument whether this interpretation of the transformations from one frame of reference to another is the final one, whether we have attained the ultimate structure of the physical universe or only a more powerful mathematical apparatus for reaching higher exactitude in measurements and calculations, whose interpretation will vary with the history of mathematical physics. The Minkowski space-time is as much an hypothesis as the de Broglie wave-constitution of matter.

But the irrevocability of the past event remains even if we are uncertain what the past event was. Even the reversible character of physical processes which mathematical equations seem to disclose does not shake this character of time experience. It may be thinkable that viewed from some vast distance the order of some of what we call the same events might differ in different perspectives, but within any perspective what has passed cannot recur. In that perspective what has happened has happened, and any theory that is presented must make room for that order in that perspective. There is an unalterable temporal direction in what is taking place and if we can attach other processes to this passage we can give to them as much of certainty as the degree of attachment justifies. Given a certain value for the velocity of a moving body in a certain frame of reference, we can determine where the body will necessarily be. Our problem is to determine just what it is that has preceded what is taking place so that the direction of temporal progress may determine what the world is going to be. There is a certain temporal process going on in experience. What has taken place issues in what is taking place, and in this passage what has occurred determines spatio-temporally what is passing into the future. So far then as we can determine the constants of motion we can follow that determination, and our analysis seeks to resolve the happening in so far as may be into motion. In general, since passage is itself given in experience, the direction of changes that are going on partly conditions what will take place. The event that has taken place and the direction of the process going on form the basis for the rational determination of the future. The irrevocable past and the occurring change are the two factors to which we tie up all our speculations in regard to the future. Probability is found in the character of the process which is going on in experience. Yet however eagerly we seek for such spatiotemporal structures as carry with them deducible results, we none the less recognize relations of things in their processes which can not be resolved into quantitative elements, and although as far as possible we correlate them with measurable characters we in any case recognize them as determining conditions of what is taking place. We look for their antecedents in the past and judge the future by the relation of this past to what is taking place. All of these relationships within the ongoing process are determining relations of what will be, though the specific form of that determination constitutes the scientific problem of any particular situation. The actuality of determination within the passage of direct experience is what Hume by his presuppositions and type of analysis eliminated from experience, and what gives such validity as it has to Kant's deduction of the categories.

It is the task of the philosophy of today to bring into congruence with each other this universality of determination which is the text of modern science, and the emergence of the novel which belongs not only to the experience of human social organisms, but is found also in a nature which science and the philosophy that has followed it have separated from human nature. The difficulty that immediately presents itself is that the emergent has no sooner appeared than we set about rationalizing it, that is, we undertake to show that it, or at least the conditions that determine its appearance, can be found in the past that lay behind it. Thus the earlier pasts out of which it emerged as something which did not involve it are taken up into a more comprehensive past that does lead up to it. Now what this amounts to is that whatever does happen, even the emergent, happens under determining conditions—especially, from the standpoint of the exact sciences, under spatio-temporal conditions which lead to deducible conclusions as to what will happen within certain limits, but also under determining conditions of a qualitative sort whose assurances lie within probability only—but that these conditions never determine completely the "what it is" that will happen. Water as distinct from combinations of oxygen and hydrogen may happen. Life and so-called consciousness may happen. And quanta may happen, though it may be argued that such happening stands on a different "level" from that of life and consciousness. When these emergents have appeared they become part of the determining conditions that occur in real presents, and we are particularly interested in presenting the past which in the situation before us conditioned the appearance of the emergent, and especially in so presenting it that we can lead up to new appearances of this object. We orient ourselves not with reference to the past which was a present within which the emergent appeared, but in such a restatement of the past as conditioning the future that we may control its reappearance. When life has appeared we can breed life, and given consciousness, we can control its appearance and its manifestations. Even the statement of the past within which the emergent appeared is inevitably made from the standpoint of a world within which the emergent is itself a conditioning as well as a conditioned factor.

We could not bring back these past presents simply as they occurred—if we are justified in using the expression—except as presents. An exhaustive presentation of them would amount only to reliving them. That is, one present slipping into another does not connote what is meant by a past. But even this statement implies that there were such presents slipping into each other, and whether we regard them from that standpoint or not we seem to imply their reality as such, as the structure within which the sort of past in which we are interested must lie, if it is an aspect of the real past. Passing by the ambiguities which such a statement carries within it, what I want to emphasize is that the irrevocability of the past does not issue from this conception of the past. For in our use of the term irrevocability we are pointing toward what must have been, and it is a structure and process in the present which is the source of this necessity. We certainly cannot go back to such a past and test our conjectures by actually inspecting its events in their happening. We test our conjectures about the past by the conditioning directions of the present and by later happenings in the future which must be of a certain sort if the past we have conceived was there. The force of irrevocability then is found in the extension of the necessity with which what has just happened conditions what is emerging in the future. What is more than this belongs to a metaphysical picture that takes no interest in the pasts which arise behind us.

In the analysis which I have undertaken we come then, *first,* to passage within which what is taking place conditions that which is arising. Everything that is taking place takes place under necessary conditions. *Second,* these conditions while necessary do not determine in its full reality that which emerges. We are getting interesting reflections of this situation from the scientist's criticism of his own methods of reaching exact determination of position and velocity and from the implications of quanta. What appears in this criticism is that while the scientist never abandons the conditioning of that which takes place by that which has gone on, expressed in probability, he finds himself quite able to think as emergent even those events which are subject to the most exact determination. I am not attempting to previse what later interpretation will be put upon the speculations of de Broglie, Schroeder, and Planck. I am simply indicating that even within the field of mathematical physics rigorous thinking does not necessarily imply that conditioning of the present by the past carries with it the complete determination of the present by the past.

*Third,* in passage the conditioning of that which is taking place by that which has taken place, of the present by the past, is *there.* The past in that sense is in the present; and, in what

we call conscious experience, its presence is exhibited in memory, and in the historical apparatus which extends memory, as that part of the conditioning nature of passage which reflects itself into the experience of the organic individual. If all objects in a present are conditioned by the same characters in passage, their pasts are implicitly the same, but if, to follow out a suggestion taken from the speculations about quanta, one electron out of two thousand sets energy free, when there are no determining conditions for the selection of this electron over against the other nineteen hundred and ninety nine, it is evident that the past as exhibited in the conduct of this electron will be of a sort that will not even implicitly be the same as that of the others in that group, though its jump will be conditioned by all that has gone before. If of two thousand individuals under disintegrating social conditions one commits suicide where, so far as can be seen, one was as likely to succumb as another, his past has a peculiarly poignant nature which is absent from that of the others, though his committing of suicide is an expression of the past. The past is there conditioning the present and its passage into the future, but in the organization of tendencies embodied in one individual there may be an emergent which gives to these tendencies a structure which belongs only to the situation of that individual. The tendencies coming from past passage, and from the conditioning that is inherent in passage, become different influences when they have taken on this organized structure of tendencies. This would be as true of the balance of processes of disruption and of agglomeration in a star as in the adjustment to each other of a living form and its environment. The structural relationship in their reciprocal balance or adjustment arranges those passing processes which reflect backward and lead us to an account of the history of the star. As Dewey has maintained, events appear as histories which have a *dénouement,* and when an historical process is taking place the organization of the conditioning phases of the process is the novel element which is not predictable from the separate phases themselves, and which at once sets the scene for a past that leads to this outcome.[4] The organization of any individual thing carries with it the relation of this thing to processes that occurred before this organization set in. In this sense the past of that thing is "given" in the passing present of the thing, and our histories of things are elaborations of what is implicit in this situation. This "given" in passage is there and is the starting point for a cognitive structure of a past.

*Fourth,* this emergent character, being responsible for a relationship of passing processes, sets up a given past that is, so to speak, a perspective of the object within which this character appears. We can conceive of an object such as, say, some atom of hydrogen, which has remained what it is through immeasurable periods in complete adjustment to its surroundings, which has remained real in the slipping of one present into another, or, better, in one unbroken, uneventful passage. For such an object there would have been unbroken existence but no past, unless we should revert to the occasion on which it emerged as an atom of hydrogen. This amounts to saying that where being is existence but not becoming there is no past, and that the determination involved in passage is a condition of a past but not its realization. The relationship of passage involves distinguishable natures in events before past, present and future can arise, as extension is a relationship which involves distinguishable physical things before structurable space can arise. What renders one event distinguishable from another is a becoming which affects the inner nature of the event. It seems to me that the extreme mathematization of recent science in which the reality of motion is reduced to equations in which change disappears in an identity, and in which space and time disappear in a four dimensional continuum of indistinguishable events which is neither space nor time is a reflection of the treatment of time as passage without becoming.

What then is a present? Whitehead's definition would come back to the temporal spread of the passage of the events that make up a thing, a spread which is extended enough to make it possible for the thing to be what it is.[5] That of an atom of iron would not need to be

longer than the period within which the revolution of each of its electrons around the nucleus is completed. The universe during this period would constitute a duration from the point of view of the atom. The specious present of a human individual would presumably be a period within which he could be himself. From the standpoint which I have suggested it would involve a becoming. There must be at least something that happens to and in the thing which affects the nature of the thing in order that one moment may be distinguishable from another, in order that there may be time. But there is in such a statement a conflict of principles of definition. From one standpoint we are seeking for what is essential to a present; from the other we are seeking for the lower limit in a process of division. I will refer to the latter first, for it involves the question of the relation of time to passage—to that within which time seems to lie and in terms of whose extension we place time and compare times. The thousandth part of a second has a real significance, and we can conceive of the universe as foundering in a sea of entropy within which all becoming has ceased. We are dealing here with an abstraction of the extension of mere passage from the time within which events happen because they become. In Whitehead's treatment this is called "extensive abstraction," and leads up to an event-particle as mathematical analysis leads up to the differential. And an event-particle should have the same relationship to something that becomes that the differential of a change such as an accelerating velocity has to the whole process. In so far, extensive abstraction is a method of analysis and integration and asks for no other justification than its success. But Whitehead uses it as a method of metaphysical abstraction and finds in the mere happening the event, the substance of that which becomes. He transfers the content of what becomes to a world of "eternal objects" having ingression into events under the control of a principle lying outside of their occurrence. While, then, the existence of what occurs is found in the present, the "what it is" that occurs does not arise out of happening, it happens to the event through the metaphysical process of ingression. This seems to me to be an improper use of abstraction, since it leads to a metaphysical separation of what is abstracted from the concrete reality from which the abstraction is made, instead of leaving it as a tool in the intellectual control of that reality. Bergson refers, I think, to the same improper use of abstraction, in another context, as the spatialization of time, contrasting the exclusive nature of such temporal moments with the interpenetration of the contents of "real" duration.

If, on the contrary, we recognize what becomes as the event which in its relation to other events gives structure to time, then the abstraction of passage from what is taking place is purely methodological. We carry our analysis as far as the control of subject matter requires, but always with the recognition that what is analysed out has its reality in the integration of what is taking place. That this is the result of defining the event as that which becomes, is evident, I think, in the application and testing of our most abstruse hypotheses. To be of value and to be accredited these must present new events springing out of old, such as the expansion or contraction of the universe in Einstein's and Weyl's speculations on the seeming recessions at enormous velocities of distant nebulae, or the stripping of electrons from atomic nuclei in the center of stellar bodies in Jeans' speculations upon the transformation of matter into radiation. And these happenings should so fit into our experimental findings that they may find their reality in the concretion of what is taking place in an actual present. The pasts which they spread back of us are as hypothetical as the future which they assist us in prevising. They become valid in interpreting nature in so far as they present a history of becomings in nature leading up to that which is becoming today, in so far as they bring out what fits into the pattern that is emerging from the roaring loom of time, not in so far as they erect metaphysical entities which are the tenuous obverse of mathematical apparatus.

If, in Bergson's phrase, "real duration" becomes time through the appearance of unique events which are distinguishable from each other through their qualitative nature, a something that is emergent in each event, then bare passage is a manner of arranging these events. But what is essential to this arrangement is that in each interval which is isolated it must be possible that something should become, that something unique should arise. We are subject to a psychological illusion if we assume that the rhythm of counting and the order which arises out of counting answer to a structure of passage itself, apart from the processes which fall into orders through the emergence of events. We never reach the interval itself between events, except in correlations between them and other situations within which we find congruence and replacement, something that can never take place in passage as such. We reach what may be called a functional equality of represented intervals within processes involving balance and rhythm, but on this basis to set up time as a quantity having an essential nature that allows of its being divided into equal portions of itself is an unwarranted use of abstraction. We can hypothetically reconstruct the past processes that are involved in what is going on as a basis for the cognitive construction of the future which is arising. What we are assured of by the experimental data is that we comprehend that which is going on sufficiently to predict what will take place, not that we have attained a correct picture of the past independent of any present, for we expect this picture to change as new events emerge. In this attitude we are relating in our anticipation presents that slip into others, and their pasts belong to them. They have to be reconstructed as they are taken up into a new present and as such they belong to that present, and no longer to the present out of which we have passed into the present present.

A present then, as contrasted with the abstraction of mere passage, is not a piece cut out anywhere from the temporal dimension of uniformly passing reality. Its chief reference is to the emergent event, that is, to the occurrence of something which is more than the processes that have led up to it and which by its change, continuance, or disappearance, adds to later passages a content they would not otherwise have possessed. The mark of passage without emergent events is its formulation in equations in which the so-called instances disappear in an identity, as Meyerson has pointed out.[6]

Given an emergent event, its relations to antecedent processes become conditions or causes. Such a situation is a present. It marks out and in a sense selects what has made its peculiarity possible. It creates with its uniqueness a past and a future. As soon as we view it, it becomes a history and a prophecy. Its own temporal diameter varies with the extent of the event. There may be a history of the physical universe as an appearance of a galaxy of galaxies. There is a history of every object that is unique. But there would be no such history of the physical universe until the galaxy appeared, and it would continue only so long as the galaxy maintained itself against disruptive and cohesive forces. If we ask what may be the temporal spread of the uniqueness which is responsible for a present the answer must be, in Whitehead's terms, that it is a period long enough to enable the object to be what it is. But the question is ambiguous for the term "temporal spread" implies a measure of time. The past as it appears with the present and future, is the relation of the emergent event to the situation out of which it arose, and it is the event that defines that situation. The continuance or disappearance of that which arises is the present passing into the future. Past, present and future belong to a passage which attains temporal structure through the event, and they may be considered long or short as they are compared with other such passages. But as existing in nature, so far as such a statement has significance, the past and the future are the boundaries of what we term the present, and are determined by the conditioning relationships of the event to its situation.

The pasts and futures to which we refer extend beyond these contiguous relations in passage. We extend them out in memory and history, in anticipation and forecast. They are preëminently the field of ideation, and find their locus in what is called mind. While they are in the present, they refer to that which is not in that present, as is indicated by their relation to past and future. They refer beyond themselves and out of this reference arises their representational nature. They evidently belong to organisms, that is to emergent events whose nature involves the tendency to maintain themselves. In other words their situation involves adjustment looking toward a past, and selective sensitivity looking toward a future. What may be called the stuff out of which ideas arise are the attitudes of these organisms, habits when we look toward the past, and early adjustments within the act to the results of their responses when we look toward the future. So far these belong to what may be termed the immediate past and future.

This relation of the event to its situation, of the organism to its environment, with their mutual dependence, brings us to relativity, and to the perspectives in which this appears in experience. The nature of environment answers to the habits and selective attitudes of organisms, and the qualities that belong to the objects of the environment can only be expressed in terms of sensitivities of these organisms. And the same is true of ideas. The organism, through its habits and anticipatory attitudes, finds itself related to what extends beyond its immediate present. Those characters of things which in the activity of the organism refer to what lies beyond the present take on the value of that to which they refer. The field of mind, then, is the larger environment which the activity of the organism calls for but which transcends the present. What is present in the organism, however, is its own nascent activity, and that in itself and in the environment which sustains it, and there is present also its movement from the past and beyond the present. It belongs to the so-called conscious organism to complete this larger temporal environment by the use of characters found in the present. The mechanism by which the social mind accomplishes this I will discuss later; what I wish to bring out now is that the field of mind is the temporal extension of the environment of the organism, and that an idea resides in the organism because the organism is using that in itself which moves beyond its present to take the place of that toward which its own activity is tending. That in the organism which provides the occasion for mind is the activity which reaches beyond the present within which the organism exists.

But in such an account as this I have been implicitly setting up this larger period within which, say, an organism begins and completes its history as there seemingly in independence of any present, and it is my purpose to insist upon the opposite proposition that these larger periods can have no reality except as they exist in presents and that all their implications and values are there located. Of course this comes back, *first,* to the evident fact that all the apparatus of the past, memory images, historical monuments, fossil remains and the like are in some present, and, *second,* to that portion of the past which is there in passage in experience as determined by the emergent event. It comes back, *third,* to the necessary test of the formulation of the past in the rising events in experience. The past we are talking about lies with all its characters within that present.

There is, however, the assumed implication that this present refers to entities which have a reality independent of this and any other present, whose full detail, though of course beyond recall, is inevitably presumed. Now there is a confusion between such a metaphysical assumption and the evident fact that we are unable to reveal all that is involved in any present. Here we stand with Newton before a boundless sea and are only gathering the pebbles upon its shore. There is nothing transcendent about this powerlessness of our minds to exhaust any situation. Any advance which makes toward greater knowledge simply extends the horizon of experience, but all remains within conceivable experience. A greater mind than Newton's or Einstein's would reveal in experience, in the world that is there, structures and processes that we cannot find nor even adumbrate. Or take Bergson's conception of all our memories, or all occur-

rences in the form of images, crowding in upon us, and held back by a central nervous system. All of this is conceivable in a present whose whole richness should be at the disposal of that very present. This does not mean that the aeons revealed in those structures and processes, or the histories which those images connote would unroll themselves in a present as temporally extended as their formulation implies. It means, in so far as such an unbridled conception or imagination can have meaning, that we should have an inconceivable richness offered to our analysis in the approach to any problem arising in experience.

The past in passage is irrecoverable as well as irrevocable. It is producing all the reality that there is. The meaning of that which is, is illuminated and expanded in the face of the emergent in experience, like $(a + b)$ to the 25th power by the binomial theorem, by the expansion of the passage which is going on. To say that the Declaration of Independence was signed on the 4th of July 1776 means that in the time system which we carry around with us and with the formulation of our political habits, this date comes out in our celebrations. Being what we are in the social and physical world that we inhabit we account for what takes place on this time schedule, but like railway time-tables it is always subject to change without notice. Christ was born four years before A.D.

Our reference is always to the structure of the present, and our test of the formulation we make is always that of successfully carrying out our calculations and observations in a rising future. If we say that something happened at such a date, whether we can ever specify it or not, we must mean that if in imagination we put ourselves back at the supposed date we should have had such an experience, but this is not what we are concerned with when we work out the history of the past. It is the import of what is going on in action or appreciation which requires illumination and direction, because of the constant appearance of the novel from whose standpoint our experience calls for a reconstruction which includes the past.

The best approach to this import is found in the world within which our problems arise. Its things are enduring things that are what they are because of the conditioning character of passage. Their past is in what they are. Such a past is not eventual. When we elaborate the history of a tree whose wood is found in the chairs in which we sit, all the way from the diatom to the oak but lately felled, this history revolves about the constant re-interpretation of facts that are continually arising; nor are these novel facts to be found simply in the impact of changing human experiences upon a world that is there. For, in the first place, human experiences are as much a part of this world as are any of its other characteristics, and the world is a different world because of these experiences. And, in the second place, in any history that we construct we are forced to recognize the shift in relationship between the conditioning passage and emergent event, in that part of the past which belongs to passage, even when this passage is not expanded in ideation.

The outcome of what I have said is that the estimate and import of all histories lies in the interpretation and control of the present; that as ideational structures they always arise from change, which is as essential a part of reality as the permanent, and from the problems which change entails; and that the metaphysical demand for a set of events which is unalterably there in an irrevocable past, to which these histories seek a constantly approaching agreement, comes back to motives other than those at work in the most exact scientific research.

# Appendix[7]

Durations are a continual sliding of presents into each other. The present is a passage constituted by processes whose earlier phases determine in certain respects their later phases. Reality then is always in a present. When the present has passed it no longer is. The question arises whether the past arising in memory and in the projection of this still further backwards, refers to events which existed as such continuous presents passing into each other, or to that conditioning phase of the passing present which enables us to determine conduct with reference to the future which is also arising in the present. It is this latter thesis which I am maintaining.

The implication of my position is that the past is such a construction that the reference that is found in it is not to events having a reality independent of the present which is the seat of reality, but rather to such an interpretation of the present in its conditioning passage as will enable intelligent conduct to proceed. It is of course evident that the materials out of which that past is constructed lie in the present. I refer to the memory images and the evidences by which we build up the past, and to the fact that any reinterpretation of the picture we form of the past will be found in a present, and will be judged by the logical and evidential characters which such data possess in a present. It is also evident that there is no appeal from these in their locus of a present to a real past which lies like a scroll behind us, and to which we may recur to check up on our constructions. We are not deciphering a manuscript whose passages can be made intelligible in themselves and left as secure presentations of that portion of what has gone before, to be supplemented by later final constructions of other passages. We are not contemplating an ultimate unchangeable past that may be spread behind us in its entirety subject to no further change. Our reconstructions of the past vary in their extensiveness, but they never contemplate the finality of their findings. They are always subject to conceivable reformulations, on the discovery of later evidence, and this reformulation may be complete. Even the most vivid of memory images may be in error. In a word our assurances concerning the past are never attained by a congruence between the constructed past and a real past independent of this construction, though we carry this attitude at the back of our heads, because we do bring our immediate hypothetical reconstructions to the test of the accepted past and adjudge them by their agreement with the accepted record; but this accepted past lies in a present and is subject, itself, to possible reconstruction.

Now it is possible to accept all this, with a full admission that no item in the accepted past is final, and yet to maintain that there remains a reference in our formulation of the past event to a something that happened which we can never expect to resuscitate in the content of reality, something that belonged to the event in the present within which it occurred. This amounts to saying that there is behind us a scroll of elapsed presents, to which our constructions of the past refer, though without the possibility of ever reaching it, and without the anticipation that our continual reconstructions will approach it with increasing exactness. And this brings me to the point at issue. Such a scroll, if attained, is not the account that our pasts desiderate. If we could bring back the present that has elapsed in the reality which belonged to it, it would not serve us. It would be that present and would lack just that character which we demand in the past, that is, that construction of the conditioning nature of now present passage which enables us to interpret what is arising in the future that belongs to this present. When one recalls his boyhood days he cannot get into them as he then was, without their relationship to what he has become; and if he could, that is if he could reproduce the experience as it then took place, he could not use it, for this would involve his not being in the present within which that use must take place. A string of presents conceivably existing as presents would never constitute a past. If then there is such a reference it is not to an entity which could fit into any past, and I cannot believe that the reference, in the past as experienced, is to a something which would not have the function or value that in our experience belongs to a past. We are not referring to a real past event which would not be the past event we are seeking. Another way of saying this is that our pasts are always mental in the same manner in which the futures that lie in our imaginations ahead of us are mental. They differ, apart from their successive positions, in that the determining conditions of interpretation and conduct are embodied in the past as that is found in the present, but they are subject to the same test of validity to which our hypothetical futures are subject. And the novelty of every future demands a novel past.

This, however, overlooks one important character of any past, and that is that no past which we can construct can be as adequate as the situation demands. There is always a reference to a past which cannot be reached, and one that is still consonant with the function and import of a past. It is always conceivable that the implications of the present should be carried further than we do actually carry them, and further than we can possibly carry them. There is always more knowledge which would be desirable for the solution of any problem confronting us but which we cannot attain. With the conceivable attainment of this knowledge we should undoubtedly construct a past truer to the present within which the implications of this past lie. And it is to this past that there is always a reference within every past which imperfectly presents itself to our investigation. If we had every possible document and every possible monument from the period of Julius Caesar we should unquestionably have a truer picture of the man and of what occurred in his life-time, but it would be a truth which belongs to this present, and a later present would reconstruct it from the standpoint of its own emergent nature. We can then conceive of a past which in any one present would be irrefragable. So far as that present was concerned it would be a final past, and if we consider the matter, I think that it is this past to which the reference lies in that which goes beyond the statement which the historian can give, and which we are apt to assume to be a past independent of the present.

## Notes

1. For a fuller account of this theory of knowledge see "A Pragmatic Theory of Truth," (1929), SW 320–344].
2. Arthur Stanley Eddington, *Space, Time, and Gravitation: An Outline of the General Relativity Theory* (Cambridge: Cambridge Univ. Press, 1920. p. 51)

3. Mead's recurrent discussion of Whitehead is based mainly on *An Enquiry Concerning the Principles of Natural Knowledge* (Cambridge: Cambridge Univ. Press, second ed. 1925) and *The Concept of Nature* (Cambridge: Cambridge Univ. Press, 1920), with some reference also to *Science and the Modern World* (Cambridge: Cambridge Univ. Press, 1926). He did not include *Process and Reality* (Cambridge: Cambridge Univ. Press, 1929) in his discussion.

4. Cf. John Dewey, *Experience and Nature*, chapters 3 and 7.

5. Cf. Whitehead, *An Enquiry Concerning the Principles of Natural Knowledge*, pp. 22 ff.

6. Emile Meyerson, *Identity and Reality* (New York: MacMillan, 1930), passim.

7. These pages were found among Mr. Mead's papers after his death. They seem to have been written later than the chapter to which they are here appended, possibly as a result of a critical discussion of it at the University of Chicago Philosophy Club meeting in January 1931.

## *Suggestions for Further Reading*

### Works by Mead

*The Philosophy of the Present,* ed. Arthur E. Murphy, (Chicago: University of Chicago Press, 1932).

*Mind, Self and Society from the Standpoint of a Social Behaviorist,* ed. Charles W. Morris, (Chicago: University of Chicago Press, 1934).

*Movements of Thought in the 19th Century,* ed. Merritt H. Moore, (Chicago: University of Chicago Press, 1936).

*The Philosophy of the Act,* ed. Charles W. Morris, et al., (Chicago: University of Chicago Press, 1938).

*The Individual and the Social Self,* ed. David L. Miller, (Chicago: University of Chicago Press, 1982).

### Anthologies

*Selected Writings: George Herbert Mead,* ed. Andrew J. Reck, (Chicago: University of Chicago Press, [1964] 1981).

*George Herbert Mead: Essays on His Social Philosophy,* ed. John W. Petras, (New York: Teachers College Press, 1968).

### Essential Works on Mead

Mitchell Aboulafia, *The Mediating Self: Mead, Sartre, and Self-Determination* (New Haven: Yale University Press, 1986).

Mitchell Aboulafia, ed., *Philosophy, Social Theory, and the Thought of George Herbert Mead* (Albany: SUNY Press, 1991).

James Campbell, *The Community Reconstructs: The Meaning of Pragmatic Social Thought* (Urbana: University of Illinois Press, 1992).

Gary A. Cook, *George Herbert Mead: The Making of a Social Pragmatist* (Urbana: University of Illinois Press, 1993).

Walter R. Corti, ed., *The Philosophy of George Herbert Mead* (Winterthur: Amriswiler, 1973).

Andrew Feffer, *The Chicago Pragmatists and American Progressivism* (Ithaca: Cornell University Press, 1993).

Hans Joas, *G. H. Mead: A Contemporary Re-examination of His Thought* (Cambridge: MIT Press, 1985).

David L. Miller, *George Herbert Mead: Self, Language, and the World* (Chicago: University of Chicago Press, [1973] 1980).

Sandra B. Rosenthal and Patrick L. Bourgeois, *Mead and Merleau-Ponty: Toward a Common Vision* (Albany: SUNY Press, 1991).

Darnell Rucker, *The Chicago Pragmatists* (Minneapolis: University of Minnesota Press, 1969).

# PART III
## CONTEXTS

# FEMINISM AND THE WRITINGS OF AMERICAN WOMEN

## Introduction by Charlene Haddock Seigfried

When William James described philosophy as the ability "to fancy everything different from what it is," as seeing "the familiar as if it were strange, and the strange as if it were familiar," as rousing "us from our native 'dogmatic slumber'" and breaking up "our caked prejudices," he was simply expressing in vivid prose Plato's and Aristotle's well-known dictum that philosophy begins in wonder.[1] But when John Dewey said that he learned from Jane Addams "the enormous value . . . of tearing away the armor-plate of prejudice, of convention, isolation that keeps one from sharing to the full in the larger and even the more unfamiliar and alien ranges of the possibilities of human life and experience," he acknowledged a genuinely new presence in philosophic reflection.[2] Ironically, the range of experiences Addams introduces into philosophy are predominately those of women, the working classes, and ethnic minorities. They can be alien and unfamiliar only to those who do not share in these experiences, either because they are men, middle or upper class, or an actual majority or privileged elite. In order to realize what has been missing in philosophic discourse, the overwhelming androcentric, ethnic, and class biases of conventional philosophizing have to be recognized and overcome. The presence of women, members of the working class, and disadvantaged ethnic minorities, including African Americans, in the discipline of philosophy wrenched the meaning of 'dogmatic slumbers' away from formalist debates over the validity of epistemological claims and toward the recognition of the legitimacy and fertility of alternative viewpoints, underscoring the pervasiveness of oppressive practices and biased perspectives.

Few women attained the prominence of the male philosophers who make up the canon of American philosophy, and those women who did enjoy a considerable reputation at the time were soon forgotten in academic circles, and their books often went out of print. Many factors worked against them: women who studied and got their degrees in philosophy often went on to make their mark in other fields; well into the twentieth century the most prestigious universities would not grant doctorates to women even when they earned them; philosophy departments did not accept women as professional equals and therefore seldom hired or promoted them; few colleges or universities would employ or retain married women; and rules against nepotism were applied to exclude women rather than men. Given their precarious academic status, women philosophers were not usually in a position to mentor graduate students who would in turn keep their work alive from one generation to the next by teaching it or referring to it in publications. Clearly, these factors are the expression of a pervasive misogyny and the sexual division of labor that made intellectual pursuits the prerogative of men. Despite the odds, there were nonetheless women who not only persisted in doing philosophy but who also made significant contributions.

Some of the better-known women—and the classical American philosophers they influenced, and were influenced by—are: Margaret Fuller and the transcendentalists; Christine Ladd-Franklin and Charles Sanders Peirce; Mary Whiton Calkins, Ethyl Puffer Howes, and William

James, Josiah Royce, and the other Cambridge philosophers; Jane Addams, Ella Flagg Young, and John Dewey; Jessie Taft, Kate Gordon, Helen Thompson Wooley and George Herbert Mead and the other Chicago pragmatists. Some, like Calkins and Ladd-Franklin continued developing theories that ignored gender. Others, like Gilman, Addams, and Howes developed original feminist theories. In either case, they both drew on, and influenced, the work of classical American philosophers. Their writings still have much to offer current debates that involve both feminists and pragmatists. These issues include: the anti-essentialist, relational self; the value of reciprocity, especially when the participants are unequally situated; and the importance of uniting theory and practice, intellect and emotion.

As long as thinkers and issues sanctioned by the canon dominated philosophy, women were discouraged from seeing themselves in the role of academic philosophers and had little incentive to look to philosophy for guidance in their lives as women. Yet according to pragmatists, by contrast, theory arises out of experience and is developed interactively. John Dewey, especially, issued a clarion call for philosophers to get beyond their continual recapitulation of traditional canonical texts and their fascination with arcane professional debates and to focus on experience and the actual problems that trouble individuals and societies. This pragmatic reconstruction of philosophic theory and practice opened a space for issues of vital concern to women. Moreover, intelligence, so understood, is not the monopoly of "a refined class or capitalistic possession of a few learned specialists," but "the slow cooperative work of a humanity guided by reflective intelligence."[3] It is not surprising that women who became acquainted with pragmatism in its formative years would reflect on, evaluate, and make proposals concerning their own situation as women, and introduce feminist issues into pragmatist discourse. Although privileged in some ways, as by Anglo-Saxon ethnicity, skin color, class, and educational advantages, early generations of college-educated women in elite schools were still speaking from the margins (of power, influence, and recognition). Not only was the way that theory influences practice and practice theory a matter of personal emancipation and social urgency for them, but the concrete specificity of their analyses meant that the obstacles, as well as the promise of such an emphasis on reciprocity (a reciprocity of unequally positioned subjects), could be recognized and assessed.

Pragmatists take seriously the way individual persons experience and interpret the world and they recognize the historical constraints and intersubjective constitution of such interpretations. They also developed a methodology for distinguishing between distorted, prejudicial beliefs and emancipatory ones, as well as between empty generalities and effective hypotheses. They rejected the ideal of a neutral, detached rationality and replaced it with the model of an understanding that is experimental and transformative, in which thinking is an instrument of action, and the results obtained feed back to further articulate, refine, or reject the original beliefs. Such an approach has much to offer to women who are determined to challenge stereotypes and develop their full potential. Those who took up the offer contributed to formulating, and further developing, such pragmatist themes as: the origin of thinking in the early socialization of children; the impact of gender, ethnicity, and class on the cultivation or stunting of individuality in social relations; the criticism of individualistic ethics and development of a dynamic social ethics; and a cooperative problem-solving methodology that takes into consideration the unequal positioning of the participants.

Many women both inside and outside academia had already independently reflected on the disparity between received views and their own experiences. Mary Church Terrell and Ida B. Wells, for example, tirelessly and courageously brought home to a white-dominated society, which did not want to acknowledge it, the widespread practice of lynching in the post-Civil War South. They publicized the fact that lynching and inflammatory charges of black rape of white women were used as methods to terrorize blacks and return them to servile status. But in the more rarified realm of the discipline of philosophy, in which authority was traditionally vested in classic texts, virtually all of them written by men, women could appeal for the first time to the authority of their own experience as a legitimate philosophic approach. The women who were already exploring the conjunction of theory and practice in innovative ways attracted the attention of academic pragmatists, both as an independent confirmation of pragmatic views on the nature and purpose of thinking and as original insights. These women include: the experimental educational theory of Ella Flagg Young, Alice Dewey, and the other teachers at the Laboratory School, as well as Lucy Sprague Mitchell at Bank Street College of Education; Myrtle McGraw's theory on infant development; Helen Thompson Wooley's work on sex differences being due to experience rather than physiology; Charlotte Perkins Gilman on the unacknowledged economic importance of women's work and how women's lesser economic opportunities affect their lives; and Ethyl Puffer Howe, Jessie Taft, and Jane Addams on the negative effects of the social, religious, legal, and other restrictions on women's human development and the benefits that accrue to all of society when women's contributions are recognized and encouraged.[4]

Feminists in a variety of disciplines have pointed out that a common theme in many women's writings from the past to the present is the dissonance between what they experience and how it is interpreted in both high and low culture, in institutional forms, in science, religion, and the government. As a consequence of their subordinate status and marginality, women are well situated to recognize the mechanisms by which a dominant perspective is maintained and enhanced. According to Margaret Fuller, for example, in *Woman in the Nineteenth Century,* it is hypocritical for men to appeal to chivalry or the need to protect the weaker sex (as reasons to restrict women's activities and opportunities), when they approve of the exhausting field work forced on black women (even during pregnancy) or the killing labor of seamstresses.[5] Men call women who excel in intellectual accomplishments masculine, thereby implying that such powers are beyond the ordinary power of women and discouraging women from striving after such unfeminine goals. Furthermore, despite protestations of concern for women, men rarely use their greater opportunities actively, to help them but instead protect the territory carved out for themselves. In sum, men believe that women are made for men, and do not encourage them to be autonomous beings.

Gilman argued that men both appropriated human characteristics, such as intelligence and sociality, as defining male characteristics and exaggerated what is only biologically male as the ideal measure of human development in every sphere.[6] This masculinization of religion, education, the arts, literature, sports, marriage, law, and economics accounts for many of their negative features, such as immoderate aggressiveness in sports, wife and child abuse in marriage, politics as the civilian equivalent of physical combat, the excessive accumulation of wealth by some, and the impoverishment of women and children in economics. Although male privilege and power have encouraged male development while stunting women's, they have also distorted men in ways that contribute to many social ills. Taft sees women as being caught between contradictory expectations: if they fulfill one they are or are taken to be unfit to pursue the other.[7] Most contradictions of these stem from the strict demarcation of the privacy of family life from the public sphere. Given societal arrangements, women have to choose "between a crippled life in the home or an unfulfilled one out of it;" between family ties and legal, governmental, and business expectations; and between expectations of chastity and sexual satisfaction due to a double standard. These problems, in turn, are attributed to the effects of industrialization, which have left the home and women's roles in a feudal state, while encouraging rapid social changes outside it.

Consider the insights Jane Addams provides. Around the turn of the century, the inner-city settlement house founded by Addams and Ellen Gates Starr (1889) provided a challenging alternative to domestic life for the growing number of young women graduating from college at a time when there were few outlets for their skills. Nothing in their educational background could have prepared them for the enormity of the problems they encountered, including rapid urbanization, industrialization without any social safety nets, the influx of non-English speaking immigrants into overcrowded neighborhoods, political corruption, rampant prejudice, and class divisions. Addams' and Starr's reflective, cooperative, and experimental approaches to these problems attracted the attention of the philosophers Dewey and Mead, as well as William Isaac Thomas and many of the social scientists at the University of Chicago, who worked with them while developing sociology as a discipline.[8] A particularly robust form of pragmatism, developed out of this collaboration in which theory and practice were continuous.

Dewey's repeated attacks on the incoherence of the model of classical liberal individualism, for example, are even more persuasive when seen in the context of Addams's model of the inter-subjective constitution of the individual. Her model derives from her astute observations of the residents of the Hull House settlement. These women's expectations, beliefs, and sense of self changed dramatically over time through their interactions with their immigrant neighbors. These neighbors, in turn, changed their habits and beliefs as they worked with settlement residents to transform their physical and social surroundings. Dewey credits Addams with developing the thesis that democracy is a way of life, a position that is central to his own theorizing. But Addams also contributes to the pragmatist model of the reconstruction of experience by her demonstrations of the complex ways gender, ethnicity, and class interact in experience and how ignoring their influence distorts our interpretation of events and, consequently, our ability to resolve problematic situations fairly and completely.

Hull House residents combined the pragmatist theses of learning from experience, perspectival views of knowledge, and anti-elitism into a democratic, multicultural perspective. Their own experiences working among the immigrant poor led them to emphasize the uniqueness of each person, and made them mistrust grand theory about the masses and ideological claims about irreconcilable animosities. Addams's insistence that reciprocity ought to characterize the relationship between teacher and student, social worker and client, the privileged and the under-privileged classes, and her testimony that she daily learned as much from the poor among whom she chose to live as she taught them, were neither *a priori* deductions from moral principles nor idle platitudes, but conclusions reached from reflections on her own experience. She constantly tested her own beliefs in her interactions with others and discarded or revised them as needed. Her perspectivism and pluralism are concretely grounded. She was more explicit than the male pragmatists about the value of the insights of women and of disadvantaged groups.

In "A Function of the Social Settlement" (1899), for example, Addams identifies democracy as the guiding value for the settlement house movement. In doing so, she embraces the classical pragmatist understanding of democracy as linking belief in the intrinsic dignity of the individual with the social aim of cooperative empowerment. But she adds to that tradition a sharp realization that the failure to realize a truly democratic society is reflected in class divisions, which most Americans would rather not acknowledge. She undercuts the social Darwinist claim that the more powerful classes rule because of superior accomplishments by attributing their success to better economic and social opportunities and educational advantages that should by right be extended to all classes. But even so admirable a goal as reconstructing society to give equal opportunity to everyone would not explain what separates her settlement approach from philanthropy. She is as determined to prevent the perception that Hull House activity is a form of charity as she is to distinguish its method of systematically gathering data as a preliminary step to proposing solutions to social problems from academic social science research.

Addams explains the difference by explicitly appealing to James's and Dewey's pragmatic theories of knowledge as rules or methods of action in which the value of knowledge is determined by its success in resolving the real life problems that give rise to reflective inquiry. Hull House was conceived of as a deliberate experiment to employ effectively knowledge in human conduct by testing its validity and discovering the best conditions for its realization. Since the lived experience of the women of Hull House was consciously both communally interactive and experimental, it can provide a working model to replace the now largely discredited one of theory as a neutral attitude detached from practice. Unlike other pragmatist approaches, Addams's method involved a group of women actually living together in a settlement house in the midst of a community whose problems they intended to address. Among the advantages that Addams delineates regarding her approach to social problems are: (1) the opportunity to harmonize one's life and theory, thought and action; (2) the concrete realization that "the good we secure ourselves is precarious and uncertain . . . until it is secured for all of us and incorporated into our common life;" and (3) the provision of an outlet for young women who desire to participate more fully in the life of the larger society and support for rejecting the family claim restricting their accomplishments to the private sphere.[9]

The historical conditions necessitating such a method of communal living have changed. It is now acceptable for women to live alone or to pursue a career single mindedly or to seek public service inside as well as outside marriage. But Hull House was a living arrangement that was deliberately organized outside of the traditional heterosexual family. It was an intentional community with stated goals and protocols, which revised procedures in accordance with explicit experimental guidelines, and which recorded the methods as well as the results of its social projects. Addams' settlement house sufficiently resembles the conditions of a social science laboratory experiment for its contributions to have more than historic value. These contributions have value in philosophy as exemplars of the pragmatist experimental method in action. Hull House's very uniqueness provides a foil for reflecting on whether the failures of some of our contemporary approaches to social problems stem in part from ignoring insights gained through a pragmatically inspired community that rigorously tested its theory in practice and used its practice to revise its theory.

What were the pragmatist principles guiding the Chicago settlement house movement? In *Twenty Years at Hull-House*, Addams explains that Hull House was founded on the premise that not only are the various classes interdependent, but that "the social relation is essentially a reciprocal relation."[10] Addams took such a pragmatist avowal of reciprocity out of the purely theoretic sphere by developing a method for overcoming social barriers that were seldom even acknowledged at the time as making any difference. The method of living together and working in the inner city slums of Chicago meant that Hull House women could not ignore the differences of class, race, language, creed, gender, and tradition that underlay the mutual hostilities dividing society into the privileged and the underprivileged.[11] One of the biggest barriers was the middle and upper class background and privileged ethnic status of the settlement workers themselves. How this distorted their ability to take in the reality of the poor and working class situations in which they found themselves and limited their options had first to be recognized before it could be addressed. Addams often invoked the pragmatist experimental approach and advocated flexibility not only because such a recognition of one's own prejudices took time and repeated efforts, but also because such awareness was most directly the result of failure to secure the ends sought. The work also required settlement women's sensitivity to how their neighbors interpreted their efforts and respect for their neighbors' opinions. Recognizing that solutions that were one-sidedly imposed from the top down neither worked nor were justified by democratic standards, Addams's method of inquiry involved "living quietly side by side with their neighbors, until they grow into a sense of relationship and mutual interests." Not only did the women need to accumulate facts patiently before working toward resolutions, but they rejected the dominant positivist approach of neutrality as necessary to scientific objectivity, and instead practiced a sympathetic cooperative approach "as one of the best instruments for that accumulation."[12]

In *Democracy and Social Ethics,* Addams argues that morality has hitherto been too individualistic and ought to give way to a social morality. As such, morality's temper will be democratic "for it implies that diversified human experience and resultant sympathy which are the foundation and guarantee of Democracy."[13] She attributes "much of the insensibility and hardness of the world . . . to the lack of imagination which prevents a realization of the experiences of other people." She rather surprisingly claims that "we are under a moral obligation in choosing our experiences, since the result of those experiences must ultimately determine our understanding of life." Limiting the range of our acquaintances to our own familiar class, ethnicity, religion, nationality, etc., limits the scope of our ethics.[14] But such experiences could lead to overcoming barriers to understanding and to mutually working together to solve personal and community problems, or to reproducing the inequities of power and the biases of an unquestioned dominant position. When Addams encourages us to ask whether our experiences have any value, she is encouraging the development of a critical pragmatic spirit of inquiry that will lead to the sort of personal growth and social betterment that reflects democratic values.

Earlier emphases in feminist theory on joining with other women in the common cause of overcoming women's oppression has been criticized as privileging white, middle class women's experiences. Blacks, Hispanics, lesbians, and third world women have reconfigured feminist theory so that much of it now takes into account the diversity of women's experiences; the intertwining of racial, class, nationalistic, and homophobic biases with sexism, and the variety rather than homogeneity of women's issues. From its origins, pragmatist theory rejected essentialism and emphasized the multiple relationships through which identities are developed and concrete problems are resolved. According to Dewey, democracy as a central value of pragmatism "means faith in the potentialities of human nature as that nature is exhibited in every human being irrespective of race, color, sex, birth and family, of material or cultural wealth." But "racial, color or other class prejudice" remain obstacles to realizing one's potential and must be dealt with if the conditions necessary for these capacities to reach fulfillment are to be realized in fact and not just in theory.[15] Recent developments in feminist theory can find an ally in pragmatism's theoretical and practical integration of philosophy and everyday life, knowledge with values, reflection with politics, intellectual and ethical principles with maximum inclusivity, and objectivity with perspectivism. On the other hand, the abstract nature of the appeal to a pluralism of perspectives by classical American philosophers becomes more apparent in light of decades of feminist research and theory into the specifics of gender, sexuality, nationality, and race. Reflections by Jane Addams, W.E.B. Du Bois, Alain Locke, and others on how class, racial, and sexual bias distorts theory and undermines social and political reforms have only recently been recognized as making contributions to pragmatist theory. How that theory will change in light of their contributions has yet to be determined. Pragmatists argue that knowledge and values are limited and distortive to the extent they are developed from one or a few perspectives, while feminists demonstrate just what those limitations are and how knowledge and values change when other perspectives are explored. Unless and until pragmatists incorporate these feminist insights, they have not yet carried out their own agenda.

## Notes

1. William James, *Some Problems of Philosophy* (Cambridge: Harvard University Press, 1979), p. 11.
2. John Dewey, "In Response," *LW,* 5:421.
3. "The Need for a Recovery of Philosophy," *MW,* 10:45, 20.

4. See Seigfried, *Pragmatism and Feminism* (Chicago: University of Chicago Press, 1996).
5. Margaret Fuller, *Woman in the Nineteenth Century* (Columbia, SC: University of Southern Carolina Press, 1980).
6. Charlotte Perkins Gilman, *The Man-Made World; or, Our Androcentric Culture* (New York: Charlton, 1911).
7. Jessie Taft, *The Woman Movement from the Point of View of Social Consciousness* (Menasha, WI: The Collegiate Press, George Banta Pub. Co., 1915).
8. Hull House settlement work predated the founding of a department of sociology at the University of Chicago, and it has recently been suggested that Jane Addams's role in the origins of sociology has not been properly recognized by the profession. For an assessment of the issues involved, see Dorothy Ross, "Gendered Social Knowledge: Domestic Discourse, Jane Addams, and the Possibilities of Social Science," in Helene Silverberg, ed., *Gender and American Social Science: The Formative Years* (Princeton University Press, forthcoming).
9. Jane Addams, *Twenty Years at Hull-House* (New York: Signet Classic, 1981), pp. 91–95.
10. Ibid., p. 76.
11. Ibid., p. 89.
12. Ibid., p. 98.
13. Addams, *Democracy and Social Ethics,* ed. Anne Firor Scott (Cambridge, MA: Belknap Press of Harvard University Press, 1964), p. 7.
14. Ibid., pp. 9–10.
15. "Creative Democracy—The Task Before Us," *LW,* 14:226.

# *Jane Addams:* Charitable Effort

All those hints and glimpses of a larger and more satisfying democracy, which literature and our own hopes supply, have a tendency to slip away from us and to leave us sadly unguided and perplexed when we attempt to act upon them.

Our conceptions of morality, as all our other ideas, pass through a course of development; the difficulty comes in adjusting our conduct, which has become hardened into customs and habits, to these changing moral conceptions. When this adjustment is not made, we suffer from the strain and indecision of believing one hypothesis and acting upon another.

Probably there is no relation in life which our democracy is changing more rapidly than the charitable relation—that relation which obtains between benefactor and beneficiary; at the same time there is no point of contact in our modern experience which reveals so clearly the lack of that equality which democracy implies. We have reached the moment when democracy has made such inroads upon this relationship, that the complacency of the old-fashioned charitable man is gone forever; while, at the same time, the very need and existence of charity, denies us the consolation and freedom which democracy will at last give.

It is quite obvious that the ethics of none of us are clearly defined, and we are continually obliged to act in circles of habit; based upon convictions which we no longer hold. Thus our estimate of the effect of environment and social conditions has doubtless shifted faster than our methods of administrating charity have changed. Formerly when it was believed that poverty was synonymous with vice and laziness, and that the prosperous man was the righteous man charity was administered harshly with a good conscience; for the chari-

From *Democracy And Social Ethics* (New York: Macmillan, 1902), pp. 13–70.

table agent really blamed the individual for his poverty, and the very fact of his own superior prosperity gave him a certain consciousness of superior morality. We have learned since that time to measure by other standards, and have ceased to accord to the money-earning capacity exclusive respect; while it is still rewarded out of all proportion to any other, its possession is by no means assumed to imply the possession of the highest moral qualities. We have learned to judge men by their social virtues as well as by their business capacity, by their devotion to intellectual and disinterested aims, and by their public spirit, and we naturally resent being obliged to judge poor people so solely upon the industrial side. Our democratic instinct instantly takes alarm. It is largely in this modern tendency to judge all men by one democratic standard, while the old charitable attitude commonly allowed the use of two standards, that much of the difficulty adheres. We know that unceasing bodily toil becomes wearing and brutalizing, and our position is totally untenable if we judge large numbers of our fellows solely upon their success in maintaining it.

The daintily clad charitable visitor who steps into the little house made untidy by the vigorous efforts of her hostess, the washerwoman, is no longer sure of her superiority to the latter; she recognizes that her hostess after all represents social value and industrial use, as over against her own parasitic cleanliness and a social standing attained only through status.

The only families who apply for aid to the charitable agencies are those who have come to grief on the industrial side; it may be through sickness, through loss of work, or for other guiltless and inevitable reasons; but the fact remains that they are industrially ailing, and must be bolstered and helped into industrial health. The charity visitor, let us assume, is a young college woman, well-bred and open-minded; when she visits the family assigned to her, she is often embarrassed to find herself obliged to lay all the stress of her teaching and advice upon the industrial virtues, and to treat the members of the family almost exclusively as factors in the industrial system. She insists that they must work and be self-supporting, that the most dangerous of all situations is idleness, that seeking one's own pleasure, while ignoring claims and responsibilities, is the most ignoble of actions. The members of her assigned family may have other charms and virtues—they may possibly be kind and considerate of each other, generous to their friends, but it is her business to stick to the industrial side. As she daily holds up these standards, it often occurs to the mind of the sensitive visitor, whose conscience has been made tender by much talk of brotherhood and equality, that she has no right to say these things; that her untrained hands are no more fitted to cope with actual conditions than those of her broken-down family.

The grandmother of the charity visitor could have done the industrial preaching very well, because she did have the industrial virtues and housewifely training. In a generation our experiences have changed, and our views with them; but we still keep on in the old methods, which could be applied when our consciences were in line with them, but which are daily becoming more difficult as we divide up into people who work with their hands and those who do not. The charity visitor belonging to the latter class is perplexed by recognitions and suggestions which the situation forces upon her. Our democracy has taught us to apply our moral teaching all around, and the moralist is rapidly becoming so sensitive that when his life does not exemplify his ethical convictions, he finds it difficult to preach.

Added to this is a consciousness, in the mind of the visitor, of a genuine misunderstanding of her motives by the recipients of her charity, and by their neighbors. Let us take a neighborhood of poor people, and test their ethical standards by those of the charity visitor, who comes with the best desire in the world to help them out of their distress. A most striking incongruity, at once apparent, is the difference between the emotional kindness with which relief is given by one poor neighbor to another poor neighbor, and the guarded care with which relief is given by a charity visitor to a charity recipient. The neighborhood mind is at once confronted not only by the difference of method, but by an absolute clashing of two ethical standards.

A very little familiarity with the poor districts of any city is sufficient to show how primitive and genuine are the neighborly relations. There is the greatest willingness to lend or borrow anything, and all the residents of the given tenement know the most intimate family affairs of all the others. The fact that the economic condition of all alike is on a most precarious level makes the ready outflow of sympathy and material assistance the most natural thing in the world. There are numberless instances of self-sacrifice quite unknown in the circles where greater economic advantages make that kind of intimate knowledge of one's neighbors impossible. An Irish family in which the man has lost his place, and the woman is struggling to eke out the scanty savings by day's work, will take in the widow and her five children who have been turned into the street, without a moment's reflection upon the physical discomforts involved. The most maligned landlady who lives in the house with her tenants is usually ready to lend a scuttle full of coal to one of them who may be out of work, or to share her supper. A woman for whom the writer had long tried in vain to find work failed to appear at the appointed time when employment was secured at last. Upon investigation it transpired that a neighbor further down the street was taken ill, that the children ran for the family friend, who went of course, saying simply when reasons for her non-appearance were demanded, "It broke me heart to leave the place, but what could I do?" A woman whose husband was sent up to the city prison for the maximum term, just three months, before the birth of her child found herself penniless at the end of that time, having gradually sold her supply of household furniture. She took refuge with a friend whom she supposed to be living in three rooms in another part of town. When she arrived, however, she discovered that her friend's husband had been out of work so long that they had been reduced to living in one room. The

friend, however, took her in, and the friend's husband was obliged to sleep upon a bench in the park every night for a week, which he did uncomplainingly if not cheerfully. Fortunately it was summer, "and it only rained one night." The writer could not discover from the young mother that she had any special claim upon the "friend" beyond the fact that they had formerly worked together in the same factory. The husband she had never seen until the night of her arrival, when he at once went forth in search of a midwife who would consent to come upon his promise of future payment.

The evolutionists tell us that the instinct to pity, the impulse to aid his fellows, served man at a very early period, as a rude rule of right and wrong. There is no doubt that this rude rule still holds among many people with whom charitable agencies are brought into contact, and that their ideas of right and wrong are quite honestly outraged by the methods of these agencies. When they see the delay and caution with which relief is given, it does not appear to them a conscientious scruple, but as the cold and calculating action of a selfish man. It is not the aid that they are accustomed to receive from their neighbors, and they do not understand why the impulse which drives people to "be good to the poor" should be so severely supervised. They feel, remotely, that the charity visitor is moved by motives that are alien and unreal. They may be superior motives, but they are different, and they are "agin nature." They cannot comprehend why a person whose intellectual perceptions are stronger than his natural impulses, should go into charity work at all. The only man they are accustomed to see whose intellectual perceptions are stronger than his tenderness of heart, is the selfish and avaricious man who is frankly "on the make." If the charity visitor is such a person, why does she pretend to like the poor? Why does she not go into business at once?

We may say, of course, that it is a primitive view of life, which thus confuses intellectuality and business ability; but it is a view quite honestly held by many poor people who are obliged to receive charity from time to time. In moments of indignation the poor have been known to say: "What do you want, anyway? If you have nothing to give us, why not let us alone and stop your questionings and investigations?" "They investigated me for three weeks, and in the end gave me nothing but a black character," a little woman has been heard to assert. This indignation, which is for the most part taciturn, and a certain kindly contempt for her abilities, often puzzles the charity visitor. The latter may be explained by the standard of worldly success which the visited families hold. Success does not ordinarily go, in the minds of the poor, with charity and kindheartedness, but rather with the opposite qualities. The rich landlord is he who collects with sternness, who accepts no excuse, and will have his own. There are moments of irritation and of real bitterness against him, but there is still admiration, because he is rich and successful. The good-natured landlord, he who pities and spares his poverty-pressed tenants, is seldom rich. He often lives in the back of his house, which he has owned for a long time, perhaps has inherited; but he has been able to accumulate little. He commands the genuine love and devotion of many of poor soul, but he is treated with a certain lack of respect. In one sense he is a failure. The charity visitor, just because she is a person who concerns herself with the poor, receives a certain amount of this good-natured and kindly contempt, sometimes real affection, but little genuine respect. The poor are accustomed to help each other and to respond according to their kindliness; but when it comes to worldly judgment, they use industrial success as the sole standard. In the case of the charity visitor who has neither natural kindness nor dazzling riches, they are deprived of both standards, and they find it of course utterly impossible to judge of the motive of organized charity.

Even those of us who feel most sorely the need of more order in altruistic effort and see the end to be desired, find something distasteful in the juxtaposition of the words "organized" and "charity." We say in defence that we are striving to turn this emotion into a motive, that pity is capricious, and not to be depended on; that we mean to give it the dignity of conscious duty. But at bottom we distrust a little a scheme which substitutes a theory of social conduct for the natural promptings of the heart, even although we appreciate the complexity of the situation. The poor man who has fallen into distress, when he first asks aid, instinctively expects tenderness, consideration, and forgiveness. If it is the first time, it has taken him long to make up his mind to take the step. He comes somewhat bruised and battered, and instead of being met with warmth of heart and sympathy, he is at once chilled by an investigation and an intimation that he ought to work. He does not recognize the disciplinary aspect of the situation.

The only really popular charity is that of the visiting nurses, who by virtue of their professional training render services which may easily be interpreted into sympathy and kindness, ministering as they do to obvious needs which do not require investigation.

The state of mind which an investigation arouses on both sides is most unfortunate; but the perplexity and clashing of different standards, with the consequent misunderstandings, are not so bad as the moral deterioration which is almost sure to follow.

When the agent or visitor appears among the poor, and they discover that under certain conditions food and rent and medical aid are dispensed from some unknown source, every man, woman, and child is quick to learn what the conditions may be, and to follow them. Though in their eyes a glass of beer is quite right and proper when taken as any self-respecting man should take it; though they know that cleanliness is an expensive virtue which can be required of few; though they realize that saving is well-nigh impossible when but a few cents can be laid by at a time; though their feeling for the church may be something quite elusive of definition and quite apart from daily living: to the visitor they gravely laud temperance and cleanliness and thrift and religious observance. The deception in the first instances arises from a wondering inability to understand the ethical ideals which can require such impossible virtues, and from an innocent desire to please. It is easy to trace the development of the mental suggestions thus received. When A discovers that B, who is very little worse off than he, receives good things from an inexhaustible supply intended for the poor at large, he feels that he too has a claim for his share, and step by step there is developed the competitive spirit which so horrifies charity visitors when it shows itself in a tendency to "work" the relief-giving agencies.

The most serious effect upon the poor comes when dependence upon the charitable society is substituted for the natural outgoing of human love and sympathy, which, happily, we all possess in some degree. The spontaneous impulse to sit up all night with the neighbor's sick child is turned into righteous indignation against the district nurse, because she goes home at six o'clock, and doesn't do it herself. Or the kindness which would have prompted the quick purchase of much needed medicine is transformed into a voluble scoring of the dispensary, because it gives prescriptions and not drugs; and "who can get well on a piece of paper?"

If a poor woman knows that her neighbor next door has no shoes, she is quite willing to lend her own, that her neighbor may go decently to mass, or to work; for she knows the smallest item about the scanty wardrobe, and cheerfully helps out. When the charity visitor comes in, all the neighbors are baffled as to what her circumstances may be. They know she does not need a new pair of shoes, and rather suspect that she has a dozen pairs at home; which, indeed, she sometimes has. They imagine untold stores which they may call upon, and her most generous gift is considered niggardly, compared with what she might do. She ought to get new shoes for the family all round, "she sees well enough that they need them." It is no more than the neighbor herself would do, has practically done, when she lent her own shoes. The charity visitor has broken through the natural rule of giving, which, in a primitive society, is bounded only by the need of the recipient and the resources of the giver; and she gets herself into untold trouble when she is judged by the ethics of that primitive society.

The neighborhood understands the selfish rich people who stay in their own part of town, where all their associates have shoes and other things. Such people don't bother themselves about the poor; they are like the rich landlords of the neighborhood experience. But this lady visitor, who pretends to be good to the poor, and certainly does talk as though she were kind-hearted, what does she come for, if she does not intend to give them things which are so plainly needed?

The visitor says, sometimes, that in holding her poor family so hard to a standard of thrift she is really breaking down a rule of higher living which they formerly possessed; that saving, which seems quite commendable in a comfortable part of town, appears almost criminal in a poorer quarter where the next-door neighbor needs food, even if the children of the family do not.

She feels the sordidness of constantly being obliged to urge the industrial view of life. The benevolent individual of fifty years ago honestly believed that industry and self-denial in youth would result in comfortable possessions for old age. It was, indeed, the method he had practised in his own youth, and by which he had probably obtained whatever fortune he possessed. He therefore reproved the poor family for indulging their children, urged them to work long hours, and was utterly untouched by many scruples which afflict the contemporary charity visitor. She says sometimes, "Why must I talk always of getting work and saving money, the things I know nothing about? If it were anything else I had to urge, I could do it; anything like Latin prose, which I had worried through myself, it would not be so hard." But she finds it difficult to connect the experiences of her youth with the experiences of the visited family.

Because of this diversity in experience, the visitor is continually surprised to find that the safest platitude may be challenged. She refers quite naturally to the "horrors of the saloon," and discovers that the head of her visited family does not connect them with "horrors" at all. He remembers all the kindnesses he has received there, the free lunch and treating which goes on, even when a man is out of work and not able to pay up; the loan of five dollars he got there when the charity visitor was miles away and he was threatened with eviction. He may listen politely to her reference to "horrors," but considers it only "temperance talk."

The charity visitor may blame the women for lack of gentleness toward their children, for being hasty and rude to them, until she learns that the standard of breeding is not that of gentleness toward the children so much as the observance of certain conventions, such as the punctilious wearing of mourning garments after the death of a child. The standard of gentleness each mother has to work out largely by herself, assisted only by the occasional shame-faced remark of a neighbor, "That they do better when you are not too hard on them"; but the wearing of mourning garments is sustained by the definitely expressed sentiment of every woman in the street. The mother would have to bear social blame, a certain social ostracism, if she failed to comply with that requirement. It is not comfortable to outrage the conventions of those among whom we live, and, if our social life be a narrow one, it is still more difficult. The visitor may choke a little when she sees the lessened supply of food and the scanty clothing provided for the remaining children in order that one may be conventionally mourned, but she doesn't talk so strongly against it as she would have done during her first month of experience with the family since bereaved.

The subject of clothes indeed perplexes the visitor constantly, and the result of her reflections may be summed up somewhat in this wise: The girl who has a definite social standing, who has been to a fashionable school or to a college, whose family live in a house seen and known by all her friends and associates, may afford to be very simple, or even shabby as to her clothes, if she likes. But the working girl, whose family lives in a tenement, or moves from one small apartment to another, who has little social standing and has to make her own place, knows full well how much habit and style of dress has to do with her posi-

tion. Her income goes into her clothing, out of all proportion to the amount which she spends upon other things. But, if social advancement is her aim, it is the most sensible thing she can do. She is judged largely by her clothes. Her house furnishing, with its pitiful little decorations, her scanty supply of books, are never seen by the people whose social opinions she most values. Her clothes are her background, and from them she is largely judged. It is due to this fact that girls' clubs succeed best in the business part of town, where "working girls" and "young ladies" meet upon an equal footing, and where the clothes superficially look very much alike. Bright and ambitious girls will come to these down-town clubs to eat lunch and rest at noon, to study all sorts of subjects and listen to lectures, when they might hesitate a long time before joining a club identified with their own neighborhood, where they would be judged not solely on their own merits and the unconscious social standing afforded by good clothes, but by other surroundings which are not nearly up to these. For the same reason, girls' clubs are infinitely more difficult to organize in little towns and villages, where every one knows every one else, just how the front parlor is furnished, and the amount of mortgage there is upon the house. These facts get in the way of a clear and unbiassed judgment; they impede the democratic relationship and add to the self-consciousness of all concerned. Every one who has had to do with down-town girls' clubs has had the experience of going into the home of some bright, well-dressed girl, to discover it uncomfortable and perhaps wretched, and to find the girl afterward carefully avoiding her, although the working girl may not have been at home when the call was made, and the visitor may have carried herself with the utmost courtesy throughout. In some very successful down-town clubs the home address is not given at all, and only the "business address" is required. Have we worked out our democracy further in regard to clothes than anything else?

The charity visitor has been rightly brought up to consider it vulgar to spend much money upon clothes, to care so much for "appearances." She realizes dimly that the care for personal decoration over that for one's home or habitat is in some way primitive and undeveloped; but she is silenced by its obvious need. She also catches a glimpse of the fact that the disproportionate expenditure of the poor in the matter of clothes is largely due to the exclusiveness of the rich who hide from them the interior of their houses, and their more subtle pleasures, while of necessity exhibiting their street clothes and their street manners. Every one who goes shopping at the same time may see the clothes of the richest women in town, but only those invited to her receptions see the Corot on her walls or the bindings in her library. The poor naturally try to bridge the difference by reproducing the street clothes which they have seen. They are striving to conform to a common standard which their democratic training presupposes belongs to all of us. The charity visitor may regret that the Italian peasant woman has laid aside her picturesque kerchief and substituted a cheap street hat. But it is easy to recognize the first attempt toward democratic expression.

The charity visitor finds herself still more perplexed when she comes to consider such problems as those of early marriage and child labor; for she cannot deal with them according to economic theories, or according to the conventions which have regulated her own life. She finds both of these fairly upset by her intimate knowledge of the situation, and her sympathy for those into whose lives she has gained a curious insight. She discovers how incorrigibly bourgeois her standards have been, and it takes but a little time to reach the conclusion that she cannot insist so strenuously upon the conventions of her own class, which fail to fit the bigger, more emotional, and freer lives of working people. The charity visitor holds well-grounded views upon the imprudence of early marriages, quite naturally because she comes from a family and circle of professional and business people. A professional man is scarcely equipped and started in his profession before he is thirty. A business man, if he is on the road to success, is much nearer prosperity

at thirty-five than twenty-five, and it is therefore wise for these men not to marry in the twenties; but this does not apply to the workingman. In many trades he is laid upon the shelf at thirty-five, and in nearly all trades he receives the largest wages in his life between twenty and thirty. If the young workingman has all his wages to himself, he will probably establish habits of personal comfort, which he cannot keep up when he has to divide with a family—habits which he can, perhaps, never overcome.

The sense of prudence, the necessity for saving, can never come to a primitive, emotional man with the force of a conviction; but the necessity of providing for his children is a powerful incentive. He naturally regards his children as his savings-bank; he expects them to care for him when he gets old, and in some trades old age comes very early. A Jewish tailor was quite lately sent to the Cook County poorhouse, paralyzed beyond recovery at the age of thirty-five. Had his little boy of nine been but a few years older, he might have been spared this sorrow of public charity. He was, in fact, better able to well support a family when he was twenty than when he was thirty-five, for his wages had steadily grown less as the years went on. Another tailor whom I know, who is also a Socialist, always speaks of saving as a bourgeois virtue, one quite impossible to the genuine workingman. He supports a family consisting of himself, a wife and three children, and his two parents on eight dollars a week. He insists it would be criminal not to expend every penny of this amount upon food and shelter, and he expects his children later to care for him.

This economic pressure also accounts for the tendency to put children to work overyoung and thus cripple their chances for individual development and usefulness, and with the avaricious parent also leads to exploitation. "I have fed her for fourteen years, now she can help me pay my mortgage" is not an unusual reply when a hard-working father is expostulated with because he would take his bright daughter out of school and put her into a factory.

It has long been a common error for the charity visitor, who is strongly urging her "family" toward self-support, to suggest, or at least connive, that the children be put to work early, although she has not the excuse that the parents have. It is so easy, after one has been taking the industrial view for a long time, to forget the larger and more social claim; to urge that the boy go to work and support his parents, who are receiving charitable aid. She does not realize what a cruel advantage the person who distributes charity has, when she gives advice.

The manager in a huge mercantile establishment employing many children was able to show during a child-labor investigation, that the only children under fourteen years of age in his employ were protégés who had been urged upon him by philanthropic ladies, not only acquaintances of his, but valued patrons of the establishment. It is not that the charity visitor is less wise than other people, but she has fixed her mind so long upon the industrial lameness of her family that she is eager to seize any crutch, however weak, which may enable them to get on.

She has failed to see that the boy who attempts to prematurely support his widowed mother may lower wages, add an illiterate member to the community, and arrest the development of a capable workingman. As she has failed to see that the rules which obtain in regard to the age of marriage in her own family may not apply to the workingman, so also she fails to understand that the present conditions of employment surrounding a factory child are totally unlike those which obtained during the energetic youth of her father.

The child who is prematurely put to work is constantly oppressed by this never ending question of the means of subsistence, and even little children are sometimes almost crushed with the cares of life through their affectionate sympathy. The writer knows a little Italian lad of six to whom the problems of food, clothing, and shelter have become so immediate and pressing that, although an imaginative child, he is unable to see life from any other standpoint. The goblin or bugaboo, feared by the more fortunate child, in his mind, has come to be the need of coal which caused his father hysterical and demonstrative grief when it carried off his mother's inherited linen, the mosaic of St. Joseph, and, worst of all, his own rubber boots. He once came to a party at Hull-House, and was interested in nothing save a gas stove which he saw in the kitchen. He became excited over the discovery that fire could be produced without fuel. "I will tell my father of this stove. You buy no coal, you need only a match. Anybody will give you a match." He was taken to visit at a country-house and at once inquired how much rent was paid for it. On being told carelessly by his hostess that they paid no rent for that house, he came back quite wild with interest that the problem was solved. "Me and my father will go to the country. You get a big house, all warm, without rent." Nothing else in the country interested him but the subject of rent, and he talked of that with an exclusiveness worthy of a single taxer.

The struggle for existence, which is so much harsher among people near the edge of pauperism, sometimes leaves ugly marks on character, and the charity visitor finds these indirect results most mystifying. Parents who work-hard and anticipate an old age when they can no longer earn, take care that their children shall expect to divide their wages with them from the very first. Such a parent, when successful, impresses the immature nervous system of the child thus tyrannically establishing habits of obedience, so that the nerves and will may not depart from this control when the child is older. The charity visitor, whose family relation is lifted quite out of this, does not in the least understand the industrial foundation for this family tyranny.

The head of a kindergarten training-class once addressed a club of working women, and spoke of the despotism which is often established over little children. She said that the so-called determination to break a child's will many times arose from a lust of dominion, and she urged the ideal relationship founded upon love and confidence. But many of the women were puzzled. One of them remarked to the writer as she came out of the club room, "If you did not keep control over them from the time they were little, you would never get their wages when they are grown up." Another one said, "Ah, of course she (meaning the speaker) doesn't have to depend upon her children's wages. She can afford to be lax with them, because even if they don't give money to her, she can get along without it."

There are an impressive number of children who uncomplainingly and constantly hand over their weekly wages to their parents, sometimes receiving back ten cents or a quarter for spending-money, but quite as often nothing at all; and the writer knows one girl of twenty-five who for six years has received two cents a week from the constantly falling wages which she earns in a large factory. Is it habit or virtue which holds her steady in this course? If love and tenderness had been substituted for parental despotism, would the mother have had enough affection, enough power of expression to hold her daughter's sense of money obligation through all these years? This girl who spends her paltry two cents on chewing-gum and goes plainly clad in clothes of her mother's choosing, while many of her friends spend their entire wages on those clothes which factory girls love so well, must be held by some powerful force.

The charity visitor finds these subtle and elusive problems most harrowing. The head of a family she is visiting is a man who has become black-listed in a strike. He is not a very good workman, and this, added to his agitator's reputation, keeps him out of work for a long time. The fatal result of being long out of work follows: he becomes less and less eager for it, and gets a "job" less and less frequently. In order to keep up his self-respect, and still more to keep his wife's respect for him, he yields to the little self-deception that this prolonged idleness follows because he was once blacklisted, and he gradually becomes a martyr. Deep down in his heart perhaps—but who knows what may be deep down in his heart? Whatever may be in his wife's, she does not show for an instant that she thinks he has grown lazy, and accustomed

to see her earn, by sewing and cleaning, most of the scanty income for the family. The charity visitor, however, does see this, and she also sees that the other men who were in the strike have gone back to work. She further knows by inquiry and a little experience that the man is not skilful. She cannot, however, call him lazy and good-for-nothing, and denounce him as worthless as her grandmother might have done, because of certain intellectual conceptions at which she has arrived. She sees other workmen come to him for shrewd advice; she knows that he spends many more hours in the public library reading good books than the average workman has time to do. He has formed no bad habits and has yielded only to those subtle temptations toward a life of leisure which come to the intellectual man. He lacks the qualifications which would induce his union to engage him as a secretary or organizer, but he is a constant speaker at workingmen's meetings, and takes a high moral attitude on the questions discussed there. He contributes a certain intellectuality to his friends, and he has undoubted social value. The neighboring women confide to the charity visitor their sympathy with his wife, because she has to work so hard, and because her husband does not "provide." Their remarks are sharpened by a certain resentment toward the superiority of the husband's education and gentle manners. The charity visitor is ashamed to take this point of view, for she knows that it is not altogether fair. She is reminded of a college friend of hers, who told her that she was not going to allow her literary husband to write unworthy potboilers for the sake of earning a living. "I insist that we shall live within my own income; that he shall not publish until be is ready, and can give his genuine message." The charity visitor recalls what she has heard of another acquaintance, who urged her husband to decline a lucrative position as a railroad attorney, because she wished him to be free to take municipal positions, and handle public questions without the inevitable suspicion which unaccountably attaches itself in a corrupt city to a corporation attorney. The action of these two women seemed noble to her, but in their cases they merely lived on a lesser income. In the case of the working-man's wife, she faced living on no income at all, or on the precarious one which she might be able to get together.

She sees that this third woman has made the greatest sacrifice, and she is utterly unwilling to condemn her while praising the friends of her own social position. She realizes, of course, that the situation is changed by the fact that the third family needs charity, while the other two do not; but after all, they have not asked for it, and their plight was only discovered through an accident to one of the children. The charity visitor has been taught that her mission is to preserve the finest traits to be found in her visited family, and she shrinks from the thought of convincing the wife that her husband is worthless and she suspects that she might turn all this beautiful devotion into complaining drudgery. To be sure, she could give up visiting the family altogether, but she has become much interested in the progress of the crippled child who eagerly anticipates her visits, and she also suspects that she will never know many finer women than the mother. She is unwilling, therefore, to give up the friendship, and goes on bearing her perplexities as best she may.

The first impulse of our charity visitor is to be somewhat severe with her shiftless family for spending money on pleasures and indulging their children out of all proportion to their means. The poor family which receives beans and coal from the county, and pays for a bicycle on the instalment plan, is not unknown to any of us. But as the growth of juvenile crime becomes gradually understood, and as the danger of giving no legitimate and organized pleasure to the child becomes clearer, we remember that primitive man had games long before he cared for a house or regular meals.

There are certain boys in many city neighborhoods who form themselves into little gangs with a leader who is somewhat more intrepid than the rest. Their favorite performance is to break into an untenanted house, to knock off the faucets, and cut the lead pipe, which they sell to the nearest junk dealer. With the money thus procured they buy beer and drink it in little free-booter's groups sitting in the alley. From beginning to end they have the excitement of knowing that they may be seen and caught by the "coppers," and are at times quite breathless with suspense. It is not the least unlike, in motive and execution, the practice of country boys who go forth in squads to set traps for rabbits or to round up a coon.

It is characterized by a pure spirit for adventure, and the vicious training really begins when they are arrested, or when an older boy undertakes to guide them into further excitements. From the very beginning the most enticing and exciting experiences which they have seen have been connected with crime. The policeman embodies all the majesty of successful law and established government in his brass buttons and dazzlingly equipped patrol wagon.

The boy who has been arrested comes back more or less a hero with a tale to tell of the interior recesses of the mysterious police station. The earliest public excitement the child remembers is divided between the rattling fire engines, "the time there was a fire in the next block," and all the tense interest of the patrol wagon "the time the drunkest lady in our street was arrested."

In the first year of their settlement the Hull-House residents took fifty kindergarten children to Lincoln Park, only to be grieved by their apathetic interest in trees and flowers. As they came back with an omnibus full of tired and sleepy children, they were surprised to find them galvanized into sudden life because a patrol wagon rattled by. Their eager little heads popped out of the windows full of questioning: "Was it a man or a woman?" "How many policemen inside?" and eager little tongues began to tell experiences of arrests which baby eyes had witnessed.

The excitement of a chase, the chances of competition, and the love of a fight are all centred in the outward display of crime. The parent who receives charitable aid and yet provides pleasure for his child, and is willing to indulge him in his play, is blindly doing one of the wisest things possible; and no one is more eager for playgrounds and vacation schools than the conscientious charity visitor.

This very imaginative impulse and attempt to live in a pictured world of their own, which seems the simplest prerogative of childhood, often leads the boys into difficulty. Three boys aged seven, nine, and ten were once brought into a neighboring police station under the charge of pilfering and destroying property. They had dug a cave under a railroad viaduct in which they had spent many days and nights of the summer vacation. They had "swiped" potatoes and other vegetables from hucksters' carts, which they had cooked and eaten in true brigand fashion; they had decorated the interior of the excavation with stolen junk, representing swords and firearms, to their romantic imaginations. The father of the ringleader was a janitor living in a building five miles away in a prosperous portion of the city. The landlord did not want an active boy in the building, and his mother was dead; the janitor paid for the boy's board and lodging to a needy woman living near the viaduct. She conscientiously gave him his breakfast and supper, and left something in the house for his dinner every morning when she went to work in a neighboring factory; but was too tired by night to challenge his statement that he "would rather sleep outdoors in the summer," or to investigate what he did during the day. In the meantime the three boys lived in a world of their own, made up from the reading of adventurous stories and their vivid imaginations, steadily pilfering more and more as the days went by, and actually imperilling the safety of the traffic passing over the street on the top of the viaduct. In spite of vigorous exertions on their behalf, one of the boys was sent to the Reform School, comforting himself with the conclusive remark, "Well, we had fun anyway, and maybe they will let us dig a cave at the School; it is in the country, where we can't hurt anything."

In addition to books of adventure, or even reading of any sort, the scenes and ideals of the theatre largely form the manners and morals of the young people. "Going to the theatre" is indeed the most common and satisfactory form of recreation. Many boys who conscientiously give all their wages to their mothers have returned each week ten cents to pay for a seat in the gallery of a theatre on Sunday afternoon. It is their one satisfactory glimpse of life—the moment when they "issue forth from themselves" and are stirred and thoroughly interested. They quite simply adopt as their own, and imitate as best they can, all that they see there. In moments of genuine grief and excitement the words and the gestures they employ are those copied from the stage, and the tawdry expression often conflicts hideously with the fine and genuine emotion of which it is the inadequate and vulgar vehicle.

As in the matter of dress, more refined and simpler manners and mode of expressions are unseen by them, and they must perforce copy what they know.

If we agree with a recent definition of Art, as that which causes the spectator to lose his sense of isolation, there is no doubt that the popular theatre, with all its faults, more nearly fulfils the function of art for the multitude of working people than all the "free galleries" and picture exhibits combined.

The greatest difficulty is experienced when the two standards come sharply together, and when both sides make an attempt at understanding and explanation. The difficulty of making clear one's own ethical standpoint is at times insurmountable. A woman who had bought and sold school books stolen from the school fund,—books which are all plainly marked with a red stamp,—came to Hull House one morning in great distress because she had been arrested, and begged a resident "to speak to the judge." She gave as a reason the fact that the House had known her for six years, and had once been very good to her when her little girl was buried. The resident more than suspected that her visitor knew the school books were stolen when buying them, and any attempt to talk upon that subject was evidently considered very rude. The visitor wished to get out of her trial, and evidently saw no reason why the House should not help her. The alderman was out of town, so she could not go to him. After a long conversation the visitor entirely failed to get another point of view and went away grieved and disappointed at a refusal, thinking the resident simply disobliging; wondering, no doubt, why such a mean woman had once been good to her; leaving the resident, on the other hand, utterly baffled and in the state of mind she would have been in, had she brutally insisted that a little child should lift weights too heavy for its undeveloped muscles.

Such a situation brings out the impossibility of substituting a higher ethical standard for a lower one without similarity of experience, but it is not as painful as that illustrated by the following example, in which the highest ethical standard yet attained by the charity recipient is broken down, and the substituted one not in the least understood:—

A certain charity visitor is peculiarly appealed to by the weakness and pathos of forlorn old age. She is responsible for the well-being of perhaps a dozen old women to whom she sustains a sincerely affectionate and almost filial relation. Some of them learn to take her benefactions quite as if they came from their own relatives, grumbling at all she does, and scolding her with a family freedom. One of these poor old women was injured in a fire years ago. She has but the fragment of a hand left, and is grievously crippled in her feet. Through years of pain she had become addicted to opium, and when she first came under the visitor's care, was only held from the poorhouse by the awful thought that she would there perish without her drug. Five years of tender care have done wonders for her. She lives in two neat little rooms, where with her thumb and two fingers she makes innumerable quilts, which she sells and gives away with the greatest delight. Her opium is regulated to a set amount taken each day, and she has been drawn away from much drinking. She is a voracious reader, and has her head full of strange tales made up from books and her own imagination. At one time it seemed impossible to do anything for her in Chicago, and she was kept for two years in a suburb, where the family of the charity visitor lived, and where she was nursed through several hazardous illnesses. She now lives a better life than she did, but she is still far from being a model old woman. The neighbors are constantly shocked by the fact that she is supported and comforted by a "charity lady," while at the same time she occasionally "rushes the growler," scolding at the boys lest they jar her in her tottering walk. The care of her has broken through even that second standard, which the neighborhood had learned to recognize as the standard of charitable societies, that only the "worthy poor" are to be helped; that temperance and thrift are the virtues which receive the plums of benevolence. The old lady herself is conscious of this criticism. Indeed, irate neighbors tell her to her face that she doesn't in the least deserve what she gets. In order to disarm them, and at the same time to explain what would otherwise seem loving-kindness so colossal as to be abnormal, she tells them that during her sojourn in the suburb she discovered an awful family secret,—a horrible scandal connected with the long-suffering charity visitor; that it is in order to prevent the divulgence of this that she constantly receives her ministrations. Some of her perplexed neighbors accept this explanation as simple and offering a solution of this vexed problem. Doubtless many of them have a glimpse of the real state of affairs, of the love and patience which ministers to need irrespective of worth. But the standard is too high for most of them, and it sometimes seems unfortunate to break down the second standard, which holds that people who "rush the growler" are not worthy of charity, and that there is a certain justice attained when they go to the poorhouse. It is certainly dangerous to break down the lower, unless the higher is made clear.

Just when our affection becomes large enough to care for the unworthy among the poor as we would care for the unworthy among our own kin, is certainly a perplexing question. To say that it should never be so, is a comment upon our democratic relations to them which few of us would be willing to make.

Of what use is all this striving and perplexity? Has the experience any value? It is certainly genuine, for it induces an occasional charity visitor to live in a tenement house as simply as the other tenants do. It drives others to give up visiting the poor altogether, because, they claim, it is quite impossible unless the individual becomes a member of a sisterhood, which requires, as some of the Roman Catholic sisterhoods do, that the member first take the vows of obedience and poverty, so that she can have nothing to give save as it is first given to her, and thus she is not harassed by a constant attempt at adjustment.

Both the tenement-house resident and the sister assume to have put themselves upon the industrial level of their neighbors, although they have left out the most awful element of poverty, that of imminent fear of starvation and a neglected old age.

The young charity visitor who goes from a family living upon a most precarious industrial level to her own home in a prosperous part of the city, if she is sensitive at all, is never free from perplexities which our growing democracy forces upon her.

We sometimes say that our charity is too scientific, but we would doubtless be much more correct in our estimate if we said that it is not scientific enough. We dislike the entire arrangement of cards alphabetically classified according to streets and names of families, with the unrelated and meaningless details attached to them. Our feeling of revolt is probably not unlike that which afflicted the students of botany and geology in the middle of the last century, when flowers were tabulated in alphabetical order, when geology was taught by colored charts and thin books. No doubt the students, wearied to death, many times said that it was all too scientific, and were much perplexed and worried when they found traces of structure and physiology which their so-called scientific principles were totally unable to account for. But all this happened before science had become evolutionary and scientific at all, before it had a principle of life from within. The very indications and discoveries which formerly perplexed, later illumined and made the study absorbing and vital.

We are singularly slow to apply this evolutionary principle to human affairs in general, although it is fast being applied to the education of children. We are at last learning to follow the development of the child; to expect certain traits under certain conditions; to adapt methods and matter to his growing mind. No "advanced educator" can allow himself to be so absorbed in the question of what a child ought to be as to exclude the discovery of what he is. But in our charitable efforts we think much more of what a man ought to be than of what he is or of what he may become; and we ruthlessly force our conventions and standards upon him, with a sternness which we would consider stupid indeed did an educator use it in forcing his mature intellectual convictions upon an undeveloped mind.

Let us take the example of a timid child, who cries when he is put to bed because he is afraid of the dark. The "soft-hearted" parent stays with him, simply because he is sorry for him and wants to comfort him. The scientifically trained parent stays with him, because he realizes that the child is in a stage of development in which his imagination has the best of him, and in which it is impossible to reason him out of a belief in ghosts. These two parents, wide apart in point of view, after all act much alike, and both very differently from the pseudo-scientific parent, who acts from dogmatic conviction and is sure he is right. He talks of developing his child's self-respect and good sense, and leaves him to cry himself to sleep, demanding powers of self-control and development which the child does not possess. There is no doubt that our development of charity methods has reached this pseudo-scientific and stilted stage. We have learned to condemn unthinking, ill-regulated kind-heartedness, and we take great pride in mere repression much as the stern parent tells the visitor below how admirably he is rearing the child, who is hysterically crying upstairs and laying the foundation for future nervous disorders. The pseudo-scientific spirit, or rather, the undeveloped stage of our philanthropy, is perhaps most clearly revealed in our tendency to lay constant stress on negative action. "Don't give;" "don't break down self-respect," we are constantly told. We distrust the human impulse as well as the teachings of our own experience, and in their stead substitute dogmatic rules for conduct. We forget that the accumulation of knowledge and the holding of convictions must finally result in the application of that knowledge and those convictions to life itself; that the necessity for activity and a pull upon the sympathies is so severe, that all the knowledge in the possession of the visitor is constantly applied, and she has a reasonable chance for an ultimate intellectual comprehension. Indeed, part of the perplexity in the administration of charity comes from the fact that the type of person drawn to it is the one who insists that her convictions shall not be unrelated to action. Her moral concepts constantly tend to float away from her, unless they have a basis in the concrete relation of life. She is confronted with the task of reducing her scruples to action, and of converging many wills, so as to unite the strength of all of them into one accomplishment, the value of which no one can foresee.

On the other hand, the young woman who has succeeded in expressing her social compunction through charitable effort finds that the wider social activity, and the contact with the larger experience, not only increases her sense of social obligation but at the same time recasts her social ideals. She is chagrined to discover that in the actual task of reducing her social scruples to action, her humble beneficiaries are far in advance of her, not in charity or singleness of purpose, but in self-sacrificing action. She reaches the old-time virtue of humility by a social process, not in the old way, as the man who sits by the side of the road and puts dust upon his head, calling himself a contrite sinner, but she gets the dust upon her head because she has stumbled and fallen in the road through her efforts to push forward the mass, to march with her fellows. She has socialized her virtues not only through a social aim but by a social process.

The Hebrew prophet made three requirements from those who would join the great forward-moving procession led by Jehovah. "To love mercy" and at the same time "to do justly" is the difficult task; to fulfil the first requirement alone is to fall into the error of indiscriminate giving with all its disastrous results; to fulfil the second solely is to obtain the stern policy of withholding, and it results in such a dreary lack of sympathy and understanding that the establishment of justice is impossible. It may be that the combination of the two can never be attained save as we fulfil still the third requirement—"to walk humbly with God," which may mean to walk for many dreary miles beside the lowliest of His creatures, not even in that peace of mind which the company of the humble is popularly supposed to afford, but rather with the pangs and throes to which the poor human understanding is subjected whenever it attempts to comprehend the meaning of life.

## Suggestions for Further Reading

Jane Addams, *Jane Addams: A Centennial Reader,* ed. Emily Cooper Johnson (New York: Macmillan, 1960).

Jane Addams, *Democracy and Social Ethics,* ed. Anne Firor Scott (Cambridge, Mass.: Harvard University Press, 1964 [1902]).

Jane Addams, *The Social Thought of Jane Addams,* ed. Christopher Lasch (Indianapolis, Ind.: Bobbs-Merrill, 1965).

Jane Addams, *Twenty Years at Hull House* (New York: Penguin, 1981 [1910]).

Joyce Antler, *The Educated Woman and Professionalization: The Struggle for a New Feminine Identity, 1890–1920* (New York: Garland, 1987).

Mary W. Calkins, "Community of Ideas of Men and Women," *Psychological Review,* 3, 1896.

Elsie Ripley Clapp, *Community Schools in Action* (New York: Viking, 1939).

Mary Jo Deegan, *Jane Addams and the Men of the Chicago School* (New Brunswick, N.J.: Transaction Books, 1988).

Ellen Fitzpatrick, *Endless Crusade: Women Social Scientists and Progressive Reform* (New York: Oxford University Press, 1990).

Eugenie Gatens-Robinson, "Dewey and the Feminist Successor Science Project, *Transactions of the Charles S. Peirce Society,* 27, 1991.

Charlotte Perkins Gilman, *Charlotte Perkins Gilman: A Non-fiction Reader,* ed. Larry Ceplair (New York: Columbia University Press, 1991).

Charlotte Perkins Gilman, *The Man-made World; or, Our Androcentric Culture* (Minneapolis: University of Minnesota Series in American Studies, 1971 [1911]).

Charlotte Perkins Gilman, *Women and Economics: A Study of Economic Relations Between Men and Women as a Factor in Social Evolution,* ed. Carl Degler (New York: Harper and Row, 1966 [1898]).

Mary A. Hill, *Charlotte Perkins Gilman: The Making of a Radical Feminist, 1860–1896* (Philadelphia: Temple University Press, 1980).

Emma Goldman, *Anarchism and Other Essays* (New York: Dover, 1971 [1910]).

Florence Kelley, *Some Ethical Gains Through Legislation,* ed. R. Ely (New York: Macmillan, 1905).

John T. McManis, *Ella Flagg Young and a Half-century of the Chicago Public Schools* (Chicago: A. C. McClurg, 1916).

Marjorie C. Miller, "Feminism and Pragmatism," *Monist,* 75, 1992.

M. M. Randall, *John Dewey and Jane Addams* (Philadelphia: Women's International League for Peace and Freedom, 1959).

Richard Rorty, "Feminism and Pragmatism," *Michigan Quarterly Review,* 30, 1991.

Charlene Haddock Seigfried, ed., "Feminism and Pragmatism" Special Issue, *Hypatia,* 8, 1993.

Charlene Haddock Seigfried, *Pragmatism and Feminism: Reweaving the Social Fabric* (Chicago: University of Chicago Press, 1996).

Jessie Taft, *The Woman Movement from the Point of View of Social Consciousness* (Menasha, Wis.: Collegiate Press, 1915).

Ella Flagg Young and John Dewey, *Contributions to Education* (Chicago: University of Chicago, 1901–1909).

# AMERICAN IDEALISM
# AND PERSONALISM

## Introduction by Thomas O. Buford

Personalism in American thought is more than 100 years old, first having been fully formulated under that name by Borden Parker Bowne in his *Metaphysics,* published in 1882. Bowne wrote, "I am a *Personalist,* the first of the clan in any thoroughgoing sense."[1] And, Personalism is reputed to be the "first complete and comprehensive system of philosophy developed in America which has had lasting influence and which still counts some of our outstanding thinkers among its adherents."[2] What are its roots and its distinguishing tenets?

American Personalism is planted in the soil of German Idealism. Before the mid-nineteenth century, few in America discussed the thought of German philosophers such as Kant, Fichte, Schelling, and Hegel. After that, the conversation grew for many reasons. As the demands of academic life increased, young American philosophers completed their philosophic preparation with a year or two of study in Germany. When they returned, no longer embracing the old Scottish orthodoxy, they enthusiastically explored idealistic philosophy. Further, many Europeans familiar with German Idealism migrated to the United States. Also, a group of nonacademic American students of German Idealism gathered to form the St. Louis Hegelians. By the 1870s some American philosophers, deeply influenced by the needs of the new American culture, reworked insights from German Idealism. Along with the St. Louis Hegelians—Henry Brokmeyer, William Torry Harris, Denton J. Snider, Thomas Davidson, and George Holmes Howison (who later taught at the University of California at Berkeley)—this group of American idealists included: Josiah Royce, Harvard University; George Sylvester Morris, University of Michigan; Alfred Henry Lloyd, University of Michigan; Edgar A. Singer, University of Pennsylvania; William Ernest Hocking, Harvard University; and James Edwin Creighton, Sage School of Philosophy at Cornell University. In this rich loam, Personalism, a distinctive form of American Idealism, took root and flowered, brilliantly nurtured by George Holmes Howison, William Ernest Hocking of Harvard, and Borden Parker Bowne, Edgar Sheffield Brightman, and Peter A. Bertocci, all of Boston University.[3]

To grasp Personalism in its classical American form, we turn to Borden Parker Bowne (1847–1910). Think of him at Boston University, making his way among the complex currents of late nineteenth-century thought. The issues that attracted Bowne revolved around the hub of science and religion. Science, both theoretical and commercialized, engaged popular thought. Intellectuals were intrigued with scientific naturalism, and were heavily indebted to Darwin, Chauncey Wright, and Herbert Spencer. Religion, deeply influenced by the criticism of German biblical scientists, lost its appeal to many in America. Some in the religious community who supported religious fundamentals and a biblical literalism withdrew from the intellectual conversation of the day, confident that they knew better. Bowne, a devout Christian and staunch Methodist, neither set aside his faith nor fell silent in the intellectual conversation.

Bowne wrote amid great optimism that science could solve America's social and economic problems. Scientific principles applied to local, national, and international problems would, according to the popular opinion of the day, result in peace and well-being for all. Responding in kind, Bowne wrote books crafted for the intelligent reader (philosophic journals were only in their infancy). Like William James, he directed his salvos primarily at Herbert Spencer, the great popularizer of evolution.[4] Bowne's calling was "making religion intellectually possible in a time when all the classical supports for religion seemed to be cracking."[5] Devoted to faith, science (but not scientific naturalism), the Bible, community, and the philosophic study of reality, he developed an intellectual structure that made the Protestant Christian religious life reasonable. Moreover, he played a key role in formulating the liberal-Protestant consensus that permeated American life, especially in higher education.[6] Though he worked out his epistemology, metaphysics, and ethics in *Thought and Knowledge* (1897), *Metaphysics* (1882), *Principles of Ethics* (1892), and *Kant and Spencer, a Critical Exposition* (1912), his *Studies in Christianity* (1909) and *Personalism* (1908) were popular statements of his philosophy and theology directed to a wide audience. In Bowne's thought, the central tenets of Personalism emerge, tenets developed and debated by those who continued the school of thought. These tenets are personal living as the philosophic starting point, radical empiricism, knowledge, Person as key to reality, and ethics.

## 1.  Personal Living as Philosophic Starting Point

Persons living in the world: This is for Bowne the starting point for any adequate philosophy. This does not mean that one starts with some kind of universal essence or Cartesian homunculus. Each of us begins doing philosophy in the context of our living in the world. All philosophies must start there, and in doing so they find common ground for discussion. Consider Bowne's words, "We find such common ground in the following postulates:—First, the coexistence of persons. It is a personal and social world in which we live, and with which all speculation must begin. We and the neighbors are facts which cannot be questioned. Secondly, there is a law of reason valid for all and binding upon all. This is the supreme condition of any mental community. Thirdly, there is a world of common experience, actual or possible, where we meet in mutual understanding, and where the great business of life goes on."[7] In this Bowne and William James agree. James wrote in a letter to Bowne, "I think we fight in exactly the same cause, the reinstatement of the fullness of practical life, after the treatment of it by so much past philosophy as spectral. . . . [I]t is that our emphatic footsteps fall on the *same spot*. You, starting near the rationalist pole, and boxing the compass, and I traversing the diameter from the empiricist pole, reach practically very similar positions and attitudes."[8]

To understand how Bowne understands our life in the world, consider his view of person or self (person, personality, and self are used interchangeably). One of Bowne's recurring claims is that in the process of living, persons change. For that change to be recognized as change, there must be a self-conscious cognitive unity persisting through that change. That means ". . . to be a person is to be an indivisible, self-conscious unity that itself exists through, and knows, succession."[9] This self-identifying unity includes ". . . selfhood, self-consciousness, self-control, and the power to know."[10] Our thoughts and feelings are inalienably our own. Through our power of self-control or self-direction, we are relatively independent, though we are neither self-sufficient nor independent in any absolute sense. Finally, persons are agents. They do not have changeless souls independent of experience and known only through conscious activities. Rather, persons are centers of activity that cannot be understood by, or reduced to, any mechanistic scheme. This is an agent theory of the self, not a causal one.[11] Bowne contends that to be is to act and to be acted upon. He says that ". . . the self itself as the subject of the mental life and knowing and experiencing itself as living, and as one and the same throughout its changing experiences, is the surest item of knowledge we possess."[12] Personality ". . . can only be experienced as a fact. . . . Whenever we attempt to go behind this fact we are trying to explain the explanation."[13]

What is the significance of this starting point? Simply that we ". . . are in a personal world from the start, and that the first, last, and only duty of philosophy is to interpret this world of personal life and relations."[14] To that we now turn.

## 2.   Radical Empiricism as Transcendental Empiricism

Bowne's philosophic insight is situated within a deep commitment to a thoroughgoing empiricism, a commitment that places him in large agreement with James and Dewey and in disagreement with Descartes.[15] This means that he denies that "the distinction between subjectivity and non-subjectivity is the most fundamental distinction in an inquiry, . . . the most fundamental tool for dividing up what is."[16] Philosophers know this axis as spawned by the competing interests of modern science, religion, and skepticism, and enshrined in philosophy by Descartes. We might simply call it systemic dualism, whether epistemic or metaphysical.

For those deeply committed to empiricism, the starting point for all philosophic study is *within* experience, broadly conceived. Bowne says, "We begin with experience, which is real and valid in its way. This is the world of things and persons about us, and the general order of life. Now in serious thought there can never be any question as to the validity and truth of this experience."[17] But how is this understood by Bowne? The question is not *whether* things exist in the world, but *how* they come to be there for us. Beginning with a radical empiricism, issues of knowledge and conduct that arise as our individual experiences within our overall lived experience conflict with each other and thus require recognition, interpretation, and action. In this way Bowne seeks to silence the Cartesian skeptic.

However, following Kant and against Hume, Bowne believes that the mind is not passive in its empirical life but is actively engaged in it from the outset. And the mind engages "in accordance with certain principles immanent in the mind, according to which it organizes the impressions of sense into the connected forms of the understanding, and thus only reaches an articulate and connected system of experience."[18] In this sense Bowne's radical empiricism is a transcendental one, in crucial contrast to James.[19]

## 3.   Knowledge and Epistemic Realism

Like experience, knowledge is *for us* constituted by the active intellect. We find in Bowne the same basic pattern we find in Kant: sensation, understanding, and the self (transcendental unity of the apperception). However, to Kant's scheme of categories Bowne adds time, space, and purpose. For Bowne, all experience is constructed temporally and spatially, and the conditions for this lie in the categories of time and space. These categories along with number, motion, quantity, being, quality, identity, causality, necessity, and possibility are the principles in terms of which we recognize and interpret our experience and build our knowledge. However, alone they leave isolated things and events; they do not provide for orderly unification within experience and for knowledge. To accomplish this unification, Bowne calls attention to the category of purpose. In purpose we find "the elevation of causality to intelligent and volitional causality, with its implication of plan and purpose."[20] Whereas Kant appeals to the transcendental unity of the apperception to account for the unity of experience and knowledge, Bowne extends this doctrine to include the purposive agent. What can account for the unity and systematic organization of experience and knowledge? Only a purposive causal agent. Does this lead us to an essence, a substance? No, Bowne claims; "back of experience we find no truly real of the noumenal type, but we infer or affirm a cause which is founding and maintaining the order of experience."[21] Implicit in Kant's insight, but more fully developed in Bowne's philosophy, is the experiencing, knowing, purposive agent.

Bowne is deeply sympathetic with Kant, and he modifies and extends the Kantian scheme. Yet he parts company with Kant at two crucial points. First, for Kant the self is phenomenal only; the noumenal self is beyond our knowing grasp, except possibly through the rational will. Bowne rejects this view. He says, "A phenomenon which is not an appearance for somebody is a logical impossibility. It is possible to look upon things as phenomenal only; but to look upon the self which views these phenomena as itself phenomenal in the same sense is altogether impossible. Where there is no perceiving subject there can be no phenomena; and when we put the subject among the phenomena, the doctrine itself disappears."[22] Again, the self is neither noumenal (a kind of soul substance) nor phenomenal. Rather person is agency, or causality. This view stems from Bowne's contention that all thought about reality must be rooted in experience, that apart from experience we can never be sure that our conceptions represent anything or not, and that in the "self-conscious causality of free intelligence we find the meaning of causality and the assurance that it represents a fact."[23] This also leads him to call his view "transcendental empiricism," as pointed out above.[24]

Bowne also contends with Kant's interpretation of how experience is possible, because the creative, constitutive mind tends to lose its way in its own idealistic, solipsistic world. No doubt we make the world as it exists for us, *but we cannot make it anything we please.* Bowne contends that we cannot "fill space with all manner of objects at [our] pleasure, or invert the laws of the outer world at will."[25] Our cognitive constructs necessarily objectively refer to an order other than they; our knowledge never stands alone, isolated from the world. Bowne's epistemic realism manifests itself in his belief that for all philosophies things hang together in certain ways, such as orders of "likeness and difference, of coexistence and sequence, and concomitant variation among the facts of experience. These are revealed only in experience, and whether we like them or not, and whether we can make anything out of them or not, they are undeniably there."[26]

In his attempt to give an account of this belief, Bowne appeals to the doctrine of objective reference. In its constructive activity, the knowing mind refers beyond itself to the content existing apart from its own perceptive act. "All thinking has this objective reference. It claims not to produce but to reproduce a content existing apart from the knowing act itself."[27] If there were no harmony between the inner constructions of the mind and outer objects and events other than the mind, the mind could neither impose its laws and forms on experience nor could know objects and events; we cannot account for knowledge of the world and also hold to Kant's view of the constructive, knowing mind.

On Bowne's understanding of our knowledge of the world "the mind has the key in itself, but there must also be an objective order and fixed meaning as the presupposition of interpretation. Otherwise we should be seeking to understand mere noises or random scratches, which would be absurd. When this thought is carried out it implies an objective rational order parallel to our subjective thinking."[28] This order is no static system—either of things and relations existing in some kind of natural order, or of ideas related within some cosmic mind. It is a realm of orderly change. Our lives in this world are never fixed, and neither is our knowledge of it. Our knowledge is open to change as we gain new experiences. There is no absolute randomness in it, however. As we experience it there is change, but there is also orderliness. At this point Bowne is very close to William James; in Bowne there is clearly a pragmatic element.[29]

## 4.   Person as Key to Reality

Bowne asks an important question based on his understanding of the order of the outer world as necessarily correlated to the order of our inner world: How best account for systematic change in the world? Neither naturalistic impersonalism nor idealistic impersonalism can account for this. The reason is simply that neither view includes a causal, organizing power sufficient to explain the systematic character of the world. For example, Spencer's evolution finally relies on a basal notion of dispersed matter or a fiery cloud to explain all subsequent evolutionary change. Unfortunately, there is nothing in these notions that can adequately account for the living, personal world.

Bowne believes these problems can be overcome by raising the problem to the personal plane. First, we find in the identity and unity of the self the key insight necessary to answer the central metaphysical problem: the relation of permanence and change. "Thus identity is entirely intelligible as the self-identification of intelligence in experience. . . . Again, unity is entirely intelligible as the unity of the self in the plurality of its activities."[30] It is no weakness that the self is not picturable. To attempt to appeal to some such picture requires that the picture be a picture for a self. This self reappears as the root of our experience and as necessary for all understandings of it. But if we look to the self, we find there *experientially* a unity and identity amid change. Though the self is the key to understanding the relation of permanence and change, we are still faced with the problem of accounting for *orderly* change.

Second, in our search for the key to understanding the kind of causality that can adequately account for the orderly changing world, we turn to the person. The only cause we know anything about that can accomplish this task is the causal activity of the personal purposive agent. This insight, Bowne argued, is rooted in the principle of sufficient reason and in the distinction between mechanical and volitional (agent) causality. If the world we know is orderly, changing, and law-like, we must hold to the view that the world is the expression of a purposive agent.

On both counts—1) the appeal to person as the key to resolving the problem of permanence and change, and 2) the recognition of the necessity of purposive agency to account for systematic change in the world—we have no alternative other than to draw the theistic conclusion. The only unity amid diversity that has its roots firmly planted in the soil of experience is that of the person, and the only purposive agent we know is person. Thus, the cause of the world must be Person, and Person is the solution to the problem of the relation of permanence and change. This Person we know as God. Our existence as we understand it can only spring from a personal source. In Bowne's language, ". . . our existence does not really abut on, or spring out of, an impersonal background; it rather depends on the living will and purpose of the Creator. And its successive phases, so far as we may use temporal language, are but the form under which the Supreme Person produces and maintains the personal finite spirit."[31]

Bowne is arguing from analogy. Does this mean that the infinite Person has all the limitations of the finite person? This question originates in a lack of understanding of person. We must remember that "the essential meaning of personality is selfhood, self-consciousness, self-control, and the power to know. . . . Any being, finite or infinite, which has knowledge and self-consciousness and self-control, is personal."[32] However, only in God can we find the complete and perfect selfhood and self-possession that are necessary to the fullness of personality. As we think of God, the Supreme Person, "we must beware of transferring to him the limitations and accidents of our human personality, which are no necessary part of the notion of personality, and think only of the fullness of power, of knowledge, and selfhood which alone are the essential factors of the conception."[33]

## 5. The Ethical Life

Given this view of experience, knowledge, and reality, how does a Personalist understand the ethical life? It is best grasped in terms of the development of morals of individuals living instinctually within institutions. At birth, the human being is a "candidate for humanity," a goal that must be won.[34] To win this goal, in a way reminiscent of Plato's philosophy, the lower must be subordinated to the higher. Humans have a body of instincts which are supplemented by rationality and the activity of the free spirit. But unlike Plato's philosophy, Bowne believes that these instincts do not by their nature drag humans to the lowest moral level. Rather, they "give our life a certain form and direction on their own account. [They] . . . initiate us into life, and prepare the way for the higher moral and rational activity."[35]

The development of the ethical life of each individual person begins in the context of prerational relations of social institutions held together by a herding instinct, analogous to that of cattle. Bowne thinks that "this instinct binds men together, and subjects them to the general law of the herd; and it does this so well that, in the lower ranges of society, the individual has no rights, and even no thought of rights, as against the tribe. This utter subjection of the individual is the only thing that saves rudimentary societies from anarchy. There being no proper thought or knowledge, the instinct, or consolidated experience, of the mass is a far safer guide than the whimsey of the individual."[36] And supplemented by rationality, the moral activity of the free spirit, and conscious of his aims, an individual he ". . . sets himself to perfect and complete that development which begins automatically, but is carried on only by freedom. Here the constitutional becomes moral; and the natural rises to the plane of the spiritual. To effect this change. . . . is the normal function of freedom in human life."[37] The ideal is the fully developed personality, one that is like the Cosmic Person.

Bowne can be called the founder of Personalism in America. This personalism is one of two distinctive American philosophies; pragmatism is the other. Formed in the late nineteenth century, it bears similarities with James's and Dewey's thought, particularly their devotion to a radical empiricism and their celebration of the freedom of the individual. But Bowne differed in his emphasis on the importance of the person as agent and interpreter of experience. As an idealist, Bowne has many similarities with Royce. However, there is an important difference: Bowne resists subjugating the individual to the Absolute, and holds to the self as a free moral agent. Bowne's vision in metaphysics, epistemology, ethics, and philosophy of religion, articulated during the classical period of American thought, helped set an agenda for many thinkers throughout the twentieth century, including Edgar Sheffield Brightman and Peter A. Bertocci, two leading personalist philosophers at Boston University, and Martin Luther King Jr., the immensely influential civil rights leader.

## Notes

1. Paul Deats and Carol Robb, eds., *The Boston Personalist Tradition in Philosophy, Social Ethics, and Theology* (Macon, Ga.: Mercer University Press, 1986), p. 4. However, Ralph Barton Perry writes that George Holmes Howison is the founder of personalism: "His prior title to it is clearly valid." *The Present Conflict of Ideals* (New York: Longmans Green and Co., 1929) p. 203.
2. W. H. Werkmesiter, *A History of Philosophical Ideals in America* (Westport, Conn.: Greenwood, 1981 [1949], p. 103.

3. The Boston University version of personalism was the fullest, richest philosophical statement. Howison, though a founder of American personalism, did not write a fully developed metaphysics, epistemology, and ethics. Hocking's work, though brilliant and richly textured, lacked final metaphysical expression. Nevertheless, the themes developed here are common to American personalists.

4. For example, in critique of Spencer's psychology, James wrote that "consciousness, however, little, is an illegitimate birth in any philosophy that starts without it, and yet professes to explain all facts by continuous evolution. *If evolution is to work smoothly, consciousness in some shape must have been there at the very origin of things.*" *Principles of Psychology,* vol. 1 (Cambridge, Mass.: Harvard University Press, 1981 [1890]), p. 152.

5. Thomas F. Trotter, "Boston Personalism's Contributions to Faith and Learning," *The Boston Personalist Tradition in Philosophy, Social Ethics, and Theology,* p. 17.

6. George Mardsen and Bradley J. Longfield, eds., *The Secularization of the Academy* (New York: Oxford University Press, 1992), p. 33. The great American Baptist preacher in New York City, Harry Fosdick asserted in his autobiography, *The Living of These Days,* that reading Bowne saved his intellectual life." "Boston Personalism's Contributions to Faith and Learning," p. 18.

7. Borden Parker Bowne, *Personalism* (New York: Houghton, 1908), pp. 20–21.

8. William James, "Letter to Bowne, August 17, 1908," in *Representative Essays of Borden Parker Bowne,* ed. Warren Steinkraus (Utica, N.Y.: Meridan Publishing Co., 1980), p. 190.

9. Peter A. Bertocci, "Borden Parke Bowne and His Personalistic Theistic Idealism," *The Boston Personalist Tradition in Philosophy, Social Ethics, and Theology,* p. 58.

10. Borden Parker Bowne, *Personalism,* p. 266.

11. Bowne distinguishes between mechanical and volitional causality. *Personalism,* pp. 159–216.

12. Ibid., p. 88.

13. Ibid., p. 264.

14. Ibid., p. 53.

15. Herbert W. Schneider, "Bowne's Radical Empiricism," *Representative Essays of Borden Parker Bowne,* pp. xi–xv.

16. Lawrence E. Cahoone, *The Dilemma of Modernity: Philosophy, Culture, and Anti-Culture* (Albany, State University of New York Press, 1988), pp 19, 20.

17. Borden Parker Bowne, *Kant and Spencer: A Critical Exposition* (Boston: Houghton Mifflin, 1912), p. 131. Here Bowne and James, the radical empiricist and humanist, agree.

18. Ibid., p. 10.

19. For example, James writes: "The generalized conclusion is that therefore the parts of experience hold together from next to next by relations that are themselves part of experience. The directly apprehended universe needs, in short, no extraneous trans-empirical connective support, but possesses in its own right a concatenated or continuous structure." *The Meaning of Truth: A Sequel to Pragmatism* (Cambridge, Mass.: Harvard University Press, 1975 [1909]), p. 7.

20. Borden Parker Bowne, *Theory of Thought and Knowledge* (New York: Harper, 1897), p. 104.

21. Borden Parker Bowne, *Kant and Spencer: A Critical Exposition,* pp. 146–147.

22. Borden Parker Bowne, *Personalism,* p. 88.

23. Ibid., 104.

24. Ibid.

25. Borden Parker Bowne, *Kant and Spencer: A Critical Exposition,* p. 19.

26. Borden Parker Bowne, *Personalism,* p. 36.

27. Ibid, p. 27.

28. Ibid., p. 76.

29. For Bowne's relation to pragmatism, see Francis J. McConnell, *Borden Parker Bowne: His Life and His Philosophy* (New York, Abingdon, 1929). See also recent studies by Douglas Anderson, Donald W. Dotterer, and John J. Stuhr in "Personalism and Pragmatism," ed. Thomas O. Buford, *The Personalist Forum,* 5 (2), 1990.

30. Borden Parker Bowne, *Personalism,* p. 260

31. Ibid., p. 265.

32. Ibid., p. 266.

33. Ibid., p. 267.

34. Borden Parker Bowne, *Principles of Ethics* (New York: Harper, 1892), p. 125.

35. Ibid.

36. Ibid., p. 127.

37. Ibid., p. 125.

# *Borden Parker Brown:* The Failure of Impersonalism

Impersonalism might rightly be ruled out, on the warrant of our previous studies. We have seen that when our fundamental philosophic principles are impersonally and abstractly taken, they disappear either in contradiction or in empty verbalism. In all our thinking, when critically scrutinized, we find self-conscious and active intelligence the presupposition not only of our knowledge but of the world of objects as well. We might, then, rest our case and demand a verdict. Pedagogically, however, it seems better to continue the case. The naturalistic obsession is not easily overcome, and it takes time to form right habits of thinking, even when the truth is recognized. The present lecture, then, is devoted to showing somewhat more in detail the shortcomings of impersonal philosophy.

Impersonalism may be reached in two ways. The sense-bound mind sees a great variety of extra-mental, impersonal things in the world about us, and these very naturally bulk large in thought. Thus things, with of course such modifications of the conception as a superficial reflection may suggest, tend to become the basal fact of existence. In this way naturalism arises, with its mechanical way of thinking and its materialistic and atheistic tendencies. This is one form of impersonalism.

The other form of impersonalism arises through the fallacy of the abstract. Uncritical minds always attempt to explain the explanation, thus unwittingly committing themselves to the infinite regress. Accordingly when they come to living intelligence as the explanation of the world, they fancy that they must go behind even this. We have the categories of being, cause, identity, change, the absolute, and the like; and intelligence at best is only a specification or particular case of these more general principles. These principles, then, lie behind all personal or other existence, as its presupposition and source, and constitute a set of true first principles, from which all definite and concrete reality is derived by some sort of logical process or implication. This is a species of idealistic impersonalism. In its origin it is antipodal to naturalism, but in the outcome the two often coincide. Strauss said of the Hegelian idealism that the difference between it and materialism was only one of words; and this was certainly true of Hegelianism of the left wing.

These two forms of impersonalism we have now to consider, and we begin with naturalism.

As is the case with so many other terms, naturalism may have two meanings. It may be a principle of scientific method, and it may be a philosophic doctrine. In the former sense it is about identical with science itself, and is full of beneficence. By making the notion and fact of law prominent, it has given us control over the world and ourselves, and has freed the human mind from endless superstition and ignorance. Nature is no longer the seat of arbitrary caprice; and life no longer swarms with omens, portents, and devils. One must read at length in the history of humanity to recognize our debt to naturalism in this sense. We live in peace and sanity where our ancestors lived among dangerous and destructive obsessions, because a wise naturalism has displaced the false supernaturalism of earlier times. When, therefore, we speak of the failure of naturalism, we do not mean the failure of scientific naturalism, for this is one of humanity's best friends.

But philosophical naturalism is another thing. This is not a science, but a philosophy, and it has to be subjected to philosophical criticism in order to estimate its value. This general view is closely allied to commonsense realism, and is indeed but a kind of extension

From *Personalism.* Boston: Houghton Mifflin Company, 1908. pp. 106–146.

or refinement of it. As the untrained mind is naturally objective in its thinking, the things and bodies about us are taken for substantial realities as a matter of course, and they tend in advance of reflection to become the standard by which all else must be measured and to which all else must conform. Things that we can see and handle are the undeniable realities. About them there can be no question; but things invisible are, for common sense, doubtful; and as these things of sense experience by an easy generalization may be gathered under the one head, matter, and their activities ascribed to the one cause, force, matter and force come to be the supreme and basal realities of our objective experience. When their realm is extended, they often come to be viewed as the sole realities. But these realities are in space and time, which are looked upon as undoubted facts of a sort, and when they are combined with matter and force we get the fundamental factors of the scheme. Space and time furnish the scene; matter furnishes the existence; and force, manifesting itself in motion, furnishes the causality. These five factors constitute nature, and from them nature is to be construed and comprehended. Mr. Spencer presents them as the factors on which an interpretation of the world must rest, and according to him cosmic processes consist in an integration of matter and concomitant dissipation of motion. Here space and time are implied, matter and motion are expressed, and force, as the back-lying causality, is understood; and all interpretation of nature, it is said, must be in terms of these factors. This might be called the programme of philosophic naturalism. It aims to explain all the higher forms of experience, including life and society, in terms of matter and force working in space and time under the forms of motion. To what extent this is a coherent and consistent system we have now to consider, and for a time we shall limit our inquiry to its explanation of the objective world of bodies, postponing any inquiry into its explanation of life and mind and society.

This system, as said, is allied in its beginnings with common-sense realism, and never gets entirely away from it. Whatever changes may be made in the common-sense view in the direction of transfigured realism, it still commonly holds on to the conception of an impersonal order of things; and even when it transforms things themselves into phenomena or processes, it still affirms the existence of energy under mechanical laws, producing a series of impersonal effects and moving from phase to phase according to the parallelogram of forces. It is an attempt to explain the world by impersonal and mechanical principles. Of course there is no suspicion that transfigured realism and phenomenalism are veritable Trojan horses for the theory.

This view was perfectly natural and almost necessary for spontaneous thought, when it became a little reflective and sought to unfold the implications of its crude sense metaphysics. But in this view we have a double abstraction. First, the objects of experience, which are given only in experience and which analysis shows are conceivable only as functions of intelligence, are abstracted from all relation to intellect as the veritable fact in itself which is later to explain intellect. This is as much as if one should abstract language from intelligence and then adduce language as the explanation of intelligence. The second abstraction is that even in experience itself only one aspect is fixed on, that of extension and motion, and this is supposed to be the real. All else is accidental and subordinate, but matter and motion are beyond any question. The world of qualities, all that gives life to experience, is ignored, and only the quantitative aspect is retained. But this is another product of fiction. There is no such world except among the abstractions of physicists. It is as little real as the forms of abstract mechanics by which we represent the relations of phenomena, without, however, pretending to reproduce the actual causality. Oddly enough, there is a strong idealistic factor in this naturalistic mechanism. Looking at the moving atoms with critical eye, nothing but quantitative distinctions and relations are discovered to exist. Qualitative distinctions and relations are contributed by the spectator, and they are the chief part of the real problem. According to the theory, the fact would be a great multitude of elements falling apart and together according to the laws of motion, but then there is very much more than this in experience. Indeed, this is not experience at all. A mind which could completely grasp the moving elements as they are in themselves and not in the appearance, would miss the most important part in the system, that is, the whole world of sense qualities and distinctions, in the midst and enjoyment of which we live. Thus the most important part of experience is not explained at all, but is handed over to a kind of subjective experience somewhere in consciousness, while the theoretical explanation applies only to abstractions. Thus we invert the true order of fact. We discredit the real experience, or ignore it, and triumphantly solve an imaginary problem. As pointed out in a previous lecture, we are shut up by this way of thinking to transfigured realism and all its fictitious problems, with the result that the world we experience becomes more and more subjective, while the alleged real world becomes less and less accessible and less and less worth knowing. This result we reach quite apart from the phenomenality of the whole mechanical scheme.

A further reflection on this view as it commonly appears in popular discussion is that on its own realistic ground it is throughout ambiguous. There are two entirely different types of explanation in logic, explanation by classification and explanation by causality; and naturalism oscillates confusedly between them. At times we are told that explanation consists entirely in discovering the uniformities of experience, and that the ultimate explanation must consist in discovering the most general uniformity of experience. At other times, however, the causal idea shuffles in and the attempt is made to explain by causality. We must consider both types in our criticism.

Explanation by classification always remains on the surface. Things are grouped together by means of some common factor of likeness, but we never get any insight into the inner nature of things in this way. Such explanation has only a formal convenience, but we never can reach causes or reasons by this road. We merely unite similar things in groups or series, and thus rescue them from their isolation and get a common name for them all. Such explanation merely drops out the differences of things and retains the point or points in which they are similar, and then regards that as their true explanation. How little this in itself helps us to insight is manifest upon reflection. We may gather all living things under the one head, organism, but in this case we simply find a common term for a multitude of things, which are not identified in any way by the classification, but simply brought under a simple head for purposes of logical convenience. Organism applies to every living thing whether animal or vegetable, spore or tree, microbe or elephant; and these differences, which are really the essential things in the case, are simply dropped out of sight, and we have the one term, organism, by which we are to understand the multitudinous plurality of living things. In the same way we may regard all objects as cases of matter and motion. But we get by such classification exceedingly little information. The generalization is so vague as to include all things at the expense of meaning practically nothing. We get very little valuable insight by classing all the products of human invention in the world as machines, or by classing all living organisms as integrations of matter and motion. It may be that they all come under the head of matter and motion in some aspects of their being, but even then we have no valuable information. It is, indeed, possible that some sciences would need to consider only the matter and motion aspect, just as a shoemaker might consider men only as shoe-wearing animals, and no harm would be done if this aspect were seen in its partial and superficial character. In some respects our human life is a case of matter and motion, and in some other respects it is not a case of matter and motion. There may be matter and motion in connection with thought, but thought is not matter and motion.

If the naturalistic formula, then, confines itself simply to such classification, it is plain that it might be in a way true, and equally plain that it would be at best only a partial view and might be worthless, inasmuch as it would leave all the differences of things, which constitute their special peculiarities and the leading problem in dealing with them, out of consideration, and merely find their explanation in some one point in which they should agree. It would be scarcely more absurd if we should decide to explain all human bodies by the fact that they all had noses and ears, and should then leave out of consideration the multitudinous personal peculiarities whereby each is constituted a separate and incommunicable individual.

It is plain, then, that if the naturalistic explanation is to be of any use to us, it must go beyond these superficial generalities of classification, and must descend into the realm of causation, and also give account of the specific peculiarities or differentia of concrete things. And here difficulties begin to thicken.

Objects in space, large or small, can be pictured, and it seems at first as if the naturalistic view admitted of being really conceived. We can easily imagine a variety of bodies in space variously grouped and moving, and these bodies might conceivably be very small, so as to give us the molecules or atoms of theoretical physics. These also admit in a way of being pictured in their spatial relations or combinations; but when we come to add to these the notion of causality, so as to explain the order of spatial and temporal change, we find grave difficulties arising. With bodies of the kind described, the only thing we can explain is amorphous masses; that is, with bare lumps we can explain only heaps. Unless we assume a mover without, we must posit moving forces within; and unless these forces are under some structural law, they will explain only amorphous masses again. Simply pulling and pushing in a straight line, as central forces are supposed to do, make no provision for organization. Assuming, then, the existence of such forces, we have a double order of facts, one of spatial change and one of a metaphysical nature. The former is a change among things; the latter is a change in things. The former

depends on the latter. All substantial changes among things must be viewed as translations into phenomenal form of dynamic relations in things, and the spatial system can be understood only through the dynamic system. No spatial change explains itself or anything else until it is referred to a hidden dynamism. If we subtract a chemical element from a given molecule no one can see the slightest reason in that fact for the resulting chemical change, unless we assume a system of dynamic relations within the elements themselves which determines the form of their manifestation and interaction, and this system must be as complex and various as the phenomena themselves.

If we had a great mass of type no one would be dull enough to suppose that that would explain literature, even in its mechanical expression. It might indeed be said that literature in its mechanical form arises through the differentiation and integration of type; but while this would be true it would hardly pay expenses, for the work of the compositor cannot be done by polysyllabic words. But if we were determined to get along without the typesetter, we should have to endow the type with highly mysterious forces if they are to be equal to their task. Plain pushes and pulls would simply give us type in heaps or scattered about, as the pushes or pulls predominated, and this would not meet the case. We must have type which will pull and push themselves into the order demanded by the thought. Thus if the type were to set up *Paradise Lost,* they would have to be such that sundry type would come to the front and arrange themselves in the following order:

*Of man's first disobedience and the fruit*
*Of that forbidden tree whose mortal taste*
*Brought death into our world and all our woe,*
*Sing, heavenly muse.*

The other type must likewise march to their proper positions in order to make up the work. But in that case it is plain that the idea of the work is already immanent in the constitution of the type, otherwise we should be seeking to explain the orderly result by the chance jostlings of the type. That this is impossible everyone can see in the case of typesetting. Everyone sees here that the arrangement of the type is as much a part of the problem as their existence, and that the existence does not imply the arrangement. But if we insist on making the existence imply the arrangement, we must carry the arrangement into the existence in the form of "subtle tendencies" and "mysterious potentialities"; and these, in addition to being of exceedingly elusive meaning, do not illumine the problem at all, but rather darken it. To complete the parallel we must suppose that the type themselves were not originally given in their separate character, but only an indefinite, incoherent, unknowable homogeneity, which through continuous differentiations and integrations produced the type with all their specific characters and subtle tendencies and mysterious potentialities. This gives us an idea, on the naturalistic basis, of the necessity of a hidden dynamism for the explanation of spatial grouping and also of its unmanageable complexity.

This invisible dynamic system is overlooked altogether by spatial thought. Such thought has only the atoms and the void as data, and it can easily conceive the atoms as variously grouped within this void. The spatial imagination serves for this insight and nothing more is demanded; but when thought is clarified to the point of seeing the necessity of forming an unpicturable dynamism behind the system of spatial changes, then the dark impenetrability of our physical metaphysics begins to appear. Spatial combination we can picture; volitional causality we experience; but what that is which is less than the latter and more than the former is an exceedingly difficult problem. The fact is, we are simply using formal counters here, and are unable to tell whether there is anything whatever corresponding to them. We believe that there must be cause and ground, and then we suppose that the atoms themselves can be causes; but when we attempt to think the matter through, then we soon find that we are applying the categories, as Kant would say, in a region where

we have no experience, or rather no intuition. The result is, our thought may be in a way formally correct, but we have no assurance that it represents any actual fact whatever. This, then, shows first of all the dark unpicturability of naturalistic metaphysics from the dynamic side; and remembering the results of the discussion of the previous lecture, we find reason for saying that this metaphysics is entirely fictitious. It is an attempt to apply the notion of causality under circumstances, and in a form, which it is impossible for us to construe.

Can life and mind and morals and society be explained on a naturalistic basis? These questions were warmly debated in the last generation, but seldom understood. How naive it all was, is manifest as soon as we look at the matter from a more critical standpoint. The space and time world of phenomena explains nothing; it is rather the problem itself. The real account of anything must be sought in the world of power; and this world eludes us altogether, unless we raise power to include intelligence and purpose. The unpicturable notions of the understanding, as substance, cause, unity, identity, etc., elude all spatial intuition, and vanish even from thought when impersonally taken. Concerning life and mind and man, it is permitted to look for all the uniformities we can find among their antecedents and concomitants, but this is only classification and reveals no causality. And any fairly clearminded critic is willing to have anything whatever discovered in the space and time realm; for he knows that the only question of any real importance is that of causation. Those persons who expect to find matter to be the sufficient cause of life, and those who fear it may be, reveal thereby such profound ignorance of the true state of the problem that, while charity is called for, they merit no further consideration. Even if so-called spontaneous generation proved to be a fact, it would only mean that living things may arise under other phenomenal conditions than those that generally obtain; it would not mean that "material causes" are able to themselves to produce living beings. The wonder would lie altogether in the phenomenal realm, and would leave the question of the power at work as obscure as ever. Thus as soon as we distinguish the question of classification and spatial arrangement from that of causality, we see how superficial naturalistic philosophy has been. Classification has passed for identification, phenomena have been made into things, and sequence has been mistaken for causality. This naïve confusion has made speculation very easy.

But supposing this dynamic difficulty in a way removed, we next meet another puzzle arising from overlooking the distinction between concrete and exhaustive thinking and symbolic or short-hand thinking. In other words, popular naturalism assumes that we have the simple physical elements in simple spatial relations, and that they are endowed with certain central forces of no very complex kind, but such that they admit of producing a great variety of complications, thus passing from the simple to the complex and from the homogeneous to the heterogeneous. Everyone will recall at this point the current formula of evolution, which claims to proceed from the like to the unlike, from the simple to the complex, from homogeneity to heterogeneity, through continuous differentiations and integrations. This difficulty is only a specification in detail of the tautology which inheres in every mechanical doctrine of causation, as pointed out in the last lecture.

This fancy is almost the sum of naturalistic philosophizing. If the infinite complexity of the concrete problem, in spite of all the simplifications and identifications of words, were seen, naturalism would lose all credit. The fancy in question is simply the fallacy of the universal, and rests upon mistaking the logical process for an ontological one, or from mistaking logical application for ontological implication. The class term applies to every member of the class, but it implies no one of them. Thus the term man applies to every human being, but it does not imply any living human being whatever. But this is overlooked by the speculator, and he thinks it very possible to pass from complexity to simplicity, from heterogeneity to homogeneity, and in this way he succeeds in reaching some simple,

almost contentless, terms, and these, which are really the last terms of logical abstraction, are supposed to be the first terms of real existence. Then these terms, because very simple and vague and indefinite in themselves, seem to raise no questions and excite no surprise. They may well, then, be taken as original starting points for world building and similar cosmological exploits. In this way, then, such abstractions as matter and force are reached, and they take the place of the physical elements, which are the only realities in the case. But in all this we simply forget the concrete facts. They remain as complex and multiform as ever. There is no simple thing, matter, and no simple fact, motion, to be distributed, but rather an indefinite number of moving things of various quantity and quality and in the most complex and mysterious dynamic relations. When we pass to the concrete we see the difference between the logical concept and the concrete reality, and we also see that logical simplification does not affect the reality at all. When, then, we replace the physical elements by the logical abstraction, matter, we do not reach anything indefinite or incoherent or homogeneous. Each of these elements has its own definite qualities definitely related in a definite system of definite law. There is no incoherency in the real system, and no progress toward greater coherency, except in relation to standards which we impose upon the system. If we take the solar system as a standard, we may call the nebulous period incoherent. If we take a solid body as a standard, we may call a gas incoherent. If we take a mature organism as a standard, we may call the embryo incoherent. But in all these cases the incoherency is relative to an assumed standard, and is non-existent for the underlying nature of things and the system of law. The homogeneity and heterogeneity, the coherence and incoherence, are relative to the speculator and his point of view, and in fact are but shadows of himself.

We may, then, admit the evolution formula as a description of the order in which things come along, such that the earlier forms were simple and homogeneous and the later forms more complex and differentiated; but we cannot admit that this represents any possible order of mechanical causality or any simplification of the concrete problem. We can never by classification reduce our problem to lower terms. If we begin with the complex no logic will enable us to escape into the simple on the impersonal plane, and if we begin with the simple we can never advance to the complex. Whatever we begin with, we are compelled to retain, however far back we may reason. The law of the sufficient reason compels us to find in the premises full and adequate preparation for the conclusion; and if the conclusion be complex, then there must be corresponding complexity in the premises. We may call it potential rather than actual, but all the same we are compelled to make our antecedents such that when they are exhaustively understood they are seen to contain, even to the minutest detail, all that will ever appear in the conclusion. The logical equivalence of cause and effect in any necessary scheme to which we referred in the last lecture makes this absolutely necessary, and hence makes it forever impossible to look upon the evolutionary doctrine as valid in causation. If we suppose a cause apart from the movement, which is successively manifesting a plan beginning with the early and simple forms and then proceeding to higher and more complex and differentiated forms, we can understand that by assimilating it to our own intellectual life; but apart from that the doctrine is absolutely impossible. We are compelled on the impersonal plane to assume everything either actually or potentially at the beginning, or, if there was no beginning, then to assume it from everlasting.

The two conceptions of evolution, evolution as a description of the phenomenal order and evolution as a doctrine of causation, have never been sufficiently distinguished by the rank and file of speculators in this field. They have taken the phenomenal order for the causal order, and have seldom raised the question as to what their evolution really means and what its conditions may be. Accordingly we have the proposition to evolve the atoms, with all the familiar formulas about passing from the homogeneous to the heterogeneous, etc. Nowadays that the supposedly fixed elements seem to be combinations of something simpler, this attempt is frequently met with. It is suggested that the atoms of those substances which lie in the same chemical group are perhaps built up from the same ions, or at least from ions which possess the same mass and electric charge, and that the differences which exist in the materials thus constituted arise more from the manner of the association of the ions in the atom than from differences in the fundamental character of the ions which build up the atoms. Well, here we have the same thing—the attempt to explain qualitative by quantitative difference, and the same failure to inquire what the attempt really presupposes.

If we should conceive a half-dozen bricks placed one at each angle of a pentagon and one at the centre, and should then conceive an additional brick added so as to have one at each angle of a hexagon and one at the centre, we see no reason whatever for any particular change of quality of the combination arising from the addition of the new brick. And that is all that bare quantity can do. No variations of quantity contain any explanation of qualitative change, unless we assume a qualitative system in connection with the quantity. We can add elements to atomic groups or subtract them; but unless the elements themselves stand in definite dynamic relations which imply particular groups and qualities, to the exclusion of other groups and qualities, we cannot deal with the problem at all. If the atoms are not in such relations, the problem is of course insoluble; and if they are in such relations, we assume the fact to be explained from the start. It is then conceivable that our present elements might be analyzed into other elements which might be called simpler, but the thing which is not possible is by such an analysis to escape from the complexity of the existing system, because we should have to trace into those antecedents which are to produce the present complexity and difference the same complexity and difference in one from or another.

Moreover, in thinking the matter through we should have to inquire whether evolution as such assumes anything or not. Does it begin with something vague, formless, and lawless, or does it begin with a definite system and reign of law, so that everything is determined in its place and relation? In the former case we can take no step whatever in the way of understanding anything. It would be simply the notion of pure being, which is nothing, and which, if it were anything, could never be used for the understanding of experience. But if we begin with a definite system of law, in which all the factors are subject to the reign of law, then it is plain we never can introduce anything new into the system, for everything is determined from the beginning; and if there was no beginning, everything was determined from everlasting. In any mechanical system, under the law of the logical equivalence of cause and effect, it is forever impossible to make new departures or to reach anything essentially new. We can only oscillate between the present actuality and the past potentiality, potentializing the present as we go back in our thought, and actualizing the potentiality as we come forward in our thought, but always so that potential plus actual must remain a constant quantity. In popular thought about this matter there is a continual oscillation, for the most part unsuspected, between the two points of view. We try to explain everything by antecedents, and so by the aid of the fallacy of the universal as we go backward we succeed in reaching to our satisfaction some indefinite, incoherent homogeneity. But logic forthwith shows the emptiness of this notion and the impossibility of reaching it. Then we begin again, mindful this time of the reign of law, and assume an order of law, and then fail to notice that as soon as we do that, on the impersonal plane we have determined everything for all future time, so that nothing new may hereafter be introduced without some irruption from without. No new departures are possible in a mechanical scheme.

The same difficulty appears when we work the question forward instead of backward. Here again the naturalistic speculator has commonly been under the influence of sense bondage and has tacitly assumed that what he could not see was not there, so that differences which did not manifest themselves to the senses might be regarded as nonexistent. But the same law which we have been referring to makes it clear that no developing thing can ever be understood or defined by what it momentarily is, but only by all that which it is to become. It can be explained, then, not by reference to its crude beginnings, but only by reference to the finished outcome. Aristotle reached this insight two thousand years ago. When, then, the biological speculator tells us, as if it were a very conclusive fact, that the embryos of many of the higher animals look alike in their earliest stages, we are not so much impressed as perhaps we are expected to be; for, however much things may look alike, if they are under different laws of development they are, to the eye of reason, even in the earliest phases, unlike with all the unlikenesses that later appear. The human embryo, when it is undistinguishable by sight from the embryo of a dog or sheep, is after all a human embryo, and not the embryo of a sheep. It is already under the law of human development, and when it quickly passes into the human form this is not something adventitiously taken on through some verbal hocus-pocus about differentiation and integration, but is simply the manifestation of the immanent organic laws under which it holds its existence and its development takes place.

The whole question of the transformation of species has been equally confused in naturalistic discussion. There are really two questions to be considered. One is, Can existing organic forms be genetically traced to earlier forms so that the lines of descent as we go backward converge to some common origin, as the branches of a tree all meet in a common trunk? The other question is, What are the individual things themselves, and what is the power that produces them? The former question belongs to science, the latter belongs to philosophy.

The former question has only a subordinate interest, and philosophy is content to have the answer fall out as it may, provided fact and logic be duly regarded. Its supposed importance is due to the implicit assumption of a self-running nature which does a great many unintended things on its own account, and to the fancy that such genetic connection would mean identity of nature in the successive members of the series.

The second question is the only one of any real importance. In considering it we must first note the nominalism of the doctrine of descent.

A species as such is nothing but a group of individuals which more or less closely resemble one another. In the case of the more prominent living species we should probably add the notion of genetic connection, but this would in no way affect the nominalism of the doctrine. If, then, the so-called transformation of species took place, the objective fact, apart from our logical manipulation, would be this: If individuals were taken from points widely apart in a line of descent, they would be so unlike that we should not class them together. But this would not identify individuals, or higher and lower forms. The fact would be a power producing individuals in such a way that they could be variously classified, possibly on an ascending scale and in adaptation to higher and fuller life. In that case we should have the familiar progress from the simple to the complex, from the low to the high, and all the rest; but it would be entirely free from all those fearsome identifications of man with the monkey, etc., which have so infested the popular imagination. For one holding the phenomenality of nature and the volitional character of all so-called natural causality, there is nothing to excite alarm in any permissible doctrine of the transformation of species.

We find naturalism, then, entirely in its right when it seeks to give a description of the phenomenal order according to which things have appeared, but we find it as a philosophy exceedingly superficial and uncritical. Apart from the critical doubts which we have discovered in the previous lecture respecting mechanical causality in general, and the necessity of lifting the problem of causation to the personal plane in order to keep it from vanishing in the Heraclitic flux, we find that this doctrine vanishes in complete and barren tau-

tology as soon as we take it concretely and exhaustively, instead of symbolically and in a shorthand way. This way of thinking is compelled to carry the present into the past, or into its machinery of whatever sort, in such a way as to empty it of all progress of any kind. When, then, in such a scheme we make a cross-section of the cosmic flow or any part of it anywhere, we are compelled to find potentially or actually present all that ever will be; and if we choose to carry the regress never so far back, the same necessity attends us; and if at last we reach some nebulous period of dispersed matter or a fiery cloud, even there, when we look around upon the situation with our eyes open, we are compelled to find latent and potential all that will ever emerge in all the future through which the system may endure. In addition, when naturalism becomes mathematical and seeks to reduce all qualitative distinctions to quantitative ones, it leaves the real world altogether, and becomes a pure abstraction like the world of abstract mechanics. Like that world, it has only representative value, and is never to be mistaken for the world of real existence.

These are the leading difficulties of naturalism as a philosophy. There are numberless difficulties of detail, but into these we forbear to enter. The doctrine is sufficiently convicted and judged by its doctrine of causality, and the hopeless tautology and endless regress to which it is condemned, and also by the impossibility of verifying as actual any of its leading conceptions. They must forever remain, at best, mere conceptual forms, to which no reality can be shown to correspond.

Naturalism may be dismissed as a failure. It remains to show that impersonalism as idealism is equally so. When we approach the metaphysical problem from the side of knowledge, it is easy to overlook the fact of will and causality in existence, and conclude that things are only ideas. And then, since the mind also is an object of knowledge, it is easy in the same way to reach the conclusion that it too is only an idea or group of ideas. The next thing is to eliminate the personal implication from these ideas, and then we forthwith reach the conclusion that the mind itself is a function of impersonal ideas. Thus impersonalism is once more installed.

It is easy to see how this view arises. The epistemological interest makes us unwilling to admit anything that cannot be conceptually grasped. Accordingly it seeks to make ideas all-embracing. At the same time it is clear that this view is a tissue of abstractions. The impersonal idea is a pure fiction. All actual ideas are owned, or belong to someone, and mean nothing as floating free. We have already seen that the various categories of thought, apart from their formal character as modes of intellectual procedure, get any real significance only in the concrete and self-conscious life of the living mind. Apart from this, when considered as real they become self-destructive or contradictory. The idealism of the type we are now considering assumes that these categories admit of being conceived in themselves, and that they are in a measure the preconditions of concrete existence, and in such a way that we might almost suppose that a personal being is compounded of being plus unity plus identity plus causality, etc. Thus personal existence appears as the outcome and product of something more ultimate and fundamental. The fictitious nature of this view has already appeared. When we ask what we mean by any of these categories, it turns out, as we have seen, that we mean the significance we find them to have in our self-conscious life. In the concrete the terms have no meaning except as it is abstracted from our own personal experience. The only unity we know anything about, apart from the formal unities of logic, is the unity of the unitary self; and the only identity we know anything about is no abstract continuity of existence through an abstract time, it is simply the self-equality of intelligence throughout its experience. And the change which we find is not an abstract change running off in an abstract time, but is simply the successive form under which the self-equal intelligence realizes its purpose and projects the realizing activity against the background of its self-consciousness. Similarly for being itself; in the concrete it means the passing object of perception, or else it means existence like our own.

So much for the nature of the categories. But still graver difficulties arise when we inquire concerning the place of their existence and the ground of their combination and movement. If we suppose them to precede personality, we must ask where they exist. The only intelligent answer that can be given would be that they exist either in space and time, or in consciousness. The former supposition would turn them into things, and then they would dissolve away in the dialectic of spatial and temporal existence; the latter is contrary to the hypothesis, which is that they are preconditions of consciousness. Thus they retreat into some kind of metaphysical $n$th dimension, where we cannot follow them because they mean nothing.

A further difficulty emerges when we ask for the ground of grouping and movement of these ideas. If we conceive their relations to be purely logical we should make immediate speculative shipwreck. The intellect conceived of as merely a set of logical relations is totally incapable of explaining the order of experience, for logic is non-temporal. Conclusions coexist with the premises. There is no before or after possible in the case. If, then, the universe as existing were a logical implication of ideas, it and all its contents would be as eternal as the ideas. There would be no room for change, but all their implications would rigidly coexist. In this view also finite minds, with all their contents, as implications of eternal ideas, would be equally eternal, and as error and evil are a manifest part of these contents, it follows that they likewise are necessary and eternal. Hence we should have to admit an element of unreason and evil in the eternal ideas themselves; and by this time the collapse of the system would be complete. There is no escape from this result so long as we look upon the intellect as a logical mechanism of ideas. Only a living, active, personal intelligence can escape this fatalism and suicidal outcome of the impersonal reason. A purely logical and contemplative intellect that merely gazed upon the relations of ideas, without choice and initiative and active self-direction, would be absolutely useless in explaining the order of life.

The claim that thought must comprise everything is itself unclear in its meaning. In our human thinking of course there is a world of objects which we do not make but find, and this dualism can never be eliminated from our thinking. But this world of objects is retained within the thought sphere by being made the product and expression of intelligence, and as such it is open to apprehension and comprehension by intelligence. But when it comes to the self-knowledge of intelligence, there is always an element which mere conceptual knowing can never adequately grasp. We have seen that concepts without immediate experience are only empty forms, and become real only as some actual experience furnishes them with real contents. Hence there is an element in self-knowledge beyond what the conceptions of the understanding can furnish. This is found in our living self-consciousness. We conceive some things, but we not only conceive, we also live ourselves. This living indeed cannot be realized without the conception, but the conception is formal and empty without the living. In this sense intelligence must accept itself as a datum, and yet not as something given from without, but as the self-recognition of itself by itself. Intelligence must always have a content for its own recognition. The recognition would be impossible without the content, and the content would be nothing without the recognition. In this fact the antithesis of thought and being finds recognition and reconciliation; but the fact itself must be lived, it cannot be discursively construed. Thought and act are one in this matter, and neither can be construed without the other.

In closing this discussion we recall once more our doctrine of transcendental empiricism. The meaning and possibility of these terms must finally be found in experience itself, and not in any abstract philosophizing. When the terms are abstractly taken without continual reference to experience, it is easy to develop any number of difficulties and even contradictions in our fundamental ideas. No better proof of this can be found than Mr. Bradley's work on Appearance and Reality. This is a work of great ability, but written from the abstract standpoint. The result is that it might almost be called a refutation of impersonalism, although such refutation was far enough from Mr. Bradley's purpose. He finds all the categories and relations of thought abounding in contradiction. Inherence, predication, quality, identity, causality, unity, space, time, things, and even the self, swarm with contradictions. Mr. Bradley seems to think that these difficulties are all removed in the absolute, but he fails to see that his logic would pursue him even into the absolute, unless it be personally conceived. Otherwise the absolute is simply a *deux ex machina* kept strictly behind the scenes, and worked only by stage direction from the manager.

But the difficulties urged by Mr. Bradley do exist for all impersonal philosophy; and they can be removed only as the problem is raised to the personal plane, and we take the terms in the meaning they have in living experience. Thus identity is entirely intelligible as the self-identification of experience in intelligence. We can easily give identity a meaning according to which the soul is not identical, but there is no loss in this, as we have no interest speculative or practical in such identity. Again, unity is entirely intelligible as the unity of the self in the plurality of its activities. Here again it is easy to define unity in such a way as to exclude plurality; but here also nothing is lost, for we have no interest of any sort in such a unity. The same may be said of the other categories. They may easily be defined in such a way as to involve contradictions or make them worthless, but philosophy is not concerned over the fact of such abstractions; it cares only to know the forms the categories take on in living experience. And here we find, as we pointed out in discussing freedom, that many things which when abstractly taken seem contradictory prove quite compatible in the concrete.

Finally, the notion of the self can easily be taken in such a way as to be worthless. We are asked of what use the self is, after all, in explaining the mental life. How does its unity explain the plurality and variety of consciousness? And the answer must be that in some sense it does not explain it, and yet the unity is no less necessary. For the consciousness of plurality is demonstrably impossible without the fact of conscious unity. This unity does not indeed enable us to deduce plurality, and hence the plurality must be viewed as an aspect of the unity, but not as an aspect of an abstract unity without distinction or difference, but a living, conscious unity, which is one in its manifoldness and manifold in its oneness. Taken verbally this might easily be shown to be contradictory, but taken concretely it is the fact of consciousness, and none the less so because our formal and discursive thought finds it impossible to construe it. And in general the self taken abstractly is indeed worthless, as all causes are on the impersonal plane. The law of the sufficient reason, which is supposed to demand causation, always shuts us up to barren tautology when impersonally taken. In such cases all our explanations only repeat the problem. But the self is not to be abstractly taken. It is the living self in the midst of its experiences, possessing, directing, controlling both itself and them; and this self is not open to the objection of barrenness and worthlessness, being simply what we all experience when we say me or mine. This self can never be more than verbally denied, and even its verbal deniers have always retained the fact. The language of the personal life would be impossible otherwise.

On all of these accounts, then, we affirm that impersonalism is a failure whether in the low form of materialistic mechanism or in the abstract form of idealistic notions, and that personality is the real and only principle of philosophy which will enable us to take any rational step whatever. We are not abstract intellects nor abstract wills, but we are living persons, knowing and feeling and having various interests, and in the light of knowledge and under the impulse of our interests trying to find our way, having an order of experience also and seeking to understand it and to guide ourselves so as to extend or enrich that experience, and thus to build ourselves into larger and fuller and more abundant personal life.

The metaphysics of impersonalism is certainly impossible, but it may be objected that personalism itself is open to at least equal objection. Some of these have become traditional and conventional, and seem to call for a word in passing.

In cruder thought the attempt is always made to solve the problem by picturing, and this ends by confounding the person with the physical organism. Of course it is easy to show that personality as thus conceived is impossible. The more significant objections arise from an abstract treatment of the subject and an attempt to construe personality as the outcome of impersonal principles. But abstraction can do nothing with the question, as the indications of living experience are the only source of knowledge in this matter. Personality can never be construed as a product or compound; it can only be experienced as a fact. It must be possible because it is given as actual. Whenever we attempt to go behind this fact we are trying to explain the explanation. We explain the objects before the mirror by the images which seem to exist behind it. *There is nothing behind the mirror.* When we have lived and described the personal life we have done all that is possible in sane and sober speculation. If we try to do more we only fall a prey to abstractions. This self-conscious existence is the truly ultimate fact.

Of course our human existence, with its various limitations and its temporal form, readily lends itself to the thought that personality develops out of the impersonal. If we should allow this to be the fact in our own case, we should still have to admit that the impersonal out of which our personality develops has already a coefficient of personality as the condition of the development. The essentially impersonal can never by any logical process other than verbal hocus-pocus, which is not logical after all, be made the sufficient reason for a personal development. But our existence does not really abut on, or spring out of, an impersonal background; it rather depends on the living will and purpose of the Creator. And its successive phases, so far as we may use temporal language, are but the form under which the Supreme Person produces and maintains the personal finite spirit.

The objections to affirming a Supreme Person are largely verbal. Many of them are directed against a literal anthropomorphism. This, of course, is a man of straw. Man himself in his essential personality is as unpicturable and formless as God. Personality and corporeality are incommensurable ideas. The essential meaning of personality is selfhood, self-consciousness, self-control, and the power to know. These elements have no corporeal significance or limitations. Any being, finite or infinite, which has knowledge and self-consciousness and self-control, is personal; for the term has no other meaning. Laying aside, then, all thought of corporeal form and limitation as being no factor of personality, we must really say that complete and perfect personality can be found only in the Infinite and Absolute Being, as only in Him can we find that complete and perfect selfhood and self-possession which are necessary to the fullness of personality. In thinking, then, of the Supreme Person we must beware of transferring to him the limitations and accidents of our human personality, which are no necessary part of the notion of personality, and think only of the fullness of power, knowledge, and selfhood which alone are the essential factors of the conception.

Thus impersonalism appears as doubly a failure. If we ask for the positive foundation of its basal conceptions, we find that there is none. They are empty forms of thought to which no reality can be shown to correspond, and upon criticism they vanish altogether. If we next ask what insight impersonalism gives into the problems of experience, we find nothing but tautology and infinite regress. Such a theory surely does not pay expenses. The alternative is personalism or nothing.

## Suggestions for Further Reading

Bertocci, Peter A. "The Essence of a Person." *The Monist* 61.1:28–41.

———. *Introduction to the Philosophy of Religion.* Englewood Cliffs: Prentice-Hall, Inc., 1951.

———. *The Person God Is.* London: Allen and Unwin, 1970.

———. "The Person, His Personality, and Environment." *Review of Metaphysics* 32 (1979): 605–621.

———. *The Person and Primary Emotions.* New York: Springer-Verlag, 1988.

Bertocci, Peter A. and Richard M Millard. *Personality and the Good.* New York: David McKay Company, Inc., 1963.

Bowne, Borden Parker. *Kant and Spencer: A Critical Exposition.* Boston: Houghton Mifflin, 1912. (posthumous).

———. *Metaphysics: A Study in First Principles.* New York: Harper and Brothers, 1882.

———. *Personalism.* New York: Houghton Mifflin, 1908.

———. *Principles of Ethics.* New York: Harper and Brothers, 1887.

———. *Theism.* New York: The American Book Company, 1902.

———. *Theory of Thought and Knowledge.* New York: Harper and Brothers, 1897.

Brightman, E. S. *Moral Laws.* New York: Abingdon Press, 1933.

———. *The Finding of God.* New York: Abingdon Press, 1931.

———. *Is God a Person?* New York: Association Press, 1932.

———. *Person and Reality.* New York: Ronald Press, 1958.

———. *A Philosophy of Religion.* Englewood Cliffs, N.J.: Prentice-Hall, Inc. 1940.

———. *The Problem of God.* New York: Abingdon Press, 1930.

Buford, Thomas O., ed. "Personalism and Pragmatism." *The Personalist Forum.* 5.2 (Fall 1990).

——. "Peter Anthony Bertocci." *The Personalist Forum.* 7.1 (Spring 1991)

Cunningham, G. Watts. *The Idealistic Argument in Recent British and American Philosophy.* New York: The Century Co., 1933.

Deats, Paul and Carol Robb. *The Boston Personalist Tradition.* Macon, Georgia: Mercer University Press, 1988.

Flewelling, Ralph Tyler. *Creative Personality.* New York: Macmillan Co., 1926.

——. *The Person.* Los Angeles: Ward Ritchie Press, 1952.

Howison, George Holmes. (ed.) *The Conception of God: A Philosophical Discussion Concerning the Nature of the Divine Idea as a Demonstrable Reality.* New York: Macmillan, 1898.

——. *The Limits of Evolution and Other Essays Illustrating the Metaphysical Theory of Personal Idealism.* New York: Macmillan Co., 1901.

——. *The Origin of Evolution.* New York: Macmillan Co., 1905.

Knudson, Albert C. *The Philosophy of Personalism.* New York: Abingdon Press, 1927.

Lavely, John. "Personalism." *The Encyclopedia of Philosophy.* Paul Edwards (ed.). Vol. 6. New York: Macmillan Publishing Co., 1967: 107–110.

Steinkraus, Warren E. (ed.). *Representative Essays of Borden Parker Bowne.* Utica, New York: Meridian Publishing Company, n.d.

Steinkraus, Warren E. and Robert N. Beck (eds.). *Studies in Personalism. Selected Writings of Edgar Sheffield Brightman.* Utica, New York: Meridian Publishing Company, n.d.

# AFRICAN-AMERICAN PHILOSOPHY

## Introduction by Leonard Harris

The history of African-American philosophy is a genre of the history of American philosophy—it begins in the ecstasy and infamy of the eighteenth century. There were numerous sailors, servants, and explorers of African descent who settled the nascent Americas. As the nation state, "America," developed in the eighteenth century, tremendous differences came to separate vast numbers of descendants of Africans from vast numbers of descendants of Europeans.

By the early eighteenth century, the infamy of conceiving persons as inherently members of a racial group, embodying separate spiritual potentials, informed American thought. Conceptions of humanity as racially separate entities helped legitimate colonial expansion against Native Americans, as it legitimated racial slavery. White racial supremacy held that racial membership determined, without fail, etiologies and teleologies. Persons were divided along lines of socially constructed definitions of race. Whether polytheists or monotheists, Christian or Muslim, sailors or servants, every person was encoded in a race. All Africans, despite personal histories, were defined as Negroes and any offspring having one Negro parent was defined as Negro. And all Negroes in America were progressively forced to be slaves or were potentially slaves.

The same early American traditions that promoted individual freedom also promoted slavery.[1] Freedom in America entailed pursuit of profits by treating people as expendable, laboring commodities. The same laws that protected individual rights to practice a faith, also allowed forced conversion to Christianity. Slavers, whether indigenous Africans, Europeans, or Americans calculated the cost of predictable deaths during transit to points of sale, during life on plantations or life in mines, for the purpose of assuring an acceptable profit.

Concepts of rights, community, citizenship, loyalty, persons, justifiable methods of change, teleology, character, experience, and truth were developed by African Americans in the context of a ubiquitous American reality of racial slavery, segregation, and discrimination. Appeals based on religion, particularly those emanating from Congregationalist, Methodist, and Baptist quarters, often informed arguments for the abolition of slavery. Increasingly, however, these appeals utilized secular accounts.

The stalwart abolitionists David Walker, Frederick Douglass, and Martin R. Delany represent three radically different secular approaches to abolition. Walker advocated and practiced insurrection. Insurrection is justified for Walker because race-based slavery usurps labor, debases a person's sense of self-worth, undermines true Christianity, and perpetuates rapes, murders, and theft.[2] Moreover, there is a positive moral duty to revolt. This duty occurs because racial slavery was intended as a system that perpetually usurps assets, preventing the transferring of assets across generations, based on the heinous criterion of race.

Douglass promoted nonviolent political agitation. Douglass was a representative of the moral suasionist tradition.[3] That tradition held that persons are endowed with a conscience, too often suppressed or uninformed. Awakening that conscience best occurs through nonviolent forms of agitation, especially when other options might prove unsuccessful.

Delany became noted for his commitment to the ascendancy of the race through African development and the emigration of African Americans to Africa, relinquishing claims to an America that fundamentally excluded the African.[4] The possibility of change for Delany was not conditioned on an awakened American conscience, but rather on the possibility of equal powers of coercion, wealth, and military acumen.

Important changes in the focus of philosophic arguments occurred after the abolition of American slavery in 1865. Arguments over moral and pragmatic methods of change had to be justified in relation to seeking economic and political inclusion, rather than seeking entitlement to self-ownership. In addition, the relationship between universal principles and particular cultural contexts was very often troubling to African-American scholars. If, for example, one argued that universal principles should inform social life, does such a claim entail that there should be one culture and all others are warrantedly less meritorious? If, on the other hand, there are no warranted principles that can evaluate competing cultures, is it impossible to morally condemn slavery with no more moral authority than saying that slavery seems incompatible with a particular contextual or cultural orientation? These problems posed special concern for African Americans, because by the early twentieth century a distinctive African-American culture had emerged.

One way to appreciate the new social changes in twentieth-century America is to consider the relationship between an African-American pragmatist and other philosophers. Alain L. Locke is the most noted African-American pragmatist. Locke was born in Philadelphia, the only child of Pliny Ishmael Locke, a Howard University educated lawyer and Mary Hawkins Locke, a teacher and member of the Felix Adler Ethical Society. Locke was raised an Episcopalian, but later was attracted to the Baha'i faith. Locke was the first African-American Rhodes Scholar at Oxford, England (1907). He also attended lectures at the University of Berlin (1910–11), before returning to the United States and joining the Howard University faculty in 1912. As a student, Locke was associated with other students who would also become luminaries; for example, Horace M. Kallen, with whom the concept of cultural pluralism emerged; H. E. Alaily, president of the Egyptian Society of England; Pa Ka Isaka Seme, Black South African law student and founder of the African National Congress; and Har Dayal, nationalist and Marxist from India. Locke received his doctorate in Philosophy from Harvard in 1918, and by 1925 was a major force in creating and directing the Harlem Renaissance.

Locke's sentinel book, *The New Negro* (1925), announced the Harlem Renaissance and set forth Locke's promotion of cultural pluralism.[5] *The New Negro* was a collage of works attesting to the vibrancy of culture and its value for destroying racial stereotypes. The anthology includes such works as the art of Winold Reiss and Aaron Douglass; pictures of African artifacts portrayed as art; articles by such authors as J. A. Rogers, E. Franklin Frazier, Charles S. Johnson, Melville J. Herskovits, and W.E.B. Du Bois; poetry by Countee Cullen, Langston Hughes, Arna Bontemps, and Angela Grimke; and spirituals and short biographies. The Harlem Renaissance, under Locke's influence, represented the integration of the aesthetic into the arena of public consciousness as a political force.

*When Peoples Meet* (1942), edited by Locke with Bernhard J. Stern, was intended as a way of forcing recognition of cultural diversity; a diversity that compels us to consider the importance of tolerance, respect, and the need for reciprocity.[6] *When Peoples Meet* was Locke's last major anthology.

Locke is a highly honored philosopher. There is, for example, an Alain Locke Elementary School in Philadelphia; an Alain Locke Building at Howard University; an Alain Locke Prize at Harvard University, founded in 1993 by Henry L. Gates, Jr. for the highest grade point average in African-American Studies; a Phi Beta Sigma Presidential Futures—Alain Locke Scholarship

Program for a high grade point average and sincere interest in the corporate environment; an honorary republication of Locke's articles concerned with education in "The Crescent," Phi Beta Sigma; an Alain L. Locke Society that publishes the Alain L. Locke *Newsletter,* Purdue University; and an Alain L. Locke web page.[7]

Locke was introduced to James's work by Horace Kallen, a Jewish graduate student responsible for a Greek class Locke attended. At Harvard, as Rhodes Scholars at Oxford, and again back in the United States, Kallen and Locke would have conversations, recalled by Kallen, about the role of racial and cultural differences.[8] As an undergraduate student, Locke immersed himself in James's writing.[9] However, as a graduate student, Locke was interested in the theory of value and value classification. Wilbur Urban, Christian F. von Ehrenfels, and the Austrian School of values were his interests.[10]

There are traces of Jamesian themes in Locke's work; for example, the value of the intellectual as a socially committed person, perceiving reality as unfinished and persons as agents impacting on its course. "The unfinished business of democracy then," argued Locke, "is the American Negro and all culturally, socially, economically, and politically oppressed groups."[11] The importance of values, as provisional, was also a Jamesian theme in Locke's works when he addressed how we should approach a culture or academic disciplines.

Locke frequently warns against value dogmatism as a source of prejudice, another theme associated with James's work. In "Pluralism and Ethical Democracy," he writes: "In a pluralist frame of reference value dogmatism is outlawed. A consistent application of this invalidation would sever the trunk nerves of bigotry and arbitrary orthodoxy all along the line, applying the religious, ideological and cultural as well as the political and social values. Value profession or adherence on this basis would need to be critical and selective and tentative (in the sense that science is tentative) and revisionist in procedure rather than dogmatic, final and en bloc. One can visualize the difference by saying that with any article of faith, each article should need independent scrutiny and justification and would stand, fall or be revised, be accepted, rejected or qualified accordingly. Fundamentalism of the 'all or none' or 'this goes with it' varieties could neither be demanded, expected nor tolerated. Value assertions would thus be a tolerant assertion of preference, not an intolerant insistence of agreement or finality. Value disciplines would take on the tentative and revisionist procedure of natural science."[12] It would be misguided to think that Locke emphasized these themes because he was influenced by James. There is no archival evidence suggesting that Locke was so influenced. Rather, Locke developed his views in an intellectual world in co-peership with others, inclusive of James.

The lives of Locke (1885–1954) and John Dewey (1859–1952) provide an interesting parallel of co-peership.[13] Both Locke and Dewey were socially committed public philosophers. Both saw science as a form of art, and emphasized experimental attitudes and tested consequences. Yet, they had radically different social realities. Locke defends cultural specificity and was a representative of the African-American community; Dewey strove to be a generalist and found suspicious Horace Kallen's dedication to specificity. Locke considered race as the vortex of social problems; Dewey tended to see it as a consequence or as a feature of social problems. They also radically differed in their personal lives. Dewey was a married heterosexual with little direct association with persons with different sexual orientations and preferences. Locke was a homosexual with international associations within the homosexual world. Dewey enjoyed the privileges of white identity, such as the ability to sit in the front of the bus or reside in hotels when traveling; all of Locke's travel accommodations were within a segregated world. Locke is a central pragmatist, but race-based scholarship often ignores his role.

Locke was unique among pragmatists in several other respects. In Earnest Mason's account, Locke was unique in emphasizing that we should promote feelings that tended to bring people together and consider negative those sentiments that promoted separation.[14] Locke's emphasis on art, as a way of conveying humanist sensibilities, is arguably a manifestation of this view. Locke was also unique because he developed a constructivist view of ontological entities, and applied this view in relationship to race, culture, and biology. Races, for Locke, were socially defined groups rather than natural consequences of biology; cultural and racial identities are distinct; and social identities are always in transition, transposition, and transvaluation.

Contemporary American philosophy continues to pursue the issues so central to Locke's concerns. The relationship of philosophy and social action, race and conceptions of reality, and the need aggressively, to change reality, continue as important dynamics of doing philosophy from the standpoint of appreciating the African American experience.

## Notes

1. Orlando Patterson, *Freedom* (New York: Basic Books, 1991). *Slavery and Social Death* (Cambridge: Harvard University Press, 1982). Elizabeth Fox-Genovese, *Within the Plantation Household* (Chapel Hill: University of North Carolina Press, 1988).
2. David Walker, *Appeal to the Coloured Citizens of the World* (Maryland: Black Classic Press, 1993). Peter P. Hinks, *To Awaken My Afflicted Brethren* (Pennsylvania: University of Pennsylvania Press, 1997).
3. Frederick Douglasss, *The Life and Writings of Frederick Douglasss,* 4 vol. (New York: International Publishers, 1950). Robert S. Levine, *Martin Delany, Frederick Douglass, and the Politics of Representative Identity* (Chapel Hill: University of North Carolina Press, 1997).
4. Martin Delany, *The Condition of Colored People* (Baltimore: Black Classics Press. 1993).
   _____ *The Origin of Races and Color* (Baltimore: Black Classics Press, 1991).
5. Alain L. Locke, ed., Arnold Rampersed, "Introduction," *The New Negro* (New York: Maxwell Macmillan, 1992, pp. ix–xxiii).
6. Locke, Alain L. and Bernhard J. Stern, *When Peoples Meet* (New York: Progressive Education Association, 1942).
7. *The Crescent,* Phi Beta Sigma Fraternity, Washington DC.
8. Sarah Schmidt, "A Conversation with Horace Kallen: The Zionist Chapter of His Life," *Reconstructionist* (November 1975) 29.
9. Jeffrey Stewart, "Introduction," *The Critical Temper of Alain Locke* (New York: Garland Pub. Co., 1983, p. 397).
10. See Leonard Harris, "Introduction: Rendering the Text," *Philosophy of Alain Locke* (Philadelphia: Temple University Press, 1983, pp. 1–27).
11. Marcus C. Bruse, "Alain Locke and the Revaluation of the Negro," *The Unfinished Universe: William James, Pragmatism, and the American Intellectual* (Yale University, Dissertation, May 1990, p. 240).
12. Alain Locke, "Pluralism and Intellectual Democracy," Conference on Science, Philosophy and Religion, Second Symposium, New York, 1942, in Leonard Harris, *The Philosophy of Alain Locke* p. 57. Also see Locke, "Values and Imperatives," 1935, 31–50; "Cultural Relativism and Ideological Peace," 1944, pp. 67–78.
13. "The Characterization of American Philosophy: The African World as a Reality in American Philosophy," *Quest: Philosophical Discussions* 11:1 (June 1988) 25–36.
14. Ernest D. Mason, "Alain Locke's Philosophy of Value," *Alain Locke,* Russell J. Linneman (Baton Rouge: Louisiana State University, 1982, pp. 1–16).
    Also George Hutchinson, *The Harlem Renaissance in Black and White* (Cambridge: Harvard University Press, 1995) pp. 41–41, 78–80.

# *Alain Locke:* The Ethics of Culture

I am to speak to you on the ethics of culture. Because I teach the one and try to practice the other, it may perhaps be pardonable for me to think of them together, but I hope at least not to leave you without the conviction that the two are in a very vital and immediate way connected. In my judgment, the highest intellectual duty is the duty to be cultured. Ethics and culture are usually thought out of connection with each other—as, in fact, at the very opposite poles. Particularly for our country, and the type of education which generally prevails, is this so. Quite unfortunately, it seems, duty toward the beautiful and the cultural is very generally ignored, and certainly, beauty as a motive has been taken out of morality, so that we confront beautiless duty and dutiless beauty. In an issue like this, it behooves education to try to restore the lapsing ideals of humanism, and to center more vitally in education the duty to be cultured.

It follows if there is any duty with respect to culture, that it is one of those that can only be self-imposed. No one can make you cultured, few will care whether you are or are not, for I admit that the world of today primarily demands efficiency—and further the only reward my experience can offer you for it is the heightened self-satisfaction which being or becoming cultured brings. There is, or ought to be, a story of a lad to whom some rather abstract duty was being interpreted who is said to have said, "If I only owe it to myself, why then I really don't owe it at all." Not only do I admit that culture is a duty of this sort, but I claim that this is its chief appeal and justification. The greatest challenge to the moral will is in the absence of external compulsion. This implies, young ladies and gentlemen, that I recognize your perfect right not to be cultured, if you do not really want to be, as one of those inalienable natural-born privileges which so-called "practical minded," "ordinary" Americans delight to claim and exercise. As a touchstone for the real desire and a sincere motive, the advocates of culture would not have it otherwise.

The way in which duty comes to be involved in culture is this: culture begins in education where compulsion leaves off, whether it is the practical spur of necessity or the artificial rod of the school master. I speak to a group that has already chosen to be educated. I congratulate you upon that choice. Though you have so chosen for many motives and with very diverse reasons and purposes, I fear that education for most of you means, in last practical analysis, the necessary hardship that is involved in preparing to earn a better living, perhaps an easier living. It is just such narrowing and truncating of the conception of education that the ideals and motives of culture are effective to remove or prevent. Education should not be so narrowly construed, for in the best sense, and indeed in the most practical sense, it means not only the fitting of the man to earn his living, but to live and to live well. It is just this latter and higher function of education, the art of living well, or, if I may so express it, of living up to the best, that the word *culture* connotes and represents. Let me offer you, if I may, a touch-stone for this idea, a sure test of its presence. Whenever and wherever there is carried into education the purpose and motive of knowing better than the practical necessities of the situation demand, whenever the pursuit of knowledge is engaged in for its own sake and for the inner satisfaction it can give, culture and the motives of culture are present. I sense immediately that you may have quite other and perhaps more authoritative notions of culture in mind. Culture has been variously and beautifully defined. But I cannot accept for the purpose I have in view even that

From *Howard University Record,* 17, 1923, pp. 178–185.

famous definition of Matthew Arnold's. "Culture is the best that has been thought and known in the world," since it emphasizes the external rather than the internal factors of culture. Rather is it the capacity for understanding the best and most representative forms of human expression, and of expressing oneself, if not in similar creativeness, at least in appreciative reactions and in progressively responsive refinement of tastes and interests. Culture proceeds from personality to personality. To paraphrase Bacon, it is that, and only that, which can be inwardly assimilated. It follows, then, that, like wisdom, it is that which cannot be taught, but can only be learned. But here is the appeal of it, it is the self-administered part of your education, that which represents your personal index of absorption and your personal coefficient of effort.

As faulty as is the tendency to externalize culture, there is still greater error in over-intellectualizing it. Defining this aspect of education, we focus it, I think, too much merely in the mind, and project it too far into the abstract and formal. We must constantly realize that without experience, and without a medium for the absorption and transfer of experience, the mind could not develop or be developed. Culture safeguards the educative process at these two points, and stands for the training of the sensibilities and the expressional activities. Mentioning the former as the neglected aspect of American education, former President Eliot contends that, since it is the business of the senses to serve the mind, it is reciprocally the duty of the mind to serve the senses. He means that properly to train the mind involves the proper training of the sensibilities, and that, without a refinement of the channels through which our experience reaches us, the mind cannot reach its highest development. We too often expect our senses to serve us and render nothing back to them in exchange. As a result they do not serve us half so well as they might: coarse channels make for sluggish response, hampered impetus, wastage of effort. The man of culture is the man of trained sensibilities, whose mind expresses itself in keenness of discrimination and, therefore, in cultivated

interests and tastes. The level of mentality may be crowded higher for a special effort or a special pursuit, but in the long run it cannot rise much higher than the level of tastes. It is for this reason that we warrantably judge culture by manners, tastes, and the fineness of discrimination of a person's interests. The stamp of culture is, therefore, no conventional pattern, and has no stock value: it is the mold and die of a refined and completely developed personality. It is the art medallion, not the common coin.

On this very point, so necessary for the correct estimation of culture, most of the popular mistakes and misconceptions about culture enter in. Democracy and utilitarianism suspect tastes because they cannot be standardized. And if I should not find you over-interested in culture or over-sympathetic toward its ideals, it is because of these same prejudices of puritanism and materialism, which, though still typically American, are fortunately no longer representatively so. Yet it is necessary to examine and refute some of these prevalent misconceptions about culture. You have heard and will still hear culture derided as *artificial, superficial, useless, selfish, over-refined,* and *exclusive.* Let us make inquiry into the reasons for such attitudes. It is not the part of loyal advocacy to shirk the blow and attack of such criticism behind the bastions of dilettantism. Culture has its active adversaries in present-day life, indeed the normal tendencies of life today are not in the direction either of breadth or height of culture. The defense of culture is a modern chivalry, though of some hazard and proportional glory.

The criticism of culture as artificial first concerns us. In the mistaken name of naturalism, culture is charged with producing artificiality destructive of the fine original naturalness of human nature. One might as well indict civilization as a whole on this point; it, too, is artificial. But perhaps just a peculiar degree of artificiality is inveighed against—to which our response must be that it is just that very painful intermediate stage between lack of culture and wholesomeness of culture which it is the object of further culture to remove. All arts have their awkward stages: culture itself is its own cure for this. Closely associated, and touched by the same reasoning, is the argument that culture is superficial. Here we encounter the bad effect of a process undertaken in the wrong order. If the polished surface is, so to speak, the last coat of a consistently developed personality, it lends its final added charm to the total worth and effect. If, on the contrary, beginning with the superficial as well as ending with the superficial, it should be merely a veneer, then is it indeed both culturally false and artistically deceptive. No true advocacy of an ideal involves the defense or extenuation of its defective embodiments. Rather on the contrary, culture must constantly be self-critical and discriminating, and deplore its spurious counterfeits and shallow imitations.

More pardonable, especially for our age, is the charge of uselessness. Here we need not so much the corrective of values as that of perspective. For we only need to appreciate the perennial and imperishable qualities of the products of culture to see the fallacy in such depreciation. Fortified in ideas and ideals, culture centers about the great human constants, which, though not rigidly unchangeable, are nevertheless almost as durable as those great physical constants of which science makes so much. Indeed, if we count in the progressive changes of science through discovery, these are the more constant—the most constant then of all the things in human experience. Moreover, there is their superior representativeness by which posterity judges each and every phase of human development. Through their culture products are men most adequately represented; and by their culture-fruits are they known and rated. As we widen our view from the standpoint of momentary and partial judgment, this fact becomes only too obvious.

I take seriously, and would have you, also, the charge that culture is selfish. Being unnecessarily so is to be unduly so. Yet there is a necessary internal focusing of culture because true culture must begin with self-culture. Personality, and to a limited extent character also, are integral parts of the equation. In the earlier stages of the development of culture there is pardonable concentration upon self-cultivation. Spiritual capital must be accumulated; indeed, too early spending of the meager resources of culture at an early stage results in that shallow and specious variety which means sham and pretense at the start, bankruptcy and humiliation at the finish. Do not begin to spend your mental substance prematurely. You are justified in serious self-concern and earnest self-consideration at the stage of education. And, moreover, culture, even when it is rich and mature, gives only by sharing, and moves more by magnetic attraction than by transfer of material or energy. Like light, to which it is so often compared, it radiates, and operates effectively only through being self-sufficiently maintained at its central source. Culture polarizes in self-hood.

Finally we meet the criticism of exclusiveness, over-selectness, perhaps even the extreme of snobbery. Culture, I fear, will have to plead guilty to a certain degree of this: it cannot fulfill its function otherwise. Excellence and the best can never reside in the average. Culture must develop an elite that must maintain itself upon the basis of standards that can move forward but never backwards. In the pursuit of culture one must detach himself from the crowd. Your chief handicap in this matter as young people of today is the psychology and "pull" of the crowd. Culturally speaking, they and their point of view define vulgarity. As Professor Palmer says, "Is this not what we mean by the vulgar man? His manners are not an expression of himself, but of somebody else. Other men have obliterated him." There is no individuality in being ordinary: it is the boast of sub-mediocrity. Who in the end wishes to own that composite of everybody's average qualities, so likely to be below our own par? Culture's par is always the best: one cannot be somebody with everybody's traits. If to be cultured is a duty, it is here that that element is most prominent, for it takes courage to stand out from the crowd. One must, therefore, pay a moral as well as an intellectual price for culture. It consists in this: "Dare to be different—stand out!" I know how difficult this advice will be to carry out: America's chief social crime, in spite of her boasted freedoms, is the psychology of the herd, the tyranny of the average and mediocre; in other words, the limitations upon cultural personality. Strive to overcome this for your own sake and, as Cicero would say, "for the welfare of the Republic."

I am spending too much time, I fear, in pointing out what culture is when I would rather point out the way to its attainment. I must not trespass, however, upon the provinces of my colleagues who are to interpret culture more specifically to you in terms of the art of English speech, the fine arts, and music. I content myself with the defense of culture in general, and with the opportunity it gives of explaining its two most basic aspects—the great amateur arts of personal expression—conversation and manners. These personal arts are as important as the fine arts; in my judgment, they are their foundation. For culture without personal culture is sterile—it is that insincere and hypocritical profession of the love of the beautiful which so often discredits culture in the eyes of the many. But with the products of the fine arts translating themselves back into personal refinement and cultivated sensibilities, culture realizes itself in the fullest sense, performs its true educative function and becomes a part of the vital art of living. We too often estimate culture materialistically by what has been called "the vulgar test of production." On the contrary, culture depends primarily upon the power of refined consumption and effective assimilation; it consists essentially in being cultured. Whoever would achieve this must recognize that life itself is an art, perhaps the finest of the fine arts—because it is the composite blend of them all.

However, to say this is not to commit the man of culture to hopeless dilettantism, and make him a Jack of the arts. Especially for you, who for the most part work toward very practical professional objectives and who lack as Americans of our time even a modicum of leisure, would this be impossible. But it is not necessary to trouble much about this, for, even were it possible, it would not be desirable.

There are, of course, subjects which are primarily "cultural" and subjects which are not, but I am not one of those who bewail altogether the departure from the old-fashioned classical program of education and the waning appeal of the traditional "humanities." Science, penetratingly studied, can yield as much and more culture than the humanities mechanically studied. It lies, I think, more in the point of view and the degree of intrinsic interest rather than in the special subject-matter or tradition of a subject. Nevertheless, to be sure of culture, the average student should elect some of the cultural studies; and, more important still, in his outside diversions, should cultivate a steady and active interest in one of the arts, aiming thereby to bring his mind under the quickening influence of cultural ideas and values. Not all of us can attain to creative productiveness and skill in the arts, though each of us has probably some latent artistic temperament, if it only expresses itself in love and day-dreaming. But each of us can, with a different degree of concentration according to his temperament, cultivate an intelligent appreciation of at least one of the great human arts, literature, painting, sculpture, music or what not. And if we achieve a high level of cultivated taste in one art it will affect our judgment and interest and response with respect to others.

May I at this point emphasize a peculiarly practical reason? In any community, in any nation, in any group, the level of cultural productiveness cannot rise much higher than the level of cultural consumption, cannot much outdistance the prevalent limits of taste. This is the reason why our country has not as yet come to the fore in the production of culture-goods. And as Americans we all share this handicap of the low average of cultural tastes. As educated Americans, we share also and particularly the responsibility for helping raise this average. A brilliant Englishman once characterized America as a place where everything had a price, but nothing a value, referring to the typical preference for practical and utilitarian points of view. There is a special need for a correction of this on your part. As a race group we are at the critical stage where we are releasing creative artistic talent in excess of our group ability to understand and support it. Those of us who have been concerned about our progress in the things of culture have now begun to fear as the greatest handicap the discouraging, stultifying effect upon our artistic talent of lack of appreciation from the group which it represents. The cultural par, we repeat, is always the best: and a group which expects to be judged by its best must live up to its best so that that may be truly representative. Here is our present dilemma. If the standard of cultural tastes is not rapidly raised in the generation which you represent, the natural affinities of appreciation and response will drain off, like cream, the richest products of the group, and leave the mass without the enriching quality of its finest ingredients. This is already happening: I need not cite the painful individual instances. The only remedy is the more rapid development and diffusion of culture among us.

It follows from this that it is not creditable nor your duty to allow yourselves to be toned down to the low level of average tastes. Some of you, many of you, I hope, will be making your life's work in sections of this country and among groups that are fittingly characterized as "Sabaras of culture," that know culture neither by taste nor sight. You betray your education, however, and forego the influence which as educated persons you should always exert in any community if you succumb to these influences and subside to the mediocre level of the vulgar crowd. Moreover, you will find that, like knowledge or technical skill, culture to be maintained must be constantly practiced. Just as we saw that culture was not a question of one set of subjects, but an attitude which may be carried into all, so also we must realize that it is not a matter of certain moments and situations, but the characteristic and constant reaction of a developed personality. The ideal culture is representative of the entire personality even in the slightest detail.

I recall an incident of visiting with a friend a celebrated art connoisseur for his expert judgment upon a painting. He examined with a knife and a pocket magnifying glass a corner of the canvas. I perhaps thought for a moment he was searching for a signature, but it was not the signature corner. Without further scrutiny, however, he gave us his judgment: "Gentlemen, it is not a Holbein." The master painter puts himself into every inch of his canvas, and can be told by the characteristic details as reliably, more reliably even than by general outlines. Culture likewise is every inch representative of the whole personality when it is truly perfected. This summing up of the whole in every part is the practical test which I want you to hold before yourselves in matters of culture. Among cultivated people you will be judged more by your manner of speech and deportment than by any other credentials. They are meant to bear out your training and your heritage, and more reliably than your diplomas or your pedigree will they represent you or betray you. Manners are thus the key to personal relations, as expression is the key to intellectual intercourse. One meets that element in others which is most responsively tuned to a similar element in ourselves. The best fruits of culture, then, are the responses it elicits from our human environment. And should the environment be limited or unfavorable, then, instead of compromising with it, true culture opens the treasuries of art and literature, and lives on that inheritance.

Finally I must add a word about that aspect of culture which claims that it takes several generations to produce and make the truly cultured gentleman. Exclusive, culture may and must be, but seclusive culture is obsolete. Not all that are well-born are well-bred, and it is better to be well-bred. Indeed, one cannot rest satisfied at any stage of culture: it has to be earned and re-earned, though it returns with greater increment each time. As Goethe says, "What thou hast inherited from the fathers, labor for, in order to possess it." Thus culture is inbred—but we ourselves are its parents. With all of the possible and hoped for spread of democracy, we may say that excellence of this sort will always survive. Indeed, when all the other aristocracies have fallen, the aristocracy of talent and intellect will still stand. In fact, one suspects that eventually the most civilized way of being superior will be to excel in culture.

This much, then, of the ideals of humanism must survive; the goal of education is self-culture, and one must hold it essential even for knowledge's own sake that it be transmuted into character and personality. It must have been the essential meaning of Socrates' favorite dictum—"Know thyself"—that to know, one must be a developed personality. The capacity for deep understanding is proportional to the degree of self-knowledge, and by finding and expressing one's true self, one somehow discovers the common denominator of the universe. Education without culture, therefore, ignores an important half of the final standard, "a scholar and a gentleman," which, lest it seem obsolete, let me cite in those fine modern words which former President Eliot used in conferring the arts degree. "I hereby admit you to the honorable fellowship of educated men." Culture is thus education's passport to converse and association with the best.

Moreover, personal representativeness and group achievement are in this respect identical. Ultimately a people is judged by its capacity to contribute to culture. It is to be hoped that as we progressively acquire in this ener-getic democracy the common means of modern civilization, we shall justify ourselves more and more, individually and collectively, by the use of them to produce culture-goods and representative types of culture. And this, so peculiarly desirable under the present handicap of social disparagement and disesteem, must be for more than personal reasons the ambition and the achievement of our educated classes. If, as we all know, we must look to education largely to win our way, we must look largely to culture to win our just reward and recognition. It is, therefore, under these circumstances something more than your personal duty to be cultured—it is one of your most direct responsibilities to your fellows, one of your most effective opportunities for group service. In presenting this defense of the ideals and aims of culture, it is my ardent hope that the Howard degree may come increasingly to stand for such things—and especially the vintage of 1926.

## Notes

1. [A freshman lecture course at Howard University, for whom, at the time, "ethics" included matters of custom, speech, dress, manners, and language.]

# *Alain Locke:* Values and Imperatives

All philosophies, it seems to me, are in ultimate derivation philosophies of life and not of abstract, disembodied "objective" reality; products of time, place and situation, and thus systems of timed history rather than timeless eternity. They need not even be so universal as to become the epitomized *rationale* of an age, but may merely be the lineaments of a person-ality, its temperament and dispositional attitudes projected into their systematic rationalizations. But no conception of philosophy, however relativistic, however opposed to absolutism, can afford to ignore the question of ultimates or abandon what has been so aptly though skeptically termed "the quest for certainty." To do that is not merely to abdicate tra-

From *American Philosophy Today and Tomorrow* eds. Horace M. Kallen and Sidney Hook (New York: Books for Libraries Press, 1968 [1935] pp. 313–333.

ditional metaphysics with its rationalistic justification of absolutes but also to stifle embryonic axiology with its promising analysis of norms. Several sections of American thought, however, have been so anxious to repudiate intellectualism and escape the autocracy of categoricals and universals that they have been ready to risk this. Though they have at times discussed the problems of value, they have usually avoided their normative aspects, which has led them into a bloodless behaviorism as arid as the intellectualism they have abandoned or else resulted in a completely individualistic and anarchic relativism which has rightly been characterized recently as "philosophic Nihilism." In dethroning our absolutes, we must take care not to exile our imperatives, for after all, we live by them. We must realize more fully that values create these imperatives as well as the more formally super-imposed absolutes, and that norms control our behavior as well as guide our reasoning. Further, as I shall later point out, we must realize that not in every instance is this normative control effected indirectly through judgmental or evaluational processes, but often through primary mechanisms of feeling modes and dispositional attitudes. Be that as it may, it seems that we are at last coming to the realization that without some account of normative principles, some fundamental consideration of value norms and "ultimates" (using the term in a non-committal sense), no philosophical system can hope to differentiate itself from descriptive science or present a functional, interpretive version of human experience.

Man does not, cannot, live in a valueless world. Pluralism has merely given temporary surcease from what was the central problem of monism,—the analysis and justification of these "ultimates," and pragmatism has only transposed the question from the traditional one of what ends should govern life to the more provocative one of how and why activity creates them. No philosophy, short of the sheerest nominalism or the most colorlessly objective behaviorism, is so neutral that it has not some axiological implications. Positivism least of all; for in opposing the traditional values, positivism has set up countervalues bidding us find meaning in the act rather than project meaning from the plane of reason and the subjective approach; and further, as pragmatism and instrumentalism, has set up at the center of its philosophy a doctrine of truth as itself a functional value. So, by waiving the question of the validity of value ultimates as "absolutes," we do not escape the problem of their functional categorical character as imperatives of action and as norms of preference and choice.

Though this characteristically American repudiation of "ultimates" was originally made in the name of the "philosophy of common sense," common sense and the practical life confronts us with the problem all the more forcefully by displaying a chronic and almost universal fundamentalism of values in action. Of this, we must at least take stock, even if we cannot eventually justify it or approve of it. The common man, in both his individual and group behavior, perpetuates the problem in a very practical way. He sets up personal and private and group norms as standards and principles, and rightly or wrongly hypostasizes them as universals for all conditions, all times and all men. Whether then on the plane of reason or that of action, whether "above the battle" in the conflict of "isms" and the "bloodless ballet of ideas" or in the battle of partisans with their conflicting and irreconcilable ways of life, the same essential strife goes on, and goes on in the name of eternal ends and deified ultimates. Our quest for certainty, motivated from the same urge, leads to similar dilemmas. The blind practicality of the common man and the disinterested impracticality of the philosopher yield similar results and rationalizations. Moreover, such transvaluations of value as from time to time we have, lead neither to a truce of values nor to an effective devaluation; they merely resolve one dilemma and set up another. And so, the conflict of irreconcilables goes on as the devisive and competitive forces of our practical imperatives parallel the incompatibilities of our formal absolutes.

We cannot declare for value-anarchism as a wishful way out, or find a solution in that other alternative blind alley of a mere descriptive analysis of interests. That but postpones the vital problems of ends till the logically later consideration of evaluation and post-valuational rationalizations. To my thinking, the gravest problem of contemporary philosophy is how to ground some normative principle or criterion of objective validity for values without resort to dogmatism and absolutism on the intellectual plane, and without falling into their corollaries, on[1] the plane of social behavior and action, of intolerance and mass coercion. This calls for a functional analysis of value norms and a search for normative principles in the immediate context of valuation. It raises the question whether the fundamental value modes have a way of setting up automatically or dispositionally their end-values prior to evaluative judgment. Should this be the case, there would be available a more direct approach to the problem of value ultimates, and we might discover their primary normative character to reside in their functional rôle as stereotypes of feeling-attitudes and dispositional imperatives of action-choices, with this character reenforced only secondarily by reason and judgment about them as "absolutes." We should then be nearer a practical understanding of the operative mechanisms of valuation and of the grounds for our agreements and conflicts over values.

Normally, one would expect a philosophical tradition dominated, as contemporary American thought has been, by an activist theory of knowledge, to have made a problem like this central. We might very profitably pause for a moment to take stock of the reasons why this has not been so. In the first place, in the reaction away from academic metaphysics, there has been a flight to description and analysis too analogous to science and too committed to scientific objectivism. It is impossible to reach such problems as we have before us effectively in terms of pure positivism, of the prevalent objectivism, or of the typical view that until quite recently has dominated American value theory,—the view namely that end-values exist only in so far as values are rationalized and mediated by processes of evaluation and formal value judgments. Added to this, is our characteristic preoccupation with theories of meaning limited practically to the field of truth and knowledge. Because of this logicoexperimental slant, we again have made common cause with the current scientific attitude; making truth too exclusively a matter of the correct anticipation of experience, of the confirmation of fact.[2] Yet truth may also sometimes be the sustaining of an attitude, the satisfaction of a way of feeling, the corroboration of a value. To the poet, beauty is truth; to the religious devotee, God is truth; so the enthused moralist, what ought-to-be overtops factual reality. It is perhaps to be expected that the typical American philosophies should concentrate almost exclusively on thought-action as the sole criterion of experience, and should find analysis of the emotional aspects of human behavior uncongenial. This in itself, incidentally is a confirming example of an influential value-set, amounting in this instance to a grave cultural bias. When we add to this our American tradition of individualism, reflecting itself characteristically in the value-anarchism and *laissez faire* of which we have already spoken, it is easy to explain why American thought has moved tangent to the whole central issue of the normative aspects and problems of value.

In saying this, do we say anything more than that values are important and that American philosophy should pay more attention to axiology? Most assuredly;—we are saying that but for a certain blindness, value-theory might easily have been an American forte, and may still become so if our predominantly functionalist doctrines ever shed their arbitrary objectivism and extend themselves beyond their present concentration on theories of truth and knowledge into a balanced analysis of values generally. Ironically enough, the very type of philosophy which has insisted on truth as a value has, by rigid insistence on the objective criterion and the experimental-instrumental aspects of thought, disabled itself for pursuing a similarly functional interpretation of the other value modes and their normative principles.

Human behavior, it is true, is experimental, but it is also selectively preferential, and not always in terms of outer adjustments and concrete results. Value reactions guided by emotional preferences and affinities are as potent in the determination of attitudes as pragmatic consequences are in the determination of actions. In the generic and best sense of the term 'pragmatic,' it is as important to take stock of the one as the other.

Fortunately, within the last few years a decided trend toward axiology and the neglected problems of value has developed, properly enough under the aegis of the *International Journal of Ethics,* promising to offset this present one-sidedness of American philosophical interests. Once contemporary American thought does turn systematically to the analysis of values, its empirical and functionalist approach will be considerably in its favor. Such a philosophic tradition and technique ought to come near to realizing the aim of Brentano, father of modern value-theory, to derive a functional theory of value from a descriptive and empirical psychology of valuation and to discover in value-experience itself the source of those normative and categorical elements construed for centuries so arbitrarily and so artificially in the realm of rational absolutes.

There is little or no hope that this can be obtained *via* a theory of value which bids us seek whatever objectivity and universality values may have outside the primary processes of valuation, whether in the confirmations of experience or the affirmations of evaluative judgments. For these positions lead only, as far as the direct apprehension of value goes, to Protagorean relativism,—each man the measure and each situation the gauge of value, and then an abysmal jump to the objective criterion of the truths of science, valid for all situations, all men and all times.

What seems most needed is some middle ground between these extremes of subjectivism and objectivism. The natural distinctions of values and their functional criteria surely lie somewhere in between the atomistic relativism of a pleasure-pain scale and the col-

orless, uniformitarian criterion of logic,—the latter more of a straight-jacket for value qualities than the old intellectualist trinity of Beauty, Truth and Good. Flesh and blood values may not be as universal or objective as logical truths and schematized judgments, but they are not thereby deprived of some relative objectivity and universality of their own. The basic qualities of values should never have been sought in logical classes, for they pertain to psychological categories. They are not grounded in types of realms of value, but are rooted in modes or kinds of *valuing.*

In fact, the value-mode establishes for itself, directly through feeling, a qualitative category which, as discriminated by its appropriate feeling-quality, constitutes an emotionally mediated form of experience. If this be so, the primary judgments of value are emotional judgments—(if the inveterate Austrian term *"feeling-judgments"* is not allowable philosophical English), and the initial reference for value prediction is based on a form-quality revealed in feeling and efficacious in valuation through feeling. Though finally validated in different ways and by different criteria, beauty, goodness, truth (as approval or acceptance), righteousness are known in immediate recognitions of qualitative apprehension. The generic types of value are basic and fundamental feeling-modes, each with its own characteristic form criterion in value perception. For the fundamental kinds, we can refer to inveterate commonsense, which discriminates them with approximate accuracy—the moral and ethical, the aesthetic, the logical and the religious categories with their roughly descriptive predicates. For an empirical psychology of values, however, they need to be approached directly from the side of feeling and value-attitudes, and re-descriminated not in terms of formal definition but in terms of technical description of their affective-volitional dimensions and factors.

Normally a value-mode is conveyed while the value is being apprehended. Otherwise the quality of the value would be indeterminate, and this is usually contrary to fact. Though we may still be in doubt regarding its validation, its quantity, place in the value series and other specific issues of the value situation, we are usually certain of the value-mode. This is why we should think of a value-quality primarily in terms of feeling or attitude and not of predicates of judgment; why we should speak of a value-reference rather than a value claim. And if the value type is given in the immediate apprehension of the particular value, some qualitative universal is given. It supplies the clue to the functional value norm,—being felt as good, beautiful, etc.—and we have this event in mind when we say that in the feeling-reference to some value-mode, some value ultimate becomes the birthmark of the value. If values are thus normatively stamped by form-qualities of feeling in the original value experience, then the evaluative judgment merely renders explicit what was implicit in the original value sensing, at least as far as the modal quality of the value is concerned. This could only be true on one of two assumptions, *viz.,* that some abstract feeling-character functioned dispositionally as a substitute for formal judgment, or that the feeling-attitude itself moulded the value-mode and reflected sympathetically its own pattern. If the latter be the case, a value-type or category is a feeling-mode carved out dispositionally by a fundamental attitude.

Of course, this notion of a feeling-reference or form-quality constituting the essential identity and unity of a value-mode is not easily demonstrable; it may be just a hypothetical anticipation of what an experimental analysis of valuation might later establish and prove. However, the main objection to such a conception of a value form-character has been undermined, if not overthrown, by the Gestalt psychology, which has demonstrated the factual reality of a total configuration functioning in perceptual recognition, comparison and choice. There is therefore nothing scientifically impossible or bizarre in assuming a form-quality felt along with the specific value context and constituting its modal value-quality and reference. In the absence of direct evidence of this configurational element in valu-

ation, the most corroborative circumstantial evidence is to be found in the interchangeability or rather the convertibility of the various kinds of value. The further we investigate, the more we discover that there is no fixity of content to values, and the more we are bound, then, to infer that their identity as groups must rest on other elements. We know that a *value-genre* often evades its definition and breaks through its logical barriers to include content not usually associated with it. The awe-inspiring scene becomes *"holy,"* the logical proof, *"beautiful,"* creative expression, a "duty," and in every case the appropriate new predicates follow the attitude and the attitude cancels out the traditionally appropriate predicates. For every value coupled by judgmental predication, thousands are linked by identities of feeling-mode; for every value transformed by change of logical pre-suppositions, scores are switched by a radical transformation of the feeling-attitude. We are forced to conclude that the feeling-quality, irrespective of content, makes a value of a given kind, and that a transformation of the attitude effects a change of type in the value situation.

In this connection, a competent analyst concludes[3]: "We are compelled to recognize that in the aesthetic value situation anything animate or inanimate, natural or artificial, deed or doer, may be the object. This consideration alone makes it clear that beauty and goodness cannot always, if ever, be the same." Yet with all this qualitative distinctness, the artist may feel duty toward his calling, obligation toward his unrealized idea, because when he feels conflict and tension in that context, he occupies an entirely different attitude toward his aesthetic material. Instead of the repose or ecstasy of contemplation or the exuberant flow of creative expression, he feels the tension and pull of an unrealized situation, and feeling obligation and conflict, senses along with that a moral quality. The changed feeling-attitude creates a new value; and the type-form of the attitude brings with it its appropriate value category. These modes co-assert their own relevant norms; each sets up a categorical imperative of its own, not of the Kantian sort with rationalized universality and objectivity, but instead the psychological urgency (shall we say, necessity?) to construe the situation as of a particular qualitative form-character. It is this that we term a functional categorical factor, since it operates in and through feeling, although it is later made explicit, analyzed and validated by evaluative processes of judgment and experiential test.

The traditional way of accounting for the various kinds of value, on the other hand, starting out as it does from the side of evaluation, leans too heavily upon logical definition. It substitutes the terminology of predicates for the real functional *differential*. A comparison, even in incomplete, suggestive outline, between a logical and a psychological classification of values will show how much more neatly a schematization of values in terms of the mechanics of value-feelings facts the facts than the rough approximations of the traditional logical classification. More than this, such a classification not only states the basis on which the primary value groups generically rest, but reveals the process out of which they genetically arise.

Taking feeling-modes as the basic factor of differentiation, the religious and ethical, moral, logical and aesthetic types of value differentiate very neatly on the basis of four fundamental feeling-modes of exaltation, tension, acceptance, and repose of equilibrium. There are sub-divisions for each value-mode determined by the usual polarity of positive and negative values, and also for each mode a less recognized but most important sub-division related to the directional drive of the value-feeling. This latter discriminates for each type of value an 'introverted' and an 'extroverted' variety of the value, according as the feeling-reference refers the value inward toward an individualized value of the self or projects it outward toward value-sharing and the socialized plane of action. We may illustrate first in terms of the moral values. Every definition of the moral or ethical situation recognizes the characteristic element of conflict between alternatives and the correlated sense of tension. The classification we are discussing would transpose a typical pragmatic definition such as "the conflict of mentally incompatible goods defines a moral situation" into a psychological category of value grounded in the form-feeling of tension, inducing the moral attitude toward the situation irrespective of content. Where the value reference is introverted or directed inwardly toward the self, this tension expresses itself as a compulsion of inner restraint or as "conscience": where an extroverted reference directs the tension toward a compulsion outward to action, the tension becomes sensed as "duty" or obligation. Or, to illustrate again, in the mode of the religious values, we have the mechanisms of introverted exaltation determining positively the ecstasy and sense of union of the religious mystic and negatively his sense of sin and separation, with the outward or extroverted form of the religious value expressing itself in the convictions of "conversion" and salvation (active union with God) and the salvationist crusade against evil (the fear and hate of Satan).

This view, if correct, leads to the conclusion that there is a form-feeling or form-quality characteristic of each fundamental value-type, and that values are discriminated in terms of such feeling factors in the primary processes of valuation. The view further regards these modalities of feeling as constituting the basic kinds of value through the creation of stereotyped and dispositional attitudes which sustain them. The substantial agreement of such a table with the traditional classification of values merely indicates that the established scheme of value judgments has traced the basic value modes with fair correctness. However, there are differences more significant than the similarities. These differences not only make possible a more accurate classification of the types of value, but make evident a genetic pattern of values by which we may trace more accurately their interrelations, both of correlation and of opposition.

Tabular illustration follows:

| Modal Quality<br>Form-Quality and Feeling-<br>Reference | Value<br>Type or<br>Field | Value<br>Predicates | Value Polarity | |
|---|---|---|---|---|
| | | | *Positive* | *Negative* |
| **Exaltation:** (Awe-Worship)<br>a. Introverted: (Individualized):<br>    Inner Ecstasy<br>b. Extroverted: (Socialized):<br>    Religious Zeal | *Religious* | Holy—Unholy<br>Good—Evil | Holiness<br>Salvation | Sin<br>Damnation |
| **Tension:** (Conflict-Choice)<br>a. Inner Tension of "Con-<br>    science"<br>b. Extrovert: Outer Tension of<br>    "Duty" | *Ethical*<br><br>*Moral* | Good—Bad<br><br>Right—Wrong | Conscience<br><br>Right | Temptation<br><br>Crime |
| **Acceptance** or **Agreement:**<br>(Curiosity—Intellectual Satisfac-<br>tion)<br>a. Inner Agreement in Thought<br>b. Outer Agreement in Experi-<br>    ence | *Logical Truth*<br>*Scientific Truth* | True (Correct)<br>and Incorrect<br>True—False | Consistency<br>Certainty | Contradiction<br>Error |
| **Repose** or **Equilibrium**<br>a. Consummation in Contem-<br>    plation<br>b. Consummation in Creative<br>    Activity | *Aesthetic*<br><br>*Artistic* | Beautiful—Ugly<br><br>Fine—Unsatisfac-<br>tory | Satisfaction<br><br>Joy | Disgust<br><br>Distress |

*a: Value: introverted type.*

*b: Value: extroverted type.*

Over and above greater descriptive accuracy in value analysis, then, this view may be expected to vindicate itself most effectively in the field of the genetics and the dynamics of values. Here it is able to account for value conversions and value opposition in terms of the same factors, and thus apply a common principle of explanation to value mergings, transfers and conflicts. It is with this range of phenomena that the logical theories of value experience their greatest difficulties. We are aware of instances, for example, where a sequence of logical reasoning will take on an aesthetic character as a "beautiful proof" or a "pretty demonstration," or where a moral quality or disposition is appraised not as "good" but as "noble," or again, where a religious ritual is a mystical "reality" to the convinced believer but is only an aesthetic, symbolic show to the noncredal spectator. The logical way of explaining such instances assumes a change of the judgmental presuppositions mediating the values, or in other cases, puts forward the still weaker explanation of the transfer of value predicates through metaphor and analogy. But by the theory that values are constituted by the primary modal quality of the actual feeling, one does not have to go beyond that to explain the accurate appropriateness of the unusual predicates or the actuality of the attitude in the valuation.

They are in direct functional relation and agreement. As a *quod erat demonstrandum,* the proof or demonstration is an enjoyed consummation of a process, and is by that very fact aesthetic in quality. Likewise, the contemplation of an ethical deed, when the tension of the act is not shared, becomes a detached appreciation, though it needs only the sharing of the tension to revert to the moral type of valuation. In fact, moral behavior, when it becomes dispositional, with the smooth feeling-curve of habit and inner equilibrium, normally takes on a quasi-aesthetic quality, as reflected in the criterion of taste and *noblesse oblige* rather than the sterner criterion of "must" and of "duty." And of course, to the disinterested spectator, the religious ritual is just like any other work of art,—an object of reposeful, equilibrated projection. Once a different form feeling is evoked, the situation and the value type are, *ipso facto,* changed. Change the attitude, and, irrespective of content, you change the value-type; the appropriate new predicates automatically follow.

The same principles hold, moreover, in explaining the conflicts and incompatibilities of values as value-groups. Of course, there are other types of value conflicts, means-ends and value-series problems, but what concerns us at this point are those graver antinomies of values out of which our most fundamental value problems arise. One needs only to recall the endless debate over the *summum bonum* or the perennial quarrel over the respective merits of the value Trinity. How, even after lip service to the parity of Beauty, Truth and Good, we conspire for the priority of one pet favorite, which usually reflects merely our dominant value interest and our own temperamental value bias. The growth of modern relativism has at least cooled these erstwhile burning issues and tempered the traditional debate. Indeed from our point of view, we see these grand ultimates, for all their assertion of fraternal harmony, as doomed to perpetual logical opposition because their basic value attitudes are psychologically incompatible. Repose and action, integration and conflict, acceptance and projection, as attitudes, create natural antinomies, irresolvable orders of value; and the only peace a scientific view of value can sanction between them is one based not upon priority and precedence but upon parity and reciprocity.

As we dispose of this traditional value feud, we become aware of the internal value conflicts within the several value fields, those schisms within common value loyalties which are becoming all the more serious as the traditional value quarrel subsides. There is the feud between the mystic and the reformer in religion, between the speculative logician and the inductive experimentalist in the pursuit of truth, yes,—even the one, less sharp and obvious, between the aesthete and the artist. An affective theory of valuation throws these internal dilemmas into an interesting and illuminating perspective. In each of these cases, the modal value-feeling is, of course, held in common and the same ideological loyalties shared, but these sub-groups are still divided by the basic difference in their orientation toward their common values. Here we see the functional importance of that distinction in feeling-reference or feeling-direction which so closely parallels the Jungian polarity of introversion and extroversion that these terms have been adopted to describe it. These directional drives, determined emotionally in the majority of cases, deciding whether the value is focussed inwardly or outwardly, individuated or socialized, are of the utmost practical importance. For they are the root of those civil feuds within the several value provinces between the saint and the prophet, the mystic and the reformer, the speculative theorist and the practical experimentalist in the search for truth, the aesthete and dilettante versus the creative and professional artist, and finally between the self-righteous moral zealot and the moral reformer. And as each of these attitude-sets becomes dispositional and rationalized, we have the scientific clue to that pattern of value loyalties which divides humanity into psychological sub-species, each laying down rationalizations of ways of life that, empirically traced, are merely the projections of their predominant value tendencies and attitudes.

Thus our varied absolutes are revealed as largely the rationalization of our preferred values and their imperatives. Their tap-root, it seems, stems more from the will to power than from the will to know. Little can be done, it would appear, either toward their explanation or their reconciliation on the rational plane. Perhaps this is the truth that Brentano came near laying hands on when he suggested a love-hate dimensionality as fundamental to all valuation. Certainly the fundamental opposition of value-modes and the attitudes based upon them has been one of the deepest sources of human division and conflict. The rôle of feeling can never be understood nor controlled through minimizing it; to admit it is the beginning of practical wisdom in such matters. As Hartmann[4] has well observed,—"Every value, when once it has gained power over a person, has a tendency to set itself up as a sole tyrant of the whole human *ethos,* and indeed at the expense of other values, even of such as are not inherently opposed to it." We must acknowledge this, though not to despair over it, but by understanding how and why, to find principles of control from the mechanisms of valuation themselves. Without doubt many value attitudes as separate experiences are incompatible and antithetic, but all of us, as individuals, reconcile these incompatibilities in our own experience when we shift, for variety as often as for necessity, from one mode of value to the other. The effective antidote to value absolutism lies in a systematic and realistic demonstration that values are rooted in attitudes, not in reality and pertain to ourselves, not to the world. Consistent value pluralism might eventually make possible a value loyalty not necessarily founded on value bigotry, and impose a truce of imperatives, not by denying the categorical factors in valuation, which, as we have seen, are functional, but by insisting upon the reciprocity of these norms. There is not necessarily irresolvable conflict between these separate value modes if, without discounting their emotional and functional incommensurability, we realize their complementary character in human experience.

At the same time that it takes sides against the old absolutism and invalidates the *summum bonum* principle, this type of value pluralism does not invite the chaos of value-anarchy or the complete *laissez faire* of extreme value individualism. It rejects equally trying to reduce value distinctions to the flat continuum of a pleasure-pain economy or to a pragmatic instrumentalism of ends-means relations. Of course, we need the colorless, common-denominator order of factual reality and objectivity (although that itself serves a primary value as a mechanism of the coordination of experience), but values simply do not reduce to it. To set values over against facts does not effectively neutralize values. Since we cannot banish our imperatives, we must find some principle of keeping them within bounds. It should be possible to maintain some norms as functional and native to the process of experience, without justifying arbitrary absolutes, and to uphold some categoricals without calling down fire from heaven. Norms of this status would be functional constants and practical sustaining imperatives of their correlated modes of experience; nothing more, but also nothing less.

Such "ends" totalize merely an aspect of human experience and stand only for a subsistent order of reality. They should not confuse themselves with that objective reality nor attempt to deny or disparage its other value aspects and the subsistent orders they reflect. This totalizing character is purely functional in valuation, and it is a mockery of fact either to raise it to the level of transcendental worship or to endow it with objective universality. This conceded, there is little sense and less need to set facts and values over against each other as antagonistic orders; rather should we think of reality as a central fact and a white light broken up by the prism of human nature into a spectrum of values. By proposing these basic value-modes as coordinate and complementary, value pluralism of this type proposes its two most important corallaries,—the principles of reciprocity and tolerance. As derivative aspects of the same basic reality, value orders cannot reasonably become competitive and rival realities. As creatures of a mode of experience, they should not construe themselves in any concrete embodiment so as to contradict or stultify the mode of which they are a particularized expression.

Should such a view become established,—and I take that to be one of the real possibilities of an empirical theory of value, we shall then have warrant for taking as the proper center of value loyalty neither the worship of definitions or formulae nor the competitive monopolizing of value claims, but the goal of maximizing the value-mode itself as an attitude and activity. The attitude will itself be construed as the value essence,—which it really is, and not as now the intellectualized *why* or the traditional and institutionalized *how* associated with the value category. In such a frame of reference, for example, romanticism and classicism could not reasonably think of themselves as monopolizing the field of art, nor Protestantism, Catholicism or even Christianity conceive themselves the only way to salvation. In such a perspective, Nordicism and other rampant racialisms might achieve historical sanity or at least prudential common-sense to halt at the natural frontiers of genuinely shared loyalties and not sow their own eventual downfall through forced loyalties and the counter-reactions which they inevitably breed. Social reciprocity for value loyalties is but a new name for the old virtue of tolerance, yet it does bring the question of tolerance down from the lofty thin air of idealism and chivalry to the plane of enlightened self-interest and the practical possibilities of effective value-sharing. As a working principle, it divorces proper value loyalty from unjustifiable value bigotry, releases a cult from blind identification with creed and dogma, and invests no value interest with monopoly or permanent priority.

However, no one can sensibly expect a sudden or complete change in our value behavior from any transformation, however radical, in our value theory. Relativism will have to slowly tame the wild force of our imperatives. There will be no sudden recanting of chronic, traditional absolutisms, no complete undermining of orthodoxies, no huge, overwhelming accessions of tolerance. But absolutism is doomed in the increasing variety of human experience. What over a century ago was only an inspired metaphorical flash in the solitary universal mind of a Goethe,—that phrase about civilization's being a fugue in which, voice by voice, the several nations and peoples took up and carried the interwoven theme, could in our day become a systematic philosophy of history like Pareto's. His historical and functional relativism of cultural values, with persistent normative constants ("residues") and variable and contingent specific embodiments ("derivatives"), is but an indication of the possibilities of relativism extended to historical and social thought. Cultural relativism, to my mind, is the culminating phase of relativistic philosophy, and it is bound to have a greater influence than any other phase of relativism upon our conception and practise of values.

Our present way of socializing values on the basis of credal agreement, dogmatic orthodoxies, and institutionally vested interests is fundamentally unsound and self-contradictory. As a practise, it restricts more than it protects the values that have called institutions into being. Organized for value-sharing and value promotion, they often contradict their own primary purposes. One way of reform undoubtedly is to combat the monopolistic tradition of most of our institutions. This sounds Marxian, and is to an extent. But the curtailing of the struggle over the means and instrumentalities of values will not eliminate our quarrels and conflicts about ends, and long after the possible elimination of the profit motive, our varied imperatives will still persist. Economic classes may be absorbed, but our psychological tribes will not thereby be dissolved. So, since there may be monopolistic attitudes and policies with respect to ends and ideals just as well as monopolies of the instrumentalities of human values—(and of this fact the ideological dogmatism of contemporary communism is itself a sad example), it may be more effective to invoke a non-Marxian principle of maximizing values.

Contrary to Marxian logic, this principle is non-uniformitarian. It is the Roycean principle of "loyalty to loyalty," which though idealistic in origin and defense, was a radical break with the tradition of absolutism. It called for a revolution in the practise of partisanship in the very interests of the values professed. In its larger outlines and implications it proclaimed a relativism of values and a principle of reciprocity. Loyalty to loyalty transposed to all the fundamental value orders would then have meant, reverence for reverence, tolerance between moral systems, reciprocity in art, and had so good a metaphysician been able to conceive it, relativism in philosophy.

But if reciprocity and tolerance on the large scale are to await the incorporation of the greater community, the day of our truce of values is far off. Before any such integrations can take place, the narrowness of our provincialisms must be broken down and our sectarian fanaticisms lose some of their force and glamor. A philosophy aiding this is an ally of the larger integration of life. Of this we may be sure, such reconstruction will never bring us to a basis of complete cultural uniformity or common-mindedness about values. Whatever integrations occur, therefore, whether of thought or social system,—and undoubtedly some will and must occur,—cultural and value pluralism of some sort will still prevail. Indeed in the atmosphere induced by relativism and tolerance, such differentiation is likely to increase rather than just continue. Only it is to be hoped that it will be less arbitrary, less provincial and less divisive.

One thing is certain,—whatever change may have occurred in our thinking on the subject, we are still monists and absolutists mainly in our practise of value, individual as well as social. But a theoretical break has come, and seems to have set in simultaneously from several quarters. Panoramically viewed, the convergence of these trends indicates a new center for the thought and insight of our present generation, and that would seem to be a philosophy and a psychology, and perhaps too, a sociology, pivoted around functionalistic relativism.

## Notes

1. Compare Professor Frank H. Knight's comment on Charner Perry's,—*The Arbitrary as Basis for Rational Morality*—Inter. Journal of Ethics, Vol. 53—No. 2—Jan., 1933—p. 148:—"In the present situation of the western mind, the crying need is to substantiate for social phenomena a middle ground between scientific objectivity and complete skepticism. On the one hand, as Scylla, is the absurdity of Behaviorism. . . . On the other side is the Charybdis of Nihilism, perhaps momentarily the nearer and more threatening of the two reefs. Of course, the two are related; nihilism is a natural correlate of "scientificism." . . . In any case, there is no more vital problem (pragmatically) than that of distinguishing between utterance that is true or sound and that which is effective in influencing behavior."

2. Compare Dewey—*The Quest for Certainty,*—p. 21:—"Are the objects of desire, effort, choice, that is to say, everything to which we attach value, real? Yes,—if they can be warranted by knowledge; if we can know objects having their value properties we are justified in thinking them real. But as objects of desire and purpose they have no sure place in Being until they are approached and validated through knowledge."

3. "Beauty and Goodness"—Herbert E. Cory—*International Journal of Ethics,* July, 1926.

4. Hartmann, *Ethics,* Vol. II, p. 423.

## *Suggestions for Further Reading*

Norm R. Allen, Jr., *African-American Humanism: An Anthology* (Buffalo, N.Y.: Prometheus, 1991).

Molefi K. Asante and Abu S. Abarry, eds., *African-American Intellectual Heritage: A Book of Sources* (Philadelphia: Temple University Press, 1996).

Houston Baker, *Modernism and the Harlem Renaissance* (Chicago: University of Chicago Press, 1987).

Francis Broderick and August Meier, *Negro Protest Thought in the Twentieth Century* (Indianapolis, Ind.: Bobbs Merrill, 1965).

Lydia Marie Child, *An Appeal in Favor of that Class of Americans Called Africans,* ed. Carolyn L. Karcher (Amherst, Mass.: University of Massachusetts Press, 1996 [1883]).

Martin Delany, *The Condition, Elevation, Emigration, and Destiny of the Colored People of the United States* (New York: Arno Press, 1968 [1852]).

Frederick Douglass, *Narrative of the Life of Frederick Douglas, an American Slave,* ed. W. Andrews and W. McFeely (New York: W. W. Norton, 1997 [1845]).

W. E. B. DuBois, *Dusk at Dawn: An Essay Toward an Autobiography of a Race Concept* (New York: Harcourt, Brace, and Co., 1940).

W. E. B. DuBois, *The Negro* (New York: H. Holt & Co., 1915).

W. E. B. DuBois, *The Oxford W. E. B. DuBois Reader,* ed. E. J. Sundquist (New York: Oxford University Press, 1996).

W. E. B. DuBois, *The Souls of Black Folks* (New York: Bantam, 1989 [1903]).

William Lloyd Garrison, *Selections from the Writings and Speeches of William Lloyd Garrison* (Boston: R. F. Wallcut, 1852).

William Lloyd Garrison, *Thoughts on African Colonization* (New York: Arno Press, 1986 [1832]).

Marcus Garvey, *Aims and Objects of Movement for Solution of Negro Problem Outlined* (New York: Universal Negro Improvement Association, 1924).

Marcus Garvey, *The Philosophy and Opinions of Marcus Garvey; or, Africa for the Africans* (Dover, Mass.: Majority Press, 1986 [1923]).

Marcus Garvey, *The Tragedy of White Injustice* (Baltimore: Black Classic Press, 1935).

Leonard Harris, ed., *Alain Locke and Values* (New York: Rowman & Littlefield, 1999).

Leonard Harris, ed., *Philosophy Born of Struggle* (Dubuque, Ia.: Kendall Hunt, 1983).

Leonard Harris, *The Philosophy of Alain Locke* (Baton Rouge, La.: Louisiana State University Press, 1982).

James Weldon Johnson, *Autobiography of an Ex-Colored Man* (New York: New American Library, 1948 [1927]).

Robert S. Levine, *Martin Delany, Frederick Douglass, and the Politics of Representative Identity* (Chapel Hill, N.C.: University of North Carolina Press, 1997).

Alain Locke, *The New Negro* (New York: A. & C. Boni, 1925).

Alain Locke, *The Philosophy of Alain Locke: Harlem Renaissance and Beyond,* ed. Leonard Harris (Philadelphia, Temple University Press, 1989).

Alain Locke, *World View on Race and Democracy* (Chicago: American Library Association, 1943).

Marable Manning, *W. E. B. DuBois: Black Radical Democrat* (Boston: Twayne, 1986).

August Meier and Elliott Rudwick, *The Making of Black America: Essays in Negro Life and History* (New York: Atheneum, 1969).

Lucius Outlaw, *On Race and Philosophy* (New York: Routledge, 1996).

John Pittman, ed., *African-American Perspectives and Philosophical Traditions* (New York: Routledge, 1997).

Jack Salzman, David Lionel Smith, and Cornel West, *Encyclopedia of African American Culture and History* (New York: Macmillan, 1996).

Crispin Sartwell, *Act Like You Know: African-American Autobiography and White Identity* (Chicago: University of Chicago Press, 1998).

Booker T. Washington, *The Future of the American Negro* (Boston: Small, Maynard, & Co., 1900).

Booker T. Washington, *Up From Slavery,* ed. W. L. Andrews (New York: Oxford University Press, 1995 [1901]).

Cornel West, *Keeping Faith: Philosophy and Race in America* (New York: Routledge, 1993).

Cary D. Wintz, ed., *African American Political Thought, 1860–1930* (Armonk, N.Y.: M. E. Sharpe, 1996).

Carter G. Woodson, ed., *Negro Orators and Their Orations* (Washington, D.C.: The Associated Publishers, Inc., 1961).

# AMERICAN NATURALISM

## Introduction by John Ryder

A naturalistic frame of mind has always been a part of the attempt to understand the world. Although, it has been more common for philosophers to regard the natural world as requiring an origin or explanation outside itself, there have also been others who have avoided the distinction between nature and the supernatural, and have made an attempt to understand reality in all its complexity, including all facets of human life, as entirely "natural." Just what it means to say that all of reality is "natural," and why there is good reason to say so, is precisely what constitutes naturalist philosophy.

Many classical Greek philosophers were to some extent naturalists in this sense, as were some classical Indian and Chinese writers. Among the Greeks, Aristotle was probably the one philosopher who most systematically developed a philosophic perspective strongly influenced by the naturalistic frame of mind. Aristotle's naturalism can be seen in the fact that he objected to Plato's idea that the Form of anything is entirely separate from its material characteristics. Form, Aristotle argued, is never divorced from natural objects, but rather always occurs in particulars. This means that to understand any particular thing one can not simply study its ideal "supernatural" Form, as Plato had argued, but one has to study the thing in its natural home, and in the processes and changes that it undergoes. This attempt to avoid a sharp distinction between nature and a non- or super-nature, which is one of the fundamental characteristics of naturalist philosophy, reappears in the philosophy of Spinoza, who used the terms "god" and "nature" synonymously to refer to the one "substance," as he put it, of which all kinds of real things and all particulars are modifications. Spinoza also importantly avoided the traditional sharp distinction between mind and body, arguing instead that both mind and body are attributes of nature. This was a direct challenge to a strongly held view that what is distinctive about being human, in this case "mind," can not be understood on natural terms. Spinoza argued, and in this respect he prefigures many contemporary philosophers, that mind is no less natural than is anything else. The naturalistic philosophy that developed in the United States in the twentieth century is the direct heir of these earlier forms of naturalism. American naturalist philosophers from Santayana through Roy Wood Sellars, John Herman Randall, Jr. to Justus Buchler have all felt this naturalistic heritage, and each has expressed it in his or her own unique vision.

American philosophic naturalism also has its roots in aspects of American thought and culture. While in its earliest expressions, American philosophy was distinctly theistic, specifically in the work of the seventeenth- and early eighteenth-century Puritan writers, it developed in much more secular directions during the Enlightenment of the latter half of the eighteenth century. When the culture as a whole began to pay more attention to social and political issues than to establishing a biblical city on a hill, philosophic direction not surprisingly changed with it. The cultural and intellectual focus shifted from the eternal to the temporal, and philosophers and scientists began to take seriously the task of understanding nature on its own terms. At the conceptual level people like Benjamin Rush, a friend of Thomas Jefferson and one of the signers of the Declaration of Independence, began to explore a secular psychology. Others, such as

Thomas Cooper and Jefferson himself, argued fairly explicitly for a materialistic understanding of nature, in which respect they were following influential materialist philosophers in France. At the political level, social and governmental relations were understood not on the basis of a compact with God, but as grounded in natural rights and popular sovereignty. American thinkers and political activists, specifically Jefferson and James Madison, went so far as to argue, and write into law, that government does not require any connection to religious institutions or for that matter to religious belief at all, an idea that has been institutionalized in the first amendment to the U.S. Constitution. This secular inclination is expressed again in a variety of ways in twentieth-century naturalist philosophy.

## People and Ideas

American naturalism can be said to begin in the work of George Santayana, one of the critical figures in American philosophy in the first half of the twentieth century. In 1905, he began to publish his five volume *Life of Reason,* the first volume of which is titled *Reason in Common Sense.* In this work Santayana articulates a number of points of view that characterize naturalist philosophy: that the natural is exhaustive of what there is; that human beings are fully natural and at home, so to speak, in nature; and that mind and reason are entirely natural processes. Santayana also, even in this early work, expresses a certain point of view that became characteristic of American naturalism—its pluralism. Santayana was not interested in limiting what could be said to exist, nor in defining anything out of existence. In other words, Santayana's philosophy was not "eliminative," as more recent forms of materialism have been. On the contrary, Santayana argues explicitly for the existence of spirit, for example, and even for a somewhat Platonic conception of essence.

The distinguishing factor for naturalism is not that this or that does not exist, or that only this or that exists, but that whatever exists is continuous with the rest of what there is. The naturalist's concern is not so much whether the world includes a "this" or a "that," for example "mind" or "matter." The naturalist's focus rather is that if there is reason to regard the world as including mind or matter, what is that like and how is that related to what else we know about the world? John Herman Randall, Jr. put the point this way: "The significant question is, not whether anything is 'real' or not, but how and in what sense it is real, and how it is related to and functions among other reals." This pluralistic sensibility is common among American naturalist philosophers, and it appears as early as Santayana's first books.

Santayana described himself, famously, as a materialist. He quipped that he was "apparently the only one living." In 1923, when Santayana made that remark, a younger contemporary took exception, since he had been advocating a version of materialism at that time. Roy Wood Sellars would in fact be the primary advocate of materialism within the naturalist camp throughout his career at the University of Michigan, from the early years of the century, through his retirement in 1950, and in fact until his death in 1973. The shape of naturalistic materialism is important to note, both because it has a noteworthy place under the naturalist umbrella, and because it differs in fact from much of the materialistic thinking that preceded it and that has come since. Throughout the history of philosophy, materialists, with some exceptions, have tended to argue that to exist at all is to be matter in some form. Ancient materialists argued this way, as did the materialist philosophers of the seventeenth and eighteenth centuries. Even Jefferson in a letter to John Adams said that "to talk of immaterial existences, is to talk of nothings." In recent years, materialist philosophers still tend to hold that matter has an exclusive claim on reality. Contemporary materialist philosophers of mind, for example, hold the view that what appear to be "mental" phenomena or events are in fact material events, such as brain processes.

Sellars's materialism differed a great deal from this. In his view, matter is the fundamental constituent of reality in the sense that whatever else there may be is a result of material properties and processes. But to say this is not to "reduce" anything else to the material, and in fact Sellars was explicit about not wanting to be reductive in this way. He argued, in fact, for an "emergent" materialism, by which he meant that nature is such that different kinds of reality emerge from others, for example the biological emerges from chemical properties and processes of the physical. The animate, biological world is *dependent* on the inanimate, physical world in the sense that one arises from the other, but the characteristics of the biological world are not *reducible* to the chemical and physical properties of the inanimate. In this way, Sellars preserves a conception of the rich variety of nature while arguing for a materialist ontology that seems to him to make more sense than any other. Naturalists have in fact been criticized by some hostile opponents as being little more than materialists in disguise. In an article originally published in 1944, in response to such a critic, Ernest Nagel, Sidney Hook, and John Dewey answered the question *Are Naturalists Materialists?* in the affirmative, in the process articulating a conception of materialism much like Sellars's.

The contrast between naturalism's nonreductive view of materialism and other, common eliminative forms has an analog in naturalism itself. Though American naturalism throughout the twentieth century has been pluralistic in the senses described here, this has to be contrasted with a currently popular conception of naturalism that is quite different. In this other view, naturalism means that the only cognitively meaningful claims are those of the natural sciences, or that only the propositions of the sciences can be said to convey knowledge. Not only is this view eliminative, but it also gives to the natural sciences a special place which American naturalists on the whole have not accorded it. Santayana, for example, believed that the poetic is no less an avenue to an understanding of nature than is the scientific. More recently, Justus Buchler argued that human beings interact with the world in three ways, or, in his technical language, that there are three modes of judgment: assertive, exhibitive, and active. For the most part, the propositions of the sciences, and for that matter of philosophy, are assertive judgments, while literary or poetic judgments will tend to be exhibitive. Buchler's point is that the exhibitive and the active are no less human renderings of natural material than are the assertive, and that there is no good reason to limit the cognitive only to the assertive, let alone only to the sciences. So while American naturalism values the natural sciences, from Santayana at the beginning of the century to Buchler at the end, it has also insisted on a conception of nature and the human activity within it that is capable of encompassing the richness of natural phenomena and of human experience.

Naturalist philosophic work was being done all over the country, but by the middle decades of the twentieth century, New York City had become the center of the naturalist frame of mind. While several important naturalist philosophers were working in various New York City universities, for example Morris Cohen at City College and Sidney Hook and New York University, the primary focus of naturalist thinking was Columbia University. What came to be referred to as "Columbia Naturalism" in fact had its origins early in the century, when, in 1902, F.J.E. Woodbridge was appointed Professor of Philosophy at Columbia. From that time until his death in 1940, Woodbridge influenced an entire generation of philosophers through his position as Dean of Graduate Faculties, as a founding editor of the *Journal of Philosophy,* and through his lectures and writings. One of the most important of the latter was his *Essay on Nature,* in which he explored problems of knowledge within a broadly, and interestingly classical, philosophic framework.

Woodbridge's naturalism was aided by the fact that in 1905 John Dewey joined the faculty at Columbia, and his most important naturalistic works were written while there and after his retirement, in fact for some forty five more years. Dewey's work emphasized the place of experience within nature, such that many of the dichotomies of traditional philosophy are broken down and their terms brought together in a new way. Traditional distinctions between matter and mind, for example, or between nature and culture, or nature and human being, or even the secular and religious, received new interpretations in Dewey's naturalism. From the earliest years of the century, Woodbridge and Dewey, the former through his influence at the university itself and the latter with a far broader reach, spawned an entire school of thought at Columbia. Sidney Hook, who had worked with Morris Cohen at City College, was also a student of Dewey's at Columbia. Though Hook went on to spend his career at New York University, many other students of Woodbridge and Dewey remained at Columbia. John Herman Randall, Jr., Ernest Nagel, and Justus Buchler, the most important of the Columbia naturalists, all received their graduate degrees at Columbia and spent most or all of their careers on its faculty.

Nagel's approach to naturalism was different from Randall's and Buchler's. Nagel was primarily a logician and philosopher of science, and he therefore came into direct contact with logical positivism and the conceptions of scientific method being developed within that context. Nonetheless, in the 1930s and 1940s Nagel, reflecting the influence of Dewey and others, argued for an explicitly instrumentalist approach, especially to logic and mathematics. Randall had different interests from Nagel. Randall brought his considerable skills as a philosophic writer and intellectual historian to bear on problems of metaphysics, on history, and on religion. The latter might seem surprising for a naturalist, since an insistence on the continuity of nature would seem to preclude any traditional conception of God. Indeed, it probably does preclude a traditional conception, but then the religious impulse is no less a feature of human life, and therefore a phenomenon of nature, than is anything else. An adequate naturalism will neither hide from it nor attempt to argue it away. Randall, quite appropriately, looked to understand religion within a naturalistic context, and to develop a meaningful conception of it. In this respect he shared an interest with Santayana, Dewey, and others. Concerning metaphysics and the philosophy of history, one of Randall's most important sets of essays was his *Nature and Historical Experience,* while the rest of his most influential works had to do with the history of philosophy and intellectual history.

Justus Buchler too was interested in metaphysics, and particularly in a naturalistic understanding of experience and the general character of human being. In an early book, *Toward a General Theory of Human Judgment,* he explored the latter question, while later on he developed a systematic naturalist metaphysics in his *Metaphysics of Natural Complexes,* first published in 1967. In this work Buchler develops a relational, what he called an ordinal, theory of natural phenomena. Randall had said that the metaphysician's question concerns how things are related to one another, and Buchler took this issue seriously. He developed a theory according to which whatever exists is constituted by its relational structure, and that all things exist or prevail in networks or complexes of relations that he called "orders." Buchler tried, with this ordinal view, to capture the complexity of nature within the general context of a naturalistic understanding of the continuity of reality.

The American naturalist tradition in recent years appears healthy and now pushes in new directions. One of the factors that has most contributed to the tradition's current vibrancy is that the American Philosophical Association established in the mid-1980s the annual Patrick Romanell Lecture in American Naturalism. Several important contemporary naturalist philosophers have delivered addresses in that series, including Abraham Edel, John McDermott, John Lachs, Thelma Levine, and Peter Manicas. The range of their work indicates the breadth of focus within the naturalist tradition, from technical questions of metaphysics and issues in the social sciences to commentary on the contemporary philosophic world as a whole.

## Naturalism and Other Philosophical Perspectives

The realm of philosophic ideas is a complicated affair, as any student of philosophy and intellectual history knows very well. Ideas and groups of ideas interact with one another, sometimes with hostility and sometimes to their mutual advantage. American naturalism has had as varied a history of interaction with other sets of ideas as has any other vibrant philosophic perspective. In the context of the history of American philosophy in the twentieth century, the most significant relationship has been between naturalism and pragmatism, since pragmatism is easily the most influential of American philosophic perspectives. With respect to more current concerns, though the relation of naturalism to pragmatism remains of interest, there is also the issue of naturalism's relation to postmodernism.

As a distinct philosophic perspective, pragmatism is a slightly older sibling of naturalism, having its origins in the 1870s in essays by Charles Sanders Peirce, or at least it has been so dated by William James. Pragmatism began to flourish, though, in the early years of this century, due primarily to the work of James and John Dewey. What is the relationship between the two sets of ideas? They are indeed close relatives, since they share several fundamental conceptions. First, both were alternatives to certain strains of thought then prominent, primarily idealism of the Hegelian or Kantian varieties. Second, both desired to make sense of the world as experienced rather than to force it into *a priori* constructs, as much of traditional philosophic system building has done. A third point is that they shared a cultural and intellectual heritage, a fact that is expressed in more than one way. One of the shared bits of background is American thought in general, from the Puritans through the middle and late nineteenth century, on which both traditions could draw. Another is the fact that in important ways both pragmatism and naturalism reacted to developments in the natural sciences. The methods and the results of work in the sciences have been so significant that, increasingly, philosophers realized that any philosophic conception of things would have to take the sciences seriously. This point has been true in fact of many important philosophic trends in the twentieth century, from logical positivism to more recent work in the philosophy of mind and in the area of artificial intelligence. It is interesting to note, though, that both pragmatism and naturalism have been able to avoid the scientism, that is a reductionism and over-emphasis on science, that has characterized these other views.

Despite such similarities, though, there are differences between naturalism and pragmatism that it would be misleading to overlook. One of the most basic is that, as James has pointed out, pragmatism is primarily a method. He and Peirce may have disagreed about what the method is able to determine, in James's case truth and in Peirce's case meaning, but still it is primarily a method. That is the reason James could use his corridor metaphor so easily: James's corridor can open onto any number of rooms, and virtually anything could be going on in those rooms, depending on the writer's taste. With respect to content, then, pragmatism—understood as a method—has no particular or specific commitments. Pragmatists are united, then, by perhaps nothing more than their method of philosophic inquiry.

Naturalism is importantly different from this. Certain general conceptions of things are necessary features of a naturalist world view. To give the most striking example, James's pragmatist corridor might well have a room in which someone is writing a theology that relies heavily on supernaturalist characteristics. Such a theology, though, could have no place under the naturalist umbrella. That is not to say that no theology could reside there, but simply that, no matter which areas naturalists investigate—theology, ethics or anything else,—their naturalism includes a certain constellation of ideas that excludes others. This is not necessarily true of pragmatism—again, understood as a method. As it happens, it is quite possible for a pragmatist also to be a naturalist, as is the case with Dewey. Dewey's instrumentalism was an integral aspect of his naturalistic approach to questions about nature, knowledge, ethics, aesthetics, religion, and social and political issues. One might be able to make a similar case for James, though it would be less obvious, and it is probably not true at all for Peirce. On the other side, Santayana's naturalism did not incline him to find pragmatism very attractive.

This same point also applies to what is now called neo-pragmatism—for example, the work of Richard Rorty. While Rorty shares with naturalism a general humanism, he, like many of the earlier pragmatists, is deeply suspicious of traditional philosophic pursuits—far more suspicious in fact than naturalists tend to be. The point has already been made that in many respects naturalism pursues traditional philosophic questions about nature and knowledge, and naturalists have not been averse to undertaking metaphysical and epistemological inquiries. The neo-pragmatist, by contrast, is likely to regard such metaphysical and epistemological pursuits as pointless and misguided intellectual exercises. A philosopher's time, Rorty might argue, is far better spent considering the cultural issues of the day in a more direct way, since in any case the sense of objective truth toward which traditional philosophic inquiry aimed is in the end illusory.

Contemporary neo-pragmatism is one version of a broader set of ideas loosely, and perhaps inaccurately, referred to as postmodernism. This loose set of ideas exerts a good deal of influence in contemporary intellectual circles, so it would be wise to consider naturalism in relation to it. To paint with very broad strokes, postmodernism is a response to certain basic features of modernist philosophy, specifically the attempt to uncover the foundations of knowledge, the pursuit of certainty, the idea that the mind can be understood as reflecting reality more or less accurately, and the assumption that there is in fact an objective truth into which philosophy can inquire. The postmodernist alternative to these traditional conceptions is that the pursuit of knowledge is always perspectival, in the sense that inquiry is always undertaken from some perspective or other, so that a pure "reflection" of reality is quite impossible. If "reflection" is the wrong metaphor, it is replaced by "construction." Through the process of inquiry, to some degree we *construct* knowledge of the world rather than simply *find* it. Moreover, in a similar sense, we even construct the world as found. Postmodernism, in other words, abandons the ideas of objective reality and objective knowledge that underlie so much of traditional philosophy.

Naturalism has an interesting place in the disagreement between traditional and postmodernist philosophy. On the one hand, naturalists would not as a rule simply dismiss out of hand the modernist, indeed classical, view that there is a world that to a considerable extent is not of our own making, and that some degree of clarity about that world is possible. As Buchler once put it, "The world judged is not a product. It is the judging alone that is the product. A judgment about the world is a finding, sometimes in the form of a shaping, but what is found is not the finding." In other words, granted that our inquiry, indeed our judgment in general, is a way of manipulating features of the world, the fact remains that the world has traits of its own that are being shaped, or found, and therefore the traditional idea of an "objective" reality can not be dismissed as postmodernism is inclined to do. The same point applies to knowledge, in the sense that though knowledge is surely perspectival and conditional, it does not follow that we can not thereby acquire accurate, objective knowledge of the world. In fact, it may well be that some perspectives provide greater accuracy than others.

But if naturalism does not endorse the postmodernist rejection of the tradition, it does not simply dismiss the objections either. In fact, one would find that American naturalists have tended to anticipate many of the important insights of postmodernism. Santayana, for example, argued against the modernist epistemological enterprise by suggesting that human inquiry is necessarily grounded in what he called "animal faith," the lived contexts and perspectives of actual human existence. He also rejected directly the modernist metaphor of mind as a mirror reflecting reality. Santayana, like Dewey after him, had a more constructivist understanding of inquiry and knowledge. And, also like Dewey, his naturalism allowed him to unite a sense of the human impact on the world without abandoning the traditional view that there is a world on, and in, which humans do have an impact. Randall, Buchler, and other naturalists inherited the same subtle sensibilities from their teachers, thereby enabling their naturalism to make a unique contribution to contemporary debates about philosophy and the world it investigates.

## Randall and Pluralistic Naturalism

This important contribution is evident in Randall's "Empirical Pluralism and Unifications of Nature," Published in 1958 in it *Nature and Historical Experience,* and included in this volume. Among the many virtues of this essay is the fact that it displays an extraordinary intellect at work. Randall's command of the history of philosophy was second to none, and here he carefully placed his sense of nature and its general character against both influential historical traditions and the philosophic trends prevalent as he wrote. Moreover, it is here that Randall articulates several claims that were later taken up by his younger colleague, Justus Buchler, and which have been a central feature of philosophic naturalism: the proposition that existence or reality consists of whatever there is, in whatever way it is, and that the term "nature" refers distributively to all that there is. If nature is whatever there is, then nature is something quite complex. There are physical features of nature, as there are chemical and biological features; nature has elements that are conscious, as well as elements that are fictional; it contains the more or less mutable and the more or less stable; it contains the material and it contains the spiritual. Metaphysics, on the view Randall defends here, is the study of nature as nature, that is to say nature not in any of its more specific characteristics, but with regard to those traits that all aspects of nature share. It is the study of nature taken generically.

While nature is to be understood as whatever there is, Randall here makes what may be the surprising point that it would be a mistake to regard nature as a "whole" in any sense. There is no "whole" of nature, he argues, in the sense that nature is not to be understood as a single process or a single system in which everything is related or into which everything is subsumed. Nature is irreducibly plural in this view. If there is no overarching system or process, no final unity of nature, then it becomes a philosophic question for the naturalist metaphysician to investigate the source and character of nature's many unities. This is precisely the issue Randall addresses in this essay. By approaching nature directly, as Randall puts it, he attempts to understand nature in all its complexity and coherence, and in doing so he is careful to take account both of nature's independent traits and of those it has by virtue of the activities of human beings. In this respect, Randall demonstrates the significance the naturalist philosophic tradition can have for the contemporary world and philosophic reflection about it.

# John Herman Randall, Jr.
# Empirical Pluralism and Unifications of Nature

## I

I am here proposing to approach Nature directly, and with none of that preliminary methodological discussion which is so much in the current mode. For I share the distaste of many for those desert sands that stretch on endlessly toward the mirage of confirmability; though I also believe that sand is an important ingredient in the hard roads that can take us places. But I am here inviting neither to excursions, nor to tours to distant scenes. I am proposing rather to explore the old homestead, the familiar Nature with whose accustomed features we have long lived in harmony and compatibility.

The Nature we encounter exhibits a thoroughgoing diversity or plurality. It is a fundamental metaphysical fact that Nature is radically and ineradicably manifold. Since William James's insistence on the "pluriverse" we live in, metaphysical inquiry has rejected all idealistic monism. Some form of ontological pluralism has come to be accepted again by most responsible metaphysicians, just as they have once more come to take time "seriously."

But it is likewise a fundamental metaphysical fact that Nature can *become* unified in human vision. Again and again the world has provoked man to many a different scheme of unification. From the beginning men have seen the world whole, through the vision that is myth and symbol, through the great creation myths of primitive cultures. More recently, some have tried to see it entirely through the vision that is knowledge and science, through the working out of progressively more unified general ideas and theories, that seem to point to an eventual unification in a single unified formula—a unified field theory, perhaps.

Whether in the end "knowledge" and "science" operate to unify Nature in a way that is fundamentally different from the way of myth and symbol—whether science is, as we say, less "symbolic" and more "literal"—has been a vexed philosophical issue, especially in modern times. I have tried to frame the question—and I might indeed claim that this is one fruit of the metaphysical leading principles here set forth—in such a way as to transform what has been an "issue" to be interminably debated, into a problem that can be inquired into, with some hope that inquiry can bring to light pertinent facts. Knowledge and science are certainly no less—and no more—"human" than are myths and symbols; and no less—and no more—"natural." Both ways of seeing the world whole employ characteristic instruments of unification. In their unifying function, scientific hypotheses, theories, and systems, together with myths and symbols, "regulative ideas" and human ideals, and such complex elaborations of symbols as mathematics, logic, and theology, and the greatest of all, discourse and language itself—all these varied instruments of unification seem to possess much in common. They all seem to enjoy the same happy ontological status: they all fall, in my metaphysical classification of "predicables," or ways of functioning,[1] into the group called "Connectives" or "Conjunctions." They are all "functionally real," they are all "real" as functioning to institute objective relations. They are all human ways of cooperating with other natural processes. Their distinctive ways of functioning, their characteristic behavior, at times their misbehavior, is a matter for detailed inquiry into facts.

The position here being developed may hence be called a "functional realism." So

From *Nature and Historical Experience* (New York: Columbia University Press, 1958). pp. 121–140.

important are Connectives in any unification of Nature that their status demands an initial clarification. In general, the structures and characters grasped and formulated in knowledge and "warranted discourse" have a determinate status in the world encountered. They are "there," in Substance—in the language of medieval realism, they are "in re." They are discoverable "there" in Substance experienced, in its complex cooperation of powers—they are there in the universe of action or the situation. Now, certain structures and factors can be said to be "there," and to be discoverable, even when the factor of which they are the structure is not functioning in a process. Examples of such structures would be the physico-chemical structure of the seed, the mechanical structure of the sewing machine, the psychological structure of human nature, or the musical structure of the symphony. Such structures we have called "formal" or "constitutive" structures, and have found them as the frames of mechanisms and materials that can, on occasion, function as means or powers in processes. Other structures and characters are not "there," are not discoverable, unless these factors are functioning as means in a process—unless the seed is growing, the sewing machine sewing, the men acting, the symphony being performed and heard. Such characters and structures we have called "functional structures."

But such functional structures enjoy an equally determinate status in the world encountered, in Substance. They are equally discoverable in its process, they are equally "real," equally "in re." Their locus is *not* in things apart from their functioning, but in that functioning of powers; they are "there," they are "real," in their functioning in a specific cooperation of powers. They are "real" as belonging to and as discoverable in that cooperation. Their "reality" can be said to be precisely their functioning. They can be said to be "functionally real," and to enjoy a "functional" status. In general, that is "real" which functions determinately and discoverably in the complex of processes that is Substance.

Now, much that is in this sense "functionally real," that has its locus and status and is discoverable in a cooperation of powers, is not operative or "actual" if because of the absence of certain necessary conditions the cooperation does not take place—if the seed does not grow, but remains a mere set of powers, or if the symphony remains a mere score. And likewise, there is much that is "functionally real" and discoverable in Substance encountered that is not operative or "actual" in the absence of the participation of *human* activities in Substance. It is here that Connectives belong. Thus the so-called "values" that function in human experience of the world, in action, art, and science, are not operative in the absence of that human participation—when they are not functioning as means to human ends. But when, with man as one factor in the situation, they are so operative, they are then "functionally real" and "objective"; they are not "subjective," but are objectively determinable—they are "good for" in the perfectly objective sense of being "good for men." The same holds true for all Connectives. Thus, in the chief Connective, language, the structures of discourse are not functioning factors unless men are talking and communicating. But they have their locus and status, they are "functionally real," in the process of communication—in Substance expressed and communicated, in Substance reflectively experienced, in Substance participated in through discourse. Just how these various factors function in Substance—i.e., how they act—how precisely they are "real"—is in each case an objective for inquiry. And the answer is always relative to the process or situation in which they are functioning as cooperating factors.

It is in this sense that the Connectives that operate in unifications of Nature can be said to be "functionally real."

## II

I want to push a little further what is implied in each of the two aspects of Nature emphasized:

the fact that the world is encountered as *plural,* and the fact that it lends itself to *unifications* through the functioning of Connectives.

I start with the fact that Substance is radically plural. Substance, it will be recalled, is defined as "the encountered context, or situation," within which reflective experience can distinguish a variety of processes and structures. Substance is always encountered as specific and determinable, and this means as "relative"—relative to the direction or end the encountering itself generates. The field or situation can be extended indefinitely, as that end makes more and more of Nature relevant to itself. But we never reach or encounter "the ultimate field, context, or situation." We encounter only the field, situation, or context that is "ultimate for" that particular substance or situation.

This suggests certain further implications of the metaphysical pluralism here being explored—the Aristotelian pluralism of "determinate substances," expressed in the language of the philosophies of being, and the Deweyan pluralism of "specific situations," expressed in the language of the philosophies of experience. Every substance, every situation, every universe of action and experience—whatever name we choose to give the complex of cooperating processes that is encountered—is always encountered as something specific and determinable—as a substance, a situation, a universe of interaction. We never encounter "*the* Universe"; we never act toward, experience, or feel being or existence as "a whole." Despite Santayana and others of like habit of speech, "pure being" seems to be pure bunk. Our encountered and experienced world is always selective and determinate. We can indeed *talk* significantly about "the Universe." But when we do, we are talking distributively, about *every* universe of action and experience, about *every* situation, substance, or field. We are not talking about some unified, all-embracing Substance or Field.

There is hence no discoverable "ultimate context," no "ultimate substance." There is only the widest context that is relevant to any

particular activity, process, or specific cooperation of processes, and is hence "ultimate for" that cooperation. "Ultimate," that is, is always relative, never "absolute"; it is always "ultimate for." Talking, discourse, has the widest context of all: we can talk significantly of any or all universes of discourse, and these universes of discourse tend to become more and more unified in the talking. The only sense in which we can speak meaningfully of "the Universe" is as the widest "Universe of discourse." But there is no discoverable "ultimate context" of discourse, save all the *other* contexts: there is no discoverable "context of contexts." In other words, Spinoza was wrong, and Kant was right: we can say nothing valid about "the Universe as a whole," or as a "totality," because we can never encounter or experience it as a whole or a totality, even in reflective experience. We possess no "adequate knowledge of the infinite and eternal essence of Nature." This may be called the "empirical principle": its fundamental character justifies calling this metaphysical pluralism an "empirical pluralism."

Hence "the Universe," or "Nature," is not "a process"—a single process—though any "Universe of action and experience" is a complex of processes. Nor has "the universe," or "nature," any "meaning"—any single meaning—as a whole, save as the sheer *locus* of all processes, contexts, and meanings. Every process has a context or field of other cooperating processes, in terms of which it has a discoverable meaning—a "meaning *for*" that context. The "meaning" of any process is the way it functions in its context. What has no context can have no function, and hence no "meaning."

Now of course it is quite possible to take "the Universe" as a single process, with a single "meaning." Most of the greatest philosophies have done just this, to say nothing of a multitude of religious schemes. But when this is done, we find that we must then invent a further "context" for "the Universe," or Nature. We must go beyond metaphysics to *philosophical theology.* We can indeed thus generalize and unify our analysis of determinate processes, as many a philosopher and philosophic theologian has done. Finding, for instance, that every particular process is always directed toward a correlative objective or "stimulus" *external* to that process—χωριστός—in the context of other cooperating processes, we may then, with Aristotle, generalize that external objective or stimulus to be found in every determinate process, into an objective or stimulus—a unified "Unmoved Mover"—external to all determinate processes. Or, finding that every process is always conditioned by its context, we may then, with Spinoza, generalize that conditioning context of every determinate process into an "Unconditioned Conditioner" of all processes. Again, finding that every process has a "source" or "origin" in antecedent processes, we may then generalize that circumstance into a Source or Origin of all processes—into a "First Cause" antecedent to all "secondary causes."

But in terms of the empirical principle, apart from their function as unifying devices, there *is* no discoverable or implied Unmoved Mover, there *is* no Unconditioned Conditioner, there *is* no Source or Origin of "the Universe." Such generalizations of factors revealed by analysis in particular processes are "metaphysical myths."[2] They are logical constructions or extrapolations, like physical theories, and they possess similar functions. In their ontological status, they are what I have called unifying Connectives or "Conjunctions." Metaphysics can say nothing about "the Universe"; it can speak only of *any* "universe of interaction." It can say nothing about "the ultimate context" or "the ultimate field"; it can speak only of *any* context or field. This our philosophies of experience, from Kant down, have taught us. The attempt so to speak leads to the invention and deployment of myths or Connectives.

Now, such myths are very far from being "meaningless." Like all Connectives, they have a perfectly definite function which can be objectively inquired into. They may well be basic in the living of human life, which often enough gets *its* "meaning" from their use—or

rather, which uses them to find and express its "meaning." It may even be true that though "the Universe" has no meaning in terms of a context external to itself, human life derives its meaning by making use of just such a "mythical" context—just such a metaphysical myth, or Connective. It may be true, as Woodbridge puts it, that though Nature has no "justification," man is "justified" by "the Supernatural"—that is, by the Ideal. The pursuit of knowledge, he maintains, does not and cannot take us beyond Nature; but the pursuit of happiness does. This may indeed be true: as Woodbridge puts it, the "judgment of the race" has maintained it. But nevertheless, Woodbridge insists, "it is faith, and not knowledge, that 'justifies.'" And no very intelligible meaning seems to be involved in saying that "the Supernatural" or "the Ideal" lies "outside Nature," or "outside history," as is often said by theologians nowadays. To be sure, "the Supernatural" certainly can be said to lie "outside" this or that particular human life, until it "comes into" it—in theological terms, until it "breaks through"—and it may well "extend beyond" all human life, and thus be "transcendent." All these ways of speaking seem to refer to facts that are familiar to those who have some sense of the religious dimension of experience.

But if this be indeed so, then "Nature" must find some secure place in her domain for "the Ideal," "the Transcendent," and even for "the Supernatural." Indeed, it is clear that any adequate philosophical "naturalism" must have room for all the genuine and obvious facts that such Connectives as "the Supernatural" have referred to; and in that sense, must find some place for "the Supernatural" itself.

Such myths or Connectives—of "the meaning" of "the Universe" in the mythical context of the Unmoved Mover, of the Unconditioned, of the Supernatural, of the Ideal, of God—are not, so long as metaphysics maintains the empirical principle, parts of metaphysical knowledge. Metaphysics can only inquire, What is implied in the fact that human life can employ them to give "meaning" to itself? How do they function to organize the values of existence? How is the actual unified in the light of the Ideal?

I am by no means suggesting that a wise philosophy will of necessity confine itself to what metaphysics can exhibit and denote, and will refuse to go on to "philosophical theology" and its myths. I have myself a great respect for philosophical theology—far more than most theologians today, who seem to have rejected it for an exclusive emphasis on kerygmatic theology. I find men today do not *know* nearly enough about God—not even those who talk to Him with the greatest familiarity. But philosophical theology is a different discipline from metaphysics. Metaphysics has nothing to say about "God" or "the Universe" as the "ultimate context" of existence. But it has much to say about the way such myths or Connectives function in the particular contexts of human living—about any "God," or any "Universe as a whole." For such metaphysical myths or Connectives are factors encountered in Substance. They are "objective facts"; and what they do, how they work, what values they achieve, are likewise objective "facts." Myths and Connectives have a natural and objective function to perform in Nature's complex cooperation of processes. To function as a Connective, or a myth, is one of the fundamental ways in which natural processes can function.

### III

This empirical pluralism, implied in the fact that what is encountered as Substance, as a situation or universe of action, is always encountered or experienced as specific and determinate—or determinable—even in reflective experience or discourse, does not deny the possibility or the value of the search for unification, so intimately bound up with the search for control, for the power of manipulation. I now wish to turn to the other aspect of Nature, to examine those unifications she brings about, and some of the ways in which they are achieved.

The demand for unification is impressive. It is persistent, and doubtless ineradicable. We have only to reflect on the tremendous kick the most unlikely men manage to get out of "Oneness" and "Unity." What do our hard-boiled and skeptical positivists today cherish above all other concerns? Nothing other than "Unity"—the unity of science. I am sure any good *Existenzphilosoph* could find this craving for "unity" and "integrity" rooted in "the human situation," springing from the disunities and "dialectical tensions" to which the contemporary German "soul" at least has fallen prey. Gilbert Murray has sought to explain it by another myth: he calls it "the groping of a lonely-souled gregarious animal to find its herd or its herd-leader." But however we attempt to account for the craving for unity, it seems to be a deeply rooted human demand. Like James's "sentiment of rationality," which is indeed but a particular variant of it, it is a sentiment and a demand long before it is justified by any discovered facts.

Logically, of course, the demand for unification and unity is a colossal assumption. Consider the insistence that existence, what is encountered, be found somehow to be a system and order, despite the inexhaustible and ineradicable variety and individuality it exhibits. Man requires that existence exhibit a common set of principles and laws, as the very condition of being found "intelligible" to the human mind. When imposing philosophies, like those of Thomas or Kant, in the process of working out an adjustment between two different sets of beliefs which for historical reasons have come into conflict, arrive at a division between different sets of principles for different "realms" of experience, this neat partition always seems unsatisfactory, and inevitably proves unstable. In the next generation these two sets of principles are unified in a common system, in the thought of a Duns Scotus or a Hegel. When a Descartes—or a Kant—divides the world between the two realms of what his intellectual method can deal with, and what it cannot, that soon appears as a methodological inadequacy, and men like Spinoza and Leibniz—or the whole generation of post-Kantians—set to work to develop a more adequate method that will not clash with the required unity of knowledge. The great historic dualisms, based on the distinction between what a given method can handle and what it cannot—Platonic, Cartesian, or Kantian—always tend toward unification—even if only by making the latter the "appearance" or the "expression" of the former.

Or consider those unifications accomplished not through a logical system of principles, but through a temporal scheme of history. There are the great creation myths, which achieve unification through deriving existence from a common source and origin. There is that most imaginative of all temporal myths, the idea of "evolution." When we ask why it is that men have so often turned to history in their craving for unification, the answer seems clear. Time itself is indeed the great unifier. For historical understanding is always unified in the focus of the present or the future. Consider the power of the "Christian epic" and its unification of the world in the eschatological myth of the Last Judgment—or of its Marxian variant, the revolution that will produce the "classless society."

Then too there is the practical motive for unification, embodied in the demand for a unity of Nature that will sustain a continuity of method: the conviction so strong in our own Augustinian and Baconian tradition, that power and control will come from the universal application of the method that has proved successful within some particular field. There must be a universal method—the Platonic dialectic, the Cartesian mathematical interpretation of Nature, the Baconian induction—that will render men the masters and possessors of Nature. And so men pass lightly over the specific conditions of different subject matters. Consider the many earnest attempts to carry over into human affairs the different methods developed in the successive stages of the enterprise of natural science, from the "geometrical method" of Spinoza in the seventeenth century to the statistical methods of our sociologists today, or the hypothetico-experimental method of Dewey. Or take the drive to make politics into a human engineering, to be treated by technological methods—despite the

inadequacy of what has so far been achieved, in comparison with the continued power of the age-old political and religious methods for enlisting for what has to be done the cooperative support and action of men.

But though these various demands for unification rest upon faith rather than proof, it is a faith that has flowered in good works. That both understanding and power do come with increasing unification is scarcely to be denied. To be sure, it never turns out to be quite so simple a matter as we assume, whether in our logical schemes of laws and principles, in our historical unifications through myths, or in our universalized methods. In the variety of Nature's riches, all these schemes inevitably leave out of account those traits and characters they are unable to handle. That is why they require constant and unremitting criticism, an ever-renewed confrontation with Substance encountered, with Nature in the raw, before she has been washed and brushed and tidied up, her hair done in the latest fashion and her nose carefully powdered. Ceaseless vigilance is the price of metaphysical adequacy.

And inevitably these schemes of unification demand the use of unifying Connectives of one sort or another—of myths and symbols, of logical constructions like physical theories, of philosophies of history, of social and political ideals. All these varied types of Connectives function to unify different substances and situations that are in fact encountered as plural and disparate. The "unity" of experience, or of the world, is not a simple discovery. It is rather a process—a *process of unification,* whose achievement demands a heavy reliance on Connectives—on myths, symbols, hypotheses, theories, ideals.

These unifications that Nature achieves in cooperation with man are clearly not "merely human"; above all, they are not "subjective," in that sense that divorces man from Nature and leaves him in splendid isolation in an alien world. To be sure, those unifications attained in vision and in knowledge all involve human cooperations with other natural operations. But it is not man alone—above all, it is not man descending from another realm and trailing clouds of glory—who connects and unifies and brings Nature to a focus in his transcendent lens. It is Nature herself, existence cooperating with men. These unifying Connectives, like the greatest of all, Discourse herself, and her noble daughter Mathematics, are factors in Substance, and function in interaction with other factors in its complex transactions. They are, as we have insisted, functionally real and objective. They may be conventional, but they are not arbitrary.

## IV

In preliminary summary, then:

1. Nature is not a "unity"—of substances.

2. Nature is a *continuity*—of natural process, making possible a continuity of analysis, of knowledge, and of scientific methods.

3. But Nature is not a continuity of ends or outcomes, in any sense that would obliterate encountered distinctions of value. Uniqueness and individuality are characteristic of Nature's productions. Nature exhibits a variety of "dimensions" in her achievements: she is not "one-dimensional"—though this is often said by those whose primary interest lies in realms of being that lie "beyond" Nature, and are thus in the literal sense "supernatural." Nature is rather "multi-dimensional": she possesses, and exhibits in her products and outcomes, all those varied "dimensions" she is found to display.

This fact is sometimes expressed: Nature exhibits many different "levels." But this doctrine of "levels" has for the most part been captured by the supernaturalists, alas!, who are concerned to deny the continuity of the mechanisms by means of which Nature effects her ends, and the consequent continuity of analysis, which has led to the triumphs of scientific inquiry. Here it is insisted that Nature exhibits different "levels" of ends and outcomes, and at the same time a continuity of means and mechanisms: the former is in no wise incompatible with the latter circumstance. The greatest conceivable difference in value between the ends of Nature's productiv-

ity sets no limits to the discovery of as much continuity as we can find between the mechanisms on which that production depends. There are no antecedent limits set to the experimental exploration of the structure of means.

This would seem not to be controversial. Yet in the same mail there were received two papers, controverting it from opposed positions. One was a defense, naive and revealing, of "materialism," by a college instructor. It ran, "Only matter exists"—that is, only means and mechanisms exist. "Love" and "beauty" do not "exist": they are "words only, for material states and situations." What is effected by mechanisms—activities, processes, outcomes, eventuations—these do not "exist." In the rendition of a violin sonata, all that can be said to "exist" is "the dragging of the tail of a dead horse across the entrails of a dead cat." Of course, the music is "delightful," it is "important," it may even be called "real"; and the author goes on to distinguish between "what exists in a simple location"—his criterion of "existence"—and "what is merely 'real.'"

Insofar as this is not a mere quibble about the meaning of the term "exist," and an undue restriction of that meaning, this illustrates where one gets when one does not take activities and processes as primary and irreducible subject matter. A sound metaphysics would say, activities, operations, and processes "exist," and are effected by means of mechanisms distinguished as facts involved in those processes. "Materialism" locates the means and mechanisms involved, then, by reductive analysis, holds that *only* these mechanisms can be said to "exist"—what they *do* does not "exist," but is merely something else.

The other paper was a defense, likewise naive and revealing, of "dualism." It happened to be by another instructor at the same college: there has never been any unity of knowledge at this seat of learning. This paper ran: Because man acts in certain distinctive ways, not encountered as the ways of acting of any other being, and therefore distinctively human ways (the paper was defending the "Humanism" of Irving Babbitt) he must perform these acts by means of a mechanism specifically different from the continuity of mechanisms by which all other natural processes are effected. The argument runs: Man perceives universals, therefore man must "have" a "simple unextended immaterial spiritual principle," by means of which to do it. This argument starts with an activity, which *is* distinctive and of "unique" value, and then assumes a mechanism not only distinctive, like all specific mechanisms, but also unanalyzable ("simple") and discontinuous with all other natural mechanisms. Where can such an argument stop? with a unique and discontinuous mechanism for each distinctive way of acting encountered in the world? The author, being a Catholic, goes on from what he calls "Dualistic Integral Humanism" to "Trialistic Supernaturalized Humanism": certain human activities demand a third unique mechanism, the "grace of God." And so on, *ad infinitum.*

Does Nature, in addition to this continuity of mechanisms, display also a continuity of genesis, as the early evolutionists believed? The last generation was much concerned to set forth how human experience, in all its manifold variety and complexity, might have "arisen" out of a prehuman and subhuman "experience" in the evolutionary process. Much indeed of the evolutionary emphasis is left over in the thought of those who, like Dewey, in their own lifetime fought through these intellectual battles of the Darwinian age.

Today, the question of the "genesis" of human experience out of lower forms has pretty much ceased to be a debatable issue. It is accepted on every hand as an undoubted fact; the details have become a problem for factual inquiry. But at the same time we have come to have grave doubts about the validity of the speculative anthropology in which our fathers so easily engaged—Dewey among the best of them! We realize we were not there when it all happened, and have doubts as to whether that prehistory can be recovered. And we have come to have even graver doubts of the explanatory value of such an account of the way in which our familiar experience "arose," even if we had accurate details. Our human problem, we have come to feel, is to understand things in terms of the way they function and operate now; that is at least something that is experimentally observable. The genetic problem of how things came to be as they are, is, after all, Nature's problem of Creation—or God's. Man's primary problem, our generation holds, is rather to understand the ways in which what is, however it may have been created, continues to operate and function.

When we approach this human problem, in sober truth, the structures distinguished in Substance by reflective experience, and formulated in discourse and knowledge, are found to be bound up with and involved in structures of other substances and situations. These relatednesses, this continuity of structure, can be explored and followed on indefinitely; and in such inquiry and discourse they tend to become more and more unified. In this process of exploration, we find structures that are not functions of any particular universe of action or any particular encountered complex of processes, but seem to be involved in all processes, in all actions and cooperations. These structures are found to be "invariant" throughout a great variety of contexts. They can hence be "isolated" from any particular context: they "transcend" the limitations of any determinate situation or substance. This fact makes them of fundamental importance for human knowledge and action. A knowledge of such structures proves to be of the widest instrumental value in all contexts. These "invariant" structures can be used, and must be conformed to, in *any* "universe of interaction," in *any* situation.

Expressing this fact as an experimental discovery, we may say, the exploration of the continuity of mechanisms by which Nature operates has led us to formulate these ways of operating in terms of physical and chemical laws. It would perhaps be more accurate to say, that those structures that are invariant through the widest diversity of contexts constitute a delimitation of the subject matter of physico-chemical inquiry. We find also, of course, structures that obtain in more limited types of context, that possess a more limited range of invariance. And these structures are formulated as the "laws" of more restricted "fields," more limited ways of acting, in other sciences.

This encountered unification of structures of a certain type has suggested to many not only a factually verifiable continuity of processes in Nature, but also an eventual "unity" of discovered structure. Such a thoroughgoing unity of the objective of knowledge, making possible the eventual unification of knowledge into a single system, possesses great value as an ideal of knowledge and of formulated discourse—as what Kant calls a "regulative idea." It also unquestionably possesses great dangers, and conceals many pitfalls. Witness the "Unity" of the Neoplatonic dialectic, which came to be elevated above the subject matter of which it was originally taken to be the "Unity," and set over against it, making of what it was at first intended to organize a "mere appearance." Witness also the "Absolute" of the post-Kantians, like F. H. Bradley, and the many purely dialectical and hence completely unreal problems in which it involves its adherents.

We may, then, with due caution, envisage an eventual unification of structure. But the process of the encountered continual unification of structure does not suggest any "unity of substance"—even "eventually." This is not even a "regulative idea." Spinoza's use of the term "Substance" to designate the unified structure of the universe—the "Order of Nature"—is perverse and misleading—even when repeated in so good a pluralistic Aristotelian as Woodbridge.[3] To avoid obliterating a fundamental distinction, it is well to follow Aristotle on this basic point. "Substance," the subject matter encountered in any universe of action, is *never* a comprehensive, all-embracing Unity, Whole, or Totality. It remains a particular and τόδε τι.[4]

## V

In conclusion, I should like to raise certain questions about one of the most characteristic ways in which Nature achieves unification—through cumulative temporal development, in the many *histories* she brings to pass. These unifications I find of peculiar interest. For when man cooperates with other natural processes to push further Nature's temporal unifications in the unifying focus of his own history, he and Nature find themselves compelled to employ that particular variety of Connective we call in the more precise sense "myths." The way in which Nature achieves unification through the operation of "myths" has been far less explored than the way she gains it through logical constructions and mathematical theories.

Now the "history" of anything—the history that a thing possesses as the outcome of its fortunes among the other impinging processes of Nature, the "history" that historical knowledge attempts to understand, not the "history" that is that understanding itself—is the significant or relevant past of that thing, the past that is relevant for what it now is. A thing's history is those processes and events that have contributed to its being, gathered into a focus in the present.[5]

Nature is full of such temporal "gatherings into a focus," such "historical unifications," such cumulative outcomes and achievements. Galaxies and stars, mountain ranges and forests, as well as human societies, institutions, and ideas, are all what they are because of their respective pasts. They are "concretions" and "cumulative conservations" of the cooperations of processes into which they have previously entered. If Nature were in truth mere "flux," if she did not exhibit countless patterns of historical unification, and hosts of teleological structures of means and eventuations with a temporal spread, then human histories would indeed be wholly anomalous. Men's unification of their own history, their discovery of the significance of their own past, through knowledge or vision, would be quite impossible. So likewise would be any discovery of "the meaning" of the world, or of human life.

But Nature being what she inescapably is, such human unifications in knowledge or vision are but a pushing further of nature's own unifying powers. So important is this ability of men to extend further the cumulative unifications of Nature that, in order to be emphatic about it, some have said that this power of man to understand his own history "transcends Nature"—forgetting that it is a fundamental character of Nature to be forever "transcending" herself, to be productive, and creative of new outcomes—nowhere more clearly than in her human parts.

When men bring Nature to a focus in the discovered "meaning"of human history, the past becomes unified in the perspective of the present, and is understood as leading up to our own goings on, to our own ideas and problems. Such a temporal unification of the life of man in Nature we usually call a "philosophy of history." These attempts to find an interpretation of "history as a whole" involve an appraisal of the present in the light of the future it suggests. They interpret the past, whose deposit constitutes our resources, in terms of the envisaged future. The nature of the world and of human societies is such as to generate philosophies of history.

A philosophy of history attempting to construe history "as a whole" thus involves two kinds of unification. History can be unified in terms of its materials and resources, of the significant past; and it can also be unified in terms of its envisaged future. Thus philosophies of history normally employ two somewhat different kinds of unifying Connectives or myths: myths of origin and myths of outcome, creation myths and eschatological myths. The origin myths serve primarily to reveal the character of the materials of history: the nature of men and their behavior, or the nature of those groups that play the role of dramatic protagonists in history—races, nations, or classes. Thus we are led to see history whole in terms of the fall of man, or of the state of nature, or of primitive communism. For centuries we could not understand our history except as beginning in a "state of nature." Today we are more apt to call it "primitive society," and to go to anthropology to find the significance of the history of our own institutions. When the Germans used to do it, and discoursed passionately of blonde beasts, we smiled—or swore—according to the degree of our philosophical resignation. When we do it ourselves, and dwell upon the Kwakiutls, the bushmen, the Andaman Islanders, and coming of age in Samoa, we are sometimes convinced that in drawing upon the anthropologists for an understanding of our own history, we are being very "scientific" indeed.

In their purest form these origin myths describe the emergence of human nature from nonhuman nature. When we used to consider man a fallen angel, the meaning of human history depended on the history and fall of the angels. Now that we are inclined to look on him rather as a great ape that has almost made good, the meaning of human history clearly depends on the history of the success story of the great apes—on the history of the "evolution of mankind." These prehuman histories are wonderfully illuminating—in both cases, that of the angels and that of the apes. The only problem is how this "pre-history" can be so illuminating, since we know hardly anything about it: our actual knowledge of the history of the apes is about as sketchy as that of the angels. Human history as a whole, clearly, seems to take on a meaning only when we view it as springing full-blown out of an antecedent myth.

On the other hand, a philosophy of history can also achieve its unification by considering the present in terms of the possible future, of the ends implicit in it, and the means to their attainment. It is selective in its focus: it involves a choice among the determinate possibilities of the present of that "tendency," or predicted future, which we judge to be "dynamic" or "controlling." This choice of focus involves a choice of allegiance, a faith—the faith that the future will display a certain character. Normally again this faith in one kind of outcome is expressed in terms of a myth—the millennium, the kingdom of God, the classless society, or the triumph of social intelligence.

Both origin myths and outcome myths are instruments for unifying our history; for bringing it to a focus from which it can be understood as a whole, and can reveal its significance and meaning. The actual way these myths function is very complex, and demands careful exploration. The two kinds seem to operate rather differently, yet both are clearly involved in historical unifications. There seems to be no discoverable "meaning of history as a whole" without some outcome myth—without some "ideal," which is another name we give to such Connectives. We can no more find the significance of "history as a whole" without an ideal than we can find the significance of life—or of the world—without one. History would then indeed be as meaningless and futile as would life, a meaningless "flux."

But history, life, or Nature herself is a "flux" only to ignorance. Each is full of implicit ends or ideals, full of values, because each alike is an affair of processes, of mechanisms producing outcomes, of causes and necessary conditions of results, of means and ends. They are all alike full, that is, of things that are "better" and "worse" for other things. Nature is in truth teeming with "entelechies"; and it takes but a single flower to refute the absurd contention that there are no "values" in Nature, no achievement of ends through valuable means. We can even say that it is obviously "good for" the planet to go round and round.

Of course, neither the flower nor the planet can be said to "find" it good: in our experience, only men "find" anything. But surely it does not follow that because only men find anything, what they find is not found. The finding is a genuine cooperation of men with Nature. Ideal Connectives are not "fictions," not "imaginary" or "arbitrary." They are as "natural," as "objective," as any other way in which existence functions in Substance. They all, to be sure, involve human cooperations with other natural operations. Without man's activities, they would remain as powers of Substance. But it is not man alone who connects and unifies: it is existence cooperating with men. And the powers of existence to connect and be connected, to unify and become unified in vision, are essential to the character of existence.

Of course, it is the significance of *our* history *for us* that we discover through the unify-

ing foci of myths or ideals—just as it is the meaning of the world for us that any Connective can generate. A star might well find a different meaning—or a being from Mars. However, there is no evidence that stars find anything significant; and if there be Martians, their philosophies remain unknown. But the fact that we must understand Nature from a human focus is not only a fact about human understanding—and, since human understanding is the only one we know of, a fact about all understanding; it is also a fact about Nature. Nature is brought to a selective unification only in a focus an ideal, that Nature has herself generated in revealing her possibilities to men. Likewise, the fact that we must understand our history in the light of a selective unification, an outcome myth, that history has itself generated, does not mean that we cannot understand it.

We can understand it best, in the degree to which the suggested focus or outcome is based on knowledge—in which it unifies what we are, what we are doing, and what we still can and must do. It is sometimes said that the ideal which reveals the significance of our history must itself stand "outside history." What this means seems clear: it must be a genuine ideal. But unless that ideal stands at the same time "inside history"—unless it is *our* ideal, rooted in what we are and in what we can become, and relevant to our problems—it will not give us a genuine understanding, or reveal the significance and pattern of our history. Nature, and history, can achieve genuine unification only through Connectives and myths which, though they be conventional, are nevertheless not arbitrary, but are rooted in the very nature of things.

If we start with the world as a *unity,* it is impossible to get from that unity to the encountered plurality of things, which remains therefore a mystery. Only God has been able to turn that trick, and he has not revealed how he has done it: human theologians have never been able to explain the process, not even the evolutionists. But if we start with the encountered plurality, there is nothing to prevent us from tracing as much of *unification* as we may.

Such unity as has been achieved, in our vision or in our knowledge, is the outcome of our processes of unification.

## Notes

1. See chapter 6, "Substance as a Cooperation of Processes," pp. 176, 194, in John Herman Ran-

dall, Jr., *Nature and Historical Experience* (New York: Columbia University Press, 1958).
2. See the classification of myths in *ibid.*, p. 262.
3. See F. J. E. Woodbridge, *Nature and Mind* (New York, 1937), "Structure," pp. 148–59.
4. For a fuller treatment of unities in knowledge, see Epilogue, "Unifications of Knowledge," in J. H. Randall, Jr., *Nature and Historical Experience,* pp. 296–309.
5. See *ibid.*, pp. 35–36.

## Suggestions for Further Reading

John P. Anton, *Naturalism and Historical Understanding: Essays on the Philosophy of John Herman Randall, Jr.* (Albany: State University of New York Press, 1967).

Justus Buchler, *Metaphysics of Natural Complexes,* eds. Kathleen Wallace, Armen Marsoobian, and Robert Corrington (Albany: State University of New York Press, 1990 [1966]).

Justus Buchler, *Nature and Judgment* (New York: Columbia University Press, 1955).

Justus Buchler, *Toward a General Theory of Human Judgment* (New York: Columbia University Press, 1951).

Morris R. Cohen, *Reason and Nature* (New York: Dover, 1978 [1931]).

Abraham Edel, *Ethical Judgment* (New York: Free Press, 1964).

Marvin Farber, *Naturalism and Subjectivism* (Albany: State University of New York Press, 1959).

Horace M. Kallen and Sidney Hook, eds., *American Philosophy Today and Tomorrow* (Freeport, N.Y.: Books for Libraries Press, 1968 [1935]). See especially the essays on naturalism by Irwin Edman, Sidney Hook, Ernest Nagel, and John Herman Randall.

Yervant H. Krikorian, ed., *Naturalism and the Human Spirit* (New York: Columbia University Press, 1944).

Sterling P. Lamprecht, *The Metaphysics of Naturalism* (New York: Appleton-Century-Crofts, 1967).

Kai Nielsen, *Naturalism Without Foundations* (Amherst, N.Y.: Prometheus Books, 1996).

Ralph Barton Perry, *Present Philosophical Tendencies: A Critical Survey of Naturalism, Idealism Pragmatism and Realism, Together With a Synopsis of the Philosophy of William James* (Westport, Conn.: Greenwood Press, 1972 [1912]).

John Herman Randall, Jr., *Nature and Historical Experience* (New York: Columbia University Press, 1958).

John Ryder, ed., *American Philosophic Naturalism in the Twentieth Century* (Amherst, N.Y.: Prometheus Books, 1994). The most comprehensive anthology.

George Santayana, *The Life of Reason,* 5 vols. (New York, Charles Scribner's Sons, 1933–34).

George Santayana, *Realms of Being* (New York: Charles Scribner's Sons, 1937–38).

George Santayana, *Scepticism and Animal Faith* (New York: Charles Scribner's Sons, 1923).

Roy Wood Sellars, *Principles of Emergent Realism,* ed. W. Preston Warren (St Louis: Warren H. Green, Inc., 1970 [1944]).

Beth J. Singer, *Ordinal Naturalism: An Introduction to the Philosophy of Justus Buchler* (Lewisburg, Penn.: Bucknell University Press, 1983).

F. J. E. Woodbridge, *An Essay on Nature* (New York: Columbia University Press, 1940).